JOHN HUSTON

a guide to references

and resources

A
Reference
Publication
in
Film

Richard J. Finneran
Editor

JOHN HUSTON

*a guide to references
and resources*

ALLEN COHEN
HARRY LAWTON

G. K. Hall & Co.
An Imprint of Simon & Schuster Macmillan
New York

Prentice Hall International
London   Mexico City   New Delhi   Singapore   Sydney   Toronto

G.K. Hall & Co.
An Imprint of Simon & Schuster Macmillan
1633 Broadway
New York, NY 10019

Library of Congress Catalog Card Number: 97–26286

Printed in the United States of America

Printing Number

1 2 3 4 5 6 7 8 9 10

Library of Congress Cataloging-in-Publication Data

Cohen, Allen, 1935–
    John Huston : a guide to references and resources / Allen Cohen, Harry Lawton.
        p.   cm. — (A reference publication in film)
    Filmography: p.
    Includes bibliographical references and index.
    ISBN 0–8161–1619–9 (alk. paper)
    1. Huston, John, 1906– —Criticism and interpretation. 2. Huston, John, 1906– —Credits.
3. Huston, John, 1906– —Bibliography. I. Lawton, Harry, 1938– . II. Series.
PN1998.3.H87C65   1997
791.43'0233'092—dc21   97–26286
                                                                                                            CIP

The paper used in this publication meets the requirements of ANSI/NISO Z39.48–1992 (Permanence of Paper).

ALLEN COHEN
For Hinda, and in memory of Mom and Richard

HARRY LAWTON
For Kitty and Diana

Contents

Contents

Preface

"Laugh, Curtin, old boy. It's a great joke played on us by the Lord or fate or by nature . . . whichever you prefer, but whoever or whatever played it, certainly had a sense of humor. The gold has gone back to where we got it. Laugh my boy, laugh. It's worth ten months of labor and suffering . . . this joke is."

—HOWARD (WALTER HUSTON) AT THE END OF *THE TREASURE OF THE SIERRA MADRE* (1948)

John Huston died in 1987, and it has taken a lifetime plus ten for him to achieve a full measure of respect. A clear token of that respect is the fact that this book is the third scholarly effort concentrated on Huston since 1993.[1] That year saw the publication of the collection of essays *Reflections in a Male Eye,* edited by Gaylyn Studlar and David Desser (Washington, D.C.: Smithsonian Institution Press), and in 1994 G. K. Hall released a compilation of critical writings on Huston, *Perspectives on John Huston,* edited by Stephen Cooper. *John Huston: A Guide to References and Resources* has a more pragmatic purpose. A guide to writings on Huston and his films, it includes synopses of all the movies he directed; a review of his career as a writer, director, and actor; information on unrealized projects; and a guide to archival resources and collections pertinent to his work. It does not purport to break new ground on Huston criticism, but attempts to gather together the critical work undertaken by others. It may serve as an introduction to a study of the director and his complete career in the movie industry. It is intended as a guide and encouragement to all who are moved to undertake research on any stage or aspect of his life and career.

What the above publishing history proves is that within ten years of Huston's death those engaged in film criticism have begun to reevaluate seriously the director's contribution to cinema and to make up for the decades in which they too casually dismissed or damned him with faint praise. In approaching Huston, these critics must come to terms with the awkward fact that, in a directing career stretching back to the early 1940s (his writing and his acting career on the stage and in film start in the 1920s), he produced a body of work that included titles that most filmgoers would put on their "Ten Most Exciting" list or their "Ten Most Entertaining" list—titles, in short, that are considered standards in the film repertory. Furthermore, there is the suspicion that just below the surface of these thrillers or adventure stories or ironical comedies (films produced with the frank expectation of commercial success) lurks something a little deeper than just a good yarn—maybe the germ of an idea, the suggestive pattern of a philosophy, or a provocative concept that spectators may take with them on leaving the cinema.

The contradiction between the storyteller and the man of ideas that turned a master storyteller into an intellectual provocateur has in its time repelled critics, while it has also created a body of loyal admirers, drawing them back again and again to the movies both for their entertainment value and to tease out just one more level of meaning. Huston was both a rebel against the studio system and one of its most enduring servants, with most of his films being delivered on time and within budget and earning their money back. While preferring the life of exile and adopting a more European outlook in his dabbling in existentialism (one of his directorial productions on Broadway was a version of Jean-Paul Sartre's *No Exit,* 1946), in his exploration of Freudian psychology, and in his mockery of the myth of success, Huston also proved to be a deeply American director in choice of theme and viewpoint. After long periods of absence he regularly startled the public with significant returns to the U.S. scene, both metaphorically and geographically, in such films as *Moby Dick* (1956; a cultural return, of course), *The Misfits* (1961), and *Fat City* (1972).

Even where he did not receive screen credit for his screenplays, in every film that he directed Huston played a major role in the script's composition (see chapter 16, "Screenplays in Collections"). Amusingly, his involvement in the writing of his films did not gain Huston fame as an "auteur." Such acclaim became the test of judgment for directors in the sixties—following the success of the French New Wave and the school of criticism formed in its wake—and Huston fell short because his detractors saw him as a maker of potboilers who dashed from project to project without reflection and without a sense of intellectual propriety. Where was the consistency, the dedication to a carefully worked-out set of referents, the personal film language? Of course it did not help Huston's reputation during that period that his films after *Moby Dick* (1956) through *The Kremlin Letter* (1970) amounted to the longest of bad patches.

If the myth of the dilettante hovers about Huston, it is partly his fault or his design. In interviews and conversations over the years (although there are some honorable exceptions), he often preferred to discuss hunting and horses or painting rather than the business of filmmaking. He could at times be very serious about films, but he often hid it. When the screenwriter Richard Brooks, who had dashed off a treatment of *The Mackintosh Man* (1973) in a matter of days, joined him in Ireland to discuss it, Brooks found a jovial old philosopher who saw filmmaking as a strictly secondary activity to painting or novel writing and was not afraid to say so. Yet, some fourteen years later that same director signed off his own career with *The Dead* (1987). The almost literary surge of Huston's films in the last fifteen years of his life revived a feverish interest in almost every aspect of his work. As a result he achieved an academic respectability, and for John Huston that is probably the finest joke that the posthumous life could play.

For the most part this book follows the established pattern of A Reference Publication in Film series. It might deviate a bit because we concentrate on Huston's complete career, not only as a director, but also as a writer and an actor. The book begins with a biography of Huston. With regard to this, we acknowledge Lawrence Grobel, whose comprehensive *The Hustons* (New York: Scribners, 1989) certainly contributed to an increased interest in both John Huston himself and his family. If that section is longer than some, it is because his life was richer in incident than most and packed with activity year by year.

We follow the biography with a critical survey of the oeuvre. Next is a chronology of his life and a filmography with synopses of the films he directed (including the wartime documentaries and his contributions to directing where others were involved), of his important writing assignments (especially at Warner Brothers), of early writing assignments at Universal, and of two important films in which he was solely an actor: *Chinatown* (1974) and *Winter Kills* (1979). (His other acting activity is indicated elsewhere.) Then we present an annotated bibliography of some important writing on Huston; general citations on the movie industry and Huston; and articles and reviews to specific films (both realized and unrealized). We follow these works with more specific citations related to Huston, including interviews and writings of his; a section on Huston in fiction; citations to people connected with him in his various capacities; obituaries; a section on the movie industry; and studio histories. Next is information on the various films that he was involved with as actor, writer, and director, with additional activity as indicated in the archives of the Academy of Motion Picture Arts and Sciences; awards and honors; his screenplays in various archival collections; his theatrical activity; audio recordings; various archival production files related to the films he was connected with; the John Huston Collection at the Academy of Motion Picture Arts and Sciences; archival resources for people connected with him; a directory of archival institutions; Huston-related films on film, video, and laser disc, with a directory of their suppliers; and bibliographical and reference sources.

Harry Lawton wrote the biographical and critical chapters. Allen Cohen was responsible for all the archival research on this project. As becomes quite apparent, any research on John Huston requires time spent in Los Angeles. Other places and institutions in the United States have important information on Huston and the people related to him, but the collections at the Academy of Motion Picture Arts and Sciences, the University of California at Los Angeles, and the University of Southern California are indispensable.

No book of this nature could be completed without the generous and timely help and advice from many librarians, friends, colleagues, and all those encountered en route. For their unstinting help the authors would thus like to thank in particular:

The Academy of Motion Picture Arts and Sciences: Linda Mehr, Sam Gill, Faye Thompson, Howard Prouty, Ed Carter, Lisa Epstein, Val Almendarez, Sandra Archer, and the rest of the wonderful staff

The British Film Institute: Graham Melville

California State University, Los Angeles: Roy Liebman

The Library of Congress: Rosemary Hanes

The Museum of Modern Art: Charles Silver, Ron Magliozzi, Mary Corliss

The National Archives: Jill Abraham

The New York Public Library for the Performing Arts: Christine Karatnytsky

The New York State Archives: Dick Andress

The State Historical Society of Wisconsin: Laura Jacobs

University of California at Los Angeles: Brigitte Kueppers, Raymond Sotto

University of California at Santa Barbara, Davidson Library: Becky Eldridge, Carol Beth Gibbens, Patrick Dawson, Lucia Snowhill, Marilyn Cordray, Scott Hathaway, Gary Johnson, Vellaurit Rivera

University of California at Santa Barbara, Film Studies Department: Kathy Carnahan, Marti Mangan

University of California at Santa Barbara, French and Italian Department: Jody Hoppe, Roxanne Lapidus

University of Iowa: Robert McKown

University of Southern California: Ned Comstock, Stuart Ng, Noelle Carter, Bill Wittington

University of Tennessee: Nick Wyman

University of Texas: Charles Ball

University of Wyoming, American Heritage Center: Jennifer King

Wisconsin Center for Film and Theatre Research: Maxine Fleckner-Ducey.

And thanks also to Brendan Searls of Video Shmideo, Santa Barbara, who generously made available many of the John Huston films from the video rental store's wonderful collection; to Bob Sivers, who provided some help in getting through the vagaries of computers; and to our editors and indexer—Desirée Bermani, Marilyn Bliss, Catherine Carter, and Vicki Chamlee—all of whom made it happen.

NOTE

1. Scheduled for publication in 1997 is Lesley Brill's *John Huston's Filmmaking* (New York: Cambridge University Press, Cambridge Studies in Film).

I
The Life of John Huston

John Huston directed forty-two films (including three documentaries), wrote at least as many screenplays, won two Oscars (both for the same film), had five wives, enjoyed three houses he could call his own, and inspired two novels, written by screenwriters who worked on two of his most important films. These are *White Hunter, Black Heart* (1953) by Peter Viertel, who worked on *The African Queen* (1951–52), and *Green Shadows, White Whale* (1992) by Ray Bradbury, who wrote the original screenplay of *Moby Dick* (1956). Among all the statistics that imperfectly sum up Huston's life, it is the last one that gives the researcher pause, for many other distinguished Hollywood directors (D. W. Griffith, Von Stroheim, John Ford, and Alfred Hitchcock, among others) have been subject to biographical scrutiny without inspiring works of fiction. Viertel and Bradbury nonetheless found in Huston qualities that moved him beyond the confines of standard biography, and they concluded that he belonged as much to the world of fiction as to that of fact.

Most of the writing on Huston until recently reflects a biographical bias. Some of these studies do yield valuable information as to how Huston worked and created; but whether you turn to Lillian Ross's *Picture* (New York: Rinehart, 1952) or James Agee's "Undirectable Director"[1] (originally published in *Life,* September 18, 1950; see also chapter 5, "Annotated Bibliography") or Lloyd Nolan's *King Rebel* (Los Angeles: Sherbourne Press, 1965), mixed in with a dose of hagiography, you are reading more about the life of the man than about the temperament of the artist. In the 1960s, journalistic accounts of the making of *The Misfits* (1961) and *The Night of the Iguana* (1964) concentrated exclusively on the private lives of the stars and on the squabbles on the set that these writers prayed they would witness firsthand. They excluded the fact that in both cases Huston was working with the two foremost writers for the American stage: Arthur Miller and Tennessee Williams.

The director himself did not discourage this emphasis. He was never one to hide from the curiosity of journalists, drawing attention with his flamboyant behavior and his insouciant flouting of convention. By tossing sops of biographical snacks to devouring columnists, Huston always granted himself the freedom to do his most serious work of adaptation and writing in private. He was also a conscious promot-

1

er of his own mythology, adopting at will the various roles of lover, adventurer, master of the hunt, lord of the manor, and guru to the young seeking guidance. Plenty in his family history engendered such patterns.

His maternal grandmother was Adelia Gore. Her father, Gen. William Richardson, lost an arm at Chancellorsville in the Civil War. His sword remained in the family for generations, and John used it in *The Red Badge of Courage* (1951). Adelia was an accomplished frontier journalist, typesetter, and editor in the late nineteenth century, and her daughter, Rhea (John's mother), inherited her mother's talent for writing and management. She herself graduated to a senior position on the *New York Post* in the 1920s and 1930s and was still a working journalist at her death in 1938.

The males from that branch of the family were more problematical. John Huston's maternal grandfather, John Gore, was a drunk with an inveterate restlessness that prohibited him from laying down roots. As soon as he had established himself and his family in one of the Western communities springing up like mushrooms on the late-nineteenth-century frontier, Gore would be lured even farther West, usually leaving his wife and baby daughter behind. In later years he would also occasionally take off on periodic drunks, and he finally died of drink alone in a hotel room in Waco, Texas, when his only grandson was three years old.[2]

It was nevertheless John Gore who made an interesting offer to Rhea and Walter Huston (John's parents) in the fall of 1905. They had been married for about a year, and Walter had yet to establish himself as an actor. His great-grandfather, Thomas Huston, had emigrated to Canada from County Armagh, Ireland, in the mid-nineteenth century. The youngest of four children, Walter had grown up in Toronto. Interest in the arts ran in the family, and his sister, Margaret, was a talented opera singer with an international reputation. John Gore was now the owner of the Public Utilities Company of Nevada, Missouri (family folklore asserted he had won it in a poker game). Gore offered his son-in-law the post of superintendent, despite his youth and inexperience. It was in Nevada, Missouri, during this brief period of stability for the Huston household that their only son was born on August 5, 1906. Rhea and Walter named him John Marcellus Huston, after his grandfather. This period of domestic security in Nevada, however, came to an abrupt end when the town's inadequate water system collapsed under pressure one night on Walter's watch. The Hustons left town immediately, and Walter informed his father-in-law (then on a binge in St. Louis) that he no longer owned the Nevada Public Utilities Company. Walter managed other power and light companies in St. Louis and Waterford, Texas, for the next four years, but his heart was never in the work. In 1909 he decided to try his luck once more on the stage, and he and Rhea separated.

Within three years of their divorce, Walter and Rhea had each remarried: Walter to his stage partner, Bayonne Whipple, and Rhea to Howard Stevens of St. Paul, Minnesota, a senior engineer for the Northern Pacific Railroad and a widower with two children from his first marriage. The stable home life that Rhea had hoped to secure for John with this marriage was not to be. A local doctor detected signs of an enlarged heart in twelve-year-old John and symptoms of nephritis. Stevens agreed that John and Rhea should move to a warmer climate, and mother and son were on the road again, passing through New Orleans and Texas (where they visited John Gore's tomb in Waco) and finally ending up on the West Coast in Los Angeles. In Phoenix, Arizona, when John was confined to bed, wondering whether his illness was terminal, his reaction was to steal out of the house every night, chance his luck in a nearby canal, and throw himself over a waterfall. This challenge to medical authority (misguided, as it happens) and even to death itself denotes a pattern of recklessness and self-confidence that marked the remainder of his life and career.[3]

Rhea never did return to live with Stevens, preferring her professional independence and her role as a mother who alone would be responsible for her son's upbringing. John's health markedly improved in Southern California, and it was apparent that any heart abnormality would be taken care of by a healthy diet and exercise. In Los Angeles the adolescent Huston discovered two passions that never left him: boxing and art. While enrolled at Lincoln Heights High School—and in defiance of his mother's strict orders—he began to fight as an amateur and train at the L.A. Athletic Club. With his height and reach, he was good enough to win the California junior lightweight championship with twenty-three wins and only two losses (and a broken nose in the bargain). A later self-portrait of Huston kitted out for a fight, plus a couple of boxing stories he sold to *The American Mercury,* testify to the intersection of art and boxing that marks a proportion of his future career.

Meanwhile, in 1924, at age forty, Walter was about to emerge as a major actor on the New York stage. He was helped by his sister, Margaret Huston Carrington, who now taught voice training to singers and actors. John was present at rehearsals of Eugene O'Neill's *Desire Under the Elms,* in which Walter scored a notable triumph as the patriarch Ephraim Cabot. At this point John was very attracted to the theater and was also reestablishing his bond with his father, whom he had rarely seen since his parents' divorce in 1909. Following a mastoid operation that John underwent in 1926, his father financed a vacation to Mexico, a country to which John would remain attached for the rest of his life. In 1926 in Mexico City the younger Huston gambled, went horseback riding, and finally ended up with a commission in the Mexican cavalry. But things got out of hand when he was challenged to a duel over another man's mistress, and his mother hurried him back to Los Angeles.

On his return from a second trip to Mexico and over the objections of both sets of parents, in 1926 Huston married his first wife, Dorothy Harvey (then studying philosophy in college), in Los Angeles. The young couple settled down in Malibu, both bent on writing careers. John managed to sell a boxing story, "Fool," to H. L. Mencken's *American Mercury.* (Walter had sent a copy to Ring Lardner Jr., who sent it on to Mencken.) John and Dorothy then moved to New York, where Walter and Rhea (who relocated to New York in 1927) moved independently through the city's literary circles. Walter and Rhea could count among their friends Thomas Wolfe, Eugene O'Neill, Ring Lardner Jr., and Sinclair Lewis. John befriended the actor Sam Jaffe, whom he later directed in *The Asphalt Jungle.* Jaffe introduced John to George Gershwin and his circle and improvised some music for a marionette version of *Frankie and Johnny,* which Huston wrote (and which was published by Boni and Liveright in 1930). The publishers paid John five hundred dollars, and the attention he received led to a position as a contract writer for the Samuel Goldwyn Studios in Hollywood. Thus, he said good-bye to the New York

3

literary life and entered the world of commercial cinema, for which his talent and temperament were better suited.

Huston soon left the Goldwyn Studios for Universal, where he worked with William Wyler on the screenplay of *A House Divided* (1931), which starred Walter. Wyler was to remain a lifelong friend and colleague. John then worked on *Law and Order,* also starring his father. This was a western based on a novel by one of his favorite authors, W. R. Burnett, who also wrote *The Asphalt Jungle.* But as John's career advanced, his marriage deteriorated. Left at home, Dorothy turned more and more to drink and descended into alcoholism. The crisis came in February 1933, when John was involved in a car crash and convicted of drunk driving. In the car with him was Zita Johann, the actress wife of theater director John Houseman. Dorothy accepted an invitation from a friend, Greta Nissen, to join her in London where she was making a film. This move relieved John of the immediate responsibility of dealing with his wife. He was to join Dorothy sooner than expected, however, after a far more serious incident in September that same year. This time Brazilian dancer Tosca Roulien stepped out in front of a car Huston was driving along Sunset Boulevard and was killed. Although Huston was cold sober at the time and innocent of any wrongdoing, the publicity in the wake of his previous history threatened his career. This time Dorothy threw him a lifeline from London, where her contacts included Mark Ostrer, the head of Gaumont-British Studios. He offered Huston a job at three hundred dollars per week.

Huston's parenthetical stay in London was neither happy nor successful, although it anticipated his final exile from Hollywood some seventeen years later. On a personal level, Dorothy's condition deteriorated to the point where she had to return to the United States. Huston left virtually no impression at Gaumont-British. All his suggestions for scripts were turned down, and his salary—at about three times the going rate for his British colleagues—only caused resentment. When he offered to resign a few months after arriving in London, he was surprised to learn that the Balcon brothers, who were in charge of the studio, accepted his offer with alacrity. Only two film projects survive from this period: *Three Strangers* and *Death Drives Through.* The first, actually proposed to and turned down by Alfred Hitchcock, was eventually scripted by Howard Koch and filmed by Warners in 1946. The second was a motor-racing melodrama, concocted by Huston and fellow American expatriate Eddy Kahn, and produced by Gaumont-British in 1935. The project earned Huston enough money so that he would not have to sleep in parks and allowed him to spend some time in Paris, where he could study the paintings that he had hitherto only seen reproduced. He was back in the United States in 1935, in time to see *Dodsworth,* one of Walter Huston's greatest screen successes. It would still be some years before the son joined his father in a position of equal primacy in the industry.

Before resuming his Hollywood career, Huston accepted the lead role in a Works Progress Administration (WPA) theatrical production in Chicago by up-and-coming playwright Howard Koch. The play was *The Lonely Man,* and Huston played Abraham Lincoln, reincarnated among mineworkers in a contemporary Depression setting. Later Koch was to write the scripts for *Casablanca* and *Mission to Moscow* (starring Walter Huston) as well as John's London story, *Three*

Strangers. In Chicago John met a young Irish woman, Leslie Black, who, in late 1937, became his second wife. She at first resisted the impecunious young actor. However, the offer of a contract from Jack Warner, the chance to work with William Wyler again, and a five-thousand-dollar check to revise the *Three Strangers* allowed Huston to reestablish himself in Hollywood, to travel to New York at the end of the year, to meet Leslie and her family, and to marry her.

In the late 1930s, Huston worked on two important films by William Wyler: *Jezebel* (1938), starring Bette Davis; and *Wuthering Heights* (1939), for which he reshaped the original Charles MacArthur–Ben Hecht draft but did not receive any screen credit. For Warners he also scripted *The Amazing Dr. Clitterhouse* (1938) and *Juarez* (1939) with Paul Muni. Edward G. Robinson played the criminal psychologist Doctor Clitterhouse as well as the lead in *Dr. Ehrlich's Magic Bullet* (1940, another Huston script), the story of the Nobel prizewinner who discovered a cure for syphilis. In 1948 Robinson would work for Huston the director in *Key Largo.* These were years of increasing professional success, marred by loss and tragedy on the family front. First Walter's sister, Margaret (then living in Santa Barbara with her second husband, theatrical designer Bobby Jones), was dying of cancer; John arranged for her to spend her last months back in Connecticut, where she died. Then John's mother, Rhea, died in November 1938 from an inoperable brain tumor. His mother's death was a heavy blow to John. It was she who had raised him, had nursed him through sickness, and had never been slow to condemn him for his shortcomings, notably in his treatment of women. With her passing he grieved for the things left unsaid between them.

The Warner Brothers contract allowed him to purchase land in Tarzana, where he designed and built a house for himself and Leslie, and to indulge his passion for horses. A further blow, however, occurred in January 1939, when Leslie gave birth to a stillborn baby daughter. Leslie never fully recovered from her loss, and this misfortune marked the beginning of the end of their marriage.

Huston was now almost ready to direct. His script for Raoul Walsh's *High Sierra* (1941) earned him an Oscar nomination, brought him into contact with W. R. Burnett, the author of the novel, and marked a turning point in the career of the film's star, Humphrey Bogart. The producer was Mark Hellinger, who would later call on Huston's services for the 1946 screen adaptation of Ernest Hemingway's *The Killers.* Paul Kohner had been both John's and Walter's agent since 1938, and he remained a lifelong friend and partner. It was he who inserted into John's Warner Brothers contract a clause committing the studio to offer his client a chance to direct when the opportunity arose. The Oscar nomination for the *High Sierra* script gave John that chance.

For his first film Huston chose Dashiell Hammett's *The Maltese Falcon* (1941), which had twice generated inferior adaptations in the thirties, both produced by Warners. The summit of Huston's ambition was to improve on these mediocre predecessors. His meticulous preparation paid off. The result was a film that remains a model of its genre and the first of a new wave of American cinema: "film noir." The success of *The Maltese Falcon* owes much to the casting; indeed, Huston began to create a small nucleus of actors he would call on in later years. Most notably it included Humphrey Bogart, who as Sam Spade indelibly fixed his persona in the mind of the public, and Sydney Greenstreet, Peter Lorre, and Mary Astor gave weight to the supporting roles. The director and his leading lady embarked on an affair that brought his marriage to Leslie closer to dissolution.

Europe was at war and the Japanese attack on Pearl Harbor was in the offing, but before joining the army, Huston still had to complete a series of assignments for Warners. He wrote the script for the patriotic *Sergeant York* (1941), starring Gary Cooper and Joan Leslie (from *High Sierra*). That same year he directed his second feature, *In This Our Life* (1942), a southern melodrama and a vehicle for Bette Davis. The film also starred Olivia de Havilland, with whom Huston began an affair that continued sporadically throughout the war years. His third feature, *Across the Pacific* (1942), was a contribution to the war effort, but it was equally a kind of buddy movie that appealed to Huston. For this project he was able to assemble much of *The Maltese Falcon* cast (Bogart, Greenstreet, and Astor). The movie was not quite finished when he reported for military duty in April 1942.

John Huston had a good war. World War II was a man's game, providing a steady supply of strong male society and available and desirable women along with the freedom to enjoy their company away from domestic ties. He was commissioned as a lieutenant in the Signal Corps, which had recruited a number of Hollywood directors to record the progress of the war and the heroism of the ordinary soldier. Most notable among his colleagues was Frank Capra, who produced the educational and propaganda series *Why We Fight*.

In the next three years Huston came of age as a director, making three outstanding documentaries on the subject of war. Together they form a remarkable triptych of men at war, men in combat, and the recuperation of the survivors. *Report from the Aleutians* (1943) chronicled the building of an airbase in the most adverse conditions in the Pacific and the air war over two Japanese islands, Attu and Kiska. He was helped by a minimal camera crew of Ray Scott and Jules Buck, and his professional association with the latter lasted through the 1960s. *The Battle of San Pietro* (made in the fall and winter of 1942–43 and released in 1945) thrust him into the Italian campaign. The English novelist Eric Ambler helped to prepare the script, and Jules Buck was cameraman and driver. What began as a simple public relations film ended as a bloody battle diary. The German forces, who had retreated from the village of San Pietro at the head of the Liri River Valley about forty kilometers south of Rome, were entrenched in the surrounding mountains and were perfectly capable of fending off direct Allied assaults by land and air. The U.S. command decided on a frontal attack and sent in the 143d Infantry regiment, which promptly lost twelve out of sixteen tanks. In the bloody battle that ensued, Huston and company found themselves in the thick of the carnage. What emerges is a film that pays tribute to the heroism of the infantrymen who fought and died there and stands as a powerful antiwar statement. It did not please the Washington top brass, however, who deemed it bad for morale. The film was eventually released on orders of General George C. Marshall, but in severely truncated form. Today only thirty minutes remain of what James Agee in *The Nation* called the best film of 1945.

Finally, *Let There Be Light* (1946) documented the difficult adjustment to civilian life of servicemen who bore the psychological scars of war. Working closely with the staff at Mason General Hospital on Long Island, for months Huston followed a select group of veterans with varying degrees of debilitating psychoses, charting their progress and noting the success of their treatment. Within two months those patients had recovered most of their capacity to resume civilian life. Again the film met extreme resistance by the military establishment, which balked at footage showing men broken by war. Military authorities banned a private screening at New York's Museum of Modern Art, and once more James Agee in *The Nation* defended Huston and denounced the military's interference. *Let There Be Light* was first shown to the public in 1980. Together *The Battle of San Pietro* and *Let There Be Light* mark a crucial chapter in Huston's career. Apart from the antiwar statements implicit in each and the humane liberality of his vision, these films reveal a director overcoming the most arduous circumstances to produce his work and at ease on location, at a safe distance from the studio.

Five years after World War II Huston was on the eve of producing two of his most enduring films, and as he was consolidating his position in Hollywood, he was also contemplating a break with the established film community. While his career flourished, his private life was in turmoil. Leslie Black had filed for divorce in April 1944. Recognizing the Lothario side of his character, Olivia de Havilland had abruptly broken up with him. In these circumstances, he capriciously embarked on a third marriage to Evelyn Keyes, who had played Vivien Leigh's younger sister in *Gone With the Wind.* Following his divorce from Leslie, Huston kept his house in Tarzana as the base for his operations.

Work continued to engage the serious side of his nature. For Mark Hellinger and Universal, Huston and Anthony Veiller adapted Ernest Hemingway's *The Killers* (1946), which was directed by Robert Siodmak. He then took a brief sabbatical from Hollywood to produce Jean-Paul Sartre's *Huis Clos* (*No Exit,* in Paul Bowles's translation) for the New York stage. All this work helped prepare him for filming *The Treasure of the Sierra Madre* (1948). Huston had begun a draft treatment of the novel during the war and had entered into correspondence with B. Traven, the novel's elusive author, who apparently lived in Mexico and who thoroughly approved of Huston's final adaptation. A major difficulty was with Jack Warner over Huston's determination to shoot the film in Mexico. The battle was really over creative control, and it came at a time when, amid the increasing tensions of the cold war, when anyone's loyalty and patriotism could be called into question, American artists and intellectuals had reason to fear the loss of intellectual freedom. Shooting on location was a reminder of all Huston had learned while making his wartime documentaries. With all logistical difficulties finally surmounted, *Treasure* boasted major performances from Humphrey Bogart as Fred C. Dobbs and Walter Huston as the old prospector Howard. Walter had played a silent cameo in *The Maltese Falcon* and had narrated *Let There Be Light,* but this part was his first and only major role in a film made by his son. At the Academy Awards ceremonies in 1948 Walter won an Oscar for Best Supporting Actor, and John awards for Best Director and Best Screenplay.

John returned from Mexico with an offering for Evelyn: an adopted son, Pablo Albaran, a waif who had been hanging around the set doing odd jobs. Friends presumed that John needed a mascot or, more likely, an instant heir. He left the responsibilities of raising Pablo almost exclusively to Evelyn, who understandably felt exploited. Pablo's life weaves in and out of the Huston family's history for the next thirty years, but his appearance in Tarzana in 1948 was simply a wedge driven between Evelyn and John.

At the height of the cold war Hollywood was under fire and the film community was under investigation from the House Un-American Activities Committee (HUAC), which was intent on sniffing out the remotest connection of anyone in the industry to communist activities. Huston was sufficiently aroused to organize, with the help of William Wyler and Philip Dunne (screenwriter for *How Green Was My Valley*, 1940), the Committee for the First Amendment. Huston held no brief for the group of Hollywood writers and directors—the Hollywood Ten, which did include several unrepentant Communists and ex-Communists in its ranks—originally indicted by the committee. What appalled him was the assault on free speech that the committee's activities represented. He and his allies then organized a delegation to go to Washington to express their collective outrage before HUAC. They had not counted on the behavior of the studio heads, who were only too eager to cooperate with the committee and were at the same time drawing up a blacklist of those they regarded as left-wing sympathizers. Nor was the Committee for the First Amendment's cause helped by the militant and polemical behavior of the Ten themselves. Huston soon realized that his venture into American politics was essentially a fiasco, and he and his committee wisely decided to retreat. The episode highlighted for him the poisonous atmosphere of political life in the era of McCarthyism and fed his misgivings about continuing to work in Hollywood.

Huston got back to work on the last film he would direct for Warner Brothers. *Key Largo* (1948) was based on a verse play by Maxwell Anderson, whose hero was a survivor from the Spanish Civil War. At the suggestion of Richard Brooks, Huston's co-screenwriter, the character became a veteran of World War II (and a survivor of the battle of San Pietro). This change made more sense to a contemporary American audience, and the part went to Humphrey Bogart, here in romantic tandem with his new wife, Lauren Bacall. Edward G. Robinson gave a stellar performance as the gangster Johnny Rocco, and Claire Trevor won an Oscar for Best Supporting Actress as Rocco's drink-sodden mistress.

Huston now announced his independence from the studios by entering into an agreement with producer Sam Spiegel to start up their own production company, Horizon Pictures. Spiegel knew of Huston's dissatisfaction with the studio system, and Huston was prepared to overlook Spiegel's unreliable reputation, committing himself to their first film, *We Were Strangers* (1949). Thematically this picture was an audacious choice, in part arising out of Huston's recent bitter experience in Washington. The film shows the failure of a revolutionary plot against a Cuban dictator at a time when the United States had friendly relations with the Cuban government. It was actually shot in Cuba and anticipates the successful Cuban revolution thirteen years later. The plot illustrates the common Huston theme of a good cause gone wrong. The revolutionaries included John Garfield (who had been under investigation by the HUAC) and Jennifer Jones.

By 1950 Huston's marriage with Evelyn Keyes had finally broken up, and he had met the woman who was to become his fourth wife. She was Enrica (Ricki)

Soma, a seventeen-year-old aspiring ballerina and actress whose face had graced the cover of *Life* magazine two years earlier. Soon after they were married Ricki announced she was pregnant, presenting Huston with an heir after three fruitless marriages. Walter Anthony Huston was born on April 16, 1950, named after the grandfather he would never know. Walter had died in Hollywood nine days earlier, after failing to attend the birthday party John had arranged for him. Once again, as at his mother's passing, life and death were intimately entwined.

In the wake of these events, in spring 1950, Huston began filming *The Asphalt Jungle,* based on W. R. Burnett's novel, with a script coauthored by Ben Maddow. This project concluded Huston's first decade as a film director on a very high note and brought to an end his film noir period. The casting was ideal: Huston's old friend Sam Jaffe as criminal strategist "Doc" Riedenschneider; Sterling Hayden as the hoodlum, Dix; Jean Hagen as his girl, Doll; and Louis Calhern as the crooked lawyer, Emmerich. Huston also gave Marilyn Monroe her first film role as Emmerich's mistress, Angela.

His next project, the film version of Stephen Crane's *The Red Badge of Courage* (1951), was an artistic success but a commercial failure. This mixed reception was in part due to the timing of producing this antiwar fable at the height of the cold war and during the Korean conflict. There was also major opposition to the film at MGM, where Louis B. Mayer battled with Huston's producer, Dore Schary, over the casting of unknowns (including Audie Murphy, America's most decorated soldier during World War II, here playing a man who runs away from battle). Sensing adverse public reaction, the studio insisted on cutting Huston's version of two hours and fifteen minutes down to sixty-five minutes; however, when these cuts were made Huston was not present to defend his work. He was in London making the financial arrangements for his second Horizon film, *The African Queen* (1952).

For the rest of the decade Huston made eight films in as many countries and established a home in Ireland at a time when many Americans in the film industry, often out of the HUAC's coercion, were plying their trade abroad. *The African Queen* was shot in the Congo under often appalling conditions. Huston and Spiegel entered into a joint venture with Romulus Films of London, founded by John Woolf and James Woolf. James Agee, a longtime Huston admirer, got to work on the first draft of the script. Peter Viertel wrote up the tribulations of the venture in his novel *White Hunter, Black Heart* and stated that Huston's prime motive in shooting the film was to kill an elephant. The movie that emerged from these turbulent months immediately became a fixture in the American canon. The public embraced the love story of the riverboat captain and the missionary as interpreted by Humphrey Bogart and Katharine Hepburn. The actress wrote her own version of the events in which her professional horror at the director's seeming flippancy grew to admiration for his unflappable calm.[4]

This project brought to an end Huston's partnership with Sam Spiegel, who had simply not been paying his bills and who had failed to send regular checks to Ricki (who was pregnant again in Malibu during this period). Huston finally settled for just his salary for *African Queen,* sacrificing a percentage of the box office for his biggest commercial success so far. He took some consolation in Ricki's announcement of the birth of Anjelica Huston (July 9, 1951).

John Huston

Huston next announced he would film, for the Woolf brothers, Pierre La Mure's novelized life of the painter Henri de Toulouse-Lautrec, *Moulin Rouge* (1953). José Ferrer, long an admirer of both Walter and John, held the rights to the book and ended up playing the lead. What really sold Huston on the film, which was shot in Paris, was the challenge of reproducing on screen the colors Toulouse-Lautrec developed for his paintings and posters. For this feat he hired an English cameraman, Oswald (Ossie) Morris, who remained his favorite cinematographer for more than twenty years. Another relationship was established during the filming: that between Huston and the French actress Suzanne Flon, who played Myriamme Hayen. They remained close friends for many years. The film mostly received plaudits for its color but also proved a popular success. While Huston received an Oscar nomination for direction, the film won Oscars for Art Direction and Costume Design.

On a visit to Ireland in 1952 John and Ricki discovered a crumbling mansion on an estate called St. Clerans in Galway. Profits from *Moulin Rouge* allowed him to purchase the place at auction for ten thousand dollars. He spent the next decade restoring what were in fact two houses and creating a proper setting for his burgeoning art collection from travels abroad. It was really St. Clerans that kept John and Ricki together through the sixties. For Huston it represented a return to his roots, a retreat between movie projects, a place where his children could grow up and where he could ride horses, and a backdrop for the image he wanted to present of himself as master of the hunt and lord of the manor. He became an Irish citizen in 1964.

From Ireland came the idea for his next movie, *Beat the Devil* (1954). This comedy-thriller was written by a neighbor, James Helvick (nom-de-plume for Claud Cockburn). This tale of larcenous misfits trying to corner uranium deposits in central Africa had echoes of *The Maltese Falcon* and persuaded Humphrey Bogart to play the lead and acquire the property for his own independent production company. Huston also signed up Peter Lorre and Robert Morley, taking over for Sidney Greenstreet. Gina Lollobrigida and Jennifer Jones played the two female roles. Ossie Morris shot the picture in black and white in Ravello, Italy. Huston brought in Truman Capote to improve on two earlier drafts of the script, and his cooperation unearthed the situation's hidden comedy. *Beat the Devil* was ahead of its time and came into its own in the sixties when the tongue-in-cheek approach of the James Bond movies and Joseph Losey's *Modesty Blaise* (1965) became fashionable.

Huston returned to Ireland to shoot *Moby Dick* (1956), the most ambitious movie of his career. Since his earliest days as a director Huston had dreamed of adapting Herman Melville's novel for the screen. He had always imagined his father as Ahab, but had to settle for Gregory Peck. Financing came from the Mirisch brothers, who had successfully invested in *Moulin Rouge,* and Warner Brothers was responsible for distribution. Ray Bradbury, who had approached Huston, was invited to write the screenplay. His initial adulation for the director turned to fear and loathing after a lengthy stay at St. Clerans, but between them they produced an elegant reduced version of the novel. The film was shot off the coasts of Ireland and Wales and in the Atlantic in some of the worst winter weather of the century. On more than one occasion the *Pequod* almost capsized, and the film crew lost their expensive mechanical whales, designed by Stephen Grimes, a young Englishman entering the Huston circle for the first time. He would continue to work for Huston on and off for the rest of his career until *The Dead* (1987). On camera Ossie Morris devised an appropriately desaturated color. A strong cast included Orson Welles as Father Mapple, Leo Genn as Starbuck, Harry Andrews as Stubb, and Richard Basehart as Ishmael. Production difficulties drove up the cost from the original three million dollars to four million dollars, and the Mirisch brothers saw their *Moulin Rouge* profits swallowed up in the Atlantic waters.

While a central film in the Huston canon, *Moby Dick* remains to this day more a critical than a popular success. Making this film sapped Huston's creative energy, a fact reflected in the quality of his work for the rest of the decade. Initially certain projects—for example, the idea of filming Melville's *Typee* in Tahiti—fell through. Another shelved project was the film version of Rudyard Kipling's *The Man Who Would Be King,* which would finally be made twenty years later. Huston postponed the project in 1957, after Humphrey Bogart, one of Huston's two protagonists, died that January. Huston's agent, Paul Kohner, managed to arrange for him a three-film deal with Universal, thanks to the approval of Buddy Adler, a friend from the war days and then the studio's head of production. The films were *Heaven Knows, Mr. Allison* (1957), *The Barbarian and the Geisha* (1958), and *The Roots of Heaven* (1958). They were made successively in Tobago, Japan, and the French Cameroons. *Heaven Knows, Mr. Allison* seemed like a genuine vacation after the trials of *Moby Dick.* A return to the format of *The African Queen,* it starred Deborah Kerr and Robert Mitchum as a nun and a marine thrown together on a Pacific island during World War II. The tone was light, and love received more emphasis than battle. Mitchum and Huston became close friends, and to an extent the actor filled some of the void left by Bogart's death.

In the case of *The Barbarian and the Geisha,* however, there was little compatibility between the director and the star, John Wayne. This movie is the story of Townsend Harris, America's first ambassador to Japan in the nineteenth century. Buried in the scenario is the serious theme of the clash between cultures and the steps to be taken to reconcile them. The role as conceived by Huston was too subtle for Wayne, who disapproved of his director's refusal to give his actors precise direction and of Huston's affair with his leading lady, Eiko Ando (the geisha of the title). History repeated itself when Huston left for Paris as soon as the shooting was over. In Hollywood, meanwhile, Wayne threatened to tear up his contract with Universal unless several scenes were reshot in order to enhance his role. The result was a film that Huston would have preferred to disown.

It is odd to see Huston the hunter making a film protesting the slaughter of African elephants, but that is the theme of his last Universal project, *The Roots of Heaven,* based on Romain Gary's novel. The crew lost sight of the seriousness of the thesis while enduring the appalling conditions under which the film was made; it was shot in French West Africa, where daytime temperatures climbed to 135 degrees in a land virtually without shade. The cast included Trevor Howard as the idealistic Morel and Errol Flynn (in what was to be his last movie) as the hard-drinking Forsythe. Eddie Albert and Juliette Greco (signed up at the insistence of the producer, Darryl Zanuck) played supporting roles. There was even some work for Orson Welles. Ossie Morris and Stephen Grimes were cinematographer and art director, respectively. One person with positive memories of the experience was Huston's longtime production assistant, Angela Allen, who had ambitions as a director and was given a chance to shoot some second unit work.

Next Huston was offered a chance to shoot a western in Mexico (*The Unforgiven,* 1960) for a new independent company, Hecht-Hill-Lancaster (Harold Hecht, James Hill, and Burt Lancaster). Lancaster himself was to head a cast including Audie Murphy, Lillian Gish, and, inexplicably, Audrey Hepburn as the part-Indian daughter. On the production side, Huston had two members of his regular team: Angela Allen as production assistant and Stephen Grimes as cinematographer. Tom Shaw joined the crew as assistant director, marking the beginning of a professional association that was to last the rest of Huston's life. What might have made an interesting western on the theme of race relations was flawed from the beginning because of Huston's complete disengagement from the project and of his competing preoccupations. He accepted the assignment because he wanted to work in Mexico. Here his rather disreputable friend, the ex-jockey Billy Pearson, was on the scent of some very tempting pre-Columbian artifacts from an archaeological site. Huston's adopted son, Pablo (who had now settled back in Mexico with his Irish wife), was supposed to help spirit the loot away from the site to a private airstrip and then out of the country. This heist was eventually pulled off, but put the parties involved in danger. Pablo found himself one step ahead of the police and a rival gang of smugglers. The only fruits of *The Unforgiven* were the life-size pre-Columbian statues that found a new home in St. Clerans.[5]

In 1958 Huston had received a short story written by Arthur Miller. Miller had written the story in Nevada while waiting for a divorce from his first wife and had since turned it into a screenplay, adding the role of a divorcee with his then-current wife, Marilyn Monroe, in mind. His story served as the basis of *The Misfits* (1961). Miller saw Nevada as a state populated by people at a loss, suspended between relationships, afraid of future commitments, and tempted by the manly lifestyle of the West that was often a cover for fear and failure. Huston saw the film as a chance to return and work in the United States and to respond to his critics who saw his recent work—most notoriously *The Unforgiven*—as proof of a career in terminal decline. He also decided to buck commercial wisdom and shoot the film in black and white. *The Misfits,* however, generated far more interest for the private crises of its stars than for the quality of the screenplay's content. In what turned out to be her last film, Marilyn Monroe was on the verge of divorce from Arthur Miller and was dependent on tranquilizers and her drama coach, Paula Strasberg. Montgomery Clift was very highly strung and recovering from a serious car accident. The project was also the last for Clark Gable, who had health problems and clearly suffered from the physical toll of the mustang roping sequences at the end of the film. Huston himself paid more attention to this film than to any since *Moby Dick,* for he, too, had serious worries. The bills for St. Clerans had come in, amounting to one million dollars; the film went over budget to four million dollars; and on a visit to Nevada Ricki told him that she and the children were moving to London. Life seemed to be imitating art. By chance Huston also found himself pre-

12

siding over the end of an era in American cinema. He had ushered in Marilyn Monroe's career, and after *The Misfits* she bowed out. Then Gable had a heart attack right after the shooting was over and died ten days later. Huston did, however, see a new era dawn in American politics that November with the election of President John Kennedy.

Buoyed by encouraging reviews for *The Misfits,* Huston turned to a study of Freud for his next film, which would be produced for Universal by his old associate Wolfgang Reinhardt. Huston had always been interested in the study of the mind, and interest now sharpened by the character studies of *The Misfits* and his observations of his stars' behavior. Before finishing his last film, he had offered the role of Freud to Montgomery Clift and had invited Jean-Paul Sartre to St. Clerans as early as October 1959 to work on a script. Sartre received twenty-five thousand dollars for that script, which was several hundred pages long and would have resulted in a seven-hour film. Eventually Huston and Reinhardt boiled it down to a manageable two hours and fifteen minutes.

Meanwhile, Huston's private life had taken a turn. In Paris, in the spring of 1961, an aspiring Anglo-Indian actress named Zoe Ismail visited Huston to ask for a part in *Freud* (1962). Huston and she became lovers, and before shooting began in Germany in the fall of 1961, Zoe was pregnant. He only informed Ricki shortly before the baby was due.

Casting Clift as Freud was a serious mistake. Although a committed actor, he was seriously ill as a result of drug and alcohol abuse and was weighed down by a guilt complex over his homosexuality. He should have been a patient of rather than the interpreter of the master of psychoanalysis. Huston was well aware of Clift's problems but did not change his plans. Instead, his homophobic impatience with his star exploded on the set in the form of calculated acts of vindictiveness. (There is very little indication of this behavior in his autobiography.)[6] The set became a battleground over Huston's treatment of Clift, with the women—notably Susannah York, who played Cecily—generally siding with the actor.

Christmas 1961 at St. Clerans brought mixed feelings. While it provided welcome relief from the tensions of *Freud,* Huston had to reflect that this holiday might be the family's last Irish Christmas together. Also on his mind was the expected birth of Zoe's and his child. Meanwhile, Tony and Anjelica were anxiously preparing for a new life and new schools in London. Freud was completed in Vienna in February 1962, and Huston battled Universal for a strong publicity campaign to back the film. The studio was at first reluctant, but it eventually released the film under a new title: *Freud: The Secret Passion.* Huston himself spoke the narration linking the disparate episodes, thus effectively undermining Clift's role. The reviews were decidedly mixed, but Huston was satisfied that a coherent film had been salvaged from the wreckage.

In May 1962 Zoe (using the surname Sallis after John's middle name, Marcellus) gave birth to Danny in Rome, her new home. She resolved not to encroach on Ricki's territory in London, gave up ideas for an acting career, and resigned herself to occasional visits from John and summer holidays with Danny in Ireland. Ricki, in London and with John's financial support, remained solely responsible for the upbringing of Tony and Anjelica. In her new life she soon became

13

known as a stylish hostess. Regular visitors to her London home included the actors James Fox and Dirk Bogarde and the poet Stephen Spender and his family. Through Spender she and the children met W. H. Auden and Henry Moore.

In a turnabout, in December 1963, Ricki announced to John that she was pregnant. The father was John Julius Norwich, the son of British diplomat Duff Cooper and Lady Diana Cooper. Norwich was a professional historian, married, with connections with the royal family. Ricki hoped he would divorce his wife, marry her, and propel her into the British peerage, but John Julius had no such intentions. Ricki's daughter Allegra was born in August 1964, when Huston was at work on *The Bible*. He reacted with the anger of a betrayed husband to both the announcement of the pregnancy and Allegra's birth; however, he also assumed responsibility for Allegra, paying for her upbringing and schooling. It was Huston who pressured Norwich into paying for a share of Allegra's education when she went to Oxford in the 1980s.

Following the traumas of *Freud: The Secret Passion,* Huston's next project was more recreational. *The List of Adrian Messenger* (1963) was based on a mystery by Philip MacDonald. While some principal photography was shot at Universal Studios, Huston moved the action to Ireland for the film's hunting sequences. In part the movie's success depended on the gimmick of inviting such Hollywood celebrities as Robert Mitchum, Burt Lancaster, Tony Curtis, and Frank Sinatra to play cameos, heavily disguised, and encouraging the public to guess who was behind the mask. Kirk Douglas played the villain, donning a different disguise for almost each episode. Acting for Huston for the first time was George C. Scott as the aristocratic detective, Gethryn. Tony Huston was taken out of school to play the heir of the Bruttenholms.

In 1962 Huston began to act in other people's films, establishing a lucrative secondary career, but he stated he had no intention of emulating his father. That year he played a cigar-smoking prince of the church in Otto Preminger's *The Cardinal* and was nominated for Best Supporting Actor. In the years to come he would appear in *Candy* (1968), as Buck Loner in *Myra Breckinridge* (1970), in Richard Sarafian's *Man in the Wilderness* (1971), and *Battle for the Planet of the Apes* (1973). Probably his most memorable portrayal was that of Noah Cross in Roman Polanski's *Chinatown* (1974). He is also remembered as the patriarch in William Richert's *Winter Kills* (1979).

The theme of religion dominates in Huston's next two projects. First, Ray Stark of Seven Arts approached him with the idea of screening Tennessee Williams' *The Night of the Iguana* (1964). This tale of a defrocked Protestant priest trying to put his shattered life together appealed to Huston, as did the prospect of shooting the film in Mexico, where once again he could be in touch with Pablo and his family. The public's interest was piqued by the idea of a flock of Hollywood's brightest stars gathered in the same obscure Mexican port under Huston's pastoral care. Richard Burton (chaperoned by Elizabeth Taylor) played Lawrence Shannon. Huston persuaded Ava Gardner to play Maxine, and Deborah Kerr was the spiritual Hannah Jelkes. Playing Shannon's adolescent temptress, Sue Lyon found herself in a similar role to Lolita. Williams was on hand to suggest emendations to Anthony Veiller's script, and although there were disagreements over the ending (which Huston made more hopeful than the original), the director was grateful for the writer's ideas on particular scenes. *Iguana* was ultimately famous for putting the sleepy village of Puerto Vallarta on the map for tourists and developers. Fifteen years later Huston would buy a plot of land just down the coast, accessible only by boat; and here he would build his last home at a place called Las Caletas.

In 1964 Huston became an Irish citizen. It was almost inevitable after so many years of residency in Ireland; but President Kennedy's assassination in November 1963 deepened his disillusionment with the United States. Meanwhile, he continued to juggle ideas and proposals, beginning with *The Bible* (1966), to be produced by Dino De Laurentiis. The original proposal was grandiose: an invitation to some of the world's major directors, including Robert Bresson, Luchino Visconti, Federico Fellini, and Orson Welles, each to contribute an episode. By August 1964 that idea had been radically scaled down, with Huston as the single director. The action would include the Creation, the Flood, the destruction of the Tower of Babel and Sodom and Gomorrah, and the sacrifice of Isaac. Huston was not only drawn to the project for its size, but for the idea of the Bible as the world's greatest compendium of enduring myths. The film also appealed to the visual artist in him. For the Creation he sent photographer Ernst Haas around the world to capture the most striking natural phenomena. He asked sculptor Giacomo Manzu to create earth sculptures to evoke the emergence of man. Apart from the roles of Adam and Eve, an all-star cast was assembled: Richard Harris (Cain), Peter O'Toole (the Angelic Messenger), Ava Gardner (Sarah), George C. Scott (Abraham). To Zoe Sallis, who had hoped to play Sarah, Huston gave the role of Hagar, her handmaiden. Huston himself played Noah in perhaps the most impressive episode, the Flood, where, using his legendary touch with animals, he managed to steer the animal couples into the Ark with minimal fuss. While the critics were not universally enthusiastic over *The Bible,* Huston won praise for doing more than present an inflated spectacle and for his aesthetic taste as evidenced in the opening sequences.

Dino De Laurentiis actually proposed another epic to Huston: this time a twenty-million-dollar version of the battle of Waterloo, starring Peter O'Toole. Instead, for the first three months of 1966 Huston took a sabbatical from film to direct an opera at la Scala: *The Mines of Sulphur* by Richard Rodney Bennett. (He could not help thinking of his Aunt Margaret, who had had a distinguished operatic career and who would have been proud of her nephew's work.) Another diversion was provided by his old friend Charles Feldman, who was producing Ian Fleming's *Casino Royale* (1967). Several directors were involved, and Huston directed the first episode, a harmless send-up of the Bond saga, starring Deborah Kerr and David Niven and with Huston himself playing M.

In the second half of 1966 he turned to a much more audacious project (one suggested to him by producer Ray Stark two years earlier): the adaptation of Carson McCullers's novel, *Reflections in a Golden Eye.* The first treatment had been done by Francis Ford Coppola and the second by Christopher Isherwood. Not quite satisfied, Huston brought in a Scottish novelist, Chapman Mortimer, and then worked over the third version with Gladys Hill. The action takes place in an army camp just after World War II, and the theme is repressed homosexuality in the military; but in 1967 any ironical reference to the behavior of those thrust into close proximity in a

15

military environment evoked the then-current turmoil over Vietnam. Huston first approached Montgomery Clift for the role of Major Penderton, and amazingly, given the experience of *Freud: The Secret Passion,* Clift accepted. When Clift died of a heart attack in New York in July 1966, Huston then offered the part to Marlon Brando, who would have to play against type. After an initial hesitation Brando accepted. Elizabeth Taylor played the sexually provocative Mrs. Penderton, and Brian Keith her lover. Julie Harris completed the major quartet as Keith's neurotic wife. Warner Brothers, which put up much of the production money, insisted the film be shot in Italy, but Huston was still able to secure the services of Ossie Morris and Stephen Grimes. Morris once more devised a desaturated color to reflect the neuroses and claustrophobia of the characters. The studio, however, withdrew this version after only ten days of distribution, and few have ever seen it.

By the mid-1960s Huston had been diagnosed with emphysema, and although he had given up cigarettes, he still smoked five cigars a day. While making *Reflections,* he often had to rest to regain his breath, and more than once Stephen Grimes (who was also second unit director) took over for him.

Huston's next film was a picaresque romp called *Sinful Davey* (1969). Set in Scotland, but filmed largely in Ireland, it was based on the diary of David Haggart, a nineteenth-century deserter whose ambition was to outdo the roguish exploits of his father, who had ended up on the gallows. John Hurt as Davey and Robert Morley as the Duke of Argyll gave nice performances, and the film tried to cash in on the success of Tony Richardson's *Tom Jones* (1963). The producer, Walter Mirisch, had the film recut after some negative previews, from which, Huston felt, it never recovered.

Anjelica made her film debut in *A Walk with Love and Death* (1969), a dark romance set against the background of the Hundred Years War. Ricki objected to her daughter's absence from school, and Anjelica herself hesitated, for she had auditioned for the lead in Zeffirelli's *Romeo and Juliet* (1968). The story, adapted for the screen by Dale Wasserman from a novel by Hans Koningsberger, seems to turn its back on the turbulent events of the late sixties. A young producer from Twentieth Century-Fox, Carter De Haven, approached Huston with the idea, and both the tale and the contractual arrangements suited the director very well. As the years have passed, however, critics have come to see the film as a chance for Huston, as director and actor (he plays the part of Robert the Elder in the film), to establish a dialogue with the younger generation. Certainly the menacing undercurrents of his day are reflected in the images of peasant revolt in the screenplay. Chaotic conditions in France in 1968, for example, forced Huston to shoot the film in Austria and northern Italy. Anjelica's costar was Assaf Dayan, the son of Israeli general Moshe Dayan. The inexperience of the two principal actors showed, but as shooting progressed they settled more comfortably into their roles. British and American critics largely trashed the movie, but more recently French critics have tried to situate it in its era and point out that the film partly reflects the turbulence of the 1960s and the confusion of the young. The film did nothing to launch Anjelica Huston's film career, but this debut does anticipate her later stunning collaboration with her father in *Prizzi's Honor* (1985) and *The Dead* (1987).

A Walk with Love and Death ended with the young lovers awaiting death, and at the end of the decade death seemed to stalk John Huston as life again began to imitate art. John Steinbeck, a good friend and a visitor to St. Clerans, died before Christmas 1968. From Los Angeles came the grim news of the abduction and murder of the daughter of another close friend and former lover, Eloise (Cherokee) Hardt. She had known John since the Tarzana days, and she had been on hand for the shooting of some scenes for A *Walk with Love and Death* in Ireland. Worse was to come. In late January 1969 Ricki set out on a European road trip with Brian Anderson Thomas, a Jamaican musician she had recently met. On January 29, just north of Dijon, with Anderson at the wheel, their car skidded across the road into the path of a northbound van. Ricki died instantly.

John received the news in Rome, where he was working on *The Kremlin Letter* (1970). Forbidden to fly by his doctors, he went to London by train to be with the children, who had been radically shaken by their mother's death. All of Ricki's close friends felt that her passing had left a hole in their lives, and all remember exactly where they were when they heard the news. Dirk Bogarde and Joan Buck (Jules Buck's daughter and Anjelica's close friend) both later stated that for them life after January 1969 would never quite be the same.[7]

As often happens in a crisis, work provided a palliative. Huston resumed work on the spy-thriller *The Kremlin Letter* (1970). This cynical tale of double-dealing and espionage was based on a novel by Noel Behn and written jointly by Huston and Gladys Hill. Carter De Haven produced the film for Twentieth Century-Fox. Huston saw this film as a chance for a commercial success after two financial flops. It also offered, to an extent, an indictment of the cynicism born of the cold war that atrophied all shades of moral conscience. Filming began in mid-winter in Helsinki (standing in for Moscow) and later moved to the milder climate of Rome. Fox spent a large amount of money on locations and on the international cast of such veterans as Bibi Andersson, Max von Sydow, George Sanders, Richard Boone, Patrick O'Neal, and Orson Welles. But finally neither sets nor stars could overcome the bizarre complications of the plot. The film was not the success Huston had hoped for. Thus, he finished the sixties with his career in a trough and with enough warnings of declining health to induce thoughts of retirement.

Given the financial responsibilities to his family—Allegra's upbringing, Danny's education, Tony's lack of a career—and his own compulsion to work, retirement was out of the question. Thus, he accepted an offer to direct an inferior male adventure film in Spain, *The Last Run* (1971), to be produced for MGM by the thirty-two-year-old Robert Littman and to star George C. Scott. Given the problems that Scott had caused Huston during the making of *The Bible,* it is odd that the latter would have accepted the assignment. Even with Gladys Hill on the script, Sven Nykvist on camera, and the ubiquitous Stephen Grimes as art director, Huston immediately clashed with Scott on the shape of the film and left the production, sacrificing his salary. At this point he really did consider ending his career, but after a brief vacation in Morocco he returned to Spain and received an offer from the young Richard Sarafian, who was directing *Man in the Wilderness* (1971) for Warner Brothers. He was invited to play the sadistic explorer Captain Henry, an

Ahab-like character he had really been playing all his life. Richard Harris was his costar, and the experience offered him a necessary interlude to review his career as well as his priorities and to prepare for what would be his most creative decade since the 1940s.

Eleven years after *The Misfits,* Huston returned to Stockton, California, to make *Fat City* (1972) from a novel by Leonard Gardner (who also wrote the script) about a boxer past his prime. This film was to be among the most personal movies Huston ever made, taking him back to his adolescent passion and the start of his writing career. After acting in *Man in the Wilderness* (1971) in Spain, Huston also found his principal actors there: Stacy Keach, just on the verge of stardom, to play Billy Tully, and Jeff Bridges, whom John had recently seen in *The Last Picture Show* (1971), as Ernie Munger. With veteran cinematographer Conrad Hall, Huston contrived a grainy, shabby look to reflect the diminished lives of his characters. All involved with the film had the feeling that they were working on a minor classic, whatever its fate at the box office. The beating the characters, and actors, took in the ring reflected the director's parlous state of health during the production. Huston frequently had to use an oxygen machine, by now a part of his life, and on the screen and the set people were pushing their bodies to the limit. *Fat City* premiered at the Museum of Modern Art in New York in July 1972. It went on to the Edinburgh International Film Festival, where Huston was feted as a reborn grand master. In Europe and the United States, critics marveled at the artist's return to the arena after a series of drubbings, yet still in full command of his creative faculties.

Between *Fat City* and *The Life and Times of Judge Roy Bean* (also 1972), Cherokee Hardt introduced Huston to his fifth wife, Celeste (Cici) Shane, who was thirty years his junior. Cici had a handicapped son, Colin, from a previous marriage, and a house in Pacific Palisades. While all who witnessed the union declared it a mismatch from the start, doubtless advancing age, ill health, the dispersal of his family, and the obvious attractions of a younger woman turned Huston's thoughts toward marriage. What he eventually got out of it, however, was Cici's maid and confidante (and Colin's nanny), a young Mexican woman called Maricela Hernandez, who became his companion. Because of Cici he eventually sold St. Clerans. She spent the summer of 1972 in Ireland and was forced to share John with Zoe Sallis (on vacation with Danny), Betty O'Keefe (a mainstay on the estate since John purchased it who was nominally in charge of the horses), and Gladys Hill (who that summer was working on preproduction of *The Mackintosh Man*). Zoe's presence in particular provoked Cici's ultimatum: John had to choose between Cici or St. Clerans. For the rest of his life he regretted selling the great house, which denied him the retreat he had come to count on and his children the birthright they had come to expect. The decision to sell may have been inevitable, but it neither brought happiness nor saved his marriage.

John Milius, who wrote the script for *The Life and Times of Judge Roy Bean,* had already written two scripts for Clint Eastwood: *Dirty Harry* (1971) and *Jeremiah Johnson* (1972). He saw this tale of the ex-bandit who established the Texas town of Langtry and set himself up as the representative of law and order as a sardonic fable of frontier (and maybe American) justice. Huston possessed his own vein of satire, but drawing on the tall tales of his own roistering grandfather

John Gore, he turned the film more toward caricature. Paul Newman, delighted to be working with Huston, brought to the role of the judge some of the humor he injected into *Butch Cassidy and the Sundance Kid* (1969). Victoria Principal played his common-law Mexican wife, and Ava Gardner was invited to walk on at the end of the film as Lily Langtry. Huston also found roles for his pal Billy Pearson and Stacy Keach (who simply had a hole blown through his midriff). Cici was in Arizona for most of the production, and her presence undoubtedly reduced her husband's concentration on the film. While *Judge Roy Bean* is a lesser achievement, its portrayal of a brutal male society and its sardonic humor are reminders of Huston's more authentic work.

Paul Newman so enjoyed working for Huston that he immediately agreed to star in a second movie under his direction—*The Mackintosh Man* (1973), made for Warner Brothers and produced by Carl Foreman. The novel was written by Desmond Bagley and adapted by Walter Hill (later a director of action movies). At the time Hill was an apprentice screenwriter who dashed off *The Mackintosh Man* in order to get out of a contract with Warner. He was amazed that anyone, let alone those of Newman's and Huston's stature, would option the work. He nevertheless found himself in the summer at St. Clerans, before Huston sold it, discussing the film, but mostly art and life. Huston had insisted that as much as possible of the film be shot in Ireland close to his home, and indeed the Irish sequences are beautifully evoked. Much credit here goes to Ossie Morris, working on his first Huston film since *Reflections in a Golden Eye,* and he was distressed not only by his friend's deteriorating health, but also by his level of detachment from the film. Apart from Newman's workmanlike performance, there is a nice oily performance by James Mason as a double-dealing, titled English member of Parliament.

In the mid-1970s Huston finally got the chance to direct the film he had been thinking about for at least twenty years: *The Man Who Would Be King* (1975). He had imagined his father in one of the leading roles, then Bogart and Cooper, then Gable and Mitchum. In the sixties he thought of Burton and O'Toole. In the end he was fortunate to find Michael Caine for Peachy Carnehan and Sean Connery for Daniel Dravot. John Foreman revived his interest in the project, but there ensued a two-year wait until the stars were free and the money had been raised. During the interim, as an actor, Huston gave a memorable performance as Noah Cross in Roman Polanski's *Chinatown* (1974), with Jack Nicholson.

Eventually, approaching his seventies, he made the film that synthesized all the elements of the Huston universe, taking himself and his audience back to the movies that had made his reputation. The code of camaraderie that kept the characters Daniel and Peachy together on their quest was in evidence in the making of the film, with Huston surrounding himself with his most trusted collaborators. Gladys Hill was coauthor of the excellent script. Ossie Morris was on hand to shoot his last film for Huston. Angela Allen returned as script supervisor. Stephen Grimes selected locations in Morocco and (although uncredited) actually wrote certain scenes for the script. The family was also represented by Tony Huston, who contributed some of the music, while the whole score is credited to Maurice Jarre. Production was complicated in part by Huston's continuing health problems, by the irregular flow of money from the investors, and by Cici's sudden appearance during the shooting.

She interfered and vetoed the casting of Zoe, who had been promised the role of Roxanne, Daniel Dravot's virgin queen. Eventually Shakira Caine (Michael Caine's wife) took the nonspeaking role. Caine himself, despite work-related tensions and sickness, remembers the period as exciting and adventurous, and he and Connery recall Huston with great respect. Here was a film executed as it had been conceived. Although a little old-fashioned for a post-sixties audience, the critics admired it and recognized in its style the signature of the best Huston films, such as *The Treasure of the Sierra Madre* and *The African Queen.*

Huston and Cici were divorced in August 1977. By this time he was living with Maricela Hernandez, who would remain with him for the rest of his life as a spouse, companion, and nurse. With his still demanding schedule and worsening health, Huston needed a helpmate with him at all times. The fiercely loyal Maricela defended him from the importunate. The couple decided to move to Mexico, which seemed a logical choice, for two reasons: they would still be close to Los Angeles, where agent Paul Kohner still took care of Huston's business interests; and living on the other side of the border also relieved them of the U.S. tax burden. In 1976 they moved to Puerto Vallarta. Mexico had been part of Huston's life for half of a century. He had plundered its archaeological sites, had served in its cavalry, and had made three movies—two among his best—in the country. Puerto Vallarta, however, was no longer a sleepy little backwater. Across the bay he discovered a clearing in the jungle right on the coast, accessible only by boat. Here he built his last home, which he called Las Caletas. He swapped the seigneurial opulence of St. Clerans for simplicity and isolation, adopting the role of swami in a Mexican ashram. Those who needed to see him had to brave the sea and put up with often primitive conditions on arrival, but many continued to come.

Huston remained busy. As part of the U.S. bicentennial celebrations he made a short film, *Independence* (1976), for the National Park Service. He also appeared in William Richert's *Winter Kills,* released in 1979. He began the screenplay, along with Gladys Hill, for a film version of Hemingway's *Across the River and into the Trees* with Richard Burton in mind, but Burton's death led to the project's cancellation. In 1977 a young southerner named Michael Fitzgerald and his wife, Kathy, approached Huston to film Flannery O'Connor's novella *Wise Blood,* for which Fitzgerald's brother, Benedict, had written the screenplay. Although Huston was intrigued, he advised Fitzgerald that the film would probably never be made. That question became instantly moot as health problems intervened. In Cedars-Sinai Hospital in the fall of 1977 he underwent three operations for the removal of an aneurysm, normally a relatively routine procedure, but complicated in Huston's case because of what one surgeon called "mammoth emphysema." He had come perilously close to death, but was given a lease on life.

Back in Puerto Vallarta, he began work on his autobiography, *An Open Book.* He had recovered sufficiently the following year to attend Tony's wedding to Lady Margot Cholmondeley in Norfolk, England. Tony had married into the higher ranks of the British aristocracy. His father-in-law was a member of the Queen's household, and the young couple went to live in Houghton Hall in Norfolk, a present from the bride's grandmother.

Michael Fitzgerald, meanwhile, had managed to raise the minimum amount required to finance *Wise Blood* (1979), but it clearly had to be made on a shoestring. No major stars could be hired and Huston would have to accept a minimum salary of $125,000. Impressed by Fitzgerald's tenacity, as well as by the story, Huston accepted and journeyed to Macon, Georgia, into the territory of apocalyptic southern religion. The hero, Hazel Motes, the hot-eyed fanatic who tries to found the Church without Christ, was played by Brad Dourif, one of the inmates in *One Flew Over the Cuckoo's Nest* (1975). Harry Dean Stanton played the "blind" preacher Asa Hawks, and Amy Wright, his daughter Sabbath Lily. Ned Beatty gave a bravura performance as Hoover Shoates, a con-man evangelist. Tony Huston also worked on *Wise Blood* as second assistant director. This story of a blasphemous cult and a forlorn quest drew Huston to it as surely as *Moby Dick*. Critics have spotted in Hazel Motes a provincial Ahab trying to beat the devil while driven by his own personal demons. Once again Huston had produced a small masterpiece by going to small-town America, by exploring its marginal and eccentric characters, and by discovering a tenacious energy among the misfits. At the 1980 Cannes Film Festival the film earned a rapturous reception.

Wise Blood was followed by two forgettable flops: *Phobia,* shot in Toronto in the last months of 1979, and *Victory,* made in Budapest in 1980. The first was intended as a psychological thriller and was never released commercially. The second was a wartime escape movie with some big stars (Michael Caine, Max von Sydow, Sylvester Stallone), but it is only remembered for the spectacular goal the legendary Brazilian star, Pelé, scored in the climactic soccer match.

Such films were not mentioned when Huston was feted for his contributions to cinema at a gala tribute dinner, which he attended with Gladys Hill, at the Lincoln Center, New York, in May 1980. Beyond the standard praise and familiar anecdotes, the speeches allowed for some serious reflections on what had been, after all, a remarkable and extraordinarily fertile career. The *New Yorker*'s Brendan Gill wrote a lengthy appreciative essay in the form of a playbill for the event. Rather more interestingly, Andrew Sarris in *The Village Voice* wrote an article in which he completely revised his earlier critical dismissals of Huston's achievements.[8]

Although these tributes are usually paid to a director at the end of his career, Huston was still hard at work. He set aside time to be interviewed by Bill Moyers for the PBS series *Creativity.* He accepted Ray Stark's invitation to direct his first musical, *Annie* (1982), for Columbia that, at forty million dollars, was by far the most expensive movie he had ever directed. They hoped to capitalize on the success of the 1976 Broadway show, and Ray Stark even toyed with the idea of Huston playing Daddy Warbucks. Health problems, however, ruled that out.

Tragedy interrupted the preparations for *Annie* when Gladys Hill suddenly died in New York in April 1981. She had worked with Huston for twenty years, after having previously worked with Sam Spiegel. She had taken charge of John's personal and professional life as no one else could, and she had been closer to him than many of his wives. An indispensable professional colleague, she had helped him to vet almost all the scripts he received (she cowrote the script for *The Man Who Would Be King*). Her death was as harsh for Huston as it was sudden. Work on

Annie, however, had to go on. Albert Finney was signed to play Daddy Warbucks, modeling certain gestures and mannerisms on his director. His performance was closely monitored by a young German producer, Wieland Schulz-Keil, who had come to speak to Huston about shooting Malcolm Lowry's cult novel *Under the Volcano,* which is set in Mexico and based on the last day of the life of a despairing British consul. For Schulz-Keil, Finney was born to take that role. Thus, it was within the parenthetical, and largely unsuccessful, *Annie* that a far more serious and inviting idea was hatched, a recurrent pattern in the career of a director who never stopped working. After New York Huston returned to Las Caletas to prepare for *Under the Volcano* (1984).

Turning Lowry's meandering narrative into a concise and coherent two-hour screenplay presented major problems. Many had made the effort over the years and failed (including, apparently, Gabriel Garcia Marquez). Huston liked the approach of an untried screenwriter from New York, Guy Gallo, who eliminated several minor characters, combined two lovers of the consul's wife into one (the half-brother Hugh, played by Anthony Andrews), and compressed the action into a final twenty-four hours. The consul is a heightened version of previous Huston characters. He has some of the compulsions of Dobbs, the madness of Ahab, the demons of Shannon. Albert Finney invests the role with a Faustian pain, making it clear from the start that this character is not just another screen drunk. The film was shot in Mexico with Gabriel Figueroa, once Luis Buñuel's cameraman, and Gunther Gerzso as art director. Tom Shaw was once again production assistant. Danny, who had graduated from the International Film School in London, produced the film's title shot. Again, working outside the studio system in awkward conditions, while battling ill health, Huston astounded the critics by producing such a complex work at age seventy-eight. At Cannes in 1985 he received yet another standing ovation, along with enthusiastic reviews in the French press. In the United States the reaction was more tepid. Critics were divided between those who admired the ambition of the film and those who saw it as a fashionable exercise in despair.

That darker side of Huston's vision had been noted in March 1983 in Los Angeles when the American Film Institute gave Huston a Lifetime Achievement Award. In an evening of glitter and laughter and some sycophantic reminiscing, anyone who had had anything to do with him during the past forty years turned out to pay tribute to him. In his remarks to the guests Orson Welles referred to Huston as "part Renaissance prince, part gentleman cardsharp" and as "Mephistopheles to his own Faust."[9]

Prizzi's Honor (1985), based on Richard Condon's novel, was first brought to Huston by his daughter Anjelica, who hoped for major roles for herself and Jack Nicholson. Huston passed on the suggestion to his producer, Carl Foreman, and turned to Janet Roach to write the script. (She had been Bill Moyers's assistant on "Creativity," had seen Huston at work on *Annie,* and had visited Las Caletas.) *Prizzi's Honor* was a family affair in that it was about a Mafia family and involved Huston's own clan. In his last two films he gathered about him his children and some of his closest associates as if offering them a legacy and bidding them farewell. *Prizzi's Honor* is a send-up of *The Godfather* (1972) in which a loyal hit man (Nicholson) falls for a killer (Kathleen Turner) from outside the clan and then must kill her to preserve the family honor. In the seventeen years since *A Walk with Love and Death* Anjelica had matured as an actress. Her portrayal of Maerose is something of an allegory of her own Hollywood career. Her character's gradual emergence as an independent force mirrors her own slow emergence from her father's shadow. Her triumph was also his, however, when she received an Oscar for Best Supporting Actress. Although it had taken Foreman some time to strike a deal with ABC, the result was a major box-office hit, with critics again admiring Huston's resilience and seemingly inexhaustible energy and wit.

John Huston spent his last Christmas (1986) at Las Caletas surrounded by his family, with the exception of Anjelica. In August that year he had been rushed to Cedars-Sinai Hospital in Los Angeles suffering from pneumonia, and on his release from the hospital, the doctors had told him not to travel beyond their reach. Huston had defied their orders, gone home, and resumed work on a series of projects. He did abandon a film to have been called *Haunted Summer,* the account of the period Lord Byron and Percy Bysshe Shelley spent in Byron's villa on Lake Geneva, when Mary Shelley had conceived *Frankenstein.* Meanwhile, Wieland Schulz-Keil, the producer of *Under the Volcano,* had purchased the film rights to James Joyce's *The Dead* from the Joyce estate, and that project seemed feasible. By October 1986 Schulz-Keil had raised $3.5 million for the project. Tony, eager to prove himself and work creatively with his father, began writing the script and by late fall had produced a workable first draft from difficult material. Huston had wanted to film in Dublin, but even he recognized that that was out of the question. In the end Joyce's snowy Dublin and cozy interiors were reproduced in a converted warehouse in Valencia, California.

Thus, for his final film Huston returned to his roots (he had been devoted to Joyce since receiving a copy of *Ulysses* from his mother shortly before his first marriage) and gathered his family around him. Anjelica played the wife, Gretta, speaking in the accent of her childhood. Danny, who was planning a film of his own, regularly visited the set. Much of Huston's creative family was also assembled. Tommy Shaw was his faithful production assistant. Roberto Silvi, who had edited *Wise Blood, Victory,* and *Under the Volcano,* was his editor. Dorothy Jeakins, whose association with Huston went back to *The Unforgiven* (1960), designed the costumes. Stephen Grimes, working on his fourteenth Huston film, was the art director. Major roles were played by Abbey Theatre veterans Cathleen Delany, Helena Carroll, Donal McCann, and Donal Donnelly, flown in from Dublin. All these elements and talents made *The Dead* a remarkable sign-off to a complete career. Huston completely dissipated any fears for his frailty on the set with his careful concentration on the script, his authoritative suggestions to actors and technicians, and his attention to detail. He remained to the end quietly in command. *The Dead* in more than one sense was a masterful performance. Two more details can be added: The film earned an Oscar nomination for Tony Huston and was dedicated to Maricela.

Although exhausted from making *The Dead,* in the spring of 1987 Huston worked with Tony on a script for a film called *Revenge,* which would eventually be made with Anthony Quinn and Kevin Costner, and he began discussions with Robert De Niro about the actor starring in a film version of Melville's *Benito Cereno.*

Huston had also promised to take part in Danny Huston's first film, *Mr. North* (1988), to be shot in Newport, Rhode Island, and Heritage Entertainment had backed the film on the condition of his participation. He now had the satisfaction of having helped all of his children in their careers. John also took the precaution of asking Robert Mitchum to step in for him should he fall ill. It was a prudent move, for he was obliged to enter the Charlton Memorial Hospital in Fall River, Massachusetts, on July 28, 1987. Old friends like Robert Mitchum and Marietta Tree visited him, and he received a telegram from President and Mrs. Ronald Reagan.

Huston celebrated his eighty-first birthday on August 5 with his family around his bedside. He recovered enough to be moved to a rented house overlooking the harbor and to send messages to old friends like Lillian Ross. Among those present during his last days were Zoe, who was in the States to be with Danny; Maricela, who looked after him around the clock; and Janet Roach, who was writing the script for *Mr. North* and needed his advice. On August 27 he began to fade, and he died quietly that night, with Maricela alone at his bedside. She waited hours until dawn to call the family and Tom Shaw, who always knew what to do.

Huston's body was flown to Los Angeles on August 28, and the family funeral was held three days later. Huston wished to be cremated and had instructed that his ashes were to be placed in his mother's grave and beside his grandmother's grave at Hollywood Memorial Park. Hollywood paid its tribute on September 12 at a memorial service arranged by the Directors Guild and presided over by Jack Nicholson and Richard Brooks. Dozens of old friends and associates who had known and worked with Huston since the days of *The Maltese Falcon* attended. Among those offering eulogies were Lauren Bacall; Gottfried Reinhardt; Huston's longtime agent, Paul Kohner; Robert Mitchum; and Jack Nicholson. They showed clips from his major movies and finally played a recording of Walter Huston singing *September Song*. John's choice to be buried with his mother rather than his father was a tribute to all that he owed her and to the things left unsaid between them. He had, like Tennyson's Ulysses, lived life to the lees, and the ashes in the ground would not soon erase the legacy he had left on the screen.

NOTES

1. James Agee's "Undirectable Director" first appeared in *Life* magazine, September 18, 1950. It was reprinted in *Agee on Film* (New York: McDowell, Obolensky, 1958). Also in Gaylyn Studlar and David Desser, eds., *Reflections in a Male Eye* (Washington, D.C.: Smithsonian Institution Press, 1993), 255.

2. For a revealing comment by Rhea Gore Huston on her father, see the paragraph from an unpublished memoir found after her death and quoted by Lawrence Grobel in *The Hustons* (New York: Scribners, 1989), 47.

3. Agee, *Agee on Film,* 321, and John Huston, *An Open Book* (New York: Scribners, 1980), 20.

4. Katharine Hepburn, *The Making of* The African Queen: *Or How I Went to Africa with Bogart, Bacall and Huston and Almost Lost My Mind* (New York: New American Library, 1987).

5.   For more details on Huston's search for art treasures while making *The Unforgiven* and on the misadventures of Pablo Huston and Billy Pearson, read Grobel, *The Hustons*, 458ff.

6.   The relevant pages in Huston's autobiography, *An Open Book*, on the making of *Freud: The Secret Passion* are pages 299–303. See also Grobel, *The Hustons*, 509–17.

7.   Grobel, *The Hustons*, 614.

8.   See Andrew Sarris's "John Huston" in *The American Cinema* (New York: Dutton, 1968). In this book Sarris places Huston among those directors who are "Less Than Meets the Eye." Reprinted in Stephen Cooper, ed., *Perspectives on John Huston* (New York: G. K. Hall, 1994). Also in Studlar and Desser, *Reflections in a Male Eye*, 269. Studlar and Desser's volume also includes Sarris's *Village Voice* article, "Johnny, We Finally Knew Ye" (May 19, 1980), 273.

9.   Grobel, *The Hustons*, 736.

II
Critical Survey of Oeuvre

LITERARY SOURCES

John Huston, virtually self-taught and with little formal schooling, is an anomaly in Hollywood as the most literary of American directors. Every film he made (with the exception of the wartime documentaries) is based on literature. He included more popular genres, such as war stories, adventure fiction, westerns, and detective novels (the basis of such films as *Heaven Knows, Mr. Allison; The Unforgiven; The Mackintosh Man;* and *The Asphalt Jungle*). He frequently turned to the more distinguished examples of a popular genre that occupies that elusive territory between pulp fiction and literature (for example, Dashiell Hammett's *The Maltese Falcon,* B. Traven's *The Treasure of the Sierra Madre,* Leonard Gardner's *Fat City*). And Huston did not shy away from classic fiction—thus risking the inevitable clamor from a critical chorus extolling the superiority of the book to the film—making *Moby Dick, Under the Volcano* (a cult classic, agreed), and *The Dead.* These last three examples are strictly "unfilmable" stories for which Huston and his screenwriters found a suitable structure and a form. In choosing from among the best of modern American fiction, he on occasion turned to elusive writers outside the mainstream: Carson McCullers (*Reflections in a Golden Eye*) and Flannery O'Connor (*Wise Blood*). He also worked with two of America's leading playwrights on converting their original material for the screen: Arthur Miller with *The Misfits* and Tennessee Williams with *The Night of the Iguana.* The American author with whom Huston acknowledged the greatest affinity is Ernest Hemingway, yet ironically he never directed any of Hemingway's fiction. He came close when he wrote the excellent script for Robert Siodmak's *The Killers* from a Hemingway story. He also began work on *A Farewell to Arms* for David Selznick, but irreconcilable differences with the producer made that impossible. Much later in his career he was drafting a script for *Across the River and into the Trees* to feature Richard Burton, but he canceled the project upon Burton's death. Nonetheless, Hemingway's terse style and manly code suited his own, and the writer's ideal of grace under pressure was matched by the director's coolness in the most trying of circumstances during filmmaking. Thematically the Huston variation is laughter in the face of a debacle.

Huston's choice of eclectic material caused his reputation to sag while directors who have consciously constructed a worldview over a cycle of films have seen theirs rise. In the post–World War II world of film, to base one's work on books became unfashionable, and moving casually from genre to genre according to one's availability or the size of the offer was even less correct. Huston himself rather mocked the idea of imposing his viewpoint on someone else's material. Nevertheless, his literary choices over a lengthy career reveal a distinct taste and the appeal of certain narrative patterns. He was, for example, drawn to the structure of the quest that is initially for riches or glory, then turns sour, and proves to have been subconsciously animated by less tangible motives (*The Maltese Falcon, The Treasure of the Sierra Madre, Moby Dick, The Man Who Would Be King*). His heroes are misfits, unsuited to regular lives, or exiles in distant lands, frequently self-destructive (*Beat the Devil, The Misfits, Under the Volcano*). He told love stories but preferred the offbeat story of a mismatched couple in which the woman is almost one of the boys (*The African Queen, Heaven Knows, Mr. Allison*). In his later years the theme of death becomes more prevalent (*Under the Volcano, The Dead*).

GROUP ENDEAVORS

Above all, it is in the making of a John Huston movie that we find clues to the film's meaning. From his first film he began to gather a central core of actors and technicians on whom he would call in the years to come. While he could not possibly create his own company within the heart of the Hollywood system, that was what he attempted. Filmmaking (always a collective effort) involved a camaraderie with mostly like-minded men, united by the task at hand and by their isolation in often uncomfortable or dangerous places. Naturally a select group of women played fundamental roles in Huston's professional life: Angela Allen, his script supervisor; Dorothy Jeakins, a frequent costume designer; and Gladys Hill, his personal assistant and general factotum. Men, however, always formed his inner circle, and many—including cinematographer Ossie Morris, art director Stephen Grimes, assistant director Tom Shaw, and editors like Russell Lloyd and Roberto Silvi—worked with him steadily for a great number of years. He also preferred to work with certain actors, cast in the manly mold: until his death, primarily Humphrey Bogart; then Robert Mitchum, Clark Gable, Paul Newman, Sean Connery, and Michael Caine. For him working required that bond of comradeship that his films themselves reflect and enshrine. The on-screen jokiness and badinage are frequently extensions of the off-screen practical (often cruel) jokes and drinking sessions with which the anecdotal histories of the productions abound.

The film crew is similar to a group of adventurers risking uncharted seas or terrain in search of possible treasure. The enterprise's success depends on their solidarity and loyalty. Equally a sense of humor and the ability to take a joke binds them together. The group is essentially masculine in which women play little or no part. They are the Penelopes left behind on the quay (*Moby Dick*) or the wife back at the farm (the letter scene in *Treasure of the Sierra Madre*) while the men leave on their Ulyssean mission.

Occasionally the Hustonian group may be a couple thrown together by chance, where the woman may prove herself equal to, or even stronger than, the man. In the case of *The African Queen* and *Heaven Knows, Mr. Allison,* the woman must exhibit manly qualities and accept discomfort and danger to gain respect. The rewards of such a union may be love. Where the woman infiltrates the male group, which reluctantly admits her as an outsider, she may prove to be the most treacherous, for she has learned the ways of male deviousness to which she can add female seductiveness. Only the hardest and most alert men can resist her. Sam Spade is such a man, making Brigid O'Shaughnessy take the fall in *The Maltese Falcon.* The woman Roslyn Taber is the most dangerous character in *The Misfits,* not because of her deviousness, but rather as a result of her frankness. She openly challenges the actions and code of the male group.

Howard Hawks is another director who focuses on groups of hard-bitten or highly trained professionals operating in worlds that women rarely enter (fliers, journalists, lawmen). However, a comparison between the two directors yields interesting differences. On the question of humor, Hawks has the more gentle touch. He created a body of light, even screwball, comedies (for example, *Twentieth Century,* 1934; *Bringing up Baby,* 1941; and *Ball of Fire,* 1941) that from the start left no doubt as to the happy ending. Apart from *Beat the Devil,* Huston did not make comedies; and the humor in his films serves as an ironic summation of what looks like failure. At the end of *The Maltese Falcon* Spade says that the bird in his hands is the stuff that dreams are made of, and the second half of *Prizzi's Honor* is an elaborate joke Maerose plays to bring Charley Partanna back into the fold. The happy ending of a Hawks comedy reflects the optimistic American credo of success, or true love. Huston's films, through comedy or not, are more likely to pose a challenge to that belief, often concluding with a reflection on failure. Compared to Hawks's polished professionals, Huston's ragtag adventurers look like bumbling amateurs (except for the thieves of *The Asphalt Jungle*) who may stumble into success (Charlie Allnut), but they usually have to come to terms with failure. They do so with a laugh.

HUMOR

Humor is not the first quality one would apply to a Huston movie, but laughter constantly ripples through even his most serious work. French critics have emphasized a particular quality of humor in his films that takes the form of irony, an ironic riff on reality, or a reminder that nothing should be taken too seriously, including the business of filmmaking. Jean-Claude Allais refers to Huston's "Homeric laughter," most memorably at the conclusion of *The Treasure of the Sierra Madre.*[1] In an existentialist study of contemporary cinema Jean Leirens lists four major existentialist themes, the last of which—the notion of the absurd—serves as an appreciation of Huston's work up to *Beat the Devil.*[2]

What these critics are talking about is Huston's acceptance of a cockeyed universe in which universal forces are consistently stacked up against the individual, happiness and success are largely a matter of chance, and justice is delivered by accident. Furthermore, challenges to a divine order are looked on askance by those who persuade themselves that they inhabit an ordered universe. The victorious conclusion to *The African Queen,* for instance, is so patently implausible (the producers' choice, not Huston's) that it has to be a mockery of the truth. Hazel Motes's death at the end of *Wise Blood* is the only way Motes knows to escape the bland domestic comforts offered by his patient landlady. This consistently ironical vision is encapsulated by laughter in three particular films: *The Treasure of the Sierra Madre, Beat the Devil,* and *The Man Who Would Be King.*

The laughter at the end of *Treasure* comes from Howard, the oldest and wisest of the prospectors. He sees that the gold dust he and his partners wrested so laboriously from the mountain has been dumped on the ground by the bandits who disposed of Dobbs and who consider mules and hides more valuable than gold. Howard understands that the dust has been blown back toward the mountain; so perhaps the world is not as cockeyed as it seems. Comic symmetry is at play here, with the survivors grasping the empty pouches, dumped at their point of departure. Howard decides to appreciate the joke played on them by "God, nature or fate" and bursts into laughter. He is shortly followed by the younger Curtin, who acknowledges they have lost far less than the wretched Dobbs and that they can start over. When the gods mock, laughter is man's way of responding. It indicates a kind of humility that may be rewarded with a second chance.

Laughter also appropriately ends *Beat the Devil.* Here Huston took a relatively straightforward yarn and turned it into a parody not only of itself, but of his own beginnings. The casting looks like a lighthearted echo of *The Maltese Falcon* with the inclusion of Humphrey Bogart and Peter Lorre, and Robert Morley nimbly stepping in for Sydney Greenstreet. It is fitting that Bogart, given a violent death in *Treasure,* should end this film in a burst of laughter as he reads the telegram from Harry Chelm, who has played the British twit throughout and who has indeed found uranium in central Africa. The fool has pulled the wool over the eyes of the professional thieves, who are being led away in handcuffs through the piazza while Billy Dannreuther expresses his appreciation of the joke. Bogart may have had another reason to laugh, if wryly. As coproducer of the film, he had sunk $500,000 into it and was facing probable failure at the box office. It only began to make money after his death in 1957.

Laughter is salvation in *The Man Who Would Be King.* The rogue heroes (fated to be underlings in the Imperial Army) decide to reshape their fate in the light of their own interests. In the upper wastes of the Himalayas they find themselves marooned amid the snows. With Danny actually snow-blind, they listen to the roar of the avalanches, which sound like arguments among the gods. As they wait for death, Peachy begins to reminisce and remind his friend of their more ribald moments in their service to the Queen. In the laughter that ensues the reverberations of their merriment set the snows in motion, reestablishing a snow bridge over the ravine that had cut them off. They are literally saved by laughter. The gods, blessing the humor with which the men had approached their end, have granted them a second chance—a chance to perpetrate a gigantic hoax on the descendants of Alexander.

THE HUSTON HERO

The Huston hero is a gambler, like the director himself. Who among his protagonists has a nine-to-five job? Sam Spade looks like one of few gainfully employed, and he inhabits a shadowy world, treading a fine line between the criminal and the legal. Spending so much time in the underworld, much of it has rubbed off on him, and he has virtually severed ties with the district attorney's office and the police department. Spade does not automatically get involved in matters of life and death in the name of justice. He does it for the money, sometimes for a dame, but always for the thrill of the chase.

Huston's heroes certainly work but only in the hope of striking it so rich that they will never have to work again. They prospect for gold in *The Treasure of the Sierra Madre,* sniff out uranium deposits in *Beat the Devil,* plan a jewel heist in *The Asphalt Jungle,* hunt whales in *Moby Dick,* box (for an absurdly low purse) in *Fat City,* and challenge orthodox religion in *Wise Blood.* Most significantly, they seek both treasure and a kingdom in *The Man Who Would Be King.* The taste for the irregular life is rooted in the vagabondage to which Huston himself was dedicated and that he had in part inherited from his Grandfather Gore. While he accepted the responsibilities toward his family (paying alimony and for his children's upkeep), he lived and worked abroad, preferring life on the road to the domestic routine. Not surprisingly, he understands the appeal of the life of crime, which might seem a shortcut to riches. Alonzo Emmerich, the crooked lawyer in *The Asphalt Jungle,* declares that "crime is, after all, a left-handed form of endeavor." It is a dark parody of the regular life. Huston sees as much professionalism in the successful execution of a jewel robbery as in the manufacture and marketing of those jewels. His sympathies are democratic. Doc Riedenschneider, the architect of the plot; Louis Ciavelli, the expert safecracker; and Dix, the honest aide-de-camp, are workers in the field. They deserve respect while the smooth and hypocritical upscale lawyer, Emmerich, does not.

"It beats wages," Gay Langland reminds Guido Dellini in *The Misfits,* speaking for every Huston protagonist who goes to bed when he feels like and rises when others are returning from work. Wages betoken a fixed schedule and confinement, hence a form of servitude. When we first see Gay, he is at the station putting a divorcée back on a train for the Midwest. She makes him an offer he finds easy to refuse: a stake in the "second largest laundry in St. Louis." He would rather chance his arm (or his whole body) at the rodeo, for he has a cowboy mentality and requires space to roam around in and pursue freedom. Hence Huston used vast spaces to symbolize that search: the desert of *The Misfits,* the mesas of *The Treasure of the Sierra Madre,* the ocean of *Moby Dick.* In a metaphysical sense, Hazel Motes of *Wise Blood* throws over the meaner limits of conventional religion and the parasitic variations of evangelism. Only the promise of an untried atheism offers appeal. Huston was no singer of the suburbs.

This drive for individual freedom is not always noble. In *The Misfits* Gay, Guido, and Perce drive into the high desert to hunt for the region's few remaining wild mustangs. At best this activity is dubious because the men's determination to make money that is "not wages" will mean captivity for the noble animals, which themselves represent freedom along a receding frontier. Gay and his friends are not simply hunting mustangs, they intend to sell the horses to dog food manufacturers. This final squalor of the operation triggers the film's crisis, with Roslyn challenging the group's ethos. Huston's irony is seen in familiar light here. Along with Arthur Miller, he used a popular setting and genre (the western) only to expose it. Behind the romantic appeal of space and freedom, he revealed a cruder reality of petty greed, diminished conscience, and squandered energies.

Among the mythical heroes, Huston's first choice would have been Prometheus, who stole fire from the gods and challenged their authority in the name of human autonomy. The closest parallel he found in literature was Melville's Ahab. It was as though Huston had spent the first fifteen years of his career preparing to make *Moby Dick* (1956). For him Melville's novel was no mere whaling saga, nor adventure story, nor romance. It was a blasphemy set in motion by one man's obsession. Ahab, marked forever by a malicious adversary, believes he has looked on the face of God and found Him to be vengeful and bloodthirsty, bent on the ruthless persecution of mankind. Driven by his mutinous conviction, Ahab draws his unsuspecting crew with him in his quest, convinced that in slaying Moby Dick he will release all mankind from divine subservience and tear the mask off the face of the divinity. In his madness he takes the crew down with him to a watery grave, and he remains lashed to his enemy in an image of eternal strife. That final image indicates simultaneously a defeat and a victory, for the Huston hero may gain existentially while failing in his intent.

THE BOGART FACTOR

In the history of cinema some actors work so closely with a director that over time they come to embody much of his viewpoint. They become a sort of alter ego, even a part of the director's film language, whereby he signals a mood or a theme. What was true of the relationships between Marcello Mastroianni and Federico Fellini, Marlene Dietrich and Josef von Sternberg, John Wayne and John Ford was true of Humphrey Bogart and John Huston.

They first met on the Warner Brothers' lot when Huston was cowriting the script of *The Amazing Dr. Clitterhouse* (1938). They met again on *High Sierra* (1941), which Huston cowrote with W. R. Burnett and in which Bogart starred as the fugitive Roy Earle. When George Raft later turned down the role of Sam Spade in *The Maltese Falcon,* Bogart was available. Bogart's interpretation changed his career and clinched his artistic relationship with Huston. Bogart went on to star in five more movies for Huston, all but one of which play an important part in the canon: *Across the Pacific* (1942), *The Treasure of the Sierra Madre* (1948), *Key Largo* (1948), *The African Queen* (1952), and *Beat the Devil* (1954). In 1957 Huston had wanted to cast him in *The Man Who Would Be King,* but Bogart died during the planning and Huston postponed the film for twenty years.

Up until *High Sierra* Bogart had often been typecast as a heavy, adopting a snarling gangster pose in films like *The Petrified Forest* (1935) or *The Roaring Twenties* (1939). While there is plenty of villainy in the part of *High Sierra*'s Roy (Mad Dog) Earle, he also exhibits civility and even courtesy; in short, a depth of

31

character that Bogart would display in the future. As he started to work with Huston, Bogart's persona and screen career underwent a transformation. As Sam Spade he crossed a line from criminal to crime fighter. He may not have exactly joined the establishment, but he discarded much of the coarseness of his previous roles. Spade has his own sort of integrity, but he is not completely admirable. With his capacity for ruthlessness and harshness, there are hints at ambiguities in his character, and he sets the standard for almost every celluloid private detective since. The darker side of Spade's nature drew Huston to the character; and in Bogart he found the actor to embody an antihero who stood at the center of Huston's universe.

The most outstanding characteristics of Bogart's screen persona are a reluctance to commit oneself and the instinct to downplay or deny a generous act once it is done. The character who most clearly embodies this reluctance to get involved, however, is not in a Huston film. It is Rick, the nightclub owner in Michael Curtiz's *Casablanca* (1942). Rick once fought for the Republicans in Spain and worked against the Nazis, but he never discusses these matters. He is a man without a past, having drawn a veil over it. Of course, he eventually does the right thing. He organizes the clandestine departure of his former love, Ilsa Lund, and her husband, Victor Laszlo, out of Morocco, so that Victor can continue the struggle against the Axis, which is much more important than an old love story. Rick's noble act is downplayed and carried out in the middle of the night on a deserted airstrip in the fog. It may just be possible to give Huston some credit for the genesis of *Casablanca's* Rick. Earlier that same year he hired Bogart to play another Rick (Leland) in *Across the Pacific,* a distinctly inferior vehicle for anti-Japanese propaganda in the post–Pearl Harbor period. Here Bogart is a courageous patriot who pretends to be a disgruntled army officer in order to penetrate a gang of enemy agents planning to blow up the Panama Canal. His line of antiestablishment cynicism and his witty verbal fencing with Sydney Greenstreet are still precisely in tune with the type of characters we expect him to play.

For Huston the pleasure in making *The Treasure of the Sierra Madre* was in being able to take a top Hollywood star (with Bogart's active compliance), roll him in the gutter, deny him the price of a meal, and force him to sleep in a doss-house. It looks like a mocking gesture toward the studio bosses who, until the film proved successful at the box office, were horrified to see their star looking like a ruffian, behaving like a madman, and dying in a ditch. The mockery of the star system (and by extension of the whole Hollywood way of making movies, on a controlled set without allowing a production out of town) is in plain view in the scene where Huston, dressed in an immaculate white suit, presses a silver coin into the palm of the pestering Dobbs and warns, "From now on you will have to make your way in life without me." It is a beautiful send-up of the star's dependence on the director and perhaps of both on the studio.

In the films Huston and Bogart made together after *Treasure* one can almost judge their meaning and intent according to the state of Bogart's laundry. He is clean and well-groomed in *Key Largo* (1948) and disheveled in *The African Queen* (1951). In the first he plays a man who has done his duty; and in the second, a man running away from responsibility. Despite appearances, these men are closely related. Frank McCloud (of *Key Largo*) feels he has done enough and is most reluctant to take a stand against the gangster Rocco. Charlie Allnut has come to Africa to hide away. It is his rotten luck that war erupts all around him and that his shipmate is Rose Sayer. Both McCloud and Allnut are finally redeemed by their women, following the ancient code that the reward of courage is love. In McCloud's case, his love for Nora Temple significantly reconstituted for the filmgoing public America's most popular movie couple, Bogart and Bacall, and for Allnut, love and a clean shave prove Rose's point: nature "is what we are put into this world to rise above."

Huston spruced Bogart up for the last movie they made together, *Beat the Devil,* but here, too, appearances are deceptive. Billy Dannreuther is debonair all right, but in spite of an old Rolls Royce and connections with some of Europe's elite, he has a murky past and louche acquaintances. *Beat the Devil* is also a bit like an appetite that increases while eating, for the full extent of its comedy was only discovered during the filming. There was a sense that everyone was having his leg pulled, including the director, who may have been sending up his own early manner. Bogart's roar of laughter that concludes the film was most apt. It was on one level in appreciation of the cunning of the fool, Harry Chelm, but it went beyond plot. Bogart was coproducer of the film, and he had put a great deal of money into it with little hope of seeing a return on his investment. Like a gambler in the Huston mold, all Bogart could do was to laugh it off. That realization takes us back to Huston's scene in *Treasure.* That simple coin pressed into the palm of the hand may have been all one could expect if he went into business with John Huston.

VISUAL STYLE

Generally critics agree that Huston was as eclectic stylistically as he was in his choice of subject matter; that is, while each individual film has its own look, the same is not true of his oeuvre as a whole. He himself declared that the look of a particular film was always dictated by the content and mood of the story.[3] In short, there is a chameleon-like quality to his pictures, with the style subordinating itself to the requirements of plot and theme. In the first decade of his directorial career, from *The Maltese Falcon* to *The Asphalt Jungle,* when he was shooting exclusively in black and white, his films were identified as film noir. After World War II French critics noted that in the Hollywood features of the forties (notably from Warner Brothers) he concentrated on urban vices and a somber mood. Visually the equivalent was found in the low-key lighting, the stifling interiors, and the deep shadows in which the film was cast. These elements could be traced to the earlier tradition of German expressionism of the 1920s and 1930s, but Huston did not simply borrow from an established tradition in his "noir" period. Rather, the early date of *The Maltese Falcon* (1941) shows him as something of an initiator. Other directors would follow his lead.

In *The Maltese Falcon* Huston preferred a closed interior to indicate a sealed-off world, with only an occasional view of the ceiling to signify confined space (a prominent feature of Orson Welles's *Citizen Kane,* released the same year). Huston was a very literary director who not only showed great respect for the original text, but believed that the script came first. Thus, he shot *Falcon* like a play, giving great weight to the dialogue. He kept the camera largely at a middle distance to include all participants in a dialogue and something of the room's decor. During the lengthy sequence in Spade's apartment in the film's final act he underlined the shifting relationships between the characters by carefully including or excluding certain individuals in each shot. Occasionally he cut away to a single character (Wilmer or Brigid, for example) to indicate isolation. This focus is not stylish but pragmatic filmmaking, conditioned by the requirements of the drama.

In *The Asphalt Jungle,* made about a decade later, Huston's style had evolved, in part, out of his experience in making the wartime documentaries outside and on location. He allowed a greater spaciousness, signaled by the opening montage of grimy city streets at dawn that signified his intent to set his drama in a particular milieu and to present (or hint at) a social framework. The action does not occur in a vacuum. The opening montage is balanced at the movie's tragic close by the spacious and lyrical motifs of Dix's death in a field where he is nuzzled by horses. Here his dream, to which his stake in the robbery led him, ends. It is also worth noting that Huston actually started a trend in the genre as the result of the detail and screen time he lavished on the theft itself. This film was to become a model for heist movies in the fifties (most notably Jules Dassin's *Rififi,* 1955). What the audience witnesses here is actually work (even if a left-handed form). As noted previously, on regular occasions in Huston's movies he provided pause to observe people at work or exercising a manual skill. It began with the accounts of the fliers and soldiers in *Report from the Aleutians* and *The Battle of San Pietro,* but he also filmed mining sequences for *The Treasure of the Sierra Madre,* a tunneling sequence for *We Were Strangers,* and whaling scenes for *Moby Dick.*

Huston's attachment to black and white cinematography goes far beyond his first entry into the world of color in *The African Queen.* He still remained faithful to filming in black and white, even when he had to argue strenuously with producers to get his way. It has to stand for a fidelity to the documentary tradition to which he had so memorably contributed in the three major war time films, and in which the viewer, rightly or wrongly, attributes to the black and white images a higher seriousness, a devotion to truth, a pursuit of ideas. Huston felt that sort of seriousness linked the movie with the tradition of information and, by extension, the documentary, which up to that period was a black and white medium. In the sixties he made four black and white films in succession (and at least two are among his most memorable): *The Misfits, Freud: The Secret Passion, The List of Adrian Messenger,* and *The Night of the Iguana.* In no case was his use of black and white photography dictated by economic considerations alone. Back in 1951, for example, when he made *The Red Badge of Courage,* he thought like an artist and wanted to reproduce some of the qualities of Matthew Brady's Civil War photographs and his own war documentaries, which were also shot in black and white.

To use the process in *The Misfits,* with its galaxy of stars, was certainly going against the grain; however, along with Arthur Miller and his cinematographer Russell Metty, what Huston did not want was glamour. He sought to emphasize the bleakness and aridity of the Nevada desert, which could be beautiful and forbidding and serve as a backdrop for the characters' desolate lives. Black and white also seemed a logical choice for *Freud: The Secret Passion* (1962) for two reasons: primarily for period reconstruction—all photography would have been in black and white in late-nineteenth-century Vienna—and, furthermore, in Huston's view the narrower chromatic range allowed him to pass more smoothly from one state of mind to another, from a physical reality to the dream state, with a less obvious sense of dislocation. (A more subtle illustration of a similar process is seen in Fellini's *8 1/2*, filmed by Gianni di Venanzo in 1961.)

Black and white was also his choice for the entertainment that followed: *The List of Adrian Messenger* (1963). Here Huston used a contemporary setting, but struck an old-fashioned mood, harking back to the tweedy, clubby world of the gentleman sleuth of the days of Conan Doyle and John Buchan. Again for these echoes from a lost world, black and white was appropriate. Finally, while one can well imagine *The Night of the Iguana* (1964) in color, Huston saw Reverend Lawrence Shannon's crisis in terms as bleak as *The Misfits'* problems of unfulfilled dreams. Also, Huston felt it was important not to paint Mexico in the primary colors of the travel brochures. Furthermore, he was working with the Mexican cinematographer Gabriel Figueroa, who had filmed *Los Olvidados* and *Nazarin* in beautiful black and white for Luis Buñuel, and Huston wanted to work in that tradition.[4]

As color became the norm in filmmaking in the fifties, the notion of Huston as a chameleon director becomes more persuasive, for as a practicing artist and an art collector he always looked for ways of weaving color into the narrative and psychological texture of his work. This search for the color equivalent of a mood often led to charges of aestheticism and even dilettantism against Huston, frequently from those quarters that had applauded the austerity and consistency of his film noir period. *Moulin Rouge* incited such criticism, and it is true that the color attracted Huston to the subject in the first place. The challenge was to develop a color scheme that reproduced the painter's palette and the tones of French impressionism, including the colors of Paris, to evoke the period of *la belle époque*. Huston intended to put Toulouse-Lautrec's colors on the screen, flattening and rendering them in solid planes. He hired *Life* photographer Eliot Elisofon, who had been doing interesting experiments in still color photography, and had him work closely with Oswald (Ossie) Morris, who was working on his first film for Huston and was always his favorite cinematographer thereafter. The success Huston and his team achieved in producing their effects horrified the executives at Technicolor who were proud of their ripe primaries and what Huston called "the garish hues of bad billboards." Huston won his point, however, and the film did attract most attention for its subtle color.[5]

Moby Dick (1956) required a quite different approach, although here the problem was more easily solved. Again working with Oswald Morris, Huston aimed for an 1840s look to fit the novel's time frame. Specifically he wanted to reproduce the watery hues of old whaling prints of the period. Whereas in *Moulin Rouge* they had highlighted the pastels with vibrant blocks of color in the foreground, now their emphasis was on a desaturation of color, resulting in a watery pallor. Morris worked with still photographs and then had the laboratory prepare two prints, one in black and white, the other in color. They were then printed together to produce the desired aging effect.[6]

Reflections in a Golden Eye (1967) also involved experiments in color. Out of respect for Carson McCullers's intentions, Huston was looking for a visual equivalent of the mood of repression that afflicted all of her characters. Again Ossie Morris came up with a solution. Although Aldo Tonti was the official cinematographer and Morris received no credit, the latter did most of the principal photography and worked with the laboratory. The process he developed involved a desaturation of the image, reducing the color range to shades of pink and gold. Only at the film's climax did he revert to using primary colors. The film's characters were virtual prisoners on their military base, and Huston saw them as neurotic products of a distorted environment. The color Morris came up with would alert the audience to the estrangement of every character in the film. The producers, Warner Brothers, were not happy with the results. Fearful of lukewarm reviews and public disinterest, the desaturated version was withdrawn after about ten days of distribution and replaced by conventional Technicolor prints. Very few people have seen the original print.[7]

LATE-FLOWERING HUSTON

After the disappointing sixties—he made a series of mediocre movies that ranged from some interesting failures to downright flops, and his wife Ricki died in 1969—Huston confounded those critics who had been announcing his demise with a full-blooded return to the height of his powers. His next film, *Fat City,* was no flash in the pan. In fact it started the richest season in Huston's career since his remarkable debut decade of the 1940s. There was a trough between 1980 and 1984, but in the last fifteen years of his life Huston directed six films that any other director might have claimed as an "oeuvre" in themselves.

In his autumnal flowering Huston returned to the themes that had always attracted him. The literary texts that he drew from in these last years were frequently challenging and elusive and certainly from the higher ranks of the canon (Malcolm Lowry, Flannery O'Connor, James Joyce), not at all the light reading of a man preparing for retirement. The themes include boxing and the physical definition of manhood (*Fat City*), a return to the idea of the doomed quest (*The Man Who Would Be King*), the search for a new faith out of the ashes of the old (*Wise Blood*), the human capacity for self-destruction (*Under the Volcano*), crime and its rewards and punishments (*Prizzi's Honor*), and a meditation on lost love and mortality (*The Dead*).

Huston handled these themes with a relaxed irony that comes only after decades of experience in life and art. Style was no longer a problem. His mastery of the form was complete. His attention to detail remained meticulous, even finicky, and all of his collaborators agreed that in these last films he seemed more engaged in the project at hand. On films like *Fat City* and *Wise Blood* he worked with limited budgets, adapting to the conditions of independent productions with a readiness and vigor that would be rare in a much younger director. As for the mood he evoked, it is darker but not despondent; the humor is blacker; and one feels his melancholy conviction that all men are losers with an inborn predilection to toss the pearl away or to fail to recognize treasure and contentment close at hand. But there remains the Hustonian faith shining through the dark vision, that the thrill of the chase is after all worthwhile and that to strain every sinew in order to test oneself is nobler than complacent resignation. Occasionally, even, there are glimpses of true love. Huston's vision is more Olympian in these films. As he passed through his seventies, stoically battling emphysema and refusing to stop working, he may frequently have been appalled at what he saw, but he was moved more to amusement than to anger at the human spectacle. We are never far from an outburst of Homeric laughter (which in a literal sense only bursts forth once, in *The Man Who Would Be King*).

Fat City was a kind of homecoming for Huston, his first American movie since *The Misfits* ten years earlier. Saved from the presence of demanding stars, it was also more powerful for being more modest in its intent. What pleasure the film must have given him as he returned to one of the great passions of his youth and the sport that had even set him on his literary career. Huston metaphorically climbed into the ring himself on this occasion, tossing down a gauntlet to those critics who had always failed to appreciate him in the way many French critics had, even in his leaner periods. He also returned to the style most congenial to him: that urban realism that casts its shadow over some of his best films, like *The Maltese Falcon* and *The Asphalt Jungle*. Conrad Hall, the cinematographer, perfectly captured the dusty ennui of the streets and the dark bars of Stockton, the sweat of the gyms and crowded auditoriums, and the life-sapping heat of agricultural labor. Nothing else in Huston's work really caps his final image of the two fighters, Billy and Ernie (superbly interpreted performances by Stacy Keach and Jeff Bridges), as they contemplate their coffee cups, the late-night loafers, and then the old man behind the counter and wonder if he is happy.

The Man Who Would Be King more obviously conforms to the Huston pattern of the quest gone wrong, whose most powerful expression heretofore was seen in *The Treasure of the Sierra Madre*. Huston had wanted to film this Kipling story at least twenty years earlier, and through the years he had envisioned most major Hollywood stars in the lead roles. He was fortunate to end up with Sean Connery and Michael Caine, who played to perfection the pair of lovable rogues and doomed fortune hunters who overreach themselves and approach death with such dignity. Daniel Dravot and Peachy Carnehan fit precisely into the Huston mold of adventurers who refuse to be held back by convention or tradition. They rebelled against the military order that gave them a chance to escape the Victorian poverty of their birthright and the British Army that would make them eternal subordinates, but from that very hierarchy they inherited a sense of superiority. (Peachy explains: "We are not gods, but Englishmen, which is the next best thing.") Thus, they have no scruples about ruling the primitives of Kafiristan, and beyond the reach of European law they want to live as kings. It might have worked, too, had they both always remembered that they were, after all, men. Dravot actually succumbs to the belief that he may be divine while Peachy's feet are more firmly planted on the ground, and for that reason he is allowed to survive to tell the tale. The gods respond to their laughter and good humor in the face of death and restore their way forward, but the gods cannot tolerate mortals who claim divinity. For those who commit that sort of heresy there is retribution. Daniel and Peachy are worthy descendants of Ahab. They refuse the sedentary acceptance of destiny—that is, class confinement—and are prepared to act out a blasphemy, dueling with the gods.

Blasphemy is also the central theme of *Wise Blood*, in which another obsessed protagonist, Hazel Motes, determines to found the Church without Christ. Hazel

wages open warfare against Sunday-morning Christians and those who parasitical-
ly leech onto the body of Christ to squeeze out a living by false prophesy and dire
predictions of damnation, such as the blind preacher Asa Hawks. As played by
Brad Dourif, Hazel is possessed by a humorless righteousness and attracts everyone
within earshot who is unloved and without a compass, like the lonely museum
attendant Enoch Emery. He draws women, too, who feel the need to mother and
protect him (for example, Sabbath Lily, who finally cannot stand his masochism,
and his landlady, who, being older, has faith in her staying power). Hazel is the
closest Huston character to Ahab. He, too, wants to tear the mask off the face of
God, revealing either malice or emptiness. He spends the movie trying to round up
a crew that never signs on, all in the heart of Flannery O'Connor's south with its
profusion of religious fanatics, eccentrics, and hucksters. At seventy-three years old
Huston did not hesitate to accept this unusual project, based on the work of a highly respected writer who was outside the mainstream. The proposal was made to him
by a husband and wife, Michael and Kathy Fitzgerald, who had no experience in
the film business and yet assumed Huston would be approachable. Huston at first
assumed the Fitzgeralds would not raise the money but was nonetheless prepared to
travel to Georgia and work at a minimum salary with a nonunion crew and lesser-
known actors. *Wise Blood* never made much money, but its excellent reviews, some
from critics who were not Huston fans, plus the standing ovation he received at
Cannes, were sweet vindication.

In his last three films, which show little sign of flagging energy, Huston not
only revisited scenes from his past, but the familiar psychic territory of his career.
These films are not mere repetitions, however, but often ambitious reworkings of
the familiar; in the case of his last film, *The Dead,* we see the breaking of new
ground.

Under the Volcano, itself a very complicated text, seemed to be waiting for
Huston to turn it into a film. Like the protagonist (and the author, Malcolm Lowry)
Huston was an exile in Mexico, and this project was his third filmed in Mexico. The
central figure, Consul Firmin, is a man who drinks both to quiet a nagging conscience and to blot out a world determined on perdition. (Perhaps time has blunted
some of the historical references, for Huston retained the 1930s setting of Mexico
and the Nazi influence spreading in Central America.) The consul is a kind of drunk-
en Ahab, denouncing the occasional injustice but really courting death. The action
covers the last twenty-four hours of his life during the Festival of the Day of the
Dead. Geoffrey Firmin, superbly played by Albert Finney, has much in common
with Lawrence Shannon (*The Night of the Iguana*), but the consul cannot be saved.
The prostitutes and thieves in the Farolito Bar, presided over by the manic dwarf,
René Luiz, are a reminder of the bandits who finally murder Dobbs (*The Treasure of
the Sierra Madre*), and the consul does not fare much better. Another odd reminder
of an earlier period of Huston's career comes when the consul pauses to watch a
scene or two from the silent classic *The Hands of Orlac,* about a doomed pianist
with the hands of a killer, starring Peter Lorre, who appeared in *The Maltese Falcon*
and *Beat the Devil.* This descent into hell is brilliantly photographed by Gabriel
Figueroa, once Buñuel's cinematographer (*Los Olvidados* and *Nazarin*), and the
final phantasmagoric scenes have a whiff of Buñuel's brimstone.

The novel *Prizzi's Honor* was written by Richard Condon, who had shown a talent for imagining such dark and paranoid political thrillers as *The Manchurian Candidate* and *Winter Kills*. In the film version of the latter (released in 1979), Huston played the political patriarch. He appreciated Condon's grim vein of humor, which corresponded with his own jocular irony. In *Prizzi's Honor* Huston revisited the Mafia, but with less respect than Francis Ford Coppola had granted the Corleone clan in *The Godfather* a decade earlier, for the last thing the Prizzis have is honor. For the appearance and the facade of honor, however, they are prepared to go to war. Family cohesion is threatened at a wedding by the appearance of the blond Irene (Kathleen Turner), who has been invited to do a hit for the Prizzis and then disappear. That is business. It becomes bad for business when Charley Partanna (Jack Nicholson), a trusted Prizzi lieutenant and member of the inner circle, falls in love with this outsider. Stung by jealousy, Maerose Prizzi determines to win Charley back, ostensibly in the name of family solidarity but in reality for herself.

Anjelica Huston, as Maerose, comes of age in *Prizzi's Honor*. She first appears as the family's black sheep who has established her independence by becoming an interior decorator, but then she causes the family to line up against Irene, all while maneuvering her father toward retirement. The film makes knowing references to her personal history—for example, her on-again, off-again relationship with Nicholson. More important, one can sense in her character, and in her as an actress, a growing independence, a move her father anoints in his penultimate film. For this achievement Anjelica Huston received that year's Oscar for Best Supporting Actress.

Huston's turn to James Joyce for the source of his final film was a remarkable act of symmetry, even if it was an unconscious choice. In many ways *The Dead* heralds a return, for Huston had read Joyce since his twenties, when the United States officially banned *Ulysses*. The film was also in part a gift to Tony Huston (who, with his father's help, converted this essentially ruminative story into dramatic and cinematic form), while Anjelica Huston breathed life into the regal but melancholy Gretta. *The Dead* was the perfect vehicle to bring Huston's career to a close, since it is a private and intimate tale, with the characters gathered under one roof and with very few scene changes. The action is found in the words, in the exchanges of dialogue, and in the songs and toasts—all perfectly designed for a director obliged to conduct the performance from his wheelchair. Above all *The Dead* is a meditation, for the attentive spectator, for the director, and for all who helped to make it. Love and death are its central motifs, even though there is no denouement. There is a powerful confession, but without a rupture. Gabriel's thoughts about his Aunt Kate's death, bringing not only a life but a tradition to an end, reflect those of Huston (who would be dead within the year) wondering about the span of his life. Gretta's confession about her true love for the lad who died young makes Gabriel realize that he has been married for years to a woman who has never fully loved him. Here, too, Huston's must have thought back to his various wives: How much had he loved them, and how much had they loved him? Ultimately, as the film ends, all are united in death.

Critics often accused Huston of making films beneath his capacity or taste and of failing to develop a consistent outlook, let alone a recognizable style. He was accused of promoting an altogether too masculine vision that dealt with action more than thought, but that is what the cinema does best. A study of his last films, however, yields intriguing variations on themes developed throughout his career as well as subtle personal undercurrents and echoes, without them ever becoming films à clef. As for the charge of aggressive masculinity (a charge more appropriate for the first part of his career), we note rather the tact with which he makes boxers acknowledge their limitations, the discretion with which he follows a man down the road to despair, and the delicacy with which he shows how a simple song can trigger a memory, open a heart, and release a confession. *The Dead* is a notable signature to a unique career pursued flamboyantly and yet completed with enviable understatement.

NOTES

1. Jean-Claude Allais, *John Huston* (Lyon: Serdoc, 1960), 3.

2. Jean Leirens, *Le Cinema et la crise de notre temps* (Paris: Editions du Cerf, 1960), 79–90.

3. John Huston, *An Open Book* (New York: Scribners, 1980), 360.

4. Gabriel Figueroa would work for Huston again (in color) on *Under the Volcano* (1984).

5. Gerald Pratley, *The Cinema of John Huston* (South Brunswick, N.J.: A. S. Barnes, 1977), 95; Stuart Kaminsky, *John Huston: Maker of Magic* (Boston: Houghton, Mifflin, 1978), 93–94; and Lawrence Grobel, *The Hustons* (New York: Scribners, 1989), 388–89.

6. Kaminsky, *John Huston,* 107; Scott Hammen, *John Huston* (Boston: Twayne, 1985), 80; and Grobel, *The Hustons,* 423.

7. Pratley, *The Cinema of John Huston,* 162; Kaminsky, *John Huston,* 175; and Grobel, *The Hustons,* 578.

III
Chronology

1906   John Marcellus Huston born August 5, 1906, in Nevada, Missouri, to Rhea Gore (a.k.a. Rhea Juare, journalist) and Walter Huston (actor). Parents separate in 1909 and divorce in 1912.

1909   Makes first show business appearance on stage in Dallas as "Yankee Doodle Dandy."

1918   Diagnosed with heart condition and hospitalized.

1921–23   Lincoln Heights High School, Los Angeles.

Amateur welterweight boxer, wins twenty-three of twenty-five bouts.

Drops out of high school and enrolls as an art student at the Smith School of Art and Art Student's League.

1923   *The Acquittal,* Universal, writer, continuity (questionable credit). (*See* chapter 14, "Huston on Film and Other Projects.")

1924   Leaves Los Angeles and moves to New York.

1925   *The Triumph of the Egg,* play, Provincetown Playhouse Theater, New York, actor. Professional debut as actor.
Ruint, play, Provincetown Playhouse Theater, New York, actor.

Adam Solitaire, play, Provincetown Playhouse Theater, New York, actor.

1926   Mastoid operation.

Trip to Mexico.

Honorary commission in the Mexican cavalry.

Marries Dorothy Jeanne Harvey (divorces in 1933).

1929   Reporter, *New York Graphic.*

The Legend of Frankie and Johnny, marionette play, Republic Theater, New York, author.

The Shakedown, Universal, actor, bit part, uncredited.

Two Americans, Paramount, actor.

American Mercury publishes his story "Fool," March 16.

1930 Contract writer (six months), Goldwyn Studios (presumably no assignments).

Contract writer, Universal Pictures, 1930–33.

Hell's Heroes, Universal, actor, bit part, uncredited.

The Storm, Universal, actor, bit part, uncredited.

1931 Short story, "Figures of Fighting Men," published in *American Mercury,* May.

A House Divided, Universal, writer, first screen credit.

1931–32 *Steel,* Universal, unproduced, writer.

1931–33 *Laughing Boy,* Universal, writer, uncredited (released by MGM, 1934).

Marius, Universal, unproduced, writer.

1932 *Black Rust,* Universal, unproduced, writer.

Destry Rides Again, Universal, writer, uncredited.

The Hero, Universal, unproduced, writer.

The Hunchback of Notre Dame, writer, uncredited (released by RKO, 1939).

The Invisible Man, Universal, writer, uncredited (released in 1933).

Jack of Diamonds, Universal, unproduced, writer.

Law and Order, Universal, writer.

Nagana, Universal, writer, uncredited (released in 1933).

U-Boat, Universal, unproduced, writer.

Murders in the Rue Morgue, Universal, writer.

1933 *Forgotten Boy,* Universal, unproduced, writer.

The Mighty Barnum (P. T. Barnum), Twentieth Century-Fox, writer, uncredited (released in 1934).

Wild Boys of the Road, Warner Brothers, writer, uncredited.

1935 Trip to Great Britain and Paris.

Death Drives Through (Great Britain), writer.

It Happened in Paris (Great Britain), writer.

Storm Child, play, New York, author (?). (*See* chapter 17, "Theatrical Activity.")

Editor, *Mid-Week Pictorial.*

1936 *Rhodes of Africa* (*Rhodes*), British-Gaumont, writer, uncredited.

1937 Marries Leslie Black (divorces in 1944).

The Lonely Man, play, WPA Theater, Chicago, actor (author, Howard Koch).

Shadows Pursuing, play, uproduced, author. Based on *Dark Tumult* by Hugh Walpole.

1938	Mother dies.
	Contract writer, Warner Brothers (1938–41).
	Jezebel, Warner Brothers, writer.
	The Amazing Dr. Clitterhouse, Warner Brothers, writer.
1939	*Disraeli,* Warner Brothers, writer, assignment. (Early version released by Warner, 1929.)
	Juarez, Warner Brothers, writer.
	The Roaring Twenties (The World Moves On), writer, uncredited.
	Underground, Warner Brothers, writer, uncredited (released in 1941).
	Wuthering Heights, Goldwyn/United Artists (UA), writer, uncredited.
1939–40	*The Constant Nymph,* writer, uncredited (released by Warner Brothers, 1943).
1940	*Captain Horatio Hornblower,* writer, uncredited (released by Warner Brothers, 1951).
	Dr. Ehrlich's Magic Bullet, Warner Brothers, writer.
	Mr. Skeffington, writer, uncredited (released in 1944).
	A Passenger to Bali, play, Ethel Barrymore Theater, New York, director. Walter acted in play.
1941	*Danger Signal,* writer, uncredited (released by Warner Brothers, 1945).
	High Sierra, Warner Brothers, writer.
	The Maltese Falcon, Warner Brothers, director, writer.
	Sergeant York, Warner Brothers, writer.
	In Time to Come, play, Broadway, coauthor with Howard Koch.
1942	*Across the Pacific,* Warner Brothers, director, writer (uncredited).
	The Hard Way, writer, uncredited (released by Warner Brothers, 1943).
	In This Our Life, Warner Brothers, director, writer (uncredited).
1942–45	Military service in World War II.
1943	*Background to Danger,* Warner Brothers, writer, uncredited.
	Report from the Aleutians, U.S. Army Pictorial Service, director, writer.
	Tunisian Victory, U.S. Army Pictorial Service, assists in remake of film.
1944	*Tomorrow the World,* United Artists, director, unrealized.
1945	*The Battle of San Pietro,* U.S. Army Pictorial Service, director, writer, narrator.
	Cheyenne, writer, unrealized (released by Warner Brothers, 1947).
	Here Is Germany, U.S. Army Pictorial Service, contributing writer.
	Know Your Enemy: Japan, U.S. Army Pictorial Service, writer.
	The Story of G.I. Joe, UA, writer (?), uncredited.

1945, 1949 *Reminiscences of a Cowboy,* director, writer (unrealized). (Released by Columbia in 1958 as *Cowboy.*)

1946 Marries Evelyn Keyes (divorces in 1950).

Adopts son Pablo.

Three Strangers, Warner Brothers, writer.

Let There Be Light, U.S. Army Pictorial Service, director, writer (released December 16, 1980).

The Stranger, RKO, writer, uncredited.

The Killers, Universal, writer, uncredited.

No Exit (*Huis Clos*), play, New York, director. Play by Jean-Paul Sartre, adaptation by Paul Bowles.

1947 Forms Committee for the First Amendment to counteract House Un-American Activities Committee (HUAC) investigations.

1948 *The Treasure of the Sierra Madre,* Warner Brothers, director, writer. Academy Awards for Best Director and Best Screenplay.

On Our Merry Way (*A Miracle Can Happen*), director, uncredited.

Key Largo, Warner Brothers, director, writer.

1949 *Quo Vadis,* director (unrealized), writer (uncredited; released by MGM, 1951).

We Were Strangers, Horizon/Columbia, director, writer, actor (uncredited).

Receives "One World" Award.

1950 Walter dies.

Marries Enrica (Ricki) Soma (Ricki dies in 1969).

Son Tony born.

The Asphalt Jungle, MGM, director, writer.

Prelude to Freedom, unrealized project, director, writer.

1950–52 *The Disenchanted,* unrealized project, director, writer.

1951 Daughter Anjelica born.

The Prowler, producer (?).

The Red Badge of Courage, director, writer, actor (cut out).

1952 Moves to Ireland.

The African Queen, Horizon-Romulus/UA, director, writer.

1952–54 *Matador,* unrealized project, director.

1953 *Moulin Rouge,* Romulus/UA, director, writer.

Richard III, unrealized project, director.

1954 *Alouette,* unrealized project, director.

Beat the Devil, Romulus-Santana/UA, director, writer.

1955   *Goya,* unrealized project, director.

         Judas, unrealized project, director.

1956   *Moby Dick,* Warner Brothers, director, writer.

         The Prince and the Showgirl, director, unrealized (released by Warner Brothers, 1957).

1956–57   *Typee,* unproduced, director, writer.

1957   *By Love Possessed,* director, unrealized (released by UA, 1961).

         A Farewell to Arms, Twentieth Century-Fox, director (withdrew), writer (uncredited).

         Hassan, unrealized project, director.

         Heaven Knows, Mr. Allison, Twentieth Century-Fox, director.

         Montezuma, unrealized project, director.

1958   *The Barbarian and the Geisha,* Twentieth Century-Fox, director, writer (uncredited).

         Bolívar, director, unrealized (?).

         The Roots of Heaven, Twentieth Century-Fox, director, writer (uncredited).

         Taras Bulba, UA, director, unrealized (released in 1962).

1960   *John Huston's Nobel Prize Theater*—proposed TV series on Nobel Prize laureates in literature that Huston would supervise—unrealized.

         Lysistrata, unrealized project, director.

         The Quare Fellow, director, unrealized (released in 1962).

         The Unforgiven, UA, director, writer (uncredited).

         Who Was That Lady? Columbia, director, unrealized.

1961   *The Misfits,* Seven Arts/UA, director, writer (uncredited).

1961–63   *The Lonely Passion of Judith Hearne,* unrealized project, director, writer (released by Handmade Films, 1987).

1962   Son Danny born (to Zoe Sallis).

         Becket, director, unrealized (released by Paramount, 1964).

         Freud: The Secret Passion, Universal, director, writer (uncredited), narrator.

1962–63,

1967   *Harrow Alley,* unrealized project, director.

1963   Dartmouth College Retrospective, 1963–64.

         The Directors, short film, produced by Nat Greenblat, interviewed.

         Frankie and Johnny, unrealized, director, writer. (Huston wrote, produced, and published a play of the same name in 1930.)

         The List of Adrian Messenger, Universal, director, writer (uncredited), actor (uncredited).

         United in Progress, United States Information Agency, narrator.

1964   Becomes citizen of Ireland.

Adopts Allegra (daughter of Ricki Soma).

The Cardinal, Gamma/Columbia, actor.

The Night of the Iguana, MGM, director.

"On Location: *The Night of the Iguana,*" TV production on making the film.

La Porta de S. Pietro de Giacomo Manzu, directed by Glauco Pellegrini, narrator, English-language version.

Return to the Island, documentary (United Kingdom), appearance.

1965   *Man of La Mancha,* director (?), unrealized (released by UA, 1972).

On the Trail of the Iguana, directed by Ross Lowell, documentary on making the film.

1965–66   *Shoes of the Fisherman,* director, unrealized (released by MGM, 1968).

Will Adams, unproduced, director, writer.

1965–68   *Patton,* director, unrealized (released by Twentieth Century-Fox, 1970).

1966   *The Bible,* De Laurentiis/Twentieth Century-Fox, director, writer (uncredited), actor, narrator.

"In Sure and Certain Hope," produced by Jules Power and Three Crown Productions, proposed TV documentary on James Agee, narrator.

"The Life and Times of John Huston, Esq.," Alan King and Associates, TV production, NET/BBC/CBC, documentary.

A Man for All Seasons, Columbia, proposed actor, unrealized.

This Property Is Condemned, Paramount, director, unrealized.

1967   *Casino Royale,* Famous Artists/Columbia, director, writer (uncredited).

"The Legend of Marilyn Monroe," Wolper Productions, TV production, ABC Stage 7, narrator.

Reflections in a Golden Eye, Warner Brothers, director, writer (uncredited).

1967–68   *Waterloo,* director, unrealized (released by Paramount, 1970).

1968   *Candy,* Selmur, actor.

The Heart Is a Lonely Hunter, Warner Brothers, director, unrealized.

"The Rocky Road to Dublin," TV production, produced and directed by Peter Lennon, interviewed.

Walking with Love and Death (*Ride This Way, Gray Horse*). Knight Films (United Kingdom). Documentary on making the film *Walk with Love and Death.*

Eire Society of Boston, Thirty-first Annual Dinner, May 4, 1968, gold medalist and guest speaker, John Huston.

1968–69   *A Terrible Beauty,* unproduced, director, unrealized.

1969 Ricki Soma dies.

De Sade, American International, actor.

The Madwoman of Chaillot, Warner, director (withdrew), writer (uncredited).

Sinful Davey, UA, director, writer (uncredited).

A Walk with Love and Death, Twentieth Century-Fox, director, writer (uncredited), actor.

1969–70 *Bullet Park,* unrealized project, director, writer.

Portrait of the Artist as a Young Man, Mystic Fire, director, unrealized (released in 1977).

1970 *Borstal Boy,* unrealized project, director.

The Hostage, unrealized project, director, writer.

"The Journey of Robert F. Kennedy," TV production, ABC/David Wolper Productions, narrator.

"Kenyan National Parks Safari with John Huston," TV production, host.

The Kremlin Letter, Twentieth Century-Fox, director, writer.

Myra Breckinridge, Twentieth Century-Fox, actor.

Nina, unproduced, proposed actor, unrealized.

Honorary degree, Trinity College, reported in the *Irish Times,* February 26, 1970.

Honorary degree, University of Dublin, July 10, 1970.

1970–75 *The Other Side of the Wind,* directed by Orson Welles, not released, actor.

1971 *The Bridge in the Jungle,* Sagittarius/Capricorn, actor.

The Deserter, Dino De Laurentiis, actor.

The Last Run, MGM, director (withdrew), writer (uncredited).

Man in the Wilderness, actor.

1971–72 *The Horse of Selene,* unrealized project, producer, director, writer.

1972 Marries Celeste Shane (divorces in 1977).

"Appointment with Destiny: The Crucifixion of Jesus—An Historical Document," TV production, CBS-TV/David Wolper Productions, narrator.

The Life and Times of Judge Roy Bean, National General Pictures, director, writer (uncredited), actor.

Rufino Tamayo: Sources of His Art, WCBS-TV (New York, Camera Three), documentary, narrator.

Fat City, Columbia, director, writer (uncredited).

San Francisco Retrospective, San Francisco International Film Festival.

1973 *Battle for the Planet of the Apes,* Twentieth Century-Fox, actor.

The Mackintosh Man, Warner Brothers, director.

1974   *Chinatown,* Paramount, actor.

"The Saga of the American Revolution," TV production, Sam Thomas Productions, unrealized, director.

1975   *Breakout,* Columbia, actor.

The Man Who Would Be King, Allied Artists, director, writer.

The Wind and the Lion, MGM/UA, actor.

1975–76 *Across the River and into the Trees,* unrealized, director, writer.

1976   *Hollywood on Trial,* documentary, narrator.

Independence, National Park Service, director, writer (uncredited).

"Sherlock Holmes in New York," TV production, John Cutts for Twentieth Century-Fox/NBC-TV, actor.

1977   *Angela,* Zev Braun Productions, Canafox Films, actor.

The Blue Hotel, unrealized project, director.

Circasia, documentary, appearance.

"The Hobbit," TV production, Rankin-Bass Productions/NBC-TV, voice-over.

"The Rhinemann Exchange," TV production, Universal TV/NBC-TV, actor.

Tentacles, American International, actor.

1978   "B. Traven: A Mystery Solved," TV production, produced by Will Wyatt (United Kingdom), interviewed.

Bermuda Triangle, Concacine/Nucleo, actor.

Hymn to Aton, short film, Phoenix/BFA Films, Huston reads prayer.

Love and Bullets, ITC, director, withdrew.

"The Word," TV production, David Manson for CBS-TV/Charles Fries Productions/Stonehenge, actor.

1978–79 *High Road to China,* director, unrealized (released by Golden Harvest/Pan Pacific, 1983).

1979   Cannes Film Festival career award.

Los Angeles Film Critics Association Career Achievement Award.

The Battle of Mareth/The Greatest Battle, Titanus/Dimension, actor. (Also has 1977 release date.)

Head On (Fatal Attraction), Greentree Productions, actor (released in United States, 1985).

Jaguar Lives, American International, actor.

Winter Kills, Avco Embassy, actor, writer (uncredited).

Wise Blood, New Line, director, writer (uncredited), actor.

1980   Los Angeles County Museum of Art, the Films of John Huston, retrospective.

Agee (James Agee project), documentary, interviewed.

Lincoln Center Film Society, "Live from Lincoln Center Honors John Huston," TV production, PBS.

"Marilyn, the Untold Story," TV production, ABC-TV, fictional account with John Ireland playing Huston.

"Moviolo: This Year's Blonde," TV production, fictional account with William Franfather as Huston.

Phobia, Paramount, director, writer (uncredited).

"Return of the King," TV production, ABC-TV, voice-over.

The Visitor, International Picture Show, actor.

1981   "Creativity with Bill Moyers," TV production, PBS, interviewed.

"John Huston: A War Remembered," TV production, Rastar TV/KCET-TV. Huston discusses his wartime documentaries.

"John Huston's Dublin," TV production, Eire TV, host and narrator.

To the Western World, directed by Margy Kinmouth (United Kingdom), documentary, narrator.

Victory (*Escape to Victory*), Paramount, director, writer (uncredited).

1982   Directors Guild of America, Special Weekend Tribute.

La Cinémathèque Française, hommage à John Huston, retrospective.

Annie, Columbia, director, voice-over.

Cannery Row, MGM/UA, narrator.

The Directors Guild Series: John Huston, Maddox-Tarrow Productions/ DGA Educational and Benevolent Foundation.

"Lights! Camera! Annie!" TV production, KCET-TV, on making the film *Annie.*

1983   American Film Institute Life Achievement Award.

"American Film Institute Salute to John Huston," TV production, CBS-TV.

Lovesick, Ladd/Warner, director (unrealized), actor.

Minor Miracle (*Young Giants*), Entertainment Enterprises, actor.

1984   *George Stevens: A Filmmaker's Journey,* Castle Hill Productions, inter-viewed.

"Luis Buñuel," TV documentary, TVE/Nitra S.A., interviewed.

Notes from Under the Volcano, documentary on making of film.

Observations Under the Volcano, Christian Blackwood Productions, making of the film.

Under the Volcano, Universal, director, writer (uncredited).

1985   David Wark Griffith Award for Career Achievement.

Deutsches Filmmuseum, retrospective.

"Alfred Hitchcock Presents: Man from the South," TV production, Universal/NBC-TV, actor.

"American Caesar," TV production, voice-over.

Black Cauldron, Buena Vista, narrator.

"Herman Melville, Damned in Paradise," TV production, narrator.

The Lions of Kora, documentary, narrator.

Prizzi's Honor, ABC/Twentieth Century-Fox, director, writer (uncredited).

1986   *Directed by William Wyler: A Film Portrait of the Man and His Works,* Topgallant Productions, PBS, interviewed.

Haunted Summer, director, withdrew (released by Pathé/Cannon, 1988).

Mr. Corbett's Ghost, TV production (United Kingdom), actor.

Momo, Cinecitta-Sacis-Tialto-Iduna, actor.

1987   Santa Fe Film Festival, retrospective.

The Dead, Vestron, director, writer.

"John Huston and the Dubliners," Liffey Films, documentary on making *The Dead.*

Revenge, director, writer (unrealized; Columbia, 1989).

Died August 28, 1987, in Middletown, Rhode Island, at eighty-one.

1988   *Mr. North,* executive producer, writer.

1989   "John Huston: The Man, the Movies, the Maverick," TV documentary, subject.

1993   John Huston Award for Artists' Rights established by Anjelica, Donny, and Tony Huston.

1995   "Orson Welles: The One-Man Band," TV, scenes from *The Other Side of the Wind.*

IV
Filmography

This chapter is divided into three parts: Huston's activity as a director, as a screen-writer (including some of his important work and earlier activity at Universal), and as an actor. Huston's other stints as a director (unrealized), writer (uncredited or unrealized projects), and actor (in his own films and others) are indicated in different sections of this book. The credits listed are as they appeared in the film's final released version. Credits are from the screen, official studio credit lists, or standard reference works.

HUSTON AS A DIRECTOR

1 *The Maltese Falcon* (1941)

Director	John Huston
Screenplay	John Huston, based on the novel by Dashiell Hammett
Executive Producer	Hal B. Wallis
Associate Producer	Henry Blanke
Director of Photography	Arthur Edeson, A.S.C.
Dialogue Director	Robert Foulk
Film Editor	Thomas Richards
Art Director	Robert Haas
Sound	Oliver S. Garretson
Gowns	Orry-Kelly
Makeup Artist	Perc Westmore
Music	Adolph Deutsch
Musical Director	Leo F. Forbstein
Cast	Humphrey Bogart (Sam Spade), Mary Astor (Brigid O'Shaughnessy), Gladys Cooper (Iva Archer), Peter Lorre (Joel Cairo), Barton MacLane (Lieutenant Dundy), Lee Patrick (Effie Perine), Sydney Greenstreet (Kasper

	Gutman), Ward Bond (Detective Tom Polhaus), Jerome Cowan (Miles Archer), Elisha Cook Jr. (Wilmer Cook), James Burke (Luke), Murray Alper (Frank Richman), John Hamilton (Bryan), Emory Parnell (Mate of the *La Paloma*), Walter Huston (Captain Jacobi, uncredited). *Bits:* Robert Homans (Policeman), Creighton Hale (Stenographer), Charles Drake (Reporter), Bill Hopper (Reporter), Hank Mann (Reporter), Jack Mower (Announcer)
Filmed	at Warner Brothers Studios, Burbank, California
Running Time	100 minutes, black and white
Release Date	October 3, 1941; production began June 10, 1941; completed September 11, 1941*

Other titles: *The Gent from Frisco* (working title), *Le Faucon maltais, Il Mistero del falco*

SYNOPSIS

The opening statement says: "In 1539 the Knights of Templars of Malta paid tribute to Charles V of Spain by sending him a Golden Falcon encrusted from beak to claw with rarest jewels—but pirates seized the galley carrying this priceless token and the fate of the Maltese Falcon remains a mystery to this day." The film opens with scenes of San Francisco and the Golden Gate Bridge from different angles and then focuses on the window of the offices of Spade and Archer. Effie, the secretary, announces a beautiful woman, a Miss Wonderly. Miss Wonderly says that someone at her hotel referred her to Sam Spade and that she is looking for her sister, Corrine, who ran away with Floyd Thursby. Her parents, who are in Hawaii, will be very upset if they come back and her sister is gone. She sent letters to her sister in care of the General Post Office, but received no response. When she went to the post office, she ran into Thursby, who was picking up the mail. He said that Corrine didn't want to see her, but he would try to convince her to come to Miss Wonderly's hotel that evening. Sam's partner, Miles Archer, enters the office at this time. They continue the conversation while Miles Archer makes eyes at Miss Wonderly. Miss Wonderly wants the investigators to get her sister away from Thursby if the couple shows up that night. Archer says that he will take care of tailing her and Thursby and Corrine, and they will try to get her sister away from Thursby. Wonderly gives them a generous retainer. The men talk about her when she leaves.

---

*This film was the third version of the story produced by Warner Brothers. A 1931 version with the same title was directed by Roy Del Ruth. A 1936 version with the title *Satan Met a Lady* was directed by William Dieterle and starred Bette Davis.

That evening Miles Archer, with a shocked look on his face, is shot point blank. Spade is awakened that night and told about his partner's murder. He calls Effie and tells her to break the news to Iva, Archer's wife, and to keep Iva away from him. He then goes to scene of crime and discusses the situation with Detective Polhaus. Polhaus indicates that Archer's gun was tucked away on his hip and hadn't been fired, that his overcoat was buttoned, and that he had money on him. Spade tries to phone Miss Wonderly at her hotel and is told that she has checked out.

Soon afterward Polhaus and Lieutenant Dundy arrive, question Spade, and try to pin Archer's murder on him. They tell him that Thursby is dead, also, having been shot four times in the back. Dundy tells Spade: "Well, you know me, Spade. If you did it, or if you didn't, you'll get a square deal from me, and most of the breaks."

The next morning Sam goes to the office. Miles's widow, Iva, is there in black. They kiss. She asks him to be kind to her, implying that he killed her husband for her. He gets sarcastic and sends her away. He then takes a call from a Miss LeBlanc. He goes to her address and finds Miss Wonderly. She admits that the story she had told him the day before was just that—a story. Her name is not Wonderly or LeBlanc, but Brigid O'Shaughnessy. She acts sad about Archer. Spade tells her not to worry, for Archer had ten thousand dollars in insurance, no kids, and a wife who didn't like him. Brigid tells Spade that she needs his protection but is unwilling to tell him why. She flirts with him. He tells her that she won't need any help; she's too good. "It's chiefly your eyes and the throb in your voice." He realizes that she is really dangerous. She asks whether he thinks she had anything to do with Archer's death. He takes five hundred dollars from her.

Spade then goes back to the office. Effie brings in Joel Cairo's card, which smells of gardenia. Cairo enters and asks whether Archer's death and Thursby's death are related and states he is interested in recovering an ornament—a black figure of a bird—that has been mislaid. He is prepared to pay five thousand dollars for its recovery. Then Cairo draws his pistol and tells Spade that he intends to search his office. Spade knocks Cairo out, searches his wallet, and discovers a number of passports, foreign coinage, and a ticket to the Geary Theater. When Cairo comes to, Spade takes a retainer of two hundred dollars. When Cairo gets his gun back he sticks Spade up again and insists on searching the office for the bird. Spade laughs, telling him to go ahead.

Spade leaves the office and realizes that he is being tailed. He eludes the person and goes to Brigid's apartment. Spade feels he is beginning to figure her out. He tells her that he saw Joel Cairo, who offered five thousand dollars to retrieve something for him. She admits that she knows Cairo, also. Spade gets angry with her when she says that five thousand dollars is more than she could ever offer him if she had to bid for his loyalty. He replies that all she has ever given him was money, that she has never told him the truth, and that she has tried to buy his loyalty only with money. When Brigid asks, "What else is there I can buy you with?" he kisses her. She tells him that she wants to see Cairo. Spade then makes arrangements for them to meet.

Spade and Brigid go to Spade's apartment. Iva Archer sees them going in. Spade spies the man who was trailing him standing outside. Cairo enters. Brigid tries to bargain with him by cutting herself in on the five thousand dollars if she gets the bird and turns it over to Cairo, but he says that he doesn't have the money right now. She indicates that she will have the bird in another week. She claims that Floyd Thursby had the bird, and she is willing to sell it because she is afraid that she will be murdered, too. She makes some comment about Istanbul, and Cairo responds, at which point she attacks him. Meanwhile, the police arrive to question Spade, but he doesn't allow them in. While they talk in the hallway, they hear someone calling for help and go into the apartment. Brigid has attacked Joel. The police and Cairo leave. Brigid is reluctant to say anything about the bird. She tempts Sam by asking whether he will do something wild and unpredictable if she doesn't tell him anything, and he replies that he might. She explains the complicated attempts to get the bird. He accuses her of lying, and she admits that she has always been a liar.

The next morning finds Spade in Cairo's hotel lobby. He sees Wilmer Cook, who has been following him. Spade confronts him, asks where Cairo is, and tells him that he is going to have to speak to Cairo and that Wilmer can tell that to the fat man. Then Spade gets the house dick to eject Wilmer. Cairo shows up, and Spade says that Brigid knows where the bird is.

Spade goes to his office, where Effie tells him that a number of people are interested in contacting him, including Gutman, who indicated that Wilmer gave him Spade's message. Brigid is also waiting in the office. Sam is having trouble figuring out what is going on. He asks Effie what her woman's intuition is about Brigid. Effie says she has a good impression, and he asks Effie to put her up for a few days. Iva comes in and tells him that she put the police on to him the previous night because she was jealous.

Spade gets a call from Gutman and goes to his apartment. Wilmer answers the door. Gutman asks whether Spade is Brigid's representative. Spade responds that he represents himself. Gutman plays a cat and mouse game with Spade with regard to what the bird is and how much it is worth. Spade gives Gutman the impression that he knows where the bird is. Gutman doesn't go along, and Spade gets angry. It turns out Spade was bluffing for Spade laughs to himself when he leaves the apartment. He goes to the district attorney's office and gets angry when he feels the D.A. is putting pressure on him, but apparently Spade is bluffing again.

Outside the D.A.'s office, Wilmer sticks a gun in Spade's back and forces him to go back to Gutman's apartment. While in the hallway Spade turns on Wilmer, takes his gun, and gives it to Gutman when they enter the apartment. Gutman tells Spade about the Maltese Falcon. In exchange for the Island of Malta, each year Emperor Charles requested the tribute of a falcon. For the knights the Crusades were just an excuse for accumulating wealth, and for the first year's tribute they decided to give him a glorious golden falcon encrusted from head to foot with the finest jewels from their coffers. The bird never reached Charles because it was stolen by pirates. Gutman then tells Spade its history through 1923, when Gutman found out that a Greek dealer had it. Then, seventeen years ago, he had read in the paper that the Greek had been murdered and the bird stolen. It had then turned up in the home of a Russian general in an Istanbul suburb. When he refused to sell it, Gutman sent some agents to steal it from him, but they didn't get it. Gutman asks when Spade can produce the bird and offers him a generous amount to get the bird, while doctoring his drink. When Spade collapses Wilmer starts kicking him. Then Cairo shows up, and the three of them leave.

After Spade awakens, he calls Effie and learns that Brigid is no longer with her. He starts searching Gutman's apartment and sees a circled item in the newspaper that *La Paloma* from Hong Kong is arriving at 5:35 P.M. Spade goes to the port to find the ship is in flames.

Back at the office Spade tells Effie the story as he knows and understands it. Captain Jacobi of the *La Paloma* stumbles into the office with a package. He then dies. Spade opens the package to find the bird. Brigid calls, begging Spade to come to her location. Effie tells him to go. He agrees, but he tells her to call the police. He takes the bird and goes to the railroad station, where he checks it in a locker and sends the ticket to a post office box. He then goes to Brigid's address, but she's not there. He goes home, where Brigid is waiting for him outside. They go into his apartment, and Gutman and Cairo are also there. They try to get the falcon from Spade, who tells them that they have to find someone to take the fall for the murders. Spade wants Gutman to use Wilmer as the fall guy, but Gutman thinks of Wilmer as his son. Then Spade has another idea: Give the police Cairo. Spade pushes Wilmer too far, and another fight ensues in which Wilmer is knocked out. Brigid picks up a gun and Spade takes it from her with a smile. Gutman agrees to give up Wilmer. Spade says he won't be able to get the bird until the next morning. Gutman suggests that they all stay together until Spade can get the bird. Gutman admits that they killed Thursby, Brigid's ally. Gutman also figured out that Brigid gave the bird to Captain Jacobi to bring to the States for her. Gutman, Wilmer, and Cairo had gone to see Captain Jacobi, and when they arrived, Brigid was already there. They thought that they came to terms, but the bird slipped through their fingers. He admits that Wilmer set the fire on *La Paloma*. They then discovered Jacobi in Brigid's apartment and say that Wilmer shot Jacobi. During the discussion, Wilmer wakes up, and Gutman tells him that he is to be sacrificed.

That morning Spade arranges to have the bird brought to his apartment. Gutman opens the package, grabbing the bird and finally bringing it into full view. He takes a knife and starts scraping, but discovers it's not the real falcon—it's lead, a fake. Gutman and Cairo start cursing one another. They think that Kemidov, the Russian general, fooled them. Gutman, optimistic, persuades Cairo to go to Istanbul with him in further pursuit of the bird. Meanwhile, Wilmer has left the apartment unnoticed. Gutman demands his money back from Spade, who refuses, indicating that he held up his end of the bargain. Spade does return the money but keeps a retainer. Gutman then suggests that Spade go with them to Istanbul, but he refuses. Gutman and Cairo leave. Spade calls the police. He tells them that Wilmer killed Jacobi and Thursby and where they can find the thieves.

Spade then turns on Brigid and accuses her of killing Miles Archer. Archer was too experienced to get caught flat-footed in a dark alley with his gun in his holster, but he was just dumb enough to go into the alley with her. She could have stood close to him and killed him with the gun she had taken from Thursby. Spade figures that if Brigid killed Archer with Thursby's gun then Thursby would be arrested and sent up. When Thursby was shot, however, she knew Gutman was in town, so she came back to Spade for protection. He tells her that with a good break she'll be out of Tahatchapi in twenty years and she can come back to him. She thinks he's joking, but he's not. He tells her she's taking the fall. She turns on him, accusing him of not loving her. He replies that he won't play the sap for her and insists that he won't walk in Thursby's footsteps. He tells her that since she killed Miles, she has to go down for it. According to Spade, when a man's partner is killed, he is supposed to do something about it. Moreover, in the detective business, it's bad business to let the killer get away. She doesn't believe him. Spade sees no reason why he should trust her. If he lets her go, she'll have something on him that she can use whenever she wants. He can't be sure that she wouldn't shoot him sometime. "Maybe I'll have some rotten nights," he tells her, but he realizes that she has manipulated him just as she had all the others. She asks him whether he would turn her in if the bird was real, and he tells her that she shouldn't be so sure that he is as crooked as he is supposed to be. They kiss.

The cops and Detective Polhaus come in. They announce that they captured Gutman, Wilmer, and Cairo. Spade hands over Brigid. He tells the police about the whole deal and what happened. He convinces them that he didn't do any of the killings. He gives them the gun and the thousand dollars, saying that the crooks tried to bribe him. He shows them the black bird. The cops thought they had Spade as part of the conspiracy. Taking Brigid, they leave. Polhaus picks up the bird. It's heavy. He asks what it is, and Sam Spade says that it is "the stuff that dreams are made of." They go into the hall. Brigid and the police go into the elevator. She turns and looks straight ahead, not at Spade. He watches her. The elevator door closes. He goes down the stairs with the bird.

2 *In This Our Life* (1942)

Director	John Huston
Screenplay	Howard Koch, based on the novel by Ellen Glasgow
Executive Producer	Hal B. Wallis
Associate Producer	David Lewis
Director of Photography	Ernie Haller, A.S.C.
Film Editor	William Holmes
Art Director	Robert Haas
Sound	Robert B. Lee
Dialogue Director	Edward Blatt
Gowns	Orry-Kelly
Special Effects	Byron Haskin, A.S.C., and Robert Burks, A.S.C.
Makeup Artist	Perc Westmore
Orchestral Arrangements	Hugo Friedhofer
Musical Director	Leo F. Forbstein
Assistant Director	Jack Sullivan
Unit Manager	Lou Baum

Cast*	Bette Davis (Stanley Timberlake), Olivia de Havilland (Roy Timberlake), George Brent (Craig Fleming), Dennis Morgan (Peter Kingsmill), Charles Coburn (William Fitzroy), Frank Craven (Asa Timberlake), Billie Burke (Lavinia Timberlake), Hattie McDaniel (Minerva Clay), Lee Patrick (Betty Wilmoth), Mary Servoss (Charlotte Fitzroy), Ernest Anderson (Parry Clay), William B. Davidson (Kim Purdy), Edward Fielding (Doctor Buchanan), John Hamilton (Inspector), William Forrest (Forest Ranger), Walter Huston (Bartender, uncredited).
Filmed	at Warner Brothers Studios, Burbank, California
Running Time	97 minutes, black and white
Release Date	May 8, 1942; production began October 13, 1941; completed January 8, 1942; postproduction through February 13, 1942

Other titles: *In Questa nostra vita*

SYNOPSIS

There is considerable activity in the Timberlake household. The family mansion, once the center of a great plantation, is now surrounded by stores and apartments, and there are plans to tear it down. Stanley Timberlake is to be married to the attorney Craig Fleming. Asa Timberlake, her father, is the nominal head of the family. His wife, Lavinia, is the niece of William Fitzroy, the richest man in town. Lavinia is a bedridden hypochondriac, and Asa has found that their marriage is dominated by Fitzroy. Fitzroy adores Stanley and spoils her, his latest gift being a new car. Her sister, Roy, is married to Peter Kingsmill, a young surgeon. Three days before Stanley is to marry Craig, she runs off with Peter. Roy gets a divorce. Stanley and Peter go to Baltimore, where he gets a job in a hospital. For her this escapade is nothing more than an exciting adventure.

Roy and Craig, meanwhile, have become close. His interests are in civil liberties. Roy brings to his attention Parry Clay, a young black man who wants to be a lawyer. Craig and Roy fall in love.

Stanley's frivolous antics drive Peter crazy, and he commits suicide. After Peter's suicide, Stanley is brought home in a state of hysteria. She is so disturbed that everyone is solicitous and forgiving toward her. Uncle Fitzroy had cut Stanley out of his will when she ran away. Now he is very ill, and she tries to get in his good

---

*In *The Hustons* (page 224), Lawrence Grobel writes that "on the first day of shooting certain players from *The Maltese Falcon* turned up to make uncredited cameo appearances. When the script called for a shadow of a man on an office door, Humphrey Bogart cast his."

graces. She also tries to win back Craig, attempting to get him to meet her at a roadside inn, but he doesn't show up. She gets drunk and speeds off in her car. She runs over a child and her mother, killing the child and seriously injuring the mother. She refuses to accept responsibility for her actions and blames Parry Clay. The police arrest him.

Roy visits Minerva Clay, Parry's mother, who tells her that Parry was home the night of the accident. Roy asks Craig to defend him. He is a bit reluctant. Roy then confronts Stanley, who still refuses to accept the blame. Craig comes in with Stanley's key ring, which was found in her car. He asks her to come to the police with him. Stanley rushes off to her uncle, but he is at death's door and too distracted to even hear what she is saying. Stanley, in desperation, jumps into her car and drives off. Her car skids and overturns, and she is killed.

3 *Across the Pacific* (1942)

Director	John Huston
Screenplay	Richard Macaulay, from the *Saturday Evening Post* serial by Robert Carson
Producers	Jerry Wald and Jack Saper
Director of Photography	Arthur Edeson, A.S.C.
Film Editor	Frank Magee
Art Directors	Robert Haas and Hugh Reticker
Sound	Everett A. Brown
Special Effects	Byron Haskin, A.S.C., and Willard Van Enger, A.S.C.
Music	Adolph Deutsch
Musical Director	Leo F. Forbstein
Montages	Don Siegel
Gowns	Milo Anderson
Makeup Artist	Perc Westmore
Unit Manager	Chuck Hansen
Assistant Director	Lee Katz
Cast	Humphrey Bogart (Rick Leland), Mary Astor (Alberta Marlow), Sydney Greenstreet (Doctor Lorenz), Charles Halton (A. V. Smith), Sen Yung (Joe Totsuiko), Roland Got (Sugi), Lee Tung Foo (Sam Wing On), Frank Wilcox (Captain Morrison), Paul Stanton (Colonel Hart), Lester Matthews (Canadian Major), John Hamilton (Court-martial President), Tom Stevenson (Unidentified Man), Roland Drew (Captain Harkness), Monte Blue (Dan Morton), Chester Gan (Captain Higoto), Richard Loo (First Officer Miyuma), Keye Luke (Steamship Office Clerk), Kam Tong (T. Oki), Spencer Chan

	(Chief Engineer Mitsuko), Rudy Robles (Assassin). *Bits:* Bill Hopper, Frank Mayo, Garland Smith, Dick French, Charles Drake, Will Morgan, Roland Drew, Jack Mower, Eddie Dew, Frank Faylen, Ruth Ford, Eddie Lee, Dick Botiller, Beal Wong, Philip Ahn, Anthony Caruso, James Leong, Paul Fung
Filmed	at Warner Brothers Studios, Burbank, California
Running Time	97 minutes, black and white
Release Date	September 5, 1942; began production March 2, 1942; completed April 18, 1942

Other titles: *Griffes jaunes, Agguato ai tropici*

SYNOPSIS

Dismissed from the service after a court-martial verdict, Captain Rick Leland of the U.S. Army, a lonely, disgraced man, walks across the deserted army post's parade grounds. A few minutes later, he tells his friend, Captain Morrison, that he is leaving for Halifax to enlist in the Canadian Artillery; but in Halifax his identity is established by the Canadian Army Command, which gives Leland a cold, official refusal. He goes then to the N.Y.K. Japanese Steamship company, where he obtains passage on the freighter *Genoa Maru,* bound for Yokohama by way of New York, Panama, and Honolulu. That night as the *Genoa Maru* sails, Rick boldly introduces himself to Alberta Marlow, an attractive young woman. Rick also encounters another passenger, Doctor H. F. C. Lorenz, who identifies himself as a sociologist headed for the Philippines. Doctor Lorenz reveals his affinity for the Japanese and points out that they are a "wonderful, greatly misunderstood" people. The doctor has a Japanese manservant, Oki. Later in bed in the stateroom, Rick sees a Japanese face spying on him through a porthole.

The next day at lunch, Rick and Alberta meet Captain Higoto, Chief Engineer Mitsuko, and First Officer Miyuma. Alberta wishes for rough weather and an exciting voyage and eats too much bread pudding. On deck afterward, Rick kisses her. She becomes seasick and asks Rick if that always happens to girls he kisses. In the saloon, Rick meets Lorenz again. The doctor buys him a drink, and Rick admits that he is broke but expects to get some money in New York. That night over the whiskey bottle, and under Lorenz's sly persuasions, Rick tells him that he was dishonorably discharged from the army. Rick also shows a surprising knowledge of U.S. military affairs, especially related to the Canal Zone. Then it's his turn to get seasick.

Rick and Alberta leave the *Genoa Maru* when it docks at New York Harbor and take a cab to Grand Central Station, where Rick deposits the girl while he goes to borrow some money from a friend on Wall Street. After avoiding a man who is obviously shadowing him, Rick presents himself at an establishment, ostensibly the Atlas Finance Company. Ushered into a private office, he meets Colonel Hart, U.S.

Army, who greets Rick warmly. From their conversation, it becomes apparent that Rick is actually in the army's secret service and that Doctor Lorenz is the man they are after. Colonel Hart also warns Rick to watch the girl. When he rejoins Alberta, Rick finds it necessary to threaten a stranger who has been shadowing her. Back at the *Genoa Maru,* Rick saves Lorenz's life when the doctor is attacked by a Filipino assassin. A new passenger comes aboard the vessel before it leaves New York: Joe Totsuiko, a nisei and a wise-cracking college kid.

The following day, Lorenz approaches Rick with a deal, whereby Rick will be well paid for certain information about military installations in the vicinity of the Panama Canal. Rick accepts some money and Lorenz's promise that he will receive more when he delivers the information to Lorenz. When the *Genoa Maru* docks at Colón, Rick, Alberta, and Lorenz register at the Pan-American Hotel, where Rick establishes contact with Sam, the Chinese proprietor and a loyal American. Later at the International Bar, Rick accuses Alberta of complicity with the Lorenz gang. She is about to confess something when she is called to the phone. She doesn't return.

Back at the hotel, Rick searches her room and discovers a photograph of the Bountiful Plantation, signed "Dad." In his own room Rick finds Lorenz waiting for him, and in the altercation that follows, the doctor canes Rick. Rick staggers downstairs into Sam's office, where Sam tends his wound and advises him to go to the Ewa Theater at 10 P.M. In the darkened theater, a man slides into the seat next to Rick's and tells him to go to the Bountiful Plantation at once. Then the informer is stabbed to death, and Rick flees in the confusion, escaping through the back of the theater in a hail of gunshots.

At the Bountiful Plantation, Rick is captured by Oki and Joe Totsuiko. There he finds Alberta, Lorenz, and Dan Morton, who is the girl's father. Alberta explains that her father had fled to Panama following an embezzlement scandal and that she was reluctant to confide in Rick for fear that he was an F.B.I. man. Rick overcomes his guards and escapes with the girl and her father, but not until he learns from the unwary Joe of Lorenz's plans to blow up the Panama Canal's Gatun Locks with torpedoes from a Japanese-piloted plane. Next the three escapees are in the tropical countryside, where they watch a plane being loaded with torpedoes. Rick moves closer, draws a bead on one of the torpedoes, and fires. The plane explodes. Rick also captures Lorenz on the spot. Then Rick and Alberta watch a U.S. battleship go through the locks and a line of war craft putting out to sea.

4 *Report from the Aleutians* (1943)

Director and Writer	John Huston
Producer	Army Pictorial Service, U.S. Signal Corps, U.S. War Department
Narration	Walter Huston and John Huston
Photography	Jules Buck, Ray Scott, John Huston, Freeman C. Collins, Buzz Ellsworth, and Herman Crabtree
Music	Dimitri Tiomkin
Filmed	in the Aleutian Islands
Running Time	47 minutes, Technicolor

Release Date   July 1943*
Other title: *Les Aleoutiennes*

SYNOPSIS

The documentary stresses the military importance of the Aleutian Islands and of the air missions to secure this theater of the war along with goals of harassing the Japanese. In early June 1942, the Japanese launched an all-out attempt to secure absolute domination of the entire Pacific Ocean, dispatching two invasion fleets. They failed. In late August 1942, a large detachment of U.S. troops landed on Adak, an island several hundred miles out along the Aleutian chain and less than two hours flight by bomber from Kiska, an island under enemy control. Adak is bleak and of no value other than its strategic position. Eleven days after the occupation an airfield was completed, and the first U.S. bombers touched down to start missions against Kiska. The sound of their engines warming up starts before dawn, and every day the bombers take off on at least one mission. If the airfield is the heart of Adak, the harbor is its hungry mouth. Its defenses are strong, and the island is secure. Supply services provide everything for the men stationed on Adak; except for drinking water everything must be brought in. The manpower of Adak is constantly augmented, rising to thousands of troops. Weather conditions are extreme, changing every few minutes.

Most air missions do return. The greatest aircraft casualties occur from anti-aircraft fire over Kiska. As a rule the bombers make it back, but often they are crippled, with wounded and dead aboard. The return of the day's mission is the highlight of each twenty-four hours, especially when six bombers go out and six come back. Anyone who has gone out will say that the most wonderful ride in the world is the ride back from Kiska. Immediately upon landing, servicing the plane begins, and crews are debriefed. A photographic ship accompanies missions to Kiska. Its task: to follow the bombers over their targets and to record the immediate results of the bombardment. The objectives of any mission from Adak are threefold: to destroy enemy shipping en route to Kiska, to demolish installations on the island, and to harass enemy personnel.

Sundays are like any other day, with missions going out. The type of bombs the crews use depends on the target. Belts of ammunition are brought to machine guns and threaded into receivers, ready for firing. Pilots are given final instructions. Three flights—two of B-24s and one of B-17s—are to go over the target. A bomber crew is a team, and the longer it is together, the better the teamwork. The men share a mutual responsibility. The safety of the ship and the lives of all the men may depend on any single crewman. Trust and respect are implicit in such a relationship if it is to endure. The former high school kids in their hopped-up jalopies have become the pilots, men of great daring in highly dangerous circumstances. Each one has flown many missions and shoulders a great burden. The machine is expensive, but his many men are also his responsibility. Behind the success of their flights are enormous amounts of work from support groups.

*No credits are indicated on the released film.

The mission proceeds toward Kiska, about an hour and forty-five minutes from Adak. The pilots fly at 160 miles per hour. Trial rounds are fired. Many pilots and crews have made the flight twenty-five or thirty times. They look out for enemy planes. They say they always get a funny feeling over Kiska: "We're way up there, out of this world, and it's like it was trying to destroy us, and us it, before we can even get back down to it." The planes go into a bombing run. They fly in an absolutely straight line toward the target. As they approach Kiska, each plane veers off toward its target and encounters heavy antiaircraft fire. "The object is to hit the target, not to avoid antiaircraft . . . you are just as liable to run into it as away from it. The best way is to forget what's happening outside, and make the run by instruments. That way, if it comes, you just look over your shoulder and you see a man with a long beard, and you say, 'Good morning, Father Abraham.'" Kiska's hangars are destroyed, after the U.S. bombers find their targets. Nine bombers came out, and nine are going home.

5 *Battle of San Pietro* (1945)

Director, Writer, and Narrator	John Huston
Prologue	Gen. Mark Clark
Producer	Army Pictorial Service, Signal Corps, U.S. War Department
Production Supervisor	Frank Capra
Cameramen	John Huston, Jules Buck, Wilbur Bradley, Roland Mead, Sam Tischler, A. I. Moroshnik, Gordon Frye, Leonard Ryan
Editor	Edward Mann
Music	Dimitri Tiomkin
Recorded	Army Air Force Orchestra, Mormon Tabernacle Choir, Children's Choir of St. Brendan's Church
Filmed	at field of action, Italy
Running Time	30 minutes, black and white*

*Information in the John Huston Collection located in the Academy of Motion Picture Arts and Sciences, Beverly Hills, states that Huston and the group of combat cameramen started shooting late in the fall of 1943. They exposed approximately sixty thousand feet of film, and the finished film was eventually cut down to three thousand feet. The film took five months to shoot. Information from the Museum of Modern Art (MOMA) indicates that the film was cut by the War Department from five reels to three. MOMA says that Kit Parker Films has available a four-reel "Capra cut" of October 12, 1944, as well as a shorter version minus General Mark Clark's foreword. An information sheet in the Huston Collection specifies that the film was released through the Office of War Information, distributed by the War Activities Committee, Motion Picture Industry, through its Exchange Area Distribution Chairmen. Various studios were responsible for distribution in different cities: Columbia, MGM, Paramount, Twentieth Century-Fox, United Artists, Universal, and Warner Brothers. No credits are listed on the released film.

Filmography

Released   May 3, 1945; opened at Fifty-fifth Street
                            Theater, New York City, on July 11, 1945
Other titles: *San Pietro, La Bataille de San Pietro*

SYNOPSIS

The documentary opens with a statement by Gen. Mark Clark regarding the military situation in Italy and the strategic importance of San Pietro, located in the Liri River Valley, some sixty miles from Naples and some forty miles south of Rome. The valley is a wide flat corridor, completely surrounded by high mountains, which are covered with snow in winter. The valley, rich farm country with many olive groves, is green all year round, but the last year saw little farming because of the war.

At the foot of the valley sits the seven-hundred-year-old town of San Pietro with its historic fifteenth-century church, now in ruins. With a narration spoken by John Huston the documentary shows vivid scenes of the battles to gain control of the mountains, their ridges, and the town from the Germans. The fierce fighting took place at the end of 1943. The battle lines were as haphazard as the terrain itself, with its flood-swollen rivers making movement extremely treacherous. One approach to town is through a narrow pass or via a scenic road over the mountains.

In this second phase of the Italian campaign, each peak and ridge had to be fought yard by yard. The foot soldier, the men with rifles and bayonets, had to capture these positions, with the enemy in heavily entrenched positions looking down on the Americans. The approaches were covered with barbed wire, and the land was heavily mined with devices that flew up at a footfall, exploding beneath the groin. Attempts to take some of the mountains proved costly. The men constantly went on patrol to ascertain enemy positions and to capture prisoners for additional information. In some cases patrols went out and no men returned. Plans were to move men up the mountains and along the ridges in the dark to take enemy positions. Some of the troops had been fighting daily with no rest since landing in Salerno. As the troops prepared to move, there was heavy bombardment and rain. The troops also encountered fierce resistance. The enemy's mortar and artillery fire was very accurate, and many Americans died.

As more reserves were brought up, the advance moved forward beyond six hundred yards. Attacks on other mountains were more successful, but the Germans mounted costly counterattacks. While the toll of enemy dead mounted, captured German soldiers told the Americans that their orders were to retake positions at any cost. More American troops were thrown into the battle. Air cover helped and massive Allied artillery barrages were laid down, but even so enemy planes bombed American positions. Next tanks were brought in to enter the town of San Pietro. Sixteen tanks took the high road into the town, which was under enemy observation. Only three reached the outskirts of San Pietro. Two were then destroyed, and the last one was missing.

Troops now paid for ground gained at the cost of a man a yard. Through successive waves of attacks, one of the main mountains was captured. With its capture

63

the enemy decided to withdraw, but not without some violent counterattacks. In these encounters some American troops lost all of their officers. Enlisted men came forward to rally their comrades. For hours the earth trembled from the guns. Finally the Americans took the town of San Pietro.

Troops were tremendously depleted, with one regiment requiring eleven hundred replacements. During scenes of a large cemetery created for the dead, the narrator states that these fallen troops gave their precious lives for their country, their loved ones, and most certainly themselves. More than one hundred decorations for acts of valor above and beyond the call of duty were awarded following the battle of San Pietro. The film then shows surviving soldiers, stating that many will join their comrades as the war moves northward, "for ahead lay San Vittori, the Rapido River, and Cassino, and beyond Cassino more rivers, more mountains, and more towns, more San Pietros, greater or lesser, a thousand more."

As the battle moved on, the townspeople came out of their hiding places. Most were old people, women, and children. Some dug their loved ones out of the rubble. The film also depicts a woman carrying a coffin on her head, women nursing babies, a woman washing clothes in a stream, a man leading his two cows through the ruined town. Women and men clear the rubble to rebuild the town. American troops distribute food. Many children smile for the cameras, but some cry, and others are serious. The narrator assures that they are able to forget quickly: "Tomorrow will be as if the bad things never happened."

As for the battle itself, its prime military objective was met and it freed the people. The fields are planted again, with a good crop anticipated in the coming season. The people pray to Saint Peter for those who came, liberated the town, and fought northward. The film ends with a picture of the Liberty Bell and the "V" symbol.

6 *Let There Be Light* (1946)

Director	John Huston
Producer	Army Pictorial Service, Signal Corps, U.S. War Department
Screenplay	Charles Kaufman and John Huston
Editor	Gene Fowler Jr.*
Photography	Stanley Cortez, George Smith, Lloyd Fromm, John Doran, Joseph Jackman
Narration	Walter Huston
Filmed	at Mason General Hospital, Long Island, New York
Running Time	59 minutes (some sources indicate 45 or 58 minutes)

*Some sources indicate that John Huston was involved in the editing. The film was produced in 1945. No credits are indicated on the released print. *Film Dope* indicates that in 1948 the Signal Corps released a reconstruction of the film, using professional actors, called *Shades of Gray,* directed by Joseph Henabery. Huston had no connection with this later project.

Released   December 16, 1980 (the film was suppressed
                                  by the government for thirty-four years)
Other titles: *Que la lumière soit*

SYNOPSIS

The film's introduction indicates that 20 percent of all wartime casualties are of a psychiatric nature. A troopship enters the harbor, and patients disembark. Some show evidence of their wounds while for others no wounds are visible. The narrator states that every man has his breaking point, and in the fulfillment of their duties these men were forced beyond the limit of human endurance.

The psychiatric patients are transported to Mason General Hospital on Long Island, New York. The admission officer tells the patients that they should not be alarmed by the cameras, which will make a photographic record of their progress. The narrator describes some of the cases: men who tremble, men who cannot sleep, men with pains or who are paralyzed with no apparent physical cause, men who can not remember. Generally, all of them have an unceasing fear and apprehension, a sense of impending disaster, a feeling of hopelessness and utter isolation. The patients are interviewed by psychiatrists, and their one overpowering fear appears to be the fear of death. The patients tell the psychiatrists about the circumstances that led them to this point. They pour their hearts out. They tell of seeing too many of their buddies die. "I figured the next one was me, and a man can only stand so much out there."

Next, there are scenes of the men calling home and settling down in the dormitories. The narrator indicates that modern psychiatry makes no sharp distinction between mind and body. In one session a patient is given a Rorschach test. Another patient cannot walk, but his paralysis is purely psychological. The patient is given a drug that induces a hypnotic state during which the causes of his paralysis are explored. The roots of his paralysis appear to be conflicts with his parents. Coming out of hypnosis the patient is able to walk. The narrator cautions that even though the patient can walk, that doesn't mean that his neurosis is cured. The door has been opened, but it will take time.

Other patients are seen in occupational therapy. They also engage in sports activities. A doctor indicates that the activities provide a basis for normalcy. Patients at various times talk about their upbringing and relationships with their parents. A patient reveals that he never spoke until he was seven. One doctor treats a patient with amnesia. Under hypnosis the patient relates his experiences on Okinawa and the bombing from the Japanese. This experience appears to have been the cause of his amnesia. His memory returns, and he remembers who he is. Another patient has an extreme case of stuttering, which the narrator says was caused by battle tension. With the help of drugs the patient is able to speak, and he becomes ecstatic at the prospect.

The narrator indicates that as the weeks pass therapy begins to show its effects. The shock and stress of war are beginning to wear off, for these men are blessed with the natural regenerative powers of youth. Now they are living less in the past and more in the present. The patients take classes on entering private life, receive visits, and participate in group therapy sessions. Some patients wonder about the public's reaction to their mental conditions. The doctors try to assure the patients that their condition is not much different from people in civilian life who undergo severe stress and develop the same symptoms and mental conditions. They talk about their lives outside, about getting jobs, and about whether to tell their prospective employers that they have mental problems. The doctors try to reinforce their situations, reminding them that there is nothing to hide, that they got something out of being in the service, and that they learned new skills. The long days in the hospital lead to normal activities, including normal gripes about the food and the movies shown. In a group therapy session a doctor stresses that children growing up must have safety and confidence. If a child doesn't have either, he must find someone that he esteems and learn to feel safe so that he can feel worthwhile and important to someone. If the child doesn't enjoy those feelings as a child, he will need to be fed acceptance and to find safety as an adult.

A baseball game is in progress. The patients that were suffering various stages of mental disorder are now playing as normal human beings. After eight weeks the men are discharged and returned to their families. The officer tells them that, as they reenter civilian life, on their shoulders falls much of the responsibility for the postwar world. As they leave the grounds the men wave from buses to the nurses and to some of the newer patients.

7 *On Our Merry Way* (1948)

Directors (credited)	King Vidor and Leslie Fenton
Directors (uncredited)	John Huston and George Stevens*
Producers	Benedict Borgeaus and Burgess Meredith
Production Company	Borgeaus–United Artists
Screenplay	Laurence Stallings, Lou Breslow, and John O'Hara (for the Stewart-Fonda sequence)
Original Story	Arch Obler
Photography	John Seitz
Cast	Paulette Goddard (Martha Pease), Burgess Meredith (Oliver Pease), James Stewart (Slim), Henry Fonda (Lank), Harry James (Guest Star), Dorothy Lamour (Gloria Manners), Victor Moore (Ashton Carrington), Fred MacMurray (Al), William Demarest

*In this anthology film, James Stewart and Henry Fonda teamed for the first time in the first segment, which John O'Hara wrote for them. Their choice of director was John Huston, who started shooting the sequence. According to the literature Huston had completed one segment when work had to stop because of Fonda's previous commitments. When he returned Huston was no longer available. The actors' choice to direct the rest of their section was George Stevens. Neither Stevens or Huston received screen credit.

(Floyd), Hugh Herbert (Elisha Hobbs), Charles D. Brown (Mr. Sadd), Eduardo Ciannelli (Maxim Cordova), Betty Caldwell (Cynthia), Eilene Janseen (Peggy Thorndike), Carl Switzer (Zoot), Dorothy Ford (Lola), Frank Moran (Bookie), David Whorf (Sniffles Dugan)

Filmed	at Hollywood, California
Running Time	107 minutes, black and white
Released	February 3, 1948

Other titles: *A Miracle Can Happen*

SYNOPSIS, HUSTON AND STEVENS SEGMENT

Oliver Pease is a mousy, mild-mannered man who makes twenty-five dollars a week working in the want ad department of a daily newspaper. To make himself important in the eyes of his bride, Martha, he has given her the impression that he is the newspaper's roving reporter and makes fifty dollars per week. To keep up appearances he has mortgaged the furniture in their apartment. Martha tells Oliver she will leave him unless he asks his boss for a raise, and she suggests a question for the roving reporter: "What great influence has a little child had upon your life?" Martha's ultimatum leads to his impersonating the roving reporter, being chased by a big lug after the money he owes, and his running into a pool hall. There Slim and Lank, two down-and-out jazz musicians, tell him their story based on the roving reporter's question. Their band was stranded in a small California seacoast town after their bus broke down. The local garage man informed them that it would take five hundred dollars to repair the bus. They decided to raise funds by giving a concert on the local pier, but the mayor wouldn't allow such concerts. The mayor's zoot-suited son was a lousy trumpet player. The musicians convinced him to talk his father into letting them give the concert, where they held a local talent contest. They conspired to let the son win. A double cross was executed when the garage man entered his "baby daughter," Lola—a beauty and very talented—in the contest. Despite their efforts she won the contest, took their band, and forced them to become her musicians.

8 *The Treasure of the Sierra Madre* (1948)

Director	John Huston
Producer	Henry Blanke
Screenplay	John Huston, based on the novel by B. Traven
Photographer	Ted McCord, A.S.C.
Art Director	John Hughes
Film Editor	Owen Marks
Sound	Robert B. Lee
Technical Advisers	Ernesto A. Romero and Antonio Arriaga
Set Decorations	Fred M. MacLean
Special Effects	William McGann, director, and H. F. Koenekamp

Makeup	Perc Westmore
Music	Max Steiner
Orchestral Arrangements	Murray Cutter
Musical Director	Leo F. Forbstein
Assistant Director	Dick Mayberry
Unit Manager	Don Page
Unit Publicist	Bob Fender
Cast	Humphrey Bogart (Fred C. Dobbs), Walter Huston (Howard), Tim Holt (Curtin), Bruce Bennett (Cody), Barton MacLane (McCormick), Alfonso Bedoya (Gold Hat), A. Soto Rangel (Presidente), Manuel Donde (El Jefe), Jose Torvay (Pablo), Margarito Luna (Pancho), Jacqueline Dalya (Flashy Girl), Bobby Blake (Mexican Boy). *Smaller Parts and Bits:* Spencer Chan, Julian Rivero, John Huston (White Suit), Harry Vejar, Pat Flaherty, Clifton Young, Jack Holt, Ralph Dunn, Guillermo Calleo, Roberto Canedo, Ernesto Escoto, Ignacio Villalbajo, Manuel Donde, Ildefonso Vega, Francisco Islas, Alberto Valdespino, Manuel Bautista, Sabino Garcia Perez, Mario Mancilla, Martin Garral
Filmed	in Mexico and at Warner Brothers, Burbank, California
Running Time	126 minutes, black and white
Release Date	January 6, 1948; production began March 17, 1947; completed July 22, 1947

Other titles: *Le Trésor de la Sierra Madre, Il Tesòro della Sierra Madre*

SYNOPSIS

Fred C. Dobbs, a down-and-out American drifter in the Mexican town of Tampico, rips up a losing lottery ticket. He starts panhandling and puts the touch on an American tourist in a white suit (John Huston in an uncredited role). In a bar a persistent Mexican kid sells him a portion of a lottery ticket. On a park bench he meets Curtin, another destitute American. Dobbs puts another touch on the man in the white suit. With the money he gets a haircut and shave and hires a prostitute. He puts another touch on the same white suit, who is getting a bit exasperated with him and asks Dobbs why he only approaches him. Dobbs, very apologetic, tells the man that he never looked at his face. The man tells Dobbs that from now on he will have to make his way through life by himself.

Dobbs then puts the touch on McCormick, who offers him a job working on an oil rig. He and Curtin go along and for weeks work hard. When the partners return, McCormick disappears, leaving them almost penniless. With what money they do have they go to the Orso Negro, a fleabag hotel to sleep and meet Howard, an old gold miner. He is very talkative and tells them about his many years as a gold prospector. "I know what gold does to men's souls," he tells them. The next day Dobbs and Curtin spot McCormick. They demand their money. They get into a fight, beat him up, and take from his wallet what he owes them. Then they decide that they want to give gold mining a shot, especially after hearing Howard's tales. In addition Dobb's lottery ticket is a winner, so they have enough money to stake an expedition. Dobbs is generous, laying out much of the money. Back at the Orso Negro, they persuade Howard to join their expedition.

On their way into the hinterlands, their train is attacked by bandits. The Federales chase the bandits off. When the would-be prospectors get to a town they buy supplies and burros. On their trek into the mountains, Howard, almost old enough to be their father, has more energy than they do and outpaces them. At one point Dobbs and Curtin think they have found gold, but Howard assures them that it is fool's gold and that they shouldn't waste water washing it. Water is more precious than gold in these parts, he advises them. When they become so exhausted and run-down that they want to give up and go back, Howard berates them and starts doing a jig. He has found what looks like a vein, but he tells them that they have to go up farther into the mountain to find where it is the richest. They try to hide their activity by camping farther down the mountain. They decide to tell anyone who comes by that they are hunters.

On one of his trips into town for supplies Curtin is questioned by Cody, another American. He tries to hook up with Curtin, who thinks he has put him off, but Cody ends up following him. As they talk around the fire that night the stranger, Cody, shows up. He tries to join up with them, knowing what they are about. At first they are reluctant, but they agree when they see they have little choice in the matter. The next morning they are attacked by bandits. They fight them off, but Cody is killed. When they search his effects, they discover that he has a wife and children back in Texas.

At one point the main mine shaft caves in, trapping Dobbs. At first Curtin is tempted to leave him there, but he eventually rescues his partner. Howard and Curtin realize that Dobbs is going crazy. He talks to himself and insists that they split up the pooled gold on a daily basis. He is convinced the others want to rob him and thinks that Howard and Curtin have discovered where he is hiding his gold. Having accumulated a large stake, they decide to break camp. Howard insists that they put the mountain back the way they found it, for they have wounded it. Going back to the town they are confronted by Indians who ask Howard to go with them. A little boy has apparently drowned, but he is not dead. Howard brings the boy around. They insist that he stay with them. He tells Curtin to take care of his goods until he can meet them again in the town. On the trip Dobbs become more dangerous. He tries to kill Curtin, leaving him for dead, but Curtin survives. The Indians find Curtin and bring him to their village, where Howard takes care of him. They decide to go after Dobbs, who now has everybody's gold.

Dobbs is incapable of going it alone. His burros die on him. He finally comes to a water hole and is confronted by bandits who kill him for his shoes and the remaining burros. They do not realize that the bags he carries are worth a small fortune. They think that they are full of dirt. When the bandits go into town and try to sell the burros, the animals' markings give them away. The bandits are arrested and shot by the Federales about the same time that Howard and Curtin arrive. They anxiously inquire about their bags of gold, and the son of the man who originally sold the burros and equipment to them tells them that he overheard the bandits talk about bags of dust. Howard and Curtin ask him to show them where they left the bags.

When they arrive at the spot outside the town, they see some torn bags and realize that the gold dust has blown off into the wind. Howard starts to laugh hysterically. Curtin at first thinks him crazy, then realizes the joke, and joins in the laughter. Howard says, "Laugh, Curtin, old boy. It's a great joke played on us by the Lord or fate or by nature . . . whichever you prefer, but whoever or whatever played it, certainly had a sense of humor. The gold has gone back to where we got it. Laugh, my boy, laugh. It's worth ten months of labor and suffering . . . this joke is." Howard decides to go back to the Indians, who consider him a god, and he figures he'll just live out his years there. He tells Curtin to sell the burros and whatever equipment and supplies are left, to take his share, and to go to Texas and see Cody's wife.

9 *Key Largo* (1948)

Director	John Huston
Producer	Jerry Wald
Screenplay	Richard Brooks and John Huston, based on the play by Maxwell Anderson
Photography	Karl Freund
Special Effects	William McGann and Robert Burks
Film Editor	Rudi Fehr
Art Direction	Leo K. Kuter
Sets	Fred MacLean
Music	Max Steiner
Musical Orchestration	Murray Cutter
Sound	Dolph Thomas
Wardrobe	Leah Rhodes
Makeup	Perc Westmore
Unit Manager	Chuck Hansen
Assistant Director	Art Lueker
Cast	Humphrey Bogart (Frank McCloud), Edward G. Robinson (Johnny Rocco), Lauren Bacall (Nora Temple), Lionel Barrymore (James Temple), Claire Trevor (Gaye), Thomas Gomez (Curley), Harry Lewis (Toots), John Rodney (Deputy Sawyer), Marc Lawrence (Ziggy), Dan Seymour (Angel), Monte Blue (Ben Wade), Jay Silverheels and Rodric Redwing (Osceola Brothers). *Small Parts and Bits:* Joe P. Smith (Bus Driver), Albert Marin (Skipper), Pat Flaherty (Man), Felipa Gomez (Old Indian Woman), Jerry Jerome, John

Phillips, and Lute Crockett (Ziggy's
Henchmen)
Filmed   at Warner Brothers Studios, Burbank and
Florida
Running Time   101 minutes, black and white
Release Date   July 31, 1948; production began December 19,
1947; completed March 13, 1948
Other titles: *L'Isola di corallo*

SYNOPSIS

Frank McCloud, a WWII veteran and drifter, travels to Key West. On his way he
stops at the hotel in Key Largo that is owned by Temple, the father of his commanding officer, who was killed in the Italian campaign. His commanding officer's
wife, Nora, also lives there. When he enters the hotel he is met by some despicable
types who are rude to him. All he wants is a drink. They refuse to give him one.
Gaye, a woman in the bar who is brutalized by these men, berates them, and they
give him a beer. Temple and Nora insist that McCloud stay overnight. While talking to them, the sheriff comes and asks whether they have seen two Indians who
have escaped from jail. The sheriff can't understand why they did this when they
had only thirty days left on their sentence. Temple replies that for an Indian thirty
days is like thirty years. McCloud then relates to Temple and Nora how the younger
Temple died, how brave he was, and where he is buried. Temple says that maybe
dying is not so important and tells Nora that maybe they will take a trip to Italy to
see his grave. They ask McCloud why he came down to this part of the country, and
McCloud reckons that maybe he will do some deep-sea fishing. A storm starts up,
and McCloud shows his knowledge of boats by securing the Temples' boat. In the
bar Curley and Toots, two of Rocco's gang, start eyeing Nora.

    Upstairs Johnny Rocco is taking a bath. Curley enters the bathroom and tells
Johnny what is going on downstairs. Downstairs Temple calls for Mr. Brown,
Johnny's alias. Before going down, Johnny looks at a prone body on the bed. When
it stirs, Johnny slaps it.

    Downstairs Johnny Rocco tells everyone that he doesn't want any trouble
from them, that he and his friends will be gone in a couple of hours. McCloud recognizes Mr. Brown as the gangster Johnny Rocco, who was deported. Temple says
that he shouldn't have been deported, that he should have been exterminated.
Rocco, overhearing this exchange, is surprised at the reception and rejoins that he is
not a dirty Red. He tells them that he was a big man at one time and will come back.
McCloud talks about fighting to rid the world of his type. Rocco taunts Nora, who
slaps him. Rocco kisses her hard on the lips. The captain of the boat that will take
Rocco and his gang back to Cuba tells them that the boat will have to be moved to
be better secured. Rocco refuses. A group of Indians asks to come to the hotel to get
out of the storm, but Rocco refuses to let them in. Rocco makes some obscene gestures to Nora. She spits in his face. Rocco is infuriated by the insult and discusses
with his gang whether they should kill her. McCloud, who doesn't want to get

involved, tells Rocco that he will have to kill all of them to get rid of witnesses. The man who was on the bed upstairs staggers in, and he turns out to be the deputy sheriff, who discovered who Rocco was before being subdued. Gaye, Johnny's girlfriend, is an alcoholic. She staggers in and commiserates with Nora. Rocco again brags to McCloud about what an important man he is and how he will be on top once more. McCloud says that he thought he fought a war to get rid of the Roccos, and yet here he still was, and wonders whether it was worth all the effort. Rocco tries to provoke McCloud into killing him, by giving him a gun, but McCloud refuses, saying that one Rocco more or less is not worth it. Nora calls McCloud a coward. The deputy grabs for the gun and is shot dead. It turns out that the gun Rocco gave McCloud was empty. Ziggy, the gangster from Miami, calls, and Rocco tells him he had better be in Key Largo by 10:00 P.M.; otherwise their deal is off. Gaye wants a drink, and Rocco tells her she will get one if she sings. She sings, but Rocco still refuses to give her a drink. McCloud pours her one. Rocco starts slapping him around.

Rocco becomes nervous about the storm. Meanwhile, Nora apologizes to McCloud for calling him a coward, and Temple prays that the storm will destroy Rocco. The Indians who were left outside during the storm return and berate Temple for mistreating them. The gangsters want McCloud to take them to Cuba. After banging on the door, the sheriff comes in, looking for Deputy Sawyer. He says that Sawyer called him from the hotel when he was looking for the fugitive Indian brothers. When he leaves he discovers the deputy's body. Rocco lies, saying that the Indians killed him. The sheriff sees the Indians running off and shoots them. He goes back into the hotel and attacks Temple for lying to him and protecting the Indians. He starts to take down the names and addresses of everyone in the room. The gangsters give a hotel in Milwaukee as their address.

After the sheriff departs, Ziggy comes in with his henchmen. Curley shows him their counterfeit money, which they consider to be first-class merchandise. Gaye and Nora tell McCloud that Rocco will kill him before they get to Cuba. Ziggy leaves. Rocco coerces McCloud into going with him to Cuba. After making lewd gestures to Nora, Rocco refuses to take Gaye along. Gaye embraces him and begs to be taken, all the while lifting Rocco's gun from his pocket and sneaking it to McCloud. McCloud, Rocco, and his gang leave. Gaye and Nora watch from the door.

On the boat Curley talks to Rocco about not taking Gaye. He thinks she might squeal on Ziggy, but Rocco doesn't care. McCloud plans his move. He pushes one man overboard and shoots another, but is wounded. Rocco realizes that his gun is missing and that all of the gang is finished off except him. He tries to bargain with McCloud. He also tries to dupe McCloud into thinking that he has tossed out the bag of money and his gun, but McCloud is not taken in. He kills Rocco. Then McCloud turns the boat around and heads back to Key Largo.

In the hotel Temple talks about the injustice done to the Indians, how they trusted him, and how everything went wrong. The phone rings. Nora picks it up, talks to McCloud, and says, "Thank God." She tells Temple that McCloud is all right and that he is coming back to them. She opens the window, and light comes in. McCloud, on the boat coming back to shore, is smiling.

10 *We Were Strangers* (1949)

Director	John Huston
Producer	S. P. Eagle
Screenplay	Peter Viertel and John Huston, based on an episode in the novel *Rough Sketch* by Robert Sylvester
Director of Photography	Russell Metty, A.S.C.
Art Director	Cary Odell
Film Editor	Al Clark
Set Decorator	Louis Diage
Special Scenes	Lawrence Butler
Assistant Director	Carl Hiecke
Miss Jones's Costumes	Jean Louis
Hairstyles	Larry Germain
Sound Engineer	Lambert Day
Dialogue Director	Gladys Hill
Music Score	George Antheil
Musical Director	M. W. Stoloff
Associate Producer	Jules Buck
Cast	Jennifer Jones (China Valdes), John Garfield (Tony Fenner), Pedro Armendariz (Armando Ariete), Gilbert Roland (Guillermo), Ramon Novarro (Chief), Wally Cassell (Miguel), David Bond (Ramón), Jose Perez (Toto), Morris Ankrum (Bank Manager), Tito Rinaldo (Manolo), Paul Monte (Roberto), Leonard Strong (Bomb Maker), Robert Tafur (Rubio), John Huston (Clerk, uncredited)
Filmed	at Horizon Productions, Columbia Pictures, Los Angeles
Running Time	106 minutes, black and white
Release Date	April 27, 1948

Other titles: *Les Insurges, Stanotte sorgera il sole*

SYNOPSIS

The events take place in Cuba in 1933, eight years after the dictatorship has been established. The mock legislature is in session and is forced to pass a law forbidding people to assemble in public. Those legislators who want to speak up are intimidated. During riots in the street, people are randomly beaten by the police. China Valdez's brother, a student, tells her that he has to stand for his principles and although she asks him to wait, he insists that he cannot. He doesn't know whether a wounded comrade has betrayed him, so he goes into hiding. They plan to meet the next day, but he is murdered in cold blood by Armando Ariete, the chief of police. At her brother's funeral China tells his comrades that she knows who killed her brother and will avenge his death. Her brother's friends warn her that the secret police are after everyone who is against the president. Nevertheless, she joins the rebels. She goes to a secret meeting on a boat and meets a Tony Fenner. Because she works for one of the banks, she is told to take care of a certain matter for Fenner at the bank. He travels with false credentials as a theatrical agent, but he is really a revolutionary leader.

In the bank where China works, Chief of Police Ariete, her brother's murderer, arrives and goes into the bank manager's office. China is then asked to join them, and she first thinks that a connection has been made with her brother. But she is asked to bring new American accounts to the office. Ariete wants to know if any American have conducted any unusual activity.

Later on, China attends a meeting where Fenner lays the plans for the assassination of everone in the government. The group debates the killing of innocent people. Fenner's plan involves digging a tunnel from China's house to the cemetery across the street, killing a cabinet minister, planting a bomb underneath the cabinet minister's grave, and at his funeral blowing the mourners up. They then decide who the "hyena" (that is, the cabinet minister) will be. One of the conspirators becomes edgy because his family is close to that of the government official who will be assassinated. The group starts digging the tunnel.

The chief of police calls on China and tries to make a play for her. He is crass and vulgar and makes himself at home without being invited. Not knowing exactly who Fenner is but knowing that he and China have some sort of relationship, Ariete questions what she sees in him. Ariete doesn't like Americans. He feels that the dollars that they bring are not worth putting up with them. He stuffs his mouth with food as he brags about himself. He boasts about how everyone fears him, but a real man fears nothing, he says. He even plays Russian roulette in front of her. He wants her, but collapses in a drunken stupor. His aides take him away. Fenner arrives, and he and China embrace. He wonders if anything will be all right ever again, and she says no. He proposes to her, telling her that they will live in a free country one day and have kids. They kiss.

The work on the tunnel proceeds with great difficulty. They now have to dig through a poorer part of the cemetery, and the stench is overpowering. One of the group, Ramón, the one whose family is connected with the "hyena," goes raving mad and starts talking to himself. He wanders the streets, wanting to tell people about the assassination. Without looking, he runs across the street and is struck down by a truck.

In the bank China is again called into the manager's office. Ariete is there. She is accused of being part of the conspiracy. Ariete tells her that Fenner is really a Cuban. He slaps her and threatens her, but she refuses to give him any information.

The diggers, meanwhile, finally reach the Contertas family tomb, and they plan to kill Vincente Contertas, a high government official. The whole plot goes awry after he is killed, because the family decides to bury him outside the city. The plotters are beside themselves. Two old ladies change their minds about a burial site, and their chances are blown. But, they remind themselves, it is not a disgrace to fail; it is a disgrace not to have tried at all. Guillermo, one of the comrades, wants to blow up the presidential palace instead. Fenner knows that he must escape from Cuba, because he is known to the secret police. If caught he might be tortured and betray everyone. He feels guilt-ridden. He raised money in Spanish Harlem, New York, from poor people and doesn't think he can go back and face them. China plans to leave with him. She cashes his check in the bank. When she sees the police at the door, she goes back into the bank and gives the money to a colleague. She is called into the manager's office and is fired for cashing the check. The teller calls the police.

The police follow China to her house. Weary, she breaks down. Fenner comes into her room. He wants to die with her. The house is surrounded. Fenner tells her that either way they will die, and it would be better to die with her than in prison. A battle erupts between the revolutionaries and the police. China runs down into the cellar for dynamite. Tony is shot. She continues to shoot at the police. Tony implores her to stay close to him. He tells her that he wants to make up for all the years he didn't know her. Bells begin to ring. The dictatorship is overthrown. Tony dies in China's arms.

11 *The Asphalt Jungle* (1950)

Director	John Huston
Producer	Arthur Hornblow Jr.
Screenplay	Ben Maddow and John Huston, from the novel by W. R. Burnett
Director of Photography	Harold Rosson
Sound	Douglas Shearer and Robert B. Lee
Music	Miklos Rozsa
Art Directors	Cedric Gibbons and Randall Duell
Set Decoration	Edwin B. Willis and Jack D. Moore
Makeup	Jack Dawn and Law Lacava
Hairstyles	Sydney Guilaroff and Elaine Ramsey
Production Manager	Lee Katz
Assistant Director	Jack Greenwood
Script Supervisor	John Banse
Film Editor	George Boemler
Cast	Sterling Hayden (Dix Handley), Louis Calhern (Alonzo D. Emmerich), Jean Hagen (Doll Conovan), James Whitmore (Gus Minissi), Sam Jaffe (Doc Riedenschneider), John McIntire (Police Commissioner Hardy), Marc Lawrence (Cobby), Barry Kelley (Lieutenant Ditrich), Anthony Caruso (Louis Ciavelli), Teresa Calli (Maria Ciavelli), Marilyn Monroe (Angela Phinlay), William Davis (Timmons), Dorothy Tree (May Emmerich), Brad Dexter (Bob Brannon), Alex Gerry (Maxwell), Thomas Browne Henry (James X. Connery), James Seay (Janocek), Dan Haggerty

| | (Andrews), Henry Rowland (Franz Schurz), Helene Stanley (Jeannie), Raymond Roe (Tallboy), Charles Courtney (Red). *Minor Parts and Bits:* Jean Carter, Ralph Dunn, Pat Flaherty, Tim Ryan, Strother Martin, Henry Corden, Frank Cady, Jack Shea, Benny Burt, Fred Graham, David Hydes, Saul Gross, Wilson Wood, Constance Weiler, John Cliff, Joseph Darr Smith, William Washington, Leah Wakefield, Judith Wood, Kerry O'Day, Eloise Hardt, Patricia Miller, Albert Morin, Fred Marlow, Ray Teal, Howard Mitchell, Ray Bennett, George Lynn, David Bond, Gene Evans, Wesley Hopper, Jack Stoney, Ralph Montgomery, William Haade, Jeff York, David Clark, John Maxwell, Harlan Warde, John Crawford, Charles Sherlock, Lewis Smith, Harry Cody, Mack Chandler, J. J. Smith, Harry G. Burcher, Mary Anderson, Ethel Lyons |

Filmed	at MGM, Culver City, California
Running Time	112 minutes, black and white
Release Date	June 8, 1950; production completed December 21, 1949

Other titles: *Quand la ville dort, Giungla d''asfalto*

SYNOPSIS

Credits run with the city in the background. The camera then shows a car drive by, empty streets, a police car, and a man walking past and eluding police (probably Dix). There is a police report of a robbery and a suspect, who appears to be Dix. He goes into a café owned by his friend, Gus, who hides Dix's gun in the cash register. The police come in and arrest Dix. He's put in lineup but is not identified. While the commissioner of police bemoans the high crime rate, Lieutenant Ditrich says that they know Dix is guilty. The commissioner is also bothered that Doc Riedenschneider, a master criminal, has come to the city, but the police don't know where he is.

Doc Riedenschneider gets out of a taxi cab in a shady part of town and enters a bookie joint. He identifies himself, and the bookmaker, Cobby, gets excited and welcomes him. He offers Doc a drink. Doc tells him that he has a scheme that will make $500,000, but he needs $50,000 to make his plans. He thought that maybe Mr. Emmerich, a crooked lawyer, might be interested. Doc heard about him in jail and was told that he could get in touch with Emmerich through Cobby. Cobby calls Emmerich. Dix comes in, wanting to make a bet. Cobby reminds him that he owes him $2,300, and Dix is insulted that Cobby only wants his money. He runs out. He insists on paying his debt to preserve his self-respect. Dix's pal, Gus, raises the money for him. Then Doll comes to Dix's apartment. She has no place to go, having been locked out of her room, and asks whether she can stay with Dix. He says that she can, but she shouldn't get any ideas.

Doc has a meeting with Emmerich and tells him about the plan to rob a safe in a jewelry store. Doc needs $50,000 to pay the three men needed for the job. Emmerich says that he would be the fence for the job also. Doc jests that after this take he plans to go to Mexico and chase the pretty girls. Emmerich appreciates Doc's comment, for he has a girlfriend, Angela, on the side. To raise money for the caper, he calls Brannon, a private detective, and asks him to come over, take a list of outstanding debtors, and try to collect.

Dix reminisces about the farm in Kentucky that his family lost. Dix vows to make a killing and head home. He brings the $2,300 to Cobby, who introduces him to Doc. Doc reveals that he heard that Emmerich is broke. When Lieutenant Ditrich attempts to bust Cobby, he bribes Ditrich, who just tells him to keep low because the commissioner is putting pressure on Ditrich to close up illegal activities. Meanwhile, Brannon tells Emmerich that he couldn't collect anything. Emmerich panics and tells Brannon that he is broke. The two of them plan to double-cross Doc, Dix and the gang after the heist.

Doc puts together the men for the robbery: Dix, Cobby, and a safecracker named Ciavelli. The caper is pulled off. The explosion to open the safe in the jewelry store sets off alarms throughout the neighborhood, but the men decide to complete the job. Police cars arrive on the block. The robbers are ready to leave through the back door when the watchman comes in. As they knock him out, his gun goes off, and Ciavelli is hit. He goes home while Doc and Dix go in another car to Emmerich's house, where Emmerich and Brannon are waiting for them. Emmerich admits that he doesn't have their $50,000 and tries to make excuses. He suggests that he hold the jewels. He is visibly nervous. Brannon pulls his gun and is killed in the ensuing shoot-out by Dix, who is also wounded. Emmerich breaks down, desperate. Doc suggests that Emmerich go to the insurance company and try to sell the jewels back to them.

Across town Ciavelli is dying. Gus, the café owner, tries to console his wife. She wants to take him to the hospital, but Gus says if they wheel him into the operating room she will never seem him again. They wait for a doctor, who never comes.

Dix refuses to go to a doctor with his wound. Cobby complains about everybody getting shot and about being out the money that he—not Emmerich—put up for the heist. Gus calls and warns them that the police are out and that they should go hide out at a safe place. Doc also gets a call: Emmerich was able to get the insurance company to settle. Emmerich then plays cards with his bedridden wife. He is interrupted, however, by two policemen who have come to question him. In the next room they tell him that they have found his associate, Brannon, and the list of people that he was trying to collect from. They ask him where he was during the robbery. He maintains that he was with his girlfriend, Angela. When the cops leave, Emmerich calls Angela for an alibi. He tells her that it is just politics, good old, dirty politics. He goes back into his wife's bedroom. He is as pale as a ghost. She tells him that he is in contact with the wrong element. He responds that crime is only a left-handed form of human endeavor.

As Doc tries to convince Dix to escape with him to Mexico and its pretty young girls, the police are looking for Doc, because they know he is the only one who could pull off this job. At the police station everyone is coming in with tips, hoping to collect a reward. One of them is the taxi driver who took Doc to Cobby's place. When Dix and Doc leave their hideout, they are confronted by a policeman who recognizes them. Dix knocks the cop out. They go to Doll's apartment. Doc laments that everything that should have gone right went wrong. He talks about blind accident and how his greed in wanting more money led to his trust of Emmerich and their current state of affairs.

The police get a break when the taxi driver makes a connection to Cobby. Lieutenant Ditrich goes to the bookie joint and manhandles Cobby, who confesses. The police then go to Angela's apartment to arrest Emmerich. Angela breaks down and admits that she lied to give Emmerich an alibi. Emmerich asks whether he can write a note to his wife, who will worry about him. He starts to write a note but cannot finish it. He takes a gun from the drawer and kill himself. The police then bring Gus into prison. He sees Cobby and tries to kill him through the bars. Next the police break into Ciavelli's apartment, but they walk in on his wake.

Meanwhile, Doc reconsiders his plans and says that he will go to Cleveland. He asks Dix to lend him $1,000 and to take the jewels in exchange. Dix gives him the money without any strings. Dix's wound starts to bleed. They find a taxi driver, a fellow German, who agrees to take Doc to Cleveland. Doll buys a car. Dix wants to go home, and Doll wants to go with him. He knows that she loves him, but he can't quite understand it.

Doc and the taxi driver stop at a diner. Teenagers are dancing. Doc is taken with a young, attractive girl. The teenagers run out of money, and Doc gives them many nickels to play the jukebox. The girl starts dancing with one of the boys. Then she dances alone. Doc is smitten as she dances a very sexy dance. Outside, the cops are looking in. The taxi driver tells Doc that it is getting late and they should go, but Doc says there is plenty of time. When they leave the diner, the police accost Doc, take his coat, and feel the jewels sewn into the lining. Doc asks the police how long they were waiting outside. He then says that it is not important. They tell him that it was about two or three minutes.

Dix and Doll are on the road. He collapses. She finds a doctor who begins to treat him and says that he has lost a lot of blood. The doctor calls the sheriff when he sees that Dix has a gunshot wound. Dix overhears the doctor and pulls the syringe out of his arm. Dix and Doll drive away. The doctor says that Dix won't get too far, because he doesn't have enough blood to keep a chicken alive. Dix and Doll drive into horse country. He talks to himself about the horses on the family farm, the black one being the best. He mumbles that if Pa just hangs onto the black colt everything will be all right. They stop. He opens a fence gate and walks onto the field, where horses are grazing. Doll runs after him. He falls. She rushes to him. The horses come and nuzzle the dead Dix.

12 *The Red Badge of Courage* (1951)

Director	John Huston
Producer	Gottfried Reinhardt

Screenplay	John Huston, based on the novel by Stephen Crane
Adaptation	Albert Band
Music	Bronislau Kaper
Director of Photography	Harold Rosson, A.S.C.
Art Directors	Cedric Gibbons and Hans Peters
Film Editor	Ben Lewis
Recording Supervisor	Douglas Shearer
Set Decorations	Edwin B. Willis and Fred MacLean
Special Effects	Warren Newcombe
Makeup	William Tuttle
Cast	Audie Murphy (Youth), Bill Mauldin (Loud Soldier), Douglas Dick (Lieutenant), Royal Dano (Tattered Man), John Dierkes (Tall Soldier), Arthur Hunnicutt (Bill Porter), Robert Easton Burke (Thompson), Smith Ballew (Captain), Glenn Strange (Colonel), Andy Devine (Cheery Soldier). *Minor Parts and Bits:* Tim Durant, Edwin J. Breen, Dick Haynes, Robert A. Fisher, Robert Davis, Obed Pickard Jr., John Riffle, Jimmy Clark Stevens, Emmett Lynn, Stanford Jolley, William (Bill) Phillips, House Peters Jr., Frank Sully, George Offerman Jr., Joel Martson, Robert Nichols, Lou Nova, Fred Kohler Jr., Dick Curtis, Guy Wilderson, John Keating, Buddy Roosevelt, David Clarke, Strother Martin, Hurb Roy Latimer, Jim Hayward, James H. Harrison, Gloria Eaton, Robert E. Nichols, Eugene Gericke, Robert Cavendish, Robert Cherry, Whit Bissell, Joe Haworth, Robert Board, Hugh Thomas, John Cliff, Dan White, Frank McGrath, Leldon Martin, Benny Burt, Casey MacGregor, Norman Kent, Joe Brown Jr., William Phipps, Ed Hinton, Dennis Dengate, Joe Schrapp, Mack Chandler, Mickey Simpson, Duke York, Norman Leavitt, William Gruenberg, William Schallert, Gregg Barton, Ivan A. Parry, Bill Roberts, Billy Dix, Todd Karns, John Crawford, Jimmy Dobson, Frank Melton, Lynn Farr, Tennessee Jim, William Hale, Lyle Clark, Wilson Wood, Allen O'Locklin, Bert Davidson, Lee J. Roberts
Filmed	at MGM Studios, Culver City, California
Running Time	69 minutes, black and white

Release Date   October 18, 1951; production began August 25, 1950

Other titles: *La Prova del fuoco, La Charge victorieuse*

SYNOPSIS

In spring 1862, war for the troops is a matter of waiting and endless training. Union soldiers talk among themselves, go fishing, and wash clothes. Soldiers hear that part of the troop will move the next day. They'll go up the river and come around the rebels. The Youth, privately doubts his courage, whereas his comrades seem to welcome war. He writes a letter home, hoping that his family will be proud of him. Men talk about how the regiment will do. Henry asks whether anyone will run. They ask Henry if he is scared. Jim, another soldier, indicates that he might run if the others do; otherwise he will stand and fight. Henry gets defensive when they ask him if he will run. That night he stands guard duty and has a conversation with a rebel sentry on other side of river. The rebel tells him to get out of the light so that he doesn't get a "red badge." The rebel sees no point in opposing sentries shooting at one another. Two soldiers start a fist fight. There is an announcement that they are going into battle. Henry is afraid and feels that he is a mental outcast.

The regiment moves out. Soldiers on the march talk about the upcoming fight. One wonders what the battle will be called. They stop by a farmhouse and see a soldier trying to steal a pig. When the soldiers taunt him, he drops the pig and joins the troop. Henry goes off by himself. His friend comes after him, asking him what's the matter. Henry asks his friend how he knows he won't run. His friend reassures him that he will do his share of the fighting, but Henry is very upset.

The regiment crosses the river. On the other side they can hear artillery. As they march closer to the battle, they become silent. They pass a dead soldier on the road. Henry stops but is told to get back in the ranks. The troop moves through the woods. They start running and taking up positions. The men use their bayonets to create a mound from which to shoot. The soldiers are then told to move on, and they can't understand what is going on. They get closer to the battle and come to an open field. The colonel tells them that the "rebs" are on a hill, and they should try and take it. They watch the cavalry charging. Explosions are all about them. Henry's regiment stands behind a mound, while other troops move on. A comrade tells Henry that he feels that it is his last battle and gives him a watch to give his folks. The troop that was charging retreats, running back. The rebels are coming. They can hear them shouting. They are told that they have to hold the rebels. At first they can't see them through the smoke. Then they see them. A shooting battle erupts. One of the soldiers starts to run away but is stopped by the lieutenant. The rebels are stopped, and they retreat. Henry and his comrades talk about never seeing anyone killed. They don't think that there will be another fight. Henry feels that he has overcome his fear and listens to the birds singing, but he then sees the wounded moving back to the rear. Then the rebels come again. There is more shooting. This time the rebels come closer. Some soldiers start running, including Henry. He runs in a panic through the woods. He overhears a general talking to his officers and a report that the second charge was held. The general is jubilant.

Henry is despondent because, unlike him, his comrades did not run. He wanders. He comes upon a long line of wounded soldiers and envies them, wishing that he also had a "red badge of courage." He joins the line of wounded. A wounded soldier tells him that it was a great fight. An officer is carried in a hammock, flaunting a superior tone to the soldiers. Henry then comes across Jim, who is wounded. Jim tells Henry that he is afraid that if he stops moving he will die. Henry tries to assure him that he will take care of him. Jim staggers and then runs up a hill. Jim rambles on, telling Henry to let him be. And then he dies.

Henry wanders alone through the woods. He again hears the birds and more shooting. He sees other soldiers running. When he stops a soldier and asks what is happening, the soldier hits him. Henry is stopped by another soldier, who brings him back to his troop. The soldier remarks that it doesn't make much of a difference if they get killed, for the birds will sing anyhow. Henry tells his friend that he has been shot in the head. The soldiers all thought he had been killed. He tells his friend that he was unconscious and might have a bullet in his head. His friend replies that it looks more as if he was hit over the head. Henry tells his friend that Jim is dead. It looks like the men were scattered and fighting with other regiments, but now they regroup. Henry gives back the watch that he was supposed to give to his friend's folks if he was killed. He has made his mistakes in the dark, so he is still a man—so says the narrator. He actually begins to brag about his accomplishments.

The men march off to the line and take up their positions. They see in the distance the rebels coming toward them. The artillery starts firing. Everybody is fighting, and someone mentions blood and destruction. Henry yells that the rebels had better watch out. He charges and keeps running. He has a great passion to destroy the enemy. He is told to get back into the line. The lieutenant says that if a soldier gets mad, you'll win the whole war. The men are thirsty, so Henry and his friend take canteens to get water. They overhear the general talking about another charge. The general goes through the line, and asks each group of men what they will be eating for supper. They all say hardtack and sourbelly, and the general invites himself to dinner with each group.

The next day there is another charge. The men pick up speed. Shells explode around them. Men fall. Henry urges the others on. He grabs the flag and runs forward. The rebel cavalry attacks them. They charge. Henry runs through with the flag while men fall around him. Henry comes across a rebel soldier holding the confederate flag. The confederate soldier falls and Henry holds both flags in his hands. Some confederate soldiers are captured. They talk and learn that the confederates are from Tennessee. The Union soldiers are from Ohio. Another soldier comes and tells them that he heard that they were being praised.

Henry now confesses to his friend that he ran away yesterday. His friend tells Henry that he started to run also, but he was caught by the captain. The men move to the rear. One soldiers says that for all the fighting they did, he wishes they could stay by the wall that they won. The country is pretty nice when there isn't any fighting going on. The men wonder if they will be home for spring planting. They hear the birds singing and remark that the birds sing as soon as the smoke clears. Having rid himself of fear, Henry can face his future without shame.

13   *The African Queen* (1952)

Director	John Huston
Producer	Sam Spiegel
Screenplay	James Agee and John Huston, based on the novel by C. S. Forester
Director of Photography	Jack Cardiff
Art Director	Wilfred Shingleton
Second Unit Photography	Ted Scaife
Music	Allan Gray
Music Direction	Norman Del Mar
Editor	Ralph Kemplen
Production Managers	Leigh Aman and T. S. Lyndon-Haynes
Assistant Director	Guy Hamilton
Assistant Art Director	John Hoesli
Makeup	George Frost
Costumes	Doris Langley Moore
Continuity	Angela Allen
Special Effects	Cliff Richardson
Sound Editor	Eric Wood
Cast	Humphrey Bogart (Charlie Allnut), Katharine Hepburn (Rose Sayer), Robert Morley (The Brother, Reverend Samuel Sayer), Peter Bull (Captain of the *Louisa*), Theodore Bikel (First Officer, *Louisa*), Walter Cotell (Second Officer, *Louisa*), Gerald Onn (Petty Officer, *Louisa*), Peter Swanick (First Officer, *Shona*), Richard Marner (Second Officer, *Shona*)
Filmed	at locations in Africa; a Horizon-Romulus Production, distributed by United Artists, a Trans-Lux release
Running Time	105 minutes, Technicolor
Release Date	February 20, 1952; shooting completed November 1, 1951

Other titles: *La Regina d'Africa, La Reine africaine*

SYNOPSIS

The jungle sounds are suddenly overwhelmed by the cacophony of natives in a jungle church, the First Methodist Church of Kungusa, where the Reverend Samuel Sayer is leading congregants in a hymn that they don't understand. Rose, his sister, plays the organ and joins in the singing. The service is interrupted by the *African Queen* coming into the landing. Its skipper, Charlie Allnut, is unkempt and puffs on a cigar. He speaks with the natives in their own language. He approaches the church and throws his cigar on the ground, which causes a riot as the natives run to get it. Allnut delivers the Sayers' letters and some rose trees. They politely invite him to tea. He is embarrassed because his stomach is growling. He tells them that a war has broken out between Germany and England, so he probably won't be back for another two months. He warns that the Germans will probably hold up their mail.

After Allnut leaves, German forces arrive. They go into the huts and round up the native men. Sayer protests, and they manhandle him. The Germans set fire to the huts and burn down the church. Sayer has a nervous breakdown and doesn't know where he is. He rambles that he is studying hard, but if he doesn't pass he will have to become a missionary, and that Rose, while not comely, has her place in God's work.

Rose sits on the porch. She hears the *African Queen* coming. As Allnut approaches the house, she tries to make herself presentable. Allnut can't believe what he is seeing: The Germans are planning to make all the natives into soldiers to take over Africa. Rose tells Allnut that her brother died that morning. They bury her brother and leave on the boat. Allnut asks Rose to take the tiller. They stop at a remote spot along the river. He says that he wants to sit out the war. When she insists on doing something, he tells her that the *Louisa,* a one hundred-ton German ship, is on the lake. She asks him about one of the rivers, and he informs her that a German fort is overlooking the shore. She then asks him about the blasting powder and cylinders on the boat and whether he can make a torpedo. She tells him about her idea to put a torpedo on the *African Queen*'s prow and sink the *Louisa.* When he dismisses the idea she accuses him of not supporting his country.

They go farther down the river, with her steering. He starts drinking, which upsets her. He offers her tea: "It'll be a little rusty, but we can't have everything." She tells him that she and her brother were out in Africa ten years, and she still misses the Sunday afternoons in England. Allnut remarks that he was always "sleeping it off" on Sunday afternoons and that he came to Africa to work on the Zambesi Bridge. He then decides to have a bath and goes up to the front of the boat, telling Rose that she can use the stern. Later it begins to rain, and he is drenched trying to sleep outside while she is under the canopy. When he comes in under the canopy she becomes enraged and orders him out. Realizing that it is raining, she invites him to come in out of the rain.

The next day they come to the river's rapids, and Allnut negotiates them. Rose never knew the rapids could be so stimulating. She claims the only time she has been so excited was during one of her brother's sermons and that she looks forward to more rapids. She is beginning to love boating. That night Allnut gets drunk. He belittles her plan to go down the river. She accuses him of being a liar and a coward. He accuses her of being a psalm-singing, skinny old maid. He reminds her that it is his boat. He drinks even more.

He wakes up the next morning to see Rose taking the bottles of Gordon's gin and pouring them into the river. He is in no shape to stop her, so the river fills with empty gin bottles. He shaves. He admits to her that it is good to have a woman around; otherwise, he lives like a hog. He tries to be ingratiating, but she refuses to talk to him. He asks how she can call herself a Christian and then completely ignore him. When he tells her that it is human nature to take a drink, she replies, "Nature is what we are put in this world to rise above." She is angry with him, not because of his drunkenness but because of his withdrawing his promise to go down the river. He gives in, as they will become supper for the crocodiles if they stay put. He tells her that he is not worried, that he already gave himself up for dead. They come into sight of the German fort and stay down, but the Germans spy them and start shooting at the boat, damaging its engine. They get past the fort and encounter much more violent rapids. Miraculously, they get through. Allnut happily embraces her. Then he kisses her. When he forages for wood ashore, he gets a thorn in his foot that she takes out. He puts his hand on her shoulder, and she takes his hand. He kisses her.

The next morning while Allnut is asleep Rose makes him tea. When he wakes she asks him what his first name is. They have become lovers. Later they approach even more terrible rapids. The boat is swamped. He goes down to survey the damage and sees that the shaft is bent out of shape. Rose encourages him to try and fix the shaft, which they do. He tells her that he hasn't just lost his mind, but also his heart. Then they are attacked by insects. "What a time we've had, Rosie, what a time," he remarks. When they get bogged down in narrow channels, he starts going a bit crazy. He jumps out of the boat and pulls it in the water, where he is attacked by leeches. After they get stuck again, he realizes he has no choice but to go back in the water and risk the leeches again. It is so bad Rose goes in to the water and hacks away at the vegetation while he pulls the boat free. Afterward he gets very sick. She proclaims that he is the bravest man alive. He tells her that he is not one bit sorry he came. It was worth it. Rose prays, asking the Lord to judge them not for their weakness, but for their love.

A rain storm frees the boat, and while Allnut and Rose are asleep it drifts toward the lake. They awake and spot the *Louisa* coming toward them. They go back into the reeds, where they argue. Allnut doesn't want Rose to come with him when he goes after the *Louisa,* but then they agree that they'll go together. At dark they start into the lake. It starts to storm again, and the boat starts to sink. They are picked up by the *Louisa*'s crew. The Germans sentence Allnut to death and Rosie, also, after she admits their purpose for being on the lake and their intention to blow up the *Louisa.* The German officers cannot believe the couple made their way down the river, but decide to hang them both. Charlie makes a last request, that the captain marry them. Rose thinks it is a wonderful idea. The captain marries them and proceeds with the execution. Just then the *African Queen* surfaces, rams the *Louisa,* which explodes, and promptly sinks. Charlie and Rose swim off to the shore and safety.

14 *Moulin Rouge* (1953)

Director	John Huston
Producer	John Huston
Associate Producer	Jack Clayton
Screenplay	John Huston and Anthony Veiller, from the novel by Pierre La Mure
Photography	Oswald Morris

Art Direction	Paul Sheriff and Marcel Vertes
Color Consultant	Eliot Elisofon
Music	Georges Auric
Film Editor	Ralph Kemplen
Costume Design	Marcel Vertes
Cast	José Ferrer (Toulouse-Lautrec), Colette Marchand (Marie Charlet), Suzanne Flon (Myriamme), Zsa Zsa Gabor (Jane Avril), Katherine Kath (La Goulue), Claude Nollier (Countess de Toulouse-Lautrec), Georges Lannes (Patou), Mary Clare (Madame Loubet), Lee Montague (Zidler), Harold Gasket (Maurice Joyant), Muriel Smith (Aicha), Jill Bennet (Sarah), Maureen Swanson (Denise), Jim Gerald (Père Cotelle), Rupert John (Chocolat), Tutti Lemkow (Aicha's Partner)
Filmed	at Romulus Films, Ltd.; released by United Artists
Running Time	119 minutes, Technicolor
Release Date	February 10, 1953; world premiere, Fox Wilshire, December 23, 1952

SYNOPSIS

It is Paris in the 1890s, and at the Moulin Rouge, Henri de Toulouse-Lautrec drinks cognac and sketches the dancers. A gallery owner stops and tells him that he has a customer who will buy his paintings. Dancers fight. Zidler, the owner of the Moulin Rouge, offers Lautrec free drinks for a month if he does a poster. Jane Avril comes out and sings and then talks to him about her love. She wishes that he were tall. Then the show is over and people leave. Lautrec gets up, revealing his stunted growth. He walks through the streets of Paris and is taunted by a drunk. He recollects his childhood and his father: Children in his family's palace are dancing. The men go fox hunting. Lautrec shows a talent for art. His father is somewhat dissolute. Lautrec has an accident. After falling down the stairs and breaking both legs, he is crippled. His legs will never grow. (Part of his problem is genetic, for his parents are first cousins.) Lautrec devotes himself to drawing. Girls reject him. His one girlfriend taunts him and cruelly tells him that he is ugly, and that no girl will ever marry him. His mother tries to reassure him that he will find a woman who will love him.

Lautrec goes to Paris to become a painter. He meets a street walker, Marie Charlet, who asks him for help when the police arrest her. He protects her, takes her to his apartment, and allows her to stay. She thinks that this arrangement means he can have her, but he doesn't want to make love with her. She asks him about his infirmity and he gets angry. He has difficulty dealing with her crudeness. She lives with him, and he takes care of her, giving her money to buy dresses. Whenever she leaves, she says that she will be back in an hour, but stays away for long periods of time. He desperately loves her, but she rejects him. She finally leaves him. He tracks her down and begs her to come back to him, but she tells him that she only lived with him to support her lover.

Lautrec goes back to the one place where he is happy, the Moulin Rouge. The dancers become the basis for his drawings, paintings, and posters. He works with a famous lithographer to bring the dancers' exciting world to life. He becomes a success. His father, however, berates him for becoming an artist and disgracing the family name. The difficulties between Lautrec and his father become serious. Lautrec goes on to become the star of the Moulin Rouge. The owner keeps him supplied with drink. Lautrec has found his métier in the demimonde of Paris: the Moulin Rouge, the cafés, the streets, the bordellos. He enjoys successful exhibitions of his work.

Entering his life is Myriamme, who knows that he needs the love of a woman, while he can help her achieve her goal of rising in society. Remembering how other women have exploited him, he is wary but eventually comes to love her. Their relationship, however, grows tense. He becomes difficult and jealous. She decides to leave him and marry someone else.

Lautrec's life goes downhill. His drinking and debauchery take their toll. He collapses in the street. The police take him home. As the dancer Patou and the concierge talk, he staggers out of the room, stands at the top of the stairs, and falls down. Dying, Lautrec is brought home to the family castle. His father is beside himself and begs his son's forgiveness. He informs his son that he has been honored as the first living artist to be given an exhibition at the Louvre. In a final dream sequence he has a vision of all of his friends from the Moulin Rouge entering his room and dancing up to his bed. Jane Avril tells him that they had to come and say good-bye to him.

15 *Beat the Devil* (1954)

Director	John Huston
Producer	John Huston
Executive Producer	Humphrey Bogart
Associate Producer	Jack Clayton
Production Manager	William Kirby
Location Manager	James Ware
Screenplay	John Huston and Truman Capote, based on the novel by James Helvick (pseudonym of Claud Cockburn)
Music	Franco Mannino
Music Director	Lambert Williamson
Photography	Oswald Morris, B.S.C.
Operating Cameraman	Freddie Francis, B.S.C.
Still Photography	Robert Capa
Film Editor	Ralph Kemplen
Art Director	Wilfred Shingleton
Sound Recording	George Stephenson and Red Law
Wardrobe	Vi Murray and May Walding
Makeup	Connie Reeve
Hairdresser	Betty Lee

Assistant Director	John Arnold
Cast	Humphrey Bogart (Billy Dannreuther), Jennifer Jones (Gwendolyn Chelm), Gina Lollobrigida (Maria Dannreuther), Robert Morley (Petersen), Peter Lorre (O'Hara), Edward Underdown (Harry Chelm), Ivor Barnard (Major Ross), Bernard Lee (C.I.D. Inspector), Marco Tulli (Ravello), Mario Perroni (Purser), Alex Pochet (The Manager, Hotel Bristol), Aldo Silvani (Charles), Giulio Donnini (Administrator), Saro Urzi (Captain), Juan De Landa (Hispano-Suiza Driver), Manuel Serano (Arab Officer), Mimo Poli (The Barman)
Filmed	at locations in Italy; a Santana/Romulus Films Ltd. Production, a United Artists release
Running Time	92 minutes, black and white
Release Date	November 24, 1953 (London), March 12, 1954 (New York)

Other titles: *Plus fort que le diable, Il Tesòro dell' Africa*

SYNOPSIS

The action starts in a small Italian port city, where four men— Petersen, O'Hara, Major Ross, and Ravello, all associates of Billy Dannreuther—are being led off by the police. In a flashback, Billy then relates how his former associates got to this point in the story.

Gwendolyn Chelm and her husband, Harry Chelm, are also in the port city. The Chelms, Billy, and his associates are waiting on the repairs of an old tramp freighter, whose captain is a drunk, to go to Africa. Having a vivid imagination, Gwendolyn tells her husband that the men she sees wandering around the city must be desperate, for they are not looking at her legs.

Billy and his wife, Maria, are in their room overlooking the town square. Maria reads the paper and learns that a colonial official whom they knew in London has been killed. Billy gets upset and tells his wife that this death is the work of Billy's associates. He is sure that they killed the colonial official to keep him quiet about their upcoming trip to East Africa, where they hope to make an illegal fortune mining uranium deposits. He goes down to the café, where he sees Major Ross arriving in a taxi. Immediately Billy suspects that Ross is the murderer. Gwendolyn and Harry are in the café playing chess, and they strike up a conversation with Billy. Gwendolyn thinks that Billy and his associates are strange because they are all of different nationalities. She is convinced that they are all doctors on their way to Africa to perform evil experiments on the natives for the advancement of science. Billy invites Gwendolyn and Harry to dinner with Maria and him. He is interrupted by the major, who tells Billy to come to a meeting of the committee; that is, of his associates. At the meeting the men complain that they are getting tired of the delays in their departure for Africa, and they want Billy to notify his contacts there about their delay, fearing the contacts will start negotiations with someone else.

That night the Dannreuthers and Chelms drive to a villa and restaurant in the hills, in a specially built limousine once owned by a matador friend of Billy's. Dannreuther relates that he himself once owned the villa and restaurant. Harry divulges that he and Gwendolyn are going to East Africa because he inherited a coffee plantation from a cousin. Harry has a suspect pedigree himself, acting like a country squire, when he really is the son of boardinghouse owners in Earl's Court.

The next morning the Chelms are planning a trip into the country with Billy, but Harry claims to have a chill on his liver and insists that Gwendolyn go on the trip with Billy. While they are gone, Maria goes to Harry's room, bringing him tea. A bit of an Anglophile, she is falling for Harry.

On a beautiful point overlooking the sea, Gwendolyn reveals to Billy that her husband is really going to Africa to exploit uranium deposits. Her vivid imagination is at work again, but what she says coincides with Billy and his associates' plans. By chance, above them, and also sightseeing, is O'Hara, who overhears Gwendolyn's tale and runs off to alert the other members of the gang.

When the couple gets back to town, Petersen and company stop Billy, for they suspect that he is out to double-cross them with the Chelms. O'Hara comes to Billy's room. Billy makes fun of his Irish name when he is so obviously German. O'Hara angrily retorts that many Germans in Chile have the name O'Hara. He also suspects that Billy will betray them to the Chelms and tells him that they are all in it together. When he leaves Billy becomes irate that his associates think of him as their hired man. His wife reminds him that he is, which doesn't improve his temper.

Down in the hotel lobby Harry Chelm invites Billy for a drink. Petersen confronts Gwendolyn Chelm, who tells him about her husband's great position and wealth and that the reason he is going to Africa is to resolve his spiritual problems. In the bar Billy and Harry encounter Major Ross, who starts expressing his enthusiasm for Hitler and Mussolini and picks a fight with Billy. The major is interrupted by a phone call from Petersen, who directs him to a committee meeting. At the meeting Petersen expresses his concerns about the Chelms. From Gwendolyn's various stories, he believes the couple will beat them to Africa and the uranium deposits. He insists that Billy join him on a preemptive flight to Africa and orders O'Hara to make inquiries in London about the Chelms.

On their way to the airport, the matador's limousine breaks down on the winding coast road. The chauffeur, Billy, and Petersen get out to push, but the car gets away from them, leaves the road, and falls into the sea below. Billy and Petersen start walking back to the hotel.

Back at the hotel Harry informs Maria and Gwendolyn that Billy's car was seen crashing into the sea. Both women are distraught. Billy's remaining associates start to form new alliances. Ravello tries to bring Harry into their scheme while O'Hara tries to ingratiate himself with Maria. Suddenly Billy and Petersen appear. Gwendolyn, who a moment ago was hysterical and had even claimed that she loved Billy, now says she knew Billy would be all right, because her old Spanish nurse had once told her that if she counted thirteen backward a number of times a miracle would happen. The group is interrupted by the ship's mate, who informs them that the ship has been repaired and will sail at midnight. At the dock Harry makes a big fuss about a metal box that belongs to him and is assured that it is in his cabin. Gwendolyn asks Billy to run off with her, but he refuses, saying he needs more money to make his life worthwhile and that they will have plenty of time together in Africa.

On board the ship Petersen, ecstatic about the fresh air, wishes he could figure a way to bottle it and make a fortune. In his jovial mood, he leads his associates in a round of sailing songs. They receive a cable indicating that Harry Chelm is neither a squire nor wealthy. They steal his metal box from his cabin and confirm that he is nothing but the son of boardinghouse owners. Harry is irate when he discovers the theft of his metal box, and the ship's mate tells him that he saw the major take it. Harry brings the major before the drunken captain, who tries to make light of Harry's accusations. He reveals that he knows what the group is up to, and threatens to report them to the authorities. The major suggests that they kill Harry. Maria later tries to convince Harry to drop his threats against the group. Harry, however, does not want to compromise.

The passengers are then informed that the ship's engine has broken down. Harry volunteers to fix the oil pump. It appears he has fixed it, but then the engine explodes. The passengers gather in the saloon. Upset that his wife is associating with Billy, Harry leaves. The major goes after him and tries to kill him, but Billy intervenes and saves Harry. Back in the saloon Gwendolyn accuses her husband of being crazy. The ship's crew overpowers him and handcuffs him to a post. After another explosion, they are all told to abandon ship. Billy and Gwendolyn go to rescue Harry, but he has escaped from the handcuffs and has apparently dived overboard. Petersen, O'Hara, Ravello, the Major, Billy, Maria, and Gwendolyn get into a lifeboat. They land on the African coast and are captured by Arabs. An Arab official suspects that they have come to incite a revolution. Petersen tells him that they are in Africa to sell vacuum cleaners to the natives. While they are imprisoned, Billy ingratiates himself with the Arab official, who is a fan of Rita Hayworth. Billy convinces him to go into partnership with him. All the prisoners are then put on a boat and returned to the Italian port.

There the group is approached by a Scotland Yard detective, who suspects one of them is behind the murder of the colonial official in London. They seem to be putting a fast one over on the detective, when Gwendolyn blurts out to him the whole scheme of going to Africa to secure the uranium deposits. Petersen, Ravello, O'Hara, and the major are led off. Gwendolyn then receives a cable from Harry, who not only safely arrived in Africa but gained the mineral rights that the group was originally after. He asks his wife to join him. When Billy reads the cable, he breaks out in laughter, indicating that this is the end.

16 *Moby Dick* (1956)

Director and Producer	John Huston
Associate Producer	Lehman Katz
Screenplay	Ray Bradbury and John Huston, based on the novel by Herman Melville

Director of Photography	Oswald Morris, B.S.C.
Art Director	Ralph Brinton
Assistant Art Directors	Stephen Grimes and Geoffrey Drake
Film Editor	Russell Lloyd
Recording Supervisor	Harold King
Sound Recording	John Mitchell and Len Shilton
Sound Effects	Leslie Hodgson
Continuity	Angela Allen
Music	Philip Sainton
Conductor	Louis Levy
Production Manager	Cecil Ford
Casting Director	Robert Lennard
Second Unit Director of Photography	Freddie Francis
Costumes	Elizabeth Haffenden
Makeup	Charles Parker
Hairdresser	Hilda Fox
Technical Adviser on Whaling	Robert Clarke
Cast	Gregory Peck (Ahab), Richard Basehart (Ishmael), Leo Glenn (Starbuck), James Robertson Justice (Captain Boomer), Harry Andrews (Stubb), Bernard Miles (Manxman), Noel Purcell (Carpenter), Edric Connor (Daggoo), Mervyn Jones (Peleg), Joseph Tomelty (Peter Coffin), Francis De Wolff (Captain Gardiner), Philip Stainton (Bildad), Royal Dano (Elijah), Seamus Kelly (Flash), Friedrich Ledebur (Queequeg), Ted Howard (Blacksmith), Tamba Alleney (Pip), Tom Clegg (Tashtego), Orson Welles (Father Mapple)
Filmed	at locations in New England; Moulin Pictures/Warner Brothers; made at Associated British Studies, Elstree, Hertfordshire, England
Running Time	116 minutes, Technicolor
Release Date	World premiere in New Bedford, Massachusetts, on June 27, 1956; released in the United States, July 3 through July 31, 1956

SYNOPSIS

It is 1842. A man walks down a hill, saying, "Call me Ishmael." He walks past waterfalls, indicating that he is out of sorts and that he heeds an inner call to the sea. There is magic in water for all men. He comes to New Bedford, Massachusetts, and enters an inn, where the whalers look him over. One, Stubb, expounds about his theory that if God wanted to be a fish he would be a whale. He would pick his teeth with the oars from men's boats. Captain Ahab passes by outside. The whalers sing and dance. Ishmael decides to rent a bed and is horrified to learn that he must share it with Queequeg, the harpooner, a tattooed cannibal from the South Seas.

A chapel scene shows the chapel's walls filled with memorial tablets for all those lost at sea. Father Mapple climbs into the pulpit, which is a ship's prow, and bases his sermon on the story of Jonah.

The next day Ishmael goes down to the harbor and is questioned by ship owners about his intentions. Ishmael is confronted by the mad prophet, Elijah. Women stand by the dock and watch the *Pequod* being readied. The *Pequod* sets sail. The crew comes from all races and different parts of the world. They include Starbuck, a stern and righteous New Englander; the irrepressible Stubb; and the nimble cabin boy, Pip. Captain Ahab appears. He asks his men what do they do when they see a whale? He tells them that they must look for the white whale, Moby Dick, who took off Ahab's leg and tore his body and soul. Ahab brings the men to a frenzy. "Death to Moby Dick!" they shout. The crewmen talk about famous whales, and Moby Dick is the greatest. He has been spotted all over the oceans, sometimes in sightings one thousand miles apart on the same day. The crew spot a whale and pursues it. Although it is not Moby Dick, they harpoon it. They prepare its blubber and oil for the lamps of the houses on the mainland. The men celebrate.

In his quarters Ahab reflects that his bed is a coffin. He tells Starbuck, the first officer, that they are bound for the Pacific. Ahab explains that whales are predictable. They could slay a record number of whales, but first Ahab wants to find Moby Dick. Starbuck doubts they will, but Ahab is insistent.

The crew sees many whales. Another ship comes by, and its crew says that they have seen Moby Dick. Ahab stops the *Pequod*'s whaling activities and pursues Moby Dick. The men are bothered. They don't want to chase Moby Dick when the whaling is so rich. "This is an evil voyage," says Starbuck, who fears the wrath of God. "Our goal in life is to whale and Ahab is perverting that goal." Starbuck reminds the crew that they have a right to take over the ship if the captain persists in his obsession.

In April with the new moon the *Pequod* enters the waters where Ahab expects to find Moby Dick. A man falls overboard and disappears immediately. The ship is in a calm, hot sea, and the men swelter. They throw a gold coin into the sea as a ransom. Maybe the sea will come alive. Queequeg tosses little whale bones on the deck and in them sees his doom. He has the ship's carpenter make him a coffin and tells him it should be as watertight as a boat. He won't eat or drink. Ahab orders the men to lower the whaleboats and to pull the ship out of the calm waters. Meanwhile, the sailors taunt Queequeg. Ishmael challenges a sailor to a fight to protect his dying friend, but when it appears he (Ishmael) might be killed, Queequeg is roused to save him. When the men suddenly spy Moby Dick, the whale seems of such gigantic and menacing proportions that they wonder if he could be real. The men get into the lowered whaleboats and go after him, with Ahab commanding one of the boats. It is very quiet. Many birds are overhead. "He's near, very near. Be ready for him," Ahab cautions. "He is no whale. He is a great white God." Moby Dick comes up briefly. Then he disappears. Disappointed, the men in the whaleboats return to the ship.

A sudden wind blows. Ahab offers the crew his 10 percent share of the profits if they kill Moby Dick. Another ship appears and asks for help, but Ahab refuses because of his compulsion to pursue the whale. A storm comes up. The *Pequod*'s sails rip, but Ahab won't lower them. He guesses they are three days behind Moby Dick and thinks the wind will allow them to catch up with him. New sails are raised. Starbuck and Ahab confront each other in an eerie light. Starbuck is angry. He believes Ahab has snatched the crew members' souls, that he is a madman begetting more madmen.

After the storm everything is calm. Ahab talks about his life as a whaler and how old he feels. Starbuck implores him to stop his mad pursuit. Starbuck is ready to kill Ahab, but thinks better of it. Birds appear again. They spot Moby Dick. The men pursue him in the whaleboats. Harpoons are cast. Moby Dick rises and capsizes a boat. Ahab grabs hold of the whale and strikes at him. The whale goes under the water. When he rises Ahab is strapped to the whale. Ahab appears to beckon to the men, although he is dead. Starbuck urges the men to pursue the whale. The whaleboats are all capsized, and all aboard drown. Moby Dick then attacks the *Pequod* and sinks it.

Ishmael is the only survivor and floats to safety on Queequeg's coffin. He is finally rescued by the *Rachel.*

17 *Heaven Knows, Mr. Allison* (1957)

Director	John Huston
Producers	Buddy Adler and Eugene Frenke
Screenplay	John Lee Mahin and John Huston, based on the novel by Charles Shaw
Music	Georges Auric
Conductor	Lambert Williamson
Director of Photography	Oswald Morris
Art Director	Stephen Grimes
Film Editor	Russell Lloyd
Costumes	Elizabeth Haffenden
Sound	Basil Fenton-Smith
Production Manager	Leigh Aman
Assistant Director	Adrian Pryce-Jones
Camera Operator	Arthur Ibbetson
Makeup	George Frost
Continuity	Angela Allen
Sound Editors	Leslie Hodgson and Malcolm Cooke
Cast	Deborah Kerr (Sister Angela), Robert Mitchum (Mr. Allison)
Filmed	at locations in the Caribbean and at Twentieth Century-Fox
Running Time	107 minutes, DeLuxe color
Release Date	November 7, 1956

Other titles: *Dieu seul le sait, L'Anima e la carne*

SYNOPSIS

Behind the credits a dinghy drifts in the Pacific. Finally the camera reveals an exhausted soldier within, and then the shoreline of an island from the soldier's point of view. He hauls himself ashore and dives for cover in the trees. He finds the ruins of a village and a grave. Behind a house he is amazed to discover a church. A nun in a white habit appears on the veranda. The soldier asks her if anyone else is alive on the island. She assures him she is quite alone and introduces herself as Sister Angela. Inside the chapel he sinks into an exhausted sleep.

Later he is awakened by the sound of her prayers. Seeing the lighted candles on the altar, he extinguishes them, reminding her of the blackout rules. Over supper she tells him that she came with her superior, Father Phillips, to rescue Father Ryan, who had been in charge of the mission here. On arriving they discovered that Father Ryan had already been captured by the Japanese, and Father Phillips died of a heart attack a day later. His is the grave by the church. She offers the priest's pipe and some tobacco to her guest, Allison, a Marine and the lone survivor of a Japanese raid on a reconnaissance mission.

Allison finds the island is a tropical paradise with an abundance of fruit and bamboo that can be sharpened for spearing fish. One day they even spot a turtle, give chase in the dinghy, and finally capture it after a lengthy pursuit, during which Allison is pulled overboard. Sister Angela has to pull him from the sea and secure the line. Over dinner Allison tells Sister Angela his life story: an illegitimate child, he was brought up in a series of orphanages and reform schools until adolescence, when he joined the Marines. The military has been his salvation. The corps for him represents family and mission. Sister Angela sees they have something in common: a sense of belonging to a form of faith. Allison also raises the possibility of escaping to Fiji (about three hundred miles away). Reluctantly Sister Angela agrees to go along, knowing he won't be dissuaded.

Their preparations, however, are brutally interrupted by a Japanese air raid, during which they must take cover in a cave. The raid demolishes the rubber dinghy and the wooden church. Among the debris Allison later discovers the Sister's crucifix.

Shortly thereafter the Japanese occupy the island to install both a weather station and a storage depot. Without housing, Sister Angela and Allison retreat to their cave. Feeling she might be a burden to him, Sister Angela suggests she ought to surrender to the Japanese. Allison insists on her staying, in part because she is necessary for boosting his own morale. He points out that they can still, with caution, fish and forage. He, in fact, does go fishing, and is forced to hide in the surf from a Japanese patrol. Although he returns with a large fish, they must eat it raw. Realizing that the Sister can not survive long on this fare, Allison decides to raid the Japanese camp.

Allison slips out of the cave at dawn, while Angela is sleeping. He finds the commissary and begins to help himself to a shelf of canned goods. He is then trapped in the hut by two unwitting off-duty soldiers, who settle into a game of cards and a few drinks. Allison is forced to spend the night locked in the commissary, but then manages to escape with his booty. Sister Angela, in the meantime, has

93

heard shots from a Japanese hunting party and is convinced that he has been caught and shot. She regards his return as little short of miraculous and makes him promise that he will never leave again without telling her.

Allison makes Sister Angela a comb out of wood, and while she is touched by his gift, she explains she cannot use it, for her hair is cropped. She nonetheless accepts it graciously. In a conversation that follows, Sister Angela explains that nuns who enter a religious order hardly ever change their minds, but they have five years before making their final vows. She is to make hers the following month. Consequently, they both know that there is still time for her to change her mind. This intimate dialogue full of unspoken feelings is followed by the sound of a huge naval battle over the horizon. Allison and the Sister follow the progress of the conflict, with Allison offering a commentary on the outcome based on his identification of the sound of the guns. The U.S. fleet appears to be the victor, for later that day Allison observes that the camp has been abandoned.

Allison and Sister Angela gleefully take advantage of the situation to bathe, eat, and sleep in relative luxury. He takes her by the arm and dances with her to the tune of "Don't Sit under the Apple Tree with Anyone Else But Me," a leitmotiv in the movie. As they prepare to dine off the food left in the commissary, Allison very hesitantly broaches the subject of their relationship. There is no one waiting for him at home, he says, and the chances of the navy rescuing them from the island in the near future are remote. He hopes very much she will not take those final vows. In short, this is a declaration of love and a proposal of marriage. Touched, she replies that she is already pledged to Christ (she shows him her silver ring), and at her final vows she will receive a gold band, symbolizing eternal troth.

The next morning Allison joins Sister Angela on the beach and apologizes for speaking so openly the night before. She later discovers a bottle of sake in a sack of rice, and Allison proceeds to get drunk. In frustration he asks why she has to be so young and pretty. And why can they not see the island as Eden, with themselves as Adam and Eve? At one point he throws Father Phillips' pipe and breaks it. She tries to distract him with a game of Japanese draughts, but in a final attempt to get away from him she runs out into a thunderstorm outside. He runs after her and tries to bring her back for her own protection, but she evades him and spends the night outside in the rain and wakes the next day with a fever. The Japanese return to occupy the island. Allison must steal water and blankets to nurse Sister Angela. During his sortie he is discovered by a Japanese soldier, whom he stabs to death, dropping the body in the sea. When Sister Angela wakes up after two days of delirium, she finds herself lying under the blankets, her habit hanging from a tree. Allison, feeling responsible for her fever, begs her forgiveness. She replies that she was not running away from him, but from "the truth." Meanwhile, the Japanese have discovered the body of their dead comrade and are combing the island for his killer. Thus, Sister Angela learns Allison has had to kill for those blankets.

They are saved from being taken by the Japanese by a U.S. air raid and a well-aimed bomb. They now await the U.S. landing. It then occurs to Allison, as if God told him so, that he can help both his comrades and himself if he can neutralize the heavy artillery pieces the Japanese have placed on the hillside above the landing area. He succeeds in dismantling the guns single-handedly, hurling the firing mechanism into the sea, but, coming under fire, he is hit by shrapnel in the shoulder. Back at the cave Sister Angela tends his wound, and they exchange their final confidences. He tells her it is a privilege to have known her, and she tells him that he will be her "dear companion always." By now the U.S. forces have landed without difficulty. As two officers try to figure out why the Japanese did not manage to fire their cannons, Allison is brought down to the shore on a stretcher, accompanied by Sister Angela clutching her crucifix. From here both will be placed aboard a landing craft and taken to safety.

18 *The Barbarian and the Geisha* (1958)

Director	John Huston
Producer	Eugene Frenke
Screenplay	Charles Grayson
Story	Ellis St. Joseph
Music	Hugo Friedhofer
Director of Photography	Charles Clarke, A.S.C.
Art Direction	Lyle R. Wheeler and Jack Martin Smith
Set Decoration	Walter M. Scott and Don B. Greenwood
Executive Wardrobe Designer	Charles LeMaire
Makeup	Webb Overlander
Film Editor	Stuart Gilmore
Assistant Director	Joseph E. Rickards
Sound	W. D. Flick and Warren B. Delaplain
Script Supervisor	Teinosuke Kinugasa
Dialogue Coach	Minoru Inuzuka
Technical Supervisor	Mitsuo Hirotsu
Technical Art Adviser	Kisaku Itoh
Japanese Technical Adviser	Kampo Yoshikawa
Assistant to the Producer	Paul Nakaoka
Cast	John Wayne (Townsend Harris), Eiko Ando (Okichi), Sam Jaffe (Henry Heusken), So Yamamura (Tamura), Norman Thomson (Ship Captain), James Robbins (Lieutenant Fisher), Morita (Prime Minister), Kodaya Ichikawa (Daimyo), Hiroshi Yamato (Shogun), Tokujiro Iketaniuchi (Harusha), Fuji Kasai (Lord Hotta), Takeshi Kumagai (Chamberlain). *Bits:* Rintaro Kaga, Henry Pong, Viraig Amosin, Jun Ohtomo, Koichi Umino, Shingo Osawa, Sanjo Akaozeki, Tsutomu Mitani, Koji Sawa, Kichiro Iwaki, Takashi Yoshikawa, Hiroshi Idaida, Hitoshi Komaki, Hiroya Morita, Tadashi Nagoaka, Ryo Futami, Shinjo Hayama, Kajiro Fujimatsu, Eitaro Aishijimi, Minanogawa, Shizu Yamanaga, Miyoshi

John Huston

	Jingu, Rollin Moriyama, Robert Okazaki,
	Frank Kumagai, Edo Mita, Fiji, Tetsu Koman
Filmed	at locations in Japan; Twentieth Century-Fox
Running Time	105 minutes, DeLuxe color
Release Date	October 2, 1958; production completed
	January 10, 1958

Other titles: *Le Barbare et la geisha, Il Barbaro e la geisha*

SYNOPSIS

A prefatory note states that this film tells the story of Townsend Harris, the first American consul appointed to Japan, in 1856, and the first American to enter the Forbidden Empire. A pre-credit sequence, narrated by the heroine, Okichi, shows a village festival, with the locals dancing and singing in honor of their ancestors.

As the film begins, a foreign ship is sighted in the harbor to the consternation of the villagers, and a messenger is dispatched to the governor of Shimoda. The next morning the governor and the villagers witness Americans rowing ashore in defiance of Japanese admonitions not to. Townsend Harris announces to Governor Tamura that he has been sent to Japan to represent the United States in accordance with the terms of a treaty negotiated two years earlier by Commodore Matthew Perry. The governor responds that such appointments require the approval of both governments. Harris rejoins that either government may appoint its representative, according to its need, and that the problem lies in the Japanese translation of the treaty.

The governor accepts Harris and his deputy/interpreter, Henry Heusken, as private citizens and leads them to what he claims is the only accommodation available—a ruined house above the harbor. One of Harris's first acts is to raise the American flag, but the governor prohibits it. Tamura also sends out the word that no local townspeople are to have any dealings with the foreigners. Thus, all forms of trade and social contact are prohibited. The Americans are to be completely ostracized.

Harris protests this treatment to the governor in person and puts to him the American position that, since Japan sits at the crossroads between East and West, it must enter the modern world of international trade. The governor steadfastly defends his country's right to isolation. Harris's main objective is to present his credentials to the shogun in Edo. He leaves his letter of accreditation with the governor, urging him to arrange an appointment in the capital. The governor invites Harris and his deputy to dinner, where the American consul first sets eyes on Okichi, a geisha under the protection of Governor Tamura. She sings for the guests.

Tamura sends Okichi to live at Harris's house, to offer him whatever services he requires, and to spy on him. She is amazed when the American does not come to her room. Harris and Okichi exchange cultural information about their respective countries. While she sings to him or arranges flowers, she observes a wind gauge and such icons as a picture of George Washington. Harris even shows her a conjuring trick with a dollar. She begins to learn some English.

96

One day an American vessel arrives in the harbor, but it cannot land, for there is cholera aboard. The captain has come for medical help, but there is no doctor in the village. Several crewmen jump ship and swim ashore, where, in spite of Harris's attempts to stop them, they are surrounded by villagers who become stricken with the disease. During the cholera epidemic that follows Harris works tirelessly to contain the spread of the disease. He resorts to burning the clothing, bedding, and even the houses of the sick. The villagers naturally turn on him in anger. Okichi also falls sick, but recovers through his devoted ministrations. In the name of the angry villagers, Tamura puts Harris and Heusken under house arrest and threatens to send them home on the first ship. Harris ironically summarizes their achievements so far: "We have brought in a cholera ship, started an epidemic, burned their houses, and have been placed in custody."

In the end he is vindicated. The epidemic passes, the fishermen return to work, and Harris receives a delegation of villagers who offer him their thanks. The governor, too, comes to thank the consul and offers to arrange the long-sought visit with the shogun. The villagers themselves decide to accompany Harris to the capital as a sign of their complete acceptance of the foreigner.

Once inside the palace at Edo, the Americans prepare for their audience with the shogun the next day. The shogun is a young man in white robes. Harris appears in full diplomatic regalia and in the name of the American people presents his host with tokens of goodwill: a chair, a telescope, bottles of bourbon. Before presenting the terms of a new treaty of friendship between the two governments, Harris addresses the shogun and his Council of Nobles on the benefits of contact between peoples. Nations no less than individuals, he argues, need neighbors. The United States offers its hand in friendship, in the name of its own inhabitants and their prosperity, Harris continues, and asks Japan to join the community of nations in an era of expanding international trade.

Three days later he and Heusken are summoned to a banquet at which Harris must submit to questions from the members of the council. These questions reveal the deep divisions in the country's ruling class on the question of relations with other countries. They ask Harris about the size of the American navy, about the number of wars in the West, about slavery in the United States, and about the meaning of progress. To the last question, Harris replies that it can mean many things, including not putting girl babies to death in time of famine. The council adjourns before the final vote, and Harris is entertained by a remarkable demonstration of archers on horseback, whose skills have been perfected by a thousand years of tradition. Tragically, however, one archer assassinates Lord Hotta, a respected elder who was planning to vote for the new treaty presented by Harris and who was a powerful voice of moderation and compromise. At this moment of crisis Lord Tamura of Shimoda, still hostile to the idea of an alliance with America, visits Harris and begs him to leave. He feels Harris's continued presence can only deepen the rifts between the ruling families of Japan. The treaty is nonetheless passed by one vote in the council.

Triumph now turns toward disaster as the result of a palace plot. Lord Tamura, Okichi's protector, summons her and in a temple in the shadow of the

Buddha demands her help. According to feudal tradition, she cannot deny him. He wants her services in a plot to assassinate Harris. She is to mark the door of the room where he sleeps with a red scarf.

That very evening Harris declares his love to Okichi. Though he must now return to the United States, he intends to return to Japan as a private citizen and marry her. They will live, he says, in a house in the mountains, far from all neighbors. Okichi retires in tears, tying the red scarf to the handle of her own door.

Later, armed with his ancestral sword, Tamura enters her room and discovers her beneath the covers, but cannot bring himself to slay her. Nor can he kill Harris, whom he then confronts in the corridor outside. He cries out to him, "Take back your life!" Dishonored, he commits suicide in the palace courtyard.

The following day, Okichi is gone. She has left Harris a comb and mirror—the former to symbolize separation; the latter, her soul. Later that day Harris is borne on a litter through the streets of Edo to the cheers of the crowds, while Okichi, hidden in the thick of the multitude, observes his triumph. She is swathed in black and remains behind as the public presses forward to follow the procession.

19 *Roots of Heaven* (1958)

Director	John Huston
Producer	Darryl F. Zanuck
Screenplay	Romain Gary and Patrick Leigh-Fermor, based on the novel by Romain Gary
Music	Malcolm Arnold
Minna's Theme	Henri Patterson
Director of Photography	Oswald Morris
Associate Producer	Robert Jacks
Art Director	Stephen Grimes
Associate Art Director	Raymond Gabutti
Editor	Russell Lloyd
Production Manager	Guy Longo
Second Unit Photography	Skeete Kelly, Henri Persin, Gilles Bonneau
Technical Adviser	Claude Hettier de Boislambert
Assistant Director	Carlo Lastricati
Sound	Basil Fenton-Smith
Special Photographic Effects	L. B. Abbott, A.S.C.
Makeup	George Frost
Set Decorator	Bruno Avesani
Costume Designer	Rosine Delamare
Special Effects	Fred Etcheverry
Script Girl	Angela Allen
Cast	Errol Flynn (Forsythe), Juliette Greco (Minna), Trevor Howard (Morel), Eddie Albert (Abe Fields), Orson Welles (Cy Sedgewick), Paul Lukas (Saint Denis), Herbert Lom (Orsini), Gregoire Aslan (Habib), André Luguet (Governor), Friedrich

	Ledebur (Peer Qvist), Edric Connor (Waitari), Olivier Hussenot (Baron), Pierre Dudan (Major Scholscher), Marc Doelnitz (De Vries), Dan Jackson (Madjumba), Maurice Cannon (Haas), Jacques Marin (Cerisot), Habib Benglia (Korotoro), Bachir Touré (Yussef), Alain Saury (A.D.C.), Roscoe Stallworth (N'Dolo), Assane Fall (Inguele), Francis de Wolff (Father Fargue)
Filmed	interiors photographed at Studios de Boulogne, Paris; locations filmed in Africa; Twentieth Century-Fox
Running Time	131 minutes, DeLuxe color
Release Date	October 15, 1958

Other titles: *Le Radici del cielo, Les Racines du ciel*

SYNOPSIS

The film opens with elephant tracks, jungle sounds, and close-ups of elephants and an elephant herd. One sees a hunter, and hears a shout which distracts the elephants.

Next, at a bar a Land Rover appears. Morel asks for Habib. Morel then tells Minna that he lives with elephants and would give anything to become an elephant. Morel is extremely agitated by hunters who kill. At the rate they are killing elephants, he says there will be nothing else left on earth save men, who will then kill one another. He shows Minna a petition to stop the slaughter. He also has a present for her boss, Habib, and drags out a beaten-up hunter who works for Habib. Minna tells Morel he should get the governor to sign his petition, but the governor refuses to sign. Later, a priest also refuses to sign, saying that he is more concerned about human suffering than that of animals. Morel then learns that Cy Sedgewick, a famous television personality and columnist, is arriving for a big safari and game hunt.

Later on in a nightclub people sarcastically berate Morel about his ridiculous cause. He gets virtually no sympathy for his fight, except from Minna and Forsythe, a former British Army officer and a drunk. When Morel leaves, Minna goes after him and relates her shaky life up until that time. A bond is formed between them.

Morel begins an underground war against hunters, zoo collectors, and poachers. A zoo collector gets buckshot in the behind when he keeps a baby elephant in a stockade away from its mother. The local ivory hunter is tied to a tree and sees his business go up in flames. And Sedgewick also gets a load of buckshot in the behind after he brags about getting his first elephant. The governor apologizes to Sedgewick, who to the surprise of the governor indicates that he is impressed by Morel's one-person crusade and that when he returns to New York he will support Morel on his TV programs. Sedgewick says, "He spits on me, and I like him." Visitors talk about Morel and his cause, and the governor is bothered by the bad publicity. The governor begins to plot against Morel. The governor sends Saint Denis into the hills to find Morel and offer him amnesty if he will give up his cause.

Saint Denis finds Morel and his group of followers. One of his followers, Waitari, a black nationalist, admits to Saint Denis that he is just using Morel because of the publicity that Morel is getting. Saint Denis tells Morel that he will go back and tell the governor what the authorities are up against. It appears that Saint Denis might be coming around to Morel's viewpoint.

Minna asks Saint Denis not to tell where Morel is. She even offers to pay him to keep quiet. Morel is guilty of the greatest crime—too much faith in human beings—Saint Denis tells Minna. Furthermore, if he continues his crusade, Saint Denis feels, Morel will be shot by either his associates or the police.

Minna has an idea where Morel is hiding. She recruits Forsythe to help her look for him. They go in search of Morel with ammunition and supplies. During their trek Forsythe confesses to Minna that once he betrayed his friends, and they died. He lived by betraying, and now he has become nothing but a drunk.

With the help of a witch doctor Minna and Forsythe find Morel. They also learn that Waitari and Habib will betray Morel, for the men have decided that Morel will be more valuable to Waitari dead than alive.

That night Morel confides in Minna that his interest in saving elephants started in a German prison camp. What kept him going was the thought of the elephants' freedom as they move across the African veldt. Morel and his group go to the office of the publisher and game hunter, Orsini, and demand that he print their manifesto in his newspaper. He readily agrees. They then go to Orsini's home, where a party is going on. There Morel reads his statement. He then confronts Madame Orisini, a big game hunter, and spanks her before the startled guests.

Waitari is angry that Morel's manifesto contains nothing about his nationalist movement. His men steal the truck and kill one of Morel's followers, forcing Morel and his followers to trek on foot to their hideaway. As they approach a lake they come upon a huge herd of elephants. Morel reveals that the greatest elephant slaughter on record occurred here thirty years before. They then spot a small plane, which crashes. The pilot is killed, but Abe Fields, a photographer, is saved. Fields has been looking for Morel and is happy at his one spot of luck.

The next day Waitari, Habib, De Vries (another associate), and some Sudanese mercenaries come to the lake to slaughter the elephants. They plan on using their tusks to finance Waitari's movement. However, just as they are surrounding the elephants, Morel and his group stampede the herd. One of Waitari's band attempts to kill Morel, but is himself killed by the elephants. Forsythe is killed. Morel is captured. Waitari chides Morel that the Congo Conference on Fauna did not even act on protecting the elephants. Morel is completely disillusioned. He throws his papers and petitions away. Fields convinces Waitari to free his captives by offering to take pictures of Waitari and by convincing him that he will get bad publicity for his movement if he keeps or harms Morel. Morel and the last of his group start walking again to their hideout. One of Waitari's men is supposed to kill Morel, but he cannot do it.

Minna is sick. Morel tells her that when she gets back home all this strife will seem a nightmare. Minna corrects him: what she goes back to will be the nightmare. Minna's condition worsens, and he decides to take her to the nearest hospital, even though he knows that he will be arrested. When they are spotted, however, the local official and his African soldiers line up on both sides of the road to give Morel and his motley group a hero's welcome. Morel leaves Minna at the hospital and marches off into the bush with his followers.

20 *The Unforgiven* (1960)

Director	John Huston
Producer	James Hill
Screenplay	Ben Maddow, based on a novel by Alan LeMay
Photography	Franz Planer
Production Designer	Stephen Grimes (Art Director)
Film Editor	Russell Lloyd
Wardrobe Designer	Dorothy Jeakins
Executive Production Manager	Gilbert Kurland
Assistant Director	Thomas F. Shaw
Sound Recording	Basil Fenton-Smith
Music	Dimitri Tiomkin
Special Effects	Dave Koehler
Makeup Artists	Frank McCoy and Frank Larue
Cast	Burt Lancaster (Ben Zachary), Audrey Hepburn (Rachel Zachary), Audie Murphy (Cash Zachary), John Saxon (Johnny Portugal), Charles Bickford (Zeb Rawlins), Albert Salmi (Charles Rawlins), Lillian Gish (Mattilda Zachary), Joseph Wiseman (Abe Kelsey), Kipp Hamilton (Georgia Rawlins), Arnold Merritt (Jude Rawlins), June Walker (Hagar Rawlins), Carlos Rivas (Lost Bird), Doug McClure (Andy Zachary)
Filmed	at locations in the West; Hecht-Hill-Lancaster, a James Production, released through United Artists
Running Time	125 minutes, Technicolor
Release Date	April 6, 1960

Other titles: *Le Vent de la plaine, Gli inesorabilli*

SYNOPSIS

In the Texas panhandle in the mid-1870s Rachel Zachary is in the family sod house with Mattilda Zachary, the family matriarch. Ben Zachary, the eldest son and family spokesman, is away hiring hands for a cattle drive. Cash, the middle brother, and Andy, the youngest, are out on the range. Near the house Rachel encounters an eccentric stranger, Abe Kelsey. He questions her about her family and frightens her. Later, rifle in hand, Mattilda has a grim interview with the eccentric, who shouts of "revenge," but she cannot bring herself to kill him.

Ben returns with the cowhands. Among them is Johnny Portugal, a handsome half-breed, whom Cash dislikes on sight. Rachel greets her brother Ben with more than sisterly affection. Trouble brews when the brothers imagine Johnny is becoming too familiar with Rachel.

Zeb Rawlins, a neighbor and cattle partner of the Zacharys, calls with Hagar, his wife, and their three children—Georgia, Charlie, and Jude. Zeb wants Ben's blessing, for Charlie desires Rachel's hand. Georgia, in turn, expresses her hopes that Cash will propose to her. Ben wants time to think about it. During the party Mattilda tells Ben about Kelsey, and this news worries him.

After the Rawlinses leave, Ben and Cash steal out in search of Kelsey. They overtake him in a windstorm and wound him, but he escapes. As preparations begin for the cattle drive, Cash finds Kelsey is spreading a rumor that is poisoning the minds of the neighbors. According to this rumor, Rachel is not a white girl, but a Kiowa Indian who was kidnapped to replace a little girl Mattilda lost in childbirth. The neighbors fear that the Zacharys' insistence on keeping her will bring the Kiowas' wrath on them all.

A party of Kiowas, inspired by Kelsey's rumor, comes to the sod house. The chief offers to "buy" Rachel back. Ben refuses. The Kiowas ride off, shouting that they will return to take by war what they could not buy in peace. Preparations for the drive continue. Charlie Rawlins visits the Zachary house to ask Ben's permission to court Rachel. Coquettishly and perhaps to arouse Ben's jealousy, she goes along. Ben agrees to the match. While returning home, Charlie is killed by prowling Kiowas. Zeb and Hagar Rawlins, distraught by the death of their son, blame Rachel. They denounce her as an Indian, saying it was she who brought down the Kiowas' fury on their son.

To set the accusation to rest, Ben and a posse ride out after Kelsey, who is lurking in the vicinity. Johnny Portugal brings him in, and from Kelsey's own words the neighbors convict him of complicity in Charlie's death. But even with the rope around his neck Kelsey insists that Rachel is a Kiowa. Shouting that Kelsey is grief-maddened over the murder of his own son by the Kiowa many years before, Mattilda puts an end to matters. She strikes his horse with a firebrand, causing it to bolt, thus tightening the noose around Kelsey's neck and hanging him. The neighbors, however, still believe Kelsey's story, leaving an open break between them and the Zacharys.

Returning to the sod house, Mattilda admits that Kelsey's story is true and tells the story of the changelings. Rachel and the boys, particularly Cash, are shocked. In a drunken rage, he renounces his family and rides off.

A large and fanatical Kiowa war party appears at the house and demands Rachel's return. The Zacharys refuse and secure the house. The Indians attack. The battle is long and fierce, but the besieged Zacharys hold out. Then the Indians drive some cattle over the sod house's roof, causing it to collapse. It appears that all is lost, and the family prepares to die together. At this point Rachel and Ben realize that they are in love. Ben sets fire to the house to drive the cattle off. The enraged Indians attack again and Mattilda is killed. By this time the fight has decimated the Indians, and the battle becomes more equal. Its course changes when a remorseful Cash returns to stand with his family. The remaining Kiowas are finally beaten off.

The Zacharys are once again united. Mourning their mother, they resolve to face the future together. Rachel and Ben plan to marry, and their neighbors will have to accept them as they are.

21 *The Misfits* (1961)

Director	John Huston
Producer	Frank E. Taylor
Screenplay	Arthur Miller
Music	Alex North
Director of Photography	Russell Metty, A.S.C.
Production Manager	C. O. (Doc) Erickson
Second Unit Director	Tom Shaw
Assistant Director	Carl Beringer
Art Direction	Stephen Grimes and William Newberry
Set Decoration	Frank McKelvy
Film Editor	George Tomasini, A.C.E.
Sound Recording	Philip Mitchell
Assistant to the Producer	Edward Parone
Miss Monroe's Wardrobe	Jean Louis
Hairstyling	Sydney Guilaroff and Agnes Flanagan, C.H.E.
Makeup	Allan Snyder; Frank Prehoda, S.M.A.; and Frank Larue
Script Supervision	Angela Allen
Wrangler	Billy Jones
Cast	Clark Gable (Gay Langland), Marilyn Monroe (Roslyn Taber), Montgomery Clift (Perce Howland), Thelma Ritter (Isabelle Steers), Eli Wallach (Guido), James Barton (The Old Man in the Bar), Estelle Winwood (The Church Lady), Kevin McCarthy (Raymond Taber), Dennis Shaw (Young Boy in Bar, Lester), Philip Mitchell (Charles Steers), Walter Ramage (Old Groom), Peggy Barton (Young Bride), J. Lewis Smith (Fresh Cowboy in Bar), Marietta Tree (Susan, at Railroad Station), Bobby LaSalle (Bartender), Ryall Bowker (Man in Bar), Ralph Roberts (Ambulance Attendant)
Filmed	at locations in and around Reno and Dayton, Nevada; Seven Arts, released through United Artists
Running Time	124 minutes, black and white
Release Date	February 1, 1961

Other titles: *Les misfits, Les desaxes, Gli spostati*

SYNOPSIS

Guido, in a pickup truck from Jack's Reno Garage, arrives at Isabelle's house to check out a brand-new, but damaged, Cadillac. Isabelle and Roslyn have to meet a lawyer prior to Roslyn's divorce proceedings, Isabelle says, and Roslyn wants to sell the car, a divorce present from her husband. Guido is flabbergasted at the damaged car's mileage—only twenty-three miles. Isabelle explains that men kept running their cars into Roslyn's just to meet her. Isabelle goes inside to fetch Roslyn, who is in her room putting on makeup and trying to memorize the lines that she will have to say in court to get her divorce. It is all false to her, the charges of cruelty and so forth, she says. She asks, "Why can't I just tell the judge that I touched him, but he wasn't there?" When Guido catches sight of Roslyn, he is smitten. Roslyn refuses to ride in the Cadillac again, and Guido agrees to take them to the courthouse in his garage pickup truck.

Roslyn's husband, Raymond Taber, is waiting on the courthouse steps. He wants a reconciliation, but she refuses. Roslyn informs Raymond that if she's going to be alone she wants to be by herself.

Guido drives to the railroad station, where his friend, Gay, is seeing off one of his lady friends. She is heartbroken. She tries to tempt him by saying that her family owns the second largest laundry in St. Louis. Gay says good-bye and goes over to Guido, telling him that they should get out into the country and away from it all. He even berates Guido for being on the job for two months. Guido rides off, shouting that he'll see him at Harrah's later and that he met the sweetest little lady that day.

Roslyn and Isabelle go into Harrah's after the divorce for a drink. Roslyn laments her terrible upbringing with a mother who didn't care. Isabelle urges her not to leave Reno, to stay around. She reminds Roslyn that she used to teach social dancing, and she could do it again. Gay and Guido are at the bar. The women join them. Roslyn can't make up her mind whether she will go back East. Guido offers her his house in the country.

Roslyn rents a car, and she and Isabelle follow Gay and Guido out to the ranch. Guido's house isn't finished. He informs them that his pregnant wife died there. When she was ready to have the baby, he had a flat tire and no spare. Guido tells Roslyn that his wife stood by him 100 percent. Roslyn replies that maybe that's what killed her. She feels a little complaining helps sometimes. They drink and dance. Gay reveals he would like Roslyn to stay on, and they continue to dance, while Guido fumes. They all go outside of the house. Guido tries to kiss her. Instead Roslyn does a strange dance by herself as they watch her, all of them sad and sullen.

Gay drives Roslyn home. He flatters her, saying that she is a beautiful woman, that she shines in his eyes, and that it's an honor to know her; but she is also the saddest girl he has ever met. She says she doesn't feel the same loving way about him, but he is not discouraged. He asks her to stay for a while and see what happens. When she asks Gay whether he has a home, he simply points to the country.

Roslyn and Gay start living together in Guido's house. He works on the unfinished house and tends the garden. They go riding and swimming. Gay discovers that a rabbit is eating the lettuce, which angers him. As he prepares to shoot it, Roslyn gets upset, maintaining that he doesn't respect her feelings.

Guido arrives in his plane with Isabelle, who tells Gay that he has finally met a real woman. Gay admits his deep feelings for Roslyn. He tells her that she has the gift of life, that when she smiles it's like the sun coming up. Guido tells Gay that he spotted some fifteen horses in the canyons and suggests that they do some mustanging. They figure they will need a third man and decide to look for him at the local rodeo.

As they are driving to the rodeo. they spot Perce Howland, a down-and-out rodeo rider, sitting by a phone booth. The phone rings, and it's his mother calling. His face is fine, just like new, he tells his mother in their tortured conversation. Gay and Guido recruit him for their mustanging expedition. It's better than wages, they say, and they put up the ten dollars he needs to enter the competitions at the rodeo. In a bar Gay offers to marry Roslyn. She thanks him, but tells him that he doesn't have to.

At the rodeo Roslyn is bothered by the cruelty to the animals. Perce enters horse and bull competitions, but is thrown from the horse and is badly shaken up. Roslyn is kind and gentle with Perce. He tells her that she has such trust in her eyes, as if she were just born, and he falls in love with her. He tells her the sad story of his life, of his father dying suddenly, his mother marrying shortly afterward, his being mistreated by his stepfather, who offered to pay him wages on land that rightfully was his. Then Gay's kids show up, and he wants to introduce them to Roslyn, but they disappear.

Guido takes them all home, but he is drunk and drives too fast, greatly upsetting Roslyn. He talks about being a bombardier during the war and laments killing people without knowing them. Guido then asks for Roslyn's comfort. Gay, Guido, and Perce are misfits who need someone, he observes, to look after them, and she might be the right person. Gay asks whether she wants a baby with him, but she turns away. She say that she recognized a strange look on his face that she didn't like, the look that he would leave her.

The next morning the four leave by truck to go mustanging. At night they camp out. The men still can't quite believe that Roslyn is such a caring person. She claims that she is just nervous. Guido replies that if it wasn't for nervous people like her they would all be crazy. She is horrified to learn that the horses that they're after will be sold and killed for dog food. Gay again tells her it is the alternative to wages, but she retorts that a kind man would not kill. When he argues that if he didn't do it, someone else would, she says, "But then it wouldn't be you." He tries to calm her by saying that he doesn't want to lose her, that he wants to be with her.

The next morning Guido flies off in his plane, finds the horses, and starts herding them toward Gay and Perce. There are not as many horses as they had thought—only a stallion, four mares, and a foal—but, Gay tells Perce, six are still better than wages. They lasso the horses with ropes tied to old tires to slow the animals down. They subdue the horses so the dealers can pick them up. Roslyn is terribly upset. Gay tells Guido and Perce that he is ready to give her the horses, but she doesn't hear him and offers to buy the horses from them. Gay then gets offended and refuses. Guido makes a desperate attempt to win Roslyn's affection by telling her that he is willing to stop the sale if Roslyn will go with him. She accuses him of being false. The men determine how much they will get from the dealer—a piddling six cents a pound, split three ways. Roslyn screams at them, saying they are three dead men, liars, who say that they love their country and yet behave outrageously. Guido, meanwhile, wants Gay to go into business with him and says that they'll get a good plane and go wherever there are mountains and plenty of horses. Perce approaches Roslyn, offering to let the horses loose. Roslyn cautions him that doing so will cause a fight, but he wants to do it anyhow.

Gay is desperate, and he fights with the stallion to subdue it. He succeeds and then lets the stallion go. Exhausted, he tells Roslyn that he doesn't want anyone to make up his mind for him. He'll just have to find another way to live. God bless you, girl, he says. The horses gallop back to the canyons. Roslyn and Gay drive home.

22 *Freud: The Secret Passion* (1962)

Director	John Huston
Producer	Wolfgang Reinhardt
Associate Producer	George Golitzin
Screenplay	Charles Kaufman and Wolfgang Reinhardt
Story	Charles Kaufman
Photography	Douglas Slocombe
Art Director	Stephen Grimes
Sound	Basil Fenton-Smith and Renato Cadueri
Music	Jerry Goldsmith
Electronic Music Sequences	Henk Badings
Music Supervision	Joseph Gershenson
Film Editor	Ralph Kemplen
Costume Designer	Doris Langley Moore
Makeup	Robert Schiffer and Raimund Stangl
Production Manager	C. O. Erickson
Medical Consultant	David Stafford-Clark, M.D., F.R.C.P., D.P.M.
Technical Adviser	Earl A. Loomis Jr., M.D.
Associate to Mr. Huston	Gladys Hill
Title Backgrounds and Foreword Paintings	James Leong
Assistant Directors	Ray Gosnell Jr. and Laci von Ronay
Cast*	Montgomery Clift (Sigmund Freud), Susannah York (Cecily Koertner), Larry Parks (Dr. Joseph Breuer), Susan Kohner (Martha Freud), Eileen Herlie (Frau Ida Koertner), Fernand Ledoux (Professor Charcot), David McCallum (Carl von Schlosser), Rosalie Crutchley (Frau Freud), David Kossoff (Jacob

*John Huston was the film's narrator.

Filmography

Freud), Joseph Furst (Jacob Koertner),
Alexander Mango (Babinsky), Leonard Sachs
(Brouhardier), Eric Portman (Dr. Theodore
Meynert)

Filmed	at locations in England; Universal-International
Running Time	139 minutes, black and white
Release Date	December 12, 1962

Other titles: *The Secret Passion; Freud, Passions secrètes; Freud, Passioni segrete*

SYNOPSIS

The film opens with the statement: "When the theories of Sigmund Freud were first presented half a century ago the shocked world called him a monster of depravity. But modern psychiatry is built upon those theories. And Freud is universally celebrated as the discoverer of a region almost as dark as hell itself—man's unconscious mind. This picture does not attempt to present the biographical facts of his life so much as to follow his tortuous descent into the underworld of man's unconscious mind and his wanderings through its mazes."

In Vienna, 1885, a group of doctors are making the rounds of a mental ward of a hospital and stop at a patient's bed. Doctor Freud says that the patient is hysterical. Contradicting Freud, the head doctor says that the patient is escaping her responsibilities in life. Freud sticks a pin in the patient, who shows no reaction, to prove his contention that the woman is in a state of hysterical withdrawal. The attending physician is infuriated and demands that the patient be removed from the hospital.

Freud's mother suggests that he leave the hospital. He obtains a traveling grant to go to Berlin to study with Doctor Charcot, who has been doing experiments with hysteria. Freud is impressed with Charcot and his techniques and the use of hypnosis. He sees demonstrations of patients being cured under hypnosis of disturbances that appear to be physical but are really mental. (Anticipating Freud's development of the theory of the Oedipus complex, one day on the train his father's watch falls and breaks.) With Charcot, hysteria is strictly a mental condition. He maintains that the patient remembers nothing and is in psychological trauma. With hypnosis, Charcot is able to treat the symptoms. He demonstrates the powers of suggestion and the power to create hysterical symptoms.

Freud and Martha Bernays get married. When Freud delivers a lecture on the unconscious, he is publicly ridiculed by Dr. Theodore Meynert. Dr. Joseph Breuer defends him. Breuer tells Freud about a young patient of his, Cecily Koertner, and how he has used hypnosis to get to the root of her mental condition, which developed after her father's death. Freud goes with Breuer to Cecily's apartment and sees how her symptoms are relieved after hypnosis. With more observation, Freud begins to develop his various theories. Breuer urges Freud to pursue the study of hysteria. The film's narrator explains that psychic memory protects the body from unpleasant things. Freud begins to think about how the human mind is able to repress intolerable memories. He is summoned to the home of Carl von Schlosser, a deeply disturbed man, who under hypnosis reveals his hatred for his father and love for his mother. Freud himself is shaken by what he is beginning to develop as the Oedipus complex when he himself has a dream in which his feelings for his mother emerge. Freud drops his research.

Then Meynert calls him to his deathbed and prods him to continue his research. He tells him to go after the demons in the heart of man's darkness and hunt them out. Freud returns to the von Schlosser house but is told that Carl died six months ago. Freud despairs because he ran away from the truth. He develops the theory that all neuroses can be linked to sexual traumas. Breuer is doubtful. Freud works with Cecily again. Under hypnosis Cecily reveals a dream in which doctors come, take her to the hospital, and ask her to identify her dead father. In her dream the hospital becomes a brothel; the doctors become policemen. On awakening she is cured of various symptoms and is able to see and walk, but she turns on Freud and screams at him to leave. Breuer is summoned once again to Cecily's house when she develops a new symptom of false pregnancy. Breuer drops her case.

When Freud's father dies, Freud collapses at the funeral. He sees this episode as an hysterical symptom and analyzes himself. He decides that he has been repressing a hatred for his father. It occurs to him that neuroses may start in childhood, before the emergence of sexual feelings, thus changing his theory of neurosis.

Cecily is ill again. This time Freud does not use hypnosis to treat her. Instead he uses free association to evoke memories. Her memory is one of her father preferring prostitutes to her. He lied to her, so she hated him and, by extension, all men.

Freud discusses with Breuer some of his new thinking. Freud believes experience is not repressed at the time, only later, and the memory arouses sexual desires. Society does not allow such thinking, so the mind projects these thoughts into physical symptoms. Breuer is impressed.

At another session with Cecily she reveals that her father sexually molested her when she was a child. While temporarily cured of her symptoms, Cecily goes to Red Tower Street and dresses as a prostitute. She tries to induce Freud to make love to her. Freud discovers that Cecily is revolted by what she related to him and that she lied to satisfy his theories. He admits that he is the guilty one, she calms down, and he takes her home.

Freud then tries to analyze the parent-child relationship from his own life. He remembers that as a little boy the family took a trip and in the hotel he was frightened. His mother gave him a piece of jewelry and promised to join him in bed, but when his father arrived he took his mother away. He then wished his father dead and thought of a plot of his father committing a crime against his little sister, who wasn't even born yet. Freud has difficulty accepting all of these developing thoughts, but his wife urges him on. He realizes that from error to error one discovers the truth; progress is like learning to walk, and the untruth is often the truth standing on its head. Suddenly he understands that Cecily's father did not desire her, but that she desired him. She loved her father and was jealous of her mother. And for him, as a man, the opposite was true: He loved his mother and was jealous of his father. Cecily is cured, and they determine that her love for Freud is really Cecily's transferring her pursuit of her father onto Freud.

Breuer is shocked by Freud's theory of infantile sexuality, and when Freud determines to lecture on the subject, Breuer warns that it will be the end of his career. The audience is outraged by his lecture on the Oedipus complex. Freud is left alone, abandoned by all his colleagues.

Freud goes to the cemetery and visits his father's grave, at peace with himself.

23 *The List of Adrian Messenger* (1963)

Director	John Huston
Producer	Edward Lewis
Screenplay	Anthony Veiller, based on a story by Philip MacDonald
Photography	Joe MacDonald, A.S.C.
European Photography	Ted Scaife
Art Directors	Alexander Golitzen, Stephen Grimes, and George Webb
Set Decorations	Oliver Emert
Sound	Waldon O. Watson and Frank H. Wilkinson
Music	Jerry Goldsmith
Music Supervision	Joseph Gershenson
Makeup	Bud Westmore
Film Editor	Terry O. Morse, A.C.E.
Hairstylist	Larry Germain
Unit Production Manager	Richard McWhorter
Assistant Director	Tom Shaw
Cast	George C. Scott (Anthony Gethryn), Dana Wynter (Lady Jocelyn Bruttenholm), Clive Brook (Marquis of Gleneyre), Kirk Douglas (George Brougham), Gladys Cooper (Mrs. Karoudjian), Herbert Marshall (Sir Wilfred Lucas), Jacques Roux (Raoul Le Borg), John Merivale (Adrian Messenger), Marcel Dalio (Anton Karoudjian), Bernard Archard (Inspector Pike), Walter Anthony Huston (Derek). *Bits:* Roland D. Long (Carstairs), Anita Sharp-Bolster (Mrs. Slattery), Alan Callou (Inspector Seymour), John Huston (Lord Ashton), Noel Purchell (Countryman), Richard Peel (Sergeant Flood), Bernard Fox (Lynch), Nelson Welch (White), Tim Durant (Hunt Secretary), Barbara Morrison (Nurse), Jennifer Raine (Student Nurse), Constance Cavendish (Maid), Eric Heath (Orderly), Anna Van Der Heide (Stewardess), Delphi Lawrence

(Airport Stewardess), Stacy Morgan (Whip Man), Joe Lynch (Cyclist), Mona Lilian (Proprietress). *Cameo Appearances:* Tony Curtis (Italian Organ Grinder), Kirk Douglas (Various Parts), Burt Lancaster (Woman), Robert Mitchum (Jim Slattery), Frank Sinatra (Gypsy Stableman)

Filmed — at locations filmed in Ireland, Joel Productions–Universal Pictures

Running Time — 98 minutes, black and white

Release Date — May 29, 1963

Other titles: *Le Dernier de la liste, I cinque volti dell'assassino*

SYNOPSIS

Before the credits, the camera shows a man walking in a London street, who stops in front of an apartment house. He sees the lights go out in an apartment on the top floor, and he quickly walks into the building, jams the elevator door, and goes down into the basement to jimmy the elevator's mechanism. At the same time the occupant of the apartment keeps ringing for the elevator. When the man releases the elevator, it goes up to the top floor. The man walks out into the street, stops, and turns. Inside the building the elevator descends at a fast pace as the occupant screams, and then the elevator crashes to the bottom. In the street the man pulls out a piece of paper and crosses off a name. The name "Adrian Messenger" is also on the list.

The credits come up, first with a montage of faces of characters who will appear in the film and then the names of those who will have cameo roles: Kirk Douglas, who will also be a main character; Tony Curtis; Burt Lancaster; Robert Mitchum; and Frank Sinatra. Question marks also swirl around the faces and names. Next the "main" credits, as such, appear.

In the following scene, a cleric (Douglas as George Brougham in disguise) cycles to the estate of the marquis of Gleneyre, a passionate fox hunter and shooter. At the end of one of the fox hunts everyone gathers in the living room, including Adrian Messenger. Someone remarks that the marquis and his grandson, Derek, who will inherit the estate since his father was killed in the Korean War, are so much alike. Another mentions that the marquis had a brother who went off to Canada and is presumed dead. Adrian Messenger is the cousin of Derek's mother, Lady Jocelyn Bruttenholm. Adrian pulls aside a family friend, Anthony Gethryn, who is a retired secret agent for the government, and asks him for a favor. Adrian tells Anthony that he cannot let him know too much, but he would like him to track down the people on a list that he has and see if they are still alive. Gethryn agrees to help and to get the information to Adrian after Adrian returns from a U.S. book tour.

At the airport Adrian checks in. Behind him is the "cleric" who appeared at the estate. The cleric's suitcase is over weight. Because Adrian's case is under weight, he offers to take the cleric's extra weight on his allowance. Rather than going on the plane, however, the cleric goes into the lavatory and peels off his disguise, thus revealing to the audience that it is Kirk Douglas. He dons another disguise, and leaves. His name is paged, but he does not respond. When the airplane is airborne, the camera focuses on the cleric's suitcase, which explodes and brings the plane down over the ocean. One of the few crash survivors, Raoul Le Borg, a Frenchman, grasps some wreckage with Adrian. Adrian, delirious and fatally wounded, mumbles some words to Le Borg and then dies.

The authorities are highly suspicious of the explosion and think that it is sabotage. Gethryn is called in to help in the investigation. He visits Le Borg, with whom, it turns out, he had worked in the Resistance during World War II. Lady Bruttenholm also visits Le Borg to thank him for helping her cousin. This visit marks the beginning of their budding romance. Le Borg is able to recall Adrian's last words, but not all of it makes much sense. Adrian did mumble something about a photograph of someone named George in a manuscript he had written that was in his home.

In Adrian's apartment George, disguised as a Mr. Pythian and claiming to be Adrian's neighbor, snoops around for the manuscript. He substitutes a page of text and takes the name and address of the woman who did the typing for Adrian. At that moment Lady Bruttenholm arrives to take care of Adrian's cat. Mr. Pythian tells her that he was doing just that. He then leaves.

Gethryn and Le Borg come in looking for George's picture and the manuscript, which is about Adrian's wartime experiences. Gethryn realizes that there is something wrong with the manuscript. They go to the typist's house and find her murdered.

In the government office one of the investigators for Gethryn suggests that the common thread for the names on the list is that they all served in Burma, but they were all in different regiments. The last name on the list is Jim Slattery. To follow him they assign an undercover agent, who assumes the disguise of an Italian organ grinder. Jim Slattery is confined to a wheelchair and is a dissolute drunk who lives with his mother and runs a small shop. Gethryn and Le Borg visit him and question him about his wartime activities. Jim claims that he was on the European front and that his brother had served in Burma, but he is dead. When Gethryn and Le Borg leave, he gets out of the wheelchair and reveals that he is the brother who was in Burma. He disguises himself as his brother so that he can collect his brother's disability insurance. Later that night after he leaves a pub, Brougham, in yet another disguise, follows Slattery and kills him.

Gethryn and Le Borg then visit the widow of one of the men on the list. She relates that during the war her husband was a prisoner of the Japanese in Burma. A group of British prisoners planned an escape and were betrayed by a Canadian, but she doesn't know his name.

Meanwhile, Derek, the young grandson of the marquis, is in the estate's barn and is approached by a gypsy with a beautiful white horse. The gypsy tells Derek that the horse is a gift from Adrian. He was told to train the horse, and now that Adrian is dead he presents the horse to him. He tells Derek that the horse knows two commands in the gypsy language: go and stop.

At the next fox hunt, George Brougham shows up as himself and without a disguise. He introduces himself to the marquis as his nephew from Canada. The family is happy to see him and invites him into their home. The marquis asks whether his brother is still alive. George indicates that he is not, and the marquis is able to state the exact date that his brother died. He tells his nephew and grandson that whenever a Brougham dies the foxes on the estate bark.

Gethryn and Le Borg put the pieces together and suspect that Brougham has murdered many people. From Adrian's last mumbled words, they now surmise that the reason for George's machinations is that he would be next in line to inherit the title and estate should the marquis, who is in his eighties, and his young grandson die. Gethryn and Le Borg set a trap for George. Gethryn shows him the changed page of the manuscript, and George fears that he will be found out. Under false pretenses he departs for London on some legal business. That night he sneaks back to the estate; captures a fox, which he puts in a sack; and drags the sack over a course to ensure that the hunt dogs will follow the scent the next day. Behind one of the walls that the horses will jump, he places a harrow on which Derek might fall and be impaled.

The next morning as the hunt begins a group of protesters against blood sports shows up and follows the fox hunters. In the course of the hunt someone removes the piece of farm machinery from behind the wall. When the fox hunters discover that they have been following the false scent of a fox, Gethryn reveals that early that morning he used one of the dogs to go over the course and that he found the farm machinery behind the wall. He also tells the hunters and protesters that a dog will now reveal who has a fox scent. The dog stops at one of the protesters, who is George in another of his disguises. George bolts, jumps on Derek's horse, and is ready to jump another wall, when Derek commands the horse to stop. The horse stops short, and George flies over the wall and is impaled on the harrow. As he lies there in agony and the crowd watches, he rips off his disguise to reveal his identity. As the marquis and his nephew walk away they hear the barking of the foxes.

The picture ends with the various actors revealing who they are: Tony Curtis as the organ grinder, Burt Lancaster as the woman protesting fox hunting, Robert Mitchum as Jim Slattery, Frank Sinatra as the gypsy who gave Derek the horse, and Kirk Douglas, as George, in the various disguises that he assumed throughout the film.

24 *The Night of the Iguana* (1964)

Director	John Huston
Producer	Ray Stark
Screenplay	Anthony Veiller and John Huston, based on the play by Tennessee Williams
Director of Cinematography	Gabriel Figueroa
Camera Operator	Manuel Gonzales
Music	Benjamin Frankel
Associate Director	Emilio Fernandez
Production Executive	Abe Steinberg
Associate Producer	Alexander Whitelaw
Production Manager	Clarence Eurist
Assistant Director	Tom Shaw

Second Assistant Director	Terry Morse Jr.
Associate to Mr. Huston	Gladys Hill
Script Supervisor	Angela Allen
Art Director	Stephen Grimes
Film Editor	Ralph Kemplen
Assistant Film Editor	Eunice Mountjoy
Costumes	Dorothy Jeakins
Sound	Basil Fenton-Smith
Continuity	Angela Allen
Hairstyles	Sydney Guilaroff and Agnes Flanagan
Makeup	Jack Obringer and Eric Allwright
Cast	Richard Burton (Rev. T. Lawrence Shannon), Ava Gardner (Maxine Faulk), Deborah Kerr (Hannah Jelkes), Sue Lyon (Charlotte Goodall), James Ward (Hank Prosner), Grayson Hall (Judith Fellowes), Cyril Delevanti (Nonno), Mary Boylan (Miss Peebles), Gladys Hill (Miss Dexter), Billie Matticks (Miss Throxton), Eloise Hardt (Teacher), Thelda Victor (Teacher), Betty Proctor (Teacher), Dorothy Vance (Teacher), Liz Rubey (Teacher), Bernice Starr (Teacher), Barbara Joyce (Teacher), Fidelmar Duran (Pepe), Roberto Leyva (Pedro), C. G. Kim (Chang)
Filmed	at locations in Mexico; Seven Arts Productions, distributed by MGM
Running Time	125 minutes, black and white
Release Date	August 6, 1964

Other titles: *La Notte dell'iguana, La Nuit de l'iguane*

SYNOPSIS

The Reverend T. Lawrence Shannon, the grandson of two bishops and the son of a clergyman, has what appears to be a nervous breakdown on the pulpit, driving his congregants out of the church and into the rain. He is removed from his parish and falls on hard times, drinking and getting into trouble with young girls.

Shannon is hired by a sleazy tour company in Texas and becomes its tour guide, accompanying a group of women teachers from a Christian college on their August vacation trip to Mexico. Among the tourists is Charlotte, who has been sent along by her parents to remove her from an embarrassing entanglement with a boy back home. She is chaperoned by the prim Miss Fellowes, who soon emerges as the Reverend Shannon's nemesis. Charlotte makes a play for Shannon, which infuriates Miss Fellowes, and she resolves to get Shannon fired. He becomes frantic, because he is at loose ends and, as despicable as his job is, it is the only one that he could get.

At a hotel one night Charlotte sneaks into his room, while he is downstairs in the lobby desperately trying to compose a letter to his bishop, pleading to be reinstated. When he enters his room, Charlotte confronts him, and he allows himself to be seduced against his better judgment. Miss Fellowes breaks into the room and vows to call her brother, the judge, in Texas the next day.

The next morning Shannon tries to get on the women's better side and waits for them in the lobby with souvenirs, which they refuse to accept. Miss Fellowes steps out of the telegraph office, having just sent a cable about Shannon to her brother. The group is scheduled to stop that day at a fancy, air-conditioned hotel, but in an attempt to prevent Miss Fellowes from receiving a reply about his background, Shannon takes over the bus-driving and drives past the fancy hotel. He takes them instead to the isolated seacoast hotel of his friends, Fred Faulk and his wife, Maxine.

On arriving Shannon removes the distributor cap from the motor, thus disabling it and preventing his assistant, Hank Prosner, from driving the women back to town. From Maxine, Shannon learns that Fred died a short time ago. Maxine is living with two muscular Mexican boys who constantly play the castanets or run after wild iguanas. At first she refuses to take the ladies in—the hotel is closed in August—but then she relents out of friendship and love for Shannon. She then makes every attempt to sidetrack Miss Fellowes from getting the information on Shannon from Texas.

When Maxine shaves Shannon as he lies in a hammock, she notices that his shoes are worn through and offers him a pair of Fred's. Shannon declines, saying that he doesn't want to walk in Fred's shoes, but Maxine replies that he could do worse. They hear Hannah Jelkes and her grandfather, Nonno, the world's oldest living poet, arrive up the hill. While very distinguished, they are actually penniless wanderers. Hannah does quick sketches of hotel guests, and the grandfather occasionally recites his poetry, last published when McKinley was assassinated (1901). Maxine agrees to let them stay one night.

While Maxine is in the kitchen preparing lunch, Hannah comes in and offers to help. She decapitates the fish with great determination. Maxine talks to her about Fred, who was twenty-eight years her senior. After a while he had no interest in sex. So she took up with the Mexican beach boys, but Fred did not seem to care. He just went fishing all the time.

Shannon, meanwhile, is still being pursued by Charlotte. Her determination greatly disturbs him, because at the same time he is also tormented by his demons, is in great mental and spiritual crisis, and is extremely fearful of losing his position with the travel company. Charlotte comes into his room as he is trying on his clerical collar. He wants to prove to everyone that he was not defrocked and to recapture his lost self-esteem. When he sees Charlotte he breaks a glass and then unknowingly walks on the shattered glass in his bare feet. Charlotte is shocked. Shannon tells her that she has the power to destroy him, and he can not accept her. She claims she loves him and wants to marry him. She says she will even walk on the broken glass, which she does, but he will still not have anything to do with her. He finally carries her out of the room, and she screams that she hates him now.

Hannah, noticing his bleeding feet, dresses the wounds. While they talk her grandfather falls down, and they take care of him. Hannah is clearly upset. They go outside. She starts to take a cigarette from her frock, thinks twice about it, and

puts it back. He asks her for a cigarette. When she gives him the pack, he promptly throws it away, telling her that they are the worst Mexican cigarettes, made
from the butts thrown away by other people. He offers her one of his own better
cigarettes and compliments her on her generosity and goodness. When she asks
how he can figure that from such a little thing, he reminds her that it is precisely
such little things that count. He points out that she was saving her last two cigarettes because she could not afford to buy more, and she readily gave them to him
when he asked. He confesses to her his problems with his parishioners and the
charges of fornication and conduct unbecoming. He adds that it is not man's inhumanity against man that bothers him, but man's inhumanity to God; and how
badly they treat one another, the environment, and all creatures. If he loses this
job, Shannon confides, he either goes back to the church or "takes the big swim to
China."

Maxine tries to play the generous hostess before lunch by serving drinks on
the house, but the ladies decline. Seeing Hannah and Shannon together, she
becomes extremely jealous. In her mind she feels she is no competition for Hannah.
Maxine gets into a childish fight with Shannon and then turns on Hannah, who
defends Shannon. Hannah points out that his sorry state is due only to unfortunate
circumstances; it is not reflective of the real man.

Then they discover that Charlotte has disappeared. They find her at a beach
bar, dancing with the beach boys. Hank, the tour bus driver, comes running to the
rescue, but the beach boys make a fool of him and beat him up. Charlotte now gives
her affection to Hank because he came to her aid, as inept as he was. Shannon,
meanwhile, takes a call from his employer and learns he is fired. In his moment of
despair and distraction, Charlotte grabs the distributor cap from him, and Hank
announces to the ladies that they will be off shortly. Maxine then explodes with a
volley of cruel insults aimed at all her unwelcome guests, singling out Miss
Fellowes, whom she denounces as a smug, sex-starved puritan. Shannon, however,
comes to Miss Fellowes's rescue and stops Maxine.

When Miss Fellowes leaves he states that she is a moral person. He tells
Maxine that if she found out about herself Miss Fellowes would be devastated.
Shannon then has another crisis of "the spooks." He tears off the cross around his
neck, thus breaking his one tie with the church, and decides to walk out into the
ocean. The beach boys dive after him, bring him back, and tie him up in a hammock. It will not be an easy night, for Shannon is hysterical, frantic, and close to a
breakdown. He becomes vicious and cruelly insults everyone, including Maxine and
Hannah.

Later, as Maxine makes love to the beach boys down at the beach, but then
realizes that it is meaningless, Hannah and Shannon talk about life and its crises.
She finally unties him because his spook has been exorcised. She discloses that she
herself was once spooked by her blue devil. She could not afford to lose, emphasizes that our every action is an attempt to give our demons the slip. They then free
a captive iguana. As Shannon puts it, they are playing God.

As Maxine returns she sees that Shannon has just cut loose one of God's creatures, so that it can at last be free. Hannah's grandfather announces that he has finished his poem. Nonno recites his poem as Hannah writes it down. He finishes,

saying that he'd like to pray. Then he dies. After a brief pause, Maxine picks up Hannah's notebook, reads Nonno's poem, and is moved by it.

The next morning Maxine, in disgust and desperation, is packing up, having decided to leave the hotel. Shannon is dressed up. When he sees that Hannah is leaving, he proposes that they travel together. Hannah declines, saying that it will not work out and ultimately will be an embarrassment to both of them. Maxine makes a proposition to them both: Admitting defeat and willing to give up Shannon to Hannah, Maxine offers to let them run the hotel for her. Hannah refuses. She tries to give Shannon back his cross, but he insists that she keep it and sell it for passage back to the States. Maxine is furious, but he surprises her and asks whether he can stay. He says that he can get down to the beach, but he doesn't know whether he can get back up the hill. Relieved, she tells him that she'll always help him back up.

25 *The Bible ... in the Beginning* (1966)

Director	John Huston
Producer	Dino De Laurentiis
Associate Producer	Luigi Luraschi
Screenplay	Christopher Fry
Assisted by	Jonathan Griffin, Ivo Perilli, and Vittorio Bonicelli
Consultants	W. M. Merchant and Salvatore Garofalo
Music	Toshiro Mayuzumi
Conductor	Franco Ferrara
Art Director	Mario Chiari
Director of Photography	Giuseppe Rotunno
Costumes	Maria De Matteis
Second Unit Director, "The Creation"	Ernst Haas
Production Supervisor	Bruno Todini
Film Editor	Ralph Kemplen
Sound Record Supervisor	Fred Hynes
Sound Recorders	Basil Fenton-Smith and Murray Spivak
Sound Editor	Leslie Hodgson
Music Editor	Gilbert Marchant
Choreography	Katherine Dunham
Unit Managers	Romano Dandi and Giorgio Morra
Assistant Directors	Vana Caruso and Ottavio Oppo
Set Dressers	Enzo Eusepi and Bruno Avesani
Special Effects	Augie Lohman
Makeup	Alberto De Rossi
Hairdresser	Elda Magnanti
Narration	John Huston
Casting Director	Guidarino Guidi
Associate to John Huston	Gladys Hill
Assistant to Producer	Ralph Serpe
Associate Art Director	Stephen Grimes

Continuity	Yvonnie Axworthy
Still Photographers	Paul Ronald and Louis Oldman
Zoological Consultant	Angelo Lombardi
Cast	Michael Parks (Adam), Ulla Bergryd (Eve), Richard Harris (Cain), John Huston (Noah), Stephen Boyd (Nimrod), George Scott (Abraham), Ava Gardner (Sarah), Peter O'Toole (The Three Angels), Zoe Sallis (Hagar), Gabriele Ferzetti (Lot), Eleonora Rossi Drago (Lot's Wife). *Costarring:* Franco Nero, Robert Rietty, Grazia Maria Spina, Claudie Lange, Adriana Ambesi, Alberto Lucantoni, Luciano Conversi, Pupella Maggio, Peter Heinze, Angelo Boschariol, Anna Maria Orso, Eric Leutzinger, Gabriella Pallotta, Rosanna De Rocco
Filmed	at locations in Rome, Sicily, Sardinia, and northern Egypt; Dino De Laurentiis Cinematografica, distributed by Twentieth Century-Fox, Seven Arts Pictures
Running Time	174 minutes, Technicolor
Release Date	September 28, 1966; filming completed around February 1966

Other titles: *The Bible, La Bible . . . au commencement des temps, La Bibbia—in principio*

SYNOPSIS

The film portrays the first twenty-two chapters of Genesis, depicting the stories of the Creation; Adam and Eve; the expulsion from Eden; Cain and Abel; Noah and the Flood; Nimrod and the Tower of Babel; Abraham, his wife Sarah, her hand-maiden Hagar, and the birth of Ishmael; the destruction of Sodom and Gomorrah; and Abraham and Isaac.

John Huston narrates the Creation: "In the beginning God created the heavens and the earth. . . ." The creation of the earth, waters, and creatures are depicted. Huston continues: "And then God said, 'Let us make man in our image, after our likeness.'" Adam emerges from the earth, and he opens his eyes to consider the mystery and strangeness of everything about him. Since "it is not good that man should be alone," Eve is created. They wander through the Garden of Eden. They can eat of any tree except that of the Tree of Knowledge of Good and Evil. Eve is tempted by the Serpent. She tastes the forbidden fruit and her innocence is lost. She persuades Adam to also eat of the fruit. Judgment follows swiftly: The serpent is cursed, Eve will conceive in sorrow, and Adam will have to work to feed himself.

Banished from Eden, Eve gives birth to Cain and Abel. Cain is a tiller of the ground while Abel keeps the flocks. Both sacrifice to the Lord, but only Abel's offerings are accepted. Cain, in anger born of jealousy and humiliation, murders his brother and runs away guiltily. When the Lord asks him where his brother is, he answers, "Am I my brother's keeper?" Cain is condemned to roam the earth as a fugitive. The narrator says that from the generation of Cain came men who did evil and turned from God.

Another son, Seth, is born. And several generations later, from this seed, Noah is born. The Lord, angry at men who are filled with idolatry and violence, decides to destroy the world. But he will save Noah and his family. "For thee have I seen righteous before me in this generation," the Lord says, and He instructs Noah to build an ark and bring aboard two of every animal. Noah carries out these instructions in spite of the mockery of his neighbors and the doubts of his family. When the earth is deluged for forty days and nights, Noah and those in the ark are the only ones saved.

After the flood the human race replenishes itself. From Noah's son Ham comes Nimrod, who becomes a king. He decides to build a tower that will soar like his pride and will reach heaven. The Lord is angry with Nimrod. At that time all people speak one language, but the Lord makes the people building the tower start to speak in different languages so they cannot understand one another. Thus, the Tower of Babel is built, but left unfinished. The people with different languages spread throughout the world.

After ten generations Abraham is born. In time the Lord sends him to a new land and tells him that he will be given all the land for his seed forever. His wife, Sarah, is barren, but her handmaiden bears Abraham a son, Ishmael. Sarah is jealous and humiliated. The Lord promises that she will also have a son.

Messengers of the Lord come to pass judgment on the evil cities of Sodom and Gomorrah. Lot, Abraham's nephew, is told that his family will be spared as long as they do not look back on the evil city. Lot's wife does look back, however, and is turned into a pillar of salt.

Finally Sarah, very old, does conceive a son, Isaac. The Lord tells Abraham to take Isaac into the mountains and prepare a sacrifice. When they get there they don't see a ram, and Abraham learns that it is Isaac who is to be sacrificed. He is in anguish, but follows the orders of the Lord. As he is ready to sacrifice Isaac the Lord stops him. He is pleased that Abraham fears Him. "I have tried thee like metal in a furnace," He tells Abraham. "Now I shall multiply thee . . . innumerable."

26 *Casino Royale* (1967)

Directors	John Huston (first half hour), Ken Hughes, Val Guest, Robert Parrish, and Joseph McGrath
Producers	Charles K. Feldman and Jerry Bresler
Associate Producer	John Dark
Additional Sequences	Val Guest
Second Unit Director	Richard Talmadge and Anthony Squire
Screenplay and Adaptation	Wolf Mankowitz and John Law
Writer	Michael Sayers
Additional Writers (uncredited)	Billy Wilder, Ben Hecht, John Huston, Val Guest, Joseph Heller, and Terry Southern
Photography	Jack Hildyard

Additional Photography	John Wilcox and Nicolas Roeg
Art Directors	John Howell, Ivor Beddoes, and Lionel Couch
Set Dresser	Terence Morgan
Production Designer	Michael Stringer
Film Editor	Bill Lenny
Cast in Huston Segment	David Niven (Sir James Bond), Deborah Kerr (Agent Mimi, alias Lady Fiona), William Holden (Ransome), Charles Boyer (Le Grand), Kurt Kaznar (Smernov), John Huston (McTarry/M)
Filmed	at locations in England, Ireland, and France; Famous Artists Productions, distributed by Columbia Pictures
Running Time	130 minutes, Technicolor
Release Date	April 28, 1967

SYNOPSIS, FIRST HALF HOUR

Four cars converge at a crossroads in an isolated area of England. Three men exit their vehicles, enter the fourth, and are chauffeured down a road. These men—McTarry (M), Ransome, Le Grand, and Smernov—represent the secret services of the United Kingdom, the United States, France, and the Soviet Union. M expounds on the qualities of good spies, saying that a good spy is a pure spy. He waxes nostalgic about Sir James Bond, the spy par excellence, who has retired and now lives in splendid isolation in the country, playing Debussy every dusk until it is too dark to read the music, standing on his head, eating royal jelly, and letting down his bowels every day and washing them by hand. They arrive at Bond's mansion, and the old retainer announces the guests. They compliment Bond on how well he looks. He replies that spying was an honorable profession and an alternative to war. He cannot stand these modern-day spies and their crazed sex drives. He criticizes all the joke-shop tricks that are used in Aston Martins, fountain pens, and so on. He is also bothered by all the phony 007s. M agrees that things are very bad. All of the secret services have lost a great deal of men, M adds, and they desperately need his help. Even an inducement from the Queen will not change Bond's mind, however; he will not go back into the service. Having heard that, M signals an army artillery unit in the distance, which proceeds to destroy Bond's house and, at the same, time kills M.

At the headquarters of SMERSH officials announce that James Bond is back in service. He is on his way to pay condolences to Mrs. McTarry, who, it turns out, is really the Agent Mimi of SMERSH. The reason they recruited her was that she was the only agent with a creditable Scottish accent.

Bond arrives at the McTarry house and finds it full of beautiful women (also spies?). Mimi announces that in true McTarry fashion there will be indulgence that night—eating, dancing, and in the morning grouse shooting. When Bond observes that grouse are not in season, Mimi responds that when a McTarry dies the grouse go into season.

Bond goes into his room, and two of M's "daughters" help him off with his clothes. They inform him that M had eleven daughters, but there are only three years between all of them. Some of us are adopted, they explain. He sees that all the rooms are occupied by beautiful girls. They lead him to the bath. A beautiful girl is in the bathtub, testing the temperature. She says she always did this for Dad, who called her his "little thermometer." Bond gets in and she scrubs his back. When he asks what form she is in, she tells him he can check for himself. While he is having his bath, two French girls sew two buttons—homing devices—onto his shooting jacket.

Bond attends the wild McTarry funeral rites. Everyone else drinks themselves into a stupor and collapses, but Bond takes a decanter and goes to his bedroom. As he lounges in bed, Agent Mimi comes in, closes the door, and offers herself to him, asking him to comfort her. She claims that it is her due as a widow, according to McTarry tradition. He refuses. She gets angry and tells him he must pay. Some strong men enter the bedroom and challenge him to the *wassal,* a heavy concrete ball. The men and girls all go downstairs. At Agent Mimi's command, the men all lift up the wassal, but don't have the strength to toss it to Bond. Thus, Bond is the only survivor. Mimi is smitten and falls in love with Bond. She thinks he's more than a man—he's a god. Having betrayed the SMERSH plan to undo Bond, she is locked up in her room.

The next morning Bond goes grouse shooting. Some of the SMERSH girls pull up in a van that is fitted with electronic missiles that are shaped like grouse. While Bond shoots away at grouse, Mimi escapes from her room down a drainpipe. The SMERSH girls start firing the "grouse" toward Bond. Bond shoots at them, and they explode. Mimi comes to him and pulls off his homing-device buttons. He takes off his suspenders, and they use them as a slingshot to shoot at the missiles. She confesses that her plan was to corrupt him, and failing that, to kill him. Then it appears that Mimi may have been mortally wounded. She tells him to think of her as the second woman in his life and implores him to kiss her good-bye. She says that she is not dying, but going to another life in a convent over the hill. They wave good-bye. (End of half hour.)

In the rest of the film, to outsmart SMERSH Bond has all agents designated as "Bond" and "007." He recruits some master spies, and they all engage in a number of Bond-like adventures, until everyone is blown up except Bond.

27 *Reflections in a Golden Eye* (1967)

Director	John Huston
Producer	Ray Stark
Screenplay	Chapman Mortimer and Gladys Hill, based on the novel by Carson McCullers
Director of Photography	Aldo Tonti
Production Designer	Stephen Grimes
Art Director	Bruno Avesani
Film Editor	Russell Lloyd
Set Direction	William Kiernan
Associate Producer	C. O. (Doc) Erickson
Production Manager	Mario Del Papa

Music	Toshiro Mayuzumi
Music Director	Marcus Dods
Costumes	Dorothy Jeakins
Sound	Basil Fenton-Smith and John Cox
Sound Editor	Leslie Hodgson
Hairstyles for Elizabeth Taylor	Alexandre of Paris
Assistant Director	Vana Caruso
Cast	Elizabeth Taylor (Leonora Penderton), Marlon Brando (Maj. Weldon Penderton), Brian Keith (Lt. Col. Morris Langdon), Julie Harris (Alison Langdon), Zorro David (Anacleto), Gordon Mitchell (Stables Sergeant), Irvin Dugan (Captain Weincheck), Fay Sparks (Susie), Robert Forster (Private Williams)
Filmed	at locations in Rome; Warner Brothers–Seven Arts International
Running Time	109 minutes, Technicolor[*]
Release Date	October 11, 1967

Other titles: *Riflessi in un occhio d'oro, Reflets dans un oeil d'or*

SYNOPSIS

The following statement appears on the screen: "There is a fort in the South where a few years ago a murder was committed."

One October morning Major Weldon Penderton summons Private Williams, a horse lover, to clean up his lawn. At the same time his wife, Leonora Penderton, has gone horseback riding with Lieutenant Colonel Morris Langdon, her lover. When she returns she engages in idle conversation with Williams, inviting him to have a drink.

Penderton teaches a class on warfare. When he comes home he accuses his wife of being a whore. She taunts him and gets undressed in front of him, infuriating him. She walks upstairs. From outside the house Williams watches her walk up the stairs. Penderton goes to his study and takes out a secret box from a drawer. It contains a picture of Adonis and a silver spoon that he stole from a Jewish officer, Captain Weincheck. It appears from his behavior that Penderton has no sexual relationship with his wife.

---

[*]In initial engagements, prints were specially treated so that the color appeared washed-out and sepia-toned. Later engagements featured full Technicolor prints. The Academy of Motion Picture Arts and Sciences Film Archives has an example of the original colored print. See also chapter 23, "Huston-Related Films on Film, Video, and Laser Disc." *Film Dope* indicates that Huston's voice is heard at the beginning of the film. In at least the U.S. video release, the film opens with a statement attributed to Carson McCullers that appears on the screen without a voice-over. The film ends the same way, with the statement appearing on the screen and no voice-over.

That evening the Pendertons entertain the Langdons. Alison Langdon is mentally and physically ill. We later learn that among other things she has cut off her nipples. Alison's chief consolation is her effete Filipino houseboy, Anacleto.

The next morning Leonora, Penderton, and Langdon go horseback riding. While in the woods they see Williams riding a horse, and he is stark naked. Penderton becomes furious at the sight.

Williams, obsessed with Leonora, stalks the Penderton house at night. That evening Penderton undresses his wife, who has become quite drunk, puts her to bed, and then goes off to his own room. Williams sneaks into the house and into Leonora's room. He stays most of the night, watching her as she sleeps. Later that night Alison Langdon goes to her window, sees Williams leaving the Penderton house, and mistakes him for her husband. She tells Anacleto that she is going to divorce Langdon.

The next day Penderton takes his wife's horse out. He rides the horse in an uncontrolled fashion. He rides past the private, who is once again nude. Penderton falls off the horse, beats it, and breaks down. Williams comes and leads the horse away. When Leonora finds out what her husband has done to her horse she whips him across the face with a riding crop.

In the middle of the night Alison cannot sleep and once again thinks that she sees someone leaving the Penderton house. That same night the Pendertons and Langdon go to a boxing match. After the fight Penderton makes some excuse and follows Williams. The private discards a candy wrapper, and Penderton takes it and adds it to his secret box. Later that night Alison awakes with a start, and from her window she sees somebody sneaking into the Penderton house. She puts on a coat and rushes after the dark figure. Bursting into Penderton's study, she tells him that her husband has gone up to Leonora's bedroom. She rushes upstairs and sees the private instead. Unwilling to provoke a direct confrontation, Penderton eases Alison back to her own house, where they are greeted at the door by her husband and Anacleto. Alison confronts her husband with the news that his mistress is deceiving him with an enlisted man. With Anacleto's assistance she begins packing up her belongings, intent on getting a separation and divorce. Her husband thinks she needs treatment and arranges for her to be committed to a sanitarium. Shortly after he learns that she has died of a heart attack. He grieves for his wife.

During a class, Penderton cannot go through with one of his lectures. He meanders and finally dismisses the class. At a card game later, Penderton asks whether it is better, because it is morally honorable, for the square peg to keep scraping around the round hole rather than to discover the unorthodox square made for it. Langdon says yes, but facing himself at last, Penderton disagrees.

Penderton becomes obsessed with Williams, and he stalks the private. It starts to rain. Williams gets into a fight in the barracks and then leaves the quarters. Penderton spots the private lurking around his house. He waits for him. The private enters the house and goes upstairs. The colonel enters his wife's room and shoots the private dead.

The story ends as it began: "There is a fort in the South where a few years ago a murder was committed."

28 *Sinful Davey* (1969)

Director	John Huston
Producer	William N. Graf
Executive Producer	Walter Mirisch
Personal Assistant to Director	Gladys Hill
Screenplay	James R. Webb, based on *The Life of David Haggart* by David Haggart
Associate Producer	William Kirby
Directors of Photography	Freddie Young and Edward Scaife
Music	Ken Thorne
Production Designer	Stephen Grimes
Costume Designer	Margaret Furse
Art Director	Carmen Dillon
Film Editor	Russell Lloyd
Sound	Basil Fenton-Smith
Sound Editor	Les Hodgson
Assistant Directors	Tom Pevsner and John O'Connor
Casting	Robert Lennard
Special Effects	Richard Parker
Camera Operators	Ken Withers and Ernest Day
Set Dresser	Josie MacAvin
Continuity	Constance Willis
Choreography	Alice Dalgarno
Construction Engineer	Gus Walker
Makeup	Neville Smallwood
Hairdresser	Joan Smallwood
Master of the Horse	Frank Hayden
Wardrobe Supervisor	Elsa Fennell
Cast	John Hurt (Davey Haggart), Pamela Franklin (Annie), Nigel Davenport (Chief Constable Richardson), Ronald Fraser (MacNab), Robert Morley (Duke of Argyll), Fidelma Murphy (Jean Carlisle), Maxine Audley (Duchess of Argyll), Fionnuala Flanagan (Penelope), Donal McCann (Sir James Graham), Allan Cuthbertson (Captain Douglas), Eddie Byrne (Yorkshire Bill), Niall MacGinnis (Boots Simpson), Noel Purcell (Jock), Judith Furse (Mary), Francis de Wolff (Andrew), Paul Farrell (The Baliff of Stirling), Geoffrey Golden (Warden McEwan), Leon Collins (Doctor Gersham), Mickser Reid (Billy the Goat), Derek Young (Bobby Rae), John Franklin (George Bagrie), Eileen Murphy (Mary Kidd)

Filmed	at locations in Ireland; Mirisch-Webb Productions, distributed by United Artists
Running Time	95 minutes, Eastman color
Release Date	May 7, 1969

Other titles: *The Sinful Adventures of Davey Haggart* (working title), *Davey des grands chemins, La Forca puo attendere*

SYNOPSIS

Following in the footsteps of his notorious highwayman father, who was hanged at the gallows, Davey Haggart deserts the army. He joins forces with MacNab, a pickpocket. Davey's goal is to become the greatest criminal in Scotland. On their way to their exploits they meet Davey's childhood friend, Annie, who was raised in the orphanage with him. She wants Davey to go back to the army, but he refuses. He is determined to follow his dream.

During some of Davey's and MacNab's exploits they are caught by a Doctor Gresham, who agrees not to turn them in if they will steal a body from the grave for him so that he can continue his medical research. They come up with the body of Tom Pepper, a criminal who was hanged. In the process of stealing the body, however, Davey and MacNab are caught and end up in jail. There Davey goes under the name Zacharia Pennyfeather, is beaten up by a dwarf, and breaks into the women's quarters, where an orgy ensues. When Annie bails him out, he feels that he will now be beholden to her and runs away.

Davey, on his own, robs a stage. The chief constable realizes that Davey is out to follow in his father's footsteps. He vows to bring him to the same gallows as his father.

After some additional adventures with rogues and scoundrels, Davey comes to the rescue of Sir James Graham, who has been set upon by a bunch of thugs. Although Davey proceeds to pick the man's pocket, they become good friends. Davey learns that Sir James is also the nephew of the Duke of Argyll. At the Argyll Grand Ball Davey ingratiates himself to the duke, makes love to his niece, and, along with some associates, plans a big robbery. Annie, posing as a maid, approaches Davey and pleads with him not to get involved with this caper; but he rebuffs her.

As Davey robs the guests of their jewels during the ball, he drops the loot into the ballroom fireplace. His cohorts, ensconced on the roof, use a fishing reel and nab the jewels. They then pass the jewelry down to the ground. When they go to retrieve it, much to their dismay they discover that the loot has disappeared. Annie has taken the jewelry and returned it. Then the constable spots Davey, and the chase is on. Davey rides into a fox hunt and is then knocked out by a golf ball.

At his trial Annie pleads with the judge to send Davey to Australia. Although the duke stands by him, Davey is condemned to hang. He writes his memoirs awaiting his death.

Annie goes to the duke and asks him to supply a proper coffin for Davey. The duke plays the bagpipes for Davey in the jail and then knocks out the hangman. Davey is led to the gallows. He realizes that the hangman is his friend and his other friends are waiting for him below the gallows to stop his fall. They put him into the coffin and drive away in a hearse. At the graveyard they celebrate. Davey and Annie go off into the fields.

29 *A Walk with Love and Death* (1969)

Director	John Huston
Producer	Carter De Haven
Screenplay and Associate Producer	Dale Wasserman
Adaptation	Hans Koningsberger, based on his novel
English Lyrics and Associate to John Huston	Gladys Hill
Music	Georges Delerue
Director of Photography	Ted Scaife, B.S.C.
Production Designer	Stephen Grimes
Art Director	Wolfgang Witzeman
Set Decorator	Josie MacAvin
Editor	Russell Lloyd
Production Manager	Laci von Ronay
Assistant Directors	Richard Overstreet and Wolfgang Glattes
Sound	Basil Fenton-Smith
Sound Editor	Leslie Hodgson
Assistant Editor	Eunice Mountjoy-Beharrel
Costumes	Leonor Fini
Costumes Executed	Rotislav Doboujinsky
Wardrobe Supervisor	Annalisa Rasalli-Rocca
Makeup	Neville Smallwood
Hairdresser	Margarete Pitter
Camera Operator	Kenneth Withers
Casting Director	Robert Lennard
Script Supervisor	Lucie Lichtig
Unit Manager	Wolfgang Odelgn
Cast	Anjelica Huston (Claudia), Assaf Dayan (Heron of Foix), Anthony Corlan (Robert), John Hallam (Sir Meles), Robert Lang (Pilgrim Leader), Guy Deghy (Priest), Michael Gough (Mad Monk), George Murcell (Captain), Eileen Murphy (Gypsy Girl), Anthony Nicholls (Father Superior), Joseph O'Connor (Saint Jean), John Huston (Robert the Elder), John Franklin (Whoremaster), Francis Heim (Knight Lieutenant), Melvin Hayes (First Entertainer), Barry Keegan (Peasant Leader), Nicholas Smith (Pilgrim), Antoinette Reuss (Charcoal Woman), Eugen Ledebur (Goldsmith), Otto Dworak (Inn Keeper), Max Sulz (Peasant), John Veenebos

	(Monk), Dieter Tressler (Major Domo), Paul Hoer (Peasant Boy), Myra Malik (Peasant Girl), Michael Baronne (Soldier), Yvan Strogoff (Soldier), Gilles Segal, Med Hondo, and Luis Masson (Entertainers)
Filmed	at locations in Austria and Italy; Twentieth Century-Fox
Running Time	90 minutes, DeLuxe color
Release Date	October 5, 1969

Other titles: *Di Pari passo con l'amore e la morte, Promenade avec l'amour et la mort*

SYNOPSIS

In fourteenth-century France, during the Hundred Years War, Heron leaves his university and becomes a wanderer. During his travels through the country he sees bodies in the fields. He buys some wine from a peasant. As he approaches a house, the soldiers inside want to kill him. He buys his own safety with money, but watches as the soldiers kill an old man.

As he wanders on he hears a girl singing and comes upon her. He asks for shelter, but she replies that only love gives shelter, and since it doesn't last, he should take it where he can. He goes on to a castle and tells the people about Paris, where wolves dig up graves and dead bodies are everywhere. Heron feels that there is peace at the castle. He eats and sleeps. He sees Claudia for the first time. When he leaves the castle Claudia joins him. She identifies herself as the lady of the house. He tells her that he is going to the sea and gives her his poetry. She agrees to become his patroness, giving him a blue scarf as a token before he departs.

A band of pilgrims returning from Jerusalem invite Heron to travel on their boat. They are starting a new sect, they explain, and he must forswear female companionship. He refuses because of his love for Claudia. He then hears that peasants have destroyed the castle.

In a nearby church Heron finds Claudia and learns that her father has been killed. She steals some candlesticks so that they can buy food. They decide to go to her uncle's castle, and they run into her cousin, Robert the Younger. Her uncle, Robert the Elder, has joined the peasants, and he tells them to eat and gorge themselves, throw up, and then eat again, for there may not be another meal. God has turned his face away, he laments. Once everything was in its place; now the nobility are wolves who prey upon peasants. Who can blame them for rebelling?

Upset, Claudia wants Heron to kill her uncle to avenge her father's death. She flees to a nearby ruin. Heron follows her, and they travel on. They are then captured by peasants. When the knights attack the peasants and free Claudia and Heron, the two join the knights' force. The whole countryside is ablaze.

They decide to go back to Claudia's uncle's castle. There, for a brief moment, they live an idyllic life as lovers. They profess their love for one another and their desire to go to the sea or die. Claudia's cousin returns and doesn't know whether his father is still alive. The knights approach the castle with reports that Robert the Elder is dead. Infuriated, her cousin leaps upon the knights, and he is dispatched.

The young lovers escape through a secret tunnel. They go to a monastery, where they are expected to follow the mortification and purification ceremonies and be separated. The priest refuses to marry them. They decide to marry themselves without the priest. Then they go to bed. They hear the sound of peasants marching toward the monastery. They know death is near, but they are not afraid.

30 *The Kremlin Letter* (1970)

Director	John Huston
Producers	Carter De Haven and Sam Weisenthal
Screenplay	John Huston and Gladys Hill, based on the novel by Noel Behn
Music	Robert Drasnin
Director of Photography	Ted Scaife
Production Designer	Ted Haworth
Editor	Russell Lloyd
Production Manager	David Anderson
Art Director	Elven Webb
Set Director	Dario Simoni
Casting Director	Bob Lennard
Script Supervisor	Lucie Lichtig
Sound Mixer	Basil Fenton-Smith
Sound Editor	Les Hodgson
Assistant Directors	Gus Agosti and Carlo Cotti
Costume Designer	John Furniss
Makeup Supervisor	George Frost
Cast	Bibi Andersson (Erika), Richard Boone (Ward), Nigel Green (Janis), Dean Jagger (Highwayman), Lila Kedrova (Sophie), Michael MacLiammoir (Sweet Alice), Patrick O'Neal (Charles Rone), Barbara Parkins (B.A.), Ronald Radd (Potkin), George Sanders (Warlock), Raf Vallone (Puppet Maker), Max von Sydow (Kosnov), Orson Welles (Bresnavitch), Sandor Eles (Grodin), Niall MacGinnis (Erector Set), Anthony Chinn (Kitai), Guy Deghy (Professor), John Huston (Admiral), Fulvia Ketoff (Sonia), Vonetta McGee (The Negress), Marc Lawrence (The Priest), Cyril Shaps (Police Doctor), Christopher Sandford (Rudolph), Hana-Maria Pravda (Mrs. Kazar), George Pravda (Kazar), Ludmilla Dudarova (Mrs. Potkin), Dimitri Tamarov (Ilya), Pehr-Olof Siren

	(Receptionist), Daniel Smid (Waiter), Victor Beaumont (The Dentist), Steve Zacharias (Dittomachine), Laura Forin (Elena), Saara Rannin (Mikail's Mother), Sacha Carafa (Mrs. Grodin)
Filmed	at locations in Rome, Mexico, New York, and Finland; Twentieth Century-Fox
Running Time	116 minutes, DeLuxe color
Release Date	February 1, 1970

Other titles: *La Lettre du Kremlin, Lettera al Kremlino*

SYNOPSIS

On a speeding train, Charles Rone becomes involved in a plan to go to Russia in order to retrieve the "Kremlin Letter," a secret plan between U.S. intelligence and the Soviets to attack Communist China. Rone learns previous attempts have been thwarted by Colonel Kosnov, head of Russian intelligence. Other agents are also recruited: Janis, known as the "Whore," who has connections with the underworld; Warlock, a transvestite; and B.A., a master safecracker. The group's leader is Ward.

The agents enter Russia, and in Moscow they start making contact with the underworld. They learn that a big government official, Bresnavitch, is plotting to overthrow Kosnov. In order to have a base in Moscow, Ward blackmails Potkin, Kosnov's agent in New York, into lending them his apartment.

In a raid Kosnov traps Warlock and Janis. Then B.A. is also captured.

Part of Rone's job is to seduce Kosnov's wife, Erika. She falls in love with him and divulges all she knows about Kosnov.

Later, Rone tells Bresnavitch that he knows about his sordid past. Bresnavitch agrees to let Rone and his colleagues leave Russia; however, he tells him that only Ward is alive.

Meanwhile, Ward brutally murders Erika. Thinking that Rone killed Erika, Kosnov prepares to kill him, but Ward stops him. Ward then confronts Kosnov about all the agents he has destroyed. He reveals that the Kremlin Letter has always been in Peking and that Ward set up the whole scheme to wreak revenge against Kosnov. He then kills Kosnov. Ward will save B.A., who is in love with Rone, but only if Rone agrees to say that Ward is dead and if he goes to New York and kills Potkin's wife and daughters. Otherwise, Ward tells Rone, he will kill B.A.

31 *Fat City* (1972)

Director	John Huston
Producer	Ray Stark
Screenplay	Leonard Gardner, based on his novel
Director of Photography	Conrad Hall
Production Designer	Richard Sylbert
Associate Producer	David Dworski
Casting	Fred Roos and Jennifer Shull

Supervising Film Editor	Margaret Booth
Unit Production Manager and Assistant Director	Russ Saunders
Assistant to John Huston	Gladys Hill
Script Supervisor	Marshall Schlom
Wardrobe Designer	Dorothy Jeakins
Properties	Richard M. Rubin
Set Decorator	Morris Hoffman
Unit Publicist	Denny Shanahan
Music Editor	Ken Hall
Music Supervision	Marvin Hamlisch
Makeup	Jack Young
Hairstyles	Virginia Jones
Titles	Wayne Fitzgerald
Sound	Tom Overton and Arthur Piantadosi
Special Effects	Paul Stewart
Cast	Stacy Keach (Tully), Jeff Bridges (Ernie), Susan Tyrrell (Oma), Candy Clark (Faye), Nicholas Colasanto (Ruben), Art Aragon (Babe), Curtis Cokes (Earl), Sixto Rodriguez (Lucero), Billy Walker (Wes), Wayne Mahan (Buford), Ruben Navarro (Fuentes)
Filmed	at locations in Bakersfield, California; Columbia Pictures and Rastar Productions
Running Time	100 minutes, Eastman color
Release Date	July 26, 1972

Other titles: *Citta amara, La Dernière chance*

SYNOPSIS

The film opens, revealing the run-down parts of Stockton, California. In a seedy hotel in the middle of the day, Tully, a worn-out boxer, is still in bed. He takes out his last cigarette, but can't find a match. After looking out the window, trying to decide what to do, he dresses, walks down the dreary corridor, and leaves the hotel. He bobs to some inner tune, then tosses the unlit cigarette, goes back into his room for his bag, and heads out for the local gym. The only other person there, Ernie, an aspiring boxer, is working out. Tully, too, starts to work out. Then Tully asks Ernie whether he wants to spar. When Ernie asks him whether he is a pro, Tully admits he used to be and offers to teach him a few things. Tully compliments Ernie, telling him that he looks pretty good. They box until Tully pulls a muscle. He tells Ernie that he's been out of the ring for a year and a half. Ernie rejoins that he's never been in the ring. Saying Ernie's got it, Tully advises him not to waste his good years. He tells him to go over to the Lido Gym; see his manager, Ruben, and tell him that Tully sent him.

Later Tully sits in a bar. Oma sits next to him, asking whether he ever goes home. Her African-American friend, Earl, sits with her. She tells Tully how much she loves Earl, but constantly bawls him out. Tully explains that he tried to get into training, but before he could turn around, he pulled a muscle. He also talks about the kid, Ernie, being such a good boxer; a natural. Oma, meanwhile, acts belligerent with everyone.

Following Tully's advice, Ernie goes to the Lido Gym and introduces himself to Ruben. As soon as Ernie says that Tully sent him, Ruben seems interested and tells the kid to show him what he has. He reminisces about what a great fighter Tully was and talks about Tully's rise and fall. Ernie learns from Ruben that Tully was married, but his wife ruined him by destroying his peace of mind.

That night in bed with his wife, Ruben describes the white kid's potential. He doesn't have anything against blacks, he says, but there are too many of them, and Anglos don't want to see two black guys fighting.

Early in the morning, men gather to hire themselves out for a day's labor in the fields and groves of the San Joaquin Valley. Pickers talk about how little they make after working all day. An old guy asks Tully why he doesn't get a real job. When he replies that he was fired from his real job, the guy behind him says he'll try to get it. "I was a cook," says Tully. After the guy declares that he can't cook, Tully admits, "I can't, either."

Ernie and his girlfriend are in his car. It's pouring rain. They are stuck in the mud, and he has to get out and push the car. Later she becomes very affectionate, telling him that she is glad that she is not a virgin anymore. She thought she would see the world through different eyes, she continues, but she doesn't. When she inquires whether he'll call her the next day, he asks, "Why?"

The next day Ruben takes his fighters to Monterey. Ernie is the first fighter in the amateur boxing match. The announcer introduces him as Irish, and Ernie tells Ruben that he's not. Ruben shrugs; not to worry, as long as he's white. Ernie's opponent is a Mexican fighter. In the second round Ruben begins to worry when the Mexican draws blood. Ernie loses on a technical knockout (TKO). Every fighter loses, and Ruben and his assistant make excuses.

Tully is back in the bar. Oma tells him that Earl is in prison, and they decide to live together.

Ernie is in another fight and loses in twenty-three seconds. Later, Ernie is in his car with his girlfriend, who tells him she is pregnant and wants to get married.

Tully tells Oma that he'll just have to start boxing again. He knows that he can't cook, that he's just a bum, but he goes back to hoeing the fields. Back in the bar he talks about his fighting in Panama. He vows to start running again and says that if he can get in shape he can get a fight.

Another early morning Tully is at the shape-up for harvesting jobs and sees Ernie. The two of them pick walnuts. Afterward, Tully and Ernie go to the Lido Gym and speak to Ruben. Tully tells him that he wants to start training. Ruben tries to arrange a fight for Tully. Meanwhile, Earl gets out of prison, and Tully is thrown out of Oma's place. Ruben sets up a fight for Tully with a Mexican boxer, Lucero, who himself is in bad shape. Lucero arrives in Stockton by bus. He goes straight to his hotel room and then to the bathroom. When he urinates, there is blood in the toilet bowl. Tully wins the fight by a TKO. After the fight Lucero leaves on his own. Ruben takes Tully home, and they have a violent argument when Tully learns that all he will receive for his win is one hundred dollars. Tully feels he has been taken and is outraged.

Later, Ernie encounters Tully, who is drunk in the street. They go to a restaurant and sit at the counter. After commenting on an old Chinese waiter, wondering whether he is happy, Tully says, "Maybe we were all happy once." A blank look comes over Tully. Both men sit there with nothing more to say.

32 *The Life and Times of Judge Roy Bean* (1972)

Director	John Huston
Producer	John Foreman
Associate Producer	Frank Caffey
Screenplay	John Milius
Music	Maurice Jarre
Director of Photography	Richard Moore
Editor	Hugh S. Fowler, A.C.E.
Art Director	Tambi Larsen
Costumes	Edith Head
Casting	Lynn Stalmaster
Assistant Director	Mickey McCardle
Unit Production Manager	Arthur S. Newman Jr.
Sound	Larry Jost
Sound Editor	Keith Scrafford
Makeup	William Tuttle and Monty Westmore
Hairstylist	Jane Shugrue
Assistant to John Huston	Gladys Hill
Assistant to Producer	Annabelle King
Special Photographic Effects	Butler-Glouner
Stunt Coordinator	James Arnett
Set Decorator	Robert Benton
Assistant Editor	Richard Wahrman
Script Supervisor	John Franco
Cast	Paul Newman (Judge Roy Bean), Victoria Principal (Marie Elena), Barbara J. Longo (Fat Lady), Anthony Perkins (Reverend LaSalle), Frank Soto (Mexican Leader), Ned Beatty (Tector Crites), Jim Burk (Bart Jackson), Matt Clark (Nick the Grub), Steve Kanaly (Whorehouse Lucky Jim), Bill McKinney (Fermel Parlee), Tab Hunter (Sam Dodd), Neil Summers (Snake River Rufus Krile), Jack Colvin (Pimp), John Huston (Grizzly Adams), Howard Morton (Photographer), Stacy Keach (Bad Bob), Billy Pearson (Miner/Station Master), Roddy McDowall (Frank Gass), Stan Barrett (Killer), Don Starr (Opera House

John Huston

	Manager), Alfred G. Bosnos (Opera House Clerk), Anthony Zerbe (Hustler), John Hudkins (Man at Stage Door), David Sharpe (Doctor), Jacqueline Bisset (Rose Bean), Ava Gardner (Lily Langtry). *Outlaws:* Roy Jenson, Gary Combs, Fred Brookfield, Ben Dobbins, Deck Farnsworth, LeRoy Johnson, Fred Krone, Terry Leonard, Dean Smith. *Whores:* Margo Epper, Jeannie Epper, Stephanie Epper. *Marshals' Wives:* Francesca Jarvis, Karen Carr, Dolores Clark, Lee Meza
Filmed	at First Artists Production, National General Pictures release, from Cinerama Releasing (UK) Ltd.
Running Time	124 minutes, Technicolor
Release Date	December 18, 1972

Other titles: *Juge et hors-la-loi*

SYNOPSIS

Roy Bean rides into Vinegaroon, Texas, a wanted man, with charges of robbery and rape on his head. A collection of outlaws beat, rob, and humiliate him. A Mexican girl, Marie Elena, helps him, and he returns to the saloon, where he kills his tormentors. After burying his victims, Bean proclaims himself judge of Vinegaroon. He vows to bring order with guns and a hanging rope. The bar becomes Bean's courtroom. He hangs up a picture of his ideal woman, Lily Langtry. A bunch of hooligans ride into town, and Judge Bean swears them in as his marshals. Within a few days their first outlaw is hanged, the judge reads the funeral oration, and the outlaws' possessions are confiscated to pay for court costs.

As the years pass Bean's fame grows along with the number of hangings. He and Marie Elena are close, but he is devoted to Lily Langtry. Grizzly Adams rides into town and presents the judge with a grizzly bear as a present. The bear is pleasant as long as it has enough beer. Frank Gass, a lawyer, rides into town and claims that he holds a deed entitling him to the judge's property; however, he changes his mind after a session in the bear's cage. He then becomes the town's defense attorney. He hires a killer to dispatch the judge, but his scheme is foiled by the bear.

The ladies of the town turn on the judge and Marie Elena when she becomes pregnant. Roy Bean goes to San Antonio to see Lily Langtry, but is unsuccessful. When he returns he finds Marie Elena dying, having given birth to their daughter. He rides out of town a defeated man.

Twenty years later oil has been discovered. Lawyer Gass is prosperous and, with a gang of hired hands, runs the town ruthlessly. Rose Bean, the judge's daughter, is faced with eviction and has decided to defend her father's property. Her father returns and rounds up his motley crew of marshals. A big gun battle ensues, and Bean is victorious. As he stands on a balcony and declares the town for Texas and Lily Langtry, an oil derrick falls on him and finishes him off.

Years later, a train stops in the desolate town of Langtry. Lily Langtry gets off the train, escorted by the two remaining residents, and visits the museum in the bar. She sees the poster of her on the wall and admiringly declares that Roy Bean must have been some man.

33 *The Mackintosh Man* (1973)

Director	John Huston
Producer	John Foreman
Screenplay	Walter Hill, based on the novel *The Freedom Trap* by Desmond Bagley
Director of Photography	Oswald Morris
Production Designer	Terry Marsh
Editor	Russell Lloyd
Art Director	Alan Tomkins
Set Dresser	Peter James
Sound Recordists	Basil Fenton-Smith and Gerry Humphreys
Sound Editors	Les Hodgson and Don Sharp
Associate Producer	William Hill
Music	Maurice Jarre
Second Unit Director	James Arnett
Assistant to Producer	Arthur S. Newman Jr.
Assistant to Mr. Huston	Gladys Hill
Wardrobe Supervisor	Elsa Fennell
Continuity	Penny Daniels
Makeup	George Frost and Hugh Richards
Hairdresser	A. G. Scott
Special Effects	Cliff Richardson and Ron Ballinger
Assistant Director	Colin Brewer
Cast	Paul Newman (Rearden), Dominique Sanda (Mrs. Smith), James Mason (Sir George Wheeler), Harry Andrews (Mackintosh), Ian Bannen (Slade), Michael Hordern (Brown), Nigel Patrick (Soames-Trevelyan), Peter Vaughan (Brunskill), Roland Culver (Judge), Percy Herbert (Taafe), Robert Lang (Jack Summers), Jenny Runacre (Gerda), John Bindon (Buster), Hugh Manning (Prosecutor), Wolfe Morris (Malta Police Commissioner), Noel Purcell (O'Conovan), Donald Webster (Jervis), Keith Bell (Palmer), Niall MacGinnis (Warder)
Filmed	at locations in Europe; Warner Brothers
Running Time	105 minutes, Technicolor
Release Date	July 25, 1973

Other titles: *Le Piege, L'Agente Speciale Mackintosh*

SYNOPSIS

The film opens with Sir George Wheeler giving a patriotic speech before the House of Commons. In the balcony Mackintosh, head of one of the secret service branches, watches him. Rearden, an undercover agent posing as an Australian criminal, goes to Mackintosh's office. They stage an elaborate diamond heist so that Rearden is set up and arrested.

In prison Rearden is approached by Soames-Trevelyan, who offers to help him escape from prison if Rearden agrees to pay half of his take in the jewel heist. Rearden pays a deposit. His background is checked, and he is informed that there will be a jail break that Saturday. Rearden will also have a companion—Slade, a Soviet spy who is serving a long term in the same prison.

On Saturday a diversion is created. Prisoners start fighting. Smoke bombs and what looks like dynamite are tossed into the prison yard. The guards and prisoners panic. A net attached to a big crane comes over the wall. Slade and Rearden cling to it and are hoisted above the prison walls. They are taken by motorcycle to a moving van, sedated, and placed in an ambulance.

Rearden wakes from a long drugged sleep and finds he and Slade are locked in a room. From the window he sees bogs and heath country with old walls. He can't figure out where he is. He is brought to a Mr. Brown, who demands the rest of the money for the escape. Brown tells him that in a week they will move him.

Mackintosh meets Wheeler in the House of Commons and tells him that the secret service is planning to expose the scheme to get the Soviet spies out of the country. He knows that Wheeler is part of the scheme and forces his hand. Later Mackintosh is run over and killed by a hit-and-run driver.

Rearden is beaten up by Mr. Brown and his henchmen. Through an elaborate scheme, Rearden escapes and burns down the mansion. He learns that he is in a remote area of Ireland and goes into the town. There he calls Mrs. Smith (Mackintosh's daughter), who tells him about her father's accident. Meanwhile, Wheeler enters the harbor on his yacht. He makes a show of great hospitality toward the townspeople, offering to pay for all of their drinks in the pub. One of the townspeople is not taken in by the rich Englishman.

Rearden meets Mrs. Smith at a remote airfield. She gives him a new identity. It becomes apparent that Wheeler is a master spy for the Soviets and that Slade is hidden on the boat. Rearden and Mrs. Smith then learn that Wheeler is planning to go to Malta. There, they assume, Slade will be transferred to a Russian trawler. As they drive away from the airport in Malta they are followed by a mysterious car. After a long chase, the driver chasing them finally loses control and crashes over the cliffs into the sea.

In Malta, Wheeler is giving a party. Mrs. Smith sneaks in, but one of the guests recognizes her as Mackintosh's daughter. Before Wheeler catches and drugs her, she snoops around the boat and finds Slade in one of the rooms. Rearden goes to the police station and tries to convince the police that Slade is aboard Wheeler's boat. The police commissioner is extremely skeptical, but they take him to Wheeler's boat, which the owner allows them to search. Rearden, seeing that Wheeler has turned the tables on him, and not knowing where Mrs. Smith is, breaks away, dives overboard, and evades the police. He later swims back to the boat, enters through one of the portholes, overpowers the radioman, and finds out that Wheeler, Slade, and Mrs. Smith are holed up in a local church.

Rearden goes to the church. Inside, a standoff occurs between Rearden and Wheeler, who holds Mrs. Smith. Rearden and Wheeler agree to put down their guns and go their separate ways. As Wheeler and Slade leave the church, Mrs. Smith picks up the guns and kills both Wheeler and Slade. She then puts the guns in the dead men's hands to make it look like they shot one another. She berates Rearden for letting them go, saying that she should have killed him also. She leaves the church and stands there for a moment, regretting among other things that she has fallen in love with Rearden. She walks off by herself into the night. Rearden comes out of the church and stands there for a moment, listening to the clicking of her shoes as she moves off in the dark. He starts walking in the opposite direction.

34 *The Man Who Would Be King* (1975)

Director	John Huston
Producer	John Foreman
Screenplay	John Huston and Gladys Hill, based on the short story by Rudyard Kipling
Associate Producer and Stunt Director	James Arnett
Assistant to John Huston	Gladys Hill
Production Supervisor	Ted Lloyd
Directory of Photography	Oswald Morris
Production Designer	Alexander Trauner
Wardrobe Designer	Edith Head
Art Director	Tony Inglis
Camera Operator	Eric Van Haren-Noman
Editor	Russell Lloyd
Assistant Director	Bert Batt
Continuity	Angela Allen
Assistant to the Producer	Annabelle King
Makeup	George Frost
Hairdresser	Pat McDermott
Wardrobe Supervisor	John Wilson Apperson
Production Assistant and Secretary	Barbara Allen
Sound Mixer	Basil Fenton-Smith
Production Accountant	Ron Allday
Horsemaster	Bob Simmons
Special Effects	Dick Parker
Still Photographer	Ian Coates
Publicist	Brian Doyle
Music	Maurice Jarre
Cast	Sean Connery (Daniel Dravot), Michael Caine (Peachy Carnehan), Christopher Plummer

	(Rudyard Kipling), Saeed Jaffrey (Billy Fish), Karroum Ben Bouih (Kafu-Selim), Jack May (District Commissioner), Doghmi Larbi (Ootah), Shakira Caine (Roxanne), Mohammed Shamsi (Babu), Paul Antrim (Mulvaney), Albert Moses (Ghulam), Kimat Singh (Sikh Soldier), Gurmuks Singh (Sikh Soldier), Yvonne Ocampo (Dancer), Nadia Atbib (Dancer), Graham Acres (Officer), the Blue Dancers of Goulamine
Filmed	at locations in Morocco; Allied Artists Pictures
Running Time	129 minutes, Technicolor
Release Date	December 17, 1975

Other titles: *L'Homme qui voulut être roi, L'Uomo che volle farsi re*

SYNOPSIS

In India in the 1880s, Daniel Dravot and Peachy Carnehan have a chance encounter with Rudyard Kipling that reveals a common bond of Freemasonry. The two former army sergeants, who have remained in India after their terms of service, turn up at Kipling's newspaper office to ask him to witness a contract. Tired of life as disreputable con men, they plan to venture beyond the Northwest Frontier into the Kafiristan—they will be the first Europeans to set foot there since Alexander the Great—and win fame and fortune by setting themselves up as kings. Unable to dissuade them, Kipling witnesses their contract wherein they pledge mutual loyalty and swear off women and drink until they achieve their goal. Then he gives them his Masonic seal for luck.

After many adventures Dravot and Carnehan reach Kafiristan, acquire an interpreter, and use smuggled rifles to subdue the warring tribes—all according to their plan. When Dravot is hailed as a god by the natives after emerging unscathed when hit by an arrow, he and Carnehan take advantage of the situation to collect tributes.

Eventually they are summoned to the holy city of Sikandergul by the high priest. Dravot is saved from having his immortality tested by arrows, however, when Kipling's Masonic seal is recognized as the emblem of Sikander, and Dravot is duly enthroned as the descendant of Alexander, who has come to claim his kingdom and a fortune in gold and jewels. Free to leave with his fortune if he chooses, Dravot takes his regal role so seriously that he ignores Carnehan's warnings and determines to take a queen—the beautiful Roxanne.

At the wedding ceremony, frightened by the legend that claims that Sikander will consume his bride with fire, the terrified Roxanne bites Dravot. His bleeding reveals that he is no god, but a mortal man. Led by the priests of this primitive theocracy, the people of Sikandergul rise up against the interlopers. Carnehan urges Dravot, along with their devoted companion, the ex-Gurka rifleman Billy Fish, to "brass it out," and they fight their way to the suspension bridge that Dravot himself had ordered built to link the ancient city to the outside world. When Dravot reaches halfway across the bridge, he turns to face his assailants and defiantly sings a hymn. The people sever the ropes tying the bridge, and Dravot is hurled to his death in the gorge. Then they crucify Carnehan, but ultimately release him.

Driven mad by his torture and all he has had to endure, Carnehan manages to make his way back to Kipling's office in Lahore. There he tells his sorry tale and leaves Dravot's crowned head as proof.

35 *Independence* (1976)

Director	John Huston
Producers	Joyce Ritter and Lloyd Ritter
Screenplay	Joyce Ritter, Lloyd Ritter, and Thomas McGrath
Camera	Owen Roizman
Editor	Eric Albertson
Art Director	Stephen Grimes
Costumes	Ann Roth
Music	Jack Cortner
Sound Mixing	Christopher Newman
Rerecording	Albert Gramahlia
Second Unit Direction and Photography	Lloyd Ritter
Historical Consultant	L. H. Butterfield
Cast	William Atherton (Benjamin Rush), John Favorite (John Lansing Jr.), Pat Hingle (John Adams), Ken Howard (Thomas Jefferson), Anne Jackson (Abigail Adams), Donald C. Moore (Benjamin Harrison), Scott Mulhern (Alexander Hamilton), Patrick O'Neal (George Washington), John Randolph (Samuel Adams), Joe Ritter (Congressional Page), Paul Sparer (John Hancock), Tom Sprately (George Mason), Donald Symington (Richard Henry Lee), James Tolkin (Tom Paine), Eli Wallach (Benjamin Franklin), E. G. Marshall (Narrator)
Filmed	at locations in Philadelphia; Twentieth Century-Fox for the U.S. National Parks Service
Running Time	28 minutes, Technicolor
Release Date	March 30, 1976

SYNOPSIS

The narrator says that the ghosts of the past still live with us. Benjamin Franklin appears and says that his wish was to be immersed in a keg of Madeira wine until he was called forth again. Thus begins this tribute to the bicentennial, a short film that commemorates the war for independence, with Franklin and his colleagues called back to relive those momentous years. Franklin says that he is sixty-eight years old, and it is great to be young again. A modern-day trolley car passes, and he looks quizzically at it. Washington says that he never felt himself equal to his past. Tom Paine felt that the sun never shined on a greater cause. Dr. Benjamin Rush claims that the war may be over but the revolution is not yet finished.

They go back to 1774. Delegates from all over the colonies are protesting King George's rule and his taxes. Delegates are warned not to be too vocal, because there are Tories about. The Continental Congress meets. They address the king about their grievances, but their petitions are thrown under the table.

In 1775, instead of answering grievances, the king sends redcoats, who open fire without provocation. The colonists built their own government under the eyes of the king. John Adams proposes that they assemble an army with George Washington as its leader. The Continental Congress convened with no other authority but that of men. The Congress proclaimed that if a king let the people slip from him, he can no longer king. Abigail Adams reminds them that women must also be considered and have representation. Abigail then asks, "When will someone affirm our independence?" Jefferson prepares the written declaration.

From July 1 through July 4, 1776, the colonies declare themselves as states and the new country as the United States.

In August 1776 the delegates sign the Declaration of Independence. They all expect to be hanged. "These are the times that try men's souls"; the war of independence goes on for six brutal years. In 1781 the war is won, and the Articles of Confederation barely keep the country together.

In 1787, a nation is proposed. The Constitution is developed. It has the appearance of permanence, although nothing is certain except death and taxes, as Franklin contends.

Franklin admonishes the viewing audience that it is up to them to keep the Constitution alive. In 1797 there is the first election. A group of tourists come into Independence Hall in 1976.* Tom Paine said that we have the power to start the world anew, reminds the narrator. We have a republic if we can keep it.

36 *Wise Blood* (1979)

Director	John Huston**
Producers	Michael Fitzgerald and Kathy Fitzgerald
Associate Producer	Hans Brockmann
Screenplay	Benedict Fitzgerald, from the novel by Flannery O'Connor
Photography	Gerald Fisher
Camera Operator	Bernie Ford

*The film is shown on a continuous basis at Independence Hall, Philadelphia, Pennsylvania.
**At the beginning of the film, John's name is spelled "Jhon": "Jhon Huston's *Wise Blood*," "Jhon Huston as Grandfather," and "Directed by Jhon Huston."

Editor	Roberto Silvi
Music	Alex North
Costumes and Sets	Sally Fitzgerald
Wardrobe	Uta Frewald
Makeup	Al Apone
Title Stills	Barbara McKenzie
Sound Recording	Collin Charles
Production Manager and Assistant Director	Tom Shaw
Assistant Director	Gene Anderson Jr.
Cast	Brad Dourif (Hazel Motes), Ned Beatty (Hoover Shoates), Harry Dean Stanton (Asa Hawks), Daniel Shor (Enoch Emory), Amy Wright (Sabbath Lilly Hawks), Mary Nell Santacroce (Landlady, Mrs. Flood), John Huston (Hazel's Grandfather), William Hickey (Preacher). *Bits:* J. L. Parker, Marvin Sapp, Richard Earle, Herb Kossover, Betty Lou Groover, John Tyndall, Gillaaron Houck, Philip Mixer, Sharon Johnson, Joe Dorsey, Stratton Leopold, Leonard Holmes, Daniel Albright, Tommy Alson, Harold Horne, Jim Barbee, Gene Howard, Raymond Foskey, Vicky Dyer, Jerry Rushing, Ken Flower, Gladys Hill, Ray Wilkes
Filmed	an Ithaca-Anthea Coproduction, released through New Line Cinema
Running Time	106 minutes, Technicolor
Release Date	Screened at the Seventeenth New York Film Festival in 1979; general commercial release February 17, 1980

Other titles: *La Saggezza nel sangue, Le Malin*

SYNOPSIS

The opening scene shows a religious sign on a rural road and then a tombstone, "Jesus Called." Hazel Motes is coming home from the army. After getting a lift in a pickup, he approaches a run-down house. He wanders around the boarded-up and empty house, writes a sign on a piece of paper, and goes outside to a small cemetery. There he experiences a flashback in which his grandfather, a preacher, appears to him.

Next Hazel buys some civilian clothes at a general store and then boards a train. Sitting next to an older woman, he tells her that he is going to the city to do something that he has not done before. The woman reckons that he has been redeemed and asks if he thinks that life is an inspiration. While washing up in the station bathroom, he sees on the wall the name of a woman—Mrs. Leora Watts, hostess of "the friendliest bed in town." He has a taxi driver take him to her house. The driver thinks that Hazel is a preacher. Hazel tells him that he doesn't believe in anything.

The next day Hazel is in the street and sees the blind street preacher Asa Hawks and his daughter, Sabbath Lilly. He is also befriended by Enoch Emory, a zookeeper. Hazel follows Hawks and Lilly, and a policeman berates him for crossing the road on the red light. After an argument with Hawks and his daughter, Hazel decides to become a preacher and to start the Church without Jesus. Emory proclaims that he has "wise blood," or a sixth sense. He has more flashbacks of his youth and his grandfather.

Hazel buys a beat-up car and goes to the zoo. Emory directs him to the local museum and shows him a mummified Pygmy.

Hazel decides to pursue Hawks and his daughter, so he follows them and rents a room in the same boardinghouse. Sabbath tells her father that she wants Hazel.

Hazel starts preaching on the street about a new Jesus, which Emory says he will get for him. Hazel states that nobody with a good car needs to be justified, but Emory steals the mummy from the museum. Sabbath Lilly hides in Hazel's car, confiding that since she is illegitimate it won't make any difference if she necks with boys because she's going to hell anyhow.

One day when Hazel is out preaching, another street preacher, Hoover Shoates, approaches him and proposes that they go into business. Hazel is disillusioned. He doesn't want to take people's money or have anything to do with Shoates.

When Hazel returns to the boardinghouse he discovers that Asa Hawks is not blind at all. He is a phony. Up in his room Hazel finds Sabbath Lilly in his bed, and she seduces him.

Emory brings Hazel the Pygmy mummy, proclaiming it the new Jesus. He says that it doesn't look like any other Jesus. Sabbath takes the mummy into the bathroom, unwraps it, and declares it "mighty cute." Hazel destroys the mummy while she yells at him.

Hoover Shoates brings along another preacher, starts preaching the same gospel as Hazel, right next to him, and ends up collecting money. Then Hazel follows the "false preacher" and runs him down with his car. He decides to leave the city and Sabbath and go elsewhere, but on the road he is stopped by the sheriff, who pushes his decrepit car into a pond.

Hazel then returns to the boardinghouse with a bag of lime with which he blinds himself. When his landlady brings him back from the hospital, she encourages him to preach again. Sabbath, meanwhile, runs off to join her father again. As a form of penance Hazel puts rocks in his shoes and wraps wire around his body. Hazel's landlady prepares his meals and keeps him company. She points out that it would be more convenient for him to move downstairs, closer to her. She then asks him who else would look after him in his condition? Since they are both alone in the world, she proposes marriage. At this Hazel simply gets dressed and walks out into the rain. The police, summoned by the landlady, later find him prone in a vacant lot. They bring him back to the landlady, who puts him in her bed. There he lies, immobile and impassive, waiting for death.

37 *Phobia* (1980)

Director	John Huston
Executive Producers	Larry Spiegel and Mel Bergman
Producer	Zale Magder
Screenplay	Lew Lehman, Jimmy Sangster, and Peter Bellwood
Story	Gary Sherman and Ronald Shusett
Assistant to Mr. Spiegel and Mr. Bergman	Judy Goldstein
Music	Andre Gagnon
Director of Photography	Reginald H. Morris, C.S.C.
Coordinator	Alice Ferrier
Production Manager	David Sheperd
Assistant	Emily Eng
Associate to Mr. Huston	Gladys Hill
First Assistant Director	David Robertson
Second Assistant Director	Richard Flower
Third Assistant Directors	Karen Pike and Louise Casselman
Production Designer	Ben Edwards
Art Director	David Jaquest
Assistant Art Director	Joe Cselenyi
Set Decorator	André Brodeur
Assistant Set Decorator	Chris Biden
Camera Operator	Murray Magder
Script Supervisor	Blanche McDermaid
Makeup	Kathy Southern
Casting Director	Vicki Mitchell
Editor	Stan Cole
Sound Editor	Peter Burgess
Special Effects	Martin Malivoire
Psychology Consultant to Mr. Huston	Melvyn Hill, Ph.D.
Cast	Paul Michael Glaser (Dr. Peter Ross), John Colicos (Inspector Barnes), Susan Hogan (Jenny St. Clair), Alexandra Stewart (Barbara Grey), Robert O'Ree (Bubba King), David Bolt (Henry Owen), David Eisner (Johnny Venuti), Lisa Langlois (Laura Adams), Kenneth Welsh (Sergeant Wheeler), Neil Vipond (Doctor Clegg), Patricia Collins (Dr. Alice Toland), Marian Waldman (Mrs. Casey), Gwen Thomas (Doctor Clemens), Paddy Campanero (Newswoman), Gerry Salsberg (First Newsman), Peter Hicks (Second Newsman), Joan Fowler (Head Nurse), John Stoneham (Security Guard, Hockey Game),

	Terry Martin (First Policeman), Ken Anderson (Second Policeman), Janine Cole (Child), Karen Pike (Hostage), Wendy Jewel (First Girl), Coleen Embry (Second Girl), Diane Lasko (Third Girl)
Filmed	at locations in Canada; Paramount
Running Time	90 minutes, Technicolor
Release Date	September 9, 1980

SYNOPSIS

Doctor Peter Ross is a controversial psychiatrist who deals with patients with extreme phobias. The film opens with a patient, Johnny Venuti, with claustrophobia, enclosed in a small space. Another of Doctor Ross's patients, Bubba King, has a terrible fear of snakes; another, a fear of crowds; and yet another, a fear of being raped. Ross's fellow doctors question his methods and whether heightening a patient's anxiety is the best way to cure him.

Ross takes the patient with a fear of crowds, Barbara Grey, out into the street to see if she can cope with her phobia. He leaves her alone, telling her to come to his house afterward. She goes into the crowded subway, where her phobia returns, and she goes to his house. He is not home, however; he is out playing hockey. As she wanders about the house, she sees a file cabinet drawer with her name on it. She opens it and is blown to pieces.

The patient with a fear of heights, Henry Owen, becomes a suspect and is harassed by the police because he is an expert on explosives. He escapes from the police station, steals a car, and climbs a building under construction. Doctor Ross is summoned. He goes up the building and tries to save him, but his patient falls to his death.

Ross's three remaining patients become distraught. The girl fearful of rape, Laura Adams, agrees to undergo a treatment of simulated rape; but she becomes hysterical. The doctor's assistant gives her a bath. When the assistant leaves for a moment the patient relaxes. Someone comes in and drowns her. The police begin to think that one of the patients is killing the others.

Doctor Ross looks for one of his patients who is missing. He contacts the patient and instructs him to go to his girlfriend's apartment. When the police arrive at the apartment, the patient jumps on top of the elevator. Somebody starts the elevator, and he is crushed to death. At this point the police begin to suspect Ross and confront him. Among other things he was a demolitions expert during the Vietnam War. But they can't figure out his motive.

The head of the hospital dismisses Ross and stops his experiments. His associate goes into Ross's office and looks through his files. His girlfriend comes in, and they discuss Ross's theories of solving patients' problems. They discuss the doctor's sister, who drowned, and how he had tried to save her. The associate thinks that Ross caused his sister's death. He is a criminal, and thus patients are criminals.

Ross's girlfriend finds him in his study with his last patient, who is dead. He rants: They wouldn't be cured, so they had to die. He threatens his girlfriend when confronted with the truth, but then turns his gun on himself and shoots himself in the head.

38 *Victory* (1981)

Director	John Huston
Producer	Freddie Fields
Screenplay	Evan Jones and Yabo Yablonsky
Story	Yabo Yablonsky, Djordje Milicevic, and Jeff Maguire
Director of Photography	Gerry Fisher, B.S.C.
Production Design	J. Dennis Washington
Editor	Roberto Silvi
Associate Producer	Annie Fargue
Executive Producer	Gordon McLendon
Music	Bill Conti
Soccer Plays Designer	Pelé
Supervising Sound Editor	Leslie Hodgson
Costumes	Tom Bronson
Unit Production Manager	Tom Shaw
First Assistant Director	Elie Cohn
Assistant to Mr. Huston	Gladys Hill
Production Coordinators	Anne Shaw and Dawne Alstrom
Production Assistant	Allegra Huston
Script Supervisor	John Franco
Dialogue Coach	Anna Korda
Sound Editors	Bonnie Koehler and Anthony Palk
Second Unit Director	Robert Riger
Cast	Sylvester Stallone (Robert Hatch), Michael Caine (John Colby), Max von Sydow (Maj. Karl Von Steiner), Tim Pigott-Smith (Rose), Daniel Massey (Colonel Waldron), Pelé (Luis Fernandez), Bobby Moore (Terry Brady), Osvaldo Ardiles (Carlos Rey), Paul Van Himst (Michel Fileu), Kazimierz Deyna (Paul Wolchek), Hallvar Thorensen (Gunnar Nilsson), Mike Summerbee (Sid Harmor), Co Prins (Pieter Van Beck), Russell Osman (Doug Clure), John Wark (Arthur Hayes), Soren Linsted (Erik Borge), Kevin O'Calloghan (Tony Lewis). *Other Cast Members:* Gary Waldhorn, George Mikell, Laurie Sivell, Arthur Brauss, Robin Turner, Michael Wolf, Jurgen Andersen, David Shawyer, Werner Roth, Amidou, Benoit Ferreux, Jean François Stevenin, Jack Lenoir, Folton Gera, Carole Laure, Julian Curry,

	Clive Merrison, Maurice Roëves, Michael Cochrane, Jack Kendrick
Filmed	at locations in Europe; Paramount–Lorimar–the Victory Company
Running Time	110 minutes, Metrocolor
Release Date	July 30, 1981

Other titles: *Fugga per la vittoria, A Nous la victoire*

SYNOPSIS

Gensdorf in 1943 is a prison for Allied officers. All the prisoners do is play soccer. Captain Colby organizes the games, having been a professional footballer before the war. An American, Captain Hatch, doesn't get the gist of this version of football and keeps tackling the other players, American style. A German officer, Major Von Steiner, suggests that the prisoners play a friendly game against German players. While Hatch, a chronic escapee, makes plans for another escape, Colby accepts Steiner's proposition and asks for better living conditions for his men if they are to play their best. The Escape Committee sees the game as an opportunity for some of the men to escape. Steiner's superiors, meanwhile, view the game as a great propaganda coup for Germany. They make arrangements for famous Allied footballers to be rounded up for the prisoners' team and play the German national team in a game to be staged in Paris.

Colby has to defend himself to the Escape Committee's head, Colonel Waldron, who accuses him of getting special privileges for his players. The players begin to arrive from all over, and the characters are acted by famous real-life soccer players. When Hatch's latest escape plans are foiled, he asks Colby whether he can be the team trainer.

Hatch, who is told to contact the French Resistance, which will help the whole team escape during the game, manages to escape. He makes contact and is told that they will use a tunnel under the stadium for the escape. To get the information back to his comrades, Hatch allows himself to be captured. He is put in solitary, but Colby gets him out, claiming that Hatch is his substitute goalie and the real goalie has been injured.

During the first half of the game the Germans are allowed to get away with brutal play and fouls. During halftime the Allied players should be ready to escape, but they are determined to finish the game and beat the Germans. They stage a great comeback. Fernandez (Pelé) performs his famous bicycle kick, and the Allied players win the game. At the game's end the Frenchmen in the stands swarm onto the field, sweeping up the Allied team and running out through the gates, where the Allied players can escape.

39 *Annie* (1982)

Director	John Huston
Producer	Ray Stark
Screenplay	Carol Sobieski

Executive Producer and Musical Sequences	Joe Layton
Director of Photography	Richard Moore
Production Design	Dale Hennesy
Costumes	Theoni V. Aldredge
Film Editor	Michael A. Stevenson
Supervising Editor	Margaret Booth
Production Executive	Howard Pine
Music Arranger and Conductor	Ralph Burns
Lyrics	Martin Charnin
Music	Charles Strouse
Musical Staging and Choreography	Arlene Phillips
Associate Producer	Carol Sobieski
Unit Production Managers	Ray Hatwick and William J. O'Sullivan
First Assistant Director	Jerry Ziesmer
Second Assistant Directors	Chris Soldo and Phil Morini
Assistant to Producer	Norman Gan
Assistant to Mr. Huston	Gladys Hill
Script Supervisor	Marshall Schlom
Men's Costumers	Ray Birdwell and Mort Schwartz
Women's Costumers	Elizabeth Pine and Geri Puhara
Makeup Artists	Ben Lane, Dan Striepeke, and Jeff Hamilton
Hairstylists	Lee Crawford and Candida Conery
Stuntmen	Bob M. Porter, Gerald E. Brutsche, and Jophery Brown
Cast	Albert Finney (Daddy Warbucks), Carol Burnett (Miss Hannigan), Bernadette Peters (Lily), Ann Reinking (Grace Farrell), Tim Curry (Rooster), Aileen Quinn (Annie), Geoffrey Holder (Punjab), Roger Minami (Asp), Edward Herrmann (Franklin D. Roosevelt), Lois DeBanzie (Eleanor Roosevelt), Peter Marshall (Bert Healy). *Other Cast Members:* Toni Ann Gisondi, Rosanne Sorrentino, Lara Burk, April Lerman, Lucie Stewart, Robin Ignacio, Loni Ackerman, Murphy Cross, Nancy Sinclair, I. M. Hobson, Lu Leonard, Mavis Ray, Pam Blair, Colleen Zenk, Victor Griffin, Jerome Callamore, John Richards, Wayne Cilento, Ken Swofford, Larry Hankin, Irving Metzman, Angela Martin, Kurtis Epper Sanders. *Dancers:* Liz Marsh, Danielle Miller, Lisa Kieldrup, Angela Lee, Tina Maria Daspary, Julie Whitman, Jan

	Mackie, Shawnee Smith, Mandy Peterson, Jamie Flowers, Cherie Michan, Janet Marie Jones, Linda Saputo, Sonja Haney, Kari Baca, Victoria Hartman
Filmed	at locations in New Jersey; Columbia Pictures, a Ray Stark Production
Running Time	128 minutes, Metrocolor
Release Date	May 20, 1982

SYNOPSIS

In New York during the Depression, determined to find her long-lost parents, Little Orphan Annie runs away from the Hudson Street Home for Girls. Promptly recaptured, Annie smuggles in Sandy, a stray dog she rescued from the dogcatcher. Eager to save Sandy from the sausage factory when he is discovered by the baleful, drink-sodden matron, Miss Hannigan, Annie charms Grace Farrell, the private secretary to billionaire tycoon Oliver Warbucks, into selecting her as the orphan to spend a week at Warbucks's mansion as part of a plan to soften the tycoon's ogre image.

When Grace shows up with Annie, Warbucks is furious. He insists that the orphan be a boy, but he relents when Annie thanks him for the joy she has already experienced and prepares to leave without a fuss. Gratified when Sandy saves him from a Bolshevik assassin, Warbucks buys out an entire performance at Radio City Music Hall so that Annie can see her first movie with himself as a sheepish escort.

As the week draws to a close, Warbucks is puzzled not only by his changing attitude toward Annie but by Annie's assurance that Grace thinks he is wonderful. Grace has little difficulty in persuading him to adopt the child. Annie then explains that her real parents promised to come back some day, and Warbucks institutes a nationwide search with a fifty-thousand-dollar reward. Innumerable false claimants are unmasked. When Miss Hannigan's jailbird brother, Rooster, and his girl, Lily St. Regis, pose as Annie's parents, who in fact died in a fire, they are armed with proof in the shape of a broken locket supplied by Miss Hannigan. (Annie still treasures the other half.) They successfully claim both Annie and the check.

Respectfully leaving with Rooster and Lily and realizing the deception only when they are joined by Miss Hannigan, Annie tears up the check and runs away. Cornered by the murderous Rooster, despite Miss Hannigan's repentant attempt to protect her, Annie is rescued thanks to a timely warning delivered by the orphanage children. Warbucks, Grace, and Annie are then happily reunited.

40 *Under the Volcano* (1984)

Director	John Huston
Screenplay	Guy Gallo, based on the novel by Malcolm Lowry
Executive Producers	Michael Fitzgerald and Kathy Fitzgerald
Producers	Moritz Borman and Wieland Schulz-Keil
Associate Producers	Hector Lopez Lechuga and Arnold Gefsky

Production Supervisors	Tom Shaw, Mauricio Rojas, and Pedro Escobedo
Production Coordinators	Anne Shaw and Luciana Cabarga
Production Manager	Jorge Jimenez B.
Second Unit Director	Danny Huston
Assistant Directors	Manuel Mueoz and Dennis Shaw
Photography	Gabriel Figueroa
Editor	Roberto Silvi
Production Designer	Gunther Gerzso
Art Director	Jose Rodriguez Granada
Set Designer	Elsa Wachter
Special Effects	Chucho Duran
Music	Alex North
Costumes	Angela Dodson
Makeup	Fernando Garcia Gonzalez, Teresa Sanchez, and Keis Maes
Supervising Sound Editor	Marvin I. Kosberg
Cast	Albert Finney (Geoffrey Firmin), Jacqueline Bisset (Yvonne Firmin), Anthony Andrews (Hugh Firmin), Ignacio Lopez Tarso (Doctor Vigil), Katy Jurado (Señora Gregoria), James Villiers (Brit), Dawson Bray (Quincey), Carlos Requelme (Bustamante), Jim McCarthy (Gringo), Rene Ruiz/Tun-Tun (Dwarf), Eliazar Garcia Jr. (Chief of Gardens), Salvador Sanchez (Chief of Stockyards), Sergio Calderon (Chief of Municipality). *Other Cast Members:* Araceli Ladewuen Castelun, Emilio Fernandez, Arturo Sarabia, Roberto Martinez Sosa, Hugo Stiglitz, Ugo Moctezuma, Isabel Vasquez, Gustavo Fernandez, Irene Diaz de Davila, Alberto Olivera, Eduardo Borbolla, Alejandra Suarez, Rudolfo de Alejandre, Juan Angel Martinez Ramos, Martin Palomares Carrion, Mario Arevalo, Ramiro Ramirez
Filmed	at locations in Mexico; Ithaca-Conacine, released by Universal
Running Time	109 minutes, Technicolor
Release Date	June 12, 1984

Other titles: *Au Dessous du volcan, Sotto il vulcano*

SYNOPSIS

On November 1, 1938, in Cuernavaca, Mexico, masses of people are encamped outside the church and cemetery on the evening of the Day of the Dead. Geoffrey Firmin walks through the crowd, wearing a tuxedo and sunglasses. He wanders into a

147

street carnival. A dog that he befriends in the cemetery follows him as he approaches a stand of ceramic skulls. He buys some food for the dog. He then goes into a cinema bar and joins a friend, Doctor Vigil, who points out that Geoffrey is wearing no socks with his tuxedo. Geoffrey asks whether any letters from his wife, Yvonne, have been found for him. He says that he received a letter from her lawyer, and they are divorced now. Only in Mexico is death an occasion for laughter, he says.

The two men go to a party for the Red Cross in a hotel, and Geoffrey continues to drink. He is introduced to the German attaché as the former British consul in Cuernavaca. Geoffrey asks him whether the Germans are financing a Nazi movement in Mexico. He is boisterous and upsets the other guests. He goes up to the bandstand and rants on about the dead. He then laments the loss of his wife. "Not even a bloody note," he says.

Doctor Vigil takes him to the church. He contemplates the image of the Virgin Mary, who takes care of all those who are alone and have no one to help them. His friend tells him to ask the Virgin for his wife back. Geoffrey cannot, insisting it would be like asking his fairy godmother for three wishes. His friend, who is as drunk as he, pleads to the Virgin for him.

A bus travels through the countryside with Yvonne on board. When the bus comes into the city, she gets off, and some peons carry her bags. She stops in the middle of the deserted road and hears Geoffrey talking inside the bar. She goes in. He turns around and sees her but continues his story, not quite believing that she is Yvonne. She asks whether he got her letters. When he rants, she realizes that he is quite drunk. He says, "It's the shakes that make life insupportable."

Geoffrey and Yvonne walk to their house. She asks him why he didn't answer her letters, but he talks about his shakes. He then asks whether she has come back to stay or if she has just come for a visit. He implies his brother, Hugh, is at the house, and she seems to be a bit shaken by the news. He alludes to his being cuckolded by Hugh and Yvonne. She asks him why he is staying in Mexico if he has resigned his position, but again he talks wildly of the shakes that he cannot control but that do not erase the fear of the abyss opening up in front of him.

Alone in a room for a moment she decides she will actually stay. In desperation he runs around the house looking for a drink. He runs into the garden and drinks the dregs of a whiskey bottle. His next-door neighbor tells him that they were kept awake half the night by the infernal howling of the Firmins' cat. He goes into the house and lies down in the bed with Yvonne. They recite the Mayan months of the year. They kiss, and he tells her how much he wanted her back. He gets passionate and then holds himself back. He apologizes by telling her that it is not any good. She cries. Geoffrey staggers into the road, starts running, and collapses.

Hugh, his half brother, appears. He and Yvonne greet one another, shaking hands and exchanging a friendly kiss. She asks him why he left Spain when the Civil War isn't over. Hugh replies that Franco has all the tanks and planes, and all the Loyalists have are the good songs. They talk about Geoffrey. They cannot tell when he is drunk and down. She informs Hugh that she thinks that Geoffrey was glad to see her, but surprised.

A fellow Britisher turns the corner in his sports car and nearly runs Geoffrey over. After he gets up, his fellow countryman gives him a very generous drink. He staggers back into the house and greets Hugh. Hugh says he can't quite understand why Yvonne has come back to Geoffrey. He would like to know what the situation is. Geoffrey acknowledges she has come back to him. He seems to accept it.

Geoffrey sees a bug in the bathroom and lets out a scream. Hugh and Yvonne run in and put him in the shower, but not before he starts drinking aftershave lotion. Geoffrey says that they should go to the fiesta. As Hugh shaves him, he asks Geoffrey whether he should leave and make it easier for Yvonne and him. Now that she is back, Hugh points out, he will be well taken care of. Geoffrey inquires whether Hugh is just fearful of his baser instincts. Yvonne comes into his bedroom. She is ravishing. She helps him put on his socks.

As soon as they are all outside they see one man carrying another man down the street. Yvonne stops to look at the distant volcano. Doctor Vigil sees them and feels that it is a miracle that Yvonne has returned. They stop to watch a street play. Hugh remarks that the next war will be for their souls. Geoffrey goes off, leaving Hugh and Yvonne alone. She says she doesn't know why he never answered her letters. Hugh thinks Geoffrey never opened them. They then talk about how they can find Geoffrey. She wants to get him away from Cuernavaca, perhaps to a farm where at least there would be work to do.

Geoffrey, who is drinking with Señora Gregoria, goes to the window and sees Yvonne at a shooting gallery with Hugh. Geoffrey gets on one of the carnival rides and is as overexcited as a child. All his money falls out, and the children pick it up and give it back.

Geoffrey, Yvonne, and Hugh take a local bus. They pass a man lying on the ground, and before they can help him he dies. A Nazi takes the dead man's money.

They go to the bullfight. Hugh borrows a guitar and sings a Spanish Loyalist song. He talks about those who stayed in Spain and expresses his guilt about leaving when his comrades stayed behind and got killed. He jumps into the ring and starts fighting the bull.

Yvonne tells Geoffrey that nothing is keeping them in Mexico. They can start over and get their marriage back again. He turns on her and demands with some bitterness whether, whenever his brother comes to visit, he should offer his wife to him. He continues to drink to excess. Yvonne denies that she has come crawling back and asks what more he wants. He replies that hell is his natural habitat and walks off. Hugh, fighting the bull, tells her not to bother going after him, for he doesn't need their help. She says that she needs his.

Geoffrey jumps on a bus and rides off, leaving them behind. He goes to El Parolito, a whorehouse that is run by a dwarf, who offers him drinks and girls and seems to like Geoffrey. The dwarf gives Geoffrey Yvonne's letters, which he reads. In her letters Yvonne had asked why he had not written and had said that his silence frightened her. The dwarf sends one of the girls over to him. She takes him to one of the rooms and undresses him. He hardly knows what's going on, he is so drunk. Hugh and Yvonne come into the bar. When Yvonne finds out that Geoffrey is with a prostitute, she gets upset and runs out into the rain with Hugh.

Geoffrey goes outside and walks over to a white horse. The Mexicans think that he wants to steal the horse, and they start to harass him. They are Mexican Nazis. An old lady tries to warn him. He insists that his name is Blackstone. As the

Mexican Nazis continue to harass him, he realizes that they killed the man on the road. He pulls a machete out of his jacket. The Mexicans shoot him, causing the white horse to panic and run off. Yvonne is trampled and killed by the horse. Hugh cradles her in his arms.

41 *Prizzi's Honor* (1985)

Director	John Huston
Producer	John Foreman
Screenplay	Richard Condon and Janet Roach, based on the novel by Richard Condon
Director of Photography	Andrzej Bartkowiak
Production Designer	Dennis Washington
Editors	Rudi Fehr, A.C.E., and Kaja Fehr
Music	Alex North
Costumes	Donfeld
Executive in Charge of Production	Herb Jellinek
Production Manager (Los Angeles)	Donald C. Klune
Production Manager (New York)	Thomas John Kane
First Assistant Director	Benjy Rosenberg
Second Assistant Director	Christopher Griffin
Production Executive	Dennis L. Judd II
Assistant to the Producer	Barbara Dreyfus
Assistant to Mr. Huston	Monique Blanke
Second Assistant Director (NY)	Randi Rosen
Production Supervisor (NY)	Jon Kilik
Art Director (NY)	Michael Helmy
Second Assistant Director (LA)	Scott Cameron
Art Director (LA)	Tracy Bousman
Cast	Jack Nicholson (Charley Partanna), Kathleen Turner (Irene Walker), Robert Loggia (Eduardo Prizzi), John Randolph (Angelo [Pop] Partanna), William Hickey (Don Corrado Prizzi), Lee Richardson (Dominic Prizzi), Michael Lombard (Filargi [Finlay]), Anjelica Huston (Maerose Prizzi), George Santopietro (Plumber), Lawrence Tierney (Lieutenant Hanley), C. C. H. Pounder (Peaches Altamont), Ann Selepegno (Amalia Prizzi), Vic Polizos (Phil Vittimizzare), Dick O'Neill (Bluestone), Sully Boyar (Casco Vascone), Antonia Vasquez (Theresa Prizzi),

	Tomasino Baratta (Opera Singer). *Other Cast Members:* John Calvani, Murray Staff, Joseph Ruskin, Ray Serra, Seth Allen, Dominic Barto, Teddi Siddall, Tom Signorelli, Raymond Iannicelli, Stanley Tucci, Themi Sapountzakis, Beth Raines, Michael Sabin, Michael Tuck, Michael Fischetti, Kenneth Cervi, Marlene Williams, Joe Kopmar, Eramus (Charlie) Alfano, Peter D'Arcy, Thomas Lomonaco, Bill Brecht, Enzo Citarelli, John Codiglia, Henry Fehren, Alexandra Ivanoff, Skip O'Brien, Theodore Theoharous, Jonathan L. Arland, Reuben Gonzalez, Luis Accinelli, Danielle Frederick
Filmed	at locations in New York and California; ABC Motion Pictures, released through Twentieth Century-Fox
Running Time	130 minutes, Technicolor
Release Date	June 13, 1985

Other titles: *L'Onore dei Prizzi, L'Honneur des Prizzi*

SYNOPSIS

At a Prizzi family wedding, Charley Partanna, a chief lieutenant in the Prizzi crime clan, sees a beautiful woman in a lilac dress—Irene Walker. They exchange glances, and she disappears. He asks a photographer to take some pictures of her and later spots her at the wedding reception. They dance, but she is suddenly called to the telephone and does not return. Maerose Prizzi, who pursues an independent career as an interior decorator, also attends the wedding. She is upset because her estranged father, Dominic Prizzi, insults her. Maerose hopes to one day get back together with Charley, her former fiancé, but Charley's thoughts are elsewhere.

Later that night Charley unsuccessfully attempts to track down the mysterious woman. Instead he is visited by members of the homicide squad inquiring into that afternoon's murder of a gangland rival of the Prizzis. Charley is swiftly released on bail, based on his alibi of attending the family wedding. Indeed, every possible Prizzi suspect was present at the wedding.

Back at home in New York he receives a phone call from Irene. She is in California, but they arrange to have lunch later that day in Los Angeles. Charley flies out and dines with Irene. She tells him about herself: She was married once; she makes good money as a tax consultant; her parents were Polish. Charley discloses that he was once engaged to Maerose, but now confesses he loves Irene. She admits that she is equally attracted to him. Later that afternoon they make love and plan to get married.

Charley returns to New York, and at a family business meeting he learns that someone has been skimming large amounts of cash off the profits of a Prizzi-owned casino in Las Vegas. An ex-partner has been murdered, and Charley has to go to

Las Vegas, clean up the mess, and recover the stolen loot. In Las Vegas he enters the house of Marxie Heller, the presumed guilty party; accuses him of conspiring to cheat the Prizzis; and then executes him in his garage. When Marxie's wife returns home with the groceries, she turns out to be Irene. Thus, Charley learns she was still married to the husband she said she was glad to have left years ago. In spite of Charley's horror that his fiancée is mixed up in this scam, Irene manages to persuade him of her complete ignorance of Marxie's plans. A bag in a closet contains $360,000, exactly half of the missing money, which Charley takes back home to New York.

While cooking dinner for his father, Angelo, Charley shows him photographs of Irene. Angelo promptly burns them in an ashtray, explaining she was the outside contractor who killed the Prizzi rival the day of the wedding.

At one o'clock in the morning Charley calls Maerose and asks if he can come over. He admits that in his despair over Irene he has broken a valuable vase Maerose gave him. Maerose wants to know if Charley wants to make love "on the oriental" (rug). Over coffee the next day, Charley tells Maerose about Irene, and Maerose's advice is to marry her. Irene is after all just doing her job and is fundamentally "a good woman" and "an American."

Back in Los Angeles Charley tells Irene he knows all about her. She admits she still has feelings of gratitude toward the late Marxie Heller, but insists she knew nothing about his plan to cheat the Prizzis in Las Vegas. They are married by a justice of the peace.

Back in New York Charley learns of another family crisis: The president of a bank in which they own 25 percent of the shares has been stealing vast sums of money. This man goes by the name of Finlay, but is actually a Neapolitan, Filargi. The family wants him punished—kidnapped, but not killed—and gives the job to Charley. Irene comes up with a plan to capture Filargi. Carrying a doll, she will wait on a landing in his apartment building. When he appears she will toss the "baby" to Filargi's bodyguard, distracting him and enabling her to kill him, thus leaving Filargi unprotected. All works perfectly until an innocent woman steps out of the elevator at the moment of confrontation. She sees Irene, who without hesitation shoots her dead. The victim is a policeman's wife, and the police vow to crack down on mob activity in the city. At a meeting of Mafia capos, a certain Bocca accuses Dominic Prizzi of bringing the police down on the families and interrupting the normal flow of business.

Meanwhile, Maerose sets in motion a plan to get rid of Irene and get Charley back. In Las Vegas she learns from a hooker that Irene killed Marxie Heller's partner. Maerose passes this information directly to her grandfather, Don Corrado Prizzi, who sees a connection to the missing $360,000. It is now time for Irene to meet the don, who greets her in the ornamental garden of his mansion and welcomes her into the family. He also mentions that he knows of her involvement in the shakedown of the Las Vegas casino, and she must make amends by paying back all the missing money plus 50 percent interest within five days.

As Dominic's fortunes in the organization have been declining for quite some time, his father plans to put him out to pasture in Las Vegas and make Charley the New York boss. Charley receives the offer over dinner and is overwhelmed by the honor, but he is also afraid. Could it be that Don Corrado is setting him up for the sin of marrying an outsider, a non-Italian?

In Los Angeles Charley voices his fears to Irene, but she knows more than he does, for Dominic already gave her a contract to execute Charley. She proposes that they both get out of the mob immediately while they are still alive. They hold a card in the kidnapped Filargi, whom they can use to pry more money out of the Prizzis before they retire. Irene wants Charley to ask the family for the money, which she feels she deserves for her services. Charley agrees to put the request to the don.

The farewell party that Don Corrado has organized for Dominic on the eve of his departure for Las Vegas is interrupted by an explosion and fire set by the Bocca gang. And Eduardo, Dominic's brother, has received a letter from Charley announcing his intention to quit the family and demanding $2 million in settlement, plus $900,000 for Irene. For this consideration Charley pledges to return Filargi. Eduardo gives Charley's letter to Dominic, who, while en route to present this negotiation to Don Corrado, is gunned down by Charley (incensed that Dominic asked his wife to kill him). Charley then makes his claim for the money directly to the don. Don Corrado replies that the couple must give up the "second man" in the Filargi kidnapping, for the police demand this price if the gangs want peace with the authorities. The don pressures Charley to remember where his first loyalties lie. His final task then is to execute his wife, the woman he loves. Even Angelo backs up the don's demands.

Charley phones Irene to say the family has agreed to everything and that she will get her $900,000. She takes the next flight to Los Angeles, intending to catch a plane to Hong Kong the next day. Charley returns to an empty apartment, reads Irene's farewell note, packs a knife in his luggage, and flies to Los Angeles. Irene welcomes him warmly, but takes a gun from her drawer before joining him in bed. Charley is an instant too fast for her as she targets him, and he pierces her neck with his knife. He then takes the suitcase with the money back to New York. After taking a long shower, he calls Maerose, who is delighted that Charley is free.

42 *The Dead* (1987)

Director	John Huston
Producers	Wieland Schulz-Keil and Chris Sievernich
Screenplay	Tony Huston, based on the short story by James Joyce
Executive Producer	William J. Quigley
Director of Photography	Fred Murphy
Production Designer	Stephen Grimes
Costumes	Dorothy Jeakins
Music	Alex North
Editor	Roberto Silvi
Production Manager and Assistant Director	Tom Shaw
Production Coordinator	Anne M. Shaw
Script Supervisor	Karen Golden
Art Director	Dennis Washington

Set Decorator	Josie MacAvin
Assistant to Mr. Huston	Marilyn LaSalandra
Second Assistant Director	John (Joe) Brooks
Sound Mixer	Bill Randall Jr.
Wardrobe Supervisor	Jennifer Parsons
Men's Costumer	John McDonald
Ladies' Costumer	Marilyn Mathews
Makeup Design	Fern Buchner
Cast	Anjelica Huston (Gretta Conroy), Donal McCann (Gabriel Conroy), Helena Carroll (Aunt Kate Morkan), Cathleen Delany (Aunt Julia Morkan), Ingrid Craigie (Mary Jane), Rachael Dowling (Lily), Dan O'Herlihy (Mr. Browne), Donal Donnelly (Freddy Malins), Marie Kean (Mrs. Malins), Frank Patterson (Bartell D'Arcy), Maria McDernottroe (Molly Ivors), Sean McClory (Mr. Grace), Katherine O'Toole (Miss Furlong), Maria Hayden (Miss O'Callaghan), Bairbre Dowling (Miss Higgins), Lydia Anderson (Miss Daly), Colm Meany (Mr. Bergin), Cormac O'Herlihy (Mr. Kerrigan), Paul Grant (Mr. Duffy)
Filmed	at Liffey Films/Zenith Productions, Valencia, California
Running Time	83 minutes, Technicolor
Release Date	December 16, 1987

Other titles: *Gens de Dublin*

SYNOPSIS

It is a snowy Dublin night, January 6, 1904, the Feast of the Epiphany, and the Misses Morkan (Kate and Julia) are throwing their annual party. The hostesses, who are aging spinsters, greet their guests at the top of the stairs. Their special guests are their nephew Gabriel Conroy, a professor of English literature at the university, and his wife, Gretta. They express some worry over Freddy Malins, who is late and who they fear will arrive drunk. His mother awaits him in the sitting room. An old friend, Mr. Browne, arrives with flowers for the ladies, and many compliments, then makes for the whiskey on the sideboard. Then Freddy arrives, and Gabriel takes charge of him, making him presentable for his mother, who greets him with great disapproval, since he failed to show up for tea at her hotel that afternoon.

The entertainment begins with Mary Jane, the third hostess and Aunt Julia's and Aunt Kate's niece, at the piano. Then Mr. Grace recites a most moving poem about love betrayed (a translation from the Irish by Lady Gregory), which makes Gretta very pensive and moves the company very much.

To change the mood, Aunt Julia calls for everyone to dance the lancers and finds a partner for Gabriel, who has been much too serious. His partner is Miss

Molly Ivors, a forthright young woman who is a Republican sympathizer and who chides Gabriel for writing a regular literary column in the *Daily Express,* an English paper. She calls him a West Briton. She says he should come with a group of friends on a trip to Ireland's west coast that summer. Gretta, who hails from the west, would love it, but Gabriel says he always goes on a bicycling holiday in Europe. Miss Ivors chides him once more for his ignorance and indifference to his country and its culture. He bursts out that frankly he is sick of his country, meaning he is bored by its provincialism.

What might have turned into an angry scene (Gretta has observed this exchange at a distance) is interrupted by Aunt Julia's prevailing on her frail sister, Kate, to sing a song for which she was once famous at Dublin musical gatherings, "Arrayed for the Bridal," by Bellini. Aunt Kate gives to the piece a lively rendition, although clearly her voice is not what it once was. Nonetheless, the company applauds enthusiastically, and Freddy, making a bit of a spectacle of himself, declares, to Aunt Kate's embarrassment, that he has never heard her in better voice. Thinking of all the hard work her sister has done with church choirs in the city, Aunt Julia indignantly erupts over how women have apparently been barred from participation in the choirs by some recent pronouncement from the pope. Imagine women's voices being replaced by those of adolescent boys! Well, she adds, maybe the pope has the dignity of Mother Church in mind, but it still does not seem fair! Before she can say any more, the maid announces that the goose is ready. The thought of food calms everyone down, and they all go in to dinner. Miss Ivors excuses herself in order to attend a Republican meeting where James Connelly is speaking.

Gabriel worries about the speech he is to make after dinner, but first he carves the goose, which meets with universal approval. After the main course, the conversation turns to music and the state of the arts in Ireland. When they ask Bartell D'Arcy, the tenor, for his opinion on a recent performance of Puccini's *La Bohème,* he replies he was disappointed because the night he went he was obliged to listen to an understudy in the role of Rodolfo. Having just returned from Italy, he observes that the arts (and above all music) in Ireland do not enjoy the respect with which they are treated in Europe. Mr. Grace speaks for many of the older guests around the table when he says that the crop of singers today can hardly compare with the masters of yesteryear. This observation prompts Aunt Julia to declare that for her there was only one real tenor, a man called Parkinson, doubtless unknown to the rest of the company, and she recalls him with such tenderness that one suspects she may even have been a bit in love with him.

The meal ends with the serving of a flaming Christmas pudding that draws much praise. Then Gabriel asks for silence and delivers his warm appreciation for the kindness and hospitality of the three hostesses, whom he describes as the Three Graces of the Dublin music scene. Even in an age of uncertainty and change, says Gabriel, their presence reassures, for they guarantee continuity, respect for the arts, and the spirit of hospitality. Aunt Kate is moved to tears by his speech, and Gabriel offers the toast to the Three Graces, followed by a chorus of "For They Are Jolly Good Fellows. . . ."

As the guests depart, D'Arcy, who has not sung all night, is suddenly persuaded to sing by Miss O'Callaghan, who is rather interested in him. He sings a traditional air, "The Lass of Aughrim." Gabriel, meanwhile, has been helping Freddy Malins, his mother, and Mr. Browne into a cab amid much confusion, for both men are drunk, and the cabman does not know the city. Then Gabriel returns to the house and sees his wife at the top of the stairs, transfixed by the song and the singing. She is clearly stirred by a deep memory.

On their way back to the hotel, Gabriel tells Gretta a funny story about his grandfather and his donkey, but she barely responds. In their room as they prepare for bed he presses her about what she is thinking. She confesses that D'Arcy's song took her back to her last night in Galway, before she came to Dublin to study with the nuns, and to a young boy called Michael Furey. He was obviously in love with Gretta. He was also in failing health, but he had a fine voice and used to sing this song. He came to see her in the middle of the night before she left and stood down at the bottom of the garden in the rain. Gretta urged him to go home, and that was the last she saw of him. He died that winter, and she is convinced that he wanted to die. Overwhelmed by the emotions of her memories, Gretta collapses on the bed, leaving Gabriel to reflect on his marriage, her past, and the events of the evening. He understands that his wife could never have loved him as she had loved the dead Michael Furey. Even though he had stated in his after-dinner speech that "our work is in the present," he also knows we are all very much attached to our dead, through memory, tradition, and emotional ties. He thinks of Aunt Kate and how frail she looked tonight, and a series of dissolves shows that this time was the last that she would help preside over that gathering of musical friends. He looks out over the snow that is falling all over Ireland, blanketing the living and the dead.

HUSTON AS A WRITER

Huston's career in the movie industry goes beyond his work as a director. His important beginning was as a screenwriter, briefly under contract to Goldwyn Studios in 1930, with Universal from 1930 to 1933, and then with Warner Brothers from 1938 until his directing career began in 1946. If he had pursued a career as a screenwriter he would have had a fairly secure place in movie history. Chapter 16, "Screenplays in Collections," provides details on his writing activity—both produced and unproduced projects. Even as a director he was deeply involved in the screenwriting of every film he directed, either credited or uncredited. This section supplies information on some of his important writing activity because in many ways this work is as significant as his directorial activity. At the end of this section are some examples of Huston's early activity at Universal. The following synopses are not as extensive as those in the directorial section, but they do give an idea of the subject matter that Huston was working on as an assigned contract writer. *Three Strangers* was an independently developed story that Warner Brothers became interested in.

Jezebel (1938)

Director	William Wyler
Executive Producer	Hal B. Wallis
Associate Producer	Henry Blanke

Screenplay   Clements Ripley, Abem Finkel, and John
                       Huston, based on the play by Owen Davis
Contributor to Treatment   Lou Edelman
Contributor to Screenplay
Construction   Robert Bruckner
Photography   Ernest Haller
Film Editing   Warren Low
Music   Max Steiner
Musical Direction   Leo F. Forbstein
Sound   Robert B. Lee
Sound Recording   B. Berry and Frank Wixel
Art Direction   Robert Haas
Costumes   Orry-Kelly
Assistant Directors   Robert Ross and Art Lueker
Cast   Bette Davis (Julie Marsden), Henry Fonda
                       (Preston Dillard), George Brent (Buck
                       Cantrell), Margaret Lindsay (Amy Branford
                       Dillard), Donald Crisp (Doctor Livingstone),
                       Fay Bainter (Aunt Belle), Richard Cromwell
                       (Ted Dillard), Henry O'Neill (General
                       Theopholus), Spring Byington (Mrs.
                       Kendrick), John Litel (Jean La Cour)
Filmed   at Warner Brothers Studios, Burbank,
                       California
Running Time   103 minutes, black and white
Release Date   March 26, 1938
Other titles: *L'Insoumise, La Figlia del vento*

SYNOPSIS

Julie is a spoiled young woman in New Orleans in the 1850s. For the Olympus Ball, even though unmarried, she decides to go to the ball in red rather than white. Her fiancé, Preston Dillard, at first refuses to take her, but then changes his mind. They go, and she shocks the assembled guests. Julie becomes embarrassed and wants to leave, but Preston, who is as strong-willed as she, refuses and forces her to dance, while everyone stands to the side.

Preston breaks off their engagement, totally demoralizing Julie, who goes into seclusion. Then Preston moves to Philadelphia to work at a bank.

Julie hears that Preston is returning to New Orleans and she is happy, but then she learns that he is bringing a wife. She tells another admirer, Buck Cantrell, that her honor has been sullied and demands that he challenge Preston to a duel. Preston's younger brother ends up taking part in the duel and killing Buck.

An epidemic of yellow fever breaks out in New Orleans. Preston is afflicted and must go to an island for those stricken. Julie, aggrieved over her own actions, convinces Preston's wife to allow her to accompany the fatally ill Preston to the island, where she will nurse him.

157

The Amazing Dr. Clitterhouse (1938)

Director	Anatole Litvak
Producer	Gilbert Miller
Executive Producers	Jack L. Warner and Hal B. Wallis
Dialogue Director	Jo Graham
Assistant Director	Jack Sullivan
Screenplay	John Wexley and John Huston
Photography	Tony Gaudio
Art Director	Carl Jules Weyl
Film Editor	Warren Low
Wardrobe	Milo Anderson
Music Director	Leo F. Forbstein
Orchestra	George Parrish
Sound	C. A. Riggs
Technical Adviser	Dr. Leo Schulman
Cast	Edward G. Robinson (Dr. Clitterhouse), Claire Trevor (Jo Keller), Humphrey Bogart (Rocks Valentine), Allen Jenkins (Okay), Donald Crisp (Inspector Lane), Gale Page (Nurse Randolph), Henry O'Neill (Judge), Thurston Hall (Grant), Maxie Rosenbloom (Butch). *Other Cast Members:* Bert Hanlon, Curt Bois, Ward Bond, Vladimir Sokoloff, Billy Wayne, Robert Homans, Irving Bacon
Filmed	at Warner Brothers Studios, Burbank, California
Running Time	87 minutes, black and white
Release Date	July 30, 1938

Other titles: *Il Sapore del delitto, Le mysterieux Docteur Clitterhouse*

SYNOPSIS

A burglar, opening a wall safe in a boudoir of the Opdyke mansion, is surprised at his work by an intruder who relieves the thief of the jewelry and departs. Moments later, a guest, Dr. Clitterhouse, is seen on the hall telephone giving directions to his nurse, Miss Randolph, to prepare a patient, Attorney Grant, for the operating table. A maid rushes downstairs, screaming about the robbery. Before all occupants are searched, Clitterhouse must leave for the hospital because of the operation.

At the hospital Randolph discovers the jewels in Clitterhouse's bag, but he explains his robberies are scientific research.

Clitterhouse gets rid of the loot through a fence, Jo Keller, and her gang, led by Rocks Valentine. Impressed with Clitterhouse's ability, they offer him a partnership, which he accepts, but he keeps his identity a secret. He starts planning the robberies and takes notes.

At one of the subsequent robberies, Rocks locks the doctor in a fur vault, but another crook frees him before the police arrive. They split the loot, and the doctor decides to call it quits. Rocks, however, learns who the doctor is, confronts him, and threatens to expose him unless Clitterhouse agrees to continue planning the successful robberies. Rocks considers the doctor's scientific notes as blackmail. Jo, Rocks, and the doctor "celebrate" the doctor's continuing criminal activities with a drink, but the doctor has poisoned Rock's drink, and he dies. Jo and Clitterhouse dispose of the body. Butch, one of the crooks, spills the beans to the police, and Clitterhouse is arrested.

At his trial when asked if he was insane during his life of crime, Clitterhouse indicates that he was not. The jury acquits him, reasoning that only a madman would claim he was not insane. The shock is too much for Grant, who falls over in a faint, and as the bailiff loudly calls, "Is there a doctor in the court?" Clitterhouse steps forward to attend his friend.

Juarez (1939)

Director	William Dieterle
Producer	Hal B. Wallis
Associate Producer	Henry Blanke
Dialogue Director	Irving Rapper
Assistant Director	Jack Sullivan and John Prettyman
Screenplay	John Huston, Wolfgang Reinhardt, and Aeneas MacKenzie
Photography	Tony Gaudio
Art Director	Anton Grot
Editor	Warren Low
Gowns	Orry-Kelly
Music	Erich Wolfgang Korngold
Sound	C. A. Riggs and G. W. Alexander
Makeup	Perc Westmore
Cast	Bette Davis (Carlotta), Paul Muni (Benito Juarez), Brian Aherne (Maximilian), Claude Rains (Napoleon III), John Garfield (Porfirio Diaz), Donald Crisp (Marchal Bazaine)
Filmed	at Warner Brothers Studios, Burbank, California
Running Time	125 minutes, black and white
Release Date	June 10, 1939

Other titles: *Il Conquistatore del messico, Juarez et Maximilian*

SYNOPSIS

In 1863 Louis Napoleon is faced with France's loss of Mexico, which is ruled by President Benito Juarez. Louis Napoleon decides to circumvent the Monroe Doctrine by staging an election that puts Maximilian on the throne of Mexico.

The idealistic Maximilian arrives with his wife, Carlotta, and cannot understand why the Mexicans don't support him. He then realizes that his French advisers expect him to retrieve the lands confiscated by Juarez and that he has been set up as a dupe. Maximilian refuses and decides to abdicate. Carlotta, however, convinces him to remain and deliver Mexico from its enemies. He offers Juarez the position of prime minister, but Juarez will not accept this compromise.

The United States orders the French out of Mexico and sends aid to Juarez. Juarez's vice president attempts to betray him, giving Maximilian the chance to become victorious. Napoleon then orders French troops out of Mexico and leaves Maximilian defenseless.

Carlotta returns to France and confronts Napoleon. She suffers a mental breakdown over her husband's situation.

Juarez again gains control and captures Maximilian and his followers. Although he can be released, Maximilian decides to stand by his men and is executed with them.

Dr. Ehrlich's Magic Bullet (1940)

Director	William Dieterle
Executive Producer	Hal B. Wallis
Associate Producer	Wolfgang Reinhardt
Dialogue Director	Irving Rapper
Assistant Director	Jack Sullivan
Screenplay	John Huston, Heinz Herald, and Norman Burnside, from an idea by Norman Burnside
Director of Photography	James Wong Howe
Special Effects	Robert Burks
Art Director	Carl Jules Weyl
Film Editor	Warren Low
Music	Max Steiner
Makeup	Perc Westmore
Cast	Edward G. Robinson (Dr. Paul Ehrlich), Ruth Gordon (Mrs. Ehrlich), Otto Kruger (Dr. Emil von Behring), Donald Crisp (Minister Althoff), Maria Ouspenskaya (Fraziska Speyer), Montagu Love (Professor Hartmann), Sig Rumann (Dr. Hans Wolfert), Donald Meek (Mittelmeyer), Henry O'Neill (Dr. Lenz), Albert Basserman (Dr. Robert Koch), Edward Norris (Dr. Morgenroth), Harry Davenport (Judge), Louis Calhern (Dr. Brockdorf), Louis Jean Heydt (Dr. Kunze), Charles Halton (Sensenbrenner), Irving Bacon (Becker)
Filmed	at Warner Brothers Studios, Burbank, California
Running Time	103 minutes, black and white

Release Date   March 2, 1940
Other titles: *Un Uomo contro la morte*

SYNOPSIS

Dr. Paul Ehrlich is released from his position at the hospital when he objects to its backward medical practices. He develops a method for identifying tuberculosis. After he is exposed to the bacillus, he goes to Egypt for his health. While treating a victim of a snake bite there he conceives the idea of antitoxins.

Returning, Ehrlich works on a serum for the treatment of diphtheria. He then pursues his goal of finding a "magic bullet" to fight invading microbes that attack the human body. He works for fifteen years on a theory of how nature fights disease. For his efforts he wins the Nobel Prize. Nonetheless, he faces attacks from the conservative elements in the medical community.

Ehrlich then works to develop a cure for syphilis and finds it. After some of his patients die, he is put on trial. He is vindicated, but the fight takes its toll on his health. The cost of finding the cure is Ehrlich's death.

High Sierra (1941)

Director	Raoul Walsh
Executive Producer	Hal B. Wallis
Associate Producer	Mark Hellinger
Assistant Director	Irving Rapper
Screenplay	John Huston and W. R. Burnett, based on the novel by W. R. Burnett
Photography	Tony Gaudio
Editor	Jack Killifer
Art Director	Ted Smith
Special Effects	Byron Haskin and H. G. Koenekamp
Music	Adolph Deutsch
Costumes	Milo Anderson
Makeup	Perc Westmore
Sound	Dolph Thomas
Cast	Humphrey Bogart (Roy Earle), Ida Lupino (Marie Garson), Alan Curtis (Babe Kozak), Arthur Kennedy (Red Hattery), Joan Leslie (Velma), Henry Hull (Doc Banton), Barton MacLane (Jake Kranmer), Henry Travers (Pa), Elisabeth Risdon (Ma), Cornel Wilde (Louis Mendoza), Minna Gombell (Mrs. Baughman), Paul Harvey (Mr. Baughman), Donald MacBride (Big Mac), Jerome Cowan (Healy)
Filmed	at locations in California and at Warner Brothers Studios, Burbank, California
Running Time	100 minutes, black and white

Release Date   January 21, 1941
Other titles: *La grande evasion, Una pallottola per Roy*

SYPNOSIS

Released from prison after serving a long stretch for bank robbery, Roy Earle is met by one of Big Mac's gang. Big Mac has planned a big jewel heist at a California resort and expects Earle to lead the robbery. He is given money and a car and told to go to a mountain resort, where he will rendezvous with two hoodlums who will take part in the robbery.

On his way west Earle stops at the Indiana farm that his family once owned. Later, as he is driving through the desert, he is almost run off the road by a jalopy driven by a crippled girl, Velma. He befriends her and her family.

Earle then goes to the mountain hideaway and meets Babe Kozak and Red Hattery. With them is one of their girlfriends, Marie, who makes a play for Earle. He is disgusted that he has to work with a couple of inexperienced punks. Louis Mendoza, their contact man inside the hotel, arrives. Suspecting that Mendoza is unreliable and possibly an informer, Earle tells the gang a story in which an informer whom he knew in the past was gunned down.

On his way to Los Angeles to meet Big Mac, Earle visits Velma and her family. When they are involved in an accident, Earle convinces the driver of the other car not to take action. Velma and her family are taken with Earle, and they invite him to come and visit any time. In a way he becomes part of their family. He then visits Big Mac, who is very sick, and the two reminisce about the good old times when criminals were criminals and not the punks they are now. An underworld doctor, Doc Banton, who treats Big Mac, tells Earle that he doesn't have much time. Earle asks the doctor whether he can cure Velma's clubfoot.

When Earle returns to the resort where the gang is hiding, he finds that Marie's boyfriend has beaten her up. Earle takes her in with him, and she begs him to be careful. He takes Marie and a mongrel dog that he found along on the caper.

At the resort they rob the guests, but things go awry when a guard is shot. Mendoza begs to escape with the robbers, fearful that he will blab if the police press him. One of the getaway cars crashes, and Babe and Red are killed. Mendoza survives and does inform on them. In Los Angeles Earle finds out that Doc Banton will fix Velma's foot, but Velma wants nothing to do with Earle. Big Mac is dead, and the crooked cop who worked for him, Jake Kranmer, wants the jewels, but Earle refuses to give them to him. They have a gun battle, and Kranmer is killed and Earle is wounded. Doc Banton fixes him up.

Earle and Marie go on the lam, waiting for a fence to take the jewels off their hands. They hole up in a small motor court but are identified because of the dog. He is proclaimed as "Mad Dog Roy Earle," which offends him. He puts Marie and the dog on a bus and heads for the High Sierra. On the way he robs a store and is then pursued by the police. He is trapped in the mountains.

When Marie hears about it, she goes to him. The police ask Marie to convince Earle that he has no way out and that he must surrender. A sharpshooter takes a position above the spot where Earle is holed up. The dog gets away and runs up to him. Earle then realizes that Marie is also there. He emerges out of the rocks and is shot dead.

Sergeant York (1941)

Director	Howard Hawks
Producers	Jesse Lasky and Hal B. Wallis
Screenplay	Abem Finkel, Harry Chandlee, Howard Koch, and John Huston, based on *The Diary of Sergeant York*
Director of Photography	Sol Polito, A.S.C.
Battle Scene Photography	Arthur Edeson, A.S.C.
Art Director	John Hughes
Film Editor	William Holmes
Sound	Oliver S. Garretson
Music	Max Steiner
Makeup	Perc Westmore
Cast	Gary Cooper (Alvin C. York), Walter Brennan (Pastor Rosier Pile), Joan Leslie (Gracie Williams), George Tobias ("Pusher" Ross), Stanley Ridges (Major Buxton), Margaret Wycherly (Mother York), Ward Bond (Ike Botkin), Noah Beery Jr. (Buck Lipscomb), June Lockhart (Rosie York), Dickie Moore (George York), Clem Bevans (Zede), Howard da Silva (Lem). *Other Cast Members:* Charles Trowbridge, Harvey Stephen, David Bruce, Charles Esmond, Joseph Sawyer, Pat Flaherty, Robert Porterfield, Erville Alderson
Filmed	at Warner Brothers Studios, Burbank, California
Running Time	134 minutes, black and white
Release Date	July 2, 1941

Other title: *Sergent York*

SYNOPSIS

In 1916 Alvin York is a mountain farmer scratching a living in Tennessee. After a hard day's work he goes drinking. The local pastor, Rosier Pile, tries to give him religion and get him off of his drinking binges. York meets Gracie Williams and falls in love with her. He tries to get some good land, so that he can marry her and still take care of his widowed mother. He works day and night to raise the money for the land, but luck works against him. By the time he gets the money together, the option has run out, and the land is sold to someone else. Furious, he leaves the house with his shotgun, but a bolt of lightning strikes the gun from his hand. For York it is an act of divine intervention. He becomes a devout church member. When war is declared, he believes strongly in the Bible's "Thou shalt not kill" admonishment and claims to be a conscientious objector. His claim is denied, and he is drafted.

At the training camp York impresses those around him with his shooting skills. Major Buxton, his superior officer, sees his sincerity in claiming to be a conscientious objector. He sends York home on a furlough.

When he returns, after reading a book on American history that Buxton gave him, York agrees to go to war. In France he single-handedly captures more than one hundred German soldiers.

He is awarded many military honors and is given boisterous receptions when he returns home. York refuses to capitalize on his fame, however, and returns to Tennessee.

Three Strangers (1946)

Director	Jean Negulesco
Producer	Wolfgang Reinhardt
Screenplay	John Huston and Howard Koch, from the story "Three Men and a Girl" by John Huston
Photographer	Arthur Edeson, A.S.C.
Art Director	Ted Smith
Film Editor	Alan Crosland
Sound	C. A. Riggs
Dialogue Director	Clifford Brooke
Set Decorations	Clarence Steensen
Technical Adviser	Fredrik T. Nyquist
Wardrobe	Milo Anderson
Makeup	Perc Westmore
Assistant Director	James McMahon
Cast	Sydney Greenstreet (Arbutny), Geraldine Fitzgerald (Crystal), Peter Lorre (Johnny West)
Filmed	at Warner Brothers Studios, Burbank, California
Running Time	92 minutes, black and white
Release Date	January 29, 1946
Other titles: *L'Idolo cinese*	

SYPNOSIS

On a street in London three strangers meet—Arbutny, a shady lawyer; Johnny West, an alcoholic small-time hood; and Crystal, a woman separated from a philandering husband. Crystal invites the two others to her apartment, where she shows them the statuette of Kwan Yin, a Chinese idol. Legend has it that at midnight on the eve of the Chinese New Year, the statue's eyes will open and a wish will be granted to three strangers. Arbutny says he would like to be admitted to an exclusive barrister's club; Johnny would like to own his own tavern; and Crystal would like her husband back.

At midnight the candles go out so they cannot see whether Kwan Yin has opened her eyes. Johnny produces a sweepstakes ticket and offers the other two a share of it. They sign the ticket with Kwan Yin's name. Perhaps they will have a bit of good luck.

Arbutny hears he is about to be exposed as an embezzler and contemplates suicide. Johnny is framed for the murder of a policeman and is sentenced to hang. Crystal's husband takes up with another woman. Johnny is saved by the deathbed confession of the real murderer.

Arbutny tries to sell his share of the sweepstakes ticket and use the money to replace what he has embezzled. Crystal resists, however, not wanting to break the statue's spell. Arbutny loses control, picks up the statue, fights with Crystal, and kills her by hitting her over the head with the statue. As Crystal dies, it is revealed that the sweepstakes ticket is a winner and now worth thirty thousand pounds. Arbutny goes completely insane and runs outside into the arms of the law. Realizing that if he tries to cash in the ticket he will be linked to Crystal's murder, Johnny burns it.

The Killers (1946)

Director	Robert Siodmak
Producer	Mark Hellinger
Screenplay	Anthony Veiller and John Huston (uncredited) from a story by Ernest Hemingway
Director of Photography	Woody Bredell, A.S.C.
Assistant to the Producer	Jules Buck
Film Editor	Arthur Hilton
Art Direction	Jack Otterson and Martin Obzina
Director of Sound	Bernard B. Brown
Set Decorations	Russell A. Gausman and E. R. Robinson
Makeup Director	Jack P. Pierce
Assistant Director	Melville Shyer
Special Photography	D. S. Horsley, A.S.C.
Music	Miklos Rozsa
Cast	Burt Lancaster (Swede), Ava Gardner (Kitty Collins), Edmond O'Brien (Riordan), Albert Dekker (Colfax), Sam Levene (Lubinsky). *Other Cast Members:* Charles D. Brown, Donald MacBride, Phil Brown, Charles McGraw, John Miljan, William Conrad, Queenie Smith, Garry Owen, Harry Hayden, Bill Walker, Vince Barnett, Jack Lambert, Jeff Corey, Wally Scott, Virginia Christine, Gabrielle Windsor, Rex Dale
Filmed	at locations in California and Universal Studios, Burbank, California
Running Time	100 minutes, black and white
Release Date	August 28, 1946

Other titles: *Les Tueurs, I Gangsters*

SYNOPSIS

Two professional killers come to a small New Jersey town to kill Swede, a boxer. The local police don't consider it a local matter and drop the case. Riordan, an insurance adjuster, finds a handkerchief with an embossed harp on the body, and it stirs a memory. His superiors give him permission to pursue the case, and Riordan sends out word through the underworld that he is interested in any information. He interviews the beneficiary of Swede's insurance policy, a maid in an Atlantic City hotel who once stopped him from leaping from a hotel window. He then interviews police lieutenant Lubinsky, a childhood friend of Swede's who once arrested him for robbery and whose wife was one of Swede's former girlfriends. Riordan learns that after a fight Swede became involved with gamblers and with a gangster named Colfax's girl, Kitty Collins, while Colfax was serving time in prison. When Kitty was caught with stolen jewelry, Swede took the fall and went to prison. When Swede got out Colfax planned a payroll holdup. In newspaper files, Riordan reads of the holdup and witnesses' reports that one of the robbers used as a mask a green handkerchief with an Irish harp on it. At the meeting to split up the take, Swede burst into the room and stole the booty from his colleagues. Swede next turned up working in a gas station in New Jersey. Colfax spotted him, and a couple of days later Swede was killed.

Riordan tracks down Colfax, now a successful building contractor in Pittsburgh, and Kitty, his respectable housewife. As Riordan speaks with her the professional killers burst in to kill him, but the police are ready. Riordan is saved. It then turns out that Kitty and Colfax had been partners in an elaborate double cross, where all of the other robbery participants were betrayed, leaving Kitty and Colfax free to go off with the loot.

The Stranger (1946)

Director	Orson Welles
Producer	S. P. Eagle
Assistant Directors	Jack Voglin and Gladys Hill
Screenplay	Anthony Veiller (credited), Orson Welles and John Huston (uncredited), from the original story by Victor Trivas and Decla Dunning
Director of Photography	Russell Metty
Editor	Ernest Nims
Art Director	Peggy Ferguson
Music	Bronislau Kaper
Cast	Edward G. Robinson (Inspector Wilson), Loretta Young (Mary Rankin née Longstreet), Orson Welles (Franz Kindler, alias Charles Rankin), Philip Merivale (Judge Longstreet), Konstantin Shayne (Konrad Meinike), Richard Long (Noah Longstreet), Byron Keith (Doctor Jeffrey Lawrence), Billy House (Mr. Potter), Martha Wentworth (Sara)

Filmography

Filmed   at International Pictures/RKO
Running Time   95 minutes, black and white
Release Date   July 10, 1946
Other titles: *Le Criminel, Lo Straniero*

SYNOPSIS

In postwar Germany the authorities release Nazi war criminal Konrad Meinike, hoping that he will lead them to his boss, Franz Kindler, a notorious war criminal. After taking a circuitous route Meinike ends up in a small New England town. All the time he is followed by Wilson, an investigator for the War Crimes Commission. Meinike makes contact with Kindler, who promptly kills him so that his cover will not be exposed. Kindler has become Charles Rankin, a college professor in the small town, a husband to the daughter of the prominent Judge Longstreet, and a passionate connoisseur of clocks, especially the bell tower clock in the local church.

Wilson learns about Rankin from the local general store owner. Posing as an antiques dealer, in time Wilson gains the confidence of the Longstreet family and is invited to dinner. Rankin launches into an anti-German tirade, convincing Wilson that Rankin is not his man.

That night Wilson calls his superior and tells him that he will be leaving the town the next day. In the middle of the night Wilson wakes up with a start. He makes a call and says, "Who but a Nazi would say that Karl Marx was not a German because he was a Jew?" This statement had slipped out of Rankin's mouth during their dinner conversation.

Wilson approaches Rankin's brother-in-law, Noah, and tells him who he is. He warns Noah of the danger his sister, Mary, is in, and solicits his help.

Beginning to feel trapped, Rankin confesses to his wife that he killed Meinike. He gives her a phony story, however, about Meinike wanting to blackmail him for something Rankin did when he was much younger.

That night Wilson arranges for Mary to come to her father's house, where he shows her, her father, and Noah pictures of the concentration camps after their liberation. He tells her that her husband is a Nazi criminal. Being so much in love with her husband, she cannot accept it and has trouble believing Wilson. She undergoes mental and emotional anguish.

Rankin, believing that he is losing his wife and that she will expose him, arranges her "accidental" death. He saws through one of the rungs on the ladder leading up to the clock tower and then gets her to go up the tower. She barely escapes alive.

When Rankin is shocked to see her at home, he confesses all. She tells him that if he wants to kill her, he should go ahead, but he should not put his hands on her. She gives him the fireplace poker.

Rankin flees to the clock tower, where Wilson confronts him. After a struggle Rankin is wounded and staggers out onto the ledge of the clock. The mechanical figures roll through as they do every hour. One, an avenging angel, has a sword held out in a horizontal position. Rankin is run through, and he and the statue fall to the ground below.

167

EARLY WRITING CAREER: UNPRODUCED PROJECTS

Following are four synopses representing John Huston's early work when he was under contract to Universal in the early 1930s. The synopses come from *Universal Pictures, Library Properties, Synopsis and Descriptive Data*, deposited at the Academy of Motion Picture Arts and Sciences Library. In these instances John Huston's name is indicated in Universal's records. The actual scripts and treatments for these films, and some others, are discussed in chapter 16, "Screenplays in Collections."

In some instances, for example, *Steel*, a number of different screenwriters worked on different treatments and scripts. The projects below were unproduced, but their synopses should provide some information on Huston's thinking in developing various stories.

Steel (Men of Steel, Steel Men, Steel Man. . .) (December 18, 1931–February 12, 1932)*

Fighting Irish foreman Liam Jones is as strong as the steel with which he works. He drives his men until month by month they continue to break records for output. At a wedding of one of his men, Jones meets sensuous Polish beauty Della Kublik, a tart from nearby Pittsburgh. He becomes involved in an affair with her that absorbs his strength and all of his attention. His work begins to fall off, and several times he is on the verge of losing his job. One night, after the twenty-mile journey to Pittsburgh to see Della, he finds her with another man. Jones threatens to kill her for cheating on him, but he marries her instead.

U-Boat (June 7, 1932)**

Ludwig Erlau, scion of a great family of shipbuilders, and his boyhood friend, Karl Strom, are fellow cadets in the submarine corps. Elsie, Strom's sister, idolizes Erlau, but he thinks of her only as a child.

Following the outbreak of World War I the two pals receive commissions and almost immediately proceed upon their first voyage aboard the U-10. Their first victim is an ironical indication of the destructive mockery of war, for it is a beautiful four-masted schooner that had been designed years ago by Erlau's own grandfather. Their next victim, a tanker, whose cargo is ignited by the sub's shell fire, spouts burning oil into the sea. It forms a lake of fire, and the U-10 submerges when pursued by a fleet of enemy destroyers. A depth bomb lodges on the submarine's deck but fails to go off, being timed for greater depth, and the submarine manages to make her narrow escape.

---

*There are numerous versions of this project by various authors. See chapter 16 under *Steel*. The Huston version is entitled *Steel Men*. "This story is incomplete. It is a treatment of *Steel* stories found in File no. 5972 and 6030."

**In Gerald Pratley's *The Cinema of John Huston* (South Brunswick, N.J.: A. S. Barnes, 1977, 27), Huston recollects working for Goldwyn Studios for a short period of time on a project "about German submarines." It is possible that Huston didn't remember that it was a project at Universal.

Three months later Strom and Erlau return to base, shocked by their experiences. Erlau perceives that Elsie is flowering into young womanhood and is attracted to her. The men's leave is short, however, and soon the friends are obliged to go to sea again.

The crippled submarine sinks to the bottom of the sea after being taken by surprise by a disguised "Q" ship, mistaken for a harmless freighter. Strom is mortally wounded. When the "Q" ship drops depth charges her captain is not deceived by the submarine commander's trick of releasing a large quantity of oil to give the appearance of the U-Boat's having been destroyed. To Erlau's horror his commander finally manages to trick the "Q" ship's captain into this belief by shooting the wounded Strom through a torpedo tube and sending him to the surface. After a voyage fraught with terrible hardship the crippled sub makes her way back to base.

On the night before he is scheduled to go to sea again, this time as the commander of his own sub, Erlau impulsively asks Elsie to marry him. Although there is no time for the ceremony, Elsie gives herself to him.

The following morning Erlau's sub embarks on the suicidal task of sinking enemy munitions ships, miraculously escaping destruction. Later, in a vicious encounter with British men-of-war, the sub with all on board sinks to the bottom of a harbor. Her engines are dead, and the crew is without any hope of rescue. His sub is well stocked with food, so Erlau orders a banquet of death, an epicurean feast. Upon the threshold of death the crew members toast each other and the Fatherland with red wine and sing a rollicking student's song.

The Hero (August 24, 1932–September 2, 1932)

Samuel Bruhl is a floorwalker in a large department store. To all appearances he is a lurid member of the august brotherhood, but underlying his imperiousness is an inherent timidity. He is almost afraid of his shadow and any kind of opposition reduces him to trembling servility. Bruhl is engaged to Miss Aubrey of the Jewelry Department.

Bruhl's entire world is about to collapse when he discovers that he bears a remarkable resemblance to gangster George (Shoe-Scar) Clinnigan, who has been taken to the hospital after a gang shooting. Bruhl, afraid that he will be mistaken for the gangster upon his release from the hospital, purchases a revolver. His belief that he will be put on the spot by Clinnigan's enemies and his thoughts of gangster prominence change his entire demeanor. He begins talking out of the side of his mouth, adopts a furtive manner, and is rude to customers. Finally he is discharged. He then shocks his adoring fiancée by announcing that they are going to honeymoon in Atlantic City without benefit of clergy. En route to the station he stops to buy "slugs" for his gun.

Clinnigan is released from the hospital and is killed by gangsters, but when they see Bruhl in an Atlantic City hotel they believe their murder plan has miscarried. The gangsters invade Bruhl's room intending to kill him, but in his role of gangster he has anticipated such a move. He ambushes them and kills all five of them in a terrific gun battle.

When he finally recovers consciousness in the hospital he finds that he is the hero of the hour. He is given the keys to the city, and he and Aubrey are married on the steps of the city hall, with the mayor officiating at the ceremony.

Jack of Diamonds (October 28, 1932)

Tilt Joplin is a big-time gambler. One night Joplin wins fifty thousand dollars when he draws the Jack of Diamonds to a straight flush. That night he encounters a bum whose face bears an amazing resemblance to the jack of diamonds. Believing that Jack, the bum, is responsible for his run of good luck, Joplin practically adopts him, and the two become inseparable. Because of his association with Jack, Joplin wins a fortune.

Joplin begins to spend his money on Icey Merman, a gold-digging dancer. Jack tries to warn him that Icey is mercenary, but Joplin refuses to listen. When he loses everything he has, Icey leaves him.

Joplin goes on a downward path and becomes a derelict. One night he again encounters Jack, and the two begin to build up a fortune together.

HUSTON AS AN ACTOR

Huston began his career in the movies as an actor. In addition, he was an actor on the stage. When he became a director, he also acted in some of his films. His most interesting role was the uncredited man in the white suit at the beginning of *The Treasure of the Sierra Madre*. Until the end of his life he acted in films, some of them under the direction of other directors. A viewing of all the films in which he acted reveals the emergence of a carefully crafted Huston persona, and the roles appeared to be written for him. Included here are probably his most famous acting roles, Noah Cross in *Chinatown* and Pa Kegan in *Winter Kills*. A side of Huston's own character comes out in *Chinatown* (in many ways he played himself) and in *Winter Kills*—an underrated film based on the novel by Richard Condon, who also wrote *Prizzi's Honor*.

Chinatown (1974)

Director	Roman Polanski
Producer	Robert Evans
Screenplay	Robert Towne
Director of Photography	John A. Alonzo, A.S.C.
Associate Producer	C. O. Erickson
Music	Jerry Goldsmith
Costume Designer	Anthea Sylbert
Film Editor	Sam O'Steen
Production Designer	Richard Sylbert
Assistant Director	Howard W. Koch Jr.
Unit Production Manager	C. O. Erickson
Art Directors	W. Stewart Campbell and Larry Jost
Cast	Jack Nicholson (J. J. Gittes), Faye Dunaway (Evelyn Mulwray), John Huston (Noah Cross), Perry Lopez (Escobar), John

	Hillerman (Yelburton), Darrell Zwerling (Hollis Mulwray), Diane Ladd (Ida Sessions), Roy Jenson (Mulvihill), Roman Polanski (Man with Knife), Belinda Palmer (Katherine)
Filmed	at Paramount Studios
Running Time	131 minutes, Technicolor
Release Date	June 20, 1974

SYNOPSIS

In Los Angeles J. J. Gittes runs a private detective agency and spends much of his time snooping on wayward husbands and other indiscretions. Ida Sessions, posing as Mrs. Mulwray, hires Gittes to investigate her husband's affair with a young girl. Gittes and his minions take photographs of Hollis Mulwray with the young girl, Katherine. At one time Gittes sees Mulwray examining the dry riverbed of the Los Angeles River, and Gittes questions a small boy who rides by on a white horse. He gives Mrs. Mulwray the photos, which then appear in a local scandal sheet.

The real Mrs. Evelyn Mulwray appears in his office and threatens to sue him for disparaging her husband's reputation. Gittes investigates Hollis Mulwray and learns that he is a water engineer. Mulwray opposes his former partner, Noah Cross, and his plan to build dams and divert water from Los Angeles to irrigate the land that Cross and his associates have been buying up cheaply, using the names of poor people in retirement homes. Hollis Mulwray is found dead, drowned in one of the canals, and Gittes has his nostrils sliced by one of Cross's gangsters (Roman Polanski). Ida Sessions, who had posed as Mrs. Mulwray, is also murdered.

Gittes discovers that Noah Cross is behind all of the murders. In addition, it turns out that he raped his own daughter, Evelyn Mulwray, and that Katherine, the young girl who was purported to be Mulwray's mistress, was really Cross's daughter and the daughter/sister of Evelyn Mulwray.

Gittes agrees to get Evelyn and Katherine out of the country. The trail leads to Chinatown, where Cross confronts them and demands control of Katherine. Evelyn wounds him. Then she and the girl drive off. The police shoot after them, killing Evelyn, as the young girl sits next to her, screaming.

Winter Kills (1979)

Director	William Richert
Producer	Fred Caruso
Executive Producers	Leonard J. Goldberg and Robert Sterling
Screenplay	William Richert, based on the book by Richard Condon
Director of Photography	Vilmos Zsigmond
Music	Maurice Jarre
Film Editor	David Bretherton, A.C.E.
Costumes	Robert De Mora
Production Designer	Robert Boyle
Art Director	Norman Newberry

John Huston

Cast   Jeff Bridges (Nick Kegan), John Huston (Pa
                         Kegan), Anthony Perkins (John Cerruti), Eli
                         Wallach (Joe Diamond), Sterling Hayden (Z.
                         K. Dawson), Dorothy Malone (Emma Kegan),
                         Tomas Milian (Frank Mayo), Belinda Bauer
                         (Yvette Malone), Ralph Meeker (Gameboy
                         Baker), Toshiro Mifune (Keith), Richard
                         Boone (Keifetz), Elizabeth Taylor (Lola
                         Comante), Irving Selbst (Irving Mentor),
                         Tomas Milian (Frank Mayo)
Filmed   at Avco Embassy
Running Time   96 minutes, Technicolor
Release Date   May 15, 1979
Other titles: *Rebu per un assassino*

SYNOPSIS

Nick Kegan—a man who grew up in the shadow of his powerful tycoon father, Pa Kegan, and who still has emotional scars from the assassination of his brother, the president—is working on one of his father's oil-drilling ships. His father's assistant, Keifetz, arrives by helicopter and has with him a terribly injured man who is close to death. Before he dies he gasps that he was one of the men who killed Nick's brother, and the rifle is hidden in an office in Philadelphia, where the assassination took place.

In Philadelphia with the help of another aide of his father and police captain, Heller, Nick discovers the gun. As they leave, a woman on a bicycle comes by with a child in the backseat. She pops the bubble gum she is chewing, and simultaneously the aide and Heller are shot dead. In a panic Nick runs across the street to call his father, and while on the phone he watches the car he had arrived in being driven away.

Nick then goes to his father's immense estate, where his father is surrounded by flunkies, political pals, and beautiful girls. His father tells him to see Z. K. Dawson, a person who hates the family and may be involved in the conspiracy.

Surrounded by Dawson's private army of tanks, Nick listens to Dawson deny that he had anything to do with the killing. Dawson tells him to see Ray Doty.

Nick goes back to New York to visit his girlfriend, Yvette Malone, a magazine editor. He gets a call from his father, who informs him that both Keifetz and the other witness to the assassin's confession on the ship are dead.

At Ray Doty's chicken ranch, Nick learns that Joe Diamond was hired to supply the assassin, a disgruntled marine named Willie Arnold. Nick goes back to New York.

While in his spacious apartment, Nick is attacked by a black maid. The butler saves him. Nick then meets Yvette and asks her to set up a meeting with someone big in the mob. She runs off, excited by the prospect of a big story for her magazine. When Nick returns to the apartment his father is there. His father tells him that he knows everything because the table in the restaurant was bugged by

172

John Cerruti, his chief of industrial intelligence. Yvette calls and indicates that a meeting has been set up in Cleveland with Irving Mentor. His father gives him a blackjack to protect himself.

In Cleveland Nick meets Irving Mentor in a restaurant. He gives him money, and Mentor tells him that Joe Diamond's contact came from Gameboy Baker. He then informs Nick about the different people involved in various aspects of the assassination. As Nick leaves the restaurant he sees the same woman who was on the bicycle just before the Philadelphia killings. Once Nick is outside, the restaurant blows up.

Nick then goes to see his father, who is in the hospital having his biannual blood change and being nursed by beautiful girls. His father says that he has arranged a meeting with Frank Mayo, a big shot in the Mafia who is in prison. Nick meets Mayo in a secure police bus. Mayo tells him that the man responsible for the assassination is Vinnie Blanik, a corrupt union official who was jailed by the president.

Afterward Nick goes to his girlfriend's magazine but learns that she doesn't work there. When he goes to her apartment building the doorman informs him that she doesn't live there. He returns to his apartment to finds Keifetz resurrected from the dead. Keifetz suggests that Nick see Cerruti for information about Yvette.

Cerruti tells him that Frank Mayo was responsible for the assassination. Lola Comante, who got girls for the president, was a go-between for Frank Mayo. Mayo gave the president an enormous contribution, Cerruti says, so the president would restore the casinos in Cuba. In order to get more information from Cerutti, Nick breaks his arms with the blackjack that his father gave him. Cerutti swears that Pa Kegan caused his son's death. He also tells Nick that if he wants to find Yvette he should go to the morgue.

Nick confronts his father, who alleges that Cerutti with his electronic empire is the real power in the whole story. He finally confesses that he is the one behind the murder of his son, because the president suddenly started to act independently and to shut his father out of the power that comes with the presidency. Keifetz bursts in, and in an ensuing fight Nick kills him. Pa Kegan runs out to the balcony and falls over the edge. Nicks sees him clinging to an enormous American flag. He loses his grip and falls to his death.

V
Annotated Bibliography

John Huston's involvement in the movie industry was extensive, as a screenwriter, director, and actor. The various sections of the bibliography attempt to cover all of these areas, including information on both realized and unrealized projects.

1950

ARTICLES

Agee, James. "Undirectable Director." *Life* 29 (September 18): 128–30.
    One of the early famous pieces on Huston in which Agee praises the director. Some feel that Huston was being "canonized prematurely" and that Agee's writing reflected in part his desire to work with Huston on *The African Queen*. The piece has been anthologized widely in Agee, *Agee on Film;* Cooper, *Perspectives on John Huston;* Studlar and Desser, *Reflections in a Male Eye;* and Denby, *Awake in the Dark.*

Lambert, Gavin. "Writer and Director: *The Wooden Horse* and *The Asphalt Jungle.*" *Sight & Sound* 19, no. 7 (November): 286–88.
    An assessment of the creative contributions of the scenarist and director in film adaptations of two popular novels. This article contains a valuable and penetrating analysis of Huston's work on *The Asphalt Jungle* (1950).

Lightman, Herb A. "Realism with a Master's Touch." *American Cinematographer* 31, no. 8 (August): 271+.
    Discusses cinematographer Hal Rosson's use of the wide-angle lens in *The Asphalt Jungle* (1950).

1952

ARTICLES

Huston, John. "The African Queen." *Theatre Arts* 36, no. 2 (February): 48+.
Huston discusses production problems and modifications of C. S. Forester's novel.

Mage, David A. "The Way John Huston Works Accounts in Large Measure for the Integrity of His Pictures." *Films in Review* (October): 394–98.
Second assistant director on *Moulin Rouge* (1953) recounts the Huston technique.

Positif, Revue Mensuelle de Cinéma, no. 3 (July–August).
The first special periodical devoted to Huston, this issue is fairly rare in the United States, as most libraries did not pick up a subscription to the periodical until later. Two copies are in the Huston Archives at the Academy of Motion Picture Arts and Sciences (AMPAS) Library, other academic libraries are in the process of acquiring copies, and a copy is also available at the British Film Institute. In this issue Huston's career is discussed with some seriousness. Articles cover *The Asphalt Jungle* (1950), *The Red Badge of Courage* (1951), *The African Queen* (1952), *The Treasure of the Sierra Madre* (1948), and *We Were Strangers* (1949). There is a piece by Jacques Demeure on Bogart and Huston. Also included are two interviews with Huston. Inserted into the issue is a filmography, biography, and bibliography. Many of the pieces in this issue are reprinted in the anthology *John Huston, Collection dirigée* (Dossier Positif Rivages, Paris, Editions Rivages, Collection Positif-Rivages, no. 2, 1988, 191 pp.), edited by Gilles Ciment. This anthology is also not readily available in most libraries, but it can be obtained through interlibrary loan. *Positif* has certainly been one of Huston's champions throughout the years. Ciment includes an excellent "Biofilmographie" (pp. 180–91) that is comprehensive in its coverage of Huston in the theater, as a screenwriter, an actor, and a director. Page 191 lists "Autre textes sur John Huston dans *Positif.*"

BOOKS

Reisz, Karel. "Substance into Shadow." In *The Cinema,* edited by Roger Manvell, 188–205. New York: Penguin Books.
The problems in adapting *The Maltese Falcon* (1941) are compared with film adaptations of *To Have and Have Not* (1945), *The Breaking Point* (1950), *Intruder in the Dust* (1949), and *A Walk in the Sun* (1946).

1953

Ross, Lillian. *Picture.* New York: Rinehart, 258 pp. (Reprints—New York: Dolphin Books, 1962; London: Gollancz, 1953. Italian edition: *Processo a Hollywood,* Milan, 1956.)

    One of the most famous accounts on the making of a Hollywood film, *The Red Badge of Courage* (1951), and perhaps a classic in the perennial debate over artistic and commercial conflict in the movie industry. "There's so much about pictures that has nothing to do with art"—Gottfried Reinhardt (p. 113). The book originally appeared as a series of articles in the *New Yorker* (May–June 1952). Ross gained the confidence of the moviemakers and followed the film through its various permutations. The book covers much territory about the making of the film, Huston's methods of filming and screenwriting ("When I put pencil to paper, I find myself sketching . . . I can't write alone—I get too lonely. I have to dictate. . . ." [p. 74]), and his personality ("John is like a race horse. You must keep him in a good mood all the time. John is a charmer, you know, but he is really very forlorn, a very lonely man. He is out of touch with human emotions. . . ." [p. 113]). Ross also documents the conflicts among Huston, Louis B. Mayer (who never wanted the film to be made), Dore Schary, and Gottfried Reinhardt. Accusations are made that Huston walked away from the film and did not defend its "integrity." The book includes information on Humphrey Bogart and how he liked working with Huston. "I like to work with John. The monster is stimulating. Offbeat kind of mind. Off center. He's brilliant and unpredictable. Never dull. When I work with John, I think about acting." (p. 149).

1953

ARTICLE

Bogart, Humphrey. "Beat the Devil." *Look* 17 (September 22): 128–29+.
    The actor's own story about the filming of *Beat the Devil* (1954).

BOOK

Nichtenhauser, Adolf, Marie Coleman, and David S. Ruhe. *Films in Psychiatry, Psychology & Mental Health.* Medical Audio-Visual Institute of the Association of American Medical Colleges. New York: Health Education Council, 269 pp.
    Discusses *Let There Be Light* (1946), pp. 151–55. Article includes production and distribution data; content description; appraisal of content, presentation, and effectiveness; and utilization.

1954

ARTICLE

Houston, Penelope. "The Ambassadors." *Sight & Sound* (April): 178.
Huston's work in Europe is discussed in an article dealing with the deterioration of the work of many of America's best directors once they left Hollywood.

BOOK

Viertel, Peter. *White Hunter, Black Heart.* London: W. H. Allen, 319 pp.
The novel is a *roman à clef* based on Huston's asking Viertel to help him get the screenplay of *The African Queen* (1952) in shape for shooting. (Viertel also worked with Huston on *We Were Strangers,* 1949). The plot revolves around Huston's desire to go to Africa to hunt elephants. Viertel only slightly disguises the characters, with John Wilson as Huston. The novel is successful and important in depicting the "true" Huston, with all his good and bad points. Viertel also gives good insights into Huston's philosophy, themes, screenwriting and revision techniques, directing, and relationships with the people who worked with him on pictures.

1955

ARTICLE

Gallez, Douglas. "Patterns in Wartime Documentaries." *Quarterly of Films, Radio & TV* 10, no. 2 (Winter): 125+.
Huston's wartime trilogy is discussed. An analytical survey of the best U.S. wartime documentaries, in which Huston's three are considered in relation to, among others, *The Battle of Midway* (1942, John Ford)*, The Fighting Lady* (1944, Louis de Rochemont), *The Memphis Belle* (1944, William Wyler), and Frank Capra's *Why We Fight* series (1942–45). The author feels that only Huston and Capra followed true documentary tradition. Their social consciousness evoked compassion as they attempted to educate the public on the question of war.

BOOK

Borde, Raymond, and Etienne Chaumeton. *Panorama du film noir américain.* Paris: Editions du Minuit, 279 pp.
This study of film noir is a classic, published a decade after the war. For many French critics, the forties were Huston's most creative period, and the

1956

book reserves respectful space for *The Maltese Falcon* (1941) and *The Asphalt Jungle* (1950), with a brief reference to *Key Largo,* 1948. *The Maltese Falcon* is cited as the first authentic example of this new film tendency, and the study singles out Humphrey Bogart's portrayal of Sam Spade and the strong performances of all supporting actors, notably Sydney Greenstreet. *The Asphalt Jungle* is praised for the careful portraiture of all the members of the gang and the fatality of the failure of each man's dream.

1956

ARTICLES

Alpert, Hollis, "Quest of Captain Ahab" (p. 28), and Arthur Knight, "The Director" (pp. 29–30). *Saturday Review* 39 (June 9).
    The cover story, with Huston's picture on front cover, is in two parts; a double article. Includes an insert of actors in the film *Moby Dick* (1956), their photographs, and a statement about the characters.

Barnes, P. "The Director on Horseback." *Quarterly of Film, Radio & Television* 10, no. 3 (Spring): 281–87.
    Huston's Hollywood films compared to his later films. The British film writer suggests John Huston's directing quality declined because he made too many films away from the United States.

Hill, Derek. "*Moby Dick* Sets New Style in Color Photography." *American Cinematographer* 37, no. 9 (September): 534–35+.
    On Oswald Morris's cinematography.

1957

ARTICLE

Hawkins, Robert F. "No *Farewell to Arms* in Italy; World War I Carnage is Reenacted for Movie of Hemingway Book." *New York Times,* May 12. (Reprinted in *New York Times Encyclopedia of Film, 1952–1957,* edited by Gene Brown, New York, Times Books, 1984.)
    On the making of the film on location, and comments on the falling-out between Huston and Selznick.

1958

ARTICLE

Grenier, C. "Huston at Fontainebleau." *Sight & Sound* 27, no. 6 (Autumn): 280–85.
> Grenier visits the shooting of *Roots of Heaven* (1958).

1959

ARTICLE

Archer, Eugene. "John Huston and the Hemingway Tradition in American Film." *Film Culture* 19:66–101.
> Perhaps the longest study in English of Huston's career to this date. Archer analyzes the influence of the Hemingway persona, ethos, and style on Huston's cinema, particularly the early work, pointing out the masculine strengths above all of *The Maltese Falcon* (1941), *Across the Pacific* (1942), *The Treasure of the Sierra Madre* (1948), and *The Asphalt Jungle* (1950). Strangely, Archer does not refer to the uncredited script Huston wrote for Robert Siodmak's *The Killers* (1946), but he does mention the preliminary work done on *A Farewell to Arms* (1957), which Huston left because of his conflict with David O. Selznick (cf. the AMPAS John Huston Collection Production File and Script Material on *Across the River and into the Trees,* an unrealized project). The article includes useful and detailed analyses *of The Maltese Falcon, The Treasure of the Sierra Madre, The Asphalt Jungle, The African Queen* (1952), and *Moby Dick* (1956). The critic finds the last an honorable failure, ambitious in scope and intention, but ultimately lacking in dramatic intensity. He attributes this deficiency in part to Gregory Peck's inadequacies as Ahab and in part to Huston's tendency to back away from the shipboard drama.

1960

PAMPHLET

Allais, Jean-Claude. *John Huston.* (Premier Plan series, no. 6.) Lyon: Société d'Etudes, de Recherches et du Documentation Cinématographiques (Serdoc).
> This early summary of Huston's career as a director takes us from *The Maltese Falcon* (1941) to *Roots of Heaven* (1958). Allais is a Huston enthusiast who does not see a decline in his career following *The Asphalt Jungle* (1950). He discovers several lines of thematic consistency in the better films

of the 1950s, notably *The Red Badge of Courage* (1951), *The African Queen* (1952), *Beat the Devil* (1954), and *Moby Dick* (1956). Allais particularly admires Huston's sense of the absurd in both existence and human nature, and his "Homeric laughter." He singles out *Moby Dick* as the director's masterpiece (to that point), praising the boldness in adapting that unwieldy classic and the interpretation of the story as an allegory of blasphemy.

BOOK

Leirens, Jean. *Le Cinema et la crise de notre temps.* Septième Art. Paris: Editions du Cerf, 133 pp.

This book may be read either as an existential guide to cinema or as a cinematic guide to existentialism. Leirens takes four basic concepts central to existentialist thought (alienation, ennui, solitude, and the notion of the absurd) and applies the last to the cinema of Huston, who is the subject of chapter 4. Like several other French critics, Leirens sees Hustonian heroes as dreamers who are driven by hopes of adventure and fortune and doomed to failure. Aware of the odds against them, they are braced for defeat and can accept loss with good grace, even greeting their failure with laughter. The author singles out *The Treasure of the Sierra Madre* (1948) and *Beat the Devil* (1954) for detailed analysis. Leirens suggests that Huston's affinity with those who risk all and shrug off their losses with a laugh can be read as a mockery of the cult of success in American culture. In this formula the loser is more worthy of study than the winner.

1961

ARTICLES

Alpert, Hollis. "*Saturday Review* Goes to the Movies: Arthur Miller, Screenwriter." Saturday Review 4 (February 4): 27+.
  Discussion of the book, the movie, and Miller's experience in the making of *The Misfits* (1961).

Bachmann, Gideon. "Eli Wallach on *The Misfits.*" Film, no. 29 (Summer): 13–15.
  The actor discusses the making of the film.

McIntyre, A. T. "Making *The Misfits,* or Waiting for Monroe, or Notes from Olympus." *Esquire* 55 (March) 74–81.
  Chronicle of the shooting on location.

Weatherby, W. J. "*The Misfits:* Epic or Requiem?" *Saturday Review* 4 (February 4): 26–27.
  The feature writer for the *Manchester Guardian* spent several weeks covering the filming of *The Misfits* (1961).

1963

BOOK

Goode, James. *The Story of* The Misfits. Indianapolis: Bobbs-Merrill, 331 pp. (Reprint—*The Making of* The Misfits. New York, Limelight Editions, 1986.) An account of making the film.

PROGRAM

"The Films of John Huston." Introduction by David Stewart Hall. Dartmouth Daily Film Program, Fall–Winter, 14 pp.

Program of one of the many retrospectives mounted in John Huston's honor; includes a substantial body of his work as director and writer up until that time. Each film reviewed includes brief notes and partial cast. This particular program is among the personal papers of John Huston now housed at the Academy of Motion Picture Arts and Sciences Library (Beverly Hills). The films viewed were *The Amazing Dr. Clitterhouse* (1938), *Across the Pacific* (1942), *In This Our Life* (1942), *The Asphalt Jungle* (1950), *The Kremlin Letter* (1970), *Jezebel* (1938), *We Were Strangers* (1949), *Dr. Ehrlich's Magic Bullet* (1940), *Moulin Rouge* (1953), *High Sierra* (1941, as writer), *The African Queen* (1952), *Beat the Devil* (1954), *Sergeant York* (1941, as writer), *Moby Dick* (1956), *Three Strangers* (1946, as writer), *Roots of Heaven* (1958), *The Barbarian and the Geisha* (1958), *The Misfits* (1961), *Heaven Knows, Mr. Allison* (1957), and *The Unforgiven* (1960).

1964

ARTICLE

Ardagh, John. "Huston in Eden." *Sight & Sound* 33, no. 4 (Autumn): 173+.

On the making of *The Bible* (1966). Huston comments on filming the American-Italian production in Rome.

BOOK

Jacob, Gilles. *Le Cinéma moderne. Part II: L'homme et la société*. Lyon: Serdoc, 232 pp.

Chapter 4, "Pour une morale du dérisoire" (pp. 93–100), is devoted to Huston. The author follows the line taken by Leirens (see under 1960) in placing Huston in an existentialist tradition, even though his heroes are men of action, not contemplation. An essential link between the varied works is the self-mocking humor, represented by bursts of often sardonic laughter. Huston earns praise for his appreciation of the absurd. Jacob finds the best of Huston in the line that extends from *The Maltese Falcon* (1941) to *The Asphalt Jungle* (1950) and regrets what he sees as a decline in quality in many of Huston's films of the fifties. Jacob does, however, acknowledge what he sees as splendid exceptions, such as *Beat the Devil* (1954) and *The Misfits* (1961), so full of simultaneous striving and disillusion that one feels that the characters have ultimately realized themselves in their efforts, rather than having to admit defeat.

1965

ARTICLES

Bachmann, Gideon. "How I Make Films: An Interview with John Huston." *Film Quarterly* 19, no. 1:3–13.
    This interview was conducted on the set of *The Bible* (1966), while Huston, as Noah and director, was filming the sequence of the animals going into the ark. The discussion centers almost entirely on the development of the script and Huston's ideal of working with just one writer. Bachmann provides some interesting revelations. For example, Huston says he wants to continue working on *The Man Who Would Be King* (1975) once *The Bible* is over. He also defines *Moby Dick* (1956) as a "great blasphemy." Huston admits that his choice of literary material (Hammett, Melville, Kipling) does indicate a preference (a masculine world of adventure and challenge) and an outlook, but he insists he would never impose his own view on a literary work. Ideally he tries to figure out the author's intent and remain faithful.

Ross, Lillian. "Our Far-Flung Correspondents: *The Bible* in Dinocitta." *New Yorker* 41 (September 25): 185–212.
    The on-the-set account of John Huston's *The Bible* (1966).

BOOK

Nolan, William F. *John Huston: King Rebel.* Los Angeles: Sherbourne Press, 247 pp.
    A breezy Hollywood biography, weighted more toward anecdote and legend and less toward achievement and art. It begins with the death of Walter Huston in 1950 and ends with the preparations for *The Bible* (1966) and Huston contemplating the idea of *The Man Who Would Be King* (1975). The portrait of Huston is that of the gentleman dilettante who sees filmmaking as a means of travel, enjoyment, and associating with like-minded companions. Nolan promotes the image of the Huston circus in such films as *The African Queen* (1952), *Beat the Devil* (1954), and *The Night of the Iguana* (1964). A filmography and bibliography are included.

1966

BOOKS

Benayoun, Robert. *John Huston: Textes et propos de John Huston, extraits de découpages, panorama critique, témoignages, filmographie, théâtrographie, bibliographie, documents iconographiques.* Cinéma d'aujourd'hui, no. 44. Paris: Seghers, 188 pp.

Benayoun's monograph was the first full-length study of Huston in any language and covered his work up to *The Bible* (1966). It includes a brief biography, chapters on each film, an eclectic selection of passages from other critics, and statements from Huston himself, taken from interviews, on filmmaking. A few extracts from screenplays, a filmography, and a bibliography complete the text. See revised edition under 1985.

Buache, Freddy. *John Huston.* (Premier Plan, no. 41.) Lyon: Société d'Etudes, de Recherches et du Documentation Cinématographiques (Serdoc), 130 pp.

This comprehensive anthology of major reviews, culled from a variety of French journals, covers all Huston's films up to *The Night of the Iguana* (1964). Associated with many of the critics of *Positif,* who are largely Huston enthusiasts, Buache also includes those critics antagonistic to the director who lament his shifts of direction following *The Asphalt Jungle* (1950). These include Georges Sadoul, Eric Rohmer, and Jacques Doniol-Valcroze, who pass negative judgments on *Moby Dick* (1956). Buache himself writes on this and all films since and finds strengths and ambitions realized in *Freud: The Secret Passion* (1962) and *The Night of the Iguana,* which came under critical fire on both sides of the Atlantic.

1967

ARTICLE

Barsness, John. "A Question of Standard." *Film Quarterly* 21, no. 1 (Fall): 32–37.

Contrasts *High Noon* (1952) and *The Misfits* (1961) as westerns.

1969

ARTICLES

Koningsberger, Hans. "From Book to Film via John Huston." *Film Quarterly* 22, no. 3 (Spring): 2–4.

1971

The author's reactions to Huston's adaptation of Koningsberger's novel *A Walk with Love and Death* (1969).

Taylor, John Russell. "John Huston and the Figure in the Carpet." *Sight & Sound* 38, no. 2 (Spring): 70–73.

A balanced look at Huston's work following the release of *Reflections in a Golden Eye* (1967). Huston's "cool, noncommittal distance" may be the key to his "aesthetic abstraction" not only visually, but in his scripts. Taylor argues that Huston in each film is "meeting and matching each problem as it comes up."

1971

ARTICLE

Villelaur, Anne. "*The African Queen* de John Huston." In *Dossiers du cinéma. Films I.* Paris: Casterman, 4 pp.

Commentary on the film, with a biographical sketch, synopsis, critical opinion, bibliography, and credits.

BOOK

The New York Times Film Reviews: A One-Volume Selection, 1913–1970. New York: Arno Press, 495 pp.

Chosen from the seven-volume set with an introduction and six original essays by George Amberg. Includes *The Asphalt Jungle* (1950), *Beat the Devil* (1954), *The Maltese Falcon* (1941), *The Red Badge of Courage* (1951), and *The Treasure of the Sierra Madre* (1948).

1972

ARTICLE

Robinson, David. "The Innocent Bystander." *Sight & Sound* 42, no. 1 (Winter): 20–21.

Notes during the production of *The Mackintosh Man* (1973). On the set, John Huston talks about his previous films and how he selects actors for his films.

BOOKS

McArthur, Colin. *Underworld USA.* Cinema One Series, no. 20. New York: Viking Press, 176 pp.

Chapter 6 is devoted to Huston, who is presented as a puzzle because of the eclectic nature of his themes and genres and who hardly fits into the definition of an auteur. Only the films of the first decade (the film noir period) are discussed, up until *The Asphalt Jungle* (1950). McArthur's pattern is objective and pessimistic. A consistency is discovered in the following formula: "In the films of this period effort is futile, betrayal is likely, failure is certain." The films most admired by McArthur are *The Maltese Falcon* (1941), *The Treasure of the Sierra Madre* (1948), and *The Asphalt Jungle*. The last is singled out for its humanization of the characters and the director's sympathy for the gang members.

Selznick, David O. *Memo from David O. Selznick.* Edited by Rudy Behlmer. New York: The Viking Press, 518 pp.

With an introduction by S. N. Behrman, includes selections from the memos to John Huston regarding *A Farewell to Arms* (1957), including excerpts from the "famous" sixteen-page memo of March 19, 1957, in which Huston left the production. This memo is now located in the Selznick papers at the University of Texas at Austin.

1973

ARTICLES

Benoit, C. "Pat Garrett et Billy the Kid. . . . U.S.A." *"Pat Garrett et Billy the Kid. Juge et hors-la-loi.* En deux westerns l'itinéraire des U.S.A." *Jeune Cinéma* 74 (November): 34–43.

Explores tendencies in the American western, as exemplified by *Pat Garrett and Billy the Kid* and *The Life and Times of Judge Roy Bean* (1972).

"Cinematographer Conrad Hall." *American Film Institute Dialogue on Film* 3, no. 1 (October): 1–24.

An interview with Conrad Hall, cinematographer on *Fat City* (1972), held at the American Film Institute as part of six cinematography seminars at the AFI's Center for Advanced Film Studies. Included is the seminar's transcript printed in full.

Gleason, Ralph. "The Mackintosh Man." *Rolling Stone* (October 11): 9.

Follows closely the book's (*Freedom Trap,* 1973) theme that the individual man is trapped into thinking that each successive breakout in life will lead to a place of freedom.

Kunert, Arnold R. "Ray Bradbury on Hitchcock, Huston and Other Magic of the Screen." *Take One* 3, no. 11 (September): 15–23.

Ray Bradbury talks about his work as a scriptwriter, his collaboration with John Huston (*Moby Dick,* 1956), and the adaptation of his books for film and television.

1974

Naremore, James. "John Huston and *The Maltese Falcon.*" *Literature/Film Quarterly* 1, no. 3 (Summer): 239–49. (Reprinted in Studlar and Desser, *Reflections in a Male Eye,* 119–35).

    Argues that Huston successfully adapted Dashiell Hammett's novel with great visual style.

BOOK

Wilson, Arthur, ed. *The Warner Brothers Golden Anniversary Book: The First Complete Filmography.* New York: Film and Venture Corp., A Dell Special, 192 pp.

    With a critical essay by Arthur Knight and an introduction by Willard Van Dyke. An excellent chronological survey of all Warner Brothers activity from 1917 through 1972; includes month and year of release, credits, and cast. Thus, much of Huston's credited activity with Warner Brothers is reflected here.

1974

ARTICLES

Atkins, Thomas R. "The Illustrated Man: An Interview with Ray Bradbury." *Sight & Sound* 43, no. 2 (Spring). (Reprinted in *The Classic American Novel and the Movies,* edited by Gerald Peary and Roger Shatzkin, 42–51, New York, Frederick Ungar.)

    Bradbury refers to two earlier versions of *Moby Dick,* made in the silent and early sound eras, both starring John Barrymore. He says that the major problem in adapting the novel to film was boiling down the sprawling narrative into a comprehensible drama that would fit into a two-hour space. Bradbury refers to the need to tone down both melodrama and rhetoric in film to avoid seeming absurd. He saw his task as building toward a climax scene by scene, rather than simply emphasizing the drama of individual scenes. This construction required changing some of the order of events as presented in the novel. He also points out that he and Huston agreed that the ending had to be changed. All the crew had to be converted to Ahab's point of view, and Ahab himself had to be lashed to the whale, while his dead arm beckoned to Starbuck and the rest to follow him. Like other commentators, Bradbury states that Gregory Peck could not project the madness that Huston saw in Ahab.

Stewart, Garrett. "'The Long Good-bye' from 'Chinatown.'" *Film Quarterly* 28, no. 2 (Winter): 25–32.

A comparison of the two films in terms of the detective genre as a whole.

1975

ARTICLES

Alonzo, J. A. "Behind the Scenes of *Chinatown*." *American Cinematographer* 56, no. 5 (May): 526–29.

Alonzo discusses the photographic style he used for *Chinatown* (1974) as well as some of the incidents that occurred during production.

Bachmann, Gideon. "Huston in Morocco." *Sight & Sound* 44, no. 3 (Summer): 161–65. Interview. (Translated into French: "John Huston au Maroc," *Ecran* 46 [April 1976]: 28–32.)

Diary of the shooting of the film *The Man Who Would Be King* (1975) during March in Morocco.

McGinnis, W. D. "*Chinatown:* Roman Polanski's Contemporary Oedipus Story." *Literature/Film Quarterly* 3, no. 3:249–51.

Suggests similarities between *Chinatown* (1974) and Sophocles' *Oedipus Rex.*

Oliver, Bill. "'The Long Good-bye' and 'Chinatown'": Debunking the Private Eye Tradition." *Literature/Film Quarterly* 3, no. 3:240–48.

Describes how the value of positive action in the old private-eye tradition is denied or satirized in two recent detective films.

Riger, Robert. "Details from the Master's Painting." *Action* 10, no. 5 (September–October): 6–14.

Discussion of the filming of *Independence* (1976).

1976

ARTICLES

Alley, K. D. "*High Sierra*—Swan Song for an Era." *Journal of Popular Film* 5, nos. 3 & 4:248–62.

A detailed description of *High Sierra* (1941) and an analysis of the transitional times between Hollywood's Depression "gangster films" and the beginnings of World War II.

1977

Bachmann, Gideon. "Watching Huston." *Film Comment* 12, no. 1 (January–February): 21+.
    John Huston discusses his various attempts to make the film *The Man Who Would Be King* (1975) and the aspects of the story that attracted him.

Gill, Brendan. "The Man Who Would Be Kipling." *Film Comment* 12, no. 1 (January–February): 23+.
    Discussion of Huston's interest in and affinity for the themes and style of Kipling and the manifestation of Huston's interpretations in *The Man Who Would Be King* (1975).

Roizman, O. "Photographing *Independence* Where It Happened." *American Cinematographer* 57, no. 7 (July): 748+.
    Roizman discusses his experiences as the cinematographer on the film.

1977

ARTICLES

Palmer, R. B. "*Chinatown* and the Detective Story." *Literature/Film Quarterly* 5, no. 2 (Spring): 112–17.
    Argues that the perverse world Polanski creates in *Chinatown* (1974) is especially appealing to the America of the early 1970s, despite the film's violation of essential conventions of the detective genre.

Sturhahn, L. "Hollywood on Trial." *Filmmakers' Newsletter* 10, no. 5 (March): 23–27.
    Director David Helpern and writer Arnold Reisman discuss how they obtained their sources and put together their film *Hollywood on Trial* (1976). From a symposium at the San Francisco Film Festival.

BOOKS

French, Brandon. "Lost at Sea." In *The Classic American Novel and the Movies,* edited by Gerald Peary and Roger Shatzkin, 52–61. New York: Frederick Ungar Publishing Co.
    French stays staunchly loyal to the literary achievement of the novel, *Moby Dick* (1851), which he sees as a search both for a new form of meaning (of life?) and a new dimension of language. The novel posits a "multiplicity of meanings." Thus, Huston's and Bradbury's attempts (1956) to wrest from the book two or three clear meanings—that Ahab is mad, that he sees in the whale the malevolent face of God, and that he is committed to this blasphe-

my—betray the book's complexity and amount to a form of heresy. French writes that there are deep mysteries and ambiguities in Melville that defy the nature of cinema, which operates on the level of the visible.

Pratley, Gerald. *The Cinema of John Huston.* New York: A. S. Barnes & Co.; London: The Tantivy Press, 223 pp.

This book compiles interviews with Huston conducted at the time he was editing *The Mackintosh Man* (1973) and presents detailed discussions with Huston of his early life and career up through *Independence* (1976). He describes his vagabond upbringing and his early passions of boxing and art. He narrates his beginnings as a contract writer in the studio system and how he first came to direct. He goes on to describe the war years and the making of the documentaries. There is an account of his break from Warner Brothers after *Key Largo* (1948) and his move to independent production. Much is anecdotal and there are many reminiscences about personalities, but there are also interesting technical discussions (the experiments with color on *Moulin Rouge,* 1953; *Moby Dick,* 1956; *Reflections in a Golden Eye,* 1967; and the making of the model whales in *Moby Dick*). The volume includes a synopsis of the plot and credits for each film. Much of the discussion appears to be punctuated with laughter.

Samuels, Charles Thomas. "How Not to Film a Novel." In *Mastering the Film and Other Essays,* edited by Lawrence Graver, 190–97. Knoxville, TN: University of Tennessee Press.

Fat City (1972) is discussed. (Originally appeared in *American Scholar* 42, no. 1 [1972–73]: 148–54.)

1978

BOOKS

Bathrick, Serafina Kent. "Independent Woman, Doomed Sister." In *The Modern American Novel and the Movies,* edited by Gerald Peary and Roger Shatzkin, 143–55. New York: Frederick Ungar Publishing.

Ellen Glasgow's Pulitzer Prize–winning novel, *In This Our Life* (1942) was intended as a portrait of the modern South, represented by a family split by internal differences and external financial pressures. The Hollywood version, scripted by Howard Koch and Huston (uncredited) and directed by John Huston, was little more than a melodramatic potboiler made to display the contrasting talents of Bette Davis and Olivia de Havilland. Huston and Koch, however, are given credit for developing a black character (falsely accused of running over a white child) sympathetically and without caricature.

1978

Kaminsky, Stuart. "Gold Hat, Gold Fever, Silver Screen." In *The Modern American Novel and the Movies,* edited by Gerald Peary and Roger Shatzkin, 53–62. New York: Frederick Ungar Publishing.

    This piece is almost the same as the chapter "Amigos" in Kaminsky's *John Huston: Maker of Magic* (see below). Here he concentrates more on the novel *The Treasure of the Sierra Madre* (1934) itself. Kaminsky summarizes several elements of B. Traven's mystery. He notes episodes of the novel that were eliminated from the screenplay and Huston's editing-out of the philosophical ruminations and political comments of the committed author. Huston's emphasis is on existential adventure and on character. Kaminsky refers to Huston's respect for the character Howard as wise, tough, and yet humble, and to the way Dobbs is presented not as a brute, but as a man with fundamental flaws who cracks under pressure. These portraits, notes the critic, are indelibly etched on the viewer's memory by the performances of Walter Huston and Humphrey Bogart.

————. *John Huston: Maker of Magic.* Boston: Houghton Mifflin Company, 237 pp.

    A biography of Huston through his films, interwoven with lengthy summaries of each film. Includes information about the preproduction and the development of the ideas, as well as physical problems of each production. While much of the material is interesting and useful, it adds little to what we already know of Huston and belongs to that category of books that contribute to the Huston legend. Kaminsky, who contributed the concise Huston biography to *The International Dictionary of Films and Filmmakers,* vol. 2 (Chicago: St. James Press, 1997, 459–463), is a genuine Huston enthusiast. He admits to admiring even the supposed failures and films the director rejected. Includes a filmography, credits, films in which Huston appeared as an actor only, and a selected bibliography.

Naremore, James. *The Magic World of Orson Welles.* New York: Oxford University Press, 310 pp.

    Compares ways the camera is used to create space in *Citizen Kane* (1939) and *The Maltese Falcon* (1941), with *Kane* having a wide-angle perspective and *Falcon* distorting space even more. Naremore makes some interesting observations about Huston functioning within the constraints of the studio system so that even though his cinematographer used "offbeat" photography, the space seems cramped: "Nearly the whole action is played out in a series of little rooms with actors gathered in tight, three-figured compositions." Reference is also made to Huston's role as an uncredited writer of *The Stranger* (1946), and he and producer Sam Spiegel's borrowing from Hitchcock's *Shadow of a Doubt* (1943) for a number of elements in the film.

1979

BOOK

Beja, Morris. *Film and Literature.* New York: Longman, 335 pp.
Compares film with literature and adaptations. Includes essays on *The Treasure of the Sierra Madre* (1948) and other films.

1980

ARTICLES

Hammen, Scott. "At War with the Army." *Film Comment* 16, no. 2 (March–April): 19–23.
Discusses Huston's war trilogy—*Report from the Aleutians* (1943), and *Battle of San Pietro* (1945)—and censorship of *Let There Be Light* (1946). "Taken together, these three works form a cohesive personal statement on the experience of combat that compares favorably to any other film, fictional or documentary, to come out of the Second World War."

Jameson, Richard T. "John Huston." *Film Comment* 16, no. 3 (May–June): 25–56.
A special "Midsection" of *Film Comment.* Jameson's lengthy appreciation of John Huston (reprinted in Cooper, *Perspectives on John Huston*) coincides with the tribute paid to Huston by the Film Society of Lincoln Center in 1980. It assesses his major films up to *The Man Who Would Be King* (1975). Jameson takes issue with the auteurist critics who undervalue Huston for not presenting a consistent worldview or not developing a recognizable personal style. On the question of thematic consistency, Jameson points out that Huston always turns to literary sources that offer themes congenial to his world-weary viewpoint, and in his analyses, Jameson quotes a raft of familiar leitmotivs: the quest that goes wrong, an ironical view of the world and human nature, the testing of the self against the odds, laughter in the face of failure, and so on. Jameson provides very detailed analysis of key films, for example, *The Maltese Falcon* (1941), *The Treasure of the Sierra Madre* (1948), *The Asphalt Jungle* (1950), *The African Queen* (1952), *Freud: The Secret Passion* (1962), *Reflections in a Golden Eye* (1967), and *The Man Who Would Be King.* The article amounts to a monograph and serves as a reinstatement of Huston as a director worthy of serious consideration.

1980

BOOKS

Burnett, W. R. "Afterward." In *The Asphalt Jungle: A Screenplay,* by Ben Maddow and John Huston and edited Matthew J. Bruccoli, 145–47. Carbondale, Ill.: Southern Illinois University Press.

Burnett reflects on his experience in making the film (1950) from his novel thirty years after the fact. He indicates that a number of his books have been turned into films, "but not one of them pleased me as much as *The Asphalt Jungle.*" He ascribes his good fortune to the foresight of Dore Schary, then head of production at MGM. It could have been a disaster because he turned over the project to Arthur Hornblow, a contract producer who was used to making a different type of film; but the project was turned over to John Huston as director. Burnett feels that Huston caught the essence of his thoughts. A couple of points disappointed Burnett, but for the most part he was pleased with the results.

Haver, Ronald. *David O. Selznick's Hollywood.* New York: Knopf, 425 pp.

Includes a fairly detailed account of the conflicts between Huston and Selznick that finally led to Huston's departure from the film *A Farewell to Arms* (1957).

Huston, John. *An Open Book.* New York: Knopf, 389 pp. (Reprint—New York: Da Capo Press, 1994, 389 pp.)

Huston's autobiography, which he wrote shortly after completing *Wise Blood* (1979), reveals him in a confident mood, following three major critical successes in the 1970s. Very anecdotal, often rambling, but always elegant, it reminds us that Huston was, after all, a writer. The book is more selective than open, and Huston admits in his conclusion that this is not the whole story. He takes some pleasure, however, in stating in the first chapter, "Writing, directing and acting in more than sixty pictures, I fail to see any continuity in my work from picture to picture—what's remarkable is how different the pictures are, one from another. Nor can I find a thread of consistency in my marriages. No one of my wives has been remotely like any of the others—and certainly none of them was like my mother. They were a mixed bag: a schoolgirl; a gentlewoman; a motion-picture actress; a ballerina; and a crocodile." (p. 5) While he provides detailed accounts of the adventures and misadventures of filming on remote and exotic locations, he discloses little about his family or matrimonial life (except for the above comment). There is plenty to sustain the Huston legend of adventurer, *bon vivant,* and connoisseur of drink, horses, and travel. He also reflects on the art (or trade) of filmmaking. In conclusion Huston describes his retreat at Las Caletas and his animal companions. While admitting his story is incomplete, he adds a list of errors he would correct if he could live his life over.

1980

Miller, Gabriel. "The Wages of Sin." In *Screening the Novel: Rediscovered American Fiction in Film,* edited by Gabriel Miller, 84–115. New York: Frederick Ungar Publishing.
    In this collection of essays eight novels and films are discussed. Chapter 5 deals with *The Treasure of the Sierra Madre* (1948). Each chapter is divided evenly between considerations of the novel (its history and assessment) and of its film version. Miller does not go much beyond previous critics and in fact is indebted to Brandon French's essay on *Moby Dick* (1956; see under 1977) and Stuart Kaminsky's biography on John Huston (see under 1978). Miller begins by observing Huston's constant reference to literature and making thematic comparisons between *Treasure* and *Moby Dick* (the quest gone wrong). Like Huston's other critics, he emphasizes Huston's tendency to reduce the novel he is working from, to simplify and clarify, and to let little stand in the way of action and excitement. Miller points out that, whereas Huston can be grimmer than most Hollywood directors, he is less pessimistic than B. Traven. Thus, Huston's Tampico and the Orso Negro rooming house are far removed from the hell on earth and the end of the road described in the novel. His characters, too, seem rather more likable, and even more decent, than they appear in the book. The critic spends time (like Kaminsky) discussing the visual compositions of the film that summarize the relationships between the characters, and he finally connects the film with other major films in the Huston canon.

PROGRAM

"The Films of John Huston." Los Angeles County Museum of Art, Leo S. Bing Theater, October–December, 14 pp.
    From one of the most comprehensive retrospectives of John Huston's work until that time, this program is located in Huston's personal papers in the Academy of Motion Picture Arts and Sciences Library. The individual program notes can be found in the collections of some specialized libraries. In addition to this program, notes were issued for each of the individual screenings. The information provided includes descriptions and some analysis of the films, partial credits, and running times. The films included in the retrospective were:

Across the Pacific (1942), *The Treasure of the Sierra Madre* (1948), *We Were Strangers* (1949), *Key Largo* (1948), *Three Strangers* (1946, as writer), *The Red Badge of Courage* (1951), *A Walk with Love and Death* (1969), *The Battle of San Pietro* (1945), *The African Queen* (1952), *The Barbarian and the Geisha* (1958), *Beat the Devil* (1954), *The List of Adrian Messenger* (1963), *Moulin Rouge* (1953), *Moby Dick* (1956), *Heaven Knows, Mr. Allison* (1957),

1981

Roots of Heaven (1958), *The Unforgiven* (1960), *The Life and Times of Judge Roy Bean* (1972), *The Misfits* (1961), *Freud: The Secret Passion* (1962), *Fat City* (1972), *Wise Blood* (1979), *The Bible* (1966), *Chinatown* (1974, as actor), *Myra Breckinridge* (1970, as actor), *The Night of the Iguana* (1964), *Reflections in a Golden Eye* (1967), *The Asphalt Jungle* (1950), *The Man Who Would Be King* (1975), and *Winter Kills* (1979, as actor).

1981

ARTICLES

Aghed, J. "Jesus var en Lognare." *Chaplin* 23, no. 3:115–18.
    Deals mainly with the relationship between Flannery O'Connor's novel *Wise Blood* and Huston's film based on the book.

Beckerman, Jim. "On Adapting 'The Most Audacious Thing in Fiction.'" In *The English Novel and the Movies,* edited by Michael Klein and Gillian Parker, 180–86. New York: Frederick Ungar Publishing Co.
    In this chapter on *The Man Who Would Be King* (1975), Beckerman reminds us that Kipling's tale was written when he was twenty-one years old and was from the start regarded as more than a tall tale of treasure-seeking adventurers. Its early readers and admirers read it as both parable and parody of empire, for the rogue heroes—Peachy and Danny, themselves trained in England's Imperial Army—feel that India is "not big enough for such as us" and turn the art of imperial conquest on the natives of remote Kafiristan. Huston, too, is drawn to the tale for its patterns of irony, quite apart from the adventurous elements, and obviously finds motifs that take him back to some of his most famous films, for example, *The Treasure of the Sierra Madre* (1948) and *Moby Dick* (1956). The adventurers overreach themselves when Danny forgets that he is just a thief, and Peachy, escaping to tell the tale, is reduced to a life of wandering and madness. In the film Kipling himself is changed from a youthful beginner to a wiser, slightly skeptical, middle-aged observer. Beckerman points out the essential fidelity of Huston and Gladys Hill to the original tale, as well as the differences that improve on Kipling in the film adaptation.

Corliss, Richard. "The Disasters of Modern War." *Time* 117 (19 January): 80.
    Let There Be Light (1946) is seen in the context of directors like John Ford, George Stevens, William Wyler, and John Huston, who recall the war as artists-combatants. Corliss considers the three wartime documentaries that Huston produced as one and believes the films should be seen as a single work.

Crespi, Alberto. "Fuga per la vittoria." *Cineforum,* December, 51–60.
    Under the guise of a critical piece on *Victory* (1981), a detailed filmography on Huston's work as a director through *Wise Blood* (1979) is included. The December 1987 issue (pp. 27–32) continues the filmography through *The Dead* (1987) and includes filmographies of Huston as screenwriter, producer, and actor; his theatrical work; and his unrealized projects.

Linderman, L. "Oedipus in *Chinatown.*" *Enclitic* 5–6, nos. 1 & 2 (Fall–Spring): 190–203.
    Linderman analyzes *Chinatown* (1974) as an oedipal text in an attempt to define what is loosely called the "classical text."

Menides, Laura Jehn. "John Huston's *Wise Blood* and the Myth of the Sacred Quest." *Literature/Film Quarterly* 9, no. 4:207–12.
    Explores the film's parallels to elements in *The Grapes of Wrath* (1940) and their common theme of the hero's mythic journey.

Mostacci, J. J. *Film News* 38 (Spring): 16.
    Questions the long suppression of *Let There Be Light* (1946), when many commercially released films after the war were dealing with the same subject. Mostacci claims the film is a professionally moving experience, showing the reality of how wars destroy not only the bodies but also the hearts and minds of those who fought them. He does criticize the facile portrayal of quick cures, with no failures shown.

Nugent, Jo. "What War Can Do to Men." *New West,* April, 53.
    Recollections of Stanley Cortez, cinematographer, on making *Let There Be Light* (1946).

Sarris, Andrew. "Hobgoblins of Reality." *Village Voice* 26 (January 21–27): 45.
    Sarris quotes extensively from James Agee's writings regarding *Let There Be Light* (1946) and his fight to have it released. Sarris's reaction is one of mystification, for Agee's eloquence did not prepare him for the conventionality and unoriginality of the work. Highly critical Sarris feels that the film should be subtitled "Song of Sigmund" and that *The Story of G.I. Joe* (1945) is a more powerful depiction of war's horror. Sarris does acknowledge the film's noble self-effacement and notes that its concern for blacks was way ahead of its time. Reprinted in *Film Review Annual 1982.*

Wittenberg, Clarissa K. "*Let There Be Light:* A Film Review." *Psychiatric News* 16, no 3 (July 3).
    Let There Be Light (1946) is conceived as a help to families for the return of mentally injured veterans and eliminates any stigma attached to men-

1982

tal illness connected with war experience. Wittenberg describes the film as a valuable document in psychiatric history.

1982

ARTICLES

American Cinematographer, June, 556+.
    Two articles dealing with the making of *Annie* (1982). Provides background information on its filming, locations used, sets, props, and so forth. Also included is an interview with Richard Moore, the cinematographer ("Behind One Camera for Filming of *Annie,*" 560+), who describes how the movie was filmed.

Benson, Sheila. *Los Angeles Times,* Calendar, sect. 4, May 21: 1.
    Article on bad reviews of *Annie* (1982).

Fultz, J. R. "Classic case of collaboration . . . *The African Queen.*" *Literature/Film Quarterly* 10, no. 1:13–14.
    Details the collaboration of James Agee and John Huston in adapting C. S. Forester's novel.

Horowitz, S. "Carol Burnett Gets a Kick out of *Annie.*" *American Film* 7, no. 7 (May): 46.
    Discusses Carol Burnett's career as a television comedienne and her transition to film, focusing on her role in *Annie* (1982).

Jacobson, H. "Stark Reality." *Film Comment* 19, no. 4 (July–August): 47–48.
    Deals with negotiations that Ray Stark went through to get rights to the film *Annie* (1982).

Schepelern, P. "Fra Monterey til Hollywood." *Kosmorama* 28 (October): 162–65.
    On Steinbeck's work in and relationship with Hollywood. Schepelern also covers adaptations made from Steinbeck's books and includes a review of *Cannery Row* (1982).

Turan, Kenneth. "Hollywood Puts Its Money on *Annie:* Ray Stark & John Huston Comment." *New York Times Magazine,* sect. 4, May 2, 40–43.
    On the making of the film.

1983

ARTICLES

Film Dope, no. 26 (January): 19–24.
  The estimable British periodical devotes each issue to film personalities, major and minor, and provides excellent information on their activities. John Huston is the subject of no. 767, with a running chronology. It includes a brief biographical note, followed by information about his various activities, some of which is obscure. His television work is covered, including miscellaneous work as a director, fictional representation on television, and films about him. The issue ends with a critical piece on Huston. Interestingly, the piece on Walter Huston, no. 768, follows. It is the policy of *Film Dope* to do updates, but the one on John Huston has not been issued to date.

Harmetz, Aljean. "John Huston Takes on Lowry's *Volcano.*" *Los Angeles Herald Examiner,* August 25: C1–C3.
  Article on challenges to filmmakers in turning great novels into artistically successful movies. Harmetz discusses the movie versions of Bernard Malamud's *The Natural* (1984) and Malcolm Lowry's *Under the Volcano* (1984).

1984

ARTICLES

Hachem, Sachem. "Under the Volcano." *American Cinematographer* 65, no. 10 (October): 58–63.
  Huston and cinematographer Gabriel Figueroa discuss the problems of bringing Malcolm Lowry's novel to the screen.

Hamill, Pete. "Against All Odds." *American Film* 9, no. 9 (July–August): 18–26+.
  Production article on *Under the Volcano* (1984). Hamill reports on the long production history of film. He includes an interview with Albert Finney in which Finney talks about film acting.

Klein, Michael. "Visualization and Signification in John Huston's *Wise Blood:* The Redemption of Reality." *Literature/Film Quarterly* 12, no. 4 (October): 230–36.
  Comparison between Flannery O'Connor's novel and Huston's film.

1985

McCarthy, Todd. "Cracking the Volcano." *Film Comment* 20, no. 4 (July–August): 59–63.
    Various people involved with the production Retsin & Dusert of *Under the Volcano* (1947) give their thoughts on Malcolm Lowry's novel. Collaborators John Huston, Wieland Schulz-Keil, and Guy Gallo discuss their adaptation of the novel.

1985

ARTICLES

Buckley, Michael. "John Huston." *Films in Review* 36, no. 1 (April): 210–20.
    On the occasion of John Huston's receipt of the David Wark Griffith Award for Career Achievement (1985), Buckley presents a concise summary of Huston's life and career both in the theater and movies. Excerpts from previous interviews (in *Films in Review*) with Claire Trevor and Gregory Peck are referred to where they talk about their experiences working with Huston. Buckley touches on Huston's philosophy of directing. The article is followed with a comprehensive filmography, compiled by Alvin H. Marill, that covers Huston's career as a writer and director through *Minor Miracle* (1986).

Combs, Richard. "The Man Who Would Be Ahab: The Myths and Masks of John Huston." *BFI/Monthly Film Bulletin* 52, no. 623 (December): 370–74.
    A stylistic analysis of symbols, motifs, and ideas behind John Huston's films.

Fernandez, Enrique. "Less Than Divine: *Under the Volcano* and *A Passage to India* Make It to Screen without Him." *Village Voice* 30 (January 22): 49–50.
    Comparison of novel to film. Fernandez speculates on the "what if" of Joseph Losey's attempt to do *Under the Volcano* and Huston's handling of the subject matter, which he feels in some aspects is successful and in others is not. There is a comparison to *The Night of the Iguana* (1964), with both taking place in Mexico and dealing with "divine" figures who are "losers."

BOOKS

Benayoun, Robert. *John Huston: La grande ombre de l'aventure.* (Nouvelle Edition. Mise à Jour. Collection Cinéma Classique. Série les Cinéastes.) Paris: L'herminier, 191 pp.
    This 1985 edition is revised from the 1966 study and includes films through *Under the Volcano* (1984). Thus, even this second book devoted to Huston by his most enthusiastic French critic does not quite round out

Huston's career. This extended edition follows the same format as the first, including the same choice of extracts from critical essays, selections from the screenplays, and an up-to-date filmography and bibliography. Notable is Benayoun's discovery of a resurgence of creative energy in the best films of the 1970s: in the gritty urban realism of *Fat City* (1972), the adventure fable *The Man Who Would Be King* (1975), and the apocalyptic *Wise Blood* (1979).

Boyum, Joy Gould. *Double Exposure: Fiction into Film.* New York: New American Library, 287 pp.
    Boyum wrote the book in defense of literary adaptations on film and presents adaptation as a form of art. Huston is represented with *Wise Blood* (1979, pp. 175–82) and *Under the Volcano* (1984, pp. 205–12). Boyum begins with the premise that Flannery O'Connor's novella, *Wise Blood,* is an "unfilmable" text, but she then goes on to show how "filmable" it seems in Huston's hands. Huston made the film much more accessible by (1) rooting it in a recognizable reality by way of shooting on location and using some non-professional actors and (2) by humanizing his characters, adding flashes of humor without patronizing them. The result is a film that does betray the author's intentions and links the finished product with Huston's other works that explore the religious quest and delve into dark humor. Boyum sees *Under the Volcano* as less successful, although the boldness of the decision to make the attempt is admired. She offers a brief history of the appeal of Malcolm Lowry's novel to many important directors, all of whom despaired at the idea of adapting it for the screen. Huston and his screenwriter, Guy Gallo, are credited with simplifying the narrative and giving it a coherent structure. But what they gain in coherence, Boyum adds, they lose in terms of interior vision and poetic resonance. She sees a contradiction between Huston's statement that a film "resembles a poem more than it resembles a book" and his deletion of most of the poetic and symbolic elements from his version. While he achieved that fusion in *Wise Blood,* this critic feels, he fell short in *Under the Volcano.*

Hammen, Scott. *John Huston.* Boston: Twayne Publishers, 163 pp.
    A useful introductory study of Huston's films and the varied directions of his career until *Under the Volcano* (1984). Hammen makes clear from the start that this book is not a biography, that he wants to try and see the direc-tor's films clearly and not the man's life through the art. He deals with Huston's drive for independence and his desire to free himself from a Hollywood contract as soon as possible. Thus, he emphasizes Huston's fre-quent choice of challenging and difficult books to film, as long as they stimu-lated him. In contrast Huston also regularly pursued popular success and the lure of the box office, which led him to less than stellar productions, for exam-ple, *The Kremlin Letter* (1970) and *The Mackintosh Man* (1973). Hammen

pays close attention to Huston's last fifteen or so years, from *Fat City* (1972). Here he finds the successes that had eluded the director in the late fifties and in the sixties. In films like *Wise Blood* (1979) and *Under the Volcano* he finds Huston working with the energy of a young independent director on a shoe-string budget and putting all those working on run-of-the-mill Hollywood blockbusters to shame.

Thompson, David. *Suspects.* New York: Knopf, 274 pp.
    "Fictionalized" accounts of the lives of characters in *Chinatown* (1974), *Beat the Devil* (1954), *High Sierra* (1941), *The Killers* (1946), and *The Maltese Falcon* (1941).

1986

BOOK

Friedrich, Otto. *City of Nets: A Portrait of Hollywood in the 1940s.* New York: Harper, 495 pp.
    Discussion of Dashiell Hammett, various versions of *The Maltese Falcon,* and Huston's own 1941 version.

1987

ARTICLES

Cineforum, no. 270 (December): 21–36.
    Dossier in Italian of reviews and critical articles on *The Dead* (1987).

Edgerton, Gary. "Revisiting the Records of Wars Past: Remembering the Documentary Trilogy of John Huston." *Journal of Popular Film and Television* 15, no. 1 (Spring): 27–41. (Reprinted in Studlar and Desser, *Reflections in a Male Eye,* 33–61.)
    On Huston's wartime documentaries as a record of personal growth.

Huston, Tony. "Family Ties." *American Film* 12, no. 10 (September): 16–19+.
    Account of making the film *The Dead* (1987) with his father, John Huston.

Schulz-Keil, Wieland. "Huston." *Film Comment* 23, no. 5 (September–October): 18–26. (Reprinted in Cooper, *Perspectives on John Huston,* 207–15.)
    The producer of *The Dead* (1987) and *Under the Volcano* (1984) discusses John Huston's approach to filmmaking.

Wiener, David John. "*The Dead:* A Study in Light and Shadow." *American Cinematographer* 68, no. 11 (November): 62+.

Fred Murphy, cinematographer on *The Dead* (1987), discusses working with Huston and creating a period look with lighting.

BOOKS

Gardner, Gerald, ed. *The Censorship Papers: Movie Censorship Papers from the Hayes Office, 1934–1968.* New York: Dodd, Mead, 226 pp.

Discusses *The African Queen* (1952) and *The Maltese Falcon* (1941). As noted elsewhere, the Academy of Motion Picture Arts and Sciences Library houses the complete files of the Hayes Office. Files on virtually all the films that Huston was involved with during this period are covered. Not only the censorship documents are included; the files cover such information on the films as cast and synopsis.

Hepburn, Katharine. *The Making of the African Queen, or How I Went to Africa with Bogart, Bacall and Huston and Almost Lost My Mind.* New York: Knopf, 129 pp.

Good background information on Hepburn's involvement in the project. She also includes some good behind-the-scenes photographs.

1988

ARTICLES

Abramson, L. H. "Two Birds of a Feather: Hammett's and Huston's *Maltese Falcon.*" *Literature/Film Quarterly* 16, no. 2:112–18.

Notes on Huston's cinematic approach to his adaptation of *The Maltese Falcon* (1941).

Barby, F.-R. "John Huston: Le noir et le blanc comme l'argile du sculpteur." *Cinéma* (Paris) 447 (June 22): 13.

During the debate on colorization the author uses as an example *The Asphalt Jungle* (1950) and argues that this film is much more successful in black and white than in any attempt to colorize it.

Dassanowsky, Robert. "*Casino Royale* Revisited." *Films in Review* 39, nos. 6 & 7 (June–July): 336–49.

Critical reassessment in which the author claims the 1967 film should be considered a milestone.

1989

Fenyez, G. "John Huston." *Film und Fernsehen* 16, no. 2 (February): 38–44.
    Interview with John Huston in which he talks about his film *The Dead* (1987) and James Joyce.

BOOKS

Ciment, Gilles, ed. *John Huston, collection dirigée.* Dossier Positif Rivages. Paris: Editions Rivages (Collection Positif-Rivages, no. 2), 191 pp.
    This anthology offers a complete study of Huston's work, including reviews of *Prizzi's Honor* (1985) and *The Dead* (1987). It includes writings by a broad selection of French critics on all aspects of Huston's work, interviews with the director, and a selection of writings by Huston himself, with a short story ("Fool," 1929), an appreciation of Eugene O'Neill, and a tribute to Humphrey Bogart. The last two-thirds of the book provides detailed reviews of twenty-six major movies directed by John Huston. All reviews have been selected from *Positif* (including its rare special issue—no. 3, 1952—which was devoted to Huston), whose writers have shown a consistent appreciation of Huston's work since the 1950s.

1989

ARTICLES

Cooper, Stephen. "Sex/Knowledge/Power in the Detective Genre." *Film Quarterly* 42, no. 3:23–31.
    Four detective films—*The Maltese Falcon* (1941), *The Big Heat* (1953), *Chinatown* (1974), and *Angel Heart* (1987)—are used to discuss characteristics of male-female relationships within the genre, notably the woman's withholding of knowledge sought by the man.

Engell, John. *"The Treasure of the Sierra Madre:* B. Traven, John Huston and Ideology in Film Adaptation." *Literature/Film Quarterly* 17, no. 4 (October): 245–52.
    Engell argues that, in his adaptation of B. Traven's novel, John Huston made significant alterations to the original text's ideology.

Maxfield, J. F. "La Belle Dame Sans Merci and the Neurotic Knight: Characterization in *The Maltese Falcon.*" *Literature/Film Quarterly* 17, no. 4 (October): 253–60.
    Draws parallels between Huston's version and the imagery in John Keats's poem, "La belle dame. . . ."

1989

Shout, J. D. "Joyce at Twenty-Five, Huston at Eighty-One: *The Dead.*" *Literature/Film Quarterly* 17, no. 2 (April): 91–94.
  Discussion of Huston's treatment of James Joyce's story, *The Dead* (1987) in his last film. Shout considers the film's success and John Huston's adaptation.

BOOKS

Brady, Frank. *Citizen Welles: A Biography of Orson Welles.* New York: Scribners, 655 pp.
  Discusses Welles's attempts to adapt *Moby Dick* (1851) to the stage and his acting as the preacher, Father Mapple, in Huston's film version (1956). Brady also writes about the unfinished *Other Side of the Wind* (1970–1975) and John Huston's acting, which some considered to be of Academy Award quality. A note indicates that Huston found it somewhat aberrant, but rewarding, to face Welles on the other side of the camera after directing Welles in three films: *Roots of Heaven* (1958), *Moby Dick* (1956) and *The Kremlin Letter* (1970).

Grobel, Lawrence. *The Hustons.* New York: Scribners, 812 pp. (Reprint—New York: Avon Books, 1990, 812 pp.)
  The most complete Huston biography to date, it covers a history of three generations of Hustons: Walter, John, and John's children—Angelica, Tony, and Danny—with John decidedly the central figure. While not intended as a correction to the selective confessions of John Huston's own *An Open Book, The Hustons* does serve to revise impressions and allows us to see more than one view of the events in Huston's life. Grobel is a lucid and objective narrator, but the most interesting passages come from conversations conducted with those who have been directly involved with Huston's long life, such as family members (and ex-wives), friends, collaborators, and business partners. Their statements often come in the form of letters or telephone conversations. Among the interesting revelations are the real reasons behind the making of *The Unforgiven* (1960), Huston's treatment of Clift during the making of *Freud: The Secret Passion* (1962), the motivation behind selling St. Clerans, and candid accounts of the deterioration of Huston's health during his last twenty years. Huston was open with his biographer (revealing more than he had in his autobiography). The result is a compelling portrait of a complex man who worked hard at his art while never letting it interfere with his zest for living.

Scorsese, Martin. *Scorsese on Scorsese.* Edited by David Thompson and Ian Christie. London: Faber and Faber, 254 pp.
  With an introduction by Michael Powell. Huston is mentioned during Scorsese's discussion about *The Last Temptation of Christ* (1988) and Huston's *The Bible* (1966).

1990

ARTICLES

Dunant, C. "Visions of Paris." *Sight & Sound* 60, no. 1 (Winter): 42–47.
Reflections on four films set in Paris during the period of "la belle époque": *French Can Can* (1955), *Moulin Rouge* (1953), *Madame de . . .* (1953), and *Gigi* (1957).

Positif, no. 351 (May): 2–16.
A series of articles by Robert Benayoun, E. Eyquem, and M. Ciment in which *White Hunter/Black Heart* (1990) is discussed. Clint Eastwood's role in the film and Huston's character and his love of hunting are discussed. The articles include an interview with Eastwood, a review of the film, and an interview with Peter Viertel, whose novel was the basis of the film and who collaborated on writing the film's screenplay.

Proteus: The Film Career of John Huston, 77, no. 2 (Fall): whole issue, 43 pp.
This special edition of the journal *Proteus,* devoted entirely to Huston, is based on a week-long colloquium on his work, held three years after his death in October 1990. It includes Lesley Brill's article on *The Misfits* (1961), Leonard Engel on *Prizzi's Honor* (1985), and two studies of *The Dead* (1987), by Paul Frizler and John F. Carson, respectively, that focus on Huston's fidelity to Joyce and his ability to turn a personal and even abstract story into a delicate film accessible to a wide audience. Greg Garrett pays tribute to the documentary *Let There Be Light* (1946), tying it to the forties' climate of film noir. The most interesting pieces are by Molly Haskell, who looks at Huston through the lens of gender, and Lawrence Grobel, reminiscing about his encounters with the director, taken from his comprehensive 1989 biography, *The Hustons.* All told, here is further proof that Huston has attained academic respectability.

Woolf, Sir John. "Letter." *The Times* (London), August 23, x2.
Letter from Sir John Woolf, Chairman of Romulus Films and producer of *The African Queen* (1952), refuting comments made by Clint Eastwood in an interview in the *Saturday Review,* August 18, regarding the making of *White Hunter/Black Heart* (1990) and its budget. Woolf contends that Huston was responsible, and not irresponsible, as depicted in "a rather dull film" (that is, *White Hunter/Black Heart*) and that Huston "was a truly great man."

BOOKS

Behlmer, Rudy. *Behind the Scenes: The Making of . . . Hollywood.* Hollywood, Calif.: Samuel French, 343 pp. (Reprint of *America's Favorite Movies: Behind the Scenes,* New York: Ungar, 1982.)

Utilizing archival and primary resources, including interviews with some of the principals, Behlmer supplies the background stories to sixteen famous films. Included are *The African Queen* (1952) and *The Maltese Falcon* (1941). Bibliographies for the particular films and filmographical information are provided. (The other fourteen films are *Singing' in the Rain, Snow White and the Seven Dwarfs, Stagecoach, A Streetcar Named Desire, Tarzan and His Mate, The Adventures of Robin Hood, All About Eve, Casablanca, Frankenstein, The Grapes of Wrath, Gunga Din, High Noon, Laura,* and *Lost Horizon.*)

McCarty, John. *The Complete Films of John Huston.* New York: Carol Publishing, 256 pp.

There were two editions of *The Films of John Huston* (by John McCarty, New Jersey, Citadel Press, 1987, 256 pp.) with the same title page, imprint, date, table of contents, paging, and ISBN number. The cover and spine even had the same title, *The Complete Films of John Huston.* The "earlier" edition (not specified as such), however, only covered Huston's films through *Prizzi's Honor* (1985), while the "later" edition (also not specified as such) included his last directed film, *The Dead* (1987). To keep the same number page count in the second edition, the publisher deleted several full-page stills from the first edition's "Huston as an Actor" chapter. The table of contents in both editions are exactly the same, with the later edition's not including *The Dead.*

1991

ARTICLES

Hagen, W. M. "Under Huston's Volcano." *Literature/Film Quarterly* 19, no. 3 (July): 138–49.

Considers the success of Huston's 1984 adaptation of Malcolm Lowry's "unfilmable" novel.

Gariel, M. K. "An American Tragedy: *Chinatown.*" *Bucknell Review* 35, no. 1:209–31.

An intertextual analysis.

Niney, F. "Le Scenario Freud." *Cahiers du Cinéma* 440 (February): 52–53.

Notes on *Freud: The Secret Passion* (1962) and *Geheimnisse einer Seele* (1926) films dealing with psychoanalysis.

1992

ARTICLE

Nielsen, Ray. "Ray's Way: Interviews with the Stars—Jan Merlin in *The List of Adrian Messenger.*" *Classic Images,* no. 199 (January): 40.

Merlin was an uncredited actor who, according to this interview, actually played the roles of some of the famous actors who made cameo appearances in *The List of Adrian Messenger* (1963).

BOOKS

Bradbury, Ray. *Green Shadows, White Whale.* New York: Knopf, 271 pp.

In this novel, Bradbury tries to convey his experience with John Huston in writing the screenplay for *Moby Dick* (1956); however, the novel is as much about Bradbury and his experiences with the Irish while he was in Ireland working with Huston on the script. Interestingly Bradbury uses John's name for the Huston character and does not attempt to disguise him at all. Those parts of the book in which Huston appears do not show Huston in the best light. The title can probably be seen as a takeoff on Peter Viertel's *White Hunter, Black Heart* (1954), which more successfully depicts Huston's true character.

Richardson, Carl. *Autopsy: An Element of Realism in Film Noir.* Metuchen, N.J., and London: The Scarecrow Press, 247 pp.

As the title states, Richardson studies the cycle, or tradition, of film noir in the context of cinematic realism and social commentary, illustrated by comparative essays on John Huston's *The Maltese Falcon* (1941), Jules Dassin's *The Naked City* (1948), and Orson Welles's *Touch of Evil* (1958). The first and third films open and close this period of film history. The chapter on *The Maltese Falcon,* entitled "Film Noir in the Studio" (pp. 37–75), provides a literary prehistory of the film, the work of Dashiell Hammett, and his portrait of San Francisco. It includes references to two previous Warner Brothers versions of the novel and the enthusiastic reception of Huston's treatment by contemporary reviewers. Richardson points out that neither the commercial considerations of the studio (for example, Hal Wallis's [the producer's] continuous calls for "more action") nor the interference of the censor, Joseph Breen (with whom Huston agreeably complied), could completely eliminate the film's consistent irony, its critical tone, and its implied contradiction of Hollywood's rosy vision of the world and human nature. These elements of Huston's film help to define the impact and appeal of film noir. Richardson also supplies useful sections on writing and direction. In the first he points out the influence of the hard-boiled school of detective stories on Huston's way of writing dialogue and on his cinematic style. In the second he praises Huston for producing a commercially successful film that satisfied the studio bosses and still retained enough subversive elements to allow the film to outlast its own era.

Silver, Alain, and Elizabeth Ward, eds. *Film Noir: An Encyclopedic Reference to the American Style.* 3d ed., rev. Woodstock, N.Y.: Overlook Press, 479 pp.

A major reference work with coverage of *The Asphalt Jungle* (1950), *Chinatown* (1974), *Key Largo* (1948), *Danger Signal* (1941), *High Sierra* (1941), *The Killers* (1946), *The Maltese Falcon* (1941), and *The Stranger* (1946). Each entry includes full credits, a synopsis, and an analysis.

1993

ARTICLES

Chankin, D. O. "The Representation of Psychoanalysis in Film: John Huston's *Freud.*" *Persistence of Vision* 10:134–43.

Examines the cinematic representation of psychoanalysis in *Freud: The Secret Passion* (1962).

Pilipp, F., and A. Pederson. "Narrative Devices and Aesthetic Perception in Joyce's and Huston's *The Dead/The Dead:* A Study of Adaptation." *Literature/Film Quarterly* 21, no. 1 (January): 61–70.

Two considerations of Huston's success in adapting James Joyce's story.

Studlar, Gaylyn. "Narrating Outside the Canon: Questions of Materiality, (Other) Meaning, and the Female Voice." *Persistence of Vision* 10:34–35.

Discusses the sound of the female voice in films in terms of psychoanalytic feminist theory, using such Hollywood films as *Enchanted April* (1991), *All This & Heaven Too* (1940), and *Jezebel* (1938).

BOOK

Studlar, Gaylyn, and David Desser, eds. *Reflections in a Male Eye: John Huston and the American Experience.* Washington, D.C.: Smithsonian Institution Press, 311 pp.

This volume is a milestone in the history of Huston criticism (in English), and the first shot in a renewed attempt at a serious reassessment of Huston's career six years after his death. The book addresses two particular aspects of Huston's art: the question of masculinity and the peculiarly American quality of his work and outlook. Regarding the latter question David Desser and Gary Edgerton each wrote essays on the significance of Huston's wartime documentaries. An essay by Robert Sklar revives interest in *We Were Strangers* (1949) and points out that it was ahead of its time. Stephen Cooper's article on *Reflections in a Golden Eye* (1967) contrasts Huston's study of repression on an army base against the climate of the Vietnam War. On the question of masculinity, Virginia Wright Wexman and Gaylyn Studlar address the image of the male body and perceptions of male contexts using *Moulin Rouge* (1953) and *Fat City* (1972), respectively, as examples. The concept of the Huston hero comes into question in chapters by James Naremore and Martin Rubin. The book also includes some standard texts on Huston: James Agee's idolizing "Undirectable Director" and Andrew Sarris's initial assault, reprinted from his 1968 *The American Cinema,* and his later retraction. Studlar and Desser also provide the two boxing stories Huston sold to *The American Mercury:* "Fool" (1929) and "Figures of Fighting Men" (1931). A filmography and selected bibliography are included.

PROGRAM

"Drawings into Film—Directors' Drawings: Sergei Eisenstein, Alfred Hitchcock, John Huston . . . et al." Essay by Annette Michelson, curated by Marc Glimcher and Mark Pollard. Pace Gallery, New York, March 26–April 24, 102 pp.

That Huston should be included in this art exhibit is interesting, as he may have certainly seen himself more as an artist than a film personality and perhaps would have preferred to have followed that direction in his life. He did have talent, as can be seen from the illustrations that appear in this catalog and in other books. Another significant source of his artistic talent is evident in his personal papers located in the Academy of Motion Picture Arts and Sciences. On scripts, letters, and other documents Huston would draw and doodle, perhaps during times of stress and pressure.

1994

BOOK

Cooper, Stephen, ed. *Perspectives on John Huston.* New York: G. K. Hall, 248 pp.

This is the second valuable collection of old and new essays on Huston to be published within two years (see also Studlar and Desser, *Reflections in a Male Eye,* 1993), a reminder of sustained interest in the director. The book opens with the editor's useful summary of the then-current state of Huston studies (although little reference is made to his enthusiastic admirers in *Positif*). Following that are some famous praise and brickbats from James Agee, Manny Farber, and Andrew Sarris. Far more comprehensive is Richard Jameson's essay from *Film Comment* (1980; see under that year), which provides detailed analysis of most of the major movies. Stephen Cooper contributes an essay on the art of adaptation as it applies to *The Maltese Falcon* (1941). An interesting aspect of this volume is a dual reassessment of *Freud: The Secret Passion* (1962) by way of Ernest Callenbach's early review and a lengthy study by Norman Holland, a professor of psychiatry. Gideon Bachmann's interview with Huston discusses how he approaches a movie and the writing of it and the importance of the script. There is also an appreciation of Huston, written just after his death, by Wieland Schulz-Keil, who persuaded him to do *Under the Volcano* (1984) and who also produced *The Dead* (1987). The book includes a selected bibliography, filmography, and rental sources.

1995

ARTICLE

Brill, Lesley. *"The African Queen* and John Huston's Filmmaking." *Cinema Journal* 34, no. 2 (Winter 1995): 3–21.

Brill offers a lengthy analysis of *The African Queen* (1952), placing the film well within the boundaries of the Huston canon and emphasizing the synthesis of romance and comedy, which nourish the theme (unusual for Huston) of the power of true love to overcome all obstacles. Brill points out that the unqualified happy ending and the clear triumph of love and virtue are almost unique in Huston's work, with the exception of *Annie* (1982, a notably inferior production). Huston did include these motifs in *Heaven Knows, Mr. Allison* (1957), but he separated the couple in the end. Brill acknowledges that Huston's vision, while never misanthropic, is generally too ironic to accommodate the pervasive good humor and harmony that grace *The African Queen.* He recommends an auteurist approach to Huston's films to yield fruitful results. Major themes, such as the search for love, the concept of the quest, religion and the suppression of instinct, and the exuberance of natural forces, are part of the texture of *The African Queen.* Although these themes also surface in such later movies as *The Treasure of the Sierra Madre* (1948), *The Night of the Iguana* (1964), *The Misfits* (1961), and *Under the Volcano* (1984), they are in different forms and usually evoke tension, contradiction, and trouble. *Note:* Lesley Brill's monograph *John Huston's Filmmaking* (New York: Cambridge University Press) for the Cambridge Studies in Film series is scheduled for publication in 1997.

BOOK

Luhr, William , ed. *The Maltese Falcon: John Huston, Director.* Rutgers Films in Print. New Brunswick, N.J.: Rutgers University Press, 1995, 210 pp.

The twenty-second in the series, this volume includes the film's complete continuity script; sections dealing with "Context, Reviews, and Commentaries";

and the writings of Dashiell Hammett, Rudy Behlmer, Bosley Crowther, Otis Ferguson, Nino Frank, James Agee, James Naremore, Jean-Loup Bourget (writing as Jacques Segond), Ilsa J. Bick, and the editor. Rounding out the volume are the filmography and selected bibliography. (Unfortunately there is no index). William Luhr's contributions are *"The Maltese Falcon:* The Detective Genre and Film Noir," "John Huston: A Biographical Sketch," and "Tracking *The Maltese Falcon:* Classical Hollywood Narration and Sam Spade." His "Tracking" essay shows the way in which the film's plot illustrates the tradition of classic Hollywood narration. Of particular interest is Luhr's first essay. He places the film precisely in both a literary and film history context, points out how the film proved a turning point in the careers of Huston and Humphrey Bogart, and summarizes the film's critical reception in the United States and France. In this last respect, the reader is recommended to read the volume's two reviews by Nino Frank, published on the occasion of the film's first appearance in Paris in 1946. Another later French appreciation of the film is that of Jean-Loup Bourget, whose "On the Trail of Dashiell Hammett" is reprinted from a 1975 issue of *Positif.*

1996

ARTICLE

Gale, Steven H. *"The Maltese Falcon:* Melodrama or Film Noir?" *Literature/ Film Quarterly* 24, no. 2 (April 1996):145–47.
    The author distinguishes between the basic elements of melodrama (intense sentiment, exaggerated emotion, emphasis on the sensational, and "conflict over an object that has no intrinsic value") and the content of film noir, which projects the focus on the individual to connect the dark psyches of the characters with certain social conventions or the state of society at a given historical moment. Following these lines, Gale maintains that Huston, who established himself as a major director in this remarkable debut, clearly breaks through the limits of melodrama to project *The Maltese Falcon* (1941) into the film noir arena precisely because of the link between the characters and a wider world and its particular moral climate. Much of Gale's article dwells on the establishing shots of the movie that place Spade against the San Francisco skyline and hint that, should anything happen to Spade's partner (Archer), Spade would feel bound to bring the guilty party to justice.

1997

ARTICLE

Richards, Peter. "The Kremlin Letter." *Film Comment* 33, no. 31 (January–February 1997): 74–81.

The author's intention is to rescue *The Kremlin Letter* from the critical limbo into which it fell after its distribution in 1970. For the studio, Twentieth Century-Fox, it was a six-million-dollar flop, and for most critics it was further proof of Huston's declining powers. Nonetheless, Richards quotes several distinguished writers on film, such as Dilys Powell, John Russell Taylor, Richard Collins, and Jean-Paul Melville, who found great merit in the picture. Richards discusses Huston's use of familiar features in the plot's design (largely male adventurers, the hunt for a false grail, the preference for living outside social legalities) and his placement of the film well within a familiar universe. He does note one unpleasant distinguishing feature: a pervasive cynicism about human behavior, in which varieties of treachery provide the means for the triumph of malice. Richards concludes that the film "presents a scathing critique of our senseless world with a clarity too painful for acceptance."

VI
General Works on John Huston

This chapter supplements the Annotated Bibliography and other bibliographical chapters. In some cases there may be some overlap between citations in this chapter and others. A number of these articles are in the production files of the Academy of Motion Picture Arts and Sciences (AMPAS), Museum of Modern Art (MOMA), and New York Public Library (NYPL), and are so indicated.

Agee, James. "Undirectable Director." *Life* 29 (September 18, 1950): 128+. (Reprinted in Cooper, *Perspectives on John Huston;* James Agee, *Agee on Film: Reviews and Comments,* New York, McDowell, Obolensky, 1958; Studlar and Desser, *Reflections in a Male Eye;* David Denby, *Awake in the Dark,* New York, Vintage, 1977; and *The Maltese Falcon: John Huston, Director,* edited by William Luhr, New Brunswick, N.J., Rutgers University Press, 1996.) AMPAS.
————. "Agee on Huston." *Films and Filming* 9, no. 11 (August 1963): 35–38.
————. "Ohjaaja Jota ei Hjailla." *Filmihullu,* no. 6 (1985): 4–9.
Alion, Y. "John Huston a fond la caisse." *Revue du Cinéma,* no. 397 (September 1984): 6.
Allais, Jean-Claude. *John Huston.* Premier Plan, no 6. Lyon: Société d'Etudes, de Recherches et de Documentation Cinématographiques (Serdoc), 1960.
The American Film Institute. John Huston. The Eleventh Annual American Film Institute Life Achievement Award, March 3, 1983. Los Angeles, 1983. NYPL.
Anderson, Ernie. Huston in Ireland: John Huston's Galway Years, Remembered by Ernie Anderson. An Gael, from the Irish Arts Center, n.d.
Anttila, Eila. "John Huston. Muistot Elavat." *Filmihullu,* no. 4 (1988): 6–13.
Archer, Eugene. "John Huston—The Hemingway Tradition in American Film." *Film Culture,* no. 19 (1959): 66–101. (Also issued in the United Kingdom as "Taking Life Seriously," *Films and Filming* 5, no. 12 [September 1959]: 13+; and 6, no. 1 [October 1959]: 9+. Also cited as "A Monograph of John Huston: Part 1—A Touch of Hemingway," *Films and Filming* 5, no. 12 [September 1959]: 13+; and "Small People in a Big World: A Monograph on John Huston, Part 2—A Touch of Melville," *Films and Filming* 6, no. 1 [October 1959]: 9+.)
Arias, R. "Master Movie Maker John Huston Finds Unwedded Bliss as Mentor to

His Caretaker Maricela Hernandez." *People's Weekly,* March 1985, 45–46.

Aristarco, Guido. "L'Anticonformismo di Huston." *Ferrania* 4, no. 10 (1950).

Armitage, Peter. "Reflections on the Critical Eye." *Film,* Autumn 1972. NYPL.

Arnold, Gary. "Salute to John Huston." *Washington Post,* October 5, 1971.

"The Art of John Huston." *MD Cinema,* April 1966. AMPAS.

Audibert, L., and J.-C. Bonnett. "Dossier: L'argent au cinema—Trois regards critiques." *Cinématographe,* no. 6 (April 1977): 15–19.

Audibert, L., et al. "Gardes-fous." *Cinématographe,* no. 123 (October 1986): 34–35.

Autera, Leonardo. "Anche ad Hollywood operano i poeti." *L'eco del cinema e dello spettacolo* 3, no. 28 (July 1952).

———. "Il sole (qualche volta) sorge ancora." *Cinema* 6, no. 106 (March 31, 1953).

———. "Huston e la critica; bibliografica." *Bianco e Nero* 18, no. 4 (April 1957): 35–47.

Bagh, P. von. "Kaksi Ikaluokkaa." *Filmihullu,* no. 6 (1985): 3.

———. "Muistinpanoja: Ohjaajasta Jota ei Ohjailla." *Filmihullu,* no. 6 (1985): 10–15.

Barnes, Peter. "The Director on Horseback." *Quarterly of Film, Radio & Television* 10, no. 3 (April 1956): 281–87.

Barry, David. "Poker as Metaphor, cf. John Huston: Beats the Devil out of Boredom." *California Magazine,* May, 1984, 129–30. AMPAS, MOMA.

Barry, N. "John Huston's Best of All Worlds." *House & Garden,* December 1964, 140–47.

"Beating the Devil, John Huston." *Vanity Fair* 46, no. 1 (March 1983): 76+. MOMA.

Benayoun, Robert. *John Huston: Textes et propos de John Huston, extraits de découpages, panorama critique, témoignages, filmographie, théâtrographie, bibliographie, documents iconographiques.* Cinéma d'aujourd'hui, no. 44. Paris: Seghers, 1966.

———. *John Huston: La grande ombre de l'aventure.* Collection cinéma classique. Série les cinéastes. Nouvelle Edition Mise à Jour. Paris: L'herminier, 1985.

Bernardi, S. "Joyce ed Ejzenstejn: Simbolo, cosa figura." *Filmcritica* 39, no. 384 (April–May 1988): 187–207.

Bester, A. "John Huston's Unsentimental Journey." *Holiday,* May 1959, 111–18.

Bianchi, Pietro. "John Huston o dell'Ironia." *La Patria,* January 18, 1953.

Bo, F. "La Piu bella delle cause perdute." *Filmcritica,* nos. 381 & 382 (January–February 1988): 22–24.

Bogdanovich, Peter. *Pieces of Time.* New York: Arbor House, 1985.

———. *Who the Devil Made It: Conversations with Various Directors.* New York: Knopf, 1997.

Boyle, Hal. "Free Soul Huston." *Los Angeles Times,* June 18, 1969.

Bressi, J. F. "Huston and Bogart." *Mise-en-scène,* no. 1 (1976): 66–70. NYPL.

Brill, Lesley. *John Huston's Filmmaking.* Cambridge Studies in Film. New York: Cambridge University Press, 1977.

Brochier, Jean-Jacques. "John Huston." *Cinéaste,* 1971, 125[–28]. MOMA.

Bruno, Edorado. "Huston, témoin d'une société." *Positif,* no. 3 (July–August 1952): 22–24.

Buache, Freddy, et al. *John Huston.* Premier Plan, no. 41. Lyon: Serdoc, 1966. NYPL.

Buckley, Michael. "John Huston." *Films in Review* 36, no. 4 (April 1985): 210–20. NYPL.

Buckner, Garth. "A Director's Progress: Huston in Perspective." *Film Journal* (Australia), no. 4 (1954?), Huston issue.

Bulnes, J. "Les immortels du cinéma: John Huston." *Cine Revue,* no. 62 (October 21, 1982): 26–28.

Byron, Stuart, and Elizabeth Weis, eds. *Movie Comedy.* New York: Grossman, 1977.

Calderoni, Franco. "Un altro 'processo a Hollywood.'" *Bianco e Nero* 18, no. 4 (April 1957): 1–4.

Canby, Vincent. "John Huston—A Master of His Art." *New York Times,* June 23, 1985. AMPAS.

———. "John Huston: Spinner of Late-Night Tales." *New York Times,* September 6, 1987, sect. 2, 15+. MOMA.

Capa, Robert. "The Little Monster Returns to Paris: Photo Essay by Robert Capa." Produced by Rupert Allan and Jack Hamilton. *Look,* October 7, 1952, 57–63.

Capara, V. "Il Ritorno del Grande Vecchio." *Revista del Cinematografo,* no. 54 (January 1981), 13–15.

Castello, Giulio Cesare. "I registi: John Huston." *Cinema* (Milan) 3, no. 43 (July 30, 1950).

———. "Dicci anni di cinema americano (1939–1949)." *Bianco e Nero* 11, no. 12 (December 1950).

Cecchini, Riccardo. *John Huston.* I Saggi, no. 5. Prato: Virdiana, 1969.

Champlin, Charles. "Huston Before, Behind Camera." *Los Angeles Times,* Calendar, August 4, 1974, 1–2. AMPAS.

———. "John Huston, a Time-Honored Filmmaker." *Philadelphia Inquirer,* June 23, 1985, 2. MOMA.

Chardière, Bernard. "Pour un juste hommage." *Positif,* no. 3 (July–August 1952): 28–30. (Reprinted in *John Huston, Collection dirigée,* edited by Gilles Ciment, 11–13, Dossier Positif Rivages, Paris, Editions Rivages, Collection Positif-Rivages, no. 2, 1988.)

Cieutat, Michel. *Les Grands thèmes du cinéma américain.* 2 vols. Paris: Les Editions du Cerf, 1988.

Ciment, Gilles, ed. *John Huston, Collection dirigée.* Dossier Positif Rivages. Paris: Editions Rivages, Collection Positif-Rivages, no. 2, 1988.

Cohen, Keith. "John Huston and Film Noir." In *Perspectives on John Huston,* edited by Stephen Cooper, 133–44. New York: G.K. Hall, 1994.

Combs, Richard. "The Man Who Would Be Ahab: The Myths and Masks of John Huston." *BFI/Monthly Film Bulletin* 52, no. 623 (December 1985): 370–74.

———. "John Huston—An Account of One Man Dead." *BFI/Monthly Film Bulletin* 54, no. 647 (December 1987): 356–57.

Cooper, Stephen. "Toward a Theory of Adaptation: John Huston and the

Interlocutive." Ph.D. diss., University of Southern California, Los Angeles, 1991.

———, ed. *Perspectives on John Huston.* New York: G.K. Hall, 1994. (Reviews of book: N. Dakovic, *Historical Journal of Film, Radio & Television* 15, no. 3 [August 1995]: 446–47; and Betsy A. McLane, *DGA* 19, no. 5 [October–November 1994]: 26–27.)

Croft, J. J. "Impressive Direction of John Huston." *Classic Images,* no. 188 (February 1991): 42.

Culhane, J. "John Huston: Hollywood's Giant." *Reader's Digest,* November 1987, 136–43.

Current Biography 10, no. 2 (February 1949). MOMA.

Custer, Elizabeth Penn. "John Huston, 1906–1987." *Proteus,* Fall 1990, vi–viii.

Davay, Paul. *John Huston.* Paris: Club du Livre de Cinéma, 1957.

Demeure, Jacques. "La fin d'un croque-mitaine: Humphrey Bogart et John Huston." *Positif,* no. 3 (July–August 1952): 31–39.

Denby, David. "A Good Man Is Hard to Find." *Premiere,* July 1990, 36–38.

Denvers, L. "John Huston: Le vieil homme et l'enfant." *Visions,* no. 36 (February 1986): 26–29.

De Santis, S. "An American Portrait: Director John Huston." *Popular Mechanics,* January 1987, 82.

Desser, David. "John Huston: A Biographical Sketch." In *Reflections in a Male Eye,* edited by Gaylyn Studlar and David Desser, 201–6. Washington, D.C.: Smithsonian Institution Press, 1993.

Desternes, J. "John Huston et l'intimisme de l'aventure." *La Revue du Cinéma,* no. 3 (October 1948): 18.

Di Giammatteo, Fernaldo. "John Huston Americano." *Bianco e Nero* 18, no. 4 (April 1957): 5–15.

"Director John Huston: A Remarkable Man and the Movies in 1956." *Newsweek,* January 9, 1956, 67–70.

"Director's Drawings." *Dance Ink* (New York) 5, no. 1 (Spring 1994): 16–21.

Dortmund, Erhard K. "Huston: First and Last." Four Quarters 7, no. 1 (Spring 1993): 15–22.

Downer, Alan S. "The Film Style of John Huston." *University—A Princeton Quarterly,* no. 29 (Summer 1966): 24–28. NYPL.

Drew, Bernard. "John Huston: At 74 No Formulas." *American Film* 5, no. 10 (September 1980): 38+. AMPAS.

Dufours, D. "John Huston: Helden en *Misfits." Film en Televisie,* no. 368 (January 1988): 10–12.

———. "Huston's Mannenmelodramas: Tussen Hoogmoed en Fatalisme." *Film en Televisie,* no. 369 (February 1988): 26–29.

Edelman, Rob. "John Huston." In *International Dictionary of Film and Filmmakers.* Vol. 3, *Actors and Actresses,* edited by Amy L. Unterburger, 585–89. 3d ed. Detroit: St. James Press, 1997.

Evans, Peter. "John Huston: *A Walk with Love and Death." Vogue,* October 1, 1968, 137+.

Farber, Manny. "Hollywood's Fair-Haired Boy." *Nation,* June 4, 1949, 642.

215

―――. "John Huston, 1950." In *Negative Space: Manny Farber on the Movies,* 32–37. New York: Praeger, 1971. (Reprinted in Cooper, *Perspectives on John Huston,* 30–34.)

Fava, C. G. "John Huston: Vecchio Amico di Gioventu." *Bianco e Nero* 48, no. 4 (October–December 1987): 82–86.

Fernandez Heredero, Carlos. *John Huston.* Coleccion Directores de Cine. Madrid: Ediciones JC, 1984 (?).

Fernandez Torres, A. "Cinefilos de todos los paises. . . !" *Contracampo,* no. 22 (June–July 1981): 39–43.

Film Comment 9, no. 3 (May–June 1973): 6–19. (Several articles.) NYPL.

Film Dope, no. 26 (January 1983): 19–24. Bio-filmography.

Filmlexicon Degli Autori e Delle Opera. Roma: Bianco e Nero, 1959. (Piece on John Huston, including filmography through 1958, and bibliography.)

Film Quarterly, Fall 1965, Huston issue.

The Film Society of Lincoln Center Presents a Tribute to John Huston, May 5, 1980. NYPL.

Finslo, Y. "John Huston Avskjedsgave." *Film og Kino,* no. 3 (1988): 12–14.

Fitzgerald, Gerald Edmund. "John Huston: Hollywood Writer-Director—A Study of the Early Career, the Period 1941–1948." Master of arts diss., University of California, Los Angeles, 1968.

Fornara, B. "Un cinéma che non divide, una Biennale che Svicola." *Cineforum* 27, no. 268 (October 1987): 8–13.

Fowler, Dan. "Walter Huston's Bad Boy John." *Look,* May 1949, 40–47.

Frank, A. "Huston: The Last Movie." *Photoplay,* December 1987, 46–47.

Garel, A. "La Matière dont on fait les rêves." *Revue du Cinéma,* no. 434 (January 1988): 58–66.

Gaston, R. "Huston at 80." *Film Directions* 8, no. 31 (1986): 5.

Gehr, R. "Huston." *Video,* September 1988, 106–9+. MOMA.

Gerosa, Guido. "Il cinema hollywoodiano." *Bianco e Nero* 13, no. 1 (1952).

Giannetti, Louis. "Roughing It: The Cinema of John Huston." In *Masters of the American Cinema,* edited by Louis Giannetti, 237–66. Englewood Cliffs, N.J.: Prentice-Hall, 1981.

Gobbers, E. "Heaven Knows, Mr. Huston." *Sinema,* no. 62 (October 1984): 10–12.

Golightly, B. "A Director's Director." *Horizon,* December 1984, 44.

Gonzalez Rubio, J. "John Huston: El de los inadaptados con esperanza." *Dicine,* no. 22 (November–December 1987): 16–17.

Griffith, R. "Wyler, Wellman and Huston: Three Directors with a Past and a Future." *Films in Review* 1, no. 1 (February 1950): 1. NYPL.

Grobel, Lawrence. *The Hustons.* New York: Scribners, 1989. (Reprint—New York: Avon Books, 1990. Excerpted in *American Way,* April 1, 1990, 76–84. Reviews of book: *Film & TV,* October 1989, D. Dufour; *Film Monthly,* July 1990, P. Wilson; *Film Quarterly,* no. 4 [1990], J. Fell; *Films in Review,* March 1990, J. Nangle; *Los Angeles,* October 1989, Merrill Shindler; *New Republic,* January 29, 1990, D. Thomson; *New Statesman,* May 11, 1990, V. Radin; *New York Times,* October 27, 1989, M. Kabutani; *New York Times,* November 10, 1989, N. Johnson; *Philadelphia Inquirer,* December 3, 1989, Desmond Ryan;

Premiere, January 1990, D. Goldman; *Sight & Sound* 59, no. 3 [1990], John Pym; *Variety,* November 29, 1989. *Note:* Clippings of reviews in MOMA.)

———. "Talent to Burn." *Movieline,* March 1990, 24–25.

———. "We Were All John's Children." *Proteus,* Fall 1990, 5–8. (Reprints the introduction to *The Hustons.*)

———. "John Huston: Mercurial Director of *The Maltese Falcon* and *The Dead* at St. Clerans." *Architectural Digest* 49, no. 4 (April 1992): 202–5+.

Hamblett, Charles. "The Year of the Bear." *Guardian,* March 3, 1972.

Hamilton, W. "The Master at St. Clerans." *House & Garden,* May 1983, 32+.

Hammen, Scott. *John Huston.* Boston: Twayne Publishers, 1985. (Review of book: *Film Quarterly,* Summer 1986, 42–43.) NYPL.

Harmetz, Aljean. "John Huston Honored by Film World." *New York Times,* March 5, 1983, 44. MOMA.

———. "Five Nominated for Directors' Guild Award." *New York Times,* January 30, 1986, C18.

———. "Patient: John Huston. Rx: Film." *New York Times,* March 8, 1987. AMPAS.

———. "John Huston Is Not Well." *Chicago Tribune,* March 12, 1987.

Haskell, Molly. "John Huston's Heart of Light and Darkness." *Proteus,* Fall 1990, 1–4.

Haun, Harry. "John Huston." *New York Daily News,* May 4, 1990, 3+.

Hendrich, V. "John Huston, ve Stylu Pokeroveho Hrace." *Film a Doba* 35, no. 10 (October 1989): 558–67.

Heredero, Carlos. *See* Fernandez Heredero, Carlos.

Higham, Charles. *Hollywood in the Forties.* New York: A. S. Barnes, 1968.

Hill, Gladwin. "John Huston—A Bull in the China Shop." *New York Times,* January 16, 1949B. (Reprinted in *The New York Times Encyclopedia of Film, 1947–1951.*) AMPAS.

Hilton, Pat. "Commercial Prospects Aren't Why John Huston Directs Films." *Drama-Logue* 8 (1985): 8–14. AMPAS.

Hodenfield, January. "A Welcome Fat Success." *New York Post,* August 5, 1972, 13. MOMA.

"Hospital Releases Huston after 22 Days." *New York Times,* August 20, 1987, C25.

Houston, Penelope. "The Ambassadors." *Sight & Sound,* April 1954, 178.

"Huston." *Lumière du Cinéma,* March 2, 1977, 80.

"Huston Honored by the AFI." *Photoplay,* July 1983, 8.

"Huston Honored in Venice." *New York Times,* September 1, 1987, C15.

"Huston: I Want to Keep On Going." *New York Times,* December 11, 1979. AMPAS.

"Huston Is Hospitalized: His Condition Is Good." *New York Times,* July 30, 1987, C17.

"Huston: Madman, Myth or Magician." *Close-up,* November 6, 1958, 3–4.

"Huston's Fight with Errol Flynn." *New York Times,* April 30, 1945. AMPAS.

"Huston's Hectic 72 Hours in New York." *Life,* February 14, 1955, 163. AMPAS.

"Huston's Marriage to Evelyn Keyes." *Los Angeles Times,* July 23, 1946.

Jacob, Gilles. "Du Côte de chez Huston." *Cahiers du Cinéma* 2, no. 12 (May 1952): 6–17. MOMA.

————. *Le Cinéma moderne.* Lyon: Serdoc, 1964.

James, Caryn. "When Film Becomes a Feast of Words (Language in Filmmaking)." *New York Times,* July 20, 1989, H11.

————. "Filmmakers' Youth: Outsiders Looking In. (Autobiographies by Directors Martin Scorsese, John Huston and Ingmar Bergman.)" *New York Times,* January 3, 1990, B1.

————. "John Huston: The Director as Monster." *New York Times,* August 9, 1992, sect. 17, 17.

Jameson, Richard T. "John Huston." *Film Comment* 16, no. 3 (May–June 1980): 25–56. (Reprinted in Cooper, *Perspectives on John Huston.*) AMPAS.

"John Cardinal Huston." *Life,* November 22, 1963, 61–62.

"John Huston." *Films and Filming* 1, no. 1 (October 1954): 3.

"John Huston." *Positif* 299 (January 1986): 2–9. (Special section.)

"John Huston: Addio all'Italia." *Bianco e Nero* 18, no. 4 (April 1957): 1–57.

"John Huston Antologia." *Casablanca* 35 (November 1983): 38–46. (Special section.)

"John Huston Designs His Own House." *Harper's Bazaar,* July 1947. AMPAS.

"John Huston Gets Film Society Honor." *Variety,* February 13, 1980, 26.

"John Huston Honored by Film Society of Lincoln Center." *Variety,* May 7, 1980, 4.

"John Huston: Musing on *Fat City* & Other Pursuits." *New York Times,* August 5, 1972. MOMA.

"John Huston 1906–1987: Favoritfilm." *Kosmorama,* Autumn 1988, 23–30.

"John Huston on Location." *Film News* (Ontario Film Institute), no. 3 (Summer 1977). MOMA.

"John Huston: There Will Never Be Another like Him." *Directors Guild of America. The Newsletter,* October 1987, 5. MOMA.

"John Huston to Receive AFI Achievement Award." *Classic Images,* no. 90 (December 1982): 75.

"John Huston Will Be Honored by the Film Society of Lincoln Center on May 5 for His Accomplishments." *New York Times,* February 6, 1980, sect. 3, 25.

Johnston, Ian. "Final Bequests and Promising Starts." *Sunday Times,* December 27, 1985.

Jolivet, Pierre. "Tribute to Huston by French director Pierre Jolivet." *Premiere,* no. 131 (February 1988).

Jones, DuPre. "Beating the Devil: Thirty Years of John Huston." *Films and Filming* 19, no. 4 (January 1973): 26–32. AMPAS, NYPL.

Joubert, Alain. "La Saga sagace de John Huston." *Positif,* no. 50 (March 1963). (Reprinted in *John Huston, Collection dirigée,* edited by Gilles Ciment, 16–20, Dossier Positif Rivages, Paris, Editions Rivages, Collection Positif-Rivages, no. 2, 1988.)

Kael, Pauline. "Note." *New Yorker,* November 10, 1969. MOMA.

Kaminsky, Stuart. *John Huston: Maker of Magic.* Boston: Houghton, Mifflin, 1978. (Review of book: *New York Times,* April 30, 1978; *Cinemonkey,* no. 1 [1979]; *Skoop,* December 1978–January 1979.)

————. "John Huston." In *International Dictionary of Films and Filmmakers.* Vol. 2, *Directors,* edited by Christopher Lyon and Susan Doll, 265–68. Chicago: St.

James Press, 1984. (Updated in Vol. 2, *Directors,* edited by Nicholas Thomas, 400–4, 2d ed, Chicago, St. James Press, 1991; and in Vol. 2, *Directors,* edited by Laurie Collier Hillstrom, 459–63, 3d ed, Detroit, St. James Press, 1997.)

Kantrowitz, Barbara. "He Believes Heroes Ought to Stand Still." *Philadelphia Inquirer,* October 10, 1980. MOMA.

Kelly, Seamus. "Seamus Kelly Pays a Visit to John Huston's Home in the West." *Irish Times,* January 2, 1960. AMPAS.

Kemp, Philip. "John Huston." In *The Oxford History of World Cinema,* edited by Geoffrey Nowell-Smith, 448–49. Oxford, U.K.: Oxford University Press, 1996.

Kezich, Tullio. "Le Tentazioni di un ribelle." *Bianco e Nero* 18, no. 4 (April 1957): 16–34.

Kilday, G. "How Huston Beats the Hollywood Odds." *Saturday Review,* January 1981, 12–16. MOMA.

King, Paul. "John Huston, Still in There Slugging." *Toronto Star,* October 13, 1979. MOMA.

Kissel, Howard. "The Real-life Adventures of John Huston." *Women's Wear Daily,* December 22, 1975, 20.

Knelman, Martin. "John Huston." *Los Angeles Herald Examiner,* January 13, 1980. AMPAS.

———. "John Huston." *Los Angeles Herald Examiner,* January 30, 1980. MOMA.

———. "*The Lion in Winter:* The Man Who Would Be Huston." *Boston Phoenix,* May 5, 1980. MOMA.

Koszarski, Richard. *Hollywood Directors, 1941–1976.* New York: Oxford University Press, 1977.

Lasoff, Sam. "Reviewing: Hollywood Misfit?" *Boston Real Paper,* May 17, 1980, 20.

Leader, Raymond. "The Great Huston." *A.B.C. Film Review,* December 1954, 10–11. AMPAS.

Lennon, Peter. "Huston in Focus on Film Industry." *Los Angeles Times,* September 16, 1967.

Leydon, Joe. "Huston on Huston." *Houston Post,* December 29, 1985, 13+.

Llinas, F. "Huston, la Warner y las ideas previas." *Contracampo,* no. 22 (June–July 1981): 44–47.

Lord, Rosemary. "John Huston." *Transatlantic Review,* no. 50 (Autumn–Winter 1974): 140–45.

Luhr, William. "John Huston: A Biographical Sketch." In *The Maltese Falcon: John Huston Director,* edited by William Luhr. New Brunswick, N.J.: Rutgers University Press, 1996.

McCarthy, Todd. "Accolades for John Huston." *Variety,* March 4, 1980, 4.

———. "AFI's Huston Tribute Appropriately Boisterous, Funny, Unsentimental." *Variety,* March 9, 1983, 22.

———. "Major Retro on John Huston Slated for Santa Fe Film Fest." *Variety,* July 8, 1987, 17.

———. "The Many John Hustons Lauded During Memorable DGA Tribute." *Variety,* September 16, 1987, 18.

McCarty, John. *The Films of John Huston.* New York: Citadel Press, 1987.

———. *The Complete Films of John Huston.* New York: Carol Publishing, 1990. (*Note:* This edition includes *The Dead.*)

McDonough, John. "John Huston: The Cinema's Grand Old Man." *Wall Street Journal,* June 30, 1987, 30 (West Coast edition), 28 (East Coast edition).

MacNamara, Paul. "A Little Visit to John Huston in Mexico." *Los Angeles,* September 1986, 158–63. MOMA.

MacTrevor, J. "John Huston était entre vivant dans la légende." *Cine Revue,* no. 37 (September 10, 1987): 37+.

Madsen, Axel. *John Huston: A Biography.* New York: Doubleday, 1978. (Review of book: *New York Times,* December 17, 1978.)

"Maestro Huston." *Newsweek,* March 7, 1966, 89.

Magny, Joel. "Huston et les mythes." *Cahiers du Cinéma,* no. 495 (October 1995): 8.

Maheo, M. "Stimulant John Huston: La vitalité et la quête." *Cinéma* (Paris), no. 418 (December 2–9, 1987): 7–9.

"A Man of Unsatorial Splendor: John Huston Makes a Name in Films—But Not for Dress." *New York Times,* January 25, 1942. (Reprinted in *The New York Times Encyclopedia of Film, 1941–1946.*) AMPAS.

Mann, Roderick. "John Huston, Still Casting a Long Shadow." *Los Angeles Times,* April 9, 1978. AMPAS.

Manvell, Roger. *New Cinema in the U.S.A.: The Feature Film Since 1946.* New York: E. P. Dutton, 1968.

Marill, A. H. "The Films of John Huston." *Films in Review,* April 1985, 215–20.

Matthews, Jack. "Film Clips: Huston Documentaries—Only Following Orders." *Los Angeles Times,* September 11, 1985, 1+.

Meyer, William R. *Warner Brothers Directors.* New York: Arlington House, 1978.

Meyerson, Peter. "The Incredible John Huston." *Pageant,* July 1960, 14–22. MOMA, NYPL.

Michaelis, Bo. "Tao. Fra Sam Spade til Sigmund Freud: To film af John Huston." *Litteratur og Samfund* 41 (May 1986): 102–12.

Miller, Gabriel. "John Huston." *Sight & Sound* 50, no. 3 (Summer 1981): 203–5.

Moilanen, H. "Kuusi kertaa Huston ja Bogart." *Filmihullu,* no. 6 (1985): 16–25.

Morandini, Morando. *John Huston.* 2d ed. Il Castoro cinema, no. 74. Rome: Il Castoro, 1995. (*Note:* First edition published in 1980.)

Morris, George. "Homage to Huston." *Soho News,* April 30, 1987, 47. MOMA.

Murcia, Claude, and Jean Lelaidier. *Litterature et cinéma.* La Revue la licorne, no. 26. Poitiers, France: La Licorne (UFR langues litteratures Poitiers), 1993.

Murray, Edward. *Nine American Film Critics.* New York: Ungar, 1975.

Natale, Richard. "Just Call Him 'Papa Huston.'" *Los Angeles Herald Examiner,* March 20, 1986.

Negulesco, Jean. "John Huston: L'artiste qui a du punch." *Positif,* no. 308 (October 1986): 56–58.

The New York Times Encyclopedia of Film: June 7, 1942; September 30, 1945A; March 23, 1947; October 23, 1947B; October 24, 1947; October 27, 1947A; May 9, 1948; June 9, 1949A; September 18, 1949; January 8, 1950B; October 16, 1950; April 15, 1951A; November 16, 1952A; January 16, 1953; January 25, 1953A;

August 29, 1953A; February 28, 1960; August 28, 1960; January 28, 1962A; July 7, 1964; November 22, 1964; March 25, 1966; July 5, 1966; July 6, 1966; December 4, 1966; June 30, 1968; January 11, 1970; January 31, 1970; June 20, 1971; August 12, 1971; October 24, 1971; July 26, 1972; April 15, 1973; May 20, 1973; July 25, 1973; June 2, 1974A; July 18, 1974; December 15, 1974; January 26, 1975; July 27, 1975; September 17, 1976; October 17, 1976C; December 27, 1977A.

(*Note:* These citations are from the *New York Times*—reprinted in *The New York Times Encyclopedia of Film,* 13 vols., New York, Times Books, 1984—and cover news reports on the movies between 1896 and 1979. They exclude material on specific films, which are indicated elsewhere.)

"Newsreel: Rothschild's New Wine Seller." *American Film,* December 1984, 9.

Nolan, William F. *John Huston: King Rebel.* Los Angeles: Sherbourne Press, 1965.

Oliva, L. "John Huston: Proti proudu." *Film a Doba* 27, no. 8 (August 1981): 472–73.

———. "John Huston: Proti proudu." *Film a Doba* 32, no. 10 (October 1986): 592–93.

———. "John Huston: Ve stylu pokeroveho hrace." *Film a Doba* 35, no. 10 (October 1989): 558–67.

"On miert keszit filmeket?" *FilmVilag* 30, no. 11 (1987): 52–58.

Paolini, Pier Francesco. "Profili: John Huston." *Bianco e Nero* 14, no. 3 (March 1953).

Peck, Tom. "Huston Meets the Eye: A New Look at the Director." *Film Comment,* May 1973, 6–11.

Pelko, S. "John Huston." *Ekran* 13, no. 2 (1988): 26–27.

Perkins, V. F. *Film as Film.* Baltimore: Penguin, 1972.

Pirie, David, ed. *Anatomy of the Movies.* New York: Macmillan, 1981.

Place, J. A., and L. S. Peterson. "Some Visual Motifs of Film Noir." *Film Comment,* January, 1974.

Porfirio, Robert. "No Way Out: Existential Motifs in the Film Noir." *Sight & Sound,* Autumn 1976.

———. "Dark Age of American Film: A Study of American Film Noir (1940–1960)." Unpublished Ph.D. diss., Yale University, New Haven, Conn., 1979.

Positif, no. 3 (July–August 1952). Special edition on Huston. (*Note:* Two copies of this rare, early special issue on Huston are located in AMPAS John Huston Archive.)

Positif, no. 20 (January 1957). Special edition on Huston.

Positif, no. 283 (September 1984): 26–43. Interview and articles with references to *Under the Volcano* and *Freud: The Secret Passion.*)

Positif, no. 299 (January 1986): 2–9 (Includes articles by subject and a review of *Prizzi's Honor* and *Reflections in a Golden Eye.*) NYPL.

Positif, no. 323 (January 1988): 5–12. Special section.

Pratley, Gerald. *The Cinema of John Huston.* New York: A. S. Barnes & Co.; London: Tantivy Press, 1977.

Pratty, Gerald. "John Huston on Location." *Film News* (Ontario Film Society), no. 3 (Summer 1977).

Premi, no. 127 (October 1987): 38–39, 163–65. Tribute and filmography.

Proteus 7, no. 2 (Fall 1990). Entire issue devoted to Huston's films.

"Questions." *New Yorker,* June 4, 1949, 21.

Quinlan, David. "Huston's Honor." *Photoplay,* November 1985, 12–15.

Rainer, Peter. "John Huston: Turning Simple Pleasure into Art." *Los Angeles Herald Examiner,* September 7, 1979, 24.

———. "John Huston Gives Longevity a Good Name." *Los Angeles Herald Examiner,* March 20, 1983. AMPAS.

Rasmussen, S. "Tykhuder." *Levende Billeder,* June 1990, 12–15.

Ravn, K. "Bedre sent end aldrig." *Levende Billeder,* March 1981, 35.

Raymond, Will. "Alt davanti alle barricate." *Cinema* (Milan) 6, no. 116 (August 31, 1953).

Real, James. "Huston as Huston." *Los Angeles Times West Magazine,* March 24, 1970. AMPAS.

Reck, T. "Huston Meets the Eye." *Film Comment* 9 (May–June 1973): 6–11.

"Revisited." *New Yorker,* February 25, 1980, 31–34. AMPAS.

Reynaert, P. "Aliez, Huston! A nous la victoire." *Amis,* no. 307 (December 1981): 33.

Robb, D. "Huston Blasts Colorizing." *Variety,* November 19, 1986, 4+.

Roberts, Jerry, and Steven Gaydos, eds. *Movie Talk from the Front Lines: Filmmakers Discuss Their Works with the Los Angeles Film Critics Association.* Jefferson, N.C.: McFarland, 1995.

Robertson, Nan. "Artists in Old Age: The Fires of Creativity Burn Undiminished." *New York Times,* January 22, 1986, C1+.

Rosenfield, Paul. "The Master Huston." *Los Angeles Times,* Calendar, February 22, 1987. AMPAS.

Rubin, Mann. "Sundays with John Huston." *Creative Screenwriting* 1, no. 4 (Winter 1994):36–40.

Rubin, Martin. "Heroic, Antihero, Aheroic: John Huston and the Problematical Protagonist." In *Reflections in a Male Eye,* edited by Gaylyn Studlar and David Desser, 137–56. Washington, D.C.: Smithsonian Institution Press, 1993.

St. Pierre, Brian. "John Huston: As He Was, Is and Probably Always Will Be." *New York Times,* September 25, 1966, 130.

Sarris, Andrew. "John Huston: Young at Heart." *Show,* January 1970, 28–29.

———. "The Festival: Films in and out of Focus—Mamma Mia, Mr. B!" *Village Voice,* October 8, 1979, 37+.

———. "Johnny, We Finally Knew Ye." *Village Voice,* May 19, 1980, 49. (Reprinted in Studlar and Desser, *Reflections in a Male Eye,* 273–76). AMPAS.

———. "Films in Focus: Leone and Huston at Cannes—Old Lions at Bay." *Village Voice,* June 5, 1984, 59–60.

"Le scepticisme, la dérision et l'amour: John Huston." *Amis,* no. 201 (February 1973): 34–35.

Scobie, William. "Huston & a Matter of Honor." *Observer Magazine,* October 20, 1985. AMPAS.

Schmedel, Scott R. "The Fat Man, Egad, Would Bid More than the IRS for John Huston's Treasures." *Wall Street Journal,* July 8, 1987, 1.

Seidenberg, R. "John Huston." *American Film,* June 1989, 66–67.

Sibilla, Giuseppe. "John Huston elementi per un profilo critico." *L'eco del cinema e dello spettacolo* 4, no. 41 (January 1953).

———. "E' andato in vacanza?" *L'eco del cinema e dello spettacolo* 5, no. 83 (October 31, 1954).

———. "America dopoguerra: Le voci muove." *Nevista del cinema italiano* 4 no. 1 (January–March 1955).

Sinyard, Neil. "Character in Action—the Films of John Huston." *Film Illustrated,* December 1981, 90–95.

Slodowski, J. "John Huston: Ostatni z wielkich." *Iluzjon,* no. 3 (1987): 5+.

Sperber, A. M., and Eric Lax. *Bogart.* New York: Morrow, 1997.

Stoop, Norman McLain. "John Huston: A Master of Foxhounds Talks about Motion Pictures." *After Dark,* August 1973, 35–40. AMPAS, MOMA.

Studlar, Gaylyn. "Life Achievement Award, John Huston." In *Magill's Cinema Annual, 1984: A Survey of 1983 Films,* edited by Frank N. Magill, 1–10. Englewood Cliffs, N.J.: Salem Press, 1984.

Studlar, Gaylyn, and David Desser, eds. *Reflections in a Male Eye: John Huston and the American Experience.* Washington, D.C.: Smithsonian Institution Press, 1993. (Review of book: *Film Criticism* 19, no. 2 [Winter 1994–95]: 103–8, D. Polan; *Film Quarterly* 47, no. 4 [1994]: 52–53, Doug K. Holm; and *Sight & Sound* 3, no. 8 [August 1993]: 36, Peter Matthews.)

Sutherland, C. "John Huston Remembers." *Ladies Home Journal,* April 1986, 98+.

Takacs, F. "A dudarc igezete." *FilmVilag* 30, no. 12 (1987): 36–41.

"Talk of the Town." *New Yorker,* June 14, 1969, 31–32.

Taylor, John Rusell. "John Huston: The Director Who Is Always Five Years Ahead." *London Times,* August 17, 1968, 15. AMPAS.

———."John Huston: The Film-maker as Dandy." *Films and Filming,* no. 383 (August 1986): 23–26. NYPL.

———. "John Huston and the Figure in the Carpet." *Sight & Sound* 38, no. 2 (Spring 1969): 70–73. MOMA, NYPL.

Telotte, J. P. *Voices in the Dark: The Narrative Patterns of Film Noir.* Urbana. Ill.: University of Illinois Press, 1989.

Tesi, G. "Sempre rosso l'emblema del coraggio?" *Cinema* (Milan) 6 no. 124 (December 30, 1953).

Tessier, Max, and A. Garel. "John Huston (1906–1987)." *Revue du Cinéma,* no. 434 (January 1988): 56–66.

Tessier, Max, and J.-C. Rohmer. "Huston, auteur et acteur." *Ecran,* no. 46 (April 1976): 32–33.

Thomas, Kevin. "Hollywood's Roman à Clef-Director John Huston." *Los Angeles Times,* September 16, 1979. AMPAS.

———. "The Adventurous Life of Director John Huston." *Los Angeles Times,* October 14, 1979. MOMA.

Toll, Roger C. "The Private World of John Huston." *House & Garden,* February 1984, 98–107. MOMA.

Touchant, J. L. "Naissance du héros hustonien." *Positif,* no. 3 (July–August 1952): 25–27. (Reprinted in *John Huston, Collection dirigée,* edited by Gilles Ciment,

14–15, Dossier Positif Rivages, Paris, Editions Rivages, Collection Positif-Rivages, no. 2, 1988.)

Tozzi, Romano. *John Huston: Hollywood's Magic People.* New York: Falcon Enterprises, 1971. (Cover title: *John Huston: A Pictorial Treasury of His Films.*) "Triple West Coast Honors for Huston." *Variety,* October 9, 1985, 5+.

Tuhus, Oddvar Bull. "Derfor elsker vi John Huston." *Samtiden,* no. 2 (1986): 67–69.

Tuska, Jon. *Encounters with Filmmakers: Eight Career Studies.* New York: Greenwood Press, 1991. (John Huston, pp. 139–87.)

Vallant, A. "John Huston." *Amis,* nos. 218 & 219 (July–August 1974): 43.

Viertel, Peter. *Dangerous Friends: At Large with Hemingway and Huston in the Fifties.* New York: Doubleday, 1992. (Review of book: *Cineaste* 20, no. 1 [1993]: 59, Patrick McGilligan; *New York Times,* September 10, 1992, Janet Maslin; and *Variety,* August 10, 1992, 71, T. Schactman.)

Vitenberg, S. "Hvis tid er penge er liv heller ikke andet." *Levende Billeder,* September 1, 1987, 26–27.

Viviani. C. "John Huston: Promenade, avec amour, après la mort." *Positif,* no. 323 (January 1988): 5–7. (Reprinted in *John Huston, Collection dirigée,* edited by Gilles Ciment, 21–24, Dossier Positif Rivages, Paris, Editions Rivages, Collection Positif-Rivages, no. 2, 1988.) NYPL.

"Who's Who in Hollywood." *Film Daily,* May 29, 1952.

Williams, P. "North West Group: The Films of John Huston—Residential Course." *Film,* February 1984, 4.

Wood, Robin. "John Huston." In *Cinema: A Critical Dictionary—The Major Filmmakers,* edited by Richard Roud. 2 vols. New York: Viking Press, 1980.

World Film Directors. Vol. 1, *1890–1945.* New York: Wilson, 1987. (John Huston, pp. 484–93.)

Wyatt, Ernest, and Ginny Rowden. "John Huston's Obsessive Characters." *Proteus,* Fall 1990, 34–41.

Yarrow, Andrew. "Huston in Hospital, Marks 81st Birthday." *New York Times,* August 6, 1987. AMPAS.

Ystavani, J. "Agee: John Huston." Translated by P. von Bagh. *Filmihullu,* no. 6 (1975): 21.

VII
Articles and Reviews of Films

This chapter includes bibliographical references to many of the films—both realized and unrealized—that John Huston was involved with as an actor, a director, and a screenwriter. Huston's lifelong love for literature is reflected in many of these projects. Consult other bibliographic sections for additional citations. The more important works are Stephen Cooper's *Perspectives on John Huston* (New York: G.K. Hall, 1994); Lawrence Grobel's *The Hustons* (New York: Scribners, 1989); John Huston's *An Open Book* (New York: Knopf, 1980); John McCarty's *The Complete Films of John Huston* (New York: Carol Publishing, 1990); Gerald Pratley's *The Cinema of John Huston* (New York: A. S. Barnes; London: Tantivy Press, 1977); Gaylyn Studlar and David Desser's *Reflections in a Male Eye* (Washington, D.C.: Institution Press, 1993, unfortunately without an index); and scheduled for publication in 1997 is Lesley Brill's *John Huston's Filmmaking* (New York: Cambridge University Press, 1997, for the Cambridge Studies in Film). Many *New York Times* articles are reprinted in *The New York Times Encyclopedia of Film* (New York: Times Books, various years.)

Each film's entry is divided into two parts: articles, including parts of monographs related to the films, and reviews. In some cases the articles and reviews are interfiled. Reviews are chiefly from newspaper and magazine pieces at the time of the film's release and are arranged alphabetically by publication title, followed by the reviewer, when known. For the most part books and articles about the film start with the writer's name and the article title. Some citations in reference sources show whether the piece has illustrations, credits, and so on, which we have retained with the usual abbreviations (for example, bio, bibliog, creds, and so forth). Articles and reviews that are in the production files of the Academy of Motion Picture Arts and Sciences (AMPAS), Museum of Modern Art (New York City) Film Library (MOMA), or New York Public Library's Performing Arts Library (NYPL) are so indicated after the citations. Reprints of reviews in the *New York Times Reviews* are signified by NYTR and *Variety Film Reviews* by VR. Some reviews have been reprinted in the following monographic publications and are indicated: *Full reviews reprinted in *Film Review Annual;* **Full reviews reprinted in *Selected Film Criticism;* ***Reprints (some condensed) in *Film Review Digest.*

225

THE ACQUITTAL. 1923. (Writer.)

ARTICLES AND REVIEWS

The American Film Institute Catalog: Feature Films, 1921–1930. New York: R. R. Bowker, 1971, 3.

Harrison's Reports, October 10, 1923, 170.

Kinematograph Weekly 867 (December 6, 1923): 50.

Morning Telegraph, September 19, 1923.

New York Times, December 12, 1923, 24. NYTR.

Variety, December 20, 1923. Skig. VR.

Note. *The American Film Institute Catalog* indicates that Huston was a contributing writer, but this assertion is extremely doubtful. (*See* chapter 14, "Huston on Film and Other Projects," for details.)

ACROSS THE PACIFIC. 1942. (Director.)

ARTICLES

Cinéma (Paris) 228 (December 1977): 64–65.

"Corralled in a Mountain Lair." *New York Times,* September 6, 1942. (Reprinted in *The New York Times Encyclopedia of Film, 1941–1946.*)

Guerif, F. *Lumière du Cinéma* 6 (July–August 1977): 72–77, creds, illus.

Halliwell, Leslie. *Halliwell's Hundred: A Nostalgic Choice of Films from the Golden Age.* New York: Scribners, 1982.

Hammen, Scott. *Film Notes.* Louisville, Ky.: Hamilton Printing Co., 1979.

Hollywood Reporter, January 4, 1943.

Kinematograph Weekly 1,855 (November 5, 1941).

Kinematograph Weekly 2,388 (April 1953): 33.

McCarthy, Todd. "The Films of John Huston" [Program notes]. Los Angeles County Museum of Art, October 10, 1980.

McCarty, Clifford. *The Complete Films of Humphrey Bogart.* Secaucus, N.J.: Citadel Press, 1965, 103–105. (Reprint—New York: Carol Publishing Group, 1995.)

Magill's Survey of Cinema: Second Series 1 (1980): 8–10. Rob Edelman.

Michael, Paul. *Humphrey Bogart: The Man and His Films.* Indianapolis: Bobbs-Merrill, 1965.

Morella, Edward, Z. Epstein, and John Griggs. *The Films of World War II.* Secaucus, N.J.: Citadel Press, 1973.

Motion Picture Guide 1 (1985): 9–10.

New York Times, October 19, 1942, 15.

"An Ounce of Prevention." *New York Times,* June 7, 1942. (Reprinted in *The New York Times Encyclopedia of Film, 1941–1946.*)

"Our Movies Leave Germans Hostile." *New York Times,* July 23, 1946. (Reprinted in *The New York Times Encyclopedia of Film, 1941–1946.*)

Sperber, A. M., and Eric Lax. *Bogart.* New York: Morrow, 1997.

Today's Cinema 6,725 (March 26, 1953): 10.

"When Films 'Quote' Films, They Create a New Mythology." *New York Times,* September 25, 1977. (Reprinted in *The New York Times Encyclopedia of Film, 1977–1979.*)

REVIEWS
Commonweal 36 (August 28, 1942): 448.
Film Daily, August 18, 1942, 6.
Harrison's Reports, August 22, 1942, 135.
Hollywood Reporter, August 8, 1942, 63. AMPAS.
London Times, November 2, 1942, 6.
Motion Picture Daily, August 14, 1942.
Motion Picture Exhibitor 28, no. 16 (August 26, 1942): 1,080.
Newsweek 20 (September 7, 1942): 80.
New York Times, September 5, 1942, 9. Bosley Crowther. NYPL, NYTR.
Theatre Arts 26 (November 1942): 693.
Time 40 (August 17, 1942): 42.
Today's Cinema 59 (October 30, 1942): 4,795.
Variety, August 19, 1942, 8. Walt. AMPAS, VR.

ACROSS THE RIVER AND INTO THE TREES. 1975–76. (Director; Writer, unrealized project.)

ARTICLES
Oliver, Charles M., ed. *A Moving Picture Feast: The Filmgoer's Hemingway.* New York: Praeger, 1989.
Phillips, Gene D. *Hemingway and Film.* New York: Ungar, 1980.

THE AFRICAN QUEEN. 1952. (Director, Writer.)

ARTICLES
Appleton, Jane Scovell. "Where Have All the Garbos Gone?" *New York Times,* April 15, 1973. Comments about how Huston handled the love scenes in the film. (Reprinted in *The New York Times Encyclopedia of Film, 1972–1974.*)
Archer, Eugene. "John Huston—The Hemingway Tradition in American Film." *Film Culture,* no. 19 (1959): 66–101.
———. "Bogart: Man and Superman." *New York Times,* January 3, 1965. (Reprinted in *The New York Times Encyclopedia of Film, 1964–1968.*)
Bacall, Lauren. "Hollywood vs. Africa." *Los Angeles Mirror,* March 31, April 1 and April 2, 1952.
Behlmer, Rudy. *Behind the Scenes: The Making of. . . .* Hollywood: Samuel French, 1990. (Reprint of *America's Favorite Movies: Behind the Scenes,* 234–52. New York, Ungar, 1982.)
Bergreen, Laurence. *James Agee: A Life.* New York: E. P. Dutton, 1984.
Braun, D. "A Look at *The African Queen.*" *Classic Images,* no. 191 (May 1991): 54.
Brill, Lesley. "The African Queen and John Huston's Filmmaking." *Cinema Journal* 34, no. 2 (Winter 1995): 3–21.

Brode, Douglas. *Films of the Fifties.* Secaucus, N.J.: Citadel Press, 1976, 59–60.

Cadet, Roger. "The African Queen." *Fiche filmographique IDHEC,* no. 76.

Cardello, J. A. "Observation Post: *The African Queen." Classic Images,* no. 117 (March 1985): 56. illus, stills.

"Carter Vetoes New Films Request *African Queen." Box Office* 111 (June 27, 1977).

Corry, John. "John Huston: Musings on 'Fat City' and Other Pursuits." *New York Times,* August 5, 1972, interv. (Reprinted in *The New York Times Encyclopedia of Film, 1972–1974.*)

Cowie, Peter. *Seventy Years of Cinema.* South Brunswick, N.J.: A. S. Barnes, 1969, 190.

Crowther, Bosley. *Reruns: Fifty Memorable Films.* New York: Putnam, 1978, 82–86.

Demeure, Jacques, and Michel Subiela. "Le bateau de Sisyphe." *Positif* 3 (July–August 1952): 14–17. (Reprinted in *John Huston, Collection dirigée,* edited by Gilles Ciment, 89–92, Dossier Positif Rivages, Paris, Editions Rivages, Collection Positif-Rivages, no. 2, 1988.)

de Selva, Lucrèce. "African Queen." *La Revue du Cinéma /Images & Son* 331 (1978): 11–16, biblio, creds, filmog. (Dossier.) Synopsis, extracts from French press reviews; bio-filmography of John Huston; analysis of the film by de Selva and others.

Dickens, Homer. *The Films of Katharine Hepburn.* New York: Citadel Press, 1971, 147–150.

Eyquem, O. "Entretien avec Peter Viertel, scénariste." *Positif* 351 (May 1990): 12–16, interv, stills.

Farber, Stephen. "Hollywood Takes on 'The Last Tycoon.'" *New York Times,* March 21, 1976. (Reprinted in *The New York Times Encyclopedia of Film, 1975–1976.*)

Film Daily, December 26, 1951, 11.

Filmkritik 10 (October 1958): 206.

Film Music 11, no. 4 (March–April 1952): 19.

Films and Filming 6 (October 1959): 10.

Films et Documents 15 (April 1954): 78.

Fultz, James R. "James Agee's Film Scripts: Adaptation and Creation." Ph.D. diss., the University of Nebraska at Lincoln, 1979. (Reprinted in *Dissertation Abstracts International [DAI],* 39 [1979]: 3884A.)

———. "Classic Case of Collaboration: *The African Queen." Literature/Film Quarterly* 10, no. 1 (1982): 13–24, illus. Details on the collaboration of James Agee and John Huston in the adaptation of Forester's novel. NYPL.

Gamarekian, Barbara. "'Gone With the Wind' Voted Greatest." *New York Times,* November 18, 1977. (Reprinted in *The New York Times Encyclopedia of Film, 1977–1979.*)

Garbicz, Adam, and Jacek Klinowski. *Cinema: The Magic Vehicle—A Guide to its Achievement. Journey Two: The Cinema in the Fifties.* New York: Schocken Books, 1983, c. 1975–79, 79–80.

Gardner, Gerald, ed. *The Censorship Papers: Movie Censorship Papers from the Hayes Office, 1934–1968.* New York: Dodd, Mead, 1987. *The African Queen* discussed.

Gerst, L. *Audience* 5 (June 1973): 1–2.

Hammel, William Muller. "James Agee and Motion Pictures." Ph.D. diss., the University of Texas, Austin, 1975. (Reprinted in *Dissertation Abstracts International [DAI]*, 35 [1975]: 5,568A.)

Hammen, Scott. *Film Notes.* Louisville, Ky.: Hamilton Printing Co., 1979. Discusses film.

Hawkins, Robert F. "'Noah' Huston's Genesis." *New York Times,* February 21, 1965, interv. (Reprinted in *The New York Times Encyclopedia of Film, 1964–1968.*)

Henry, Catherine. "The African Queen." In *International Dictionary of Films and Filmmakers.* Vol. 1, *Films,* edited by Christopher Lyon, 13–14. Chicago: St. James Press, 1984. (Reprinted in *International Dictionary of Films and Filmmakers,* vol. 1, *Films,* 2d ed., edited by Nicholas Thomas, 12–14, Chicago, St. James Press, 1990; and in 3d ed., edited by Nicolet V. Elert and Aruna Vasudeven, 10–12, Detroit, St. James Press, 1997.)

Hepburn, Katharine. *The Making of* The African Queen, *or How I Went to Africa with Bogart, Bacall and Huston and Almost Lost My Mind.* New York: Knopf, 1987. (Reviews of book: James Harvey, "The Making of *The African Queen,*" *New York Times Review of Books* 35, no. 11 [June 30, 1988]: 23–27; Edwin McDowell, "Hepburn Writes a Book about *The African Queen,*" *New York Times* 136 [February 17, 1987]: C16.)

———. "The Arts: *The Making of* The African Queen." *Newsweek* 110 (August 31, 1987): 53–55, illus, port.. Excerpt from book. MOMA.

"Humphrey Bogart et John Huston: La fin d'un croque-mitaine." *Positif* 3 (July–August 1952): 31–39.

Huston, John. "Story Behind a Safari: Director of 'African Queen' Finds Film Work in Jungle Tough but Rewarding." *New York Times,* February 3, 1952A. (Reprinted in *The New York Times Enclyclopedia of Film, 1952–1957.*)

———. "The African Queen." *Theatre Arts* 36, no. 2 (February 1952): 48–49+. Huston discusses production problems and modifications of Forester's novel. MOMA.

———. "Ladylike Kate." *American Film* 5 (September 1980): 40.

Jameson, Richard T. "John Huston," *Film Comment* [Midsection] 16, no. 3 (May–June 1980): 40–43.

Jamison, Barbara Berch. "You Can't See the Jungle for the Stars." *New York Times,* October 19, 1952. (Reprinted in *The New York Times Encyclopedia of Film, 1952–1957.*)

Kael, Pauline. *Kiss Kiss Bang Bang.* New York: Bantam Books, 1969, 281–82.

Kast, Pierre. "Fiançailles avec le notarie (notes sur Conrad et le cinéma)." *Cahiers du Cinéma* 2, no. 12 (May 1952).

Kuhns, William, and John Carr. *Teaching in the Dark: Resource Guide for Movies in America.* Dayton, Ohio: Pfalum, 1973, 54–59. Discusses film adaptation of *The African Queen.*

Libby, Bill. *They Didn't Win the Oscars.* Westport, Conn.: Arlington House, 1980. Discusses *The Maltese Falcon, The Treasure of the Sierra Madre,* and *The African Queen.*

"Life Goes on on Location in Africa." *Life* 31 (September 17, 1951): 172–76+.

Lindsey, Robert. "Even Good Films Don't Know When to Stop." *New York Times,* February 27, 1977. (Reprinted in *The New York Times Encyclopedia of Film, 1977–1979.*)

McCarty, Clifford. *The Complete Films of Humphrey Bogart.* Secaucus, N.J.: Citadel Press, 1965, 161–62. (Reprint—New York: Carol Publishing Group, 1995.)

McDowell, E. "Hepburn Writes a Book about 'African Queen.'" *New York Times,* February 17, 1987, C16, port.

Magill's Survey of Film, First Series 1 (1980): 22–25. Ellen J. Snyder.

Malcolm, Andrew H. "Huston: 'I Want to Keep Right on Going.'" *New York Times,* December 11, 1979. (Reprinted in *The New York Times Encyclopedia of Film, 1977–1979.*)

Michael, Paul. *Humphrey Bogart: The Man and His Films.* Indianapolis: Bobbs-Merrill, 1965, 159.

Motion Picture Guide 1 (1985): 27.

New York Times Magazine, February 10, 1952, 20–21.

Niven, David. *Bring on the Empty Horses.* New York: Putnam, 1975, 337–38.

Ohlin, Peter. *Agee.* New York: Ivan Obolensky, 1966.

Sadoul, George. *Dictionary of Films.* Translated, edited, and updated by Peter Morris. Berkeley: University of California Press, 1972, 3.

Schmidt, M. A. "Battling Bogart's Saga, or an Appraisal of Humphrey Bogart's Rebellious Climb up the Ladder." *New York Times,* September 6, 1953. (Reprinted in *The New York Times Encyclopedia of Film, 1952–1957.*)

Silberberg, Elliot David. "The Celluloide Muse: A Critical Study of James Agee." Ph.D. diss., the University of Wisconsin, 1974. (*Dissertation Abstracts International [DAI]* 34 [1974]: 6,662A.)

Siniscalo, Marco. "La regina d'Africa." *Ressagna de film* 2, no. 10 (January 1953).

Snyder, Stephen. "From Word to Images: Five Novelists in Hollywood." Canadian *Review of American Studies* 8, no. 2 (Fall 1997): 206–13.

Sperber, A. M., and Eric Lax. *Bogart.* New York: Morrow, 1997.

Thomas, Tony. *Great Adventure Films.* Secaucus, N.J.: Citadel Press, 1976, 162–65.

Viertel, Peter. *White Hunter, Black Heart.* London: W. H. Allen, 1954.

Villelaur, Anne. "*The African Queen* de John Huston." In *Dossiers du Cinéma. Films I.* Paris: Casterman, 1971, 4 p., bio, biblio, comment, creds, synopsis. MOMA.

Watters, Jim. "John Huston on Kipling, Hemingway and Jack Daniels." *New York Times,* February 15, 1976. (Reprinted in *The New York Times Encyclopedia of Film, 1975–1976.*)

Wilmington, Richard. *Film Criticism and Caricature, 1943–1953.* London: Paul Elek, 1975, 135–36.

Woolf, Sir John. "Letter." *The Times* (London), August 23, 1990, 2. From the chairman, Romulus Films, and producer of *The African Queen.*

Zakowski, S., and P. de Maeyer. *Klassierkers Sinema,* no. 38 (April 1982): 27–28.

REVIEWS

BFI/Monthly Film Bulletin 19, no. 217 (February 1952): 15.

Casablanca 35 (November 1983): 40.

Catholic World 174 (March 1952): 457–58.

Celluloide 27, no. 341 (November 1982): 22–23, creds. E. Nunes.

Christian Century 69 (March 19, 1952): 351.

Commonweal 55 (March 14, 1952): 566.

Films in Review 3, no. 2 (February 1952): 81–84, illus. Henry Hart.

Harrison's Reports, December 29, 1951, 207.

Hollywood Reporter, December 26, 1951, 3.

Les lettres françaises, no. 351, April 10, 1952. Georges Sadoul, "The African Queen."

Manchester Guardian Weekly, January 24, 1952. AMPAS.

Motion Picture Herald Product Digest 185, no. 13 (December 29, 1951): 1,169.

Motion Picture Daily, December 26, 1951.

New Republic 126 (March 10, 1952): 21.

New Statesman and Nation, January 12, 1952. AMPAS.

**New Yorker* 28 (February 23, 1952): 85. John McCarten. AMPAS.

New York Times, February 21, 1952, 24. Bosley Crowther. NYTR.

New York Times, February 24, 1952, sect. 2, 1.

L'Observateur, April 3, 1952. Jacques Doniol-Valcroze.

Saturday Review 35 (February 23, 1952): 29 Gilbert Seldes.

Scholastic 60 (March 12, 1952): 24.

Sight & Sound 21, no. 4 (April–June 1952): 172. Clarissa Bowen.

Spectator 188 (January 11, 1952): 44.

Theatre Arts 36 (March 1952): 45+. Arthur Knight. MOMA.

Time 59 (February 25, 1952): 68. MOMA.

Variety, December 26, 1951, 6. Brog. NYPL, VR.

Video 17 (January 1994): 86, illus. T. Soter.

Village Voice, February 16, 1988. Andrew Sarris and Tom Allen, "Revivals in Focus: A Critical Guide." MOMA.

AGEE. 1980. TV Documentary. (Interviewed.)

ARTICLES AND REVIEWS

Boston Real Paper, February 12, 1981, 33. Kathy Huffhines.

Cinéaste 10, no. 3 (Summer 1980): 39. G. Crowdus.

Film News 37 (Summer 1980): 22+. B. Flynn, "Agee."

Films in Review 30, no. 8 (October 1979): 499–500. Marsha McCreadie. AMPAS.

Literature/Film Quarterly 9, no. 4 (1981). J. R. Fultz.

Los Angeles Herald Examiner, September 15 1980, B2. AMPAS.

Los Angeles Times, September 15, 1990, part 4, 2. Kevin Thomas. AMPAS.

Maland, Charles. "*Agee:* A Film." *Southern Quarterly* 19, nos. 3 & 4 (Spring–Summer 1981): 225–28. (Also issued as *The South and Film,* edited by Warren French, 225–28, Jackson, Miss., University of Mississippi, 1981.)

New Republic, November 3, 1979. Robert Coles.

New York, November 24, 1980. David Denby.

New York Times, November 14, 1980, C7. Vincent Canby. AMPAS.

Spears, Ross. "Regional Filmmaking: The James Agee Project." *Southern Quarterly* 19, nos. 3 & 4 (Spring–Summer 1981): 223–25. (Also issued as *The South and Film,* edited by Warren French, 223–25, Jackson, Miss., University of Mississippi, 1981.)

Variety 300 (September 24, 1980): 18+. Cart (T. McCarthy). AMPAS.

Village Voice 25 (November 12, 1980): 52, creds, illus., stills. C. Rickey.

Village Voice 26 (January 21–27, 1981): 45. Andrew Sarris.

Wall Street Journal, March 13, 1981, 23. Jay Gould Boyum. AMPAS.

ALFRED HITCHCOCK PRESENTS: MAN FROM THE SOUTH. TV. 1985. (Actor.)

ARTICLES AND REVIEWS

Anderson, Nancy. "Master of Suspense Returns with Remakes of Huston's Classics." *New York City Tribune,* May 2 1985, 5B.

Farber, Stephen. "Old Hitchcock TV Episodes Remade into Movie." *New York Times,* January 29, 1985, C16. NYPL.

"Pilot, Segments, Includes 'Man from the South,' and Four Other Episodes." Ruth, Daniel. "A Hitchcock Resurrection: NBC Brings the Thriller Back from Dead." *Chicago Sun Times,* May 3, 1985, 8+. NYPL. *Variety,* May 8, 1985, 158.

Village Voice, May 14, 1985, 45. Elvis Mitchell. NYPL.

Women's Wear Daily, May 1, 1985, 26. NYPL.

THE AMAZING DR. CLITTERHOUSE. 1938. (Writer.)

ARTICLES

The American Film Institute Catalog: Feature Films, 1931–1940. Berkeley: University of California Press, 1993, p. 48.

Bookbinder, Robert. *Classics of the Gangster Film.* Secaucus, N.J.: Citadel Press, 1985, 59–62.

Clarens, Carlos. *Crime Movies: An Illustrated History.* New York: Norton, 1980, 147–49.

Hill, Gladwyn. "John Huston—A Bull in the China Shop." *New York Times,* January 16, 1949. (Reprinted in *The New York Times Encyclopedia of Film, 1947–1951.*)

McCarty, Clifford. *The Complete Films of Humphrey Bogart.* Secaucus, N.J.: Citadel Press, 1965, 58–59. (Reprint—New York: Carol Publishing Group, 1995.)

Michael, Paul. *Humphrey Bogart: The Man and His Films.* Indianapolis: Bobbs-Merrill, 1965, 80–82.

Motion Picture Guide 1 (1985): 55.

Parish, James Robert, and Alvin H. Marill. *The Cinema of Edward G. Robinson.* New York: A. S. Barnes, 1972, 115–17.

Parish, James Robert, and Michael R. Pitts. *The Great Gangster Pictures.* Metuchen, N.J.: Scarecrow Press, 1976, 20–22.

Sennett, Ted. *Lunatics and Lovers.* New York: Limelight Editions, 1985, 277+.

Trent, Paul. *Those Fabulous Movie Years: The 30s.* Barre, Mass.: Barre Publications, 1975, 144.

REVIEWS

BFI/Monthly Film Bulletin 5, no. 57 (September 1938): 220.

Commonweal 28 (August 5, 1938): 390.

Esquire 10 (November 1938): 171–72.

Film Daily, June 21, 1938, 5.

Film Weekly 20, no. 527 (November 19, 1938): 23.

Harrison's Reports, July 16, 1938, 115.

Hollywood Reporter, June 28, 1938, 3.

Look, August 2, 1938, 20, illus.

Motion Picture Daily, June 20, 1938.

Motion Picture Herald, June 25, 1938, 47+.

The New Masses 28 (July 5, 1938): 29–30.

New Republic 96 (August 10, 1938): 18. Otis Ferguson. (Reprinted in *The Film Criticism of Otis Ferguson,* edited by Robert Wilson, 228–29, Philadelphia, Temple University Press, 1971.)

Newsweek 12 (July 4, 1938): 26.

New York Daily Mirror, July 21, 1938.

New Yorker 14 (July 23, 1938): 53. John Mosher. NYPL.

New York Herald Tribune, July 21, 1938. Howard Barnes.

New York Times, July 21, 1938, 14. Frank S. Nugent. NYTR.

Picturegoer 8, no. 399 (January 14, 1939): 22.

Rob Wagner's Script 19 (August 16, 1938): 22.

The Spectator 161 (December 2, 1938): 945.

The Tattler 150 (November 30, 1938): 378.

Time 32 (July 18, 1938): 20.

Today's Cinema 51, no. 4,001 (August 27, 1938).

Today's Cinema 51, no. 4,004 (August 31, 1938).

Variety, June 22, 1938, 14. Wear. VR.

World Film News 3 (October 1938): 266–67.

AMERICAN CAESAR. TV. 1985. (Voice-over: Huston speaks some of the quotes of Douglas MacArthur).

REVIEWS

Christian Science Monitor 74 (June 11, 1982): B1.

New York Times 27, March 3, 1985, sect. 2, 27. John Corry.

Variety 318 (March 20, 1985): 120, creds. Tone (T. Scott).

Wall Street Journal, March 4, 1985, 22 (West Coast ed.), 24 (East Coast ed.). George V. Higgins.

AMERICAN FILM INSTITUTE LIFE ACHIEVEMENTS AWARDS: JOHN HUSTON. 1983.

ARTICLES AND REVIEWS

"AFI Gives Life Achievement Nod to John Huston." *Hollywood Reporter,* October 29, 1982. AMPAS.

Champlin, Charles. "Are They Fated to Be Fatal?" *Los Angeles Times,* February 26, 1983, sect. 6.

Christian Science Monitor 75 (March 22, 1983): 23. Arthur Unger.

Hollywood Reporter, March 7, 1983. Robert Osborne, "Huston Honored at the 11th AFI Lifetime Achievement Awards." AMPAS.

Los Angeles Herald Examiner, March 5, 1983. Betty Goodwin, "For Huston, an Award and Praise." AMPAS.

Los Angeles Herald Examiner, March 20, 1983. Peter Rainer.

Los Angeles Times, March 3, 1983, part 3, 1–2. Dave Pollack, "John Huston: Direct Hit on Award of a Lifetime." AMPAS.

New York Times, October 30, 1982, 13.

New York Times, March 5, 1983, 14. Aljean Harmetz, "John Huston Honored by Film World." AMPAS.

Philadelphia Inquirer, March 23, 1983. Rick Lyman.

Pollack, Dave. "Huston to Receive AFI's Life Award." *Los Angeles Times,* October 29, 1982. AMPAS.

———. "John Huston: Reminiscing with a Hollywood Treasure." *Los Angeles Times,* March 5, 1983. AMPAS.

Variety March 9, 1983, 3. Todd McCarthy, "Huston Gains AFI Achievement Award: Colleagues Sing Praises." AMPAS.

Washington Post, March 5, 1983, C1. Kenneth Turan.

ANGELA. 1977. (Actor.)

ARTICLES AND REVIEWS

Cine Revue 58 (March 2, 1978): 14–17, creds, stills. J. MacTrevor.

Copie Zero 4 (1979): 7–8, creds, stills.

Hollywood Reporter 243, no. 36 (October 22, 1976): 12.

Motion Picture Guide 1 (1985): 70.

Variety, April 11, 1984, 18. Lor. AMPAS, VR.

ANNIE. 1982. (Director.)

ARTICLES

American Cinematographer 58, no. 6 (June 1982): 556+. Two articles dealing with the making of *Annie* include background information on its filming, locations used, sets, props, and an interview with Richard Moore, the cinematographer, who describes how the movie was filmed.

Arenson, K. W. "Market Place: *Annie,* the Prospects." *New York Times,* May 21, 1982, D6.

Caufield, D. Los Angeles Times, May 16, 1982, Calendar. AMPAS.

Dangaard, C. "Comment l'histoire de la petite orpheline Annie est devenue le film au plus gros budget de l'histoire du cinéma!" *Cine Revue* 62 (June 24, 1982): 10–11.

Di Nubila, D. "Shrewd Promo Linking 'Annie' Arg. TV Star Boosts Pic's B.O." *Variety* 309 (December 29, 1982): 26.

Harmetz, Aljean. "Annie Finds Its Screen Annie." *New York Times,* January 15, 1981, C17, illus. MOMA.

Hinds, Michael de Courcy. "A Mansion for Daddy Warbucks." *New York Times,* June 25, 1981, sect. 3, C1. MOMA.

Horowitz, S. "Carol Burnett Gets a Kick out of *Annie.*" *American Film* 7, no. 7 (May 1982): 46–49, illus. NYPL.

Homan, H., and R. Kruthof. "*Skoop* enquete scenario-seminar 'ze nemen liever her heisje van de buren dan een echte sciptschrijver.'" *Skoop* 18 (December 1982–January 1983): 20–24.

Jacobson, H. "Stark Reality." *Film Comment* 18, no. 4 (July–August 1982): 47–48. NYPL.

"John Huston, 74, Health Problems, Rush Pre-prod. & Start Filming Early in May." *New York Times,* January 26, 1981, sect. 3, 23.

Kaminsky, R. "Columbia Hyping Mega-musical 'Annie' Like There's No Tomorrow." *Film Journal* 85 (May 3, 1982): 3, illus.

Klain, S. "'Annie' O'seas Xmas Push Tries Rare Total Dub-job in 6 Lingos; Japan, Brazil in Non-reader Bid." *Variety* 309 (November 4, 1982): 3+.

Los Angeles Herald Examiner, May 19, 1982. Making of *Annie.* AMPAS.

Los Angeles Times, November 15, 1981. Article on trouble with Teamsters in making film. AMPAS.

Los Angeles Times, May 21, 1982. Article on bad reviews of *Annie.* AMPAS.

Los Angeles Times, May 26, 1982, Calendar. Piece on *Annie.*

McCarthy, Todd. "Huston Chides 'Annie' Reviews." *Variety* 307 (May 26, 1982): 15.

Magill's Cinema Annual, 1983, 56–59. Irene Kahn Atkins.

Mariani, J. "Bringing 'Annie' to the Screen." *Millimeter* 10 (May 1982): 52–54+, illus, stills. NYPL.

Masson, Alain. "Le petite rousse de la bibliothèque rose." *Positif* 264 (February 1983): 74–76, creds, stills. NYPL. (Reprinted in *John Huston, Collection dirigée,* edited by Gilles Ciment, 162–64, Dossier Positif Rivages, Paris, Editions Rivages, Collection Positif-Rivages, no. 2, 1988.)

Matthews, Jack. "After 40 Years, He's Directing a Musical." *Philadelphia Inquirer,* February 27, 1982. MOMA.

Motion Picture Guide 1 (1985): 77.

New York Times, August 8, 1982. AMPAS.

Quindlen, A. "The Film *Annie* Speaks Her mind." *New York Times,* May 16, 1982): sect. 2, 1+, illus, interv, stills.

"Showmandiser: 'Annie' Tie-ins and Merchandising." *Box Office* 118, April 1982, 80, illus.

Turan, Kenneth. "Hollywood Puts Its Money on *Annie.* Ray Stark & John Huston Comment." *New York Times Magazine,* May 2, 1982, sect. 4, 40–43. AMPAS, MOMA.

REVIEWS

Atlantic Monthly 249 (June 1982): 88–89, illus. S. Schiff.
*BFI/Monthly Film Bulletin 49, no. 583 (August 1982): 164–65, creds, stills. Tom Milne.
Boston Globe, June 18, 1982, 63. Michael Blowen.
Boston Phoenix, no. 3 (June 22, 1982): 2. Alan Stern.
Box Office 118 (June 1982): 62–63. D. Linck.
Cahiers du Cinéma, no. 344 (February 1983): 62, stills. M. Chion.
Casablanca 26 (February 1983): 56, illus.
Celluloide 28, no. 348 (May 1983): 137. N. Viana.
Chicago, August 1982, 105–6. Dave Kehr.
Christian Century 99 (June 9–16, 1982): 708–9. J. M. Wall.
Christianity Today 26 (August 6, 1982): 61.
*Christian Science Monitor, June 10, 1982, 18. David Sterritt.
Cineforum 23, no. 222 (March 1983): 75–76, creds, illus. E. Comuzio.
Cinéma (Paris) 289 (January 1983): 49–50, creds, illus. A. Tarqui. NYPL.
Cine Revue 62 (June 10, 1982): 9. F. Dhont.
Cine Revue 62 (November 25, 1982): 20–23, stills. F. Dhont and M. MacTrevor.
Cine Revue 62 (December 16, 1982): 40, creds, stills.
Coming Attractions, July–August 1982, 88+. Jake Paris.
Commonweal 109 (June 4, 1982): 338–39. C. L. Westerbeck.
Commonweal 109 (June 18, 1982): 371–72. C .L. Westerbeck.
Contemporary Review 241 (November 1982): 267–68. D. Shipman.
Dance Magazine 56 (June 1982): 52–56, stills. Norman McLain Stoop, "Why Annie Isn't Annie Anymore."
Ecran Fantastique, no. 30 (January 1983): 76–77. NYPL.
Epoca, December 24, 1983, 88. Nuccio F. Marera. MOMA.
Fantas 12, nos. 5 & 6 (1982): 86. D. Bartholomew and S. Rebello.
Film Bulletin 43 (July 1982), creds. D. Munroe.
Filmcritica 34, no. 331 (January 1983): 27–29, stills. G. Turroni.
Film en Televisie, no. 307 (December 1982): 10–11, creds, illus, stills. Ronnie Pede.
Film en Televisie, no. 307 (December 1982): 26–27, illus. R. Pede, "Filmmuziek."
Film Journal 85 (May 3, 1982): 9, creds, stills. J. Curry.
Films 2, no. 7 (June 1982): 25–29. Photo section.
Films 2, no. 9 (August 1982): 33, creds, illus. Harlan Kennedy.
Films 2, no. 10 (September 1982): 35, creds. S. Button.
Films and Filming, no. 335 (August 1982): 29–30, creds, illus. T. Vallence. NYPL.
FilmVilag 30, no. 2 (1987): 55, creds.
Fortune 105 (June 28, 1982): 31.
Hollywood Reporter 271, no. 42 (May 12, 1982): 3.
Horizon 25 (April 1982): 37.

Inquiry, June 1982, 53. Stephen Harvey. MOMA.
Kultura 33, no. 2 (1987): 80–81, port, stills.
Levende Billeder 8 (July 15, 1982): 31–33. K. Schumacher.
Levende Billeder 8 (December 15, 1982): 28–30, stills. U. Breuning.
Los Angeles Times, May 21, 1982, Calendar, sect. 6, 1. Sheila Benson. AMPAS.
Maclean's 95 (May 31, 1982): 57.
MD, March 6, 1982. MOMA.
Motion Picture Product Digest 9, no. 25 (June 1982): 97–98.
New Republic 186 (June 9, 1982): 22–23. Stanley Kauffmann.
Newsday, May 21, 1982, 11. Joseph Gelmis.
New Statesman, 104 (July 9, 1982): 28. John Coleman.
Newsweek 99 (May 24, 1982): 82+. David Ansen.
New York 15 (May 31, 1982): 79–80, stills. David Denby. AMPAS, MOMA.
New York Daily News, May 21, 1982, 5+. Kathleen Carroll. MOMA.
New Yorker 58 (May 31, 1982): 82–84. Pauline Kael. AMPAS. (Reprinted in Pauline
    Kael's *Taking It All In,* 341–47, New York, Holt, Rinehart and Winston, 1984.)
New York Post, May 21, 1982, 49. Archer Winsten.
New York Times, May 21, 1982, sect. 3, C4, creds, stills. Vincent Canby. NYTR.
Penthouse 13 (August 1982): 46–47. R. Greenspun.
Philadelphia Inquirer, June 18, 1982, 26. Desmond Ryan. MOMA.
Photoplay 33, no. 6 (June 1982): 64–65, stills. M. Branford, "A Preview of Annie."
Photoplay 33 (August 1982): 25+, creds, stills. D. Smith.
La Revue du Cinéma 379 (January 1983): 22, creds, stills. Gilles Colpart. NYPL.
La Revue du Cinéma , hors serie 28 (1983): 25, creds. R. Bassan.
Saturday Review 9 (June 1982): 64–65, stills. Judith Crist.
Screen International 346 (June 1982): 20.
Segnocinema 3, no. 8 (May 1983): 59, creds, illus. A. Morsiani.
Séquences 110 (October 1982): 58–60, creds, stills. M. Petrowski.
Skoop 18, nos. 9 & 10 (December 1982–January 1983): 18–19, stills. J. Voeten.
Time 119 (May 24, 1982): 75, stills. Richard Corliss.
Variety 307, no. 2 (May 12, 1982): 11, creds. "Har" [J. Harwood]. AMPAS, VR.
Village Voice 27 (June 1, 1982): 51+, stills. Andrew Sarris. AMPAS.
Wall Street Journal, May 21, 1982, 25 (West Coast ed.), 31 (East Coast ed.). Jay
    Gould Boyum.
Washington Post, June 18, 1982, C1. Gary Arnold.
Washington Post, June 18, 1982, Weekend, 15. Judith Martin.
Women's Wear Daily, May 18, 1982, 24. Howard Kissel.

APPOINTMENT WITH DESTINY . . . THE CRUCIFIXION OF JESUS. 1972. (Narrator.)

ARTICLES AND REVIEWS
Films in Review 32, no. 10 (December 1981): 633.
Hollywood Reporter 220, no. 38 (April 4, 1972): 8.
New York Times, February 6, 1972, sect. 2, 19. NYTR.
Variety, April 5, 1972.

THE ASPHALT JUNGLE. 1950. (Director, Writer.)

ARTICLES

Archer, Eugene. "John Huston—The Hemingway Tradition in American Film." *Film Culture,* no. 19 (1959): 66–101.

Barby, F.-R. "John Huston: Le noir et le blanc comme l'argile du sculpteur." *Cinéma* (Paris) 447 (June 22, 1988).

Bookbinder, Robert. *Classics of the Gangster Film.* Secaucus, N.J.: Citadel Press, 1985, 188–94.

Brode, Douglas. *The Films of the Fifties.* Secaucus, N.J.: Citadel Press, 1976, 39–42.

Burnett, W. R. "Afterward." In *The Asphalt Jungle: A Screenplay,* by Ben Maddow and John Huston and edited by Matthew J. Bruccoli, 145–47. Carbondale, Ill.: Southern Illinois University Press, 1980.

Cinéma (Paris) 447 (June 22, 1988): 13.

Conway, Michael, and Mark Ricci. *The Films of Marilyn Monroe.* Secaucus, N.J.: Citadel Press, 1964, 38–41.

Cowie, Peter. *Seventy Years of Cinema.* South Brunswick, N.J.: A. S. Barnes, 1969, 178.

Crowther, Bosley. *Reruns: Fifty Memorable Films.* New York: G. P. Putnam, 1978, 72–76.

Delaume, G. "The Broadcasting of a Colourized Version of a Film." *EBU Review* 41, no. 1 (January 1990): 14–15. John Huston's heirs brought an injunction against French TV channel La Cinq for broadcasting a colorized version of *The Asphalt Jungle.*

Dufour, F. "Monsieur Lapsus." *Cinéma* (Paris) 167 (June 1972): 22–24, illus. Critique of an introduction by Henri Verneuil to an ORTF screening of *The Asphalt Jungle.*

Edward, R. "Jurisprudence." *Film Echange* 51, no. 3 (1990): 48–51. Lawsuit regarding coloring of *The Asphalt Jungle.*

"Film colories: La nouvelle conjuration des imbeciles." *La Revue du Cinéma* 445 (January 1989): 3.

"French Appeals Court Lets Turner Distribute Colorized Huston Film." *Wall Street Journal,* July 10, 1989, B5.

"A French Court Blocks an Altered Huston Film." *New York Times,* July 11, 1988, C13.

Garbicz, Adam, and Jacek Klinowski. *Cinema: The Magic Vehicle—A Guide to Its Achievement. Journey Two: The Cinema in the Fifties.* New York: Schocken Books, c. 1975–79, 53.

Gerard, Olivier. "Les Gangsters ne sont plus des gangsters: *Asphalt Jungle.*" *Raccords,* no. 7 (Spring 1951).

Hammen, Scott. *Film Notes.* Louisville, Ky.: Hamilton Printing Co., 1979.

Hawkins, Robert F. "'Noah' Huston's Genesis." *New York Times,* February 21, 1965A. (Reprinted in *The New York Times Encyclopedia of Film, 1964–1968.*)

Jaffe, Sam. "This World: Behind the Scenes at the Making of the Film." *San Francisco Chronicle,* June 18, 1950, 20+. AMPAS.

Holly, Ellen. "Where Are the Films about Real Black Men and Women?" *New York Times,* June 2, 1974. (Reprinted in *The New York Times Encyclopedia of Film, 1972–1974.*)

Jameson, Richard T. "The Asphalt Jungle." *Film Comment* [Midsection] 16, no. 3 (May–June 1980): 38–40.

Jamison, Barbara Birch. "Body and Soul: A Portrait of Marilyn Monroe Showing Why Gentlemen Prefer That Blonde." *New York Times* July 12, 1953. (Reprinted in *The New York Times Encyclopedia of Film, 1952–1957.*)

Kast, Pierre. "Fiançailles avec le notaire (notes sur Conrad et le cinéma)." *Cahiers du Cinéma* 2, no. 12 (May 1952).

Kemp, Philip. "The Asphalt Jungle." In *International Dictionary of Films and Filmmakers.* Vol. 1, *Films,* 2d ed., edited by Nicholas Thomas, 60–61, Chicago, St. James Press, 1990; and in 3d ed., edited by Nicolet V. Elert and Aruna Vasudeven, 69–70, Detroit, St. James Press, 1997.)

Lightman, Herb A. "Realism with a Master's Touch." *American Cinematographer* 31, no. 8 (August 1950): 271.

Lottman, Herbert R. "France Gets 'Moved Right' Ruling. (Cast Involving the Right to Broadcast the Color-enhanced Version of John Huston's 'Asphalt Jungle'). *Publisher's Weekly* 238, no. 32 (July 25, 1991): 9.

Magill's Survey of Cinema: Second Series 1:124–26. Carl F. Macek.

Malcolm, Andrew. "Huston: 'I Want to Keep Right on Going.'" *New York Times,* December 11, 1979. (Reprinted in *The New York Times Encyclopedia of Film, 1977–1979.*)

Massie, Brenda. "Cinemateque Notes: *The Asphalt Jungle.*" New York: Columbia University, n.d. MOMA.

Motion Picture Guide 1 (1985): 101–2.

Parish, James Robert, and Michael R. Pitts. *The Great Gangster Pictures.* Metuchen, N.J.: The Scarecrow Press, 1976, 27–28.

Peck, Seymour. "It Must Be More than Sex." *New York Times,* September 14, 1958A. (Reprinted in *The New York Times Encyclopedia of Film, 1958–1963.*)

Poulos, Phil Johnston. "Benighted Eyes: W. R. Burnett and Film Noir (CA)." Ph.D. diss., University of Tulsa, Oklahoma, 1983. (*Dissertation Abstracts International [DAI]* 44 [1983]: 1,451–52A.) *High Sierra* and *The Asphalt Jungle* discussed.

Riding, A. "Filmmakers Are Victors in Lawsuit on Coloring." *New York Times,* August 25, 1991, 60.

Sadoul, Georges. *Dictionary of Films.* Translated, edited, and updated by Peter Morris. Berkeley: University of California Press, 1972, 15.

Silver, Alain, and Elizabeth Ward, eds. *Film Noir: An Encyclopedic Reference to the American Style.* 3d ed., rev. Woodstock, N.Y.: Overlook Press, 1992. *The Asphalt Jungle* (pp. 13–15) and includes full credits, synopsis, and analysis.

Simon, John. "From Fake Happyendings to Fake Unhappyendings." *New York Times,* June 8, 1975. (Reprinted in *The New York Times Encyclopedia of Film, 1975–1976.*)

Toronto Film Society. Program Notes on *The Asphalt Jungle.* 1969. MOMA.

Tuska, Jon. *Dark Cinema: American Film Noir in Cultural Perspective.* Westport, Conn.: Greenwood Press, 1984.

Vives, Madeleine. "De l'homme, *Asphalt Jungle.*" *Positif,* no. 3 (July–August 1952): 2–9. (Reprinted in *John Huston, Collection dirigée,* edited by Gilles Ciment, 78–84, Dossier Positif Rivages, Paris, Editions Rivages, Collection Positif-Rivages, no. 2, 1988.)

Watters, Jim. "John Huston on Kipling, Hemingway and Jack Daniels." *New York Times,* February 22, 1976. (Reprinted in *The New York Times Encyclopedia of Film, 1975–1976.*)

Wilmington, Richard. *Film Criticism and Caricatures, 1943–1953.* London: Paul Elek, 1975, 114–15.

You, D. "Le droit moral des auteurs américains." *Film Echange,* no. 45 (1989): 51–64. Judgment of the Court of Appeals in Paris authorizing the transmission of the colorized version of *The Asphalt Jungle.*

Zinman, David. *Fifty from the Fifties: Vintage Films from America's Mid-Century.* New York: Arlington House, 1979, 17–26.

REVIEWS

BFI/Monthly Film Bulletin 17, no. 200 (September 1950): 134. Penelope Houston.
Brooklyn Eagle, June 9, 1950. Jane Corby. AMPAS.
Casablanca 10 (October 1981): 54, illus. M. Marinero.
Christian Century 67 (July 5, 1950): 831.
Cinema (Milan) 3, no. 45 (August 30, 1950). Guido Aristarco.
Cinéma (Paris) 269 (May 1981): 88–89, creds. G. Haustrate.
Cinématographe 67 (May 1981): 49–50, creds, illus. L. Audibert.
Combat, January 5, 1957. R.-M. Arlaud. (Originally in *Positif,* no. 3 [July–August 1952]: 45.)
Commonweal 52 (June 16, 1950): 249.
Contracampo, nos. 25 & 26 (November–December 1981): 80. J. Vega.
Daily Compass, June 9, 1950. Seymour Peck. AMPAS.
Daily Worker, June 9, 1950. Jose Yglesias. AMPAS.
Film Daily, May 5, 1950, 8.
Filmkritik 23, no. 6 (June 1979): 259–61, illus. P. Nav.
Filmkritik 24, no. 1 (January 1980): 28–29. H. Bitowsky.
Films and Filming 6 (October 1959): 9–10.
Films in Review 1, no. 5 (July–August 1950): 15–17. Arthur Knight.
**Fortnight* 8, no. 3 (June 23, 1950): 32.
Good Housekeeping 131 (July 1950): 17.
Harrison's Reports, May 6, 1970, 70.
**Hollywood Reporter* 108, no. 49 (May 5, 1950): 3+.
Listener 116, no. 2,973 (August 14, 1986): 28. R. Combs.
Los Angeles Times, June 21, 1950. Edwin Schallert. AMPAS.
Motion Picture Daily, May 5, 1950.
Motion Picture Herald Product Digest, May 6, 1950, 285.
The Nation 171 (July 15, 1950): 65.
The Nation 171 (October 28, 1950): 397.
New Republic 122 (June 26, 1950): 23.

New Statesman and Nation 40 (October 28, 1950): 395.
Newsweek 35 (June 12, 1950): 88. AMPAS.
New York Daily News, June 9, 1950. Kate Cameron. AMPAS.
New Yorker 26 (June 17, 1950): 54. Pauline Kael. (Reprinted in Kael's *Going
    Steady,* Boston, Little, Brown, 1970.)
New York Herald Tribune, June 9, 1950. Howard Barnes. AMPAS.
New York Journal American, June 9, 1950. Rose Pelswick. AMPAS.
New York Times, June 9, 1950, 29. Bosley Crowther. AMPAS, NYPL, NYTR.
New York Times, June 18, 1950, sect. 2, 1. (Also reprinted in *The New York Times
    Film Reviews. A One-Volume Selection, 1913–1970,* edited by George Amberg,
    New York, Arno Press, 1971.)
New York Times, March 23, 1986, H30. Vincent Canby.
New York World Telegram, June 9, 1950. Alton Cook. AMPAS.
Saturday Review 33 (June 24, 1950): 34.
*Séquence 12 (Autumn 1950): 40–42. Derrick Grigs.
Sight & Sound 19, no. 7 (November 1950): 286–88, illus. Gavin Lambert, "Writer
    and Director: *The Wooden Horse* and *The Asphalt Jungle.*"
Time 55 (June 19, 1950): 92. AMPAS.
Time Out 469 (April 13, 1979): 47.
Today's Cinema 75 (August 10, 1950).
Variety, May 5, 1950, 3+.
Variety, May 10, 1950. Brog. VR.

B. TRAVEN: A MYSTERY SOLVED. 1978. TV (U.K.). (Interviewed.)

ARTICLES
"The Mystery of B. Traven Unraveled by BBC Team." *New York Times,* December
    22, 1978, C30.
Wyatt, Will, and Robert Robinson, "Who Was B. Traven?" *The Listener,* January 4,
    1979.
———. "The Identity of B. Traven." *The Listener,* January 11, 1979.

BACALL ON BOGART. 1988. TV. (Appearance.)

REVIEWS
New York, March 14, 1988. John Leonard.
New York Times 137 (March 6, 1988): H33. Jamie James.
New York Times 137 (March 11, 1988): C34. John O'Connor.
Variety, April 27, 1988.

BACKGROUND TO DANGER. 1943. (Writer, uncredited.)

ARTICLES AND REVIEWS
Film Index (Australia) 31 (1975): 263.
Harrison's Reports, June 12, 1943, 94.
Motion Picture Guide 1 (1985): 122–23.
New Yorker, July 10, 1943.

New York Times, July 3, 1943, 11. Bosely Crowther. NYTR.
Time, July 19, 1943.
Today's Cinema 60, no. 4,895 (June 25, 1943): 20.
Variety, June 9, 1943. Walt. AMPAS, VR.

THE BARBARIAN AND THE GEISHA. 1958. (Director.)

ARTICLES AND REVIEWS

America 100 (October 18, 1958): 89.
BFI/Monthly Film Bulletin 25, no. 298 (November 1958): 139.
Catholic World 188 (December 1958): 241.
Commonweal 69 (October 17, 1958): 73.
Daily Cinema 8,066 (October 13, 1958): 6.
Falk, Ray. "Shooting a 'Barbarian': Townsend Harris Biography Is Filmed at
     Authentic Japanese Locales." *New York Times,* January 12, 1958. (Reprinted in
     The New York Times Encyclopedia of Film, 1958–1963.)
Film Daily 114 (September 30, 1958): 6.
Filmfacts 1 (November 5, 1958): 181–82.
Film Quarterly 12, no. 2 (Winter 1958): 42–45. Arlene Croce.
Films 1 (1958): 181, creds.
Films and Filming 5, no. 3 (December 1958): 22, illus. Peter G. Baker.
Films in Review 9, no. 8 (October 1958): 462. I. Tanaka.
Harmetz, Aljean. "Notes: Hustling 'Lipstick,' Chopping Classics, Rating
     Previews." *New York Times,* May 9, 1976. (Reprinted in *The New York Times
     Encyclopedia of Film, 1975–1976.*)
Harrison's Reports, October 4, 1958, 158.
Hollywood Reporter 151, no. 44 (September 30, 1958): 3.
"John Huston Hits a Double." *Look* 22 (November 25, 1958): 106+.
Kinematograph Weekly 2,670 (October 16, 1958): 16.
Motion Picture Daily, September 30, 1958.
Motion Picture Guide 1 (1985): 139.
Motion Picture Herald 213, no. 2 (October 11, 1958): 11.
Nason, Richard W. "Huston Hits High with 'Heaven' and 'Geisha.'" *New York
     Times,* September 28, 1958, interv. (Reprinted in *The New York Times
     Encyclopedia of Film, 1958–1963.*)
New Republic 139 (November 3, 1958): 21–22.
Newsweek 52 (October 6, 1958): 90–91.
New Yorker 34 (October 11, 1958): 94.
New York Herald Tribune, September 28, 1958, sect. 4, 3. Richard C. Wald, "The
     World Is a Motion Picture Set to John Huston, a Traveling Director." MOMA.
New York Herald Tribune, October 3, 1958, 3. Paul Beckley.
New York Times, September 25, 1958, 32.
New York Times, October 3, 1958, 25. Bosley Crowther. NYTR.
St. Pierre, Brian. "John Huston: As He Was, Is, and Probably Always Will Be."
     New York Times, September 25, 1966. (Reprinted in *The New York Times
     Encyclopedia of Film, 1964–68.*)

Saturday Evening Post 230 (May 10, 1958): 28–29+. Keyes Beech, "Hollywood's Oriental Fad." MOMA.

Saturday Review 41 (October 11, 1958). AMPAS.

Time 72 (October 6, 1958): 89.

Variety, October 1, 1958, 6. Powe. VR.

Zmijewsky, Steve, Boris Zmijewsky, and Mark Ricci. *The Complete Films of John Wayne.* Secaucus, N.J.: Citadel Press, 1986, 220–22.

BATTLE FOR THE PLANET OF THE APES. 1973. (Actor.)

ARTICLES AND REVIEWS

BFI/Monthly Film Bulletin 40, no. 475 (August 1973): 163–64.

Cinefantastique 3, no. 1 (Autumn 1973): 29. Dale Winogura.

Cinema TV Today 10,041 (July 21, 1973): 19, creds, illus. D. Winogura.

Filmfacts 16, no. 3 (1973): 61–63, creds, illus.

Films and Filming 20, no. 2 (November 1973): 59, creds A. Stuart.

Films in Review 24, no. 7 (August–September 1973): 440.

Hollywood Reporter 226, no. 22 (May 1973): 3.

Kosmorama 20, no. 120 (April 1974): 221, illus. P. Schepelern.

Motion Picture Guide 1 (1985): 147.

New York Times, July 13, 1973, 9. Vincent Canby. NYTR.

Variety, May 23, 1973, 28. Murf. VR.

Village Voice, August 16, 1973, 65. Gerald Weeles.

BATTLE OF SAN PIETRO. 1945. (Director, Writer, Narrator.)

ARTICLES

Barnes, Nancy. "Art of the Forties" [Program notes]. Museum of Modern Art: Department of Film, March 12, 1991.

Barsam, Richard Meran. *Nonfiction Film: A Critical History.* New York: Dutton, 1973.

Beal, Greg. *CinemaTexas Program Notes* 12, no. 2 (1977), biblio, creds, filmog.

Bertelsen, L. "*San Pietro* and the 'Art' of War." *Southwest Review* 74 (Spring 1989): 230–56, illus.

Bigio, Denise. "Huston Goes to War." *International Documentary,* December 1985. AMPAS.

Champlin, Charles. "Huston Wartime Films on KCET." *Los Angeles Times,* April 30, 1981.

Crowther, Bosley. "Hollywood Defended: An American View." *New York Times,* September 30, 1945. (Reprinted in *The New York Times Encyclopedia of Film, 1941–1946.*)

Culbert, David. "The Making of John Huston's *The Battle of San Pietro.*" Paper presented at the University Seminar on Cinema and Interdisciplinary Interpretation. Museum of Modern Art, New York, February 23, 1984.

———, ed. *Film & Propaganda in America.* Westport, Conn.: Greenwood Press, 1990.

Desser, David. "The Wartime Films of John Huston: Film Noir and the Emergence of the Therapeutic." In Gaylyn Studlar and David Desser, *Reflections in the Male Eye,* 19–32. Washington, D.C.: Smithsonian Institution Press, 1993.

Edgerton, Gary. "Revisiting the Records of Wars Past: Remembering the Documentary Trilogy of John Huston." *Journal of Popular Film and Television* 15, no. 1 (Spring 1987): 27–41. (Reprinted in Studlar and Desser, *Reflections in a Male Eye,* 33–61.)

Gallez, Douglas. "Patterns in Wartime Documentaries." *Quarterly of Film, Radio & TV* 10, no. 2 (Winter 1955): 125+.

Garner, Jack. "John Huston's Frank Look at War Finally Released." *Rochester* (New York) *Democrat and Chronicle* 27 (August 9, 1981): F6–F7.

Garrett, G. "John Huston's 'The Battle of San Pietro.'" *War Literature & Arts* 5, no. 1 (1993): 1–12, biblio.

Gleiberman, Owen "'Let There Be Light' and 'The Battle of San Pietro.'" *Boston Phoenix,* May 19, 1981.

Hammen, Scott. *Film Notes.* Louisville, Ky.: Hamilton Printing Co., 1979.

———. "At War with the Army." *Film Comment* 16, no. 2 (March–April 1980): 19–23, illus.

Hill, Gladwyn. "John Huston—A Bull in the China Shop." *New York Times,* January 16, 1949. (Reprinted in *The New York Times Encyclopedia of Film, 1947–1951.*)

Hölbling, Walter. "Patriotische Pflicht und die Veroflichtung zur Dokumentation: John Ford, John Huston und US Dokumentarfilme zum Zweiten Weltkreig." In *Der Krief der Bilder: Ausgewahlte Dokumentarfilme zum Zweiten Weltkrieg und zum Vietnamkrieg,* edited by Michael Barchet, Maria Diedrich, and Walter Hölbling, 25–40. (Crossroads: Studies in American Culture, Bd. 8.) Trier: Wissenshchaftlicher Verlag Trier, 1993. Abstract in English.

Hughes, Robert, ed. "The Courage of Men: An Interview with John Huston." In *Film: Book 2, Films of Peace and War,* 22–35. New York: Grove, 1962.

Jacobs, Lewis. *The Documentary Tradition: From Nanook to Woodstock.* New York: Hopkinson and Blake, 1971.

Jameson, Richard T. "San Pietro and Let There Be Light." *Film Comment* [Midsection] 16, no. 3 (May–June 1980): 32–33.

MacCann, Richard Dyer. "Documentary Film and Democratic Government: An Administrative History from Pare Lorentz to John Huston." Ph.D. diss., Harvard University, Cambridge, Massachusetts, 1951. Basis for *The People's Films.*

———. *The People's Films. A Political History of U.S. Government Motion Pictures.* New York: Hastings House, 1973.

Matthews, Jack. "Huston Documentaries: Only Following Orders." *Los Angeles Times,* September 11, 1985, interv. Discussion on Huston's experiences making war trilogy. AMPAS.

Rotha, Paul. *Documentary Film.* London: Faber & Faber, 1952.

Weiler, A. H. "Random Notes about the Screen: 'San Pietro' Battle Film to Be Released This Week—Other Items." *New York Times,* April 29, 1945. (Reprinted in *The New York Times Encyclopedia of Film, 1941–1946.*)

Youra, Steven. "James Agee on Film and the Theater of War." *Film Criticism* 10, no. 1 (Fall 1985): 18–31.

REVIEWS
Aufbau (New York), August 3, 1945.
Black Oracle 7 (Fall 1973): 29–30, creds. J. E. Parnum.
Cinema TV Today 9,995 (August 26, 1972): 24.
Motion Picture Daily, July 11, 1945.
Motion Picture Herald 158 (March 1945): 10.
**The Nation,* May 26, 1945, 608. James Agee.
New Yorker, July 21, 1945.
New York Post, July 21, 1945.
New York Times, July 15, 1945. Bosley Crowther, *"San Pietro* Is Given 'A Bell.'" MOMA; July 12, 1945, 8. NYTR.
PM, July 12, 1945. Seymour Peck.
Time, May 21, 1945, 94.
Time, January 19, 1981, 80.
Village Voice 18 (August 16, 1973): 65. G. Weales.
Washington Star, May 1, 1945. Jay Carmody.

BEAT THE DEVIL. 1954. (Director, Writer.)

ARTICLES
American Film 5 (September 1980): 45. "Stalling for Time." Excerpt from *An Open Book.*
Bogart, Humphrey. "Beat the Devil." *Look* 17 (September 22, 1953): 128–29+. AMPAS.
———. "Movie Making Beats the Devil: As Told to Joe Hyams." *Cue,* November 28, 1953, 14–15.
Castello, Giulio Cesare. "Il tesoro dell'Africa." *Cinema* (Milan) 6, no. 124 (December 30, 1953).
Champlin, Charles. "Beat the Devil." In *Movie Comedy,* edited by Stuart Byron and Elisabeth Weis. New York: Grossman, 1977. (Reprinted in *Produced and Abandoned: The Best Films You've Never Seen,* edited by Michael Sragow, San Francisco, Mercury House, 1990.)
Chardière, Bernard. "Ne soyons jamais sérieux." *Positif* 14–15 (November 1955): 33–41. (Reprinted in *John Huston, Collection dirigée,* edited by Gilles Ciment, 93–96, Dossier Positif Rivages, Paris, Editions Rivages, Collection Positif-Rivages, no. 2, 1988.)
CinemaTexas Program Notes 19, no. 1 (September 2, 1980), 5 p., biblio, creds, filmog.
Considine, Shaun. "The Men Who Work as the Director's Eyes." *New York Times,* April 8, 1979. (Reprinted in *The New York Times Encyclopedia of Film, 1977–1979.*)
Fernandez Torres, A. "Cinefilos de todos los paises . . . !" *Contracampo* 22 (June–July 1981): 39–43.
Garbicz, Adam, and Jacek Klinowski. *Cinema: The Magic Vehicle—A Guide to Its Achievement. Journey Two: The Cinema in the Fifties.* New York: Schocken Books, c. 1975–79, 180–81.

Greenfield, Josh. "Truman Capote, the Movie Star?" *New York Times,* December 28, 1975. (Reprinted in *The New York Times Encyclopedia of Film, 1975–1976.*)

Hawkins, Robert F. "Observations on the Italian Picture Scene: The John Huston–Humphrey Bogart Team Busily 'Beat the Devil'—Other Items." *New York Times,* April 5, 1953. (Reprinted in *The New York Times Encyclopedia of Film, 1952–1957.*) AMPAS.

———. "'Noah' Huston's Genesis." *New York Times,* February 21, 1965. (Reprinted in *The New York Times Encyclopedia of Film, 1964–1968.*)

Jameson, Richard T. "Beat the Devil." *Film Comment* [Midsection] 16, no. 3 (May–June 1980): 43–45.

McCarty, Clifford. *The Complete Films of Humphrey Bogart.* Secaucus, N.J.: Citadel Press, 1965, 170–72. (Reprint—New York: Carol Publishing Group, 1995.)

Magill's Survey of Cinema: Second Series 1 (1981): 190–92. Ed Hulse.

Malcolm, Andrew. "Huston: 'I Want to Keep Right on Going.'" *New York Times,* December 11, 1979. (Reprinted in *The New York Times Encyclopedia of Film, 1977–1979.*)

Maltin, Leonard. "American Film Comedy" [Program notes]. Museum of Modern Art: Department of Film, October 12, 1976.

Michael, Paul. *Humphrey Bogart: The Man and His Films.* Indianapolis: Bobbs-Merrill, 1965, 164–66.

Moshier, W. Franklyn. *The Films of Jennifer Jones.* San Francisco: The author, 1978, 117–22.

Motion Picture Guide 1 (1985): 155.

Plimpton, George. "Truman Capote, Screenwriter." *Paris Review* 38, no. 138 (Spring 1996): 125–31.

"A Portrait of Jennifer: The Films of Jennifer Jones" [Program notes]. Los Angeles County Museum of Art: Film Department, August 28, 1992.

Pryor, Thomas. "Hollywood Report." *New York Times,* September 27, 1953. (Reprinted in *The New York Times Encyclopedia of Film, 1952–1957.*)

St. Pierre, Brian. "John Huston: As He Was, Is, and Probably Always Will Be." *New York Times,* September 25, 1966A. (Reprinted in *The New York Times Encyclopedia of Film, 1964–1968.*)

Schmidt, M. A. "Battling Bogart's Saga, or an Appraisal of Humphrey Bogart's Rebellious Climb up the Ladder." *New York Times,* September 6, 1953. (Reprinted in *The New York Times Encyclopedia of Film, 1952–1957.*)

Sragow, Michael, ed. *Produced and Abandoned: The Best Films You've Never Seen.* San Francisco: Mercury House, 1990.

Sperber, A. M., and Eric Lax. *Bogart.* New York: Morrow, 1997.

Thompson, David. *Suspects.* New York: Knopf, 1985. "Fictionalized" accounts of the lives of characters in *Chinatown, Beat the Devil, High Sierra, The Killers,* and *The Maltese Falcon.*

Younkin, Stephen D., James Bigwood, and Raymond G. Cabana. *The Films of Peter Lorre.* Secaucus, N.J.: Citadel Press, 1982, 205–7.

REVIEWS
BFI/Monthly Film Bulletin 21, no. 240 (January 1954): 2.
Casablanca 5 (May 1981): 43–44, creds, illus. Miguel Marias.
Catholic World 179 (April 1954): 63–64.
Commonweal 59 (March 19, 1954): 600.
Coronet 35 (April 1954): 6.
Farm Journal 78 (May 1954): 137.
Film Daily, March 3, 1954, 10.
Films in Review 5, no. 3 (March 1954): 143–44. B. G. Marple.
Film Society Review, January 1966, 13. Philip Chamberlin.
Harrison's Reports, March 6, 1954, 38.
Hollywood Reporter, May 15, 1953, 21.
Hollywood Reporter, March 2, 1954, 3. Milton Luban.
Kinematograph Weekly 2,422 (November 1953): 18.
London Sunday Times, November 29, 1953. Dilys Powell. AMPAS.
Los Angeles Times, May 6, 1954. AMPAS.
Millimeter 3, no. 12 (December 1975): 56–57, illus. Charles Champlin.
Motion Picture Daily, March 4, 1954.
Motion Picture Herald, September 28, 1966, 13+. Richard Gerner.
Motion Picture Herald Product Digest 194, no. 10 (March 6, 1954): 2,205–6.
National Parent-Teacher 48 (April 1954): 38.
New Statesman and Nation 46 (December 5, 1953): 715.
Newsweek 43 (March 8, 1954): 82. AMPAS.
New Yorker 30 (March 20, 1954): 118. Pauline Kael. AMPAS. (Reprinted in
   Pauline Kael, *Kiss Kiss Bang Bang,* 290–91, New York, Bantam Books, 1969.)
New Yorker, May 4, 1992. AMPAS.
New York Times, March 13, 1954, 11. Howard Thompson. NYPL, NYTR.
   (Reprinted in *The New York Times Film Reviews: A One-Volume Selection,
   1913–1970,* edited by George Amberg, New York, Arno Press, 1971.)
New York Times 135 (June 15, 1986): H30. Vincent Canby.
Saturday Review 37 (March 13, 1954): 28. AMPAS.
Senior Scholastic 64 (March 10, 1954): 27.
Sight & Sound 23, no. 2 (October–December 1953): 77, illus.
Sight & Sound 23, no. 3 (January–March 1954): 147–48. Lindsay Anderson.
Time 63 (March 8, 1954): 94+. AMPAS.
Today's Cinema 81, no. 6,894 (November 1953): 8.
Variety, December 2, 1953, 6. Myro. VR.
Variety, December 4, 1953. AMPAS.

BERMUDA TRIANGLE (*Diabolico Triangulo de las Bermudas,* Mexico/Italy/USA). 1978. (Actor.)

REVIEWS
Cineforum 174 (May 1978): 314–18. Y. Alion.
La Revue du Cinéma 332 (October 1978): 195–96. G. Gauthier.

Note. An American film with the same title, directed by Richard Friedenberg, was released in 1979.

THE BIBLE . . . IN THE BEGINNING. 1966. (Director, Actor, Narrator.)

ARTICLES

The American Film Institute Catalog: Feature Films, 1961–1970. New York, R. R. Bowker, 1976, 83–84.

Ardagh, John. "Huston in Eden." *Sight & Sound* 33, no. 4 (Autumn 1964): 173+.

"Ark that John Built: Filming *The Bible.*" *Life* 59 (August 13, 1965): 43. AMPAS.

Berlanger, Terry. [Study Guide to *The Bible*], n.d. NYPL.

"Bible as Living Technicolor: The Filming of *The Bible.*" *Time* 85 (January 15, 1965): 70.

Bonicelli, Vittorio. *La Bibbia (The Bible).* Verona, Italy: A. Mondadori, 1966.

Cox, Harvey. "How to Kill God: Film Upsets Leading American Theologian." *Look* 30 (October 18, 1966): 104+.

Culkin, John M., Society of Jesus. "A Study Guide for Classroom Discussion." (1966?) illus. NYPL.

Hawkins, Robert. "Noah Huston's Genesis." *New York Times,* February 21, 1965. (Reprinted in *The New York Times Encyclopedia of Film, 1962–1964.*) AMPAS.

Huston, John. "La parola a John Huston." In *La Bibbia,* by Vittorio Bonicelli, 9–10. Verona, Italy: A. Mondadori, 1966.

Knight, Arthur. "The King John Version: John Huston's *The Bible* in Production." *Saturday Review* 49 (October 1, 1966): 34. AMPAS.

"A Literal View of the Bible in Huston's New Movie Noah." *Look,* 29 (July 27, 1965): 21–26 AMPAS.

Motion Picture Guide 1 (1985): 187.

"Movies Abroad: No, but I Saw the Picture." *Time,* January 26, 1962. On location.

Osborne, Robert, ed. *The Bible . . . in the Beginning: Photographs from the Dino De Laurentiis Motion Picture Production of* The Bible. Publisher, Marvin Miller; art director, Roger LaMana. Covina, Calif.: Collectors Publications, 1966.

Pollock, Eileen, and Robert Mason Pollock. "The Making of Eve." *Show* 4 (October 1964) 64–65+.

"Problems in Paradise." *Newsweek* 64 (September 14 1964): 90.

Ross, Lillian. "Our Far-flung Correspondents: '*The Bible* in Dinocitta.'" *New Yorker* 41 (September 25, 1965): 185–212. AMPAS.

Sage, T. "Giraffe in Piazza del Popolo." *National Review* 17 (February 9, 1965): 105–6.

St. Pierre, Brian. "John Huston: As He Was, Is, and Probably Always Be." *New York Times,* September 25, 1966A. (Reprinted in *The New York Times Encyclopedia of Film, 1964–68.*)

Scorsese, Martin. *Scorsese on Scorsese.* Edited by David Thompson and Ian

Christie, with an introduction by Michael Powell. London: Faber and Faber, 1989.

Sequin, Louis. "En ses mains redoutables." *Positif* 84 (May 1967): 47. (Reprinted in *John Huston, Collection dirigée,* edited by Gilles Ciment, 127–29, Dossier Positif Rivages, Paris, Editions Rivages, Collection Positif-Rivages, no. 2, 1988.)

Sunday Times (London) *Magazine,* April 4, 1965, 22–29, illus.

REVIEWS

America 115 (October 8, 1966): 433–35. Moira Walsh.

BFI/Monthly Film Bulletin 33, no. 394 (November 1966): 163.

Bianco e Nero 28, no. 2 (February 1967): 68.

Box Office, October 3, 1966, 12. Frank Legendecker.

Box Office, December 12, 1966.

Cahiers du Cinéma (in English), no. 5 (1966): 7–8.

Catholic World 204 (October 1966): 64.

Christian Century 83 (September 7, 1966): 1,083. Malcolm Boyd.

Christian Century 83 (November 16, 1966): 1,410. Letter to editor.

Christian Science Monitor (Western ed.), October 10, 1966, 6.

Cinema 3, no. 4 (December 1966): 47. Axel Madsen.

Commonweal 85 (October 21, 1966): 79. Philip T. Hartung.

Cue, October 1, 1966.

Film Daily 129, no. 26 (September 28, 1966): 38–39.

Filmfacts 9 (1966): 213, creds.

Film Quarterly 20, no. 4 (Summer 1967): 11–22. Stephen Farber.

Films and Filming 13, no. 2 (November 1966): 10–11. Robin Bean.

Films in Review 17, no. 8 (October 1966): 517–19, illus. Henry Hart.

Harper's Magazine 17 (October 1966): 517–19.

Hollywood Reporter 192, no. 33 (September 28, 1966): 3–4. AMPAS.

Illustrated London News 249 (October 8, 1966): 11.

Life 61 (October 7, 1966): 22 Richard Schickel.

Los Angeles Times, October 2, 1966, Calendar, 9. Philip K. Scheuer.

Motion Picture Herald, October 19, 1966.

Motion Picture Herald Product Digest 17, no. 8 (September 28, 1966): 614–15.

The National Observer, September 26, 1966.

National Review 19 (April 18, 1967): 428–30.

New Republic 155 (October 22, 1966): 30–32.

Newsweek 68 (October 3, 1966): 105.

New York Daily News, September 26, 1966. AMPAS.

New Yorker 42 (October 1, 1966): 194–95. Pauline Kael. AMPAS. (Reprinted in *Kiss Kiss, Bang Bang,* by Pauline Kael, Boston, Little, Brown, 1968, 131–34; and *For Keeps,* 91–94, New York, E. P. Dutton, 1994.)

New York Herald Tribune, October 16, 1966, 28. Judith Crist. (Reprinted in *The Private Eye, the Cowboy and the Very Naked Girl,* by Judith Crist, 198–201, New York, Holt, 1968.)

New York Post, September 29, 1966. Archer Winsten. AMPAS.

New York Times, September 29, 1966, 60. Bosley Crowther. NYTR.

New York World Journal Tribune, September 29, 1966. AMPAS.
Playboy 13 (November 1966): 32+.
Reed, Rex. *Big Screen, Little Screen.* New York: Macmillan, 1971, 367–70.
Reporter 35 (November 3, 1966): 56.
Senior Scholastic 89 (November 11, 1966): 26.
Sight & Sound 35, no. 4 (Autumn 1966): 199–200. John Gillett.
Spectator 217 (October 14, 1966): 487.
Time 88 (October 7, 1966).
Variety, September 28, 1966, 6. Murf. AMPAS, VR.
Vogue 148 (October 1, 1966): 162.
Women's Day, October 1966, 10+. Hollis Alpert. MOMA.

BLACK CAULDRON. 1985. (Prologue Narrator.)

ARTICLES AND REVIEWS
Adamson, Joe. "What's Cooking in the *Black Cauldron.*" *American Cinematographer* 66 (July 1985): 60–68, illus, stills. AMPAS.
Allombert, G. "Brève recontre avec Ted Berman." *La Revue du Cinéma* 411 (December 1985): 32.
Animator 15 (Spring 1986): 22–23, stills. B. Sibley.
**BFI/Monthly Film Bulletin* 52, no. 621 (October 1985): 305–6, creds, stills. Nigel Floyd.
Back Stage, July 26, 1985. Howard Beckerman. AMPAS.
Box Office 121 (September 1985): R106–7, creds. J. Summers. AMPAS.
California Magazine 10 (August 1985): 57. Kenneth Turan.
**Christian Science Monitor,* July 26 1985, 23. David Sterritt. AMPAS.
Cinefantastique 15, no. 3 (1985): 15, stills. M. Rebeaux.
Cinéma (Paris) 331 (November 27–December 3, 1985): 5, creds, stills. P. Dumont.
Cinéma (Paris) 335 (December 24, 1985): 6–7, bio-filmog, illus.
Cine Revue [65] (June 20, 1985): 9–11, port, stills. J. MacTrevor.
Cine Revue [65] (November 28, 1985): 24–25, stills. J. MacTrevor.
City Limits 210 (October 11, 1985): 23.
EPD Film 3, no. 1 (January 1986): 31, creds.
Fantasy and Science Fiction 69 (October 1985): 109.
Film en Televisie 342 (November 1985): 4–5, creds, stills. C. Moens.
Film Journal 88 (August 1985): 15, creds, stills. M. Meisel.
Films and Filming 373 (October 1985): 34, creds, stills. V. Miles.
Grand Angle 13, no. 80 (February 1986): 37–38, biblio, creds, stills. M. Lequeux.
Hollywood Reporter 287, no. 48 (July 22, 1985): 3. AMPAS.
Los Angeles Daily News, July 29, 1985, 16. Kirk Honeycutt. AMPAS.
**Los Angeles Times,* July 24, 1985, sect. 6, 1. Charles Solomon.
Los Angeles Times, July 27, 1985, part 5, 1–2. Charles Champlin.
Los Angeles Weekly, August 26, 1985. Michael Dare. AMPAS.
Maclean's 98 (August 1985).
Magill's Cinema Annual, 1986, 75–76.
Midnight Marquee 34 (Fall 1985): 37. G. J. Svehia.

Motion Picture Guide, 1986 Annual, 18.
Movieline, July 26–August 1, 1985, 28+. Ski Ferderber.
*Newsday, July 26, 1985, sect. 3, 3. Peter Goodman.
*New Statesman 110 (October 11, 1985): 38.
*Newsweek 106 (August 12, 1985): 71. L. Shapiro. AMPAS.
New York Herald Tribune, October 16, 1966, 28. Judith Crist. MOMA.
New York Post, July 26, 1985, 21. Rex Reed.
New York Times, July 26, 1985, C5, creds. Walter Goodman. AMPAS, NYTR.
Philadelphia Magazine 76 (October 1985): 85.
Photoplay 36 (October 1985): 46, stills. D. Quinlan.
Positif 300 (February 1986): 126. M. Cieutat.
La Revue du Cinéma 411 (December 1985): 30–32, creds, stills. A. Garel.
La Revue du Cinéma, hors serie 33 (1986): 116–17, creds. G. Colpart.
Robley, L. P. "Computer Graphics Aid Animation Rebirth." *American Cinematographer* 67 (October 1986): 73–76, illus, stills.
Scapperotti, D. "Not the Hoped-for Fantasy Epic, but Still the Best in Animation." *Cinefantastique* 16, no. 1 (1986): 40, creds, stills.
Screen International 519 (October 19, 1985): 416.
Segnocinema 6, no. 23 (May 1986): 90, creds, stills. P. Cherchi Usai.
Séquences 122 (October 1985): 60–62, creds, stills. Patrick Schupp.
Sightlines 19, no. 2 (1985–86): 10–13. C. Solomon, "Disney Today."
Smith, L. "Sound Design for the *Black Cauldron.*" *Cinefantastique* 16, no. 1 (1986): 41.
Soundtrack 4, no. 16 (December 1985): 12–13. Steven J. Lehti.
*Time 126 (July 29, 1985): 68. R. Schickel. AMPAS.
Time 126 (August 5, 1985): 68.
Time Out 790 (October 10, 1985): 67.
USA Today 114 (November 1985): 93–97, stills. K. R. Hey.
Variety, July 22, 1985 (D).
Variety, July 24, 1985 (W), creds. Har. VR.
*Village Voice 30 (August 6, 1985): 56, stills. J. Hoberman. AMPAS.
Visions 34 (December 1985): 30–31, illus, stills. C. H. Felix.
Wall Street Journal, July 23, 1985, 26 (West Coast ed.); 30 (East Coast ed.).
Washington Post, July 25, 1985, B8. Paul Attanasio.
Washington Post, July 26, 1985. Rita Kempley.

THE BLUE HOTEL. 1977. (Director [?]. Unrealized project.)

ARTICLE
Fultz, James R. "Heartbreak at the Blue Hotel: James Agee's Scenario of Stephen Crane's Story." *Midwest Quarterly* 21, no. 4 (Summer 1980): 423–34.

BREAKOUT. 1975. (Actor.)

ARTICLES AND REVIEWS
BFI/Monthly Film Bulletin 42, no. 497 (June 1975): 130, creds. T. Milne.

Boston Real Paper, June 11, 1975. AMPAS.
"'Breakout' in Two Weeks Has Scored $12,711,224." *Box Office* 107 (June 16, 1975): 11.
Cinema (Romania) 13 (December 1975): 13, creds, stills. A. Darian.
Cinéma (Paris) 198 (May 1975): 135. M. Grisolia.
Cinema TV Today 10,135 (May 24, 1975): 14.
Cine Revue 55 (March 27, 1975). P. Sariat. Photo essays.
"Columbia Launches Massive Campaign to Promote *Breakout* Nationwide." *Box Office* 107 (May 19, 1975): 4.
Cosmopolitan, March 1969. AMPAS.
Cue, June 2, 1975. Donal Mayerson. AMPAS.
Davidson, Bill. "America Discovers a 'Sacred Monster.' On Location with Bronson on the Shooting of 'Breakout.'" *New York Times,* September 22, 1974. (Reprinted in *The New York Times Encyclopedia of Film, 1972–1974.*)
Films and Filming 21, no. 10 (July 1975): 41–42, creds, stills. Derek Elley. AMPAS.
Films Illustrated 4 (June 1975): 370, creds. J. Williams.
Hollywood Reporter 236, no. 11 (April 29, 1975): 3. Arthur Knight. AMPAS.
Independent Film Journal 75, no. 10 (May 28, 1975): 10, creds.
Iskusstvo Kino, 6 (June 1979): 177–80.
Los Angeles Herald Examiner, May 22, 1975, C3. Bridget Byrne. AMPAS.
Los Angeles Times, May 22, 1975. Kevin Thomas. AMPAS.
Motion Picture Guide 1 (1985): 288.
Motion Picture Product Digest, July 9, 1975. Richard Gertner. AMPAS.
Movietone News 42 (July 1975): 42, creds. R. T. Jameson.
New York, June 2, 1975. Judith Crist. AMPAS.
Positif 169 (May 1975): 67. P.-L. Thirard.
La Revue du Cinéma 296 (May 1975): 78–79, creds. G. Colpart.
La Revue du Cinéma 299 (October 1975): 124, creds. G. Colpart.
Saturday Review, January 11, 1969. AMPAS.
Variety, April 28, 1975. VR.
Variety 278, no. 13 (May 7, 1975): 52, creds. Murf (A. D. Murphy).

THE BRIDGE IN THE JUNGLE. 1971. (Actor.)

REVIEWS

Hollywood Reporter 210 (March 6, 1970): 9–10.
Variety, October 27, 1970 (D).
Variety, November 4, 1970 (W). Rick. AMPAS, VR.

BRIDGE OF SAN LUIS REY. 1929; 1944. (Unrealized project?)

ARTICLES AND REVIEWS

The American Film Institute Catalog: Feature Films, 1921–1930. New York: R. R. Bowker, 1971, 86.
Film Daily, October 27, 1928, 12.

Film Daily, April 28, 1929, 9.
Film Daily, February 3, 1944, 4.
Harrison's Reports, May 25, 1929, 83.
Harrison's Reports, February 5, 1944, 22.
Hollywood Reporter, February 1, 1944, 7.
Magill's Cinema Annual, 1982, 408–11.
Motion Picture Guide 1 (1985): 295 (for both 1929 and 1944 versions).
New Yorker 20 (March 4, 1944): 46+.
New York Times, May 20, 1929, 22. NYTR.
New York Times, March 4, 1944, 11. NYTR.
Outlook 152 (June 5, 1929): 235.
Scholastic 44 (March 27, 1944): 38.
Variety, May 22, 1929, 16.
Variety, February 2, 1944, 18. VR.

BY LOVE POSSESSED. 1961. (Unrealized project.)

ARTICLES AND REVIEWS

The American Film Institute Catalog: Feature Films, 1961–1970. New York: R. R. Bowker, 1976, 136.
Harrison's Reports, June 10, 1961, 90.
Motion Picture Guide 1 (1985): 323.
New York Times, July 30, 1961, 32. NYTR.
Variety, June 14, 1961. VR.

CANDY. 1968. (Actor.)

ARTICLES AND REVIEWS

BFI/Monthly Film Bulletin 36, no. 423 (April 1969).
Box Office, January 6, 1969. AMPAS.
"*Candy* Had No Sweet Path to Screen; Zoref Explains Preproduction Problems." *Variety,* February 7, 1968. AMPAS.
Dassanowsky-Harris, Robert von. "The Southern Journey: *Candy* and *The Magic Christian* as Cinematic Picaresques." *Studios in Popular Culture* 15, no. 1 (1992): 95–111.
Film and Television Daily, December 18, 1968. Edward Lipton. AMPAS.
Films and Filming, March 1969. Photo essay. AMPAS.
Films and Filming, April 1969, 38. Brian Murphy.
Films in Review 20, no. 1 (January 1969): 56. Janet Hall.
Kinematograph Weekly 3,202 (February 22, 1969): 26.
Los Angeles Herald Examiner, December 20, 1968, C4. Dale Munroe.
Los Angeles Times, December 21, 1968. Charles Champlin. AMPAS.
Life, March 8, 1968. AMPAS.
Motion Picture Guide 2 (1985): 343.
Motion Picture Herald, January 1, 1969. Lee Schwartz.
Newsweek, December 30, 1968, 61.

New Yorker, January 14, 1969. Pauline Kael. AMAPS, MOMA.
New York Morning Telegraph, December 18, 1968. Leo Mishkin.
New York Times, December 18, 1968, 54. NYPL, NYTR.
Saturday Review, January 11, 1969. Hollis Alpert.
Shenker, Israel. "Good Grief—It's Candy on Film." *New York Times Magazine,* February 11, 1968, 50–60. AMPAS, MOMA. (Reprinted in *The New York Times Encyclopedia of Film, 1964–1968.*)
Time, December 27, 1968, 56. AMPAS, MOMA.
Today's Cinema 9,639 (February 21, 1969): 13.
Variety, December 17, 1968 (D). Murf.
Variety, December 18, 1968 (W). Murf. VR.
Village Voice 14, no. 11 (December 26, 1968): 45. Andrew Sarris.

CANNERY ROW. 1982. (Narrator.)

ARTICLES AND REVIEWS

American Cinematographer 62, no. 4 (April 1981): 336+. Sven Nykvist. Production article by film's cinematographer.
Bell, Arthur. "Raquel's *Cannery Row.*" *Village Voice,* February 4–10, 1981, 42. AMPAS.
———. "A Hard 'Row' to Hoe." *Village Voice,* February 11–17, 1981, 56. AMPAS.
*BFI/Monthly Film Bulletin 50, no. 596 (September 1983): 253+, creds, stills. Paul Taylor.
Box Office 118 (March 1982): 62–63, creds. J. Summers. AMPAS.
Chicago Sun Times, February 12, 1982, 41+. Roger Ebert.
Film en Televisie 308 (January 1983): 19, creds, stills. Karin Seberechts.
Film Journal 85 (February 15, 1982): 38, creds, stills. M. Kane. AMPAS.
Hollywood Reporter 270, no. 23 (February 3, 1982): 3. AMPAS.
Levende Billeder 8 (August 16, 1982): 44–45, creds, stills. E. Suszkiewicz.
Los Angeles Herald Examiner, February 13, 1982, B1+. Peter Rainer.
*Los Angeles Times, February 12, 1982, sect. 6, 1+. Kevin Thomas. AMPAS.
Macleans 95 (February 22, 1982): 56.
Magill's Cinema Annual, 1983, 95–99. Paul H. Broeske.
Millichap, Joseph. *Steinbeck on Film.* New York: Frederick Ungar, 1983, 172–75.
Morsberger, Robert E. "Cannery Row Revisited." *Steinbeck Quarterly* 16 (1983): 89–95.
Motion Picture Guide 2 (1985): 343.
Motion Picture Product Digest 9, no. 19 (March 3, 1982): 75. Richard Guertner. AMPAS.
*Newsday, February 12, 1982, sect. 2, 9. Alex Keneas.
*New York Post, February 12, 1982, 53. Archer Winsten.
New York Times, February 12, 1982, C10, creds. Vincent Canby. NYTR.
Oceans 15 (May–June 1982): 60.

Orth, Maureen. "The Gamblers of *Cannery Row.*" *Rolling Stone,* April 2, 1981, 16–22. AMPAS.
Prevue 47 (April–May 1982): 52–53.
San Francisco Examiner, February 12, 1982. Nancy Scott.
*Saturday Review 9 (March 19, 1982): 54–55, stills. J. Crist.
Schepelern, P. "Fra Monterey til Hollywood." *Kosmorama* 28, no. 161 (October 1982): 162–65, biblio, illus. On Steinbeck's work in and relationship with Hollywood, adaptations made from his books, and review of *Cannery Row.*
Screen International 279 (February 14, 1981): 4.
Taylor, Paul. "Stung! The Misadventures of a Young Writer [David S. Ward] on Litigation Row." *BFI/Monthly Film Bulletin* 50 (September 1983): 260, bio, filmog, illus.
Tibbets, J. "It Happened in Monterrey: John Steinbeck's *Cannery Row.*" *Literature/Film Quarterly* 10, no. 2 (1982): 82–84, creds, stills.
*Time 119 (February 15, 1982): 64. Richard Schickel. AMPAS.
Variety, February 1, 1982 (D), 3.
Variety, February 3, 1982 (W), 18, creds. Cart. VR.
**Village Voice,* March 16, 1982, 48, stills. Carrie Rickey.
Washington Post, February 12, 1981, 63. Gary Arnold.

CAPTAIN HORATIO HORNBLOWER. 1951. (Writer, uncredited.)

ARTICLES AND REVIEWS
BFI/Monthly Film Bulletin 18 (May 1951): 258.
Biette, Jean-Claude. "Au creux des scénarios." *Cahiers du Cinéma,* nos. 371 & 372 (May 1985): xv–xvi.
Catholic World 174 (October 1951): 64.
Christian Century 68 (September 19, 1951): 1,087.
Film Daily, June 15, 1951, 6.
Films in Review 2 (August–September 1951): 43.
Griggs, John. *The Films of Gregory Peck.* Secaucus, N.J.: Citadel Press, 1984, 111–13.
Harrison's Reports, June 10, 1951, 95.
High Fidelity 29 (October 1979): 125.
Hollywood Reporter, April 13, 1951, 4.
Hollywood Reporter, June 14, 1951, 4.
Motion Picture Guide 2 (1985): 350.
Motion Picture Herald Product Digest, June 16, 1951, 886.
Newsweek 38 (September 24, 1951): 87.
New Yorker 27 (September 22, 1951): 91.
New York Times, September 14, 1951, 21. NYTR.
Thomas, Tony. *The Great Adventure Films.* Secaucus, N.J.: Citadel Press, 1976, 156–61.
Time 58 (September 10, 1951): 96.
Variety, April 18, 1951, 6. VR.
Variety, June 20, 1951, 6.

THE CARDINAL. 1963. (Actor.)

ARTICLES AND REVIEWS

America 110 (January 4, 1963): 27.

The American Film Institute Catalog: Feature Films, 1961–1970. New York: R. R. Bowker, 1976, 147.

Annunciation 9, no. 2 (February 1964): 18.

Archer, Eugene. "Introduction to an Irish Individualist." *New York Times,* September 30, 1962. (Reprinted in *The New York Times Encyclopedia of Film, 1958–1963.*)

———. "Moviemaker Clarifies 'The Cardinal' Issues." *New York Times,* December 8, 1963. (Reprinted in *The New York Times Encyclopedia of Film, 1958–1963.*)

BFI/Monthly Film Bulletin 31, no. 361 (February 1964): 18.

Box Office, October 27, 1963, 13. Frank Leyendecker. AMPAS.

Cahiers du Cinéma 26, no. 154 (April 1964): 61.

Catholic World 198 (February 1964): 327–28.

Catholic World 198 (March 1964): 365–71.

Cinema 1, no. 6 (November–December 1963): 4–9, illus.

Cinema 2, no. 1 (February–March 1964): 48, illus.

Commonweal 79 (December 20, 1963): 371–72.

Cue, December 14, 1963.

Daily Cinema 8,853 (December 18, 1963): 14.

Ebony 19 (December 1963): 126–28.

Esquire 61 (March 1964): 24. Dwight McDonald. AMPAS.

Film Daily 123, no. 75 (October 17, 1963): 3.

Filmfacts 6 (December 19, 1963): 281–84.

Film Ideal 136 (January 15, 1964): 68.

Films and Filming 10, no. 5 (February 1964). Allen Eyles.

Films in Review 15, no. 1 (January 1964). Adelaide Comerford.

"The Films of Otto Preminger" [Program notes]. Museum of Modern Art: Department of Film. December 16, 1971.

Hollywood Reporter 177, no. 27 (October 1963).

"John Cardinal Huston: Tough Director Portrays a Church Prince." *Life,* November 12, 1963, 61+. AMPAS.

"John Huston, Actor." *Newsweek* 61 (March 18, 1963), por.

Kinematograph Weekly 2,934 (December 26, 1963): 7.

Listener 111, no. 2,850 (March 22, 1984): 33. P. Oakes.

Los Angeles Herald Examiner, December 20, 1963. Harrison Carroll.

Motion Picture Guide 2 (1985): 357.

Motion Picture Herald 230, no. 11 (October 30, 1963): 9+.

Motion Picture Herald 230, no. 12 (November 13, 1963).

Moviegoer 2 (Summer–Autumn 1964): 55.

National Review 16 (January 28, 1964).

New Republic 149 (December 21, 1963): 29. AMPAS.

New Statesman 66 (December 20, 1963): 921.

Newsweek 62 (December 16, 1963): 90.

New Yorker 39 (December 14, 1963): 198.

New York Herald Tribune, December 13, 1963. Judith Crist.

New York Times, December 13, 1963, +41. Bosley Crowther. NYTR.

New York Times, December 15, 1963, sect. 2, 3. Bosley Crowther.

New York Times, February 7, 1988, H28. Glenn Collins.

Pratley, Gerald. *The Cinema of Otto Preminger.* New York: A. S. Barnes, 1971, 146–47.

Preminger, Otto. *"The Cardinal* & I." *Films and Filming* 10, no. 2 (November 1963), illus.

Pryor, Thomas. "Random Notes Concerning Pictures and People." *New York Times,* September 10, 1950. (Reprinted in *The New York Times Encyclopedia of Film, 1947–1951.*)

Raines, Halsey. "Half-way around the World with Otto Preminger." *Motion Picture Herald* 229, no. 10 (May 15, 1963).

Reed, Rex. "Like They Could Cut Your Heart Out." *New York Times,* August 21, 1966. (Reprinted in *The New York Times Encyclopedia of Film, 1964–1968.*)

Reporter 30 (February 13, 1964): 44.

La Revue du Cinéma 172 (April 1964).

St. Pierre, Brian. "John Huston: As He Was, Is, and Probably Always Will Be." *New York Times,* September 25, 1966. (Reprinted in *The New York Times Encyclopedia of Film, 1964–1968.*)

Saturday Review 46 (December 7, 1963): 32. Hollis Alpert. AMPAS.

Sight & Sound 33, no. 1 (Winter 1963–64): 39–40, illus. Richard Roud. AMPAS.

Time 82 (December 13, 1963): 97–98. AMPAS.

Variety, October 14, 1963.

Variety, October 16, 1963, 6+. Pry. VR.

Village Voice 9, no. 8 (December 12, 1963): 23. Andrew Sarris.

CASINO ROYALE. 1967. (Director, Actor, Writer.)

ARTICLES AND REVIEWS

Ager, Ceclia. "Katharine Hepburn: 'Come, I Want You to Meet My Niece.'" *New York Times,* June 18, 1967. (Reprinted in *The New York Times Encyclopedia of Film, 1964–1968.*)

Allen, Woody. "The Girls of *Casino Royale.*" *Playboy,* February 1967.

America 116 (May 20, 1967): 764.

The American Film Institute Catalog: Feature Films, 1961–1970. New York: R. R. Bowker, 1976, 153–54.

Bart, Peter. "Hollywood's Trend to Remakes Worrying Creative Filmmakers." *New York Times,* April 22, 1966. (Reprinted in *The New York Times Encyclopedia of Film, 1964–1968.*)

———. "Where the Action Isn't." *New York Times,* July 31, 1966. (Reprinted in *The New York Times Encyclopedia of Film, 1964–1968.*)

Bensen, Raymond. *James Bond's Bedside Companion.* New York: Dodd, Mead, 1984, 238–39.

BFI/Monthly Film Bulletin 34, no. 401 (June 1967): 87–88.

Brode, Douglas. *Woody Allen: His Films and Career.* Secaucus, N.J.: Citadel Press, 1985, 67–76.

Brosnan, John. *James Bond in the Cinema.* San Diego: A. S. Barnes, 1981, 283–86.

Cahiers du Cinéma (in English) 5 (1966): 7–8.

"Columbia Pictures: A Diamond Jubilee Celebration" [Program notes]. Los Angeles County Museum of Art, December 20, 1984. Program notes consist of credits and review from *Variety* (April 19, 1967).

Commonweal 86 (May 19, 1967): 264.

Daily Cinema 9,356 (April 1967): 3.

Denby, David. "The Art of Screenwriting: An Interview with Wolf Mankewitz." *Filmmaker News* 7, no. 4, (February 1974): 26–29, illus.

Esquire 68 (August 1967). Wilfred Sheed. (Reprinted in *Film 67/68: An Anthology by the National Society of Film Critics,* edited by Richard Schickel and John Simon, 150–51, New York, Simon & Schuster, 1968.)

Film Daily 130, no. 83, (May 1, 1967): 8. AMPAS.

Filmfacts 10 (1967): 116, creds.

Film Quarterly 20, no. 4 (Summer 1967): 77–78. Stephen Farber.

Films in Review 18, no. 6 (June–July 1967): 367–68. Elaine Rothschild.

Films in Review 39, no. 6–7 (June–July 1988). Robert Dassanowsky.

Garrett, Gerard. *The Films of David Niven.* Secaucus, N.J.: Citadel Press, 1976, 206–11.

Harris, R. D. "*Casino Royale* Revisited." *Films in Review* 39, nos. 6 & 7 (June–July 1988): 336–49.

Heller, Joseph. "How I Found James Bond." *Holiday* 41 (June 1967): 123–25+.

Hollywood Reporter 195, no. 33 (May 1, 1967): 3. AMPAS.

Kinematograph Weekly 3,106 (April 22, 1967): 15.

Life 62 (April 21, 1967): 108–10.

"Little Cleopatra." *Time* 87 (May 6, 1966): 86.

London Life, April 23, 1966, 8.

London Life, April 30, 1966, 27.

London Life, May 7, 1966, 22.

London Life, December 17, 1966, 12–14.

Los Angeles Times, July 9, 1967. AMPAS.

MD, August 1967, 231–32.

Motion Picture Guide 2 (1985): 374.

Motion Picture Herald Product Digest 237, no. 19 (May 10, 1967): 681. AMPAS.

New Republic, July 15, 1967. AMPAS.

Newsweek 69 (May 15, 1967): 94. AMPAS.

New Yorker 43 (May 6, 1967). AMPAS.

New York Post, April 29, 1967. NYPL.

New York Times, May 22, 1966, sect. 2, 11.

New York Times, October 5, 1966, 38.

New York Times, April 29, 1967, 25. NYTR.

Quirk, Lawrence J. *The Films of William Holden.* Secaucus, N.J.: Citadel Press, 1973, 226–28.

La Revue du Cinéma 446 (February 1989): 33, creds, stills. Y. Alion.
Rubin, Steven Jay. *The James Bond Films.* New York: Arlington House, 1981.
Saturday Review 50 (May 20, 1967): 65. Arthur Knight. AMPAS.
Stone, Judy. "Woody, This Is Your Dream Life." *New York Times,* September 22, 1968. (Reprinted in *The New York Times Encyclopedia of Film, 1964–1968.*)
Time 89 (May 12, 1967): 100. AMPAS.
U.S. Camera 30 (August 1967): 61.
Variety, April 17, 1967.
Variety, April 19, 1967, 6. VR.
Variety, May 13, 1987. Rich (R. Gold).
Video 18 (February 1995): 67–68. T. Soter.
Village Voice 12 (June 15, 1967): 41. Andrew Sarris.
"Who Is the Real James Bond Anyhow?" *Look* 30, November 15, 1966, 50–54+.

CATHOLICS. 1973. TV Movie. (Director; Actor, unrealized.)

ARTICLE
New York Times, August 22, 1972. MOMA.

CHEYENNE. 1947. (Writer, unrealized.)

REVIEWS
Harrison's Reports, April 27, 1947, 66.
Motion Picture Guide 2 (1985): 409.
New York Herald Tribune, June 15, 1947. Otis L. Guernsey.
New York Times, June 7, 1947. Bosley Crowther. NYTR.
Variety, April 23, 1947. Brog. VR.

CHINATOWN. 1974. (Actor.)

ARTICLES
Alonzo, J. A. "Behind the Scenes of *Chinatown.*" *American Cinematographer* 56, no. 5 (May 1975): 526–29. AMPAS.
Alvarez, A. "Can Polanski Make a Star of Polanski?" *New York Times,* February 22, 1976. (Reprinted in *The New York Times Encyclopedia of Film, 1975–1976.*)
Andersson, W. "Josef K i Amerika." *Filmrutan* 18, no. 1 (1975): 36–42, stills.
Atlas, Jacoba. "The Facts behind *Chinatown.*" *LA Free Press,* September 27, 1974, 23. AMPAS.
Beal, Greg. *CinemaTexas Program Notes* 11, no. 1 (September 2, 1976): 17–23, biblio, creds, filmog.
Belton, John. "Language, Oedipus, and 'Chinatown.'" *MLN* 106, no. 5 (December 1991): 993–1,010.
Benelli, D. "Contemporary Film Noir: Questing in Chinatown's Maze." *Cinemonkey* 4, no.4 (1978): 20–23, stills.
Bisplinghoff, Gretchen, and Virginia Wright Wexman. *Roman Polanski: A Guide to References and Resources.* Boston: G.K. Hall, 1979, 31–33.

Bookbinder, Robert. *Films of the Seventies.* Secaucus, N.J.: Citadel Press, 1982, 107–10.

Bottigi, W. D. "The Importance of 'C——-ing' in Earnest: A Comparison of *The Maltese Falcon* and *Chinatown.*" *Armchair Detective* 14, no. 1 (1981): 86–87.

Burke, Tom. "The Restoration of Roman Polanski." *Rolling Stone,* July 18, 1974, 40–46.

Butler, Ivan. *The Cinema of Roman Polanski.* New York: A. S. Barnes, 1970.

Cawelti, John G. "*Chinatown* and Generic Transformation in Recent American Films." In *Film Genre Reader II,* edited by Barry Keith Grant, 227–45. Austin: University of Texas Press, 1995. (Originally appeared in *Film Genre Reader,* edited by Barry Keith Grant, 183–201, Austin, University of Texas Press, 1986.)

Cooper, Stephen. "Sex/Knowledge/Power in the Detective Genre." *Film Quarterly* 42, no. 3 (Spring 1989): 23–31, biblio, stills.

Cremonini, G. "Le 'Esche' in *Chinatown* di Roman Polanski." *Cineforum* 27, no. 266 (August 1987): 62–72.

"The Current Scene—America: Polanski on *Chinatown.*" *Films* 2, no. 19 (October 1974): 20.

"Dialogue on film: Robert Towne—Interview with Towne." *American Film* 1 (December 1975): 33–48, stills.

English, Priscilla. "*Chinatown:* Two Wrongs Make a Right." *Los Angeles Times,* May 5, 1974. AMPAS.

Farber, Stephen. "Movies that Reflect Our Obsession with Conspiracy and Assassination." *New York Times* 123 (August 11, 1974): sect. 2, 11+.

———. "L. A. Journal." *Film Comment* 10, no. 6 (November–December 1974): 2+.

Fawell, John. "Cruel Fates: Parallels between Roman Polanski's *Chinatown* and Sophocles' *Oedipus Rex.*" *Armchair Detective* 29, no. 2 (Spring 1996): 178–85.

Gariel, M. K. "An American Tragedy: 'Chinatown.'" *Bucknell Review* 35, no. 1 (1991): 209–31.

Graham, Olive. *CinemaTexas Program Notes* 14, no. 4 (May 3, 1978): 89–94.

Gussow, Mel. "Only Faye Dunaway Knows What She's Hiding." *New York Times,* October 20, 1974. (Reprinted in *The New York Times Encyclopedia of Film, 1972–1974.*)

Higham, Charles. "Polanski: 'Rosemary's Baby' and After." *New York Times,* September 23, 1973. (Reprinted in *The New York Times Encyclopedia of Film, 1972–1974.*)

Horowitz, Mark. "Fault Lines." *Film Comment* 26, no. 6 (November–December 1990): 52+, filmog, illus.

Jameson, Richard T. "Film Noir: Today, Son of Noir." *Film Comment* 10 (November–December 1974): 30–33, illus.

Kahan, Saul. "Polanski Talks about *Chinatown.*" *Los Angeles Herald Examiner,* July 3, 1974.

Kavanagh, James. "*Chinatown:* Other Places, Other Times." *Jump Cut* 3 (September–Octoctober 1974): 1+, illus.

Laguna, P. "Tajemnice chinskiej dzielnicy." *Kino* 17, no. 4 (July 1983): 25–33.

Levy, S. "Forget it? Never—It's *Chinatown!*" *Box Office* 126 (February 1990), stills. AMPAS.

Lewis, Jon H. *CinemaTexas Program Notes* 19, no. 2 (November 6, 1980): 73–76, biblio, creds, discussion, Polanski filmog.

Linderman, A. "Oedipus in *Chinatown.*" *Enclitic* 5–6, nos. 1 & 2 (Fall 1981–Spring 1982): 190–203, stills.

Lippert, R. "Was is los mit Mrs. Mulwray?" *Frauen und Film,* no. 48 (March 1990): 44–55, biblio, creds, stills.

Lorenz, A. "Reader's Right: *Chinatown.*" *Film Illustrated* 5 (June 1976): 386–87.

Lyons, David. "Flaws in the Iris." *Film Comment* 29, no. 4 (July–August 1993): 44+.

McCarty, John. "Chinatown." In *International Dictionary of Film and Filmmakers.* Vol. 1, *Films.* Detroit: St. James Press, 1997, 204–5.

McGinnis, W. D. "'Chinatown': Roman Polanski's Contemporary Oedipus Story." *Literature/Film Quarterly* 3, no. 3 (1975): 249–51, stills.

McGowan, John. "Oedipus at the Movies." *Southern Humanities Review* 20, no. 1 (Winter 1986): 1–11.

Magill's Survey of Cinema: First Series 1 (1980): 332–35. Charles Albright Jr.

Mancini, M. "Vuoto e fiction (Wyler, Polanski, Peckinpah)." *Filmcritica* 26, no. 251 (January–February 1975): 8–11.

Maxfield, James. "'The Injustice of It All': Polanski's Revision of the Private Eye Genre in *Chinatown.*" In *The Fatal Woman: Sources of Male Anxiety in American Film Noir, 1941–1991,* edited by James Maxfield, 120–31. Madison, N.J.: Farleigh Dickinson University Press, 1996.

Motion Picture Guide 2 (1985): 418.

Oliver, Bill. "'The Long Good-bye' and 'Chinatown': Debunking the Private Eye Tradition." *Literature/Film Quarterly* 3, no. 3 (1975): 240–48, stills.

Palmer, R. Barton. "*Chinatown* and the Detective Story." *Literature/Film Quarterly* 5, no. 2 (Spring 1977): 112–17.

Polanski, Roman. "The Day I Gave Jack Nicholson a Bloody Nose." *Gentleman's Quarterly,* February 1984, 178+. (Reprinted from Roman Polanski, *Roman by Polanski,* New York, Morrow, 1984.) AMPAS.

———. "A Matter of Perception." *Index on Censorship* 24, no. 6 (November–December 1995): 84–90.

Rosenbaum, J. "Paris-London Journal." *Film Comment* 10, no. 6 (November–December 1974): 4+, illus.

Sayre, Nora. "Two New Films Focus on California and Californians." *New York Times* 123 (September 1, 1974): sect. 2, 9+. AMPAS.

Silver, Alain, and Elizabeth Ward, eds. *Film Noir: An Encyclopedic Reference to the American Style.* 3d ed., rev. Woodstock, N.Y.: The Overlook Press, 1992, 56–58, analysis, creds, illus, synopsis.

Sinyard, Neil. "Roman Polanski." *Cinema Papers* 35 (November–December 1981): 438–43, illus, interv, stills.

———. *Classic Movies.* Fort Lee, N.J.: Salem, 1985, 128–31.

Slade, Tony. "Chinatown." In *International Dictionary of Films and Filmmakers.* Vol. 1, *Films,* edited by Christopher Lyon, 90–91. Chicago: St. James Press, 1984. (Updated in 2d ed., edited by Nicholas Thomas, 179–80, Detroit, St. James Press, 1990.)

Sperber, M. "*Chinatown:* 'Do as Little as Possible'; Polanski's Message and Manipulation." *Jump Cut* 3 (September–October 1974): 9–10.

Stewart, Garrett. "'The Long Good-bye' from 'Chinatown.'" *Film Quarterly* 28, no. 2 (Winter 1974–75): 25–32, illus.

Telotte, J. P. "The Detective as Dreamer: The Case of the Lady in the Lake." *Journal of Popular Film and Television* 12, no. 1 (Spring 1984): 4–15.

Thompson, David. *Suspects.* New York: Knopf, 1985.

Wexman, Virginia Wright. *Roman Polanski.* Boston: Twayne, 1985, 91–108.

Wood, G. "A New Look at an Old Genre." *University Film Association Journal* 27, no. 2 (1975): 39+.

"Written for the Screen" (Film notes). Los Angeles County Museum of Art, September 30, 1983.

Zinman, David. *Fifty Grand Movies of the 1960s and the 1970s.* New York: Crown, 1986, 155–58.

REVIEWS
Amis du Film et de la Télévision 223 (December 1974): 11, illus. J. Belmans.
Audience 7 (November 1974): 8–9. C. Canham.
BFI/Monthly Film Bulletin 41, no. 487 (August 1974): 171–72, creds. R. Combs.
Box Office, July 8, 1974.
Bright Lights, no. 12 (Spring 1994): 44+.
Cahiers du Cinéma, no. 256 (February–March 1975): 63–66. P. Kane.
Celluloide 18 (April 10, 1975): 20. J. C. Costa.
Chaplin 8, no. 135 (1974): 284–85, illus. L.-O. Lothwall.
Christian Century 91 (September 18, 1974): 860–61. G. Forshay.
Cinéaste 6, no. 3 (1974): 38–39, creds. F. Kaplan.
Cinefantastique 4, no. 1 (1975): 32, creds. J. Thingvall.
Cineforum 140 (January 1975): 81–90, creds, stills. M. Porro.
Cinema Nuovo 24, no. 233 (January–February 1975): 58–59, creds. S. Piro.
Cinema Papers 2 (March–April 1975): 51–52, creds, stills. M. Randall.
Cinéma (Paris), no. 194 (January 1975): 142–43, creds, stills. M. Cluny.
Cinématographe 11 (January–February 1975): 2, creds, stills. D. Offroy.
Cinema TV Today 10,096 (August 17, 1974): 14.
Cine Revue 54 (July 25, 1974): 4–5. Photo essay.
Commentary 58 (September 1974): 70–72.
Commonweal 100 (July 26, 1974): 405. C. L. Westerbeck Jr.
Cue, June 24, 1974. W. W.
Ecran 32 (January 1975): 63–64, creds, stills. M. Tessier.
Esquire 82 (October 1974): 14+. John Simon. (Reprinted in his *Reverse Angle,* 156–57, New York, C. N. Potter, 1982.) AMPAS.
Film a Doba 21 (May 1975): 280–81, stills. E. Hepnerova.

Filmcritica 26, no. 251 (January–February 1975): 13–17. Cappabianca, A. "L'occhio e il ragno. Note su 'Chinatown' e 'Il Fantasma Della Liberta.'"
Filmcritica 26 (March 1975): 64–67. C. Tiso.
Filmcritica 26, no. 256 (August 1975): 263–64.
Film Heritage 10, no. 1 (Fall 1974): 44–46. D. Elliott.
Films 2, no. 18 (September 1974): 18, creds, illus. P. Cargin.
Films and Filming 20 (August 1974): 25–27. Photo essay. AMPAS.
Films and Filming 21, no. 1 (October 1974): 38–39, creds, illus. G. Gow. AMPAS.
Films Illustrated 3, no. 36 (August 1974): 472, creds, illus. M. Whitman.
Films Illustrated 4 (September 1974): 28–29.
Films in Review 25, no. 7 (August–September 1974): 442, illus. C. P. Reilly.
Films in Review 25, no. 9 (November 1974): 560–63. P. Cook.
Film und Fernsehen 4, no. 9 (1976): 26–27. Photo essay.
Film und Fernsehen 5, no. 3 (March 1977): 34–35, creds, stills. W. Lange.
Hablemos de Cine 68 (1976): 35, stills. F. De Cardenas.
Hollywood Reporter 231, no. 46 (June 19, 1974): 3. Alan Howard.
Independent Film Journal 74 (June 26, 1974): 7–8, creds, illus.
Jeune Cinéma 84 (February 1975): 38–40, illus, stills. C. Benoit.
Jugend Film Fernsehen 19, no. 3 (1975): 181–82, creds. W. Knorr.
Kino 10, no. 6 (June 1975): 56–57. creds, illus, stills. J. Plazewski.
Kino 10, no. 6 (June 1975): 58–59, stills. B. Michalek.
Kosmorama 21, no. 126 (1975): 151–52, illus. P. Hirsch.
London Sunday Telegraph, August 11, 1974.
London Sunday Times, August 11, 1974.
London Telegraph, August 9, 1974. Keith Nurse.
London Times, August 9, 1974. Penelope Houston.
Los Angeles Herald Examiner, June 21, 1974. Bridget Byrne. AMPAS.
Los Angeles Times, June 21, 1974, 1+. Charles Champlin.
Motion Picture Product Digest, July 3, 1974. Richard Gertner.
Movietone News 33 (July 1974): 1–8+, creds, illus. R. T. Jameson.
Movietone News 34 (August 1974): 37–38, creds. A. Paxton.
The Nation 219 (July 6, 1974): 29–30. R. Hatch.
New Leader, August 5, 1974, 23–24. Marcia Cavell.
New Republic 171 (July 20, 1974): 16+. S. Kauffmann. AMPAS.
New Statesman 88 (August 9, 1974): 197–98. J. Coleman.
Newsweek 89 (July 1, 1974): 74. P. D. Zimmerman. AMPAS.
New Times, July 26, 1974. Frank Rich. AMPAS.
New York 7 (July 8, 1974): 74–75. J. Crist. AMPAS.
New York 7 (August 26, 1974): 54. M. Sragow. AMPAS.
New Yorker 50 (July 1, 1974). Penelope Gilliatt. AMPAS.
New York Times, June 21, 1974, 26. Vincent Canby. NYTR.
Observer, August 1974. Russell Davies.
Partisan Review 41, no. 4 (1974): 581–85. J. Baumbach.
Penthouse 6 (September 1974). R. Hofler.
Positif 164 (December 1974): 51–54, creds, illus. J. Segond.
Progressive 38 (September 1974): 53–54.

Real Paper (Boston), July 17, 1974, 24. Stuart Byron.
La Revue du Cinéma, no. 293 (February 1975): 88–90 creds, stills. R. Lefevre.
La Revue du Cinéma, no. 299 (October 1975): 6, creds. R. Lefevre.
Saturday Review/World 1 (July 27, 1974): 46. H. Alpert. AMPAS.
Séquences 19, no. 78 (October 1974): 34–35, creds, illus. A. Ruszkowski.
Sight & Sound 43, no. 4 (Autumn 1974): 243–44, illus. Tom Milne.
Skoop 10, no. 9 (December 1974): 28–32, illus. C. Boost.
Social Policy 5 (November–December 1974): 48–49. H. J. Gans.
Society 12 (November–December 1974): 73–77. M. Walling.
Take One 4, no. 4 (July 1974): 32. M. S. Cohen.
Telecine 197 (March 1975): 29–30. M. Grange.
Time 104 (July 1, 1974): 42, illus. J. Cocks. AMPAS.
Time Out 232 (August 1974): 20–21.
Variety 275, no. 6 (June 19, 1974): 16, creds. Murf. (A. D. Murphy). VR.
Velvet Light 13 (Autumn 1974): 13–16, illus. M. Wilmington.
Village Voice 19 (August 1, 1974): 63. Andrew Sarris.
Village Voice 19 (November 7, 1974): 85. Andrew Sarris.
Wall Street Journal, July 1, 1974. Jay Gould Boyum. AMPAS.
Washington Post, June 27, 1974, B1+. Gary Arnold. AMPAS.
Women's Wear Daily, June 20, 1974. Howard Kissel.

CIRCASIA. 1977. Documentary. (Appearance.)

ARTICLE
Screen International, no. 79 (March 19, 1977): 21.

THE CONSTANT NYMPH. 1943. (Writer, uncredited.)

ARTICLES AND REVIEWS
Commonweal 38 (August 13, 1943): 421.
Film Daily, June 30, 1943, 6.
Films in Review, June–July 1970.
Films in Review, February 1974.
Harrison's Reports, July 3, 1943, 107.
Hollywood Reporter, June 29, 1943, 3.
Magill's Survey of Cinema: Second Series 2 (1981): 511–14. Ronald Bowers.
Motion Picture Guide 2 (1985): 480–81.
Motion Picture Herald Product Digest, July 13, 1943, 1,401.
New Republic 109 (August 23, 1943): 255.
Newsweek 22 (August 9, 1943): 85.
New York Times, July 24, 1943, 8. NYTR.
Thomas, Tony. *The Films of the Forties.* Secaucus, N.J.: Citadel Press, 1975, 88–89.
Time 42 (August 9, 1943): 96.
Variety, June 6, 1943, 8.
Variety, June 30, 1943. VR.

Younkin, Stephen D., James Bigwood, and Raymond G. Cabana. *The Films of Peter Lorre.* Secaucus, N.J.: Citadel Press, 1982, 157–59.

CREATIVITY WITH BILL MOYERS: JOHN HUSTON. 1981. TV. (Interviewed.)

ARTICLES AND REVIEWS

McBryde, Susan. "Producing 'Creativity' . . . An Exercise in Ingenuity." *Millimeter* 10, no. 4 (April 1982): 152–19.

New York Times 131 (March 26, 1982): C26. John O'Connor, "TV Weekend: Wisdom of John Huston."

DANGER SIGNAL. 1945. (Writer, uncredited.)

ARTICLES AND REVIEWS

Harrison's Reports, November 17, 1945, 183.
Motion Picture Guide 2 (1985): 554.
New York Times, November 22, 1945, 39. NYTR.
Variety, November 14, 1945. VR.

THE DEAD. 1987. (Director, Writer.)

ARTICLES

Ahlund, J. "Huston's sista verk—subtil Joyce—filmatisering." *Chaplin* 30, no. 1 (1988): 16–17.

Allison, David. "Entretien avec John Huston." *Positif,* no. 320 (October 1987): 5–7, biblio, illus, interv, stills. (Reprinted in *John Huston, Collection dirigée,* edited by Gilles Ciment, 46–47, Dossier Positif Rivages, Paris, Editions Rivages, Collection Positif-Rivages, no. 2, 1988.)

Baechler, L. *James Joyce Quarterly* 25 (Summer 1988): 521–27.

Barolsky, P. "Joyce's Distant Music." *Virginia Quarterly Review* 65 (Winter 1989): 118–19.

Benayoun, Robert. "La leçon de tenebres de John Huston." *Positif,* no. 323 (January 1988): 8–10. (Reprinted in *John Huston, Collection dirigée,* edited by Gilles Ciment, 176–78, Dossier Positif Rivages, Paris, Editions Rivages, Collection Positif-Rivages, no. 2, 1988.)

Broadcast, December 19, 1986, 11.

Burgess, Anthony. "The Task of Turning Joyce's Prose to Film Poetry." *New York Times,* January 3, 1988, *sect.* 2, 15+, stills. AMPAS, MOMA, NYPL.

Cardullo, Bert. "Epiphanies." In *Film Chronicle: Critical Dispatches from a Forward Observer, 1987–1992,* by Bert Cardullo, 81–91. New York: Peter Lang, 1994.

Carr, Jay. ["The Dead."] In *Produced and Abandoned: The Best Films You've Never Seen,* edited by Michael Sragow. San Francisco: Mercury House, 1990.

Carson, John F. "John Huston's *The Dead:* An Irish Encomium." *Proteus,* Fall 1990, 26–29.

265

Ciment, Michel. "Epitaphe et codicille." *Positif,* no. 320 (October 1987): 3–4, creds, stills. (Reprinted in *John Huston, Collection dirigée,* edited by Gilles Ciment, 174–75, Dossier Positif Rivages, Paris, Editions Rivages, Collection Positif-Rivages, no. 2, 1988.)

Cineforum, no. 270 (December 1987): 22–36. "Speciale—*The Dead.*" Includes pieces by E. Martini (22–29), A. Piccardi (30–33), and M. Sesti (33–36). NYPL.

City Limits 323 (December 10, 1987): 20.

Curtis, David. "To John Huston, after Seeing 'The Dead' (poem)." *Literature/Film Quarterly* 17, no. 2 (April 1989): 141.

Deane, Paul. "Motion Picture Techniques in James Joyce's 'The Dead.'" *James Joyce Quarterly* 6 (1969): 231–36.

Harmetz, Aljean. "Patient: John Huston. Rx: Film." *New York Times,* March 8, 1987, sect. 2, 1+, illus, interv, port. MOMA.

———. "John Huston Is Not Well." *Chicago Tribune,* March 12, 1987, D1–D2, interv.

———. "Designer with an Affinity for the Past." *New York Times,* March 13, 1988, sect. 2, 23–24, stills.

Hart, Clive. "Joyce, Huston and the Making of *The Dead.*" The Princess Grace Irish Library. Lectures: 5. Buckinghamshire, U.K.: Colin Smythe Ltd., 1988.

Huston, Tony. "Family Ties." *American Film* 12, no. 10 (September 1987): 16+, illus, port.

———. "My Father's Last Film." *Telegraph Sunday Magazine,* December 13, 1987, 33.

———. "The Dead: Huston Jr. over Huston Sr." *Skoop* 24, no. 2 (February 1988): 12–17, filmog, illus.

James, Caryn. "Film View: When Film Becomes a Feast of Words." *New York Times,* July 30, 1989, sect. 2, 11+, stills.

Kakutani, Michiko. "John Huston's Last Legacy." *New York Times,* December 13, 1987, 1+, stills. AMPAS, MOMA, NYPL.

Magill's Cinema Annual 1988, pp. 95–99. R. C. Dale.

Martini, Emanuela. "Di parl passo con l'amore e la morte." *Cineforum* 27, no. 12 (December 1987): 22–29, creds, filmog, illus, stills.

Maslin, Janet. "Film Critics' Group Honors *The Dead.* (Voted Best Film of 1987 by the National Society of Film Critics)." *New York Times,* January 4, 1988, C18.

Motion Picture Guide Annual, 1988, 61–62.

Naremore, James. "Return of *The Dead.*" In *Perspectives on John Huston,* edited by Stephen Cooper, 197–206. New York: G.K. Hall, 1994. (Update of "Return of the Living Dead," *The James Joyce Literary Supplement,* Spring 1991.)

Neil, Philippe. "Obrazy ucztuowania na ekranach." *Kino* 23, no. 11 (November 1989): 39–42. (Reprinted in French translation: *Positif,* no. 334 [December 1988]: 48–51.)

Norman, Barry. "Barry Norman on. . . ." *Radio Times* 273, no. 3,567 (May 9, 1992): 42.

O'Haire, Patricia. "Requiem for a Heavyweight." *New York Daily News,* December 13, 1987, 3.

O'Shea, Michael J. "'Raiders and Cineman Too': Joyce on Video." *James Joyce Literary Supplement* 4, no. 1 (Spring 1990): 21–23.

Pederson, Ann. "Uncovering *The Dead:* A Study of Adaptation." *Literature/Film Quarterly* 21, no. 1 (1993): 69–70.

Piccardi, Adriano. "Riconoscersi soli." *Cineforum* 27, no. 12 (December 1987): 30–33.

Pilipp, Frank. "Narrative Devices and Aesthetic Perception in Joyce's and Huston's *The Dead.*" *Literature/Film Quarterly* 21, no. 1 (1993): 61–68.

Rockett, Kevin, Luke Gibbons, and John Hill. *Cinema and Ireland.* New York: Syracuse University Press, 1988.

Rosenfield, Paul. "The Master Huston." *Los Angeles Times,* February 22, 1987, Calendar, A1+. AMPAS.

Sabouraud, Frederic. "Le plan irlandais." *Cahiers du Cinéma* 400 (October 1987): 34, port. NYPL.

Schulz-Keil, Wieland. "Huston." *Film Comment,* September–October 1987, 18–23. (Reprinted in Cooper, *Perspectives on John Huston,* 207–15.)

Screen International 555 (July 5, 1986): 6.

Screen International 579 (December 20, 1986): 4.

Screen International 619 (September 1987): 27.

Sesti, Mario. "La morte, la sua voce." *Cineforum* 27, no. 12 (December 1987): 33–36.

Shout, J. D. "Joyce at Twenty-five, Huston at Eighty-one." *Literature/Film Quarterly* 17, no. 2 (April 1989): 91–94.

Silverman, Stephen. "John Huston Lives: Tony Huston Interviewed on Making *The Dead.*" *New York Post,* December 21, 1987, 39. NYPL.

Sinyard, Neil. *Filming Literature: The Art of Screen Adaptation.* London: Croom Helm, 1986.

Stills 30 (March 1987): 79.

Thomas, Bob. "At 80 John Huston Takes on Another Film Project: No. 45." *Philadelphia Inquirer,* March 22, 1987, 2–I.

Time Out 899 (November 11, 1987): 22. Interview with Anjelica Huston on film and her father, John Huston.

Variety, August 31, 1987. AMPAS.

Varjola, M., and H. Bacon. "Elava kuollut musiikin muistot." *Filmihullu* 4 (1988): 4+.

Verdone, M. "Cinema senzo il cinema in James Joyce." *Filmcritica* 38, no. 379 (November 1987): 571–80.

Walker, Beverly. "Anjelica." *Film Comment* 23, no. 5 (September 1987): 24–26.

Wall, James H. "Universal Connections among Living and Dead." *Christian Century* 105, no. 2 (January 20, 1988): 43–44. Editorial.

Walsh, M. "John Huston Raises *The Dead.*" *Time,* March 16, 1987, 92–93, illus, port.

Wiener, David John. "*The Dead*—A Study in Light and Shadow." *American Cinematographer*, 68, no. 11 (November 1987): 62+. AMPAS, NYPL.

"Zenith and Huston to Team on 'Dead." *Variety,* December 17, 1986, 7+.

REVIEWS
America 158 (February 20, 1988). Robert A. Blake.
*BFI/Monthly Film Bulletin, 56, no. 647 (December 1987): 355–56, creds, stills. Tom Milne.
Box Office 124 (February 1988): 26 [p. R16]. T. Matthews.
Cahiers du Cinéma 403 (January 1988): 20–21, creds, stills. I. Katsahnias.
Chaplin 30, nos. 2 & 3 (215–216) (1988): 143–144, creds, stills. S. Farran-Lee.
Chicago Sun Times, January 4, 1991, "Weekend Plus," 3. Joe Pixler. NYPL.
Christian Century 105 (January 20, 1988): 43–44, illus. J. M. Wall.
*Christian Science Monitor, January 15, 1988, 19. David Sterritt. AMPAS, NYPL.
Cine-Bulletin 7, no. 4 (1988): 10–11, ports, stills. Y Rousseau.
Cinéma (Paris) 424 (January 13, 1988): 7–8, filmog, illus. A.-M. Baron. NYPL.
Cinema Nuovo 36, no. 310 (November–December 1987): 8–19. M. M. Gazzano.
Cinema Nuovo 37, no. 311 (January–February 1988): 40–42, creds, illus, stills. L. Termine.
Cinema Papers 69 (May 1988): 54–55, creds, illus, stills. B. Routt and D. Routt.
Commonweal 114 (December 18, 1987): 748–49. Tom O'Brien. AMPAS.
Dicine, no. 36 (September 1990): 20–21, creds, stills. N. Yehya.
Ekran 13, no. 2 (1988): 29, creds, stills. S. Pelko.
Film (London) 3, no. 10 (December 1987): 9. P. Cargin. NYPL.
Film & Kino, no. 3 (1988): 12–14, port, stills. Y. Finslo.
Filmcritica, nos. 381 & 382 (January–February 1988): 22–24. F. Bo.
Film-Echo/Filmwoche 54 (September 25, 1987): 15.
Film en Televisie 368 (January 1988): 9, creds, stills. D. Dufour.
Film Journal 91 (January 1988): 45, creds. C. Gagne.
Filmrutan 31, no. 3 (1988): 32–33, creds, illus. S. Andersson.
Films and Filming 399 (December 1987): 23–24, creds, stills. B. Baxter. NYPL.
*Films in Review 39, no. 1 (January 1988): 43–44. Michael Scheinfeld. NYPL.
Film und Fernsehen, no. 2 (1988): 38–44, illus. G. Fenyez.
FilmVilag 31, no. 5 (1988): 58–60, port, stills. Ollozo, "Joyce es a film."
Grand Angle 15, no. 101 (January 1988): 18–19, biblio, creds, illus. M. Septon.
Hollywood Reporter 296, no. 20 (March 1987): 16, creds.
Hollywood Reporter 296, no. 37 (August 31, 1987): 3. AMPAS.
Hudson Review 41, no. 4 (Winter 1989): 710–13. B. Cardullo.
James Joyce Quarterly 25, no. 4 (Summer 1988): 521–27. Lea Baechler and A. Walton Litz.
James Joyce Quarterly 25, no. 4 (Summer 1988): 527–33, Richard Gerber.
Jeune Cinéma 184 (November–December 1987): 32–34, creds, stills. Bernard Nave.
Kosmorama 34, no. 185 (Autumn 1988): 21–22, creds, stills. D. Nissen.
Levende Billeder 4 (September 1988): 12–14, port, stills. U. Breuning.
Listener 118, no. 3,043 (December 31, 1987): 29, illus. Margaret Walters.
London Times, September 5, 1987, 18. David Robinson.
London Times Literary Supplement, December 18, 1987, 1,405. NYPL.
Los Angeles Herald Examiner, December 18, 1987, 6. Peter Rainer. AMPAS, MOMA.

Los Angeles Times, December 17, 1987, Calendar, 1. Sheila Benson. AMPAS.

Los Angeles Weekly, December 12–24, 1987, 61. F. K. Feeney.

Maclean's 100 (December 14, 1987). Lawrence O'Toole.

Medien 32, no. 1 (1988): 19–26, biblio, creds, illus, stills. P. Kremski.

Metro, no. 76 (May 1988): 52, creds, stills. F. Calvert.

National Review 40 (January 22, 1988): 64–65. John Simon. MOMA.

New Republic, 197 (December 21, 1987): 26–28. Stanley Kauffmann. AMPAS, MOMA, NYPL.

*Newsday, December 17, 1987, part 2, 9. Mike McGrady. NYPL.

*Newsweek, December 21, 1987, 68, stills. David Ansen.

*New York 21 (January 18, 1988): 59–60, stills. David Denby. AMPAS, MOMA, NYPL.

New York Daily News, December 17, 1987, 9. Kathleen Carroll. NYPL.

New Yorker 63 (December 14, 1987): 144+. Pauline Kael, "Irish Voices." (Reprinted in Pauline Kael, *Hooked,* 402–9, New York, E. P. Dutton, 1989;. and in Pauline Kael, *For Keeps,* 1,155–59, New York, Dutton, 1994.) AMPAS.

New Yorker, December 28, 1992. AMPAS.

New Yorker 68 (December 28, 1992–January 4, 1993): 48.

New York Native, December 21, 1987, 30. Joel Weinberg. NYPL.

*New York Post, December 17, 1987, 56. V. A. Musetto. NYPL.

New York Review of Books 35 (March 3, 1988): 18–19, stills. Dennis Donoghue.

New York Times 138 (December 4, 1988): H32.

New York Times, December 17, 1987, C19, creds, stills. Vincent Canby. AMPAS, MOMA, NYTR.

Photoplay 38 (December 1987): 46–47, port, stills. A. Frank.

People Weekly 29 (January 11, 1988): 10+, illus. Peter Travers.

Playboy 35 (February 1988): 28–29, stills. B. Williamson.

Positif, no. 323 (January 1988): 5–10, creds, biblio. Robert Benayoun. (Reprinted in *John Huston, Collection dirigée,* edited by Gilles Ciment, 174–75, Dossier Positif Rivages, Paris, Editions Rivages, Collection Positif-Rivages, no. 2, 1988.)

Premiere 1 (December 1987): 82, stills. L. Sante.

La Revue du Cinéma, no. 35 (1988): 50, creds. F. Chevassu. NYPL.

La Revue du Cinéma, no. 34 (January 1988): 56–66, creds, illus, stills. Max Tessier and A. Garel.

Segnocinema 8, no. 31 (January 1988): 66–67, creds, stills. Adelina Preziosi.

Séquences 134 (June 1988): 48–49, creds, stills. Jean Beaulieu.

*Sight & Sound 57, no. 1 (Winter 1987–88): 67–68. Tim Pulleine. NYPL.

Skrien 158 (February–March 1988): 21, illus. Ivo de Kock.

*Time 131 (January 4, 1988): 64, stills. Richard Schickel. AMPAS, MOMA.

Time Out 903 (December 9 1987): 35.

24 Images 37 (Spring 1988): 48, creds, port. M. Tourigny.

Variety 328, no. 6 (September 2, 1987): 14, creds. 'Cart,' "Venice Festival Reviews: Reviewed–Out of Competition." VR.

Video Review, December 1988. Andrew Sarris.

*Village Voice 32 (December 22, 1987): 94, stills. Katherine Dieckmann. AMPAS, MOMA, NYPL.

Wall Street Journal, December 17, 1987, 26 (West Coast ed.), 28 (East Coast ed.). Julie Salamon.
Washington Post, December 18, 1987, G1. Hal Hinson.
Washington Post, December 18, 1987, Weekend, 49. Desson Howe.
*Women's Wear Daily, December 18, 1987, 16. Kevin Haynes. NYPL.
Z 6, no. 2 (n24) (1988): 14–15, creds, illus, stills. T. Lundemo.

DEATH DRIVES THROUGH. 1935. (Writer.)

REVIEWS
BFI/Monthly Film Bulletin 15, no. 170 (February 1948): 15.
Kinematograph Weekly 2,125, (January 22, 1948).
Motion Picture Guide 2 (1985): 602.
Pathscope Monthly, December 1936, 8–9.
Today's Cinema 70, no. 5,599 (January 21, 1948).

DE SADE. 1969. (Actor.)

ARTICLES AND REVIEWS
The American Film Institute Catalog: Feature Films, 1961–1970. New York: R. R. Bowker, 1976, 237.
BFI/Monthly Film Bulletin 38, no. 445 (February 1971): 2,021.
Box Office, October 13, 1969. AMPAS.
Canby, Vincent. "Bye, Bye, Beach Bunnies." *New York Times,* March 2, 1969. (Reprinted in *The New York Times Encyclopedia of Film, 1967–1971.*)
Cinema 4, no. 4 (December 1968): 20–21. George Clayron.
Cinéma (Paris), no. 169 (September–October 1972): 142. Raymond Lefevre.
Entertainment World, October 3, 1969, 28. Nat Freedland.
Films and Filming 16, no. 5:63–66, illus. Robert Joseph.
Films and Filming 17, no. 7 (April 1971): 50. George Gow.
Film TV Daily, September 26, 1969. Gene Arneel. MOMA.
Harmetz, Aljean. "The Dime-store Way to Make Movies—and Money. If What AIP Peddles Is Trash, It Is Trash with an Eager Market." *New York Times,* August 4, 1974A. (Reprinted in *The New York Times Encyclopedia of Film, 1972–1974.*)
Hollywood Reporter 203, no. 33 (November 1968): 14, creds.
Hollywood Reporter 207, no. 48 (September 29, 1969): 3. John Mahoney. AMPAS.
Interview, January 2, 1969. Robert Weiner.
Kinematograph Weekly 3,300 (January 1971): 14.
Koeting, Christopher. "The A.I.P. X Files." *Filmfax,* no. 56 (May–June 1996): 59+.
Los Angeles Herald Examiner, September 27, 1964. Michael Ross. AMPAS.
Los Angeles Times, September 29, 1969. Charles Champlin. AMPAS.
Motion Picture Guide 2 (1985): 589.
Motion Picture Herald, October 15, 1969.
New Yorker, October 10, 1969. AMPAS.
New York Times, September 26, 1969, 40. NYTR.

Playboy, June 1969.
Positif, no. 142 (September 1972): 120.
Saturday Review, October 11, 1969.
Time, October 24, 1969, 106. MOMA.
Variety, October 1, 1969 (W), 17.
Variety, September 29, 1969 (D). Rick. AMPAS, VR.
Village Voice 14, no. 52 (October 9, 1969): 56. Richard McGuinness.

THE DESERTER. 1971. (Actor.)

REVIEWS
BFI/Monthly Film Bulletin 38, no. 454 (November 1971).
Bianco e Nero 16, nos. 1 & 2 (January–February 1955), creds.
Box Office, June 21, 1971.
Cinema d'Oggi, December 14, 1970, 4.
Filmfacts 14, no. 14 (1971): 350. AMPAS.
Hollywood Reporter 215, no. 36 (April 7, 1971): 3. AMPAS.
Intermezzo 25, nos. 23 & 24 (December 21, 1970): 12.
Kinematograph Weekly 3,334 (September 4, 1971): 8.
Motion Picture Exhibitor, April 7, 1971.
Motion Picture Exhibitor, May 17, 1971.
Motion Picture Guide 2 (1985): 624–25.
New York, June 21, 1971.
New York Daily News, June 10, 1971. Ann Guarino.
New York Post, June 10, 1971. Archer Winsten.
New York Times, June 10, 1971, 49. NYTR.
Today's Cinema 9,936 (September 1971): 8.
Variety, April 7, 1971, 18. Murf. AMPAS, MOMA, VR.
Village Voice 16 (July 8, 1959): 27. Michael Kerbel.

DESTRY RIDES AGAIN. 1932; 1939. (Writer, uncredited.)

ARTICLES AND REVIEWS
The American Film Institute Catalog: Feature Films, 1931–1940. Berkeley:
  University of California Press, 1993, 491.
Cinéma (Paris), no. 290 (February 1983): 48–49.
Cinématographe, no. 85 (January 1983): 45.
Commonweal 31 (December 15, 1939): 187.
Crowther, Bosley. *Reruns: Fifty Memorable Films.* New York: Putnam, 1978.
Dickens, Homer. *The Films of Marlene Dietrich.* New York: Citadel Press, 1968,
  140–43.
Druxman, Michael B. *Make It Again, Sam: A Survey of Remakes.* South Brunswick,
  N.J.: A. S. Barnes, 1975, 45–49.
Enclitic 5, no. 2 (Fall 1981–Spring 1982): 55–65.
Film Daily, November 30, 1939, 10.

Halliwell, Leslie. *Halliwell's Island: A Nostalgic Choice of Films from the Golden Age.* New York: Scribners, 1982, 65–68.

Harrison's Reports, April 16, 1932, 62.

Harrison's Reports, December 9, 1939, 195.

Hochman, Stanley, ed. *From Quasimodo to Scarlett O'Hara: A National Board of Review Anthology, 1920–1940.* New York: Ungar, 1982, 335.

Hollywood Reporter, November 29, 1939, 3.

Hollywood Spectator 14 (December 9, 1939): 6.

Jones, Ken D., Arthur F. McClure, and Alfred E. Twomey. *Character People.* South Brunswick, N.J.: A. S. Barnes, 1970, 76–79.

Kael, Pauline. *Kiss Kiss Bang Bang.* New York: Bantam Books, 1969, 317–18.

Magill's Survey of Cinema: First Series 1 (1980): 436–39 (1939 version). Julia Johnson.

Motion Picture Guide 2 (1985): 634 (1932; 1939).

Motion Picture Herald, December 2, 1939, 41.

The Nation 149 (December 9, 1939): 662.

National Board of Review Magazine 15 (January 1940): 23.

New Masses 33 (December 19, 1939): 29–30.

Newsweek 14 (December 11, 1939): 33.

New Yorker 15 (December 9, 1939): 97.

New York Times, November 30, 1939, 25. NYTR.

Parish, James Robert, and Michael R. Pitts. *The Great Western Pictures.* Metuchen, N.J.: Scarecrow Press, 1976, 83–86.

Positif, no. 263 (January 1983): 70–72. F. Vitoux.

Radio Times 273, no. 3,563 (April 11, 1992): 38. Barry Norman.

La Revue du Cinéma, no. 379 (January 1983): 40. Gilles Colpart.

Rob Wagner's Script 21 (January 13, 1940): 16.

Spectator 164 (February 16, 1940): 213.

Time 34 (December 18, 1939): 76.

Tuska, Jon. *The Filming of the West.* Garden City, N.Y.: Doubleday, 1976, 390–91.

Variety, December 6, 1939. VR.

Vermilye, Jerry. *The Films of the Thirties.* Secaucus, N.J.: Citadel Press, 1982, 250–52.

DIRECTED BY WILLIAM WYLER. 1986. (Interviewed.)

ARTICLES AND REVIEWS

Film Comment 22 (December 1986): 50+, stills. S. Harvey, "The 24th NY Film Festival."

Hollywood Reporter, July 7, 1986.

Hollywood Reporter, October 7, 1986, 46. George Christy.

New York, September 22, 1986. Jesse Kornbluth.

New York Times, September 20, 1986, 9, creds. Vincent Canby. NYTR.

Variety 324, no. 5 (August 27, 1986): 16, creds. Strat. VR.

Washington Post, June 5, 1986, interv. Elizabeth Kastor.

DIRECTORS GUILD OF AMERICA SERIES: JOHN HUSTON. 1982.

ARTICLE

McCarthy, Todd. "Listen as Well as He Talks: John Huston's DGA Weekend." *Variety* 307 (June 2, 1982): 6+, interv.

DISRAELI. 1921, 1929. (Assigned writer, November–December 1939.)

ARTICLES AND REVIEWS

The American Film Institute Catalog: Feature Films, 1921–1930. New York: R. R. Bowker, 1971, 190.

**Cinema* 1, no. 1 (January 1930): 42. James Shelley Hamilton.

Commonweal 11 (February 5, 1930): 399.

Exhibitor's Herald-World, December 14, 1929, 44.

Film Daily, October 13, 1929, 8.

**Film Mercury* 10, no. 11 (November 1, 1929): 6. Richard Watts Jr.

Harrison's Reports, October 12, 1929, 162.

Literary Digest 105 (April 12, 1929): 19.

Magill's Cinema Annual, 1982, 429–31.

Motion Picture Guide 2 (1985): 667.

New York Times, August 22, 1921, 13.

New York Times, October 3, 1929, 27. NYTR.

Outlook 153 (October 16, 1929): 273.

**Photoplay* 20, no. 6 (November 1921): 61.

Variety, August 26, 1921.

Variety, October 9, 1929. VR.

DR. EHRLICH'S MAGIC BULLET. 1940. (Writer.)

ARTICLES AND REVIEWS

The American Film Institute Catalog: Feature Films, 1931–1940. Berkeley: University of California Press, 1993, 515–16.

Commonweal 31 (March 1, 1940): 412.

Churchill, Douglas W. "Hollywood Goes Historical." *New York Times,* August 4, 1940. (Reprinted in *The New York Times Encyclopedia of Film, 1937–1940.*)

Crowther, Bosley. "Wives of Great Men." *New York Times,* February 18, 1940. (Reprinted in *The New York Times Encyclopedia of Film, 1937–1940.*)

Documentary News Letter 1, no. 6 (June 1940): 9.

Documentary News Letter 1, no. 12 (December 1940): 21.

Film Daily, February 2, 1940, 6. AMPAS.

Harrison's Reports, February 17, 1940, 27.

Hollywood Reporter, February 2, 1940, 3.

Hygeia 18 (February 1940): 138–39.

Kinematograph Weekly 1,725 (May 9, 1940.)

Life 8 (March 4, 1940): 74–77. AMPAS.

Look, March 26, 1940, 54+, illus.

Lorentz, Pare. *Lorentz on Film: Movies, 1927–1941.* New York: Hopkinson and Blake, 1975, 187–89.

Magill's Survey of Cinema: First Series 1 (1980): 454–56. Timothy W. Johnson.

Motion Picture Daily, February 5, 1940. Charles S. Aaronson.

Motion Picture Guide 2 (1985): 674–75.

The Nation 150 (March 9, 1940): 346.

New Republic 102 (March 25, 1940): 409.

Newsweek 15 (February 26, 1940): 30+.

New Yorker 16 (February 24, 1940): 67. John Mosher. AMPAS.

New York Herald Tribune, February 24, 1940. Howard Barnes.

New York Times, February 15, 1940, sect. 9, 5.

New York Times, February 24, 1940, 9. NYTR.

New York Times, May 19, 1950. "Heyday for the Research Experts." (Reprinted in *The New York Times Encyclopedia of Film, 1937–1940.*)

Parish, James Robert, and Alvin H. Marill. *The Cinema of Edward G. Robinson.* New York: A. S. Barnes, 1972, 124–26.

Photoplay 54 (May 1940): 69.

Robinson, Edward G. "The Role I Liked Best." *Saturday Evening Post,* February 16, 1946.

Scholastic 36 (February 19, 1940): 38.

Time 35 (February 19, 1940): 80+.

Today's Cinema 54, no. 4,412, (May 8, 1940).

Variety, February 2, 1940. Preview.

Variety, February 7, 1940, 14. AMPAS, VR.

Wilson, Robert, ed. *The Film Criticism of Otis Ferguson.* Philadelphia: Temple University Press, 1971, 291–93.

A FAREWELL TO ARMS. 1957. (Director, withdrew.)

ARTICLES

Arnold, Robert, Nicholas Humy, and Ana Lopez. "Rereading Adaptations: *A Farewell to Arms.*" *Iris,* no. 1 (1983): 101–13.

Calderoni, Franco. "Un altro 'processo a Hollywood.'" *Bianco e Nero* 18, no. 4 (April 1957): 1–4.

"David O. Selznick's Hollywood" [Program notes]. Museum of Modern Art: Department of Film, April 12 and April 14, 1980.

Haver, Ronald. *David O. Selznick's Hollywood.* New York: Knopf, 1980.

Hawkins, Robert F. "No *Farewell to Arms* in Italy. World War I Carnage Is Re-enacted for Movie of Hemingway Book. On the Making of the Film, on Location, and Comments on the Falling out of Huston and Selznick." *New York Times,* May 12, 1957. (Reprinted in *The New York Times Encyclopedia of Film, 1952–1957.*)

Horrigan, William. "Dying without Death: Borzage's *A Farewell to Arms.*" In *The Classic American Novel and the Movies,* edited by Gerald Peary and Roger Shatzkin, 297–304. New York: Frederick Ungar, 1977.

"Huston Leaves Production." *Bianco e Nero* 18, no. 3 (March 1957): 1.

Laurence, Frank M. *Hemingway on Film*. Jackson, Miss.: University Press of Mississippi, 1981, 6–16.

Magill's Survey of Cinema: First Series 2 (1980): 524–26. Carl F. Macek.

Marcus, Mordecai. "*A Farewell to Arms:* Novel into Film." *Journal of the Central Mississippi Valley American Studies Association* 2 (1961): 69–71.

Moshier, W. Franklyn. *The Films of Jennifer Jones*. San Francisco: The author, 1978, 149–54.

Motion Picture Guide 3 (1986): 816–17.

Oliver, Charles M., ed. *A Moving Picture Feast: The Filmgoer's Hemingway*. New York: Praeger, 1989.

Phillips, Gene D. *Hemingway and Film*. New York: Frederick Ungar, 1980.

Ranieri, Tino. "Hemingway e il cinema: Due strade diverse." *Bianco e Nero* 18, no. 4 (April 1957): 48–57.

Roud, Richard "Two Cents on the Rouble." *Sight & Sound* 27, no. 5 (Summer 1958): 245–47.

Selznick, David O. *Memo from David O. Selznick*. Selected and edited by Rudy Behlmer, with an introduction by S. N. Behrman. New York: The Viking Press, 1972.

"To: Whom It May Concern, From: David O. Selznick, Subject: Making a Memo. Selection of Memos from Selznick to Those Involved in Making of the Movie, Including Huston." *Life,* March 17, 1958, 93+.

REVIEWS

America 98 (January 25, 1958): 495–96.

BFI/Monthly Film Bulletin 25, no. 292 (May 1958): 56.

Commonweal 67 (February 7, 1958): 488.

Daily Cinema 7,975 (March 7, 1958): 3.

Film Daily 112, no. 118 (December 19, 1957): 11.

Film Daily, April 1958, 21.

Films and Filming 4, no. 7 (April 1958): 21, illus. Paul Rotha.

Films in Review 9, no. 1 (January 1958): 29–30. Henry Hart.

Harrison's Reports, December 21, 1957, 202.

Hollywood Reporter 147, no. 46 (December 19, 1957): 3. James Powers. MOMA.

Kinematograph Weekly 2,638 (March 6, 1958): 25.

Motion Picture Herald 210, no. 1 (January 4, 1958): 666.

Motion Picture Herald Product Digest, December 21, 1957, 14.

New Republic 138 (February 17, 1958): 22.

Newsweek, December 16, 1957.

Newsweek 50 (December 30, 1957): 61.

New Yorker 33 (February 1, 1958): 65. John McCarten.

New York Herald Tribune, January 25, 1988. William Zinsser.

New York Times, January 25, 1958, 14. Bosley Crowther. NYTR.

New York Times, February 2, 1958, sect. 2, 1. Bosley Crowther, "Farewell to Arms: Picture Misses Point of Hemingway Novel."

Saturday Review 61 (February 1, 1958): 27. Hollis Alpert. MOMA.
Time 71 (February 3, 1958): 80. MOMA.
Variety, December 25, 1957, 6. VR.

FAT CITY. 1972. (Director; Writer, uncredited.)

ARTICLES

Aghed, Jan, and Michel Ciment. "Deux soirées avec John Huston." *Positif* 142 (September 1972): 93–104. Interview with director, review.

Bell, Arthur. "Days of Brine & Pizzazz: *Fat City*'s Susan Tyrell." *Village Voice,* August 10, 1972. NYPL.

Benayoun, Robert. "La part de l'ombre." *Positif* 142 (September 1972): 89–92, illus. (Reprinted in *John Huston, Collection dirigée,* edited by Gilles Ciment, 141–43, Dossier Positif Rivages, Paris, Editions Rivages, Collection Positif-Rivages, no. 2, 1988.)

Bount, Roy Jr. "Poom & I'll Go Pow." *Sports Illustrated,* February 14, 1972, 29–37. MOMA.

Braucourt, G. "Entretien avec John Huston." *Ecran* 10 (1972): 61–63, illus.

Canby, Vincent. "Huston's Fine, Lean *Fat City.*" *New York Times,* August 6, 1972, sect. 2, 1. AMPAS, NYPL, NYTR.

Champlin, Charles. ["Fat City."] In *Film 72–73: An Anthology by the National Society of Film Critics,* edited by David Denby, 23–25. Indianapolis: Bobbs-Merrill, 1973.

———. ["Fat City."] In *Produced and Abandoned: The Best Films You've Never Seen,* edited by Michael Sragow. San Francisco: Mercury House, 1990.

"Cinematographer Conrad Hall." *American Film Institute Dialogue on Film* 3, no. 1 (October 1973): 1–24.

Corry, John. "John Huston: Musing on *Fat City* and Other Pursuits." *New York Times,* August 5, 1972, interv. (Reprinted in *The New York Times Encyclopedia of Film, 1972–1974.*) AMPAS, MOMA, NYPL.

Head, Anne. "John Huston's *Fat City* Wins Praise at Cannes Festival." *Hollywood Reporter* 221, no. 17 (May 15, 1972): 1+. AMPAS. (*Note:* Three copies of this piece are in AMPAS John Huston Archive.)

Hodenfield, Jan. "John Huston, a Welcome Fat Success." *New York Post,* August 5, 1972. AMPAS.

Jameson, Richard T. "Fat City." *Film Comment* [Midsection] 16 (May–June 1980): 52–55.

Klemesrud, Judy. *"Fat City*'s Susie—Oh, oh, What a Girl." *New York Times,* August 13, 1972, sect. 2, 1. (Reprinted in *The New York Times Encyclopedia of Film, 1972–1974.*) AMPAS.

Lewis, Grover. *Academy All the Way.* San Francisco: Straight Arrow, 1974. Includes "Up in *Fat City* with Stacy Keach and John Huston." (Reprinted from *Rolling Stone,* September 30, 1971, 20.) MOMA.

McCarthy, Todd. "The Films of John Huston" [Program notes]. Los Angeles County Museum of Art, November 14, 1980, creds.

Magill's Survey of Cinema: Second Series 2 (1980): 763–65. Michael Shepler.

Malmkjaer, P. "Fat City." *Kosmorama,* 19, no. 111 (October 1972): 32–35, illus.
Moore, Thomas. "John Huston Fights His Way Back to *Fat City.*" *Life* 73 (August 4, 1972): 69, illus, interv, port. MOMA.
Motion Picture Guide 3 (1986): 821.
Natale, Richard. "Going Back to Huston." *Women's Wear Daily,* July 27, 1972, 12. MOMA, NYPL.
Porro, M., ed. "Citta Amara. *Fat City.*" *Cineforum* 14, no. 130 (February–March 1974): 137–50, creds, illus. Fiche.
Samuels, Charles Thomas. "How Not to Film a Novel." In *Mastering the Film and Other Essays,* 190–97. Knoxville, Tenn.: University of Tennessee Press, 1977. (Originally in *American Scholar* 42, no. 1 [1972–73]: 148–54.)
Sarris, Andrew. ["Fat City."] In *Film 72–73: An Anthology by the National Society of Film Critics,* edited by David Denby, 25–27. Indianapolis: Bobbs-Merrill, 1973.
Shecter, Leonard. "Craft Beat Art by a T.K.O.: The Making of *Fat City.*" *Look* 35 (October 19, 1971): 88–90. AMPAS.
Studlar, Gaylyn. "Shadowboxing: *Fat City* and the Malaise of Masculinity." In *Reflections in a Male Eye,* edited by Gaylyn Studlar and David Desser, 177–98. Washington, D.C.: Smithsonian Institution Press, 1993.

REVIEWS
America 127 (September 2, 1972): 126.
BFI/Monthly Film Bulletin 39, no. 465 (November 1972): 211.
Casablanca, no. 35 (November 1983): 44.
Chaplin 14, no. 6 (1972): 228, illus. K. Freund.
Christian Science Monitor, July 29, 1972, 6. NYPL.
Cinema (Bucharest) 11, no. 10 (October 1973): 19–20, illus. O. Tiroiu.
Cinéma (Paris), no. 173 (February 1973): 102–3, illus. M. Amiel.
Cinema Nuovo 23, no. 228 (March–April 1974): 133–34, creds. S. P[iro].
Cinema Quebec 2, no. 3 (November 1972): 44–45, illus. A. Leroux.
Cinema TV Today 9,996 (September 2, 1972): 20.
Commentary 54 (November 1972): 82–83.
Commonweal 97 October 6, 1972): 15–16. Colin L. Westerbeck Jr. MOMA.
Ecran, no. 10 (December 1972): 61–63. Claude Beylie.
Filmfacts 23 (1972): 507.
Film Information, September 1972. Peter P. Schillaci.
Film International, September 19, 1972. Peter P. Schillaci. NYPL.
Filmkritik 26 (February 1982): 80–90, bio. John Huston, "Einfalt."
Films and Filming 19, no. 1 (October 1972): 67–69. Portfolio of photos from *Fat City.* NYPL.
Films and Filming 19, no. 2 (November 1972): 52–53. G. Gow.
Films in Review 23, no. 8 (October 1972): 507–8. D. Leach. NYPL.
Hollywood Reporter 223, no. 44 (November 5, 1972): 9. AMPAS.
Image & Son 270 (March 1973): 106–8. P. Gaulier and J. Chevallier.
International Herald Tribune, October 8, 1972. Quinn Curtiss. NYPL.
Jeune Cinéma, no. 69 (March 1973): 34–35, illus. A. Tournes.

Life 73 (August 25, 1972): 20. Richard Schickel.
Listener 116, no. 2,969 (July 17, 1986): 32. R. Combs.
Los Angeles Times, November 22, 1972. Charles Champlin. AMPAS.
Lumière 24 (June 1973): 29–30. L. Clancy.
Lumière 26 (August 1973): 33. G. Gardner.
Newark Evening News, July 27, 1972, 15. Bruce Bahrenburg. NYPL.
New Republic 167 (August 19, 1972): 25.
Newsweek 80 (August 7, 1972): 61. Paul Zimmerman. NYPL.
New York, July 31, 1972, 50. Judith Crist. NYPL.
New York Daily News, July 27, 1972. Kathleen Carroll.
New York Daily News, July 28, 1972, 64. Rex Reed. NYPL.
New Yorker 48 (July 29, 1972): 53. Penelope Gilliatt. AMPAS, MOMA, NYPL.
New Yorker, August 5, 1972. "Revels, Talk of the Town: *Fat City.*" AMPAS.
New Yorker, September 30, 1972, 115.
New York Post, July 27, 1972, 22. Archer Winsten. AMPAS, NYPL.
New York Times, July 27, 1972, 20. Vincent Canby. MOMA, NYTR.
The Observer, August 27, 1972, 24. Tom Milne. NYPL.
Punch, August 30, 1972, 281. Richard Mallett. NYPL.
La Revue du Cinéma 276 & 277 (October 1973): 146–47, creds.
La Revue du Cinéma 270 (March 1973): 106–8. P. Gaulier and J. Chevallier.
Rolling Stone, September 14, 1972. Paul Nelson. MOMA.
Saturday Review 55 (September 2, 1972): 61. Arthur Knight. AMPAS, MOMA.
Sight & Sound 16, no. 3 (Summer 1972): 168–69, illus. John Russell Taylor. MOMA.
Skoop 8, no. 8 (1973): 2–7, illus. G. Vanderwildt.
Skrien, no. 165 (April–May 1989): 66–67, stills. S. Vander Laan.
Spectator, September 27, 1972, 366. Christopher Hudson.
Take One 3 (October 1971): 24–25. John Kane.
Time 100 (August 7, 1972): 76. Jay Cocks. AMPAS, MOMA, NYPL.
Time Out 133 (September 1, 1972): 41.
Travelling 40 (January–February 1974): 52–54, creds. E. Steiner.
Variety, May 19, 1972. AMPAS.
Variety, May 24, 1972, 19. Mosk. VR, NYPL.
Variety, May 1988, 56. Jim Farber. NYPL.
Village Voice, August 17, 1972, 53. Jonas Mekas, "Movie Journal." MOMA, NYPL.
Village Voice, September 21, 1972, 73. Andrew Sarris. MOMA, NYPL.
Washington Post, September 27, 1972. Gary Arnold.
Women's Wear Daily, July 27, 1972, 12. Howard Kissel. NYPL.

FREUD: THE SECRET PASSION. 1962. (Director, Narrator; Writer, uncredited.)

ARTICLES

The American Film Institute Catalog: Feature Films, 1961–1970. New York: R. R. Bowker, 1976, 376.
Archer, Eugene. "Code Amended to Allow Films to Deal with Homosexuality."

New York Times, October 4, 1961. (Reprinted in *The New York Times Encyclopedia of Film, 1958–1963.*)

Callenbach, Ernest. "Freud." *Film Quarterly* 16, no. 4 (Summer 1963): 50–51. (Reprinted in *Perspectives on John Huston,* edited by Stephen Cooper, 161–63, New York: G.K. Hall, 1994.)

Chankin, Donald O. "The Representation of Psychoanalysis in Film: John Huston's *Freud.*" *Persistence of Vision* 10 (1993): 134–43.

Cieutat, Michel. "*Freud, passion secrète:* La perfection de l'inaccompli." *Positif* 264 (February 1983): 83–84, creds, stills. (Reprinted in *John Huston, Collection dirigée,* edited by Gilles Ciment, 120–22, Dossier Positif Rivages, Paris, Editions Rivages, Collection Positif-Rivages, no. 2, 1988.)

———. "Le scenario *Freud* de Jean-Paul Sartre ou l'Oedipe-cinéma." *Positif* 283 (September 1984): 40–42, illus.

Crinkley, Richmond. "Metamorphoses: John and Jean-Paul." *Film Comment* 20 (November–December 1984): 78–79.

Edelman, Lee. "Plasticity, Paternity, Perversity: Freud's Falcon, Huston's *Freud.*" *American Image: Studies in Psychoanalysis* 34, no. 2 (Spring 1994): 69–104.

"Family of Freud Protests Film Opening in London." *New York Times,* August 28, 1963. NYPL.

"*Freud* e il cinema." *Cinema Nuovo* 33, no. 289 (June 1984): 19. On the collaboration between director John Huston and writer Jean-Paul Sartre on a film about Freud.

"Freud Film Not to Liking of Kin, Others in Vienna." *Variety,* November 1961. NYPL.

"Freud's Son Asks Film Carry Disclaimer." *Variety,* April 24, 1963. NYPL.

Hamblett, Charles. "Film Analysis of Sigmund Freud." *New York Times,* October 29, 1961. (Reprinted in *The New York Times Encyclopedia of Film, 1958–63.*) AMPAS.

Holland, Norman. "How to See Huston's *Freud.*" In *Perspectives on John Huston,* edited by Stephen Cooper, 164–81, New York, G.K. Hall, 1994.

Hollywood Reporter 168, no. 14 (December 19, 1961): 11.

Huston, John. "Focus on 'Freud' Huston Analyzes His Own Motivations in Making a Psychiatric Biography." *New York Times,* December 24, 1962. (Reprinted in *The New York Times Encyclopedia of Film, 1958–1963.*) AMPAS, NYPL.

Jameson, Richard T. "Freud." *Film Comment* [Midsection] 16, no. 3 (May–June 1980): 50–51.

Kass, Judith M. *The Films of Montgomery Clift.* New York: Citadel Press, 1979.

Koch, Gertrud. "Sartre's Screen Projection of Freud." *October,* no. 57 (Summer 1991): 3–17.

LaGuardia, Robert. *Monty: A Biography of Montgomery Clift.* New York: Arbor House, 1977.

Lippe, R. "Montgomery Clift: A Critical Disturbance." *Cineaction,* no. 17 (Summer 1989): 36–42, illus, port, stills.

McCarthy, Todd. "The Films of John Huston" [Program notes]. Los Angeles County Museum of Art, November 8, 1980, creds.

Magill's Cinema Annual, 1984, 535–41. Gaylyn Studlar.

Meer, J. "Freud: The Movie." *Psychology Today* 21 (June 1987): 67–68.

Motion Picture Guide 3 (1986): 939.

Niney, F. "Le scénario Freud." *Cahiers du Cinéma* 440 (February 1991): 52–53, illus, stills. Notes on *Freud: The Secret Passion* and *Geheimnisse einer Seele* (1926), films dealing with psychoanalysis.

Ronning, Helge. "John Huston, Jean-Paul Sartre, Marilyn Monroe og Freud." *Samiden* 93, no. 5 (1984): 57+.

Schumach, Murray. "Film Code Change Vexes Producers." *New York Times,* October 23, 1961. (Reprinted in *The New York Times Encyclopedia of Film, 1958–1963.*)

Shortland, Michael. "Screen Memories: Toward a History of Psychiatry and Psychoanalysis in the Movies." *British Journal for the History of* Science 20, no. 67 (October 1987): 421–52, part 4.

Simon, John. *Private Screenings.* New York: Macmillan, 1967, 55–57.

Walker, Janet, and Diane Waldman. "John Huston's *Freud* and Textual Repression: A Psychoanalytic Feminist Reading." In *Close Viewing: An Anthology of New Film Criticism,* edited by Peter Lehman, 282–99. Tallahassee, Fla.: Florida State University Press, 1990.

REVIEWS

America 108 (January 26, 1963): 153.

BFI/Monthly Film Bulletin 30, no. 357 (October 1963): 140–41.

Catholic World 196 (February 1963): 327–28.

Cinématographe 86 (February 1983): 63–64, creds. D. Goldschmidt.

Cinématographie Française 2,024 (July 13, 1963): 15.

Commonweal 77 (January 4, 1963): 389.

Cue, December 22, 1962, 18. NYPL.

Daily Cinema 8,805 (August 28, 1963): 97.

Ekran 5, nos. 9 & 10 (1980): 40–41, creds, stills. B Lesnik.

Esquire, June 1963. MOMA, NYPL.

Figaro, June 8, 1954. Clovis Chauvat. NYPL.

Film-Blaetter 28 (July 6, 1963): 549.

Film Comment 16 (May–June 1980): 50–51.

Film Daily 121, no. 113 (December 13 1962): 11. Mandel Herbstman. AMPAS, MOMA.

Film-Echo/Filmwoche 54 (July 6, 1963): 11.

Filmfacts 5 (January 4, 1962): 315–17, creds.

Film Quarterly 16 (Summer 1963): 50–51.

Films and Filming 10, no. 1 (October 1963): 22–23, creds, illus. Richard Whitehall. AMPAS.

Films in Review 14, no. 1 (January 1963): 44–46, illus. Ellen Fitzpatrick. NYPL.

High Fidelity & Musical America 28 (August 1978): 94. R. S. Brown.

Hollywood Reporter 173, no. 15 (December 13, 1962): 3. MOMA.

Illustrated London News 243 (September 14, 1963): 396, illus.

Jeune Cinéma 1 (September–October 1964): 13.

Kinematograph Weekly 2,917 (August 29, 1963): 12.

Life 54 (January 4, 1963): 51A–51B. AMPAS, NYPL.
Listener 115, no. 2,959 (May 8, 1986): 30. Richard Combs.
Los Angeles Times, December 13, 1962. AMPAS.
Los Angeles Times, January 22, 1963. AMPAS.
Motion Picture Herald Product Digest 228, no. 13 (December 26, 1962): 71.
The Nation 196 (January 19, 1963): 59.
New Republic 148 (January 5, 1963): 19–20. AMPAS.
New Statesman 66 (September 6, 1963): 297.
Newsweek 60 (December 24, 1962): 63.
New Yorker 38 (December 22, 1962): 77–78.
New York Herald Tribune, December 9, 1962. NYPL.
New York Times, December 13, 1962, 37. Bosley Crowther. AMPAS, NYPL NYTR.
Observer, September 1, 1963. P. Gilliatt. NYPL.
Reporter 28 (January 31, 1963): 50. NYPL.
La Revue du Cinéma 467 (January 1991): 44, creds, stills. Yves Alion.
Saturday Review 46 (January 5, 1963): 30. Arthur Knight. AMPAS.
Show, February 1963. NYPL.
Sight & Sound 32 (Autumn 1963): 196–97. Elizabeth Sussex.
The Society of Film & Television, no. 14 (Winter 1963–64). Roger Manvell and Geoffrey Bell.
Time 80 (December 28, 1962): 60. AMPAS, MOMA.
Variety, December 19 1962, 6. Tube. AMPAS, MOMA, NYPL, VR.
Villager, December 20, 1962. Walter J. Carroll. NYPL.
Village Voice 8, no. 9 (December 20, 1962): 17. Jonas Mekas. NYPL.
Washington Post, February 28, 1963, C26+. Richard Coe. NYPL.

GEORGE STEVENS: A FILMMAKER'S JOURNEY. 1984. (Interviewed.)

ARTICLES AND REVIEWS
Box Office 121 (June 1985): R73, creds. M. Moss.
Chicago Sun Times, June 5, 1985. Roger Ebert.
Chicago Tribune, June 5, 1985. Gene Siskel.
Christian Century 102 (July 17–24, 1985): 684–85. J. M. Wall.
Christian Science Monitor, May 2, 1985, 35. David Sterritt.
Commonweal 112 (May 31, 1985): 343–34. T. O'Brien. AMPAS.
EPD Film 3, no. 6 (June 1986): 37. H. Gassen.
Film Comment 21 (July–August 1985): 66–69, illus, interv, stills. R. Haver, "George II on George I" (George Stevens Jr. discusses production of the film).
Film Journal 88 (July 1985): 18, creds. K. Lally.
Films in Review 36, nos. 8 & 9 (August–September 1985): 420–21. L. Taubman.
Hollywood Reporter, April 12, 1985. AMPAS.
International Herald Tribune, September 12, 1984. Thomas Quinn Curtiss. MOMA.
Listener 107, no. 2,998 (February 12, 1987): 31. Richard Combs.

Los Angeles Herald Examiner, April 13, 1985, B1+. David Chute. AMPAS.
Los Angeles Times, April 11, 1985, 1+. Sheila Benson. AMPAS.
Los Angeles Weekly, April 19, 1985. F. X. Feeney.
Films in Review 36 (August–September 1985). L. Taubman.
New York Times, May 3, 1985, C8, creds, stills. Vincent Canby. AMPAS, MOMA, NYTR.
New York Times, May 6, 1985, C13, interv, port, stills. E. B. Fein, "'George Stevens': A Son's Tribute."
New York Times, August 18, 1988, C22. Eleanor Blau.
Philadelphia Inquirer, July 31, 1985. Desmond Ryan. MOMA.
Philadelphia Inquirer, August 4, 1985, 2J. Desmond Ryan, "Son Honors His Father, the Director."
"Stevens Jr. to Donate Color War Footage to French National Archives." *Variety* 320 (September 4, 1985): 1+.
Time 125 (May 6, 1985): 86. R. Corliss. AMPAS.
Variety 316, no. 8 (September 19, 1984): 20+, creds. Len. MOMA. VR.
Village Voice 30 (April 30, 1985): 53. Andrew Sarris. AMPAS.
Wall Street Journal, August 9, 1985, 30 (West Coast ed.), 26 (East Coast ed.). Julie Salman.
Wall Street Journal, August 22, 1988, 11. Martha Bayles.
Washington Post, May 17, 1985, B1. Paul Attansio.
Washington Post, May 17, 1985, Weekend. Rita Kempley.
Women's Wear Daily, May 1, 1985. Mort Sheinman. AMPAS.

THE GREATEST BATTLE. 1977, 1979. (Actor.)

ARTICLES AND REVIEWS
Cinema 235 (July 1978): 122.
Films and Filming 337 (October 1982): 36–37.
La Revue du Cinéma 332 (October 1978): 129–30, creds. P. Mérigeau.
Variety 290 (February 8, 1979): 36, interv. H. Werba, "Ital Prod Martino Long in "B" Arena Shifts to Bigger Pix in Line with Changing Times."

THE HARD WAY. 1942. (Script doctor.)

ARTICLES AND REVIEWS
Commonweal 37 (February 26, 1943): 471.
Film Daily, September 21, 1942, 6.
Harrison's Reports, September 19, 1942, 152.
Hollywood Reporter, September 21, 1942, 3.
Magill's Cinema Annual, 1985, 555–60.
Motion Picture Guide 4 (1986): 1,160.
Motion Picture Herald Product Digest, September 19, 1942, 923.
The Nation, February 20, 1943, 283.
New Republic 108 (March 29, 1943): 414.
New York Times, March 13, 1943, 9. NYTR.

Thomas, Tony. *The Films of the Forties.* Secaucus, N.J.: Citadel Press, 1975, 82–84.
Time, March 1, 1943, 46+.
Variety, September 23, 1942. VR.

HARROW ALLEY. 1962–63, 1967. (Director, unrealized project.)

ARTICLE
Wilson, John M. "One of Hollywood's Most Celebrated 'Lost Scripts.'" *New York Times,* January 8, 1978. (Reprinted in *The New York Times Encyclopedia of Film, 1977–1979.*)

HAUNTED SUMMER. 1988. (Director, withdrew.)

ARTICLES AND REVIEWS
BFI/Monthly Film Bulletin 56, no. 664 (May 1989): 136–37, creds, stills. Tom Milne.
Cahiers du Cinéma 412 (October 1988): 25. S. Toubiana.
"Cannon Signs John Huston to Direct Film." *Variety,* May 7, 1986.
City Limits 392 (April 6, 1989): 18.
Film Bulletin 46, no. 3 (March 1977): 24.
Film Journal 92 (February–March 1989): 62–63, creds. D. Noh.
"*Haunted Summer:* Huston Was to Direct." *Variety,* May 2, 1986.
Hollywood Reporter 295, no. 36 (January 27, 1987): 20, creds.
Hollywood Reporter 297, no. 19 (May 26, 1987): 27, creds.
Hollywood Reporter, December 13, 1988, 4+. Kirk Honeycutt.
"Huston Declared Not Well Enough to Direct, by His Doctors." *Screen International,* July 19, 1986, 2.
"Ivan Passer Takes over Directorial Reins on Cannon's *Haunted Summer* (from the Recouping John Huston)." *Variety,* July 16, 1986.
"John Huston Will Direct, to Start in August." *Los Angeles Times,* May 24, 1966.
Kinematograph Weekly 3,328 (July 24, 1971): 13. Was to have been made at Chillon castle in Switzerland.
Los Angeles Herald Examiner, December 18, 1988, 9. David Ehrenstein.
Los Angeles Times, December 16, 1988, part 4, 21. Michael Wilmington.
New York Times, July 5, 1989, C14, creds. Caryn James. MOMA, NYTR.
Noble, Peter. "Ivan Passer to Direct." *Screen International,* August 23, 1986, 6.
Reader, December 16, 1988. Henry Sheehan.
Screen International, May 17, 1986, 8.
Screen International, May 31, 1986.
Screen International, October 25, 1986, 38, creds.
Screen International, June 13, 1987, 16, creds.
Screen International, September 19, 1987, 31.
Screen International, April 8, 1989, 18–19.
Soundtrack 8, no. 32 (December 1989): 16. Randall D. Larson reviews film score.
Time Out 972 (April 5, 1989): 34, illus.

Variety, September 8, 1988, 3. Venice Film Festival review, Strat.
Variety, September 14, 1988, 23+, creds. D. Stratton. VR.

HEAD ON. 1979. (Actor.)

ARTICLES AND REVIEWS
Cinema Canada 69 (October–November 1980), creds, stills. G. Flahive.
Cinema Canada 89 (June 1982): 18–19. M. Bradden.
Cinemag 25 (October 29, 1979): 14, creds.
Continental Film & Video Review 30, no. 10 (August–September 1983): 31.
Hollywood Reporter 288, no. 34 (September 12, 1985): 2.
"Low Budget Big as Grant & Simmonds Meet *Head On.*" *Cinemag* 26 (November 12, 1979): 6.
Motion Picture Guide 4 (1986): 1,177.
Screen International 202 (August 11, 1979): 17.
Screen International 210 (October 6, 1979): 6.
Variety 300, no. 9 (October 1, 1980): 22+. Klad (L. Klady). VR.
Video Viewer 3, no. 3 (September 1983).

THE HEART IS A LONELY HUNTER. 1968. (Director [?]. Unrealized project.)

ARTICLES AND REVIEWS
Aldridge, Robert. "*The Heart Is a Lonely Hunter:* Two Planetary Systems." In *The Modern American Novel and the Movies,* edited by Gerald Peary and Roger Shatzkin, 119–30. New York: Frederick Ungar, 1978.
Atlantic 222 (October 1968): 147–49.
BFI/Monthly Film Bulletin 36 (July 1969): 140–41.
Christian Science Monitor (Western Edition), August 23, 1968, 4.
Cinema (Bucharest) 10, no. 5 (May 1972): 17. E. Havas.
Commonweal 88 (September 6, 1968): 598.
Esquire 70 (November 1968): 24.
Film Daily, July 30, 1968, 4.
Filmfacts 11 (August 15, 1968): 207–9.
Films and Filming 15 (August 1969): 38+.
Films in Review 19 (October 1968): 519.
Hollywood Reporter, July 30, 1968, 3.
Life 65 (August 30, 1968): 8.
Listener 81 (June 19, 1969): 873.
Look 32 (April 2, 1968): M14–M16.
Mademoiselle 67 (October 1968): 72.
Magill's Survey of Cinema 3, no. 2 (1981): 1,002–4.
Motion Picture Herald Product Digest, July 31, 1968, 835.
New Republic 159 (September 14, 1968): 41.
Newsweek 72 (August 12, 1968): 80.
New Yorker 44 (August 3, 1968): 72–74.

New York Times, August 1, 1968, 24. NYTR.
New York Times, December 10, 1967, 19.
Sarris, Andrew. "The Heart Is a Lonely Hunter (My Foolish Heart)." *Film Comment* 27, no. 1 (January–February 1991): 42–46.
Saturday Review 51 (August 10, 1968): 43.
Senior Scholastic 93 (October 11, 1968): 24.
Sight & Sound 38 (Summer 1969): 156–57.
The Spectator 222 (June 14, 1969): 794.
Time 92 (August 9, 1968): 82.
Variety, July 31, 1968, 6. VR.
Vogue 152 (September 1, 1968): 276.

HEAVEN KNOWS, MR. ALLISON. 1957. (Director, Writer.)

ARTICLES AND REVIEWS
America 96 (March 23, 1957): 716.
BFI/Monthly Film Bulletin 24, no. 280 (May 1957): 55.
Catholic World 185 (May 1957): 145.
Commonweal 65 (March 29, 1957): 661.
Daily Film Renter 7,359 (April 11, 1957): 3.
Deschner Donald, ed. "The Films of John Huston" [Program notes]. Los Angeles County Museum of Art, November 1, 1980, creds. Includes Huston's comments in his autobiography, *An Open Book.*
Film Daily 111, no. 51 (March 15, 1957): 4.
Films and Filming 3 (June 1957): 23, creds. John Cutts.
Films in Review 8, no. 4 (April 1957): 176–77. Anne F. Murphy.
French, Brandon. *On the Verge of Revolt.* New York: Ungar, 1978, 121–36.
Good Housekeeping 144 (April 1957): 17.
Harrison's Reports, March 16, 1957, 44.
Hollywood Reporter 144, no. 1 (March 15, 1957): 3.
Kiley, Bridget. "The Films of Robert Mitchum" [Program notes]. Los Angeles County Museum of Art, March 26, 1983, creds.
Kinematograph Weekly 2,591 (April 11, 1957): 17.
Kyrou, A. "Le sabre et le goupillon." *Positif,* nos. 25 & 26:79–81. (Reprinted in *John Huston, Collection dirigée,* edited by Gilles Ciment, 107–9, Dossier Positif Rivages, Paris, Editions Rivages, Collection Positif-Rivages, no. 2, 1988.)
Life 42 (March 25, 1957): 99–100. NYPL.
Listener 119, no. 3,049 (February 11, 1988): 28.
Magill's Survey of Cinema: Second Series 3 (1981): 1,008–11. Elizabeth McDermott.
Marill, Alvin H. *Robert Mitchum on the Screen.* South Brunswick, N.J.: A. S. Barnes, 1978, 159–60.
Motion Picture Guide 4 (1986): 1,185.
Motion Picture Herald Product Digest 206, no. 11 (March 16, 1957): 297.
**Newsweek* 49 (March 25, 1957): 110. NYPL.
New York Daily News, March 18, 1957, 51. Kate Cameron. NYPL.

New Yorker 33 (March 23, 1957): 103. NYPL.

New York Herald Tribune, March 15, 1957. William Zinsser. NYPL.

New York Times, November 8, 1956, sect. 2, 8.

New York Times, March 15, 1957, 22. Bosley Crowther. NYTR.

New York Times, March 24, 1957, sect. 2, 1. NYPL.

Observer, June 9, 1957, 11. L. A. Lejeune. NYPL.

Positif 3, nos. 25 & 26 (Rentrée 1975): 79.

Robertson, Nan. "On the Tumult in Tobago for 'Mr. Allison.'" *New York Times,* November 18, 1956. (Reprinted in *The New York Times Encyclopedia of Film, 1952–1957.*) NYPL.

St. Pierre, Brian. "John Huston: As He Was, Is, and Probably Always Be." *New York Times,* September 25, 1966. (Reprinted in *The New York Times Encyclopedia of Film, 164 –1968.*)

Sarris, Andrew. "Revival in Focus. A Critical Guide." *Village Voice,* September 29, 1987, 96. NYPL.

Saturday Review 40 (April 6, 1957): 27.

Senior Scholastic 70 (April 12, 1957): 35.

Time 69 (March 25, 1957): 106. MOMA.

Variety, March 20, 1957, 6. VR.

HELL'S HEROES. 1930. (Actor, uncredited.)

ARTICLES AND REVIEWS

The American Film Institute Catalog: Feature Films, 1921–1930. New York: R. R. Bowker, 1971, 338.

Bioscope 82, no. 1,215 (January 15, 1930): 34.

Film Spectator 9, no. 3 (January 18, 1930): 10–11.

Harrison's Reports, January 4, 1930, 3.

Motion Picture Guide 4 (1986): 1,199.

New York Times, December 28, 1929, 11. NYTR.

Variety, January 1, 1930. VR.

HERE'S LOOKING AT YOU, WARNER BROTHERS. TV. 1992. (Interviewed.)

REVIEWS

New York Post, March 26, 1993, 80. David Bianculli.

New York Times 142 (March 26, 1993): C28. Walter Goodman.

HERMAN MELVILLE: DAMNED IN PARADISE. TV. 1985. (Narrator.)

ARTICLES AND REVIEWS

Herman Melville: Damned in Paradise, A Companion Guide. Washington, D.C.: The Film Company, 1985.

New York Times, May 12, 1985, H2, 31, illus. port. Herbert Mitang.

New York Times, May 15, 1985, C22. Richard F. Shepard. MOMA.

Wall Street Journal, May 15, 1985, 32 (West Coast ed.), 28 (East Coast ed.). Jane Mayer.

Washington Post, May 15, 1985, B1. Lois Romano.

HIGH ROAD TO CHINA. 1983. (Director, unrealized.)

ARTICLES AND REVIEWS

BFI/Monthly Film Bulletin 51, no. 602 (March 1984): 79–80, creds, illus. Tony Rayns.

Box Office 119 (May 1983): 82–83, creds, stills. Jimmy Summers. AMPAS.

Cinéma (Paris) 294 (June 1983): 49, illus. P. Borker.

Cine Revue 63 (April 21, 1983): 20–23, stills. J. MacTrevor and F. Dhont.

Cine Revue 63 (May 12, 1983): 68, creds, stills.

City Limits 131 (April 6, 1984): 26.

Filmfaust 34–35 (June–September 1983): 36–37, creds, illus.

Film Journal 86 (March 25, 1983): 11–12, creds, stills. M. Kearns.

Films and Filming 355 (April 1984): 38, creds, illus.

Hollywood Reporter, March 1, 1983, 5–6. Robert Osborne.

Levende Billeder 9 (October 15, 1983): 62–63, creds, stills. P. B. Christensen.

Los Angeles Times, March 19, 1983, sect. 5, 1. Sheila Benson.

Motion Picture Guide 4 (1986): 1,227.

Motion Picture Product Digest 10–20 (March 30, 1983): 77–78. Richard Gertner.

New York Times, March 18, 1983, C4, creds. Vincent Canby. NYTR.

Positif 269–270 (July–August 1983): 117. A. Garsault.

Prevue 50 (December–January 1983): 18–21.

Prevue 51 (March–April 1983): 43–49 Larry Schott.

La Revue du Cinéma 30–31, no. 28 (1963), creds. P. Ross.

Screen International 188 (May 5, 1979): 35, creds.

Screen International 336 (March 27, 1982): 124.

Screen International 434 (February 25, 1984): 16. Marjorie Bilbow.

Sinema 50 (June 1983): 18–19, stills. M. Holthof.

Sinema 50 (June 1983): 37–38, stills. E. Kloeck.

Soundtrack 3, no. 9 (March 1984): 28–29. T. Macy. On John Barry's score for the film.

Starburst 51 (November 1982): 8.

Variety, March 1, 1983 (D).

Variety, March 9, 1983, 18 (W), creds. Har. MOMA, VR.

Village Voice 28 (March 29, 1983): 45. Andrew Sarris. AMPAS.

Washington Post, March 18, 1983, D3. Gary Arnold.

HIGH SIERRA. 1941. (Writer.)

ARTICLES AND REVIEWS

American Film 9, no. 4 (January–February 1984): 19. NYPL.

The American Film Institute Archives. *The American Film Heritage.* Washington, D.C.: Acropolis Books, 1972.

Archer, Eugene. "Bogart: Man and Superman." *New York Times,* January 3, 1965. (Reprinted in *The New York Times Encyclopedia of Film, 1964–1968.*)

Armchair Detective 17, no. 1 (1984): 69–72, stills. T. Godfrey, "The Armchair Detective at the Movies."

Canham, Kingsley. *Michael Curtiz, Raoul Walsh, Henry Hathaway.* Vol. 1, *The Hollywood Professionals.* London: Tantivy Press; New York: A. S. Barnes, 1973.

Cargin, P. "Adventures of Robin Hood, High Sierra, Green Pastures." *Film* 82 (February 1980): 8.

Casablanca, February 2, 1981, 40.

Celluloide 26, nos. 324 & 325 (September. 1981): 16. E. Nunes, "O ultimo refugio."

Commonweal 33 (January 21, 1941): 376.

Conley, Tom. "High Sierra." In *International Dictionary of Films and Filmmakers.* Vol. 1, *Films,* 2d ed., edited by Nicholas Thomas, 387–88. Chicago: St. James Press, 1990. (Updated in 3d ed., edited by Nicolet V. Elert and Aruna Vasudeven, 440–42, Detroit, St. James Press, 1997.)

Druxman, Michael B. *Make It Again, Sam: A Survey of Movie Remakes.* South Brunswick, N.J.: A. S. Barnes, 1975, 69–74.

Ecran 7 (July 1972): 9, illus.

Enclitic 5–6, nos. 1 & 2 (1981–82): 66–74. M. B. Haralovich and C. R. Klaprat, "'Marked Woman' and 'Jezebel': The Spectator in the Trailer."

Filmihullu, nos. 3 & 4 (1986): 19, stills. O. Peltonen, "'High Sierra' asfolttividakko."

Film Comment 19 (January–February 1983): 58–68+, bio, illus, interv, port, stills. K. Mate, P. McGilligan, and P. Burnett.

Film Culture 34 (Fall 1964): 35–37. Harris Dienstfrey.

Film Daily, January 20, 1941, 5.

Gardner, Paul. "A Vanishing Breed of Film Director." *New York Times,* November 5, 1973. (Reprinted in *The New York Times Encyclopedia of Film, 1972–1974.*)

Gomery, Douglas. "Introduction: Reworking the Classic Gangster Film." In *High Sierra,* edited by Douglas Gomery, 9–26. Wisconsin/Warner Bros. Screenplay Series. Madison, Wis.: University of Wisconsin Press, for the Wisconsin Center for Film and Theater Research, 1979.

Harrison's Reports, January 25, 1941, 14.

Hermann, R. "He's from Back Home." *Movietone News* 45 (November 1975): 34–37.

Higham, Charles. "He Directed 'Em All—from Doug Fairbanks to Bogey." *New York Times,* April 14, 1974. (Reprinted in *The New York Times Encyclopedia of Film, 1972–1974.*)

Hill, Gladwin. "John Huston—A Bull in the China Shop." *New York Times,* January 16, 1949. (Reprinted in *The New York Times Encyclopedia of Film, 1947–1951.*)

Hogue, P. "Big Shots." *Movietone News* 45 (November 1975): 14–21, creds, stills.

Hollywood Reporter, January 22, 1941.

Journal of Popular Film 5, nos. 3–4 (1976): 248–62, stills. K. D. Alley, *"High Sierra*—Swan Song for an Era."

Kauffmann, Stanley. *American Film Criticism: From the Beginnings to Citizen Kane.* New York: Liveright, 1972, 100–3.

Krutnik, Frank. *In a Lonely Street: Film Noir, Genre, Masculinity.* London: Routledge, 1991.

Laemmle, Ann. *CinemaTexas Program Notes* 16, no. 2 (April 5, 1979): 97–102, biblio, creds, discussion.

London Times, August 4, 1941, 80.

McCarty, Clifford. *The Complete Films of Humphrey Bogart.* Secaucus, N.J.: Citadel Press, 1965, 89–91. (Reprint—New York: Carol Publishing Group, 1995.)

Magill's Survey of Cinema: First Series 2 (1980): 748–50. Michael Shepler.

Michael, Paul. *Humphrey Bogart: The Man and His Films.* Indianapolis: Bobbs-Merrill, 1965, 108–9.

Motion Picture Exhibitor, January 22, 1941, 677+.

Motion Picture Guide 4 (1986): 1,228.

Motion Picture Herald 142, no. 4 (January 25, 1941).

New Republic 104 (February 1941): 180. Otis Ferguson. (Reprinted in *The Film Criticism of Otis Ferguson,* edited by Robert Wilson, Philadelphia, Temple University Press, 1971.)

New York Times, January 25, 1941, 11. NYTR.

Picturegoer 11, no. 540 (November 1, 1941): 14.

Poulos, Phil Johnston. "Benighted Eyes: W. R. Burnett and Film Noir." Ph.D. diss., University of Tulsa, Oklahoma, 1983. (*Dissertation Abstracts International,* 44 [1983]: 1,451–52A.)

Shadoian, Jack. *Dreams and Dead Ends: The American Gangster/Crime Film.* Cambridge, Mass.: MIT Press, 1977. Discusses *High Sierra* and *The Killers.*

Schraeder, Paul. "Notes on Film Noir." *Film Comment* 8 (Spring 1972): 8–13.

Silver, Alain, and Elizabeth Ward, eds. *Film Noir, an Encyclopedic Reference to the American Style.* 3d ed., rev. Woodstock, N.Y.: The Overlook Press, 1992, 125–26, full analysis, creds, illus, synopsis.

Simon, John L. "Henry on Bogie: Reality and Romance in 'Dream Song no. 9' and *High Sierra."* *Literature/Film Quarterly* 5, no. 3 (Summer 1977): 269–72.

Sperber, A. M., and Eric Lax. *Bogart.* New York: Morrow, 1997.

Thompson, David. *Suspects.* New York: Knopf, 1985.

Time, February 17, 1941, 16.

Today's Cinema 56, no. 4,574 (May 28, 1941).

Variety, January 22, 1941, 16. Sho. VR.

Walsh, Raoul. *Each Man in His Time: The Life Story of a Director.* New York: Farrar, 1974.

"Warner Library Brings $21,000,000." *New York Times,* March 2, 1956. (Reprinted in *The New York Times Encyclopedia of Film, 1952–1957.*)

Warshow, Robert. "The Gangster as Tragic Hero." In *The Immediate Experience,* 127–33. Garden City, N.Y.: Doubleday, 1964.

THE HOBBIT. 1977. (Voice.)

ARTICLES AND REVIEWS

Cinefantastique 5, no. 3 (Winter 1977): 37.

Cinefantastique 7, no. 2 (Summer 1978): 28+, creds, stills. D. Hutchinson.

Funnyworld, no. 18 (Summer, 1978): 53. Mike Barrier.

Hardy, Gene. *"The Hobbit:* More than a Magic Ring." In *Children's Novels and the Movies,* edited by Douglas Street, 131–40. New York: Frederick Ungar, 1983.

Hollywood Reporter 246, no. 2 (April 7, 1977): 12, creds.

Hollywood Reporter 249, no. 14 (November 29, 1977): 4.

Library Journal 116, no. 13 (August 1991): 160.

Variety 289 (November 30, 1977): 36, creds. Mick (L. Michie). VR.

HOLLYWOOD ON TRIAL. 1976. (Narrator.)

ARTICLES AND REVIEWS

BFI/Monthly Film Bulletin 46, no. 544 (May 1979): 97. Richard Combs.

Boston Phoenix, October 5, 1976, 4+. David Denby, "Backlisting on Trial."

Bosworth, Patricia. "Daughter of a Blacklist that Killed a Father." *New York Times,* September 27, 1992, H1.

Cinema Papers 13 (July 1977): 80–81, creds, stills. K. Connolly.

Cocks, J. "Hat in the Morning." *Time* 109 (January 17, 1977): 40.

Commentary 63 (January 1977): 72–75. W. S. Pechter, "American Activities."

"Comments on 'The Blacklist': Letters on the Kramer article." *New York Times,* October 17, 1976. (Reprinted in *The New York Times Encyclopedia of Film, 1975–1976.*)

Film en Televisie+Video 238 (March 1977): 26–27, creds, interv, port. R. Pede.

Filmmakers' Newsletter 10, no. 5 (March 1977): 23–27. L. Sturhahn. NYPL.

Film Quarterly 30, no. 4 (Summer 1977): 32–34, stills. E. Callenbach.

Hollywood Reporter 243, no. 33 (October 19, 1976): 3.

Kramer, Hilton. "The Blacklist and the Cold War." *New York Times,* October 3, 1976.

Screen International 160 (October 14, 1978): 25.

Take One 5, no. 3 (August 1976): 14–15.

Variety, June 9, 1976, 22+. Holl. VR.

Village Voice 22 (December 5, 1977): 50, stills. Tom Allen, "Ten Who Dared."

A HOUSE DIVIDED. 1931. (Writer.)

ARTICLES AND REVIEWS

The American Film Institute Catalog: Feature Films, 1931–1940. Berkeley: University of California Press, 1993, 965.

Anderegg, Michael A. *William Wyler.* Boston: Twayne, 1979, 31–34.

Bioscope 90, no. 1,319 (January 13, 1932): 84.

Film Daily, January 10, 1932, 9.

Harrison's Reports, January 16, 1932, 10.

Hollywood Reporter, November 13, 1931, 3.

Hollywood Spectator 12, no. 11 (February 1932): 6.

Judge 102 (February 6, 1932): 22.
Kern, Sharon. *William Wyler: A Guide to References and Resources.* Boston: G.K. Hall, 1979, 68–70.
Motion Picture Guide 4 (1986): 1,290.
Motion Picture Herald, November 28, 1931, 44.
New Yorker 7 (January 16, 1932): 53.
New York Times, January 9, 1932, 21. NYTR.
New York Times, January 17, 1932, 4.
Picturegoer 2, no. 55 (June 11, 1930): 20.
Rob Wagner's Script 6, no. 7 (November 21, 1931): 31.
Variety, January 12, 1932, 28. VR.
"Who's Who This Week in Pictures." *New York Times,* October 16, 1932. (Reprinted in *The New York Times Encyclopedia of Film, 1929–1936.*)

THE HUNCHBACK OF NOTRE DAME. 1939. (Writer, uncredited.)

ARTICLES AND REVIEWS

The American Film Institute Catalog: Feature Films, 1931–1940. Berkeley: University of California Press, 1993, 976.
Commonweal 31 (January 12, 1940): 266.
Druxman, Michael B. *Make It Again, Sam: A Survey of Movie Remakes.* South Brunswick, N.J.: A. S. Barnes, 1975, 81–87.
Film Daily, December 15, 1939, 4.
Harrison's Reports, December 23, 1939, 202.
Hollywood Reporter, December 15, 1939, 3.
****Hollywood Spectator* 14, no. 18 (December 23, 1939): 15. Welford Beaton.
Life 8 (January 1, 1940): 37–39.
Magill's Survey of Cinema: First Series 2 (1980): 786–92. Robert E. Morsberger.
Motion Picture Guide 4 (1986): 1,313.
Motion Picture Herald, December 23, 1939, 37+.
New Republic 102 (January 22, 1940): 116.
Newsweek 15 (January 8, 1940): 37.
New Yorker 15 (December 30, 1939): 47.
New York Times, January 1, 1940, 29. NYTR.
Photoplay 53 (January 8, 1940): 66–67.
La Revue du Cinéma, no. 452 (September 1989): 47.
****Rob Wagner's Script* 22, no. 535 (December 23, 1939): 17.
Spectator 164 (February 16, 1940): 213.
Studio 119 (May 1940): 179.
Taylor, John Russell. *Graham Greene on Film: Collected Film Criticism, 1935–1940.* New York: Simon & Schuster, 1972, 271.
Theatre Arts 23 (November 1939): 804.
Time 35 (January 8, 1940): 37.
Variety, December 20, 1939, 14. VR.
Wilson, Robert, ed. *The Film Criticism of Otis Ferguson.* Philadelphia: Temple University Press, 1971, 282.

INDEPENDENCE. 1976. (Director.)

ARTICLES AND REVIEWS

Box Office 107 (September 29, 1975): 54. "*Independence* Bows October 4 in Philly; *Independence* Costs Are Higher than Anticipated."

Cinematographer 57, no. 7 (July 1976): 48–49+, illus.

Coffin, Howard A. "Philadelphia Streets Make History: The Making of *Independence.*" *Philadelphia Inquirer,* June 1, 1975, sect. K.

Films in Review 28, no. 1 (January 1977): 21–22.

Naedere, Walt. "Bicentennial Film Clears One Legal Hurdle." *Philadelphia Evening Bulletin,* August 8, 1975, 49. MOMA.

Newsweek 87 (April 26, 1976): 103. K. Ames. NYPL.

Philadelphia Daily News, June 30, 1975. MOMA.

Philadelphia Daily News, October 7, 1975.

Philadelphia Inquirer, June 30, 1975. MOMA.

Philadelphia Inquirer, July 6, 1975.

Philadelphia Inquirer, October 3, 1975, Weekend, sect. C.

Philadelphia Magazine 67 (January 1976): 48+.

Positif 341–342 (July–August 1989): 74–76, illus. P. Pernod.

Riger, Robert. "Details from the Master's Painting." *Action* (Director's Guild of America) 10, no. 5 (September–October 1975): 6–14. AMPAS, MOMA, NYPL.

Roizman, O. "Photographing *Independence* Where It Happened." *American Cinematographer* 57, no. 7 (July 1976): 748+.

Ryan, Desmond. "Bicentennial Film: A Few Liberties Were Taken." *Philadelphia Inquirer,* October 6, 1975, 5-B. NYPL.

Variety, July 9, 1975. MOMA, NYPL.

Variety, October 15, 1975, 2+. "Huston Bicentennial Film Gets the Ballyhoos but Actors No-show." NYPL.

Variety, April 7, 1976, 26+, creds. [G] Prat[ley]. VR.

IN THIS OUR LIFE. 1942. (Director, Writer, uncredited.)

ARTICLES

Asheim, Lester. "From Book to Film: Simplification." *Hollywood Quarterly* 5, no. 3 (Spring 1951): 291–22.

Bathrick, Serafina. *The Female Colossus.* Los Angeles: Routledge, 1990.

———. "*In This Our Life:* Independent Women, Doomed Sister." In *The Modern American Novel and the Movies,* edited by Gerald Peary and Roger Shatzkin, 143–55. New York: Ungar, 1978.

Brady, Thomas F. "Hollywood Notes: Films-Television Issue Growing Hotter—Two of a Kind—Bette Davis Mellows." *New York Times,* May 23, 1948. (Reprinted in *The New York Times Encyclopedia of Film, 1947–1951.*)

Brown, C. F. "Movies Then: American Gothic." *Bijou* 1 (Spring 1977): 63+, stills.

Campbell, Edward D. C., Jr. *The Celluloide South: Hollywood and the Southern Myth.* Knoxville, Tenn.: University of Tennessee Press, 1981.

Crowther, Bosley. "Cleaving the Color Line." *New York Times,* June 6, 1943. (Reprinted in *The New York Times Encyclopedia of Film, 1941–1946.*)

"The Films of Bette Davis: *In This Our Life*" [Program notes]. Los Angeles County Museum of Art, June 7, 1980.

"A Man of Unsartorial Splendor: John Huston Makes a Name in Films—but Not for Dress." *New York Times,* January 25, 1942. (Reprinted in *The New York Times Encyclopedia of Film, 1941–1946.*)

Motion Picture Guide 4 (1986): 1,377.

Nacache, Jacqueline. "John Huston: La vitalité et le mystère." *Cinéma* (Paris) 426 (January 27, 1988): 7, illus.

Noble, Peter. *The Negro in Film.* London: Skelton & Robinson, 1949.

"An Ounce of Prevention." *New York Times,* June 7, 1942. (Reprinted in *The New York Times Encyclopedia of Film, 1941–1946.*)

Patterson, Lindsay, ed. *Black Films & Filmmakers: A Comprehensive Anthology from Stereotype to Superhero.* New York: Dodd, Mead, 1975.

Ringgold, Gene. *Bette Davis: Her Films and Career.* Secaucus, N.J.: Citadel Press, 1985, 115–16.

Variety, August 19, 1942. MOMA.

Watters, Jim. "John Huston on Kipling, Hemingway and Jack Daniels." *New York Times,* February 15, 1976. (Reprinted in *The New York Times Encyclopedia of Film, 1975–1976.*)

REVIEWS

Bijou 1 (April 1977): 63+.

Commonweal 36 (May 22, 1942): 112–13.

Film Daily, April 7, 1942, 4.

Harrison's Reports, April 11, 1942, 59.

Hollywood Reporter, April 7, 1942, 3. AMPAS.

Kinematograph Weekly 1,845 (August 27, 1942).

London Times, September 18, 1942, 6.

Motion Picture Exhibitor, April 22, 1942, 494.

Motion Picture Herald Product Digest 147, no. 2 (April 11, 1942): 597.

Musician 47 (May 1942): 76.

Newsweek 19 (May 18, 1942): 50.

New York Daily News, May 9, 1942. Kate Cameron. MOMA.

New York Herald Tribune, May 9, 1942. Howard Barnes. MOMA, NYPL.

New York Post, May 9, 1942. Archer Winsten. MOMA.

New York Times, May 9, 1942, 10. Bosley Crowther. NYPL, NYTR.

New York World Telegram, May 9, 1942.

Positif 327 (May 1988): 69–70, creds, illus. J.-P. Bleys.

La Revue du Cinéma, no. 35 (1988): 57–58, creds. R. Bassan.

La Revue du Cinéma, no. 436 (March 1988): 46.

Time 39 (May 11, 1942): 88.

Today's Cinema 59, no. 4,765 (August 21, 1942).

Variety, April 8, 1942, 8+. VR.

THE INVISIBLE MAN. 1933. (Writer, uncredited.)

ARTICLES AND REVIEWS

The American Film Institute Catalog: Feature Films, 1931–1940. Berkeley: University of California Press, 1993, 1,033–34.

Cahiers du Cinéma 346 (April 1983): 57–58. M. Chion.

Cahiers du Cinéma Hors serie (1993): 63. Jean François Rauger.

Cinéma (Paris) 292 (April 1983): 39. P. Dumont.

Cinématographe 87 (March 1983): 54. B. Philbert.

Commonweal 19 (December 29, 1933): 246.

Curtis, James. *James Whale.* Metuchen, N.J.: Scarecrow Press, 1982, 102–8.

Film Daily, November 18, 1933, 4.

Friedman, Favius. *Great Horror Movies.* New York: Scholastic Book Services, 1974, 45–46.

Harrison's Reports, November 25, 1933, 186.

Hollywood Reporter, October 27, 1933, 3.

Judge 106 (January 1934): 12.

Kauffmann, Stanley. *American Film Criticism: From the Beginnings to Citizen Kane.* New York: Liveright, 1972, 293–94.

Magill's Survey of Cinema: Second Series 3 (1981): 1,169–74. Stephen L. Hanson.

Motion Picture Guide 4 (1986): 1,402.

Motion Picture Herald, November 4, 1933, 37–38.

**The Nation* 137 (December 13, 1933): 688. William Troy.

New Statesman and Nation 7 (February 10, 1934): 191.

Newsweek 2 (November 25, 1933): 33.

New Yorker 9 (November 25, 1933): 57.

New York Times, November 18, 1933, 18. NYTR..

New York Times, November 26, 1933, 5.

New York Times, December 3, 1933, 8.

Pohl, Frederick. *Science Fiction Studies in Film.* New York: Ace Books, 1981, 68–72.

Positif 268 (June 1983): 66–68. Christian Viviani.

La Revue du Cinéma 381 (March 1983): 43. P. Mérigeau.

Sadoul, George. *Dictionary of Films.* Translated, edited, and updated by Peter Morris. Berkeley: University of California Press, 1972, 159–60.

Spectator 152 (February 2, 1934): 159.

Time 22 (November 20, 1933): 37.

Variety, November 21, 1933. VR.

IT HAPPENED IN PARIS. 1935. (Writer.)

ARTICLES

Motion Picture Guide 4 (1986): 1,421.

Wapshot, Nicholas. *The Man Between: A Biography of Carol Reed.* London: Chatto & Windus, 1990.

JAGUAR LIVES. 1979. (Actor.)

ARTICLES AND REVIEWS

BFI/Monthly Film Bulletin 47, no. 553 (February 1980): 23–24, creds. P. Taylor.
Film Bulletin 48 (September 1979), creds. D. Silk.
Hollywood Reporter 251, no. 36 (May 23, 1978): 8.
Levende Billeder 6 (March 1980): 44–45, creds, stills. P. A. Berg and P. Tolstoy.
Motion Picture Guide 4 (1986): 1,443.
La Revue du Cinéma 294, no. 24 (1980), creds. J.-L. Cros, "Nom de Code: *Jaguar.*"
Screen International 144 (June 24, 1978): 16.
Screen International 146 (July 8, 1978): 8, creds.
Screen International 220 (December 15, 1979): 30.
Variety, 296, no. 5 (September 5, 1979): 20, creds. Cart. MOMA, VR.

JEZEBEL. 1938. (Writer.)

ARTICLES AND REVIEWS

The American Film Institute Catalog: Feature Films, 1931–1940. Berkeley: University of California Press, 1993, 1,064–66.
Anderegg, Michael A. *William Wyler.* Boston: Twayne, 1979, 85–95.
Brady, Thomas. "Peace Comes to the 'Little Foxes.'" *New York Times,* June 22, 1941. (Reprinted in *The New York Times Encyclopedia of Film, 1941–1946.*)
Cahiers du Cinéma 497 (December 1995): 17.
Castoro Cinema 2, no. 36 (July–August 1988): 10–13.
Churchill, Douglas W. "A House Divided: The Warner-Goldwyn Dispute Headlines Hollywood's All-Star Word Battle." *New York Times,* June 1, 1941. (Reprinted in *The New York Times Encyclopedia of Film, 1941–1946.*)
Classic Images 161 (November 1988): 14. L. E. Ward, "The Great Films."
Crisler, B. R. "Film Gossip of the Week." *New York Times,* January 16, 1938. (Reprinted in *The New York Times Encyclopedia of Film, 1937–1940.*)
———. "Footnotes on Film Personalities." *New York Times,* March 13, 1938. (Reprinted in *The New York Times Encyclopedia of Film, 1937–1940.*)
Crowther, Bosley. "Scanning the Film Sales." *New York Times,* May 23, 1937. (Reprinted in *The New York Times Encyclopedia of Film, 1937–1940.*)
Delehanty, Thornton. "Snarls in Dighting a Jade." *New York Times,* March 13, 1938. (Reprinted in *The New York Times Encyclopedia of Film, 1937–1940.*)
Dyer, Richard. "White." *Screen* 29, no. 4 (Autumn 1988): 44–64. (An abridged version appears in *Frauen und Film* 54–55 [April 1994]: 64–80.)
Esquire 9 (June 1938): 89.
"An Expert's View of It." *New York Times,* July 3, 1938. (Reprinted in *The New York Times Encyclopedia of Film, 1937–1940.*)
Film Comment 6 (Fall 1970): 18–24.
Film Daily, March 11, 1938, 6.
Film Weekly 20, no. 497 (April 23, 1938): 23.
Gussow, Mel. "Bette Davis: One of the First to Look Like 'a Real Person.'" *New*

York Times, January 19, 1977. (Reprinted in *The New York Times Encyclopedia of Film, 1977–1979.*)

Haralovich, Mary Beth, and C. R. Klapart. *"Marked Woman* and *Jezebel:* An Investigation of the Processes Operative in Film Trailers with Special Reference to the Trailers for *Marked Woman* and *Jezebel." Enclitic* 5, no. 2 (Fall 1981–Spring 1982): 66–74, illus.

Harrison's Reports, March 26, 1938, 50.

Hill, Gladwyn. "John Huston—A Bull in the China Shop." *New York Times,* January 16, 1949. (Reprinted in *The New York Times Encyclopedia of Film, 1947–1951.*)

Hochman, Stanley, ed. *From Quasimodo to Scarlett O'Hara: A National Board of Review Anthology, 1920–1940.* New York: Ungar, 1982, 279–82.

Hollywood Reporter, March 8, 1938, 3.

Jeter, Ida. *"Jezebel* and the Emergence of the Hollywood Tradition of a Decadent South." *The Southern Quarterly* 19, nos. 3 & 4 (Spring–Summer 1981): 31–46. (Also issued in *The South and Film,* edited by Warren French, 31–46, Jackson, Miss., University of Mississippi Press, 1981.)

Johnson, Grady. "Back to Broadway in Triplicate." *New York Times,* December 7, 1947. (Reprinted in *The New York Times Encyclopedia of Film, 1947–1951.*)

Kael, Pauline. *Kiss Kiss Bang Bang.* New York: Bantam Books, 1969, 361.

Kern, Sharon. *William Wyler: A Guide to References and Resources.* Boston: G.K. Hall, 1979, 95–99.

Kinematograph Weekly 1,617 (April 14, 1938).

Life 4 (March 28, 1938): 44–46+.

Magill's Survey of Cinema: First Series 2 (1980): 870–73. Cheryl Karnes.

Mason, James. "Mr. Mason Names Five 'Six Best Actresses.'" *New York Times,* November 30, 1947. (Reprinted in *The New York Times Encyclopedia of Film, 1947–1951.*)

Motion Picture Guide 4 (1986): 1,457–58.

Motion Picture Herald 130, no. 11 (March 12, 1938): 36.

Motion Picture Herald 169, no. 5 (November 1, 1947).

The Nation 146 (March 26, 1938): 365.

National Board of Review Magazine 13 (April 1938): 13.

New Statesman and Nation 15 (April 23, 1938): 688.

Newsweek 11 (March 21, 1938): 25.

New York Daily News, March 11, 1938, 52. Kate Cameron.

New Yorker 14 (March 19, 1938): 57–58.

New York Herald Tribune, March 11, 1938, 14. Howard Barnes.

New York Times, March 11, 1938, 15. Frank Nugent. NYTR.

Ringgold, Gene. *Bette Davis: Her Films and Career.* Secaucus, N.J.: Citadel Press, 1985, 84–87.

Rob Wagner's Script 19 (March 26, 1938): 10.

Schatz, Thomas. "A Triumph of Bitchery: Warner Brothers, Betty Davis, and *Jezebel." Wide Angle* 10, no. 1 (1988): 16–29, biblio, illus.

Sight & Sound Supplement 14 (March 1948): 10.

Springer, John. *The Fondas: The Films and Careers of Henry, Jane and Peter Fonda.* New York: Citadel Press, 1970, 76–78.

Studlar, Gaylyn. "Narrating Outside the Canon: Questions of Materiality (Other) Meaning, and the Female Voice." *Persistence of Vision* 10 (1993): 34–35, illus.
The Tattler 148 (April 27, 1938): 152.
Thomas, Tony. *The Films of Henry Fonda.* Secaucus, N.J.: Citadel Press, 1983, 66–69.
Time 31 (March 28, 1938): 33.
Trent, Paul. *Those Fabulous Movie Years: The 30s.* Barre, Mass.: Barre Publications, 1975, 138–39.
Variety, March 8, 1938.
Variety, March 16, 1938, 15. Abel. VR.
Vermilye, Jerry. *The Films of the Thirties.* Secaucus, N.J.: Citadel Press, 1982, 204–7.
Wanger, Walter. "Mr. Wanger on the Stand: The Prominent Producer Has His Say about American and Foreign Films." *New York Times,* May 15, 1938. (Reprinted in *The New York Times Encyclopedia of Film, 1937–1940.*)
Wide Angle 3, no. 4 (1986): 19.
World Film News 3 (May–June 1938): 89.
World Film News 3 (July 1938).

JOAN (The Lark). (Unrealized project? *See* chapter 14, "Huston on Film and Other Projects.")

ARTICLE
"Wanted to Shoot *The Lark.*" *Time,* December 2, 1955. MOMA.

JOHN HUSTON AND THE DUBLINERS. 1987. Documentary. (Subject.)

REVIEWS
Chaplin 30, no. 1 (214) (1988): 16–17, illus, stills. J. Ahlund.
Films in Review 40, no. 1 (January 1989): 28.
Hollywood Reporter 299, no. 47 (November 19, 1987): 7.
Newsday, March 19, 1988, part 2, 7. Mike McGrady. NYPL.
New York Times, October 30, 1982, 13.
New York Times, March 19, 1988, 8. Janet Maslin. NYPL, NYTR.
New York Times, July 18, 1988, C16. John O'Connor. NYPL.
Variety 328, no. 5 (August 26, 1987): 18, creds. Lor. NYPL, VR.
Village Voice 33 (March 22, 1988): 72, stills. A. Taubin.

JOHN HUSTON: THE MAN, THE MOVIES, THE MAVERICK. 1989. TV Documentary. (Subject.)

ARTICLES AND REVIEWS
American Film 14, no. 8 (June 1989): 66–67, port. R. Siedenberg. Background article about the documentary John Huston.
Hollywood Reporter 307, no. 48 (June 12, 1989): 4+.

Los Angeles Herald Examiner, June 11, 1989. Bill Higgins.

Los Angeles Times, June 7, 1989, part 6, 7. Sheila Benson.

Program Booklet, TNT-TV, 1989. Issued for the premiere of the screening, June 12, 1989, unpaged. Includes production notes, background information on the making of the film, and interviews with producers Levin and Martin.

Variety September 26, 1988 (D), 3+.

Variety September 28, 1988 (W), 16, creds. Kimm. VR.

Wilson Library Bulletin 64, no. 8 (April 1990): 81.

JOHN HUSTON'S DUBLIN. 1981. TV Documentary.

REVIEW

Variety, June 26, 1989, 64. Tone.

THE JOURNEY OF ROBERT F. KENNEDY. 1970. TV Documentary. (Narrator.)

REVIEWS

Entertainment World, February 13, 1970, 19+. Ray Loynd.

Hollywood Reporter 209, no. 47 (February 11, 1970): 11.

New York Times 95 (February 18, 1970): 3. NYTR.

Variety, February 18, 1970.

JUAREZ. 1939. (Writer.)

ARTICLES AND REVIEWS

The American Film Institute Catalog: Feature Films, 1931–1940. Berkeley: University of California Press, 1993, 1,073.

Appleton, Jane Scovell. "Where Have All the Garbo's Gone?" *New York Times,* April 15, 1973. (Reprinted in *The New York Times Encyclopedia of Film, 1972–1974.*)

Churchill, Douglas W. "The Coming of 'Gone.'" *New York Times,* April 23, 1939. (Reprinted in *The New York Times Encyclopedia of Film, 1937–1940.*)

Commonweal 30 (May 12, 1939): 77.

Crowther, Bosley. "A Man Who Means to Make a Dent." *New York Times,* December 18, 1938. (Reprinted in *The New York Times Encyclopedia of Film, 1937–1940.*)

———. "The Myth of the Trend: Hall B. Wallis of Warner Brothers Point out the Facts of the Matter." *New York Times* March 3, 1940. (Reprinted in *The New York Times Encyclopedia of Film, 1937–1940.*)

Documentary News Letter 1 (January 1940): 12.

Druxman, Michael B. *Paul Muni: His Life and His Films.* South Brunswick, N.J.: A. S. Barnes, 1974, 172–77.

Film and History 5, no. 1 (February 1975): 15–18.

Film Daily, April 26, 1939, 7.

Film Weekly 22, no. 570 (September 16, 1939): 26.

Gelman, Howard. *The Films of John Garfield.* Secaucus, N.J.: Citadel Press, 1975, 61–64.

Greene, Graham. *Graham Greene on Film: Collected Film Criticism, 1935–1940.* Edited by John Russell Taylor. New York: Simon & Schuster, 1972, 254–55.

Grindon, L. "Romantic Archetypes & Political Meaning in the Historical Fiction Film." *Persistence of Vision* 3–4 (Summer 1986): 15–22.

Harrison's Reports, May 13, 1939, 75.

Hill, Gladwyn. "John Huston—A Bull in the China Shop." *New York Times,* January 16, 1949. (Reprinted in *The New York Times Encyclopedia of Film, 1947–1951.*)

Hochman, Stanley, ed. *From Quasimodo to Scarlett O'Hara: A National Board of Review Anthology, 1920–1940.* New York: Ungar, 1982, 305–8.

Hollywood Reporter, April 26, 1939, 3.

Hollywood Spectator 14 (May 13, 1939): 8–9.

"Juarez on Democracy," *New York Times,* May 28, 1939. (Reprinted in *The New York Times Encyclopedia of Film, 1937–1940.*)

Kinematograph Weekly 1,679 (June 22, 1939).

Magill's Survey of Cinema: Second Series 3 (1981): 1,232–35. Lewis Larchbald.

Motion Picture Daily, April 26, 1939. Charles S. Aaronson.

Motion Picture Guide 4 (1986): 1,483.

Motion Picture Herald 135, no. 3 (April 22, 1939).

Motion Picture Herald 135, no. 4 (April 29, 1939): 15.

The Nation 148 (May 6, 1939): 539–40.

National Board of Review Magazine 14 (May 1939): 14.

The New Masses 31 (May 9, 1939): 27–28.

The New Masses 31 (May 23, 1939): 28–29.

New Republic 99 (May 10, 1939): 20. Otis Ferguson. (Reprinted in *The Film Criticism of Otis Ferguson,* edited by Robert Wilson, 254, Philadelphia, Temple University Press, 1971.)

New Statesman and Nation 18 (November 25, 1939): 756.

Newsweek 13 (May 8, 1939): 22–23.

New Yorker 15 (April 29, 1939): 94–95.

New York Herald Tribune, April 26, 1939. Howard Barnes.

New York Times, April 23, 1939. "Excavating 'Juarez' from the Ruins." (Reprinted in *The New York Times Encyclopedia of Film, 1937–40.*)

New York Times, April 26, 1939, 27. Frank S. Nugent. NYTR.

North American Review 247 (June 1939): 379–81.

Nugent, Frank S. "A Critic's Adventures in Wonderland." *New York Times,* February 5, 1939. (Reprinted in *The New York Times Encyclopedia of Film, 1937–1940.*)

Photoplay 53 (May 1939): 22–23+.

Photoplay 53 (July 1939): 62.

Picturegoer 9, no. 450 (January 6, 1940): 22.

Ringgold, Gene. *Bette Davis: Her Films and Career.* Secaucus, N.J.: Citadel Press, 1985, 94–95.

Rob Wagner's Script 21 (May 20, 1939): 16–17.
Scholastic 34 (May 13, 1939): 33.
Schulberg, Budd Wilson. "Hollywood's Second Generation." *New York Times,* July 2, 1939. (Reprinted in *The New York Times Encyclopedia of Film, 1937–1940.*)
Sight & Sound 8 (Summer 1939): 74–75.
The Spectator 163 (November 24, 1939): 744.
Time 33 (May 8, 1939): 66.
Vanderwood, Paul J. "Introduction: A Political Barometer." In *Juarez,* edited with an introduction by Paul J. Vanderwood, 9–41. Madison, Wis.: University of Wisconsin Press, for the Wisconsin Center for Film and Theater Research, 1983.
Variety, April 26, 1939, 12. VR.
Weiler, A. H. "Reverie on a Pastrami Sandwich." *New York Times,* August 10, 1941. (Reprinted in *The New York Times Encyclopedia of Film, 1941–1946.*)

KEY LARGO. 1948. (Director, Writer.)

ARTICLES

Archer, Eugene. "Bogart: Man and Superman." *New York Times,* January 3, 1965. (Reprinted in *The New York Times Encyclopedia of Film, 1964–1968.*)
Aristarco, Guido. "'Stanotte sorgera il sole' e 'L'isola di corallo.'" *Cinema* (Milano) 2, no. 29 (December 30, 1949).
Bartnett, Edmond J. "Presenting the Peregrinating Pip: John Mills Traveled Far to Attain His 'Great Expectations.'" *New York Times,* July 6, 1947. (Reprinted in *The New York Times Encyclopedia of Film, 1947–1951.*)
Bergman, Andrew. *We're in the Money: Depression America and Its Films.* New York: New York University Press, 1971.
"Blue Penciled." *New York Times,* November 9, 1947. (Reprinted in *The New York Times Encyclopedia of Film, 1947–1951.*)
Conforti, A. "I tesoro della Sierra Madre: L'isola di corallo." *Cineforum* 28, no. 277 (September 1988): 63–70.
Cowie, Peter. *Seventy Years of Cinema.* South Brunswick, N.J.: A. S. Barnes, 1969, 167.
Di Giammatteo, Fernaldo. "*We Were Strangers* e *Key Largo.*" *Bianco e Nero* 2, no. 2 (February 1950).
Film Culture, no. 19 (1959). Eugene Archer.
"The Films of John Huston" [Program notes]. Los Angeles County Museum of Art, October 17, 1980, creds.
Gabree, John. *Gangsters: From* Little Caesar *to* The Godfather. New York: Pyramid, 1973.
Hammen, Scott. *Film Notes.* Louisville, Ky.: Hamilton Printing Co., 1979.
Hill, Gladwyn. "John Huston—A Bull in the China Shop." *New York Times,* January 16, 1949. (Reprinted in *The New York Times Encyclopedia of Film, 1947–1951.*)
Kaminsky, Stuart. *American Film Genres.* 2d ed. Chicago, Ohio: Nelson-Hall, 1985.
Laskas, Kristin. *CinemaTexas Program Notes* 10, no. 3 (April 13, 1976): 103–8, biblio, creds, filmog.

Magill's Survey of Cinema, First Series 2 (1980): 885–88. Lawrence Fargo Jr.
Motion Picture Guide 4 (1986): 1,512–14.
Nichols, Nina. *CinemaTexas Program Notes* 17, no. 2 (October 22, 1979): 28–33,
biblio, creds, filmog.
Radio Times 234, no. 3,044 (March 13, 1982): 11. Roger Woodis.
Reijnhoudt, B. "Robinson, Cagney, Bogart: de snoevende, snauwendegansters van
Warner Bros." *Skoop* 14 (June 1978): 13–17, illus, stills.
Seguin, Louis. "Richard Brooks ou la sincérité." *Positif* 2, no. 17 (June–July 1956): 11–18.
Sight & Sound 21 (January–March 1952): 30–32, interv. Karl Reisz.
Silver, Alain, and Elizabeth Ward, eds. *Film Noir: An Encyclopedic Reference to
the American Style.* 3d ed., rev. Woodstock, N.Y.: The Overlook Press, 1992,
150–51, analysis, creds, illus, synopsis.
Sperber, A. M., and Eric Lax. *Bogart.* New York: Morrow, 1997.
Spinard, Leonard. "Whodunit First?" *New York Times,* May 9, 1948. (Reprinted in
The New York Times Encyclopedia of Film, 1947–1951.)
Weinraub, Bernard. "London: Film-Buffs' Nightly Queue." *New York Times,* July
31, 1972. (Reprinted in *The New York Times Encyclopedia of Film, 1972–1974.*)

REVIEWS
Casablanca 35 (November 1983): 39.
Christian Science Monitor, January 6, 1948. Frank Daugherty. NYPL.
Commonweal 48 (July 30, 1948): 379.
Ecran Français, August 22, 1949. Jean Nery. (Excerpt of review in *Positif,* no. 3
[July–August 1952]: 45.)
Films in Review, November 1963, 54. NYPL.
**Fortnight* 5, no. 3 (July 30, 1948): 30.
Harrison's Reports, July 10, 1948, 111.
**Hollywood Reporter* 99, no. 30 (July 7, 1948): 3–4. AMPAS.
Liberty, September 1948. NYPL.
Life, September 18, 1950. James Agee.
Look, August 3, 1948. NYPL.
Los Angeles Examiner, July 17, 1948. AMPAS.
Modern Screen, August 1948. Jean Kincaid. NYPL.
Motion Picture Herald 172, no. 2 (July 10, 1948).
The Nation, July 31, 1948, 137. James Agee.
The Nation, June 4, 1949. Manny Farber.
New Republic 119 (August 2, 1948): 30.
Newsweek 32 (July 26, 1948): 84–85. NYPL.
New Yorker 24 (July 24, 1948): 38. AMPAS, NYPL.
New York Herald Tribune, July 17, 1948. Otis Guernsey Jr. NYPL.
New York Times, July 17, 1948. Bosley Crowther. NYTR.
Séquence, no. 7 (Spring 1949): 34–36. Peter Ericsson.
Time 52 (August 2, 1948): 72+.
Today's Cinema 72, no. 5,776 (March 11, 1949).
Variety, July 7, 1948. Brog. AMPAS, NYPL, VR.
Women's Home Companion 75 (September. 1948): 10–11.

THE KILLERS. 1946. (Writer, uncredited.)

ARTICLES AND REVIEWS

Adams, Val. "*The Killers* to Have Double Exposure." *New York Times,* October 18, 1959, sect. 2, 19.

Alloway, Lawrence. *Violent America: The Movies, 1946–1964.* New York: Museum of Modern Art, 1971.

Beal, Greg. *CinemaTexas Program Notes* 11, no. 2 (October 7, 1976): 43–49.

BFI/Monthly Film Bulletin 48, no. 573 (October 1981): 208, creds. S. Jenkins.

Cinématographe 112 (July 1985): 54–55. D. Goldschmidt.

Classic Images 165 (March 1989): C12+. D. Fury.

Cohen, Mitchell S. "Film Noir: The Actor, Villains and Victims." *Film Comment,* November–December 1991.

Conley, Tom. "The Killers." In *International Dictionary of Films and Filmmakers.* Vol. 1, *Films,* 2d ed., edited by Nicholas Thomas, 466–67. Chicago: St. James Press, 1990. (Updated in Vol. 1, 3d ed., edited by Nicolet V. Elert and Aruna Vasudeven, 523–24, Detroit, St. James Press, 1997.)

Ecran 7 (July 1972): 14.

EPD Film 7, no. 8 (August 1990): 28–29, creds, stills. H. Gassen.

Film Culture 28 (Spring 1963): 22. Andrew Sarris, "Esoterica."

Film Daily, August 12, 1946, 6.

Garbicz, Adam, and Jacek Klinowski. *Cinema: The Magic Vehicle—A Guide to Its Achievement. Journey One: The Cinema through 1949.* New York: Schocken Books, 1983, ca. 1975–79, 432–33.

Godfrey, T. "TAD at the Movies." *Armchair Detective* 18, no. 2 (1985): 196–99, stills.

Harrison's Reports, August 24, 1946, 135.

Hollywood Reporter, August 7, 1946, 3.

Hotchner, A. E. "Drawn from a Master's Original: Fashioning Hemingway Stories into Drama Was Touchy Task." *New York Times,* July 22, 1962. (Reprinted in *The New York Times Encyclopedia of Film, 1958–1963.*)

Kaminsky, Stuart M. "Hemingway's *The Killers.*" *Take One* 4, no. 6 (November 1974): 17–19. Discussion of both movie versions: 1946 and 1964.

———. "Literary Adaptation: *The Killers*—Hemingway, Film Noir, and the Terror of Daylight." In *American Film Genres,* 2d. 3d., 81–96. Chicago: Nelson-Hall, 1985. (Reprinted in *A Moving Picture Feast: The Filmgoer's Hemingway,* edited by Charles M. Oliver, 125–34, New York, Praeger, 1989.)

Kinematograph Weekly 2,066 (November 21, 1946).

Krutnik, Frank. *In a Lonely Street: Film Noir, Genre, Masculinity.* London: Routledge, 1991.

Laurence, Frank. *Hemingway and the Movies.* Jackson, Miss.: University Press of Mississippi, 1982, 173–205.

Life 21 (September 2, 1946): 59–61.

Lillich, Richard B. "Hemingway on the Screen." *Films in Review* 10 (April 1959): 208–18.

Magill's Survey of Cinema, Series I, 3 (1980): 1,254–56.

Marshman, D. "Mister Siodmak." *Life* 23 (August 25, 1947): 208–18.

Motion Picture Daily, August 8, 1946. Thalia Bell.

Motion Picture Guide 4 (1986): 1,526.

Motion Picture Herald 164, no. 6 (August 10, 1946).

Motion Picture Herald Product Digest, August 17, 1946, 3,150.

Narducy, Ray. "The Killers." In *International Dictionary of Film and Filmmakers.* Vol. 1, *Films,* edited by Christopher Lyon, 38–39, Chicago, St. James Press, 1984.

The Nation 163 (September 14, 1946): 305. James Agee.

New Republic 115 (September 30, 1946): 405.

Newsweek 28 (September 9, 1946): 106.

New Yorker 22 (September 7, 1946): 52. John McNulty.

New York Times, August 29, 1946, 24. Bosley Crowther. NYTR.

New York Times, September 1, 1946, sect. 2, 1.

Nolan, Jack Edmond. "Robert Siodmak." *Films in Review* 20 (April 1969): 218–32.

Phillips, Gene D. *Hemingway and Film.* New York: Ungar, 1980, 66–75.

Pryor, Thomas M. "Leap to Stardom: Burt Lancaster, Ex-Acrobat, Scales Film Heights with the Greatest of Ease." *New York Times,* October 17, 1948. (Reprinted in *The New York Times Encyclopedia of Film, 1947–1951.*)

Ranieri, Tino. "Hemingway e il cinema I due strade diverse." *Bianco e Nero* 18, no. 4 (April 1957): 48–57.

Rob Wagner's Script 32 (September 28, 1946): 13.

Sadoul, George. *Dictionary of Films.* Translated, edited, and updated by Peter Morris. Berkeley: University of California Press, 1971, 176.

Schatz, Thomas. *Hollywood Genres: Formulas, Filmmaking, and the Studio System.* New York: Random House, 1981, 140–42.

Selby, Spencer. *Dark City: The Film Noir.* Jefferson, N.C.: McFarland, 1984, 39–44.

Shadoian, Jack. *Dreams and Dead Ends: The American Gangster/Crime Film.* Cambridge, Mass.: MIT Press, 1977, 83–114.

Silver, Alain, and Elizabeth Ward, eds. *Film Noir: An Encyclopedic Reference to the American Style.* 3d ed., rev. Woodstock, N.Y.: The Overlook Press, 1992, 153–54, analysis, creds, synopsis.

Siodmak, Robert, and Richard Wilson. "Hoodlums: The Myth and the Reality." *Films and Filming* 5 (June 1959): 10+.

"Siodmak's 'Whistle.'" *New York Times,* October 14, 1951. (Reprinted in *The New York Times Encyclopedia of Film, 1947–1951.*)

Taylor, J. Russell. "Encounter with Siodmak." *Sight & Sound* 28 (Summer–Autumn 1959): 180–82.

Telecotte, J. P. "A Consuming Passion: Food & Film Noir." *Georgia Review* 39, no. 2 (1985): 397–410.

Theatre Arts 30 (October 1946): 603.

Thompson, David. *Suspects.* New York: Knopf, 1985. "Fictionalized" accounts of the lives of characters in *Chinatown, Beat the Devil, High Sierra, The Killers,* and *The Maltese Falcon.*

Time 48 (September 9, 1946): 100.

Today's Cinema 67, no. 5,422 (November 15, 1946).

Tuska, Jon. *Dark Cinema: American Film Noir in Cultural Perspective.* Westport, Conn.: Greenwood Press, 1984.

Variety, August 7, 1946, 15. VR.

Vermilye, Jerry. *Burt Lancaster: A Pictorial Treasury of His Film.* New York: Falcon Enterprises, 1971, 30–31.

Village Voice 9, no. 47 (September 10, 1964): 17. Andrew Sarris.

Wald, Malvin. "Richard Brooks and Me." Creative Screenwriting 1, no. 2 (Summer 1994): 56–58.

Weiler, A. H. "By Way of Report." *New York Times,* June 13, 1948. (Reprinted in *The New York Times Encyclopedia of Film, 1947–1951.*)

KISS THE BLOOD OFF MY HANDS. 1948. (Unrealized project? *See* chapter 14, "Huston on Film and Other Projects.")

ARTICLES AND REVIEWS

Harrison's Reports, October 16, 1948, 167.

Motion Picture Guide 4 (1986): 1,551.

New York Times, October 30, 1948, 10. NYTR.

Variety, October 20, 1948. VR.

THE KREMLIN LETTER. 1970. (Director, Writer, Actor.)

ARTICLES AND REVIEWS

Aba, Markia. "Huston Back in Stream with *Kremlin.*" *Los Angeles Times,* May 11, 1969, 24–25.

Astor, Gerald. "The Man Who Delivered *The Kremlin.*" *Look,* March 24, 1970, interv.

The American Film Institute Catalog: Feature Films, 1961–1970. New York: R. R. Bowker, 1976, 587–88.

BFI/Monthly Film Bulletin 37, no. 438 (July 1970): 139.

Christian Science Monitor, February 9, 1970, 6. Louise Sweeney. MOMA, NYPL.

Commentary 50 (November 1970): 91–92.

Entertainment World, February 20, 1970. Nat Freedland.

Film Bulletin 39, no. 2 (January 26, 1970): 9. AMPAS.

Films in Review 21, no. 3 (March 1970): 179–80, illus. Norman Cecil. NYPL.

Friendly, Alfred, Jr. "Luck of the Bored—Rome: On the Set of *The Kremlin Letter.*" *New York Times,* April 27, 1969, 14D, interv. AMPAS, NYPL. (Reprinted in *The New York Times Encyclopedia of Film, 1969–1971.*)

Hollywood Reporter, March 7, 1969, 11, creds.

Hollywood Reporter, April 8, 1969. AMPAS.

Hollywood Reporter, February 23, 1970, 3. AMPAS.

Joyce, Jean. "Day on a Film Set: Shooting of *Kremlin Letter.*" *Newark Evening News,* August 24, 1969, 28–34. NYPL.

Kinematograph Weekly 3,268 (May 30, 1970): 8.

Life 68 (February 27, 1970): 61. Richard Schickel. AMPAS, MOMA, NYPL.

London Times, June 28, 1970, 27. Penelope Mortimer. NYPL.

Los Angeles Herald Examiner, March 6, 1970. AMPAS.

Los Angeles Times, March 5, 1970. AMPAS.

McCarthy, Todd. "The Films of John Huston" [Program notes]. Los Angeles County Museum of Art, November 28, 1980, creds.

Monogram, no. 1 (April 1971): 18–19. Richard Collins.

Motion Picture Exhibitor, February 11, 1970.

Motion Picture Guide 4 (1986): 1,561–62.

Motion Picture Herald 240, no. 6 (February 11, 1970): 371.

Newark Evening News, February 2, 1970, 3. Alan Branigan. NYPL.

New York Daily News, February 2, 1970, 48. Kathleen Carroll. NYPL.

New Yorker, June 14, 1969, 31–33. "Takes: Shooting Scenes for *The Kremlin Letter;* an Interview with John Huston."

New Yorker, February 7, 1970, 91–93. Pauline Kael. AMPAS, MOMA, NYPL.

New York Magazine 3 (February 9, 1970): 55. Judith Crist. NYPL.

New York Morning Telegraph, February 2, 1970, 3. Joe Rosen. NYPL.

New York Post, February 2, 1970, 26. Archer Winsten. NYPL.

New York Times, February 2, 1970, 26. Vincent Canby. MOMA, NYPL, NYTR.

Punch, July 1 1970, 36. Richard Marttett. NYPL.

Richards, Peter. "John Huston's *The Kremlin Letter.*" *Film Comment* 33, no. 1 (January–February 1997): 74–80.

Saturday Review 53 (February 14, 1970): 82. Roland Gelatt. AMPAS, MOMA, NYPL.

Senior Scholastic 96 (March 16, 1970): 22.

Sight & Sound 39, no. 4 (Autumn 1970): 220. John Russell Taylor. MOMA.

Silver, Alain, and Elizabeth Ward, eds. *Film Noir: An Encyclopedic Reference to the American Style.* 3d ed., rev. Woodstock, N.Y.: The Overlook Press, 1992, 162–63, analysis, creds, synopsis.

Today's Cinema 9,813 (June 12, 1970): 13.

Torok, Jean-Paul. "Comment peut-on être un espion?" *Positif* 118 (Summer 1970): .59+. (Reprinted in *John Huston, Collection dirigée,* edited by Gilles Ciment, 137–39, Dossier Positif Rivages, Paris, Editions Rivages, Collection Positif-Rivages, no. 2, 1988.) NYPL.

Variety, January 21, 1970. AMPAS, VR.

Variety, January 28, 1970, 17. Gene. MOMA, NYPL.

Village Voice 15, no. 7 (February 12, 1970): 60. Molly Haskell. MOMA, NYPL.

Watters, Jim. "John Huston on Kipling, Hemingway and Jack Daniels." *New York Times,* February 15, 1976. (Reprinted in *The New York Times Encyclopedia of Film, 1975–1976.*)

THE LAST RUN. 1971. (Director, withdrew; Writer, uncredited.)

REVIEWS

BFI/Monthly Film Bulletin 38 (December 1971): 242.

Big Reel, January 1991, B13.

Cinéma (Paris) 168 (July–August 1972): 147. M. Grisolia.
Filmfacts 14 (1971): 281–83.
Films and Filming 18, no. 7 (April 1971): 60. G. Gow.
Hollywood Reporter, June 29, 1971, 3.
Motion Picture Guide 5 (1986): 1,619.
Newsweek 78 (July 19, 1971): 79. S. R. Oberbeck.
New York Times, July 8, 1971, 30. NYTR.
Positif 142 (September 1972): 109–12. Alain Garsault.
Saturday Review 54 (July 31, 1971): 50.
Time 98 (July 26, 1971): 51. Jay Cocks.
Variety, July 7, 1971, 20. VR.
Village Voice, July 22, 1971, 60. William Paul.

LAUGHING BOY. 1934. (Writer, uncredited.)

ARTICLES AND REVIEWS

The American Film Institute Catalog: Feature Films, 1931–1940. Berkeley:
    University of California Press, 1993, 1,157–58.
Harrison's Reports, May 19, 1934, 79.
Motion Picture Guide 5 (1986): 1,626.
Variety, May 15, 1934. VR.

LAW AND ORDER. 1932. (Writer.)

ARTICLES AND REVIEWS

The American Film Institute Catalog: Feature Films, 1931–1940. Berkeley:
    University of California, Press, 1993, 1,160–61.
The Big Reel, January 1991, B13.
Bioscope 90, no. 1,323 (February 10, 1932).
Film Daily, March 6, 1932, 10.
Harrison's Reports, March 5, 1932, 39.
Magill's Survey of Cinema: Second Series 3 (1981): 1,337–39. Rob Edelman.
Motion Picture Guide 5 (1986): 1,630.
New York Times, February 29, 1932, 21. NYTR.
Parish, James Robert, and Michael R. Pitts. *Great Western Pictures.* Metuchen,
    N.J.: The Scarecrow Press, 1976, 186–88.
Picturegoer 2, no. 56 (June 18, 1932): 20.
Tuska, Jon. *Filming of the West.* Garden City, N.Y.: Doubleday, 1976, 192–93.
Variety, March 1, 1932, 21+. VR.

LET THERE BE LIGHT. 1946; released 1980. (Director, Writer.)

ARTICLES AND REVIEWS

Asayas, O. "1945: Huston interdit." *Cahiers du Cinéma* 319 (January 1981): 43–35
    (special insert "Journaldes," no. 11, January 1981, between 34 and 35, paged
    i–xvi).

Casablanca 2 (February 1981): 6. "Autorizada la exhibicion de un documental de John Huston prohibido durante treinta y cinco anos."

Champlin, Charles. "Huston Wartime Films on KCET." *Los Angeles Times,* April 30, 1981.

Chicago Sun Times, April 10, 1981, 51+. David Elliott. NYPL.

Chicago Tribune, February 14, 1981, sect. 3, 5. NYPL.

Cinema 81, nos. 271 & 272 (July–August 1981): 136. J. Roy.

CinemaTexas Program Notes 21, no. 2 (October 26, 1981). Scott Bowles.

Classic, no. 78 (November 1981): 17. J. Collura.

Corliss, Richard. "The Disasters of Modern War." *Time* 117 (January 19, 1981): 80, port, stills. NYPL.

Desser, David. "The Wartime Films of John Huston: Film Noir and the Emergence of the Therapeutic." In *Reflections in the Male Eye,* edited by Gaylyn Studlar and David Desser, 19–32. Washington, D.C.: Smithsonian Institution Press, 1993.

Edgerton, Gary. "Revisiting the Records of Wars Past: Remembering the Documentary Trilogy of John Huston." *Journal of Popular Film and Television* 15, no. 1 (Spring 1987): 27–41. (Reprinted in Studlar and Desser, *Reflections in a Male Eye,* 33–61.)

Fleming, Michael, and Roger Manvell. *Images of Madness: The Portrayal of Madness in the Feature Film.* Rutherford, N.J.: Fairleigh Dickinson University Press, 1985.

Gallez, Douglas. "Patterns in Wartime Documentaries: Huston's Trilogy Discussed." *Quarterly of Films, Radio & TV* 10, no. 2 (Winter 1955): 125+.

Garner, Jack. "John Huston's Frank Look at War Finally Released." *Rochester* (NY) *Democrat and Chronicle,* August 9, 1981, 27.

Garrett, Greg. "*Let There Be Light* and Huston's Film Noir." *Proteus,* Fall 1990, 30–33.

———. "John Huston's *The Battle of San Pietro.*" *War, Literature, and the Arts* 5, no. 1 (Spring–Summer 1993): 1–12.

Gleiberman, Owen. "*Let There Be Light* & *Battle for San Pietro.*" *Boston Phoenix,* May 19, 1981.

Grant, Alex. "Feedback: Huston's World War II Documentaries." *Take One* 3, no. 2 (November–December 1970): 4.

Hammen, Scott. "At War with the Army." *Film Comment* 16, no. 2 (March–April 1980): 19–23, illus.

Harmetz, Aljean. "Three Films that Didn't Get Nominations for Oscars: *Let There Be Light* One of Them." *New York Times,* February 19, 1981, C15+. NYPL.

Hill, Gladwyn. "John Huston—A Bull in the China Shop." *New York Times,* January 16, 1949. (Reprinted in *The New York Times Encyclopedia of Film, 1947–1951.*)

Hölbling, Walter. "Patriotische Pflicht und die Veroflichtung zur Dokumentation: John Ford, John Huston und US Dokumentarfilme zum Zweiten Weltkreig." In *Der Krief der Bilder: Ausgewahlte Dokumentarfilme zum Zweiten Weltkrieg und zum Vietnamkrieg,* edited by Michael Barchet, Maria Diedrich, and Walter Hölbling, 25–40. (Crossroads: Studies in American Culture, Bd. 8.) Trier: Wissenshchaftlicher Verlag Trier, 1993. Abstract in English.

Hughes, Robert, ed. "The Courage of Men: An Interview with John Huston." In *Film: Book 2, Films of Peace and War,* 22–35. New York: Grove Press, 1962.

Huston, John. "Focus on 'Freud.'" *New York Times,* December 24, 1962. (Reprinted in *The New York Times Encyclopedia of Film, 1958–1963.*)

"Huston's *Let There Be Light* Gets Green Light from Army." *Variety,* December 17, 1980, 7. MOMA.

"Huston's Suppressed Army Film Prompts Valenti Plea to Pentagon." *Variety,* November 19, 1980, 5. NYPL.

Jameson, Richard T. "Let There Be Light." *Film Comment* [Midsection] 16, no. 3 (May–June 1980): 32–33.

Levende Billeder 7 (March 1981): 35, port, stills. K. Ravn.

Los Angeles Times, March 25, 1981, Calendar, 1. Sheila Benson. AMPAS.

MacCann, Richard Dyer. *The People's Films: A Political History of U.S. Government Motion Pictures.* New York: Hastings House, 1973. (Originally "Documentary Film and Democratic Government: An Administrative History from Pare Lorentz to John Huston." Ph.D. diss., Harvard University, Cambridge, Massachusetts, 1951.)

McFadden, Frances. "Let There Be Light: A Commentary on John Huston's Film." *Harper's Bazaar,* May 1946.

Matthews, Jack. "Huston Documentaries: Only Following Orders." *Los Angeles Times,* September 11, 1985, interv. Discussion on Huston's experiences making his war trilogy.

Media & Methods, February 1982. NYPL.

Museum of Modern Art. "Film notes: *Let There Be Light.*" MOMA.

New Republic, 184 (January 31, 1981): 20–21 Stanley Kauffmann. NYPL.

Newsday, January 16, 1981, part 2, 7. Joseph Gelmis.

New York Daily News, January 15, 1981, 59. Ernest Leogrande. NYPL.

New York Magazine 14 (January 19, 1981): 43–44, stills. David Denby. NYPL.

New York Post, May 6, 1948. "Huston's *Let There Be Light* Hidden under Army Bushel." NYPL.

New York Times, April 13, 1946, 22.

New York Times, January 16, 1981, C6, creds. Vincent Canby. AMPAS, NYPL, NYTR.

Nichtenhauser, Adolf, Marie Coleman, and David S. Ruhe. *Films in Psychiatry, Psychology & Mental Health.* New York: Head Education Council for Medical Audio-Visual Institute of the Association of American Medical Colleges, 1953, 151–55.

Nugent, Jo. "What War Can Do to Men." *New West,* April 1981, 53. Recollections of Stanley Cortez, cinematographer. AMPAS.

Positif, nos. 244 & 245 (July–August 1981): 96–97. O. Eyquem.

Psychiatric News 16, no. 3 (July 3, 1981). Clarissa K. Wittenberg. AMPAS.

Rotha, Paul. *Documentary Film.* London: Faber & Faber, 1952.

Sacramento Bee, November 17, 1981. George Williams. (Reprinted in *Newsbank* 67 [July 1981–June 1982]: B11–B12.)

San Diego Union, August 11, 1981. Carol Olten. NYPL.

Schrader, Paul. "Notes on Film Noir." In *Film Genre Reader*, edited by Barry Keith Grant, 169–82. Austin, Tex.: University of Texas Press, 1986.
"Shell-shock WWII Vets Treatment Goes Public; Thalia NY to Unreel." *Variety*, January 7, 1981, 6.
Shortland, Michael. "Screen Memories: Towards a History of Psychiatry and Psychoanalysis in the Movies." *British Journal for the History of Science* 20, part 4, no. 67 (October 1987): 421–52.
Take One 3, no. 1 (September–October 1970): 4. David Batterson.
Telotte, J. P. *Voices in the Dark: The Narrative Patterns of Film Noir.* Urbana, Ill.: University of Illinois Press, 1989, 22.
Variety, November 12, 1980, 26+. MOMA, NYPL.
Village Voice 26 (January 21–27, 1981): 45, stills. Andrew Sarris, "Hobgoblins of Reality."
Washington Post, February 12, 1981, F1. Michael Kernan.
Winston, Archer. "Lest We Forget—Film Everyone Ought to View. Suppression of the Film Prior to Screening at MOMA." *New York Post*, July 2, 1946, 28+.

THE LIFE AND TIMES OF JOHN HUSTON, ESQ. 1966. TV Documentary. (Subject.)

ARTICLES AND REVIEWS
BFFS Newsletter 135 (December 1971): 21.
BFI/Monthly Film Bulletin 39, no. 456 (January 1972).
Variety, March 1, 1967. VR.

THE LIFE AND TIMES OF JUDGE ROY BEAN. 1972. (Director, Actor; Writer, uncredited).

ARTICLES AND REVIEWS
Amis du Film et Télévision, no. 210 (November 1973): 16–17. J. Leiveus.
Benoit, C. "'Pat Garrett et Billy the Kid.' 'Juge et hors-la-loi': En deux westerns l'itineraire des U.S.A." *Jeune Cinéma* 74 (November 1973): 34–43.
BFI/Monthly Film Bulletin 39, no. 467 (December 1972): 252.
BFI/Monthly Film Bulletin 40, no. 470 (March 1973): 64.
Boston Phoenix, March 20, 1973, 3–4. Janet Maslin. MOMA.
Bourget, J.-L. "Le dernier carre? (Huston, Mankiewicz, Cukor, Wilder)." *Positif* 149 (April 1973): 1–13.
Carragher, Bernard. "I Had a Fine Childhood, How About You?" *New York Times*, November 19, 1972. (Reprinted in *The New York Times Encyclopedia of Film, 1972–1974.*)
Chaplin 15, no. 3 (1973): 87, illus. Y. Bengtsson.
Christian Science Monitor, December 22, 1972, 4. Louise Sweeney. NYPL.
Cineforum 13, no. 121 (March 1973): 278–80, creds. E. Comuzio.
Cinéma (Paris), no. 180 (September–October 1973): 116–18. C. M. Cluny.
Cinema TV Today 10,026 (April 7, 1973): 20.
Commonweal 97 (January 12, 1973): 327–28. Colin L. Westerbeck Jr. MOMA, NYPL.

Crawdaddy, March 1973, 87+.

Cue, December 23–30, 1972. W. W. NYPL.

Deschner, Donald, ed. "The Films of John Huston" [Program notes]. Los Angeles County Museum of Art, November 7, 1980.

Ecran, no. 18 (September–October 1973): 63–64, creds, illus. J. A. Gili.

Ekran 1, nos. 9 & 10 (1976): 36, creds, stills.

Esquire, April 1973, 59–60. Thomas Berger. MOMA.

Filmcritica 24, no. 231 (January–February 1973): 45–47. R. Tomasino.

Filmfacts 15, no. 24 (1972): 607.

Film Information 3, no. 12 (December 1972): 2. NYPL.

Films and Filming 19, no. 6 (March 1973): 46, creds, illus. G. Gow. AMPAS, NYPL.

Ford, Dan. "Legend Tackles Legend: Huston, Judge Roy Bean." *Los Angeles Times,* May 28, 1972, 17+. AMPAS.

———. "Legendary Huston Views Another Legend, Roy Bean." *Philadelphia Inquirer,* June 4, 1972, 4-G. AMPAS.

Hablemos de Cine 10, no. 66 (1974): 45–46, illus. R. Bedoya.

Harmetz, Aljean. "How Do You Pick a Winner in Hollywood? You Don't." *New York Times,* April 29, 1973. (Reprinted in *The New York Times Encyclopedia of Film, 1972–1974.*)

Hollywood Reporter 224, no. 9 (December 7, 1972): 3.

Interview, no. 29 (January 1973): 41. J. Calendo.

Kosmorama 19, nos. 115 & 116 (August 1973): 300–1. A. Bodelsen.

Kosmorama 36, no. 192 (Summer 1990): 62–63, stills. Maren Pust.

Lindsey, Robert. "The New Wave of Filmmakers." *New York Times,* May 28, 1978. (Reprinted in *The New York Times Encyclopedia of Film, 1977–1979.*)

Los Angeles Herald Examiner, December 20, 1972. AMPAS.

Los Angeles Times, December 12, 1972. AMPAS.

Magill's Survey of Cinema: Second Series 3 (1981): 1,363–66. Frances M. Malpezzi and William M. Clements.

Motion Picture Daily, November 17, 1972. MOMA.

Motion Picture Guide 5 (1986): 1,667.

Motion Picture Herald, December 1972. AMPAS.

New Leader, January 22, 1973. NYPL.

New Republic 168 (January 20, 1973): 26+. Stanley Kauffmann. MOMA.

New York, December 18, 1972, 109. Judith Crist. NYPL.

New York Daily News, December 19, 1972, 68. Kathleen Carroll. NYPL.

New Yorker 48 (January 13, 1973): 86–88. Pauline Kael. (Reprinted in Pauline Kael, *Reeling,* New York, Warner Books, 1976.) AMPAS, MOMA.

New York Post, December 19, 1972, 50. Frances Herridge. MOMA, NYPL.

New York Times, December 19, 1972, 52. Vincent Canby. MOMA, NYPL, NYTR.

Observer, March 25, 1973, 34. George Melly. NYPL.

Playboy 20 (February 1973): 28.

Punch, March 28, 1973, 437. Benny Green. NYPL.

Reel Paper, March 14, 1973. Stuart Byron.

La Revue du Cinéma, no. 275 (September 1973): 129–32. F. Chevassu.

La Revue du Cinéma, nos. 288 & 289 (October 1974): 186–87. J. Zimmer.
Rolling Stone, February 15, 1973, 56–57. Jon Landau. MOMA .
Senior Scholastic 102 (February 12, 1973): 18.
Sight & Sound 42, no. 1 (1972–73): 48–49, illus. P. French.
Skoop 8, no. 8 (1973): 2–7, illus. G. Vanderwildt.
Sunday Times (London), March 25, 1973. NYPL.
Telecine 182 (November 1973): 20.
Time 100 (December 25, 1972): 75. NYPL.
Travelling 40 (January–February 1974): 52–54, creds. E. Steiner.
Variety, December 13, 1972, 20. Goff. AMPAS, MOMA, VR.
Vitoux, F. "The Life and Times of Director John Huston." *Positif* 155 (January
   1974): 46–48, creds, illus. (Reprinted in *John Huston, Collection dirigée,* edited
   by Gilles Ciment, 144–46, Dossier Positif Rivages, Paris, Editions Rivages,
   Collection Positif-Rivages, no. 2, 1988.)
Wall Street Journal, December 29, 1972. Jay Gould Bryan. MOMA.
Women's Wear Daily, December 19, 1972, 16. NYPL.

THE LIST OF ADRIAN MESSENGER. 1963. (Director, Actor; Writer, uncredited.)

ARTICLES AND REVIEWS
America 109 (August. 3, 1963): 123.
The American Film Institute Catalog: Feature Films, 1961–1970. New York: R. R.
   Bowker, 1976, 617–18.
BFI/Monthly Film Bulletin 30, no. 354 (July 1963): 95.
Commonweal 78 (June 21, 1963): 354.
Esquire, October 1963. Dwight McDonald. NYPL.
Film Daily 122, no. 104 (May 29, 1963): 5. AMPAS.
Filmfacts 6 (1963): 115, creds.
Films and Filming 9, no. 10 (July 1963): 25–26, creds. Raymond Durgnat.
Films in Review 14, no. 6 (June–July 1963): 364–65, illus. Henry Hart. NYPL.
"The Films of John Huston" [Program notes]. Los Angeles County Museum of Art,
   October 25, 1980.
Hollywood Reporter 175, no. 30 (May 29, 1963): 3. AMPAS.
Kinematograph Weekly 2,903 (May 23, 1963): 19.
Listener 124, no. 3,182 (September 13, 1990): 43.
Los Angeles Times, May 30, 1963. AMPAS.
Magill's Survey of Cinema: Second Series 3 (1981): 1,386–89. Patricia King
   Hanson.
Marill, Alvin H. *Robert Mitchum on the Screen.* South Brunswick, N.J.: A. S.
   Barnes, 1978, 182–84.
Motion Picture Guide 5 (1986): 1,686–87.
Motion Picture Herald 229, no. 11 (May 29, 1963): 817. AMPAS.
New Republic 148 (June 15, 1963): 33. AMPAS.
Newsweek 61 (June 10, 1963): 105. NYPL.
New Yorker 39 (June 8, 1963): 166. Brendan Gill. AMPAS, NYPL.

New York Herald Tribune, May 30, 1963. Judith Crist. NYPL.
New York Mirror, May 30, 1963. J. G. NYPL.
New York Post, August 31, 1963. NYPL.
New York Times, May 30, 1963, 20. NYTR.
Nielsen, Ray. "Ray's Way: Jan Merlin in *The List of Adrian Messenger.*" *Classic Images,* no. 199 (January 1992): 40. Merlin was an uncredited actor who, according to this interview, actually played the roles of some of the famous actors who made cameo appearances.
Richards, Peter. "Huston's Killer Comedy." *Film Comment,* 27, no. 3 (May–June 1991): 66+, illus.
Ringgold, Gene, and Clifford McCarty. *The Films of Frank Sinatra.* Secaucus, N.J.: Citadel Press, 1980, 192–94.
Show, August 1963, 23–24. NYPL.
Sight & Sound 32, no. 3 (Summer 1963): 146–77. Penelope Houston.
Silver Screen 29, no. 1 (October 1963): 10.
Thomas, Tony. *The Films of Kirk Douglas.* Secaucus, N.J.: Citadel Press, 1972, 194–97.
Time 81 (June 14, 1963): 98+. MOMA, NYPL.
Variety, May 29, 1963, 6. Tube. AMPAS, NYPL, VR.
Vermilye, Jerry. *Burt Lancaster: A Pictorial Treasury of His Films.* New York: Falcon Enterprises, 1971, 120–21.
Washington Post, May 31, 1963. Richard Coe. NYPL.
Wilson, John M. "One of Hollywood's Most Celebrated 'Lost Scripts.'" *New York Times,* January 8, 1978. (Reprinted in *The New York Times Encyclopedia of Film, 1977–1979.*)
Yeager, Robert. "Irish Tally-Ho. . . . (On Location for Shooting of Film)." *New York Times,* October 28, 1962, 11, 7. NYPL.

THE LONELY PASSION OF JUDITH HEARNE. 1987. (Director, unrealized project.)

ARTICLES AND REVIEWS
BFI/Monthly Film Bulletin 55, no. 652 (May 1988): 143–44. John Pym.
Blau, Eleanor. "Judith Hearne at Last." *New York Times,* December 25, 1987, C6.
Clarke, J., and L. Alster. "Jack Clayton back on Track." *Films and Filming,* November–December 1988, 9+.
Film (Italy), no. 5 (May–June 1989): 38. L. Leconte.
Film en Televisie, no. 382 (March 1989): 27. Hilde Van Gaelen.
Films in Review 39, no. 4 (April 1988): 236–37.
Gaelen, Hilde Van. "Jack Clayton: Een droom van een kwart eeuw." *Film en Televisie,* no. 394 (March 1990): 38.
Listener 121, no. 3,095 (January 5, 1989): 31. Margaret Walters.
McIlroy, B. "Tackling Aloneness: Jack Clayton's *The Lonely Passion of Judith Hearne.*" *Literature/Film Quarterly* 21, no. 1 (January 1993): 33–37.
Motion Picture Guide Annual Issue, 1988, 168.

New Republic, January 25, 1988. Stanley Kauffmann. MOMA.
New Yorker 63 (December 28, 1987): 92–95. Pauline Kael.
New York Times, December 23, 1987, C15. Janet Maslin. MOMA, NYTR.
New York Times, October 23, 1988, H28.
Skrien, no. 168 (September–October 1989): 28–29.
Time, February 17, 1987. MOMA.
Variety, December 16, 1987, 11. Cart. (T. McCarthy). MOMA, VR.

LOVE AND BULLETS. 1978. (Director, withdrew.)

ARTICLES AND REVIEWS
BFI/Monthly Film Bulletin 46, no. 543 (April 1979): 74, creds. Richard Combs.
Box Office 115 (November 12, 1979): 17, creds. J. K. Loutzenhiser.
Film Bulletin 48 (September 1979), creds. D. Munroe.
Film en Televisie 268 (September 1979): 33–34, creds, stills. Gaston Weemaes.
Film Illustrated 8 (April 1979): 290. D. Castell.
La Revue du Cinéma 343 (October 1979): 112. H. Béhar.
Motion Picture Guide 5 (1986): 1,742–43.
New Yorker 55 (September 24, 1979): 132–33. Donald Barthelme.
New York Times, September 14, 1979, C5, creds. Janet Maslin. NYTR.
Positif 223 (October 1979): 73. H. Niogret.
La Revue du Cinéma 343 (October 1979): 112, creds. H. Baher.
La Revue du Cinéma , no. 24 (1980): 41–42, creds. F. Guerif.
Variety 294, no. 8 (March 28, 1979): 20+. Simo. VR.
Village Voice 24 (September 17, 1979): 50, creds, stills. T. Allen.

LOVESICK. 1983. (Actor.)

ARTICLES AND REVIEWS
*BFI/Monthly Film Bulletin 50, no. 591 (April 1983): 101, creds, stills. Geoff
   Brown.
Box Office 119 (April 1983): 53, creds, stills. J. Summers.
Christian Science Monitor (March 10, 1983): 18. David Sterritt.
Continental Film and Video Review 30, no. 6 (April 1983): 10.
Dawson, L. "'I Was Always Desperate to Be Loved,' Says Dudley Moore Who
   Stars in *Lovesick.*" *Photoplay* 35 (May 1983): 27–29, illus, port, stills.
Film Journal 86 (February 18, 1983): 38–39, creds. J. H. Burns.
Films and Filming 345 (June 1983): 35, stills. D. Shipman.
*Films in Review 34, no. 3 (March 1983): 177+. Kenneth M. Chanko.
Hollywood Reporter 275, no. 32 (February 14, 1983): 3–4.
*Los Angeles Times, February 21, 1983, Calendar, sect. 5, 6. Sheila Benson.
Maclean's 96 (February 28, 1983): 50.
Motion Picture Guide 5 (1986): 1,766.
Motion Picture Product Digest 10, no. 11 (February 23, 1983): 70.
New Republic 188 (March 14, 1983): 24–25. Stanley Kauffmann.
*Newsday, February 18, 1983, sect 2, 6. Alex Keneas.

New Statesman 105 (April 1, 1983): 25–26. John Coleman.

Newsweek 101 (February 21, 1983): 61, stills. David Ansen.

New York, February 21, 1983. David Denby.

New Yorker 59 (March 7, 1983): 128–29. Pauline Kael.

New York Post, February 18, 1983, 45. Archer Winsten.

New York Times, February 18, 1983, C19, creds. Vincent Canby. NYTR.

Penthouse 14 (June 1983): 54, stills. Roger Greenspun.

Photoplay 34 (June 1983): 20, creds, stills. D. Castell.

Screen International 387 (March 26, 1983): 29.

Stills 7 (July–August 1983): 83.

Variety 310 (February 9, 1983): 23, creds. Loyn (R. Loynd). VR.

Village Voice 28 (March 1, 1983): 45, stills. Andrew Sarris.

Women's Wear Daily, February 18, 1983, 11. Howard Kissel.

MACKINTOSH MAN. 1973. (Director.)

ARTICLES AND REVIEWS

After Dark, September 1973. NYPL.

America 129 (August 4, 1973): 76.

BFI/Monthly Film Bulletin 40, no. 479 (December 1973): 252.

Box Office, August 6, 1973. AMPAS.

Casablanca 35 (November 1983): 44–45.

Chaplin 15, no. 8 (1973): 292, illus. K. Freund.

Christian Science Monitor, July 26, 1973, 14. Louise Sweeney. NYPL.

Cinéma (Paris) 188 (June 1974): 145–46, creds, illus. T. Renaud.

Cinématographe, no. 8 (June–July 1974): 4, creds, illus. C. Bechtold.

Cinema TV Today 1,005 (November 3, 1973): 12.

Crawdaddy, November 1973, 85.

Cue, July 30, 1973. W. W. NYPL.

Ecran 25 (May 1974): 71–72, creds, illus. M. Tessier.

Ekran 13, nos. 9 & 10 (1976): 36, illus.

Filmcritica 25, no. 244 (April 1974): 157. G. Turroni.

Filmcritica 25, no. 245 (May 1974): 193–96, creds. G. Frezza.

Films in Review 24, no. 9 (November 1973): 567. W. Avery.

Hollywood Reporter 227, no. 16 (July 23, 1973): 3. AMPAS.

Jeune Cinéma 79 (June 1974): 43–44. C. Benoit.

Kosmorama 20, no. 121 (June 1974): 273, illus.

London Observer, November 11, 1973, 35. NYPL.

Los Angeles Herald Examiner, August 1, 1973. AMPAS.

Los Angeles Times, August 1, 1973, sect. 5, 14. Kevin Thomas. AMPAS.

McKee, Allen. "Huston: Has He Declined or Material?" *New York Times,* December 20, 1972, 17.

Motion Picture Guide 5 (1986): 1,787.

Motion Picture Product Digest, August 8, 1973. NYPL.

Movietone News, no. 27 (November 1973). Robert Cumbow. NYPL.

New Republic 169 (September 1, 1973): 35. Stanley Kauffmann.

New Statesman 86 (November 16, 1973): 747–48. J. Coleman.
Newsweek 82 (August 13, 1973): 94. Charles Michener. AMPAS, NYPL.
New York Daily News, July 21, 1973, 54. Rex Reed. NYPL.
New York Daily News, July 26, 1973, 72. Kathleen Carroll. NYPL.
New Yorker 49 (August 6, 1973): 70–71. Penelope Gilliatt. MOMA, NYPL.
New York Magazine 6 (August 13, 1973): 60+. Chris Chase. NYPL.
New York Post, July 26, 1973. Archer Winsten. NYPL.
New York Times, July 26, 1973, 44. Vincent Canby. AMPAS, MOMA, NYPL, NYTR.
Playboy 20 (November 1973): 48.
PTA Magazine 68 (October 1973): 8.
La Revue du Cinéma 294 (May 1974): 98–99, creds, illus. G. Allombert.
Robinson, David. "The Innocent Bystander." *Sight & Sound* 42, no. 1 (Winter 1972–73): 20–21. NYPL.
Rolling Stone, no. 143 (September 13, 1973): 72–73, illus. J. Landau. AMPAS, MOMA.
Rolling Stone, October 11, 1973, 9. Ralph Gleason.
Segond, Jacques. "D'un manoir l'autre." *Positif* 159 (May 1974): 67–69, creds, illus. (Reprinted in *John Huston, Collection dirigée,* edited by Gilles Ciment, 147–49, Dossier Positif Rivages, Paris, Editions Rivages, Collection Positif-Rivages, no. 2, 1988.)
Séquences, no. 74 (October 1973): 40–41, creds, illus. A. Ruszdowski.
Sight & Sound 43, no. 1 (Winter 1973–74): 52–53, illus. Tom Milne.
Silver, Alain J., and Elizabeth Ward. "Scriptwriter & Director: Interview with Walter Hill." *Movie,* no. 26 (Winter 1978–79): 29–42, bio, creds, filmog, stills.
Time 102 (August 27, 1973): 50+. Richard Schickel. AMPAS, NYPL.
Variety 271 (August 1, 1973): 18, creds. [Murf] A. D. Murphy. VR.
Villager, July 26, 1973, 10. Roger Dooley. NYPL .
Village Voice 18 (October 4, 1973): 69. Michael McKegney. MOMA, NYPL.
Wall Street Journal, August 10, 1973. AMPAS.
Watters, Jim. "John Huston on Kipling, Hemingway and Jack Daniels." *New York Times,* February 15, 1976. (Reprinted in *The New York Times Encyclopedia of Film, 1975–1976.*)
Women's Wear Daily, July 26, 1973, 10. Howard Kissel. NYPL.

THE MADWOMAN OF CHAILLOT. 1969. (Director, replaced.)

ARTICLES AND REVIEWS
America 121 (October 18, 1969): 40–41.
The American Film Institute Catalog: Feature Films, 1961–1970. New York: R. R. Bowker, 1976, 661.
BFI/Monthly Film Bulletin 36, no. 430 (November 1969): 233.
Christian Science Monitor, October 13, 1969, 6. Louise Sweeney.
Commonweal 91 (October 3, 1969): 21–22.
Dickens, Homer. *The Films of Katharine Hepburn.* New York: Citadel Press, 1971, 196–99.

Film Daily 132, no. 38 (February 26, 1968): 3.
Film Daily, June 24, 1969, 11.
Films and Filming 16, no. 3 (December 1969): 40. Margaret Tarratt.
Films in Review 20, no. 8 (October 1969): 514–15. Henry Hart.
Good Housekeeping 169 (October 1969): 76.
Holiday 46 (November 1969): 20.
Hollywood Reporter 199, no. 46 (March 1, 1968): 11, creds.
Hollywood Reporter 206, no. 31 (June 24, 1969): 3.
Life 67 (October 31, 1969): 20.
Kinematograph Weekly 3,220 (June 28, 1969): 5+.
Kinematograph Weekly 3,238 (November 1, 1969): 12.
Motion Picture Guide 5 (1986): 1,800–1.
Motion Picture Herald 239, no. 27 (July 2, 1969): 221.
New Republic 161 (October 25, 1969): 20. Stanley Kauffmann.
Newsweek 74 (October 27, 1969): 125. Paul Zimmerman.
New Yorker 45 (October 18, 1969): 196. Pauline Kael. (Reprinted in Pauline Kael,
     Deeper into Movies, Boston, Little, Brown, 1973, 25–26.)
New York Times, October 13, 1969, 54. Vincent Canby. NYTR.
New York Times, October 24, 1971. Byron Forbes discusses working on *Madwoman*
     after taking over from Huston.
Popular Photography 65 (October 1969): 117.
Reed, Rex. *Big Screen, Little Screen.* New York: Macmillan, 1971, 245–47.
Saturday Review 52 (October 18, 1969): 34.
Shenker, Israel. "Hepburn: The World Has Gone Cuckoo." *New York Times,* April
     28, 1968. On making the film. (Reprinted in *The New York Times Encyclopedia
     of Film, 1962–1964.*)
Simon, John. *Movies into Film.* New York: Dial Press, 1971, 51–52.
Time 94 (October 31, 1969): 91.
Today's Cinema, no. 9,743 (October 31, 1969): 10.
Variety, June 25, 1969, 6. VR.
Village Voice 14, no. 55 (October 30, 1969): 63. Richard McGuinness.
Vogue 154 (October 1, 1969).

THE MAGNIFICENT YANKEE. 1950. (Unrealized project? *See* chapter 14, "Huston on Film and Other Projects.")

ARTICLES AND REVIEWS
BFI/Monthly Film Bulletin 18 (August 1951): 308.
Christian Century 68 (May 16, 1951): 623.
Commonweal 53 (January 26, 1951): 399.
Film Daily, November 15, 1950, 3.
Films in Review 2 (February 1951): 33–35.
Harrison's Reports, November 8, 1950, 182.
Hollywood Reporter, November 15, 1950, 3.
Motion Picture Guide 5 (1986): 1,810.

Motion Picture Herald Product Digest, November 18, 1950, 569–70.
The Nation 172 (February 3, 1951): 114.
New Republic 124 (January 29, 1951): 22.
Newsweek 37 (January 22, 1951): 83.
New Yorker 26 (January 27, 1951): 58.
New York Times, January 19, 1951, 21. NYTR.
Saturday Review 34 (February 10, 1951): 29.
Senior Scholastic 57 (January 10, 1951): 30.
Time 57 (January 8, 1951): 72.
Variety, November 15, 1950. VR.

THE MALTESE FALCON. 1941. (Director, Writer.)

Warner Brothers produced three versions of *The Maltese Falcon:* 1931, 1936 (*Satan Met a Lady*), and the 1941 Huston version. Because of similarities between the 1931 version (directed by Roy Del Ruth) and the Huston version, citations are provided for both.

ARTICLES AND REVIEWS (1931)

The American Film Institute Catalog: Feature Films, 1931–1940. Berkeley: University of California Press, 1993, 1,288. (*See also* p. 1,862: *Satan Met a Lady,* 1936 version).
Druxman, Michael B. *Make It Again, Sam: A Survey of Movie Remakes.* South Brunswick, N.J.: A. S. Barnes, 1975, 114–19.
Everson, William K. *The Detective in Film.* Secaucus, N.J.: Citadel Press, 1972, 39–41.
Film Daily, May 31, 1931, 10.
Hollywood Reporter, April 8, 1931, 3.
Judge 100 (June 20, 1931): 20.
Life 97 (June 26, 1931): 18.
Motion Picture Herald, April 18, 1931, 40.
New Masses 22 (January 12, 1937): 27.
New Yorker 7 (June 6, 1931): 70.
New York Times, May 29, 1931, 26. NYTR.
Outlook and Independent 158 (June 24, 1931): 247.
Parish, James Robert, and Michael R. Pitts. *The Great Gangster Pictures.* Metuchen, N.J.: Scarecrow Press, 1976, 265–67.
Sadoul, George. *Dictionary of Films.* Translated, edited, and updated by Peter Morris. Berkeley: University of California Press, 1972, 206.
Time 17 (June 8, 1931): 30.
Variety, June 2, 1931, 15. VR.

ARTICLES (1941)

Abrahams, Paul P. "On Rereading *The Maltese Falcon.*" *Journal of American Culture* 18, no. 1 (Spring 1995): 97–108.
Abramson, L. H. "Two Birds of a Feather: Hammett's and Huston's *Maltese Falcon.*" *Literature/Film Quarterly* 16, no. 2 (1988): 112–18, biblio, illus.

Anderson, John Robert. "Hidden Fires: The Dimensions of Detection in American Literature and Film." Ph.D. diss, Yale University, New Haven, Connecticut, 1983. (*Dissertation Abstracts International [DAI]* 44 [1984]: 2,808A.)

———. "The World of *The Maltese Falcon.*" *Southwest Review* 73 (Summer 1988): 376–97.

Archer, Eugene. "John Huston—The Hemingway Tradition in *American Film.*" *Film Culture* 19 (1959): 66–101.

———. "Bogart: Man and Superman." *New York Times,* January 3, 1965. (Reprinted in *The New York Times Encyclopedia of Film, 1964–1968.*)

———. "Where Are the Stars of Yesteryear?" *New York Times,* May 30, 1965. (Reprinted in *The New York Times Encyclopedia of Film, 1964–1968.*)

Asheim, Lester, and Sara I. Fenwick, eds. *Differentiating the Media: Proceedings of the 37th Annual Conference of the Graduate Library School, August 5–6, 1974.* Chicago: University of Chicago Press, 1975, 46–55.

Astor, Mary. "Talkies? 'They Can't Last'" *New York Times,* October 15, 1967. (Reprinted in *The New York Times Encyclopedia of Film, 1964–1968.*)

Barbour, Alan G. *Humphrey Bogart.* New York: Pyramid Publications, 1973, 80–84.

Bauer, S. F., et al. "The Detective Film as Myth: *The Maltese Falcon* & Sam Spade." *American Imago* 35, no. 3 (1978): 275–96, biblio.

Behlmer, Rudy. "The Stuff that Dreams Are Made Of." In *American Favorite Movies: Behind the Scenes,* 135–53. New York, Frederick Ungar, 1982. (Reprinted as *Behind the Scenes,* Los Angeles, S. French, 1989. Chapter reprinted in *The Maltese Falcon: John Huston, Director,* edited by William Luhr, New Brunswick, N.J., Rutgers University Press, 1996.)

Beja, Morris. *Film and Literature: An Introduction.* New York: Longman, 1979, 129–36.

Benayoun, Robert. "Le faucon maltais." *Avant-Scene* 233 (October 1, 1979): 28.

Benequist, L. "Function and Index in Huston's *Maltese Falcon.*" *Film Criticism* 6, no. 2 (Winter 1982): 45–50.

Bick, Ilsa J. "The Beam that Fell and Other Crises in *The Maltese Falcon.*" In *The Maltese Falcon: John Huston, Director,* edited by William Luhr, New Brunswick, N.J., Rutgers University Press, 1995.

Blake, Rich. *Screening America: Reflections on Five Classic Films.* Mahwah, N.J.: Paulist Press, 1991.

Bogart, Humphrey. "Bogart Balks at Bogey." *New York Times,* November 28, 1948. (Reprinted in *The New York Times Encyclopedia of Film, 1947–1951.*)

Borde, Raymond, and Etienne Chaumeton. *Panorama du film noir américain.* Paris: Les Editions du Minuit, 1995.

Bordwell, David, and Kristin Thomson. *Film Art: An Introduction.* Reading, Mass.: Addison-Wesley, 1979, 166–70.

Bottigi, W. D. "The Importance of 'C——ing' in Earnest: A Comparison of *The Maltese Falcon* and *Chinatown.*" *Armchair Detective* 14, no. 1 (1981): 86–87, stills.

Brady, Thomas. "The Hollywood Scene." *New York Times,* January 11, 1942. (Reprinted in *The New York Times Encyclopedia of Film, 1941–1946.*)

Cahill, Marie. *The Maltese Falcon.* New York: Smithmark, 1991.

Canby, Vincent. "Freed from Code Shackles, Movies Still Limp Along." *New York Times,* March 9, 1986, 19. Discussion including *Prizzi's Honor* and *The Maltese Falcon.*

Cooper, Stephen. "Flitcraft, Spade, and *The Maltese Falcon:* John Huston's Adaptation." In *Perspectives on John Huston,* edited by Stephen Cooper, 117–32. New York: G.K. Hall, 1994.

———. "Sex/Knowledge/Power in the Detective Genre: Four Detective Films— *The Maltese Falcon, The Big Heat, Chinatown, Angel Heart.*" *Film Quarterly* 42, no. 3 (Spring 1989): 23–31, biblio, illus.

Corliss, Richard. "Have You Read Any Good Movies Lately?" *New York Times,* February 8, 1976. (Reprinted in *The New York Times Encyclopedia of Film, 1975–1976.*)

"Corralled in a Mountain Lair." *New York Times,* September 6, 1942. (Reprinted in *The New York Times Encyclopedia of Film, 1941–1946.*)

Corry, John. "John Huston: Musings on 'Fat City' and Other Pursuits." *New York Times,* August 5, 1972. (Reprinted in *The New York Times Encyclopedia of Film, 1972–1974.*)

Cowie, Peter. *Seventy Years of Cinema.* South Brunswick, N.J.: A. S. Barnes, 1969, 143, illus.

Crowther, Bosley. *The Great Films: Fifty Golden Years of Motion Pictures.* New York: Putnam, 1967, 153–56.

Deming, Barbara. *Running away from Myself.* New York: Grosset, 1969, 144–54.

Domeyne, Pierre. "Le falcon maltais/The Maltese Falcon." In *Dossiers du Cinéma Film II.* Paris: Casterman, 1972. MOMA.

Douin, Jean-Luc. "Hammett, noir d'encore." *Télérama* 2,267 (June 23, 1993): 72–73.

Druxman, Michael B. *Make It Again, Sam: A Survey of Movie Remakes.* South Brunswick, N.J.: A. S. Barnes, 1975, 114–19.

Edelman, Lee. "Plasticity, Paternity, Perversity: Freud's Falcon, Huston's *Freud.*" *American Imago: Studies in Psychoanalysis* 51, no. 1 (Spring 1994): 69–104.

Eder, Richard. "At the Movies." *New York Times,* July 9, 1976. (Reprinted in *The New York Times Encyclopedia of Film, 1975–1976.*)

Everson, William K. *The Detective in Film.* Secaucus, N.J.: Citadel Press, 1972.

——— "Rediscovery." *Films in Review* 31, no. 3 (March 1980): 160–62.

Eyles, Allen. "The Maltese Falcon." *Films and Filming* 11, no. 2 (November 1964): 45–50.

Film Comment 29, no. 5 (September–October 1993): 74. Selection of ten cameos.

Film News 30 (October 1973): 18.

Film Society Review (New York), February 1966, 21–22.

Friedrich, Otto. *City of Nets: A Portrait of Hollywood in the 1940s.* New York: Harper, 1986.

Gale, Steven H. "'The Maltese Falcon': Melodrama or Film Noir?" *Literature/Film Quarterly* 24, no. 2 (April 1996): 145–47.

———. "The Stuff Dreams Are Made Of: How Chance Created a Classic." *Washington Post,* June 14, 1987, H1.

Gardner, Gerald, ed. *The Censorship Papers: Movie Censorship Papers from the Hayes Office, 1934–68.* New York: Dodd, Mead, 1987.

Godfrey, Lionel. "Martinis without Olives." *Films and Filming* 14, no. 7 (April 1968): 10–14.

Gow, Gordon. "Pursuit of the Falcon." *Films and Filming* 20, no. 6 (March 1974): 56–58.

Greenberg, Harvey. "*The Maltese Falcon*—Even Paranoids Have Enemies." In *The Movies on Your Mind,* by Harvey Greenberg, 53–78. New York: Saturday Review Press/E. P. Dutton, 1975. (Reprinted in *Screen Memories: Hollywood Cinema on the Psychoanalytic Couch,* by Harvey Greenberg, 67–92, New York, Columbia University Press, 1993, with an afterword [pp. 91–92].)

Guerif, F. "Le faucon maltais." *Lumière du Cinéma* 2 (March, 1977): 60–65, creds, illus.

Halliwell, Leslie. *Halliwell's Hundred: A Nostalgic Choice of Films from the Golden Age.* New York: Scribners, 1982.

Hammen, Scott. *Film Notes.* Louisville, Ky.: Hamilton Printing Co, 1979.

Harmetz, Aljean. "Huston Protests Coloring of *Falcon.*" *New York Times,* November 14, 1986, C36. NYPL.

Hawkins, Robert F. "'Noah' Huston's Genesis." *New York Times,* February 21, 1965. (Reprinted in *The New York Times Encyclopedia of Film, 1964–1968.*)

Hill, Gladwyn. "John Huston—A Bull in the China Shop." *New York Times,* January 16, 1949. (Reprinted in *The New York Times Encyclopedia of Film, 1947–1951.*)

Hollywood Reporter 292, no. 6 (May 20, 1986): 4. "Film to be Colorized and Syndicated to TV under the Color Classic Network Banner."

Jameson, Richard T. "The Maltese Falcon." *Film Comment* [Midsection] 16, no. 3 (May–June 1980): 27–32.

Johnson, W. "Sound & Image." *Film Quarterly* 43, no. 1 (1989): 24–35, stills.

Kinematograph Weekly 2,388 (April 2, 1953): 33.

Joly, André. "Pour une analyse systematique des modialités non verbales de la communication." In *Communiquer et Traduire/Communication and Translation: Hommages à Jean Dierickx,* edited by G. Debusscher and J. P. van Noppen, 121–41. Bruxelles: Faculté de Philosophe et Lettres, 1985.

Kaminsky, Stuart. "The Maltese Falcon." In *International Dictionary of Films and Filmmakers.* Vol. 1, *Films,* edited by Christopher Lyon, 275–76. Chicago: St. James Press, 1984. (Reprinted in *International Dictionary of Films and Filmmakers,* vol. 1, *Films,* 2d ed., edited by Nicholas Thomas, 540–41, Chicago, St. James Press, 1990; and in 3d ed., edited by Nicolet V. Elert and Aruna Vasudeven, 608–10, Detroit, St. James Press, 1997.)

Krutnik, Frank. *In a Lonely Street: Film Noir, Genre, Masculinity.* London: Routledge, 1991.

Leff, Leonard J. *Film Plots: Scene by Scene Narrative.* Vol. 1. Ann Arbor, Mich.: Perian Press, 1983.

Libby, Bill. *They Didn't Win the Oscars.* Westport, Conn.: Arlington House, 1980.

Listener 107, no. 2,749 (February 25, 1982): 32. Gavin Millar.

Listener 116, no. 2,967 (July 3, 1986): 37.

Lloyd, Ann, ed. *Good Guys & Bad Guys.* New York: Galahad Bks, n.d. (Originally published by Orbis Publications in 1982.)

Luhr, William. "Tracking *The Maltese Falcon:* Classical Hollywood Narration and Sam Spade." In *Close Viewings: An Anthology of New Film Critics,* edited by Peter Lehman. Tallahassee, Fla: State University Press, 1990. (Reprinted in *The Maltese Falcon: John Huston, Director,* edited by William Luhr, Rutgers Films in Print, vol. 22, New Brunswick, N.J., Rutgers University Press, 1996.)

———. "*The Maltese Falcon,* the Detective Genre and Film Noir." In *The Maltese Falcon: John Huston, Director,* edited by William Luhr. Rutgers Films in Print, vol. 22. New Brunswick, N.J.: Rutgers University Press, 1996.

McVay, D. "Revival: 'The Maltese Falcon' and 'Casablanca.'" *Focus on Film,* no. 30 (June 1978): 4–7, creds, stills.

Magill, Frank, ed. *The Novel into Film.* Pasadena, Calif.: Salem Press, 1980, 299–302.

Magill's Survey of Cinema: First Series 3 (1980): 1,049–52. William H. Brown Jr.

Malcolm, Andrew H. "Huston: 'I Want to Keep Right on Going." *New York Times,* December 11, 1979. (Reprinted in *The New York Times Encyclopedia of Film, 1977–1979.*)

"A Man of Unsartorial Splendor: John Huston Makes a Name in Films—but Not for Dress." *New York Times,* January 25, 1942. (Reprinted in *The New York Times Encyclopedia of Film, 1941–1946.*)

Marcus, Fred H. *Film and Literature: Contrasts in Media.* Scranton, Penn.: Chandler Publishing Co, 1971.

Marks, Martin. "Music, Drama, Warner Brothers: The Cases of *Casablanca* and *The Maltese Falcon.*" *Michigan Quarterly Review* 35, no. 1 (Winter 1996): 112–42.

Masterson, Peg. *CinemaTexas Program Notes* 11, no. 1 (September 16, 1976): 59–66, biblio, creds, discussion, filmog.

Maxfield, J. F. "La Belle Dame Sans Merci and the Neurotic Knight: Characterization in *The Maltese Falcon.*" *Literature/Film Quarterly* 17, no. 4 (October 1989): 253–60. (Reprinted in *The Fatal Woman: Sources of Male Anxiety in American Film Noir, 1941–1991,* edited by J. F. Maxfield, 15–25, Madison, N.J., Farleigh Dickinson University Press, 1996.)

Michael, Paul. *Humphrey Bogart: The Man and His Films.* Indianapolis: Bobbs-Merrill, 1965, 112–13.

Michaels, Bo Tao. "Fra Sam Spade til Sigmund Freud: To film af John Huston." *Literature og Samfund* 41 (1986): 102–12.

Miller, Don. "Private Eyes: From Sam Spade to J. J. Gittes." *Focus on Film* 22 (1975): 15–35.

Motion Picture Guide 5 (1986): 1,821–24.

Movietone News, no. 26, October 1973. Robert C. Cumbow. NYPL.

Naremore, James. "Dashiell Hammett and the Poetics of Hard-boiled Fiction." In *Essays on Detective Fiction,* edited by Bernard Benstock. New York, London: Macmillan, 1983.

———. "John Huston and *The Maltese Falcon.*" *Literature/Film Quarterly* 1, no. 3 (July 1973): 239–40. (Reprinted in *Reflections in a Male Eye,* edited by Gaylyn

Studlar and David Desser, 119–35, Washington, D.C., Smithsonian Institution Press, 1993.)

Nason, Richard W. "Huston Hits High with 'Heaven' and 'Geisha.'" *New York Times,* September 28, 1958. (Reprinted in *The New York Times Encyclopedia of Film, 1958–1963.*)

Nolan, William. *Dashiell Hammett: A Casebook.* Santa Barbara, Calif.: McNally and Loftin, 1969.

"Painting the Backdrops." *New York Times,* September 28, 1941. (Reprinted in *The New York Times Encyclopedia of Film, 1941–1946.*)

Palmer, R. Barton. *Hollywood's Dark Cinema: The American Film Noir.* New York: Twayne, 1994.

Parish, James Robert, and Michael R. Pitts. *The Great Detective Pictures.* Metuchen, N.J.: Scarecrow Press, 1990, 309–14.

Pitts, Michael R. *Famous Movie Detectives.* Metuchen, N.J.: Scarecrow Press, 1979.

Ponder, Eleanor Anne. "The American Detective Form in Novels and Film, 1929–1947." Ph.D. diss., University of North Carolina at Chapel Hill, 1980. (*Dissertation Abstracts International* [*DAI*] 40 [1980]: 4,599A–600A.)

Reeves, Jimmie L. *CinemaTexas Program Notes* 21, no. 1 (October 20, 1981): [73]–78, biblio, filmog.

Reisz, Karel. "Substance into Shadow." In *The Cinema,* 188–205. New York: Penguin Books, 1952.

Richardson, Carl. *Autopsy: An Element of Realism in Film Noir.* New York: Scarecrow Press, 1992, 33–70. (Originally Ph.D. diss., Columbia University, New York, 1989.)

Robb, David. "Huston Blasts Colorizing." *Variety,* November 19, 1986, 4.

Roche, Gilbert. "John Huston à la poursuite du *faucon maltais.*" *Libération,* August 4, 1990, 19.

Schatz, Thomas. *Hollywood Genres.* New York: Random House, 1981.

Schmidt, Dana Adams. "Our Movies Leave Germans Hostile." *New York Times,* July 23, 1946. (Reprinted in *The New York Times Encyclopedia of Film, 1941–1946.*)

Schmidt, M. A. "Battling Bogart's Saga." *New York Times,* September 6, 1953. (Reprinted in *The New York Times Encyclopedia of Film, 1952–1957.*)

Schrader, Paul. "Notes on Film Noir." *Film Comment,* Spring 1972, 8–13.

Schumach, Murray. "Hollywood Usage: Experts Analyze Pros and Cons of Time-Tested 'Master' Scene." *New York Times,* August 28, 1960. (Reprinted in *The New York Times Encyclopedia of Film, 1958–1963.*)

———. "Hollywood Joust: Rising Status of Scenarist-Director May Stir Rivalry among Companies." *New York Times,* January 28, 1962A. (Reprinted in *The New York Times Encyclopedia of Film, 1958–1963.*)

Segond, J. "Sur la piste de Dashiell Hammett (les trois versions de 'Faucon Maltais')." *Positif* 171–172 (July–August 1975): 13–18, creds, stills. (Reprinted as "On the Trail of Dashiell Hammett [The Three Versions of *The Maltese Falcon*]." by Jean-Loup Bourget [writing as Jacques Segond] and translated by

Articles and Reviews of Films

Connor Hartnett. In *The Maltese Falcon, John Huston, Director,* edited by William Luhr, New Brunswick, N.J., Rutgers University Press, 1996.)

Selby, Spencer. *Dark City: The Film Noir.* Jefferson, N.C.: McFarland, 1984, 7–12.

Silver, Alain, and Elizabeth Ward, eds. *Film Noir: An Encyclopedic Reference to the American Style.* 3d ed., rev. Woodstock, N.Y.: Overlook Press, 1992, 181–82, analysis, credits, illus, synopsis.

Siniscalco, L. "Il mistero del falco." *Rivista del Cinematografo* 63, no. 4 (April supplement, 1993), creds, stills.

Sinyard, Neil. *Classic Movies.* Salem, N. H.: Salem House, 1985, 158–59.

Sklar, Robert. *Movie-Made America: A Social History of American Movies.* New York: Random House, 1975.

Solomon, Stanley J. *Beyond Formula: American Film Genres.* New York: Harcourt, 1976.

Sperber, A. M., and Eric Lax. *Bogart.* New York: Morrow, 1997.

Spinard, Leonard. "Whodunit First?" *New York Times,* May 9, 1948. (Reprinted in *The New York Times Encyclopedia of Film, 1947–1951.*)

Tailleur, Roger. "Les jumeaux du crime." *Positif* 75 (May 1966): 139. (Reprinted in *John Huston, Collection dirigée,* edited by Gilles Ciment, 68–71, Dossier Positif Rivages, Paris, Editions Rivages, Collection Positif-Rivages, no. 2, 1988.)

Taylor, John Russell. "John Huston and the Figure in the Carpet." *Sight & Sound* 28, no. 38/2 (Spring 1969) : 70–73. MOMA, NYPL.

Telecine, no. 215 (February 1977): 13–14. G. Colpart.

Telotte, J. P. *Voices in the Dark: The Narrative Patterns of Film Noir.* Urbana, Ill.: University of Illinois Press, 1989.

Teréus, R. "Riddarfalken fran Malta." *Filmrutan,* 36, no. 2 (1993): 16–17.

Thomson, David. *Suspects.* New York, Knopf, 1985. "Fictionalized" accounts of the lives of characters in *Chinatown, Beat the Devil, High Sierra, The Killers,* and *The Maltese Falcon.*

Today's Cinema 80, no. 6,725 (March 26, 1953): 10.

Toeplitz, J. "Opowiesc o Sokole Maltanskim." *Iluzjon* 1, no. 45 (January–March 1992): 30–34, illus. Analysis of *The Maltese Falcon* and its historical background.

Tomasulo, Frank P. "The Maltese Phallcon: The Oedipal Trajectory of Classical Hollywood Cinema, Authority and Transgression." In *Literature and Film,* edited by Bonnie Braendlin and Hans Braendlin, 78–87. Gainsville, Fla.: University of Florida, 1996.

Tuska, Jon. *Dark Cinema: American Film Noir in Cultural Perspective.* Westport, Conn.: Greenwood Press, 1984.

Velvet Light Trap, no. 20 (Summer 1983): 2–9.

"Warner Library Brings $21,000,000." *New York Times,* March 2, 1956. (Reprinted in *The New York Times Encyclopedia of Film, 1952–1957.*)

Watters, Jim. "John Huston on Kipling, Hemingway and Jack Daniels." *New York Times* February 15, 1976. (Reprinted in *The New York Times Encyclopedia of Film, 1975–1976.*)

Weiler, A. H. "Random Notes about the Screen." *New York Times,* April 29, 1945. (Reprinted in *The New York Times Encyclopedia of Film, 1941–1946.*)

Wexman, Virginia Wright. "The Transfer from One Medium to Another: *The Maltese Falcon,* from Fiction to Film." *Library Quarterly* 45 (1975): 46–55, biblio.

————. "Kinesics and Film Acting: Humphrey Bogart in *The Maltese Falcon* and *The Big Sleep.*" *Journal of Popular Film & Television* 7, no. 1 (1978): 42–55.

————. *Creating the Couple: Love, Marriage, and Hollywood Performance.* Princeton, N.J.: Princeton University Press, 1993, 25–32.

Whitten, A. P. [Program notes.] Toronto Film Society, October 6, 1969, 3 p.

Wilson, Robert, ed. *The Film Criticism of Otis Ferguson.* Philadelphia: Temple University Press, 1971, 390.

Yost, Elwy. *Magic Moments from the Movies.* Garden City, N.Y.: Doubleday, 1978, 100–1.

Younkin, Stephen D, James Bigwood, and Raymond G. Cabana Jr. *The Films of Peter Lorre.* Secaucus, N.J.: Citadel Press, 1982, 140–44.

Zinman, David. "They Used to Save the Best Line for Last." *New York Times,* July 6, 1975. (Reprinted in *The New York Times Encyclopedia of Film, 1975–1976.*)

REVIEWS (1941)

Baltimore Sun, December 6, 1941. Gilbert Kanour and Donald Kirles. NYPL.

Brooklyn Citizen, October 4, 1941. Edgar Price. NYPL.

Brooklyn Daily Eagle, October 4, 1941.

Casablanca 35 (November 1983): 38–39.

Christian Science Monitor, October 14, 1941. JDB. NYPL.

Christian Science Monitor, July 26, 1983, 18. David Sterritt.

Commonweal 34 (October 17, 1941): 614.

Cue, October 4, 1941. NYPL.

Daily Worker, October 6, 1941. Milton Meltzer. NYPL.

Dallas Morning News, December 21, 1941. John Rosenfield. NYPL.

L'Ecran Français, no. 61 (August 28, 1946): 8. Nino Frank. (Reprinted in English translation by Connor Hartnett in *The Maltese Falcon: John Huston, Director,* edited by William Luhr, New Brunswick, N.J., Rutgers University Press, 1996.)

Film Daily, September 30, 1941, 8.

Harrison's Reports, October 4, 1941, 159.

Hollywood Reporter, September 30, 1941, 3. AMPAS.

Kinematograph Weekly 1,826 (April 16, 1942): 24.

London Times, June 22, 1942, 8.

Motion Picture Daily, September 30, 1941. Edward Greif.

Motion Picture Exhibitor 26, no. 23 (October 15, 1941): 871–72.

Motion Picture Herald Product Digest 145, no. 1 (October 4, 1941): 298.

New Republic 105 (October 20, 1941): 508. Otis Ferguson. (Reprinted in *The Film Criticism of Otis Ferguson,* edited by Robert Wilson, Philadelphia, Temple University Press, 1977; and in *The Maltese Falcon: John Huston, Director,* by William Luhr, New Brunswick, N.J., Rutgers University Press, 1996.)

Newsweek, 18 (October 13, 1941): 66. NYPL.

New York Daily Mirror, October 4, 1941. Lee Mortimer. NYPL.

**New Yorker* 17 (October 4, 1941): 63–64. John Mosher. AMPAS.

New York Herald Tribune, October 4, 1941. Howard Barnes. NYPL.
New York Herald Tribune, October 12, 1941. Howard Barnes.
New York Journal American, October 4, 1941. Rose Pelswick. NYPL.
New York Post, October 4, 1941. Archer Winsten. MOMA, NYPL.
New York Sun, October 4, 1941. Eileen Creelman. NYPL.
New York Times, October 4, 1941, 18. Bosley Crowther. NYTR. (Reprinted in *The New York Times Film Reviews: A One-Volume Selection, 1913–1970,* edited by George Amberg, New York, Arno Press, 1971; and in *The Maltese Falcon: John Huston, Director,* by William Luhr, New Brunswick, N.J., Rutgers University Press, 1996.)
New York Times, October 12, 1941, sect. 9, 5.
New York Times, April 19, 1987, H22. Vincent Canby.
New York World Telegram, October 4, 1941. William Boehnel. NYPL.
**PM,* October 5, 1941, 19. Louise Levitas. AMPAS, NYPL.
Scribner's Commentator 11 (December 1941): 108.
Theatre Arts 25 (December 1941): 886.
Time 38 (October 20, 1941): 100.
Today's Cinema 58, no. 4,709 (April 14, 1942).
University Film Association Journal 27 (1975): 39+. G. Wood, "A New Look at an Old Genre."
Variety, September 30, 1941.
Variety, October 1, 1941. AMPAS, NYPL, VR.

MAN IN THE WILDERNESS. 1971. (Actor.)
ARTICLES AND REVIEWS
BFI/Monthly Film Bulletin 39, no. 458 (March 1972): 54–55.
Cinema (Bucharest) 11, no. 7 (July 1973): 14, illus. J. Tintea.
Cinéma (Paris) 166 (May 1972): 144. M. Grisolia.
Cinema TV Today 9,968 (February 19, 1972): 25.
Ecran 7 (July–August 1972): 71–72, illus. Jean-A. Gili.
Filmfacts 14, no. 23 (1971): 643–66.
Filmrutan 15, no. 1 (1972): 30–31, illus. B. Oijer, "Zach bass-mannen i vildmarken. Ett analysforslag."
Films and Filming 18, no. 7 (April 1972): 50–51. G. Gow.
Hablemos de Cine 8, no. 63 (January–March 1972): 77. Vigil R. Gonzalez.
Hollywood Reporter 215, no. 28 (March 26, 1971): 12, creds.
Hollywood Reporter 218, no. 46 (November 24, 1971): 3.
Jeune Cinéma 63 (May–June 1972): 25–34, illus. C. Benoit, "Richard Sarafian."
New York Times, August 20, 1972. Allen McKee, "So Close to Disaster, But They Just Don't Care." (Reprinted in *The New York Times Encyclopedia of Film, 1972–1974.*)
Motion Picture Guide 5 (1986): 1,843.
New Yorker, December 11, 1971, 36–137. Pauline Kael.
New York Times, November 25, 1971, 53. Howard Thompson. NYTR.

Photoplay 23, no. 1 (January 1972): 22–23.
Positif 139 (June 1972): 45–47, illus. Michel Sineux, "Crepuscule des dieux."
La Revue du Cinéma 262 (June–July 1972): 106. J.-J. Dupuich.
Time, December 6, 1971.
Today's Cinema 9,877 (February 1971): 9, creds.
Variety, November 24, 1971, 16. VR.
Village Voice 16, no. 50 (December 16, 1971): 85. Foster Hirsch. MOMA.

THE MAN WHO WOULD BE KING. 1975. (Director, Writer.)

ARTICLES

Bachmann, Gideon. "En écoutant Huston." *Ecran* 46 (April 1976): 26–28, illus. (French translation of "Huston in Morocco." *Sight & Sound* 44, no. 3 [Summer 1975]: 161–65.) NYPL.

———. "Watching Huston." *Film Comment,* 12, no. 1 (January– February 1976): 21–22, illus.

Beckerman, Jim. "The Man Who Would Be King: On Adapting the Most Audacious Thing in Fiction." In *The English Novel and the Movies,* edited by Michael Klein and Gillian Parker, 180–86. New York: Ungar, 1981.

Benoit, C. "Cinéma-catastrophe? Non: Cinéma d'aventures." *Jeune Cinéma* 109 (March 1978): 21–26.

Bookbinder, Robert. *The Films of the Seventies.* Secaucus, N.J.: Citadel Press, 1982, 134–35.

Boost, C. "Eigenzinnig regisseur die geen slechte film kan maken." *Skoop* 12, no. 5 (May 1976): 5–10, creds, filmog, illus.

"British Gentleman, Michael Caine" [Film notes]. Los Angeles County Museum of Art, June 28, 1984.

Ebert, Roger. "Caine and Connery on Films, Booze, Pubs and Sex." *Chicago Sun-Times,* February 8, 1976, 1–2.

Film Review 25, no. 12 (December 1975): 18–19.

Films and Filming 22, no. 4 (January 1976): 17–19. Portfolio of photos. AMPAS, NYPL.

Focus on Film no. 23 (Winter 1975–1976): 10–12, creds, stills. Allen Eyles.

Gill, Brendan. "The Man Who Would Be Kipling." *Film Comment* 12, no. 1 (January–February 1976): 23+.

Grella, George. "The Colonial Movie and *The Man Who Would Be King.*" *Texas Studies in Literature and Language* 22 (1980): 246–62.

Jameson, Richard T. "The Man Who Would Be King." *Film Comment* [Midsection] 16, no. 3 (May–June 1980): 55–56.

Kozloff, Sarah. "Taking Us Along on *The Man Who Would Be King.*" In *Perspectives on John Huston,* edited by Stephen Cooper, 184–96. New York: G.K. Hall, 1994.

Lehti, S. J. "The Epic Film Music of Maurice Jarre: *The Man Who Would Be King.*" *SCN* 10 (July 1991): 20, illus.

Lindsay, Robert. "Critics of the Movie Business Find Pattern of Financial

Irregularities." *New York Times,* January 29, 1978. (Reprinted in *The New York Times Encyclopedia of Film, 1977–1979.*)

Magill's Survey of Cinema: First Series 3 (1980): 1,063–66. Marie Soule.

Malcolm, Andrew. "Huston: 'I Want to Keep Right on Going." *New York Times,* December 11, 1979. (Reprinted in *The New York Times Encyclopedia of Film, 1977–1979.*)

Mills, Bart. "On the Far Side of the Kyber with Connery and Caine." *Chicago Tribune,* October 5, 1975. (Reprinted in *Newsbank* 60:D10–D12.)

Minetree, Harry. "On Location with John Huston for the Shooting on the *Man Who Would Be King." People,* April 21, 1975, 61–65. NYPL.

Motion Picture Guide 5 (1986): 1,859–60.

New Yorker 68 (February 1, 1993): 27. "Royal Flush."

Photoplay 26, no. 5 (May 1975): 44–45.

Photoplay 27, no. 1 (January 1976): 14–15.

Ronan, Margaret. *The Man Who Would Be King. A Study Guide for Classroom Discussion and Analysis of a Major Motion Picture,* n.d., 4 p. AMPAS.

Segond, Jacques. "Le fils d'Alexandre." *Positif* 181 (May 1976): 60–64, creds, stills. (Reprinted in *John Huston, Collection dirigée,* edited by Gilles Ciment, 150–54, Dossier Positif Rivages, Paris, Editions Rivages, Collection Positif-Rivages, no. 2, 1988.)

Spiegal, A. "John Huston as Survivor of the Second Generation." *Salagamundi,* no. 35 (Fall 1976): 141–52.

Stars & Cinema (1975): 32–33.

Tessier, M. "Sur John Huston et 'L'homme qui voulut être roi.'" *Ecran* 46 (April 1976): 22–26.

Thomas, Tony. *The Great Adventure Films.* Secaucus, N.J.: Citadel Press, 1976.

Tuohy, William. "Three Musketeers in Morocco." *Los Angeles Times,* March 2, 1975, 1+.

Watters, Jim. "John Huston on Kipling, Hemingway & Jack Daniels." *New York Times,* February 15, 1976, sect. 2, 1+, bio, interv, port. (Reprinted in *The New York Times Encyclopedia of Film, 1975–1976.*) AMPAS, MOMA, NYPL.

Wolf, William. "Can Huston Cap Career with Another Great Film?" *Cue,* November 22, 1975, 25.

REVIEWS

Amis du Film et de la Télévision, nos. 242 & 243 (July–August 1976): 35. J. Leirens.

***BFI/Monthly Film Bulletin* 43, no. 505 (February 1976): 32, creds. Tom Milne.

Casablanca 35 (November 1983): 45–46.

***Christian Science Monitor,* January 14, 1976, 22. David Sterritt. NYPL.

Cine al Dia 22 (November 1977): 34–35, creds, illus. M. San Andres.

Cinéaste 7, no. 2 (Spring 1976): 52. NYPL.

Cineforum 16, no. 155 (June 1976): 397–98. P. Mereghetti.

Cinéma (Paris) 109 (May 1976): 118–19, creds. C-.M. Cluny.

Cinema Papers, March–April 1976, 366, creds, stills. J. Murphy.

Cinema TV Today 1,011 (January 11, 1975): 9, creds.

***Commonweal,* January 30, 1976, 83–84. Colin L. Westerbeck Jr.
Film & TV, no. 230–231 (July–August 1976): 31. L. Mees.
Film Bulletin 45 (January 1976): 24–25. D. Bartholomew.
Film Comment 12, no. 1 (January–February 1976): 23+.
***Film Information,* January 1976. Charles M. Austin.
Film Monthly 2 (January 1991): 29. P. Cliff. Sound track review .
Films and Filming 22, no. 5 (February 1976): 36, creds. G. Gow. AMPAS, NYPL.
Films Illustrated 5, no. 52 (December 1975): 139–42.
Films Illustrated 5, no. 53 (January 1976): 162.
***Films in Review* 27 (February 1976): 122. Michael Buckley.
Hablemos de Cinema 13, no. 69 (1977–1978): 56, stills. Miguel Marias.
Hartford Courant, January 24, 1976. Malcolm Johnson, "John Huston's *Man Who Would Be King.*" (Reprinted in *Newsbank* 76 [8]:C4.)
Hollywood Reporter 239, no. 18 (December 12, 1975): 3+. AMPAS.
Independent Film Journal 77 (December 24, 1975): 35–36.
***Jump Cut* 12, no. 13 (Winter 1977): 17–18, stills. Robert L. Greene.
Kosmorama 22, no. 129 (Spring 1976): 82, stills. P. Schepelern.
Listener 117, no. 3,022 (July 30, 1987): 26–27, illus.
***London Times,* December 19, 1975. David Robinson.
***London Times,* December 21, 1975. Dilys Powell.
Los Angeles 21 (January 1976): 112+.
***Los Angeles Times,* December 18, 1975, sect. 4, 1. Charles Champlin.
Mademoiselle 82 (March 1976): 38. P. Ranier.
Motion Picture Herald Product Digest, December 31, 1975, 58.
Movietone News 48 (February 1976): 38–39, creds, stills. R. C. Cumbow.
Movietone News 49 (April 18, 1976): 41–42, creds. R. Hermann.
New Republic 174 (January 31, 1976): 24–25. Stanley Kauffmann. (Reprinted in *Before My Eyes: Film Criticism and Comment,* by Stanley Kauffmann, 193–95, New York, Harper, 1980.) NYPL.
New Statesman 90 (December 19, 1975): 799–800. J. Coleman.
***Newsweek* 86 (December 29, 1975): 50–51. Charles Michener. AMPAS.
New Times 6 (January 23, 1976): 56+.
New York Daily News, December 18, 1975. Kathleen Carroll. NYPL.
New Yorker 51 (January 5, 1976): 52–55. Pauline Kael. (Reprinted in *When the Lights Go Down,* by Pauline Kael, 107–12, New York, Holt, Rinehart and Winston, 1980; and in *For Keeps,* by Pauline Kael, New York, E. P. Dutton, 1994.) MOMA, NYPL.
***New York Magazine* 9 (January 12, 1976): 58–59. John Simon. AMPAS, NYPL.
***New York Post,* December 18, 1975, 46. Frank Rich. NYPL.
New York Times, December 18, 1975, 62. Vincent Canby. AMPAS, MOMA, NYPL, NYTR.
Observer (London), December 21, 1975, 22. Philip French. NYPL.
Penthouse 7 (March 1976): 48–49, stills. Roger Greenspun. NYPL.
Philadelphia Magazine 67 (February 1976): 48.
Photoplay 26, no. 12 (December 1975): 14–15.

Playboy 23 (March 1976): 24.
La Revue du Cinéma, no. 306 (May 1976): 74–77, creds, stills. H. Béhar.
La Revue du Cinéma, nos. 309 & 310 (October 1976): 172, creds. G. Dagneau.
***Saturday Review 3 (January 24, 1976): 49–50. Judith Crist. AMPAS, MOMA, NYPL.
Screen International 16 (December 20, 1975): 21.
Senior Scholastic 108 (February 24, 1976): 42.
Séquences 21, no. 84 (April 1976): 42–43, creds, stills. R.-C. Berube.
****Sight & Sound* 45, no. 2 (Spring 1976): 122–23, stills. Geoff Brown.
Soho Weekly, December 18, 1975, 32. Roger Greenspun. NYPL.
Time 106 (December 29, 1975): 38, illus. Jay Cocks. MOMA, NYPL.
Variety 281, no. 5 (December 10, 1975): 26, creds. R. B. Frederick. MOMA, NYPL, VR.
***Village Voice 21 (January 12, 1976): 99–100, illus. Andrew Sarris. AMPAS, NYPL.
****Women's Wear Daily,* December 16, 1975, 28. Howard Kessel. NYPL.

MARILYN: THE UNTOLD STORY. 1980. TV Production. (Fictional account with John Ireland as Huston.)

REVIEWS
BFI/Monthly Film Bulletin 48, no. 573 (October 1981): 203, creds. Jenkins.
Films and Filming 326 (November 1981): 40, creds, illus. D. Shipman.
New York Times, September 26, 1980, C33. J. J. O'Connor, "TV Weekend: *Marilyn Story,* Electronic Evangelists."

THE MIGHTY BARNUM. 1934. (Writer, uncredited.)

ARTICLES AND REVIEWS
The American Film Institute Catalog: Feature Films, 1931–1940. Berkeley: University of Califronia Press, 1993, 1,381–82.
DeMille, Cecil B. "It's Tough, but the Show Must Go On." *New York Times,* December 3, 1950. (Reprinted in *The New York Times Encyclopedia of Film, 1947–1951.*)
Film Daily, November 23, 1934, 10.
Film Weekly 13, no. 325 (January 4, 1935): 30.
"Fox Film to Merge with 20th Century." *New York Times,* May 28, 1935. (Reprinted in *The New York Times Encyclopedia of Film, 1929–1936.*)
Harrison's Reports, December 29, 1934, 206.
Hollywood Reporter, November 22, 1934, 2.
Literary Digest 119 (January 15, 1935): 31.
Motion Picture Guide 5 (1986): 1950.
Motion Picture Herald, December 1, 1934, 38.
The Nation 140 (January 23, 1935): 112.
Newsweek, December 22, 1934, 24.

New York Times, December 24, 1934, 17. NYTR.
Nugent, Frank. "The Tailor-Made Actor." *New York Times,* December 23, 1934. (Reprinted in *The New York Times Encyclopedia of Film, 1929–1936.*)
Picturegoer 5, no. 225 (September 14, 1935): 26, creds, synopsis.
Time 24 (December 31, 1934): 15.
Variety, December 25, 1934. VR.

MINOR MIRACLE (Young Giants). 1983. (Actor.)

ARTICLES AND REVIEWS
BFI/Monthly Film Bulletin 50, no. 598 (November 1983): 313–14, creds, stills.
City Limits 106 (October 14, 1983): 26.
Motion Picture Guide 9 (1987): 3,975. (Under *Young Giants.*)
Photoplay 34 (December 1983): 18, creds, stills. D. Quinlan.
Screen International 396 (May 28, 1983): 20.
Screen International 417 (October 22, 1983): 19.
Time Out 686 (October 13, 1983): 41.

THE MISFITS. 1961. (Director; Writer, uncredited.)

ARTICLES
Alpert, Hollis. "Arthur Miller: Screenwriter." *Saturday Review* (February 4, 1961): 27+. AMPAS, NYPL.
The American Film Institute Catalog: Feature Films, 1961–1970. New York: R. R. Bowker, 1976, 711
Bachman, Gideon. "Eli Wallach on *The Misfits.*" Film 29 (Summer 1961): 13–15.
Barbaro, Nick. *CinemaTexas Program Notes* 10, no. 4 (May 4, 1976), biblio, creds, filmog.
Barnes, Brooks. *CinemaTexas Program Notes* 26, no. 4 (March 11, 1968): [45]–52, biblio, filmog.
Barsness, John. "A Question of Standards." *Film Quarterly* 21, no. 1 (Fall 1967): 32–37.
Bergan, Ronald. *Sports in the Movies.* London: Proteus Books, 1982.
Brill, Lesley. "*The Misfits* and the Idea of John Huston's Films." *Proteus* 7, no. 2 (Fall 1990): 9–17. (Reprinted in *Perspectives on John Huston,* edited by Stephen Cooper, 145–60, New York, G.K. Hall, 1994.)
Cawlti, John. *The Six-Gun Mystique.* Bowling Green, Ohio: Bowling Green State University Popular Press, 1971.
Cieutat, Michel. "Les faux désaxés de la nouvelle frontière." *Positif* 260 (October 1982): 67–69, creds, stills. (Reprinted in *John Huston, Collection dirigée,* edited by Gilles Ciment, 117–19, Dossier Positif Rivages, Paris, Editions Rivages, Collection Positif-Rivages, no. 2, 1988.)
Cinéma (Paris) 422 (December 30, 1987–January 6, 1988): 8, illus. "Miller + Huston = *Les Misfits.*"
Conway, Michael, and Mark Ricci. *The Films of Marilyn Monroe.* Secaucus, N.J.: Citadel Press, 1972, 153–58.

Copeland, Roger. "When Films 'Quote' Films, They Create a New Mythology." *New York Times,* September 25, 1977. (Reprinted in *The New York Times Encyclopedia of Film, 1977–1979.*)

Cowie, Peter. *Seventy Years of Cinema.* South Brunswick, N.J.: A. S. Barnes, 1969, 242, illus.

Crowther, Bosley. "Last of a Legend: Clark Gable Bows out in *The Misfits." New York Times,* February 5, 1961, sect. 2, 1.

———. "Setting Stars." *New York Times,* May 21, 1961. (Reprinted in *The New York Times Encyclopedia of Film, 1958–1963.*)

Essoe, Gabe. *The Films of Clark Gable.* New York: Citadel Press, 1970, 250–53.

"Film Buff Series 'A': 1981–82." Programme 7. Toronto Film Society, January 24, 1982. (Notes excerpted from *BFI/Monthly Film Bulletin.*)

"The Films of John Huston" [Program notes]. Los Angeles County Museum of Art, November 8, 1980.

Garfield, Brian. *Western Films: A Complete Guide.* New York: Rawson Associates, 1982.

Gaven, Jack. "Miller Impressed with *Misfits,* Initial Film Effort." *New York Morning Telegraph,* January 26, 1961.

Goode, Charles. "Famous Pair and a Finale." *Life* 50 (January 13, 1961): 53–54B. NYPL.

Goode, James. *The Story of* The Misfits. Indianapolis: Bobbs-Merrill, 1963. (Reprinted as *The Making of* The Misfits, New York, Limelight Editions, 1986. Reviews of book: *Film Culture* 34 [Fall 1964]: 65. Andrew Sarris; and *New York Times Book Review,* July 20, 1986, 28, Patricia O'Connor.)

———. "The Making of *The Misfits." Nevada,* November–December 1986, 113–17.

Hamblett, Charles. "Profile of Huston at Time of Making Film." *Men Only,* March 1960, 32–35. AMPAS.

Hardy, Phil. *The Western: The Film Encyclopedia.* New York: Morrow, 1983.

Illustrated London News 243 (September 14, 1963): 396, illus.

Jameson, Richard T. "The Misfits." *Film Comment* [Midsection] 16, no. 3 (May–June 1980): 46–49.

Jeune Cinéma 187 (April–May 1988): 35–37, illus. M. Borgese.

Kaminsky, Stuart M. *American Film Genres.* 2d ed. Chicago, Ohio: Nelson-Hall, 1985.

Kass, Judith M. *The Films of Montgomery Clift.* New York: Citadel Press, 1979.

Lippe, Richard. "Montgomery Clift: A Critical Disturbance." *Cine Action,* no. 17 (Summer 1989): 36–42, illus, port, stills.

———. "The Misfits." In *International Dictionary of Films and Filmmakers.* Vol. 1, *Films,* edited by Nicolet V. Elert and Aruna Vasudeven, 654–56. Detroit: St. James Press, 1997.

Listener 116, no. 2,976 (September 4, 1986): 37.

Listener 120, no. 3,086 (October 27, 1988): 41.

MacDonald, Dwight. *On Movies.* New York: Da Capo Press, 1981, 285–86.

McDonald, Thomas. "Staking 'The Misfits,' Production Unit Treks to 'Biggest

Little City' for Colorful Canvas." *New York Times,* August 21, 1960. (Reprinted in *The New York Times Encyclopedia of Film, 1958–1963.*)

McIntyre, A. T. "Making *The Misfits.*" *Esquire* 55 (March 1961): 74–81.

Magill's Survey of Cinema: First Series 3 (1980): 1,117–20. Pat H. Broeske.

Malcolm, Andrew. "Huston: 'I Want to Keep Right on Going." *New York Times,* December 11, 1979. (Reprinted in *The New York Times Encyclopedia of Film, 1977–1979.*)

Mathison, R. "Who's a Misfit?" *Newsweek* 56 (September 12, 1960): 102–3.

Meyer, William R. *The Making of the Great Westerns.* New York: Arlington House, 1979.

Miller, Arthur. *Timebends: A Life.* New York: Grove Press, 1987.

———. "Monroe & Miller: Magnificent Misfits—Shooting John Huston's Picture Was a Nightmare." *Washington Post,* December 13, 1987, M1.

———. "Leben mit Marilyn." *Film und Fernsehen* 18, no. 3 (1990): 28–32, illus, stills.

Motion Picture Guide 5 (1986): 1,969.

Murray, Edward. *Cinematic Imagination: Writers & the Motion Pictures.* New York: F. Ungar, 1972.

O'Grady, Gerald. "The Dance of *The Misfits:* A Movie Mobile." *The Journal of Aesthetic Educations* 5, no. 2 (April 1971): 75–89.

Oms, Marcel. "Marilyn, Miller, Huston et l'amour." *Positif* 41 (September 1961): 53–58. (Reprinted in *John Huston, Collection dirigée,* edited by Gilles Ciment, 112–16, Dossier Positif Rivages, Paris, Editions Rivages, Collection Positif-Rivages, no. 2, 1988.)

Press, David P. "The Misfits: The Western Gunned Down." *Studies in the Humanities* 8, no. 1 (1980): 41–44.

Ross, Don. "Arthur Miller Writes His First Film." *New York Herald Tribune,* July 17, 1960, sect. 4, 1+. NYPL.

San Francisco Chronicle, September 28, 1960. AMPAS.

San Francisco Chronicle, September 29, 1960. AMPAS.

Sarris, Andrew. "Fallen Idols." *Film Culture* 28 (Spring 1963): 30. MOMA.

Schumach, Murray. "Hollywood Usage: Experts Analyze the Pros and Cons of Time-Tested 'Master' Scene." *New York Times,* August 28, 1960. (Reprinted in *The New York Times Encyclopedia of Film, 1958–1963.*)

———. "Hollywood Flop." *New York Times,* August 19, 1962. (Reprinted in *The New York Times Encyclopedia of Film, 1958–1963.*)

"Show Business: Marilyn and the Mustangs on Location." *Time,* August 8, 1960, 57. MOMA, NYPL.

Signoret, Simone. "Marilyn without Makeup." *New York Times,* May 7, 1978. (Reprinted in *The New York Times Encyclopedia of Film, 1977–1979.*)

The Theatre, February 1961. NYPL.

Thomas, Bob. "Huston tells King Gable's Last Act in *Misfits.*" *New York World-Telegram Sun,* January 15, 1961, 12.

Variety, June 27, 1956, 6.

Variety, February 10, 1960, 30. Hy Hollinger. Preproduction information. AMPAS.

Weatherby, W. J. "Conversation at St. Clerans between Arthur Miller and John Huston." *The Guardian,* February 25, 1960. AMPAS.

———. "Making *The Misfits:* Author—back to Life, Director—back to People, Actress—away from Hollywood." *The Guardian,* November 3, 1960, 8. MOMA.

———. *"The Misfits:* Epic or Requiem." *Saturday Review,* February 4, 1961, 26–27. Study of John Huston's film in production. AMPAS, NYPL.

———. "Conversation with Miller. Article II: *The Misfits.*" *New York Post,* April 20, 1976, 33. NYPL.

Whitcomb, Jon. "Marilyn Monroe—The Sex Symbol Versus the Good Wife." *Cosmopolitan,* December 1960, 52+.

Wood, Thomas. "Arthur Miller Shifts Target." *New York Herald Tribune,* January 29, 1961. On location of the film. NYPL.

REVIEWS

America 104 (February 18, 1961): 676+.
BFI/Monthly Film Bulletin 28, no. 330 (July 1961): 92–93.
Casablanca 35 (November 1983): 42–43.
Christian Century 78 (April 5, 1961): 424–45.
Christian Science Monitor 88, no. 165 (July 22, 1996): 11. David Sterritt.
Commentary 31 (May 1961): 433–36.
Commonweal 73 (February 17, 1961): 532.
Cue, February 4, 1961. NYPL.
Daily Cinema 8,466 (June 2, 1961): 6.
Film Daily 118, no. 21 (February 1, 1961): 6. Mandel Herbstman. AMPAS.
Filmfacts 4 (1961): 11, creds.
Film Quarterly 14, no. 3 (Spring 1961): 51–53, illus. Lawrence Grauman Jr.
Films and Filming 7, no. 9 (June 1961): 21, creds, illus. C. A. Lejeune.
Films in Review 12, no. 2 (February 1961): 102–3, illus. Henry Hart.
Harrison's Reports, February 4, 1961, 18.
Hollywood Reporter 163, no. 42 (February 1, 1961): 3. AMPAS.
Jeune Cinéma 187 (April–May 1988): 35–37. M. Borgese.
Kinematograph Weekly 2,800 (June 1, 1961): 21.
Listener 116, no. 2,967 (July 3, 1986): 37, illus.
Los Angeles Times, February 2, 1961. AMPAS.
McCall's 88 (April 1961): 6+.
Modern Photographer 25 (May 1961): 24–25.
Motion Picture Herald 222, no. 3 (February 4, 1961): 4. AMPAS.
The Nation 192 (February 18,1961): 154–55.
National Review 10 (May 20, 1961): 321.
New Republic 144 (February 20, 1961): 26+. Stanley Kauffmann. AMPAS.
Newsweek 57 (February 6, 1961): 84. AMPAS, MOMA.
New York Daily News, February 2, 1961. Kate Cameron. AMPAS.
New Yorker 36 (February 4, 1961): 86+. Roger Angell. AMPAS, NYPL.
New York Herald Tribune, February 5, 1961. Paul V. Beckley. AMPAS, NYPL.
New York Journal American, February 2, 1961. AMPAS.
New York Mirror, February 2, 1961. Justin Gilbert. AMPAS.
New York Post, February 2, 1961. Archer Winsten. AMPAS, NYPL.

New York Times, February 2, 1961, 24. Bosley Crowther. AMPAS, NYPL, NYTR.
New York World Telegram Sun, February 2 1961. Alton Cook. AMPAS.
Reporter 24 (March 21, 1961): 46–47.
Sight & Sound 30, no. 3 (Summer 1961): 142–44, illus. Arlene Croce.
Time 77 (February 3, 1961): 68. AMPAS.
Variety, February 1, 1961. AMPAS, VR.
Village Voice, February 9, 1961, 6. Jonas Mekas.

MR. CORBETT'S GHOST. 1986. (Actor.)

ARTICLES AND REVIEWS

Hollywood Reporter, May 14, 1986. Regarding financing of the film. AMPAS.
Screen International, no. 538 (March 8, 1986): 4. Background on making of film. AMPAS.
Screen International, no. 540 (March 22, 1986): 21.
Screen International, March 29, 1986, 17, creds. AMPAS.
Screen International, no. 544 (April 19, 1986): 73. On making of the film. AMPAS.
Screen International, no. 546 (May 3, 1986): 4. John Paul Getty Jr.
Screen International, June 7, 1986. Background on making of the film. AMPAS.

MR. NORTH. 1988. (Executive Producer, Writer.)

ARTICLES AND REVIEWS

Backstage, August 28, 1987, 57.
BFI/Monthly Film Bulletin 56, no. 661 (February 1989): 54–55, creds, stills. R. Combs.
Box Office 124 (October 1988): bet 89 and 100 [R90], creds. T. Matthews.
Cineforum 28, no. 280 (December 1988): 93–94. B. Fornara.
City Limits 385 (February 16, 1989): 21.
Film & Kino 8 (1988): 12–13, stills. Y. Finslo, "Forfriskende *Mr. North.*"
Film Journal 91 (January 1988): 80+, interv, port, stills. C. Gagne, "A Family Heritage Continues with Danny Huston's *Mr. North.*"
Film Journal 91 (August 1988): 27, creds. D. Noah.
Films and Filming 412 (February 1989): 35–36, creds, stills. M. Sutton.
Hollywood Reporter 298, no. 13 (July 28, 1987): 14, creds.
Hollywood Reporter 303, no. 16 (July 1988): 3+.
Interview 18 (March 1988): 128–30, illus. K. P. Buckley, "Movies: All about Betty."
Levende Billeder 5 (March 1989): 47, creds, stills. H. Jul-Hansen.
Listener 121, no. 3,102 (February 23, 1989): 42.
Motion Picture Guide. Annual Issue, 1989, 112.
New York Times, August 6, 1987, C17. Andrew L. Yarrow.
New York Times, July 22, 1988, C8, creds, stills. Vincent Canby. MOMA, NYTR.
New York Times, January 1, 1989, H28. Stewart Kellerman.
Philadelphia Inquirer, August 3, 1988, 3C. Desmond Ryan.

Photoplay 40 (March 1989): 20, creds, stills. M. Bilbow.
Positif 340 (June 1989): 78. P. Pernod.
La Revue du Cinéma 447 (March 1989): 30. D. Roth-Bettoni.
Screen International 608 (July 11, 1987): 2.
Screen International 612 (August 8, 1987): 8. Mitchum replaces John Huston.
Screen International 666 (August 20, 1988): 37.
Sight & Sound 58, no. 2 (Spring 1989): 136, stills. A. Stanbrook.
Time Out 965 (February 15, 1989): 13. Comments from Danny Huston.
Time Out 965 (February 15, 1989): 35.
Variety 327 (July 8, 1987): 3+. "Danny Huston to Direct Dad in Theophilus Pic."
Variety 328 (August 5, 1987): 4+. D. Kimmel, "Ailing Huston Exits Role in *Mr. North;* Mitchum Steps In."
Variety 331 (July 20, 1988): 12, creds. Cart (T. McCarthy). MOMA, VR.
Village Voice 33 (July 26, 1988): 66. Katherine Dieckmann. MOMA.
Wall Street Journal, July 14, 1988, 24. Julie Salamon.
(*Note*: Huston was to act, but illness prevented him from doing so, and Robert Mitchum took over the role.)

MR. SKEFFINGTON. 1944. (Writer, uncredited.)

ARTICLES AND REVIEWS

Agee, James. *Agee on Film: Reviews and Comments.* New York: McDowell, Obolensky, 1958. (Reprint—as Vol. 1, New York:Grosset & Dunlap, 1967, 95–96.)
Commonweal 40 (June 9, 1944): 184–85.
Film Daily, May 31, 1944, 10.
Harrison's Reports, May 27, 1944, 87.
Hollywood Reporter, May 26, 1944, 3.
London Times, August 9, 1945, 6.
Magill's Survey of Cinema: First Series 3 (1980): 1,125–27. Cheryl Karnes.
Motion Picture Exhibitor 32, no. 1 (May 17, 1944): sect. 2, 1, 518.
Motion Picture Guide 5 (1986): 1,990.
Motion Picture Herald Product Digest, May 27, 1944, 1,909.
The Nation 158 (June 3, 1944): 661.
New Republic 111 (June 31, 1944): 133.
Newsweek 23 (June 5, 1944): 90.
New Yorker 20 (May 27, 1944): 61.
New York Times, May 26, 1944, 23. NYTR.
New York Times, June 19, 1988, H30. Richard F. Shepard.
Nugent, Frank S. "How Long Should a Movie Be?" *New York Times,* February 18, 1945. (Reprinted in *The New York Times Encyclopedia of Film, 1941–1946.*)
Ringgold, Gene. *Bette Davis: Her Films and Career.* Secaucus, N.J.: Citadel Press, 1985, 126–28.
Time 43 (June 5, 1944): 94+.
Variety, May 31, 1944, 20. VR.

MOBY DICK. 1956. (Director, Writer.)

ARTICLES

Alpert, Hollis. "Quest of Captain Ahab." *Saturday Review* 39 (June 9, 1956): 28+.

Archer, Eugene. "Small People in a Big World: A Monograph on John Huston, pt. 2: A Touch of Melville." *Films and Filming* 6, no. 1 (October 1959): 9+.

Atkins, Thomas. "An Interview with Ray Bradbury." *Sight & Sound* 43, no. 2 (Spring 1974). (Reprinted in *The Classic American Novel and the Movies,* edited by Gerald Peary and Roger Shatzkin, 42–51, New York, Unger, 1977.)

Baar, Stephen Ronald. "Novel into Film: The Adaptation of American Renaissance Symbolic Fiction." Ph.D. diss., University of Utah, 1973. (*Dissertation Abstracts International [DAI]* 34 [1974]: 4,186A.)

Barron, Arthur. "The Intensification of Reality." *Film Comment* 6 (Spring 1970): 20–23.

Berger, Meyer. "About New York." *New York Times,* October 22, 1956. (Reprinted in *The New York Times Encyclopedia of Film, 1952–1957.*)

Bradbury, Ray. *Green Shadows, White Whale.* New York: Knopf, 1992. Fictionalized account of writing the script.

Brady, Frank. *Citizen Welles: A Biography of Orson Welles.* New York: Scribners, 1989.

Cinema Nuovo 8, no. 89 (September 1956): 114, interv.

Colliers 135 (March 4, 1955): 70–73. Includes photo essay. Evelyn Harvey. NYPL.

Corry, John. "John Huston: Musings on 'Fat City' and Other Pursuits." *New York Times,* August 5, 1972. (Reprinted in *The New York Times Encyclopedia of Film, 1972–1974.*)

Crowther, Bosley. "Huston's *Moby Dick:* New Film Version of Melville's Novel Betokens Great Screen Artistry." *New York Times,* July 8, 1956, sect. 2, 1. AMPAS, NYPL.

De Laurot, Edouard. "An Encounter with John Huston, with Emphasis on *Moby Dick.*" *Film Culture* 2, no. 8 (1956): 1–4.

———. "John Huston on *Moby Dick.*" *Film* 10 (November–December 1956): 11–13.

Druxman, Michael B. *Make It Again, Sam: A Survey of Movie Remakes.* South Brunswick, N.J.: A. S. Barnes, 1975, 12–14.

Fieschi, J. "La religion du monstre." *Cinématographe* 18 (April–May 1976): 1,013, stills.

"Filming in Colour: The Hunting of Moby Dick. Location Shooting Abroad 19th Century Whaling Boat." *Illustrated London News* 225, no. 597 (October 9, 1954).

Films and Filming 1, no. 11 (August 1955): 4. Bill Leader.

Films and Filming 3, no. 2 (November 1956): 23, illus. Paul Rotha.

French, Brandon. "Lost at Sea." In *The Classic American Novel and the Movies,* edited by Gerald Peary and Roger Shatzgin, 52–61. New York: Ungar, 1977.

Godley, John, Lord Kilbracken. "In the Wake of the Whale, John Huston." *Vogue* 126 (November 15, 1955): 118+. AMPAS, MOMA.

————. *Living Like a Lord.* Boston: Houghton, 1956.

Griggs, John. *The Films of Gregory Peck.* Secaucus, N.J.: Citadel Press, 1984, 139–43.

Hamblett, Charles. "On Launching 'Moby Dick' in Eire: Huston Directs Latest Adaptation of Famed Novel by Melville." *New York Times,* August 15, 1954. (Reprinted in *The New York Times Encyclopedia of Film, 1952–1957*). AMPAS.

————. "'Moby Dick' Landed, or Some Footnotes to a Tough Film Stint." *New York Times,* March 6, 1955. (Reprinted in *The New York Times Encyclopedia of Film, 1952–1957.*)

Harmetz, Aljean. "The 15th Man Who Was Asked to Direct 'MASH' (and Did) Makes a Peculiar Western." *New York Times,* June 20, 1971. (Reprinted in *The New York Times Encyclopedia of Film, 1967–1971.*)

Hawkins, Robert F. "'Noah' Huston's Genesis." *New York Times,* February 21, 1965. (Reprinted in *The New York Times Encyclopedia of Film, 1964–1968.*)

Hill, Derek. "*Moby Dick* Sets New Style in Color Photography: On Oswald Morris' Cinematography." *American Cinematographer* 37, no. 9 (September 1956): 534+.

Hill, Gladwyn. "John Huston—A Bull in the China Shop." *New York Times,* January 16, 1949. (Reprinted in *The New York Times Encyclopedia of Film, 1947–1951.*)

Hillway, Tyrus. "Hollywood Hunts the Whale." *Colorado Quarterly* 5 (1957): 298–305.

Huston, John. "Harpoons Away: The Director of *Moby Dick* Finds the Great Tradition of New England Whalemen Still Alive Among the Courageous Men of Madeira." *Sports Illustrated,* June 6, 1955, 66+.

"Interview with Frank Buckingham, Director of Still Photography on Moby Dick." *Kodak View,* Summer 1955, 6+.

Jameson, Richard T. "Moby Dick." *Film Comment* [Midsection] 16, no. 3 (May–June 1980): 45–46.

Jamison, Barbara B. "Bonanza in Beards." *New York Times,* October 24, 1954. (Reprinted in *The New York Times Encyclopedia of Film, 1952–1957.*)

Kavanagh, Patrick. "Some Thoughts on 'Moby Dick.'" *Irish Times,* February 20, 1954, 5. AMPAS.

Knight, Arthur. "The Director." *Saturday Review* 39 (June 9, 1956): 29–30.

Kunert, Arnold R. "Ray Bradbury on Hitchcock, Huston and Other Magic of the Screen." *Take One* 3, no. 11 (September 1973): 15–23, filmog, illus, interv.

Kurnitz, Harry. "Captain Huston Takes *Moby Dick.*" *Holiday* 20 (July 1956): 73+. AMPAS, NYPL.

Kyrou, Ado. "La grande découverte." *Positif* 20 (January 1957): 21–24. (Reprinted in *John Huston, Collection dirigée,* edited by Gilles Ciment, 104–6, Dossier Positif Rivages, Paris, Editions Rivages, Collection Positif-Rivages, no. 2, 1988.)

Leyda, Jay. "Modesty and Pretention in Two New Films." *Film Culture* 2, no. 4 (1956): 3+, illus.

MacCann, Richard Dyer. "Peck Discusses 'Moby Dick' Role." *Christian Science Monitor,* September 13, 1955.

Magill's Survey of Cinema: Second Series 4 (1986): 1,623–25. Larry S. Rudner.

Malcolm, Andrew H. "Huston: 'I Want to Keep Right on Going." *New York Times,* December 11, 1979. (Reprinted in *The New York Times Encyclopedia of Film, 1977–1979.*)

Melvin, Edwin. "John Huston Meets Press after Filming *Moby Dick." Christian Science Monitor,* March 20, 1956. AMPAS, NYPL.

Miles, Bernard. "Moby Dick Almost Killed Me." *Daily Mail,* September 18, 1956, 4. Recollections on the making of the film.

———. "And Inside the Whale Sat a Man from the Plumbers' Union." *Daily Mail,* September 19, 1956, 4.

———. "Throw 'Em in the Sea Said Huston." *Daily Mail,* September 20, 1956, 4.

———. "Moby Dick Hits Back . . . and I Leave Two Teeth in the Ocean." *Daily Mail,* September 21, 1956, 4. AMPAS.

"*Moby Dick:* A Preview of John Huston's Film on Location in Yonghal, Ireland." *New York Times Magazine,* August 8, 1954, 42–43.

"Moby Dick Is Missing: A Life-sized Model of the Giant Whale Is Lost in North Atlantic." *Life* 37 (November 22, 1954): 52–53.

Moore, Betty. "New Bedford in Ireland for Moby Dick. Huston Films Melville Story with Peck as Captain Ahab." *Christian Science Monitor,* August 10, 1954, 4+. NYPL.

Motion Picture Guide 5 (1986): 1,999+.

"Movie Special Report: Director John Huston, a Remarkable Man and the Movies in '56." *Newsweek,* January 9, 1956, 67–70. Cover story with Huston picture on front cover, on the making of *Moby Dick.*

"The New Captain Ahab: Gregory Peck in John Huston's *Moby Dick." Films and Filming* 1, no. 5 (February 1955).

New York Times, information on *Moby Dick* (1930 version)*:* September 7, 1930; July 28, 1931; April 29, 1934; April 21, 1940. (Reprinted in *The New York Times Encyclopedia of Film, 1929–1936.*)

New York Times, August 1, 1954, sect. 1, 5. Filming notes. AMPAS.

New York Times, November 21, 1954, sect. 2, 5. Comment on filming. AMPAS.

New York Times, July 15, 1956, sect. 2, 1. Comment. AMPAS.

New York Times Magazine, May 13, 1956, 30–31. Seymour Peck, photo essay. NYPL.

"*Pequod* Portrait." *New York Times,* December 5, 1954. (Reprinted in *The New York Times Encyclopedia of Film, 1952–1957.*)

Pryor, Thomas M. "Doleful Hollywood." *New York Times,* June 3, 1956. (Reprinted in *The New York Times Encyclopedia of Film, 1952–1957.*)

Rotha, Paul. *Rotha on the Film: A Selection of Writings on the Cinema.* Fair Lawn, N.J.: Essential Books, 1958.

St. Pierre, Brian. "John Huston: As He Was, Is, and Probably Always Will Be." *New York Times,* September 25, 1966. (Reprinted in *The New York Times Encyclopedia of Film, 1964–1968.*)

Saturday Review 39 (June 9, 1956): 28+. Cover story, with Huston's picture on front cover, in two parts: Hollis Alpert, "Quest of Captain Ahab" (p. 28), and Arthur Knight, "The Director" (pp. 29–30). AMPAS, NYPL.

Scheuer, Philip. "A Town Called Hollywood: Huston Has Some Comments on Production of 'Moby Dick.'" *Los Angeles Times,* November 27, 1955, 2. AMPAS.

———. "Another Chase in 'Moby' but Exalted." *Los Angeles Times,* June 10, 1956, part 4, 1+.

Stern, Milton. "The Whale and the Minnow: Moby Dick and the Movies." *College English,* 17 (1956): 470–73.

Stone, Edward. "Ahab Gets the Girl, or Herman Melville Goes to the Movies." *Literature/Film Quarterly* 3 (1975): 172–81.

Tailleur, Roger. "Les chasses du John Huston." *Positif* 20 (January 1957): 11–20. (Reprinted in *John Huston, Collection dirigée,* edited by Gilles Ciment, 95–103, Dossier Positif Rivages, Paris, Editions Rivages, Collection Positif-Rivages, no. 2, 1988.)

Thirard, P.-L. "Bavardages autour de quelques journaux." *Positif* 20 (January 1957): 32–36.

Vasey, Margaret. "Perspectives on Narration: When Work Becomes Action in *Moby Dick.*" In *Varieties of Filmic Expressions, Proceedings,* edited by Douglas Radcliff, 142–47. From International Film Conference of Kent State University, Seventh, 1989. Umstead, Kent, Ohio: Romance Languages Department, Kent State University, 1989.

Watters, Jim. "John Huston on Kipling, Hemingway and Jack Daniels." *New York Times,* February 15, 1976. (Reprinted in *The New York Times Encyclopedia of Film, 1975–1976.*)

Zinsser, William K. "Huston 'Moby Dick': Critic's Account of Gala World Premiere Features 'Gam,' Ghost and Gregory Peck." *New York Herald Tribune,* July 1, 1956, 1+. AMPAS.

REVIEWS

America 95 (July 14, 1956): 372.

BFI/Monthly Film Bulletin 23, no. 275 (December 1956): 150.

Bianco e Nero 18, no. 2 (February 1957).

Bianco e Nero 47, no. 2 (April–June 1986): 45.

Box Office, June 30, 1956, 16. Ivan Spear. AMPAS.

Cahiers du Cinéma 12, no. 67 (January 1957). Eric Rohmer. (Reprinted in English translation *The Taste for Beauty,* edited by Eric Rohmer, 105–11, Cambridge, U.K., Cambridge University Press, 1989.)

Casablanca 35 (November 1983): 40–41.

Catholic World 183 (June 1956): 221.

Celluloide 26, nos. 324 & 325 (September 1981): 16. F. Duarte.

Cinema Nuovo 6, no. 98 (January 15, 1957): 24. Guido Aristoarco.

Commonweal 62 (June 10, 1955): 256.

Commonweal 64 (June 29, 1956): 324.

Cosmopolitan 140 (June 1956): 18.

Cue, July 7, 1956, 17. Jesse Zunser. NYPL.

Film Daily 1,09, no. 124 (June 27, 1956): 6.

Filmkritik 17, no. 7 (July 1973): 334.
Films and Filming 2, no. 9 (June 1956): 20–21.
Films and Filming 3, no. 2 (November 1956). Paul Rotha. (Reprinted in *Rotha on the Film: A Selection of Writings about the Cinema,* 189–91, Fair Lawn, N.J., Essential Books, 1958.)
Films in Review 7, no. 7 (August–September 1956): 338–41, illus. Henry Hart.
Harrison's Reports, June 30, 1956, 102.
Hollywood Reporter 140, no. 19 (June 27, 1956): 3. Mérigeau
La Revue du Cinéma 205 (1967): 109.
Kinematograph Weekly 2,569 (November 8, 1956): 17.
Life 40 (June 25, 1956): 50–53, illus. NYPL.
Listener 115, no. 2,953 (March 27, 1986): 37, illus. Richard Combs.
London Times, November 8, 1956.
Look, July 24, 1956, 86+. NYPL.
Los Angeles Examiner, July 3, 1956, sect. 4, 8. Ruth Waterbury. AMPAS.
Los Angeles Herald & Express, July 3, 1956, A14. Harrison Carroll. AMPAS.
Los Angeles Times, July 3, 1956, part 1, 12. Edwin Schallert. AMPAS.
Manchester Guardian, November 10, 1956, 5. AMPAS.
Manchester Guardian Weekly, November 15, 1956, 14. NYPL.
Motion Picture Herald 203, no. 13 (June 30, 1956): 20.
The Nation 183 (July 14, 1956): 46.
National Parent-Teacher 51 (September 1956): 40.
Newsweek 48 (July 2, 1956): 72.
New Yorker 32 (July 14, 1956): 83–84. John McCarten. AMPAS, NYPL.
New York Herald Tribune, July 7, 1956, 8. William Zinsser. NYPL.
New York Times, July 5, 1956, 18. Bosley Crowther. AMPAS, NYPL, NYTR.
New York Times, June 24, 1984, sect. 2, 24. Janet Maslin.
Observer (London), November 11, 1956. C. A. Lejeune. AMPAS, NYPL.
Quarterly of Film, Radio and TV 11, no. 2 (Winter 1956): 167–70. Andrew Mayer.
Reporter 15 (August 9, 1956): 47–48.
La Revue du Cinéma, no. 438 (May 1988): 36. M. Tessier.
Scholastic 68 (May 10, 1956): 37.
Sight & Sound 26, no. 3 (Winter 1956–57): 151–52. Tony Richardson.
Sunday Times, November 11, 1956, 15. Dilys Powell. AMPAS.
Time, July 9, 1956, 78. AMPAS.
Today's Cinema 87, no. 7,647 (November 8, 1956): 5.
Variety, June 27, 1956, 6. Land. AMPAS, VR.
Village Voice 1, no. 46 (October 17, 1956): 6. William Murray.

MOMO. 1986. (Actor.)

ARTICLES AND REVIEWS
Cineforum 26, no. 260 (December 1986): 66–67. A. Crespi.
Cinema d'Oggi 19, no. 11 (June 26, 1985): 2. Note.
EPD Film 3, no. 8 (August 1986): 32, creds, illus. Marli Feldross.

Film Bulletin 28, no. 4 (1986): 34–35, creds, stills. J. Horni.
Film-Echo/Filmwoche, October 19, 1985, 7.
Film-Echo/Filmwoche, August 1, 1986, 8.
Film Français 2,070 (January 3, 1986): 8.
Foreign Sales, Italian Movie Trade 11, nos. 7 & 8 (July–August 1985): 10.
Foreign Sales, Italian Movie Trade 11, no. 9 (September 1985): 14.
Foreign Sales, Italian Movie Trade 11, nos. 10 & 11 (October–November 1985): 48.
Kino: Filme der Bundesrepublik 2 (1986): 10, bio, creds, filmog, port, stills.
Kino: German Film 23 (Summer 1986): 14–15, creds. G. Sedlag, "*Momo:* The Saga of Michael Ende II."
Levende Billeder 3 (September 1, 1987): 26–27, stills. S. Vintergerg.
Medien und Erziehung 30, no. 6 (1986): 357–61, biblio, creds, stills. W. Schwartz.
Screen International 511 (August 24, 1985): 67.
Screen International 527 (December 14, 1985): 23.
Screen International 529 (January 4, 1986): 22–23. "John Huston Enjoys a Holiday from Responsibility on *Momo.*" AMPAS.
Segnocinema 7, no. 26 (January 1987): 74–75, creds, stills. L. Neri.
Variety 326, no. 8 (March 18, 1987): 18, creds. Binn. VR.

THE MOST ENDANGERED SPECIES . . . GEORGE ADAMSON. 1982. TV documentary. (Narrator.)

REVIEW
Christian Science Monitor, February 1, 1982, 17. Arthur Unger.

MOULIN ROUGE. 1953. (Director, Writer.)

ARTICLES
Bernstein, Barbara. "The Films of John Huston" [Program notes]. Los Angeles County Museum of Art, October 31, 1980.
Brady, Thomas F. "Toulouse-Lautrec Sits for a Film Portrait, or a Sketch of John Huston's Work in Progress on the Artist's Biography." *New York Times,* July 27, 1952. (Reprinted in *The New York Times Encyclopedia of Film, 1952–1957.*)
Castello, Giulio Cesare. "Troppi 'Leoni' al Lido." *Cinéma* (Milan) 6, no. 116 (August 31, 1953).
Champlin, Charles. "Films Huston Would Like to Remake." *Los Angeles Times,* October 30, 1969.
Chassler, S. "Great Imitation: Designs for *Moulin Rouge.*" *Colliers* 131 (February 21, 1953): 30–31. Short biography of Marcel Vertes, who helped design sets and costumes for *Moulin Rouge.*
Considine, Shaun. "The Men Who Work as the Directors' Eyes." *New York Times,* April 8, 1979. (Reprinted in *The New York Times Encyclopedia of Film, 1977–1979.*)
Corry, John. "John Huston: Musings on 'Fat City' and Other Pursuits." *New York*

Times, August 5, 1972. (Reprinted in *The New York Times Encyclopedia of Film, 1972–1974.*)

Crowther, Bosley. "Feast or Famine." *New York Times,* March 1, 1953. (Reprinted in *The New York Times Encyclopedia of Film, 1952–1957.*)

————. "The Three-Dimensional Riddle." *New York Times,* March 29, 1953. (Reprinted in *The New York Times Encyclopedia of Film, 1952–1957.*)

Doniol-Valcroze, J. "Une stile de couleur." *Cahiers du Cinéma* 6, no. 31 (January 1954).

Dunant, C. "Visions of Paris." *Sight & Sound* 60, no. 1 (Winter 1990–91): 42–47, illus. Reflections on four films—*French Can Can, Moulin Rouge, Madame de...,* and *Gigi*—set in Paris in the period of la belle epoque.

"Film Buff Series, 1983–1984" [Program notes]. Toronto Film Society, September 26, 1983. MOMA.

"Fox Houses on Coast Cancel 'Limelight' under the Threat of Picketing by Legion." *New York Times,* January 16, 1953. (Reprinted in *The New York Times Encyclopedia of Film, 1952–1957.*)

Gabor, Zsa Zsa, and Gerold Frank. *Zsa Zsa Gabor: My Story—Written for Me by Gerold Frank.* Cleveland: World, 1960.

Garbicz, Adam, and Jack Klinowski. *Cinema: The Magic Vehicle—A Guide to Its Achievement. Journey Two: The Fifties.* New York: Schocken, 1983, c. 1975–79.

Guernsey, Otis L, Jr. "Technicolor Comes of Age: *Moulin Rouge* Proves that the Camera Can Reproduce Extraordinary Tones." *New York Herald Tribune,* February 22, 1953. NYPL.

Hawkins, Robert F. "Now Farewell to Arms in Italy." *New York Times,* May 12, 1957. (Reprinted in *The New York Times Encyclopedia of Film, 1952–1957.*)

————. "'Noah' Huston's Genesis." *New York Times,* February 21, 1965. (Reprinted in *The New York Times Encyclopedia of Film, 1964–1968.*)

Hine, A. "Paris in the 90's: *Moulin Rouge* on Location." *Holiday* 13 (April 1953): 26–27+, interv.

Huston, John. "*Moulin Rouge:* An Appreciation of Toulouse-Lautrec." *Esquire,* December 1952, 103+. NYPL.

Institut des Hautes Etudes Cinématographiques. *Fiche Filmographique,* no 102, n.d. 5 p.

Joseph, Robert. "Unusual Story behind *Moulin Rouge.*" *New York Herald Tribune,* December 28, 1952, 3. NYPL.

Lawson, John Howard. *Film in the Battle of Ideas.* New York: Masses & Mainstream, 1953.

Mage, David A. "The Way John Huston Works Accounts in Large Measure for the Integrity of His Pictures." *Films in Review* 3, no. 8 (October 1952): 394–98. Second assistant director on *Moulin Rouge* recounts the Huston technique. NYPL.

Magill's Survey of Cinema: First Series 3 (1980): 1,154–58. Tanita C. Kelly.

Motion Picture Guide 5 (1986): 2,035–36.

New York Times, August 31, 1952, sect. 6, 12–13. Photo essay.

New York Times, January 4, 1953, sect. 2, 5. Comment on American Legion attack on José Ferrer and John Huston on alleged Communist links.

New York Times, February 15, 1953, sect. 2, 1. NYPL.

Pryor, Thomas M. "Hollywood Debate." *New York Times,* November 16, 1952. (Reprinted in *The New York Times Encyclopedia of Film, 1952–1957.*)

St. Pierre, Brian. "John Huston: As He Was, Is, and Probably Always Will Be." *New York Times,* September 25, 1966. (Reprinted in *The New York Times Encyclopedia of Film, 1964–1968.*)

Sadoul, George. *Dictionary of Films.* Translated, edited, and updated by Peter Morris. Berkeley: University of California Press, 1972, 229.

Thompson, Howard. "Gielgud on Cassius." *New York Times,* November 16, 1952. (Reprinted in *The New York Times Encyclopedia of Film, 1952–1957.*)

Truscott, Lucian K, IV. "Hollywood's Wall Street Connection." *New York Times,* February 26, 1978A. (Reprinted in *The New York Times Encyclopedia of Film, 1977–1979.*)

Tyler, Parker. "Toulouse-Ferrer." *Theatre Arts* 37 (March 1953): 84–85. AMPAS, MOMA.

Watts, Stephen. "Reports on Britain's Varied Movie Fronts." *New York Times,* January 24, 1960. (Reprinted in *The New York Times Encyclopedia of Film, 1958–1963.*)

Weiler, A. H. "On the Local Screen Scene." *New York Times,* January 25, 1953. (Reprinted in *The New York Times Encyclopedia of Film, 1952–1957.*)

Wexman, Virginia Wright. "Mastery through Masterpieces: American Culture, the Male Body, and Huston's *Moulin Rouge.*" In *Reflections in a Male Eye,* edited by Gaylyn Studlar and David Desser, 157–75. Washington, D.C.: Smithsonian Institution Press, 1993. (Reprinted in *Star Texts: Images and Performance in Film and Television,* edited by Jeremy G. Butler, Detroit, Wayne State University Press, 1991.)

White, Mimi. "An Extra-Body of Reference: History in Cinematic Narrative." Ph.D. diss., University of Iowa, Iowa City, Iowa, 1981. Moulin Rouge discussed.

REVIEWS

American Photographer 47 (May 1953): 4.

BFI/Monthly Film Bulletin 20, no. 231 (April 1953): 48.

Catholic World 176 (March 1953): 459–60.

Christian Century 70 (April 22, 1953): 495.

Cinema (Bucharest) 13, no. 2 (February 1975): 12, illus. D. Comsa.

Commonweal 57 (February 13, 1953): 473–74.

**Cue,* February 14, 1953, 17. Jesse Zunser.

Film Daily, 102, no. 121 (December 24, 1952): 8.

Films in Review 4, no. 3 (March 1953): 141.

Films in Review 4, no. 3 (March 1953): 142. Henry Hart.

Films in Review 4, no. 3 (March 1953): 142–48, illus. B. G. Marple.

Harrison's Reports, December 27, 1952, 206.

Hollywood Reporter, December 24, 1952, 3. AMPAS.

Illustrated London News 222 (April 4, 1953): 540.
Life 34 (January 19, 1953): 63–68, illus. NYPL.
Motion Picture Herald Product Digest 189, no. 13 (December 27, 1952): 1,661.
The Nation 176 (February 28, 1953): 193–94.
National Parent-Teacher 47 (April 1953): 40.
New Statesman & Nation 45 (March 21, 1953): 339. AMPAS.
Newsweek 41 (February 23, 1953): 96. AMPAS.
New Yorker 29 (February 21, 1953): 65. AMPAS.
New York Herald Tribune, February 11, 1953, 24. Otis Guernsey Jr. NYPL.
New York Times, February 11, 1953, 33. Bosley Crowther. NYPL, NYTR.
New York Times 139 (December 3, 1989): H34.
Picturegoer 25, no. 925 (January 24, 1953): 13.
Punch, December 27, 1972, 963. Benny Green. NYPL.
La Revue du Cinéma, nos. 320 & 321 (October 1977): 184–85. G. Dagneau.
Saturday Review 36 (February 14, 1953): 46. AMPAS.
Sight & Sound 22, no. 4 (April–June 1953): 194–95. Gavin Lambert.
Spectator 207 (March 13, 1953): 560.
The Tattler, March 25, 1953, 560.
Theatre Arts 37 (March 1953): 84–85.
Time, January 5, 1953, 61.
Today's Cinema 79, no. 6,540 (July 1952): 34.
Today's Cinema 80, no. 6,697 (February 1953): 3.
Today's Cinema 80, no. 6,714 (March 11, 1953): 15.
Variety, December 24, 1952, 6. AMPAS, VR.

MOVIOLA: THIS YEAR'S BLONDE. 1980. TV Production. (Fictional account with William Franfather as Huston.)

ARTICLES AND REVIEWS
American Cinematographer 61 (November 1980): 1,138–39, illus, interv, port, stills.
Variety, June 4, 1980, 58. Bok.
Wolcott, J. "Medium Cool: I Need a Vacation." *Village Voice* 25 (June 2, 1980): 50, stills.

MURDERS IN THE RUE MORGUE. 1932. (Writer.)

ARTICLES AND REVIEWS
The American Film Institute Catalog: Feature Films, 1931–1940. Berkeley: University of California Press, 1993, 1,447.
Bioscope 91, no. 1,333 (April 20, 1932): 16.
Bojarski, Richard. *The Films of Bela Lugosi.* Secaucus, N.J.: Citadel Press, 1977, 68–73.
"A Chat with Laemmle Jr." *New York Times,* April 3, 1932. (Reprinted in *The New York Times Encyclopedia of Film, 1929–1936.*)
Film Daily, February 14, 1932, 10.

"Film Plays and Titles." *New York Times,* February 21, 1932. (Reprinted in *The New York Times Encyclopedia of Film, 1929–1936.*)
"Frankenstein Finished." *New York Times,* October 11, 1931. (Reprinted in *The New York Times Encyclopedia of Film, 1929–1936.*)
Harrison's Reports, February 20, 1932, 30.
Hollywood Reporter, January 6, 1932, 3.
Hollywood Spectator 12, no. 12 (March 1932): 7+.
Manchester, William. "How the Movies Chased the Blues away in the Last Depression." *New York Times,* March 16, 1975. (Reprinted in *The New York Times Encyclopedia of Film, 1975–1976.*)
Motion Picture Guide 5 (1986): 2,058.
Motion Picture Herald, February 20, 1932, 34+.
New Yorker 8 (February 20, 1932): 62.
New York Times, February 11, 1932, 16. NYTR.
Picturegoer 2, no. 67 (September 3, 1932): 20.
Picture-Play Magazine 36, no. 3 (May 1932): 48+.
Scarlet Street 19 (Summer 1995): 33–34. Sean Farrell.
Taves, Brian. "Universal's Horror Tradition." *American Cinematographer* 68, no. 4 (April 1987): 36–48. Article on early horror films produced by Universal, focusing on the work of cameraman Karl Freund and writer/director Robert Florey.
Variety, February 16, 1932, 24. VR.
Video Watchdog 29 (1995): 6063. Tim Lucas.
"Who's Who This Week in Pictures." *New York Times,* October 30, 1932. (Reprinted in *The New York Times Encyclopedia of Film, 1929–1936.*)

MYRA BRECKINRIDGE. 1970. (Actor.)

ARTICLES AND REVIEWS
The American Film Institute Catalog: Feature Films, 1961–1970. New York: R. R. Bowker, 749–50.
BFI/Monthly Film Bulletin 38, no. 446 (March 1971): 54.
BFI/Monthly Film Bulletin 38, no. 448 (May 1971): 110.
Boylan, Jane. "So Now There's a New Sexy Rexy." *New York Times,* November 23, 1969. (Reprinted in *The New York Times Encyclopedia of Film, 1967–1971.*)
Burke, Tom. "Mae West Is Coming Back, Fellas." *New York Times,* July 25, 1976. (Reprinted in *The New York Times Encyclopedia of Film, 1975–1976.*)
Canby, Vincent. "Getting beyond Myra and the Valley of Junk." *New York Times,* July 5, 1970, sect. 2, 1.
Cinema e Cinema 11, nos. 40 & 41 (July–December 1984): 37–39.
Entertainment World 1, no. 1 (October 3, 1969): 14–18.
Film Bulletin 39, no. 7 (April 6, 1970): 9+.
Film Bulletin 39, no. 12 (July 6, 1970): 9+.
Film Quarterly 24, no. 2 (Winter 1970–71): 61–62.
Films and Filming 17, no. 5 (February 1971): 26–27, illus. Mike Sarne.
Films and Filming 17, no. 7 (April 1971): 59. Michael Armstrong.

Films in Review 21, no. 7 (August–September 1970): 442–43, illus. Gwenneth Britt.

Haber, Joyce. "Shell Shock on the 'Myra' Set—and It's Not a War Film." *Los Angeles Times,* October 19, 1989, Calendar.

Harmetz, Aljean. "Oh, Those Beautiful Dolls!" *New York Times,* December 21, 1969. (Reprinted in *The New York Times Encyclopedia of Film, 1967–1971.*)

Hollywood Reporter 208, no. 12 (October 1969): 11, creds.

Hollywood Reporter 211, no. 36 (June 24, 1970): 3.

Huston, John. "John Huston's Analysis of *Myra Breckinridge.*" St. Clerans [Ireland], September 3, 1969, 20 p. Unpublished. In the UCLA Twentieth Century-Fox Script Archives.

Kinematograph Weekly 3,303 (January 1971): 10–11.

Motion Picture Daily, June 25, 1970. Nick Yami.

Motion Picture Herald 240, no. 23 (July 15, 1970): 480. MOMA.

New Republic, July 18, 1970, 27. Stanley Kauffmann.

Newsweek, July 6, 1970. Joseph Morgenstern.

New York, July 13, 1970, 54. Judith Crist.

New York Times, June 25, 1970, 1. Howard Thomson. NYTR.

New York Times, December 3, 1989, H34.

Phillips, McCandlish. "U.S. Filmmakers De-emphasizing Sex." *New York Times,* April 20, 1971. (Reprinted in *The New York Times Encyclopedia of Film, 1967–1971.*)

Premiere 6 (November 1970): 56–59.

Saturday Review, July 11, 1970, 40. Hollis Alpert.

Take One 2, no. 7 (1969): 21. Bruce Pittman.

Time, July 6, 1970, 70.

Today's Cinema 9,876 (January 29, 1971): 8.

Trillin, Calvin. "Through the Muck with *Myra.*" *Life,* March 6, 1970, 50–52.

Variety, June 24, 1970, 17. VR.

Village Voice 15, no. 27 (July 2, 1970): 1+. Barbara Long.

Village Voice 15, no. 27 (July 2, 1970): 51. Richard McGuinness.

NAGANA. 1933. (Writer, uncredited.)

ARTICLES AND REVIEWS

The American Film Institute Catalog: Feature Films, 1931–1940. Berkeley: University of California Press, 1993, 1,478.

Harrison's Reports, February 25, 1933, 30.

Motion Picture Guide 6 (1986): 2,099.

New York Times, February 16, 1933, 23. NYTR.

Variety, February 21, 1933. VR.

NATIONAL GEOGRAPHIC SPECIAL: FLIGHT OF THE WHOOPING CRANE. 1984. TV Documentary. (Narrator).

REVIEWS

Christian Science Monitor, April 3, 1984, 28. Arthur Unger.

New York Times, April 4, 1984, C25. John Corry.

THE NIGHT OF THE IGUANA. 1964. (Director, Writer.)

ARTICLES

Alius, John. "Drama of *Iguana* Is Only in Spirit." *New York Journal-American,* November 3, 1963.

The American Film Institute Catalog: Feature Films, 1961–1970. New York: R. R. Bowker, 1976, 768.

Archer, Eugene. "Richard Burton: Belated Baccalaureate for a Brooding Welshman." *New York Times,* June 28, 1964. (Reprinted in *The New York Times Encyclopedia of Film, 1964–1968.*)

Bart, Peter. "Picturing Painting and Passion." *New York Times,* September 27, 1964. (Reprinted in *The New York Times Encyclopedia of Film, 1964–1968.*)

Borde, Raymond. "Les visages du hasard, de l'aventure et du désespoir." *Positif,* no. 64, (September 1964). (Reprinted in *John Huston, Collection dirigée,* edited by Gilles Ciment, 123–26, Dossier Positif Rivages, Paris, Editions Rivages, Collection Positif-Rivages, no. 2, 1988.)

Canby, Vincent. "Stark Is Basking in 'Funny Girl' Sun." *New York Times,* September 19, 1968. (Reprinted in *The New York Times Encyclopedia of Film, 1967–1971.*)

———. "Whatever Became of Richard Burton?" *New York Times,* June 13, 1971. (Reprinted in *The New York Times Encyclopedia of Film, 1969–1971.*)

Crist, Judith. "Plain Talk & Fancy Sex." *New York Herald Tribune,* July 12, 1964, 15.

Daily Express, October 14, 1963. On location. Peter Evans.

Daily Express, October 16, 1963. On location. Peter Evans.

Daily Express, October 17, 1963. On location. Peter Evans.

Daily Express, October 18, 1963. On location. Peter Evans.

Daily Express, November 17, 1963. On location. Peter Evans.

Evans, Peter. "Tennessee Wants to Unsweeten Ava: Fights Happy Ending for Night World." *New York Telegram & Sun,* October 24, 1963, 12. On location. NYPL.

Greenspan, Lou. "Hollywood vs. O'Hara—Sexpots Calling the Kettle Black." *Los Angeles Times,* November 1, 1964. (*See below* O'Hara, John.)

Kennedy, Paul. "John Huston's *Iguana.*" *New York Times,* December 1, 1963, X5. (Reprinted in *The New York Times Encyclopedia of Film, 1958–1963.*) AMPAS, NYPL.

Kerr, Deborah. "Days and Nights of the *Iguana.*" *Esquire* 61 (May 1964): 128–30+. AMPAS.

Kerr, Walter. "When the Heroes Stumble, or the Virtues of Outtakes." *New York Times,* December 27, 1977. (Reprinted in *The New York Times Encyclopedia of Film, 1977–1979.*)

Lawrenson, H. "The Nightmare of the *Iguana.*" *Show* 4, no. 1 (January 1964): 46+. NYPL.

"The Films of John Huston" [Program notes.] Los Angeles County Museum of Art, November 22, 1980, 2 p. (Film notes excerpted from *John Huston: Maker of Magic,* by Stuart Kaminsky, Boston, Houghton, Mifflin Company, 1978.)

McKee, Allen. "So Close to Disaster, but They Just Don't Care." *New York Times,*

August 20, 1972. (Reprinted in *The New York Times Encyclopedia of Film, 1972–1974.*)

Magill's Survey of Cinema: Second Series 4 (1986): 1,721–24. Anne Kail.

Malcolm, Andrew H. "Huston: 'I Want to Keep Right on Going.'" *New York Times,* December 11, 1979. (Reprinted in *The New York Times Encyclopedia of Film, 1977–1979.*)

Motion Picture Guide 6 (1986): 2,153.

Nolan, William. "Hollywood on Location." *Coronet,* ca. 1965. AMPAS.

O'Hara, John. "Hollywood Dilemma—What Do They Do for Encore?" *Los Angeles Times,* October 25, 1964. (*See above* Greenspan, Lou.)

Phillips, Gene D. *The Films of Tennessee Williams.* Cranbury, N.J.: Art Alliance, 1980.

"Stars Fell on Mismalaya: The Making of Night." *Life* 55 (December 20, 1963): 69+.

Sutton, Horace. "Roughing It with the Cognoscenti." *Saturday Review,* March 14, 1964. AMPAS.

Victor, Thelda, and Muriel Davidson. "The Drama the Cameras Missed: A Secret Diary by Richard Burton." *Saturday Evening Post,* July 11–18, 1964, 24–34. AMPAS.

Weales, Gerald. "The Beast under the Porch." *Reporter* 31 (October 8, 1964): 49–50. NYPL.

Yacowar, Maurice. *Tennesee Williams and Film.* New York: Ungar, 1977.

REVIEWS

America 111 (August 15, 1964): 116.

BFI/Monthly Film Bulletin, 31, no. 369 (October 1964): 146.

Box Office 85 (July 13, 1964): 2,844.

Cahiers du Cinéma 164 (March 1965): 77.

Casablanca 35 (November 1983): 43.

Cinema 3, no. 3 (October–November 1964): 48, illus. James Silke.

Cinéma (Paris) 294 (June 1983): 47, creds, illus. A. Tarqui.

Commonweal 80 (August 21, 1964): 580.

Cosmopolitan, February 1964. Stephen Birmingham. AMPAS.

Cue, August 8, 1964, 8. William Wolf. AMPAS, NYPL.

Daily Cinema 8,960 (September 4, 1964): 10.

Film Daily 124–127 (July 1, 1964): 3.

Filmfacts 7 (1964): 146.

Film Quarterly 18, no. 2 (Winter 1964): 50–52, illus. Stephen Taylor. NYPL.

Films and Filming 11, no. 1 (October 1964): 28+, illus. Allen Eyles. AMPAS.

Films in Review 15, no. 7 (August–September 1964): 439–41, illus. Elaine Rothschild.

Hollywood Reporter 181, no. 9 (July 1, 1964): 3.

Illustrated London News 245 (September 26, 1964): 480.

Kinematograph Weekly 2,970 (September 3, 1964): 9.

Life 57 (July 10, 1964): 11. Richard Oulahan. AMPAS, MOMA, NYPL.

Motion Picture Herald Product Digest 232, no. 1 (July 8, 1964): 81–82. AMPAS.

Newsday, July 1, 1964, 3C. Mike McGrady. NYPL.
New Statesman 68 (September 11, 1964): 370.
Newsweek 64 (July 13, 1964): 85. AMPAS, NYPL.
New York Daily News, July 1, 1964. Wanda Hale. NYPL.
New Yorker 40 (August 15, 1964): 84–85. Edith Oliver. AMPAS, NYPL.
New York Herald Tribune, July 1, 1964. Judith Crist. NYPL.
New York Morning Telegraph, July 1, 1964. NYPL.
New York Post, July 1, 1964. Archer Winsten. NYPL.
New York Times, July 1, 1964, 42. Bosley Crowther. NYPL, NYTR.
Observer, September 13, 1964. Penelope Gilliatt.
Saturday Review 47 (July 18, 1964): 22. Arthur Knight. AMPAS, NYPL.
Screen Facts 19 (1968): 35. NYPL.
Sight & Sound 25, no. 3 (Winter 1955–56): 147–48. Gavin Lambert.
Sight & Sound 33, no. 4 (Autumn 1964): 199. Elizabeth Sussex.
Sunday Times, September 13, 1964. Derek Prouse. AMPAS.
Time 82 (November 8, 1963): 69 MOMA.
Time 84 (July 17, 1964): 86+. AMPAS.
Variety, July 1, 1964. AMPAS, VR.
Variety, July 8, 1964. AMPAS, NYPL.
Villager, August 13, 1964, 12. Walter J. Carroll. NYPL.
Village Voice 9, no. 43 (August 13, 1964): 12. Andrew Sarris.
Vogue 144 (September 1, 1964): 106.
Washington Post, September 29, 1966, 24. Richard L. Coe. NYPL.

NOTES FROM UNDER THE VOLCANO. 1984. (Documentary.)

REVIEW
Variety, July 11, 1984, creds. Cart. VR.

OBSERVATIONS UNDER THE VOLCANO. 1984. (Documentary.)

ARTICLES AND REVIEWS
Hollywood Reporter 282, no. 35 (July 6, 1984): 26.
New York Daily News, November 2, 1984, 20. Ernest Legrande. NYPL.
New York Post, November 2, 1984, 43. Archer Winsten.
New York Times, November 2, 1984, C12. Janet Maslin. NYPL, NYTR.
Variety, July 11, 1984, 18. Cart.
Village Voice, November 6, 1984, 69. David Edelstein. NYPL.

ON OUR MERRY WAY (*A Miracle Can Happen*). 1948. (Director, uncredited.)

ARTICLES AND REVIEWS
Focus on Film 26 (1977).
Harrison's Reports, February 7, 1948, 23. (Reviewed as *A Miracle Can Happen.*)
Hill, Gladwyn. "Jimmy Stewart Prepares to Meet a Rabbit." *New York Times,* July
    13, 1947. (Reprinted in *The New York Times Encyclopedia of Film, 1947–1951.*)

Hollywood Reporter, February 2, 1948. (Reviewed as *A Miracle Can Happen.*)
Hollywood Reporter, February 8, 1948. Irving Hoffman.
Motion Picture Daily, February 2, 1948. (Reviewed as *A Miracle Can Happen.*)
Motion Picture Guide 6 (1986): 2,246.
Motion Picture Herald 170, no. 6 (February 7, 1948).
New Republic, February 23, 1948. Robert Hatch.
New York Herald Tribune, February 4, 1948. Otis L. Guernsy. NYPL.
New York Times, February 4, 1948. Bosley Crowther. NYPL, NYTR.
Today's Cinema 71, no. 5,700 (September 14, 1948).
Variety, February 2, 1948. (Reviewed as *A Miracle Can Happen.*) VR.
Variety, February 4, 1948.

ORSON WELLES: THE ONE-MAN BAND. 1995. TV. (Appearance.)

REVIEW
New Republic, January 6, 1997, 24–25. Stanley Kauffmann.

THE OTHER SIDE OF THE WIND. 1970–75. Unreleased Film. (Actor.)

ARTICLES
American Film 1, no. 9 (July–August 1976): 14–20.
Brechner, Kevin C. "Welles' Farewell: *The Other Side of the Wind.*" *American Cinematographer* 67, no. 7 (July 1986): 34–38. (Reprinted in *Perspectives on Orson Welles,* edited by Morris Beja, 186–92, New York, G.K. Hall, 1995.)
Ecran 33 (February 1975).
Film Comment 24, no. 5 (September–October 1988): 72+. Article looking at this film, along with other "lost" and unrealized films: *The Merchant of Venice, The Dreamers,* and *Don Quixote.*
Higham, Charles. "Orson's Back and Marlene's Got Him." *New York Times,* January 31, 1971, D15. On the making of the film. Article on the beginning of the shooting, theme of films, and at that time whether Huston would do part. (Reprinted in *The New York Times Encyclopedia of Film, 1969–1971.*)
———. "The Film that Orson Welles Has Been Finishing for 6 Years." *New York Times,* April 18, 1976, sect. 2, 1+. (Reprinted in *The New York Times Encyclopedia of Film, 1975–1976.*)
Millimeter, July–August 1976, 39. NYPL.
New York Post, December 8, 1966. In Welles's will he left the film to Peter Bogdanovich to finish, and Bogdanovich asked Huston to complete it, which he agreed to do. NYPL.
Sight & Sound 55, no. 3 (Summer 1986): 168.
Today's Cinema 9,879 (February 9, 1971): 3.
Variety, February 12, 1975, 27. Joseph McBride.

Variety, January 31, 1979. Film 96 percent completed and edited; Paris film lab under control of Iranian-owned FIDCI headed by Shah's bother-in-law.

Variety, February 13, 1980, 31. John Huston plays central role, depicted as famous U.S. director and closet homosexual. Welles describes film as attack on masochism and guilt behind drive for power.

Variety, May 27, 1991, 103.

Variety, September 18, 1995, 99. David Stratton, "The documentary *Orson Welles: The One Man Band,* which includes two sequences from *The Other Side of the Wind.*"

PHOBIA. 1980. (Director; Writer, uncredited.)

ARTICLES AND REVIEWS

Anderson, K. "Coming *Phobia* vs. *Phobia:* Two Thrillers Battle for Custody of Their Title." *Cinefantastique* 10, no. 1 (Summer 1980): 38.

BFI/Monthly Film Bulletin 48, no. 567 (April 1981): 77, creds. T. Pulleine.

Cahiers du Cinéma, no. 345 (March 1983): 75, stills. A. Philippon.

Cinefantastique 11, no. 2 (Autumn 1981): 52.

Cinéma (Paris) 291 (March 1983): 50, creds, illus. E. Caron-Lowins.

Cinema Canada 69 (October–November 1980): 34–35, creds, illus. J. G. Harkness.

Cinemag, October 1, 1979, 2.

Cinemag, October 13, 1980, 18. J. Paul Costabile.

Cine Revue 63 (February 17, 1983): 48, creds.

Film Illustrated 10 (May 1981): 286. M. Whitman.

Films 1, no. 5 (April 1981): 39, creds, illus.

Hollywood Reporter 259, no. 20 (November 27, 1979): 14, creds.

"Huston Arrives with *Phobia.*" *The Movie Works Weekly* (Toronto [Canada's international trade paper serving the entertainment industry]), n.d. AMPAS.

Jeune Cinéma 150 (April 1983): 45–46. A. Caron.

Klemesrud, Judy. "At the Movies." *New York Times,* September 14, 1979. Note about Paul Michael Glaser being signed for starring role in film. (Reprinted in *The New York Times Encyclopedia of Film, 1977–1979.*)

Knelman, Martin. "In the Arts, People Have to Be Beaten to Death." *Los Angeles Herald Examiner,* January 13, 1980, D10–D11, interv.

———. "*The Lion in Winter:* The Man Who Would Be Huston." *Boston Phoenix,* April 8, 1980, 2+, interv.

Los Angeles Times, April 14, 1983, sect 6, 1.

Malcolm, A. H. "Huston: 'I Want to Keep Right on Going.'" *New York Times,* December 11, 1979, C7, illus. MOMA.

Motion Picture Guide 6 (1986): 2,390–91.

La Revue du Cinéma 381 (March 1983): 36, stills. G. Allombert.

La Revue du Cinéma 146, no. 28 (1983), creds. G. Allombert.

Screen International 225 (January 26, 1980): 9.

Screen International 285 (March 28, 1981): 13.

Screen International, April 4, 1981. Marjorie Bilbow.

Variety 300, no. 6 (September 10, 1980): 36, creds. [G] Mosk[owitz]. VR.

THE PRINCE AND THE SHOWGIRL. 1957. (Director, unrealized.)

ARTICLES AND REVIEWS

America 97 (July 6, 1957): 392.

BFI/Monthly Film Bulletin 24 (July 1957): 84.

Clark, Colin. *The Prince, the Showgirl, and Me: Six Months on the Set with Marilyn and Olivier.* New York: St. Martin's Press, 1996.

Commonweal 66 (June 21, 1957): 303.

Film Daily 111 (May 15, 1957): 6.

Films and Filming 3 (July 1957): 21–22.

Films in Review 8 (August–September 1957): 347–48.

Harrison's Reports, May 18, 1957, 80.

Hollywood Reporter, May 15, 1957, 3.

Motion Picture Guide 6 (1986): 2,456.

Motion Picture Herald Product Digest 207 (May 18, 1957): 377.

The Nation 184 (June 29, 1957): 574.

Newsweek 49 (June 17, 1957): 111.

New Yorker 33 (June 22, 1957): 74.

New York Times, June 14, 1957. NYTR.

Saturday Review 40 (June 8, 1957): 30.

Sight & Sound 27 (Summer 1957): 409–41.

Time 69 (June 24, 1957): 84.

Variety, May 15, 1957, 6 VR.

PRIZZI'S HONOR. 1985. (Director; Writer, uncredited.)

ARTICLES

Benayoun, Robert. "John Huston: There's No Business Like Crime Business (sur *L'Honneur de Prizzi*)." *Positif* 299 (January 1986): 2–4, creds, illus, stills. (Reprinted in *John Huston, Collection dirigée,* edited by Gilles Ciment, 171–73, Dossier Positif Rivages, Paris, Editions Rivages, Collection Positif-Rivages, no. 2, 1988. Text in French.) NYPL.

Canby, Vincent. "Film View: John Huston—a Master of His Art. A Review of Huston's Career on the Occasion of *Prizzi's Honor.*" *New York Times,* June 23, 1985, sect. 2, 17–18. MOMA, NYPL.

———. "Freed from Code Shackles, Movies Still Limp Along." *New York Times,* March 9, 1986, 19. Discussion including *Prizzi's Honor* and *The Maltese Falcon.*

Caufield, Deborah. "Nicholson on the Matter of His 'Honor.'" *Los Angeles Times,* June 16, 1985, C24.

Champlin, Charles. "New 'Honor' Puts a Gleam in Huston's Eye." *Los Angeles Times,* June 15, 1985, sect. 5, 1.

Ciment, Michel. "Le quarantième film." *Positif,* no. 298 (December 1985): 48, stills. (Reprinted in *John Huston, Collection dirigée,* edited by Gilles Ciment, 169–70, Dossier Positif Rivages, Paris, Editions Rivages, Collection Positif-Rivages, no. 2, 1988.)

"Embassy Home Entertainment Has Acquired All UK Rights." *Screen International* 476 (December 15, 1984): 2.

Engel, Leonard. "Irony and Sentiment in *Prizzi's Honor:* Shades of Spade in the '80s." *Proteus,* Fall 1990, 18–25.

Ferraro, Thomas J. "Blood in the Marketplace: The Business of Family in *The Godfather* Narratives." In *The Invention of Ethnicity,* edited by Werner Sollors, 176–208. New York: Oxford University Press, 1989.

Harmetz, Aljean. "At the Movies." *New York Times,* February 7, 1986, C10, port.

Hollywood Reporter 287, no. 13 (May 31, 1985): 18.

Huston, John. "Associés cinématographiques: Sur les directeurs de la photographie." *Positif* 299 (January 1986): 5–6. (Reprinted in John Huston, *Collection dirigée,* 65–67.)

———. "Die Ehre der Prizzis." *Film und Fernsehen* 15, no. 5 (1987): 24–25, illus, stills.

"Huston to Direct 'Prizzi's Honor' Starring Nicholson for ABC Pics." *Variety* 316 (October 3, 1984): 30.

Jameson, Richard T, ed. *They Went That a Way: Redefining Film Genres—A National Society of Film Critics Video Guide.* San Francisco: Mercury House, 1994.

Karp, A. "John Huston Makes 'Prizzi's Honor' His Fortieth Film." *Box Office* 121 (July 1985): 11–13, illus, interv, port.

Klemesrud, Judy. "At the Movies: *Prizzi's* Don Is a Plum Part for William Hicky." *New York Times,* July 5, 1985, C6.

Kolodynski, A. "Honor Prizzich." *FSP* (*Filmowy Serwis Prasowy*) 32, nos. 20 & 21 (1986): 31–5, creds, filmog, interv.

Kupfer, J. H. "At the Movies: Avant-garde Entertainment." *Journal of Aesthetic Education* 20, no. 4 (1986): 75–79.

McDowell, Edwin. "Hollywood and the Novelists—It's a Fickle Romance, at Best." *New York Times,* July 14, 1985, H1.

Magill's Cinema Annual, 1986, 285–89. R. C. Dale.

Maslin, Janet. "*Prizzi's Honor* Takes a Comic View of Deadly Lovers." *New York Times,* June 9, 1985, sect. 2, 1. AMPAS, MOMA.

———. "Two Performers Who Dare." *New York Times,* August 4, 1985, sect. 2, 15.

Maxfield, James F. "Eating Their Children: The Honor of the Prizzis." In *The Fatal Woman: Sources of Male Anxiety in American Film Noir, 1941–1991,* 132–43. Madison, N.J.: Farleigh Dickinson University Press, 1996.

Motion Picture Guide, Annual Issue, 1986, 154.

Norman, N. "Laughter in the Dark." *Photoplay* 36 (October 1985): 38–39, stills.

Positif, no. 299 (January 1986): 2–9. NYPL.

Sragow, Michael. "John Huston: *Prizzi's Honor.*" In *They Went That a Way: Redefining Film Genres—A National Society of Film Critics Video Guide,* edited by Richard T. Jameson, 163–69. San Francisco: Mercury House, 1994. (Reprinted from the *Boston Phoenix,* June 18, 1985.)

Taylor, Clarke. "New Honor for Condon in *Prizzi* Success." *Los Angeles Times,* July 17, 1985, sect. 6, 1.

———. "Acting in Blood of the Don of *Prizzi's Honor.*" *Los Angeles Times,* August 20, 1985, sect. 6, 4.

Walker, Beverly. "The Bird Is on His Own." *Film Comment* 21 (May–June 1985): 53–61, illus, interv. Nicholson discusses his career with emphasis on *Prizzi.*

Walsh, Michael. "Prizzi's Opera." *Film Comment* 21 (September–October 1985): 4+. NYPL.

Zavarzadeh, M. "The New Woman as Mafia Hit Man." *North Dakota Quarterly* 56, no. 1 (1988): 154–64.

REVIEWS

American Film 10, no. 7 (May 1985): 69.

Aquarian Weekly, January 19, 1985, 8. James Verniere. NYPL.

BFI/Monthly Film Bulletin 52 (November 2, 1985): 331–22, creds, stills. Tom Milne.

Bianco e Nero 46, no. 4 (October–December 1985): 34–36, creds, stills. C. G. Fava.

Box Office 121 (August 1985): R93–R94, creds. A. Karp.

Cahiers du Cinéma 376 (October 1985): 14, illus.

Cahiers du Cinéma 379 (January 1986): 55–56, creds, stills. Antoine de Baecque. NYPL.

Chaplin 27, no. 5 (n200) (1985): 250+, creds, stills. Stig Bjorkman.

Chicago Sun Times, June 14, 1985, 17. Roger Ebert. NYPL.

Christian Century 102 (July 17–24, 1985): 684–85. J. M. Wall.

Christian Century 103 (January 29, 1986): 212+. G. Forshey and J. M. Wall.

*Christian Science Monitor, June 19, 1985, 24. David Sterritt. NYPL.

*Cinéaste 14, no. 2 (1985): 60. Richard Linnett. NYPL.

Cineforum 26, no. 3 (252) (March 1986): 59–62, creds, illus. S. Bortolussi. NYPL.

Cinéma (Paris) 336 (January 8, 1986): 3, creds, stills. A. Carbonnier. NYPL.

Cinema Papers 55 (January 1986): 62–63, creds, stills. David Stratton.

Cinématographe, no. 115 (January 1986): 32, creds, stills. G. Horvilleur.

City Limits 212 (October 25, 1985): 23.

Commonweal 112 (July 12, 1985): 407–8. Tim O'Brien. NYPL.

EPD Film 3, no. 1 (January 1986): 30, creds, illus. Gertrud Koch.

Film a Doba 33, no. 6 (June 1987): 343–45, creds, stills. V. Hendrich.

Film Bulletin 27, no. 4 (no. 143) (1985): 32–33, creds, stills. W. R. Vian.

Film en Televisie 344 (January 1986): 13, creds, illus. Dirk Michiels.

Filmfaust 11, no. 52 (April–May 1986): 9+, creds, illus. M. Reiner.

Film Journal 88 (July 1985): 13, creds, stills. K. Lally.

Filmnews 15, no. 9 (December 1985): 15.

Filmrutan 28, no. 4 (1985): 34, creds, illus. S. Andersson.

Films and Filming, no. 373 (October 1985): 44–45. John Russell Taylor.

*Films in Review 36 (August 1985): 428–29. Kenneth M. Chanko.

Glamour 83 (August 1985): 221. J. Boyum.

Grand Angle 13, no. 79 (January 1986): [17–18], biblio, creds, stills. G. Dewasse.

Hollywood Reporter 283, no. 46 (October 2, 1984): 35, creds.

Hollywood Reporter 287, no. 16 (June 5, 1985): 3+. AMPAS.

Iskusstvo Kino 2 (February 1992): 169.

Jeune Cinéma 172 (February 1986): 28–29, creds, stills. Bernard Nave.

Kosmorama 31, no. 174 (December 1985): 189–90, creds, illus, stills. P. Calum.

Levende Billeder 1 (November 27, 1985): 12–13, illus, stills. "Jack and Kathleen."
Life 8 (June 1985): 139.
Listener 114, no. 2,933 (October 31, 1985): 40.
Listener 122, no. 3,145 (December 21, 1989): 50.
Los Angeles Times, June 14, 1985, Calendar, sect. 6, 1. Sheila Benson. AMPAS.
Los Angeles Times, June 15, 1985.
Los Angeles Times, July 17, 1985. AMPAS.
Maclean's 98 (June 17, 1985): 54. L. O'Toole.
Mademoiselle 91 (October 1985): 80. R. Rosenbaum.
Mediafilm, no. 140 (Winter 1982): 48–49, creds, illus. J. Boesten.
Medien 30, no. 4 (1986): 220–23, creds, stills. H. Ettenhuber.
National Review 37 (July 26, 1985): 48–51. John Simon.
New Leader 68 (July 1–15, 1985): 20–22, illus. Daphne Merkin.
New Republic 193 (July 8, 1985): 24–25. Stanley Kauffmann. NYPL.
Newsday, June 14, 1985, part 3, 3. Leo Seligsohn.
New Statesman 110 (October 25, 1985): 33–34, stills. J. Coleman.
Newsweek 105 (June 17, 1985): 89, stills. David Ansen. AMPAS, MOMA.
New York 18 (June 24, 1985): 65–66, stills. David Denby. NYPL.
New York Daily News, June 14, 1985, 3. Kathleen Carroll. NYPL.
New Yorker 60 (October 15, 1984): 36–39. "Forty: The Making of *Prizzi's Honor.*"
New Yorker 61 (July 1, 1985): 84–86. Pauline Kael. AMPAS, MOMA, NYPL.
    (Reprinted in *State of the Art,* by Pauline Kael, 375–81, New York, E. P. Dutton,
    1985; and in *For Keeps,* by Pauline Kael, 1,065–69, New York, Dutton, 1994.)
New York Native, July 27, 1985, 47. Joel Greenberg. NYPL.
New York Post, June 14, 1985, 45. Rex Reed. NYPL.
New York Times, June 9, 1985, H21. Janet Maslin.
New York Times, June 14, 1985, sect. 3 (C), 8, creds, stills. Vincent Canby.
    AMPAS, MOMA, NYPL, NYTR.
New York Times, June 23, 1985, H17. Vincent Canby.
New York Times, July 5, 1985, C6. Judy Klemesrud.
New York Times, August 4, 1985, H15. Janet Maslin.
New York Times, December 19, 1985, C20.
New York Times, December 29, 1985, H19+. Vincent Canby.
New York Times, March 9, 1986, H19. Vincent Canby.
People Weekly 23 (June 17, 1985): 16, illus. P. Travers.
Photoplay 36 (October 1985): 44, creds, stills. M. Gray.
La Revue du Cinéma 412 (January 1986): 23–24, creds, stills. F. Guerif. NYPL.
La Revue du Cinéma 64–65, no. 33 (1986), creds. J. Valot.
San Francisco Chronicle, June 14, 1985. Peter Stack. NYPL.
Screen International 468 (October 20, 1984): 6.
Screen International 471 (November 10, 1984): 17, creds.
Screen International 520 (October 26, 1985): 18.
Segnocinema 6, no. 21 (January 1986): 66, creds, stills. Robert Pugliese.
Séquences 122 (October 1985): 50–51, creds, stills. R.-C. Bérube.
Sight & Sound 54, no. 4 (Autumn 1985): 255–57, illus, stills. Terence Rafferty.
    NYPL.

Sinema, no. 71 (January–February 1986): 52–53, creds, stills. M. Holthof.

Skoop 21, nos. 9 & 10 (December 1985–January 1986): 23. R. Proper.

*Time 125 (June 10, 1985): 83, stills. Richard Schickel. AMPAS, MOMA.

Time Out 792 (October 24, 1985): 43.

24 Images 25 (Summer 1985): 59–60, creds, stills. M. Tourigny.

USA Today 114 (September 1985): 95–96, stills. K. R. Hey.

Variety 319 (June 5, 1985): 14, creds. "Loyn" (R. Loynd). AMPAS, MOMA, NYPL, VR.

Video Review, January 1986, 84. Andrew Sarris. NYPL.

Video Review, January 1986, 122. Michael Walsh, "*Prizzi* Scores Hit: Music in *Prizzi's Honor.*" NYPL.

*Village Voice, 30 (June 18, 1985): 57, stills. Andrew Sarris. AMPAS, MOMA, NYPL.

Village Voice 30 (October 1, 1985): 68. Stuart Byron and A. Thompson.

Wall Street Journal, June 13, 1985, 28. Julie Salamon. AMPAS.

Wall Street Journal, August 13, 1985, 22 (West Coast ed.), 30 (East Coast ed.). Julie Salamon.

Wall Street Journal, August 29, 1985, 18. Julie Salamon.

Washington Post, June 14, 1985, C1. Paul Attanasio.

Washington Post, June 14, 1985, Weekend, 27. Rita Kempley.

*Women's Wear Daily, June 13, 1985, 8. Howard Kissel.

THE PROWLER. 1951. (Producer? *See* chapter 14, "Huston on Film and Other Projects.")

ARTICLES AND REVIEWS

BFI/Monthly Film Bulletin 18 (October 1951): 344.

Commonweal 54 (June 29, 1951): 286.

Film Daily, May 3, 1951, 8.

Harrison's Reports, April 28, 1951, 66.

Hollywood Reporter, April 25, 1951, 4.

Hirsch, Foster. *Joseph Losey.* Boston: Twayne, 1980, 47–51.

Motion Picture Daily, May 2, 1951. Mandel Herbst.

Motion Picture Guide 6 (1986): 2,482.

Motion Picture Herald Product Digest, April 28, 1951, 817.

The Nation 173 (July 14, 1951): 37.

The Nation 174 (January 5, 1952): 19.

New Republic 124 (June 4, 1951): 23.

New Statesman & Nation 42 (November 17, 1951): 561.

Newsweek 37 (May 21, 1951): 101.

New York Times, July 2, 1951, 16. NYTR.

Saturday Review 34 (June 9, 1951): 27.

Spectator 187 (November 16, 1951): 640+.

Time 57 (June 4, 1951): 100.

Variety, April 25, 1951. VR.

QUO VADIS. 1951. (Writer; Director, removed.)

ARTICLES AND REVIEWS

American Cinematographer 32 (October 1951): 398+.
Audio-Visual Guide 18, no. 4 (December 1951): 17.
BFI/Monthly Film Bulletin 19, no. 218 (March 1952): 32.
Catholic World 174 (January 1952): 303–4.
Christian Century 69 (March 5, 1952): 295.
Commonweal 55 (November 23, 1951): 174.
**Cue,* November 17, 1951, 18–19. Jesse Zunser.
"Film Buff Series, 1984–1985" [Program notes]. Programme 9. Toronto Film Society.
Film Daily, November 9, 1951, 3.
Films in Review 2 (December 1951): 47+.
Films in Review 3 (April 1952): 184–94.
Friedrich, Otto. *City of Nets: A Portrait of Hollywood in the 1940s.* New York: Harper, 1986.
Harrison's Reports, November 17, 1951, 182.
High Fidelity 29 (April 1979): 102.
Holiday 10 (November 1951): 24.
Hollywood Reporter, November 9, 1951, 3–4.
Illustrated London News 220 (February 9, 1952): 226.
Magill's Survey of Cinema: First Series 3 (1980): 1,411–14. Ronald Bowers.
Motion Picture Guide 6 (1986): 2,515–16.
Motion Picture Herald 185, no. 7 (November 17, 1951): 33.
Motion Picture Herald Product Digest, November 24, 1951, 1,118–19.
New York Statesman and Nation 43 (February 2, 1952): 124.
Newsweek 38 (November 19, 1951): 102.
New Yorker 27 (November 17, 1951): 108.
New York Times, November 9, 1951, 22. NYTR.
New York Times Magazine, November 4, 1951, 22–23.
Picturegoer 20, no. 809 (November 4, 1950).
Picturegoer 22, no. 865(December 1, 1951): 8.
Quarterly of Film, Radio and Television 10 (Spring 1956): 262–72.
Quirk, Lawrence J. *The Films of Robert Taylor.* Secaucus, N.J.: Citadel Press, 1975, 118–22.
Sadoul, George. *Dictionary of Films.* Translated, edited, and updated by Peter Morris. Berkeley: University of California Press, 1972, 304.
Saturday Review 34 (November 24, 1951): 29.
Séquences 177 (March–April 1995): 8.
Spectator 188 (February 1, 1952): 140.
Spiro, J. D. "Now It's for Sure: After Many False Starts Metro Finally Gets 'Quo Vadis' into Production." *New York Times,* May 7, 1950. (Reprinted in *The New York Times Encyclopedia of Film, 1947–1951.*)
Time 58 (November 19, 1951): 108.

Time 61 (March 16, 1963): 108.
Variety, November 14, 1951, 6. VR.

THE RED BADGE OF COURAGE. 1951. (Director; Actor, cut from final release; Writer.)

ARTICLES

BFI/Monthly Film Bulletin 52, no. 622 (November 1985): 331–32, creds, illus. Tom Milne.

Casablanca 35 (November 1983): 3940.

Dietz, Howard. "Case for Maligned Salesmen." *New York Times,* December 2, 1951. (Reprinted in *The New York Times Encyclopedia of Film, 1947–1951.*)

Doniol-Valcroze, J. "Huston, apologiste de la volonté?" *Positif* 3 (July–August 1952): 10–13. (Reprinted in *John Huston, Collection dirigée,* edited by Gilles Ciment, 85–87, Dossier Positif Rivages, Paris, Editions Rivages, Collection Positif-Rivages, no. 2, 1988.)

Films and Filming 373 (October 1985): 44–45, creds, illus. J. R. Taylor.

"The Films of John Huston, 1980" [Program notes]. Los Angeles County Museum of Art. October 18, 1980.

Garbicz, Adam, and Jack Klinowski. *Cinema: The Magic Vehicle—A Guide to Its Achievement. Journey Two: The Fifties.* New York: Schocken, 1983, c. 1975–79, 72–75.

Gentleman's Quarterly 2 (February 1992): 69–72, illus.

Hamblett, Charles. "On Launching 'Moby Dick' in Eire." *New York Times,* August 15, 1954. (Reprinted in *The New York Times Encyclopedia of Film, 1952–1957.*)

Hammen, Scott. *Film Notes.* Louisville, Ky.: Hamilton Printing Co, 1979.

Hollywood Reporter, July 13, 1993, 10. "Ross *Picture* Book Gets a New Polishing." AMPAS.

Kezich, Tullio. "La provo del fuoco." *Rassegna del film* 1, no. 5 (June–July 1952).

Lawson, John Howard. *Film in the Battle of Ideas.* New York: Masses & Mainstream, 1953, 29–38.

Listener 116, no. 2976 (September 4, 1986): 37.

Magill's Survey of Cinema: Second Series 5 (1981): 1,994–96. Stephanie Kreps.

Malcolm, Andrew H. "Huston: 'I Want to Keep Right on Going.'" *New York Times,* December 11, 1979. (Reprinted in *The New York Times Encyclopedia of Film, 1977–1979.*)

Max, D. T. "*Picture* Author Ross Remembers It Well." *Variety,* May 29, 1993, X3.

Motion Picture Guide 6 (1986): 2,559–60.

Nason, Richard W. "Huston Hits High with 'Heaven' and 'Geisha.'" *New York Times,* September 28, 1958. (Reprinted in *The New York Times Encyclopedia of Film, 1958–1963.*)

New York Times, September 3, 1950, sect. 2, 3.

New York Times, November 4, 1951, sect. 2, 1, comment.

Nichols, Nina. *CinemaTexas Program Notes* 18, no. 3 (April 23, 1980): 73–78, filmog, quotes from Lillian Ross's *Picture* (New York, Rinehart, 1952).

Palmer, James Wentworth. "Film and Fiction: Essays in Narrative Rhetoric." Ph.D.

diss., Claremont Graduate School, Claremont, California, 1976. (*Dissertation Abstracts International* [*DAI*], 37 [1976]: 1–2A.)

Reinhardt, Gottfried. "Sound Track Narration: Its Use Is Not Always a Resort of the Lazy or the Incompetent." *Films in Review* 4 (November 1953): 459–60. Producer of *Red Badge* emphasizes values in using narration.

Rollins, Janet Buck. "Stephen Crane on Film: Adaptation as Interpretation." Ph.D. diss., Oklahoma State University, Stillwater, Oklahoma, 1983. Chapter 3: John Huston's *Red Badge of Courage* (1951).

Ross, Lillian. *Picture.* New York: Rinehart, 1952. (Reprints—London:Gollancz, 1953; New York: Dolphin Books, 1962;. New York: Avon Books, 1969. Italian edition—*Processo a Hollywood,* Milano, 1956. Originally in *New Yorker* 28 [May 24, 1952]: 32–36+; [May 31, 1952]: 29–32+; [June 7, 1952]: 32–34+; [June 14, 1952]: 39–40+; [June 21, 1952]: 31–32+.) The classic account on the making of the film.

———. "Everything Has Just Gone Zoom." In *Film: An Anthology,* edited by Daniel Talbot. New York: Simon & Schuster, 1959.

Sadoul, George. *Dictionary of Films.* Translated, edited, and updated by Peter Morris. Berkeley: University of California Press, 1972, 307.

Schary, Dore. *Heyday.* Boston: Little, Brown, 1979.

Screen Education Yearbook. London: Society for Education in Film and Television, 1963, 61–63. N. Tucker.

Sight & Sound 21, no. 3 (January–March 1952): 124. Gavin Lambert.

Silva, Fred. "*The Red Badge of Courage:* Uncivil Battles and Civil Wars." In *The Classic American Novel and the Movies,* edited by Gerald Peary and Roger Shatzkin, 114–23. New York: Frederick Ungar, 1977.

Stevenson, James A. "Beyond Stephen Crane: *Full Metal Jacket.*" *Literature/Film Quarterly* 16, no. 4 (1988): 238–43.

"Summer Series 1980." Programme 3. Toronto Film Society, July 21, 1980, creds.

Village Voice, October 6, 1967, 72. Andrew Sarris, "Revivals in Focus." NYPL.

Watters, Jim. "John Huston on Kipling, Hemingway and Jack Daniels." *New York Times,* February 15, 1976. (Reprinted in *The New York Times Encyclopedia of Film, 1975–1976.*)

Weiler, A. H. "By Way of Report: Information on Audie Murphy and His Role in Film." *New York Times,* October 14, 1951. (Reprinted in *The New York Times Encyclopedia of Film, 1947–1951.*)

Wilmington, Richard. *Film Criticism and Caricature, 1943–1953.* London: Paul Elek, 1975, 131–33.

REVIEWS

Audio-Visual Guide 18, no. 3 (November 1951): 26.

BFI/Monthly Film Bulletin 18, no. 215 (December 1951): 373.

Catholic World 174 (October 1951): 65.

Christian Century 68 (November 21, 1951): 1,359.

Commonweal 55 (November 2, 1951): 93.

Film Daily, August 24, 1951, 6.

Films in Review 2, no. 8 (October 1951): 42–43. B. G. Marple.

Harrison's Reports, August 18, 1951, 130.
Hollywood Reporter, August 15, 1951, 3. AMPAS.
Life 31 (September 10, 1951): 102–4+. Review, photo essay, and sketches of making film by Bill Mauldin (pp. 107–8). NYPL.
Los Angeles Times, December 13, 1951. AMPAS.
Motion Picture Herald Product Digest 184, no. 7 (August 18, 1951): 981.
The Nation 173 (November 10, 1951): 49.
New Republic 125 (September 24, 1951): 21.
New Statesman & Nation 42 (November 24, 1951): 590.
Newsweek 38 (October 15, 1951). AMPAS.
New Yorker, October 27, 1951. Richard H. Rovere. NYPL.
New York Herald Tribune, October 19, 1951. Otis L. Guernsy Jr. NYPL.
New York Times, October 19, 1951. Bosley Crowther. (Reprinted in *The New York Times Film Reviews. A One-Volume Selection, 1913–1970,* edited by George Amberg, New York, Arno Press, 1971.) NYPL, NYTR.
Picturegoer 22, no. 869 (December 29, 1951): 12.
Saturday Review 34 (September 29, 1951): 31 Arthur Knight. AMPAS, NYPL.
Senior *Scholastic* 59 (October 10, 1951): 22.
Sight & Sound 20, no. 1 (May 1951): 6, illus.
Time 58 (October 8, 1951): 110. MOMA.
Variety, August 15, 1951, 6. Brog. AMPAS, NYPL, VR.

REFLECTIONS IN A GOLDEN EYE. 1967. (Director; Writer, uncredited.)

ARTICLES

The American Film Institute Catalog: Feature Films, 1961–1970. New York: R. R. Bowker, 1976, 896.
Bart, Peter. "Hollywood 'at Rest.'" *New York Times,* July 19, 1964. (Reprinted in *The New York Times Encyclopedia of Film, 1964–1968.*)
Brando, Marlon, with Robert Lindsay. *Songs My Mother Taught Me.* New York: Random House, 1994.
Canby, Vincent. "Stark Is Unfazed by Columbia Row." *New York Times,* November 14, 1966. (Reprinted in *The New York Times Encyclopedia of Film, 1964–1968.*)
———. "Filmmakers Show Less Fear of Catholic Office." *New York Times,* October 13, 1967. (Reprinted in *The New York Times Encyclopedia of Film, 1964–1968.*)
———. "Stark Is Basking in 'Funny Girl' Sun." *New York Times,* September 19, 1968. (Reprinted in *The New York Times Encyclopedia of Film, 1964–1968.*)
Carey, Gary. *Brando.* New York: Pocket Books, 1973. Section on film.
Carson, Virginia Spencer. *The Lonely Hunter: A Biography of Carson McCullers.* Garden City, N.Y.: Doubleday, 1975.
Celluloide 27, no. 331 (January 1982): 17–18, creds. E. Nunes.
Champlin, Charles. "'Reflections' Tours the Southern Gothic Style." *Los Angeles Times,* October 8, 1967, Calendar, 14–15. AMPAS.

Cooper, Stephen. "The Undeclared War: Political Reflections in a Golden Eye." In *Reflections in a Male Eye,* edited by Gaylyn Studlar and David Desser, 97–113. Washington, D.C.: Smithsonian Institution Press, 1993.

Corry, John. "John Huston: Musings on 'Fat City' and Other Pursuits." *New York Times,* August 5, 1972. (Reprinted in *The New York Times Encyclopedia of Film, 1972–1974.*)

Crowther, Bosley. "Sex, Shock and Sensibility." *New York Times,* October 22, 1967, 2C. AMPAS.

Ecran 24 (April 1974): 70, creds, illus. C. Beyle.

"The Films of John Huston" [Program notes]. Los Angeles County Museum of Art, November 22, 1980. Notes excerpted from Huston's autobiography, *An Open Book.*

Gill, Brendan. "The Current Cinema: Hard Days in Wessex." *New Yorker,* October 28, 1967, 165–66.

Hudson, Peggy. "Boudoir Battle Shifts from Wide to Home Screen." *New York Times,* December 4, 1966. (Reprinted in *The New York Times Encyclopedia of Film, 1964–1968.*)

"Huston Vexed: Thinks His Color Ideas Suppressed Unfairly by Distributor." *Variety,* May 1, 1968. AMPAS.

Jameson, Richard T. "Reflections in a Golden Eye." *Film Comment* [Midsection] 16, no. 3 (May–June 1980): 51–52.

Kael, Pauline. "The Current Cinema: Making Lawrence more Lawrentian." *New Yorker,* February 10, 1968, 100+. (Reprinted in *Going Steady,* 29–35, by Pauline Kael, Boston, Little Brown, 1970.)

Klemesrud, Judy. "Robert Forster—How to Succeed in Flops." *New York Times,* June 4, 1972. (Reprinted in *The New York Times Encyclopedia of Film, 1972–1974.*)

Laemmle, Ann. *CinemaTexas Program Notes* 21, no. 2 (November 11, 1981): [32]–36.

Lightman, Herb A. "Reflections in a Golden Eye Viewed through a Glass Darkly." *American Cinematographer* 48 (December 1967): 862–83. On Aldo Tonti's cinematography.

Listener 116, no. 2,972 (August 7, 1986): 29. MOMA.

Motion Picture Guide 6 (1986): 2,573.

Positif 299 (January 1986): 2–9, biblio. Special section.

Ramasse, François. "Le regard et la peau: Reflects dan un oeil d'or." *Positif* 299 (January 1986): 7–9, illus. (Reprinted in *John Huston, Collection dirigée,* edited by Gilles Ciment, 131–33, Paris, Dossier Positif-Rivages, 1988.)

Sarris, Andrew. *Confessions of a Cultist: On the Cinema, 1955–1969.* New York: Simon & Schuster, 1970, 321–25.

Stephens, Martha. *The Question of Flannery O'Connor.* Baton Rouge, La.: Louisiana State University Press, 1973.

Taylor, John Russell. "John Huston and the Figure in the Carpet." *Sight & Sound* 38, no. 2 (Spring 1969): 70–73. MOMA, NYPL.

Thomas, Tony. *The Films of Marlon Brando.* Secaucus, N.J.: Citadel Press, 1973, 188–97.

Thompson, Howard. "McCullers' Story Ends L.I. Filming: 'Golden Eye' Going to Rome after Mitchell Field." *New York Times,* October 17, 1966. (Reprinted in *The New York Times Encyclopedia of Film, 1964–1968.*)

Vermilye, Jerry. *The Films of Elizabeth Taylor.* Secaucus, N.J.: Citadel Press, 1976, 188–93.

Watters, Jim. "John Huston on Kipling, Hemingway and Jack Daniels." *New York Times,* February 15, 1976. (Reprinted in *The New York Times Encyclopedia of Film, 1975–1976.*)

Weiler, A. H. "Local View: 'Eye' Deal—Richardson, Seven Arts Team to Make McCullers Drama." *New York Times,* May 12, 1964.

White, Terence de Vere. "With Carson McCullers." *Irish Times,* April 10, 1967, interv.

REVIEWS

BFI/Monthly Film Bulletin 35, no. 415 (August 1968): 114.

Box Office, October 23, 1967. AMPAS.

Cinema 4, no. 1 (Spring 1968): 47. Axel Madsen.

Cinéma (Paris) 327 (October 30, 1985): 4, illus. F. Revault d'Allonnes.

Cue, October 21, 1967. W. W. NYPL.

Daily Cinema 9,510 (April 19, 1968): 9.

Daily Mail (London), April 17, 1968. Cecil Wilson. NYPL.

Film Daily 131, no. 68 (October 10, 1967): 3. AMPAS.

Filmfacts 10 (1967): 288, creds.

Film Quarterly 21, no. 2 (Winter 1967–68): 63. Margot Kernan. NYPL.

Films and Filming 14, no. 8 (May 1968): 24, creds. Allen Eyles. AMPAS.

Films in Review 18, no. 9 (November 1967): 576–77. Elaine Rothschild.

Hollywood Reporter 197, no. 45 (October 9, 1967): 3. AMPAS.

Kine Weekly 3,158 (April 20, 1968): 12.

Listener, April 25, 1968. Eric Rhode.

Listener 116, no. 2,972 (August 7, 1986): 29.

Manchester Guardian, April 25, 1968. Ian Wright.

Motion Picture Herald Product Digest 237, no. 43 (October 25, 1967): 733.

Movie 15 (Spring 1968): 25–26, illus. Paul Mayersberg.

Newsweek 70 (October 30, 1967): 94. AMPAS, MOMA, NYPL.

New Yorker, October 21, 1967, 137–38. Brendan Gill.

New York Morning Telegraph, October 12, 1967. Leo Mishkin. NYPL.

New Statesman, April 19, 1968. John Coleman.

New York Times, October 12, 1967, 59. Bosley Crowther. AMPAS, NYTR.

Nouvel-Observateur, April 10, 1968, 46.

La Nouvelle Revue Française, n.d. Henry Ragnal. AMPAS.

Observer (London), April 21, 1968, 32. Tom Milne. NYPL.

Saturday Review 50 (October 28, 1967): 26. Arthur Knight. AMPAS, NYPL.

Saturday Review, November 4, 1967. John Russell Taylor. AMPAS.

Senior Scholastic 72 (October 3, 1958): 4.

Sight & Sound 37, no. 2 (Spring 1968): 99–100, illus. John Russell Taylor.

Spectator, April 26, 1968, 570–71. Penelope Houston. AMPAS, MOMA.

Sunday Telegraph, April 21, 1968, 14. Margaret Hinxman.
Sunday Times (London), April 21, 1968, 54. Dilys Powell. AMPAS, NYPL.
Time 90 (October 27, 1967): 102+. AMPAS.
Times (London), April 18, 1968. John Russell Taylor. AMPAS.
Variety, October 11, 1967. AMPAS, VR.
Villager, January 18, 1968, 10. Maurice Blanc. NYPL.
Village Voice 13, no. 7 (November 30, 1967): 39. Andrew Sarris. NYPL.

REMINISCENCES OF A COWBOY. (Released as *Cowboy.*) 1958. (Director, unrealized.)

ARTICLES AND REVIEWS
America 98 (March 1, 1958): 643.
Baltake, Joe. *The Films of Jack Lemmon.* Secaucus, N.J.: Citadel Press, 1977, 86–90.
BFI/Monthly Film Bulletin 25 (March 1958): 31.
Commonweal 67 (March 7, 1958): 593.
Film Daily, February 13, 1958, 6.
Filmfacts 1 (March 19, 1958): 27–28.
Films in Review 9 (March 1958): 143.
Harrison's Reports, February 15, 1958, 26.
Hollywood Reporter, February 11, 1958, 3.
Los Angeles Times, February 9, 1958, sect. 5, 1.
Magill's Cinema Annual, 1982, 417–21.
Motion Picture Guide 2 (1985): 502.
Motion Picture Herald Product Digest, January 9, 1954, 2,134.
National Parent-Teacher 48 (June 1954): 38.
Newsweek 51 (February 17, 1958): 106.
New Yorker 34 (March 1, 1958): 107.
New York Times, February 20, 1958, 29. NYTR.
Saturday Review 41 (March 1, 1958): 26.
Time 71 (February 17, 1958): 64.
Variety, February 12, 1958, 6. VR.

REPORT FROM THE ALEUTIANS. 1943. (Director, Writer.)

ARTICLES AND REVIEWS
Champlin, Charles. "Huston Wartime Films on KCET." *Los Angeles Times,* April 30, 1981.
Desser, David. "The Wartime Films of John Huston: Film Noir and the Emergence of the Therapeutic." In *Reflections in a Male Eye,* edited by Gaylyn Studlar and David Desser, 19–32. Washington, D.C.: Smithsonian Institution Press, 1993.
Edgerton, Gary. "Revisiting the Records of Wars Past: Remembering the Documentary Trilogy of John Huston." *Journal of Popular Film and Television* 15, no. 1 (Spring 1987): 27–41. (Reprinted in Studlar and Desser, *Reflections in a Male Eye,* 33–61.)

Gallez, Douglas. "Patterns in Wartime Documentaries." *Quarterly of Films, Radio & TV* 10, no. 2 (Winter 1955): 125+.

Garrett, Greg. "John Huston's *The Battle of San Pietro.*" *War, Literature, and the Arts* 5, no. 1 (Spring–Summer 1993): 1–12.

Hammen, Scott. *Film Notes.* Louisville, Ky.: Hamilton Printing Co, 1979.

———. "At War with the Army." *Film Comment* 16, no. 2 (March–April 1980): 19–23, illus.

Hughes, Robert, ed. *Film: Book 2, Films of Peace and War.* New York: Grove Press, 1962.

Kinematograph Weekly 1,945 (July 27, 1944).

MacCann, Richard Dyer. *The People's Films: A Political History of U.S. Government Motion Pictures.* New York: Hastings House, 1973.

Matthews, Jack. "Huston Documentaries: Only Following Orders." *Los Angeles Times,* September 11, 1985.

New York Times, July 31, 1943. Theodore Strauss. NYPL, NYTR.

New York World Telegram, July 31, 1943. NYPL.

PM, August 4, 1943. John T. McManus. NYPL.

Rotha, Paul. *Documentary Film.* London: Faber & Faber, 1952.

Strauss, Theodore. "Delayed Report. The Signal Corps' Fine Film on Aleutians Was Held up by Lamentable Arguments." *New York Times,* August 8, 1943, sect. 2, 3. NYPL.

Time 117 (January 19, 1981): 80.

Today's Cinema 63, no. 5,062 (July 25, 1944).

Variety, July 14, 1943. NYPL, VR.

RETURN OF THE KING. 1980. TV Production. Sequel to *The Hobbit.* (Voice.)

ARTICLES AND REVIEWS

Hollywood Reporter 261, no. 35 (May 9, 1980): 6.

Library Journal 116, no. 21 (December 1991): 219.

Village Voice 25 (May 12, 1980): 50+, creds. T. Allen.

REVENGE. 1989. (Writer; Director, unrealized.)

ARTICLES AND REVIEWS

BFI/Monthly Film Bulletin 57, no. 678 (July 1990): 204–5, creds. N. Floyd.

Box Office 126 (April 1990): bet 50 and 59 [R28–R29]. T. Matthews.

Cinema Papers 80 (August 1990): 59–60, creds, stills. P. Hatching.

City Limits 455 (June 21, 1990): 32.

EPD Film [8] (February 1991): 30, creds. R. Gerz.

Film & TV 403 (December 1990): 29, creds, stills. K. Seberechts.

Film Journal 93 (March 1990): 19–20, creds. M. Meisel.

Films and Filming 410 (November–December 1988): 4, creds.

Grand Angle 133 (December 1990): 333–34, creds, stills. P. Lefebvre.

Hollywood Reporter 299, no. 22 (October 19, 1987): 4.

Hollywood Reporter 303, no. 35 (August 12, 1988): 14.
Lee, N. "*Revenge:* The Most Primitive Motive." *American Cinematographer* 71, no. 4 (April 1990): 28+, illus, stills.
Newsweek 115 (February 26, 1990): 66, stills. David Ansen.
New York 23 (March 5, 1990): 66+, stills. David Denby.
New York Times, February 16, 1990, C8, creds, stills. Vincent Canby. NYTR.
Maslin, Janet. "Film View: What If. . . ? New Movies in Other Hands—Just Suppose John Huston Had Directed 'Revenge' and David Lean, 'Mountains of the Moon.'" *New York Times,* March 11, 1990, sect. 2, 17+, stills.
Rohter, L. "Old Pro, Young Idol Team up for *Revenge.*" *New York Times,* February 11, 1990, sect. 2, 20+, stills.
SCN 9 (June 1990): 21. R. D. Larson.
Screen International 622 (October 17, 1987): 14.
Screen International 745 (February 24, 1990): 19.
Skoop 26 (September 1990): 44–45, stills. E. E. Vos.
Time Out 1,035 (June 20, 1990): 48.
24 Images 49 (Summer 1990): 81, stills. G. Privet.
Variety 338, no. 7 (February 21, 1990): 306, creds. A. Dawes. VR.
Village Voice 35 (February 27, 1990): 62, stills. G. Giddins.

THE RHINEMANN EXCHANGE. 1977. TV. (Actor.)

REVIEW
Variety 286 (March 16, 1977): 46. Bok (B. Knight).

RHODES OF AFRICA. 1936. (Writer.)

ARTICLES AND REVIEWS
Agate, James. *Around Cinemas.* New York: Arno Press, 1946, 127–29.
The American Film Catalog: Feature Films, 1931–1940. Berkeley: University of California Press, 1993, 2,578.
Canadian Magazine 85 (February 1936): 37.
Esquire 5 (May 1936): 115.
Film Daily, February 21, 1936, 13.
Film Weekly 15, no. 388 (March 21, 1936).
Greene, Graham. *Graham Greene on Film: Collected Film Criticism, 1935–1940.* Edited by John Russell Taylor. New York: Simon & Schuster, 1972, 61.
Harrison's Reports, March 14, 1936, 42.
Hollywood Reporter, February 25, 1936, 3.
**Hollywood Spectator* 10, no. 12 (March 28, 1936): 6–7.
Kinematograph Weekly 1,509 (March 19, 1936).
Kinematograph Weekly 1,519 (May 28, 1936).
Kino News 2, no. 4 (1935).
Life and Letters To-day 14, no. 4 (Summer 1936): 174.
Literary Digest 121 (March 7, 1936): 21.
Motion Picture Guide 6 (1986): 2,601.

Motion Picture Herald, March 7, 1936, 50.
The Nation 142 (March 18, 1936): 360.
National Board of Review Magazine 11 (March 1936): 13.
New Republic 86 (March 18, 1936): 166.
New Statesman & Nation 11 (March 21, 1936): 457.
New Yorker 12 (February 29, 1936): 51.
New York Times, February 23, 1936, 4.
New York Times, February 29, 1936, 11. NYTR.
**Rob Wagner's Script* 15 (March 28, 1936): 10.
Saturday Review (London) 161 (March 27, 1936): 416.
Spectator 156 (March 27, 1936): 575.
Stage 13 (February 1936): 61.
The Tattler, 139 (March 25, 1936): 562.
Time 27 (March 9, 1936): 44.
Variety, March 4, 1936, 26. VR.
Wilson, Robert, ed. *The Film Criticism of Otis Ferguson.* Philadelphia: Temple University Press, 1971, 123–24.

THE ROARING TWENTIES. 1939. (Writer, uncredited.)

ARTICLES AND REVIEWS

The American Film Institute Catalog: Feature Films, 1931–1940. Berkeley: University of California Press, 1993, 1,814.
Bookbinder, Robert. *Classics of the Foreign Film: A Pictorial Treasury.* Secaucus, N.J.: Citadel Press, 1985.
Clarens, Carlos. *Crime Movies: An Illustrated History.* New York: Norton, 1980, 155–56.
Commonweal 31 (November 10, 1939): 79.
Dickens, Homer. *The Films of James Cagney.* Secaucus, N.J.: Citadel Press, 1972, 143–46.
Draper, Ellen. *CinemaTexas Program Notes* 17, no. 1 (September 17, 1979): 29–35, filmog.
Film Daily, October 16, 1939, 6.
Hanson, Patricia King. "The Roaring Twenties." In *International Dictionary of Films and Filmmakers.* Vol. 1, *Films,* edited by Christopher Lyon, 394–95. Chicago: St. James Press, 1984. (Updated in *International Dictionary of Films and Filmmakers,* vol. 1, *Films,* 2d ed., edited by Nicholas Thomas, 760–62, Chicago, St. James Press, 1990; and in 3d ed., edited by Nicolet V. Elert and Aruna Vasudeven, 857–58, Detroit, St. James Press, 1997.)
Harrison's Reports, November 4, 1939, 43.
Hochman, Stanley, ed. *From Quasimodo to Scarlett to O'Hara: A National Board of Review Anthology, 1920–1940.* New York: Ungar, 1982, 329–29.
Hollywood Reporter, October 12, 1939, 3.
Hollywood Spectator 14 (October 28, 1939): 10–11.
McCarty, Clifford. *The Complete Films of Humphrey Bogart.* Secaucus, N.J.: Citadel Press, 71–72. (Reprint—New York: Carol Publishing Group, 1995.)

Magill's Survey of Cinema: First Series 3 (1986): 1,458–61. Dan Scapperotti.

Michael, Paul. *Humphrey Bogart: The Man and His Films.* Indianapolis: Bobbs-Merrill, 1965, 96–98.

Motion Picture Guide 6 (1986): 2,643–44.

Motion Picture Herald, October 21, 1939, 38.

Movietone News, no. 45 (November 1975): 14–21.

***National Board of Review Magazine* 14 (December 1939): 11–12.

New Masses 33 (November 21, 1939): 29–30.

New Republic 101 (December 6, 1939): 194.

Newsweek 14 (October 30, 1939): 39.

New Yorker 15 (November 11, 1939): 69.

New York Times, November 11, 1939, 12. NYTR.

On Film, no. 12 (Spring 1984): 28–36.

Parish, James Robert, and Michael R. Pitts. *The Great Gangster Pictures.* Metuchen, N.J.: Scarecrow Press, 1977, 333–35.

Photoplay 53 (December 1939): 63.

Positif 315 (May 1987): 69–71. Alain Masson.

***Rob Wagner's Script* 22 (November 4, 1939): 16–17.

Spectator 164 (March 1, 1940): 284.

Time 34 (November 13, 1939): 86.

Variety, October 25, 1939, 11. VR.

Vermilye, James. *The Films of the Thirties.* Secaucus, N.J.: Citadel Press, 1982, 244–46.

Wilson, Robert, ed. *The Film Criticism of Otis Ferguson.* Philadelphia: Temple University Press, 1971, 277–78.

THE ROCKY ROAD TO DUBLIN. 1968. Documentary. (Interviewed.)

ARTICLES AND REVIEWS
Jeune Cinéma 33 (October 1968): 15.

New York Times, July 21, 1968. Gloria Emerson.

Positif 100–101 (December 1968–January 1969): 80. Peter Lennon.

Variety, May 15, 1968, 7. VR.

ROOTS OF HEAVEN. 1958. (Director; Writer, uncredited.)

ARTICLES
Archer, Eugene. "To Cut or Not to Cut." *New York Times,* January 22, 1961. (Reprinted in *The New York Times Encyclopedia of Film, 1958–1963.*)

Canby, Vincent. "'D. Z.': The Last Tycoon." *New York Times,* March 17, 1968. (Reprinted in *The New York Times Encyclopedia of Film, 1964–1968.*)

Champlin, Charles. "Films Huston Would Like to Remake." *Los Angeles Times,* October 30, 1969. Discusses *Moulin Rouge* and *Roots of Heaven.*

Flynn, Errol. *My Wicked, Wicked Ways.* New York: Putnam, 1959.

Grenier, C. "Huston at Fontainbleau." *Sight & Sound* 27, no. 6 (Autumn 1958): 280–85.

"John Huston Hits a Double: Short Production Report on *Roots* and *Barbarian.*" *Look* 22 (November 25, 1958): 106. NYPL.

"John Huston's Big Stage: Huston Talks about His Technique While Filming *Roots* in Paris." *Newsweek* 52 (July 21, 1958): 87.

Maucerti, James. "Africa: Still Dark in Zanuck's *Roots.*" *Film Daily,* September 9, 1958, 1+.

Motion Picture Guide 6 (1986): 2,669.

Nason, Richard W. "Huston Hits High with 'Heaven' and 'Geisha.'" *New York Times,* September 28, 1958. (Reprinted in *The New York Times Encyclopedia of Film, 1958–1963.*) Interview with Huston on the opening of his two Twentieth Century-Fox films: *Heaven Knows, Mr. Allison* and *Roots of Heaven.*

St. Pierre, Brian. "John Huston: As He Was, Is, and Probably Always Will Be." *New York Times,* September 25, 1966. (Reprinted in *The New York Times Encyclopedia of Film, 1964–1968.*)

Saturday Review 41 (July 19, 1958): 36. Hollis Alpert. On making film. NYPL.

Thomas, Tony, Rudy Behlmer, and Clifford McCarty. *The Films of Errol Flynn.* New York: Citadel Press, 1969, 217–19.

Variety, June 11, 1958.

Variety, August 13, 1958.

Variety, September 10, 1958.

Variety, November 5, 1958.

Variety, November 19, 1958. NYPL.

REVIEWS

America 100 (November 1, 1958): 147.

BFI/Monthly Film Bulletin 26, no. 301 (February 1959): 15.

Bianco e Nero 47, no. 4 (October–December 1986): 31.

Casablanca 35 (November 1983): 41.

Catholic World 188 (January 1959): 327–28.

Commonweal 69 (November 7, 1958): 150.

Cue, October 25, 1958. NYPL.

Daily Cinema 8,095 (December 19, 1958): 3.

Film Daily 114, no. 75 (October 16, 1958): 6. Mandel Herbstman. AMPAS.

Filmfacts 1 (1958–59): 191, creds.

Film Quarterly 12, no. 2 (Winter 1958): 42–45. Arlene Croce, "*The Roots of Heaven* and *The Barbarian and the Geisha.*"

Films and Filming 5, no. 4 (January 1959): 20, illus.

Films and Filming 5, no. 5 (February 1959): 25–26, creds. Gordon Gow.

Films in Review 9, no. 9 (November 1958): 513–15, illus. Courtland Phipps. AMPAS.

Harrison's Reports, October 18, 1958, 166.

Hollywood Reporter 152, no. 6 (October 16, 1958): 3. AMPAS.

Kinematograph Weekly 2,680 (December 25, 1958): 14.

Life 45 (October 27, 1958): 105–6.

Los Angeles Times, November 1, 1958. AMPAS.
Motion Picture Daily, October 16, 1958.
Motion Picture Herald 213, no. 3 (October 18, 1958): 18. AMPAS.
New Republic 139 (November 3, 1958): 21–22.
Newsweek 52 (October 27, 1958): 94–95. AMPAS, MOMA.
New Yorker 34 (October 25, 1958): 192. AMPAS, NYPL.
New York Herald Tribune, October 16, 1958. AMPAS.
New York Journal American, October 16, 1958. Rose Pelswick.
New York Mirror, October 16, 1958, 44. Justin Gilbert.
New York Post, October 16, 1958, 34. Archer Winsten.
New York Times, October 16, 1958, 46. Bosley Crowther. AMPAS, NYPL, NYTR.
New York Times, October 19, 1958, sect. 2, 1. MOMA.
Observer, January 18, 1959. C. A. NYPL.
Thirard, Paul-Louis. "Adieu John?" *Positif* 30 (July 1959): 50–53. (Reprinted in
    John Huston, Collection dirigée, edited by Gilles Ciment, 110–11, Dossier
    Positif Rivages, Paris, Editions Rivages, Collection Positif-Rivages, no. 2, 1988.)
Saturday Review 41 (October 25, 1958): 25. Hollis Alpert. NYPL.
Senior Scholastic 73 (December 5, 1958): 33.
Sight & Sound 28, no. 2 (Spring 1959): 94. Derek Hill.
Time 72 (November 3, 1958). AMPAS, MOMA.
Variety, October 22, 1958. AMPAS, NYPL, VR.
Village Voice 4, no. 6 (December 3, 1958): 6. Jonas Mekas.

RUFINO TAMAYO: THE SOURCES OF HIS ART. 1972.
(Narrator.)

ARTICLE AND REVIEW
Film Library Quarterly 8, no. 2 (1975): 37–38.
New York Times (December 7, 1986): H30. Douglas C. McGill.

SERGEANT YORK. 1941. (Writer.)

ARTICLES AND REVIEWS
Barkley, Frederick B. "'Falsehood' Cry in Movie Hearing." *New York Times,*
    September 26, 1941. (Reprinted in *The New York Times Encyclopedia of Film,*
    1941–1946.)
Brady, Thomas. "Mr. Goldwyn Bows Out." *New York Times,* February 16, 1941.
    (Reprinted in *The New York Times Encyclopedia of Film, 1941–1946.*)
———. "Grist from the Hollywood Mill." *New York Times,* January 18, 1942.
    (Reprinted in *The New York Times Encyclopedia of Film, 1941–1946.*)
Catholic World 154 (October 1941): 86.
Churchill, Douglas W. "The New Production Set-up at Fox." *New York Times,*
    November 24, 1940. (Reprinted in *The New York Times Encyclopedia of Film,*
    1937–1940.)
Cinématographe Française 1974 (July 7, 1962): 22.

Classic Images 204 (June 1992): C22.

Commonweal 34 (July 1941): 306.

Crowther, Bosley. "Possible Formula for a Screen Hit." *New York Times,* March 22, 1942. (Reprinted in *The New York Times Encyclopedia of Film, 1941–1946.*)

———. "Reality or Escape?" *New York Times,* June 14, 1942. (Reprinted in *The New York Times Encyclopedia of Film, 1941–1946.*)

———. "America in Films." *New York Times,* July 12, 1942. (Reprinted in *The New York Times Encyclopedia of Film, 1941–1946.*)

———. "Living Biographies, Hollywood Style." *New York Times,* January 20, 1946. (Reprinted in *The New York Times Encyclopedia of Film, 1941–1946.*)

Dickens, Gary. *The Films of Gary Cooper.* New York: Citadel Press, 1970, 181–83.

Dietz, Howard. "Must the Movies Be 'Significant'?" *New York Times,* January 27, 1946A. (Reprinted in *The New York Times Encyclopedia of Film, 1941–1946.*)

"Eagles and the Hawks." *New York Times,* January 24, 1943. (Reprinted in *The New York Times Encyclopedia of Film, 1941–1946.*)

Film Daily, July 3, 1931, 4.

Harrison's Reports, July 12, 1941, 111.

Hawks, Howard. *Hawks on Hawks.* Berkeley: University of California Press, 1982, 93–94, 169–70.

Hollywood Reporter, July 2, 1941, 3.

"Joan Leslie Leafs Her Memory Book." *New York Times,* March 14, 1943. (Reprinted in *The New York Times Encyclopedia of Film, 1941–1946.*)

Lasky, Jesse, and Don Weldon. *I Blow My Own Horn.* Garden City, N.Y.: Doubleday, 1957.

Lee, David L. "Appalachia on Film: The Making of *Sergeant York.*" *The Southern Quarterly* 19, nos. 3 & 4 (Spring–Summer 1981): 207–21. (Also issued as *The South and Film,* edited by Warren French, Jackson, Miss., University Press of Mississippi, 1981, 207–21.)

Life 11 (July 14, 1941): 63–65.

London Times, December 1, 1941, 8.

Lorentz, Pare. *Lorentz on Film: Movies, 1927–1941.* New York: Hopkinson and Blake, 1975, 214–15.

Magill's Survey of Cinema: First Series 4 (1980): 1,509–511. Carl Macek.

Morella, Joe, Edward Z. Epstein, and John Griggs. *The Films of World War II.* Secaucus, N.J.: Citadel Press, 1973, 51–52.

Motion Picture Daily, July 3, 1941. Charles S. Aaronson.

Motion Picture Exhibitor, July 9, 1941, 786.

Motion Picture Exhibitor 26, no. 17 (September 3, 1941): sect. 2, 839.

Motion Picture Guide 7 (1987): 2,826–28.

Motion Picture Herald 144, no. 1 (July 5, 1941).

Motion Picture Herald Product Digest, April 19, 1941, 111.

New Republic 105 (September 29, 1941): 404–5.

Newsweek 18 (July 14, 1941): 61–62.

New Yorker 17 (July 5, 1941): 47.

New York Times, July 3, 1941, 15. Bosley Crowther. NYTR.

Now and Then 8, no. 3 (1991): 41. D. D. Lee. Making of *Sergeant York.*

Nugent, Frank S. "The All-American Man." *New York Times,* July 5, 1942. (Reprinted in *The New York Times Encyclopedia of Film, 1941–1946.*)

"Painting the Backdrops." *New York Times,* September 28, 1941. (Reprinted in *The New York Times Encyclopedia of Film, 1941–1946.*)

Picturegoer 11, no. 539 (October 18, 1941): 5.

Picturegoer 11, no. 547 (February 7, 1942): 14.

***Rob Wagner's Script* 27 (August 30, 1941): 14.

Scholastic 39 (September 15, 1941): 28.

Stanley, Fred. "Hollywood's Films Follow Our Battle Flags." *New York Times,* August 22, 1943. (Reprinted in *The New York Times Encyclopedia of Film, 1941–1946.*)

———. "Westerns Ride Again." *New York Times,* July 23, 1944. (Reprinted in *The New York Times Encyclopedia of Film, 1941–1946.*)

Strauss, Theodore. "Out of the Incubator." *New York Times,* June 29, 1941. (Reprinted in *The New York Times Encyclopedia of Film, 1941–1946.*)

Time 38 (August 4, 1941): 70.

Today's Cinema 57, no. 4,633 (October 14, 1941).

Variety, July 2, 1941, 12. VR.

"War Films Shoot the Girls to Stardom." *New York Times,* January 15, 1950. (Reprinted in *The New York Times Encyclopedia of Film, 1947–1951.*)

Weiler, A. H. "Reverie on a Pastrami Sandwich." *New York Times,* August 10, 1941. (Reprinted in *The New York Times Encyclopedia of Film, 1941–1946.*)

Willis, Donald C. *The Films of Howard Hawks.* Metuchen, N.J.: Scarecrow Press, 1975, 168–71.

Wilson, Robert, ed. *The Film Criticism of Otis Ferguson.* Philadelphia: Temple University Press, 1971, 385–86.

"Windfall for the Salvagers." *New York Times,* October 26, 1941. (Reprinted in *The New York Times Encyclopedia of Film, 1941–1946.*)

THE SHAKEDOWN. 1929. (Actor, uncredited.)

ARTICLES AND REVIEWS

The American Film Institute Catalog: Feature Films, 1921–1930. New York: R. R. Bowker, 1971, 702.

Bioscope 77, no. 1,159 (December 19, 1928).

Bioscope 79, no. 1,175 (April 10, 1929): 32.

Film Spectator 6, no. 12 (December 8, 1928): 6.

Harrison's Reports, April 13, 1929, 58.

Motion Picture Guide 7 (1987): 2,858.

New York Times, April 8, 1929, 32. NYTR.

Variety, April 10, 1929. VR.

SHERLOCK HOLMES IN NEW YORK. TV. 1976. (Actor.)

REVIEW

Cinema Fantastique 5, no. 3 (1976): 29, creds, stills. D. Masloski.

SINFUL DAVEY. 1969. (Director; Writer, uncredited.)

ARTICLES AND REVIEWS

The American Film Institute Catalog: Feature Films, 1961–1970. New York: R. R. Bowker, 1976, 1991.

BFI/Monthly Film Bulletin 36, no. 425 (June 1969): 112.

Christian Science Monitor, June 9, 1969. David Sterritt.

Daily Cinema 9,394 (July 12, 1967): 8.

Filmfacts 12 (1969): 302, creds.

Films and Filming 15, no. 10 (July 1969): 46, creds, illus. Peter Buckley. AMPAS.

Film TV Daily, March 13, 1969, 6. Mandel Herbstam.

Films in Review 20, no. 5 (May 1969): 319–20, illus. Wilson Derr.

Focus, no. 5 (October 1969): 34. Myron Meisel.

Hollywood Reporter 204, no. 43 (February 19, 1969): 3. AMPAS.

Kine Weekly 3,212 (May 3, 1969): 17.

Lennon, Peter. "Huston in Focus on Film Industry." *Los Angeles Times,* September 16, 1957, part 1, 17. On-location exclusive to *Los Angeles Times* from *Manchester Guardian.*

Los Angeles Times, May 29, 1969. AMPAS.

Miller, E. "You've Got to Shout to Make Yourself Heard." *Seventeen* 27 (June 1968): 90+.

Motion Picture Guide 7 (1987): 2,933.

New York Times, June 5, 1969, 54. Vincent Canby. NYTR.

Saturday Review, March 8, 1969. Arthur Knight.

Today's Cinema 9,670 (May 9, 1969): 4.

Variety, February 26, 1969, 33. VR.

THE STORM. 1930. (Actor, uncredited.)

ARTICLES AND REVIEWS

The American Film Institute Catalog: Feature Films, 1921–1930. New York: R. R. Bowker, 1971, 768.

Bioscope 84, no. 1,246 (August 20, 1930): 37.

Harrison's Reports, August 30, 1930, 139.

Motion Picture Guide 7 (1987): 3,138.

New York Times, August 23, 1930, 7 NYTR.

Variety, August 27, 1930. VR.

THE STORY OF G.I. JOE. 1945. (Writer, uncredited. *See* chapter 14, "Huston on Film and Other Projects.")

ARTICLES AND REVIEWS

Agee, James. *Agee on Film: Reviews and Comments.* New York: McDowell, Obolensky, 1958. (Reprint—as Vol. 1, New York, Grosset & Dunlap, 1967, 171–75.)

Commonweal 42 (July 27, 1945): 358.

Epstein, Edward Z., and John Griggs. *The Films of World War II*. Secaucus, N.J.: Citadel Press, 1973, 232–33.

Film Daily, June 18, 1945, 56.

Film Quarterly 1 (October 1945): 34–39.

Harrison's Reports, June 23, 1945, 98.

Hollywood Reporter, June 18, 1945, 3.

Kane, Kathryn. *Visions of War: Hollywood Combat Films of World War II*. Ann Arbor, Mich.: University of Michigan Research Press, 1982, 92–100.

Lejeune, C. A. *Chestnuts in Her Lap, 1936–1946*. London: Phoenix House, 1947, 158–59.

Life 19 (July 9, 1945): 61+.

London Times, September 27, 1945, 8.

Magill's Survey of Cinema: First Series 4 (1980):1,638–40. Leslie Taubman.

Marill, Alvin H. *Robert Mitchum on the Screen*. South Brunswick, N.J.: A. S. Barnes, 1978, 86–87.

Motion Picture Guide 7 (1987): 3,145.

Motion Picture Exhibitor 34, no. 8 (June 27, 1945): sect. 2, 1,738.

Motion Picture Herald Product Digest, June 23, 1945, 2,509.

Musician 50 (July 1945): 137.

The Nation 161 (September 15, 1945): 264–66.

New Republic 113 (August 13, 1945): 190.

Newsweek 26 (July 6, 1945): 98+.

New Yorker 21 (October 6, 1945): 85.

New York Times, October 6, 1945, 9. NYTR.

Scholastic 47 (September 24, 1945): 32.

Suid, Lawrence H. *Guts & Glory: Great America War Movies*. Reading, Mass.: Addison-Wesley, 1978, pp. 62–69.

Theatre Arts 29 (October 1945): 581–82.

Thompson, Frank T. *William A. Wellman*. With a foreword by Barbara Stanwyck. Metuchen, N.J.: Scarecrow Press, 1983, 212–15+.

Time 46 (July 23, 1945): 96.

Variety, June 20, 1945, 11. VR.

THE STRANGER. 1946. (Writer, uncredited.)

ARTICLES AND REVIEWS

Agee, James. *Agee on Film: Reviews and Comments*. New York: McDowell, Obolensky, 1958. (Reprint—as Vol. 1, New York, Grosset & Dunlap, 1967, 204–5.)

Anderegg, M. "Orson Welles as Performer." *Persistence of Vision* 7 (1989): 73–82.

Bazin, Andre. *Orson Welles: A Critical View*. New York: Harper, 1978.

Bogdanovich, Peter. *Cinema of Orson Welles*. New York: The Library of the Museum of Modern Art, 1961, 84–85.

Cahiers du Cinéma 310 (April 1980): 47–48, creds, stills. L. Perrin.

Carrere, E. "Kindler, Quinlan, MacBeth, Faust, Harry Lime, Kurtz . . .: 'The Stranger.'" *Positif,* no. 231 (June 1980): 69–71, creds, stills.

Cinéma (Paris), no. 255 (March 1980): 76–77, creds, stills. C. M. Cluny.

Cinématographe, no. 56 (April 1980): 52. creds, stills. J. Tonnerre.

Commonweal 44 (July 12, 1946): 309.

Cowie, Peter. *The Cinema of Orson Welles.* London: Zwemmer; New York: A. S. Barnes, 1965.

Douin, Jean-Luc, and A. Moreau. "Le génie musel/le criminel." *Télérama* 2,285 (October 27, 1993): 92+.

D. W. Griffith Film Center. *The Stranger* (1946). [2 p.] Discussion on making the film and Sam Spiegal's role as producer.

"Film Buff Series, 1980–1981" [Program notes]. Toronto Film Society, January 1981.

Film Daily, May 23, 1946, 7.

Harrison's Reports, May 25, 1946, 83.

Hollywood Reporter, May 21, 1946, 3. Jack D. Grant.

Life 20 (June 3, 1946): 75–78.

Kinematograph Weekly 2,046 (July 4, 1946).

Kinematograph Weekly 2,490 (March 17, 1955): 29.

Magill's Survey of Cinema, Second Series 5 (1981): 2,294–97.

Medium 7 (March 1977): 26–28, creds, stills. N. Grob.

Morella, Joe, Edward Z. Epstein, and John Griggs. *The Films of World War II.* Secaucus, N.J.: Citadel Press, 1973, 238–39.

Motion Picture Daily, May 21, 1946. Red Kann.

Motion Picture Guide 7 (1987): 3,161.

Motion Picture Herald Product Digest 163, no. 8 (May 25, 1946): 3,005.

Naremore, James. *The Magic World of Orson Welles.* New York: Oxford University Press, 1978.

————. "Between Works & Texts: Notes from the Welles Archive." *Persistence of Vision* 7 (1989): 12–23, stills.

The Nation 162 (June 22, 1946): 765.

New Republic 115 (September 16, 1946): 326–27.

Newsweek 28 (July 15, 1946): 97.

New Yorker 22 (June 29, 1946): 64.

New York Times, July 11, 1946, 18. NYTR.

Palmer, R. Barton. "The Politics of Genre in Welles' *The Stranger.*" *Film Criticism* 9, no. 2 (Winter 1984–85): 2–14. (Reprinted in *Film Criticism* 11, nos. 1 & 2 [1987]: 31–42.)

Quaderni 5 (December 1985): 28–29, creds.

**Rob Wagner's Script* 32, no. 734 (July 20, 1946): 13.

Silver, Alain, and Elizabeth Ward, eds. *Film Noir: An Encyclopedic Reference.* 3d ed., rev. Woodstock, N.Y.: Overlook Press, 1992, 268–69, analysis, creds, synopsis.

Stanley, Fred. "An Old Hollywood Costume." *New York Times,* October 21, 1945. (Reprinted in *The New York Times Encyclopedia of Film, 1941–1946.*)

Theatre Arts 30 (August 1946): 441.

Time 47 (June 17, 1946): 98. MOMA.

Today's Cinema 66, no. 5,362 (June 28, 1946).

Today's Cinema 84, no. 7,223 (March 11, 1955): 10.
Variety, May 22, 1946, 10. VR.
Video Watchdog 23 (May–July 1994): 28–39. On deleted scenes from the final version of *The Stranger* that were left out without Orson Welles's consent.

TENTACLES. 1977. (Actor.)

ARTICLES AND REVIEWS
BFI/Monthly Film Bulletin 44, no. 521 (June 1977): 129–30. creds. T. Milne.
Cinematografia 44, nos. 1 & 2 (January–February 1977): 85–86, creds.
Film Bulletin 46 (June 1977): 38. B. Klauber.
Films and Filming 23, no. 11 (August 1977): 33, creds. A. Stuart.
Films Illustrated 6 (June 1977): 364, stills.
Hollywood Reporter 247, no. 5 (June 22, 1977): 3+.
Independent Film Journal 80 (August 19, 1977): 18, creds. S. Klain.
Mano, D. K. "Mano Gets Waterlogged." *Oui* 6 (December 1977): 60+.
Motion Picture Guide 8 (1987): 3,311.
New York Times, August 4, 1977, sect. 3, 14. NYTR.
Positif 194 (June 1977): 77. G. Gressard.
La Revue du Cinéma 317 (May 1977): 124–25, stills. G. Allombert.
La Revue du Cinéma 320–321 (October 1977): 259–60, creds. A. Garel.
Screen International 88 (May 21, 1977): 16–17.
Soundtrack 10, no. 39 (September 1991): 43. Randall D. Larson.
Variety 287, no. 6 (June 15, 1977): 20, creds. Pit (J. Pitman). VR.

THREE STRANGERS. 1946. (Writer.)

ARTICLES AND REVIEWS
Brooklyn Eagle, February 23, 1946. Herbert Cohen.
Film Daily, January 28, 1946.
Harrison's Reports, February 2, 1946, 19.
Hollywood Quarterly 1, no. 2 (January 1946): 214–22. Adolph Deutch.
Hollywood Reporter, January 23, 1946.
Hollywood Review, January 28, 1946.
Kinematograph Weekly 2,015 (November 29, 1945).
Los Angeles Times, February 9, 1946. Edwin Schallert.
Motion Picture Daily, January 23, 1946.
Motion Picture Guide 8 (1987): 3,426.
Motion Picture Herald 152, no. 4 (January 26, 1946).
New York Herald Tribune, February 23, 1946. Howard Barnes.
New York Morning Telegraph, February 22, 1946. Alton Cooke.
New York Sun, February 23, 1946. Eileen Creelman.
New York Telegraph, February 23, 1946. Leo Mishkin.
New York Times, February 23, 1946, 20. NYTR.
Nielsen, Ray. "Ray's Way: Geraldine Fitzgerald on *Three Strangers.*" *Classic Images* 158 (August 1988): 52+, illus, interv, stills.

————. "Ray's Way: Joan Lorring and *Three Strangers*." *Classic Images* 159 (September 1988): 27, illus, interv.
PM, February 24, 1946. McManus.
Today's Cinema 65, no. 5,272 (November 28, 1945).
Tuska, Jon. *Dark Cinema: American Film Noir in Cultural Perspective.* Westport, Conn.: Greenwood Press, 1984.
Variety, January 30, 1946. VR.

TOMORROW THE WORLD. 1944. (Unrealized project.)

ARTICLES

Harrison's Reports, December 23, 1944, 207.
Motion Picture Guide 8 (1987): 3,485.
New York Times, December 22, 1944, 12. NYTR.
Variety, December 20, 1944. VR.

TO THE WESTERN WORLD: THE TRAVELS OF J. M. SYNGE AND JACK YEATS IN CONNEMARA IN 1905. 1981. Documentary. (Narrator.)

ARTICLES

Broadcast 1,098 (March 9, 1981): 9.
Broadcast 1,136 (November 30, 1981): 10.
Screen International 272 (December 20, 1980): 16.

THE TREASURE OF THE SIERRA MADRE. 1948. (Director, Writer, Actor.)

ARTICLES

Allen, Lillian. "On the Set with John Huston." *Cinema* (Hollywood) 2 (July 1947): 7–8.
Alpert, Hollis. "Offbeat Director in Outer Space." *New York Times,* January 16, 1966. (Reprinted in *The New York Times Encyclopedia of Film, 1964–1968.*)
Archer, Eugene. "A Monograph of John Huston: Part 1—A Touch of Hemingway." *Films and Filming,* September 1959, 13–14.
————. "Bogart: Man and Superman." *New York Times,* January 3, 1965. (Reprinted in *The New York Times Encyclopedia of Film, 1964–1968.*)
————. "Where Are the Stars of Yesteryear?" *New York Times,* May 30, 1965. (Reprinted in *The New York Times Encyclopedia of Film, 1964–1968.*)
Bachmann, Gideon. "How I Make Films: An Interview with John Huston." *Film Quarterly* 11 (Fall 1965): 3–13.
Beja, Morris. *Film and Literature: An Introduction.* New York: Longman, 1979, 168–74.
Brennan, Frederick Hazlitt. "Memo to the Moguls of Hollywood." *New York Times,* July 25, 1948D. (Reprinted in *The New York Times Encyclopedia of Film, 1947–1951.*)

Burke, Tom. "'Casting Is Everything,' Says 'Cukoo's' Director, Milos Forman." *New York Times,* March 28, 1976. (Reprinted in *The New York Times Encyclopedia of Film, 1975–1976.*)

Claro, J., and M. Stern. "Letters: Huston and the Man Who Might Be Traven." *New York Times* 136 (July 27, 1987): A18, stills.

Colbert, Claudette. "Nominations for the Late, Late—." *New York Times,* February 28, 1960. (Reprinted in *The New York Times Encyclopedia of Film, 1958–1963.*)

Conforti, A. "Il tesoro della Sierra Madre: L'isola di Corallo." *Cineforum* 28, no. 9 (September 1988): 63.

Corry, John. "John Huston: Musings on 'Fat City' and Other Pursuits." *New York Times,* August 5, 1972. (Reprinted in *The New York Times Encyclopedia of Film, 1972–1974.*)

"Costume Pictures on the Upswing." *New York Times,* September 21, 1947. (Reprinted in *The New York Times Encyclopedia of Film, 1947–1951.*)

Cowie, Peter. *Seventy Years of Cinema.* South Brunswick, N.J.: A. S. Barnes, 1969, 165–67.

Crowther, Bosley. *The Great Films: Fifty Golden Years of Motion Pictures.* New York: Putnam, 1967, 189–92.

Desternes, Jean. "John Huston et l'intimisme de l'aventure: *Le Trésor de la Sierra Madre.*" *La Revue du Cinéma* 3, no. 18 (October 1948).

Engell, John. "The Treasure of Sierra Madre: B. Traven, John Huston and Ideology in Film Adaptation." *Literature/Film Quarterly* 17, no. 4 (October 1989): 245–52, biblio, illus.

————. "Traven, Huston and the Textual Treasures of the Sierra Madre." In *Reflections in a Male Eye,* edited by Gaylyn Studlar and David Desser, 79–95. Washington, D.C.: Smithsonian Institution Press, 1993.

"Film Buff Series 'A': 1981–82" [Program notes]. Programme 7. Toronto Film Society, January 24, 1982. Notes compiled by Marcia Gillespie and Lloyd Gordon Ward, research by Helen Arthurs. Screened *The Misfits* and *Treasure.*

The Films of John Huston" [Program notes]. Los Angeles County Museum of Art, October 11, 1980. Excerpted from Tony Thomas, *The Great Adventure Films* (Secaucus, N.J., Citadel Press, 1976).

Gardner, Gerlad, ed. *The Censorship Papers: Movie Censorship Papers from the Hayes Office, 1934–1968.* New York: Dodd, Mead, 1987.

Graham, Olive. *CinemaTexas Program Notes* 16, no. 3 (May 3, 1979): [85]–88, biblio, filmog.

Greenberg, Harvey R. "*The Treasure of Sierra Madre*—There's Success Phobia in Them Thar Hills!" In *Movies on Your Mind,* Harvey R. Greenberg, 33–52. New York: Saturday Review Press/E. P. Dutton, 1975.

Hammen, Scott. *Film Notes.* Louisville, Ky.: Hamilton Printing Co, 1979.

Hardy, Phil. *The Western: The Film Encyclopedia.* New York: Morrow, 1983.

Hawkins, Robert F. "Observations on the Italian Picture Scene." *New York Times,* April 5, 1953. (Reprinted in *The New York Times Encyclopedia of Film, 1952–1957.*)

————. "'Noah' Huston's Genesis." *New York Times,* February 21, 1965. (Reprinted in *The New York Times Encyclopedia of Film, 1964–1968.*)

Hill, Gladwyn. "John Huston—A Bull in the China Shop." *New York Times,* January 16, 1949. (Reprinted in *The New York Times Encyclopedia of Film, 1947–1951.*)

Hollywood Reporter, March 25, 1949.

Institut des Hautes Etudes Cinématographiques. *Fiche Filmographique,* no. 83 [Program notes]. MOMA.

Jones, Dupre. "Beating the Devil: 30 Years of John Huston." *Films and Filming* 19 (January 1973): 26–32.

Kaminsky, Stuart. "Gold Hat, God Fever, Silver Screen." In *The Modern American Novel and the Movies,* edited by Gerald Peary and Roger Shatzkin, 53–62. New York: Ungar, 1978. (Updated as "Literary Adaptation: The Treasure of the Sierra Madre—Novel into Film." In *American Film Genres,* 2d ed., by Stuart Kaminsky, 97–105, Chicago, Nelson-Hall, 1985.)

———. "The Treasure of the Sierra Madre." In *International Dictionary of Films and Filmmakers.* Vol. 1, *Films,* edited by Christopher Lyon, 485–86. Chicago: St. James Press, 1984. (Reprinted in *International Dictionary of Films and Filmmakers,* vol. 1, *Films,* 2d ed., edited by Nicholas Thomas, 914–15, Chicago, St. James Press, 1990; and in 3d ed., edited by Nicolet V. Elert and Aruna Vasudeven, 1,025–26, Detroit, St. James Press, 1997.)

Leff, Leonard J. *Film Plots: Scene by Scene Narrative.* Vol. 2. Ann Arbor, Mich.: Perian Press, 1988

Lewis, Anthony. "TV Block Booking of Movies Barred." *New York Times,* November 6, 1962. (Reprinted in *The New York Times Encyclopedia of Film, 1958–1963.*)

Libby, Bill. *They Didn't Win the Oscars.* Westport, Conn.: Arlington House, 1980.

Life 26 (March 14, 1949): 44.

McCarty, Clifford. *The Complete Films of Humphrey Bogart.* Secaucus, N.J.: Citadel Press, 1965, 136–41. (Reprint—New York: Carol Publishing Group, 1995.)

McDougal, Stuart Y. *Made into Movies: From Literature to Film.* New York: Holt, Rinehart, 1985.

McKee, Patrick, and Jennifer McLerran. "The Old Prospector: *The Treasure of the Sierra Madre* as Exemplar of Old Age in Popular Film." *International Journal of Aging and Human Development* 40, no. 1 (January–February 1995): 1–9.

Magill's Survey of Cinema: First Series 4 (1986): 1,773–76. Leslie Taubman.

Malcolm, Andrew H. "Huston: 'I Want to Keep Right on Going.'" *New York Times,* December 11, 1979. (Reprinted in *The New York Times Encyclopedia of Film, 1977–1979.*)

Marcus, Fred H. *Film and Literature: Contrasts in Media.* Scranton, Penn.: Chandler Publishing Co, 1971.

Masterson, Peg. *CinemaTexas Program Notes* 11, no. 3 (November 9, 1976): 73–75, biblio, credits, discussion, filmog.

Michael, Paul. *Humphrey Bogart: The Man and His Films.* Indianapolis: Bobbs-Merrill, 1965, 143–44.

Miller, Gabriel. "The Wages of Sin: *The Treasure of the Sierra Madre.*" In

Screening the Novel: Rediscovered American Fiction in Film. New York: Ungar, 1980, 84–115.

Motion Picture Guide 8 (1987): 3,536–38.

Motion Picture Herald Product Digest 170, no. 2 (January 10, 1949): 4,009.

"The Mystery of B. Traven Unraveled by BBC Team." *New York Times,* December 22, 1978. (Reprinted in *The New York Times Encyclopedia of Film, 1977–1979.*)

Naremore, James. "Introduction: A Likely Project." In *The Treasure of the Sierra Madre,* edited by James Naremore, 9–32. Wisconsin/Warner Bros. Screenplay Series. Madison, Wis.: University of Wisconsin Press, 1979.

Nason, Richard W. "Huston Hits High With 'Heaven' and 'Geisha.'" *New York Times,* September 28, 1958. (Reprinted in *The New York Times Encyclopedia of Film, 1958–1963.*)

Overton, R. "'The Treasure of Sierra Madre' Poem." *Literature/Film Quarterly* 1, no. 2 (1973): 166.

"Passing of Taboos." *New York Times,* April 1, 1951. (Reprinted in *The New York Times Encyclopedia of Film, 1947–1951.*)

Photoplay 32, no. 4 (April 1981): 22.

Radio Times 250, no. 3,271 (August 2, 1986): 14.

La Revue du Cinéma, nos. 320 & 321 (October 3, 1977): 271. A. Garel.

Rotha, Paul, and Richard Griffith. *The Film Till Now.* London: Vision Press, 1949.

Ruffinelli, Jorge. "El misterio de B. Traven." *Quimera* 20 (June 1982): 26–31.

St. Pierre, Brian. "John Huston: As He Was, Is, and Probably Always Will Be." *New York Times,* September 25, 1966. (Reprinted in *The New York Times Encyclopedia of Film, 1964–1968.*)

Schumach, Murray. "Hollywood Joust." *New York Times,* January 28, 1962. (Reprinted in *The New York Times Encyclopedia of Film, 1958–1963.*)

Sperber, A. M., and Eric Lax. *Bogart.* New York: Morrow, 1997.

Spinard, Leonard. "Is There a B. Traven in the House?" *New York Times,* January 18, 1948. (Reprinted in *The New York Times Encyclopedia of Film, 1947–1951.*)

Subiéla, Michel. "Et qui rira, verra, *The Treasure of Sierra Madre.*" *Positif,* no. 3 (July–August 1952): 18–21. (Reprinted in *John Huston, Collection dirigée,* edited by Gilles Ciment, 73–75, Dossier Positif Rivages, Paris, Editions Rivages, Collection Positif-Rivages, no. 2, 1988.)

Taylor, John Russell. "John Huston and the Figure in the Carpet." *Sight & Sound* 38 (Spring 1969): 70–73.

"10th Season Programme 10" [Program notes]. Toronto Film Society, May 11, 1958.

Thomas, Tony. *The Great Adventure Films.* Secaucus, N.J.: Citadel Press, 1976.

Valenti, Peter. "*The Treasure of the Sierra Madre:* Spiritual Quest and Studio Patriarchy." In *Image & Likeness: Religious Visions in American Film Classics,* edited by John R. May, Mahwah, N.J.: Paulist Press, 1992.

Variety, March 23, 1949.

Variety, March 25, 1949. On the Academy Awards.

Watters, Jim. "John Huston on Kipling, Hemingway and Jack Daniels." *New York*

Times, February 15, 1976. (Reprinted in *The New York Times Encyclopedia of Film, 1975–1976.*0

REVIEWS

Commonweal 47 (February 6, 1948): 424.

Ecran Française, February 15, 1949. Robert Pilat. (Excerpt reprinted in *Positif,* no. 3 [July–August 1952]: 45.)

Film Daily, January 7, 1948, 7. AMPAS.

Filmihullu, no. 6 (1975): 19–20. (Translation of James Agee's piece in *The Nation,* January 31, 1948.)

**Fortnight* 4, no. 3 (January 30, 1948): 30.

Harrison's Reports, January 10, 1948, 7.

Hollywood Quarterly 3, no. 3 (Spring 1948): 316–19. Lawrence Morton.

Hollywood Reporter, January 6, 1948, 3. AMPAS.

Jameson, Richard T. "The Treasure of the Sierra Madre." *Film Comment* [Midsection]16, no. 3 (May–June 1980): 33–37.

Kinematograph Weekly 2,159 (September 16, 1948): 18.

Life 24 (February 2, 1948): 63–64.

Los Angeles Times, January 15, 1948. AMPAS.

Motion Picture Daily, January 7, 1948.

Motion Picture Herald Product Digest, January 10, 1949, 4,009.

Movie Makers 23, no. 1 (January 1948): 24.

The Nation 166 (January 31, 1948): 136–38.

**New Movies* 23, no. 2 (February–March 1948): 6. Henry Hart.

New Republic 118 (January 26, 1948): 35.

Newsweek 31 (January 26, 1948): 88. AMPAS.

New Yorker 23 (January 24, 1948): 50.

New York Herald Tribune, January 24, 1948. Howard Barnes.

New York Times, January 24, 1948, 11. NYTR.

New York Times, January 25, 1948, sect. 2, 1. (Reprinted in *The New York Times Film Reviews. A One-Volume Selection, 1913–1970,* edited by George Amberg, New York, Arno Press, 1971.)

Séquences, no. 7 (Spring 1949): 34–36. Peter Ericsson. Reviews *Key Largo* and *The Treasure of the Sierra Madre.*

Theatre Arts 32 (February 1948): 41.

Time 51 (February 2, 1948): 80–82. AMPAS, MOMA.

Today's Cinema 71, no. 5,699 (September 10, 1948).

Variety, January 6, 1948. VR.

Variety, January 7, 1948, 56. AMPAS.

Women's Home Companion 75 (March 1948): 10.

TUNISIAN VICTORY. 1943. (Director, replacement scenes; Writer.)

ARTICLES AND REVIEWS

Aldgate, T. "Mr. Capra Goes to War: Frank Capra, the British Army Film Unit, and

Anglo-American Travails in the Production of *Tunisian Victory.*" *Historical Journal of Film, Radio and Television* 11, no. 1 (March 1991): 21–39.

Coultass, Clive. "*Tunisian Victory:* A Film Too Late?" *Imperial War Museum Review* 1 (1986): 64–73.

Crowther, Bosley. "Observations on War Documentaries as Inspired by *Tunisian Victory.*" *New York Times,* April 2, 1944. MOMA, NYPL.

Cue, March 25, 1944. NYPL.

Motion Picture Daily, March 7, 1944. Charles Ryweck.

New Yorker, March 25, 1944, 77. NYPL.

New York Herald Tribune, March 19, 1944.

New York Herald Tribune, March 25, 1944. Howard Barnes. MOMA, NYPL.

New York Journal American, March 24, 1944. NYPL.

New York Morning Telegraph, March 25, 1944.

New York Times, March 24, 1944, 17. Bosley Crowther. NYTR.

New York World Telegram, March 24, 1944. NYPL.

Time, April 17, 1944. MOMA, NYPL.

"Tunisian Victory Now Being Filmed." *New York Times,* April 28, 1943.

Variety, March 8, 1944. VR.

UNDERGROUND. 1941. (Writer, uncredited.)

ARTICLES AND REVIEWS
Harrison's Reports, June 21, 1941, 9.
Motion Picture Guide 8 (1987): 3,624–25.
New York Times, June 23, 1941, 13. NYTR.
Variety, June 25, 1941. VR.

UNDER THE VOLCANO. 1984. (Director; Writer, uncredited.)

ARTICLES

Atlas, Jacobo. "Albert Finney, Jacqueline Bisset & Anthony Andrews in John Huston's *Under the Volcano.*" *Movie Magazine,* Summer 1984, 12+. MOMA.

"*Au-dessous du Volcan:* Un film de John Huston. D'apres l'oeuvre de Malcolm Lowry," n.d. Press kit for French release, n.d., [13 p.], creds. MOMA.

Benayoun, Robert. "Un fleuve de lave pour dieux jumeaux." *Positif* 283 (September 1984): 36–39, creds, stills. (Reprinted in *John Huston, Collection dirigée,* edited by Gilles Ciment, 165–68, Dossier Positif Rivages, Paris, Editions Rivages, Collection Positif-Rivages, no. 2, 1988.)

Binns, Ronald. "The Filming of *Under the Volcano.*" In *Malcolm Lowry,* by Ronald Binns, 85–88. London: Metheun, 1984.

———. "John Huston's *Under the Volcano* (I)." *Malcolm Lowry Review* 15 (Fall 1984): 45–53.

———. "Filming *Under the Volcano.*" In *Malcolm Lowry Eighty Years On,* edited by Sue Vice, 108–24. New York: St. Martin's Press, 1989.

Bonitzer, Pascal. "John Huston tourne *Under the Volcano.*" *Cahiers du Cinéma* 353 (November 1983): 4–5, illus, stills. NYPL.

Boston Globe, August 28, 1983, A1. Michel Blowen. MOMA.

Box Office 121 (May 1985): 58, 75.

Boyum, Joy Gould. "*Wise Blood:* Wise Choices and *Under the Volcano*—Looking Outward." In *Double Exposure: Fiction into Film,* 175–81, 205–11. New York: Universe Books, 1985.

Budtz, P. J. "Albert Finney: En engelsk Ole Jastrau 'Under vulkanen.'" *Levende Billeder* 10 (August 15, 1984): 22–25, stills.

Canby, Vincent. "Huston's *Volcano* Pays Homage to the Novel." *New York Times,* June 24, 1984, sect. 2, 1. AMPAS, MOMA, NYTR.

———. "Relief from Laser Duels." *New York Times,* July 22, 1984, sect. 2, 15.

Chevallier, J., and F. Guerif. "John Huston: *Au dessous du volcan.*" *La Revue du Cinéma* 397 (September 1984): 42–48, creds, illus, interv. NYPL.

Cineforum 25, no. 241 (January 1985): 73–74, creds, stills. G. Rinaldi.

City Limits 151 (August 24, 1984): 19–20, interv.

D'Elia, G. "Le due vie dell'ultimo Huston." *Cinema Nuovo* 34, no. 293 (February 1985): 3–4. Letter on the latest films by John Huston, especially *Under the Volcano* and *Wise Blood.*

Dionne, E. J. "Albert Finney's Amazing Performance." *Los Angeles Herald Examiner,* June 10, 1984. AMPAS.

———. "A Portrayal of Alcoholism Ignites 'Under the Volcano.'" *New York Times,* June 10, 1984, sect. 2, 19+, illus, stills. AMPAS, MOMA.

Fernandez, Enrique. "Less Than Divine: *Under the Volcano* and *A Passage to India* Make It to Screen without Him." *Village Voice* 30 (January 22, 1985): 49–50, port, stills. AMPAS.

Gerard, L, and J. Gerard. "Conversando con Cain." *Imagenes* 2 (1986): 11–19, illus, interv.

Gobbers, E. "Wenders & Huston: De lava en de rots." *Sinema* 63 (November 1984): 12–14, stills.

Gold, Herbert. "Huston Films a Cult Classic." *New York Times* Magazine, December 18, 1983, 60+, illus. AMPAS.

Hachem, Samir. "Under the Volcano." *American Cinematographer* 65, no. 10 (October 1984): 58–63. John Huston and cinematographer Gabriel Figueroa discuss the problems of bringing Lowry's novel to the screen.

Hagen, W. M. "John Huston's *Under the Volcano* (2)." *The Malcolm Lowry Newsletter* 15 (Fall 1984): 54–59.

———. "Under Huston's *Volcano.*" *Literature/Film Quarterly* 19, no. 3 (July 1991): 138–49.

Hamill, Pete. "Against All Odds." *American Film* 9, no. 9 (July–August 1984): 18+.

Harmetz, Aljean. "Huston Filming 'Under the Volcano' Beside Mist-shrouded Pococatepti." *New York Times,* August 23, 1983, C11, illus. MOMA, NYPL.

———. "John Huston Takes on Lowry's *Volcano.*" *Los Angeles Herald Examiner,* August 25, 1983, C1–C3. AMPAS.

———. "Lowry and Malamud Tested on Film." *New York Times,* June 14, 1984, sect. 3, C7.

"Huston Thanks Mexico for 'Volcano' but He Skips Specifics." *Variety* 315 (May 23, 1984): 7.

Insdorf, A. "The Art of Adaptation: Guy Gallo Discussed *Under the Volcano.*" *Cinéaste* 13, no. 4 (1984): 10–11. NYPL.

Lyman, Rick. "John Huston at 77: On the Set Again." *Philadelphia Inquirer,* August 28, 1983, 1L. MOMA.

McCarthy, Todd. "Huston & Fitzgerald Tackle Two Novels to Follow 'Volcano.'" *Variety* 312 (October 12, 1983): 4+.

———. "Cuernavaca Journal." *Film Comment* 20, no. 1 (January–February 1984) : 4+, illus, port.

———. "Cracking the Volcano." *Film Comment* 20, no. 4 (July–August 1984): 59–63. John Huston, Wieland Schulz-Keil, and Guy Gallo discuss their adaptation of the novel.

McGuigan, Cathleen. "Huston's Volcanic Vision." *Newsweek* 102 (October 31, 1983): 79–80.

Magill's Cinema Annual, 1985, 499–503. Michael Sprinker.

Matthews, Jack. "How Finney Inherited Burton's *Volcano.*" *USA Today,* September 14, 1984.

Mevensen, J., and K. Sebrehts. "Under the Volcano." *Film & TV,* no. 330 (November 1984): 16–17, creds, interv, stills. Huston discusses the film.

Meyer, Mark-Paul. "De consul centraal: *Under the vulcano.*" *Skrien,* no. 137 (September–October 1984): 34, stills.

Mosier, J. "Cannes 1984." *New Orleans Review* 12, no. 1 (1985): 58–89.

Mota, Miguel, and Paul Tiessen, eds. *The Cinema of Malcolm Lowry: A Scholarly Edition of Lowry's* Tender Is the Night. Vancouver: University of British Columbia Press, 1990.

"Lowry's 'Volcano' Long a Dare, to Film as U Classics Production." *Variety* 311 (June 15, 1983): 6+. Cart.

Motion Picture Guide 9 (1987): 4,116.

"Motion Picture Version of Lowry's Novel Will Be Filmed under Direction of John Huston." *New York Times,* July 11, 1983, sect. 3, 15.

Neelley, Julius. "Pursuing the 'Volcano': How Lowry's Novel Finally Became a Film." *Washington Post,* July 15, 1984, H1. (A slightly revised version appeared in "Wheels with Wheels," *The Malcolm Lowry Newsletter* 15 [Fall 1984]: 64-67.)

———. "John Huston's *Under the Volcano* (4)." *The Malcolm Lowry Newsletter* 15 (Fall 1984): 61-63.

Oliva, L. "John Huston: barva, herci a tak dale." *Film a Doba,* 30, no. 8 (August 1984): 471–72, illus.

Positif, no. 283 (September 1984): 26–43, interv. NYPL.

Schulz-Keil, Wieland. "The 67th Reading: *Under the Volcano* and Its Screenplays." In *London Conference on Malcolm Lowry. Proceedings, 1984,* edited by Gordon Bowker and Paul Tiessen, 45-61. London: Goldsmith's College, University of London, 1985. (Reprinted in *Apparently Incongruous Parts: The Worlds of Malcolm Lowry,* edited by Paul Tiessen, Metuchen, N.J., Scarecrow Press, 1990.)

————. "Huston." *Film Comment* 23, no. 5 (September–October 1987): 18–23.

Sight & Sound 54, no. 1 (Winter 1984–85): 31–33, interv. with producer.

Steward, Richard. "John Huston's *Under the Volcano* (3)." *The Malcolm Lowry Newsletter* 15 (Fall 1984): 59–61.

Tatum, C, Jr. "Notes sur une infidelité respectable." *Visions,* nos. 21 & 22 (October 1984): 24–25, illus, still.

Tiessen, Paul. "A Canadian Film Critic in Malcolm Lowry's Cambridge." *Malcolm Lowry Review,* nos. 19 & 20 (Autumn 1986–Spring 1987): 27–42. (Reprinted in *Apparently Incongruous Parts: The Worlds of Malcolm Lowry,* edited by Paul Tiessen, Metuchen, N.J., Scarecrow Press, 1990.)

Time Out 732 (August 30, 1984): 20–21. Interview with Huston.

Williams, Chris. "*Under the Volcano:* A Tragic 24-hour Binge." *BAM,* September 7, 1984. AMPAS.

Williams, Joy. "A Brick: The Movie Version of *Under the Volcano.*" *Shenandoah* 25, no. 4 (1984): 84–92.

Young, Vernon. "Other Countries." *Hudson Review* 37, no. 4 (Winter 1984–85): 584–89.

REVIEWS

America 151(September 1–8, 1984): 104. R. A. Blake.

*BFI/Monthly Film Bulletin 51, no. 606 (July 1984): 214–15, creds, stills. Tom Milne.

Boston Globe, July 13, 1984, 40.

Boston Phoenix, July 7, 1984, 4. Michael Sragow.

Box Office 120 (September 1984): R107, creds, stills. A. Karp.

Cahiers du Cinéma 360–361 (Summer 1984): 52–53, stills. S. Toubiana.

California, July 1984, 124+. Kenneth Turan.

Casablanca 35 (November 1983): 34–37. Manolo Marinero.

*Christian Science Monitor, July 5, 1984, 25. David Sterritt. AMPAS.

Cineforum 24, no. 235 (June–July 1984): 18–19, stills. P. Vecchi. NYPL.

Cineforum 25, no. 241 (January 1985): 73–74. G. Rinaldi.

Cinéma (Paris) 307–308 (July–August 1984): 20, creds, stills. C. Blanchet.

Cinema Nuovo 34, no. 293 (February 1985): 51–53, creds, stills. R. D'Andrea.

Cinématographe 103 (September–October 1984): 48–49, creds, stills. M. Celemenski.

City Limits 152 (August 31, 1984): 26.

Cine Revue 64 (May 10, 1984): 24–27, stills. F. Dhont and J. MacTrevor.

Commonweal 111 (August 10, 1984): 438–39. F. Hirsch. AMPAS.

Contemporary Review 246 (August 1985): 102–4. D. Shipman.

Ekran 11, nos. 3 & 4 (1986): 17. V. Konjar.

Film & Kino, no. 5 (1984): 168, creds, stills. K. Alnaes.

Filmcritica 36, no. 351 (June 1985): 58–60. C. Scarrone.

Film Journal 87 (July 1984): 20, creds. C. Gagne.

Film News International 39–40 (September 1984), creds, stills. R. Gehr.

Films, no. 127 (August 1984): 12, creds, illus, stills. Douglas McVay. NYPL.

Films and Filming, no. 358 (July 1984): 26, creds, stills. J. R. Taylor. NYPL.
*Films in Review 35, no. 7 (August–September 1984): 427–28. Armond White.
Hollywood Reporter 278, no. 40 (September 1983): 68, creds.
Hollywood Reporter 282, no. 22 (June 18, 1984): 4+. AMPAS.
Informer, August 1984, 8–11, stills. R. Horton, "Volcano beit."
Jeune Cinéma 160 (July–August 1984): 23–24, creds, stills. Gérard Camy.
Kino 19, no. 2 (February 1985): 48–[49], creds, illus, stills. Alicia Helman.
Kosmorama 30, nos. 169 & 170 (December 1984): 138–41, creds, stills. P. Schepelern.
Levende Billeder 10 (August 15, 1984): 6–8, stills. J. Bredsdorff.
London Observer, September 2, 1984, 18. Philip French.
London Times Literary Supplement, September 21, 1984, 1,056. Galen Strawson.
*Los Angeles Times, July 6, 1984, sect. 5, 1. Sheila Benson. AMPAS.
Los Angeles Times, July 8, 1984, C18. Sheila Benson. AMPAS.
Maclean's 97 (July 23, 1984): 45, illus. I. Pearson.
Motion Picture Product Digest 12, no. 1 (July 4, 1984): 2.
The Nation 239 (July 7–14, 1984): 26–27. A. Kopkind. AMPAS.
National Review 36 (July 27, 1984): 48–49. John Simon.
*New Leader 67 (June 11, 1984): 19–21. D. Merkin.
New Republic 190 (June 18, 1984): 24–25. Stanley Kauffman.
*Newsday, June 13, 1984, part 2, 55. Alex Keneas.
*New Statesman 108 (August 24, 1984): 27–28. John Coleman.
*Newsweek 103 (June 18, 1984): 92, illus, stills. Jack Kroll. AMPAS.
*New York 17 (June 25, 1984): 62–63, stills. David Denby. MOMA.
New York Daily News, June 13, 1984, 43. MOMA.
New Yorker 60 (July 9, 1984): 84–86. Pauline Kael. (Reprinted in *State of the Art,* by Pauline Kael, 198–201, New York, E. P. Dutton, 1985.) AMPAS.
*New York Post, June 13, 1984, 32. Rex Reed.
New York Sunday News Magazine, June 17, 1984, 8+. Marjorie Rosen.
New York Times, June 12, 1984. AMPAS.
New York Times, June 13, 1984, sect. 3 (C), 21, creds, stills. Janet Maslin. NYTR.
New York Times, June 24, 1984, H1. Vincent Canby.
New York Times, November 2, 1984, C12. Janet Maslin.
Philadelphia Inquirer, July 13, 1984, 18. Desmond Ryan. MOMA.
Photoplay 35, no. 9 (September 1984): 21, creds, stills. T. Hutchinson.
Photoplay 35, no. 9 (September 1984): 26–27, stills. L. Dewson.
Positif, nos. 281 & 282 (July–August 1984): 102, stills. L. Codelli.
Progressive 48 (August 1984): 40–41. M. H. Seitz.
Quaderni 5, no. 25 (April 1985): 46–48.
Retro 26 (December 1984–January 1985): 8.
La Revue du Cinéma 396 (July–August 1984): 38. J. Chevallier.
La Revue du Cinéma 22, no. 31 (1985), creds. G. Colpart.
Screen International 406 (August 6, 1983): 2. Note.
Screen International 413 (September 24, 1983): 6. Note on casting.
Screen International 457 (August 4, 1984): 16.

Segnocinema 4, no. 14 (September 1984): 57, creds. G. Muscio.
Segnocinema, no. 16 (January 1985): 75, creds, stills. G. Ca[nova].
Séquences, no. 117 (July 1984): 16, stills.
Séquences, no. 118 (October 1984): 49–50, creds, stills. Maurice Elia.
*Sight & Sound 53, no. 3 (Summer 1984): 226, stills. John Pym.
Skoop 20, no. 8 (November 1984): 27, creds, stills. R. A. F. Proper.
*Time 123 (June 25 1984): 68, illus, stills. Richard Schickel. AMPAS.
Time Out 732 (August 30, 1984): 47. Caption review.
24 Images 21 (Summer 1984): 36–37, stills. A. Leroux.
Variety 315 (May 23, 1984): 12, creds. Strat [D. Stratton]. AMPAS, VR.
Village Voice 29 (June 5, 1984): 59–60.
Visions, no. [20] (June 15, 1984): 6, illus, stills. P. Elhem.
Wall Street Journal, June 28, 1984, 22 (West Coast ed.), 26 (East Coast ed.). Julie Salamon. AMPAS.
Washington Post, July 13, 1984, E4. Gary Arnold.
Washington Post, July 13, 1984, Weekend, 17. Rita Kempley.
*Women's Wear Daily, June 13, 1984, 42. Howard Kissel.
Working Woman 9 (September 1984): 247–48, illus. P. Bosworth.

THE UNFORGIVEN. 1960. (Director; Writer, uncredited.)

ARTICLES AND REVIEWS
America 103 (April 30, 1960): 200–1.
BFI/Monthly Film Bulletin 27, no. 317 (June 1960): 82.
Casablanca 35 (November 1983): 42.
Commonweal 72 (April 22, 1960): 95–96.
Daily Cinema 8,317 (June 10, 1960): 5.
Deschner, Donald, ed. "The Films of John Huston" [Program notes]. Los Angeles County Museum of Art, November 7, 1980. (Notes are excerpts from Paul Kennedy, *New York Times,* February 1, 1959.)
Esquire, June 1960. Dwight MacDonald. AMPAS, MOMA.
Film Daily 117, no. 61 (March 30, 1960): 6. Mandel Herbstman. AMPAS.
Filmfacts 3 (1960): 73, creds.
Film Quarterly 13, no. 4 (Summer 1960): 61.
Films and Filming 6, no. 10 (July 1960): 20–22, creds. Gordon Gow.
Films in Review 11, no. 5 (May 1960): 287–88. Albert "Hap" Turner. AMPAS.
Hardy, Phil. *The Western: The Film Encyclopedia.* New York: Morrow, 1983.
Harrison's Reports, April 2, 1960, 54.
Hollywood Reporter 159, no. 28 (March 30, 1960): 3. James Powers. AMPAS.
Hunter, Allan. *Burt Lancaster: The Man and His Movies.* New York: St. Martin's Press, 1984, 104+.
Kauffman, Stanley. *A World on Film: Criticism and Comment.* New York: Harper, 1966, 147.
Kennedy, Paul P. "Trailing 'The Unforgiven' below the Border." *New York Times,* February 1, 1959, sect. 2, 7.
Life 48 (May 16, 1960): 77–78. AMPAS, MOMA.

London Times, June 13, 1960. NYPL.
Los Angeles Examiner, May 5, 1960, sect. 2, 6. Ruth Waterbury.
Los Angeles Times, May 5, 1960, part 1, 9. Philip K. Scheuer.
McCall's 87 (May 1960): 6.
MacDonald, Dwight. *On Movies.* Introduction by John Simon. New York: Da Capo, 1981, 283–84.
Magill's Survey of Cinema: Second Series 6 (1981): 2,593–96. Robert Mitchell.
Motion Picture Daily, March 30, 1960.
Motion Picture Guide 8 (1987): 3,630–31.
Motion Picture Herald, April 20, 1960. AMPAS.
The Nation 190 (April 9, 1960): 323.
New Republic 142 (April 25, 1960): 20.
Newsweek 55 (April 18, 1960): 113. AMPAS.
New Yorker 36 (April 16, 1960): 148. John McCartern. AMPAS, MOMA, NYPL.
New York Herald Tribune, April 17, 1960, 1+. Paul V. Beckley.
New York Times, April 7, 1960, 46. Bosley Crowther. AMPAS, NYTR.
Saturday Review 43 (April 16, 1960): 32. Arthur Knight. AMPAS.
Sight & Sound 29, no. 3 (Summer 1960): 142. Penelope Houston.
Time 75 (April 11, 1960): 69. AMPAS.
Unkefer, Linn. "Lookout from Genet's 'Balcony.'" *New York Times,* November 11, 1962. (Reprinted in *The New York Times Encyclopedia of Film, 1958–1963.*) Background on Ben Maddow.
Variety, March 3, 1960, 6. AMPAS, MOMA, NYPL, VR.
Vermilye, Jerry. *Burt Lancaster: A Pictorial Treasury of His Films.* New York: Falcon Enterprises, 1971, 84–86.
Video 17 (December 1993): 106. B. Eder.

VICTORY. 1981. (Director; Writer, uncredited.)

ARTICLES AND REVIEWS
*BFI/Monthly Film Bulletin 48, no. 572 (June 1981): 175–76, creds. Tom Milne.
Boston Phoenix, August 4, 1981, sect. 3, 4. Alan Stern.
Box Office 117 (September 1981): 48, creds. D. Linck.
Casablanca 13 (January 1982): 6+. Jos Ruiz and Manolo Marinero.
*Christian Science Monitor, July 30, 1981, 19. David Sterritt.
Cineforum 21, no. 210 (December 1981): 51–60, creds, filmog, stills. A. Crespi.
Cinéma (Paris) 275 (November 1981): 95–97, creds, stills. A. Carbonnier.
Cinema Canada, no. 77 (September 1981): 45, creds. J. P. Costabile.
Cinématographe 71 (October 1981): 50. G. Cebe.
Ekran 9, nos. 9 & 10 (1984): 37, creds, stills. V. Konjar.
Film Bulletin 30 (August 1981), creds. D. Munroe.
Film en Televisie 295 (December 1981): 15, creds, stills. C. Moens.
Film Illustrated 10 (September 1981): 444, creds, stills. D. Castell.
Film Journal 84 (July 20, 1981): 16–17, creds, stills. D. Shifren. AMPAS.
Films 1, no. 10 (September 1981): 33–34. D. Elley.
Films and Filming 325 (October 1981): 44–45, creds, stills. A. Turner. NYPL.

Films in Review 32, no. 8 (October 1981): 494–95. Gay Cowan.
FilmVilag 28, no. 5 (1985): 53. P. Snee.
Hollywood Reporter 263, no. 40 (October 7, 1980): 14, creds.
Hollywood Reporter July 20, 1981, 4. AMPAS.
Hollywood Reporter 268, no. 3 (August 11, 1981): 1+. On filming in Hungary.
Houston Chronicle, August 1, 1981, 8. Jeff Millar. AMPAS.
Jeune Cinéma 139 (December 1981–January 1982): 46–47, creds, stills. Bernard Nave.
Levende Billeder 7 (December 1981): 58–59, creds, stills. P. H. Hansen.
Listener 106, no. 2,726 (September 10, 1981): 284. Gavin Millar.
London Telegraph, September 6, 1981, 16. MOMA.
London Times, September 4, 1981, 15. MOMA.
London Times, September 6, 1981, 39. Alan Bach. MOMA.
Los Angeles Times, July 31, 1981, Calendar, 1. Sheila Benson. AMPAS.
Magill's Cinema Annual, 1982, 374–77. Betti Stone.
Mediafilm, no. 140 (Winter 1982): 50–52, creds, stills. W. Verbestel.
Motion Picture Guide 8 (1987): 3,682–83.
Motion Picture Product Digest 9, no. 4 (July 22, 1981): 15.
New Leader, August 10, 1981, 22. Robert Asahina.
New Republic 185 (September 16, 1981): 28–29. Stanley Kauffmann. AMPAS.
Newsday, July 31, 1981, part 2, 7. Joseph Gelmis.
New Statesman 102 (September 4, 1981): 25. Christopher Hitchens.
Newsweek 98 (August 10, 1981): 69, stills. David Ansen. NYPL.
New York Daily News, July 31, 1981, 3. Kathleen Carroll.
New York Times 130 (July 26, 1981): sect. 2, 1, stills. Nightingale, B. "Caine Stretches His Range: In 'Victory' He Displays His Maturing Art."
New York Times, July 31, 1981, sect. 3 (C), 6. Vincent Canby. AMPAS, MOMA, NYPL, NYTR.
New York Post, July 31, 1981, 35. Archer Winsten.
Ob*server* (London), September 6, 1981, 24. Philip French. NYPL.
Philadelphia Bulletin, August 1, 1981. John R. Cochran. MOMA.
Positif, no. 248 (November 1981): 76. P.-L. Thirard.
"Revisited: A Periodic Visit on the Part of Lillian Ross with Huston, Interviewing Him on His Activities from the Last Time They Met, 1972." *New Yorker* 56 (February 25, 1980): 31–34. AMPAS.
La Revue du Cinéma, no. 366 (November 1981): 52–53. P. Mérigeau.
La Revue du Cinéma 34, no. 26 (1982), creds. P. Mérigeau.
Rolling Stone, no. 354 (October 15, 1981): 46+, stills. M. Sragow.
San Francisco Examiner & Chronicle, July 26, 1981, 26–27. Bart Mills. (Reprinted in *Houston Post,* August 2, 1981, 12A. AMPAS.
Screen Digest, August 1981, 146.
Screen International 243 (May 31, 1980): 13. Note.
Screen International 305 (August 15, 1981): 19.
Segnocinema 1, no. 2 (December 1981): 58, creds. P. Madron.
Séquences 106 (October 1981): 47–48, creds. R. Martineau.

Sinema, no. 34 (December 1981): 40–41, creds, stills. M. Holthof.
Sports Illustrated 55 (August 10, 1981): 44.
*Time 118 (August 3, 1981): 66, stills. Richard Schickel. AMPAS, MOMA.
Times Literary Supplement (London), September 11, 1981, 1,047. Archer Hislop. NYPL.
Variety 303, no. 12 (July 22, 1981): 18, creds. "Step" (S. Klain). MOMA, NYPL, VR.
**Village Voice,* July 29–August 4, 1981, 35. Andrew Sarris. AMPAS.
Voi, P. "Fuga per la vittoria." *Revue Cinematografo* 55 (March 1982): 96–97 [xxix–xxx], stills.
Washington Post, July 31, 1981, B3. Gary Arnold.
Washington Post, July 31, 1981, Weekend, 17. Judith Martin.
**Women's Wear Daily,* July 29, 1981, 96. Howard Kissel.

THE VISITOR. 1980. (Actor.)

ARTICLES AND REVIEWS
Bianco e Nero 47, no. 4 (October–December 1986): 150, creds.
Box Office, May 5, 1978, SE-2.
Cinefantastique 10, no. 2 (Autumn 1980): 43. D. Luciano.
Hollywood Reporter 260, no. 50 (March 21, 1980): 32.
Motion Picture Guide 8 (1987): 3,698.
Philadelphia Inquirer, June 3, 1980. Desmond Ryan.
Variety 298, no. 8 (March 26, 1980): 27+, creds. Pege (P. G. Springer). VR.

A WALK WITH LOVE AND DEATH. 1969. (Director, Actor; Writer, uncredited.)

ARTICLES AND REVIEWS
America 121 (November 1, 1969): 400.
The American Film Institute Catalog: Feature Films, 1961–1970. New York: R. R. Bowker, 1976, 1,188–89.
Benayoun, Robert. "Huston le renégat." *BFI/Monthly Film Bulletin* 44, no. 517 (February 1977): 36. (Translation of review from *Positif* 118 [Spring 1970].)
BFI/Monthly Film Bulletin 44, no. 517 (February 1977): 33–34, creds. Richard Combs.
Blume, May. "Huston Directing Daughter in *Walk.*" *Los Angeles Times,* February 2, 1969, 15.
Boyer, H. "Le moyen-age au cinema: A propos de 'Promenade avec l'amour et la la mort.'" *Cahiers de la Cinémathèque* 42–43 (Summer 1985): 82–83, illus. Analysis.
Cahiers du Cinéma 229 (May–June 1971): 59–60. Pascal Kane. MOMA.
Casablanca 35 (November 1983): 43–44.
Christian Century 87 (January 7, 1970): 22+.

Cinéaste 15, no. 3 (1987): 3. H. Koning.

Devlin, Peggy. "Young and Strong with Love and War." *Vogue* 154 (September 15, 1969): 130–31+.

Ehrlich, H. "Anjelica." *Look* 32 (November 12, 1968): 66–71.

Fields, Steffi. "Background and Interview with Anjelica & Assaf." *Women's Wear Daily,* October 3, 1969, 40. MOMA.

Figaro, March 28, 1971. Louis Chauvet. AMPAS.

Film Heritage 6, no. 2 (Winter 1970–1971): 14–17, illus. Michael Dempsey.

Film Society Review 6, no. 2 (October 1970): 19.

Film Society Review 6, no. 2 (October 1970): 44–46, creds. Michael Sragow.

Films and Filming 19 (June 1973): 22–23. Photo essay.

Films in Review 20, no. 8 (October 1969): 511. Norman Cecil.

"The Films of John Huston" [Program notes]. Los Angeles County Museum of Art, October 18, 1980.

Film TV Daily, September 8, 1969. Mandel Herbstman. MOMA.

Hollywood Reporter 202, no. 14 (August 16, 1968): 12.

Hollywood Reporter 207, no. 33 (September 8, 1969): 3. AMPAS.

Koningsberger, Hans. "*A Walk with Love and Death:* From Book to Film Via John Huston." *BFI/Monthly Film Bulletin* 44, no. 517 (February 1977): 36. (Extracted from an article that appeared in *Film Quarterly* 22, no. 3 [Spring 1969]: 2–4.)

Life 67 (November 28, 1969): 20. Richard Schickel. MOMA.

Listener 97, no. 2,499 (March 10, 1977): 313.

Los Angeles Herald Examiner, October 17, 1980. AMPAS.

Los Angeles Times, November 24, 1968, 1. Sally Bass. AMPAS.

Los Angeles Times, April 24, 1970.

Manhattan Tribune, October 25, 1969, 8. Colin L. Westerbeck Jr.

Miller, E, ed. "Extraordinary Debut [Angelica]." *Seventeen* 27 (October 1968): 138–39+, illus.

Motion Picture Daily, September 5, 1969. Richard Gertner.

Motion Picture Guide 9 (1987): 3,723.

Motion Picture Herald 239, no. 37 (September 10, 1969): 69. AMPAS.

New Statesman 93 (March 11, 1977): 329. J. Coleman.

New York, October 20, 1969, 63. Judith Crist. MOMA.

New York Daily News, October 6, 1969. Kathleen Carroll. MOMA, NYPL.

New Yorker 45 (October 11, 1969): 159–60. Pauline Kael. AMPAS, MOMA.

New York Morning Telegraph, October 7, 1969, 3. NYPL.

New York Post, October 6, 1969, 12. Nicholas Meyer. MOMA, NYPL

New York Times, October 6, 1969, 56. Roger Greenspun. MOMA, NYPL, NYTR.

Nogueira, Rui. "A Walk with Love and Death." *Films Illustrated* 1, no. 3 (September 1971): 6.

Park East, October 16, 1969, 12. Nicholas Meyer. MOMA, NYPL.

Saturday Review 52 (November 1, 1969): 28. Richard Gelatt.

Seguin, Louis. "Nulle part ailleurs." *Positif* 118 (Spring 1970). (Reprinted in *John*

Huston, Collection dirigée, edited by Gilles Ciment, 134–36, Dossier Positif Rivages, Paris, Editions Rivages, Collection Positif-Rivages, no. 2, 1988.)
Senior Scholastic 95 (October 13, 1969): 21.
Time 94 (October 24, 1969): 105. AMPAS.
Variety, September 5, 1969.
Variety, September 10, 1969, 48. VR, MOMA.
The Villager, October 23, 1969, 9. Donald J. Meyerson. MOMA.

WATCH ON THE RHINE. 1943. (Director; Writer, unrealized)

ARTICLES AND REVIEWS
Commonweal 38 (September 24, 1943): 563.
Film Daily, July 27, 1943, 8.
Hollywood Reporter, July 27, 1943, 3.
Magill's Survey of Cinema. Series 1 (1980): 1,820–22.
Motion Picture Herald Product Digest, July 31, 1943, 1,454.
New Republic 109 (September 13, 1943): 364.
New York Times, August 28, 1943, 15. NYTR.
New Yorker 19 (August 28, 1943): 50.
Newsweek 22 (September 6, 1943): 96.
Sperber, A. M., and Eric Lax. *Bogart.* New York: William Morrow, 1997, 180–82.
Time 42 (September 6, 1943): 94.
Variety, July 28, 1943, 8. VR.

WE WERE STRANGERS. 1949. (Director; Actor, uncredited; Writer.)

ARTICLES AND REVIEWS
Arisarco, Guido. "'Stanotte sorgera il sole' e 'L'isola di corolla.'" ("'We Were Strangers' and 'Key Largo.'") *Cinema* (Milano) 2, no. 29 (December 30, 1949).
BFI/Monthly Film Bulletin 16, no. 188 (August 1949): 146.
Brownell, William W, Jr. "Gilbert Roland: Mucho Hombre." *New York Times,* June 28, 1953. (Reprinted in *The New York Times Encyclopedia of Film, 1952–1957.*)
Chardière, Bernard. "A propos de *We Were Strangers." Positif* 3 (July–August 1952): 40–41. (Reprinted in *John Huston, Collection dirigée,* edited by Gilles Ciment, 76–77, Dossier Positif Rivages, Paris, Editions Rivages, Collection Positif-Rivages, no. 2, 1988.)
Colliers 123 (April 2, 1949): 48.
Commonweal 50 (May 6, 1949): 95.
Cue, April 30, 1949, 26. Jesse Zunser.
Daily Worker, April 28, 1949. Jose Yglesias. AMPAS.
de Giammatteo, Fernaldo. "'We Were Strangers' e 'Key Largo.'" *Bianco e Nero* 2, no. 2 (February 1950).
Film Bulletin, June 6, 1949, 8.
Filmcritica 36, no. 385 (October 1985): 476–77. E. Bruno.

Film Daily, April 21, 1949, 8. AMPAS.
Film Quarterly, Autumn 1949. Gavin Lambert. AMPAS.
Gelman, Howard. *The Films of John Garfield.* Secaucus, N.J.: Citadel Press, 1982, 162–66.
Hammen, Scott. *Film Notes.* Louisville, Ky.: Hamilton Printing Co, 1979.
Harrison's Reports, April 30, 1949, 70.
Hollywood Reporter, April 22, 1949, 3. AMPAS.
Los Angeles Times, May 4, 1949. Edwin Schallert. AMPAS.
Manvell, Roger, ed. *Shots in the Dark.* London: Allen Wingate, 1951, 82–87. AMPAS.
Moshier, W. Franklyn. *The Films of Jennifer Jones.* San Francisco: The author, 1978, 81–84.
Motion Picture Guide 9 (1987): 3,756–57.
Motion Picture Herald Product Digest 175, no. 5 (April 30, 1949): 4,589. AMPAS.
New Republic 120 (May 9, 1949): 29.
Newsweek 33 (May 9, 1949): 90. AMPAS.
New York Daily News, April 28, 1949. Kate Cameron. AMPAS.
New Yorker 25 (May 7, 1949): 103.
New York Herald Tribune, April 28, 1949. Howard Barnes.
New York Sun, April 28, 1949. Eileen Creelman. AMPAS.
New York Times, April 28, 1948, 28. NYTR.
New York Times, May 1, 1949, sect. 2, 1. Bosley Crowther. AMPAS, MOMA.
New York World Telegram, April 27, 1949. Alton Cook. AMPAS.
Photoplay 35 (May 1949): 32.
Rotarian 75 (October 1949): 38.
*Séquences, no. 9 (Autumn 1949): 127–29. Gavin Lambert. AMPAS.
Simon, John. "From Fake Happyendings to Fake Unhappyendings." *New York Times,* June 8, 1975B. (Reprinted in *The New York Times Encyclopedia of Film, 1975–1976.*)
Sklar, Robert. "Havana Episode: The Revolutionary Situation of *We Were Strangers.*" In *Reflections in a Male Eye,* edited by Gaylyn Studlar and David Desser, 63–77. Washington, D.C.: Smithsonian Institution Press, 1993.
———. "A Second Look." *Cinéaste* 15, no. 3 (1987): 56–57, illus.
Teichner, Miriam. "Silent Lover." *New York Times,* June 12, 1949. (Reprinted in *The New York Times Encyclopedia of Film, 1947–1951.*)
Theatre Arts 33 (May 1949): 4.
Time 53 (May 2, 1949): 92+. MOMA, NYPL.
Today's Cinema 73, no. 5,835 (July 29, 1949): 7.
Variety, April 22, 1949.
Variety, April 27, 1949, 11. Wit. AMPAS, VR.
Weiler, A. H. "By Way of Report." *New York Times,* April 10, 1949. (Reprinted in *The New York Times Encyclopedia of Film, 1947–1951.*)

WHITE HUNTER, BLACK HEART. 1990. (Fictionalized account with Clint Eastwood as John Huston.)

ARTICLES AND REVIEWS

Bagley, C. "To Africa, with Bugs." *Premiere* 3 (February 1980): 45–46, illus, stills.

Benayoun, Robert. "Clint et John: Une saison infernale." *Positif* 351 (May 1990): 2–4.

BFI/Monthly Film Bulletin 57, no. 681 (October 1990): 304–5, creds, stills. Tom Milne.

Bingham, Dennis. "Masculinity, Star Reception, and Desire to Perform: Clint Eastwood in 'White Hunter, Black Heart.'" *Post Script* 12, no. 2 (1993): 40–53, biblio, illus, stills.

Box Office 126 (November 1990): 22, 31 (R84–R85).

Chicago Reader, September 28, 1990, 14+. Jonathan Rosenbaum. MOMA.

Christian Science Monitor, September 14, 1990, 12. David Sterritt.

Christian Science Monitor, May 18, 1990, 12. David Sterritt.

Ciment, M. "Entretien avec Clint Eastwood." *Positif* 351 (May 1990): 5–11, illus, interv, stills.

Cineforum 30, no. 295 (June 1990): 18–19, stills. S. Della Casa.

Cineforum 30, no. 297 (September 1990): 85–87, creds, stills. A. Piccardi.

Cinéma (Paris) 468 (June 1990): 22–23, creds, stills. S. Garel.

City Limits 465 (August 30, 1990): 25.

Commonweal 117 (December 21, 1990): 757–59. Richard Alleva.

Dufour, Dirk. "Een Afrikaanse queeste." *Film en Televisie* 396–397 (May–June 1990): 10–11, creds, illus, stills.

EPD Film 7, no. 6 (June 1990): 32, creds, stills. V. Lueken.

Eyquem, O. "Entretien avec Peter Viertel, scénariste." *Positif* 351 (May 1990): 12–16, interv, stills.

Film (Rome) 1 (September–October 1990): 26–27. S. Della Casa.

Filmihullu 5 (1990): 50–51. M. Lahti.

Film Journal 93 (October 1990): 61–62, creds, stills. C. Gagne.

Film Monthly 2 (October 1990): 12, creds, stills. T. Hutchinson.

Filmrutan 33, no. 3 (1990): 38, creds, illus. Yngve Bengtsson.

Films in Review 41, nos. 11 & 12 (November–December 1990): 552. William K. Everson.

Fuller, Graham. "The Heart of a Lonely Hunter." *Listener* 126, no. 3,180 (August 30, 1990): 28–30. Interview with Eastwood, who discusses film, story, and background.

———— "The Man Who Would Be Huston." *Interview* 20 (October 1990): 56+, interv, stills.

Geddes, H., and J. Harcourt. "About Elephants." *Eyepiece* 11, no. 4 (1990): 20–21, illus, stills.

Gentry, R. "White Hunter's Green Heart." *Millimeter* 18 (October 1990): 232, stills.

Grand Angle 128 (June 1990): [9–10], biblio, creds, stills. J. Noel.

Hollywood Reporter 307, no. 48 (June 1989): 3+.

Hollywood Reporter 308, no. 9 (June 27, 1989): 76.
Hollywood Reporter 314, no. 13 (September 14, 1990): 10+.
Hommel, M. "A Man's Gotta Do What a Man's Gotta Do." *Skrien* 173 (August–September 1990): 14–15.
In Camera, Autumn 1989, 4, creds. On film stock used.
Kosmorama 36, no. 193 (Fall 1990): 40–41, creds, stills. K. Schmidt.
Levende Billeder 6 (June 1990): 12–15.
Listener 124, no. 3,181 (September 6, 1990): 28–30.
Los Angeles Times, September 14, 1990, F20+. Michael Wilmington. MOMA.
Maslin, Janet. "Film View: Plenty Is New under the Sun at Cannes." *New York Times,* May 20, 1990, sect. 2, 17+.
Motion Picture Guide, Annual Issue, 1991, 187–88.
New York 23 (October 1, 1990): 56+, stills. David Denby. MOMA.
New York Times, May 20, 1990, H17. Janet Maslin.
New York Times, May 14, 1990, B1. Janet Maslin.
New York Times, September 14, 1990, C1, creds, stills. NYTR.
Perlez, J. "Clint Eastwood Directs Himself Portraying a Director." *New York Times,* September 16, 1990, sect. 2, 19+, stills.
Pezzotta, A. "Cinema senza centro." *Filmcritica* 41, no. 408 (September–October 1990): 410–14, biblio, stills.
Philadelphia Inquirer, September 19, 1990, 8D. Carrie Rickey. MOMA.
La Revue du Cinéma, no. 37 (1990) : 26, creds. D. Roth-Bettoni.
La Revue du Cinéma 461 (June 1990): 19–20, creds, filmog, illus, stills. Jacques Zimmer.
Rolling Stone 589 (October 18, 1990): 45, port, stills. Peter Travers.
Screen International 680 (November 26, 1988): 5.
Screen International 774 (September 15, 1990): 42.
Segnocinema 10, no. 46 (November–December 1990): 48–49. creds. Alberto Morsiana.
Seidenberg, R. "Behind Every Blockbuster." *American Film* 15, no. 9 (June 1990): 34–39, illus, ports, stills. Discusses production design, cinematography, and editing.
Sight & Sound 59, no. 4 (Autumn 1990): 278–79, stills. Richard Combs.
Sinema 98 (July–August 1990): 54–55. J. Blondeel.
Time 136 (September 24, 1990): 84. Richard Schickel.
Time Out, April 18, 1990, 16–18, illus, interv.
Time Out, August 29, 1990, 41.
Toubiana, Serge. "African King." *Cahiers du Cinéma* 431–432 (May 1990): 98–99, creds, stills.
24 Images 50 (Autumn 1990): 60, stills. M.-C. Loiselle.
24 Images 52 (November–December 1990): 83, creds, stills. Thierry Horguelin.
van Tongeren, P. "Het instinct aan de macht." *Skoop* 26 (June 1990): 8–11+, illus, stills.
Variety 339, no. 6 (May 16, 1990): 25, creds. Strat (D. Stratton). VR.
Viertel, Peter. *White Hunter, Black Heart.* Garden City, N.Y.: Doubleday, 1953.

Wilson, P. "*White Hunter, Black Heart:* Clint's Big Screen Gamble." *Film Monthly* 2 (September 1990): 39, stills.
Wall Street Journal, September 27, 1990, A10 (West Coast ed.), A16 (East Coast ed.). Julie Salamon.

WILD BOYS OF THE ROAD. 1933. (Writer, uncredited.)

ARTICLES AND REVIEWS
The American Film Institute Catalog: Feature Films, 1931–1940. Berkeley: University of California Press, 1993, 2,425.
Beal, Greg. *CinemaTexas Program Notes* 11, no. 1 (September 8, 1976): 31–39, filmog.
Film Daily, September 22, 1933, 8.
Harrison's Reports, September 30, 1933, 154.
Hollywood Reporter, September 5, 1933, 2.
Motion Picture Guide 9 (1987): 3,850.
Motion Picture Herald, September 30, 1933, 40.
The Nation 137 (October 18, 1933): 458.
Newsweek 2 (September 30, 1933): 46.
New York Herald Tribune, September 22, 1933. Richard Watts Jr.
New York Sun, September 25, 1933. John S. Cohen Jr.
New York Times, September 22, 1933, 14. NYTR.
Rob Wagner's Script 10 (October 7, 1933): 10.
Thompson, Frank T. *William A. Wellman.* With a foreword by Barbara Stanwyck. Metuchen, N.J.: Scarecrow Press, 1983, 136–41.
Time 22 (October 2, 1933): 40.
Variety, September 26, 1933, 20. VR.

THE WIND AND THE LION. 1975. (Actor.)

ARTICLES AND REVIEWS
BFI/Monthly Film Bulletin 42, no. 499 (August 1975): 185–86, creds. T. Milne.
Burke, Tom. "'Casting Is Everything,' Says 'Cukoo's' Director, Milos Forman." *New York Times,* March 28, 1976. (Reprinted in *The New York Times Encyclopedia of Film, 1975–1976.*)
Canby, Vincent. "Forgettable Names, Familiar Film Faces." *New York Times,* December 10, 1976. (Reprinted in *The New York Times Encyclopedia of Film, 1975–1976.*)
Chaplin 18, no. 2 (1976): 47–48, stills. H. Stjerne.
***Christian Science Monitor,* June 2, 1975. David Sterritt.
Cinema (Paris) 205 (January 1976): 134. D. Rabourdin.
Cinema Papers, March–April 1976, 369, creds, stills. M. Cole.
Cine Revue 55 (December 18, 1975): 11. P. Deglin. Photo essay.
"The Clean Movie." *New York Times,* May 11, 1975. (Reprinted in *The New York Times Encyclopedia of Film, 1975–1976.*)

Cocks, J., and R. Schickel. "Bully, Brown and Beige, On the Street." *Time* 105 (June 9, 1975): 60–61, illus.

Film & TV 228–229 (May–June 1976): 32. L. Mees.

***Film Information,* June 1975. Ron Henderson.

Films and Filming 21, no. 12 (September 1975): 38, creds. G. Gow.

Films Illustrated 4 (July 1975): 405, creds. S. D'Arcy.

***Films in Review* 26, no. 8 (October 1975): 502–3. George Larkin.

Films in Review 26, no. 9 (November 1975): 555–56.

Gable, J. A. "Teddy Roosevelt's Morocco Role Nothing Like 'Wind and Lion.'" *Variety* 279 (June 11, 1975): 6.

Gorman, M. J. "*The Wind and the Lion* (UA-MGM) Wins July's Blue Ribbon Award." *Box Office* 107 (September 8, 1975): 12, creds, stills.

Hollywood Reporter 233, no. 5 (September 13, 1974): 19, creds.

Hollywood Reporter 236, no. 24 (May 16, 1975): 4+.

Independent Film Journal 75 (May 28, 1975): 7, creds, stills.

Kosmorama 21, no. 128 (1975): 317–19, stills. M. Blaedel.

Lindsey, Robert. "The New New Wave of Filmmakers." *New York Times,* May 28, 1978. (Reprinted in *The New York Times Encyclopedia of Film, 1977–1979.*)

Listener 93, no. 2,413 (July 3, 1975): 26.

***London Times,* June 27, 1975. David Robinson.

***Los Angeles Times,* May 22, 1975, sect. 4, 1.

Medium 6 (March 1976): 30, creds. R.-R. Hamacher.

Morris, Edmund. "Does Teddy Roosevelt Deserve This?" *New York Times* 124 (June 15, 1975): sect. 2, 17.

———. "Historical Document." *New York Times,* July 15, 1975, sect. 2, 15.

Motion Picture Guide 9 (1987): 3,868–69.

Motion Picture Herald Product Digest, May 28, 1975, 97.

Movie 23 (June 1976): 37–38.

Movietone News 42 (July 1975): 31–33, creds. R. T. Jameson.

***New Leader,* June 23, 1975. Calvin Fentress.

***Newsweek* 86 (July 21, 1975): 66. Paul D. Zimmerman. MOMA.

New Times, June 27, 1975, 63. Frank Rich.

***New York* 8 (June 2, 1975): 71. J. Crist.

***New York Times,* May 23, 1975, 22. Vincent Canby. MOMA, NYTR.

"Notes: Of Stuntwomen, Critics and Coincidence." *New York Times,* August 17, 1975. (Reprinted in *The New York Times Encyclopedia of Film, 1975–1976.*)

Positif 176 (December 1975): 72–73, stills. J. Segond.

Prendergast, Roy M. *A Neglected Art.* New York: New York University Press, 1977, 162+.

La Revue du Cinéma 302 (January 1976): 115. H. Behar.

La Revue du Cinéma 309–310 (October 1976): 216–17, creds. A. Garel.

Rosen, Marjorie. "Isn't It about Time to Bring on the Girls?" *New York Times,* December 15, 1974. (Reprinted in *The New York Times Encyclopedia of Film, 1972–1974.*)

***Sight & Sound* 44, no. 4 (Autumn 1975): 255–56, stills. R. Combs.

Time 105 (June 9, 1975): 60.
TV Times 99, no. 24 (June 5, 1980): 4–5. David Quinlan. Preview.
Variety 279, no. 2 (May 21, 1975): 19, creds. Murf (A. D. Murphy). MOMA, VR.
Variety 279, no. 4 (June 11, 1975): 4. *"Wind and Lion* in 4, $713,653."
***Village Voice 20 (June 2, 1975): 71–72. Andrew Sarris.

WINTER KILLS. 1979. (Actor.)

ARTICLES AND REVIEWS
Anderson, Chris. *CinemaTexas Program Notes* 25, no. 1 (September 1, 1983): 11–20, biblio, creds, filmog.
BFI/Monthly Film Bulletin 52, no. 615 (April 1985): 126–27. Steve Jenkins.
Björkman, S. "Familjentriger." *Chaplin* 27, no. 5 (1985): 250+, creds, illus. Family plots in two films based on novels by Richard Condon with John Huston in a key position.
Canby, Vincent. "Film View: A Funny Paranoid Fable." *New York Times,* May 27, 1979, sect. 2, 13. AMPAS, MOMA, NYTR.
**Christian Science Monitor,* January 27, 1983, 18. David Sterritt.
Cineforum 199 (November 1980): 781–82, creds.
City Limits 179 (March 8, 1985): 21.
Film Bulletin 48 (June 1979), creds. D. Bartholomew.
Films and Filming 367 (Spring 1985): 43.
Harmetz, Aljean. "Film Took a Gamble that May Pay Off." *New York Times* 128 (May 17, 1979), C17, illus. MOMA. (Reprinted in *The New York Times Encyclopedia of Film, 1977– 1979.*)
Hollywood Reporter 254, no. 27 (December 12, 1978): 1+. Account of the resumption of shooting after two-year delay.
Jameson, Richard T. "Wild Bill." *Film Comment,* November–December 1982, 20–27.
Kaminsky, R. "Massive Ad Campaign for *Winter Kills.*" *Box Office* 114 (February 12,1979): 5.
Listener 123, no. 3,149 (January 25, 1990): 36.
Los Angeles Times, May 13, 1979, Calendar. Charles Champlin. MOMA.
**Los Angeles Times,* February 19, 1983, sect. 5, 1. Charles Champlin.
Motion Picture Guide 9 (1987): 3,878.
The Nation, June 16, 1979. R. Hatch. MOMA.
Newsweek 93 (June 4, 1979): 76, stills. David Ansen. MOMA.
New Yorker 55 (June 4, 1979): 154–55. Brendan Gill, "The Current Cinema: King John." AMPAS, MOMA.
**New York Post,* January 21, 1983, 43. Archer Winsten.
New York Times, May 18, 1979, C7, creds, stills. Janet Maslin. MOMA, NYTR.
New York Times, May 18, 1979, C18. Tom Buckley, "At the Movies."
New York Times, January 7, 1983, C8. Chris Chase.
Positif 220–221 (July–August 1979): 67. Christian Viviani, "Cannes 1979: *Winter Kills.*"

Screen International 148 (July 22, 1978): 6.
Screen International 168 (December 9, 1978): 1.
Screen International 192 (June 2, 1979): 11.
Screen International 488 (March 16, 1985): 39+.
Sight & Sound 54, no. 3: (Summer 1985): 222–23.
Stills 17 (March 1985): 61–62. Brian Case.
Take One 7, no. 8 (July 1979): 13, illus. W. Aitken.
*Time, March 7, 1983, BT8. Richard Corliss. MOMA.
Time Out 759 (March 7, 1985): 43.
Variety 295, no. 2 (May 16, 1979): 38, creds. Pol (D. Pollock). VR.
Village Voice 24 (May 21, 1979): 46. Tom Allen. MOMA.
*Village Voice, January 25, 1983, 54. J. Hoberman. MOMA.
"*Winter Kills* to Resume Lensing after Long Halt." *Box Office* 114 (January 1, 1979): 12.

WISE BLOOD. 1979. (Director, Actor; Writer, uncredited.)

ARTICLES

Aghed, J. "Jesus var en lognare." *Chaplin* 23, no. 174 (1981): 115–18, port, stills. On the relationship between O'Connor's novel and Huston's film adaptation of it.

Amiel, M. "Cannes 79: La sagesse dans le sang." *Cinéma* (Paris) 247–248 (July–August 1979): 23.

Asahina, R. "On Screen: Novels into Films." *New Leader* 62 (November 5, 1979): 23–24.

Benayoun, Robert. "Delivrez-nous de la grâce." *Positif* 225 (December 1979): 60–62, creds, illus. (Reprinted in *John Huston, Collection dirigée,* edited by Gilles Ciment, 157–61, Dossier Positif Rivages, Paris, Editions Rivages, Collection Positif-Rivages, no. 2, 1988.) NYPL.

Boyum, Joy Gould. "*Wise Blood:* Wise Choices and *Under the Volcano:* Looking Outward." In *Double Exposure: Fiction into Film,* 175–81, 205–11. New York: Universe Books, 1985.

Buckley, Tom. "At the Movies: John Huston back from Surgery and Going Strong at 72." *New York Times,* January 26, 1979, C6, illus. interv.

Canby, Vincent. "Dialogue Can Make the Difference." *New York Times,* October 7, 1979, sect. 2, 1. NYTR.

———. "Many Try, but *Wise Blood* Succeeds." *New York Times,* March 2, 1980, 19, stills. NYTR.

———. "Golden Age of Junk." *New York Times,* August 17, 1980, sect. 2, 13. NYTR.

Carter, Martin. "*Wise Blood:* From Novel to Film." *The Flannery O'Connor Bulletin* 8 (Autumn 1979): 97–115. Interview with Benedict Fitzgerald, producer.

Charlton, Linda. "Young Dreamer + Old Pro = *Wise Blood.*" *New York Times,* February 17, 1980, sect. 2, 15, port, stills. MOMA.

Cinéma (Paris) 459 (September 1989): 6, creds. S. Brisset.

Cooper, Stephen. "Literal Silences, Figurative Excess: 'Jhon' Huston's *Wise Blood.*" *The Flannery O'Connor Bulletin* 17 (1988): 40–50.

D'Elia, G. "Le due vie dell'ultimo Huston." *Cinema Nuovo* 34, no. 293 (February 1985): 3–4. (Letter on the latest films by John Huston, especially *Under the Volcano* and *Wise Blood.*)

Film-Echo/Filmwoche 15 (March 14, 1987): 13.

Film-Echo/Filmwoche 16 (March 20, 1987): 10–11.

"The Films of John Huston" [Program notes]. Los Angeles County Museum of Art, November 14, 1980. (Notes are excerpted from John Huston's autobiography, *An Open Book.*)

Henry, Michel. "La tentation de la sainteté." *Positif* 220–221 (July–August 1979): 67–68, stills. (Reprinted in *John Huston, Collection dirigée,* edited by Gilles Ciment, 155–56, Dossier Positif Rivages, Paris, Editions Rivages, Collection Positif-Rivages, no. 2, 1988.)

Jameson, Richard T, ed. *They Went That a Way: Redefining Film Genres—A National Society of Film Critics Video Guide.* San Francisco: Mercury House, 1994. Includes pieces on *Prizzi's Honor* by Richard Sragow and *Wise Blood* by Stephen Schiff.

Klein, Michael. "Visualization and Signification in John Huston's *Wise Blood:* The Redemption of Reality." *Literature/Film Quarterly* 12, no. 4 (October 1984): 230–36.

Listener 121, no. 3,108 (April 6, 1989): 39.

McKenzie, Barbara. "The Camera and *Wise Blood.*" *The Flannery O'Connor Bulletin* 10 (1981): 29–37.

Menides, Laura Jehn. "John Huston's *Wise Blood* and the Myth of the Sacred Quest." *Literature/Film Quarterly* 9, no. 4 (1981): 207–12. NYPL.

Mongin, O. "L'homme qui voulait se liberer du fanatisme." *Esprit,* no. 9 (September 1989): 77–85.

Remond, Alain. "Petit Palmares pour Grand Festival. Special Cannes." *Télérama,* no. 1,534 (June 6, 1979).

La Revue du Cinéma, no. 448 (April 1989): 43, creds, stills. Y. Alion.

Sight & Sound 54, no. 1 (Winter 1984): 31–33, interv. with producer.

REVIEWS

Amis du Film et de la Télévision, no. 282 (December 1979): 37, stills. E. Flipo.

BFI/Monthly Film Bulletin 47, no. 52 (January 1980): 13–14, creds. Richard Combs.

Books and Arts, February 8, 1980, 24–25. Marc Green.

Boston Real Paper, January 5, 1980, 22+. Gerald Peary.

Box Office 116 (April 14, 1980): 20. J. Robbins.

Cahiers du Cinéma 306 (December 1979): 62–63, stills. J.-C. Biette.

Casablanca 35 (November 1983): 46.

Christianity & Crisis 40 (April 14, 1980): 82–83.

*Christian Science Monitor, March 7, 1980, 19. David Sterritt.

Cineforum 21, no. 206 (August 1981): 67–71, bio, creds, stills. D. Ferrario.

Cinéma (Paris) 251 (November 1979): 85–86, creds, stills. C. M. Cluny. NYPL.

Cinema 2,002, no. 63 (May 1980): 33, creds. C. F. Herdero.

Cinemagic, no. 55 (February 2, 1981): 15, creds.

Cinématographe 52 (November 1979): 44, creds, illus. R. Bezombes.

Cine Revue 59 (May 23, 1979): 16–19, stills. F. Dhont and J. MacTrevor.

Contemporary Review 236 (May 1980): 270–72. J. Morton.

Contracampo 2, no. 12 (May 1980): 68, illus.

Cue, February 29, 1980. William Wolf.

Daily Telegraph, January 11, 1980. Patrick Gibbs. AMPAS.

Ecran, no. 82 (July 15, 1979): 30, creds. R. Bassan. NYPL.

Ecran, no. 85 (November 1979): 57–58, creds, stills. M. Tessier.

Film Comment 15 (November 1979): 63–64.

Film en Televisie 272 (January 1980): 23, creds, stills. M. Holthof.

Filmihullu, no. 8 (1981): 34–35, creds, stills. O. Peltonen.

Film Illustrated 9 (February 1980): 236–37, creds, stills. M. Whitman.

Film Quarterly 33, no. 4 (Summer 1980): 15–17, stills. M. Tarantino. AMPAS, NYPL. (A copy is located in the AMPAS John Huston Archive.)

Filmrutan 24, no. 3 (1981): 36, creds, illus, stills. I. Engven.

Films, no. 82 (February 1980): 11, stills.

Films and Filming 26, no. 3 (December 1979): 31, creds. Julian Fox. AMPAS.

*Films in Review 31, no. 2 (February 1980): 115–16. R. Edelman. AMPAS.

Financial Times, November 1, 1980. Nigel Andrews.

The Guardian, October 1, 1980. AMPAS.

Hablemos de Cine 10, no. 77 (March 1984): 83–84, stills. R. Bedoya.

Hollywood Reporter 255, no. 15 (February 6, 1979): 10.

Hollywood Reporter 258, no. 39 (October 12, 1979): 2. AMPAS.

Horizon 23 (June 1980): 70.

Hudson Review 33, no. 2 (1980): 251–56.

Jeune Cinéma, no. 120 (July–August 1979): 13–14, stills. R. Predal.

Kosmorama 26, no. 149 (October 1980): 195–96, creds, stills. U. S. Jorgensen.

Levende Billeder 6 (September 1980): 40–41, creds, stills. J. J. Christensen.

Liberation, October 24, 1979. Gilbert Rocher. AMPAS.

Listener 102, no. 2,626 (August 30, 1979): 280.

Listener 103, no. 2,644 (January 10, 1980): 56.

London Times, January 11, 1980. David Robinson. AMPAS.

*Los Angeles Times, December 12, 1979, sect. 4, 1. Charles Champlin. AMPAS.

Mediafilm, no. 140 (Winter 1982): 48–49, creds, illus. J. Boesten.

Motion Picture Guide 9 (1987): 3,880.

The Nation 229 (October 27, 1979): 409–11. Harold Clurman.

The Nation 230 (March 8, 1980): 283–84. T. Hatch.
National Review 32 (May 2, 1980): 543–44. John Simon. MOMA.
New Republic 182 (March 15, 1980): 24–25. Stanley Kauffmann.
*Newsday, February 18, 1980, part 2, 30. Alex Keneas.
*New Statesman 99 (January 18, 1980): 102. Geoffrey Nowell-Smith.
Newsweek, October 22, 1979, 101. AMPAS.
*Newsweek 95 (March 17, 1980): 101, stills. David Ansen. MOMA.
New West, May 5, 1980. S. Farber.
New Yorker 56 (February 25, 1980): 114–17. Roger Angell. AMPAS, MOMA.
*New York Magazine 13 (March 10, 1980): 85–86, illus. David Denby. MOMA.
*New York Post, February 18, 1980, 26. Archer Winston.
New York Times, September 29, 1979, 12, creds, stills. Vincent Canby. (Reprinted
    in *New York Times,* February 17, 1980, 68. Excerpts from Canby's review after
    film is shown at the New York Film Festival 1979.) MOMA, NYTR.
New York Times, June 24, 1984, H1. Vincent Canby.
Philadelphia Magazine 71 (April 1980): 60+.
La Revue du Cinéma, no. 24 (1980): 257–58. P. Mérigeau.
La Revue du Cinéma, no 344 (November 1979): 131–32, creds. J. Zimmer. NYPL.
Rivista del Cinematografo 54 (November 1981): 591, creds, stills. P. Pisarra.
Saturday Review, March 15, 1980. AMPAS.
Screen International 223 (January 12 1980): 15.
Séquences 103 (January 1981): 40–42, creds, stills. A. Leroux.
*Sight & Sound 49, no. 1 (Winter 1979–80): 56–57, stills. Tim Pulleine.
Skoop 17 (February 1981): 36, creds, stills. P. Cohen.
Texas Monthly 8 (May 1980): 189+. George Morris. MOMA.
*Time 115 (February 25, 1980): 50, stills. Frank Rich. AMPAS, MOMA.
Time Out 508 (January 11, 1980): 14–15. Chris Auty, "The Blind Don't See and the
    Lame Don't Walk and What's Dead Stays That Way."
Variety 195, no. 5 (June 6, 1979): 22, creds. [G.] Mosk[owitz]. AMPAS, VR.
*Village Voice 25 (February 25, 1980): 39, stills. Andrew Sarris. AMPAS, MOMA.
Wall Street Journal, February 22, 1980. Jay Gould Boyum. AMPAS.
Washington Post, May 7, 1980, C1. Gary Arnold.
Washington Post, May 7, 1980, Weekend, 17. Judith Martin.

THE WORD. 1978. TV. (Actor.)

REVIEWS
Variety, November 22, 1978.
Village Voice 23 (November 27, 1978): 72–73. S. Wolcott, "Medium Cool: Look!
    The Angel of Death."

WUTHERING HEIGHTS. 1939. (Writer, ucredited.)

ARTICLES AND REVIEWS

American Film 14, no. 6 (April 1989): 77.

The American Film Institute Catalog: Feature Films, 1931–1940. Berkeley: University of California Press, 1993, 2,476–78.

Anderegg, Michael A. *William Wyler.* Boston: Twayne, 1979, 67–76. *Avant-Scene du Cinéma* 168 (April 1976): 62–65.

Berg, Scott. "*Wuthering Heights:* Adapted from His Biography on Sam Goldwyn, 'Goldwyn, a Biography,' Knopf, 1989." *New York Times Magazine,* February 19, 1989, 47+.

Bianco e Nero 5, no. 5 (May 1941): 3. Mario Praz.

Bluestone, George. *Novels into Film: The Metamorphosis of Fiction into Cinema.* Berkeley: University of California Press, 1971, 91–114.

Catholic Film News 1, no. 8 (June 1939): 14.

Churchill, Douglas. "Mr. Goldwyn Storms the 'Heights.'" *New York Times,* January 8, 1939. (Reprinted in *The New York Times Encyclopedia of Film, 1937–1940.*)

―――. "Hollywood Prepares for the Worst." *New York Times,* June 11, 1939. (Reprinted in *The New York Times Encyclopedia of Film, 1937–1940.*)

Cinéma (Paris) 301 (January 1984): 49.

Commonweal 29 (April 21, 1939): 722.

Crisler, B. R. "Gossip of the Film." *New York Times,* August 22, 1937. (Reprinted in *The New York Times Encyclopedia of Film, 1937–1940.*)

Crowther, Bosley. "Mr. Olivier Comes Clean." *New York Times,* March 26, 1939. (Reprinted in *The New York Times Encyclopedia of Film, 1937–1940.*)

―――. "The Director Dissents." *New York Times,* April 16, 1939. (Reprinted in *The New York Times Encyclopedia of Film, 1937–1940.*)

Daniels, Robert L. *Laurence Olivier: Theatre and Cinema.* New York: A. S. Barnes, 1980, 65–72.

Druxman, Michael B. *Make It Again, Sam: A Survey of Movie Remakes.* South Brunswick, N.J.: A. S. Barnes, 1975, 210–14.

EPD Film 9, no. 5 (May 1992): 29–30. Dietrich Kuhlbrodt.

Epstein, Lawrence J. *Samuel Goldwyn.* Boston: Twayne, 1981, 80–92.

Film Daily, March 28, 1939, 9.

Film-dienst 45, no. 11 (May 26, 1992): 38–39. Hans Messias.

Films 1, no. 5 (April 1981): 40–41.

"Films from the Archive" [Program notes]. Museum of Modern Art: Department of Film, January 22–23, 1976.

Garbicz, Adam, and Jacek Klinowski. *Cinema: The Magic Vehicle—A Guide to Its Achievement. Journey One: The Cinema through 1949.* New York: Schocken Books, 1983, c. 1975–79, 318–19.

Harrington, John. "*Wuthering Heights:* Wyler as Auteur." In *The English Novel and the Movies,* edited by Michael Klein and Gillian Parker,. 67–82 New York: Ungar, 1981.

Harrison's Reports, April 15, 1939, 59.

Hirsch, Forest. *Laurence Olivier.* Boston: Twyane, 1979, 42–46.

Hochman, Stanley, ed. *From Quasimodo to Scarlett O'Hara: A National Board of Review Anthology, 1920–1940.* New York: Ungar, 1982, 295–98.

Hollywood Reporter, March 25, 1939, 3.

Ladies Home Journal 56 (June 1939): 18+.

Life 6 (April 3, 1939): 39–40.

Luhr, William. "Victorian Novels on Film." Ph.D. diss., New York University, 1979. (*Dissertation Abstracts International* [*DAI*] 39 [1979]: 7,358A.)

Magill's Survey of Cinema: First Series 4 (1980): 1,884–87. DeWitt Bodeen.

Marill, Alvin H. *Samuel Goldwyn Presents.* South Brunswick, N.J.: A. S. Barnes, 1976, 197–200.

Motion Picture Guide 9 (1987): 3,935–36.

Motion Picture Herald, April 1, 1939, 28.

The Nation 148 (April 22, 1939): 478.

**National Board of Review Magazine* 14 (April 1939): 16–17.

New Masses 31 (April 25, 1939): 29.

New Republic 98 (April 26, 1939): 336.

Newsweek 13 (April 10, 1939): 27.

New Yorker 15 (April 15, 1939): 79–80.

New York Times, April 14, 1939, 28. Frank Nugent. NYTR.

North American Review 247 (June 1939): 385–86.

Nugent, Frank S. "A Few New Faces Brighten up the 1939 Season." *New York Times,* October 15, 1939. (Reprinted in *The New York Times Encyclopedia of Film, 1937–1940.*)

Photoplay 53 (May 1939): 38–39.

Photoplay 53 (June 1939): 58.

Pryor, Thomas M. "The Fascinating Miss Fitzgerald." *New York Times,* May 21, 1939. (Reprinted in *The New York Times Encyclopedia of Film, 1937–1940.*)

Quarterly of Film, Radio and Television 11 (Winter 1956): 171–80.

Quirk, Lawrence J. *The Great Romantic Films.* Secaucus, N.J.: Citadel Press, 1974, 68–71.

***Rob Wagner's Script* 21 (April 15, 1939): 17–18.

Sadoul, George. *Dictionary of Films.* Translated, edited and updated by Peter Morris. Berkeley: University of California Press, 1972, 422–23.

Scholastic 34 (April 29, 1939): 33.

Schulberg, Budd Wilson. "Hollywood's Second Generation." *New York Times,* July 2, 1939. (Reprinted in *The New York Times Encyclopedia of Film, 1937–1940.*)

Sequence: Film Quarterly 13 (1951): 21.

Spectator 162 (May 5, 1939): 760.

Stage 16 (April 15, 1939): 22–24.

The Tattler 152 (May 10, 1939): 240.

Taylor, John Russell, ed. *Graham Greene on Film: Collected Film Criticism, 1935–1940.* New York: Simon & Schuster, 1972, 219–20.

Time 33 (April 17, 1939): 49.

Variety, March 29, 1939, 14. MOMA, VR.

Vermilye, Jerry. *The Films of the Thirties.* Secaucus, N.J.: Citadel Press, 1982, 227–29.

Wagner, Geoffrey. *The Novel and the Cinema.* Rutherford, N.J.: Fairleigh Dickinson University Press, 1975.

Wilson, Robert, ed. *The Film Criticism of Otis Ferguson.* Philadelphia: Temple University Press, 1971, 251–52.

Wolf, William, with Lillian Kramer Wolf. *Landmark Films: The Cinema of Our Century.* New York: Paddington Press, 1979, 42–47.

VIII
Interviews and Writings of John Huston

The two categories of interviews and writings are combined because in some ways they are interchangeable. Huston was very open to interviews, which in many cases read as if he wrote them. An important area of his writing was as a screenwriter, and that material is in chapter 16, "Screenplays in Collections." When copies of the following materials are in the production files of the Academy of Motion Picture Arts and Sciences (AMPAS), Museum of Modern Art (MOMA), and New York Public Library (NYPL), they are so indicated.

Aghed, Jan, and Michel Ciment. "Deux soirées avec John Huston." *Positif* 142 (September 1972): 93–104.

Allison, Davey. "Entretien avec John Huston." *Positif* 320 (October 1987): 5–7. (Reprinted in *John Huston, Collection dirigée,* edited by Gilles Ciment, 46–47, Dossier Positif Rivages, Paris, Editions Rivages, Collection Positif-Rivages, no. 2, 1988.)

Amory, Cleveland. "If I Had My Life to Live over Again: An Interview with John Huston." *Parade,* August 2, 1987. AMPAS.

Andrews, Rena. "Interview with John Huston." *Denver Post,* January 25, 1976.

Ardagh, John. "Huston in Eden." *Sight & Sound* 33, no. 4 (Autumn 1964): 173+.

Astor, Gerald. "The Man Who Delivered *The Kremlin Letter.*" *Look,* March 24, 1970.

Bachmann, Gideon. "How I Make Films: Interview." *Film Quarterly* 19, no. 1 (Fall 1965): 3–13. (Reprinted in *Perspectives on John Huston,* edited by Stephen Cooper, New York, G.K. Hall, 1994; and Andrew Sarris, *Interviews with Film Directors,* New York, Bobbs-Merrill, 1967 [reprinted as *Hollywood Voices.*])

———."En écoutant Huston." *Ecran* 46 (April 1976): 26–28. (French translation of "Huston in Morocco," *Sight & Sound* 44, no. 3 [Summer 1975]: 161–65.

———. "Watching Huston." *Film Comment* 12, no. 1. (January–February 1976): 21–22.

Bandler, Michael. "John Huston." *American Way,* October 15, 1987, 62+. MOMA.

Benayoun, Robert. "Entretien avec John Huston." *Positif,* no. 70 (June 1963).

Brandes, D. "An Interview with John Huston." *Filmmaker's Newsletter* 10, no. 9 (July 1977): 20–24. NYPL.

Braucourt, G. "Entretien avec John Huston." *Ecran,* no. 10 (December 1972): 61–63.

Buckley, Tom. "At the Movies: John Huston Back from Surgery and Going Strong at 72." *New York Times,* January 26, 1979, C6. MOMA.

Butler, Ivan. *The Making of Feature Films—A Guide.* Baltimore: Penguin Books, 1970.

Chevallier, Jacques, and F. Guérif. "John Huston: *Au dessous du volcan.*" *Revue du Cinéma,* no. 397 (September 1984): 42–48. NYPL.

Cillario, G. "Padre padrino, colloquio con John Huston." *L'Espresso,* September 1, 1985, 63–66. (Excerpt appeared as "Een gespred met John Huston" in *Skrien,* no. 146 [February–March 1986]: 58.)

Ciment, Michel. "Deux rencontres avec John Huston." *Positif,* no. 283 (September 1985): 26–35. NYPL.

———. *Passeport pour Hollywood: Entretiens avec Wilder, Huston, Mankiewicz, Polanski, Forman, Wenders.* Paris: Seuil, 1987.

Cinema Nuovo 8, no. 89 (September 1956): 114. Interview with John Huston.

Corry, John. *New York Times,* August 5, 1972. (Reprinted in *The New York Times Encyclopedia of Film, 1972–1974.*) MOMA, NYPL.

Crawley, T. "Acting up a Storm." *Photoplay* 37 (May 1986): 4–6.

Crawley, T. "The Old Man and the Sea Siren." *Films Illustrated* 9 (March 1980): 268–75.

Crist, Judith. *Take 22: Movie Makers on Moviemaking.* New York: Viking, 1984.

Decaux, E., and Villien, B. "John Huston: Souvenirs d'Hollywood." *Cinématographe,* no. 52 (November 1979): 40–43.

De Laurot, Edouard. "An Encounter with John Huston." *Film Culture,* no. 8 (1956): 1–4. (*Note:* A copy is located in the AMPAS John Huston Archive.) NYPL.

Demeure, Jacques, and Michel Subiela. "Recontre avec John Huston: 'I Like Stories, I Like Action.'" *Positif,* no. 3 (1952): 42–43. (Reprinted in *John Huston, Collection dirigée,* edited by Gilles Ciment, 25–26, Dossier Positif Rivages, Paris, Editions Rivages, Collection Positif-Rivages, no. 2, 1988.)

Dreifus, Claudia. "Conversation with John Huston." *Los Angeles Herald Examiner,* December 7, 1980. AMPAS.

Ebert, Roger. "The Man Who Would Be Huston." *New York Post,* September 30, 1975.

Edwin, Melvyn. "John Huston Meets Press after Filming *Moby Dick.*" *Christian Science Monitor,* March 20, 1956. NYPL.

Egger, Urs. "John Huston Interview." *Cinema Papers,* October 1977, 138–41+.

Elliott, David. "Interview with John Huston." *Chicago Sun-Times,* October 10, 1980. (Reprinted in *Newsbank* 75 [July 1980–June 1981]: F12–F13.)

F[altysova], H. *Film a Doba* 19, no. 6 (June 1973): 332–33.

Fenyvez, G. *Film und Fernsehen* 16, no. 2 (February 1988): 38–44. (Interviews.)

Film Comment 12, no. 1 (January–February 1976): 23+.

Ford, D. "A Talk with John Huston." *Action* 7, no. 5 (September–October 1972): 21–25. NYPL.

Franklin, Rebecca. "Interview with John Huston on Occasion of *The Misfits.*" *Birmingham News,* November 2, 1980.

Frascani, Federico. "Per andare in Africa Huston parte da Ravello." *Cinema Nuovo* 2, no. 8 (April 1, 1953).

Freudenheim, Milt. "Chatting with Director of a Reborn Smash." *Sunday Star* (Washington, D.C.), April 4, 1971, C-5. AMPAS.

"Going Back to John Huston." *New York,* May 12, 1980. AMPAS.

Greenberg, Peter S. "Saints & Stinkers: Director John Huston Talks about the Best Life in the World. And Some Who Had It. And Some Who Lost It." *Rolling Stone,* no. 337 (February 19, 1981): 21–25. (Translated into Spanish: *Contratempo,* no. 22 [June–July 1981]: 48–53.) MOMA.

Grobel, Lawrence. "Interview with John Huston." *Playboy,* Fall 1985, 63+.

Guerif, F. "Entretien avec John Huston." *Revue du Cinéma,* no. 397 (September 1984): 46–48. NYPL.

Hachem, Samir. "Under the Volcano." *American Cinematographer* 65, no. 9 (October 1984): 58–63.

———. "Motion Picture News: Interview with John Huston." *Millimeter,* no. 13 (July 1985): 44–45. NYPL

Harmetz, Aljean. "Lowry and Malamud Tested on Film." *New York Times,* June 14, 1984, C17. AMPAS.

———. "Patient: John Huston. Rx: Film." *New York Times,* March 8, 1987, 1+. MOMA.

———. "John Huston Is Not Well." *Chicago Tribune,* March 12, 1987, D1–D2.

Hendrick, Kimmis. "Huston: I Direct as Little as Possible." *Christian Science Monitor,* November 22, 1968, 6.

Hickey, Des. "The Irish Horizons of Squire Huston." *Chicago Sun-Times,* April 30, 1967, sect. 3, 4.

Hine, A. "Paris in the 90s: *Moulin Rouge* on Location." *Holiday,* April, 1953, 26–27.

Hughes, Robert, ed. "The Courage of Men: An Interview with John Huston." In *Film: Book 2,* 22–35. New York: Grove, 1962.

Huston, John. "Fool" (short story). *American Mercury* 16 (March 1929): 347–51. (Reprinted in *Reflections in a Male Eye,* edited by Gaylyn Studlar and David Desser, 239–47, Washington, D.C., Smithsonian Institution Press, 1993; and in *New Stories for Men,* edited by Charles Grayson, New York, Garden City Publishing, 1943. Translated into German: "Einfalt" [Fool], *Filmkritik* 26, no. 2 [February 1982]: 80–90; and into French: *Positif* 20 [January 1957]: 25–31, and reprinted in *John Huston, Collection dirigée,* edited by Gilles Ciment, 48–54, Dossier Positif Rivages, Paris, Editions Rivages, Collection Positif-Rivages, no. 2, 1988.)

———. *Frankie and Johnny.* Illustrated by Covarrubias. New York: A. & C. Boni, 1930. (Reprint—New York: B. Blom, 1968.)

———. "Figures of Fighting Men" (short story). *American Mercury* 23 (May 1931): 113–15. (Reprinted in *Reflections in a Male Eye,* edited by Gaylyn Studlar and David Desser, 249–53, Washington, D.C., Smithsonian Institution Press, 1993.)

———. "My Father." *Film Weekly,* May 11, 1934:10.

———. "Picture Partners." *The American Cinematographer,* December 1941. (Reprinted in *Hollywood Directors, 1941–1976,* edited by Richard Koszarski, 41–46, New York, Oxford University Press, 1977.)

————. "The Film Industry and World Peace." *Hollywood Reporter* 90, no. 4 (September 23, 1946): sect. 2.

————. "A Tribute to Robert Flaherty." *Sight & Sound* 21, no. 2 (October, December 1951): 64.

————. "The African Queen," *Theatre Arts* 36, no. 2 (February 1952): 48+. MOMA.

————. "Story behind a Safari: Director of *African Queen* Finds Film Work in Jungle Tough but Rewarding." *New York Times,* February 3, 1952. (Reprinted in *The New York Times Encyclopedia of Film,* New York, Times Books, 1984.)

————. "*Moulin Rouge:* An Appreciation of Toulouse-Lautrec." *Esquire,* December 1952, 103+. NYPL.

————. "Regarding Flaherty." *Sequence Film Review* (London) 14 (New Years' 1952): 17–18.

————. "Harpoons Away." *Sports Illustrated,* June 6, 1955, 66+.

————. "Humphrey Bogart est mort lundi matin." *Positif,* no. 21 (February 1957): 15. (Reprinted in *John Huston, Collection dirigée,* edited by Gilles Ciment, 61–64, Dossier Positif Rivages, Paris, Editions Rivages, Collection Positif-Rivages, no. 2, 1988.)

————. "Focus on Freud." *New York Times,* December 9, 1962. AMPAS, NYPL.

————. "Home Is Where the Heart Is—and so Are Films." *Screen Producers Guild Journal,* March 1963, 3–4.

————. "Monkeys I Have Known." *Pageant,* August 1965.

————. "La parola a John Huston." In *La Bibbia,* edited by Vittorio Bonicelli et al., [9–10]. Verona: A. Mondadori, 1966.

————. "John Huston's Analysis of *Myra Breckinridge.*" St. Cleran's, Ireland, September 3, 1969, 20 pp. Unpublished. In the UCLA Twentieth Century-Fox Script Archives.

————. "Eugene O'Neill, Playwright." *Action* 5, no. 3 (May–June 1970): 32. (Translated into French as "Eugene O'Neill, dramaturge," *Positif,* no. 123 [January 1971]. Reprinted in *John Huston, Collection dirigée,* edited by Gilles Ciment, 55–59, Dossier Positif Rivages, Paris, Editions Rivages, Collection Positif-Rivages, no. 2, 1988.) AMPAS, NYPL.

————. "Ladylike Katie." *American Film* 5 (September 1980): 40.

————. "Stalling for Time." *American Film* 5 (September 1980): 45.

————. "Puhen aiheena John Huston." *Filmihullu,* no. 3 (1980): 18–23.

————. *An Open Book.* New York: Knopf, 1981. (Translated into Spanish: *A libro abierto,* Madrid, Espasa Calpe, 1986; in Italian: *Cinque mogli a sessanta film,* Roma, Editori Riuniti, 1982; and in French: *John Huston par John Huston,* Paris, Pygmalion-Gérand Watelet, 1983. Reviews of the Knopf book: *New York Times* 130 [October 12, 1980]: 9, T. Buckley; *New York Times* 129 [September 18, 1980]:C19, C. Lehman-Haupt; "Les Livres," *Positif,* no. 235 [October 1980]: 78; *Positif,* nos. 269 & 270 [July–August 1983]: 125–26, H. M. Ceiutat, "John Huston par John Huston"; *Cinématographe,* no. 86 [February 1983]: 68–69, H. E. Decaux, "John Huston par John Huston"; *Cinema 83,* no. 289

[January 1983]: 6, M. Amiel, "M. Huston par Huston"; *Variety,* no. 301 [January 14, 1981]: 28; *Kosmorama* 28, no. 162 [December 1982]: 207; *Philadelphia Bulletin,* November 9, 1980, Joseph X. Dever; *Philadelphia Inquirer,* September 28, 1990, 14-H. Richard Fuller; *New York Times,* January 3, 1990, C13, Caryn James.)

———. "Einfalt." *Filmkritik* 26 (February 1982): 80–90.

———. "Dialogue on Film: John Huston." *American Film* 9, no. 4 (January–February 1984): 19+. NYPL.

———. "Associés cinématographiques sur les directeurs de la photographie." *Positif,* no. 299 (January 1986): 5–6. (Reprinted in *John Huston, Collection dirigée,* edited by Gilles Ciment, 65–67, Dossier Positif Rivages, Paris, Editions Rivages, Collection Positif-Rivages, no. 2, 1988.)

———. "Die ehre der Prizzis." *Film & Fernsehen* 15, no. 5 (1987): 24–25.

———. "Silhouettes de boxeurs." *Positif,* no. 323 (January 1988): 11–12.

Huston, John, Mark Robson, Jud Kinberg, Charles Schneer, Mitchell Kowal, and Robert Siodmak. "The Journal Looks at Hollywood away from Home." *Journal of Screen Producers Guild* (Producers Guild of America, Hollywood), March 1963, 3–14.

"Interview" (in French with Huston). *Première,* no. 5 (1984). MOMA.

"It's Really through Films that I've Seen a Large Part of the World." *Travel & Leisure,* May 1982. MOMA.

"John Huston." *Positif,* no. 283 (September 1984): 26–43. (Special section.)

"John Huston: A 78 ans je n'ai qu'une peur, c'est de mourir d'ennui." *Paris Match,* July 5, 1984. AMPAS.

"John Huston on *Moby Dick:* A Conversation with Edward Lauret." *Film* 10 (November–December 1956): 11.

"John Huston's Big Stage." *Newsweek,* July 21 1958, 87.

"John Huston, Who Will Be Guest of Honor at Lincoln Center Film Society's 9th Annual Tribute." *New York Times,* May 5, 1980, sect. 3, 4.

Kissel, Howard. *Women's Wear Daily,* December 16, 1975, 28.

Knelman, Martin. "In the Arts, People Have to Be Beaten to Death." *Los Angeles Herald Examiner,* January 13, 1980, D10–D11.

McCarthy, Todd. "Listens as Well as He Talks: John Huston's DGA Weekend." *Variety,* June 2, 1982, 6+.

———. "Cracking the Volcano." *Film Comment* 20, no. 4 (July–August 1984): 59–63.

McDonough, Charles. *Chicago Tribune,* March 20, 1983. (Reprinted in *Newsbank,* July 1982–June 1983, F7–F8).

MacNamara, Paul. "A Little Visit to John Huston in Mexico." *Los Angeles,* September 1986, 158+. AMPAS.

Maher, Mary. "John Huston on Location: An Interview in Co. Wicklow." *Irish Times,* June 17, 1967. AMPAS.

Malcolm, Andrew H. "Huston: 'I Want to Keep Right on Going.'" *New York Times,* December 11, 1979. (Reprinted in *The New York Times Encyclopedia of Film, 1977–1979.)*

Matthews, Jack. "Film Clips: Huston Documentaries—Only Following Orders." *Los Angeles Times,* September 11, 1985, 1+.

Mevensen, J., and Karen Seberechts. "Under the Volcano." *Film en Televisie* 330 (November 1984): 16–19. (Review and interview.)

Midding, G, and L. O. Beier. "Die erste Reaktion beim Sehen ein es films ist emotional." *Film Bulletin* (Switzerland) 29, no. 2 (1987): 26–39.

Minetree, Harry. "On Location with John Huston for the Shooting on *The Man Who Would Be King.*" *People,* April 21, 1975, 61–65. AMPAS, NYPL.

"Multi-talented John Huston Talks Movies (What else?)." *Box Office,* May 9, 1977, ME-2.

Nason, Richard W. "Huston Hits High with 'Heaven' and 'Geisha.'" *New York Times,* September 28, 1958.

Natale, Richard. "Going back to Huston." *Women's Wear Daily,* July 27, 1972, 12. MOMA.

New Yorker, June 4, 1949. Interview with John Huston.

Nogueira, Rui, and Bertrand Tavernier. "Encounters" (an interview with John Huston). *Positif,* no. 116 (May 1970), translated from the English by Ruth Hottell. (In Studlar and Desser, *Reflections in a Male Eye,* edited by Gaylyn Studlar and David Desser, 207–37, Washington, D.C., Smithsonian Institution Press, 1993.)

O'Dowd, B. "John Huston: Last of the Rebel Directors?" *Hollywood Studio,* no. 2 (1985): 9.

Pelko, S. "O poslu in pravilih." *Ekran* 13, no. 2 (1988): 29+.

Perisco, Joseph. "An Interview with John Huston, the Dean of American Movie Men at Seventy-five." *American Heritage,* April–May 1982, 9–14. MOMA.

Phillips, Gene D. "Talking with John Huston." *Film Comment,* May–June 1973, 15–19.

Prouse, Derek. *Sunday Times,* February 20, 1966. Interview on the occasion of Huston directing *The Mines of Sulphur* at La Scala, Milan.

"Q and A: At 75, Director John Huston Loves Life behind the Scenes." *Los Angeles Herald Examiner,* April 26, 1982. AMPAS.

Reisz, Karel. "Interview with Huston." *Sight & Sound,* no. 3 (January–March 1952): 130–32.

"Revisited." *New Yorker,* February 25, 1980, 31–34. AMPAS.

Riger, Robert. "Details from the Master's Painting." *Action* 10, no. 5 (September–October 75): 6–14.

Robinson, David. "The Innocent Bystander." *Sight & Sound* 42, no. 1 (Winter 1972–1973): 20–21.

Rochu, Gilbert. "Entretien, John Huston à la poursuite du *Faucon Maltais.*" *Libération,* August 4, 1980, 19.

Ruiz, Jos, and Manolo Marinero. "Con John Huston, Michael Caine, Sylvester Stallone y Max von Sydow, en Budapest, durante el rodaje de 'Evasion o victoria.'" *Casablanca* 13 (January 1982): 6+.

Rynning, R. "John Huston." *Filmrutan* 25, no. 4 (1982): 27–29.

———. "Jeg er med pa a lage noe som vil leve for alltid!" *Film & Kino* 52, no. 1 (1984): 22–23.

St. Pierre, Brian. "John Huston: As He Was, Is, and Probably Always Will Be." *New York Times,* September 25, 1966A. (Reprinted in *The New York Times Encyclopedia of Film, 1964–1968.*)

Schaper, M. "Man muss sich seine Freiheit erkampfen." *EPD Film* 3, no. 9 (September 1986): 25–30.

Sutherland, Christine. "John Huston Remembers." *Ladies Home Journal,* April 1986. AMPAS.

"Takes." *New Yorker* 45 (June 14, 1969): 31–33.

"The Talk of the Town: Forty." *New Yorker,* October 15, 1984, 36–39.

Taylor, Charles, and Glenn O'Brien. "Huston!" *Inter/View* 25 (September 1972): 42–45. AMPAS, MOMA.

Thomas, Barbara. "Interview." *Atlanta Journal,* May 24, 1978, B13–B14.

Thomas, Kevin. "Hollywood's Roman à Clef-Director John Huston." *Los Angeles Times,* September 16, 1979.

Tsey, Pauline. "John Huston: Prolific Film Director Discusses Career, Tips on Movies." *UCLA Daily Bruin,* October 15, 1986. AMPAS.

Turan, Kenneth. "His Last Bow." *GQ,* December 1987, 160–66.

Ventura, Michael. "John Huston: A Quick Take." *LA Weekly,* July 24–30, 1981. AMPAS.

Walsh, M. "John Huston Raises *The Dead.*" *Time,* March 16, 1987, 92–93.

Watters, Jim. "John Huston on Kipling, Hemingway & Jack Daniels." *New York Times,* February 15, 1976, sect. 2, 1+. (Reprinted in *The New York Times Encyclopedia of Film, 1975–1976.*) AMPAS, MOMA, NYPL.

Wolf, William. "Can Huston Cap Career with Another Great Film?" *Cue,* November 22, 1975, 25.

IX
The "Fictionalized" Huston

There are few Hollywood personalities whose character and personality have been so frequently the subject of fiction as has John Huston. Certainly the most famous depiction of him is in *White Hunter, Black Heart*—Peter Viertel's slightly disguised account of the making of *The African Queen* (1952)—which was made into a film by Clint Eastwood. (While one can praise Eastwood for attempting to portray Huston's character, he does not quite succeed.) Huston, however, succeeds without much help in films, where in many ways his personality comes out much more successfully than in some biographical studies. Interestingly a side of Huston emerges in some of his straight acting assignments, such as *Chinatown* (1974) and *Winter Kills* (1979). There are also some depictions of Huston in television productions, especially in fictionalized accounts of Marilyn Monroe's story.

Bradbury, Ray. *Green Shadows, White Whale.* New York: Knopf, 1992.
      Novel based on Bradbury's experiences with Huston as cowriter of *Moby Dick* (1956).

Busch, Niven. *The Actor.* New York: Simon & Schuster, 1955.
      The novel includes a character named Harold Heston presumably based on Huston.

Hamblett, Charles. *Crazy Kill.* London: Sidgwick and Jackson, 1956.
      This novel deals, in semifictional form, with the filming of *Moby Dick* (1956). Huston wrote the introduction.

Roszak, Theodore. *Flicker.* New York: Summet Books, 1991.
      A famous fictionalized European filmmaker claims to have worked in an uncredited capacity with John Huston on *The Maltese Falcon* (1941), by assisting Huston in the production.

Thompson, David. *Suspects.* New York: Knopf, 1985.
    "Fictionalized" accounts of the lives of characters in *Chinatown* (1974), *Beat the Devil* (1954), *High Sierra* (1941), *The Killers* (1946), and *The Maltese Falcon* (1941).

Viertel, Peter. *White Hunter, Black Heart.* Garden City, N.Y.: Doubleday, 1953.
    A fictionalized account of events surrounding the production of *The African Queen* (1952).

X
People Involved with John Huston

This chapter provides bibliographical citations to some of the people who were involved with Huston's personal life and those having connections with him in his capacity as a director, screenwriter, and actor. Many of these publications include references to Huston.

JAMES AGEE
Agee, James. *Letters of James Agee to Father Flye.* New York: Braziller, 1962.
Barson, Alfred T. *A Way of Seeing: A Critical Study of James Agee.* Amherst, Mass.: University of Massachusetts Press, 1972.
Bergreen, Laurence. *James Agee: A Life.* New York: E. P. Dutton, 1984.
Kramer, Victor. *James Agee.* New York: Twayne, 1975.
Moreau, Genevieve. *The Restless Journey of James Agee.* Translated from the French by Miriam Kleiger with Morty Schiff. New York: Morrow Press, 1977.
Ohlin, Peter. *Agee.* New York: Ivan Obolensky, 1966.
Seib, Kenneth. *James Agee: Promise and Fulfillment.* Pittsburgh: University of Pittsburgh Press, 1968.

BRIAN AHERNE
Aherne, Brian. *A Proper Job.* Boston: Houghton, Mifflin, 1969.
Aherne, Brian, assisted by George Sanders and Benita Hume. *A Dreadful Man.* New York: Simon & Schuster, 1979.

SAM ARKOFF
Arkoff, Sam, with Richard Trubo. *Flying through Hollywood by the Seat of My Pants.* Secaucus, N.J.: Carol Publishing, 1992.

MALCOLM ARNOLD
Poulton, Alan J. *The Music of Malcolm Arnold: A Catalog.* Boston: Faber Music in association with Faber & Faber, 1986.

MARY ASTOR
Astor, Mary. *My Story: An Autobiography.* Garden City, N.Y.: Doubleday, 1959.
———. *A Life in Film.* With an Introduction by Sumner Locke Elliott. New York: Delacorte Press, 1971.

GEORGES AURIC
Golea, Antoine. *Georges Auric.* Paris: Ventadour, 1958.

LAUREN BACALL
Bacall, Lauren. "Hollywood vs. Africa." *Los Angeles Mirror,* March 31, April 1, and April 2, 1952.
————. *Lauren Bacall by Myself.* New York: Knopf, 1979.
————. *Now.* New York: Knopf, 1994.
Buckley, K. P. "Movies: All about Betty." *Interview,* March 1988.
Quirk, Lawrence J. *Lauren Bacall: Her Films and Career.* Secaucus, N.J.: Citadel Press, 1986.
Royce, Brendan Scott. *Lauren Bacall: A Bio-bibliography.* Westport, Conn.: Greenwood Press, 1992.

LIONEL BARRYMORE
Barrymore, Lionel, as told to Cameron Shipp. *We Barrymores.* New York: Grosset & Dunlap, 1951.

S. N. BEHRMAN
Klink, William. *Maxwell Anderson and S. N. Behrman: A Reference Guide.* Boston: G.K. Hall, 1977.

CHARLES BICKFORD
Bickford, Charles. *Bulls, Balls, Bicycles and Actors.* New York: P. S. Eriksson, 1965.

THEODORE BIKEL
Bikel, Theodore. Theo. *The Autobiography of Theodore Bikel.* New York: HarperCollins, 1994.

HUMPHREY BOGART
Barbour, Alan G. *Humphrey Bogart.* New York: Pyramid Publications, 1973.
Benchley, Nathaniel. *Humphrey Bogart.* Boston: Little, Brown, 1975.
Bogart, Stephen Humphrey. *Bogart: In Search of My Father.* New York: E. P. Dutton, 1995.
Bounoure, Gaston. *Humphrey Bogart.* Premier plan, 20. Lyon: Société d'Etudes, de Recherches et de Documentation Cinématographiques, 1962.
Coe, Jonathan. *Humphrey Bogart: Take It & Like It.* London: Bloomsbury, 1991.
Eisenschitz, Bernard. *Humphrey Bogart.* Paris: Le Terrain Vague, 1967.
Eyles, Allen. *Humphrey Bogart.* London: Sphere Books Ltd., 1990.
Hyams, Joe. *Bogie: The Biography of Humphrey Bogart.* New York: New American Library, 1966.
————. *Bogart & Bacall: A Love Story.* New York: David McKay, 1975.
McCarty, Clifford. *The Complete Films of Humphrey Bogart.* New York: Carol Publishing Group, 1995. (Originally published as *Bogey: The Films of Humphrey Bogart,* New York, Citadel Press, 1965).
Meyers, Jeffrey. *Bogart: A Life in Hollywood.* Boston: Houghton, Mifflin, 1997.
Michael, Paul. *Humphrey Bogart: The Man & His Films.* Indianapolis: Bobbs-Merrill, 1965.

John Huston

Pettigrew, Terrence. *The Bogart File.* London: Golden Eagle, 1977.

———. *Bogart: A Definitive Study of His Film Career.* London: Proteus, 1981.

Ruddy, Jonah, and Jonathan Hill. *Bogey: The Man, the Actor, the Legend.* London: Souvenir Press, 1965.

Sklar, Robert. *City Boys: Cagney, Bogart, Garfield.* Princeton, N.J.: Princeton University Press, 1992.

Sperber, A. M., and Eric Lax. *Bogart.* New York: Morrow, 1997.

RAY BRADBURY

Atkins, Thomas. "The Illustrated Man: An Interview with Ray Bradbury." *Sight & Sound* 43, no. 2 (Spring 1974). (Reprinted as "*Moby Dick:* An Interview with Ray Bradbury" in *The Classic American Novel & the Movies,* edited by Gerald Peary and Roger Shatzkin, 42–51, New York, Ungar, 1977.)

Bradbury, Ray. *The Anthem Sprinters.* New York: Dial Press, 1963. A collection of short Irish plays that is dedicated to Huston, and contains comment by the author on *Moby Dick.*

———. *Green Shadows, White Whale.* New York: Knopf, 1992. Novel based on Bradbury's experiences with Huston as a cowriter of *Moby Dick* (1956).

Kunert, Arnold R. "Ray Bradbury on Hitchcock, Huston and Other Magic of the Screen." *Take One,* no. 3 (September 1973): 11.

Nolan, William. *The Ray Bradbury Companion: A Life and Career History, Photolog and Comprehensive Checklist of Writings with Facsimiles from Ray Bradbury's Unpublished and Uncollected Work in All Media.* Detroit: Gale, 1975.

MARLON BRANDO

Brando, Marlon, with Robert Londsey. *Brando: Songs My Mother Taught Me.* New York: Random House, 1994.

Carey, Gary. *Brando.* New York: Pocket Books, 1973.

Grobel, Lawrence. *Conversations with Brando.* New York: Hyperion, 1991.

Higham, Charles. *Brando: The Unauthorized Biography.* New York: New American Library, 1987.

Manso, Peter. *Brando: A Biography.* New York: Hyperion, 1994.

Schickel, Richard. *Brando: A Life in Our Times.* New York: Atheneum, 1991.

Thomas, Tony. *The Films of Marlon Brando.* Secaucus, N.J.: Citadel Press, 1973.

JEFF BRIDGES

Klemesrud, Judy. "Bridges Going Up, Going Up." *New York Times,* October 22, 1972. (Reprinted in *The New York Times Encyclopedia of Film, 1972–1974.*)

CHARLES BRONSON

Vermilye, Jerry. *The Films of Charles Bronson.* Secaucus, N.J.: Citadel Press, 1980.

RICHARD BROOKS

Roberts, Jerry, and Steven Gaydos, eds. *Movie Talk from the Front Lines: Filmmakers Discuss Their Works with the Los Angeles Film Critics Association.* Jefferson, N.C.: McFarland, 1995.

BILLIE BURKE
Burke, Billie, with Cameron Shipp. *With a Feather on My Nose.* New York: Appleton-Century-Croft, 1949.

CAROL BURNETT
Burnett, Carol. *One More Time: A Memoir.* New York: Random House, 1986.

W. R. BURNETT
Burnett, W. R. "Afterward." In *The Asphalt Jungle: A Screenplay,* by Ben Maddow and John Huston and edited by Matthew J. Bruccoli, 145–47. Carbondale, Ill.: Southern Illinois University Press, 1980.
Mate, K., and P. McGilligan. "Burnett." *Film Comment,* January–February 1983, 58–68.

RICHARD BURTON
Alpert, Hollis. *Burton.* New York: Putnam, 1986.
Archer, Eugene. "Richard Burton: Belated Baccalaureate for a Brooding Welshman." *New York Times,* June 28, 1964. (Reprinted in *The New York Times Encyclopedia of Film, 1964–1968.*)
Bragg, Melvyn. *Rich: The Life of Richard Burton.* London: Hodder & Stoughton; Boston: Little, Brown, 1988.
Stevenson, Tyrone. *Richard Burton: A Bio-bibliography.* Westport, Conn.: Greenwood Press, 1992.

MICHAEL CAINE
Andrews, Emma. *The Films of Michael Caine.* London: Barnden Castell Williams, 1974.
———. *Michael Caine: A Biography.* Surrey, U.K.: LSP Books, 1982.
Caine, Michael. *Michael Caine's Moving Picture Show.* New York: St. Martin's Press, 1988.
———. *Acting in Film.* New York: Applause, 1990.
Hall, William. *Raising Caine.* New York: Prentice-Hall, 1982.

TRUMAN CAPOTE
Brinnin, John Malcolm. *Truman Capote: Dear Heart, Old Buddy.* New York: Delacorte Press, 1986.
Capote, Truman. *Truman Capote: Conversations.* Edited by M. Thomas Inge. Jackson, Miss.: University Press of Mississippi, 1987.
Clarke, Gerald. *Capote: A Biography.* New York: Simon & Schuster, 1988.
Grobel, Lawrence. *Conversations with Capote.* Foreword by James A. Michener. New York: New American Library, 1985.
Stanton, Robert J. *Truman Capote: A Primary and Secondary Bibliography.* Boston: G.K. Hall, 1980.

FRANK CAPRA
American Film Institute. *Frank Capra: A Study Guide.* Research by Barbara Pearce Johnson, edited by Dennis R. Bohnenkamp and Sam L. Grogg. Washington, D.C.: The American Film Institute, 1979.

Bohn, Thomas. *A Historical and Descriptive Analysis of the "Why We Fight" Series.* New York: Arno Press, 1977. Dissertations on film series; with a new introduction; the Arno Press Cinema Program.

Capra, Frank. *The Name above the Title.* New York: Macmillan, 1971. (Reprint— New York, Bantam, 1972.)

Carney, Raymond. *American Vision: The Films of Frank Capra.* New York: Cambridge University Press, 1986.

Glatzer, Richard, and John Raeburn. *Frank Capra: The Man and His Films.* Ann Arbor, Mich.: University of Michigan Press, 1975.

Griffith, Richard. *Frank Capra.* London: British Film Institute, 1949?

Hanson, Patricia King, ed. *Meet Frank Capra: A Catalog of His Work.* Palo Alto, Stanford Theater Foundation; Los Angeles: National Center for Film and Video Preservation, 1990. A project of the American Film Institute Catalog of Motion Pictures Produced in the United States.

Scherle, Victor, and William Turner Levy. *The Complete Films of Frank Capra.* New York: Carol Publishing Group, 1992.

Willis, Donald. *The Films of Frank Capra.* Metuchen, N.J.: The Scarecrow Press, 1974.

Wolfe, Charles. *Frank Capra: A Guide to Reference and Resources.* Boston: G.K. Hall, 1987.

JACK CLAYTON

Gaston, George. *Jack Clayton: Guide to References and Resources.* Boston: G.K. Hall, 1981.

MONTGOMERY CLIFT

Bosworth, Patricia. *Montgomery Clift: A Biography.* New York: Harcourt, 1978.

Lippe, R. "Montgomery Clift: A Critical Disturbance." *CineAction,* Summer 1989, 36–42.

Kalfatovic, Mary. *Montgomery Clift: A Bio-bibliography.* Westport, Conn.: Greenwood Press, 1994.

Kass, Judith M. *The Films of Montgomery Clift.* Secaucus, N.J.: Citadel Press, 1979.

LaGuardia, Robert. *Monty: A Biography of Montgomery Clift.* New York: Arbor House, 1977.

SEAN CONNERY

Andrews, Emma. *The Films of Sean Connery.* New York: Beaufort Books, 1982.

Callan, Michael Feeney. *Sean Connery.* New York: Stein & Day, 1983.

Pfeiffer, Lee, with Philip Lisa. *The Films of Sean Connery.* Secaucus, N.J.: Carol Publishing Group, 1993.

Sellers, Robert. *The Films of Sean Connery.* London: Vision Press; New York: St. Martin's Press, 1991.

FRANCIS FORD COPPOLA

Johnson, Robert K. *Francis Ford Coppola.* Boston: Twayne, 1977.

Zucker, Joel S. *Francis Ford Coppola: A Guide to References and Resources.* Boston: G.K. Hall, 1984.

GARY COOPER

Dickens, Homer. *The Films of Gary Cooper.* New York: Citadel Press, 1970.

TONY CURTIS

Hunter, Allan. *Tony Curtis: The Man and His Movies.* New York: St. Martin's Press, 1985.

BETTE DAVIS

Affron, Charles. *Star Acting: Gish, Garbo, Davis.* New York: E. P. Dutton, 1977.

Davis, Bette. *The Lonely Life.* New York: Putnam, 1962.

Davis, Bette, with Michael Herskowitz. *This 'n That.* New York: Putnam. 1987.

Higham, Charles. *Bette: The Life of Bette Davis.* New York: Macmillan, 1981.

Leaming, Barbara. *Bette Davis: A Biography.* New York: Simon & Schuster, 1992.

Noble, Peter. *Bette Davis: A Biography.* London: Skelton Robinson, 1948.

Quirk, Lawrence. *Fasten Your Seat Belts: The Passionate Life of Bette Davis.* New York: Morrow, 1990.

Riese, Randall. *All about Bette: Her Life from A to Z.* Chicago: Contemporary Books, 1993.

Ringgold, Gene. *Bette Davis: Her Films and Career.* Rev. ed. New York: Citadel Press, 1985.

———. *The Complete Films of Bette Davis.* Foreword by Henry Hart, revised and updated by Lawrence J. Quirk. New York: Carol Publishing Group, 1990.

Robinson, Jeffrey. *Bette Davis: Her Film and Stage Career.* London and New York: Proteus, 1982.

Stine, Whitney. *Mother Goddam: The Story of the Career of Bette Davis, with a Running Commentary by Bette Davis.* New York: Hawthorne Books, 1974.

———. *I'd Love to Kiss You . . . Conversations with Bette Davis.* New York: Pocket Books, 1990.

OLIVIA DE HAVILLAND

De Havilland, Olivia. *Every Frenchman Has One.* New York: Random House, 1961.

Higham, Charles. *Sisters: The Story of Olivia de Havilland and Joan Fontaine.* New York: Coward, McCann, 1984.

Thomas, Tony. *The Films of Olivia de Havilland.* Foreword by Bette Davis. Secaucus, N.J.: Citadel Press, 1983.

KIRK DOUGLAS

Douglas, Kirk. *Ragman's Son: An Autobiography.* New York: Simon & Schuster, 1988.

Munn, Michael. *Kirk Douglas.* New York: St. Martin's Press, 1985.

Thomas, Tony. *The Films of Kirk Douglas.* Secaucus, N.J.: Citadel Press, 1972.

FAYE DUNAWAY

Hunter, Allen. *Faye Dunaway.* New York: St. Martin's Press, 1986.

PHILIP DUNNE

Dunne, Philip. *Take Two: A Life in Movies and Politics.* Rev. ed. New York: Limelight Editions, 1992.

CLINT EASTWOOD

Gallafont, Edward. *Clint Eastwood: Filmmaker & Star.* New York: Continuum, 1994.

Guerif, François. *Clint Eastwood.* Translated by Lisa Nesselson. New York: St. Martin's Press, 1986.

Munn, Michael. *Clint Eastwood: Hollywood Loner.* London: Robson Books, 1992.

Smith, Paul. *Clint Eastwood: A Cultural Production.* Minneapolis: University of Minnesota Press, 1993.

Thompson, Douglas. *Clint Eastwood: Riding High.* Chicago: Contemporary Books, 1992.

ALBERT FINNEY

Falk, Quentin. *Albert Finney in Character: A Biography.* London: Robson Books, 1992.

BENEDICT FITZGERALD

Martin, Carter. "*Wise Blood:* From Novel to Film." *The Flannery O'Connor Bulletin* 8 (Autumn 1979): 97–115. (An interview.)

ROBERT FLAHERTY

Calder-Marshall, Arthur. *The Innocent Eye: The Life of Robert J. Flaherty.* New York: Harcourt Brace, 1963.

ERROL FLYNN

Flynn, Errol. *My Wicked, Wicked Ways.* New York: Putnam, 1959.

Higham, Charles. *Errol Flynn: The Untold Story.* Garden City, NY: Doubleday, 1980.

Thomas, Tony, Rudy Behlmer, and Clifford McCarty. *The Films of Errol Flynn.* Foreword by Greer Garson. New York: Citadel Press, 1969.

Valenti, Peter. *Errol Flynn: A Bio-bibliography.* Westport, Conn.: Greenwood Press, 1984.

HENRY FONDA

Springer, John. *The Fondas: The Films and Careers of Henry, Jane and Peter Fonda.* New York: Citadel Press, 1970.

Sweeny, Kevin. *Henry Fonda: A Bio-bibliography.* New York: Greenwood Press, 1992.

Thomas, Tony. *The Films of Henry Fonda.* Secaucus, N.J.: Citadel Press, 1983.

CHRISTOPHER FRY

Leeming, Glenda. *Christopher Fry.* Boston: Twayne, 1990.

Roy, Emil. *Christopher Fry.* Carbondale, Ill.: Southern Illinois University Press, 1968.

CLARK GABLE

Essoe, Gabe. *The Films of Clark Gable.* Foreword by Charles Champlin. New York: Citadel Press, 1970.

Tornabene, Lynn. *Long Live the King: A Biography of Clark Gable.* New York: Putnam, 1976.

Williams, Chester. *Gable.* New York: Fleet Press Corp., 1968.

ZSA ZSA GABOR

Gabor, Zsa Zsa, and Gerold Frank. *Zsa Zsa Gabor: My Story—Written for Me by Gerold Frank.* Cleveland: World, 1960.

AVA GARDNER

Daniell, John. *Ava Gardner.* New York: St. Martin's Press, 1982.

Flamini, Roland. *Ava: A Biography.* New York: Coward, McCann, 1983.

Fowler, Karen. *Ava Gardner: A Bio-bibliography.* New York: Greenwood Press, 1990.

Gardner, Ava. *Ava: My Story.* New York: Bantam Books, 1990.

Higham, Charles. *Ava: A Life Story.* New York: Delacorte Press, 1974.

Wayne, Jane Ellen. *Ava's Men: The Private Life of Ava Gardner.* New York: St. Martin's Press, 1990.

JOHN GARFIELD

Beaver, James. *John Garfield: His Life and Films.* South Brunswick, N.J.: A. S. Barnes, 1978.

Gelman, Howard. *The Films of John Garfield.* Introduced by Abraham Polonsky. Secaucus, N.J.: Citadel Press, 1975.

McGrath, Patrick. *John Garfield: The Illustrated Career in Films and on Stage.* Jefferson, N.C.: McFarland, 1993.

Morris, George. *John Garfield.* New York: Harvest/HBJ Books, 1977.

Sklar, Robert. *City Boys: Cagney, Bogart, Garfield.* Princeton, N.J.: Princeton University Press, 1992.

Swindell, Larry. *Body and Soul: The Story of John Garfield.* New York: Morrow, 1975.

ROMAIN GARY

Gary, Romain. *Promise at Dawn.* New York: Harper, 1961. (Translated from the French, *La promesse de l'aube.*)

DOROTHY GISH

Gish, Lillian. *Dorothy and Lillian Gish.* Edited by James E. Fransher. New York: Scribners, 1973.

LILLIAN GISH

Gish, Lillian. *Dorothy and Lillian Gish.* Edited by James E. Fransher. New York: Scribnerss, 1973.

SAMUEL GOLDWYN

Berg, A. Scott. *Goldwyn: A Biography.* New York: Knopf, 1989.

Easton, Carol. *The Search for Sam Goldwyn: A Biography.* New York: Morrow, 1976.

Griffith, Richard. *Samuel Goldwyn: The Producer and His Films.* New York: Museum of Modern Art, 1956.

Marill, Alvin H. *Samuel Goldwyn Presents.* South Brunswick, N.J.: A. S. Barnes, 1976.

Marx, Arthur. *Goldwyn: A Biography of the Man behind the Myth.* New York: Norton, 1976.

SYDNEY GREENSTREET

"Corralled in a Mountain Lair." *New York Times,* September 6, 1942. (Reprinted in *The New York Times Encyclopedia of Film, 1941–1946.*)

Sennett, Ted. *Masters of Menace: Greenstreet and Lorre.* New York: E. P. Dutton, 1979.

HOWARD HAWKS

Bogdanovich, Peter. *The Cinema of Howard Hawks.* New York: The Library of the Museum of Modern Art, 1962.

Hawks, Howard. *Hawks on Hawks.* Berkeley: University of California Press, 1982.

Mast, Gerald. *Howard Hawks: Storyteller.* New York: Oxford University Press, 1982.

McBride, Joseph. *Focus on Howard Hawks.* Englewood Cliffs, N.J.: Prentice-Hall, 1972.

Poague, Leland A. *Howard Hawks.* Boston: Twayne, 1982.

Willis, Donald. *The Films of Howard Hawks.* Metuchen, N.J.: Scarecrow Press, 1975.

Wood, Robin. *Howard Hawks.* Garden City, N.Y.: Doubleday, 1968.

STERLING HAYDEN

Hayden, Sterling. *Wanderer.* New York: Knopf, 1963.

EDITH HEAD

Head, Edith. *Edith Head's Hollywood.* New York: E. P. Dutton, 1983.

Hirsch, Virginia. "Edith Head: Film Costume Designer." Ph.D. diss., University of Kansas, Lawrence, Kansas, 1975.

BEN HECHT

Getherling, Doug. *The Five Lives of Ben Hecht.* Toronto: Lester & Orpen, 1977.

Hecht, Ben. *A Child of the Century.* New York: Signet Books, 1954.

Martin, Jeffrey Brown. *Ben Hecht: Hollywood Screenwriter.* Ann Arbor, Mich.: University of Michigan Research Press, 1985.

McAdams, William. *Ben Hecht: The Man behind the Legend.* New York: Scribners, 1990.

MARK HELLINGER

Bishop, Jim. *The Mark Hellinger Story: A Biography of Broadway and Hollywood.* New York: Appleton-Century-Croft, 1952.

ERNEST HEMINGWAY

Donaldson, Scott. *By Force of Will: The Life and Art of Ernest Hemingway.* New York: Viking, 1977.

Phillips, Gene D. *Hemingway and Film.* New York: Ungar, 1980.

Laurence, Frank. *Hemingway and the Movies.* Jackson, Miss.: University Press of Mississippi, 1982.

PAUL HENREID

Henreid, Paul. *Ladies' Man.* New York: St. Martin's Press, 1984.

AUDREY HEPBURN

Harris, Warren G. *Audrey Hepburn: A Biography.* New York: Simon & Schuster, 1994.

Higham, Charles. *Audrey: The Life of Audrey Hepburn.* New York: Macmillan, 1984.

Hofstede, David. *Audrey Hepburn: A Bio-bibliography.* Westport, Conn.: Greenwood Press, 1994.

Karney, Robyn. *A Star Danced: The Life of Audrey Hepburn.* London: Bloomsbury, 1993.

Walker, Alexander. *Audrey: Her Real Story.* New York: St. Martin's Press, 1995.

KATHARINE HEPBURN

Dickens, Homer. *The Films of Katharine Hepburn.* New York: Citadel Press, 1971.

Hepburn, Katharine. *The Making of* The African Queen*, or How I Went to Africa with Bogart, Bacall and Huston and Almost Lost My Mind.* New York: Knopf, 1987.

Higham, Charles. *Kate: The Life of Katharine Hepburn.* New York: Norton, 1974.

WALTER HILL

Silver, A. J., and E. Ward. "Scriptwriter & Director: Interview with Walter Hill." *Movie,* Winter 1978–79, 29–42.

WILLIAM HOLDEN

Quirk, Lawrence J. *The Films of William Holden.* Secaucus, N.J.: Citadel Press, 1973.

TREVOR HOWARD

Munn, Michael. *Trevor Howard: The Man and His Films.* London: Robson, 1989.

ANJELICA HUSTON

Harmetz, Aljean. "Anjelica of the Hustons: Back in the Family Fold." *New York Times,* June 27, 1985, C19.

Harris, Martha. *Anjelica Huston: The Lady and the Legacy.* New York: St. Martin's Press, 1989.

Kaplan, J. "Anjelica Rising: Stardom for Another Huston." *New York Times,* February 12, 1989, 18–21.

Morrison, Mark. "Life with Father." *Los Angeles Times Magazine,* June 21, 1987.

Ross, Lillian. "Huston Chronicle." *New Yorker* 71, no. 43 (January 8, 1996): 25.

Time Out, November 11, 1987, 22. Interview with Anjelica Huston on film and her father, John Huston.

Walker, Beverly. "Anjelica." *Film Comment* 23 (September–October 1987): 24–26.

DANNY HUSTON

Radin, V. "Danny Huston: A Chip off the Old Monument." *Vogue,* September 1986, 108.

TONY HUSTON

Huston, Tony. "Family Ties." *American Film,* September 1987, 16–19.

City Limits, December 10, 1987, 20. Tony Huston talks about John Huston and his method of working during filming.

"A Huston Tribute." *New York Times,* April 1, 1988, 21.

JENNIFER JONES

Carrier, Jeffrey L. *Jennifer Jones: A Bio-bibliography.* New York: Greenwood Press, 1990.

Epstein, Edward. *Portrait of Jennifer: A Biography.* New York: Simon & Schuster, 1995.

Moshier, W. Franklyn. *The Films of Jennifer Jones.* San Francisco: The author, 1978.

DEBORAH KERR

Braun, Eric. *Deborah Kerr.* New York: St. Martin's Press; London: W. H. Allen, 1977.

EVELYN KEYES

Keyes, Evelyn. *Scarlett O'Hara's Younger Sister.* Secaucus, N.J.: Lyle Stuart, 1977.

HOWARD KOCH

Koch, Howard. "Reflections on a Golden Boy." *Film Comment,* May–June 1973, 12–14.

———. *As Time Goes By: Memoirs of a Writer.* New York: Harcourt, 1979.

PAUL KOHNER

Kohner, Frederick. *The Magician of Sunset Boulevard: The Improbable Life of Paul Kohner, Hollywood Agent.* Palos Verdes, Calif.: Morgan Press, 1974.

BURT LANCASTER

Clinch, Minty. *Burt Lancaster.* New York: Stein & Day, 1985.

Fishgall, Gary. *Against Type: The Biography of Burt Lancaster.* New York: Scribners, 1995.

Fury, David. *The Cinema History of Burt Lancaster.* Minneapolis: Artist's Press, 1989.

Hunter, Allan. *Burt Lancaster: The Man and His Movies.* New York: St. Martin's Press, 1984.

Vermilye, Jerry. *Burt Lancaster: A Pictorial Treasury of His Films.* New York: Falcon Enterprises, 1971.

Windleer, Robert. *Burt Lancaster.* New York: St. Martin's Press, 1984.

JESSE LASKY

Lasky, Jesse. *I Blow My Horn.* London: V. Gollancz, 1957.

————. *Whatever Happened to Hollywood?* New York: W. H. Allen, 1973.

PETER LORRE

Sennett, Ted. *Masters of Menace: Greenstreet and Lorre.* New York: E. P. Dutton, 1979.

Youngkin, Stephen D., James Bigwood, and Raymond Cabana. *The Films of Peter Lorre.* Secaucus, N.J.: Citadel Press, 1982.

ERNST LUBITSCH

Carringer, Robert, and Barry Sabath. *Ernst Lubitsch: A Guide to References and Resources.* Boston: G.K. Hall, 1981.

Poague, Leland A. *The Cinema of Ernst Lubitsch.* Brunswick, N.J.: A. S. Barnes, 1978.

CARSON MCCULLERS

Carr, Virginia Spencer. *The Lonely Hunter: A Biography of Carson McCullers.* Garden City, N.Y.: Doubleday, 1975.

HATTIE MCDANIEL

Jackson, Carlton. *Hattie: The Life of Hattie McDaniel.* Lanham, Md.: Madison Books, 1990.

JAMES MASON

Hirschorn, Clive. *The Films of James Mason.* London: LSP Books, 1975.

LOUIS B. MAYER

Crowther, Bosely. *Hollywood Rajah: The Life and Times of Louis B. Mayer.* New York: Holt, 1960.

BURGESS MEREDITH

Meredith, Burgess. *So Far, So Good: A Memoir.* Boston: Little, Brown, 1994.

ARTHUR MILLER

Bloom, Arthur, ed. *Arthur Miller.* New York: Chelsea House, 1987.

Centola, Steve. *Arthur Miller in Conversation.* Dallas: Northouse & Northouse, 1993.

Ferres, John H. *Arthur Miller: A Reference Guide.* Boston: G.K. Hall, 1979.

Goode, James. *The Story of* The Misfits. Indianapolis: Bobbs-Merrill, 1963.

Jensen, George. *Arthur Miller: A Bibliographical Checklist.* Columbia, S.C.: J. Faust, 1976.

Miller, Arthur. *Timebends: A Life.* New York: Grove Press, 1987.

————. *Conversations with Arthur Miller.* Edited by Matthew C. Roudane. Jackson, Miss.: University Press of Mississippi, 1987.

Savran, David. *Communists, Cowboys and Queers: The Politics of Masculinity in the Work of Arthur Miller and Tennessee Williams.* Minneapolis: University of Minnesota Press, 1992.

JOHN MILIUS

Lindsey, Robert. "The New Wave of Filmmakers." *New York Times,* May 28, 1978B. (Reprinted in *The New York Times Encyclopedia of Film, 1977–1979.*)

ROBERT MITCHUM

Belton, John. *Robert Mitchum.* New York: Pyramid Publications, 1976.

Eells, George. *Robert Mitchum: A Biography.* New York: F. Watts, 1984.

Malcolm, Derek. *Robert Mitchum.* Tunbridge Wells, Kent, U.K.: Spellmount; New York: Hippocrene Books, 1984.

Marill, Alvin H. *Robert Mitchum on the Screen.* South Brunswick, N.J.: A. S. Barnes, 1978.

Roberts, Jerry Wayne. *Robert Mitchum: A Bio-bibliography.* Westport, Conn.: Greenwood Press, 1992.

Tomkies, Mike. *The Robert Mitchum Story.* Chicago: Regnery, 1972.

MARILYN MONROE

Arnold, Eve. *Marilyn Monroe—An Appreciation.* New York: Knopf, 1987.

Conway, Michael, and Mark Ricci. *The Films of Marilyn Monroe.* Secaucus, N.J.: Citadel Press, 1964.

Guiles, Fred Lawrence. *Norma Jean: The Life of Marilyn Monroe.* New York: Bantam, 1973.

Kobal, John. *Marilyn Monroe: A Life on Film.* London and New York: Hamlyn, 1974.

McCann, Graham. *Marilyn Monroe.* New Brunswick, N.J.: Rutgers University Press, 1988.

Mailer, Norman. *Marilyn.* New York: Grosset, 1973.

Wagenknecht, Edward. *Marilyn Monroe: A Composite View.* Philadelphia: Chilton Book Co., 1969.

ROBERT MORLEY

Morley, Margaret. *Larger than Life: The Biography of Robert Morley.* London: Robson, 1979.

Morley, Robert. *Robert Morley: A Reluctant Autobiography.* New York: Simon & Schuster, 1967.

———. *The Best of Robert Morley.* London: Robson, 1981.

OSWALD MORRIS

Considine, Shaun. "The Men Who Work as the Directors' Eyes." *New York Times,* April 8, 1979C. (Reprinted in *The New York Times Encyclopedia of Film, 1977–1979.*)

Eyles, Allan. "Behind the Camera: Oswald Morris." *Focus on Film,* no. 8:28–37.

Shear, D. "There Is No Set Pattern: An Interview with Director of Photography Oswald Morris." *Film Heritage* 12, no. 3 (1977): 1–11.

PAUL MUNI

Druxman, Michael B. *Paul Muni: His Life and His Films.* South Brunswick, N.J.: A. S. Barnes, 1974.

AUDIE MURPHY
Graham, Don. *No Name on the Bullet: A Biography of Audie Murphy.* New York: Viking, 1989.

JEAN NEGULESCO
Negulesco, Jean. *Things I Did and Things I Think I Did.* New York: Linden Press, 1984. (Excerpted in *Positif* 308 [October 1986]: 56–58.)

PAUL NEWMAN
Hamblett, Charles. *Paul Newman.* Chicago: Regnery, 1975.
Quirk, Lawrence. *The Films of Paul Newman.* New York: Citadel Press, 1971.

JACK NICHOLSON
Davidson, Bill. "The Conquering Antihero." *New York Times,* October 12, 1975A. (Reprinted in *The New York Times Encyclopedia of Film, 1975–1976.*)
Flately, Guy. "Jack Nicholson—Down to the Very 'Last Detail.'" *New York Times,* February 10, 1974A. (Reprinted in *The New York Times Encyclopedia of Film, 1972–1974.*)
Gussow, Mel. "Easy Actor's Road Was Hard Riding." *New York Times,* January 2, 1976. (Reprinted in *The New York Times Encyclopedia of Film, 1975–76.*)
McGilligan, Patrick. *Jack's Life: A Biography of Jack Nicholson.* New York: Norton, 1994.

DAVID NIVEN
Garrett, Gerard. *The Films of David Niven.* Secaucus, N.J.: Citadel Press, 1976.
Niven, David. *Bring on the Empty Horses.* New York: Putnam, 1975.

PETER O'TOOLE
Flately, Guy. "Peter O'Toole: From *Lawrence* to *La Mancha.*" *New York Times,* September 17, 1972. (Reprinted in *The New York Times Encyclopedia of Film, 1969–1971.*)

BILLY PEARSON
Pearson, Billy, with Stephen Longstreet. *Never Look Back.* Introduction by John Huston. New York: Simon & Schuster, 1958.

GREGORY PECK
Griggs, John. *The Films of Gregory Peck.* Secaucus, N.J.: Citadel Press, 1984.

SAM PECKINPAH
Parill, William. *The Films of Sam Peckinpah.* Hammond, La.: Bay-Wulf Books, 1980.

ANTHONY PERKINS
Bernard Carragher. "I Had a Fine Childhood, How About You?" *New York Times,* November 19, 1972. (Reprinted in *The New York Times Encyclopedia of Film, 1972–1974.*)
Palmer, Laura Kay. *Osgood and Anthony Perkins: A Comprehensive History of Their Work in Theater, Film, and Oher Media, with Credits and an Annotated Bibliography.* Jefferson, N.C.: McFarland & Co., 1991.

ROMAN POLANSKI
Bisplinghoff, Gretchen, and Virginia Wright Wexman. *Roman Polanski: A Guide to References and Resources.* Boston: G. K. Hall, 1979.
Butler, Ivan. *The Cinema of Roman Polanski.* New York: A. S. Barnes, 1970.
Leaming, Barbara. *Polanski: A Biography.* New York: Simon & Schuster, 1981.
Polanski, Roman. *Roman by Polanski.* New York: Morrow, 1984.
Wexman, Virginia Wright. *Roman Polanski.* Boston: Twayne, 1985.

OTTO PREMINGER
Frischauer, Willi. *Behind the Scenes of Otto Preminger.* New York: Morrow, 1974.
Lourcelles, Jacques. *Otto Preminger.* Paris: Seghers, 1965.
Pratley, Gerald. *The Cinema of Otto Preminger.* New York: A. S. Barnes, 1971.
Preminger, Otto. *An Autobiography.* New York: Doubleday, 1977.

CAROL REED
Moss, Robert F. *The Films of Carol Reed.* New York: Columbia University Press, 1987.
Wapshot, Nicholas. *The Man Between: A Biography of Carol Reed.* London: Chatto & Windus, 1990.

EDWARD G. ROBINSON
Gangsberg, Alan. *Little Caesar: A Biography of Edward G. Robinson.* London: New English Library, 1993.
Higham, Charles "'Little Caesar' Is Still Punching." *New York Times,* November 5, 1972. (Reprinted in *The New York Times Encyclopedia of Film, 1972–1974.*)
Marill, Alvin H. *The Complete Films of Edward G. Robinson.* Secaucus, N.J.: Carol Publishing, 1990.

GILBERT ROLAND
Brownell, William, Jr. "Gilbert Roland: Mucho Hombre." *New York Times,* June 28, 1953A. (Reprinted in *The New York Times Encyclopedia of Film, 1952–1957.*)
Teichner, Miriam. "'Silent' Lover: Gilbert Roland, One of the Old Latin Romeos, Says Sound Ruined Romance." *New York Times,* June 12, 1949. (Reprinted in *The New York Times Encyclopedia of Film, 1947–1951.*)

DORE SCHARY
Schary, Dore. *Heyday: An Autobiography.* Boston: Little, Brown, 1979.

GEORGE C. SCOTT
Harbinson, W. A. *George C. Scott: The Man, the Actor, and the Legend.* New York: Pinnacle Books, 1977.
Reed, Rex. "George Is on His Best Behavior Now." *New York Times,* March 29, 1970A. (Reprinted in *The New York Times Encyclopedia of Film, 1969–1971.*)

DAVID O. SELZNICK
Haver, Ronald. *David O. Selznick's Hollywood.* New York: Knopf, 1980.
Selznick, David O. *Memo from David O. Selznick.* Selected and edited by Rudy Behlmer. New York: Viking Press, 1972.

Thomas, Bob. *Selznick.* Garden City, N.Y.: Doubleday, 1970.

Thomson, David. *Showman: The Life of David O. Selznick.* New York: Knopf, 1992.

DON SIEGEL

Kaminsky, Stuart. *Don Siegel: Director.* New York: Curtis Books, 1974.

Lovell, Alan. *Don Siegel: American Cinema.* London: British Film Institute, 1975.

FRANK SINATRA

Ringgold, Gene, and Clifford McCarty. *The Films of Frank Sinatra.* Secaucus, N.J.: Citadel Press, 1980.

SAM SPIEGEL

Fuchs, D. "Remembering Sam Spiegel." *Commentary,* July 1988, 53–54.

Sinclair, Andrew. *Spiegel: The Man behind the Pictures.* Boston: Little, Brown, 1987.

JOHN STEINBECK

Millichap, Joseph R. *Steinbeck on Film.* New York: Ungar, 1983.

GEORGE STEVENS

Richie, Donald. *George Stevens: An American Romantic.* New York: Museum of Modern Art, 1970.

JAMES STEWART

Eyles, Alan. *James Stewart.* New York: Stein & Day, 1984.

ELIZABETH TAYLOR

Shepard, Dick. *Elizabeth.* New York: Doubleday, 1974.

Vermilye, Jerry, and Mark Ricci. *The Films of Elizabeth Taylor.* Secaucus, N.J.: Citadel Press, 1976.

B. TRAVEN

Baumann, Michael L. *B. Traven: An Introduction.* Albuquerque: University of New Mexico Press, 1976.

Chankin, Donald O. *Anonymity and Death: The Fiction of B. Traven.* University Park, Penn.: Pennsylvania State University, 1975.

DALTON TRUMBO

Trumbo, Dalton. *Additional Dialogue: Letters, 1942–1962.* New York: Evans, 1970.

PETER VIERTEL

Viertel, Peter. *Dangerous Friends: At Large with Huston & Hemingway in the 50s.* New York: Doubleday, 1992. (Review of book: *New York Times,* September 6, 1992, Janet Maslin.)

SALKA VIERTEL

Viertel, Salka. *The Kindness of Strangers.* New York: Holt, 1969.

HAL B. WALLIS
Crowther, Bosely. "The Myth of the Trend: Hal B. Wallis of Warner Brothers Points out the Facts of the Matter." *New York Times,* March 3, 1940. (Reprinted in *The New York Times Encyclopedia of Film, 1937–1940.*)

The Museum of Modern Art. *Hal B. Wallis, Film Producer.* Edited by Adrienne Mancia. New York: Museum of Modern Art, 1970.

Wallis, Hal, and Charles Higham. *Starmaker: The Autobiography of Hal Wallis.* Foreword by Katharine Hepburn. New York: Macmillan, 1980.

RAOUL WALSH
Walsh, Raoul. *Each Man in His Time: The Life Story of a Director.* New York: Farrar, 1974.

JACK L. WARNER
Warner, Jack, with Dean Jennings. *My First Hundred Years in Hollywood.* New York: Random House, 1965.

JOHN WAYNE
Eyles, Alan. *John Wayne and the Movies.* South Brunswick, N.J.: A. S. Barnes, 1976.

Zmijewsky, Steve, Boris Zmijewsky, and Mark Ricci. *The Complete Films of John Wayne.* Secaucus, N.J.: Citadel Press, 1983.

Zolotow, Maurice. *Shooting Star: A Biography of John Wayne.* New York: Simon & Schuster, 1974.

ORSON WELLES
Bazin, André. *Orson Welles: A Critical View.* Translated by Jonathan Rosenbaum. New York: Harper, 1978.

Beja, Morris, ed. *Perspective on Orson Welles.* Perspectives on Film series. New York: G.K. Hall, 1995.

Bessy, Maurice. *Orson Welles.* New York: Crown, 1971.

Bogdanovich, Peter. *The Cinema of Orson Welles.* New York: The Library of the Museum of Modern Art, 1961.

Brady, Frank. *Citizen Welles: A Biography of Orson Welles.* New York: Scribners, 1989.

Cowie, Peter. *The Cinema of Orson Welles.* South Brunswick, N.J.: A. S. Barnes, 1973.

Gottesman, Ronald, ed. *Focus on Orson Welles.* Englewood Cliffs, N.J.: Prentice-Hall, 1976.

Higham, Charles. *The Films of Orson Welles.* Berkeley: University of California Press, 1970.

———. *Orson Welles.* New York: St. Martin's Press, 1985.

Leaming, Barbara. *Orson Welles: A Biography.* New York: Viking, 1985.

McBride, Joseph. *Orson Welles.* New York: Viking Press, 1972.

———. *Orson Welles: Actor and Director—An Illustrated History of the Movies.* New York: Harcourt, 1977.

Naremore, James. *The Magic World of Orson Welles.* Dallas: Southern Methodist University Press, 1989.

MAE WEST

Tuska, Jon. *The Films of Mae West.* Secaucus, N.J.: Citadel Press, 1973.

TENNESSEE WILLIAMS

Phillips, Gene D. *The Films of Tennessee Williams.* Cranbury, N.J.: Art Alliance, 1980.

Yacowar, Maurice. *Tennessee Williams and Film.* New York: Ungar, 1977.

WILLIAM WYLER

Anderegg, Michael A. *William Wyler.* Boston: Twayne, 1979.

Kern, Sharon. *William Wyler: A Guide to References and Resources.* Boston: G.K. Hall, 1979.

Madsen, Axel. *William Wyler: An Authorized Biography.* New York: Crowell, 1973.

DARRYL F. ZANUCK

Canby, Vincent. "D. Z.: The Last Tycoon." *New York Times,* March 17, 1968A. (Reprinted in *The New York Times Encyclopedia of Film, 1962–1968.*)

Gussow, Mel. *Zanuck: Don't Say Yes until I Finish Talking.* New York: Pocket Books, 1972.

Mosley, Leonard. *Zanuck: The Rise and Fall of Hollywood's Last Tycoon.* Boston: Little, Brown, 1984.

Zanuck, Darryl. *Memo from Darryl F. Zanuck: The Golden Years at Twentieth Century-Fox.* Selected, edited, and annotated by Rudy Behlmer, forward by Philip Dunne. New York: Grove Press, 1993.

XI
Obituaries

John Huston passed away on August 28, 1987. His importance in film worldwide can be seen from the wide coverage of his death. For example, the *New York Times* had a page one obituary, and *Variety* ran a three-page obituary. Listed are some of the many tributes that were written at the time. Copies of the tributes in the files of the Academy of Motion Picture Arts and Sciences (AMPAS), Museum of Modern Art (MOMA), and New York Public Library (NYPL) are so indicated. The name following the citation is the author of the obituary.

BFI/Monthly Film Bulletin, no. 54 (December 1987): 356–57, R. Combs.
Boston Globe. MOMA.
Boston Phoenix. MOMA.
Christian Science Monitor, September 4, 1987. AMPAS.
Cineinforme, no. 518 (September 1987): 28.
Cinéma (Paris), no. 418 (December 1987): 7–9, Maheo. NYPL.
Cinema India 4, no. 4 (1987): 6–9, E. Katz et al.
City Limits, no. 310 (September 10, 1987): 26.
Classic Images, no. 148 (October 1987): 60.
Columbus Dispatch, August 29, 1987—Ray Bradbury, "Reminiscences of Huston."
    AMPAS.
Directors Guild of America. The Newsletter, October 1987, 5.
EPD Film 4, no. 10 (October 1987): 3–5, Dietrich Kuhlbrodt.
Film (London) 3, no. 8 (October 1987): 2. NYPL.
Films and Filming, no. 397 (October 1987): 12, Tim Pulleine. NYPL.
Film & Kino, no. 7 (1987): 28–29, J. E. Holst.
Filmcritica 38, no. 379 (November 1987): 628–30, G. Barbagli.
Film Echo/Film Woche, no. 50 (September 1987): 10.
Film en Televisie, no. 365 (October 1987): 6, D. Dufour.
Film Français 2,157 (September 1987): 58+.
Films in Review 38, no. 11 (November 1987): 567, Michael Buckley. NYPL.
Film und Fernsehen 16, no. 2 (1988):38–39.
Hollywood Reporter, August 31, 1987. AMPAS.
Levende Billeder, no. 3 (October 1987): 24–25, A. Skytte.
Logbuch, no. 14 (September 1987): 50, G. Pohl.
Los Angeles Daily News, August 30, 1987. AMPAS.
Los Angeles Herald Examiner, August 29, 1987. AMPAS, MOMA.
Los Angeles Times, August 29, 1987, 1, Charles Champlin, AMPAS; August 30,
    1987, sect. 5, 4.

Maclean's 100 (September 7, 1987): 63, P. Hluchy.

Nation 245 (September 1987): 295, A. Cockburn.

National Review 39 (October 9 1987): 21–22, John Simon.

Newsweek 110 (September 7 1987): 71, David Ansen.

New York Times, August 29, 1987, 1+, Peter B. Flint. AMPAS.

People's Weekly 28 (September 14 1987): 40–41, P. Travers.

Philadelphia Inquirer, August 29, 1987, Rick Lyman. MOMA.

Positif, no. 320 (October 1987): 2–6. NYPL.

Premi 1 (December 1987): 104, S. Immergut.

Premiere 1 (December 1987): 58–63, Pete Hamill.

Revue du Cinéma, no. 431 (October 1987): 75–76, H. Moret.

Skrien, no. 156 (November–December 1987): 7.

Time 130 (September 7, 1987): 64, R. Schickel. MOMA.

Times of London, August 29, 1987, 10.

Variety, August 31, 1987, AMPAS; September 2, 1987, 4+, Todd McCarthy. AMPAS, MOMA.

Village Voice 32 (September 15, 1987): 99, Andrew Sarris. AMPAS.

Washington Post, August 29, 1987, A1, J. Y. Smith.

Z 5, no. 3 (1987): 32, T. O. Svendsen.

XII
The Movie Industry and John Huston

These citations provide information on the movie industry in which Huston worked. Many of the "general" references have discussions on Huston and his particular films. Some of the following citations are found in other chapters.

Agee, James. *Agee on Film: Reviews and Comments.* New York: McDowell, Obolensky, 1958. (Reprint—New York: Grosset & Dunlap, 1969, as Vol. 1.)

Alpert, Hollis. *The Dreams and the Dreamers.* New York: Macmillan, 1962.

Bach, Stephen. *Final Cut: Dreams and Disaster in the Making of Heaven's Gate.* New York: Morrow, 1985.

Barsam, Richard Meran. *Nonfiction Film: A Critical History.* New York: E. P. Dutton, 1973.

Barson, Michael. *The Illustrated Who's Who of Hollywood Directors.* Vol. 1, *The Sound Era.* New York: Farrar Straus and Giroux, 1995.

Baxter, John. *Hollywood in the Thirties.* New York: Paperback Library, 1970.

———. *Hollywood in the Sixties.* London: Tantivy Press, 1972.

Bazin, André. "De l'ambiguïté." *Cahiers du Cinéma,* no. 27 (October 1953).

Beja, Morris. *Film and Literature: An Introduction.* New York: Longman, 1979.

Belton, John. *American Cinema/American Culture.* New York: McGraw-Hill, 1994.

Bentley, Eric. *Thirty Years of Treason. Excerpts from Hearings before the House Committee on Un-American Activities, 1938–1968.* New York: Viking Press, 1971.

Bergan, Ronald. *A–Z of Movie Directors.* New York: Proteus, 1982a.

———. *Sports in the Movies.* London: Proteus Books, 1982b.

Bergman, Andrew. *We're in the Money: Depression America and Its Films.* New York: New York University Press, 1971.

Bernardoni, James. *The New Hollywood: What the Movies Did with the New Freedoms of the Seventies.* Jefferson, N.C.: McFarland, 1991.

Bessie, Alvah. *Inquisitions in Eden.* New York: Macmillan, 1965.

Bogdanovich, Peter. *Who the Devil Made It: Conversations with Various Directors.* New York: Knopf, 1997.

Borde, Raymond, and Etienne Chaumeton. *Panorama du film noir américain.* Paris: Editions du Minuit, 1955.

Bordwell, David, Janet Staiger, and Kristin Thompson. *The Classical Hollywood Cinema: Film Style and Mode of Production to 1960.* New York: Columbia University Press, 1985.

Bordwell, David. *Narration in the Fiction Film.* Madison, Wis.: University of Wisconsin Press, 1985.

Boyum, Joy Gould. *Authors on Film.* Bloomington, Ind.: Indiana University Press, 1972.

―――. *Double Exposure: Fiction into Film.* New York: New American Library, 1985.

Braudy, Leo, and Morris Dickstein, eds. *Great Film Directors: A Critical Anthology.* New York: Oxford University Press, 1978.

Buache, Freddy. *The Cinema of Luis Buñuel.* Translated by Peter Graham. London: Tantivy Press, 1973.

Butler, Jeremy, ed. *Star Texts: Images and Performance in Film and Television.* Detroit: Wayne State University Press, 1991.

Cahiers du Cinéma. *The 1950s.* Edited by Jim Hillier. Cambridge, Mass.: Harvard University Press, 1985.

―――. *The 1960s.* Edited by Jim Hillier. Cambridge, Mass.: Harvard University Press, 1986.

Caputo, Philip. *A Rumor of War.* New York: Ballantine Books, 1977.

Ceplair, Larry, and Steven Englund. *The Inquisition in Hollywood: Politics in the Film Community, 1930–1960.* Garden City, N.Y.: Anchor Press, 1980.

Chatman, Seymour. *Story and Discourse: Narrative Structure in Fiction and Film.* Ithaca, N.Y.: Cornell University Press, 1978.

Cogley, John. *Report on Blacklisting.* Vol. I, *Movies.* (n.p.): The Fund for the Republic, 1956.

Cohen, Keith. *Film and Fiction: The Dynamics of Exchange.* New Haven, N.J.: Yale University Press, 1979.

Cook, Pam, ed. *The Cinema Book.* London: British Film Institute, 1985.

Coursodon, Jean-Pierre, and Pierre Sauvage, ed. *American Directors.* 2 vols. New York: McGraw-Hill, 1983.

Cowie, Peter, ed. *Concise History of the Cinema.* Vol. 2, *Since 1940.* London: A. Zwemmer, 1971.

Dardis, Tom. *Some Time in the Sun.* New York: Scribners, 1976. (Originally, "Some Time in the Sun: The Hollywood Years of Fitzgerald, Faulkner, Nathanael West, Aldous Huxley, and James Agee," Ph.D. diss., Columbia University, New York, 1980.)

Denby, David. *Awake in the Dark.* New York: Vintage, 1977.

Downer, Alan S. *The Monitor Image in Man and the Movies.* Edited by W. R. Robinson with assistance from George Garrett. Baton Rouge, La.: Louisiana State University Press, 1967.

Durgnat, Raymond. "Paint It Black: The Family Tree of Film Noir." *Cinema* (U.K.), August 1970.

Edmunds, I. G., and Reiko Mimura. *The Oscar Directors.* New York: A. S. Barnes, 1980.

Ellis, Jack. *A History of Film.* 2d ed. Englewood Cliffs, N.J.: Prentice-Hall, 1979.

Fenin, George. "The Face of '63—United States." *Films and Filming* 9, no. 6 (March 1963): 55.

Fenin, George, and William Everson. *The Western, from Silents to Cinerama.* New York: Orion Press, 1962.

Ferguson, Otis. *The Film Criticism of Otis Ferguson.* Edited and preface by Robert Wilson; foreword by Andrew Sarris. Philadelphia: Temple University Press, 1971.

Finler, Joel W. *The Movie Directors' Story.* New York: Crescent Books, 1985.

Gabree, John. *Gangsters: From* Little Caesar *to* The Godfather. New York: Pyramid Communications, 1973.

Geduld, Harry M., ed. *Filmmakers on Filmmaking.* Bloomington, Ind.: Indiana University Press, 1967.

Gessner, Robert. *The Moving Image: A Guide to Cinematic Literacy.* New York: E. P. Dutton, 1968.

Gianetti, Louis. *Masters of the American Cinema.* Englewood Cliffs, N.J.: Prentice-Hall, 1981.

Giannetti, Louis, and Scott Eyman. *Flashback: A Brief History of Film.* Englewood Cliffs, N.J.: Prentice-Hall, 1986.

Giddings, Robert. *Screening the Novel: The Theory & Practice of Literary Dramatization.* New York: St. Martin's Press, 1990.

Gilles, Jacob. *Le Cinéma moderne.* Paris: Serdoc, 1964.

Gomery, Douglas. *Movie History: A Survey.* Belmont, Calif.: Wadsworth Publishing Co., 1991.

Goodman, Ezra. *The Fifty-year Decline and Fall of Hollywood.* New York: Simon & Schuster, 1961.

Grant, Barry Keith, ed. *Film Genre Reader.* Austin, Tex.: University of Texas Press, 1986.

Grover, Lewis. *Academy All the Way.* San Francisco: Straight Arrow Press, 1974.

Gunton, Sharon R., comp. and ed. *Contemporary Literary Criticism.* 20 Vols. Detroit: Gale, 1982.

Harmetz, Aljean. *Round up the Usual Suspects: The Making of Casablanca— Bogart, Bergman and WWII.* New York: Hyperion, 1992.

Hirsch, Foster. *The Dark Side of the Screen: Film Noir.* New York: A. S. Barnes, 1981.

Hochman, Stanley, ed. *American Film Directors.* New York: Ungar, 1974.

International Dictionary of Films and Filmmakers. Chicago: St. James Press, 1991.

Jacobs, Lewis. *The Documentary Tradition: From Nanook to Woodstock.* New York: Hopkinson & Blake, 1971.

———, ed. *The Movies as Medium.* New York: Farrar, 1970.

Jameson, Richard T., ed. *They Went That A Way: Redefining Film Genres—A National Society of Film Critics Video Guide.* San Francisco: Mercury House, 1994.

Kael, Pauline. *I Lost It at the Movies.* New York: Little, Brown, 1965.

———. *Kiss Kiss Bang Bang.* Boston: Little, Brown, 1968.

————. *Going Steady.* Boston: Little, Brown, 1970.

————. *Deeper into Movies.* Boston: Little, Brown, 1972.

————. *Reeling.* Boston: Little, Brown, 1976.

————. *When the Lights Go Down.* New York: Holt, Rinehart and Winston, 1980.

————. *Taking It All In.* New York: Holt, Rinehart and Winston, 1984.

————. *State of the Art.* New York: E. P. Dutton, 1985.

————. *Hooked.* New York: E. P. Dutton, 1989.

————. *5001 Nights at the Movies.* New York: Holt, 1991.

————. *For Keeps.* New York: E. P. Dutton, 1994.

Kanfer, Stefan. *A Journal of the Plague Years.* New York: Atheneum, 1973.

Karimi, Amir Massourd. *Toward a Definition of the American Film Noir.* New York: Arno Press, 1970.

Kauffman, Stanley. *A World on Film.* New York: Harper, 1967.

Klein, Michael, and Gillian Parker, eds. *The English Novel and the Movies.* New York: Ungar, 1981.

Knight, Arthur. *The Liveliest Art: A Panoramic History of the Movies.* Rev. ed. New York: Macmillan, 1978.

Koszarski, Richard. *Hollywood Directors, 1941–1976.* New York: Oxford University Press, 1977.

————, ed. *Great American Film Directors in Photography.* New York: Dover, 1984.

Lambray, Maureen. *The American Film Director.* New York: Rapoport Press, 1976.

Lawson, John Howard. *Film: The Creative Process—The Search for an Audio-Visual Language and Structure.* Preface by Jay Leda. New York: Hill & Wang, 1964.

Leff, Leonard, and Jerold Simmons. *The Dame in the Kimono.* New York: Grove Weidenfeld, 1990.

Lehman, Peter, ed. *Close Viewings: An Anthology of New Film Criticism.* Tallahassee, Fla.: Florida State University Press, 1990.

Leirens, Jean. *Le Cinéma et la crise de notre temps.* Septième Art. Paris: Editions du Cerf, 1960.

Lucas, F. L. *Tragedy.* New York: Colliers, 1962.

Luhr, William, ed. *World Cinema Since 1945.* New York: Ungar, 1987.

McBride, Joseph, ed. *Filmmakers on Filmmaking: The AFI Seminars on Motion Pictures & TV.* Los Angeles: J. P. Tarcher, 1983.

McCaffrey, Donald W. *Assault on Society: Satirical Literature to Film.* Metuchen, N.J.: Scarecrow Press, 1992.

McArthur, Colin. *Underworld USA.* New York: Viking, 1972.

McCarthy, Todd, and Charles Flynn, eds. *King of the Bs: Working within the Hollywood System—An Anthology of Film History and Criticism.* New York: E. P. Dutton, 1975.

McClintick, David. *Indecent Exposure: A True Story of Hollywood and Wall Street.* New York: Dell, 1983.

McCrandle, Joseph F., ed. *Behind the Scenes: Theater & Film Interviews—from "The Transatlantic Review."* New York: Holt, 1971.

Macdonald, Dwight. *On Movies.* Englewood Cliffs, N.J.: Prentice-Hall, 1969.

Macgowan, Kenneth. *Behind the Screen: The History and Techniques of the Motion Picture.* New York: Delacorte Press, 1965.

Mast, Gerald, and Marshall Cohen. *Film Theory and Criticism.* 3d ed. New York: Oxford University Press, 1979.

Mast, Gerald. *A Short History of the Movies.* 4th ed. New York: Macmillan, 1986.

May, John R., ed. *Image and Likeness: Religious Visions in American Film Classics.* Mahwah, N.J.: Paulist Press, 1992.

Meyer, William R. *Warner Brothers Directors.* New York: Arlington House, 1978.

Millichap, Joseph. *Steinbeck and Film.* New York: Ungar, 1983.

Mitchell, Greg. *The Campaign of the Century: Upton Sinclair's Race for Governor of California and the Birth of Media Politics.* New York: Random House, 1992.

Mordden, Ethan. *The Hollywood Studios: House Style in the Golden Age of the Movies.* New York: Knopf, 1988.

Morsberger, Robert, Stephen O. Lesser, and Randall Clark, eds. *Dictionary of Literary Biography.* Vol. 26, *American Screenwriters.* Detroit: Gale, 1984.

Mulvey, Laura. "Visual Pleasure and Narrative Cinema." *Screen* 16 (Autumn 1975): 6–18.

Navasky, Victor. *Naming Names.* New York: Viking Press, 1980.

Norman, Barry. *Talking Pictures.* London: Hodder and Stoughton, BBC Books, 1987.

O'Connor, John E., and Martin A. Jackson. *American History/American Film: Interpreting the Hollywood Image.* 2d ed. Foreword by Arthur M. Schlesinger Jr. New York: Continuum, 1981.

Oumano, Ellen. *Film Forum: Thirty-five Top Filmmakers Discuss Their Craft.* New York: St. Martin's Press, 1985.

Palmer, R. Barton. *Hollywood's Dark Cinema: The American Film Noir.* New York: Twayne, 1994.

Peary, Gerald, and Roger Shatzkin, eds. *The Classic American Novel and the Movies.* New York: Ungar, 1977.

———, eds. *The Modern American Novel and the Movies.* New York: Ungar, 1978.

Pye, Michael, and Lynda Pye. *The Movie Brats.* New York: Holt, 1979.

Quinlan, David. *The Illustrated Guide to Film Directors.* Totowa, N.J.: Barnes & Noble Books, 1983.

Rhode, Eric. *A History of the Cinema from Its Origins to 1970.* New York: Hill & Wang, 1976.

Roberts, Jerry, and Steven Gaydos. *Movie Talk from the Front Lines: Filmmakers Discuss Their Work with the Los Angeles Film Critics Association.* Jefferson, N.C.: McFarland, 1995.

Robinson, David. *The History of World Cinema.* New York: Stein & Day, 1973.

Robinson, W. R. *Man and the Movies.* Baton Rouge, La.: Louisiana State University Press, 1967.

Roddick, Nick. *A New Deal in Entertainment: Warner Brothers in the 1930s.* London: British Film Institute, 1983.

Rosten, Leo C. *Hollywood: The Movie Colony, the Movie Makers.* New York: Harcourt, 1941.

Rotha, Paul. *The Film till Now: A Survey of World Cinema.* With an additional section by Richard Griffith. London: Spring Books, 1967.

Roud, Richard, ed. *Cinema: A Critical Dictionary—The Major Filmmakers.* 2 vols. London: Secker & Warburg, 1980.

Salamon, Julie. *The Devil's Candy.* Boston: Houghton, Mifflin, 1991.

Sarris, Andrew. *The American Cinema: Directors and Directions, 1929–1968.* New York: E. P. Dutton, 1968.

Schatz, Thomas. *Hollywood Genres.* New York: Random House, 1981.

———. *The Genius of the System: Hollywood Filmmaking in the Studio Era.* New York: Pantheon Books, 1988.

———, ed. *Hollywood Voices.* New York: Bobbs-Merrill, 1971. (Reprint of *Interviews with Film Directors,* New York, Bobbs-Merrill, 1967.)

Schickel, Richard. *Movies: The History of an Art and an Institution.* New York: Basic Books, 1964.

Schwartz, Nancy Lynn. *The Hollywood Writers' Wars.* Completed by Sheila Schwartz. New York: Knopf, 1982.

Server, Lee. *Screenwriter: Words Become Pictures—Interviews with Twelve Screenwriters from the Golden Age of American Movies.* Pittstown, N.J.: Main St. Press, 1987.

Shadoian, Jack. *Dreams and Dead Ends: The American Gangster/Crime Film.* Cambridge, Mass.: MIT Press, 1977.

Sherman, Eric, comp. *Directing the Film: Film Directors on Their Art.* Boston: Little, Brown, 1976.

Shipman, David. *The Story of Cinema: A Complete Narrative History from the Beginnings to the Present.* Preface by Ingmar Bergman. New York: St. Martin's Press, 1982.

Simon, John. *Movies into Film: Film Criticism, 1967–70.* New York: Delta, 1971.

Singer, Michael, ed. *Film Directors: A Complete Guide.* Beverly Hills, Calif.: Lone Eagle Pub., 1983.

Sinyard, Neil. *Film Literature: The Art of Screen Adaptation.* London: Croom Helm, 1986.

Sklar, Robert. *City Boys: Cagney, Bogart, Garfield.* Princeton, N.J.: Princeton University Press, 1992.

Slide, Anthony. *The American Film Industry.* New York: Greenwood Press, 1986.

Suid, Lawrence H. *Guts and Glory: Great American War Movies.* Reading, Mass.: Addison-Wesley, 1978.

Taylor, John Russell. *Cinema Eye, Cinema Ear: Some Key Filmmakers of the Sixties.* New York: Hill & Wang, 1964.

Thomas, Tony. *Music for the Movies.* South Brunswick, N.J.: A. S. Barnes, 1973.

Thompson, Frank. *Between Action & Cut: Five American Directors.* Metuchen, N.J.: Scarecrow Press, 1985.

Tuska, Jon. *Encounters with Filmmakers: Eight Career Studies.* Westport, Conn.: Greenwood Press, 1991.

———, ed. *Close-up: The Hollywood Director.* Metuchen, N.J.: Scarecrow Press, 1978.

Tynan, Kenneth. *Tynan, Right and Left.* New York: Atheneum, 1967.

Wakeman, John, ed. *World Film Directors, 1890–1945.* 2 vols. New York: Wilson, 1987.

Wetta, Frank J., and Stephen J. Curley. *Celluloid Wars.* New York: Greenwood Press, 1992.

Wiseman, Thomas. *Cinema.* London: Cassell, 1964.

Wright, Basil. *The Long View.* New York: Knopf, 1974.

Wyver, John. *The Moving Image: An International History of Film, Television and Video.* Oxford, U.K.: Basil Blackwell/BFI Publishing, 1989.

XIII
Studio Histories

Listed are some of the published histories of studios for which John Huston worked in some capacity. See other chapters for additional information. Many of the histories below have references to Huston and the films that he produced.

AMERICAN INTERNATIONAL PICTURES
McGee, Mark Thomas. *Faster and Furiouser: The Revised and Fattened Fable of American International Pictures.* Jefferson, N.C.: McFarland, 1996.
Ottoson, Robert. *American International Pictures: A Filmography.* New York: Garland, 1985.

COLUMBIA PICTURES
Dick, Bernard F., ed. *Columbia Pictures: Portrait of a Studio.* Lexington, Ky.: University Press of Kentucky, 1992.
Hirschhorn, Clive. *The Columbia Story.* New York: Crown, 1990.
Larkin, Rochelle. *Hail, Columbia.* New Rochelle, N.Y.: Arlington House, 1975.
Martin, Len D. *The Columbia Checklist: The Feature Films, Serials, Cartoons, and Short Subjects of Columbia Pictures Corporation, 1922–1988.* Jefferson, N.C.: McFarland, 1991.

HORIZON PICTURES
Fuchs, D. "Remembering Sam Spiegel." *Commentary,* July 1988, 53–54.
Sinclair, Andrew. *Spiegel: The Man behind the Pictures.* Boston: Little, Brown, 1987.
Weiler, A. H. "By Way of Report: 'Third Secret,' Second Film on Horizon Slate—Tone to Direct—School Story." *New York Times,* April 10, 1949. (Reprinted in *The New York Times Encyclopedia of Film, 1947–1951.*)

METRO-GOLDWYN-MAYER (MGM)
Bart, Peter. *Fade Out: The Calamitous Final Days of MGM.* New York: William Morrow, 1990.
Carey, Gary. *All the Stars in Heaven: The Story of Louis B. Mayer's MGM.* New York: E. P. Dutton, 1981.

Crowther, Bosley. *The Lion's Share: The Story of an Entertainment Empire.* New York: E. P. Dutton, 1957.

Eames, John Douglas, and Ronald Bergan. *The MGM Story: The Complete History of Sixty-nine Roaring Years.* Rev. ed. London: Hamlyn, 1993.

Hay, Peter. *MGM: When the Lion Roars.* Atlanta: Turner, 1991.

Higham, Charles. *Merchant of Dreams: Louis B. Mayer, M.G.M., and the Secret Hollywood.* New York: D. I. Fine; London, Sidgwick & Jackson, 1993.

MGM. (BFI dossier, no. 1.) London: British Film Institute, 1980.

Montgomery, Elizabeth. *The Best of MGM.* Twickenham, U.K.: Hamlyn, 1986.

Parish, James Robert. *The MGM Stock Company: The Golden Era.* New York: Bonanza Books, 1972.

Parish, James Robert, and Gregory W. Mark. *The Best of MGM: The Golden Years (1928–59).* Westport, Conn.: Arlington House, 1981.

Thomas, Laurence B. *The MGM Years.* New York: Columbia House, 1972.

PARAMOUNT PICTURES

Eames, John Douglas. *The Paramount Story.* London: Octopus, 1985.

Edmonds, I. G. *The Best Show in Town: Paramount Pictures and the People Who Made Them.* South Brunswick, N.J.: A. S. Barnes; London: T. Yoseloff, 1980.

TWENTIETH CENTURY-FOX

Solomon, Aubrey. "The Best Fanfare in Town: An Analysis of the 20th Century-Fox Studio, 1950–1960." Master of arts thesis, University of Southern California, Los Angeles, 1975.

———. *Twentieth Century-Fox: A Corporate and Financial History.* (Filmmakers series, no. 20.) Metuchen, N.J.: Scarecrow Press, 1988.

Thomas, Tony, and Aubrey Solomon. *The Films of 20th Century-Fox: A Pictorial History.* Rev. ed. Secaucus, N.J.: Citadel Press, 1985.

Twentieth Century-Fox: 50 anni di grande cinema [catalog]. Curated by Alberto Ravaglioli and Tenato Venturelli in collaboration with comune di Roman, Assessorato alla cultura. Montepulciano, Siena: Editori del Grifo, 1985.

UNITED ARTISTS

Balio, Tino. *United Artists: The Company that Changed the Film Industry.* Madison, Wis.: University of Wisconsin Press, 1987.

Bergan, Ronald. *The United Artists Story: The Complete History of the Studio and Its 1,581 Films.* New York: Crown, 1986.

UNIVERSAL PICTURES

Fitzgerald, Michael G. *Universal Pictures: A Panoramic History in Words, Pictures and Filmographies.* New Rochelle, N.Y.: Arlington House, 1977.

Freeman, Patricia. *Universal Studios: A World within a World.* Los Angeles: Universal City Studios by Rosebud Books, 1982.

Hirschhorn, Clive. *The Universal Story.* New York: Crown, 1983.

Koszarski, Richard. *Universal Pictures: 65 Years.* New York: MCA Publishing, 1977.

Thomas, Tony. *The Best of Universal.* Vestal, N.Y.: Vestal Press, 1990.

WARNER BROTHERS
Aylesworth, Thomas G. *The Best of Warner Brothers.* Twickenham, Middlesex, U.K.: Hamlyn, 1986.
Behlmer, Rudy, ed. *Inside Warner Bros. (1935–1951).* New York: Viking, 1985; London: Weidenfield and Nicolson, 1985.
Freedland, Michael. *The Warner Brothers.* New York: St. Martin's Press, 1983.
Gustafson, Robert. "The Buying of Ideas: Source Acquisition at Warner Brothers, 1930–1949." Ph.D. diss., University of Wisconsin, Madison, 1983.
Higham, Charles. *Warner Brothers.* New York: Scribners, 1975.
———. *Warner Brothers: A History of the Studio.* New York: Scribners, 1976.
Hirschhorn, Clive. *The Warner Brothers Story.* New York: Crown, 1979.
Jerome, Stuart. *Those Crazy, Wonderful Years When We Ran Warner Bros.* Secaucus, N.J.: L. Stuart, 1983.
Meyer, William R. *Warner Brothers Directors: The Hard-boiled, the Comic and the Weepers.* New Rochelle, N.Y.: Arlington House, 1978.
Roddick, Nick. *A New Deal in Entertainment: Warner Brothers in the 1930s.* London: British Film Institute, 1983.
Sennett, Ted. *Warner Brothers Presents: The Most Exciting Years—From* The Jazz Singer *to* White Heat. Secaucus, N.J.: Castle Books, distributed to the trade by Book Sales, 1971.
Silke, James R. *Here's Looking at You, Kid: Fifty Years of Fighting, Working, and Dreaming at Warner Bros.* Boston: Little, Brown, 1976.
Wilson, Arthur, comp. and ed. *The Warner Bros. Golden Anniversary Book: The Film Complete Filmography.* With a critical essay by Arthur Knight and introduction by Willard Van Dyke. New York: Film & Venture Corp., 1973.
Yeck, Joanne Louise. "The Woman's Film at Warner Brothers, 1935–1950." Ph.D. thesis, University of Southern California, 1983. Locations: University of Southern California, Columbia University Libraries.

XIV
Huston on Film and Other Projects

Following is a summary listing of the films and other projects with which John Huston was involved. Both realized and unrealized projects are included in his capacity as a director, screenwriter, actor, and narrator. In some cases detailed information is provided, especially for unrealized projects. Those projects which he brought to fruition as a director and, in some cases, as a writer and actor are provided in greater detail in chapter 4, "Filmography/Synopsis." As a guide to information on particular projects this chapter should be used in conjunction with others. Following each citation below are abbreviations indicating that additional information is available in those chapters:

AMPAS	John Huston Collection: Production Files at the Academy of Motion Picture Arts and Sciences (other collections may be included)
ARTICLES	Articles and Reviews of Films
AWARDS	Awards and Honors
FILMOGRAPHY	Filmography/Synopsis, with such details on Huston films as full credits, running time, release date, synopsis
FILMS	Huston-Related Films on Films, Video, Laser Discs
PRODUCTION FILES	Archival information in various library collections, including AMPAS
SCREENPLAYS	Screenplays in Collections, includes those in the AMPAS Huston Archive

Abbreviations for certain institutions are:

AFI	The American Film Institute, including *The American Film Institute Catalog: Feature Films*
AMPAS	Academy of Motion Picture Arts and Sciences
BFI	British Film Institute
LC	Library of Congress
NYPL	New York Public Library
USC	University of Southern California

ACADEMY AWARDS, TWENTY-FIFTH ANNUAL. 1952.
Excerpts. Humphrey Bogart. Greer Garson presented Humphrey Bogart with the award for best actor for *The African Queen*. FILMS

ACADEMY AWARDS, FIFTY-EIGHTH ANNUAL. March 25, 1986.
Aired on ABC. Huston was a presenter. FILMS

THE ACQUITTAL. 1923.
Universal. 35 minutes. Clarence Brown. *The American Film Institute Catalog: Feature Films, 1921–1930* (p. 3) indicates that the scenario was by Jules Furthman and continuity by Dale Van Every, John Huston, Tom Reed, Tom Kilpatrick, Anthony Veiller, and Jules Furthman. This information came from company records. John Huston, however, would have been seventeen years old at that time, and there is no evidence that he worked on the project. Lawrence Grobel provides an accounting of Huston's activities during this time, but he does not include this film (*The Hustons,* New York, Scribners, 1989, 102–6]). In a conversation with Grobel, he expressed his doubts, as John Huston's role in the movies was due in part to his father's involvement, which did not occur until 1929. Also, it was about this time Huston was signed as a contract writer for Goldwyn, for a brief period of time, and then from about 1929 until 1932 as a contract writer for Universal (there is much evidence of this later activity). A search through the production files at the New York Public Library and the Academy of Motion Picture Arts and Sciences did not uncover anything, other than Jules Furthman was given credit for the script, which is based on the original work of Rita Weiman. A search through other sources, such as the literature and filmographies on John Huston, reveals no connections. Contact with the Special Collections Department of the University of Tennessee, where Clarence Brown's papers are housed, did not help. Unfortunately they do not have any of his script material prior to 1924. A filmography on Clarence Brown—*The Hollywood Professionals,* vol. 6: *Capra, Cukor, Brown,* by Allen Estrin (New York, A. S. Barnes, 1980)—indicates that the scenario was by Jules Furthman; the adaptation by Raymond L. Schrock, from the Rita Weiman stage play; and continuity by Jules Furthman and Dale Van Every. Estrin also lists the persons mentioned in *The American Film Institute Catalog* and says, "John Huston, Tom Reed, Tom Kilpatrick and Anthony Veiller as continuity writers for this film, impossible as this would seem." (p. 180) Library of Congress cataloging for the film lists only Raymond L. Schrock as the adapter, and apparently no copy of the print is available at the Library of Congress or elsewhere. ARTICLES, PRODUCTION FILES

ACROSS THE PACIFIC. 1942.
Warner Brothers. 97 minutes, black and white. Release date: September 5, 1942. Produced by Jerry Wald and Jack Saper. Screenplay by Richard Macaulay, from the *Saturday Evening Post* serial by Robert Carson. John Huston contributed to the screenplay (uncredited) and directed the film. ARTI-

CLES, AWARDS, FILMOGRAPHY, FILMS, PRODUCTION FILES, SCREENPLAYS

ACROSS THE RIVER AND INTO THE TREES. 1975–76.
Director. Unrealized project. Also as a writer with Gladys Hill. Based on Ernest Hemingway's *Across the River and into the Trees.* AMPAS, SCREENPLAYS

THE AFRICAN QUEEN. 1952.
A Horizon-Romulus Production. Distributed by United Artists. A Trans-Lux release. 105 minutes. Produced by Sam Spiegel. Screenplay by James Agee and John Huston, from the novel by C. S. Forester. Directed by John Huston. (A TV pilot film was produced in 1977 by Mark Carliner Productions, Viacom. Directed by Richard C. Sarafian. The cast included Warren Oates, Mariette Hartley, Johnny Sekka, and Clarence Thomas.) AMPAS, ARTICLES, AWARDS, FILMOGRAPHY, FILMS, PRODUC-TION FILES, SCREENPLAYS

AGEE. 1980.
A film by Ross Spears. 88 minutes. Cinematography, Anthony Forma; voice, Earl McCarroll; associate producer, Jude Cassidy. Produced, written, and directed by Ross Spears.* With John Huston, Robert Fitzgerald, Walker Evans, Dwight MacDonald, Mia Agee, Father James Flye, Olivia Wood, "Annie Mae Gudger," "Margaret Ricketts," Alma Neuman, Robert Saudek, and President Jimmy Carter. Feature documentary, featuring many of James Agee's close friends.

Note. *A transcript of the film was published by Holt, Rinehart and Winston in 1985 as *Agee: His Life Remembered,* edited by Ross Spears and Jude Cassidy, with a narrative by Robert Coles. ARTICLES, FILMS, PRODUCTION FILES

ALFRED HITCHCOCK PRESENTS: MAN FROM THE SOUTH. 1985.
Universal/NBC-TV. Produced by Stephen Cragg and Alan Barnette. Directed by Steve DeJarnatt. Teleplay by William Fay and Steve DeJarnatt, based on a story by Roald Dahl. Cast includes John Huston (The Man), Steven Bauer, Melanie Griffith, and Kim Novak. ARTICLES, PRODUC-TION FILES, SCREENPLAYS

ALOUETTE. 1954.
Director. Unrealized project. The John Huston Collection in AMPAS indicates that Huston was interested in purchasing the rights to the Jean Anouilh play. "I wish definitely to acquire and do picture and want no com-plications" (January 21, 1954). It also appears that Anouilh was interested in doing the script and that Suzanne Flon was in the stage play (French version). A translation of the play, with the title *Joan (The Lark),* is included. AMPAS, PRODUCTION FILES, SCREENPLAYS (under *Joan*)

THE AMAZING DR. CLITTERHOUSE. 1938.
Warner Brothers. 87 minutes. Produced by Gilbert Miller. Screenplay by John Wexley and John Huston, based on the play by Barre Lyndon. Directed by Anatole Litvak. AFI (*Catalog: Feature Films, 1931–1940*), ARTICLES, FILMOGRAPHY, FILMS, PRODUCTION FILES, SCREENPLAYS

AMERICAN CAESAR. 1985.
TV. Turner Program Services/Metromedia. Huston speaks some of the quotes of MacArthur in this five-hour documentary about Gen. Douglas MacArthur, based on William Manchester's biography and with readings by John Huston. Aired March 3, 1985, at various times and channels. The BFI reports the title as "The Way Back" series, "American Caesar"; production country, Canada, 1983; production company, Cineworld Productions. Ian McLeod, producer; Michael Feheley, production supervisor; series devised by Michael Maclear, from the book by William Manchester; music by Art Phillips; narrator, John Colicos; host, John Huston. ARTICLES, FILMS, PRODUCTION FILES

THE AMERICAN FILM INSTITUTE SALUTE TO JOHN HUSTON. 1983.
CBS Special. 102 minutes. Written by George Stevens Jr. and Joseph Mcbride and directed by Marty Pasetia. Broadcast by CBS on March 23, 1983, 9 P.M. ARTICLES, FILMS, SCREENPLAYS

THE AMERICAN FILM INSTITUTE SALUTE TO GENE KELLY. July 5, 1985.
CBS. 9:30 P.M. Includes clips of previous awards, including that of John Huston. FILMS

THE AMERICAN FILM INSTITUTE LIFE SALUTE TO BARBARA STANWYCK. 1987.
The BFI reports that John Huston made an appearance.

THE AMERICAN FILM INSTITUTE SALUTE TO ORSON WELLES. February 17, 1975.
CBS. 9:30 P.M. Includes clippings from *The Other Side of the Wind,* an unreleased film starring John Huston. FILMS

ANGELA (original title: *Jocasta*). 1977.
Zev Braun Productions. Canafox Films (Canada). Produced by Zev Braun and Leland Nolan. Screenplay by Charles E. Israel. Directed by Boris Sagal. Cast includes Sophia Loren, Steve Railsback, John Huston (Hogan, the underworld leader),* William Shatner, Lloyd Bochner, and John Vernon.

Note. *Reports indicate that Huston was signed as wizened cult minister, who predicts a dramatic turn of events between Loren and Railsback, her son. ARTICLES, FILMS, PRODUCTION FILES, SCREENPLAYS

ANNIE. 1982.
Columbia Pictures/A Ray Stark Production. 128 minutes. Produced by Ray Stark. Screenplay by Carol Sobieski, based on the stage musical by Thomas Meehan (book), Charles Strouse (music), and Martin Charnin (lyrics). Based on Harold Gray's comic strip character, Little Orphan Annie. Directed by John Huston. AMPAS, ARTICLES, AWARDS, FILMOGRAPHY, FILMS, PRODUCTION FILES, SCREENPLAYS

APPOINTMENT WITH DESTINY. THE CRUCIFIXION OF JESUS . . . AN HISTORICAL DOCUMENT. March 31, 1972.
CBS-TV. David Wolper Productions. 40 minutes. Directed by Robert Guenette. Ron Greenblatt as Jesus. Huston narrates. Documentary-drama, shot on location, of the last days of Jesus Christ. ARTICLES, FILMS, PRODUCTION FILES

THE ASPHALT JUNGLE. 1950.
MGM. 112 minutes. Produced by Arthur Hornblow Jr. Screenplay by Ben Maddow and John Huston from the novel by W. R. Burnett. Directed by John Huston. AMPAS, ARTICLES, AWARDS, FILMOGRAPHY, FILMS, PRODUCTION FILES, SCREENPLAYS

B. TRAVEN: A MYSTERY SOLVED. 1978.
United Kingdom. TV production. Produced by Will Wyatt. Huston interviewed. An article in the *New York Times* (December 22, 1978, C30, "The Mystery of B. Traven Unraveled by BBC Team") alludes to this project. ARTICLES

BACALL ON BOGART. 1988.
Educational Broadcasting Corp. and Turner Entertainment Co. 88 minutes. Hosted by Lauren Bacall. Written by John L. Miller. Executive producer, Jac Venza; producers, Joan Kramer and David Heeley. Directed by David Heeley. Shows clips of Huston being interviewed about his relationship with Bogart and appearing in a number of scenes directing films with which they were both involved. ARTICLES, FILMS

BACKGROUND TO DANGER (working title: *Uncommon Danger*). 1943.
Warner Brothers. Produced by Jerry Wald. Screenplay by W. R. Burnett, based on Eric Ambler's novel of the same name (New York: Knopf, 1937). Directed by Raoul Walsh. Photography by Tony Gaudio. Edited by Jack Killifer, Don Siegel, and James Leicester. Cast includes George Raft, Brenda Marshall, Sydney Greenstreet, Peter Lorre, Osa Massen, and Turhan Bey. *Film Dope* indicates that Huston did uncredited polishing on the script. The USC Warner Brothers Archive contains versions of the script, including a working script by John Huston; however, AMPAS has *Call Bureau Cast,* which does not list Huston as a writer of credit. The sole writer listed is W. R. Burnett. ARTICLES, FILMS, PRODUCTION FILES, SCREENPLAYS

THE BARBARIAN AND THE GEISHA. 1958.

Twentieth Century-Fox. 105 minutes. Produced by Eugene Frenke. Screenplay by Charles Grayson (and John Huston, uncredited), from *The Townsend Harris Story* by Ellis St. Joseph. Directed by John Huston. AMPAS, ARTICLES, FILMOGRAPHY, FILMS, PRODUCTION FILES, SCREENPLAYS

BATTLE FOR THE PLANET OF THE APES. 1973.

Twentieth Century-Fox/Apjac Productions. 86 minutes. Produced by Arthur P. Jacobs. Associate producer, Frank Capra Jr. Screenplay by John William Corrington and Joyce Hooper Corrington, from a story by Paul Dehn, and based on characters created by Pierre Boulle. Directed by J. Lee Thompson. Photography by Richard H. Kline. Edited by Alan L. Jaggs and John C. Horger. Cast includes Roddy McDowall, John Huston (The Lawgiver), Claude Akins, Natalie Trundy, Severn Darden, Lew Ayres, and Paul Williams. ARTICLES, FILMS, PRODUCTION FILES, SCREEN-PLAYS

THE BATTLE OF MARETH/THE GREATEST BATTLE/BATTLE FORCE (other titles: *The Great Battle, I Grande Attacco*). 1979.

German/Yugoslavian production: Titanus/Dimension. Directed by Hank Milestone (Umberto Lenzi). Cast includes John Huston, Henry Fonda, Stacy Keach, Samantha Egger, Helmut Berger, and Orson Welles (narrator). *Film Dope* lists this project as the same as *The Biggest Battle,* but its date is 1977. Stephen Cooper's *Perspective on John Huston* (New York, G.K. Hall, 1994) also has this citation with the same production company, release date, and director. AFI also includes it under *The Battle of Mareth.* The U.S. release was *The Greatest Battle.* Director also listed as Humphrey Longan. ARTICLES, FILMS

BATTLE OF SAN PIETRO (*San Pietro*). 1945. Army Pictorial Service of the U.S. Signal Corps. 30 minutes, black and white. Writing, directing, and narration by John Huston.*

Note. **Nostalgia WWII,* Video Library, includes *San Pietro* (1945). Part of a ten-volume video set on various films produced during the war, this project appears to be the only one with Huston's involvement. AMPAS, ARTICLES, FILMO-GRAPHY, FILMS, PRODUCTION FILES, SCREENPLAYS

BEAT THE DEVIL. 1954.

A Santana-Romulus Production, in association with Rizzoli-Haggiag. Distributed by United Artists in the United States; in the United Kingdom by Independent Film Distribution (in association with British Lion). 92 minutes. Produced and directed by John Huston; associate producer, Jack Clayton. Screenplay by Truman Capote and John Huston, from the novel by James Helvick (pseudonym of Claud Cockburn). AMPAS, ARTICLES, AWARDS, FILMOGRAPHY, FILMS, PRODUCTIONS FILES, SCREENPLAYS

BECKET. 1964.
>Paramount. Screenplay by Edward Anhalt. Directed by Peter Glenville. Huston was considered as director (unrealized). AMPAS production file for *Harrow Alley* includes a letter from Keep Films, Ltd. (United Kingdom) (dated October 11, 1962), indicating the company's desire to have Huston direct. FILMS, PRODUCTION FILES, SCREENPLAYS

THE BERMUDA TRIANGLE (other titles: *The Mystery of the Bermuda Triangle; El Triangulo diabolico de la Bermudas; Il Trinagulo diabolico de Bermudas; Triangle; The Bermuda Mystery; The Mystery of the Bermuda Triangle*). 1978.
>Concacine/Nucleo Filmca. Mexico/Italy. Producer and director, Rene Cardona Jr. Screenplay by Rene Cardona and Carlos Valdemar. Cast includes John Huston (The Father), Edward Martin, Gloria Guida, Marina Vlady, Claudine Auger, and Hugo Stiglitz. Other sources have a release date of 1977, with the original release title: *Il Triangulo diabolico de la Bermudas.* AMPAS, ARTICLES, PRODUCTION FILES, SCREENPLAYS

THE BEST OF BOGART. Warner Brothers. 19??.
>FILMS

THE BIBLE . . . IN THE BEGINNING (other titles: *La Bibbia; La Bible*). 1966.
>U.S.-Italian production. Produced by Dino De Laurentiis for Dino De Laurentiis Cinematografica. Distributed by Twentieth Century-Fox, in association with Seven Arts. 174 minutes. Screenplay by Christopher Fry (and John Huston, uncredited). Directed by John Huston, who acted (Noah). AFI (*Catalog: Feature Films, 1961–1970,* 83–84), AMPAS, ARTICLES, AWARDS, FILMOGRAPHY, FILMS, PRODUCTION FILES, SCREEN-PLAYS

BLACK CAULDRON. 1985.
>Walt Disney Productions–Silver Screen Partners II–Buena Vista Distribution Co. 80 minutes. Based on the *Chronicles of Prydain* series by Lloyd Alexander. Executive producer, Ron Miller; producer, Joe Hale; and directors, Ted Berman and Richard Rich. Executive in charge of production, Edward Hansen. With the voice talents of Grant Bardsley, Susan Sheridan, Freddie Jones, Nigel Hawthorne, and John Hurt. Additional dialogue by Rosemary Anne Sisson and Roy Edward Disney. Prologue narrated by John Huston. Story by David Jonas, Vance Gerry, Ted Berman, Richard Rich, Al Wilson, Roy Morita, Peter Young, Art Stevens, and Joe Hale. ARTICLES, FILMS, PRODUCTION FILES

BLACK RUST. 1932.
>Universal. Unproduced. While under contract to Universal as a writer (1929–33), Huston developed two treatments for this property in 1932. SCREENPLAYS

THE BLUE HOTEL. 1977.

Director (?). Unrealized project. *Cineforum* (December 1987) indicates that this film was an unrealized project of Huston's, but there is no other information regarding this in the AMPAS Huston papers or elsewhere. James Agee wrote his first script while under contract to Huntington Hartford (1948–49), but it was not produced. The TV production (Tuesday, April 19, 1977, 54 minutes) was part of NET's "American Short Story" series. Directed by Jan Kadar, teleplay by Harry M. Petrakis (based on the James Agee screenplay?), and produced by Ozzie Brown. Cast includes David Warner, James Keach, and John Bottoms. FILMS, PRODUCTION FILES, SCREENPLAYS

BOGIE: THE LAST HERO. 1980.

Charles Fries Productions. Executive producers, Charles Fries and Malcolm Stuart; producer, Philip Barry; director, Vincent Sherman; and writer, Daniel Taradash. TV movie, CBS, March 4, 1980. Fictionalized account.

BOLÍVAR. 1958.

Director (?). Unrealized project. In a letter to Huston, dated February 13, 1958, and found in AMPAS production file, someone writes that he saw in French papers information that Huston's next picture will be "Bolívar." AMPAS, PRODUCTION FILES

BORSTAL BOY.

Director. Unrealized. Book by Brendan Behan. AMPAS production file includes a July 29, 1970, letter from Irving Lazar to Huston with a passing comment asking if Huston would be interested in pursuing this project. PRODUCTION FILES, SCREENPLAYS

BREAKOUT (other titles: *Ten-Second Jail Break; The Second Jail Break*). 1975.

Persky-Bright, Vista/Columbia. Produced by Robert Chartoff and Irwin Winkler. Screenplay by Howard B. Kreitsek, Marc Norman, and Elliott Baker, from the book by Warren Hinckle, William Turner, and Eliot Asinof (*Ten-Second Jailbreak*). Directed by Tom Gries, photography by Lucien Ballard, and editing by Bud S. Isaacs. Cast includes Charles Bronson, Robert Duvall, Jill Ireland, Randy Quaid, Sheree North, Emilio Fernandez, Alejandro Rey, Paul Mantee, Roy Jenson, Alan Vint, Sidney Clute, and John Huston (Harris Wagner). ARTICLES, FILMS, PRODUCTION FILES, SCREENPLAYS

THE BRIDGE IN THE JUNGLE.* 1971.

Sagittarius/Capricorn. United Artists release. 85 minutes. Produced, directed, and written by Pancho Kohner. Screenplay based on the novel by B. Traven. Camera, Javier Cruz. Cast includes John Huston (Sleigh), Katy Jurado, Charles Robinson, Guadalupe Tellez-Chauvet, and Jorge Martinez De Hoyos.

Note. *Shown at the Santa Fe Film Festival as part of a Huston retrospective. AMPAS, ARTICLES, FILMS, PRODUCTION FILES, SCREENPLAYS

THE BRIDGE OF SAN LUIS REY.
Director. Unrealized project. AMPAS contains a screenplay by Dorothy Hodel (Huston's first wife was Dorothy Harvey). Based on Thornton Wilder's novel. MGM produced a version in 1929 and in 1944. ARTICLES, FILMS, PRODUCTION FILES, SCREENPLAYS

BULLET PARK. 1969–70.
Director, writer. Unrealized project. AMPAS contains numerous versions of a screenplay based on John Cheever's novel. Intended as a John Huston–Carter De Haven Production. PRODUCTION FILES, SCREENPLAY

BY LOVE POSSESSED. 1961.
UA/Mirisch/Seven Arts. Produced by Walter Mirisch. Screenplay by John Dennis and Charles Schnee, based on the James Gould Cozzens novel. Directed by John Sturges. Photography was by Russell Metty (*The Misfits, We Were Strangers*), and Susan Kohner (*Freud: The Secret Passion*), Paul Kohner's daughter, was one of the actors. Cast includes Lana Turner, Efrem Zimbalist Jr., Jason Robards Jr., George Hamilton, Susan Kohner, Barbara Bel Geddes, Thomas Mitchell, and Everett Sloane. AMPAS has an October 1957 letter from Mark Cohen (Huston's attorney), asking whether Huston would be interested in doing picture or *Typee* after the Zanuck film (?). Huston indicates he would be interested if the writer mentioned in the cable to Paul (Kohner, Huston's agent) does the script. (This writer is not identified, and the script is not in the AMPAS Huston Archive.) When Huston was then asked whether he would accept Howard Koch if Lillian Hellman didn't work out, Huston's response was an emphatic "NO!" AMPAS, ARTICLES, FILMS, PRODUCTION FILES, SCREENPLAYS

CANDY. 1968.
Selmur Pictures–Dear Films–Les Films Corona (U.S./French/Italian production). Distributed by Cinerama Releasing Corp. 124 minutes. Produced by Robert Haggiag and Peter Zoref. Screenplay by Buck Henry, from the novel by Terry Southern and Mason Hoffenberg. Italian screenplay version by Enrico Mediolo. Directed by Christian Marquand. Cast includes Marlon Brando, Ewa Aulin, Richard Burton, James Coburn, Walter Matthau, Ringo Starr, John Astin, Elsa Martinelli, Sugar Ray Robinson, and John Huston (Dr. Dunlap). AFI (*Catalog: Feature Films, 1961–1970*), ARTICLES, FILMS, PRODUCTION FILES, SCREENPLAYS

CANNERY ROW. 1982.
Produced by Michael Phillips. MGM/UA. 120 minutes. Screenplay and direction by David S. Ward, from the novels *Cannery Row* and *Sweet*

Thursday by John Steinbeck. Director of photography, Sven Nykvist; production designer, Richard Macdonald; editor, David Bretherton. Cast includes Nick Nolte, Deborah Winger, Audra Lindley, Frank McRae, M. Emmet Walsh, and John Huston (Narrator). AMPAS, ARTICLES, FILMS, PRODUCTION FILES, SCREENPLAYS

CAPTAIN HORATIO HORNBLOWER. 1951.
Warner Brothers. 117 minutes. Screenplay by Ivan Goff, Ben Roberts, and Aeneas MacKenzie, from the novel by C. S. Forester, who adapted it for the screen. Huston was the writer (uncredited) on assignment from July through August 1940 (with Aeneas MacKenzie), but there is evidence of his work to December 1940. Directed by Raoul Walsh. Director of photography, Guy Green; film editor, Jack Harris; art director, Tom Morahan. Cast includes Gregory Peck, Virginia Mayo, Robert Beatty, James R. Justice, and Denis O'Dea. ARTICLES, FILMS, PRODUCTION FILES, SCREENPLAYS

THE CARDINAL. 1964.
Gamma Productions. Distributed by Columbia Pictures. 175 minutes. Produced and directed by Otto Preminger. Screenplay by Robert Dozier, from the novel by Henry Morton Robinson. Photography, Leon Shamroy; editor, Louis R. Loeffler; art directors, Otto Niedermoser and Antonio Sarzi-Braga. Cast includes Tom Tryon, Carol Lynley, Romy Schneider, John Saxon, Burgess Meredith, and John Huston (Cardinal Glennon in scenes shot in Boston). AFI (*Catalog: Feature Films, 1961–1970*), AMPAS, ARTICLES, AWARDS, FILMS, PRODUCTION FILES, SCREENPLAYS

CASINO ROYALE. 1967.
Charles K. Feldman and Jerry Bresler for Famous Artists Productions. Distributed by Columbia. 130 minutes. Screenplay and adaptation by Wolf Mankowitz, John Law, and Michael Sayers. Additional writers (uncredited) were Billy Wilder, Ben Hecht, John Huston, Val Guest, Joseph Heller, and Terry Southern. Directed by John Huston (first half hour), Ken Hughes, Val Guest, Robert Parrish, and Joseph McGrath. Huston also acted (McTarry/M). AFI (*Catalog: Feature Films, 1961–1970*, 153–54), AMPAS, ARTICLES, FILMOGRAPHY, FILMS, PRODUCTION FILES, SCREENPLAYS

CATHOLICS. 1973.
Director, Actor. Unrealized. The *New York Times* (August 22, 1972, 54) indicates that Huston would direct and have a leading role in *Catholics*, a film adaptation of the Brian Moore novella. Moore did the screenplay, Sidney Glazier was to produce, and the film was scheduled for production in Ireland the following spring. A TV version was broadcast in 1979, based on the Moore novel and with Moore's script. Directed by Jack Gold. Cast includes Trevor Howard, Martin Sheen, Cyril Cusack, Andrew Keir, and Michael Gambon. ARTICLES, FILMS, PRODUCTION FILES

CHARLIE CHAPLIN'S SEVENTY-SEVENTH BIRTHDAY. April 15, 1966. London. Hearst Vault Material. FILMS

CHEYENNE (also known as *The Wyoming Kid* for television release). 1947. Warner Brothers. 100 minutes. Produced by Robert Buckner, directed by Raoul Walsh, screenplay by Alan LeMay and Thames Williamson, photographed by Six Hickox, edited by Christian Nyby, and art directed by Ted Smith. Cast includes Dennis Morgan, Jane Wyman, Janice Paige, Emily Carson, Bruce Bennett, Arthur Kennedy, and Alan Hale. ARTICLES, FILMS, PRODUCTION FILES, SCREENPLAYS, USC WARNER ARCHIVE (indicates Huston's involvement in project)

CHINATOWN. 1974.
Robert Evans for Paramount/Long Road. 131 minutes. Screenplay by Robert Towne. Directed by Roman Polanski. Cast includes Jack Nicholson, Faye Dunaway, John Huston (Noah Cross), Perry Lopez, Burt Young, and Roman Polanski. ARTICLES, FILMOGRAPHY, FILMS, PRODUCTION FILES, SCREENPLAYS

CIRCASIA. 1977.
John McCarty's *The Complete Films of John Huston* (New York: Carol Publishing Group, 1990, 253) indicates that this project was an independent film from 1976 that was directed and produced by Kevin McClory. Its cast included Sean Connery, Shirley MacLaine, John Huston, and Eric Clapton. AMPAS's information stipulates it was not a film, but a benefit by the Variety Club of Ireland (September 14, 1975) called Circasia '75, or "A Circus Fantasy," for the blind and handicapped children of Ireland. With Huston, Independent. Produced and directed by Kevin McClory. Huston served as the ringmaster, and the "cameo clowns" were Eric Clapton, Judy Geeson, Richard Harris, Shirley MacLaine, Burgess Meredith, Milo O'Shea, and Siobhan McKenna. The BFI reported *Circasia* as a film (release date ca. 1977), directed by John McColgan and Brian MacLochlainn, with the production company Kevin McClory Productions. Credits: John Huston, ringmaster; Sean Connery, clown; Shirley MacLaine, clown; Milo O'Shea, clown. Library synopsis: Happenings in a small Irish traveling circus (reference: *Screen International*, no. 79 [March 19, 1977]: 21). The article says that "the Special Jury Award of the Ninth Film Festival of the Americas recently held in the Virgin Islands has been awarded to Kevin McClory for 'Circasia.' . . . The film was produced by Kevin McClory in association with RTE and Paradise Film Productions Limited, and directed by John McColgan and Brian MacLochlainn. The film is about a small Irish traveling circus with John Huston as the Ringmaster. . . ." AMPAS, ARTICLES

THE COMMODORE MARRIES.
Unrealized project (?).AMPAS contains a play script of the play by A. H. Parsons, with a handwritten note indicating that Walter Huston was in

the play and "John Huston Contemplated Movie." PRODUCTION FILES, SCREENPLAYS

CONCERTINA.
Unrealized project (?). AMPAS includes: "'Concertina': An Original Story by John Huston and Frederick Kohner, n.d., 14 p. Treatment." SCREENPLAYS

CONSTANT NYMPH. 1943.
Warner Brothers. Screenplay by Kathryn Scola. Directed by Edmund Goulding. Huston assigned as writer from December 14, 1939, to January 13, 1940. Produced by Henry Blanke and directed by Edmund Goulding. Screenplay by Kathryn Scola, from the novel by Margaret Kennedy and the play by Margaret Kennedy and Basil Dean. Director of photography, Tony Gaudio; film editor, Davis Weisbart; art director, Carl Jules Weyl. Cast includes Charles Boyer, Joan Fontaine, Brenda Marshall, Alexis Smith, Charles Coburn, and Dame May Whitty. ARTICLES, FILMS, PRODUCTION FILES, SCREENPLAYS

COST OF LIVING.
Director. Unrealized project. According to a *New York Times* article (January 8, 1950): Van Heflin plays the field, giving up a Metro contract for freedom to select his own roles. "[H]e made a tentative commitment to appear in 'Cost of Living,' a Ben Hecht screenplay which Director John Huston plans to make independently in association with his producing partner, S. P. Eagle." No other information on Huston's involvement is available in literature or in the Huston papers in AMPAS.

CREATIVITY WITH BILL MOYERS: JOHN HUSTON. 1981.
PBS. Huston interviewed. Executive producers, Charles Grinker and Mert Koplin; directors, Janet Roach and Sidney Smith; and writer, Janet Roach (also a writer on *Prizzi's Honor* and *Mr. North*). Broadcast on WNET-TV, March 26, 1982. ARTICLES, FILMS, PRODUCTION FILES

THE CRUCIFIXION OF JESUS: APPOINTMENT WITH DESTINY. *See* APPOINTMENT WITH DESTINY: CRUCIFIXION OF JESUS.

DANGER SIGNAL. 1945.
Warner Brothers. Screenplay by Adele Comandini and Graham Baker. Directed by Robert Florey. Huston on assignment from March 10, 1941 to March 12, 1941. No indication in AMPAS Huston Archive or the USC Warner Archive of any writing work by Huston. Per the studio's credit sheet: A Warner Brothers–First National Picture. Produced by William Jacobs; directed by Robert Florey; screenplay by Adele Comandini and Graham Baker, from a novel by Phyllis Bottome; photographed by James Wong Howe; art director, Stanley Fleischer; film editor, Frank Magee. Cast includes Faye Emerson,

Zachary Scott, Dick Erdman, Rosemary DeCamp, Bruce Bennett, and Mona Freeman. ARTICLES, FILMS, PRODUCTION FILES, SCREENPLAYS

THE DEAD (*Gens de Dublin*). 1987.
Wieland Schulz-Keil and Chris Sievernich for Liffey Films. Released by Vestron Pictures. 83 minutes. Screenplay by Tony Huston and John Huston, based on the short story by James Joyce. Directed by John Huston. ARTICLES, AWARDS, FILMOGRAPHY, FILMS, PRODUCTION FILES, SCREENPLAYS

DEATH DRIVES THROUGH. 1935.
Gaumont-British. Directed by Edward L. Cahn. According to *The British Film Catalogue: 1895–1985—A Reference Guide,* by Denis Gifford (New York: Facts on File, 1986, cat. no.: 09735): Produced by Clifford Taylor for Associated British Film Distributors. Directed by Edward L. Cahn; screenplay by Katherine Strueby and John Huston; scenario by Gordon Wellesley. Cast includes Dorothy Bouchier, Robert Douglas, Miles Mander, Percy Walsh, Frank Atkinson, and Lillian Gunns. ARTICLES, FILMS, PRODUCTION FILES

A DEATH IN THE FAMILY.
Unrealized project (?).AMPAS contains the play script by Tad Mosel. PRODUCTION FILES, SCREENPLAYS

THE DECEIVERS. 1988.
Merchant-Ivory/Michael White/Cinecom/Film Four. Produced by Ismail Merchant and Tim Van Rellim. Screenplay by Michael Hirst, based on the John Masters novel. Directed by Nicholas Meyer. Huston considered as director (?). AMPAS includes memo to Huston on *The Deceivers* by John Masters and two-page synopsis by AE. M (Aeneas MacKenzie?). AMPAS, FILMS, PRODUCTION FILES

DE SADE. 1969.
American International Productions–Transcontinental Film–CCC–Filmkunst. New York open. September 25, 1969. 113 minutes. Produced by Samuel Z. Arkoff and James H. Nicholson. Distributed by American International Pictures. Screenplay by Richard Matheson and Peter Berg. Directed by Cy Endfield. Additional direction by Roger Corman and Gordon Hessler (uncredited). Cast includes Keir Dullea, Sena Berger, Lilli Palmer, Anna Massey, and John Huston (Abbe de Sade, uncle of the Marquis de Sade). *Film Dope* indicates that Huston was also an uncredited director. According to Arkoff, however, Huston was approached to finish the shooting but declined. AFI (*Catalog: Feature Films, 1961–1970*), ARTICLES, FILMS, PRODUCTION FILES, SCREENPLAYS

THE DESERTER (other titles: *La Spina Dorsae del diavolo, La Quebrada del diablo, Ride to Glory, The Devil's Backbone, The S.O.B.s*). 1971.
Dino De Laurentiis/Jadran/Heritage. Distributed by Paramount. 99 minutes. Produced by Norman Baer and Ralph Serpe. Screenplay by Clair Huffaker. Directed by Burt Kennedy. (*Film Dope* notes the Italian version directed by Niska Gulgozi). Cast includes Bekim Fehmiu, John Huston (General Miles), Richard Crenna, Chuck Connors, Ricardo Montalban, Ian Bannen, Brandon De Wilde, Slim Pickens, Albert Salmi, Woody Strode, Patrick Wayne. ARTICLES, FILMS, PRODUCTION FILES, SCREEN-PLAYS

DESTRY RIDES AGAIN. 1932.
Universal. 53 minutes. Produced by Carl Laemmle Jr. Dialogue by Robert Keith and continuity by Isadore Bernstein. From the story of Max Brand. Directed by Ben Stoloff. Cast includes Tom Mix, Claudia Dell, ZaSu Pitts, Stanley Fields, Earle Fox, Edward Piel Sr., Francis Ford, Frederick Howard, George Ernest, John Ince, Edward LeSaint, Charles K. French, and Andy Devine. Huston was assigned to the project and wrote the treatment with Randall Faye and Tom Reed, October 19, 1931. AMPAS, ARTICLES, FILMS, PRODUCTION FILES, SCREENPLAYS

DICK CAVETT SHOW: INTERVIEW WITH JOHN HUSTON. October 21–22, 1980.
Daphne Productions. WNET/Thirteen. Note also that on the Wild World of Entertainment: "The Dick Cavett Show: Katharine Hepburn Interview" on ABC-TV, October 3, 1973, 11:30 P.M., Huston appeared. Audio tapes of the interviews are available (*see* chapter 18, "Audio Recordings.") PRODUC-TION FILES

DIRECTED BY WILLIAM WYLER: A FILM PORTRAIT OF THE MAN AND HIS WORK. 1986.
Topgallant Productions, Inc., in association with Tatge Productions, Inc., presents director and editor, Aviva Slesin; narration and interviews, A. Scott Berg; producer, Catherine Tatge; executive producer, Catherine Wyler. Produced with the assistance of American Masters/WNET and the Directors Guild of America's Educational and Benevolent Foundation. Presented at the Twenty-fourth New York Film Festival—1986 on September 20, 1986, at 58 minutes. Features interviews with Bette Davis, Samantha Eggar, Greer Garson, Lillian Hellman, Audrey Hepburn, Charlton Heston, John Huston, Laurence Olivier, Gregory Peck, Ralph Richardson, Terence Stamp, Barbra Streisand, Billy Wilder, Talli Wyler, and William Wyler. Also screened on PBS, "American Masters" series, July 13, 1987. ARTICLES, FILMS, PRO-DUCTION FILES

THE DIRECTORS (Short). 1963.

Produced by Nat Greenblatt. *Film Dope* reports that, per a notice in the *New York Post* (December 20, 1963) and other sources, *The Directors*—a short subject in color centering on several of the world's leading film directors—would open at Cinema II on December 23, 1963, in league with *Ladybug, Ladybug*. Among the filmmakers featured in the short are Federico Fellini, George Stevens, Billy Wilder, David Lean, William Wyler, Pietro Germi, Michelangelo Antonioni, and Joseph Mankiewicz. Huston also appears. PRODUCTION FILES

THE DIRECTORS GUILD SERIES: JOHN HUSTON. 1982.

Maddox-Turrow Productions/DGA Educational and Benevolent Foundation. Produced by Randolph Turrow. Directed by William Crain. With John Huston and Philip Dunne. Appears to be based on the full weekend tribute to Huston by the DGA in May 1982. *See Variety* (June 2, 1982) and the video recording: Interview, John Huston, DGA interview and film clips, UCLA, 1982. ARTICLES, FILMS

THE DISAPPOINTMENT, OR THE FORCE OF CREDULITY.

Unrealized project (?). AMPAS contains a photocopy of this 1767 play. No other indication of Huston's involvement. SCREENPLAYS

THE DISENCHANTED. 1950–52.

Writer, director. Unrealized project. AMPAS contains correspondence among Bud Schulberg (whose novel of the same name [Random House, 1950]) is the basis for film), Arthur Hornblow Jr. (MGM producer), Dore Schary (MGM producer), and Paul Kohner, regarding Huston's involvement in the film. It appears that Gregory Peck was considered for the film. Schulberg suggests to Huston that he would do a first draft of the screenplay, which they could polish and refine. AMPAS, PRODUCTION FILES

DISRAELI. 1929.

Warner Brothers. Screenplay by Julian Josephson, based on a play by Louis N. Parker. Directed by Alfred E. Green. Huston assigned from November 13, 1939, to December 13, 1939 (with Michael Hogan and Aeneas MacKenzie). No information on later release. ARTICLES, FILMS, PRODUCTION FILES, SCREENPLAYS

DR. EHRLICH'S MAGIC BULLET. 1940.

Hal Wallis for Warner Brothers. 103 minutes. Original screenplay by John Huston, Heinz Herald, and Norman Burnside, based on an idea by Burnside and developed from letters and notes held by Mrs. Ehrlich. Directed by William Dieterle. AFI (*Catalog: Feature Films, 1931–1940*), ARTICLES, AWARDS, FILMOGRAPHY, FILMS, PRODUCTION FILES, SCREENPLAYS

"EDITH PIAF." 1980 (?).
Director, unrealized (?). Per a piece in *Variety* (July 30, 1980), following *Annie,* Huston would direct a Rastar (Ray Stark) biography of Edith Piaf.

A FAREWELL TO ARMS. 1957.
Twentieth Century-Fox. 151 minutes. Produced by David O. Selznick; directed by Charles Vidor; screenplay by Ben Hecht, based on Ernest Hemingway's novel; cinematography by Piero Poralupi and Oswald Morris; art design by Mario Garbuglia; edited by Gerald J. Wilson and John M. Foley. Cast includes Rock Hudson, Jennifer Jones, Vittorio de Sica, Alberto Sordi, Kurt Kaznar, Mercedes McCambridge, Oscar Homolka, and Elaine Stritch. Huston, the original director, withdrew after clashes with David O. Selznick. Huston also contributed to the screenplay. AMPAS, ARTICLES, FILMS, PRODUCTION FILES, SCREENPLAYS

FATAL ATTRACTION. *See* HEAD ON.

FAT CITY. 1972.
Ray Stark (Rastar) and Columbia Pictures. 100 minutes. Screenplay by Leonard Gardner (and John Huston, uncredited), based on Gardner's novel. Directed by John Huston. AMPAS, ARTICLES, AWARDS, FILMOGRAPHY, FILMS, PRODUCTION FILES, SCREENPLAYS

FINE SHAKEDOWN. *See* SHAKEDOWN.

FORGOTTEN BOY (other working title: *Wild Boys of the Road* [*see* under that entry]).
Universal. Unproduced. While Huston was under contract to Universal as a screenwriter (1929–33), he worked on this project with William Wyler in 1933. AMPAS (William Wyler Collection), PRODUCTION FILES, SCREENPLAYS

FRANKIE AND JOHNNY ("St. Louis Legend"). 1963.
Unrealized project. Huston wrote, produced, and published puppet play in 1930. AMPAS contains correspondence and screenplay version. The USC Warner Brothers Archive contains information regarding this project from 1939 to 1952. AMPAS, PRODUCTION FILES, SCREENPLAYS

FREUD: THE SECRET PASSION. 1962.
Wolfgang Reinhardt and John Huston for Universal-International. 139 minutes. Screenplay by Charles Kaufman and Wolfgang Reinhardt, from the story by Charles Kaufman. Directed by John Huston, who also provides the narration and is an uncredited contributor to screenplay. AFI (*Catalog:*

Feature Films, 1961–1970), AMPAS, ARTICLES, AWARDS, FILMOGRA-
PHY, FILMS, PRODUCTION FILES, SCREENPLAYS

GEORGE STEVENS: A FILMMAKER'S JOURNEY. 1984.
A Castle Hill Productions release. 113 minutes. Written, produced, and
directed by George Stevens Jr. Film editor, Catherine Shields; coproducer and
supervising editor, Susan Winslow. Fellow directors appear: Warren Beatty,
Frank Capra, John Huston, Rouben Mamoulian, Joseph L. Mankiewicz, Alan
J. Pakula, and Fred Zinnemann. Telecast on ABC-TV in 1988. ARTICLES,
FILMS, PRODUCTION FILES, SCREENPLAYS

THE GINGER MAN. Director (?).
Unrealized project. AMPAS contains a screenplay by J. P. Donleavy.
SCREENPLAYS

GOYA. 1955.
Director. Unrealized project. AMPAS contains correspondence indicating that Huston received the first treatment from Titanus Films of Rome (June
16, 1955); that is, the first-draft screenplay by Talbot Jennings (148 p.). The
script is not in the Huston collection. AMPAS, PRODUCTION FILES

THE GREATEST BATTLE. *See* THE BATTLE OF MARETH.

GREAT PERFORMANCES: LIVE FROM LINCOLN CENTER. 1980.
The Film Society of Lincoln Center's "A Tribute to John Huston."
Produced by Joanne Koch and Wendy Keyes. Broadcast on Monday, May 5,
1980, 8:30 P.M. to 10:00 P.M. on PBS.

THE HARD WAY. 1942.
Warner Brothers. 196 minutes. Screenplay by Daniel Fuchs and Peter
Viertel, based on the original story by Jerry Wald (producer). Directed by
Vincent Sherman. The USC Warner Archive includes a memo (December 3,
1941) from Jerry Wald to John Huston, asking him to comment on the Irwin
Shaw script, and Huston's reply to Hal Wallis (December 8, 1941), with his
reactions. Archive includes Wald's original story and various treatments and
versions of the screenplay by Irwin Shaw, Arch Obler, and Daniel Fuchs.
Credits: Produced by Jerry Wald, directed by Vincent Sherman, screenplay by
Irwin Shaw and Daniel Fuchs, original story by Jerry Wald. Director of pho-
tography, James Wong Howe; editor, Thomas Pratt; art director, Max Parker.
Cast includes Ida Lupino, Joan Leslie, Dennis Morgan, and Jack Carson.
ARTICLES, FILMS, PRODUCTION FILES, SCREENPLAYS

HARROW ALLEY. 1962–63, 1967.
Director. Unrealized project. AMPAS contains correspondence
(1963–63, 1967), screenplay, and indications that Huston was seriously consid-

ered to direct, and he was interested. Apparently the project failed because of a lack of financing, although Ingo Preminger, producer, attempted to get financing from CBS, ABC, MGM, and Twentieth Century-Fox. (Cf. also *New York Times,* January 8, 1978, John M. Wilson, "One of Hollywood's Most Celebrated 'Lost Scripts' [reprinted in *The New York Times Encyclopedia of Film, 1977–1979*].) AMPAS, ARTICLES, PRODUCTION FILES, SCREENPLAYS

HASSAN. 1957.
        Director. Unrealized project. An AMPAS file from December 30, 1957, indicates that Fox was interested in purchasing rights to the play and in possibly lining up a deal with Buddy Adler. Huston mentioned as director. Attachment from Nigel Balchin (screenwriter) shows actors considered for the film: Sophia Loren, José Ferrer, and James Mason. Screenplay material also included. AMPAS, PRODUCTION FILES, SCREENPLAYS

HAUNTED SUMMER. 1988.
        Pathé/Cannon. Screenplay by Lewis John Carlino. Directed by Ivan Passer. Huston was originally designated as the director, but he withdrew in 1986 because of ill health. An ad in the *Hollywood Reporter* (May 6, 1988) lists John Huston as director. Credits: Cannon Group release and production, with executive producers Menahem Golan and Yoram Globus. Produced by Martin Poll, directed by Ivan Passer, and screenplay by Lewis John Carlino, from the Anne Edwards novel. Camera, Giuseppe Rotunno; editors, Cesare D'Amico and Richard Fields; production design, Stephen Grimes.* Cast includes Philip Anglim, Laura Dern, Alice Krige, Eric Stoltz, and Alex Winter.

Note. *Huston's longtime production and art director, Stephen Grimes, had the same position in this film. ARTICLES, FILMS, PRODUCTION FILES, SCREENPLAYS

HEAD ON (other title: *Fatal Attraction,* 1979 [Canada]). 1985 (United States.)
        Greentree Productions (AFI has Michael Grant Productions.) Produced by Alan Simmonds, directed by Michael Grant, screenplay by Jim Sanderson and Paul Illidge. Photography, Anthony Richmond; production design, Antonin Dimitrov; editor, Gary Oppenheimer. Cast includes Sally Kellerman, Stephen Lack, John Huston (Clarke Hill), and Larry Dane. AMPAS, ARTICLES, FILMS, PRODUCTION FILES, SCREENPLAYS

THE HEART IS A LONELY HUNTER. 1968.
        Warner Brothers. 124 minutes. Screenplay by Thomas C. Ryan. Directed by Robert Ellis Miller. A file in AMPAS contains information that the screenplay was by Thomas C. Ryan from March 1968. Not other indication of Huston's involvement in the project. Cast includes Alan Arkin, Sandra Locke, Laurinca Barret, and Stacy Keach Jr. FILMS, PRODUCTION FILES, SCREENPLAYS

HEAVEN KNOWS, MR. ALLISON. 1957.
Buddy Adler and Eugene Frenke for Twentieth Century-Fox. 107 minutes. Screenplay by John Lee Mahin and John Huston, from the novel by Charles Shaw. Directed by John Huston. AMPAS, ARTICLES, AWARDS, FILMOGRAPHY, FILMS, PRODUCTION FILES, SCREENPLAYS

HELL'S HEROES. 1930.
Universal. 65 minutes. Screenplay and dialogue by Tom Reed, based on the novel, *The Three Godfathers,* by Peter Kyne. Directed by William Wyler and photographed by George Robinson. Cast includes Charles Bickford, Raymond Hatton, Fred Kohler, Fritzi Ridgeway, Maria Alba, Joe de la Cruz, Buck Connors, Walter James, and John Huston (a bit part, uncredited). ARTICLES, PRODUCTION FILES, SCREENPLAYS

HERE IS GERMANY (working titles: *Know Your Enemy: Germany; Lest We Forget*). September 1945.
U.S. War Department, Information and Education Division. Army Service Forces. Army Pictorial Service. Signal Corps. Official Orientation Film no. 11. Story preparation and writers, William Shirer and George Ziomer, with additional story preparation by Ernest Lubitsch; writer, Sgt. Gottfried Reinhardt. Huston, as part of this group, was an uncredited contributing writer (cf. AMPAS), although he is not listed in *Meet Frank Capra: A Catalog of His Work* (Washington, D.C.: Smithsonian Institute, 1990, 75). Credits there are producers, Col. Frank Capra and Maj. Edgar Stevenson; project officer, Maj. William Hornbeck; original production and direction, Ernst Lubitsch; story preparation and writers, William L. Shirer and George Ziomer; story preparation, Ernest Lubitsch; writer, Gottfried Reinhardt; animation, Walt Disney Productions; music, Dimitri Tiomkin; and cutters, Dorothy Spencer and Bud Sheets. FILMS, SCREENPLAYS

HERE'S LOOKING AT YOU, WARNER BROTHERS. 1992.
Documentary. Interviewed. Produced in conjunction with an exhibition at the Museum of Modern Art, New York: "Warner Brothers: Behind the Shield, June 1992–March 1993." Video produced by David L. Wolper Productions. Directed by Robert Guennete. Original running time: 140 minutes. Screened on TNT, March 27, 1993. ARTICLES, FILMS, PRODUCTION FILES

HERMAN MELVILLE: DAMNED IN PARADISE. 1985.
TV. 90 minutes. Documentary. Directed by Robert Squier. Broadcast on PBS, May 15, 1985, 9 P.M. John Huston is the narrator; F. Murray Abraham reads the words of Melville. Produced by Robert D. Squier and Karen Thomas. Writers: George Wolfe, Robert D. Squier, Patricia Ward, and Carter Eskew. ARTICLES, FILMS, PRODUCTION FILES

THE HERO. 1932.
Universal. Unproduced. According to Universal Pictures's records, the original story was by Huston, a contract screenwriter from 1929 to 1932. AMPAS contains a fourteen-page treatment by Huston from 1932. FILMO-GRAPHY, SCREENPLAYS

HIGH ROAD TO CHINA. 1983.
Golden Harvest/Pan Pacific. 120 minutes. Screenplay by Sandra Weintraub Roland and S. Lee Pogostin. Directed by Brian G. Hutton. Project started in 1976 by Hutton and Pogostin. Huston took over the project in 1978, commissioned two scripts, and scouted locations. Huston dropped out of project sometime in 1979 (cf. *Film Dope,* no. 26 [January 1983]: 20: Miscellaneous work as director). According to *Variety* (August 1, 1979), production was pushed back to the March 8, 1980, start date. Also Huston, originally set to direct, had been rumored to be departing the project, but Paul Kohner said Huston planned to proceed with the picture the following spring. Another news report indicates that film went into production in 1978 and that Huston was to direct Bo Derek and Roger Moore. Credits from the press kit: Golden Harvest and Jadran Films present a Fred Wientraub Production for City Films, a Brian G. Hutton Film. Starring Tom Selleck and Bess Armstrong. Also starring Jack Weston, Wilford Brimley, Robert Morley, Brian Blessed, and Cassandra Gava. Directed by Brian G. Hutton, produced by Fred Weintraub. Screenplay by Sandra Weintraub Roland and S. Lee Pogostin, based on the book by Jon Cleary. Executive producer, Raymond Chow; film editor, John Jympson; production designer, Robert Laing. ARTICLES, FILMS, PRODUCTION FILES, SCREENPLAYS

HIGH SIERRA. 1941.
Hal Wallis and Mark Hellinger for Warner Brothers. 100 minutes. Screenplay by John Huston and W. R. Burnett, based on Burnett's novel. Directed by Raoul Walsh. ARTICLES, AWARDS, FILMOGRAPHY, PRODUCTION FILES, SCREENPLAYS

THE HOBBIT. 1977.
Rankin-Bass Productions and NBC-TV.* 78 minutes. Teleplay by Romeo Muller, from the works of J. R. R. Tolkien. Produced and directed by Arthur Rankin Jr. and Jules Bass. Voices: John Huston, Orson Bean, Richard Boone, and Hans Conreid.

Note. *The Hobbit* broadcast in two parts with the overall title "ABC Movie Special: Return of the King" on ABC-TV on May 11, 1980; on CBS-TV on May 11, 1979; and originally broadcast November 27, 1977. ARTICLES, FILMS, PRODUCTION FILES

HOLLYWOOD ON TRIAL. 1976.
   Corinth Films. A Cinema Associates–October Films Presentation. A James Gutman–David Helpern Jr. Production. 100 minutes. Director, Helpern; producer, Guttman; associate producers, Frank Galvin and Juergen Hellwig; camera, Barry Abrams; writer, Arnie Reisman; editor, Frank Galvin. Screened at Cannes Festival, May 19, 1976. Narrator, John Huston, with appearances by Walter Bernstein, Alvah Bessie, Lester Cole, Howard Da Silva, Edward Dmytryk, Millard Lampell, Ring Lardner Jr., Albert Maltz, Ben Marolis, Zero Mostel, Otto Preminger, Ronald Reagan, Martin Ritt, Gale Sondergaard, Leo Townsend, Dalton Trumbo, and William Wheeler. ARTICLES, FILMS, PRODUCTION FILES

THE HORSE OF SELENE. 1971–72.
   Writer, director, producer. Unrealized project. AMPAS includes correspondence from July 1971 to January 24, 1972. Tim Vignoles took a two-year option on Irish author Juanita Casey's novel of the same name (Dublin: Calder & Boyars/Dolman Press, 1971) and wanted Huston to direct. Casey would prepare the first treatment. Vignoles met with Huston. Huston wanted to have Hugh Leonard do the screenplay, but he wasn't interested. Leonard felt that Huston and Casey should develop the script. Vignoles wanted Huston to be writer/director/producer. Because of other commitments Huston could not do script at that time but wanted to start shooting in late summer 1972. After January 1972 indications are that Huston may have lost interest. File includes some script material. AMPAS, PRODUCTION FILES, SCREENPLAYS

THE HOSTAGE. 1970.
   Director. Unrealized. AMPAS contains various correspondence from July to August 1970, regarding Huston's involvement in supervising the writing of the script (with remunerations indicated) and in directing the film. Huston and Ray Stark agreed that while there was no firm commitment, one month after John Osborne turned in the script, it could can be submitted to Huston for his consideration. If parties agreed Huston would direct. Otherwise no obligations. Includes draft screenplay by John Osborne. AMPAS, PRODUCTION FILES, SCREENPLAYS

A HOUSE DIVIDED (working title: *Heart and Hand*). 1931.
   Universal. 68 minutes. Carl Laemmle Jr., producer; Paul Kohner, associate producer. Screenplay by John Clymer and Dale Van Every, and dialogue by John Huston,* based on the novel, *Hearts and Hands,* by Olive Edens. Directed by William Wyler. Photography by Charles Stumar. Cast includes Walter Huston, Kent Douglass (Douglas Montgomery), Helen Chandler, Vivian Oakland, and Frank Hagney.

Note. *This project is Huston's first writing credit. AFI (*Catalog: Feature Films, 1931–1940*), ARTICLES, FILMS, PRODUCTION FILES, SCREENPLAYS

HUMPHREY BOGART. OMNIBUS SERIES. 1973.

BBC-TV. According to BFI reports, it is a documentary on Bogart. Credits include Michael Houldey, producer/writer; Andrew Faulds, narrator; and with on-screen participants John Huston, Lauren Bacall, Alistair Cooke, Art Buchwald, Nunnally Johnson, Richard Brooks, and Joseph L. Mankiewicz.

HUNCHBACK OF NOTRE DAME. 1939.

RKO. The AFI (*Catalog: Feature Films, 1931–1940*) cites a news item in the *Hollywood Reporter* (1932) that Huston was writing the first sound treatment as a vehicle for Boris Karloff. Huston wrote the early treatments. Archives include a screenplay treatment by Huston. Producer, Pandro S. Berman; director, William Dieterle; screenplay writers, Sonya Levien and Bruno Frank; cinematographer, Joseph H. August; editors, William Hamilton and Robert Wise; art director, Van Nest Polglase. Cast includes Charles Laughton, Maureen O'Hara, Cedric Hardwicke, Thomas Mitchell, Edmond O'Brien, and Harry Davenport. ARTICLES, FILMS, PRODUCTION FILES, SCREENPLAYS

HUSTON, HEMINGWAY, HEARST NEWSREEL FOOTAGE. From May 1950 to July 1961.

18 minutes. FILMS

HYMN TO ATON. 1978.

15 minutes. Per *Video Source Book* (17th ed., 1997–78): "An ancient Egyptian king's prayer to 'the one God' is visualized and highlighted." Eartha Kitt provides an introductory narrative, and John Huston reads the prayer. Produced by Nadine Markova and Larry Russell. (Video: Phoenix/BFA Films, 800–221–1274.) According to other information: director, Nadine Markova; New York, Phoenix Films, 1978. Huston is not indicated in the cataloging. FILMS

IN SURE AND CERTAIN HOPE. . . . 1966.

Proposed TV documentary on James Agee.* Unrealized. Produced by Jules Power and Three Crown Productions, featuring John Huston as the narrator.

Note. *AMPAS John Huston Collection, Script Material, includes an "outline of presentation for James Agee TV special. 5/66. 10 p." plus a one-page letter from Barry Downes.

INDEPENDENCE. 1976.

National Historic Park, National Park Service, U.S. Department of the Interior/Twentieth Century-Fox. 28 minutes. Produced by Joyce Ritter and Lloyd Ritter. Screenplay by the Ritters and Thomas McGrath. Directed by

John Huston. AMPAS, ARTICLES, FILMOGRAPHY, FILMS, PRODUC-
TION FILES, SCREENPLAYS

IN THIS OUR LIFE. 1942.
Hal B. Wallis, executive producer. Warner Brothers. 97 minutes.
Screenplay by Howard Koch (and John Huston, uncredited), from the novel
by Ellen Glasgow. Directed by Huston. ARTICLES, AWARDS, FILMOG-
RAPHY, FILMS, PRODUCTION FILES, SCREENPLAYS

IN TIME TO COME. 1941.
Play. Written by Howard Koch and John Huston, based on Woodrow
Wilson and the League of Nations. Staged and directed by Otto Preminger.
Premiered at the Manfield Theater, New York, December 28, 1941.
Unrealized screen project. AMPAS contains three versions of play script, one
of which has a Paul Kohner (Huston's agent) label, indicating that Kohner
was possibly looking for film opportunities for this play. No evidence that
screenplay material was prepared. The USC Warner Brothers Archive con-
tains a manuscript of the play by Howard Koch, with the title *Woodrow
Wilson,* along with the synopsis and a seven-page treatment from 1940.
AMPAS, PRODUCTION FILES, SCREENPLAYS

THE INVISIBLE MAN. 1933.
Universal. 71 minutes. Produced by Carl Laemmle Jr. while Huston
was a contract screenwriter for Universal (1929–32). Screenplay by R. C.
Sherriff. Contributing writer, Preston Sturges; director, James Whale. Cast
includes Claude Rains, Gloria Stuart, William Harrigan, Henry Travers, Una
O'Connor, Forrester Harvey, Holmes Herbert, E. E. Clive, Dudley Digges,
Harry Stubbs, Donald Stuart, and Merle Tottenham. Huston developed a ten-
page treatment. ARTICLES, FILMS, PRODUCTION FILES, SCREEN-
PLAYS

ISRAELI FILM PROJECT. 1971.
Unrealized. Uninventoried part of John Huston Archives contains background material. No other information found on possible project.

IT HAPPENED IN PARIS. 1935.
Great Britain. Writer. *Film Dope* has the title as *It Started in Paris,*
Huston as co-adaptor, and Robert Wyler (brother of William Wyler) as direc-
tor. Per Denis Gifford's *The British Film Catalogue, 1895–1985—A
Reference Guide* (New York: Facts on File, 1986, entry no. 09796: *It
Happened in Paris*), it was produced by Bray Wyndham for Associated
British Film Distributors. Directed by Robert Wyler and Carol Reed; story
(play) by Yves Mirande (L'Arpete); and screenplay by John Huston and H. F.
Maltby. Cast includes John Loder, Nancy Burne, Edward H. Robbins, Esme
Percy, and Lawrence Grossmith. ARTICLES, FILMS, PRODUCTION
FILES, SCREENPLAYS

JACK OF DIAMONDS.* 1932.
. Universal. Unproduced. Universal company records indicate that original story was by Huston, a contract writer at Universal from 1929 to 1932.

Note. *MGM produced a film with same title in 1967. FILMOGRAPHY, PRODUCTION FILES, SCREENPLAYS

JAGUAR LIVES. 1979.
Derek Gibson for American International. 90 minutes. Screenplay by Yabo Yablonsky. Directed by Ernest Pintoff. Camera, John Cabrera; editor, Angelo Ross; and art director, Adolfo Confino. Cast includes Joe Lewis, Christopher Lee, Donald Pleasence, Barbara Bach, and John Huston (Ralph Richards). AMPAS, ARTICLES, FILMS, PRODUCTION FILES, SCREENPLAYS

JEZEBEL. 1938.
Henry Blanke and Hal B. Wallis (executive producer) for Warner Brothers. 103 minutes. Screenplay by Clements Ripley, Abem Finkel, and John Huston, based on the play by Owen Davis. Directed by William Wyler. AFI (*Catalog: Feature Films, 1931–1940*), ARTICLES, AWARDS, FILMOGRAPHY, FILMS, PRODUCTION FILES, SCREENPLAYS

JOAN (THE LARK). *See* ALOUETTE.

JOHN HUSTON. 1961.
TV. Interviewed. The BFI reports: John Huston, interview; production country, United Kingdom. No other credit information. Huston and Montgomery Clift, interviewed. 35 mm, 1,300 feet. *The NFA Catalog*'s summary: An interview with John Huston on the making of *Freud: The Secret Passion* (1962). The house where Freud lectured and lived. Hotel room in Vienna where the interview takes place. Huston talks about how his interest in Freud developed; working on *Let There Be Light* (1946); his experience with hypnotism and its role in the film; scripts with satire; the dramatization of dreams and reminiscences and how it is done (with examples); the casting of Montgomery Clift as Freud; the relationship he had with his father and the effect this had on his career; and on dramatizing the Oedipal complex. Also contains an interview with Clift about the role of Freud and how it was necessary to experience psychoanalysis. FILMS

JOHN HUSTON. 1967.
TV. Interviewed. The BFI reports: John Huston, the Levin interview; director, Jim Pope; production country, United Kingdom; production company, Rediffusion. *The NFA Catalog*'s summary: Jim Pope, director; Bernard Levin, interviewer. FILMS

JOHN HUSTON. 1972.
TV. Inteviewed. The BFI reports: John Huston, Cinema series; director, Richard Guinea; production country, United Kingdom; production company, Granada Television. *The National Film Archive Catalogue*'s summary: Clive James interviews John Huston; Richard Guinea, director. FILMS

JOHN HUSTON AND THE DUBLINERS. 1987.
Liffey Films. 60 minutes. Produced and directed by Lilyan Sievernich. Documentary on the making of *The Dead,* with Huston, cast, and crew. Credits from *Variety:* A Liffey Films presentation (sales, Gray City Inc.); executive producers, Chris Sievernich and Wieland Schulz-Keil; produced and directed by Lilyan Sievernich; camera, Lisa Rinzler; editor, Miroslav Janek. Released August 1987. Includes John Huston, Anjelica Huston, Tony Huston, Roberto Silvi, Tom Shaw, and cast. ARTICLES, FILMS, PRODUC-TION FILES

JOHN HUSTON: A WAR REMEMBERED. 1981.
Los Angeles/Rastar Television/KCET-TV on June 13, 1981. Produced and directed by Jim Washburn. John Huston and Clete Roberts discuss Huston's three WWII documentaries, which are shown in their entirety. *TV Guide*'s announcement of the WWII trilogy: airs on channel 28, April 30, 1981. The three films shown were *Report from the Aleutians* (1943), *Battle of San Pietro* (1945), and *Let There Be Light* (1946). FILMS

JOHN HUSTON: FACE TO FACE. 1959.
BBC. The BFI reports: producer, Hugh Burnett; interviewer, John Freeman; interviewee, John Huston. Reference listing: *British National Film Catalogue,* vol. 3, 1965.

JOHN HUSTON, FRED ZINNEMANN. Unidentified films: UCLA Film and Television Archive, FILMS

JOHN HUSTON, HEARST NEWSREEL FOOTAGE. May 1950 to April 1966. 9 minutes. FILMS

JOHN HUSTON INTERVIEW. 1956.
Television interview shot in New Bedford, Massachusetts, in which a woman asks director Jon Huston about the making of *Moby Dick* (1956). Last ninety feet showing a banquet is silent. According to a letter from the Rhode Island Historical Society, this footage came from WJAR-TV: one reel, 240 feet, sound, black and white, 16-mm reference print. An AFI gift to the Library of Congress. The AFI acquired film from the Rhode Island Historical Society.

JOHN HUSTON: THE MAN, THE MOVIES, THE MAVERICK. 1989.
A Point Blank Presentation. Premier, Los Angeles County Museum of Art, June 7, 1989; television screening on TNT, June 12, 1989, 5 P.M. PST;

Encore, 8 P.M., and Sunday, June 18, 1989, 11 A.M. Executive producers, Judith Ganz and David Ganz; producer, Joni Levin; director, Frank Martin. Cast includes John Huston, Robert Mitchum, Paul Newman, Lauren Bacall, Marietta Tree, Michael Fitzgerald, Evelyn Keyes, Tom Shaw, Danny Huston, Anjelica Huston, Oswald Morris, Ray Stark, Zoe Sallis, Michael Caine, Arthur Miller, Lord Hemphill, and Lady Hemphill. Credits from *Variety:* Released as *John Huston*. A Point Blank Presentation. 126 minutes. Producer, Joni Levin; executive producers, David Ganz and Judith Ganz; director, Frank Martin; writers, Martin Beagelman and Charles Beagelman; camera, Harry Dawson; editor, Robert Sinise; production designer, Thomas A. Walsh; and art director, Jane Osmann. Screened at the Boston Film Festival on September 19, 1988. Cast includes Robert Mitchum, narrator, with Paul Newman, Lauren Bacall, Evelyn Keyes, Arthur Miller, Michael Caine, Anjelica Huston, Danny Huston, Oswald Morris, and Burgess Meredith. ARTICLES, FILMS, PRODUCTION FILES

JOHN HUSTON'S DUBLIN (other title: *John Huston in Dublin*). 1981, 1985.
EIRE-TV. Produced by John McGreevey and Pat Ferns, Toronto. 60 minutes. Directed by John McGreevy. Written by James Plunkett. Huston, host and narrator, with Niall Tobin, Gerard Gillen, and Jos Begley. Stephen Cooper's *Perspectives on John Huston* (New York: G.K. Hall, 1994) lists a release date of 1980 (as does the AFI) and describes the film as a documentary-travelogue. AMPAS contains copies of the TV script. A newspaper article (difficult to make out which one), dated October 1979, reports that "John Huston's Dublin" was scheduled for CBC broadcasting the following day at 9:30 P.M., and it is part of the "Cities" series. The BFI reports the title as "Dublin," series as "Cities," and John Huston as director (?). Producing countries, United Kingdom and Canada; cast, Niall Tobin and Brendan Behan. *Variety* (1985) credits: "John Huston's Dublin" ("Cities"), with Huston (Narrator) and Niall Tobin. Supplier: John McGreevy Productions and Neilson-Gerns International, Ltd. Producers, John McGreevy and Pat Ferns; director, McGreevy; writer, James Plunkett; music, John Hills-Cockell; photography, Ron Stannett. Broadcast on PBS. ARTICLES, FILMS, PRODUCTION FILES, SCREENPLAYS.

JOHN HUSTON'S NOBEL PRIZE THEATRE. 1960s (?).
Unrealized Project. Executive Producer, Norman B. Katz (London); Seven Arts Production International. Proposed television series, focusing on Nobel laureates in literature, that Huston would supervise. SCREENPLAYS

THE JOURNEY OF ROBERT F. KENNEDY (working title: "The Unfinished Journey of Robert F. Kennedy"). 1970.
Movie of the Week on ABC-TV. David Wolper Productions. 73 minutes. Produced by David Seltzer and directed by Mel Stuart. Broadcast on February 17, 1970. Huston, narrator. According to *Film Dope:* "The Journal of Robert F. Kennedy" (British release title?). Credits from *Entertainment*

World: "Movie of the Week: The Journey of Robert F. Kennedy," ABC-TV, February 17, 1970. David L. Wolper, executive producer; David Seltzer, associate producer; Gabriel Bayz, director; Mel Stuart and Arthur Schlesinger Jr, writers; John Huston, narrator; Elmer Bernstein, music; William T. Cartwright, editor-associate producer. ARTICLES, FILMS, PRODUCTION FILES, SCREENPLAYS (under "The Unfinished Journey of Robert F. Kennedy")

JUAREZ. 1939.

Hal Wallis for Warner Brothers. 125 minutes. Screenplay by John Huston, Aeneas MacKenzie, and Wolfgang Reinhardt, based on *Maximilian and Carlotta* by Franz Werfel and on *The Phantom Crown* by Bertita Harding. Directed by William Dieterle. AFI (*Catalog: Feature Films, 1931–1940*), ARTICLES, AWARDS, FILMOGRAPHY, FILMS, PRODUCTION FILES, SCREENPLAYS

JUDAS. 1955.

Director. Unrealized project. AMPAS contains correspondence, cables, etc. regarding Huston's interest in Marcel Pagnol's play by same name. Allied Pictures seemed to be the production company involved. Huston wanted Pagnol to develop the screenplay and Brando, Laughton, and Lancaster to appear in the film. AMPAS, PRODUCTION FILES

KATHARINE HEPBURN AND HUMPHREY BOGART IN LEOPOLDVILLE, THE BELGIAN CONGO, AFRICA. June 6, 1951.

Hearst Vault Material. FILMS

KENYAN NATIONAL PARKS SAFARI WITH JOHN HUSTON. 1970.

TV. Huston was a host for the series "The American Sportsman." AMPAS file for *The Hostage* contains an August 20, 1970, letter from Gladys Hill to Irving Paul Lazar that Huston was going to Kenya in September 1970 to do an ABC documentary on elephant conservation. AMPAS (under *The Hostage*)

KEY LARGO. 1948.

Jerry Wald for Warner Brothers. 101 minutes. Screenplay by Richard Brooks and John Huston, from the play by Maxwell Anderson. Directed by John Huston. AMPAS, ARTICLES, AWARDS, FILMOGRAPHY, FILMS, PRODUCTION FILES, SCREENPLAYS

THE KILLERS. 1946.

Mark Hellinger for Universal. 100 minutes. Screenplay by Anthony Veiller and John Huston (uncredited). Directed by Robert Siodmak. ARTICLES, AWARDS, FILMOGRAPHY, FILMS, PRODUCTION FILES, SCREENPLAYS

KISS THE BLOOD OFF MY HANDS (working title: *The Unafraid*). 1948.
Universal. 84 minutes. Screenplay by Leonardo Bercovici, with additional dialogue by Hugh Gray. Adapted by Ben Maddow and Walter Bernstein, from the novel by Gerald Butler. Directed by Norman Foster. Cast includes Joan Fontaine, Burt Lancaster, and Robert Newton. Huston: Unrealized project? AMPAS has a copy of the screenplay; otherwise, there is no other indication of Huston's involvement in film. ARTICLES, FILMS, PRODUCTION FILES, SCREENPLAYS

KNOW YOUR ENEMY: GERMANY. *See* HERE IS GERMANY.

KNOW YOUR ENEMY: JAPAN. 1945.
U.S. War Department Information and Education Division. Army Service Forces. Army Pictorial Service. Signal Corps. Project 6,017: Official Orientation Film no. 10. 63 minutes. Produced by Col. Frank Capra. Written by Joris Ivens, Pvt. Carl Foreman, Col. Frank Capra, Maj. Edgar Peterson, and Maj. John Huston. No director indicated, but as noted in *Meet Frank Capra: A Catalog of His Work* (Washington, D.C.: Smithsonian Institute, 1990, catalog no. 074, pp. 47–48), Jorge Ivens and Edgar Peterson served as the director at various times. It also specifies periods of time that Huston worked on the film. AMPAS includes versions of the screenplay. AMPAS, FILMS, PRODUCTION FILES, SCREENPLAYS

THE KREMLIN LETTER. 1970.
Carter De Haven and Sam Weisenthal for John Huston. Distributed by Twentieth Century-Fox. 116 minutes. Screenplay by John Huston and Gladys Hill, from the novel by Noel Behn. Directed by John Huston, who also acts (The Admiral). AFI (*Catalog: Feature Films, 1961–1970*), AMPAS, ARTICLES, FILMOGRAPHY, FILMS, PRODUCTION FILES, SCREENPLAYS

THE LAST RUN. MGM. 1971.
Credits from press kit: MGM. Produced by Carter De Haven, directed by Richard Fleischer, original screenplay by Alan Sharp, photography by Sven Nykvist, edited by Russell Lloyd, and art directed by Roy Walker and José Maria Tapiador. Cast includes George C. Scott, Tony Musante, Trish Van Devere, and Colleen Dewhurst. According to *Film Dope*, Huston started directing, but grew unhappy with the script changes and quit. (Information in AMPAS indicates other reasons.) Richard Fleischer took over direction, while Huston was supposed to produce, write, and act in the film. Also notes Huston's involvement (ca. December 1970 to February 1971), even conflicts he had with such principals as George C. Scott. Included are chronologies from Huston regarding his contributions to the screenplay's development. AMPAS, ARTICLES, FILMS, PRODUCTIONS, SCREENPLAYS

LAUGHING BOY. 1934.
MGM. 79 minutes. Produced by Hunt Stromberg. Screenplay by John Colton and John Lee Mahin. Directed by W. S. Van Dyke. An original

Universal project that was sold to MGM. Huston, under contract as a writer at Universal, developed the project with William Wyler. They both developed versions of the script, did research, and went on field trips (cf. Axel Madsen's *William Wyler: The Authorized Biography,* New York, Crowell, 1973, 81–82; Gerald Pratley's *The Cinema of John Huston,* New York, A. S. Barnes, 1977, 29–30; and John Huston's *An Open Book,* New York, Da Capo Press, 1994, c. 1980, 58–60). AMPAS includes versions of the screenplay. Credits from *Variety* (May 15, 1934): Metro production and release. Starring Ramon Novarro and Lupe Velez. Directed by W. S. Van Dyke. Based on the novel by Oliver La Farge. Adaptation by John Colton and John Lee Mahin. Film editor, Blanche Sewell. Cast also includes William Dickenson, Chief Thunderbird, Catalina Rambula, Tall Man's Boy, and A. Armentia. AMPAS, ARTICLES, FILMS, PRODUCTION FILES, SCREENPLAYS

LAW AND ORDER (working titles: *Saint Johnson; Bullet Proof;* reissued as *Guns a' Blazing*). 1932.
> Per the AFI, Carl Laemmle Jr. for Universal. 70 or 73 minutes. Screenplay Tom Reed, based on the novel, *Saint Johnson,* by W. R. Burnett. Adaptation and dialogue by John Huston.* Directed by Edward L. Cahn. Cinematography by Jackson Rose. Cast includes Walter Huston, Harry Carey, Russell Simpson, Russell Hopton, and Ralph Ince.

Note. *A copy of the script, previously designated "Early Scripts—Untitled," has been discovered in AMPAS. ARTICLES, FILMS, PRODUCTION FILES, SCREENPLAYS

THE LEGEND OF MARILYN MONROE. 1964.
> Wolper Productions.* 60 minutes. TV production, ABC Stage 67. Script by Theodore Strauss and Terry Sanders. Directed by Terry Sanders. John Huston, narrator.

Note. *Produced by Wolper in 1964 and aired in 1967. FILMS, SCREEN-PLAYS

LET THERE BE LIGHT. 1946.*
> Army Pictorial Service of the U.S. Signal Corps. 45 minutes. Screenplay by Charles Kaufman and John Huston, commentary by Walter Huston, editing by Gene Fowler Jr. Cinematography by Stanley Cortez, George Smith, Lloyd Fromm, John Doran, and Joseph Jackman. Directing by Huston.

Note. *The film was suppressed by the U.S. government and not released until 1980. AMPAS, ARTICLES, FILMOGRAPHY, FILMS, PRODUCTION FILES, SCREENPLAYS

THE LIFE AND TIMES OF JOHN HUSTON, ESQ. 1966.
TV. Allan King and Associates, NET/BBC/CBC. 60 minutes. Produced, directed, and written by Roger Graef. Cast includes John Huston, Anjelica Huston, Tony Huston, Gladys Hill, Evelyn Keyes, Elizabeth Taylor, Marlon Brando, and Burl Ives.

THE LIFE AND TIMES OF JUDGE ROY BEAN. 1972.
John Foreman for National General Pictures. 124 minutes. Screenplay by John Milius. Directed by John Huston who also acts (Grizzly Adams). Huston also contributed to the screenplay (uncredited). AMPAS, ARTICLES, FILMOGRAPHY, FILMS, PRODUCTION FILES, SCREENPLAYS

LIGHTS! CAMERA! ANNIE! 1982.
KCET-TV, Los Angeles/Kaleidoscope Films/Columbia/Rastar. Documentary on the making of *Annie* (1982). Produced by Margery Doppelt and Gregory McClatchey. Directed by Andrew J. Kuehn. Cast includes John Huston, Ray Stark, Aileen Quinn, Albert Finney, Carol Burnett, Tim Curry, and Bernadette Peters. FILMS

THE LIONS OF KORA. 1985.
Documentary. BBC Television Transmission Co. The BFI reports Robert Duncan, director; Harry Minetree, producer/writer; John Huston, narrator. Transmission date: January 1985. A documentary about the lions of the Kora Game Reserve in Kenya, it follows "Koretta" as she introduces her cubs to George Adamson for the first time.

THE LIST OF ADRIAN MESSENGER. 1963.
Edward Lewis and Joel Productions for Universal. 98 minutes. Screenplay by Anthony Veiller, from the novel by Philip MacDonald. Directed by John Huston, who also contributed to the screenplay (uncredited) and acted (the leader of the hunt, Lord Ashton, also uncredited). AFI (*Catalog: Feature Films, 1961–1970*), AMPAS, ARTICLES, FILMOGRA-PHY, FILMS, PRODUCTION FILES, SCREENPLAYS

THE LONELY PASSION OF JUDITH HEARNE. 1987.
Handmade Films presents a United British Artists–Peter Nelson Production. Produced by Peter Nelson and Richard Johnson; directed by Jack Clayton;* screenplay by Peter Nelson, based on the Brian Moore novel; photographed by Peter Hannan; production designed by Michael Pickwoad; edited by Terry Rawlins. Cast includes Maggie Smith, Bob Hoskins, and Wendy Hiller. AMPAS indicates Huston's interest (December 1961–July 1963): acquisition of film rights of the novel; a script of the play submitted for his consideration; a letter from Richard Widmark, expressing his interest in being in the film, which he had heard Huston was going to do with Katharine Hepburn. Includes a copy of the play script by Brian Moore and versions of the screenplay, some by Huston.

Note. *Jack Clayton was associate producer on *Beat the Devil* (1954) and *Moulin Rouge* (1953). AMPAS, ARTICLES, FILMS, PRODUCTION FILES, SCREENPLAYS

LOVE AND BULLETS. 1978.
ITC. According to *Film Dope,* Huston was to direct this film but left the project during the preproduction stage. Stuart Rosenberg took over direction. Credits per the *New York Times:* Directed by Stuart Rosenberg; an original story written for the screen by Wendell Mayes; edited by Michael Anderson, Lesley Walker, and Tom Priestly; cinematography by Fred Koenekamp and Anthony Richmond; produced by Pancho Kohner. A Lew Grade Presentation for ITC Entertainment. Cast includes Charles Bronson, Jill Ireland, Rod Steiger, Strother Martin, Henry Silva, and Bradford Dillman. ARTICLES, FILMS, PRODUCTION FILES

LOVESICK. 1983.
A Ladd Company Release through Warner Brothers. Written and directed by Marshall Brickman, produced by Charles Okun, photography by Gerry Fisher, production design by Philip Rosenberg, edited by Nina Feinberg. Cast includes Dudley Moore, Elizabeth McGovern, Alec Guinness, Christine Baranski, Gene Saks, Renee Taylor, Wallace Shawn, and John Huston (Larry Geller, M.D.) ARTICLES, FILMS, PRODUCTION FILES, SCREENPLAYS

LUIS BUÑUEL. 1984.
TVE/Nitra S. A. Project for International Communication Studies. "Annenberg/CPB Project." Directed by Rafael Cortes. Documentary on Buñuel. Performers include Carlos Saura, Federico Fellini, John Huston, and Rafael Alberti. In Spanish. FILMS

LYSISTRATA (*All's Fair*). 1960.
Unrealized project. AMPAS contains correspondence regarding the stage play, a music production of *Lysistrata* (*All's Fair,* 1961) by Gilbert Seldes, who understood that Huston was interested in doing a film version; letter by Hans Holzer (producer ?), indicating that he wanted Huston to do the stage production and film; and by Huston, who was interested but involved with *The Misfits* (1961). AMPAS, PRODUCTION FILES

THE MACKINTOSH MAN. 1973.
John Foreman for Warner Brothers. 105 minutes. Screenplay by Walter Hill, based on the novel, *The Freedom Trap,* by Desmond Bagley. Directed by John Huston. ARTICLES, FILMS, PRODUCTION FILES, SCREENPLAYS

THE MADWOMAN OF CHAILLOT. 1969.
Commonwealth United Corp. Distributed by Warner Brothers–Seven Arts Inc. An Ely Landau–Bryan Forbes Production. 132 minutes. Produced by

Ely Landau; directed by Bryan Forbes; screenplay by Edward Anhalt, based on the Jean Giraudoux play; photographed by Claude Renoir and Burnett Guffey; production designed by Ray Sims; edited by Roger Dwyer; art directed by Georges Petitot. Cast includes Katharine Hepburn, Charles Boyer, Claude Dauphin, Edith Evans, John Gavin, Paul Henreid, Oscar Homolka, Margaret Leighton, Giulietta Masina, Nanette Newman, Richard Chamberlain, Yul Brynner, Donald Pleasence, and Danny Kaye. The AFI indicates that although Huston was the original director, he was replaced by Forbes early in the filming. According to *Film Dope*, Huston directed the first seventeen days, but none of his material is in the finished film. The *New York Times* (October 24, 1971) wrote that Forbes took over from Huston ten days before shooting commenced. Forbes said that Huston had differences with the producer. "I [i.e., Huston had]assumed that they would do it my way but that wasn't what they wanted. So I withdrew" (Grobel, *The Hustons,* New York, Scribners, 1989, 595–96). AFI (*Catalog: Feature Films, 1961–1970*), AMPAS, ARTICLES, FILMS, PRODUCTION FILES, SCREENPLAYS

THE MAGNIFICENT YANKEE. 1950.
Unrealized project? AMPAS contains a copy of the play script by Emmet Lavery (1945), based on the original book by Francis Biddle on Oliver Wendell Holmes. No other indication of Huston's involvement. Produced by MGM in 1950. Directed by John Sturges. Produced by Armand Deutsch. Written by Emmet Lavery, based on his play. Cast includes Louis Calhern, Ann Harding, Eduard Franz, Philip Ober, Ian Wolfe, Edith Evanson, Guy Anderson, Richard Anderson, and James Lydon. ARTICLES, FILMS, PRODUCTION FILES, SCREENPLAYS

MAKING OF THE B-25. 1942.
Army Pictorial Service (?), U.S. Signal Corps. Writer and director, Huston (?) (cf. Grobel, *The Hustons,* 234–35). No other indication of Huston involvement. A conversation with Grobel in October 1995 did not shed any further light on this project. The National Archives came up with a number of films dealing with the B-25, but identification could not be determined from this information.

THE MALTESE FALCON. 1941.
Henry Blanke for Hal B. Wallis and Warner Brothers. 100 minutes. Screenplay by John Huston, from the novel by Dashiell Hammett. Directed by Huston. ARTICLES, AWARDS, FILMOGRAPHY, FILMS, PRODUCTION FILES, SCREENPLAYS

MAN FOR ALL SEASONS. 1966.
Columbia/Highland. 120 minutes. Screenplay by Robert Bolt, based on his play. Directed by Fred Zinnemann. AMPAS includes correspondence between Huston and Zinnemann (January to March 1966), in which Huston was seriously considered for the acting role of the Duke of Norfolk. A note

from Zinnemann, dated March 9, 1966, expresses his regret that Huston was not going to do film. Includes script material. Credits: Highland Production Company. Produced and directed by Fred Zinnemann. Screenplay by Robert Bolt, based on his play. Photography, Ted Moore; editor, Ralph Kemplen; production design, John Box; art director, Terence Marsh. Cast includes Paul Scofield, Robert Shaw, Wendy Hiller, Leo McKern, Orson Welles, Susannah York, Nigel Davenport, John Hurt, and Corin Redgrave. FILMS, PRODUC-TION FILES, SCREENPLAYS

MAN IN THE WILDERNESS. 1971.
   Sandy Howard for Warner Brothers. 105 minutes. Screenplay by Jack DeWitt. Directed by Richard C. Sarafian. Director of photography, Gerry Fisher; editor, Geoffrey Foot; art director, Gumersindo Andres. Cast includes Richard Harris, John Huston (Captain Henry), Percy Herbert, Prunella Ransome, Henry Wilcoxon, Zachary Bass, John Bindon, Ben Carruthers, and James Doohan. ARTICLES, FILMS, PRODUCTION FILES, SCREEN-PLAYS

MAN OF LA MANCHA. 1972.
   Produzioni Europee Associates/UA. Screenplay by Dale Wasserman. Directed by Arthur Hiller. Paul Kohner, Huston's agent, sent this property to Huston to determine his interest. No other indication of Huston being involved in its production. FILMS, PRODUCTION FILES, SCREENPLAYS

THE MAN WHO WOULD BE KING. 1975.
   John Foreman for Allied Artists Pictures. 129 minutes. Screenplay by John Huston and Gladys Hill, based on Rudyard Kipling's short story of the same name. Directed by Huston. AMPAS, ARTICLES, AWARDS, FIL-MOGRAPHY, FILMS, PRODUCTION FILES, SCREENPLAYS

MARILYN: THE UNTOLD STORY. 1980.
   Directed by Jack Arnold and John Flynn. A fictional account with John Ireland as Huston. *Film Dope* also indicates that a shortened version was shown theatrically. ARTICLES, FILMS, PRODUCTION FILES

MARIUS. 1931.
   France. Paramount. Screenplay by Marcel Pagnol, from his play. Directed by Alexander Korda. Unrealized project? AMPAS contains a play script by Marcel Pagnol that was adapted from the French by Robert Wyler (brother of William Wyler). No other indication of Huston's involvement. PRODUCTION FILES, SCREENPLAYS

MATADOR. 1952–54.
   Director. Unrealized project. Project based on Barnaby Conrad's "Death of a Matador." AMPAS contains correspondence regarding Huston's involvement in the project with José Ferrer. The film would be made by

Huston Productions; rights would be purchased by Huston Corporation, by way of Romulus Films, London; filming would start in the spring or summer of 1953. Rights were then sold to John Wayne productions. AMPAS, PRODUCTION FILES

THE MIGHTY BARNUM (P. T. Barnum). 1934.
Per the AFI: Twentieth Century-Fox. 87, 98, or 101 minutes. Screenplay by Gene Fowler and Bess Meredyth. Directed by Walter Lang. The AFI credits Huston as a contributing writer. *Film Dope* reports that Huston "wrote an unused script for Darryl F. Zanuck entitled 'Barnum,' circa 1931; We don't know whether any of his material survived," but chapter 16, "Screenplays in Collections," indicates that it has. Credits: Twentieth Century–UA, 1934. Directed by Walter Lang, screenplay by Gene Fowler and Bess Meredyth, camera by Peverell Marley. Cast includes Wallace Berry, Adolphe Menjou, Virginia Bruce, Rochelle Hudson, Janet Beecher, and Tammany Young. AFI (*Catalog: Feature Films, 1931–1940*), ARTICLES, FILMS, PRODUCTION FILES, SCREENPLAYS

MINOR MIRACLE (other title: *Young Giants*). 1986.
Independent. Entertainment Enterprises. 100 minutes. Directed by Terrill (Terry?) Tannen. Screenplay by Tom Moyer, Mike Lammers, and Terrill Tannen. Cast includes John Huston (Father Bud Cadenas), Pele, and David Ruprecht. Stephen Cooper's *Perspectives on John Huston* (New York: G.K. Hall, 1994) lists it as *Minor Miracle/Young Giants*. ARTICLES, FILMS, SCREENPLAYS

A MIRACLE CAN HAPPEN. *See* ON OUR MERRY WAY.

THE MISFITS.* 1961.
Frank E. Taylor for Seven Arts Productions. Distributed by United Artists. 124 minutes. Screenplay by Arthur Miller. Directed by John Huston, who also contributed to the screenplay (uncredited).

Note. *The AMPAS John Huston Archives contains information on the narration for a 16mm featurette "The Making of 'The Misfits'" (20 minutes). The AMPAS archive's inventory also reports a 16-mm publicity film (16 mm, one reel in can). AMPAS, ARTICLES, FILMOGRAPHY, FILMS, PRODUCTION FILES, SCREENPLAYS

MISS HARGREAVES.
Director. Unrealized project. The AMPAS Huston Collection's *Moulin Rouge* (1953) production file includes information that Huston was to direct "Miss Hargreaves" for Romulus and that it would star Katharine Hepburn.

MR. CORBETT'S GHOST ("Corbett's Ghost"). 1986.
TV. British production. 60 minutes. Produced by Heritage Enterprises
Productions. Screenplay by Jerry Wilson. Produced and directed by Danny
Huston and Barry Navidi.* Executive producer, Michael Fitzgerald; director
of photography, Robin Vidgeon; designer, Deborah Gillingham. Cast includes
John Huston, Paul Scofield, and Burgess Meredith.

Note. *Huston and Navidi made the film with funding from the Fuji Film
Scholarship awards in 1983. ARTICLES, FILMS, PRODUCTION FILES

MR. NORTH. 1988.
A Samuel Goldwyn Release. 92 minutes. Director, Danny Huston;
executive producer, John Huston; producers, Steven Haft and Skip Steloff.
Screenplay by Janet Roach, John Huston, and James Costigan. Based on the
novel, *Theophilus North,* by Thorton Wilder. Cast includes Anthony Edwards,
Robert Mitchum,* Lauren Bacall, Harry Dean Stanton, and Anjelica Huston.

Note. *Huston was expected to act, but his poor health prevented it. Robert
Mitchum took over his role. ARTICLES, FILMS, PRODUCTION FILES,
SCREENPLAYS

MR. SKEFFINGTON. 1944.
Warner Brothers. Screenplay by Julius Epstein and Philip Epstein.
Directed by Vincent Sherman. Stars Bette Davis, Claude Rains, Walter Abel,
Richard Waring, George Coulouris, John Alexander, and Jerome Cowan.
Huston developed the screenplay while writing under assignment at Warner
Brothers from August to December 1940. Credits from MOMA: Directed by
Vincent Sherman, produced by Julius J. Epstein and Philip G. Epstein, screen-
play by the Epsteins, adapted from the novel by "Elizabeth." Photography by
Ernest Haller, editing by Ralph Dawson, art direction by Robert Haas. Cast
includes Bette Davis, Claude Rains, Walter Abel, Richard Waring, and
George Coulouris. ARTICLES, FILMS, PRODUCTION FILES, SCREEN-
PLAYS

MOBY DICK. 1956.
John Huston for Moulin Pictures/Warner Brothers. 116 minutes.
Screenplay by Ray Bradbury and John Huston, from the novel by Herman
Melville. Directed by Huston. Per a *Film Daily* article (May 2, 1955), Huston
assembled two half-hour color films on the making of *Moby Dick,* designed
for television showing, and Huston would probably handle the narration. The
AFI/LC Catalog lists *Moby Dick: John Huston Interview,* a short film on
acetate. The AMPAS John Huston Archive's production file on *Moby Dick*
indicates that the BBC shot a documentary of the making of the film on or
about November 4, 1954, which would run about seven minutes. AMPAS,
ARTICLES, AWARDS, FILMOGRAPHY, FILMS, PRODUCTION FILES,
SCREENPLAYS

MOMO. 1986.

Produced by Horst Wendlandt. Directed by Johannes Scaaf. Cast includes Radost Bokel, Leopoldo Trieste, Bruno Stori, Ninetto Davoli, Mario Adorf, and John Huston. Press kit credits: *Momo* from the book by Michael Ende. Directed by Johannes Schaaf. In her first screen appearance, Radost Bokel as Momo. With special guest appearance of John Huston as Hora and Leopoldo Trieste, Bruno Stori, Ninetto Davoli, Mario Adorf, and Armin Muller Stahl. Screenplay by Rosemarie Fendel, Johannes Schaaf, and Marcello Coscia. Director of photography, Xavier Schwarzenberger. An Italian-German coproduction, Cinecitta-Sacis-Tialto-Iduna. Produced by Horst Wendlandt. International Distribution Sacis. ARTICLES, FILMS, PRODUC-TION FILES

MONEY AND MEDICINE. 1983.

TV Documentary. Louis Rukeyser, host and commentator. John Huston, narrator. "Transcript of the video recording" (24 p., University of California, Berkeley, holdings) specifies John Huston as narrator, which has been ascertained by examining the transcript. The cataloging of the videocassette, however, indicates Louis Rukeyser as narrator, with no mention of Huston. FILMS, SCREENPLAYS

THE MOST ENDANGERED SPECIES . . . GEORGE ADAMSON. 1982.

TV Documentary. Produced by Mafuta Mingi, in cooperation with KUHT/Houston. Narrated by John Huston. ARTICLES

MONTEZUMA ("Montezuma and Cortez"). 1956, 1960.

Director. Unrealized project. The *Hollywood Reporter* (May 3, 1960) stated that Huston was to direct, with Kirk Douglas as Cortez, the film, which would be produced by Bryna Productions (Eugene Frenke and Edward Lewis) for release by Universal. Slated to start production in the summer of 1961. AMPAS, PRODUCTION FILES, SCREENPLAYS

MOULIN ROUGE. 1953.

John Huston for Romulus. Distributed by United Artists. 119 minutes. Screenplay by Anthony Veiller and Huston, from the novel by Pierre La Mure. Directed by Huston. AMPAS, ARTICLES, AWARDS, FILMOGRAPHY, FILMS, PRODUCTION FILES, SCREENPLAYS

MOVIE DIRECTOR JOHN HUSTON TALKS. 1950.

Hearst Newsreel Footage, New York City, May 25, 1950. Stock footage originally intended for use in a Hearst news production; not used. Footage consists of one statement and several retakes of interview. Huston discusses the film *The Asphalt Jungle* (1950). FILMS

MOVIOLA: THIS YEAR'S BLONDE. 1980.

TV. David L. Wolper and Stan Margulies, producers, and Warner Brothers TV. 360 minutes. Directed by John Erman. Writers, James Lee and William Hanley, based on Garson Kanin's book. Broadcast Sunday through Tuesday, May 19–21, 1980, 9 P.M., on NBC-TV. Per *Film Dope,* "This Year's Blonde" (Marilyn Monroe) is the first episode, with Lloyd Bridges, Constance Forslund, Norman Fell, Vic Tayback, Michael Lerner, John Marley, Richard Seer, Lee Wallace, and William Frankfather (as John Huston). ARTICLES, FILMS, PRODUCTION FILES, SCREENPLAYS

MURDERS IN THE RUE MORGUE. 1932.

Universal. 62 minutes. Carl Laemmle Jr. and E. M. Asher (associate producer). Screenplay by Tom Reed and Dale Van Every, based on the short story by Edgar Allan Poe; additional dialogue by John Huston. Directed by Robert Florey, photography by Karl Freund, editing by Milton Carruth. Cast includes Bela Lugosi, Sidney Fox, Leon Waycoff (Leon Ames), Bert Roach, and Brandon Hurst. *The American Film Institute Catalog: Feature Films, 1931–1940* gives Huston credit for additional dialogue. ARTICLES, FILMS, PRODUCTION FILES, SCREENPLAYS

MYRA BRECKINRIDGE. 1970.

Robert Fryer for Twentieth Century-Fox. 94 minutes. Screenplay by Michael Sarne and David Giler, from the novel by Gore Vidal. Directed by Michael Sarne. Director of photography, Richard Moore; art directors, Jack Martin Smith and Fred Harpman; film editor, Deanford B. Greene. Cast includes Raquel Welch, Rex Reed, Mae West, Farrah Fawcett, and John Huston (Buck Loner). AFI (*Catalog: Feature Films, 1961–1970*), ARTICLES, FILMS, PRODUCTION FILES, SCREENPLAYS

NAGANA (working titles: *Animal World; Adventure Woman*). 1933.

Universal. 74 minutes (per the AFI). Screenplay by Dale Van Every and Don Ryan. Story by Lester Cohen. Directed by Ernst L. Frank. Cast includes Tala Birell, Melvyn Douglas, Miki Morita, Onslow Stevens, Everett Brown, Billy McClain, William H. Dunn, and Frank Lacteen. Huston was then under contract as a writer to Universal and developed a nine-page treatment. ARTICLES, PRODUCTION FILES, SCREENPLAYS

NATIONAL GEOGRAPHIC SPECIAL: FLIGHT OF THE WHOOPING CRANE. 1984.

TV Documentary. Narrated by John Huston. There doesn't appear to be any evidence that National Geographic issued this program on video as part of its video program. ARTICLES.

NEWS OF THE DAY 19, no. 217.

Excerpt, "Red Issue Creates Furor at House Movie Inquiry, Washington, D.C." Outtakes, 3:08 minutes. FILMS

NEXT DOOR TO HEAVEN.
Unrealized project (?).AMPAS contains screenplay material. SCREEN-
PLAYS

NIGHT FIGHTERS. *See* A TERRIBLE BEAUTY.

THE NIGHT OF THE IGUANA. 1964.
Ray Stark for Seven Arts Productions. Distributed by MGM. 125 min-
utes. Screenplay by Anthony Veiller and John Huston, from the play by
Tennessee Williams. Directed by Huston. From the Hearst Vault Material:
Lincoln Center, New York City, world premiere of *The Night of the Iguana* on
June 30, 1964. UCLA. AFI (*Catalog: Feature Films, 1961–1970*), AMPAS,
ARTICLES, AWARDS, FILMOGRAPHY, FILMS, PRODUCTION FILES,
SCREENPLAYS

NINA. 1970.
Actor. Unrealized project. AMPAS contains correspondence with
Huston that Hemdale was producing the film in the United Kingdom and
wanted Huston to play the leading role of Edward Granville. They hoped to
start shooting in August or September 1970. While no screenplay material is
in the collection, Gladys Hill indicated that it was received. ARTICLES,
FILMS, PRODUCTION FILES

NOTES FROM UNDER THE VOLCANO. 1984.
56 minutes. Produced, directed, photographed, and narrated by Gary
Conklin. Editor, Michael Toshiyuki Uno; sound, Daniel Cambi. Features John
Huston, Guy Gallo, Albert Finney, Jacqueline Bisset, Anthony Andrews,
James Villiers, and Arturo Sarabia. On the making of the film along with inter-
views with John Huston. A French version was issued on video with the title
John Huston Filming. ARTICLES, FILMS, PRODUCTION FILES

OBSERVATIONS UNDER THE VOLCANO. 1984.
A Christian Blackwood Productions release. 82 minutes. Produced,
directed, and photographed by Blackwood. Edited by Ned Bastile. Based on
the writings of Malcolm Lowry, as read by John Hurt. Features John Huston,
Albert Finney, Jacqueline Bisset, Anthony Andrews, Michael Fitzgerald,
Wieland Schulz-Keil, Guy Gallo, Gabriel Figueroa, Tom Shaw, Emilio
Fernandez, and Rene Ruiz. On the making of the film. ARTICLES, FILMS,
PRODUCTION FILES

ON LOCATION: THE NIGHT OF THE IGUANA. 1964.
David L. Wolper Productions. 26 minutes. Producer, director, and
writer, William Kronick; narrator, Joseph Cotton; music supervisor, Jack

481

Tillar; director of photography, David Blewitt; film editor, David Newhouse.
ARTICLES, FILMS, PRODUCTION FILES

ON OUR MERRY WAY (*A Miracle Can Happen*). 1948.
Borgeaus-UA. 107 minutes. Producers, Benedict Borgeaus and
Burgess Meredith. Directors (credited), King Vidor and Leslie Fenton.
Screenplay by Laurence Stallings, Lou Breslow, and John O'Hara, based on a
story by Arch Obler. O'Hara is indicated as the writer of the James
Stewart–Henry Fonda sequence. According to *Film Dope,* Huston was the
uncredited director of the Fonda-Stewart sequence, but John Huston's *An
Open Book* (New York: Knopf, 1981) and Lawrence Grobel's *The Hustons*
(New York: Scribners, 1989) do not mention Huston's involvement with the
film. John Springer, in *The Fondas: The Films and Careers of Henry, Jane
and Peter Fonda* (New York: Citadel Press, 1970, 145), writes that George
Stevens and John Huston were uncredited directors of the Fonda-Stewart
sequence, which was written by John O'Hara. "Fonda and Stewart, given their
choice of writer and director, also picked John Huston . . . But Huston had
completed only one segment of their section when work had to stop because
of previous Fonda commitments. When he returned, Huston was no longer
available. Their choice to direct the body of the section was George Stevens.
. . . At their request, neither Stevens nor Huston received screen credit but
they should have taken it—their part in the picture was a bright oasis in a
dreary desert." ARTICLES, FILMOGRAPHY, FILMS, PRODUCTION
FILES, SCREENPLAYS

ON THE TRAIL OF THE IGUANA. 1965.
Directed by Ross Lowell. Per *Motion Picture Exhibitor* (July 8, 1964)
and *Film Dope,* a thirteen-minute, 35mm color featurette was prepared for
The Night of the Iguana to be shown in theaters and on television as a key pre-
sell promotion for the film. SCREENPLAYS

THE ORSON WELLES STORY. 1982.
TV. 180 minutes. Per BFI reports: Arena Series, with alternate title
"With Orson Welles: Stories from a Life in Film." Production country, United
Kingdom; production company, BBC; Leslie Megahey, director/producer/
writer; Alan Yentob, producer; Peter Smokler, photography; Leslie Megahey,
narrator. On-screen participants: Orson Welles, John Huston, Charlton
Heston, Anthony Perkins, Jeanne Moreau, Peter Bogdanovich, Robert Wise,
and Michael MacLiammoir.

ORSON WELLES: THE ONE-MAN BAND. 1995.
Documentary. German-French-Swiss. A Medias Res Film. 90 minutes.
Produced by Dominique Antoine, Freddy Messmer, and Roland Zag.

Executive producer, Pit Riethmuller. Directed by Vassili Silovic. Made possible by Oja Kodar. Screenplay by Silovic and Zag. Reviewed in *Variety* at Venice Film Festival ("Window on Images," September 6, 1995). Includes two scenes from *The Other Side of the Wind*. ARTICLES

THE OTHER SIDE OF THE WIND. 1970–75.

Not yet released. Produced, directed, and screenplay by Orson Welles. Cast includes John Huston in the leading role as film director; Peter Bogdanovich, Lilli Palmer, Oja Kodar, Susan Strasberg, and Bob Random. Per a *New York Times* article by Charles Higham (January 31, 1971), Welles started shooting a film he wrote about a director of the Henry Hathaway–John Ford (John Huston?) mold "who comes back to Hollywood after a long exile to be confronted by the self-conscious intellectualism and Beverly Hills hippiedom of Hollywood in the 1970's. . . . It hasn't been settled whether John Huston or Welles himself will appear in the role of the director. The *New York Post* (December 8, 1966) reported that Huston would finish the film after Welles's death. In his will Welles left the film to Bogdanovich to finish. Bogdanovich asked Huston to complete it, and he agreed. ARTICLES, FILMS, PRODUCTION FILES, SCREENPLAYS

PATTON. Twentieth Century-Fox. 1970.

171 minutes. Screenplay by Francis Ford Coppola and Edmund H. North. Directed by Franklin Schaffner. AMPAS contains correspondence and other documents (October 1965 to March 1968) from Zanuck, who was extremely interested in having Huston direct the film; versions of the screenplay sent to Huston; and a cable from Darryl Zanuck to Huston (June 6, 1966): "You are my first choice provided you can be available even toward better part of 1967." AFI (*Catalog: Feature Films, 1961–1970*), AMPAS, FILMS, PRODUCTION FILES, SCREENPLAYS

PHOBIA. 1980.

Zale Magder for Paramount. 90 minutes. Screenplay by Lew Lehman, Jimmy Sangster, and Peter Bellwood, from a story by Gary Sherman and Ronald Shusett. Directed by John Huston, who also contributed to the screenplay (uncredited). AMPAS, FILMOGRAPHY, FILMS, PRODUCTION FILES, SCREENPLAYS

LA PORTA DI S. PIETRO DI GIACOMO MANZU. 1964.

Italy. Directed by Glauco Pellegrini. Huston narrates the English-language version (cf. *Film Dope*).

PORTRAIT OF THE ARTIST AS A YOUNG MAN. 1977.

Joseph Strick. Earlier unrealized project of Huston's, 1969–70. AMPAS includes correspondence and screenplays regarding this project. AMPAS, FILMS, PRODUCTION FILES, SCREENPLAYS

PRELUDE TO FREEDOM. 1939, 1950.

Unrealized project. Also developed under the titles: *Theodosia: Empress of America,* and possibly *Eight Years of Tom Jefferson.* AMPAS contains correspondence and screenplays regarding the project. The USC Warner Brothers Archive contains treatments, screenplay, memos, and other documentation under this title and one of its alternate titles: *Theodosia: Empress of America.* AMPAS, PRODUCTION FILES, SCREENPLAYS

THE PRINCE AND THE SHOWGIRL (*Sleeping Prince*). 1957.

Warner Brothers–Marilyn Monroe Productions. Screenplay by Terence Rattigan, based on his play, *The Sleeping Prince.* Directed by Laurence Olivier. AMPAS contains a file of newspaper and magazine clippings from 1956 stating that Huston was to direct the project. AMPAS, ARTICLES, FILMS, PRODUCTION FILES, SCREENPLAYS

PRIZZI'S HONOR. 1985.

An ABC Motion Pictures. Released through Twentieth Century-Fox. 130 minutes. Producer John Foreman. Screenplay by Richard Condon and Janet Roach, based on Condon's novel. Directed by Huston, who also contributed to the screenplay (uncredited). ARTICLES, AWARDS, FILMO-GRAPHY, FILMS, PRODUCTION FILES, SCREENPLAYS

THE PROWLER (*The High Cost of Living; Cost of Living*). 1951.

United Artists Release. Horizon Pictures Production. 91 minutes. Produced by Sam Spiegel. Screenplay by Hugo Butler, from the original story by Robert Thoeren and Hans Wilhelm. Director, Joseph Losey; camera, Arthur Miller; music, Lyn Murray; art director, Boris Leven; editor, Paul Weatherwax. Cast includes Van Heflin, Evelyn Keyes, John Maxwell, Katharine Warren, Emerson Tracy, and Madge Blake. *Film Dope* indicates that Horizon Productions released the picture as *The Prowler.* This film was the only Horizon production with which Huston was associated other than *The African Queen* (1952), for he left the company after the latter production. ARTICLES, FILMS, PRODUCTION FILES, SCREENPLAYS

THE QUARE FELLOW. 1962.

BLC/Bryanston. 85 minutes. Director. Unrealized project (?). Astor Pictures. Written and directed by Arthur Dreifuss, produced by Anthony Havelock-Allan. Screenplay by Arthur Dreifuss. Adaptation by Jacqueline Sundstrom and Arthur Dreifuss, based on Brendan Behan's play of the same name. Edited by Gitta Zadek, art directed by Ted Marshall, photography by Peter Hennessy. Starring Patrick McGoohan and Sylvia Syms. AMPAS has script material. FILMS, PRODUCTION FILES, SCREENPLAYS

QUO VADIS. 1951.

MGM. Screenplay by John Lee Mahin, S. N. Behrman, and Sonya Levien. Directed by Mervyn Le Roy. Huston was a writer (with others) and the director, from January 1949 until May 1949 when he withdrew. Le Roy's name began appearing in memos in March 1950. Per *Film Dope,* Huston worked on preproduction, directed some tests, and contributed to the screenplay. AMPAS includes extensive information on Huston's early involvement (February through August 1949). An *New York Times* article (May 7, 1950) indicates that Sam Zimbalist took over as producer from Arthur Hornblow Jr. and that Mervyn Le Roy was appointed to replace John Huston. Screenplay information included. Credits for release: MGM. Director, Mervyn LeRoy; producer, Sam Zimbalist; script writers, John Lee Mahin, Sonya Levien, and S. N. Behrman, based on Henryk Sienkiewicz's novel. Cinematographer, Robert Surtees and William Skall; editor, Ralph E. Winters; art directors, William Horning, Cedric Gibbons, and Edward Carfagno. Cast includes Robert Taylor, Deborah Kerr, Leo Genn, Peter Ustinov, Patricia Laffan, and Finlay Currie. AMPAS, ARTICLES, FILMS, PRODUCTION FILES, SCREENPLAYS

THE RED BADGE OF COURAGE. 1951.
Gottfried Reinhardt for MGM. 69 minutes. Screenplay by John Huston, from the novel by Stephen Crane, and adaptation by Albert Band. Directed by Huston. According to *Film Dope,* Huston had a bit role as a taunting soldier, but he was cut from final release. AMPAS, ARTICLES, AWARDS, FILMOGRAPHY, FILMS, PRODUCTION FILES, SCREENPLAYS

REFLECTIONS IN A GOLDEN EYE. 1967.
Ray Stark for Warner Brothers–Seven Arts. 109 minutes. Screenplay by Chapman Mortimer and Gladys Hill, from the novel by Carson McCullers. Directed by John Huston, who also contributed to the screenplay (uncredited). AFI (*Catalog: Features Films, 1961–1970,* 896), AMPAS, ARTICLES, FILMOGRAPHY, FILMS, PRODUCTION FILES, SCREENPLAYS

REMINISCENCES OF A COWBOY. Released as *Cowboy.* 1958.
Columbia/Phoenix. Produced by Julian Blaustein, screenplay by Edmund H. North, directed by Delmer Daves. AMPAS lists Huston as the designated director around 1949, with the film to be produced by Horizon and released by Columbia. Montgomery Clift and Walter Huston were possible leads. Another report says that Peter Viertel would write the screenplay. In an earlier letter to Huston (November 1, 1945) he says he acquired the rights to Frank Harris's *My Reminiscences as a Cowboy.* In a letter to Huston, Julian Blaustein, producer writes that Huston may have had a long relationship with this property and was perhaps one of the writers, but Huston denied this assertion. Script material included. AMPAS, PRODUCTION FILES, SCREENPLAYS

REPORT FROM THE ALEUTIANS. 1943.
Army Pictorial Service of the U.S. Signal Corps. 47 minutes. Screenplay by John Huston, commentary by Walter Huston and John Huston, and photography by Jules Buck, Ray Scott, John Huston, Freeman C. Collins, Buzz Ellsworth, and Herman Crabtree. Directed by John Huston. AMPAS, ARTICLES, FILMOGRAPHY, FILMS, PRODUCTION FILES, SCREENPLAYS

THE RETURN OF THE KING. 1980.
ABC-TV. Rankin-Bass Productions. Directors, Akiyuki Kubo, Arthur Rankin, and Jules Bass. Voices, Orson Bean, Theodore Bikel, William Conrad, and John Huston (Gandalf). Sequel to the 1977 production of *The Hobbit,* this TV animated film was screened May 11, 1980, 7 P.M. by Romeo Muller and Glenn Yarborough. *Video Source Book* lists as the third and final animated episode of J. R. R. Tolkien's Middle Earth trilogy. ARTICLES, FILMS, PRODUCTION FILES

RETURN TO THE ISLAND. 1964.
Documentary. United Kingdom. Produced by George Grafton Green. Huston appears. While *Film Dope* lists this film as "other work by Huston" and the BFI reports holdings of a copy, no other information available. FILMS

REVENGE. 1989.
Columbia Tristar/Rastar. Produced by Hunt Lowry and Stanley Rubin. Screenplay by Jim Harrison. Directed by Tony Scott. Huston intended to direct this film after *The Dead* (1987) and to work on the screenplay with his son Tony, but ill health prevented John from pursuing the project. In the *New York Times* (March 11, 1990), Janet Maslin reports that an early draft was cowritten by John Huston and Tony Huston, and Huston might have directed. (Cf. also Lawrence Grobel's *The Hustons,* New York, Scribners, 1989, various pages.) Credits at release: Columbia Pictures in association with New World Entertainment of a Rastar Production. Produced by Hunt Lowry and Stanley Rubin. Executive producer, Kevin Costner; director, Tony Scott. Screenplay by Jim Harrison and Jeffrey Fiskin, based on Harrison's novella. Camera, Jeffrey Kimball; editor, Chris Lebenzon; production designers, Michael Seymour and Benjamin Fernandez. Cast includes Kevin Costner, Anthony Quinn, and Madeleine Stowe. ARTICLES, FILMS, PRODUCTION FILES, SCREENPLAYS

THE RHINEMANN EXCHANGE. 1977.
Universal TV for NBC-TV.* Executive producer, George Eckstein; producer and writer, Richard Collins. Screenplay based on the novel by Robert Ludlum. Directed by Burt Kennedy. Cast includes Stephen Collins, Lauren Hutton, Claude Akins, Len Birman, Vince Edwards, Gene Evans, Larry Hagman, John Huston, Jeremy Kemp, Werner Klemperer, Roddy McDowall, Trisha Noble, William Prince, and José Ferrer.

Note. *Five-hour miniseries for NBC-TV's "Best Sellers." FILMS, PRODUCTION FILES

RHODES OF AFRICA (*Rhodes*). 1936.
Gaumont-British Pictures, Inc. Adaptation by Leslie Arliss and Michael Barringer. Dialogue by Miles Malleson. Directed by Berthold Viertel. Walter Huston was cast as Cecil Rhodes. According to Lawrence Grobel's *The*

Hustons (New York: Scribners, 1989, 174–75), Walter did not like the script and sent it to John, asking him to "punch it up a bit." John rewrote the script, and Walter felt it was an improvement. John's script is not in AMPAS, but a copy of Arliss and Barringer's script is available at NYPL. Cast includes Walter Huston, Oscar Homolka, Basil Sydney, Peggy Ashcroft, Frank Cellier, Bernard Lee, and Lewis Casson. ARTICLES, FILMS, PRODUCTION FILES, SCREENPLAYS

RICHARD III.* 1953.
      Director. Unrealized project. AMPAS John Huston Collection's production file contains correspondence from March 1953 to May 1953 in which Romulus sent Huston the script and asked him to direct; suggestions for the cast, including José Ferrer, Claire Bloom, Michael Redgrave or John Gielgud, Paul Scofield, and Laurence Harvey; in March, Huston's expression of interest in the film and in Brando for the lead; a letter from Brando to Huston, saying he was not interested; and Huston's reply to Brando that he probably will abandon the project if Brando turns the role down. According to a *New York Times* article (April 26, 1953), "By February [1954] he [i.e., José Ferrer] has to be in England for the film 'Richard III' to be directed by John Huston. . . ."

Note. * This film does not appear to have any relation to the Laurence Olivier film of 1955. AMPAS, PRODUCTION FILES

RIDE THIS WAY, GRAY HORSE. *See* WALKING WITH LOVE AND DEATH.

THE ROARING TWENTIES.* 1939.
      Warner Brothers. Writing assignment, May 18, 1939, to August 13, 1939, with John Wexley and Frank Donoghue, under the early working title *The World Moves On.* Writers (of credit): Jerry Wald, Richard Macaulay, and Robert Rossen. Director, Raoul Walsh. Per *The American Film Institute Catalog: Feature Films, 1931–1940:* Original story, Mark Hellinger; contributor to treatment, John Wexley; contributors to screenplay construction, Earl Baldwin and Frank Donoghue. Although there is no mention of Huston's contributions, chapter 16, "Screenplays in Collections," indicates others' contributions. Credits at release: Directed by Raoul Walsh. Executive producer, Hal B. Wallis; associate producer, Samuel Bischoff. Written by Jerry Wald, Richard Macaulay, and Robert Rossen, based on an original story by Mark Hellinger. Director of photography, Ernie Haller; editor, Jack Killifer; art director, Max Parker. Cast includes James Cagney, Priscilla Lane, Humphrey Bogart, Gladys George, and Jeffrey Lynn.

Note. *Another film with the same title, but a different story line, was produced by Fox in 1934. USC has screenplay versions of this project, which was directed by John Ford, written by Reginald Berkeley, and starred Madeleine Carroll and Franchot Tone. ARTICLES, FILMS, PRODUCTION FILES, SCREENPLAYS

THE ROCKY ROAD TO DUBLIN. 1968.
Documentary. 75 minutes. Huston interviewed by Peter Lennon. Produced and directed by Peter Lennon. According to the *New York Times* (July 21, 1968) article by Gloria Emerson, the film was first shown in Paris, France, in May 1968. ARTICLES, PRODUCTION FILES

ROOTS OF HEAVEN. 1958.
Darryl F. Zanuck for Twentieth Century-Fox. 131 minutes. Screenplay by Romain Gary and Patrick Leigh-Fermor, from the novel by Romain Gary. Directed by John Huston, who also contributed to screenplay (uncredited). AMPAS, ARTICLES, FILMOGRAPHY, FILMS, PRODUCTION FILES, SCREENPLAYS

RUFINO TAMAYO: SOURCES OF HIS ART. 1972.
WCBS-TV (New York, Camera Three) and PBS. A film by Gary Conklin; Brockway Merrill, producer; Stephen Chodorov, director; Octavio Paz, writer; Carlos Chavez, composer; James MacAndrew, host; and John Huston, narrator. Televised on various dates. ARTICLES, FILMS

THE SAGA OF THE AMERICAN REVOLUTION. 1974.
Director. Unrealized project (?). Sam Thomas Productions. TV. In a (September 12, 1974) letter attached to the script to John Huston Sam Thomas revealed he was having problems getting CBS or ABC to allocate six hours' airtime to the project. George C. Scott was being lined up as the narrator. SCREENPLAYS

SAGA OF WESTERN MAN: CHRIST IS BORN. 1986.
ABC-TV. 60 minutes. Broadcast on March 25, 1986, at 8 P.M. Huston indicated as being in cast and voice. FILMS

SATURDAY NIGHT LIVE. 1972.
NBC-TV. Broadcast on March 12, 1972, at 11:30 P.M. John Huston appeared in a commercial for RCA Color Trak. FILMS

SERGEANT YORK. 1941.
Jesse Lasky and Hal Wallis for Warner Brothers. 134 minutes. Screenplay by Abem Finkel, Harry Chandlee, John Huston, and Howard Koch, based on *War Diary of Sergeant York* by Sam. K. Cowan, *Sergeant York and His People* by Sam K. Cowan, and *Sergeant York: Last of the Long Hunters* by Tom Skeyhill. Directed by Howard Hawks. ARTICLES, AWARDS, FILMOGRAPHY, FILMS, PRODUCTION FILES, SCREEN-PLAYS

THE SHAKEDOWN (*Fine Shakedown?*). 1929
(Released March 29 with talking sequences). Robert Wyler for Universal. Story and screenplay by Charles Logue and Clarence J. Marks.

Title and dialogue by Albert De Mond. Directed by William Wyler. Cast includes James Murray, Barbara Kent, George Kotsonaros, and John Huston (a bit part, uncredited; cf. *Film Dope*). *The American Film Institute Catalog: Feature Films, 1921–1930* does not list Huston. Nor is there any indication that *Fine Shakedown* was the alternate title. ARTICLES, PRODUCTION FILES, SCREENPLAYS

SHERLOCK HOLMES IN NEW YORK. 1976.
John Cutts for Twentieth Century-Fox/NBC-TV. Teleplay by Alvin Sapinsley, based on characters created by Sir Arthur Conan Doyle. Directed by Boris Sagal. Cast includes Roger Moore, Patrick MacNee, Charlotte Rampling, David Huddleston, and John Huston (Professor Moriarity). ARTICLES, FILMS, PRODUCTION FILES, SCREENPLAYS

SHIRLEY. 1967.
Unrealized project. Uninventoried part of the AMPAS Huston Archives includes a synopsis of E. V. Cunningham's *Shirley* (New York: Doubleday, 1964). From Ray Stark to John Huston (April 10, 1967): "I thought that it would be rather interesting for Barbra Streisand." AMPAS

SHOES OF THE FISHERMAN. 1968.
MGM. AMPAS 1965–66 contains correspondence and cables from George Englund (producer) that he sent the script to Huston and that he wanted to show Huston a revised script. Presumably Englund wanted Huston to direct. Script does not appear in Huston Collection. Credits at release: MGM release of George Englund Production. Directed by Michael Anderson. Screenplay by John Patrick and James Kennaway, based on the novel by Morris L. West. Camera, Erwin Hillier; editor, Ernest Walter; art director, George W. Davis. Cast includes Anthony Quinn, Laurence Olivier, Oskar Werner, David Janssen, Vittorio De Sica, Leo McKern, and John Gielgud. AMPAS, FILMS, PRODUCTION FILES, SCREENPLAYS

SINFUL DAVEY. 1969.
William N. Graf, John Huston, and Mirisch-Webb Productions. 95 minutes. Distributed by United Artists. Screenplay by James R. Webb, based on the diary *The Life of David Haggart* by David Haggart. Directed by John Huston, who also contributed to the screenplay (uncredited). AFI (*Catalog: Feature Films, 1961–1970*), AMPAS, ARTICLES, FILMOGRAPHY, FILMS, PRODUCTION FILES, SCREENPLAYS

SOAR ON EAGLE, OR MR. PRESIDENT. 1934.
Unrealized project. The USC Warner Brothers Archive contains treatments, memos, and other documentation regarding this project. PRODUCTION FILES, SCREENPLAYS

STEEL (working titles: *Men of Steel, Steel Man; Steel Men; Disaster; Record Month*).

Universal. Unproduced. While Huston was under contract as a writer at Universal (1929–32), he worked on treatments. FILMOGRAPHY, SCREEN-PLAYS

THE STORM. 1930 (released August 22 in New York City).

Universal. Screenplay by Wells Root and Charles Logue. Dialogue by Wells Root. Directed by William Wyler. Cast includes Lupe Velez, William Boyd, Paul Cavanaugh, and John Huston (a bit part, uncredited; cf. *Film Dope*). *The American Film Institute Catalog: Feature Films, 1921–1930* does not acknowledge Huston's involvement. ARTICLES, FILMS, PRODUC-TION FILES, SCREENPLAYS

THE STORY OF G.I. JOE (original title: *G.I. Joe*). 1945.

United Artists. 100 minutes. Produced by Lester Cowan and David Hall. Screenplay by Leopold Atlas, Guy Endore, and Philip Stevenson. Directed by William Wellman. Cast includes Burgess Meredith and Robert Mitchum. AMPAS material indicates Huston's involvement with this project as a writer, but there is no other evidence in the literature of his involvement. ARTICLES, FILMS, PRODUCTION FILES, SCREENPLAYS

THE STRANGER. 1946.

S. P. Eagle (Sam Spiegel) and William Goetz (executive producer) for International Pictures/RKO. 95 minutes. Screenplay by Anthony Veiller, based on a story by Victor Trivas and Decla Dunning, with John Huston and Orson Welles (uncredited writers). Directed by Orson Welles. *Film Dope* observes that being under contract to Warner Brothers, Huston did not receive credit on this film. ARTICLES, AWARDS, FILMOGRAPHY, FILMS, PRO-DUCTION FILES, SCREENPLAYS

SUPERSTAR PROFILE: JOHN HUSTON. 1982.

France. The BFI reports the film, Thames Television Transmission Company, September 16, 1982, in the United Kingdom.

TARAS BULBA. 1962.

UA/H-H/Avala. 124 minutes. Produced by Harold Hecht. Screenplay by Waldo Salt and Karl Tunberg. Directed by J. Lee-Thompson. AMPAS contains a cable to Huston from Eugene Frenke (May 28, 1958) in which Frenke indicated that he was working on the screenplay and wanted to know if Huston was interested. Huston responded that Frenke should discuss it with Paul Kohner, his agent, and asked, "Meanwhile what about Montezuma script query?" Credits at release: Hecht-UA. Producer, Harold Hecht; director, J. Lee Thompson. Screenplay by Waldo Salt and Karl Tunberg, based on the Nikolai Gogol novel. Photography, Joseph MacDonald; art direction, Edward Carrere; film editor, William Reynolds. Cast includes Tony Curtis, Yul

Brynner, Christine Kaufmann, Sam Wanamaker, and Brad Dexter. AMPAS, FILMS, PRODUCTION FILES, SCREENPLAYS

TENTACLES (*Tentacoli*). 1977.
Samuel Z. Arkoff presents an Ovidio Assonitis Film. An American International Release. Executive producer, Ovidio Assonitis*; producer, Enzo Dioria; director, Oliver Hellman.* Written by Jerome Max, Tito Carpi, and Steve Carabatsos. Director of photography, Roberto D'Ettore Piazzoli; art director, M. Spring; film editor, A. J. Curi. Cast includes John Huston (Ned Turner), Shelley Winters, Bo Hopkins, Henry Fonda, Delia Boccardo, Cesare Danova, Alan Boyd, and Claude Akins.

Note. *Indications are that Ovidio Assonitis and Oliver Hellman are the same person. ARTICLES, FILMS, PRODUCTION FILES, SCREENPLAYS

A TERRIBLE BEAUTY (other title: *Night Fighters*). 1968–69.
File located in AMPAS (uncataloged material, box 3) includes correspondence and other information reflecting Huston's interest in doing a film on the Irish uprising of 1916, inspired by William Butler Yeats's poem "Easter 1916." A screenplay was to be written by Gerald Hanley, who developed some treatments (not located in the Huston Collection). *Cinemaforum* (December 1987) includes as an unrealized project. AMPAS, PRODUCTION FILES

THEODOSIA: EMPRESS OF AMERICA. *See* PRELUDE TO FREEDOM.

THE THIRD SECRET.
Writer. Unproduced. A *New York Times* (April 10, 1949) article indicates that after *We Were Strangers,* Sam Spiegel was ready for a second project: *The Third Secret,* based on Fyodor Dostoevsky's *The Eternal Husband.* Lewis Milestone would direct and "Ben Hecht and John Huston worked on the script." No other information on this project is in the literature or archives.

THIS PROPERTY IS CONDEMNED. 1966.
Paramount/Seven Arts/Ray Stark.* *Cineforum* (December 1987) reported that Huston may have been considered as the director. No information in AMPAS. Credits at release: Paramount Pictures release of a Seven Arts–Ray Stark presentation. Produced by John Houseman. Screenplay by Francis Ford Coppola, Fred Coe, and Edith Sommer, suggested by a one-act play by Tennessee Williams. Camera, James Wong Howe. Cast includes Natalie Wood, Robert Redford, Charles Bronson, and Kate Reid.

Note. *Appears to have been originally a Warner product that then went to Paramount. FILMS, PRODUCTION FILES, SCREENPLAYS

THREE STRANGERS. 1946.
Produced by Wolfgang Reinhardt for Warner Brothers. 92 minutes. Screenplay by John Huston and Howard Koch, based on a story John Huston wrote in 1936. Directed by Jean Negulesco. ARTICLES, FILMOGRAPHY, FILMS, PRODUCTION FILES, SCREENPLAYS

TOWARDS DEATH. 1933, 1947.
Unrealized project. The USC Warner Brothers Archive contains treatments, memos, and other documentation regarding this project. PRODUCTION FILES, SCREENPLAYS

TOMORROW THE WORLD. 1944.
AMPAS includes a version of the screenplay by Ring Lardner Jr. No other indication of Huston involvement. Credits at release: Directed by Leslie Fenton. Screenplay by Ring Lardner Jr. and Leopold Atlas, from the stage play by James Gow and Arnaud D'Usseau. Cinematographer, Henry Sharp. Cast includes Fredric March, Betty Field, Agnes Moorehead, Skip Homeier, and Joan Carroll. AMPAS, ARTICLES, FILMS, PRODUCTION FILES, SCREENPLAYS

TO THE WESTERN WORLD. 1981.
Documentary. United Kingdom. Directed by Margy Kinmonth. Huston narrates. ARTICLES, FILMS

THE TREASURE OF THE SIERRA MADRE. 1948.
Henry Blanke for Warner Brothers. 126 minutes. Screenplay by John Huston, from the novel by B. Traven. Directed by Huston, who also had an uncredited acting role at beginning of film (Tourist in White Suit). AMPAS, ARTICLES, AWARDS, FILMOGRAPHY, FILMS, PRODUCTION FILES, SCREENPLAYS

TUNISIAN VICTORY. 1943.
55, 76 minutes (*see Meet Frank Capra: A Catalog of His Work,* Washington, D.C., Smithsonian Institute, 1990, catalog no. 070; and *Film Dope*). Huston directed some replacement scenes when footage was lost, provided co-commentary, and contributed screenwriting with J. L. Hodson, Capt. Anthony Veiller, Capt. Roy Boulting, and Capt. Alfred Black. Credits from a *New York Times* review (March 24, 1944): *Tunisian Victory,* a documentary film presented by the U.S. and British governments; filmed by British and U.S. Army Film units; produced and directed by Lt. Col. Hugh Stewart of the Royal Army Film Unit and Lt. Col. Frank Capra, U.S. Army Signal Corps. Written by J. L. Hodson and Capt. Anthony Veiller; commentary spoken by Lt. Col. Leo Genn, British Army Film Unit, and Capt. Anthony Veiller. Commentary by British Tommy and American Doughboy spoken by Bernard Miles and Burgess Meredith, respectively. Distributed by the British Ministry of Information and released by MGM. *Variety* (March 7, 1944) credits: War

documentary. Metro release of feature-length official film record produced by British and U.S. Service Film units. Assembled and edited under direction of Col. Frank Capra, U.S.A., and Lt. Col. Hugh Stewart, British Northwest African Film Unit. Script prepared by J. L. Hodson, Capt. Roy Boulting, and Capt. Alfred Black of Great Britain, and Maj. Tony Veiller and Capt. John Huston for the U.S. Army. Photographed by fifty cameramen of the armed forces and two hundred other film technicians from various branches of British and U.S. services. Reviewed at Metro Studios on March 6, 1944. ARTICLES, FILMS, PRODUCTION FILES

TURN OF THE SCREW. 1942.
Unrealized project. The USC Warner Brothers Archive has an information card on Huston's screenwriting and other related activity. An entry indicates: "4/15/42, sc'play (unfin.) (from Henry James book)." Annotation on card reads "NIF [i.e., No Synopsis in Filing Cabinet]."

TWO AMERICANS. 1929.
Paramount (Famous Lasky). Directed by John Meehan or Joseph Santley. Screenplay by John Meehan. Cast includes Walter Huston and John Huston. (Cf. Lawrence Grobel, *The Hustons,* New York, Scribners, 1989, 133: this film was Huston's first acting role, although *The Shakedown* may have been the first.) *Film Dope* also indicates that some sources suggest that the director of this film was Joseph Santley. *The American Film Institute Catalog: Feature Films, 1921–1930* has no listing for this film. SCREENPLAYS

TYPEE. 1956–57.
Allied Artists. Director. Unproduced. AMPAS indicates that Huston was designated as the director. Preproduction work started and Gregory Peck was considered for the lead, but the project was indefinitely postponed in May 1957. As late as February 1962, Huston still seemed interested. Script material included. AMPAS, PRODUCTION FILES, SCREENPLAYS

U-BOAT.
Universal.* Unproduced. Universal inventory in AMPAS lists the original story by John Huston, June 7, 1932.

Note. *Per Gerald Prately's *The Cinema of John Huston* (New York: A. S. Barnes & Co.; London: The Tantivy Press, 1977, 27), Huston worked a short period of time for Goldwyn before going to Universal and recalled that Goldwyn wanted him to work on a project about German submarines. FILMOGRAPHY, SCREENPLAYS

UNDERGROUND. 1941.
Warner Brothers. Writing assignment, with Guy Endore, from August 14, 1939, until August 31, 1939. Writer of credit, Charles Grayson; director, Vincent Sherman; photography, Sid Hickox; music, Adolph Deutsch. Cast

493

includes Jeffrey Lynn, Philip Dorn, Karen Verne, Mona Maris, Frank Reicher, Martin Kosleck, and Ilka Gruning. ARTICLES, FILMS, SCREEN-PLAYS

UNDER THE VOLCANO. 1984.
Moritz Borman and Wieland Schulz-Keil for Ithaca-Conacine. A Universal release. 109 minutes. Screenplay by Guy Gallo, based on the novel by Malcolm Lowry. Directed by John Huston, who also contributed to the screenplay (uncredited). ARTICLES, AWARDS, FILMS, PRODUCTION FILES, SCREENPLAYS

THE UNFORGIVEN. 1960.
James Hill for Hecht-Hill-Lancaster. Distributed by United Artists. 125 minutes. Screenplay by Ben Maddow, from the novel by Alan LeMay. Directed by John Huston, who also contributed to the screenplay (uncredited). AMPAS, ARTICLES, FILMOGRAPHY, FILMS, PRODUCTION FILES, SCREENPLAYS

UNITED IN PROGRESS. 1963.
Directed by Charles Guggenheim for the U.S. Information Agency. Huston narrates. FILMS

VICTORY (*Escape to Victory*). 1981.
Freddie Fields for Paramount. 110 minutes. Screenplay by Evan Jones and Yabo Yablonsky, from a story by Yabo Yablonsky, Djordje Milicevic, and Jeff Maguire. Directed by John Huston, who also contributed to the screenplay (uncredited). AMPAS, FILMOGRAPHY, FILMS, PRODUC-TION FILES, SCREENPLAYS

THE VISITOR (*Il Visitore/Stridulum*). Italy. 1980.
Ovidio Assonitis for International Picture Show Co. 103 minutes. Directed by Michael J. Paradise (Giulio Paradisi). Cast includes Mel Ferrer, Glenn Ford, John Huston (Jersey Colsowitz, the visitor), Sam Peckinpah, and Shelley Winters. *Film Dope* indicates that some sources cite Jules Paradise as the director. Stephen Cooper, in *Perspectives on John Huston* (New York: G.K. Hall, 1994), lists Michael J. Paradise as the director. ARTICLES, FILMS, PRODUCTION FILES, SCREENPLAYS

WALKING WITH LOVE AND DEATH (in the United Kingdom: *The Making of A Walk with Love and Death* [also known as *Ride This Way, Gray Horse*]). 1968.
Directed by Paul Joyce. Knight Films. 5 minutes. 16mm film. Per the Library of Congress cataloging the film shows John Huston at work in Austria directing the motion picture *A Walk With Love and Death*. Shows Huston working with Anjelica Huston and Assaf Dayan. In the Twentieth Century-

Fox Film Collection of the American Film Institute Collection, Library of Congress. FILMS

A WALK WITH LOVE AND DEATH. 1969.
    Carter De Haven and John Huston. Distributed by Twentieth Century-Fox. Screenplay by Dale Wasserman, from the novel by Hans Koningsberger. Adaptation by Hans Koningsberger. Directed by John Huston, who also contributed to the screenplay (uncredited). AFI (*Catalog: Feature Films, 1961–1970*), AMPAS, ARTICLES, AWARDS, FILMOGRAPHY, FILMS, PRODUCTION FILES, SCREENPLAYS

WATCH ON THE RHINE. 1943.
    Warner Brothers. 114 minutes. Produced by Hal B. Wallis. Screenplay by Dashiell Hammett from the stage play by Lillian Hellman. Directed by Herman Shumlin. Cast includes Paul Lukas and Bette Davis. A. M. Sperber and Eric Lax's *Bogart* (New York: Morrow, 1997, 180–82) indicates Huston's interest in doing the film after *The Maltese Falcon* (1941). The USC Jack Warner Collection indicates some possible interest in his writing and directing this film.

WATERLOO. 1970.
    A Paramount Picture, Dino De Laurentiis Presents. 123 minutes. Director, Sergei Bondarchuk. Story and screenplay by H. A. L. Craig. Screenplay collaboration, Sergei Bondarchuk and Vittorio Bonicelli. Music by Nino Rota, edited by Richard C. Meyer, and designed by Mario Garbuglia. Cast includes Rod Steiger, Christopher Plummer, Orson Welles, Jack Hawkins, Virginia McKenna, Dan O'Herlihy, Ian Ogilvy, Michael Wilding, and Rupert Davies. AMPAS shows that Huston was designated as the director in 1967 or 1968, and the file contains information on script development and preproduction. According to Lawrence Grobel (*The Hustons*, New York, Scribners, 1989, 574), "The project fell through when the Russians agreed to finance it on the condition that a Russian direct." Includes script material. AMPAS, FILMS, PRODUCTION FILES, SCREENPLAYS

WE WERE STRANGERS (*Les Insurges*). 1949.
    S. P. Eagle (Sam Spiegel) and Horizon for Columbia. 106 minutes. Screenplay by Peter Viertel and John Huston, from an episode in the novel, *Rough Sketch*, by Robert Sylvester. Directed by John Huston, who also had a bit part (Bank Clerk, uncredited). AMPAS, ARTICLES, FILMOGRAPHY, FILMS, PRODUCTION FILES, SCREENPLAYS

WHITE HUNTER, BLACK HEART. 1990.
    Clint Eastwood. 112 minutes. Eastwood as Huston in the fictionalized account of the making of *The African Queen*, based on Peter Viertel's 1953 novel of the same name. Credits at release: Warner Brothers presents a Malpaso/Rastar Production. Directed and produced by Clint Eastwood.

Screenplay by Peter Viertel, James Bridges, and Burt Kennedy, based on the novel by Peter Viertel. Executive producer, David Valdes; director of photography, Jack N. Green; editor, Joel Cox; production designer, John Graysmark. Cast includes Clint Eastwood (the Huston character), Jeff Fahey, George Dzundza, Alun Armstrong, Marisa Berenson, Timothy Spall, and Mel Martin. ARTICLES, FILMS, PRODUCTION FILES, SCREENPLAYS

WHO WAS THAT LADY? 1960.

Unrealized project (?). AMPAS includes script material; otherwise, no other indication of Huston's involvement. Credits at release: Columbia Pictures. Producer, Norman Krasna; director, George Sidney. Screenplay by Norman Krasna, based on Krasna's play *Who Was That Lady I Saw You With?* Assistant director, David Silver; music, Andre Previn; photography, Harry Stradling; editing, Viola Lawrence; art direction, Edward Haworth. Cast includes Tony Curtis, Dean Martin, Janet Leigh, James Whitmore, John McIntire, and Barbara Nichols. FILMS, PRODUCTION FILES, SCREEN-PLAYS

WILD BOYS OF THE ROAD. 1933.

Warner Brothers. Screenplay by Earl Baldwin. Story by Daniel Ahearn, and Cyril Hume contributed to treatment. Directed by William Wellman. Cast includes Frankie Darro, Edwin Phillips, Rochelle Hudson, Dorothy Coonan, Sterling Holloway, Ann Hovey, Arthur Hohl, Grant Mitchell, and Ward Bond. John Huston and William Wyler worked on versions when at Universal (cf. information under *Forgotten Boy* for various possible versions). Axel Madsen, in *William Wyler: The Authorized Biography* (New York: Crowell, 1973, 83), notes that after *Laughing Boy* Wyler and Huston started working on the Universal property, Daniel Ahearn's *The Wild Boys of the Road,* which was then sold to First National. ARTICLES, FILMS, PRODUCTION FILES, SCREENPLAYS

WILL ADAMS. 1965–66.

Director. Unrealized. Paramount. AMPAS includes extensive correspondence on Huston's involvement, such as a long letter from Huston to Jules Buck (presumably producer) regarding some serious disagreements and accusations regarding Huston's seriousness on the project. (Cf. also Lawrence Grobel, *The Hustons,* New York, Scribners, 1989, 564, 568–70.) Script material included. AMPAS, PRODUCTION FILES, SCREENPLAYS

THE WIND AND THE LION. 1975.

MGM/UA. A Herb Jaffe Production. Written and directed by John Milius, produced by Herb Jaffe, photography by Billy Williams, edited by Robert L. Wolfe, production design by Gil Parrando, art directed by R. Antonio Paton. Cast includes Sean Connery, Candice Bergen, Brian Keith, and John Huston (John Hay). ARTICLES, FILMS, PRODUCTION FILES, SCREENPLAYS

WINTER KILLS. 1979.
    Fred Caruso for Avco Embassy/Richert International. 79 minutes. Directed by William Richert. Screenplay by Richert from Richard Condon's screenplay. Cast includes Jeff Bridges, John Huston (Pa Kegan), Anthony Perkins, Sterling Hayden, Dorothy Malone, and Elizabeth Taylor. AMPAS, ARTICLES, FILMOGRAPHY, FILMS, PRODUCTION FILES, SCREENPLAYS

WISE BLOOD (*Le Malin*). 1979.
    An Ithaca-Anthea Co-Production. Released through New Line Cinema. 108 minutes. Produced by Michael Fitzgerald and Kathy Fitzgerald. Screenplay by Benedict Fitzgerald and Michael Fitzgerald, based on the novel by Flannery O'Connor. John Huston served as director, an actor (The Grandfather), and a contributor to the screenplay (uncredited). At the beginning of the film, "John" is spelled "Jhon"—that is, "Jhon Huston's Wise Blood," "Jhon Huston as Grandfather," and "Directed by Jhon Huston." AMPAS, ARTICLES, AWARDS, FILMOGRAPHY, FILMS, PRODUCTION FILES, SCREENPLAYS

WOODROW WILSON. *See* IN TIME TO COME.

THE WORD. 1978.
    David Manson for CBS-TV/Charles Fries Productions/Stonehenge. 188 minutes. Teleplay by Dick Berg, Robert L. Joseph, S. S. Schweitzer, and Richard Fiedler, from the novel by Irving Wallace. Directed by Richard Lang. Serialized. Cast includes David Janssen, James Whitmore, Florinda Bolkan, Eddie Albert, John Huston (Reverend Randall), Geraldine Chaplin, Hurt Hatfield, Nicol Williamson, and Donald Moffett. ARTICLES, FILMS, PRODUCTION FILES, SCREENPLAYS

WORKING WITH ORSON WELLES. 1993.
    A film by Gary Graver. Produced by Sidney Niekirk. Issued on video in 1995. Gary Graver was Welles's longtime cameraman. Much of the documentary is about the making of *The Other Side of the Wind*. Huston appears in some still shots, and some of the people interviewed talk about the Welles-Huston relationship. No clips of the film are in this documentary. FILMS

THE WORLD MOVES ON. *See* THE ROARING TWENTIES.

WUTHERING HEIGHTS. 1939.
    Produced by Samuel Goldwyn, released by United Artists. Director, William Wyler; producer, Samuel Goldwyn. Screenplay by Ben Hecht and Charles MacArthur, from the novel by Emily Brontë. Photographer, Gregg Toland; editor, Daniel Mandel; musical director, Alfred Newman. Cast includes Laurence Olivier, Merle Oberon, David Niven, Hugh Williams, Flora Robson, Geraldine Fitzgerald, Donald Crisp, Leo G. Carroll, Cecil Kellaway, and Miles Mander. AMPAS includes script material. *The American Film*

Institute Catalog: Feature Films, 1931–1940 lists Huston as contributing writer (uncredited). ARTICLES, FILMS, PRODUCTION FILES, SCREEN-PLAYS

YOUNG GIANTS. *See* A MINOR MIRACLE.

ADDITIONAL MATERIAL IN AMPAS

MISCELLANEOUS STORIES AND SCRIPTS

During research on this material the authors were able to identify some materials, and they have been moved to titled parts of the collection.

"The Ascension," by John Huston, n.d., twelve pages (two copies). Play script.

"Casey Jones," by Dorothy Huston, n.d., twelve pages. A play script by Huston's first wife.

"The Dancing Spy," n.d. Story or treatment in same folder as "The Sad Tourists." WWI theme.

"Life's Fourth Round Table, The Tables," 1949. Contains a file that includes a fifty-page transcript with a cover letter from Eric Hodgins (June 6, 1949), saying this script is the first draft of a discussion. Huston is in the dialogue (pp. 10–11), discussing business aspects "Art and Dollar." Copies of the draft also went to Robert Rossen, Dore Schary, Jerry Wald, and Hal B. Wallis.

"A Return Engagement," n.d., five pages. Beginnings of a play with possible connection to "The Sad Tourists," in same folder and also deals with expatriates in Paris.

"The Sad Tourists," various treatments on play script or movie, n.d., various paging, including handwritten notes.

"The Seventh Cavalry," January 18, 19??, four-page treatment.

"Shadow Pursuing: A Dramatization" by John Huston, based on Hugh Walpole's novel, *Above the Dark Tumult,* n.d., various paging. Play script with some handwritten annotations on the back of the last page. Another version only includes a revised first act, which is heavily annotated and revised, n.d., various paging.

UNTITLED MATERIAL

Two versions of a story idea, with characters Mr. Dash and Captain.

Treatment about "Little Band of Mummers" during the English Restoration, n.d., four pages and two pages of dialogue.

Six-page treatment about bike racers.

Four-page treatment about the Greek gods and the Irish.

Seventeen-page treatment about Kentucky boys and a health farm.

Untitled script in two parts, n.d., v.p. At top of first section (pp. 1 and 3): Roosevelt; at top of second section: Coolidge.

Untitled full-length script on the Depression, n.d., v.p., highly annotated. This script may be a version of *Wild Boys of the Road* (1933).

File of correspondence, various treatments, and version of a story by Ruth Marton and John Huston, to be sold to a studio, about a magician who lives vicariously through a young acrobat. 1944.

An idea for a "deep" film, script "untitled," that would remain untitled and without credits since no title seemed adequate and credits seemed inappropriate to the purpose for which it is made. Script on world events starts with the death of Franklin Delano Roosevelt and includes Harry S Truman, Winston Churchill, the United Nations, Joseph Stalin, and Los Alamos; n.d., twenty-two pages.

Untitled play script by John Huston and Sam Jaffe, n.d., eighty-two pages. Action takes place in the Mallocks' home studio in Andalusia, Spain.

Stories by Dorothy Harvey (Huston's first wife) and correspondence with Huston asking his opinions on whether there are movies in them.

MISCELLANEOUS TITLED STORIES

Stories by John Huston: "Hopadeen," March 1, 1962, eight pages; and "Toward Death," n.d., fifteen pages (another copy with Paul Kohner on cover).

"Host of Ghosties" by Rhea Stevens (Huston's mother), n.d., seventy-one pages.

"Polly and Al" by E. Leahny, screenplay treatment, thirty-nine pages.

Letter to John Huston from Larry White, NBC, September 19, 1957, with outlines of Saki stories available for television.

Miscellaneous titled stories: "Don Quixote," treatment, n.d., thirty-five pages.

MISATTRIBUTIONS

"Huston, John, 1906–. 'Meditations on the Seven Last Words of Christ': for organ. New York, H. W. Gray Co.: agents for Novello, 1956." *Comment:* The cataloger at the institution attributed this to the film director John Huston. Another John Huston (1915–75) wrote the composition.

"The Two Gentlemen of Verona." 1983. Produced by BBC Television in association with Time-Life Television. New York, Time-Life Video. *Comment:* John

Huston is listed as one of the performers, when in actuality the actor was John Hudson.

Boy and the Bridge. 1959. United Kingdom. IMDB, one of the big movie web sites, indicates that Huston was an actor in this film, but this source is the only one that lists Huston as connected with this film. *Halliwell's Film Guide* (1996) has no indication of his involvement; *Variety* (August 5, 1959) does not list Huston in the cast, credited or uncredited; and *The All Movie Guide,* a CD-ROM, makes no mention of Huston. (Interestingly, Royal Dano, who was in *The Red Badge of Courage* [1951] was in *Boy and the Bridge,* but that is a stretch.)

XV
Awards and Honors

INDIVIDUAL

The American Film Institute's Life Achievement Awards: John Huston. 1983.

The Directors Guild Series: John Huston. 1982. Full weekend tribute to Huston by the DGA, May 1982.

John Huston Award for Artists' Rights. In March 1993, Anjelica, Danny, and Tony Huston joined with the Artists Rights Foundation to establish the John Huston Award for Artists' Rights. The award commemorated their father's career and honors an individual or organization that shows courage, artistic integrity, and efforts on behalf of artists' rights. The annual awards have been awarded to Fred Zinnemann, 1994; Steven Spielberg, 1995; Martin Scorsese, 1996; and Milos Forman, 1997.

John Huston Retrospective. Columbia II Theater, New York City, 1972.

The International Film Guide Directors of the Year Awards. 1974. Huston named with four other directors.

Live from Lincoln Center, the Film Society of Lincoln Center's "A Tribute to John Huston." Monday, May 5, 1980, 8:30 P.M. to 10:00 P.M., PBS.

Los Angeles County Museum of Art: The Films of John Huston. 1980. A retrospective of his films.

National Archives and Records Service, Washington, D.C.: Films at the Archives—A Salute to John Huston. 1971.

San Francisco International Film Festival, Twelfth Annual. 1969. Huston as honored guest.

Writers Guild of America: Laurel Award. 1964.

SPECIFIC FILMS

ACROSS THE PACIFIC
National Board of Review/D. W. Griffith Awards (1942): Acting, Sydney Greenstreet.

THE AFRICAN QUEEN
Academy Awards (1951): Humphrey Bogart, Best Actor; Katharine Hepburn, nominated, Best Actress; John Huston, nominated, Best Director; Huston and James Agee, nominated, Best Screenplay.

Time Magazine (1952): among twelve best films of the year.

Broadcast Information Bureau "Best Ever" Survey of Film Executives (1975): sixteenth best film ever.

American Film Institute "Best Ever" Survey (1977): among ten best American films ever.

AGEE
Academy Awards (1980), nomination: Best Feature Documentary.

ANNIE
Academy Awards (1983), nominations: Art and Set Direction.

ASPHALT JUNGLE
Academy Awards (1951), Nominations: Sam Jaffe, Best Supporting Actor; John Huston, Director; Ben Maddow and Huston, Best Screenplay; Harold Rosson, Cinematography.

National Board of Review/D. W. Griffith Awards (1950): John Huston, Best Director; Third Best American Film.

New York Times (1950): fourth best film.

Venice Film Festival Awards (1950): Sam Jaffe, Best Actor.

Director's Guild of America (1950–51): Quarterly Award to John Huston.

Mystery Writers of America (1950): Best Mystery Motion Picture, "Edgar."

BEAT THE DEVIL
National Board of Review/D. W. Griffith Awards (1954): Tenth Best Film.

Time Annual Ten Best List (1954).

THE BIBLE . . . IN THE BEGINNING
National Board of Review/D. W. Griffith Awards (1966): Fifth Best English-Language Film.

David Di Donatello Prizes ("Italian Oscars," 1965–66): Best Film; John Huston, Foreign Director.

THE CARDINAL
Academy Awards (1963), nomination: John Huston, Best Supporting Actor.

Golden Globe/Hollywood Foreign Press Association Awards (1963): John Huston, Best Supporting Actor.

THE DEAD
Academy Awards (1987), nomination: Tony Huston, Best Adapted Screenplay.

National Society of Film Critics Awards (1987): Best Film.

New York Times Annual Ten Best List (1987).

British Film Critics' Circle Award (1988): John Huston, Director.

The Independent Spirit Awards (The Indies, 1987): John Huston, Director; Anjelica Huston, Supporting Actress.

DR. EHRLICH'S MAGIC BULLET
Academy Awards (1940), nomination: John Huston, Heinz Herald, and Norman Burnside, Best Writing, Original Screenplay.

FAT CITY
Academy Awards (1972), nomination: Susan Tyrell, Best Supporting Actress.

New York Times Annual Ten Best List (1972).

Take One, the magazine's "Best of the Decade" Survey: twenty-first best American film (tie).

FREUD: THE SECRET PASSION
Academy Awards (1962), nomination: Charles Kaufman and Wolfgang Reinhardt, Best Story and Screenplay.

New York Times Annual Ten Best List (1962): ninth best film.

HEAVEN KNOWS, MR. ALLISON
Academy Awards (1957), nominations: Deborah Kerr, Best Actress; John Lee Mahin and John Huston, Best Screenplay Based on Material from Another Medium.

New York Film Critics Circle Awards (1957): Deborah Kerr, Best Actress.

HIGH SIERRA
National Board of Review/D. W. Griffith Awards (1941): Sixth Best American Film; Humphrey Bogart, Acting Award (shared); Ida Lupino, Acting Award (shared).

IN THIS OUR LIFE
National Board Review/D. W. Griffith Awards (1942): Acting awards for Ernest Anderson, Charles Coburn, and Hattie McDaniel.

JEZEBEL
Academy Awards (1938): Bette Davis, Best Actress; Fay Bainter, Best Supporting Actress; Best Film, nominated.

National Board of Review/D. W. Griffith Awards (1938): Eighth Best English-Language Film.

Venice Film Festival Awards (1938): Special Mention for Artistic Ensemble.

JUAREZ
Academy Awards (1939), nomination: Brian Aherne, Best Supporting Actor.

New York Times Annual Ten Best List (1939): fifth best film.

KEY LARGO
Academy Awards (1948): Claire Trevor, Best Supporting Actress.

THE KILLERS
Academy Awards (1946), nominations: Robert Siodmak, Best Director; Anthony Veiller, Best Screenplay.

National Board of Review/D. W. Griffith Awards (1946): Ninth Best Film.

Time (1946): 10 Best List.

THE MALTESE FALCON
Academy Awards (1941), nominations: Best Film; Sydney Greenstreet, Best Supporting Actor; John Huston, Best Screenplay.

National Board of Review/D. W. Griffith Awards (1941): Humphrey Bogart, Acting Award.

University of Southern California Performing Arts Council's "Most Significant American Films" Survey (1972): thirty-third most significant American film ever.

Broadcast Information Bureau "Best Ever" Survey of Film Executives (1975): tenth best film.

American Film Institute "Best Ever" Survey (1977): fiftieth best American film ever.

THE MAN WHO WOULD BE KING
Academy Awards (1975), nomination: John Huston and Gladys Hill, Best Screenplay Adapted from Other Material.

Time (1975): 10 Best List.

Take One (1978): seventeenth best American film of the decade.

MOBY DICK
National Board of Review/D. W. Griffith Awards (1956): John Huston, Best Director; Richard Basehart, Best Supporting Actor; Second Best American Film.

New York Film Critics (1956): John Huston, Best Direction.

New York Times Annual Ten Best List (1956): third best film.

Nastri D'Argento (Silver Ribbons, Italy, 1956): John Huston, Best Foreign Director.

Thomas Alva Edison Foundation Award (1956): "The Film Best Serving the National Interest."

Film Daily poll (1956): sixth of the "ten best pictures."

MOULIN ROUGE
Academy Awards (1952): Marcel Vertes, Best Color Costume Design. Nominations: Best Picture; John Huston, Best Director; José Ferrer, Best Actor; Colette Marchand, Best Supporting Actress.

Golden Globe Awards (1952): Colette Marchand, Most Promising Newcomers.

Time (1952): among Twelve Best Films of the Year.

National Board of Review/D. W. Griffith Awards (1953): Second Best Foreign Film.

New York Times (1953): Best Film of the Year.

Venice Film Festival (1953): Silver Prize.

THE NIGHT OF THE IGUANA
Academy Awards (1964): Dorothy Jeakins, Best Black and White Costume Design. Nomination: Grayson Hall, Best Supporting Actress.

Writers Guild (1964): Screenplay, one of five best.

PRIZZI'S HONOR
Academy Awards (1985): Anjelica Huston, Best Supporting Actress. Nominations: Best Film; John Huston, Best Direction; Jack Nicholson, Best Actor; William Hickey, Best Supporting Actor; Richard Condon and Janet Roach, Best Adapted Screenplay.

Golden Globe Awards (1985): Best Musical/Comedy; John Huston, Best Director; Jack Nicholson, Best Actor.

Los Angeles Film Critics Circle Awards (1958): Anjelica Huston, Best Supporting Actress.

National Board of Review/ D. W. Griffith Awards (1985): Sixth Best English-Language Film; Anjelica Huston, Best Supporting Actress.

National Society of Film Critics (1985): John Huston, Best Director; Jack Nicholson, Best Actor; Anjelica Huston, Best Supporting Actress.

New York Film Critics Circle (1985): Best Film; John Huston, Best Director; Jack Nicholson, Best Actor; Anjelica Huston, Best Supporting Actress.

New York Times (1985): 10 Best List.

Time (1985): 10 Best Films of the Year.

Time (1989): 10 Best List of the Decade.

Writers Guild of America (1985): Richard Condon and Janet Roach, Best Adapted Screenplay.

THE RED BADGE OF COURAGE
National Board of Review/D. W. Griffith Awards (1951): Second Best American Film of the Year.

Time (1951): Annual Ten Best List.

SERGEANT YORK
Academy Awards (1941): Gary Cooper, Best Actor; William Holmes, Best Film Editing. Nominations: Best Film; Howard Hawks, Best Director; Walter Brennan, Best Supporting Actor; Margaret Wycherly, Best Supporting Actress; Abem Finkel, Harry Chandlee, Howard Koch, and John Huston, Best Original Screenplay.

National Board of Review/D. W. Griffith Awards (1941): Gary Cooper, Acting Award.

New York Film Critics Circle Awards (1941): Gary Cooper, Best Actor.

New York Times (1941): fourth best film.

THE STRANGER
Academy Awards (1947), nomination: Victor Trivas, Writing (Original Story).

THE TREASURE OF THE SIERRA MADRE
Academy Awards (1948): John Huston, Best Director; Walter Huston, Best Supporting Actor; John Huston, Best Screenplay. Nomination: Best Film.

National Board of Review/D. W. Griffith Awards (1948): Walter Huston, Best Actor; John Huston, Best Script; Fourth Best Film of the Year.

Golden Globe Awards (1948): Best Drama; John Huston, Best Director; Walter Huston, Best Supporting Actor.

New York Film Critics Circle Awards (1948): Best Film; John Huston, Best Director.

New York Times (1948): Best Film of the Year.

Venice Film Festival Awards (1948): Max Steiner, Best Music.

Writers Guild of America/Screen Writers Guild of America Awards (1948): John Huston, Best-Written American Western.

University of Southern California Performing Arts Council's "Most Significant American Films" Survey (1972): eleventh most significant American film ever.

American Film Institute "Best Ever" Survey (1977): fiftieth best American film ever.

UNDER THE VOLCANO
Academy Awards (1984), nomination: Albert Finney, Best Actor.

Los Angeles Film Critics Circle Awards (1984): Albert Finney, Best Actor.

National Board of Review/D. W. Griffith Awards (1984): Tenth Best English-Language Film.

A WALK WITH LOVE AND DEATH
Association of French Film Critics and the Theatre of Arts and Experiment "Best Ever" Survey (1975): forty-fifth best film ever.

WISE BLOOD
New York Film Festival (1979).

New York Times Annual Ten Best List (1980).

Time (1980): Annual Ten Best List.

XVI

Screenplays in Collections

"In line with this, I can't ever remember having directed a picture on which I did not work on the screenplay. . . . The point is that my working on a script is expected of me as part of my duties."
—Letter from John Huston to Paul Kohner (Huston's long-term agent), February 6, 1971 (AMPAS John Huston Collection, Production Files: *The Last Run*).

Most bibliographies and inventories of screenplays (see chapter 24, "Bibliographical and Reference Sources") list titles without any indication of which versions are housed in the particular institution. Screenplay development involves numerous versions and revisions before the final product. At times various writers are involved in the screenplay's development, and in many cases the final credits for screenwriting as they appear in the released film do not reflect all of the writers involved. Sometimes this issue becomes contentious, and arbitration before the Writers Guild is necessary to determine credits on the film. Huston had his share of these disputes, one example being *Moby Dick* (1956), in which a certain version of the script indicates Huston's contributions, Bradbury's, and so on, because of the apparent conflict.

This chapter provides details from various collections on films both produced and unproduced with which Huston was involved. In virtually all cases each screenplay was examined and cataloged. In some cases this work was not possible, and as much information as was provided is indicated. This inventory will allow researchers to pursue Huston's involvement in screenplay development. It also provides means of examining his thinking as the project progressed, and the influence of his thinking on others as they took on the project. We might even speculate as to the form of the film had it been completed under Huston's direction (*The Last Run* [1971], for example). As some of the Huston-related films are not readily available the screenplay also gives people an idea of a film's content.

Included are both realized and unrealized films that Huston was involved with as a writer, a director, and an actor. In the instances where his role was solely as an actor, the corresponding scripts give researchers the opportunity to observe the Huston character evolving, as in many instances the role was specifically written for him, and the character represents the Huston persona to some extent.

In this inventory the screenplays are arranged alphabetically by project title. If the screenplay (usually the final version, but not in all cases) is available in published form, it is followed by the institution and the unpublished versions that are available. In some cases two or more institutions have the same version, but they may have subtle differences, because even after the supposed issuance of the final version, there may have been script changes and additions up to and into the actual shooting of the film.

Note that in virtually all instances screenplays are housed in the special collections areas of the library, which may have strict restrictions on photoduplication but none on transcribing pages of the script by hand or by computer. In at least one instance, at the University of California, Santa Barbara (UCSB), Davidson Library, the screenplay, even in unpublished format, circulates and is even available through interlibrary loan. Unpublished scripts are available from services like Script City (see chapter 24, "Bibliographical and Reference Sources," for their address).

ACROSS THE PACIFIC. 1942.

Warner Brothers. Produced by Jerry Wald and Jack Saper. Screenplay by Richard Macaulay, from the *Saturday Evening Post* serial by Robert Carson. Directed by John Huston.

AMPAS. JOHN HUSTON COLLECTION. SCRIPT MATERIAL.

1. No title page (t.p.). *Cover sheet: Across the Pacific.* Temporary, Part I, 1/13/42. (No indication of other parts.) *Cover: Across the Pacific* (handwritten), 1942. 192 p., annotated. Some pages reversed, with both sides used, and different paging (appears to be a script for another film). Verso of page 124 is a diagram for "Pet Shop Sequence," unidentified film. Some of the characters are Fiona and Sussana.

NEW YORK PUBLIC LIBRARY FOR THE PERFORMING ARTS.

1. Screenplay by Richard Macaulay, directed by John Huston, produced by Jerry Wald and Jack Saper. *Cover:* Revised final, 3/5/42. Includes pink revision pages, 3/27/42–4/24/42. 125 p.

NEW YORK STATE ARCHIVE.

1. Dialogue script.

UNIVERSITY OF SOUTHERN CALIFORNIA (USC). WARNER BROTHERS ARCHIVE.

1. Synopsis of script outline by Charles E. Blaney and Darryl Zanuck and read by A. E. MacKenzie, April 29, 1935. 7 p.
2. Copy of story "Aloha Means Good-Bye" by Robert Carson. From Myron Selznick and Co., Beverly Hills. 177 p.
3. Pages from *Saturday Evening Post,* where story appeared, June and July 1941.
4. Copy of play, Blaney Play Co., New York. 84 p., annotated.
5. Warner Brothers presents *Across the Pacific*, an epic of the Spanish-American War in the Philippines by Darryl F. Zanuck. Based on the play of the same name by Charles E. Blaney. Directed by Roy Del Ruth. Unpaged. *On cover:* March 21, 1938, (in pencil) Final.
6. No t.p. *Cover page:* Temporary, January 13, 1942–January 29, 1942. *Cover:* January 13, 1942, no author. 192 p.
7. Screenplay by Richard Macaulay; director, John Huston; producers, Jerry Wald and Jack Saper. *Cover sheet:* Rev. Temp., February 14, 1942–February 21, 1942. *Cover:* February 14, 1942. 111 p.
8. As no. 7. *Cover sheet:* Final, February 24, 1942–March 3, 1942. 134 p. Includes pink revision sheet, March 2, 1942. *Cover:* Final, February 24, 1942.
9. As no. 7. *Cover sheet:* Rev. final, March 5, 1942. Includes pink revision sheets to April 24, 1942. 125 p. *Cover:* March 5, 1942.
10. Pink changes, March and April 1942.
11. (Dialogue Transcript) 1942. Various paging.

WISCONSIN/WARNER BROTHERS SCREENPLAY SERIES. Reel 50.

1. "Aloha Means Good-bye" by Richard Macaulay.* Revised final, March 5, 1941, with revisions to April 24, 1941. 125 p.

Note. *The Wisconsin Center for Film and Theater Research, the State Historical Society of Wisconsin, which houses this collection, reports multiple versions of the screenplay.

ACROSS THE RIVER AND INTO THE TREES. 1975–76.

Writer/Director. Unrealized project. Based on Ernest Hemingway's *Across the River and into the Trees* (New York: Scribners, 1950).

AMPAS. JOHN HUSTON COLLECTION. SCRIPT MATERIAL.

1. Screenplay by Anson Bond and Samuel Marx. First draft, September 1. 158 p. Another copy, with Paul Kohner's (Huston's agent) label.
2. Screenplay by John Huston and Gladys Hill, February 27, 1976. 117 p. Some pages dated February 28, 1976; some annotations.
3. John Huston and Gladys Hill. Revised pages dated March 4, 1976. 117 p.
4. John Huston and Gladys Hill, April 2, 1976. 109p. (2 copies.)
5. *Across the River and into the Trees,* August 26, 1976. Information obtained from John Huston card in collection. Citation indicates "(coll: Gladys Hill) scply." Annotation on card indicates NIF—that is, No Synopsis in Filing Cabinet.

Additional screenplay material reported by Dartmouth College Library.

THE AFRICAN QUEEN. 1952.

Horizon-Romulus/UA. Produced by S. P. Eagle. Screenplay by James Agee and John Huston, based on Cecil Scott Forester's *The African Queen* (with new foreword by the author, New York, Modern Library, 1940 and 1963; Boston, Little, Brown, 1935; London, Heineman, 1935). Directed by John Huston.

PUBLISHED SCRIPT.

1. Agee, James. *Agee on Film.* Vol. 2, *Five Film Scripts.* Foreword by John Huston (New York: McDowell, Obolensky, 1960). Screenplay of *The African Queen,* pp. 151–259.

AMPAS. JOHN HUSTON COLLECTION. SCRIPT MATERIAL.

1. Screenplay by James Agee, John Collier, and John Huston, n.d. 137 p. Specially bound.
2. Screenplay by John Collier. *Cover sheet:* Temporary, 4–11–47. 130 p. Property of Warner Brothers. Some annotations.
3. Postproduction script—domestic version, January 3, 1952. Script includes footage notations and an additional five pages of music cue sheets.
4. Screenplay by James Agee, John Collier, and John Huston. Property of Horizon Pictures, Hollywood, in association with Romulus Films Ltd., London. 137 p. *Cover* (handwritten): John Huston.
5. Another copy, 137 p. In Huston collection, uncataloged, box 1.
6. *The African Queen.* Domestic version. Produced by S. P. Eagle, directed by John Huston, distributed by Independent Film Distributors, Ltd. Exhibition footage, 9,406 feet; number of reels, eleven; running time: 1 hr., 45 min. *Cover: The African Queen* by C. S. Forester. Postproduction script, various paging, n.d. Music cue sheets, dated January 3, 1952.

THE BRITISH FILM INSTITUTE.

1. One version of screenplay.

NEW YORK STATE ARCHIVE.

1. Cutting continuity script.

STATE UNIVERSITY OF NEW YORK AT STONY BROOK.

1. Screenplay, 137 p.

UCSB. DAVIDSON LIBRARY.

1. Screenplay by James Agee, John Collier, and John Huston, from the novel by C. S. Forester. Property of Horizon Pictures, Inc., Hollywood, California, in association with Romulus Films Ltd., London, n.d. 137 p.

ADDITIONAL SCREENPLAY MATERIAL IN THE FOLLOWING LIBRARIES.

Barrington Public Library, Capitol Regional Library, Cranston Public Library, East Greenwich Free Library, Haywood City Public Library, Indiana University, Rhode Island Department of State Library Services.

ALFRED HITCHCOCK PRESENTS: MAN FROM THE SOUTH. 1985.

Universal/NBC. Teleplay by William Fay and Steve DeJarnatt, based on a story by Roald Dahl. Directed by Steve DeJarnatt. Huston, actor, The Man.

UCLA. ARTS SPECIAL COLLECTION. TV SCRIPT COLLECTION.
1. Teleplay by William Fay and Steve DeJarnatt. Production #85952-D, December 5, 1984. 19 p.

THE AMAZING DR. CLITTERHOUSE. 1938.
Warner Brothers. Screenplay by John Wexley and John Huston, based on Barre Lyndon's *The Amazing Dr. Clitterhouse: A Play in Three Acts* (London: S. French, 1938; New York: Random House, 1937). Directed by Anatole Litvak.

AMPAS. JOHN HUSTON COLLECTION.
1. Final screenplay by John Wexley and John Huston, January 26, 1938, with revisions to March 12, 1938. 166 p. Specially bound.

MUSEUM OF MODERN ART. DEPARTMENT OF FILM.
1. Synopsis. 1 p. [While listed in the catalog, we could not locate it, October 1995.] 2. Screenplay by John Wexley and John Huston. 124 p. [While listed in the catalog, we could not locate, October 1995.]
3. [Cutting continuity] 125 p.

NEW YORK PUBLIC LIBRARY FOR THE PERFORMING ARTS.
1. Screenplay by John Wexley and John Huston. Directed by Anatole Litvak. *Cover:* Final, 1/26/38. 166 p. Includes blue revision sheets, 2/14/38–3/12/38.

NEW YORK STATE ARCHIVE.
1. Dialogue script.

USC. WARNER BROTHERS ARCHIVES.
1. Synopsis of play by Barre Lyndon, November 2, 1936. Script based on Lyndon's play.
2. Robert Lord's (producer) notes for finish, n.d. 16 p.
3. Copies of Barre Lyndon's play.
4. Screenplay by Wexley and Huston; supervisor, Lord. November 30, 1937. Part I, temporary, no. 6, A-44. 197 p.
5. John Wexley and John Huston. Revised temporary, December 29, 1937, no. 7, A-44. 178 p.
6. John Wexley and John Huston. Version to comply with Hays Office, letter of January 5, 1938. Second revised temporary. 179 p.
7. John Wexley and John Huston. Final, January 26, 1938. 166 p. Includes blue revised sheets, February–March 1938. Includes Lord's notes, annotations, insertions. (Another copy but without changes.)

WISCONSIN/WARNER BROTHERS SCREENPLAY SERIES. Reel 6.
1. Treatment by John Wexley, n.d. 116 p.
2. Screenplay by John Wexley and John Huston.* Final, January 26, 1938, with revisions to March 12, 1938. ca 165 p.

Note. *The Wisconsin Center for Film and Theater Research, the State Historical Society of Wisconsin, which houses these scripts, reports multiple versions of the screenplay.

ADDITIONAL SCREENPLAY MATERIAL IN THE FOLLOWING LIBRARIES.
Dartmouth University Library, Ohio State University Library.

THE AMERICAN FILM'S INSTITUTE SALUTE TO JOHN HUSTON. 1983.
>CBS Special. Written by George Stevens Jr. and Joseph McBride. Directed by Marty Pasetia.

WRITERS GUILD OF AMERICA, WEST. SCRIPT COLLECTION.
1. Script as Broadcast, March 23, 1983. Various paging.

ANGELA. 1977.
>Zev Braun Productions (Canada). Screenplay by Charles E. Israel. Directed by Boris Sagal. Huston, actor, Hogan.

AMPAS. GENERAL COLLECTION.
1. *Jocasta* by Benjamin Manaster. Adapted from the original Screenplay. The gift of Malcolm Hart and Tim Chester. Fifth draft. June 1976. *Cover: Jocasta* crossed out, and *Angela* written in pencil. 103 p.

ANNIE. 1982.
>Columbia. Produced by Ray Stark. Screenplay by Carol Sobieski. Directed by John Huston. Huston's voice may be on radio in Carol Burnett's room at orphanage (?).

PUBLISHED BOOKS.
1. Ehrlich, Amy. *Annie: The Storybook Based on the Movie.* New York: Scholastic Books, 1982; Random House, 1982.
2. Fleischer, Lenore. *Annie: Based on the Screenplay by Carol Sobieski.* New York: Ballantine Books, 1982.

AMPAS. JOHN HUSTON COLLECTION. SCRIPT MATERIAL.
1. *Annie* by Carol Sobieski. First draft, May 26, 1980. *Inscription:* With all my love. *Cover: Annie,* first draft, 5–26–80, property of RASTAR, Burbank. 103 p. Some annotations.
2. Carol Sobieski. Revised first draft, n.d. 112 p.
3. Carol Sobieski, August 1980. 112 p. Includes pink and blue revision pages, 8/4/80.
4. Carol Sobieski. Revised, January 22, 1981. 121 p.

THE AMERICAN FILM INSTITUTE.
1. Screenplay by Carol Sobieski. Revised first draft, n.d. 112 p.
2. Carol Sobieski. Revised as of January 30, 1981. 120 p.
3. Carol Sobieski. Revised as of March 14, 1981. Includes shooting schedule. 40 p.
4. Combined continuity, March 22, 1982. 189 p.

THE BRITISH FILM INSTITUTE.
1. A version of screenplay.

MUSEUM OF MODERN ART. FILM DEPARTMENT.
1. Screenplay by Carol Sobieski. Revised as of March 14, 1981. 124 p. Page 98 missing.

NEW YORK PUBLIC LIBRARY FOR THE PERFORMING ARTS.
1. No t.p. Top p. 1: Revised 10/20/81, no author. 120 p. Includes revised pages, March 4–June 7, 1981.
2. Screenplay by Carol Sobieski. Revised as of March 14, 1981. [124 p., page 98 missing.]

UNIVERSITY OF CALIFORNIA, LOS ANGELES (UCLA). ARTS SPECIAL COLLECTION. GENERAL COLLECTION.
1. Screenplay by Carol Sobieski, August 1980. 113 p. Revised pages dated August 4, 1980, and September 10, 1980.

USC. BOYLE COLLECTION.
1. No t.p., n.d. Dates on some revised pages, 8/4/80 and 9/10/80; some dates obliterated. Various paging.

ADDITIONAL SCREENPLAY MATERIAL IN THE FOLLOWING LIBRARIES.
Dayton and Montgomery County Public Library, Salt Lake City Public Library.

THE ASPHALT JUNGLE. 1950.
MGM. Produced by Arthur Hornblow Jr. Screenplay by Ben Maddow and John Huston, based on W. R. Burnett's *The Asphalt Jungle* (New York: Knopf, 1949; London, Macdonald, 1949). Directed by John Huston.

PUBLISHED SCRIPT.
1. *The Asphalt Jungle,* a screenplay by Ben Maddow and John Huston, from a novel by W. R. Burnett, and with an afterword by W. R. Burnett (Carbondale, Ill.: Southern Illinois Press, 1980). Includes a foreword by Matthew J. Bruccoli, editor of the series.

AMPAS. GENERAL COLLECTION.
1. Screenplay by Ben Maddow and John Huston, October 12, 1949, with changes to December 9, 1949. 136 p.

AMPAS. JOHN HUSTON COLLECTION. SCRIPT MATERIAL.
1. Reader's report of W. R. Burnett's novel. Bill Cole, 2/3/49. From Swanson Agency to M. Thorson, 2/1/49. 15 + 1 p. Includes a cover memo to Huston from Marjorie Thorson, 2–7-49, regarding her feelings about the story's quality.
2. Treatment from Ben Maddow, 5–21–49. No t.p. *Cover:* MGM label. 14 p.
3. Treatment. No t.p. *Detached cover:* From Ben Maddow, 6–7-49. MGM label. 40 p.
4. No t.p. *Cover:* Screenplay [incomplete] from Ben Maddow, 6–15–49. MGM label. 23 p.
5. No t.p., cover detached and missing. Screenplay [incomplete], 6/10/49–6/29/49. 53 p.
6. No t.p. Page 1 missing, cover detached, no authors indicated. MGM label. Dated, 6–15–49; run, 7–1-49. Temporary, complete, pp. 2–163. + 1 p, which indicates script completed, 7–16–49. Pages variously dated June through July 1949. Some annotations.
7. No t.p. *Cover:* Producer Mr. Hornblow, From Ben Maddow, 7–25–49. MGM label. Temporary incomplete. 76 p. Annotated. Pages dated July 21, 1949, to August 17, 1949.
8. No t.p. *Cover:* Okayed by Mr. Hornblow. Director: John Huston. From Ben Maddow, John Huston, 10–12–49. Complete. MGM label. Production #1479. Huston's name handwritten on cover. 136 + 1 p. *Last page:* Script completed 10–12–49. Inserted: pink changes for page 41 (four copies). 4 p. Annotated. Pages dates October 12, 1949.
9. Screenplay by Ben Maddow and John Huston, October 12, 1949, with revisions to December 6, 1949. 136 p. (Two copies: one specially bound; one unbound.)

10. No t.p. *Cover:* From Ben Maddow, John Huston, 10–12–49. MGM label. 136 + 1 p. Script completed 10–12–49. Pink changes 10–25–49 through 11-8-49. Other pages dated 10–12–49. Numerous changes stapled in. Preceding script, memo from Mr. Hornblow, 11–3-49, indicating name changes. Inserted one loose page: dialogue at the lineup between Negro and Policeman.

11. Folder includes handwritten notes, various pages for different version of script, variously dated July through September and November 1949. Includes white, yellow, and pink pages. Includes pages incorporated into no. 10 script.

12. Folder includes various pages from different version of script, including additional copies of Hornblow memo on name changes, November 3, 1949. White and pink changes, October through November 1949. Includes pages incorporated into no. 10 script.

13. *The Asphalt Jungle.* Loops 1479. [19 p.] Some pages dated 11–23–49. Annotated.

14. Folder includes various script pages, different versions, dated July through November 1949. Some pages annotated.

15. Folder of various script pages, no. 2. Some pages dated 9/49, some pages annotated. Includes five pages of Huston's handwritten notes.

16. Folder of various script pages, annotated. Includes one handwritten page by Huston.

AMPAS. TURNER/MGM COLLECTION.

1. *The Asphalt Jungle* by W. R. Burnett, from H. N. Swanson, Inc., West Hollywood. *Cover:* MGM label—File Copy, no. 5,329. No. 6 Agt's Copy. Complete mimeographed manuscript of W. R. Burnett's. 335 p. Transcription of novel.

2. Complete breakdown from Ben Maddow, 5/21/49. 13 p. *Handwritten note on cover:* Dictation interspersed. Annotated.

3. Breakdown from Ben Maddow, 5/21/49. 14 p.

4. Old pages out of 5/21/49, breakdown from Ben Maddow. 13 p.

5. From Ben Maddow, 6/7/49. Treatment. 40 p. Some pages also dated 6/8/49 and 6/10/49.

6. Old pages out of 6/7/49 treatment from Ben Maddow. 2 p.

7. Complete treatment from Ben Maddow, 6/14/49. 40 p.

8. Treatment from Ben Maddow, 6/14/49. 41 p.

9. Temporary complete, composite script. From Ben Maddow, 6/15/49; run, 7/1/49. Producer: Mr. Hornblow. *Preceding page 1:* Script completed, 7/16/49. 163 p.

10. Changes from Ben Maddow to Cp. script, 6/15/49; run, 7/1/49. Various paging. Pages dated 7/1/49 through 7/14/49.

11. Old pages out of Inc. script, dated 6/15/49; from Ben Maddow, 6/16/49 through 6/29/49. Various paging.

12. Notes (draft scenes and structure outline) from Ben Maddow, 8/9/49. Various paging. Some pages also dated 8/12/49 and 8/15/49.

13. No t.p. Two covers: inside, blue; outside, orange. *Blue:* Temporary incomplete; (penciled) Final incomplete, Producer Mr. Hornblow. From Ben Maddow (and in pencil): John Huston, with Maddow indicated as first and Huston as second, 7/21/49. *Orange:* Complete, OK script from Ben Maddow and John Huston, 8/19/49. Okayed by Mr. Hornblow. From Ben Maddow and John Huston. Director: John Huston, 8/19/49. 158 p. Heavily annotated with some changes stapled onto sections of pages. Some pages stamped 9/6/49 and 9/19/49.

14. Composite script, complete. Okayed by Mr. Hornblow. From Ben Maddow, John Huston. Director: John Huston, 8/19/49. Preceding script: (script completed 9/19/49). 151 p. Various dates on pages, through 9/19/49.

15. Complete, OK. From Ben Maddow and John Huston, 8/19/49. Preceding script: script completed 9/19/49. 151 p. Changes through 9/21/49.
16. Section of script from Ben Maddow. Changes in 8/19/49. From 9/1/49 through 9/23/49. Various paging. Heavily annotated.
17. Section of script from Ben Maddow. Changes in 9/19/49. OK script, 9/1/49–9/23/49. *In pencil:* 69 misc. pages.
18. Double orange covers. *Inside:* Okayed by Mr. Hornblow. From: Ben Maddow, John Huston. Director: John Huston, 8/19/49. Rerun 9/16/49. *Outside:* OK Script from John Huston and Ben Maddow. Okayed by Mr. Hornblow. From: Ben Maddow, John Huston. Director: John Huston, 10/12/49. 144 p. Heavily annotated. Pages have various dates, from October to November 1949.
19. Composite script, complete. Okayed by Mr. Hornblow. Director: John Huston. From: Ben Maddow, John Huston, 10/12/49. Production #1479. 136 p. Includes pink revision pages, dated through 11/8/49. Preceding page 1: Memo from Mr. Hornblow, 11/3/49, regarding name changes. (Another copy: photocopy).
20. From Legal Department, 10/10/49–11/12/49, script name changes. To Hornblow, Huston, Maddow, Strohm, Farrell, Publicity; from F. L. Hendrickson. 5 p.
21. Synopsis, 10/18/49, *The Asphalt Jungle,* by Ben Maddow and John Huston; reader, Lee Phillips. 20 p.
22. (Dialogue cutting continuity) March 17, 1950. Various paging.
23. (Music report and footage) March 17, 1950.
24. (Trailer) dialogue cutting continuity, 6/9/50. 4 p.
25. (Trailer) (footage) June 9, 1950. 1 p.
26. Trailer, international version, based on domestic script, 5/9/50. 4 p.

NEW YORK PUBLIC LIBRARY FOR THE PERFORMING ARTS.
1. No t.p. *Cover:* OK by Mr. Hornblow. Director: John Huston. From: Ben Maddow, John Huston, 10–12–49. Includes cover memo regarding name changes, 11/3/49. 136 p. Includes pink revision pages, 11/3/49 and 11/8/49.

NEW YORK STATE ARCHIVE.
1. Cutting continuity script.

UCLA. ARTS SPECIAL COLLECTION. GENERAL COLLECTION.
1 From Ben Maddow, John Huston, October 12, 1949. Complete, October 12, 1949. Includes Hornblow memo indicating name changes in OK script. 137 p. Includes penciled annotations and pink pages with story board sketches.

UCSB. DAVIDSON LIBRARY.
1. *The Asphalt Jungle,* okayed by Mr. Hornblow. Director: John Huston. From: Ben Maddow, John Huston, 10–12–49. 136 p. Includes revised pages dated 11-3-49 and 11-8-49. Preceding text of screenplay is memo from Mr. Hornblow, 11–3-49, indicating name changes.

USC. BOYLE COLLECTION.
1. From: Ben Maddow, John Huston, 10–12–49. Some changes dated 11/49. 136 p. Includes memo from Arthur Hornblow Jr. (producer), indicating name changes. Photocopy.

USC. MGM COLLECTION.
1. Mimeo, novel, manuscript (335 p.). Synopsis. 6 p.
2. Complete OK script (136 p.), October 12, 1949. Production #1479. Complete OK by Mr.

Hornblow. Director: John Huston. Reader: Lee Phillips, October 18, 1949. Synopsis and summary.
3. Transcription of novel. 335 p.
4. *Cover title:* From Ben Maddow, May 21, 1949. *Cover label:* No. 9, Breakdown. 14 p.
5. Complete treatment, Ben Maddow, June 7, 1949, no. 1. 40 p. Some pages dated June 8, 1949.
6. Treatment by Ben Maddow, June 14, 1949, no. 28. 41 p.
7. Incomplete script by Ben Maddow, June 15, 1949, no. 1. 66 p.
8. Script, Ben Maddow. Producer: Mr. Hornblow. Run: July 1, 1949. Temporary incomplete, no. 30. 163 p. Pages dated through July 16, 1949.

WRITERS GUILD OF AMERICA, WEST.
1. Screenplay by Maddow and Huston, October 12, 1949. 136 p.

ADDITIONAL SCREENPLAY MATERIAL IN THE FOLLOWING LIBRARIES.
Burke City Public Library, California Institute of the Arts, Cornell University, Dartmouth University, High Point Public Library, Indiana University, University of Illinois.

BACKGROUND TO DANGER (working title: *Uncommon Danger*). 1943.
    Warner Brothers. Screenplay by W. R. Burnett, based on Eric Ambler's *Background to Danger* (New York: Knopf, 1937). Directed by Raoul Walsh. *Film Dope* indicates that Huston did uncredited polishing on the script.

NEW YORK PUBLIC LIBRARY FOR THE PERFORMING ARTS.
1. Screenplay by W. R. Burnett; director, Raoul Walsh; producer, Jerry Wald; September 25, 1942. Cover sheets for parts I through VIII indicate Revised Final, 9/25/42–11/6/42. 140 p. Includes blue revision sheet changes, 10/2/42. p. 43.

NEW YORK STATE ARCHIVE.
1. Dialogue script.

USC. WARNER BROTHERS ARCHIVE. SCRIPT COLLECTION.
1. Treatment, July 21, 1942, no author. 23 + 1 p.
2. Story outline, no author, n.d. 11 p.
3. Treatment, July 10, 1942, no author. 21 p.
4. Treatment. *In pencil:* Collier's work, n.d. 49 p.
5. Screenplay by Fred Niblo Jr., n.d. 124 p.
6. Screenplay by Paul Gerard Smith, n.d. 125 p.
7. Screenplay by M. Coates Webster and Arthur Arent, September 13, 1941. 145 p. Annotated.
8. As no. 6, but date on title page is August 20, 1941. *Cover sheet:* Temp. 117 p.
9. Screenplay by Philip MacDonald, July 7, 1942. *Cover sheet:* Rev. Temp, July 8, 1942. *Cover:* July 9, 1942. 132 p.
10. Final script, no author, August 8, 1942. Blue revision sheets, September 2, 1942. 121 p.
11. Screenplay by W. R. Burnett, September 25, 1942. *Cover sheet:* Revised Final. Pink changes to December 5, 1942, various paging. *Note inserted in folder:* Faulkner on . . . Nov. 23, 1942–Decc. 7, 1942 (with Dan Fuchs). *In pencil:* Chgs in Rev. Final.
12. (Dialogue transcript) 1943. Various paging.
13. No t.p. *On first page:* Working script. *In margin, in Huston's hand: Background to*

Danger, from John Huston, n.d. 79 p. Yellow pages. Heavily annotated. Located in Warner Brothers Archive Story File.

THE WISCONSIN CENTER FOR FILM AND THEATER RESEARCH, THE STATE HISTORICAL SOCIETY OF WISCONSIN.
1. Versions of the screenplay.

THE BARBARIAN AND THE GEISHA. 1958.
Twentieth Century-Fox. Produced by Eugene Frenke. Screenplay by Charles Grayson. Huston contributed to screenplay (uncredited). Directed by John Huston.

PUBLISHED "SCRIPT."
1. Payne, Robert. *The Barbarian and the Geisha,* based on the screenplay by Ellis St. Joseph. New York: New American Library, a Signet Book; London: Payne Books, 1958. *Facing t.p.: The Barbarian* by Ellis St. Joseph is the screenplay which provided the basis of this novel. Includes author's note, pp. 157–60.

AMPAS. GENERAL COLLECTION.
1. Final script, September 26, 1957.
2. *The Townsend Harris Story.* Final script, October 23, 1957. No authors indicated.
3. New scenes and retakes, April 16, 1958.

AMPAS. JOHN HUSTON COLLECTION. SCRIPT MATERIAL.
1. Synopsis, *Townsend Harris* by Ellis St. Joseph. Original (78 p). Submitted by Eugene Frenke, May 17, 1956. 11 p.
2. About Townsend Harris's story, analysis, no author or date. 1 p. Stapled are some script pages, Act IV, Scene 8 [5 p.].
3. Miscellaneous analysis pages, no author or date. One page dated 11/20/57.
4. Buddy Adler to John Huston, cc: Charles Grayson, 9/18/57. Subject: *Townsend Harris,* writer's working script of September 5, 1957. 15 p.
5. Director Kinugasa's suggestions for first sequence, *The Townsend Harris Story.* 6 p. Annotated. (Two copies.)
6. Various notes sent to John Huston: Mac's notes and Gene Frenke's notes, n.d, various paging. Handwritten notes on Grayson's script on a legal pad, 4 p.
7. Script, no. t.p., no cover, separate pages. First page has in Huston's hand "John Huston's copy, 10/14.57." 133 p. Continuously paged. Some pages have "Mr. Huston" written at top. Some pages revised: 12/2/57 and 12/5/57. Another set of pages, pp. 64–95 [not same as previous]. Huston's name at top of some pages. Pages dated 1/8/58, 1/9/58, and 1/15/58. Some pages annotated. Handwritten notes verso page 93. *Note:* These pages were originally in an envelope marked "John's working script of *The Barbarian."*
8. Script pages, variously paged and dated from different versions. Some pages annotated heavily. Call sheet attached to some pages, November 14. Missing pages, 10/14/57; replaced pages, 11/4/57; pages typed from November 1; handwritten notes, doodles; revised pages, October 12.
9. Payne, Robert. *The Barbarian and the Geisha.* New York: New American Library, 1958.

NEW YORK PUBLIC LIBRARY FOR THE PERFORMING ARTS.
1. No t.p. *Cover:* New Scenes and Retakes, Apr. 16, 1958. 30 p. Dated at top of pages: Apr. 14–18, 1958. Gift of Sam Jaffe.

NEW YORK STATE ARCHIVE.
1. Cutting continuity script.

UCLA. ARTS SPECIAL COLLECTION. GENERAL COLLECTION.
1. *The Barbarian and the Geisha* (formerly *The Townsend Harris Story*), final (written in Tokyo), October 23, 1957. 89 + additional pages. Revised pages dated 1957–58. Includes retakes and added scenes (working outline), April 11, 1958. Pink and blue sheets, no authors indicated.

UCLA. ARTS SPECIAL COLLECTION. TWENTIETH CENTURY-FOX ARCHIVE.
1. *The Townsend Harris Story.* Story outline by Charles Grayson, n.d. 97 p., plus additional pages "Final outline" and pages from script dated December 1957 and January 1958. Includes annotations.
2. *Townsend Harris,* by Ellis St. Joseph, May 22, 1956. 78 p.
3. Ellis St. Joseph, writer's working script, September 5, 1956. 210 p. Preceding the script: historical authenticity of scene and dialogue, authenticity of character, October 15, 1956.
4. Ellis St. Joseph, December 8, 1956. 117 p.
5. *Townsend Harris Story,* breakdown of master scenes by John Huston and Charles Grayson, August 5, 1957. 62 p.
6. Screenplay by Charles Grayson and John Huston, writers' working script, September 5, 1957. 119 p. Memo in file, September 5, 1957: Buddy Adler (head of production) to John Huston, cc: Charles Grayson. Detailed critique of September 5 script. 15 p. Memo in file, September 25, 1957: Buddy Adler to John Huston, cc: Eugene Frenke (producer), Charles Grayson, Alfred Hayes, Lew Schreiber, David Brown, and Sid Rogell. Re: Grayson's second draft. 9 p.
7. Screenplay by Charles Grayson, final script, September 26, 1957. 113 p.
8. New scenes and retakes, April 16, 1958. Some pages dated April 15, 1958. 30 p.
9. Continuity and dialogue taken from the screen, September 11, 1958. (No writing credit for Huston.)

UNIVERSITY OF IOWA. TWENTIETH CENTURY-FOX SCRIPT COLLECTION.
1. Working outline, October 23, 1957.
2. Continuity and dialogue, September 11, 1958.
3. Continuity and dialogue, edited copy, September 18, 1958.

USC. TWENTIETH CENTURY-FOX COLLECTION.
1. Japanese text.
2. *Townsend Harris* by Ellis St. Joseph. Original copies, May 22, 1956. 78 p.
3. Ellis St. Joseph, writer's working script, September 5, 1956. *Top of p. 1:* October 15, 1956. 211 p.
4. Ellis St. Joseph, December 8, 1956. 117 p.
5. *The Townsend Harris Story.* Outline by Charles Grayson, n.d. (on some pages, July 9, 1957). Various paging. Includes some script pages at end, Grayson rewrites, variously dated, December 1957–January 1958.
6. Breakdown of master scenes by John Huston and Charles Grayson, August 5, 1957. 62 p.
7. Screenplay by Charles Grayson and John Huston, writer's working script, September 5, 1957. 119 p.
8. Conference notes on "Townsend Harris," September 18, 1957. *Contents:* Memo from Buddy Adler (production head) to John Huston, cc: Charles Grayson, on the writer's

working script of September 5, 1957. 15 p. Takes the form of a letter. Stamped: Permanent Legal Records.

9. Memorandum on revised script (incomplete and undated), dictated by Buddy Adler, September 25, 1957. *Contents:* Memo to Huston, cc: Eugene Frenke (producer), Charles Grayson, Alfred Hayes, Lew Schreiber, David Brown, and Sid Rogell. Subject: Revised script (incomplete). In form of a letter. 9 p.

10. Charles Grayson, final script, September 26, 1957. 133 p.

11. Nigel Balchin's contributions as indicated by letter, March 8, 1958. Indicates amount of work he did, various pages, dated December 1957–January 1958. In a letter he relates how impossible it was to sort out who did what: "What on earth can I say about a scene which was suggested by me, drafted by Charlie, and re-written on the floor by John and me?"

12. October 23, 1957, final, no t.p., no authors indicated. Sid Rogell's copy that he received in Japan. 89 p. Pages variously dated December 1957–January 1958. Some indicated as second revision. Some annotations.

13. New scenes and retakes, *The Barbarian and the Geisha,* April 16, 1958. No authors indicated. 30 p. Some dated: Apr. 15, 1958.

BATTLE FOR THE PLANET OF THE APES. 1973.

Twentieth Century-Fox/APAC. Screenplay by John William Corrington and Joyce Hooper Corrington. Directed by J. Lee Thompson. Huston, actor, The Lawgiver.

AMPAS. GENERAL COLLECTION.

1. Revised screenplay by John William Corrington and Joyce Hooper Corrington, December 20, 1972. With revised shooting schedule, December 28, 1972. Various paging.

UCLA. ARTS SPECIAL COLLECTION. TWENTIETH CENTURY-FOX COLLECTION.

1. Screenplay by Paul Dehn and John William Corrington and Joyce Hooper Corrington, revised, December 20, 1972. *Above title:* Revised December 29, 1972. Various paging. Includes colored revised sheets.

UCLA GENERAL COLLECTION.

1. Revised screenplay, December 20, 1972. *At top of page:* Revised, 12/29/72. 114 p. Includes revised pages, 12/27/72, 12/21/72, 1/2/73.

USC. GENERAL SCRIPT COLLECTION.

1. Script. 114 p.

BATTLE OF SAN PIETRO (*San Pietro*). 1945.

U.S. Army Signal Corps. Pictorial Service. Huston was writer, director, and commentator and was involved in photography.

AMPAS. JOHN HUSTON COLLECTION. SCRIPT MATERIAL.

1. Original script, n.d. 15 p. Heavily annotated.

2. July 25, 1944. 16 p.

3. Corrected copy. As amended, November 3, 1944, various pages.

4. Narration script, January 5, 1945. Photographic scenario. 15 p.

5. *San Pietro,* public revision, taken from Moviola of approved release print, March 16, 1945. 19 p.

6. Page with variation on closing words.

ADDITIONAL SCREENPLAY MATERIAL IN THE FOLLOWING
LIBRARIES.
Howard University Library.

BEAT THE DEVIL. 1954.

Santana-Romulus. Screenplay by Truman Capote and John Huston,
based on the novel of the same name by James Helvick (pseudonym of Claud
Cockburn.) Directed by John Huston.

PUBLISHED BOOK.
1. Helvick, James. *Beat the Devil.* Philadelphia: Lippincott, 1951.
2. Helvick, James. *Beat the Devil.* London: Hogarth Press, 1985, with new introduction by
   Alexander Cockburn.

PUBLISHED SCRIPT.
1. In Robert Gessner's *The Moving Image* (New York: Dutton, 1968), pp. 325–26 (excerpt).

AMPAS. GENERAL COLLECTION.
1. Screenplay by John Huston, Anthony Veiller, and Peter Viertel, January 8, 1953.

NEW YORK PUBLIC LIBRARY FOR THE PERFORMING ARTS.
1. Screenplay by Truman Capote. Final shooting script (edited version). Directed by John
   Huston. Copyright by Romulus Films, Ltd., London. 107 p.

NEW YORK STATE ARCHIVE.
1. Dialogue script.

BECKET. 1964.

Paramount. Screenplay by Edward Anhalt. Directed by Peter Glenville.
Huston, considered director, unrealized. *Note:* Production file for *Harrow
Alley* in AMPAS, JOHN HUSTON COLLECTION, includes a letter from
Keep Films, Ltd., U.K., October 11, 1962, indicating the company's desire to
have Huston direct.

PUBLISHED SCRIPT.
1. In Robert Gessner's *The Moving Image* (New York: Dutton, 1968), pp. 63–64 (excerpt).

AMPAS. JOHN HUSTON COLLECTION. SCRIPT MATERIAL.
1. *Becket* by Jean Anouilh (first draft), play script, various pages, n.d.

NEW YORK PUBLIC LIBRARY FOR THE PERFORMING ARTS.
1. Play script.

NEW YORK STATE ARCHIVE.
1. Cutting continuity script.

WRITERS GUILD OF AMERICA, WEST.
1. Screenplay by Edward Anhalt, 1964.

ADDITIONAL SCREENPLAY MATERIAL IN THE FOLLOWING
LIBRARIES.
University of Regina, Saskatchewan, Canada.

THE BERMUDA TRIANGLE. 1978.
    Concacine/Nucleo. Screenplay by Rene Cardona Jr. and Carlos Valdemar Directed by Rene Cardona Jr. Huston, actor, the father, Edward Martin.

UCLA. ARTS SPECIAL COLLECTION. GENERAL COLLECTION.
1. Screenplay by Kenneth Hartman, 1979. 119 p.

THE BIBLE . . . IN THE BEGINNING. 1966.
    Dino De Laurentiis Cinematografica/Twentieth Century-Fox/Seven Arts. 1966. Screenplay by Christopher Fry. Directed by John Huston, who also acted (Noah) and narrated.

BOOK BASED ON FILM.
1. Bonicelli, Vittorio. *La Bibbia.* Milan: A. Mondadori, 1966.

PUBLISHED SCRIPT.
1. *The Bible.* Original screenplay by Christopher Fry; assisted by Jonathan Griffin; special consultant, W. M. Merchant. New York: Pocket Books, 1966. 175 p.

AMPAS. JOHN HUSTON COLLECTION. SCRIPT MATERIAL.
1. Obey, André. *Noe. Pièce en 5 actes.* Paris: L'Amicale; Libraire Théâtrical, 1962. 80 p. Some annotations.
2. Translation of the above, by A. Talbot, Rome, April 28, 1964, Noah. 75 p. Bound in cardboard covers with Dino De Laurentiis, Cinematografica S.P.A., Roma, on cover.
3. Screenplay. Property of Dino De Laurentiis, Roma: "Creation," sequence no. "A," pp. 1–20, no author or date; "The Fall," sequence no. "B," pp. 21–35, no author or date; "Cain and Abel," sequence no. "C," pp. 36–57, no author or date; "The Deluge," sequence no. "D," pp. 58–94+, no author or date; "Tower of Babel," revised May 7, 1964, [no sequence indicated; no author], pp. 95–107; pp. 108–12 omitted; "Abraham," sequence no. "F," pp. 113–89. "Table of Contents" preceding "Creation" page indicates "Abraham" on pp. 113–200. *At top of this page, in pencil:* Checked against Gladys Hill script, 24/3. *Cover, in pencil:* John Huston, extra script, *The Bible.* Inserted: Discarded pages, February 8, 1965; stapled together: two lines of dialogue between Noah and Wife; followed by: "Creation," narrated by John Huston, 3/1/65, and retyped 3/17/65, 3 p.; voice test for Paul Scofield, *The Bible,* "Creation," 2 p., and "Cain and Abel," 2 p.; script heavily annotated. Some blue and pink revisions pages, indicate second and third revisions, variously dated: Apr. 1964–Feb. 1965.
4. Sequence no. "A," n.d. Revisions to February 11, 1965. 189 p. Specially bound.

THE BRITISH FILM INSTITUTE.
1. A version of the screenplay.

UCLA. ARTS SPECIAL COLLECTION. TWENTIETH CENTURY-FOX ARCHIVE.
1. No t.p., no writers or date indicated. Possibly Huston's copy. *Cover title: The Bible.* Breakdown: "Creation," sequence no. "A," pp. 1–20. Indication in text: Recorded January 3, 1965, JH. Other penciled annotations. "The Fall," sequence no. "B," pp. 21–(52), various annotations [in Huston's hand?]. Includes note to Huston about particular scene. "The Deluge," sequence no. "D," pp. 52–94a. Various annotations: Huston's name handwritten at top of p. 86B. "Tower of Babel," revised May 7, 1964, sequence "E," pp. 95–107, various annotations in hand. "Pp. 108–112 omitted." "Abraham,"

sequence no. "F," pp. 113–89, various annotations and additions in pencil and typewritten inserted.

UNIVERSITY OF IOWA. TWENTIETH CENTURY-FOX SCRIPT COLLECTION.
1. Screenplay by Christopher Fry.
2. Continuity script.
3. Continuity and dialogue.

USC. TWENTIETH CENTURY-FOX SOUND COLLECTION.
1. *The Bible.* Incomplete. (Sequence "A," "Creation"; "B," "The Fall"; "C," "Cain and Abel"; "D," "The Deluge"; "E," "Tower of Babel." No authors or dates.) 112 p.

BLACK RUST. 1932.
Universal. Unproduced.

AMPAS. UNIVERSAL LIBRARY PROPERTIES. SYNOPSIS AND DESCRIPTIVE DATA 4, no. 6,084. Unproduced. Author, Paul De Kruif; date of purchase, February 12, 1932
1. Treatment: John Huston, 2/12/32. 17 p.

AMPAS. JOHN HUSTON COLLECTION. SCRIPT MATERIAL.
1. "Black Rust" from the biography of Paul De Kruif. From: John Huston, February 12, 1932. 17 p.
2. "Mark Alfred Carleton" by John Huston, n.d. 6 p. Located in John Huston Inventory, Early Scripts and Stories—Titled, p. 39. *Note:* Lawrence Grobel, in *The Hustons* (New York: Scribners, 1989, 146), writes that "in February 1932 he [Huston] put together a treatment for a film he wanted to call *Black Rust,* based on the writings of Paul De Kruif about Mark Alfred Carleton."

THE BLUE HOTEL. 1977.
James Agee. Unrealized project (*Cineforum,* December 1987). No other information in AMPAS HUSTON ARCHIVE.

PUBLISHED SCRIPT.
1. Agee, James. *Agee on Film.* Vol. 2, *Five Film Scripts.* Foreword by John Huston. New York: McDowell, Obolensky, 1960.

BORSTAL BOY.
Book by Brendan Behan (New York: Knopf, 1959; London, Gorgi Books, 1958). Huston considered for directing. Unrealized.

AMPAS. JOHN HUSTON COLLECTION. PRODUCTION FILE.
1. In the file for *The Hostage* is a letter from Irving Lazar to Huston, July 29, 1970, asking Huston if he would be interested in "Borstal Boy."

AMPAS. JOHN HUSTON COLLECTION. SCRIPT MATERIAL.
1. Adapted for the stage by Frank McMahon, Part I, 45 p; Part II, 44 p. Annotated. *Handwritten on cover:* Corrected, n.d.

BREAKOUT. 1975.
Columbia. Screenplay by Howard B. Kreitsek, Marc Norman, and Elliott Baker, based on the book, *The 10-Second Jailbreak: The Helicopter Escape of Joel David Kaplan,* by Eliot Asinof, Warren Hinckle, and William

Turner (New York: Holt, Rinehart and Winston, 1973). Directed by Tom Gries. Huston, actor, Harris Wagner.

UNIVERSITY OF WYOMING. AMERICAN HERITAGE CENTER.

1. "Breakout" screenplay, notes, drafts, total pages, n.d., 747 p. (Howard Kreitsek Collection #6253.)

USC. BOYLE COLLECTION.

1. Screenplay by Marc Norman, November 21, 1973. 115 p.

THE BRIDGE IN THE JUNGLE. 1971.
Sagittarius/Capricorn/UA. Screenplay and direction by Pancho Kohner. Based on B. Traven's *The Bridge in the Jungle* (New York: Knopf, 1938; London, J. Cape, 1940). (Reprint—New York: Hill and Wang, 1967; translation of *Die Brucke im Dschungel*). Huston, actor, Sleigh.

AMPAS. GENERAL COLLECTION.

1. No t.p. Screenplay. Released by United Artists, 1970. 105 p.

AMPAS. JOHN HUSTON COLLECTION.

1. Screenplay by Albert Maltz, from the novel by B. Traven. Property of Paul Kohner, n.d. 105 p.
2. B. Traven's *The Bridge in the Jungle*. Screenplay by Pancho Kohner. March 1969. Capricorn Productions (Switzerland). First draft screenplay. 112 p. Includes blue revision pages, May 20.

ADDITIONAL SCREENPLAY MATERIAL IN THE FOLLOWING LIBRARIES.
Indiana University, Ohio State University, University of California, Riverside.

THE BRIDGE OF SAN LUIS REY. 1929, 1944.
Unrealized project (?).*

AMPAS. JOHN HUSTON COLLECTION.

1. Screenplay by Dorothy Hodel (*in ink:* Huston), first draft, n.d. 110p. Annotated. No other indication of Huston involvement. Huston's first wife was Dorothy Harvey.

Note. *The USC Library has versions of the screenplays produced by MGM for the 1929 and 1944 versions. Among the writers of the latter version was John Howard Lawson.

BULLET PARK. 1969–70.
Based on the novel by John Cheever (New York: Knopf, 1969). Writer, director. Unrealized project. Intended as a John Huston–Carter De Haven Production.

AMPAS. JOHN HUSTON COLLECTION. SCRIPT MATERIAL

1. Breakdown by John Huston and Gladys Hill, April 28, 1969. 47 p. (Two copies.) Loose pages included. Annotated. Includes some handwritten notes and Huston's doodles.
2. Various handwritten notes on white legal pad, with various pages dated August 21, 1969.
3. Huston and Hill, September 1, 1969–September 26, 1969. Version I. 137 p. Some annotations. Another copy marked "Working Copy." Heavily annotated.

4. Huston and Hill, September 30, 1969–October 10, 1969. Working copy. Version II. Some annotations.
5. Huston and Hill, January 15, 1970. 81 p. Some annotations.
6. Huston and Hill, April 9, 1970. 142 p. Specially bound.
7. Miscellaneous script pages, 1969–70, and discarded pages. Some annotated, some with Huston's notes and his doodles. (Three folders.)

BY LOVE POSSESSED. 1961.

UA/Mirisch/Seven Arts. Produced by Walter Mirisch. Screenplay by John Dennis and Charles Schnee, based on the James Gould Cozzens novel (New York: Fawcett, 1957). Directed by John Sturges.

AMPAS. JOHN HUSTON COLLECTION. PRODUCTION FILE.

1. Letter, October 1957, from Mark Cohen (Huston's attorney) on whether Huston would be interested in doing the picture or *Typee* after Zanuck film (?). Huston indicates he would be interested if writer mentioned in the cable to Paul (Kohner) does the script (which is not in the file). When Huston was then asked whether he would accept Howard Koch if Lillian Hellman didn't work out, he responded emphatically: NO! Credits from *Motion Picture Guide:* Produced by Walter Mirisch; directed by John Sturges; screenplay by John Dennis and Charles Schnee, based on the James Gould Cozzens novel; photography by Russell Metty; edited by Ferris Webster; art direction by Malcolm Brown. Cast includes Lana Turner, Efrem Zimbalist Jr., Jason Robards Jr., George Hamilton, Susan Kohner, Barbara Bel Geddes, Thomas Mitchell, and Everett Sloane.

USC. CLARK GABLE COLLECTION.

1. *By Love Possessed,* second draft, revised, Ketti Frings, Hollywood, California, n. d. 113 p.

CANDY. 1968.

Selmur Pictures–Dear Films–Les Films Corona. Distributed by Cinerama Releasing Corp. Produced by Robert Haggiag. Screenplay by Buck Henry, from the novel by Terry Southern and Mason Hoffenberg. Italian screenplay version by Enrico Mediolo. Directed by Christian Marquand.

THE BRITISH FILM INSTITUTE .

1. A version of the screenplay.

NEW YORK PUBLIC LIBRARY FOR THE PERFORMING ARTS.

1. Screenplay by Terry Southern, from the novel by Terry Southern and Mason Hoffenberg. First draft. Francis Productions, Inc., New York, n.d., 136 p.
2. Third draft, n.d. 139 p. Shelley Winters Collection.

CANNERY ROW. 1982.

MGM/UA. Screenplay and direction by David S. Ward, based on John Steinbeck's two novels: *Cannery Row* (New York: Viking, 1945) and *Sweet Thursday* (New York: Viking, 1954). Huston, narrator.

THE AMERICAN FILM INSTITUTE.

1. Screenplay by David Ward, February 1979. 119 p.
2. Final draft, April 22, 1980. 150 p. Includes revisions.
3. Final revised draft, October 24, 1980. 136 p. Includes revisions.

AMPAS. GENERAL COLLECTION.
1. Screenplay by David S. Ward, based on the novels *Cannery Row* and *Sweet Thursday* by John Steinbeck. Final revised draft, October 24, 1980. Various pages.

AMPAS. JOHN HUSTON COLLECTION.
1. As AMPAS. GENERAL COLLECTION. Final revised draft, October 24, 1980. 136 p. Includes blue revision sheets, November 17, 1980.

THE BRITISH FILM INSTITUTE.
1. A version of the screenplay.

NEW YORK PUBLIC LIBRARY FOR THE PERFORMING ARTS.
1. Screenplay by David S. Ward, based on the novels *Cannery Row* and *Sweet Thursday* by John Steinbeck. Final revised draft, October 24, 1980, 136 p. Includes blue, green, yellow, and revised pages, through December 29, 1980. *Cover:* Property of MGM, Producer Michael Phillips, Director David S. Ward.

UCLA. ARTS SPECIAL COLLECTION. GENERAL COLLECTION.
1. No t.p. No authors or date indicated. 118 p.
2. David S. Ward. Final draft, April 22, 1980. 150 p.
3. Revised final draft, May 27, 1980. 136 p. Includes blue revision pages, June 17, 1980.

USC. BOYLE COLLECTION.
1. Final draft, April 22, 1980. 150 p.

WRITERS GUILD OF AMERICA, WEST.
1. Revised draft, October 24, 1980.

ADDITIONAL SCREENPLAY MATERIAL IN THE FOLLOWING LIBRARIES.
Dartmouth College, Stanford University, University of Alabama.

CAPTAIN HORATIO HORNBLOWER. 1951.
> Warner Brothers. Screenplay by Ivan Goff, Ben Roberts, and Aeneas MacKenzie. With Aeneas MacKenzie, Huston, as a writer on assignment, July through August 1940 (but evidence of work to December 1940. Cf. no. 11, USC Warner Archives). Based on C. S. Forester's novel (Boston: Little, Brown, 1939).

AMPAS. JOHN HUSTON COLLECTION. SCRIPT MATERIAL.
1. Revised, March 22, 1940. 200 p. No authors indicated. Some annotations.
2. Revised temporary, July 29, 1940. 182 p. No authors indicated. Warner's copy.

NEW YORK STATE ARCHIVE.
1. Dialogue script.

USC. WARNER BROTHERS ARCHIVES. SCRIPT COLLECTION.
1. Test adaptation by MacKenzie-Klein, October 11, 1949.
2. Test adaptation with Reinhardt, January 24, 1944.
3. First version, part I, n.d. 94 p. No authors indicated, #2. 68 p.
4. Treatment by Forester, MacKenzie, and Klein, #3. 74 p. (Two copies.)
5. Script marked #4, no authors or date. 200 p.

6. Second revised temporary, #7, August 27, 1940. 162+ pages.
7. Temporary, #6, Wallis's cut version, July 12, 1940. No authors indicated. 221 p. Heavily annotated.
8. Same as no. 7. 221 p. No authors indicated.
9. Revised temporary, # 9, no authors indicated. 182 p. Production files contain memos from W. Reinhardt to Hal Wallis (7/12/40), John Huston to Hal Wallis (7/12/40), and Huston to Wallis (7/29/40), indicating Huston's involvement with script. The last memo outlines changes Huston and Aeneas MacKenzie made "as noted by you, roughed in connecting scenes where necessary, and put the material through in the form of a Revised temporary script. It amounts to 182 p."
10. Outline of action and locations in the first temporary script, #5, n.d., no authors. 21 p. Also thematic pattern of the script, #A-2. 18 p. + 7 p.
11. Second revised temporary, #48, December 17, 1940, 162 p. + 4 p. *T.p.:* Screenplay by Aeneas MacKenzie, C. S. Forester, and John Huston, from the novel by C. S. Forester. *On cover:* Do Not Give Out. See Note Inside. *Inside piece of paper stapled in* (August 12, 1949): At Mr. Warner's request all copies of the 2nd rev. temp, dated 12/17/40, in the story files and in Stenographic were given new covers with both 2nd Rev. temporary and 12/17/40 removed. Otherwise the scripts remain the same. No one is to receive a copy unless it has been altered.
12. Notes for revision of script by MacKenzie, Forester and Huston, by Ivan Goff and Ben Roberts, received October 12, 1949, pp. 1–6, complete, #8.
13. Screenplays and other treatments by Ivan Goff and Ben Roberts, October 24, 1949, through February 1950; July 1950. Complete final script, as actually shot in England, by Goff and Roberts, December 10, 1949.

THE CARDINAL. 1964.
>Gamma Productions/Columbia. Produced and Directed by Otto Preminger. Screenplay by Robert Dozier, based on Henry Morton Robinson's novel (New York: Simon & Schuster, 1950). Huston, actor, Cardinal Glennon.

AMPAS. JOHN HUSTON COLLECTION. SCRIPT MATERIAL. Uncataloged, box 1.
1. Screenplay by Robert Dozier, from the novel by Henry Morton Robinson. Gamma Productions, Inc., Otto Preminger, New York. *Cover:* An Otto Preminger film, n.d. 214 p. Includes blue revision page (page 60).

GEORGETOWN UNIVERSITY.
1. Screenplay, 214 p.

NEW YORK STATE ARCHIVE.
1. Dialogue script.

CASINO ROYALE. 1967.
>Famous Artists Productions/Columbia. Screenplay and adaptation by Wolf Mankowitz, John Law, and Michael Sayers. The AFI indicates additional uncredited writers: Billy Wilder, Ben Hecht, John Huston, Val Guest, Joseph Heller, and Terry Southern, based on Ian Fleming's novel of the same name (London: J. Cape, 1953; New York: Macmillan, 1954). Directed by John Huston (first half hour), Ken Hughes, Val Guest, Robert Parrish, and Joseph McGrath.

AMPAS. JOHN HUSTON COLLECTION.
1. Miscellaneous pages of script, typed and handwritten. One page dated 1966.
2. Miscellaneous script pages in envelope. Some revision, May 6, 1966, John Huston; "Sir James Bond in Scotland," revisions, John Huston, April 6–April 11, 1966; dungeon scene, revisions, May 17, 1966, John Huston; other various revision sheets, April–May 1966, John Huston.
3. Revisions, John Huston and W. M. (Wolf Mankowitz), March 28, 1966.
4. Revisions, Wolf Mankowitz, March 31 and April 3, 1966. Huston's doodles.
5. Folder in envelope: Sir James Bond story. Huston rewrite, per Mankowitz, March 12, 25, 26, and 27, 1966. (Rewrite, John Huston.) Other revisions, April 10, 1966; May 10, 1966; and other various dates.

CHEYENNE. 1947.
Warner Brothers. Screenplay by Alan LeMay. Directed by Raoul Walsh.

USC. WARNER BROTHERS ARCHIVE.
1. File indicates Huston was under contract to write a screenplay for film in 1945 and was paid two thousand dollars. It appears that he did not do any work on it, and Warner's demanded its money back. A memo in the files (from March 18, 1946) says that Alan LeMay, Charles Tedford, Paul Wellman, Emmet Lavery, Thames Williamson, and Pat C. Flick worked on the script, but not Huston. Files contain all of this work, July 17, 1944 through March 9, 1946.

WISCONSIN/WARNER BROTHERS SCREENPLAY SERIES. Reel 57.
1. Contains versions* by Thames Williamson, Alan LeMay, and LeMay and Williamson.

Note. *The Wisconsin Center for Film and Theater Research, the State Historical Society of Wisconsin, which houses these scripts, reports multiple versions of the screenplay.

CHINATOWN. 1974.
Paramount. Screenplay by Robert Towne. Directed by Roman Polanski. Huston, actor, Noah Cross; in earlier versions, Julian Cross.

PUBLISHED SCRIPT.
1. Screenplay by Robert Towne (Santa Barbara, Calif.: Neville Publishers, 1983).
2. Towne, Robert. *Chinatown, The Last Detail, Shampoo—The Screenplays.* New York: Grove Press, 1994.

AMPAS. GENERAL COLLECTION.
1. Screenplay by Robert Towne. Third draft, October 9, 1973. 145 p. Gift of the author.

THE AMERICAN FILM INSTITUTE.
1. Screenplay by Robert Towne. Third draft, October 9, 1973. 145 p.
2. Towne, n.d. 153 p.

MUSEUM OF MODERN ART. DEPARTMENT OF FILM.
1. Screenplay by Robert Towne. Third draft plus revisions, October 9, 1973. 146 p. Photocopy. Revision dates obliterated.

NEW YORK PUBLIC LIBRARY FOR THE PERFORMING ARTS.
1. Screenplay by Robert Towne. Third draft, October 9, 1973, 145 p.

UCSB. DAVIDSON LIBRARY.
1. Screenplay by Robert Towne, third draft, October 9, 1973, 145 p.

UCLA. ARTS SPECIAL COLLECTION. GENERAL COLLECTION.
1. Robert Towne, n.d. 153 p. *Title page:* Starring Jack Nicholson and Faye Dunaway. Noah Cross referred to as Julian Cross in this version.
2. Third draft, October 9, 1973. 145 p.
3. Second draft, September 7, 1973. 152 p. Yellow pages.

USC. GENERAL COLLECTION.
1. T.p.: *Chinatown* by Robert Towne, Director: Roman Polanski. Starring Jack Nicholson and Faye Dunaway. A Robert Evans–Paramount Pictures Production, n.d. 153p.
2. Second draft, September 7, 1973. Noah Cross is Julian Cross in this version.
3. Third draft, October 9, 1973. 146 p. Includes revised pages: 10/12/73, 10/24/73, and 11/28/73. Some annotations in script. Noah Cross character is Justin Cross in this version, but is crossed out and Noah substituted.

WRITERS GUILD OF AMERICA, WEST.
1. Screenplay by Robert Towne. 1974.

ADDITIONAL SCREENPLAY MATERIAL IN THE FOLLOWING LIBRARIES.
Brigham Young University; California State University, San Francisco; Chapman University; Columbia College; George Washington University; Hampshire College; Johns Hopkins University; Library of Congress; Los Angeles Public Library; New York University; Oklahoma State University; Orlando City Library System; San Francisco Public Library; Stanford University; Temple University; University of Alabama; University of Minnesota; University of Pennsylvania; University of St. Thomas; Wichita Public Library.

THE COMMODORE MARRIES.
Unrealized project.

AMPAS. JOHN HUSTON COLLECTION. SCRIPT MATERIAL.
1. A comedy-drama in three acts, by A. H. Parsons. *Handwritten:* With Walter Huston, John Huston Contemplated Movie. Photocopy from NYPL Collection.

CONCERTINA.
Unrealized project.

AMPAS. PAUL KOHNER [Huston's longtime agent] COLLECTION.
1. Story by John Huston and Frederick Kohner, n.d.

CONSTANT NYMPH. 1943.
Warner Brothers. Screenplay by Kathryn Scola. Directed by Edmund Goulding. Huston assigned, December 14, 1939–January 13, 1940.

NEW YORK STATE ARCHIVE.
1. Dialogue script.

NEW YORK PUBLIC LIBRARY FOR THE PERFORMING ARTS.
1. Screenplay, second revised final, 8/27/41, 123 + A-C p. Includes pink revised pages, 4/10/42, no author indicated.

2. (Script for British production), no title page, no authors or date indicated, various pages.

USC. WARNER BROTHERS ARCHIVE.

1. Script from British version, Gaumont and Play. (It appears that Warner Brothers bought rights from Gaumont.)
2. Script versions: May 29, 1940, no author; June 4, 1940, no author; June 10, 1940, no author; May 6, 1941, Edmund Goulding; August 27, 1941, no author; January 28, 1942, no author.
3. *The Constant Nymph* by John Huston, n.d. 174 p. (Two copies in file, with second copy as treatment.)
4. Continuity and dialogue from screen, February 1, 1934. British version.
5. Script by Kay Van Riper, with scenes suggested by Edmund Goulding, n.d.
6. Dialogue transcript, various paging. 1942.

THE WISCONSIN CENTER FOR FILM AND THEATER RESEARCH, THE STATE HISTORICAL SOCIETY OF WISCONSIN.

1. Versions of the screenplay.

DANGER SIGNAL. 1945.

Warner Brothers. Screenplay by Adele Comandini and Graham Baker. Directed by Robert Florey. Huston on assignment, March 10, 1941–March 12, 1941. No indication in AMPAS Huston Archive or USC Warner Archive of any writing work by Huston.

NEW YORK STATE ARCHIVE.

1. Dialogue script.

USC. WARNER BROTHERS ARCHIVE. SCRIPT COLLECTION.

1. Script work from 1940, 1941 (January, October, December) through 1945 by: Alvah Bessie; Graham Baker; Emmet Lavery; Comandini and Baker; Lionel Wiggam; Arthur Horman; Craig Rice; Alfred Neumann; Howard Koch, Anne Froelik, and Heinz Herald; Thomas Job and Jo Pagano; Leonhard Frank; John Wexley and Harriet Hinsdale; and Alfred Nuemann.

THE WISCONSIN CENTER FOR FILM AND THEATER RESEARCH, THE STATE HISTORICAL SOCIETY OF WISCONSIN.

1. Versions of the screenplay.

THE DEAD. 1987.

Liffey Films/Zenith Productions/Vestron Pictures. Screenplay by Tony Huston and John Huston. Directed by John Huston.

AMPAS. GENERAL COLLECTION.

1. Tony and John Huston. Final version, May 10, 1987. 108 p. Includes opening and closing credits.

NEW YORK PUBLIC LIBRARY FOR THE PERFORMING ARTS.

1. A screenplay by Tony Huston and John Huston, based on the novella *The Dead* from *The Dubliners* by James Joyce, ca. 1986, Wieland Schulz-Keil and Chris Sievernich, New York, starts with page 6 (no pages of script missing). 112 p. Following page 112 is another title page, providing production information, March 1986. Handwritten on page

are names of other production members, $3.5. Following are pages 1 and 2, which is a brief description of *The Dead,* its history, and production team. Following pages 5 and 6 is Synopsis.

UCSB. DAVIDSON LIBRARY.
1. Screenplay by Tony Huston and John Huston, 1986. 112 p.

ADDITIONAL SCREENPLAY MATERIAL IN THE FOLLOWING LIBRARIES.
Connecticut College, Emerson College, Colgate University, Middlebury College.

A DEATH IN THE FAMILY.
   Unrealized project (?).

AMPAS. JOHN HUSTON COLLECTION. SCRIPT MATERIAL.
1. A play in three acts by Tad Mosel. From the novel by James Agee. Property of Fred Coe, New York. *On t.p.:* #3, various pages, n.d. No indication of Huston's involvement.

DE SADE. 1969.
   American International Production/Transcontinental Film/CCC/Filmkunst. Screenplay by Richard Matheson and Peter Berg. Directed by Cy Endfield. Uncredited additional directing by Roger Corman and Gordon Hessler. *Film Dope* indicates that Huston was also an uncredited director. Producer Samuel Z. Arkoff noted that Huston was approached to finish the direction, but declined. Huston, actor, Abbe de Sade.

AMPAS. JOHN HUSTON COLLECTION. SCRIPT MATERIAL.
1. *The Marquis De Sade.* Original screenplay by Richard Matheson, n.d. 136 p. *On top of page, in pen:* Acted in.

USC. GENERAL COLLECTION. THE MARQUIS DE SADE.
1. Original screenplay by Richard Matheson. *Cover:* American International Pictures. *In pencil:* OK sj, AIP; stamped June 24, 1968. *Also in pencil:* (Vizzard?), 6/26/68. 133 p. Gen. no. 305.
2. Keir Dullea, Senta Berger, and Lilli Palmer, starring in *De Sade.* Special guest appearance, John Huston as "The Abbe." Directed by Cy Endfield, written by Richard Matheson, produced by James H. Nicholson and Samuel Z. Arkoff. Ca. 1968 by American International Pictures. *Cover:* Property of American International Productions. De Sade. 127 p.

THE DESERTER. 1971.
   Dino De Laurentiis/Jadran/Heritage/Paramount. Screenplay by Clair Huffaker. Directed by Burt Kennedy. Huston, actor, General Miles.

AMPAS. JOHN HUSTON COLLECTION. SCRIPT MATERIAL.
1. "The Devil's Backbone" by Clair Huffaker, August 1969. 151 p. Also incomplete copy of same screenplay, 98 p.

USC. CHUCK CONNORS COLLECTION.
1. *The Devil's Backbone.* Revised title: *The Deserter.* Revised first draft, April 14, 1969. 128 p. Pasted into back of front cover is a still of Chuck Connors.

DESTRY RIDES AGAIN. 1932.
Universal. Produced by Carl Laemmle Jr. Dialogue by Robert Keith. Continuity by Isadore Bernstein. Directed by Ben Stoloff.

AMPAS. UNIVERSAL PICTURES. LIBRARY PROPERTIES. SYNOPSIS AND DESCRIPTIVE DATA 4, no. 6,051. Author: Max Brand. Purchased 8/20/31; released 4/17/32.

1. Treatment: Randall Faye, Tom Reed, John Huston, 10/19/31, complete (no pages indicated). Screenplay: Randall Faye, Tom Reed, Ernst L. Frank, John B. Clymer, Isadore Bernstein, Robert Kief, and Harold Shumate.

NEW YORK STATE ARCHIVE.

1. Cutting continuity script.

THE DIRECTORS (Short). 1963.
Produced by Nat Greenblatt. Notice in *New York Post* (December 20, 1963) and an unidentified paper: *The Directors,* a short subject in color centering on several of the world's leading film directors, to open at Cinema II on December 23, 1963, in league with *Ladybug, Ladybug.* Among the filmmakers featured in the short are Fellini, Stevens, Wilder, Lean, Wyler, Germi, Antonioni, and Joseph Mankiewicz. Huston appears.

NEW YORK STATE ARCHIVE.

1. Dialogue script.

THE DISAPPOINTMENT, OR THE FORCE OF CREDULITY.
Unrealized project (?).

AMPAS. JOHN HUSTON COLLECTION.

1. A new comic opera of two acts by Andrew Barton, Esq., New York. Printed in the Year MDCCLXVII (i.e., 1767). A photocopy from the Library Co. of Philadelphia. No other indication of Huston's involvement unless related to *Independence* (cf. that entry).

DISRAELI. 1929.
Warner Brothers. Screenplay by Julian Josephson, based on a play by Louis N. Parker. Directed by Alfred E. Green. Huston assigned, November 13, 1939–December 13, 1939 (with Michael Hogan and Aeneas MacKenzie).

UCLA. ARTS SPECIAL COLLECTION. GENERAL COLLECTION.

1. *Disraeli* by Louis Parker. Adapted by Julian Josephson. 1929. 107 p. *Note:* Dialogue is final.

USC. WARNER BROTHERS ARCHIVE.

1. Final dialogue, by Louis Parker, adapted by Julian Josephson, n.d.
2. Script, December 16, 1939. 83 p. No t.p. and no authors indicated.
3. Script, October 24, 1940. MacEwan, "An Empire Was Built."
4. Scripts, December 11, 1939; April 16, 1940. Michael Hogan, *The Prime Minister.*
5. Script, Louis Parker, *Disraeli.* 1929 (?).
6. Biographical appraisement of the man, MacKenzie, n.d.
7. Scenario by Forrest Haley, n.d. 60 p. Heavily annotated.
8. *The Prime Minister.* Dialogue transcript. 1941. Screenplay by Michael Hogan and Brock

Williams. Directed by Thorold Dickinson. Stars John Gielgud and Diana Wynyard. Includes eliminations.

9. *Disraeli* (1849) screenplay and dialogue by Julian Josephson, n.d. 66p.

WISCONSIN/WARNER BROTHERS SCREENPLAY SERIES.* Reel 66.
1. Screenplay by Julian Josephson, final, n.d. 107 p.

Note. *The State Historical Society of Wisconsin, which houses these scripts, reports multiple versions of the screenplay.

DR. EHRLICH'S MAGIC BULLET. 1940.
     Warner Brothers. Screenplay by John Huston, Heinz Herald, and Norman Burnside. Directed by William Dieterle.

PUBLISHED SCRIPT.
1. Ward, Jerry, and Richard Macaulay, eds. *The Best Pictures, 1939–1940, and The Yearbook of Motion Pictures in America.* New York: Dodd, Mead, 1940. Includes screenplay for *Dr. Ehrlich's Magic Bullet.*

AMPAS. GENERAL COLLECTION.
1. Final screenplay, October 13, 1939, with blue revision pages.

AMPAS. JOHN HUSTON COLLECTION. SCRIPT MATERIAL.
1. Final screenplay, October 13, 1939, with revisions to December 7, 1939. 140 p. Specially bound.

NEW YORK STATE ARCHIVE.
1. Dialogue script.

USC. WILLIAM DIETERLE COLLECTION.
1. Background information on Ehrlich, including Marquardt piece in Robinson collection, obit, background photos of Dr. Ehrlich and his lab, and other associations. Additional background and articles on Dieterle.
2. Two loose-leaf binders of research material from Warner Brothers Research Department, October 11, 1939.
3. Test shots makeup and costumes of Robinson, Nolan, Crisp, Kruger, Basserman, Litel, Stevenson, Heydt, Love, and Children.
4. *606* (*Paul Ehrlich*), December 7, 1938. 55 p. Treatment.
5. *Test 606.* Original story and screenplay by John Huston, Heinz Herald, and Norman Burnstine (Burnside), August 12, 1939. 177 p. + additional 7 p. "Dr. Ehrlich" in pencil above title. *Cover sheet:* August 12, 1939, temporary. Annotated, handwritten notes and correct date sheet attached.
6. *Dr. Ehrlich,* September 22, 1939. No authors indicated. Revised temporary. 159 p. Annotated.
7. *Dr. Ehrlich,* October 13, 1939. Final. No authors indicated. 146 p. Additional changes, October 12, 1939. 5 p. *Cover, penciled note:* Final, October 13, 1939.

USC. EDWARD G. ROBINSON COLLECTION.
1. Marquardt, Martha. *Paul Ehrlich: The Man and the Scientist—Recollections of the Years, 1902–1915.* 1924. 79 p. Transcription and translation of *Festschrift* (originally published in German by Deutsche Verlags-Anstalt, 1924).

John Huston

2. *Paul Ehrlich,* part I, May 8, 1939. No authors indicated. First revised version. 236 p.
3. *Dr. Ehrlich* revised temporary, September 22, 1939. 159 p. Another copy, but end includes five pages of men's temporary wardrobe plot (from revised temporary). Schedules, Dieterle, September 25, 1939.
4. *Dr. Ehrlich,* October 13, 1939. Final. 146 p. Annotated.
5. *Dr. Ehrlich,* October 13, 1939. 140 p. Includes blue revised pages, October–December 1939. Specially bound copy, with Robinson's initials embossed on cover. Included in copy: congratulatory telegram, Robinson's makeup and comparison with the real Dr. Ehrlich, speech that Robinson made before scientific and doctors' group, and other biographical information.

USC. WARNER BROTHERS ARCHIVE.

1. *Ehrlich* screenplay by Norman Burnstine and Heinz Herald. Treatment, March 21, 1939. 235 p. *Cover:* Parts I and II. Heavily annotated. Also includes typescript.
2. *Paul Ehrlich: The Man and the Scientist—Recollection of the Years, 1902–1915* by Martha Marquardt. *Feschrift* on his seventieth birthday, March 14, 1924 (rough translation). 78 p. Heavily annotated. (Two copies.) Second copy dated April 3, 1939.
3. Screenplay by Burnstine and Herald. Cover date, March 18, 1939. *Over title: Life of. . . .* 238 p.
4. Screenplay by Burnstine and Herald, March 21, 1939. 235 p.
5. Treatment by Burnstine. First draft, October 8, 1938. Treatment #1, October 30, 1938. 94 p. (Three copies.) Copy 3, no date; *in pencil on cover:* October 15, 1931. Treatment #2.
6. No title page. *Cover: Paul Ehrlich; in pencil:* Huston-Herald I. Treat 4. *Lower left:* Mr. Reinhardt. Preceding screenplay: cast of characters, n.d. *On cover, in pencil:* July 8, 1939. 236 p.
7. No t.p. *Cover: 606 (Paul Ehrlich). In pencil:* Herald, December 7, 1938. Orig. 4. *Lower left:* Reinhardt. Treatment. 55 p.
8. *Test 606.* Original story and screenplay by John Huston, Heinz Herald, and Norman Burnstine. *Cover sheet:* Temp, August 12, 1939. 177 p.
9. No t.p. *Cover: Dr. Ehrlich,* September 22, 1939. Revised temporary. No authors indicated. 159 p.
10. No t.p. *Cover: Dr. Ehrlich. Penciled in above title: Life of. . . .* Final, October 13, 1939. Exclusive. No authors indicated. 140 + 1 p. Includes blue revision sheets, October 27, 1939–December 6, 1939.
11. *Dr. Ehrlich's Magic Bullet* (dialogue transcript), Warner Brothers, 1940. Various paging.

WISCONSIN/WARNER BROTHERS SCREENPLAY SERIES. Reel 68.

1. *The Life of Dr. Ehrlich* by John Huston and Heinz Herald, March 8, 1939.* 235 p.
2. *Dr. Ehrlich.** Final. No authors indicated. October 13, 1939, with revisions to December 1, 1939. 145 p.

Note. *The Wisconsin Center for Film and Theater Research, the State Historical Society of Wisconsin, which houses these scripts, reports multiple versions of the screenplay.

ADDITIONAL SCREENPLAY MATERIAL IN THE FOLLOWING LIBRARIES.
Dartmouth College.

A FAREWELL TO ARMS. 1957.
Twentieth Century-Fox. Screenplay by Ben Hecht. Huston also contributed to screenplay, based on Ernest Hemingway's novel of the same name (New York: Scribners, 1929). Directed by Charles Vidor. Huston was the original director but withdrew.

AMPAS. JOHN HUSTON COLLECTION. SCRIPT MATERIAL.
1. Screenplay by Ben Hecht, October 22, 1956. 191 p. (Two copies.)
2. Screenplay by Ben Hecht, January 26, 1957. 173 p. Pages of script inserted, annotated by John Huston. Throughout drawing and doodles by Huston. Another copy in the collection, after page 173, has five pages entitled, "Geographical and Personality Notes for the Battle of Caparetto."

THE BRITISH FILM INSTITUTE.
1. A version of the screenplay.

MUSEUM OF MODERN ART. FILM LIBRARY.
1. Combined dialogue and cutting continuity on *A Farewell to Arms*. In Cinemascope, January 10, 1958. Length of film—16,677 feet, 8 frs. 238 p.

UCLA. ARTS SPECIAL COLLECTION. GENERAL COLLECTION.
1. Screenplay by Ben Hecht, 1957. 173 p. Includes complete credits with Charles Vidor listed as director.

UCLA. ARTS SPECIAL COLLECTION. TWENTIETH CENTURY-FOX ARCHIVE.
1. Screenplay by Ben Hecht, October 22, 1956. 191 p.
2. Ben Hecht, February 7, 1957. 152 p. *Cover:* Directed by John Huston. Includes some cast members: Rock Hudson, Vittorio de Sica, and Jennifer Jones.
3. Revisions of March 7 script. Attached are scenes that are to be shot on lot. *Above title:* August 22, 1957.
4. *Cover title:* Dialogue continuity, January 7, 1958. Credits indicate Charles Vidor as director.
5. Combined dialogue and cutting continuity, January 10, 1958. 238 p.
6. Ben Hecht, Selznick Co., 1957. 176 p. Vidor as director.
7. Sixth draft, January 10, 1957. 210 p. Red underlining throughout.
8. Ben Hecht, eighth draft, January 26, 1957. 173 p. Huston indicated as director.
9. Fourth draft, October 10, 1956. Revisions: October 17, 1956, and October 19, 1956. 186 p.
10. Seventh draft, January 17, 1957. 135 p. Inserted between pages 123 and 124, handwritten annotations.
11. March 7, 1957. Tenth draft, with revised pages. Various colored sheets. Shooting script. Includes annotations and some revised dialogue (stapled in). Vidor indicated as director.
12. Combined second and third drafts, September 11–19, 1956. 190 p.
13. First draft, August 18, 1956. 108 p. Annotated underlining in red.

USC. TWENTIETH CENTURY-FOX. COLLECTION.
1. Dialogue continuity, January 7, 1958. Dialogue taken from pre-dubbed dialogue track onto tape. 76 p. Credits indicate Hecht and Vidor.
2. Combined dialogue and cutting continuity, January 10, 1958. Continuity taken from Moviola. 238 p. Credits indicate Hecht and Vidor.

ADDITIONAL SCREENPLAY MATERIAL IN THE FOLLOWING
LIBRARIES.
California State University, San Francisco; Colgate University; Detroit Public Library;
Emerson College; Evanston Public Library; Howard University; Loyola Marymount
University; Michigan State University; Milwaukee County Federated Library System;
Newberry Library; Oklahoma State University; Wichita Public Library.

FATAL ATTRACTION. *See* HEAD ON.

FAT CITY. 1972.
Columbia. Produced by Ray Stark. Screenplay by Leonard Gardner, based
on Gardner's novel of the same name (New York: Straus and Giroux, 1969).
Directed by John Huston, who also contributed to screenplay (uncredited).

PUBLISHED SCRIPT.
1. Gardner, L., and John Huston. "Nadmute mesto." *Film a Doba* 19, no. 12 (December 19,
   1973): 640–49, illus. (Script extract)—IIFP 74, p. 201.

AMPAS. GENERAL COLLECTION.
1. Screenplay by Leonard Gardner, March 17, 1971.
2. Screenplay by Leonard Gardner and John Huston, November 4, 1970.

AMPAS. JOHN HUSTON COLLECTION. PRODUCTION FILE.
1. In file on *The Hostage* a letter from Ed Pearlstein, Rastar and Columbia Pictures, to Paul
   Kohner (Huston's agent), July 29, 1970, in which Huston's involvement with *Fat City* is
   discussed. Huston would write and deliver a revision of Leonard Gardner's second draft
   script on or before November 15, 1970. Also, Huston to direct and supervise writing of
   script, with payments stipulated.

AMPAS. JOHN HUSTON COLLECTION. SCRIPT MATERIAL. Uncataloged,
box 1.
1. *Fat City.* Screenplay by Leonard Gardner and John Huston, adapted from the novel by
   Leonard Gardner, November 4, 1970. *At top of pages:* JH, November 4, 1970. Heavily
   annotated by Huston. 130 p.
2. *Fat City* by Leonard Gardner, n.d. 140 p.
3. No t.p. No author or date indicated. 131 p. Heavily annotated.
4. John Huston and Leonard Gardner, October 1970–November 1970. 134 p. Typewritten
   on loose-leaf pages. Annotated. (Two copies.)
5. Leonard Gardner, May 5, 1971. 131 p.
6. Leonard Gardner, revision, April 22, 1971. 121 p. Heavily annotated.
7. Leonard Gardner, May 18, 1971. *Cover:* Original—No Revisions. 119 p.
8. Script in folder, no author, n.d. 135 p. Huston annotations.
9. Files includes miscellaneous pages, discarded pages, pink and green revision pages,
   dated March–September 1971. Huston's handwritten notes. D. Giler, August 15, and his
   notes on Gardner to Ray Stark, July 26, 1971. "Cutting notes from John Huston," June
   27, 1971. *Fat City* added shots. Mentor Huebner. Thirteen pages of storyboard drawings.
10. Envelope marked: "Discards *Fat City.*" Includes handwritten notes; typewritten notes for
    Fat City; breakdown of *Fat City* screenplay, first version, on St. Clerans letterhead, n.d.,
    14 p.; breakdown of the book, St. Clerans, n.d., 8 p.; various script pages from Huston
    and Gardner, October 22, 1970; script pages, John Huston, October 16, 1970.

AMPAS. JOHN HUSTON COLLECTION. SCRIPT MATERIAL. Uncataloged, box 4.
1. Ray Stark's reactions to November 4, screenplay, December 21, 1970. 13 p.

ADDITIONAL SCREENPLAY MATERIAL IN THE FOLLOWING LIBRARIES.
Columbia College, Emerson College, Ohio State University.

FORGOTTEN BOY. (An early version of *Wild Boys of the Road;* cf. under that entry.)
Universal. Unproduced. Huston contract writer for Universal, 1929–32.

AMPAS. JOHN HUSTON COLLECTION. SCRIPT MATERIAL.
1. Untitled script in collection. 94 p. Based on information in Universal inventory, no. 6,244, this script is the April 18, 1933, Huston treatment. Previously listed in John Huston Inventory, Early Scripts and Stories—Untitled #2 [1932–33?], pp. 39–40. Moved to Early Scripts and Stories—Titled, A–L, pp. 39–40.

AMPAS. WILLIAM WYLER COLLECTION.
1. *My Wandering Boy: The Story of The Forgotten Boy.* An original screenplay by N. Brewster Morse, n.d., various paging. (About 80 p.) *Note:* Same characters as in Huston's work.
2. *Boys in Uniform* (Universal inventory 6,232). Screenplay by Wellman Totman. Copies, March 9, 1933. 101 p.
3. Various sequences to screenplay, no author or dates indicated. Ca. 82 p.
4. No t.p. *The Forgotten Boy* from John Huston. Copied April 18, 1933. 94 p. Some pages out. Annotated. Same as previously untitled in Huston Script Collection. Other versions of script, some with Wyler's name indicated. Versions: 82 p.; 64 p.; first draft, 94 p. (same as April 18, 1933, version); some dated April 19, 1933.
5. *Forgotten Boy* from John Huston, June 5, 1933, 373 scenes, 86 p. (Same as Universal inventory 6,244.)
6. Folders with pages marked "outs," various paging, no author or dates, handwritten notes, some pages annotated.

AMPAS. UNIVERSAL PICTURES. LIBRARY PROPERTIES. SYNOPSIS AND DESCRIPTIVE DATA 5, no. 6,244. Unproduced. Date of purchase: February 9, 1933.
1. Authors: John Huston and M. Brewster Morse. Title: "Forgotten Boy" ("My Wandering Boy"). Original: M. Brewster Morse, 2/9/33. 71 p. Treatment: John Huston, 4/18/33. 94 p. Screenplay: John Huston, 6/5/33. 373 scenes.

FRANKIE AND JOHNNY ("St. Louis Legend"). 1963.
Writer/director. Unrealized project. *Note:* Huston wrote, produced, and published a play of the same name in 1930.

AMPAS. JOHN HUSTON COLLECTION. SCRIPT MATERIAL.
1. Screenplay, June 18, 1963. 93 p. No authors indicated.
2. Screen treatment by John Huston, n.d. 69 p.
3. Screen treatment by John Huston, n.d. Revised. 41 p.
4. *St. Louis Legend: The Story of Frankie and Johnny.* A screenplay by John Huston and Anthony Veiller, based on the play by John Huston, August 5, 1963. 128 p.

5. As no. 4. *Penciled notes on t.p.:* File copy, August 5, 1963, 6, to p. 43—July 28, 1963. 128 p.
6. Envelope with various loose and clipped-together sheets from script. Some by Veiller, some by Veiller and Huston, and some by Huston. Various dates—June 1963, January 1963. Includes additional copies of treatment and screenplay version. Discarded pages.
7. Folder with additional miscellaneous script sheets. Includes discards and rewrites, July 31, 1963. Veiller, June 11, 1963.

AMPAS. PAUL KOHNER (Huston's longtime agent) COLLECTION.

1. Treatment by John Huston, n.d., 70 p.

FREUD: THE SECRET PASSION. 1962.

Universal. Screenplay by Charles Kaufman and Wolfgang Reinhardt. Directed by John Huston. Huston contributed to screenplay (uncredited) and provided narration.

PUBLISHED SCRIPT.

1. Sartre, Jean-Paul. *Le Scénario Freud.* Paris: Gallimard, 1984.
2. Sartre, Jean Paul. *The Freud Scenario.* Chicago: University of Chicago Press, 1986. 549 p. (early version). Sartre, Jean-Paul. *The Freud Scenario.* Translated by Quentin Hoare. Chicago: University of Chicago Press, 1985.
3. *Kino* (Moscow), no. 4 (1991): 157–76. V. Gul'chenko. "Freid: il scenario."

AMPAS. GENERAL COLLECTION.

1. Final screenplay, August 9, 1961. 168 p.

AMPAS. JOHN HUSTON COLLECTION. SCRIPT MATERIAL.

1. Original outline by Jean-Paul Sartre, December 15, 1958. 60 p. Verbatim translation, first draft.
2. Screenplay by Jean-Paul Sartre, parts I–III, n.d. 179 p.
3. Screenplay, French version, various paging, n.d.
4. Screenplay by Jean-Paul Sartre. Revised by Wolfgang Reinhardt. December 28, 1959. 174 p. (incomplete). Includes handwritten partial script. Heavily annotated. Marked "A" on cover and "To: Paul Kohner" and (in German) *Zweite Version, Engl.*
5. Screenplay by Jean-Paul Sartre. Revised by Wolfgang Reinhardt, January. To Paul Kohner, Hollywood, 1960. 127 p.
6. Screenplay by Jean-Paul Sartre. Revised by Wolfgang Reinhardt, January 1960. 127 p. Marked "B" on cover. *Inside cover:* 12/14/60—German statement.
7. Screenplay by Jean-Paul Sartre. Version II. 127 p. Copy 2 (uncorrected) annotated.
8. Notes on script by Wolfgang Reinhardt, February 3, 1960–December 13, 1960. Marked "C" on cover. To Paul Kohner. *Inside front cover:* Table of Contents. Rough scene sequence, February 11, 1960, Reinhardt-Huston, 2 p. "F," Part one, March 28, 1960. Reinhardt and Charles Kaufman, and scene sequence.
9. Script changes and notes by Wolfgang Reinhardt, February 6, 1961–July 28, 1961. Preproduction, "D," to Paul Kohner. "Table of Contents" inside cover. Includes miscellaneous handwritten notes.
10. Outline by Charles Kaufman, n.d. 101 p.
11. Screenplay, July 25, 1960, with revisions to August 24, 1960. 257 p. Heavily annotated. *Note on cover:* Script with additions, deletions, etc., from which "First Draft" screenplay, dated September 1, 1960, was made. Tamara Comstoci. Pages 1–200 in folder; pp. 201–57 loose.
12. First draft screenplay, original screenplay by Jean-Paul Sartre. Adapted by Charles

Kaufman and Wolfgang Reinhardt, September 1, 1960. 283 p. Property of Universal Pictures.

13. No t.p. First page: I. Scene synopsis of *Freud* script, 10/12/60, 6 p., no author; outline of screenplay for *Freud* script, 8 p., no author or date; outline for screenplay for *Freud* script—John Wexley, October–November 1960. Annotated. *Cover:* For John Huston. *Inserted:* 2 p. of Huston's notes and doodles. Also in folder: loose pages, various paging, discards (March 1960), some pages annotated.

14. Revised first draft screenplay, April 14, 1961. With revisions to April 21, 1961. 207 p. Some annotations. Author statement on t.p. crossed out: Jean-Paul Sartre, Charles Kaufman, Wolfgang Reinhardt. Annotated. Includes Huston's doodles.

15. Revised first draft screenplay, April 14, 1961. With revisions to April 26, 1961. 207 p. No t.p., no author. *Cover:* John Huston. Includes one blue revision page.

16. Final screenplay, August 9, 1961. 168 p. No authors or date. (Two copies.)

17. *Freud.* Screenplay by John Huston and Wolfgang Reinhardt. Final shooting script, February 10, 1962. 145 p. *Note:* Script marked throughout to indicate writers' contributions—Charles Kaufman (K), Jean-Paul Sartre (S), John Huston (H), and Wolfgang Reinhardt (R). Some pages are combinations: R/H, K/R/H, S/H/R.

18. Final shooting script by John Huston and Wolfgang Reinhardt, February 10, 1962. 145 p. Specially bound.

19. *Miscellaneous changes and discards, 1960–62:*
    File copy: partial of work from February through April 1961. File contains pages dated through July 1961. Also includes discards.

Reinhardt, *Freud,* 1960. Exposition continued in the omitted first sequence to be covered 12/13/60, 6 p.; Paris sequence, 12/13/60, pp. 2–6.

Patients, including Nora, March 16, 1961. Annotations.

Carl Von Schlosser. 1961. Various paging, some handwritten by Huston, March 1961, July 1961.

Breur, 1961. Various paging, March, June 1961. Some marked: "final version, second version."

Breur, 1961. Various paging, June–July 1961.

Cecily, 1961. Various paging, June 1961. Annotated.

Huston, *Freud,* May–July 1961. Also includes Huston's handwritten notes.

Martha, March 19, 1961. 3 p. *At top of page 1:* JH and WR.

Freud. First lecture, various paging, June 1961. Some pages marked "JH," some "WR/JH."

Final, Cecily-Freud, 1961–62, mostly Huston's handwritten notes.

Suicide attempt and scene after Cecily's bedroom. Huston with Reinhardt, 1961–62. Various pages, paging, and dates, 1961. Some handwritten notes. Including blue and pink revised pages.

Freud-Martha. First scene (now Freud-Mother), 1962. Various paging, various dates: Some April 4 and 5, 1961. Marked "J. Huston."

John Huston and Wolfgang Reinhardt, 1962. Blue sheets, various paging, September 8, 1961.

John Huston and Wolfgang Reinhardt, 1962. Numerous handwritten notes with Huston doodles; pages, JH and WR, September 6, 1961; some, no authors, March 1961.

AMPAS. JOHN HUSTON COLLECTION. SCRIPT MATERIAL. Uncataloged, box 2.

1. *Freud.* Screenplay by John Huston and Wolfgang Reinhardt. Final shooting script, February 10, 1962. 145 p. *Cover:* Copy 3—John Huston.

AMPAS. VERTICAL FILE COLLECTION.
1. *Freud* by Jean-Paul Sartre. *Top of page 1:* May 1959. 181 p.

NEW YORK STATE ARCHIVE.
1. Cutting continuity script.

UCLA. ARTS SPECIAL COLLECTION. GENERAL COLLECTION.
1. Screenplay by John Huston and Wolfgang Reinhardt, n.d. 122 p.

UCSB. DAVIDSON LIBRARY.
1. Original screenplay by Jean-Paul Sartre, adapted by Charles Kaufman and Wolfgang Reinhardt, n.d. 207 p.

WRITERS GUILD OF AMERICA, WEST.
1. Screenplay by Charles Kaufman and Wolfgang Reinhardt.

ADDITIONAL SCREENPLAY MATERIAL IN THE FOLLOWING LIBRARIES. Dartmouth College, Emerson College.

GEORGE STEVENS: A FILMMAKER'S JOURNEY. 1984.
Written, produced, and directed by George Stevens Jr. Huston appears and discusses Stevens.

WRITERS GUILD OF AMERICA, WEST.
1. Script, 1988.

THE GINGER MAN.
Unrealized project (?).

AMPAS. JOHN HUSTON COLLECTION. SCRIPT MATERIAL.
1. Screenplay by J. P. Donleavy, n.d. 125 p. *In pencil on t.p.:* Carter De Haven?

GOYA. 1955.
Director. Unrealized project.

AMPAS. JOHN HUSTON COLLECTION. PRODUCTION FILE.
1. Correspondence that Huston received first treatment from Titanus Films, Rome, June 16, 1955, of the first draft screenplay by Talbot Jennings (148 p.). Script not in Huston Collection.

NEW YORK PUBLIC LIBRARY FOR THE PERFORMING ARTS.
1. Screenplay by Albert Lewin, from the adaptation by Talbot Jennings, September 23, 1957. 230 p. *Cover:* A Titanus Production. Gift of Howard Atlee.

THE HARD WAY. 1943.
Warner Brothers. Screenplay by Daniel Fuchs and Peter Viertel, based on the original story by Jerry Wald (producer). Directed by Vincent Sherman.

NEW YORK PUBLIC LIBRARY FOR THE PERFORMING ARTS.
1. Screenplay by Irwin Shaw and Daniel Fuchs. Producer, Jerry Wald. Director, Vincent Sherman. *Cover sheet:* Second Revised Final, 4/9/42. 138 p.

NEW YORK STATE ARCHIVE.
1. Dialogue script.

USC. WARNER BROTHERS ARCHIVE. PRODUCTION FILE.
1. Memo from Jerry Wald to John Huston, December 3, 1941, asking him to comment on Irwin Shaw's script.
2. Memo from Huston to Hal Wallis, December 8, 1941, with Huston's reactions.
3. Original story by Wald and various treatments and versions of screenplay by Irwin Shaw, Arch Obler, and Daniel Fuchs.

THE WISCONSIN CENTER FOR FILM AND THEATER RESEARCH, THE STATE HISTORICAL SOCIETY OF WISCONSIN.
1. Multiple versions of this screenplay.

HARROW ALLEY. 1962–63, 1967.
   Huston considered as director. Unrealized.

AMPAS. JOHN HUSTON COLLECTION. PRODUCTION FILE.
1.Correspondence, 1963, 1967. Huston was seriously considered as director, and he was interested. Project failed because of a lack of financing, despite Ingo Preminger's (producer) attempt to get financing from CBS, ABC, MGM, and Twentieth Century-Fox.

AMPAS. JOHN HUSTON COLLECTION. SCRIPT MATERIAL.
1. Final screenplay by Walter Newman, n.d. 141 p. (Three copies.)

NEW YORK PUBLIC LIBRARY FOR THE PERFORMING ARTS.
1. Screenplay by Walter Brown Newman, n.d., 173 p. *Cover:* Ingo Preminger presents *Harrow Alley* by Walter Newman.

HASSAN. 1957.
   Huston considered as director. Unrealized.

AMPAS. JOHN HUSTON COLLECTION. PRODUCTION FILE.
1. December 30, 1957, letter. Fox was interested in purchasing rights to play and possibly in lining up a deal with Buddy Adler. Attachment from Nigel Balchin (screenwriter) with actors considered for film.

AMPAS. JOHN HUSTON COLLECTION. SCRIPT MATERIAL.
1. *Hassan* by James Elroy Flecker. Screenplay by Nigel Balchin, n.d. 161 p.
2. As no. 1, n.d. 74 p.

HAUNTED SUMMER. Pathé/Cannon. 1988.
   Screenplay by Lewis John Carlino. Directed by Ivan Passer. Huston originally designated as director but withdrew.

NEW YORK PUBLIC LIBRARY FOR THE PERFORMING ARTS.
1. A screenplay by Lewis John Carlino, from the book by Anne Edwards. Second draft, April 9, 1985, ca. 1986, Cannon Films. 127 p.

John Huston

UCLA. ARTS SPECIAL COLLECTION.
1. Screenplay by Carlino. Second draft, April 9, 1985. 127 p. *Handwritten on t.p.:* Cannon 1988, Ivan Passer, Dir.

USC. BOYLE COLLECTION.
1. *Haunted Summer,* a screenplay by Lewis John Carlino, second draft, April 9, 1985, from the book by Anne Edwards. Ca. 1986, Cannon Films, Inc. 127 p.

HEAD ON (*Fatal Attraction*). 1979.
Greentree Productions. Screenplay by Jim Sanderson and Paul Illidge. Directed by Michael Grant. Huston, actor, Clarke Hill.

UCLA. ARTS SPECIAL COLLECTION. GENERAL COLLECTION.
1. Screenplay by Ted Gershung. First draft, 1980. 98 p.

THE HEART IS A LONELY HUNTER. 1968.
Warner Brothers. Screenplay by Thomas C. Ryan. Directed by Robert Ellis Miller. Huston: Unrealized project (?).

AMPAS. JOHN HUSTON COLLECTION. SCRIPT MATERIAL.
1. Screenplay by Thomas C. Ryan, from the novel by Carson McCullers, the Landau Co., New York, n.d. *In pencil:* Ray Stark, March 15, 1966. 136 p. (Stark was not producer on this project.)

MUSEUM OF MODERN ART. FILM LIBRARY.
1. Screenplay by Thomas C. Ryan, produced by David Suskind. Talent Assoc., New York., n.d. 146 p.

NEW YORK PUBLIC LIBRARY FOR THE PERFORMING ARTS.
1. Screenplay by Thomas C. Ryan, from the novel by Carson McCullers, revised, Brownston Productions, New York, n.d. 144 p.

WRITERS GUILD OF AMERICA, WEST.
1. Screenplay by Thomas C. Ryan. Revised final, September 21, 1967.

HEAVEN KNOWS, MR. ALLISON. 1957.
Twentieth Century-Fox. Screenplay by John Lee Mahin and John Huston, based on the novel of the same name by Charles Shaw (London: F. Muller, 1952). Directed by John Huston.

AMPAS. GENERAL COLLECTION.
1. Revised final, August 13, 1956. Includes blue revision pages. 108 p. No author indicated, but copy from John Lee Mahin Collection.

AMPAS. JOHN HUSTON COLLECTION. SCRIPT MATERIAL.
1. Revisions to August 21, 1956. No author. 108 p. Specially bound.
2. Script, loose pages in folder. No t.p. *Note stapled to cover: Heaven Knows, Mr. Allison* script. No author indicated. Continuously paged, 108 p. Heavily annotated. Handwritten notes (verso p. 30). Some pages revised, November–December 1956; some pages marked "Second revision, 11/17/56." Huston's name at top of some pages.

AMPAS. JOHN HUSTON COLLECTION. SCRIPT MATERIAL. Uncataloged, box 2.
1. *Heaven Knows, Mr. Allison* by John Lee Mahin. Writer's working script, February 1, 1956. 115 p. Inserted are notes on conference with Legion of Decency, 2 p.

542

NEW YORK STATE ARCHIVE.
1. Dialogue script.

UCLA. ARTS SPECIAL COLLECTION. TWENTIETH CENTURY-FOX
ARCHIVE.
1. Writer's working script by John Lee Mahin, February 1, 1956. 115 p.
2. John Lee Mahin. Final, May 11, 1956. 136 p. Includes yellow revision sheets.

UNIVERSITY OF IOWA. TWENTIETH CENTURY-FOX SCRIPT COLLECTION.
1. Dialogue taken from the screen, February 11, 1957.
2. Revised final script, August 13, 1956.
3. Continuity and dialogue, March 1957.
4. Continuity and dialogue, edited copy.

USC. TWENTIETH CENTURY-FOX COLLECTION.
1. John Lee Mahin. Writer's working script, February 1, 1956. 115 p. Buddy Adler's (production head) copy. Heavily annotated with "Hold" indication by Adler. (Another annotated copy, no indication of whose.)
2. John Lee Mahin. Final, May 11, 1956. *Author's note:* Changes reflect conference with representatives from the Motion Picture Code and Legion of Decency, July 6, 1956. 136 p. Pages are white and yellow.
3. John Lee Mahin. Revised final, August 13, 1956. 108 p. Includes blue revised pages, August 1956, November 1956.

WRITERS GUILD OF AMERICA, WEST.
1. Revised final, August 13, 1956. 108 p. Includes revised pages, various dates, November 1956.

HELL'S HEROES. 1930.
Universal. Screenplay and dialogue by Tom Reed, based on the novel, *The Three Godfathers,* by Peter Kyne. Directed by William Wyler. John Huston, actor, bit part (uncredited).

NEW YORK STATE ARCHIVE.
1. Dialogue script.

HERE IS GERMANY (working titles: *Know Your Enemy: Germany; Lest We Forget*). September 1945.
U.S. War Department Information and Education Division. Army Services Forces. Army Pictorial Service. Signal Corps. Official Orientation Film no. 11. Story preparation and writers, William Shirer and George Ziomer. Additional story preparation by Ernst Lubitsch; writer, Sgt. Gottfried Reinhardt. Huston, as part of this group, was contributing writer (uncredited).

AMPAS. JOHN HUSTON COLLECTION. SCRIPT MATERIAL.
1. "Dear Jules" letter, June 14, 1944, from George Roth, on Army Service Corps, Photographic Center, LIC, New York, letterhead, indicates that four sets of pages revised by Major Veiller were enclosed and need to be inserted in the scripts. Various pages. Some pages marked "Revised June 12, 1944."
2. Script. No authors indicated, n.d. 42 p. Annotated throughout by Huston. Inserted between pages 27 and 28 are thirteen pages of handwritten notes. Note inserted in file: Nitrate Film Frame Removed November 10, 1981.

THE HERO. 1932.
Universal. Unproduced.

AMPAS. JOHN HUSTON COLLECTION. SCRIPT MATERIAL.
1. *The Hero,* from: John Huston, September 22, 1932. 14 p. Located in John Huston Inventory, Early Script and Stories—Titled, p. 39.

AMPAS. UNIVERSAL PICTURES. LIBRARY PROPERTIES. SYNOPSIS AND DESCRIPTIVE DATA 4, no. 6,182. Unproduced. Author, John Huston. Title, *The Hero* ("Amateur Gangster"). Date of purchase, August 24, 1932. $1.00.
1. Original: John Huston, 9/2/32. 14 p.

HIGH ROAD TO CHINA. 1983.
Golden Harvest/Pan Pacific. Screenplay by Sandra Weintraub Roland and S. Lee Pogostin. Directed by Brian G. Hutton. Project started in 1976 by Hutton and Pogostin. Although Huston took over project in 1978, commissioned two scripts, and scouted locations, he dropped out of the project sometime in 1979 (cf. *Film Dope,* no. 26 [January 1983]: 20: Miscellaneous work as director).

AMPAS. GENERAL COLLECTION.
1. Screenplay by S. Lee Pogostin, adapted from the novel by Jon Cleary, n.d. 131 p.

AMPAS. JOHN HUSTON COLLECTION.
1. Screenplay by S. Lee Pogostin, n.d. 131 p.
2. Screenplay by Jonathan Hales. Revised March 9, 1979. 139 p.

THE AMERICAN FILM INSTITUTE.
1. Screenplay by Jonathan Hales. Revised March 9, 1979. 139 p.

UCLA. ARTS SPECIAL COLLECTION. GENERAL COLLECTION.
1. Screenplay by Sandra Roland, n.d. 129 p.
2. Screenplay by Jonathan Hales. Revised May 1, 1979. 129 p.
3. Screenplay by S. Roland, November 10, 1980. 120 p.

HIGH SIERRA. 1941.
Warner Brothers. Screenplay by John Huston and W. R. Burnett, based on W. R. Burnett's novel (New York: Knopf, 1940). Directed by Raoul Walsh.

PUBLISHED SCRIPT.
1. Gomery, Douglas, ed. *High Sierra.* Wisconsin/Warner Brothers Screenplay Series. Madison, Wis.: University of Wisconsin Press, for the Wisconsin Center for Film and Theater Research, 1979.

AMPAS. GENERAL COLLECTION.
1. Original story by W. R. Burnett. Screenplay by John Huston and W. R. Burnett. Supervisor, Mark Hellinger. 138 p. Includes blue page revisions.

AMPAS. JOHN HUSTON COLLECTION. SCRIPT MATERIAL.
1. Final screenplay by John Huston and W. R. Burnett, July 22, 1940. 161 p. Specially bound.

NEW YORK PUBLIC LIBRARY FOR THE PERFORMING ARTS.
1. Screenplay by John Huston and W. R. Burnett. Original story by W. R. Burnett. *Cover:* Rev. final, 7/31/40. 138 p.

NEW YORK STATE ARCHIVE.
1. Dialogue script.

UCLA. ARTS SPECIAL COLLECTION. GENERAL COLLECTION.
1. Huston and Burnett. Supervisor, Mark Hellinger. Revised temporary, July 10, 1940. 166 p.
2. Huston and Burnett, revised final, July 21, 1940. 138 p.

USC. BOYLE COLLECTION.
1. Original story by W. R. Burnett, screenplay by John Huston and W. R. Burnett. Supervisor, Mark Hellinger. 1941. 167 p. Photocopy.

USC. WARNER BROTHERS ARCHIVE.
1. Screenplay by John Huston. Temporary, May 24, 1940. 160 p. Inserted: Revised cast of characters, May 27, 1940.
2. Screenplay by John Huston and W. R. Burnett. Final, July 22, 1940. 160 p.
3. Huston and Burnett. Revised final, July 31, 1940. 138 p. Includes blue revised sheets, August 20, 1940.

WISCONSIN/WARNER BROTHERS SCREENPLAY SERIES. Reel 6.
1. Screenplay by John Huston and W. R. Burnett, July 31, 1940, with revisions to September 6, 1940.* 142 p.

Note. *The Wisconsin Center for Film and Theater Research, the State Historical Society of Wisconsin, which houses this script, reports multiple versions of the screenplay.

ADDITIONAL SCREENPLAY MATERIAL IN THE FOLLOWING LIBRARIES.
Dartmouth College, Indiana University.

THE HORSE OF SELENE. 1971–72.
Writer/director. Unrealized project.

AMPAS. JOHN HUSTON COLLECTION. SCRIPT MATERIAL.
1. *The Horse of Selene,* Tim Vignoles. Author's rough notes, scene by scene, n.d. (12 p.) Filed in Huston's Inventory: Miscellaneous Stories, Scripts—Untitled Works.

THE HOSTAGE. 1970.
Director. Unrealized.

AMPAS. JOHN HUSTON COLLECTION. PRODUCTION FILE.
1. Various correspondence, July–August 1970, regarding Huston's involvement in supervising writing of script (with remuneration's indicated) and in directing the film. Huston and Ray Stark agreed that while there was no firm commitment, one month after John Osborne turned in the script, it could be submitted to Huston for his consideration. If the parties agreed, Huston would direct; otherwise, no obligations.

AMPAS. JOHN HUSTON COLLECTION. SCRIPT MATERIAL.
1. Draft screenplay by John Osborne, n.d. 135 p.

A HOUSE DIVIDED. 1931.
Universal. Produced by Carl Laemmle Jr. Paul Kohner (associate producer). Screenplay by John Clymer and Dale Van Every and dialogue by John Huston.

NEW YORK STATE ARCHIVE.
1. Cutting continuity script.

HUNCHBACK OF NOTRE DAME. 1939.
RKO. Screenplay by Sonya Levien and Bruno Frank. Directed by William Dieterle. Huston wrote early treatments.

NEW YORK STATE ARCHIVE.
1. Cutting continuity dialogue.

UCLA. ARTS SPECIAL COLLECTION. RKO SCRIPT COLLECTION.
1. File includes numerous versions of screenplay, 1939–40; dialogue continuity (October 14, 1939); cutting continuity (December 12, 1939); background material; and synopsis of various versions.

USC. DIETERLE COLLECTION.
1. *The Hunchback of Notre Dame* (from John Huston, October 27, 1932). Blue covers. *Five pages on yellow paper:* Treatment, followed by the beginnings of a script, 3 pages; followed by 2 continuous pages, stapled together; followed by additional scenes, stapled together. Various other markings on file and the names Mr. Schrager and Marion Pecht.

INDEPENDENCE. 1976.
National Historic Park, National Park Service, Department of the Interior/Twentieth Century-Fox. Produced by Joyce Ritter and Lloyd Ritter. Screenplay by the Ritters and Thomas McGrath. Directed by John Huston.

AMPAS. JOHN HUSTON COLLECTION. SCRIPT MATERIAL. Uncataloged, box 2.
1. Story outline and treatment outline. First revision, September 23, 1974. Twentieth Century-Fox Bicentennial Division, Wylde and Assoc., New York. Job #4,954, no author. 46 p. (Two copies.)
2. A script for a film for Independence. Joyce Ritter, Lloyd Ritter, Louis Solomon, and Thomas McGrath. Dramatic consultant: John Huston. Historical and editorial consultant: L. H. Butterfield. November 25, 1974. 44 p. (Two copies.) Inserted in both copies are notes from the Ritters to Huston regarding the script.
3. Joyce Ritter, Lloyd Ritter, and Thomas McGrath, May 27, 1975. 28 p. Some pages marked "Revised, June 15." Includes annotations. (Two copies.)
4. Same as no. 3. Huston's signature upper right on t.p. Revisions incorporated. 28 p.
5. Same as no. 3. "May 27, 1975" crossed out, and "15 June" written in. Gladys Hill's signature on t.p. 28 p.
6. Same as no. 3. *Handwritten:* Revised, June 15, 1975. Gladys Hill's signature. 28 p.

IN THIS OUR LIFE. 1942.

Warner Brothers. Screenplay by Howard Koch, based on Ellen Glasgow's novel of the same name (New York: Harcourt, Brace, 1941). Directed by John Huston. Huston may have been an uncredited writer, but not much evidence of this assertion exists.

AMPAS. GENERAL COLLECTION.

1. Screenplay by Howard Koch, from the novel by Ellen Glasgow, n.d. 145 p. Includes blue revisions Pages, November 8 and November 10, 1941. Annotations in different hands. Sheets inserted regarding shooting schedule and revised dialogue.

DARTMOUTH COLLEGE LIBRARY.

1. Screenplay by Howard Koch, from the novel by Ellen Glasgow, Burbank, Warner Brothers, 1941. 134 p.

NEW YORK PUBLIC LIBRARY FOR THE PERFORMING ARTS.

1. Screenplay by Howard Koch, from the novel by Ellen Glasgow. *Cover sheet:* Revised final, 10/3/41. 133 p.

NEW YORK STATE ARCHIVE.

1. Dialogue script.

USC. WARNER BROTHERS ARCHIVE.

1. Summary of the Ellen Glasgow's novel by Loralee May, February 18, 1941. 20 p.
2. Proposed screen story based on the novel, March. 28, 1941, no author indicated. 12 p.
3. Same designation as no. 2, April 17, 1941. No author indicated. 19 p. *On cover, in pencil:* Treat.
4. No t.p. *Cover:* June 18, 1941, no author indicated. 141 p. *On cover, in pencil:* Treat.
5. No t.p. *Cover:* July 9, 1941. *In pencil:* Treat. Various penciled notes on cover. Cast: Davis, Lupino (?), Travis. Special. 141 p. No author indicated. Includes undated blue revision sheets. Annotated.
6. Screenplay by Howard Koch. *Cover sheet:* September 10, 1941, Part 1, final (crossed out). *Cover:* September 9, 1941. 141 p. Includes photoduplicated and typescript pages.
7. Howard Koch. No t.p. *Cover:* Revised Final, October 3, 1941. 145 p. Blue revision sheets, various dates, November 1941–January 1942. (Two copies.)
8. Blue sheet changes, various paging, various dates, November 1941–January 1942.
9. (Dialogue transcript) 1942. Various paging.

WISCONSIN/WARNER BROTHERS SCREENPLAY SERIES. Reel 14.

1. Screenplay, final, by Casey Robinson, December 8, 1941.* 145 p.

Note. *The Wisconsin Center for Film and Theater Research, the State Historical Society of Wisconsin, which houses this script, reports multiple versions of the screenplay.

ADDITIONAL SCREENPLAY MATERIAL IN THE FOLLOWING LIBRARIES.

Colby College, Dartmouth College.

IN TIME TO COME. 1941.

Play. Written by Howard Koch and John Huston, based on Woodrow Wilson and the League of Nations. Staged and directed by Otto Preminger. Premiered at the Manfield Theater, New York, December 28, 1941. Unrealized screen project.

PUBLISHED TEXT.

1. Koch, Howard, and John Huston. "In Time to Come" (abridged, edited text). In *The Best Plays of 1941–1942,* edited by Burns Mantle. New York: Dodd, Mead and Co., 1942.

AMPAS. JOHN HUSTON COLLECTION. SCRIPT MATERIAL.

1. Three versions of play script, one of which has Paul Kohner's (Huston's agent) label. Kohner was possibly looking for film opportunities for this play. No indication of script material prepared.

USC. WARNER BROTHERS ARCHIVE.

1. *Woodrow Wilson* by Howard Koch, manuscript play, received from Mr. MacEwan, May 25, 1940. Includes one-page synopsis and seven-page treatment.

THE INVISIBLE MAN. 1933.

70–71 min. Huston as a contract writer at Universal, 1929–32. Produced by Carl Laemmle Jr. Screenplay by R. C. Sherriff. Contributing writer, Preston Sturges. Directed by James Whale.

AMPAS. JOHN HUSTON COLLECTION. SCRIPT MATERIAL.

1. *Invisible Man.* From John Huston, June 29, 1932. 10 p. Located in John Huston Inventory, Early Scripts and Stories—Titled, p. 39.

AMPAS. UNIVERSAL PICTURES. LIBRARY PROPERTIES. SYNOPSIS AND DESCRIPTIVE DATA 4, no. 6,064. Purchased, 9/22/31; released, 11/13/33.

1. Treatment: Martin Brown, James Whale, John L. Balderston, and Gouverneur Morris, John Weld; John Huston, 7/5/32, 10 p.; Richard Schayer, Gouverneur Morris. Screenplay: John Weld, Preston Sturges, R. C. Sherriff, Gouverneur Morris, John Balderston, Garrett Fort, and Laird Doyle.

THE BRITISH FILM INSTITUTE.

1. Version of the screenplay.

NEW YORK STATE ARCHIVE.

1. Cutting continuity script.

IT HAPPENED IN PARIS. 1935.

Great Britain. Writer. *Film Dope* lists the title as *It Started in Paris* and Huston as co-adaptor (no confirmation that this title is correct). Directed by Robert Wyler. Same as *April in Paris* (cf. NYPL [no indication that this is correct].) Per Denis Gifford's *The British Film Catalogue, 1895–1985: A Reference Guide* (New York: Facts on File, 1986, no. 09796: *It Happened in Paris*): Produced by Bray Wyndham for Associated British Film Distributors; directed by Robert Wyler and Carol Reed; story (play) by Yves Mirande (L'Arpete); screenplay by John Huston and H. F. Maltby.

THE BRITISH FILM INSTITUTE.

1. Screenplay in its collection.

USC. WARNER BROTHERS ARCHIVE.
1. *It Happened in Paris,* by Yves Mirande and adapted by Kay Stueby and John Huston, December 1951. Five-page treatment.

JACK OF DIAMONDS.
Universal. Unproduced. Huston contract writer, 1929–32.

AMPAS. JOHN HUSTON COLLECTION. SCRIPT MATERIAL.
1. *Jack of Diamonds* from John Huston, October 28, 1932. 3 p. (Three copies.) Located in John Huston Inventory, Early Scripts and Stories—Titles, p. 39.

AMPAS. UNIVERSAL PICTURES. LIBRARY PROPERTIES. SYNOPSIS AND DESCRIPTIVE DATA 5, no. 6,209. Unproduced. Author, John Huston.
1. Original: John Huston, 10/28/32. 3 p.

JAGUAR LIVES. 1979.
American International. Screenplay by Yabo Yablonsky. Directed by Ernest Pintoff. Huston, actor, Ralph Richards.

AMPAS. JOHN HUSTON COLLECTION.
1. "Jaguar" Lives! June 6, 1978. 119 p. *In pen on t.p.:* John Huston.

MUSEUM OF MODERN ART. FILM DEPARTMENT.
1. "Jaguar" Lives! A PSO Production, May 20, 1978. *Cover:* A Sandy Howard Production. No author, 119 p.

UCLA. ARTS SPECIAL COLLECTION. GENERAL COLLECTION.
1. Screenplay by Yabo Yablonsky. Script II, May 20, 1978. 119 p.

JEZEBEL. 1938.
Warner Brothers. Screenplay by Clements Ripley, Abem Finkel, and John Huston, based on the play by Owen Davis. Directed by William Wyler.

THE AMERICAN FILM INSTITUTE.
1. Dialogue transcript.

AMPAS. GENERAL COLLECTION.
1. Screenplay by Clements Ripley, Abem Finkel, and John Huston. Produced by Henry Blanke. Review date, March 11, 1938.
2. Screenplay, October 13, 1937. 167 p. Includes blue revision pages. Another copy, no t.p, n.d. 167 p. Includes blue revision pages.

AMPAS. JOHN HUSTON COLLECTION. SCRIPT MATERIAL.
1. Final screenplay, October 13, 1937, with revisions to December 8, 1937. 167 p. Specially bound.

MUSEUM OF MODERN ART. FILM DEPARTMENT.
1. Dialogue transcript. 50 p.

NEW YORK PUBLIC LIBRARY FOR THE PERFORMING ARTS.
1. Screenplay, no authors indicated. *Cover sheets:* Parts I–VI, 10/13/37–12/8/37. 167 p. Includes blue revision pages through 12/21/37.

John Huston

NEW YORK STATE ARCHIVE.
1. Dialogue script.

UCSB. DAVIDSON LIBRARY.
1. *Jezebel,* by John Huston, n.d. 167 p. Some pages dated 10/22/37–12/30/37.

USC. GENERAL COLLECTION.
1. No t.p. indicated. Verso of page 1: #191, *Jezebel,* 1-6-38. 170 p. Highly annotated. Blue revision pages with other dates, 10/37. Many upper right corners clipped. Includes cast members, addresses, and phone numbers. Henry Blanke's (producer) copy. Specially bound copy. Gift of Henry Blanke.

USC. WARNER BROTHERS ARCHIVE.
1. Synopsis of and comment on play by Owen Davis. Read by Jean Hollingsworth, January 4, 1934. 12 p.
2. Suggested story line for *Jezebel,* Mary C. McCall, March 30, 1935. 11 p. *Penciled on front page:* To MacEwan.
3. Copy of the play *Jezebel* by Owen Davis, n.d., various paging.
4. A treatment by Clements Ripley, July 14, 1937. 58 p.
5. First draft screenplay by Robert Buckner, April 30, 1937. 131 p. Inserted are handwritten and types notes. Notes inside front cover.
6. Revised screenplay by Abem Findel [sic] and Clements Ripley. Various dates, September 20, 1937–October 27, 1937. Some sections marked "Temporary." 174 p.
7. Final, 1937, no authors indicated. Some pages dated October 1937–December 1937. 167 p.
8. (Dialogue transcript), March 3, 1938, various paging. Located in production file.

WISCONSIN/WARNER BROTHERS SCREENPLAY SERIES. Reel 12.
1. Screenplay by Robert Buckner, April 30, 1937.* 131 p.
2. Treatment by Clements Ripley, July 14, 1937. 79 p.
3. Final screenplay, no authors indicated, October 13, 1937, with revisions to December 30, 1937. 165 p.

Note. *The Wisconsin Center for Film and Theater Research, the State Historical Society of Wisconsin, which houses these scripts, reports multiple versions of the screenplay.

ADDITIONAL SCREENPLAY MATERIAL IN THE FOLLOWING LIBRARIES.
Dartmouth College, Emerson College, Indiana University, Middlebury College.

JOAN (THE LARK).
Unrealized project (?).

AMPAS. JOHN HUSTON COLLECTION. SCRIPT MATERIAL.
1. *Joan: A Play in Two Parts* by Jean Anouilh. Translated from the French by Lucienne Hill. *In pen: The Lark,* n.d., various paging. Certain lines in script underlined in red. *Note:* This is a translation of *Alouette.*

JOHN HUSTON IN DUBLIN. 1981.
Note: Broadcast as "John Huston's Dublin" as part of the television series, "Cities."

550

AMPAS. JOHN HUSTON COLLECTION.

1. "John Huston in Dublin," written by James Plunkett, n.d. 21 p. (Two copies.) File contains background notes, letters, and proposals to Huston in order to interest him in taking part in the series "Cities." Already lined up and possibly broadcast was Ustinov's "Leningrad"; Wiesel's "Jerusalem"; Laing's "Glasgow"; Zetterling's "Stockholm"; Burgess's "Rome"; and Plimpton's "New York." File includes a letter from McGreevy to Paul Kohner, 4/12/78, expressing his interest in doing such a film within the next six months.

JOHN HUSTON'S NOBEL PRIZE THEATRE. 1960s?
Unrealized TV project.

AMPAS. JOHN HUSTON COLLECTION. SCRIPT MATERIAL.

1. Proposal, n.d. 229 p.
2. Proposal, n.d. 205 p.

THE JOURNEY OF ROBERT F. KENNEDY (The Journal of Robert F. Kennedy). *See* THE UNFINISHED JOURNEY OF ROBERT F. KENNEDY.

JUAREZ. 1939.
Warner Brothers. Screenplay by John Huston, Aeneas MacKenzie, and Wolfgang Reinhardt. Directed by William Dieterle.

PUBLISHED SCRIPT.

1. Gassner, John, and Dudley Nichols, eds. *Twenty Best Film Plays.* New York: Crown, 1943, 705–69. Includes *Juarez* by John Huston, Wolfgang Reinhardt, and Aeneas MacKenzie.
2. Huston, John, Aeneas MacKenzie, Wolfgang Reinhardt, and Abem Finkel. *"Juarez:* Scenes from a Shooting Script." *TAC* magazine 1 (March 1939): 5–12. An excerpt from the continuity of the Warner Brothers production of *Juarez* (1939).
3. Vanderwood, Paul J., ed. *Juarez.* Wisconsin/Warner Brothers Screenplay Series. Madison, Wis.: University of Wisconsin Press, for the Wisconsin Center for Film and Theater Research, 1983.

AMPAS. JOHN HUSTON COLLECTION. SCRIPT MATERIAL.

1. *Phantom Crown* screenplay by John Huston, n.d. 230 p. Specially bound.
2. *Juarez.* Screenplay by John Huston, Aeneas MacKenzie, Wolfgang Reinhardt, and Abem Finkel. *Cover sheet:* Part I, 10/29/38. Final. *Obliterated at top: The Phantom Crown,* P-50. *Cover: Juarez,* Warner Brothers. 176 + 2 p. Revisions to 1/5/39. Revisions dated 11/38–1/39. Following t.p., some production, cast, and credits information. Release date: June 10, 1939. Writers indicated as John Huston, Wolfgang Reinhardt, and Aeneas MacKenzie. Finkel not listed. Preceding page 1, blue pages: *Juarez* (to be inserted into part I, Final) D-M.
3. Script. Loose pages, but continuously paged. No. t.p., no authors or dates indicated. Handwritten dialogue inserted between pages 73 and 74. 209 p.

MUSEUM OF MODERN ART. DEPARTMENT OF FILM.

1. *Juarez* by John Huston, Aeneas MacKenzie, Wolfgang Reinhardt, and Abem Finkel. *Cover sheets:* Pt. 1, final, 10/29/38; pt. 2, 11/2/38; pt. 3, 11/4/38. 176 p.

NEW YORK STATE ARCHIVE.

1. Dialogue script.

John Huston

USC. GENERAL COLLECTION.
1. Title page includes Abem Finkel. No date, but includes blue revision pages, variously dated 11/38, 12/38, and 1/39. Henry Blanke's (producer) copy. Includes letters to J. L. Warner from Joseph Breen, 11/1/38, 11/7/38, 11/14/38, and 11/23/3; and a cast list, 11/15/38. Highly annotated, with some pages having upper right corner clipped. 176+ p.

USC. WARNER BROTHERS ARCHIVE.
1. *The Phantom Crown,* June 2, 1938. 230 p. Includes blue revision sheets, June 24, 1938–August 1, 1938. No authors indicated.
2. *Juarez* by John Huston, Aeneas MacKenzie, and Wolfgang Reinhardt, September 17, 1938. 165 p.
3. As no. 2. *Cover:* Rev. Temp. September 17, 1938. 165 p.
4. Screenplay by John Huston, Aeneas MacKenzie, Wolfgang Reinhardt, and Abem Finkel. Final, October 29, 1938–November 4, 1938. 176+ p. Includes blue revision pages, November 1938–January 1939. (Two copies.)
5. Blue sheet changes, various dates, November 1938–January 1939.

WISCONSIN/WARNER BROTHERS SCREENPLAY SERIES. Reel 67.
1. *The Phantom Crown* by Wolfgang Reinhardt. Treatment, February 15, 1938. 141 p.
2. Screenplay by Abem Finkel, October 29, 1938,* with revisions to January 9, 1939. 175 p.

Note. *The Wisconsin Center for Film and Theater Research, the State Historical Society of Wisconsin, which houses these scripts, reports multiple versions of the screenplay.

ADDITIONAL SCREENPLAY MATERIAL IN THE FOLLOWING LIBRARIES.
Indiana University Library.

KEY LARGO. 1948.
Warner Brothers. Screenplay by Richard Brooks and John Huston, from the play by Maxwell Anderson (*Key Largo: A Play in a Prologue and Two Acts,* Washington, D.C., Anderson House, 1939). Directed by John Huston.

AMPAS. JOHN HUSTON COLLECTION. SCRIPT MATERIAL.
1. Summary of Maxwell Anderson play. Read by New York office, October 31, 1939. Submitted by Brandt and Brandt. 9 p.
2. Pages from script, no t.p., no author or date. Two parts stapled together: pp. [1]–42; pp. 42–86 plus "Notes on 'Key Largo,'" 8/27/47; no author indicated. 7 p. The content of the notes would indicate that they are Huston's. Also included pink-sheet insert on procedures for calling a Coast Guard cutter, in script form; no author or date. 2 p. (Three copies.)

DARTMOUTH COLLEGE LIBRARY.
1. Screenplay by Richard Brooks, from the play by Maxwell Anderson. Warner Brothers Pictures, 1947, 119 p.

NEW YORK STATE ARCHIVE.
1. Dialogue script.

UCLA. ARTS SPECIAL COLLECTION. GENERAL COLLECTION.

1. Screenplay by Richard Brooks and John Huston, n.d. 113 p. *Note:* At bottom of p. 1, cast and credit list with the note: "Please destroy previously issued cast and credits, May 19, 1948." Complete credits indicated.

UCSB. DAVIDSON LIBRARY.

1. Screenplay by Richard Brooks and John Huston, from the play by Maxwell Anderson, n.d. 116 p. Includes revision pages, 12/19/47–3/19/48. *Cover sheet:* Rev. Final, 12–16–47. Preceding text of screenplay is a synopsis of the stageplay version, cast of characters (film version), production report for stage production (November 27, 1939), review of play (November 30, 1939), and a reader's analysis of the A. J. Cronin novel, *Grand Canary* (November 17, 1932), which does not have any relationship to *Key Largo.*

USC. WARNER BROTHERS ARCHIVE.

1. Synopsis of Maxwell Anderson play, n.d. 10 p. Another copy in production files: Read by New York office, October 31, 1939. Summary. Submitted by Brandt and Brandt. 9 p. Also in production files: Synopsis of *Key Largo,* no authors, n.d. 2 p. (Fourteen copies).
2. A treatment of the play, July 22, 1947. 46 p. *In pencil:* Jerry Wald (producer).
3. Screenplay by Richard Brooks; director, John Huston; October 1, 1947. 42 p. Received October 7, 1947, pp. 1–42.
4. Richard Brooks, October 1, 1947. 121 p.
5. Screenplay by John Huston and Richard Brooks. Temporary. Various dates: October 4, 1947–November 5, 1947. Includes pink revised pages. 121 p.
6. Huston and Brooks. Final. Various dates: November 17, 1947–December 9, 1947. Includes pink revised sheets. 119 p.
7. Huston and Brooks. Final, November 17–26, 1947. 123 p. Includes pink revised pages.
8. Huston and Brooks. Revised final, December 16, 1947. Includes pink revised sheets, December 1947 and March 19, 1948. 116 + 1 p.

THE WISCONSIN CENTER FOR FILM AND THEATER RESEARCH, THE STATE HISTORICAL SOCIETY OF WISCONSIN.

1. Dialogue script.

WRITERS GUILD OF AMERICA, WEST.

1. Revised final, December 16, 1947. 116 p.

ADDITIONAL SCREENPLAY MATERIAL IN THE FOLLOWING LIBRARIES.

Columbia College, Dartmouth College, University of Illinois.

THE KILLERS. 1946.

Universal. Screenplay by Anthony Veiller and John Huston (uncredited), based on the Ernest Hemingway story. Directed by Robert Siodmak.

THE AMERICAN FILM INSTITUTE.

1. Continuity and dialogue, August 6, 1946.

AMPAS. GENERAL COLLECTION.

1. Screenplay by Anthony Veiller, April 3, 1946. 136 p. Includes blue revision pages. Cast list including actors included.

NEW YORK STATE ARCHIVE.
1. Cutting continuity script.

UCLA. ARTS SPECIAL COLLECTION. GENERAL COLLECTION.
1. Screenplay by Anthony Veiller, April 3, 1946. 142 p. Includes blue revision pages, April 20, 1946, and April 29, 1946.

USC. GENERAL COLLECTION.
1. Continuity and dialogue trailer, August 16, 1946. Various pages.

USC. MARK HELLINGER COLLECTION.*
1. Transcription of the Ernest Hemingway story. 12 p.
2. Ernest Hemingway's "The Killers." Screenplay by Anthony Veiller. First revised draft, February 22, 1946. 122p. Also series of typewritten pages, no title, n.d., held together with metal stud. *In pencil:* First revised draft, Veiller, February 22, 1946. Pages are of various sizes. Heavily annotated.
3. Same as no. 2. Temporary, March 5, 1946. 138 p. (Two copies.) Also no author, n.d. 138 p. Include pink revised pages. Some pages folded at edge. Penciled notes on cover. Heavily annotated.
4. Same as no. 2. Final, April 3, 1946. 142 p. A copy, April 3, 1946, 136 p. Includes blue revised pages, dated April–June 1946. Preceding t.p.: Shooting schedule, April 29, 1946. *Cover:* Final. Penciled notes, including Hellinger's markings. Heavily annotated. Another copy, March 3, 1946; *crossed out and in pencil:* April 3, 1946. *In pencil:* Final. Pink and white pages of various sizes. Heavily annotated. Held together with metal stud.
5. *Cover title:* Same as no. 2. Temporary, n.d. 113 p. Heavily annotated.
6. Collection also includes loose sheets from particular scenes, with no dates or authors listed.

Note. *Scripts are labeled as the property of Mark Hellinger Productions.

USC. BURT LANCASTER COLLECTION.
1. Final, April 3, 1946, by Anthony Veiller. 142 p. Includes revised pages, April 20, 1946–June 24, 1946. Photocopy. Special leather-bound copy, with stills from the film bound in, donated to the USC Collection, as stipulated in Burt Lancaster's will.

ADDITIONAL SCREENPLAY MATERIAL IN THE FOLLOWING LIBRARIES.
Dartmouth College, Stanford University.

KISS THE BLOOD OFF MY HANDS (working title: *The Unafraid*). 1948.
Universal. Screenplay by Leonardo Bercovici, with additional dialogue by Hugh Gray. Adapted by Ben Maddow and Walter Bernstein, from the novel by Gerald Butler. Directed by Norman Foster. Unrealized project (?). No other indication of Huston involvement's in the film.

AMPAS. JOHN HUSTON COLLECTION. SCRIPT MATERIAL.
1. First treatment, no authors, n.d. 128 p.

KNOW YOUR ENEMY: GERMANY. *See* HERE IS GERMANY.

KNOW YOUR ENEMY: JAPAN. 1945.

U.S. War Department, Information and Education Division. Army Service Forces. Army Pictorial Service. Signal Corps. Project 6,017: Official Orientation Film, no. 10. Produced by Col. Frank Capra. Written by Joris Ivens, Pvt. Carl Foreman, Col. Frank Capra, Maj. Edgar Peterson, and Maj. John Huston. No director indicated, but as noted in *Meet Frank Capra* (catalog no. 074, pp. 47–48), Joris Ivens and Edgar Peterson served as director at various times. It also specifies periods of time that Huston worked on the film.

AMPAS. JOHN HUSTON COLLECTION. SCRIPT MATERIAL.
1. Script, September 11, 1944, no authors indicated. 75 p. Includes various notes, scribbles, and Huston's doodles.
2. Loose pages from script, December 18, 1944. 12 p. No authors indicated. (Two copies.)
3. Script. Restricted, War Department, Photographic Scenario, January 12, 1945. 26 p. No authors indicated. Some annotations.
4. Script. Same information as in no. 3. 44 p. *On cover, in pencil:* Pete.
5. Loose sheet. Standard form from Signal Corps, April 24, 1945. To Colonel Litvak, title, Project #1,104, copy no. 14, assigned to him. Following is script #14 (of 35), dated April 21, 1945. Project #1,104. No authors indicated. 36 p.
6. Various loose script pages, handwritten notes, with some pages heavily annotated. Some pages with Huston's doodles.

THE KREMLIN LETTER. 1970.
> Twentieth Century-Fox. Screenplay by John Huston and Gladys Hill, based on Noel Behn's *The Kremlin Letter* (London: W. H. Allen, 1966). Directed by John Huston.

THE AMERICAN FILM INSTITUTE.
1. Screenplay by John Huston and Gladys Hill. Copies, March 25, 1968. 147 p.

AMPAS. JOHN HUSTON COLLECTION. SCRIPT MATERIAL.
1. Breakdown on *The Kremlin Letter,* January 8, 1967. 49 p. At top of all pages: "GH, January 8–26, 1967." (Two copies.) Included in the folder are various additional pages: Middle Section; Third Section as in book, December 11, 1967 (4 p.); Sequence third part of screenplay (5 p.), with "JH & GH" at top of page 2. (Two copies, 1 copy annotated.)
2. Screenplay, no t.p. *Top of page 1:* Revised, July 12, 1967, JH and GH. 175 p. All pages marked "JH & GH." Revisions through July 28, 1967. Annotated. In binder.
3. Pages of script, "JH & GH," no t.p. October 16, 1967–December 27, 1967. Loose pages, continuously numbered. 47 p. Annotations. *At top of page 1:* II.
4. Screenplay, no t.p. "JH & GH," October 16, 1967–March 2, 1968. 146 p. Annotated. *At top page 1:* I.
5. Folder of handwritten notes, script pages, annotated; five-page synopsis; script pages clipped together, "JH & GH," October 22, 1967–February 24, 1968. Various pages on development of script on legal pad with dialogue and other notes.
6. Folder marked "Rewrites." Clipped to it is note marked: "Missing pages." No t.p., white and pink sheets, page-1 missions, with pages (pp. 2–144A) loose but continuous. All pages have "JH & GH" at top. Dated February 25, 1968–March 20, 1968. Annotated.
7. Revisions, loose pages, 1968–69, including handwritten notes and dialogue.
8. Numerous files: discards, April–May 1967; June–July 1967; October–December 1967; January 1968; February 1968; March 1968.

9. Screenplay by John Huston and Gladys Hill, February 25, 1968–May 22, 1969. 147 p. Specially bound.

AMPAS. JOHN HUSTON COLLECTION. SCRIPT MATERIAL. Uncataloged, box 2.

1. Remaining scenes for Rome, May 20, 1969. Includes various revised pages, some pink, February–April 1968. Some pages have "Zanuck" at upper right.
2. No t.p. *Cover: Kremlin Letter.* Screenplay by John Huston and Gladys Hill. 147 p. *Top of pages:* JH & GH, February–March 1968. Annotated.
3. John Huston and Gladys Hill. 147 p. *At top of pages:* JH & GH, February 25, 1968–March 20, 1968.

UCLA. ARTS SPECIAL COLLECTION. TWENTIETH CENTURY-FOX ARCHIVE.

1. Huston and Hill, March 25, 1968. *At top of pages:* JH and GH, various dates, February 1968–June 1969. 147 p.
2. Dialogue and continuity taken from the Moviola, February 12, 1970.
3. Combination title book, February 1970.

UNIVERSITY OF IOWA. TWENTIETH CENTURY-FOX SCRIPT COLLECTION.

1. Dialogue and continuity ("combination title book"), taken from the Moviola, February 12, 1970.

USC. GENERAL COLLECTION.

1. Screenplay copied 3–25–68. Includes blue revision pages, various dates, 3/68. Some marked as copies, 1/17/69; some with pencil annotations; and some with upper-right corner folded down. 147 p.

USC. TWENTIETH CENTURY-FOX COLLECTION.

1. Screenplay copies, 3–25–68, 147 p. Includes blue revised pages, dated through June 1969.

THE LAST RUN. 1971.

MGM. Screenplay by Alan Sharp. Directed by Richard Fleischer. Huston, the original director, withdrew. He was also supposed to produce, write, and act in the film.

AMPAS. JOHN HUSTON COLLECTION. SCRIPT MATERIAL.

1. Screenplay by Alan Sharp. Second draft. Revised, April 2, 1970. Property of MGM. 127 p.
2. Alan Sharp. Revised per John Huston's discussions, October 30, 1970. MGM, London. 103 p.
3. Alan Sharp. A John Huston–Carter De Haven Production. Revised, December 30, 1970. 68 p. Some pages annotated. *On cover, in pen:* Gladys Hill.
4. As no. 3. 74 p. Some pages annotated.
5. As no. 3. 115 p. Pages 67–115, revised January 18, 1971; pp. 36–39, revised January 21, 1971. *On cover:* Gladys Hill.
6. Third draft, no authors, n.d. 166 p.
7. Miscellaneous script pages. *At top of pages:* JH, GH, WAH (i.e., Huston, Hill, and Walter A. Huston, meaning Tony, John's son), November 24, 1970. Includes breakdown of revisions. Other pages marked "JH & GH" (i.e., Huston and Hill), November 27, 1970–December 6, 1970. Some pages annotated.

8. Loose sheets in folder labeled "Walter A. Huston [cf. no. 7], London and St. Clerans, Eire." Folder includes revised sheets, December 14, 1970, with "JH & GH" crossed out at top of some pages, but pages dated December 6, 11, and 14, 1970; the breakdown, November 16, 1970; and handwritten pages of notes on white legal pad.

9. Folder of loose revised pages, some handwritten, variously dated: December 6, 1970; January 18, 1971. Some pages with "JH & GH" at top of page, variously dated from December 1970; discards, variously dated from December 1970; and revised pages, variously dated from January 1971. Also includes Gladys Hill's notes and a letter from Paul Kohner to Gladys Hill, January 20, 1971.

10. Script pages, no authors, n.d.; handwritten notes and pages. Some pages marked "JH, GH, WAH [i.e., Huston, Hill, and Tony Huston], November 24, 1970." Some pages variously dated from December 1970 to January 1971. Some pages labeled "JH & GH, Dec. 6, 1970." Includes stapled-together breakdown on revisions, 5 p.

11. Script pages, Handwritten pages, variously dated from December 1970 to January 1971. Some marked "JH & GH." Clipped together, revised pages, December 14–30, 1970. Continuous, 72 p. No authors indicated.

USC. RICHARD FLEISCHER COLLECTION.

1. Script by Alan Sharp. Revised per John Huston's discussions, October 30, 1970. 103 p.

USC. GENERAL COLLECTION.

1. Third draft, Alan Sharp, November 2, 1970. 166 p.

LAUGHING BOY. 1934.

MGM. Produced by Hunt Stromberg. Screenplay by John Colton and John Lee Mahin. Directed by W. S. Van Dyke. An original Universal project that was sold to MGM. Huston, under contract as writer at Universal, worked with William Wyler on the project, doing research and developing scripts (cf. Axel Madsen's *William Wyler: The Authorized Biography,* New York, Crowell, 1973, 81–82; Gerald Pratley's *The Cinema of John Huston,* New York, A. S. Barnes, 1977, 29–30; and John Huston's *An Open Book,* New York, Da Capo Press, 1994, 58–60).

AMPAS. JOHN HUSTON COLLECTION. SCRIPT MATERIAL.

1. Sequences A–E. No authors, n.d. *Cover sheet:* Property of Universal. Script no. 39. Unpaged throughout, but first page indicates 132 p. Located in John Huston Inventory, Early Scripts and Stories—Titled, p. 39.

AMPAS. TURNER/MGM COLLECTION.

1. Synopsis by Julie A. Herne of the novel *Laughing Boy* by Oliver La Farge and the play *Laughing Boy* by Otis Chatfield Taylor (adapted from the novel by Oliver La Farge); 5/30/31, 11 p.; and n.d., 6 p., respectively.

2. Universal's temporary complete screenplay by Earl Haley, 3/16/32. About 150 p. Handwritten note on cover.

3. Temporary complete screenplay from John Huston, 6/11/32. About 120 p. Handwritten note on cover.

4. Complete outline by Wanda Tuchock, 5/13/33. 12 p.

5. Miscellaneous sections of dialogue, opening, and outlines by Wanda Tuchock, 5/16/33–6/24/33, 119 p. Includes blue and pink revision sheets.

6. Miscellaneous sections of dialogue, outlines, sequences, and story lines by Lynn Riggs, 5/25/33–6/22/33, 242 p.

7. Complete screenplay by Wanda Tuchock and Lynn Riggs, 7/31/33. 99 p.
8. Trailer, dialogue cutting continuity, and trailer footage, 3/30/34. Various pages.
9. Dialogue cutting continuity by Blanche Sewell (editor), music, and footage, 3/13/34. 64 p. and 12 p.

AMPAS. WILLIAM WYLER COLLECTION.
1. Sequence A–D, 310 scenes, 111 p. *Handwritten on t.p.:* Huston, 5/27/31.
2. Screenplay and dialogue by Earl Haley. 161 p. Blue page revisions, no authors, n.d. Various pages. Annotated.

NEW YORK STATE ARCHIVE.
1. Cutting continuity script.

USC. MGM COLLECTION.
1. Synopsis of Oliver La Farge's novel, no author, n.d. 6 p.
2. Synopsis of play by Otis Chatfield Taylor, May 30, 1931, no author. 11 p.
3. Synopsis of screenplay by John Colton and John Lee Mahin. Studio script #0400, November 3, 1933. 1 p.
4. Treatment by Earl Haley. From Universal, January 28, 1932. 90 p. *Note:* Bought from Universal, but didn't use.
5. Script from Earl Haley, March 1, 1932, with MGM label and an indication of previous Universal ownership. 196 p. Heavily annotated.
6. As no. 5, March 15, 1932. 161 p. MGM, formerly Universal.
7. As no. 5, March 16, 1932. 161 p. MGM, formerly Universal.
8. *Laughing Boy* "(From John Huston) (March 19, 1932)," file no: 6,060. *Handwritten on t.p.:* Mr. Ford and John Huston's doodle, a woman's face. *Cover:* Vault copy. *MGM label:* From John Huston, March 19, 1932, "Laughing Boy" script from Universal. *Handwritten:* Bought from Universal, But Never Used. Includes four sequences, 386 scenes, 141 p. Some annotations. More of Huston's doodles on back page.
9. As no. 8: "(From John Huston) (May 27, 1932)." 111 p. Some annotations.
10. As no. 8: "(From John Huston)." June 11, 1932. 136 p. Yellow pages, some annotations.
11. As no. 8: "(From John Huston) (June 24, 1932)." Universal Pictures's stamp. No. 50, file no. 6,060. *In pencil:* 139 p. *Cover:* MGM label. Bought from Universal information. Sequence, scene. 132 p. Blue pages.
12. No t.p. *Cover:* Dialogue script from Universal. Copied in MGM Script Department, April 4, 1933. *Penciled note:* Without pencil changes. MGM label. 91 p. No author indicated, but some writing is based on Huston's script no. 11.
13. As no. 12. No t.p. *Cover:* Dialogue script from Universal Studios. *Penciled note:* This copy marked with pencil changes per original—pp. 44–61–62–74–77–79–85–87–88–90. 91 p. Based on Huston script, no. 11. Bought from Universal, note indicated.
14. No t.p. *Cover:* Miscellaneous sections of dialogue. From Hunt Stromberg (producer, MGM), May 4, 1933, through February 24, 1934. 100 p.
15. Continuity outline by Wanda Tuchock, May 11, 1933. 4 p.
16. As no. 15, May 12, 1933. 20 p.
17. No t.p. First page notes outline for *Laughing Boy. Cover:* Complete outline by Wanda Tuchock, May 13, 1933. 12 p.
18. No t.p. *Cover:* Miscellaneous sections of dialogue openings and outlines from Wanda Tuchock, May 16, 1933, through June 24, 1933. 119 p. Includes yellow, blue, pink sheets.
19. No t.p. *Cover:* Miscellaneous sections of dialogue, outlines, sequences, and story lines.

From Lynn Riggs, May 25, 1933, through June 22, 1933. *Top of page 1:* Tentative outline, Mr. Riggs, May 25, 1933. 242 p.

20. Screenplay by Wanda Tuchock and Lynn Riggs, June 26, 1933. *Penciled date:* July 31, 1933. 128 p. Cover missing.

21. As no. 20. Annotations on t.p. *Top of page 1:* June 26, 1933. 177 p. *Cover:* Original cross out. Pages have tabbed indicators. Includes pages from Stromberg's treatment.

22. Version #2, Tuchcoch [sic]-Riggs, June 27, 1933, pp. 1–21.

23. Two excerpts from Arthur Hyman: June 28, 1933, 2 p. Excerpt from the Book #2 (condensed), June 28, 1933. 3 p.

24. No t.p. *Cover:* MGM label. Screenplay by Lynn Riggs and Wanda Tuchock, July 21, 1933. 99 p.

25. Pages 12–35, *in pencil:* J. Colton, M. Smith. October 19, 1933.

26. No t.p. *Cover:* Okay script by Mr. Stromberg, October 25, 1933. *In pencil:* Includes Old. No authors indicated. 14 p.

27. No t.p. *Cover:* Temp Script from Mr. Stromberg, November 1, 1933. 78 p.

28. No t.p. *Cover:* Screenplay by John Colton and John Lee Mahin. Script okayed by Mr. Stromberg, November 1, 1933. *In pencil:* 11/2, 11/6, Old, Complete. 154 p.

29. No t.p. *Cover:* Okay script, November 9, 1933. Script okayed by Mr. Stromberg. No authors indicated. 158 p.

30. Miscellaneous sections of sequences and dialogue from John Colton, January 11, 1934 through March 20, 1934. Various paging.

31. Miscellaneous sections of old and new dialogue, various dates. No author indicated. [152 p.]

32. Trailer, dialogue cutting continuity, March 30, 1934. Various paging.

33. Dialogue cutting continuity. Film editor, Blanche Sewell, March 31, 1934. Various paging.

LAW AND ORDER (working title: *Saint Johnson*). 1932.
Universal. Produced by Carl Laemmle Jr. Screenplay by Tom Reed. Adaptation and dialogue by John Huston, based on the novel, *Saint Johnson*, by W. R. Burnett. Directed by Edward L. Cahn.

AMPAS. JOHN HUSTON COLLECTION. SCRIPT MATERIAL.

1. A copy of the script is located in John Huston Inventory, Early Scripts and Stories— Untitled [1932–33?], #1, p. 39: Title page missing, various paging, n.d. *Note:* Inserted between C-14 and Sequence "D" is a receipt to John Huston for an ad placed in the *Los Angeles Evening Herald Express,* 6/16/33 (Address: Chateau Elysée) in which he apparently was searching for a "lost manuscript."

AMPAS: UNIVERSAL PICTURES. LIBRARY PROPERTIES. SYNOPSIS AND DESCRIPTIVE DATA 3, no. 5,947: released February 3, 1932.

1. Treatment, Dale Van Every; continuity, Gladys Lehman, Harrison Jacobs, Charles Logue, and Tom Reed. Continuity retakes: John Huston, 10/30/31, 11/14/31, and 11/21/31, 113 scenes. John Huston is given credit for the adaptation.

NEW YORK STATE ARCHIVE.

1. Cutting continuity script.

THE LEGEND OF MARILYN MONROE. 1964.
Wolper Productions. TV production. Script by Theodore Strauss and Terry Sanders. Directed by Terry Sanders. Huston, narrator.

UNIVERSITY OF PENNSYLVANIA LIBRARIES.

1. *The Legend of Marilyn Monroe,* teleplay by Theodore Strauss and Terry Sanders, Los Angeles, Writers Guild of America, West, 1964. 41 p.

USC. TV COLLECTION.

1. *The Legend of Marilyn Monroe,* teleplay by Theodore Strauss and Terry Sanders. Produced and directed by Terry Sanders. Wolper Productions, Hollywood, California. No date. 41 p. + page of credits: Produced, edited, and directed by Sanders.

WRITERS GUILD OF AMERICA, WEST.

1. Script, 1967.

ADDITIONAL SCREENPLAY MATERIAL IN THE FOLLOWING LIBRARIES.

Goucher College, Ohio University, Smith College, University of Pennsylvania.

LET THERE BE LIGHT. 1946.

U.S. Signal Corps. Army Pictorial Service. Screenplay by Charles Kaufman and John Huston.* Commentary by Walter Huston. Directed by John Huston.

PUBLISHED SCRIPT.

1. Hughes, Robert, ed. *Film: Book 2.* New York: Grove Press, 1962, 205–33.

THE BRITISH FILM INSTITUTE.

1. A version of the screenplay.

Note. *While the Huston Papers in AMPAS has script material from his other wartime documentaries, *Battle of San Pietro* and *Report from the Aleutians,* the files do not have script material for this documentary.

THE LIFE AND TIMES OF JUDGE ROY BEAN. 1972.

National General Pictures/First Artists. Screenplay by John Milius. Directed by John Huston, who also acted, Grizzly Adams.

PUBLISHED SCRIPT.

1. Milius, John. *The Life and Times of Judge Roy Bean: The Screenplay.* New York: Bantam Books, 1973. 180 p.

AMPAS. JOHN HUSTON COLLECTION. SCRIPT MATERIAL. Uncataloged, box 2.

1. John Milius, first draft, August 28, 1971. 138 p. Includes blue revision pages, 9/13/71.
2. Folder with various script changes: revisions, 11/13/71; notes on narration, extra cuts, and dialogue, 1/31/72; general notes, 2/22/72; breakdown as revised, 9/22/71; miscellaneous pages, various dates, October–November 1971 (heavily annotated throughout); and *Reality and Judge Roy Bean* by Dan Ford, 11 p. Revised 11/4/71; rewritten by Gladys Hill.
3. Folder includes quick breakdown of screenplay as shot, February; handwritten notes, December 4, 1971, 14 p.; pages from script, various dates, November–December 1971; and typewritten notes, February 23, 1972.

NEW YORK PUBLIC LIBRARY FOR THE PERFORMING ARTS.

1. Screenplay by John Milius, n.d. 168 p. At head of title, "Law and Order, West of the Pecos" crossed out. Property of Dick Lederer, Pacific Palisades.

UCLA. ARTS SPECIAL COLLECTION. GENERAL COLLECTION.
1. John Milius. First draft, August 28, 1971. 138 p. Includes yellow, goldenrod, pink, and blue revision sheets dated September 13, September 30, and October 1, 1971.

USC. GENERAL COLLECTION.
1. By John Milius, n.d. 168 p. Property of Dick Lederer, Pacific Palisades, California. *Above title and crossed out:* Law and Order; West of the Pecos.
2. First draft, August 28, 1971, 138 p. First Artists Production Co. Ltd./Coleytown Productions Inc. *Life and Times . . .* title used in script.

THE LIST OF ADRIAN MESSENGER. 1963.
Joel Productions/Universal. Screenplay by Anthony Veiller, based on the Philip MacDonald novel. Directed by John Huston, who also acted (uncredited), Lord Ashton.

AMPAS. GENERAL COLLECTION.
1. Screenplay by Anthony Veiller. Revised final, July 13, 1962. Includes blue revision pages.

AMPAS. JOHN HUSTON COLLECTION. SCRIPT MATERIAL.
1. MacDonald, Philip. *The List of Adrian Messenger.* New York: Bantam Books, 1959. (First published by Doubleday, 1959.) Annotated.
2. Treatment by Alec Coppel. *Cover:* Revised treatment, May 15, 1961, Bryna Productions, Inc. 63 p. Includes yellow pages through June 12, 1961. Annotated. Another copy, *cover:* Revised treatment, June 15, 1961. 62 p. Annotated.
3. Screenplay by Charles Schnee. Bryna Productions, Inc. *Cover:* Final screenplay, Mar. 5, 1962. 112 p.
4. *In pen, top of page:* Outline–John Huston–Tony Veiller, July 3, 1962. 10 p. Annotated.
5. On legal pad, breakdown of novel (as. no. 1). At top "Chapters 1–2"; other pages have other chapter designations. *In margin:* pages 1–194, with action as it appeared on various pages. 12 p.+ Following are main plot points, 1 p.
6. Revised final screenplay by Anthony Veiller. *Cover:* Revised Final Screenplay, July 13, 1962. Joel Productions, Inc. 105 p. Includes blue revision pages, 7/20/62. Following p. 79, pp. 80–115 are typescript pages, with changes, Veiller, July 25, 1962. Annotations.
7. Revised final screenplay by Anthony Veiller. *Cover:* Revised Final Screenplay, July 13, 1962, Joel Productions, Inc. *In pencil:* File copy. 128 p. Pink and blue revision pages, changes through August 3, 1962. (Two copies.)
8. Screenplay by Anthony Veiller. Revised final, July 30, 1962, with revisions to October 25, 1962. Specially bound.

NEW YORK STATE ARCHIVE.
1. Cutting continuity script.

UCLA. ARTS SPECIAL COLLECTION. GENERAL COLLECTION.
1. Screenplay by Anthony Veiller. Revised final, July 13, 1962. 128 p. Includes pink and blue revision pages, various dates, July–August, November 1962.

THE LONELY PASSION OF JUDITH HEARNE. 1987.
Handmade Films (U.K.). Screenplay by Peter Nelson. Directed by Jack Clayton. 1987.

AMPAS. HUSTON COLLECTION. PRODUCTION FILE.

1. Various indications of Huston's interest December 1961–July 1963: acquisition of films rights to novel; play script submitted for his consideration; letter from Richard Widmark, expressing his interest in being in the film, which he had heard that Huston was going to do with K. Hepburn; reply from Gladys Hill indicating that Huston would get back to him after he finished *Freud: The Secret Passion;* letter from Ray Stark to Huston, stating Hepburn didn't want to leave the country to discuss the project. Unrealized project.

AMPAS. JOHN HUSTON COLLECTION. SCRIPT MATERIAL.

1. Play by Bryan Forbes, April 1960, variously paged. Based on his novel.
2. Treatment and script. 76+ p. No authors or date indicated. In folder is a piece of paper with titles and a note: "Original, Riki Huston" (i.e., Riki Soma Huston, Huston's fourth wife).
3. Revision of no. 2. 110 p. No authors or date indicated. In folder is a piece of paper with title "Original, by J. Huston and Riki Huston."
4. First draft screenplay, December 18, 1961. 135 p. First five pages, annotated and inserted. *Cover, label:* John Huston, Title. *Another copy's cover:* Label, Title, December 20, 1961.

NEW YORK PUBLIC LIBRARY FOR THE PERFORMING ARTS.

1. Postproduction script by Peter Nelson, various paging, November 1987.

LOVESICK. 1983.

The Ladd Co./Warner Brothers. Screenplay and direction by Marshall Brickman. Huston, actor, Larry Geller, M.D.

THE AMERICAN FILM INSTITUTE.

1. Screenplay by Marshall Brickman, December 28, 1981. 129 p.

AMPAS. GENERAL COLLECTION.

1. Screenplay by Marshall Brickman. Combined continuity and master spotting list, March 8, 1983. 172 p.
2. Marshall Brickman, December 28, 1981. Title page indicates: Blue pages, January 14, 1982; pink pages, February 3, 1982. Copy contains only pink pages. 129 p.

ADDITIONAL SCREENPLAY MATERIAL IN THE FOLLOWING LIBRARIES.

Stanford University Library.

THE MACKINTOSH MAN. 1973.

Warner Brothers. Screenplay by Walter Hill, based on Desmond Bagley's *The Freedom Trap* (London: Collins, 1971; rev. ed., London: Fontana, 1973). Directed by John Huston.

UCLA. ARTS SPECIAL COLLECTION. GENERAL COLLECTION.

1. Screenplay by Walter Hill, September 7, 1972. 134 p. Revision pages dated September 15 and 19, 1972.

THE MADWOMAN OF CHAILLOT. 1969.

Ely Landau and Bryan Forbes, producers for Warner Brothers–Seven Arts, Inc. Screenplay by Edward Anhalt, Adaptation by Maurice Valency. Directed by Brian Forbes. The AFI indicates that Huston was the original director, but he was replaced by Forbes early in the filming. Per *Film Dope* Huston directed the first seventeen days, but none of his material is used in the finished film. Huston also did work on the screenplay.

AMPAS. JOHN HUSTON COLLECTION.

1. Play script by Jean Giraudoux, translated from the French. 88 p.
2. Screenplay. Second draft, May 26, 1967. 149 p. (Three copies.) *At top of page on two copies, in hand:* John Huston #6.
3. Loose sheets, various sizes and page numbers. Some have handwritten notes and annotations. Some pages marked at top: "JH & BH [i.e., William Hamilton; cf. Grobel, *The Hustons,* 595–96], Jan. 23, 1968."
   A section held together with a paper clip: III, JH and BH, Jan. 23, 1968. 23 p.; Jan. 24, 1968, pp. 20–20A.
   Test scene II, Pierre and Irma. 2 p.
   Huston's handwritten notes, including his doodles.
   Folder with various pages, Edward Anhalt, 12.7.67.

NEW YORK PUBLIC LIBRARY FOR THE PERFORMING ARTS.

1. Screenplay by Edward Anhalt, second draft, 5/26/67. 149 p, Property of the Landau/Ungar Co., New York.

ADDITIONAL SCREENPLAY MATERIAL IN THE FOLLOWING LIBRARIES.

Ohio State University Library.

THE MAGNIFICENT YANKEE. 1950.

MGM. Produced by Armand Deutsch. Screenplay by Emmet Lavery, based on his play about Oliver Wendell Holmes. Directed by John Sturges. Unrealized project (?). Play script by Emmet Lavery, based on the book by Francis Biddle and Lavery's play.

AMPAS. HUSTON COLLECTION.

1. Inventory indicates "ca. 1943" but no evidence in script.

NEW YORK PUBLIC LIBRARY FOR THE PERFORMING ARTS.

1. Teleplay for TV production, 1965.

USC. MGM COLLECTION.

1. Synopsis, E. Heyworth, 12/29/45; Jeanne Melton, 12/17/43; Helen Spencer, 7/10/50.
2. Preliminary outline from Emmet Lavery, 2/21/50. 44 p. (Two copies.)
3. Script from Emmet Lavery, 3/7/50 151 p.; 4/18/50, 120 p.; 5/29/50, 114 p.; 5/29/50, 114 p.; 6/13/50, 116 p. (John Sturges, director).
4. Test scenes, from John Sturges, 5/22/50 3 p.
5. Dialogue cutting continuity, 12/11/50.

THE MALTESE FALCON. 1941.

Warner Brothers. Screenplay and directed by John Huston.

PUBLISHED SCRIPT.

1. Anobile, Richard J., ed. *The Maltese Falcon.* Film Classic Library Series. New York: Universe Books, 1974, 256 p. Includes stills and script.

2. Luhr, William , ed. *The Maltese Falcon: John Huston, Director.* Rutgers Films in Print, vol. 22. New Brunswick, N.J.: Rutgers University Press, 1995. "The Continuity Script," pp. 27–103.

THE AMERICAN FILM INSTITUTE.
1. Final, May 26, 1941.

AMPAS. JOHN HUSTON COLLECTION. SCRIPT MATERIAL.
1. Screenplay by John Huston. Final. May 26, 1941, with revisions to June 2, 1941. 147 p. Specially bound.

NEW YORK PUBLIC LIBRARY FOR THE PERFORMING ARTS.
1. "The Maltese Falcon" from the novel by Dashiell Hammett. Screenplay by John Huston, Producer Henry Blanke, n.d. 147 p. Following title page, cast and credits. Signed by Lee Patrick.

NEW YORK STATE ARCHIVE.
1. Dialogue script.

UCLA. ARTS SPECIAL COLLECTION. GENERAL COLLECTION.
1. Screenplay by John Huston. Final, May 26, 1941. 147 p.

USC. GENERAL COLLECTION.
1. No t.p. *First page, handwritten:* 1st draft, n.d. 134 p. Some annotations throughout.

USC. WARNER BROTHERS ARCHIVE.
1. Changes, blue sheets, June 2, 1941, September 9, 1941. No author indicated, various paging.
2. *The Maltese Falcon,* from the novel by Dashiell Hammett. Screenplay by John Huston. Producer, Henry Blanke. *Cover sheet:* May 26, 1941. Final. *Cover:* Seven Arts Associated Corp. Preceding t.p. is a certificate of authenticity: Micrographic copy produced November 20, 1957. 147 p. Changes incorporated dated June 2, 1941, September 9, 1941.
3. As no. 2. Cover sheet is the same, with some handwritten notes. *Cover, in hand:* Cutting script, May 24, 1941. Final, Warner Brothers. 147+ p. Heavily annotated.
4. File marked "Camera Reports" includes continuity sheet. 3 p. (Three copies.)
5. Trailer script. 1941. 1 p.
6. (Dialogue transcription). Warner Brothers, 1941. Various paging.
7. In file designated "Picture": Screenplay, *The Clock Struck Three,* by Charles S. Belden. Based on the novel by Dashiell Hammett. 40 p. Cover sheets attached. Contracts indicate that Belden did the screenplay (incomplete) pursuant to a verbal agreement of employment commencing March 6, 1939. Screenplay is based on *The Maltese Falcon.*
8. Summary of novel, read by Kenneth Gamet, May 24, 1934. 1 p.
9. Summary of the novel, no author, n.d. 18 p.
10. Preliminary draft of analysis and argument about "Sam Spade" character in *The Maltese Falcon* (novel and films) and in "The Adventures of Sam Spade" (radio series). Developed in connection with a suit that Warners brought against CBS. Prepared by Stephen Karnot. Warner Brothers Studios, July 1949. 98 p.
11. No t.p. *Cover, in hand: The Maltese Falcon. At top, handwritten:* I. Negulesco. Treatment, n.d. 179 p.
12. Screenplay by John Huston. *Cover sheet:* May 15, 1941, temporary. Cover same with May 16, 1941, date. 168 p.

13. *The Maltese Falcon* from the novel by Dashiell Hammett. Screenplay by John Huston. Producer, Henry Blanke. *Cover sheet:* May 26, 1941, Final. *Cover:* Same. Stamp on cover indicates that this copy was used as evidence in suit that Warner Brothers brought against CBS, filed, May 15, 1951, Exhibit no. 5. *Also penciled on cover:* Complete Last Copy. Do Not Give Out. Final. Complete. May 24, 1941. 147 p. Includes blue revision sheets, June 2, 1941, and September 9, 1941.

THE WISCONSIN CENTER FOR FILM AND THEATER RESEARCH, THE STATE HISTORICAL SOCIETY OF WISCONSIN.
1. Final version of screenplay and dialogue script.

ADDITIONAL SCREENPLAY MATERIAL IN THE FOLLOWING LIBRARIES.
Art Center College of Design, Broward County Library, Columbia College, Fort Lauderdale Library, Dartmouth College, Dayton and Montgomery County Public Library, De Anza College, Howard University, Indiana University, Middlesex County College, Mississippi State University, Pennsylvania State University, Salt Lake City Public Library, Stanford University, State University of New York at Stony Brook, Syracuse University, University of Alabama, University of Massachusetts, University of North Carolina, University of South Carolina, University of Texas at El Paso, Wichita Public Library.

MAN FOR ALL SEASONS. 1966.
Columbia/Highland. Screenplay by Robert Bolt, based on his play. Directed by Fred Zinnemann.

AMPAS. JOHN HUSTON COLLECTION. PRODUCTION FILE.
1. Correspondence between Huston and Zinnemann, January–March 1966, in which Huston was seriously considered for the acting role of the duke of Norfolk. Note from Zinnemann, 3/9/66, expresses his regret that Huston was not going to do film. (Nigel Davenport did role.)

AMPAS. JOHN HUSTON COLLECTION. SCRIPT MATERIAL.
1. Final screenplay by Robert Bolt, n.d. 129 p.

UNIVERSITY OF WYOMING. AMERICAN HERITAGE CENTER.
1. *A Man for All Seasons* by Robert Bolt, n.d. 142 p. (Robert Bolt Collection #6,450.)

USC. GENERAL COLLECTION.
1. *A Man for All Seasons.* Second draft screenplay. No author or date. 132 p. Gen. no. 796.

MAN IN THE WILDERNESS. 1971.
Warner Brothers. Screenplay by Jack DeWitt. Directed by Richard Sarafian. Huston, actor, Captain Henry.

THE AMERICAN FILM INSTITUTE.
1. Screenplay by Jack DeWitt, February 2, 1971. 154 p.

UNIVERSITY OF WYOMING. AMERICAN HERITAGE CENTER.
1. *Man in the Wilderness,* n.d. 154 p. (Jack DeWitt Collection.)

John Huston

MAN OF LA MANCHA. 1972.
Produzioni Europee Associate/UA. Screenplay by Dale Wasserman. Directed by Arthur Hiller. Paul Kohner, Huston's agent, sent this property to Huston to see if he would be interested. No other indication of Huston being involved in its production.

AMPAS. JOHN HUSTON COLLECTION. SCRIPT MATERIAL.
1. Play script, New York production, premiere, November 22, 1965. A musical play by Dale Wasserman. Music by Mitch Leigh; lyrics by Joe Darion. Albert W. Selden–Hal James, New York City. 85 p. *Label on t.p.:* Paul Kohner, Hollywood, California.

THE MAN WHO WOULD BE KING. 1975.
Columbia/Allied Artists/Persky-Bright/Devon. A John Foreman Production. Screenplay by John Huston and Gladys Hill. Adapted from a short story by Rudyard Kipling. Directed by John Huston.

THE AMERICAN FILM INSTITUTE.
1. Huston and Hill, September 1968. 129 p. Annotated. Edith Head's copy.

AMPAS. GENERAL COLLECTION.
1. No t.p. Screenplay. 119 p. No indication of author or date.

AMPAS. JOHN HUSTON COLLECTION. SCRIPT MATERIAL.
1. Radio script. Suspense. CBS. "The Man Who Would Be King." William N. Robson, dir. (who became associated with the program in 1956). No author or date indicated. This version starred Dan O'Herlihy. 19 p.
2. Report on *The Man Who Would Be King* for film production. No author or date. 40 p. *Cover, label:* Property of Paul Kohner, Hollywood.
3. No t.p. *Cover:* A screenplay from the story by Rudyard Kipling. November 18, 1959. First page is a handwritten memo from Aeneas MacKenzie, January 20, 1960: "A copy of the working script to page 65 was delivered to John Huston in Hollywood on December 9, 1959. . . . Pages 66 to 115 represent the work done by me between December 14, 1959 and January 14, 1960. To date it has not been seen in any part by Mr. Huston." Following is a blue page: "Changes made in all 5 copies, pp. 7–94." *At bottom of page:* "On Mr. Huston's copy, I made above changes on page 73, 79, 84, 94. Preceding pages had already gone out to Huston." Following, yellow pages with various dates, November–December 1959.
4. Screenplay by Aeneas MacKenzie, 2–2-3–15–59. 139 p.
5. Screenplay by Aeneas MacKenzie. *In pencil:* 2nd MacKenzie version. *In pen:* First Rough draft, 2–2-3–15–59. *Cover:* Paul Kohner label. *In pencil:* II. 121 p.
6. First draft screenplay by Aeneas MacKenzie. *Cover:* May 2, 1960. Property of Universal. 157 p.
7. Screenplay by Peter Viertel. July 19, 1954. *In pencil:* John Huston, Fish guard-3208, Only Copy. 179 p. In binder.
8. Another copy of first draft screenplay, May 2, 1960. Lacks t.p. 157 p. In binder.
9. Revised first draft screenplay. No author. *Cover:* April 27, 1961. Property of Universal. *On t.p., in pencil:* Stephen Grimes. 158 p. Another copy also with "Stephen Grimes" in pencil on t.p.
10. No t.p. *First page in pencil:* Only version Veiller-Huston. 204 p. Typescript. *On cover:* July 26, 1963. (May–June 1963 crossed out.) In binder.
11. No t.p. *First page, in pencil:* John's copy, February 22, 1964, revisions. *Penciled note:*

566

T.V. leaves St. C. March 5. Penciled, various pages. Yellow larger-size pages interspersed with white pages. Heavily annotated. (Original white paged script had 169 pages.)
12. Screenplay by Anthony Veiller. Revised first draft, March 6, 1964. Seven Arts Associated Corp. 150 p. (Two copies.)
13. Script. No author or dates. Loose pages clipped together: 59 + 3 p. Two copies. Both annotated in same manner.
14. Miscellaneous script pages, including 6 p. of handwritten notes. Some pages heavily annotated, various paging, no author or dates indicated.
15. Yellow and green loose pages, no author or dates indicated: *yellow,* pp. 118–24; *green,* pp. 125–78.

AMPAS. JOHN HUSTON COLLECTION. SCRIPT MATERIAL. Uncataloged, box 3.
1. Alteration of script by Drew Smythe, pp. 66–71. Cover letter, January 10, 1975.
2. Scenes for which dialogue is required. From Bill Hill (associate producer), 5/3/74.
3. Pages of dialogue, January 18, 1975, no author. 3 p.
4. Annotated script pages, some annotated. No author, various dates.
5. John Huston and Gladys Hill, December 11, 1974. *At head of title:* Royal Service Company. 128 p. White and blue pages, different sizes. Annotated.
6. Miscellaneous script pages, no author, various paging, and various dates.
7. John Huston and Gladys Hill. *Cover, handwritten:* title, Version II, with changes, July 3 and July 5, 1974. Also dated June 25, 1974. Straightforward version, G. Hill. 127 p. Includes yellow revised pages and sketch of bridge, version, p.125.
8. John Huston and Gladys Hill, October 3, 1974, based on July 7 version. *In ink on t.p.:* Pages missing. 126 p. Inserted new page 38, n.d.
9. John Huston and Gladys Hill. *Cover, in pen:* July 5, 1974. Various paging, including yellow, pink, and blue revision pages. Some pages indicate Version I, September 16, 1974, JH and GH, July 1974, October 1974.
10. Envelope marked "Discards." Numerous pages, various paging, various dates. Some pages dated January 1975; some, handwritten; some, annotated.

THE BRITISH FILM INSTITUTE.
1. A version of the screenplay.

MUSEUM OF MODERN ART. FILM DEPARTMENT.
1. J. F. Productions. *John Huston's 'The Man Who Would Be King,'* by John Huston and Gladys Hill. Adapted from the story by Rudyard Kipling. JH-JF Productions, November 15, 1974. 131 p.

UCLA. ARTS SPECIAL COLLECTION. GENERAL COLLECTION.
1. Huston and Hill, version I. 129 p.
2. Huston and Hill, revised final version, December 11, 1974. 119 p. *Note:* Filming was completed April 3, 1975.

UCSB. DAVIDSON LIBRARY.
1. J. F. Productions. *John Huston's 'The Man Who Would Be King,'* by John Huston and Gladys Hill. Adapted from a short story by Rudyard Kipling. John Huston–John Foreman Production, November 15, 1974. 131 p.

USC. CLARK GABLE COLLECTION.
1. A letter to Gable, 9/17/57, from George Chasin, MCA, indicates that he is enclosing a

report on film's production, dated 4/24/56, by A. E. MacKenzie; copy 2 of the short story by Kipling. In the letter Chasin indicates the Mirisch Brothers' relationship with Allied Artists; reminds Gable that Huston discussed the project with him a few years before in London; and says that at that time Huston wanted Bogart and Gable for the main roles.

2. Included in the collection are:

Notes and sketches for John Huston's film of Rudyard Kipling's classic story, *The Man Who Would Be King.*

Location drawings made by the art director, Stephen Grimes, in Afghanistan, winter 1959.

"*The Man Who Would Be King:* A Report for Film Production," A. E. MacKenzie, 4/24/56. Page 1 begins: "Mr. Huston's interest in this Kipling short story derives from a conviction that its characters and situations are fundamental ones. Consequently, he has a disinclination to depart in any marked degree from the original material, or to make any major interpolations in the scripting of it as a screenplay." 41 p.

Transcription of the short story. 24 p.

WRITERS GUILD OF AMERICA, WEST.

1. Huston and Hill, October 18, 1973. 125 p.

ADDITIONAL SCREENPLAY MATERIAL IN THE FOLLOWING LIBRARIES.

Emerson College, Pennsylvania State University, University of Alabama, University North Carolina.

MARIUS. 1931.

Paramount. Screenplay by Marcel Pagnol, from his play. Directed by Alexander Korda. Unrealized project (?).

AMPAS. JOHN HUSTON COLLECTION. SCRIPT MATERIAL.

1. Play script by Marcel Pagnol. Adapted from the French by Robert Wyler (brother of William Wyler), n.d. 125 p.

AMPAS. UNIVERSAL PICTURES. LIBRARY PROPERTIES. SYNOPSIS AND DESCRIPTIVE DATA 5, no. 6,470. Unproduced. Date of purchase: June 15, 1934.

1. Author, Marcel Pagnol. *Marius: Three-Act Play.* 113 p.

THE MIGHTY BARNUM. 1934.

Twentieth Century-Fox. Screenplay by Gene Fowler and Bess Meredyth. Directed by Walter Lang. *The American Film Institute Catalog: Feature Films, 1931–1940* lists Huston as a contributing writer (uncredited).

PUBLISHED SCRIPT.

1. Fowler, Gene, and Bess Meredyth. *The Mighty Barnum Screenplay.* New York: Covici-Friede, 1934.

AMPAS. JOHN HUSTON COLLECTION. SCRIPT MATERIAL.

1. Copy of letter to Darryl F. Zanuck (cf. also USC entries), June 17, 1933, in which

Huston discusses the Barnum character. Includes an outline of the story "with several scenes worked out."

2. *P. T. Barnum.* Skeleton outline, 6–16–33. 35 p. (Located in John Huston Inventory, Miscellaneous Stories, Scripts—Untitled Works.)
   a. Jenny Lind's Apartment, Jenny Lind and Barnum, n.d. 4 p. Annotated.
   b. Love Scene of Lavinia Warren and Tom Thumb, n.d. 7 p. Annotated.
   c. A Banquet Table. . . , n.d. 3 p.
   d. A Garden: Barnum and Vivalla, n.d. 2 p.

THE BRITISH FILM INSTITUTE.
1. A version of the screenplay.

NEW YORK STATE ARCHIVE.
1. Dialogue script.

UCLA. ARTS SPECIAL COLLECTION. GENERAL COLLECTION.
1. Screenplay by Gene Fowler and Bess Meredyth. Revised final, September 12, 1934. 180 p.

USC. ERNEST LEHMAN COLLECTION.
1. Revised final by Fowler and Meredyth, September 12, 1934. 180 p.

USC. TWENTIETH CENTURY-FOX COLLECTION.
1. *The Great Barnum,* no author, n.d. *In pencil on cover:* Treatment outline. 12 p.
2. Two-page letter from John Huston to Darryl F. Zanuck on the Barnum story, June 17, 1933. Includes pages titled "P. T. Barnum, Skeleton Outline, 6–16–33," which are seventeen pages of script. Huston explains the Barnum character and indicates that he is submitting an outline and several scenes.
3. *P. T. Barnum* first treatment by John Huston, August 9, 1933. 115 p. Darryl Zanuck's signature on cover.
4. Skeleton synopsis by John Huston, October 17, 1933, 27 p.
5. Treatment by Raymond Griffith, January 24, 1934. 30 p.
6. Summary on *Barnum* from Darryl Zanuck, February 5, 1934. 7 p.
7. Rough continuity, March 4, 1934. 21 p. Zanuck's copy, with date of March 6, 1934, at end.
8. Additional notes on *Barnum,* Darryl Zanuck, March 7, 1934. 3 p.
9. Suggestions for *Barnum,* Darryl F. Zanuck, March 21, 1934. 8 p.
10. Notes on *Barnum* Conference, March 23, 1934: Zanuck, Fowler, and Meredyth. 6 p.
11. Conference with Mr. Zanuck, *The Mighty Barnum* by Bess Meredyth, April 21, 1934. 22 p. Some annotations.
12. Staff and cast, shooting schedule, call sheet, September–October 1934.
13. Dialogue continuity, *The Mighty Barnum,* November 28, 1934.

MINOR MIRACLE (*Young Giants*). 1986.
Independent. Entertainment Enterprises. Screenplay by Tom Moyer, Mike Lammers, and Terrill Tannen. Directed by Terrill Tannen. John Huston, actor, Father Bud Cadenas.

NEW YORK PUBLIC LIBRARY FOR THE PERFORMING ARTS.
1. Copy of play by Al Morgan based on his novel, n.d., various pages.

THE MISFITS. 1961.

Seven Arts Productions/UA. Screenplay by Arthur Miller, based on a short story published in Esquire in 1957. Directed by John Huston.

PUBLISHED SCRIPT.
1. Garrett, George P., O. B. Hardison Jr., and Jane R. Gelfman, eds. *Film Scripts Three.* New York: Appleton-Century-Crofts, 1972. Introductory comments indicated that the script bears notation: Revised, September 1959.
2. Miller, Arthur. *The Misfits.* New York: Viking, 1961; London, Secker & Warburg, 1961. Novelized format. *Author's note:* Written as a guide to the director and the artists in the making of the 1961 motion picture, "a story conceived as a film."
3. Miller, Arthur. *Plays Two.* London: Methuen Drama, 1994.

AMPAS. JOHN HUSTON COLLECTION. SCRIPT MATERIAL.
1. Arthur Miller. *The Misfits.* New York: Viking Press, 1957. "Dedicated to Clark Gable, who did not know how to hate." "An early version of *The Misfits* appeared as a story in *Esquire.*" Inscribed to Huston: "Dear John, Friend, here is a monument to the uses of confusion, in short, Huston, it's enough to make a man believe in Miracles. Arthur, January 1961."
2. *An Original Play for the Screen,* by Arthur Miller. (Based on the author's story, "The Misfits," published in *Esquire,* October 1957.) First draft, October 28, 1957. 164 p. Some annotations.
3. Revision, June 15, 1959. 50 p. Inserted letter from Miller to Huston, June 16, 1959: "Here is the beginning of the screenplay. . . ."
4. Revision, September 1959. 159 p. Some annotations.
5. Revision, March 1960. 139 p. plus p. 160 (blue), pp. (a)–(g). Some annotations.
6. Revisions, July 13, 1960, loose pages. 147 p. Includes blue revision pages, July 13, 16, and 18, 1960. Some annotations. This version starts with a note: "The first two pages are to be improvised and amended by the director."
7. Blue revision pages: Rev. 7–13–60, 21 plus 1 p.; Rev. 7–16–60, various paging; Rev. 7–18–60, various paging (*top of first page, in pencil:* G. Hill). Yellow revision pages: August 28, 1960, pp. 145–46; September 19, 1960, pp. 96, 96a, 96b.
8. Revision, September 1959. 163 p. (Two copies.)
9. Screenplay by Arthur Miller. July 13, 1960, with revisions to November 2, 1960. 146 p. Specially bound.

NEW YORK STATE ARCHIVE.
1. Dialogue script.

UCSB. DAVIDSON LIBRARY.
1. *The Misfits* by Arthur Miller; director, John Huston; n.d., complete script, with paging: 205–382.

USC. BOYLE COLLECTION.
1. *The Misfits* by Arthur Miller; director, John Huston; n.d. 382 p.

ADDITIONAL SCREENPLAY MATERIAL IN THE FOLLOWING LIBRARIES.
Columbia College, De Anza College, Florence County Library, Indiana University, Mississippi State University, University of Massachusetts.

MR. NORTH. 1988.

Samuel Goldwyn. Screenplay by Janet Roach, John Huston, and James Costigan. Directed by Danny Huston. John Huston, executive producer.

AMPAS. GENERAL COLLECTION.
1. Screenplay by James Costigan, n.d. 105 p.

USC. GENERAL COLLECTION.
1. *Mr. North.* Screenplay by Janet Roach and John Huston, based on the novel by Thornton Wilder. Property of Heritage Entertainment, Inc., Los Angeles, June 1987. 98 p.

MR. SKEFFINGTON. 1944.

Warner Brothers. Screenplay by Julius J. Epstein and Philip G. Epstein. Directed by Vincent Sherman. Huston was on assignment as a writer from August 23, 1940 to December 15, 1940.

AMPAS. JOHN HUSTON COLLECTION. SCRIPT MATERIAL.
1. Screenplay by John Huston. Associate producer, David Lewis. November 30, 1940. 136 p.

NEW YORK STATE ARCHIVE.
1. Dialogue script.

USC. WARNER BROTHERS ARCHIVE.
1. First treatment outline by Lenore Coffee, January 24, 1944. 52 p. *Cover:* #1, Warner Brothers, Wallis. Numerous other penciled notes on cover.
2. *Mr. Skeffington* screenplay by John Huston. Associate producer, David Lewis. Temporary, December 3, 1940. 138 p.
3. Screenplay by Julius Epstein and Philip Epstein. Revised temporary, September 26, 1942. 178 p.
4. Epstein Brothers. Final, June 25, 1943. Includes pink revision sheets, September 9, 1943. 156 p.
5. Epstein Brothers. Revised final. Various dates, October 1943–January 1944. Includes blue revision sheets. 159 p. (Two copies.)
6. Additional revised and replaced sheets, variously dated, September 1943–January 1944.

WISCONSIN/WARNER BROTHERS SCREENPLAY SERIES. Reel 15.
1. Treatment by Lenore Coffee, August 12, 1940. 52 p.
2. Temporary by John Huston, December 3, 1940. 138 p.
3. Revised final by Philip Epstein and Julius Epstein, October 5, 1943,* with revisions to January 29, 1944. 160 p.

Note. *The Wisconsin Center for Film and Theater Research, the State Historical Society of Wisconsin, which houses these scripts, reports multiple versions of the screenplay.

MOBY DICK. 1956.

Moulin Pictures/Warner Brothers. Screenplay by Ray Bradbury and John Huston, based on Herman Melville's novel. Directed by John Huston.

AMPAS. JOHN HUSTON COLLECTION. SCRIPT MATERIAL.
1. Final screenplay, n.d. 103 p. Specially bound. *Note on first page:* "Differences between

this script and one dated May 20 (last one Bradbury worked on) are noted in blue and constitute the rewrites and changes made by John Huston."

2. NBC University of the Air: "World's Great Novels: Moby Dick" by Herman Melville. Adapted by Frederick Schlick, n.d. Episodes 1–4, various paging.

3. "The Sea Beast" A Warner Brothers. Picture. 1926. From the story Moby Dick by Herman Melville. Adaptation by Bess Merdyth, Director: Millard Webb. *Cover:* Final, 1926. [124 p.]

4. *The Sea Beast.* German version. Directed by Michael Curtiz. *Cover sheet:* Sound version. English translation of German. 77 p.

5. Final dialogue. Adaptation by Oliver H. P. Garrett, dialogue by J. Grubb Alexander. *Cover:* Final script, 1930. 120 p.

6. Treatment by Gilbert Wilson, 2/26/52. 53 p.

7. Three versions for a modern music drama: Libretto by Gil Wilson, n.d. 136 p.; synopsis by Gil Wilson, n.d. 11 p.; contemporary interpretation by Gil Wilson, n.d. 66 p.

8. Screenplay by Robert Rossen. Incomplete. 1954. 117 p. Some annotations.

9. Outline, first section, Ray Bradbury, 11/11/53. Following first page: Third draft, finished November 20, 1953. 162 p. Some pages annotated. Included is a handwritten note on piece of paper: "John's script, November 20, 1953, with pages 54 to 114 missing, and his notes on pages, and 118–121 missing put in my script."

10. Third draft, finished, November 20, 1953. Bradbury. *In pencil:* II. Loose pages, but consecutively numbered. 91 p. (Two copies.) *Top of first page:* Brad, 11/11/53. Second copy has "IV" on t.p.

11. Fourth draft by Ray Bradbury, January 15, 1954. 84 p. Loose pages. variously dated, through January 20, 1954.

12. Fourth draft by Ray Bradbury, January 15, 1954. 162 p. Heavily annotated. Some pages have handwritten date, February 16, 1954. Some pages have "John" in pencil at top of page. Handwritten dialogue included. Loose pages.

13. Final by Ray Bradbury, February 5, 1954. Also dated February 22, 1954. *Cover, handwritten:* Larry Sherwood. 71 p.

14. Final by Ray Bradbury, February 22, 1954. *Cover, handwritten:* John Huston. 90 p. Annotated. Copy 2.

15. Final by Ray Bradbury, February 5, 1954. 149 p. Preceding t.p. one unnumbered page of dialogue. In binder. (Two copies.)

16. Final by Ray Bradbury, February 5, 1954. Also dated February 22, 1954. 134 p. Includes revisions dated April 14, 1954, annotated. Another copy with revision through September 30, 1954, annotated.

17. Incomplete script, 1954. 134 p. Includes revisions, March 26, 1954. Name of L. Sherwood (i.e., Lorraine Sherwood, Huston's secretary) on cover.

18. Script, February 1954, with revisions through April 14, 1954. 134 p. Copy 119.

19. Screenplay by Ray Bradbury. Typed May 20, 1954. *Cover:* Copy no. 46, 5–1954. From Lorry Sherwood. Pages numbered: Sequence A–P, pp. 1–136. Each page marked with red and blue marks. Inserted copy of letter from Lorraine Sherwood to Paul Kohner, October 25, 1955. Sherwood says that the one copy with a pink cover and dated May 20, 1954, was the last script that Bradbury worked on, and she has marked his work in red and Huston's in blue. She points out that much of it is marked in red and blue. The second screenplay is marked only in blue and shows all the work that Huston did on the script in terms of rewrites and changes. Huston wants the two scripts and the Rossen and Grayson scripts submitted to the Screenwriters Guild. Huston also requested that Kohner give the Guild Bradbury's original script (see no. 22 below). Sherwood indicates that

Bradbury has that script, which he wrote before she came on the scene. All of this discussion has to do with conflicts between Huston and Bradbury as to who should get credits for the screenplay. The Screenwriters Guild arbitrated and decided that both of them should have screenwriting credits.

Top of [p. 1]: [Red]—Bradbury; [blue]—Huston.

On Sequence A.2.: "Note: Above was written together out of the book. Narration: Bradbury."

On Sequence A.8.: "Note: Above was written and rewritten many times by both— singly and together—passed back and forth. Also part of scene was taken from R. Rossen script."

20. Screenplay by Ray Bradbury. Typed May 20, 1954. In pencil, coding indicating where scenes were to be shot, for example: S = studio; LF = location off Fishguard. 55 p. Some pages marked "Revised." Some pages stapled over originals. Loose pages.

21. Screenplay by Ray Bradbury. Typed May 20, 1954. Cover: Copy 129. 136 p. Revisions to October 8, 1954. Revised pages inserted: pp. 107–9, 111–14.

22. The other copy that L. Sherwood refers to (cf. no. 19 above). No t.p. Cover: Label: Moby Dick, screenplay by Ray Bradbury (followed in pencil: John Huston, his signature, and his initials). Final screenplay, May 20, 1954. Numerous notes in pen and pencil on cover. Copy from A. Allen (script girl): up to date, only complete copy. Also without cutting or continuity script, May 20. In blue, some shorthand notes. Copy of letter to Kohner (see no. 19 above). 118 p. Heavily annotated. Changes pasted over originals, handwritten notes, cross outs, and blue markings (Huston's work).

23. Rewrites of Father Mapple scene: June 25, 1954; July 1, 1954; July 28, 1954; and September 10, 1954. Includes handwritten notes.

24. Rewrites of Starbuck-Stubb flask scene, July 12, 1954; and Starbuck-Ahab cabin scene, July 28, 1954. Additional rewrites with cover letter to Huston from Bradbury, August 3, 1954. Also September 8, 1954, rewrite of pp. 114–15: Ahab's speech to Starbuck prior to lowering of boat; new scene with Ahab and Pip, to be inserted pp. 108–9, shots 705 to 714 inclusive. Also various other rewrite sheets and deletions.

25. No t.p. On first page, in pencil: Final [5/20/54?]. 136 p. Some pages revised through September 1954. Mr. Huston at top of some pages. Annotated. Inserted pages of dialogue. Tide table inserted. Inserted: nine pages of typed and handwritten pages on Father Mapple.

26. No t.p. Cover: Screenplay by Ray Bradbury and John Huston. Final screenplay, May 20, 1954. Copy 1. File Copy. 103 p. At top of first page: "Note: Difference between this present script and the one dated Twentieth May 1954 are noted in blue and constitute the rewrites and changes made by John Huston." Page 11: "Note: Above written by Huston—most of it edited from the book. Other annotations, paste overs and blue markings indicated." (See also nos. 19 and 22 above).

27. Analysis of script by John Kilbracken, July 29, 1954. 11 p. Revision and rearrangement, scene 279 to end, Kilbracken, August 1, 1954, various paging.

28. No t.p. No author or date. 137 p. In binder.

29. Title page missing. No author or date. 138 p.

30. No t.p. *Cover, in pencil:* Moby Dick and Huston's name. Starts with chapter 2, 114 p. *Penciled note, p. 114:* "Chapters 101–135 are being typed." Treatment (two copies.) Another treatment 144 p. plus 4 p. Some annotations.

31. Pages from script, various paging, various dates. Five files. Includes handwritten dialogue, storyboard drawings, heavily annotated pages, pages where scenes are to be shot, and pages with pasted over dialogue.

32. Envelope with handwritten note: "Dahl and Bradbury suggestions, 1954–55." Various pages, n.d. Annotated.

33. Two large envelopes of various pages and dates of script. Includes score sheets of card games between John Huston and "Sy." Includes clipped pages, with note: "Make changes in my script and Ray's." Numerous handwritten notes and pages. Annotations.

LIBRARY OF CONGRESS. RAY BRADBURY PLAYS COLLECTION.

1. A screenplay of *Moby Dick.*

NEW YORK STATE ARCHIVE.

1. Dialogue Script.

USC. GENERAL COLLECTION.

1. Screenplay by Ray Bradbury. Final, February 22, 1954. Cast and credits indicated, 1–27–56. 148 p.

USC. WARNER BROTHERS ARCHIVE.

1. Synopsis read by A. E. MacKenzie, July 26, 1937. 9 p.

2. Screenplay by Robert Rossen. *Penciled date on cover:* April 4, 1942. #1. Incomplete. 117 p.

3. Continuity outline by Charles Grayson, January 14, 1947, #2. 9 p.

4. No t.p. *Cover: Moby Dick. In pen:* Scene breakdown of novel by ?John Huston. Received December 17, 1946, to February 11, 1947. Incomplete. #3. 145 p. Begins with chapter #2. Some annotations.

5. No t.p. *Cover:* Screenplay by Charles Grayson. Received February 4, 1947–April 15, 1947. Complete, #4. 145 p.

6. No t.p. *Cover:* Screenplay by Charles Grayson. Producer, Henry Blanke. April 17, 1947. Complete #5. 137 p. Includes another copy, Jack Warner's, with his notes. *Annotated on cover:* Names of Bogart and Flynn next to title.

7. Screenplay by Charles Grayson. Producer, Henry Blanke. Received August 3, 1947. 138 p. Complete. #6.

8. Final dialogue script from earlier version, March 11, 1930. Released September 13, 1930. With John Barrymore and Joan Bennett. Adaptation by Oliver H. P. Garrett, dialogue by J. Grubb Alexander. 120 p. (pp. 44–45 and 95–99 missing).

9. Screenplay by Ray Bradbury. Final, February 22, 1954. 148 p. Includes blue revision sheets. Also cast and credits. January 27, 1956. Following page 148, inserted upside down are pages that were replaced with blue revision pages. *Note on another copy's cover, in pencil:* My Marked Copy. Do Not Give Out. (Huston?). Heavily annotated in block letters, rather than script.

10. Release script, February 1956 and August 1, 1956. Revisions. *Note in pencil:* This is dialogue transcript with brief continuity. Use final instead. Credits, same. Also, color style created by Oswald Morris and John Huston. Various paging.

11. Release script, February 1956. With revision received August 1, 1956. *Note:* Use final instead. Various paging.

12. Screenplay by Ray Bradbury. Final. *Cover:* Final (England), February 22, 1954. 134 p. (Same as no. 9 above, before changes.)

13. Release script, August 1, 1956. Various paging.

14. Trailer, June 28, 1956. transcription.

ADDITIONAL SCREENPLAY MATERIAL IN THE FOLLOWING
LIBRARIES.
California State University, San Diego; Emerson College; New York Public Library
Rare Books and Manuscripts; University of Illinois.

MONEY AND MEDICINE. 1983.
TV Documentary. Louis Rukeyser, host and commentator. John Huston
Narrator.

UNIVERSITY OF CALIFORNIA, BERKELEY.
1. "Transcript of the video recording" (24 p.) specifies John Huston as the narrator and has
been confirmed by examining the transcript. The cataloging of the videocassette, however, lists Louis Rukeyser as narrator, with no mention of Huston.

MONTEZUMA (*Montezuma and Cortez*). 1956, 1960.
Director. Unrealized project. *Hollywood Reporter* (May 3, 1960) notes
that Huston would direct, with Kirk Douglas as Cortez, and the film would be
produced by Bryna Productions (Eugene Frenke and Edward Lewis) for
release by Universal. Slated to start production in the summer of 1961.

AMPAS. JOHN HUSTON COLLECTION PRODUCTION FILE.
1. Correspondence between Paul Kohner and Eugene Frenke (August 6, 1957) regarding
Huston's role in production. Additional correspondence from July to September 1960.

AMPAS. JOHN HUSTON COLLECTION. SCRIPT MATERIAL.
1. Play by Bridget Boland, n.d, various paging.
2. *The Great Montezuma* by Joseph O'Kane Foster, n.d. 111 p plus 2 p. Inserted is a May
15, 1961, letter to Huston from Producer Edward Lewis.
3. *Montezuma* screenplay, no author, n.d.
4. Screenplay, no author, n.d. 262 p. Inserted between pages 108 and 109 and stapled
together are eight pages of Huston's drawings. *First page of "White Kiowa hills scene":*
"I'll give fifty dollars to the first man to lay hands on the stolen horse and the rider."
5. Screenplay, July 14, 1960, no author. Bryna Productions, Universal City. 256 p. (Two
copies.)

MOULIN ROUGE. 1953.
Romulus/UA. Screenplay by Anthony Veiller and John Huston.
Directed by Huston.

NEW YORK PUBLIC LIBRARY FOR THE PERFORMING ARTS.
1. Screenplay by John Huston and Anthony Veiller, based on the novel by Pierre La Mure.
May 6, 1952. 115 p. Property of Romulus Films, Ltd.

NEW YORK STATE ARCHIVE.
1. Cutting continuity script.

MOVIOLA: THIS YEAR'S BLONDE. 1980.
TV. David L. Wolper and Stan Margulies, producers, and Warner
Brothers TV. Directed by John Erman. Writers, James Lee and William
Hanley, based on Garson Kanin's book.

USC. TV COLLECTION.
1. Moviola: "This Year's Blonde" teleplay by James Lee, based on the book by Garson Kanin. Second draft, David L. Wolper/Stan Margulies Production, Warner Brothers, n.d., various paging, with revisions dated September 12, 1979. Huston appears on pp. 88–90 and 96–97, and on revised pages of same numbering. *Note:* The USC collection also contains scripts for other parts of the Moviola.

MURDERS IN THE RUE MORGUE. 1932.
Universal. Produced by Carl Laemmle Jr.; associate producer, E. M. Asher. Screenplay by Tom Reed and Dale Van Every. Additional dialogue by John Huston. Based on the short story by Edgar Allan Poe. Directed by Robert Florey.

AMPAS: UNIVERSAL PICTURES. LIBRARY PROPERTIES. SYNOPSIS AND DESCRIPTIVE DATA 4, no. 6,009. Released February 21, 1932.
1. Treatment: Leon Birinski (original treatment) and Tom Reed. 2. Screenplay: Leon Birinski, Tom Reed, Francis E. Faragoh, Dale Van Every, and John Huston, 10/8/31, 247 scenes; Tom Reed, Dale Van Every, and John Huston, 10/13/31, 260 scenes.

NEW YORK STATE ARCHIVE.
1. Cutting continuity script.

MYRA BRECKINRIDGE. 1970.
Twentieth Century-Fox. Screenplay by Michael Sarne and David Giler. Directed by Michael Sarne. Huston, actor, Buck Loner.

THE AMERICAN FILM INSTITUTE.
1. Screenplay by Michael Sarne and David Giler. Final, September 17, 1969. 146 p.

AMPAS. GENERAL COLLECTION.
1. Screenplay by Gore Vidal. First draft, July 21, 1968. 150 p.

UCLA. ARTS SPECIAL COLLECTION. TWENTIETH CENTURY-FOX COLLECTION.
1. "John Huston's Analysis of 'Myra Breckinridge,'" *St. Clerans*, September 3, 1969. 20 p. He notes that he did not intend it to be a critical evaluation of Vidal's work. Merely an analysis of those elements of the work fit for the basis of making a film and an evaluation of the two versions of the screenplay—one dated July 3, 1969, described as a revised first draft (no. 4), and the other undated, whereon no screenwriter's name is given [no. 5?].
2. Michael Sarne. First draft, April 9, 1969. 150 p.
3. Revised first draft, June 13, 1969. 160 p.
4. Revised first draft, July 3, 1969. 145 p.
5. First revised screenplay, July 24, 1969. 126 p.
6. David Giler, September 4, 1969. 166 p.
7. First draft, September 5, 1969.
8. Revised first draft, September 10, 1969. 130 p.
9. Final, September 17, 1969. 146 p.
10. Dialogue and continuity taken from the Moviola, June 30, 1970.

UNIVERSITY OF IOWA. TWENTIETH CENTURY-FOX SCRIPT COLLECTION.
1. Dialogue and continuity taken from the Moviola, June 30, 1970.

2. Dialogue and continuity ("combination title book"), August 1970.

USC. GENERAL COLLECTION.
1. First revised screenplay by Gore Vidal, July 24, 1969. *Cover:* July 3, 1969. Revised first draft. 126 p.

USC. TWENTIETH CENTURY-FOX COLLECTION.
1. Screenplay by Gore Vidal, June 1968. 154 p.
2. Gore Vidal. First draft screenplay, July 21, 1968. 150 p.
3. Screenplay by Michael Sarne. First draft, April 9, 1969. 150 p.
4. Michael Sarne. Revised first draft, June 13, 1969. 160 p.
5. Screenplay by David Giler, September 4, 1969. 166 p.
6. David Giler. First draft, September 5, 1969. 146 p.
7. David Giler. Revised first draft, September 10, 1969. 130 p.
8. Screenplay by Michael Sarne and David Giler. Revised final, September 22, 1969. Various paging. Includes blue revised pages, October–November 1969.

NAGANA (working titles: *Animal World, Adventure Woman*). 1933.
Screenplay by Dale Van Every and Don Ryan. Story by Lester Cohen. Directed by Ernst L. Frank.

AMPAS. JOHN HUSTON COLLECTION. SCRIPT MATERIAL.
1. *Nagana* from John Huston, August 22, 1932. 9 p. Located in John Huston Inventory, Early Scripts and Stories—Titled, p. 39.

AMPAS. UNIVERSAL PICTURES. LIBRARY PROPERTIES. SYNOPSIS AND DESCRIPTIVE DATA 4, no. 6,075. Released 1/26/33.
1. Author, Lester Cohen; magazine story, Dale Collins; treatment, Ernst L. Frank and John B. Clymer; John Huston, 8/22/32, 9 p.; screenplay, Dale Van Every (alone and with Don Ryan), Lester Cohen, John B. Clymer, and Edwin H. Knopf (alone and with Paul Perez).

NEW YORK STATE ARCHIVE.
1. Cutting continuity script.

NEXT DOOR TO HEAVEN.
Unrealized project (?).

AMPAS. JOHN HUSTON COLLECTION. SCRIPT MATERIAL.
1. Screenplay. No author, n.d. 155 p. (Two copies.)

NEW YORK PUBLIC LIBRARY FOR THE PERFORMING ARTS.
1.Play script by Harold Callen and Edmond Paulker, n.d., various pages.

THE NIGHT OF THE IGUANA. 1964.
Seven Arts/MGM. Screenplay by Anthony Veiller and John Huston, based on the Tennessee Williams play. Directed by Huston.

AMPAS. JOHN HUSTON COLLECTION. SCRIPT MATERIAL.
1. Screenplay. September 19, 1963, with revisions to November 13, 1963. 140 p. Specially bound.
2. Treatment, no author or date. 91 p. Seven Arts Associated Corp.
3. Treatment by Gavin Lambert. Seven Arts Associated Corp., n.d. 80 p.
4. First draft screenplay by Gavin Lambert, n.d. 139 p.

5. Final script. Seven Arts. *Cover:* no. 1, John Huston written. No author or date. 134 p. Some pages marked "Revisions, JH, Sept. 16, 1963."
6. Screenplay, September 19, 1963. Property of Seven Arts. No author. 139 p. *In pen on another copy's cover:* Veiller.
7. Folder of various pages: rewrites, Huston's handwritten notes and doodles, some pages "Veiller, 10/6/63." Some pages annotated.

AMPAS. MGM/TURNER COLLECTION.

1. First draft temporary script, no authors, Seven Arts Associated Corp. *On cover:* Received 3/25/64. 131 p.
2. Final version screenplay by Anthony Veiller and John Huston, based on the play by Tennessee Williams, 9/19/63, 140 p. Property of Seven Arts. Red line markings on side of pages in some sections.
3. Screenplay, Seven Arts Productions International Ltd., 9/19/63, no authors indicated, 148 p. *On cover:* Hold for Legal Research Dept., Latest, 6015#2, Start September 25, [19]63. Vault Copy, Sept. 19, 1963, Property of Seven Arts Productions.
4. "Dialogue Cutting Continuity," printed in England; May 1, 1964; 6 reels; 10,576 feet; reprinted in the United States, 6/4/64, 117 p.
5. Trailer's dialogue cutting continuity and trailer footage, 7/8/64, 7 p., and 1 p., respectively.
6. Teaser trailer's dialogue cutting continuity and trailer footage, 7/21/64, 2 p. and 1 p., respectively.
7. Theater announcement, trailer dialogue continuity, and trailer footage, 7/21/64, 2 p. and 1 p., respectively.

NEW YORK PUBLIC LIBRARY FOR THE PERFORMING ARTS.

1. Final script, no author, n.d. 133 p. Seven Art Assoc. Corp. Audrey Wood's name on cover. Gift of Mrs. Robert Gessner.

NEW YORK STATE ARCHIVE.

1. Cutting continuity script.

USC. WARNER BROTHERS ARCHIVE.

1. Play script by Tennessee Williams. Rehearsal version, July 24, 1961. Property of Charles Bowden, New York City. Warner Brothers' property stamp. Various paging.
2. *Noche de la Iguana.* Seven Arts Associated Corp., Beverly Hills, California, n.d. 87 p. Transcription of play into prose form. *On cover:* Final, Spanish.
3. First draft screenplay by Gavin Lambert. Seven Arts, Beverly Hills, n.d. 139 p. *Cover, handwritten:* Old version by Lambert. 139 same as 131 1st draft.
4. No author, n.d. Seven Arts, Warner. 91 p. *Cover, handwritten:* Treatment.
5. First draft, temporary script. Seven Arts, Warner Brothers. No author, n.d. 131 p. (Does not appear to be same as no. 3.)
6. No author. September 19, 1963. Seven Arts, Warner Brothers 139 p. Some pages marked as "Revised, September 23, 1963." *Cover, handwritten:* Old Version. (Does not appear to be the same as no. 3.)
7. Screenplay by Anthony Veiller and John Huston, from the play by Tennessee Williams. Final version, September 19, 1963. Revisions to December 7, 1963. 140 p. *Cover:* Final Version. (Two copies.)

WRITERS GUILD OF AMERICA, WEST.

1. Final version, September 19, 1963. 140 p.

ADDITIONAL SCREENPLAY MATERIAL IN THE FOLLOWING
LIBRARIES.
Indiana University Library.

NINA. 1970.
Unrealized project. Actor.

AMPAS. JOHN HUSTON COLLECTION. PRODUCTION FILE.
1. Correspondence with Huston indicating that Hemdale was producing the film in the
United Kingdom and wanted Huston to play the leading role of Edward Granville. They
hoped to start shooting in August or September 1970. While no screenplay material is in
the collection, Gladys Hill indicated that it was received.

NEW YORK PUBLIC LIBRARY FOR THE PERFORMING ARTS.
1. *Nina,* a comedy in three acts, by Bruno Frank, n.d., 40 p.

ON OUR MERRY WAY (*A Miracle Can Happen*). 1948.
Directed by King Vidor and Leslie Fenton. According to *Film Dope*
Huston was director (uncredited) of the Henry Fonda–James Stewart
sequences.

NEW YORK STATE ARCHIVE.
1. Dialogue script.

ON THE TRAIL OF THE IGUANA. 1965.

INDIANA UNIVERSITY LIBRARY.
1. *On the Trail of the Iguana.* American instruction list. MGM and Seven Arts Production,
1964. 31 p. Caption title. Mimeographed film script of exploitation short subject; numbered scenes and footage; action and dialogue; dated June 2, 1964.

THE OTHER SIDE OF THE WIND. 1970–75.
Not yet released. Produced, directed, and screenplay by Orson Welles.
John Huston, actor, film director. Per a *New York Times* (January 31, 1971)
article by Charles Higham, Welles had started shooting a film he wrote about a
director of the Henry Hathaway–John Ford–[John Huston?] mold "who comes
back to Hollywood after a long exile to be confronted by the self-conscious
intellectualism and Beverly Hills hippiedom of Hollywood in the 1970s. . . . It
hasn't been settled whether John Huston or Welles himself will appear in the
role of the director."

AMPAS. GENERAL COLLECTION.
1. *The Other Side of the Wind.* No author, n.d. 211 p.

USC. BOYLE COLLECTION.
1. *The Other Side of the Wind.* No author indicated. (*Handwritten:* Including revisions 28
Dec '72, 29 December '72, 30 December '72, 3 January '73; printed 7 Nov '73.) Various
paging, heavily annotated (by Welles?).

PATTON. 1970.
Twentieth Century-Fox. Screenplay by Francis Ford Coppola and
Edmund H. North. Directed by Franklin Schaffner. Huston considered for
director, October 1965 to March 1968.

NEW YORK PUBLIC LIBRARY FOR THE PERFORMING ARTS.
1. Screenplay by Francis Ford Coppola and Edmund H. North, shooting script, February 1, 1969. 155 p.

UCLA. ARTS SPECIAL COLLECTION. GENERAL COLLECTION.
1. Coppola and North, shooting script, February 1, 1969. 155 p.
2. Coppola. Writers' working script, November 10, 1965. 196 p. *Binding label:* First, Dec. 27, 1965. Gift of Tom Korman.

UCLA. ARTS SPECIAL COLLECTION. TWENTIETH CENTURY-FOX ARCHIVE.
1. Memos from Frank McCarthy (producer) to Richard Zanuck about Huston's involvement: Appears first draft screenplay, 12/27/65, was submitted to Huston for his consideration, and they met with him. Numerous other memos, 1965–68.
2. Coppola and North. Third revised screenplay, December 10, 1968. 155 p.
3. Final screenplay, January 1, 1969. 155 p. Revision pages included.
4. Coppola. Writer's working script, November 11, 1965. 196 p.
5. Coppola. First draft, December 27, 1965. Includes six weeks of revisions. 202 p. Another copy. Also included Spanish translation.
6. *Blood and Guts.* Screenplay by Jack Pearl, n.d. 186 p.
7. *Patton: A Profile* by Robert S. Allen, November 13, 1961. 174 p.
8. *Patton!* Screen treatment by Calder Willingham, July 12, 1965. 130 p. Another copy. Includes memo to McCarthy from Willingham, July 12, 1965. 4 p.
9. Summary outline of writer's working script, James R. Webb (186 p.), dated July 26, 1967. Prepared by G. Byron Sage, August 14, 1967. 22 p.
10. Coppola and North. Second revised screenplay, October 24, 1968. 171 p.
11. Continuity and dialogue taken from the Moviola.

USC. GENERAL COLLECTION.
1. Screen treatment by Calder Willingham. July 12, 1965. 130 p.
2. Shooting script, February 1, 1969. 155 p.

WRITERS GUILD OF AMERICA, WEST.
1. Screenplay by Francis Ford Coppola and Edmund H. North, 1970.

PHOBIA. 1980.
　　Paramount. Screenplay by Lew Lehman, Jimmy Sangster, and Peter Bellwood. Directed by John Huston.

AMPAS. JOHN HUSTON COLLECTION. SCRIPT MATERIAL.
1. Story by Ronald Shusett and Gary Sherman. Screenplay by Lew Lehman, James Sangster, and Peter Bellwood. Totally revised script—October 15, 1979. Borough Park Production Inc., Scarborough, Ontario. Various paging. Script is made up of yellow, pink, and blue sheets. Revisions to December 10, 1979. Various pages have "John Huston" written at top of page.

UCLA. ARTS SPECIAL COLLECTION. GENERAL COLLECTION.
1. Screenplay by Lew Lehman, James Sangster, and Peter Bellwood. Draft, January 29, 1979. Revisions: February 15, 1979; June 15, 1979; September 3, 1979. 135 p.

PORTRAIT OF THE ARTIST AS A YOUNG MAN. 1977.
　　Joseph Strick. Earlier unrealized project of Huston's (?).

AMPAS. JOHN HUSTON COLLECTION. SCRIPT MATERIAL.
1. Screenplay by Hugh Leonard. Amicus Productions, Shepperton, n.d. 109 p. (Three copies.) *On copy 2's t.p., handwritten:* Max R GR 04121 (i.e., Max Rosenberg, Vanguard Productions, New York City).

PRELUDE TO FREEDOM.
Unrealized project. Also developed under the titles: *Theodosia: Empress of America* and *Eight Years of Tom Jefferson.*

AMPAS. JOHN HUSTON COLLECTION. SCRIPT MATERIAL.
1. Original screen story by John Huston and M. L. Gunzburg. Registered Screenwriters Guild, n.d. 96 p. Preface: Story of Jefferson and birth of Americanism. Attached is a photocopy of the cover letter from Gunzburg, Gunzburg Productions, May 12, 1950, to Huston, MGM, indicating that he is sending Huston another script after six months and questions the location of the original set of scripts. He hopes that Huston will move on the project.
2. On script of *Prelude to Freedom:* An original screenplay, treatment, research, and plot structure for a motion picture dramatizing the administration of Thomas Jefferson in which Americans first found form [a form of self]. By John Huston and Lowell Brodaux [pseudonym of M. L. Gunzburg]. Registered with Screenwriters Guild, n.d. 99 p. [Following:] Where to start? What of Jefferson's life to concentrate on—his struggle to keep infant Democracy alive—they're 1932–40. Jefferson is still with us. [Following characters and suggested players:] Thomas Jefferson—Walter Huston; also John Barrymore as Burr, Bette Davis as Theodosia Burr, Jeffrey Lynn as Meriwether Lewis, Claude Rains as Alexander Hamilton. [Walter Huston died April 7, 1950.]
3. Another copy of no. 2 in loose-leaf binder: Screenwriters Guild, registered no. 15,288. 99 p. Includes screen outline by Huston and Gungzburg, n.d., 2 p., and various pages of research materials.
4. *Theodosia: Empress of America.* An original screen story by John Huston and Lowell Brodaux, n.d. 14 p. Page 14 marked "End of Part 1." *Note:* The last approximate two-thirds of *Theodosia* is suggested in the plot of *Prelude to Freedom,* an original screen story in screenplay continuity by Huston and Brodaux.

AMPAS. MILTON GUNZBURG [LOWELL BRODAUX] COLLECTION.
1. *Theodosia: Empress of America.* An original Screen story by John Huston and Lowell Brodaux, n.d. 14 p. Treatment.

AMPAS. PAUL KOHNER (Huston's longtime agent) COLLECTION.
1. *Prelude to Freedom.* An original screen story by John Huston and M. L. Gunzburg, n.d. 96 p. Paul Kohner's label on cover.
2. *Theodosia: Empress of America.* An original screen story by John Huston and Lowell Brodaux (that is, Milton Gunzburg), n.d. 14 p. Treatment.
3. *Theodosia: Empress of America.* An original screen story by John Huston and Milton Gunzburg, n.d. 16 p. Page 16 marked "End of Part One." Following is *Prelude to Freedom.* An original Screen story by John Huston and Milton Gunzburg, n.d. 99 p.
4. *The Eight Years of Tom Jefferson* by John Huston and Milo Brodaux, n.d. Various paging. *Title page:* Being the plot structure, the research material, the major characters, and background for a motion picture immortalizing the eight dramatic years of Thomas Jefferson's administration, in which America first found form—a democracy.

USC. WARNER BROTHERS ARCHIVE.
1. *Prelude to Freedom* by John Huston and Lowell Brodaux. Original from Mr. MacEwan, 5/22/39. Includes synopsis plus treatment (16 p.).
2. *Theodosia: Empress of America* by John Huston and Lowell Brodaux. Original 5/11/40. Includes treatment (1 p.). Copy received from Paul Kohner, Huston's agent.

PRINCE AND THE SHOWGIRL (*Sleeping Prince*). 1957.
Warner /Marilyn Monroe Productions. Screenplay by Terence Rattigan. Directed by Laurence Olivier. Unrealized project.

USC. WARNER BROTHERS ARCHIVE.
1. *The Sleeping Prince: An Occasional Fairy Tale* by Terence Rattigan. *Cover:* Warner Brothers Story Department. *In pencil:* Play script. No date. Various paging. (Six copies.)
2. L.O.P. presents *The Sleeping Prince* by Terence Rattigan. Final shooting script, June 11, 1956. Inserted before first page: cast and credits, 5/22/57. 176 p. *Cover, in pencil:* Final, Only copy, London Copy.
3. As no. 2, 168 p. *Cover:* Final, June 11, 1956. (Six copies.)
4. *The Prince and the Showgirl* (dialogue transcript). Copyrighted 1957 by Marilyn Monroe Productions, Inc. Presented by Warner Brothers Pictures. Various paging. *At top of t.p.:* May 1, 1957. (Numerous copies.)
5. *The Prince and the Showgirl* (trailer). June 13, 1957. 2 p. (Numerous copies.)

ADDITIONAL SCREENPLAY MATERIAL IN THE FOLLOWING LIBRARIES.
Indiana University, University of California, Los Angeles.

PRIZZI'S HONOR. 1985.
ABC Motion Pictures/Twentieth Century-Fox. Screenplay by Richard Condon and Janet Roach, based on Condon's novel of the same name (New York: Berkeley Books, 1982). Directed by John Huston.

THE AMERICAN FILM INSTITUTE.
1. February 2, 1984. 139 p. Title on script amended by hand to read: *Family Honor.*
2. Shooting script, revised, September 24, 1984. 124 p.
3. Shooting script, revised, October 1, 17, 30, 1984. 124 p.

AMPAS. GENERAL COLLECTION.
1. Story and screenplay by Richard Condon and Janet Roach. Shooting script, revised, October 1, 1984, with changes to November 14, 1984. Includes yellow and pink revision pages. 124 p. *On t.p.:* Director: John Huston, Producer: John Foreman.

THE BRITISH FILM INSTITUTE.
1. Screenplay in the collection.

MUSEUM OF MODERN ART. FILM DEPARTMENT.
1. ABC Motion Pictures. *Prizzi's Honor.* Story and screenplay by Richard Condon and Janet Roach. Shooting script, revised, 9/24/84. Director, John Huston; producer, John Foreman. 124 p.

NEW YORK PUBLIC LIBRARY FOR THE PERFORMING ARTS.
1. Story and screenplay by Richard Condon and Janet Roach, shooting script, revised, October 1, 1984. *Top of page:* ABC Motion Pictures, revised 10/17/84, 10/30/84. Director, John Huston; producer, John Foreman. 124 p.

UCLA. ARTS SPECIAL COLLECTION. TWENTIETH CENTURY-FOX COL-
LECTION.
1. Story and screenplay by Richard Condon and Janet Roach. June 1984. 118 p. *Note:* Page
46 missing. Academy has complete shooting script.

UCSB. DAVIDSON LIBRARY.
1. Story and screenplay by Richard Condon and Janet Roach. ABC Motion Pictures.
Director, John Huston; producer, John Foreman. Shooting script, revised, October 1,
1984. Title page also marked: "Rev. 10/17/84, Rev. 10/30/84." 124 p.

USC. GENERAL COLLECTION.
1. May 11, 1984. 118 p.
2. Shooting script, Rev. October 1, 1984. Other revision dates indicated on t.p—10/17/84,
10/30/84, 11/14/84—and others are noted in the text. 124 p. Partial cast listed.

WRITERS GUILD OF AMERICA, WEST.
1. Screenplay by Richard Condon and Janet Roach. Shooting script. Revised, October 1,
1984–November 14, 1984.

ADDITIONAL SCREENPLAY MATERIAL IN THE FOLLOWING
LIBRARIES.
Stanford University Library.

THE PROWLER ("The Cost of Living"). 1951.
Horizon. Produced by Sam Spiegel. Screenplay by Hugo Butler.
Directed by Joseph Losey. Per *Film Dope* (no. 26 [January 1983]: 20, Horizon
Productions: *The Prowler*), this film was the only other Horizon production
with which Huston was associated for he left the company after *The African
Queen* (1952).

AMPAS. JOHN HUSTON COLLECTION. SCRIPT MATERIAL.
1. *The Cost of Living,* no author. Screenplay, March 8, 1950. Property of Horizon Pictures.
On cover in pencil: The Prowler. Upper right: JH. Inserted are retake sheets, pp. 84–87,
April 17, 1950; revised sheets, pp. 110–13. 123 p.

NEW YORK STATE ARCHIVE.
1. Dialogue script.

THE QUARE FELLOW. 1962.
BLC/Bryanston. Produced by Anthony Havelock-Allan. Writer and
director Arthur Dreifuss. Unrealized project (?).

AMPAS. JOHN HUSTON COLLECTION.
1. *The Quare Fellow.* Film adaptation by Jacqueline Sundstrom and Arthur Dreifuss, based
on the play by Brendan Behan. Screenplay by Arthur Dreifuss. First draft, January 15,
1960. 207 p.

NEW YORK STATE ARCHIVE.
1. Cutting continuity script.

QUO VADIS. 1951.
MGM. Screenplay by John Lee Mahin, S. N. Behrman, and Sonya
Levien. Director, Mervyn Le Roy. Huston was a writer (with others) and the

director from January through May 1949, when he withdrew. Le Roy's name began appearing in memos in March 1950.

THE AMERICAN FILM INSTITUTE.
1. Complete. April 30, 1950. 187 p.

AMPAS. GENERAL COLLECTION.
1. Screenplay. April 3, 1950. 185 p. No author indicated. Another copy in John Lee Mahin Collection.

AMPAS. JOHN HUSTON COLLECTION. PRODUCTION FILES.
1. Four files of correspondence, pre- and production notes, and schedules, February–August 1949.

AMPAS. JOHN HUSTON COLLECTION. SCRIPT MATERIAL. Three files of miscellaneous script pages, virtually all yellow:
1. *February 18, 1949–May 18, 1949:* Various pages clipped together. Some have "Mr. Huston" at top of pages. Some pages have notes attached and others are heavily annotated, some in Huston's hand.
2. *May 9, 1949–October 6, 1949:* As no. 1. Includes changes. Handwritten pieces inserted. *Notes:* For Mr. Huston from Mr. Lewin. Some pages have superimposed "Permanent script File."
3. *August 22, 1949–September 6, 1949:* Two sections have notes attached from Al Lewin, September 8, 1949.

UNIVERSITY OF WYOMING. AMERICAN HERITAGE CENTER.
1. *Quo Vadis* by S. N. Behrman and Sonya Levien, August 31, 1948, 148 p. (Sonya Levien Collection #6447.)

USC. MGM COLLECTION.
1. Summaries of the novel, one by John Lee Mahin, April 7, 1950.
2. Treatment by Arthur Gregor, November 27, 1936.
3. Complete script, April 3, 1950. 187 p.
4. Cyril Hume and Walter Reisch. Temporary incomplete, September 25, 1942. 94 p.
5. Cyril Hume. Temporary incomplete, composite script, October 29, 1942. 17 p.
6. S. N. Behrman, December 11, 1942, original, 43 p.; December 23, 1942, 36 p.; and Behrman and Reisch, no. 4, 57 p. Includes various other scenes and points by Behrman, including conference notes, March 1943.
7. Miscellaneous original for old pages, out of March 17, 1943, script, Behrman and Reisch. 201 p. Heavily annotated; notes and additional pages by Sonya Levien, April 4 through April 6, 1948 (some with Behrman).
8. Notes and additional pages by Sonya Levien, April 4 through April 6, 1948 (some with Behrman).
9. Original. Behrman and Levien, August 10, 1948. Various pages, heavily annotated. Also notes by Gerald Fairlie and breakdown of novel, July 1948, Levien and Arthur Hornblow Jr., August–September 1948.
10. Section 3, script, Behrman and Levien, September 11, 1948. Various pages. Highly annotated.
11. Various revisions, notes, and breakdown by Behrman, Levien, Hugh Gray, and Caryl Ledner, September–December 1948.
12. *Quo Vadis* conference notes from Arthur Hornblow Jr., John Huston, and Sonya Levien,

February 1, 1949. Same folder includes letters on technical matters, wardrobe information, cast list, and research notes, all dated January–February 1949. (Folder 13, box 7.)

13. Script material, Sonya Levien, February 1949.

14. Notes from Hugh Gray and censors, February 1949; survey of Cine Citta Studios (Rome), March 1949.

15. Old pages out of March 10, 1949, script, from S. N. Behrman, Sonya Levien, and John Huston, March 10, 1949, through April 1, 1949, no. 7. 100 p. From S. N. Behrman, Sonya Levien, and John Huston, March 10, 1949. Various pages, heavily annotated. Some pages have other dates, March 1949. (Folder 16, box 7.)

16. From Behrman, Levien, and Huston, March 10, 1949. *In pencil on cover:* Hornblow, 2nd copy, Checked, OK, 1/23/50. 101 p. Includes pages, April 1949. *Note attached to script:* Incomplete dialogue script, nos. 2–3.

From Behrman, Levien, and Huston, March 10, 1949. 2–6. Incomplete dialogue script. 101 p. Dates up to April 1949.

Original. From Huston and Hugh Gray, March 24, 1949. *Note:* Section of script from Huston and Gray. Various pages, dates from May 1949. Heavily annotated. (Folder 17, box 17.)

17. From Huston and Gray, March 24, 1949, no. 4. Section of script, various pages.
Old pages out of March 24, 1949. Section of script from Huston and Gray, pages dated March 28, 1949, through May 17, 1949.
Section of script from Huston, Levien, and Behrman, no. 1, April 8, 1949. (Folder 18, box 7.)

18. Conference notes, Sonya Levien, April 8, 1949, no. 6.
Sonya Levien and Hugh Gray, April 11, 1949, various paging, heavily annotated.
Sonya Levien and Hugh Gray, April 11 through April 28, 1949. Some pages dated May to June 1949. Various pages, highly annotated.

19. Temporary incomplete, Sonya Levien and Hugh Gray, April 11–28, 1949, production #1,312; producer, Mr. Hornblower. 141 p. Some pages dated June 1949.
Old pages out of April 11, 1949; screen run April 28, 1949, from Sonya Levien and Hugh Gray.
Italian research notes, April 29, 1949.

20. Test scenes, May 5, 1949, revised start and finish dates, May 6, 1949. Memos from Eddie Mannix, May 13, 1949. (Huston not indicated in "cc".)

21. Various pages by Sonya Levien and Hugh Gray, May 18 through June 8, 1949. Sections of script by Gray and Levien, June 6, 1949. Some pages dated through September 1949. Heavily annotated.

Miscellaneous sections, scripts, and notes, June 6 through October 17, 1949. Old pages out of June 6, 1949, including screenplay by Gray and Levien, June 6 through October 18, 1949. Various pages. Notes on script, Hugh Gray, October through November 1949.

Details of music from Miklos Rozsa and Gray, November 1949 and March 1950. Other script changes, December 1949.

Actors suggested by Irene Howard, December 1949.

Other script changes, December 1949. Producer, Zimbalist.

Numerous other script changes: Gray, January–February 1950; John Lee Mahin, January–March 1950.

22. Conversion scene from John Huston, undated, no. 1. *Penciled note:* Sent to file, January 1950. 3 p.

Test scene, Peter Ustinov, February 15, 1950.

Technical matters, February 28, 1950.

Latin inscriptions, February 16, 1950; list of characters, March 1, 1950; list of music, March 1, 1950; cast sheet, March 8, 1950; personnel to Rome (Huston not mentioned), March 8, 1950; other test scenes, March 16, 1950; revised details of music, March 30, 1950, to April 7, 1950.

Miscellaneous memos, Hugh Gray, April 4 to April 20, 1950; blue memo from Gray, April 4, 1950, to April 20, 1950.

Songs and hymns from Hugh Gray and Miklos Rosza, April 11, 1950; old pages out of January 9, 1951; loops, January 9, 1951; frame description, November 8, 1951; music in reels, December 17, 1951.

THE RED BADGE OF COURAGE. MGM. 1951.
Screenplay and direction by John Huston. Adaptation by Albert Band, based on Stephen Crane's novel of the same name.

AMPAS. GENERAL COLLECTION.

1. From John Huston, April 20, 1950. Retakes from Mr. Reinhardt (Gottfried Rienhardt, producer), October 27, 1950. Includes retakes to October 31, 1950. *The t.p.:* Okayed by Mr. Reinhardt, Director: John Huston. 92 p.

AMPAS. JOHN HUSTON COLLECTION. SCRIPT MATERIAL.

1. Crane, Stephen. *The Red Badge of Courage.* Edited and introduced by John T. Winterich. London: The Folio Society, 1951. With Civil War photographs. (Contains very graphic photographs of dead soldiers.)

2. Folder: Summary production notes, no author or date, 20 p. Treatments: various versions, no authors, some dated 2/26/50 and 3/6/50, various paging, with some annotated and others heavily annotated, some handwritten pages.

3. *The Red Badge of Courage.* From John Huston, 3–6–50. Complete. MGM label no. 4. Some pages indicate changes, 3/8/50. Treatment. 51 p.

4. Treatment changes, 3/6/50 and 3/8/50, various paging. (Two copies.)

5. Screenplay from John Huston, April 20, 1950. Temporary complete, rerun April 20, 1950. Also dated April 26, 1950. MGM label. no. 55. 92 p. Pages variously dated, April 1950.

6. Screenplay from John Huston, 4–20–50. Okayed by Mr. Reinhardt; director, John Huston. 92 p. Includes pink revised pages through 8/26/50. Annotated. In binder. *Cover:* John Huston, 1950, *Red Badge.*

7. Folder of pages variously dated April through August 1950. Changes, April 24, 1950 (six sets); yellow pages, 6/7/50 and 7/14/50, with Huston's handwritten notes. Another folder with changes, August through October 1950.

AMPAS. TURNER/MGM COLLECTION.

1. Synopsis by Ann Doyle of radio program, 6/10/47, 3 p.

2. Treatments by John Huston and Albert Band, 3/6/50, 54 p. and 51 p., respectively. (Three copies: original #1 and #2 and retyped version; originals annotated.)

3. Complete OK screenplay by John Huston, 4/20/50 and 10/10/50. About 300 p. Annotated.
4. Complete composite OK screenplay by John Huston, 4/20/50 and 10/10/50. About 250 p.
5. Complete OK screenplay by John Huston, 4/20/50 and 10/10/50, with 10/27/50 retakes by Gottfried Reinhardt, 112 p. Also synopsis by Sheila Walker, 5/26/50, original and retyped version, 11 p.
6. Retakes by Gottfried Reinhardt, 10/27/50 and 10/30/50, 12 p. and 23 p., respectively. (Two copies: original and composite script.)
7. Comments for opening title by Gottfried Reinhardt, 3/27/51, 12 p.
8. Teaser trailer dialogue continuity and trailer footage, 7/25/51, 2 p. and 1 p., respectively.
9. Dialogue cutting continuity by Ben Lewis (editor) and footage and music report, 8/22/51, 65 p. and 9 p.
10. Trailer #1 dialogue cutting continuity and trailer footage, 8/25/51, 5 p. and 1 p.
11. Trailer #2 cutting continuity and trailer footage, 9/25/51, 4 p. and 1 p.

NEW YORK STATE ARCHIVE.
1. Cutting continuity script.

UCLA. ARTS SPECIAL COLLECTION. GENERAL COLLECTION.
1. From John Huston, April 20, 1950, with October 27, 1950, retakes from Mr. Reinhardt (Gottfried Reinhardt, producer), 91 plus 51 p.

USC. MGM COLLECTION.
1. Synopsis of radio program, Studio One, WCBS, June 10, 1947. Heard by Ann Doyle. Starring Everett Sloane. 3 p.
2. Complete OK script, John Huston (92 p.), April 20, 1950. Synopsis, 11 p. Reader, Sheila Walker, May 26, 1950.
3. *The Red Badge of Courage* from John Huston and Albert Band, March 6, 1950. Complete, treatment, no. 14, 51 p.
4. Retakes from Mr. Reinhardt (Gottfried Reinhardt, producer), October 27, 1950. Composite script, 15 p.
5. Commentation for opening title. From G. Reinhardt, March 27, 1951. 12 p.
6. Teaser trailer (dialogue cutting continuity), July 25, 1951, no. 6. 2 p.
7. Dialogue cutting continuity. Film editor, Ben Lewis, August 22, 1951.
8. Trailer no. 1, August 23, 1951; trailer no. 2, September 28, 1951.

ADDITIONAL SCREENPLAY MATERIAL IN THE FOLLOWING LIBRARIES.
California Institute of Arts, Columbia College, Lafayette College, Northern Illinois University, University of Illinois.

REFLECTIONS IN A GOLDEN EYE. 1967.
Warner Brothers–Seven Arts. Screenplay by Chapman Mortimer, Gladys Hill, and John Huston (uncredited), based on Carson McCullers's novel of the same name (Boston: Houghton, Mifflin, 1941). Directed by Huston.

AMPAS. GENERAL COLLECTION.
1. Screenplay by Chapman Mortimer, Gladys Hill, and John Huston. September 19, 1966. 143 p.

AMPAS. JOHN HUSTON COLLECTION. SCRIPT MATERIAL.

1. Screenplay by Chapman Mortimer, Gladys Hill, and John Huston. September 16, 1966, with revisions to November 2, 1966. 143 p. Heavily annotated. Specially bound.
2. Screen treatment by Francis Ford Coppola. Seven Arts, n.d. 120 p.
3. Screenplay by Coppola. First draft, n.d. 139 p. (Two copies.)
4. Screenplay by William Archibald. First draft, Seven Arts, n.d. 283 p.
5. Screenplay by Christopher Isherwood, July 27, 1964. Seven Arts. 102 p. (Three copies.)
6. Screenplay by Chapman Mortimer, April 15, 1966. 70 p. (Two copies.)
7. Screenplay by Chapman Mortimer, June 9, 1966. 145 p. (Three copies.)
8. Screenplay by Chapman Mortimer, Gladys Hill, and John Huston, n.d. 143 p. Includes blue revision sheets, 9/21/66. Dialogue and other changes inserted, 11/2/66 and 12/7/66. Another copy marked "Incomplete 3rd copy." Includes blue revision sheets.
9. Italian version: "Rifless in un occio d'oro" by Mortimer, Hill, and Huston, n.d. 216 p.

USC. GENERAL COLLECTION.

1. Screenplay by Christopher Isherwood, July 27, 1964. *Cover:* Seven Arts Associated Corp., Beverly Hills. 102 p.

USC. WARNER BROTHERS ARCHIVE.

1. Warner Brothers memo, P. D. Knecht to Curtis Kenyon, May 23, 1967: "The following writers worked on *Reflections:* William Archibald, Alfred Hayes, Francis Coppola, Christopher Isherwood, Anthony Veiller, Chapman Mortimer, Glades[sic] Hill." (Huston not mentioned.) Various other memos and communications in file indicate that Huston worked on various versions of script.
2. Screen treatment by Alfred Hayes, n.d. 30 p.
3. As no. 2, n.d. 73 p.
4. Screen treatment by Francis Ford Coppola, n.d. *Cover, in pencil:* 4/16/63. 120 p.
5. Francis Ford Coppola, n.d. 157 p.
6. Screenplay by Francis Ford Coppola. First draft, n.d. *Cover, in pencil:* (?)5/13/63. 50 p.
7. As no. 6. First draft, n.d. *Cover, in pencil:* 6/21/63. 139 p.
8. Screenplay by Christopher Isherwood, July 27, 1964. 102 p.
9. As no. 8, July 27, 1964. 95 p. Annotated. *In pencil:* 95 p. Basis of 102 p.
10. Screenplay by William Archibald. First draft, n.d. *Cover, in pencil:* August 12, 1965. 151 p. Also typescript of this version.
11. William Archibald. First draft, Paris, November 1965. 281 p. Typescript, same as no. 12.
12. William Archibald. First draft, n.d. *Cover, in pencil:* November 29, 1965.
13. Screenplay by Chapman Mortimer, April 15, 1966. 70 p.
14. Screenplay by Chapman Mortimer, Gladys Hill, and John Huston, n.d. *Cover, in pen:* X final Screenplay. 143 p. White pages have marked at top "16.9.66." Blue pages revised, September 21, 1966. Following t.p. and preceding script: cast and credits sheet. (Huston not indicated as writer of credit.)
15. Chapman Mortimer, n.d. 159 p.
16. Chapman Mortimer, Gisebo, Sweden, June 1966. *Cover, in pencil:* Basis of 159 p. Photocopy. Top parts cut off on some pages.
17. Leonora scenes: (Mrs. Pendleton), June 20, 1966. Typescript. Various paging.
18. Trailer dialogue transcript, December 28, 1967. 4 p.
19. Dialogue transcript, October 18, 1967. Various paging.

ADDITIONAL SCREENPLAY MATERIAL IN THE FOLLOWING LIBRARIES.

Indiana University, Ohio State University, Wellesley College.

REMINISCENCES OF A COWBOY (released as *Cowboy*). 1958.
Columbia/Phoenix. Produced by Julian Blaustein, screenplay by Edmund H. North, directed by Delmer Daves. Huston, director, unrealized.

AMPAS. JOHN HUSTON COLLECTION. PRODUCTION FILES.
1. Report that Huston was designated as director around 1949. Film to be produced by Horizon and released by Columbia. Montgomery Clift and Walter Huston were possible leads.
2. Another report says that Peter Viertel would do screenplay. In an earlier letter to Huston, 11/1/45, he writes that he had acquired the rights to Frank Harris's *My Reminiscences as a Cowboy.*
3. Per a letter to Huston from Julian Blaustein, producer, Huston may have had a long relationship with this property and was perhaps one of the writers.

AMPAS. JOHN HUSTON COLLECTION. SCRIPT MATERIAL.
1. *Reminiscences of a Cowboy.* First draft screenplay by Peter Viertel, n.d. 194 p. AMPAS Inventory indicates "[1948?]" but no evidence of designation of this date.

AMPAS. RANDALL MACDOUGALL COLLECTION.
1. *Reminiscences of a Cowboy.* Screenplay by Randall MacDougall. First draft, January 5, 1953. *On t.p.:* Frontier. 176 p.

NEW YORK STATE ARCHIVE.
1. Dialogue script under released title *Cowboy.*

REPORT FROM THE ALEUTIANS. 1943.
U.S. Army Pictorial Service, Signal Corps. Screenplay by John Huston and commentary by Walter Huston. Directed by John Huston.

AMPAS. JOHN HUSTON COLLECTION. SCRIPT MATERIAL.
1. Two versions of script available (three copies), no author or dates. Script broken down by reel—for example, Reel One, R/1, pp. 1–3; etc. Two of the versions are annotated. Also included are loose-leaf pages with Huston's handwritten notes, background information, doodles, and storyboard drawings with such comments as "Over these shots explain the tactical principals by which the missions are planned."

REVENGE. 1989.
Columbia Tristar/Rastar. Produced by Hunt Lowry and Stanley Rubin. Screenplay by Jim Harrison. Directed by Tony Scott. Huston intended to direct this film after *The Dead* and to work on screenplay with his son Tony, but ill health prevented John from pursuing project (cf. Grobel's *The Hustons,* various pages).

AMPAS. GENERAL COLLECTION.
1. Screenplay by Jeffrey Fiskin. Based on the novella by Jim Harrison. First draft, December 1987. 108 p.

USC. GENERAL COLLECTION.
1. *Revenge* by Jeffrey Fiskin, based on the novella by Jim Harrison. Second draft, second polish, March 4, 1988. 113 p. Gen. no. 2,049.

RHODES OF AFRICA (*Rhodes*). 1936.
Gaumont (Great Britain). Screenplay by Michael Barringer, Leslie Arliss, and Miles Malleson. Directed by Berthold Viertel. According to Lawrence Grobel (*The Hustons,* 174) Walter, who starred in the film as Rhodes, received the script, didn't like it, and turned it over to John, who rewrote it. "Walter thought [it] was an improvement."

NEW YORK PUBLIC LIBRARY FOR THE PERFORMING ARTS.
1. Dialogue sheets, n.d., 42 p. *On t.p.:* "Of Africa" crossed out; and inserted in pencil is "The Diamond Master." This version lists credits: Adaptation by Leslie Arliss and Michael Barringer; dialogue by Miles Malleson; and directed by Berthold Viertel.

NEW YORK STATE LIBRARY.
1. Dialogue script.

THE ROARING TWENTIES. 1939.
Warner Brothers. Writing assignment—May 18, 1939, to August 13, 1939—with John Wexley and Frank Donoghue, under the early working title *The World Moves On.* Writers of credit: Jerry Wald, Richard Macaulay, and Robert Rossen. Director, Raoul Walsh. Per *The American Film Institute Catalog: Feature Films, 1931–1940:* Original story, Mark Hellinger; contributor to treatment, John Wexley; contributors to screenplay construction, Earl Baldwin and Frank Donoghue. Huston not indicated. *Note:* Another film with the same title but a different story line was produced by Fox in 1934. USC has screenplay versions of this project, which was directed by John Ford, written by Reginald Berkeley, and starred Madeleine Carroll and Franchot Tone. The Wisconsin State Historical Society, which houses scripts, reports multiple versions of this screenplay.

NEW YORK STATE ARCHIVE.
1. Dialogue script.

USC. WARNER BROTHERS ARCHIVE.
1. Original story for the screen by Mark Hellinger, n.d. 51 p. (Two copies.)
2. Robert Lord's treatment, n.d. 35 p.
3. Screen story by Mark Hellinger. Screenplay by Earl Baldwin and Frank Donoghue. First draft, April 19, 1939. 90 p. *Cover sheet:* Part 1, temporary, April 20, 1939.
4. Screenplay by Jerry Wald and Richard Macaulay. *Cover sheet:* June 15, 1939. Part 1, Final, to Part IV, Final, July 5, 1939. *Cover, in pencil: Roaring Twenties.* 134 p.
5. As no. 4. *Cover sheet:* July 7, 1939, Part 1, Revised Final. *In pencil: Roaring Twenties.* 167 p. Includes blue revision sheets, July through August 1939. Includes through Part IV, July 22, 1939.
6. Changes to *The Roaring 20s.* Various dates and pages, July though August 1939.

WISCONSIN/WARNER BROTHERS SCREENPLAY SERIES. Reel 7.
1. Treatment, *The World Moves On,* by Mark Hellinger, n.d. 51 p.
2. Treatment, *The World Moves On,* by Frank Donoghue, n.d. 66 p.
3. Screenplay by Jerry Wald and Richard Macaulay.* Revised final. July 7, 1939, with revisions to August 28, 1939. 181 p.

Note. *The Wisconsin Center for Film and Theater Research, the State Historical Society of Wisconsin, which houses these scripts, reports multiple versions of the screenplay.

ROOTS OF HEAVEN. 1958.
Twentieth Century-Fox. Screenplay by Romain Gary and Patrick Leigh-Fermor, based on Gary's novel *Racines du ciel* (1958). Directed by John Huston.

AMPAS. JOHN HUSTON COLLECTION. SCRIPT MATERIAL.
1. No t.p. Huston's copy. Various paging. Revisions in hand. "May 6, 1958" at top of some pages. Includes production schedules and accommodations list, Bangui, AEF. Specially bound.
2. Galleys of novel by Romain Gary (New York: Simon and Schuster, 1958). Includes cover memo from David Brown, April 25, 1957, and a summary of the novel by Joan Southerden, April 21, 1957. 24 p.
3. Final first draft by Romain Gary, December 14, 1957. Property of Darryl F. Zanuck. 170 p.
4. Screenplay by Romain Gary and Patrick Leigh-Fermor. Third revised script, January 21, 1958. 173 p.

NEW YORK STATE ARCHIVE.
1. Cutting continuity script.

UCLA. ARTS SPECIAL COLLECTION. TWENTIETH CENTURY-FOX ARCHIVE.
1. Second revised rough draft, November 18, 1957. *On cover, handwritten:* Fermor. 125 p. Includes revised pages, November 25–28, 1957.
2. Screenplay by Romain Gary. Final 1st draft, December 14, 1957. 170 p.
3. Revised temporary script, January 8, 1958. *On cover, handwritten:* Leigh-Fermor's Version. 165 p.
4. Romain Gary. Dialogue script. 58 p.
5. Continuity and dialogue taken from the screen, October 16, 1958.

UNIVERSITY OF IOWA. TWENTIETH CENTURY-FOX SCRIPT COLLECTION.
1.Continuity and dialogue, October 16, 1958.
2. Continuity and dialogue, edited December 1, 1958.

USC. TWENTIETH CENTURY-FOX COLLECTION.
1. Screenplay by Romain Gary. Final first draft, December 19, 1957. 170 p.
2. Screenplay by Romain Gary. Revised temporary script, January 8, 1958. *On cover:* Leigh Fermor's Version. 165 p.

THE SAGA OF THE AMERICAN REVOLUTION. 1974.
Sam Thomas Productions. TV. Huston designated director. Unrealized (?). In a letter attached to the script (below) to John Huston, September 12, 1974, Sam Thomas revealed that he was having problems getting CBS or ABC to allocate six hours' time to the project. George C. Scott was being lined up as the narrator.

AMPAS. JOHN HUSTON COLLECTION. SCRIPT MATERIAL. Uncataloged, box 3.

1. *The Saga of the American Revolution,* September 6, 1974. Additional first draft material (pp. 136–94), no author. 194 p. (incomplete).

SERGEANT YORK. 1941.
    Warner Brothers. Screenplay by Abem Finkel, Harry Chandlee, John Huston, and Howard Koch. Directed by Howard Hawks.

AMPAS. GENERAL COLLECTION.

1. Screenplay by Abem Finkel, Harry Chandlee, Howard Koch, and John Huston.

AMPAS. JOHN HUSTON COLLECTION.

1. Screenplay by Abem Finkel and Harry Chandlee and John Huston and Howard Koch. Revised final, January 31, 1941, with blue revision pages to March 7, 1941. 162 p. Specially bound.

NEW YORK STATE ARCHIVE.

1. Dialogue script.

USC. WARNER BROTHERS ARCHIVE.

1. *The Amazing Story of Sergeant York* treatment. Harry Chandlee and Abem Finkel, July 11, 1940. 105 p.
2. *Sergeant York* Temp, Part I, September 17, 1940. No authors indicated. 194 p. Some penciled statements on cover. White and yellow sheets. Some annotations.
3. No t.p. *Cover: Sergeant York,* Part 1, January 10, 1941. Final. *In pencil:* Never completed. No authors indicated. Does contain Part IV, Final, January 22, 1941. 83 p.
4. *Sergeant York* original screenplay by Abem Finkel and Harry Chandlee and John Huston and Howard Koch. Cover sheets, Part I, Rev. Final, January 31, 1941; to Part II, Rev. Final, February 15, 1941. 162 + 1 p. Includes blue revision sheets to March 20, 1941.
5. Second unit script, March 11, 1941, no authors, pp. 123–45. From no. 4.
6. Blue sheet changes, January 31, 1941–March 26, 1941.
7. (Dialogue transcript). 1941.

WISCONSIN/WARNER BROTHERS SCREENPLAY SERIES.

1. *The American Rifleman* by Fred Niblo Jr. Treatment. April 29, 1940. 78 p.
2. *The Amazing Story of Sergeant York* by Harry Chandlee and Abem Finkel. Treatment. July 11, 1940. 105 p.
3. Screenplay by Abem Finkel, Harry Chandlee, John Huston, and Howard Koch.* Revised final, January 31, 1941, with revisions to March 26, 1941. 160 p.

Note. *The Wisconsin Center for Film and Theater Research, the State Historical Society of Wisconsin, which houses these scripts, reports multiple versions of the screenplay.

ADDITIONAL SCREENPLAY MATERIAL IN THE FOLLOWING LIBRARIES.
Indiana University Library.

THE SHAKEDOWN (*Fine Shakedown?*) 1929.
    (Released March 29 with talking sequences.) Robert Wyler for Universal. Story and screenplay by Charles Logue and Clarence J. Marks.

Title and dialogue by Albert De Mond. Directed by William Wyler. John Huston, actor, bit part (uncredited).

NEW YORK STATE LIBRARY.

1. Dialogue script.

SHERLOCK HOLMES IN NEW YORK. 1976.

Twentieth Century-Fox/NBC-TV. Teleplay by Alvin Sapinsley. Directed by Boris Sagal. John Huston, actor, Professor Moriarity. While screenplay material has not be ascertained, a novel based on the production has been published: D. R. Benson's *Sherlock Holmes in New York,* from the television film written by Alvin Sapinsley and adapted by D. R. Bensen (New York: Ballantine Books, 1976).

SHOES OF THE FISHERMAN. 1968.

MGM. Produced by George Englund. Screenplay by John Patrick and James Kennaway, based on the novel by Morris L. West. Directed by Michael Anderson.

AMPAS. JOHN HUSTON COLLECTION. PRODUCTION FILE.

1. Correspondence and cables from George Englund (producer), 1965–66, noting that he sent a script to Huston and that he wanted to show Huston a revised script. Presumably Englund wanted Huston to direct. Script does not appear in Huston Collection.

MUSEUM OF MODERN ART. FILM DEPARTMENT.

1. *The Shoes of the Fisherman.* No t.p. Starts with author's note by Morris L. West, n.d. 125 p.

SINFUL DAVEY. 1969.

Mirisch-Webb Productions/UA. Screenplay by James R. Webb. Directed by John Huston.

AMPAS. JOHN HUSTON COLLECTION. SCRIPT MATERIAL.

1. Screenplay by James R. Webb. Property of the Mirisch Corp. and James R. Webb Productions, n.d. *At top of t.p., handwritten:* J. Huston (crossed out, and above his name: G. Hill). Marked at top of first page, pink revision page (handwritten): "Gladys Hill." Throughout, pink and blue revision pages. Some blue pages have June 1967 date. Includes revisions through August 19, 1967. Throughout script, in various hands, annotations. 114 p. Specially bound copy.
2. *The Sinful Adventures of Davey Haggart.* Written by James R. Webb. Property of Mirisch Corp. and James Webb Productions, April 28, 1965. 131 p. Another copy.
3. Same t.p. as no. 1. Cover has Huston's name written at top. January 14, 1966. 127 p. Another copy has Gladys Hill's name written on cover. Some annotations. Another copy without any name. Another copy with typewritten pages interspersed with other pages.
4. *Sinful Davey.* Dialogue revision. *Top of p. 1:* June 1, 1967. No author indicated. 113 p. Annotated throughout, some with the date June 8, 1967.
5. Screenplay by James R. Webb, n.d. 114 p. Includes pink and blue revision pages, with handwritten dialogue, notes, and typewritten pages inserted. Some pages have at top: 1st revision (dialogue changes only) with John Huston's name written. Various other revisions and dates of June and August 1967. Call sheet inserted with Huston's doodles. In red binder.

AMPAS. JOHN HUSTON COLLECTION. SCRIPT MATERIAL. Uncataloged, box 3.
1. Additional scenes and narration, revised, 2/21/68. *Upper right on t.p.:* JRW [i.e., James R. Webb], 1/12/68. 5 p. *Cover letter:* Walter Mirish to John Huston, 2/21/68.

WRITERS GUILD OF AMERICA, WEST.
1. Screenplay by James R. Webb. 1969.

ADDITIONAL SCREENPLAY MATERIAL IN THE FOLLOWING LIBRARIES.
Dartmouth College.

SLEEPING PRINCE. *See* THE PRINCE AND THE SHOWGIRL.

SOAR ON EAGLE. 1934.
Unrealized project.

USC. WARNER BROTHERS ARCHIVE.
1. *Soar on Eagle,* or *Mr. President,* by John Huston and Leslie Swabacker. Synopsis in five acts. April 2, 1934. Also includes treatment, 4 p.

STEEL (other titles: *Men of Steel, Steel Man, Steel Men, Disaster, Record Month*). Universal. Unproduced. Huston was a writer under contract at Universal from 1929 to 1932.

AMPAS. JOHN HUSTON COLLECTION. SCRIPT MATERIAL.
1. *Steel Man* from John Huston, April 21, 1932. [9 p.]. Located in John Huston Inventory, Early Scripts and Stories—Titled, p. 39. Another copy located in Inventory—Untitled. (1932–33?), no. 1, p. 39. Another treatment included, pp. 2–19 (12/26/31?). (Cf. Universal inventory, vol. 4, no. 6,105 below).

AMPAS: UNIVERSAL PICTURES. LIBRARY PROPERTIES. SYNOPSIS AND DESCRIPTIVE DATA.
1. Volume 3, no. 5,972. Unproduced. Purchased, September 4, 1930. Author, Courtnay Terrett; play, John Wexley, 4/15/29; continuity, Courtnay Terrett, John Wexley (?), Stuart Anthony, Walton Hall Smith, and Tom Reed; original, Stuart Anthony, Tom Reed, P. J. Wolfson, and John Huston, 12/26/31, 19 p.; *Steel* (cont.), Robert Dillon, Kay Morris, and Courtnay Terrett.
2. Another version, also unproduced, found in volume 3, no. 5,972-A; date of purchase, October 21, 1930. Tom Reed indicated as screenwriter, October–December 1931.
3. Also unproduced, in volume 3, no. 6,030. Courtnay Terrett listed as screenwriter, 4/25/31.
4. Volume 4, no. 6,105, unproduced. Has a separate sheet for *Steel Men.* Author, John Huston. Date of purchase, 2/12/32, $1.00. *Original:* John Huston, 12/18/31. 11 p. *Treatment:* John Huston, 12/26/31. 19 p.; and 4/21/32, incomplete (a treatment of *Steel* stories found in file nos. 5,972 and 6,030).

AMPAS. WILLIAM WYLER COLLECTION.
1. *Steel Men* (from John Huston) (December 18, 1931), 11 p. Included is copy of memo from John Huston to John LeRoy Johnston, January 15, 1932, regarding the short outline Johnston requested. "The title is *Steel Man,* not *Steel Men.*"
2. *Steel Men.* By Owen Francis, n.d. 9 p.

3. *Disaster.* By Owen Francis, n.d. 9 p.
4. *Record Month.* By Owen Francis, n.d. 12 p.
5. File also includes background photos of steel mills and clippings of research material.

THE STORM. 1930.
Universal. Screenplay by Wells Root and Charles Logue. Dialogue by Wells Root. Directed by William Wyler. John Huston, actor, a bit part (uncredited).

NEW YORK STATE LIBRARY.
1. Dialogue script.

THE STORY OF G.I. JOE. 1945.
United Artists. Produced by Lester Cowan and David Hall. Screenplay by Leopold Atlas, Guy Endore, and Philip Stevenson. Directed by William Wellman. Huston, writer (uncredited). *Note:* While this material shows Huston's involvement with this project, there is no indication in the literature of his involvement.

AMPAS. JOHN HUSTON COLLECTION. SCRIPT MATERIAL.
1. *The Story of G.I. Joe.* Revised first draft, May 3, 1944. *On cover:* Maj. John Huston's Copy. #3A. 52 p. White and green sheets. *On back cover, handwritten note:* Johnny— Had to leave—see you tomorrow. (Name?)
2. *Cover memo, letterhead:* Lester Cowan Productions. From Martin Hourihan to Major Huston, May 31, 1944: "I am enclosing the latest script on 'G.I. Joe.'" It is in continuity to page 96. The Italian town and the marriage of Murphy are two separate sequences that are not in continuity, but only a first draft. Following:
   a. *Title page:* "Story of G.I. Joe," Major Huston.
   b. Green and yellow pages, pp. 40–96.
   c. Italian sequence, yellow pages, May 27, 1944, pp. 1–32.
   d. Marriage sequence, white pages, May 25, 1944, pp. 1–9.
3. No t.p. *Cover, handwritten, title:* 6–1944. Preceding script:
   a. Memo on character and story of Ernie Pyle (and suggested additional material), Phil Stevenson, June 5, 1944. 9 p
   b. Interview with Chris Cunningham on Ernie Pyle, Sunday, June 4, 1944. 9 p.
   c. Additional background material, including letter to Lester Cowan, May 26, 1944.
   d. Script. Revised first draft, May 3, 1944.
      Green pages, annotated, pp. 1–81.
      Yellow pages, pp. 82–105.
      Italian sequence, yellow pages, May 27, 1944, pp. 1–32.
      Bombing sequence, yellow pages, June 2, 1944, pp. 32–40. Cowan's name handwritten at top of page.
      Marriage sequence, yellow pages, pp. 41–53.
      Walker death scene, yellow pages, pp. 1–11, June 8, 1944.
   e. Conference on suggestions and on changes of script with Endore, Stevenson, and Thornton, June 7, 1944. Cowan's name handwritten on page.
4. Memo from Burgess Meredith to Lester Cowan, May 31, 1944, regarding changes: script material from Meredith, 22 p.
5. Synopsis of story, June 14, 1944. 9 p.

THE BRITISH FILM INSTITUTE.
1. Copy of screenplay.

THE STRANGER (working title: *A Date with Destiny*). 1946.
RKO. Produced by S. P. Eagle (Sam Spiegel). Screenplay by Anthony
Veiller (credited) and Orson Welles and John Huston (uncredited). Directed
by Welles.

AMPAS. JOHN HUSTON COLLECTION. SCRIPT MATERIAL.
1. File includes numerous miscellaneous script pages, no authors indicated, various dates,
   May and June 1945. Some pages heavily annotated. Includes earlier changes and ongo-
   ing continuity.
   Notes on Spiegel script, June 13, 1945, with Huston's doodles.
   Treatment of *A Date with Destiny,* heavily annotated.
   Treatment of Mary and Rankin, regarding "Red" the dog.
   Handwritten notes by Huston.

MUSEUM OF MODERN ART. FILM DEPARTMENT.
1. *The Stranger* final shooting script. Property of International Pictures, Hollywood,
   September 24, 1945. 163 p. No author indicated. Includes yellow, pink, and blue revision
   pages, 9/26/45–10/10/45.

NEW YORK STATE ARCHIVE.
1. Cutting continuity script.

UCLA. ARTS SPECIAL COLLECTION. RKO SCRIPTS COLLECTION.
1. Continuity, 88 p.

UCSB. DAVIDSON LIBRARY.
1. Temporary draft by Orson Welles and John Huston, August 9, 1945, 156 p.

UNIVERSITY OF WYOMING. AMERICAN HERITAGE CENTER.
1. *The Stranger,* December 13, 1945 (Leo Spritz Collection).

USC. BOYLE COLLECTION.
1. Temporary draft by Orson Welles and John Huston, August 9, 1945. 156 p.

TARAS BULBA. 1962.
UA/H-H/Avala. Produced by Harold Hecht. Screenplay by Waldo Salt
and Karl Tunberg. Directed by J. Lee-Thompson.

AMPAS. JOHN HUSTON COLLECTION. PRODUCTION FILE.
1. Cable from Eugene Frenke to John Huston, 5/28/58, in which Frenke wrote that he was
   working on a screenplay and wanted to know if Huston was interested. Huston responded that Frenke should discuss it with Paul Kohner, his agent, and asked, "Meanwhile
   what about Montezuma script?"

USC. MAC DAVIS COLLECTION.
1. *Taras Bulba* screenplay, from the story by Nikolai Gogol, June 6, 1961. Property of
   Harold Hecht Productions, Inc. No author indicated. (Handwritten note on t.p. regarding
   the songs written for film by Mack Davis.) 142 p. Contains various revisions.

TENTACLES (*Tentacoli*). 1976.
An American International/A-Esse Cinematografica. Screenplay by Jerome Max, Tito Carpi, Steven Carabatsos, and Sonia Molteni. Directed by Oliver Hellman (Ovidio Assosnitis). John Huston, actor, Ned Turner. File in AMPAS indicates Huston's involvement in writing script, at least his role.

AMPAS. JOHN HUSTON COLLECTION. SCRIPT MATERIAL.
1. Various pages from script included. Pages with Huston as Ned Turner. Pages annotated by Huston. Includes handwritten comments by Huston on various aspects of script, July 4, 1976. Scene with Tillie, annotated, July 22, 1976.

MUSEUM OF MODERN ART. FILM DEPARTMENT.
1. *Tentacles* rewrite by Steven W. Carabatsos, n.d. 109 p. *Cover:* Ancillary Enterprises, New York.

USC. BOYLE COLLECTION.
1. Written by Jerome Max, Tito Carpi, Steve Carabatsos, and Sonia Molteni. Rewrite by Steven W. Carabatsos, July 2, 1976. 109 p. Photocopy.

THEODOSIA: EMPRESS OF AMERICA. *See* PRELUDE TO FREEDOM.

THIS PROPERTY IS CONDEMNED. 1966.
Paramount/Seven Arts/Ray Stark. *Cineforum* (December 1987) reported that Huston may have been considered as the director. No information in AMPAS Huston Archive. Screenwriters of credit: Francis Ford Coppola, Fred Coe, and Edith Sommer, based on the Tennessee Williams play. Director of credit, Sydney Pollack. Appears to have been originally a Warner product that then went to Paramount.

USC. WARNER BROTHERS ARCHIVE.
1. Various versions in file by Robert Thom; Horton Foote; Richard Rush; Francis Ford Coppola and Fred Coe; Anthony Veiller; Charles Eastman; Coppola, Coe, and Edith Sommer; and David Rayfield. Dated June 1962 to December 1962.

ADDITIONAL SCREENPLAY MATERIAL IN THE FOLLOWING LIBRARIES.
Indiana University, Ohio State University.

THREE STRANGERS. 1946.
Warner Brothers. Screenplay by John Huston and Howard Koch, based on a story Huston wrote in 1936. Directed by Jean Negulesco.

AMPAS. JOHN HUSTON COLLECTION. SCRIPT MATERIAL.
1. *Three Strangers.* Original story and screenplay by John Huston. Supervisor, Robert Lord. Temporary, March 13, 1939. 131 p. Specially bound. Another copy, unbound, with cover sheet, temporary, 3/13/39. *Cover:* Warner Copy.
2. Original story and screenplay by John Huston. *Cover:* Temporary script, March 13, 1939. Retyped August 12, 1944. *Handwritten:* Huston. Following t.p., characters listed. 131 p. No indication of Warner copy.
3. Singapore (*Three Strangers*) by Maj. Chalky Whyte and Randall MacDougall. From the original story, "Three Strangers," by John Huston. October 1944. Producer, W.

Reinhardt. 158 p. No Warner Brothers information. Includes pages dated September 1944.

NEW YORK PUBLIC LIBRARY FOR THE PERFORMING ARTS.
1. Original story and screenplay by John Huston and Howard Koch. Revised final, 12/12/44. 132 p. Imperfect: pp. 114, 115, 120, and 121 wanting. Includes blue revision pages through 2/5/45.

NEW YORK STATE ARCHIVE.
1. Dialogue script.

USC. WARNER BROTHERS ARCHIVES.
1. *Three Men and a Girl* by John Huston. Read by Smith Dawless, September 10, 1937. Received September 10, 1937, from Mr. Lord, via Mr. MacEwan's office. Outline. 6 p.
2. Radio account of Grant National Steeplechase, March 24, 1939. No author or date indicated. 3 p.
3. *Three Strangers'* treatment #4. Major Whyte. Received August 5, 1944. Various paging.
4. *Three Men and a Girl* by John Collier, n.d. 9 p.
5. *Three Men and a Girl* by John Collier, October 14, 1942. Cover letter to Henry Blanke, outlining suggested changes. 7 p. (Appears that John Garfield was considered for role at one time.)
6. *Three Men and a Girl* by John Collier, October 9, 1942. 8 p., includes Greenstreet story. Addressed as a letter to Blanke.
7. *Three Strangers.* Synopsis, no author or date. 11 p.
8. *Three Men and a Girl* by John Collier. Cover letter to Blanke, September 18, 1942. 9 p.
9. Notes for *Three Strangers,* Lord, August 1940. 6 p.
10. Scheme for revision of *Three Strangers* script, Robert Lord, August 29, 1940. 6 p.
11. *Three Strangers.* Original story and screenplay by John Huston. Supervisor, Robert Lord. Temporary, March 13, 1939. 131 p.
12. *Three Men and a Girl.* Howard Koch. Treatment #3. Change after temporary. 135 p.
13. *Three Strangers* original story and screenplay by John Huston. First draft, treatment #1. Supervisor, Robert Lord. February 11, 1938, and February 21, 1938 [crossed out], 141 p.+ Radio account of race, 4 p. (not same as March 24, 1939, account). Some annotations indicated.
14. *Three Strangers.* Original story and screenplay by John Huston and Howard Koch. Supervisor, Robert Lord. Revised temporary, September 21, 1940. 126 p.
15. *Three Strangers.* New opening sequence, September 18, 1940. No authors indicated.
16. *Three Strangers.* Original story and screenplay by John Huston. Treatment #2, March 8, 1939.
17. *Three Men and a Girl* by John Huston, n.d. 49 p. Four copies in file. Appears to be original story.
18. Notes on rewrite of *Three Strangers* by Major Whyte, November 25, 1944, 6 p.; also includes are notes, November 11, 1944, various paging.
19. *Singapore (Three Strangers)* by Maj. Chalky Whyte and Randall MacDougall. From the original story, *Three Strangers,* by John Huston, October 1944. Producer, W. Reinhardt. Received October 7, 1944, to October 21, 1944, from Whyte. Treatment #6. 115 p.
20. *Three Strangers* by Randall MacDougall. Treatment # 7, received September 9, 1944, to October 14, 1944. 121 p.
21. *Three Strangers,* Major Whyte, received August 12, 1944, to September 30, 1944. Incomplete, treatment #5, August 1944. Producer, W. Reinhardt. 152 p.
22. *Three Strangers* original story and screenplay by John Huston and Howard Koch.

Supervisor, W. Rienhardt. Revised final, December 22, 1944. 137 p. plus radio account of race, pp. A–D. Includes blue revision sheets, January–February 1945.
23. *Three Strangers* screenplay by Frank Gruber. Producer, Henry Blanke, May 26, 1943. Revised pages dated June 1943. *Cover, in pencil:* latest version, Mr. Warner. Before final mimeograph. Other annotations.
24. *Three Strangers.* Frank Gruber. January 16, 1943. 128 p.
25. *Three Strangers.* Frank Gruber, based on the original by John Huston. Final. June 16, 1943. 130 p.
26. *Three Strangers.* Original story and screenplay by John Huston and Howard Koch. Supervisor, W. Reinhardt. Revised final, December 12, 1944. 138 p., with race account, pp. A–D. Blue revision pages, January–February 1945.
27. Dialogue transcript. 1945. *In pencil:* June 8, 1945. Various paging. Credits indicated as original screenplay by John Huston and Howard Koch.

WISCONSIN/WARNER BROTHERS SCREENPLAY SERIES. Reel 47.
1. Screenplay by John Huston.* Temporary, March 13, 1939. 131 p.
2. Screenplay by John Huston and Howard Koch. Revised final, December 12, 1944, with revisions to February 5, 1945. 140 p.

Note. *The Wisconsin Center for Film and Theater Research, the State Historical Society of Wisconsin, which houses these scripts, reports multiple versions of the screenplay.

ADDITIONAL SCREENPLAY MATERIAL IN THE FOLLOWING LIBRARIES.
Dartmouth College Library.

TOMORROW THE WORLD. 1944.
United Artists. Produced by Lester Cowan.

AMPAS. JOHN HUSTON COLLECTION. SCRIPT MATERIAL.
1. Screenplay by Ring Lardner Jr. and Leopold Atlas. Directed by Leslie Fenton. Cast includes Fredric March, Betty Field, Skip Homeier, Agnes Moorehead, and Joan Carroll. Unrealized project (?).

TOWARD DEATH. 1933, 1947.
Unrealized project.

USC. WARNER BROTHERS ARCHIVE.
1. *Toward Death* by John Huston, January 26, 1933. Treatment, 5 p.
2. *Toward Death* by John Huston, n.d. [1947?] Treatment, 17 p.

THE TREASURE OF THE SIERRA MADRE. 1948.
Warner Brothers. Screenplay and direction by John Huston, who also acted, American Tourist (uncredited). Based on B. Traven's book of the same name.

PUBLISHED BOOK.
1. Traven, B. *The Treasure of the Sierra Madre.* Translated by Basil Creighton from the original *Der Schatz der Sierra Madre.* London: Chatto and Windus, 1934; New York: Knopf, 1935.

PUBLISHED SCRIPTS.

1. Huston, John. *The Treasure of the Sierra Madre.* Edited with an introduction by James Naremore. Wisconsin/Warner Brothers Screenplay Series. Madison, Wis.: Wisconsin University of Press, for the Wisconsin Center for Film and Theater Research, 1979.
2. Thomas, Sam. *Best American Screenplays 2: Complete Screenplays.* New York: Crown, 1990.

THE AMERICAN FILM INSTITUTE.

1. Revised final, January 10, 1947. 143 p.

AMPAS. JOHN HUSTON COLLECTION. SCRIPT MATERIAL.

1. Script by John Huston, n.d. Includes pink revision pages to June 9, 1947. 143 p. Inserted in copy are eleven original stills by Max Julian, Warner Brothers. Specially bound. Also mimeographed copies of this version (two copies). One copy has cast and credits list bound in.
2. (The novel) Traven, B. *The Treasure of the Sierra Madre.* New York: Knopf, 1935.
3. Folder with conference notes, 2 p., no author or date (two copies); storyboard drawings; treatment, no author or date, 4 p. (three copies); expansion of previous treatment, 18 p. plus unnumbered pages, no author or date; first rough outline of preliminary suggestions to the screen version of B. Traven's *The Treasure of the Sierra Madre* by the author (i.e., Huston), n.d. 29 p.
4. Script by John Huston. *Cover sheet:* 8/17/46, Final. Property of Warner Brothers. 141 p. Includes blue revision pages, 8/20/46 and 8/21/46. *Note:* The famous line delivered by Huston to Bogart at the beginning of film is slightly different in this version (page 8)— "But understand from now on you are to try your best to make your way in life without my assistance."
5. Folder with miscellaneous script pages: various numbering, no particular order, some pages annotated. Includes two pages of unidentified memoir of Huston (?) on Mexico while making film. Some pages heavily annotated, with attached notes, handwritten notes, and doodles. Includes beginning pages of script, pp. 1–30, no author; some with dates July and September, pp. 131–34 and 140–57. Out of order: pp. 30–33, July. Another treatment preceded with handwritten notes of Huston, n.d. , 27 p. Heavily annotated. Additional changes, 7/21/46.

MUSEUM OF MODERN ART. FILM DEPARTMENT.

1. Screenplay by John Huston. *Cover sheet:* Revised Final. January 10, 1947. 143 p. Includes pink revision pages, March 20, 1947.

NEW YORK STATE ARCHIVE.

1. Dialogue script.

UCLA. ARTS SPECIAL COLLECTION. GENERAL COLLECTION.

1. Script by John Huston, n.d. 143 p. On spine of binding: Revised, June 9, 1947. Page 101 missing. (Two copies.)
2. Script by John Huston, n.d. 143 p. Includes changes, March 20, 1947, and June 9, 1947. Following t.p., complete cast and credits. Preceding t.p.: synopsis by David Wear III, Reader, September 16, 1941, 1 p.; detailed synopsis, September 16, 1941, 10 p.; synopsis by John K. Butler, March 21, 1934; comment by D. W. Weir, n.d., 1 p.; Warner Brothers memo, August 28, 1934, to MacEwan, from Daugherty, with a recommendation not to do the film.

UNIVERSITY OF CALIFORNIA, RIVERSIDE. SPECIAL COLLECTIONS.
1. Screenplay by Robert Rossen. First temporary, January 1, 1947, with revisions, 3/20/47–6/9/47, 143 p.

USC. BOYLE COLLECTION.
1. Screenplay by Robert Rossen. First temporary, white, January 1, 1947. 143 p.

USC. WARNER BROTHERS ARCHIVE. Many scripts, treatments, etc., designated T-91.
1. Treasure trailer, November 26, 1947.
2. Notes regarding different versions of script worked on: Rossen, Arthur Arent, Norbert Faulkner, John Huston, and Walter Gorman.
3. Reader's comments, David Wear III, September 16, 1941.
4. Screenplay by Arthur Arent and Norbert Faulkner, n.d. 30 p. #A-1.
5. Script by Robert Rossen, n.d. 18 p. #A-2.
6. Scripts by Walter Gorman: May 26, 1945, 16 p., #A-5; June 9, 1945, 22 p., #A-6; June 30, 1945, 24 p., #A-7; and July 2, 1945, 24 p., #A-7.
7. Massacre sequence by Arent and Faulkner, pp. 53–90, #B-1.
8. Robert Rossen, July 14, 1945, 53 p., #B-2. Henry Blanke's copy (producer). *On cover:* December 6, 1943 crossed out. (Two copies.)
9. Gorman, August 1–18, 1945, 23 p., #B-7. (Two copies: one dated August 1, 1945.)
10. Arent and Faulkner, January 6, 1942, 64 p., #C-1. From Blanke.
11. Arent and Faulkner, n.d. 53 p.
12. Robert Rossen, July 14, 1945, 53 p. Blanke's copy. #C-2.
13. Arent and Faulkner, June 27, 1942, 190 p. #1. Blanke's copy.
14. Arent and Faulkner. Version complete, n.d. 190 p. #1.
15. Robert Rossen, February 26, 1943, 145 p. #3.
16. Robert Rossen, n.d. 143 p. #3.
17. Robert Rossen, February 26, 1943, 132 p. #4. *Note on cover:* Version, Complete (He never finished script). Blanke's copy (another copy in file).
18. Robert Rossen, January 4, 1943–February 26, 1943. Incomplete, 132 p. #4.
19. Walter Gorman. Alternate outline, June 2, 1945, #5. Also rough draft, n.d. 22 p.
20. Character outline, June 16, 1945, 29 p. No authors.
21. John Huston, July 9, 1946, pp. 1–20. #7.
22. John Huston. Received by Blanke, August 19, 1946, 152 p. #8. Following t.p. *Cast:* Dobbs—A guy like Bogart; Howard—A guy like Walter Huston (with his teeth out); Curtin—A guy like Burgess Meredith; Lecaude [Cody]—A guy like Ronald Reagan. Another copy with no author indicated.
23. John Huston. Received by Blanke, August 17/46. Final #9. Huston's copy "Corrected and First [unclear] Original." 152 p. Cast information from no. 22, but Lecaude crossed out, and Cody substituted.
24. Screenplay, pp. 7–53, retyped on white, January 8, 1942. No authors, various pages.
25. John Huston. Final, August 17, 1946. Blanke's personal copy. Includes blue revision sheets, August 20–21, 1946. 141 p. Includes budget notes. (Two copies.)
26. John Huston, December 9, 1947, #10, 141 p. Highly annotated, with changes pasted in.
27. John Huston. Revised final, January 10, 1947. 143p. Pink revised pages, March 20, 1947, and June 9, 1947. (Another photocopy included.)
28. Henry Blanke's personal copy and shooting copy. Revised final, January 10, 1947, 143 p. Pink sheets as in no. 27. Heavily annotated. Some pages has top edge of pages clipped.

Preceding script is inserted a memo to Carl Stucke from Blanke, November 4, 1947: "Here are copies of different versions . . . the revised final I have marked accordingly. Keep safely as I might have to refer back to it." Also included is shooting schedule, March 28, 1947. Production #680. Also notes to Huston on the shooting of certain scenes.

WISCONSIN/WARNER BROTHERS SCREENPLAY SERIES. Reel 57.
1. Screenplay.* No authors indicated, n.d. 152 p.
2. Screenplay by John Huston.* Revised final, January 10, 1947. 143 p.

Note. *The Wisconsin Center for Film and Theater Research, the State Historical Society of Wisconsin, which houses these scripts, reports multiple versions of the screenplay.

WRITERS GUILD OF AMERICA, WEST.
1. Script by John Huston, n.d. 143 p. Includes pink revision sheets, March 20, 1947, and June 9, 1947.

ADDITIONAL SCREENPLAY MATERIAL IN THE FOLLOWING LIBRARIES.
Columbia College, Dartmouth College, Mississippi State University, University of California, Riverside.

TWO AMERICANS. 1929.
Paramount (Famous Lasky). Directed by John Meehan or Joseph Santley. Screenplay by John Meehan. Cast includes Walter Huston and John Huston. (Cf. Grobel, *The Hustons,* 133, in which he indicates that this project was John Huston's first acting role, although *The Shakedown* may be the first.)

NEW YORK STATE ARCHIVE.
1. Dialogue script.

TYPEE. 1956–57.
Allied Artists. Unproduced.

AMPAS. JOHN HUSTON COLLECTION. PRODUCTION FILE.
1. Reports Huston as the designated director. Preproduction work started and Gregory Peck was considered for the lead, but the project was indefinitely postponed in May 1957. As late as February 1962, Huston still seemed interested. (Cf. also Grobel, *The Hustons,* 430–33.)

AMPAS. JOHN HUSTON COLLECTION. SCRIPT MATERIAL.
1. *Typee.* Screenplay, from the novel by Herman Melville, by Nigel Balchin. August 1956. 134 p. Some pages dated August 14–15, 1956.
2. Same as no. 1, but Nigel Balchin's second version, August 3, 1956. Paul Kohner's label. 134 p.
3. Loose pages: *Typee. In hand:* by John Huston and Nigel Balchin, n.d. 108 p. Some annotations and corrections then appear in nos. 1 and 2.

UNIVERSITY OF WYOMING. AMERICAN HERITAGE CENTER.
1. *Typee* script by Wavery Production, Inc., November 10, 1957. 133 p. (Jane Powell Collection #5,573.)

U-BOAT.
Universal. Unproduced.
AMPAS. JOHN HUSTON COLLECTION. SCRIPT MATERIAL.
1. *U-Boat* story outline. From John Huston, June 7, 1932. 8 p.* Also *U-Boat,* sequence "A,"
2 p. Annotated. Located in John Huston Inventory, Early Scripts and Stories—Titled,
p. 39.

Note. *In Gerald Pratley's *The Cinema of John Huston* (New York: A. S.
Barnes, 1977, 27), Huston recollects working for Goldwyn for a short period on
a project "about German submarines." It is possible that Huston didn't remember
that it was a project at Universal.

AMPAS. UNIVERSAL PICTURES. LIBRARY PROPERTIES. SYNOPSIS AND
DESCRIPTIVE DATA 3, no. 5,982.
1. Purchased October 31, 1931. Author, Raymond Schrock, 1/6/31, 78 p.
2. Other versions, unproduced: vol. 3, no. 5,991: Frank Wead, 6/18/32; no. 5,991A: John
Thomas Neville, 4/17/31; no. 5,991B: Raymond L. Schrock, 10/31/30; no. 5,991C: John
Wexley, 2/24/31; no. 5,991D: John Huston, (date of purchase) 6/15/32 ($1.00); original,
John Huston, 6/7/32, 8 p.

UNDERGROUND. 1941.
Warner Brothers. Writing assignment, with Guy Endore, from August
14, 1939 to August 31, 1939. Writer of credit, Charles Grayson. Director,
Vincent Sherman.
NEW YORK PUBLIC LIBRARY FOR THE PERFORMING ARTS.
1. Screenplay by Charles Grayson, from a story by Edwin Justus Mayer and Oliver H. P.
Garett. *Cover sheets:* Pts I–III, January 24, 1941–February 5, 1941, 159 p.

NEW YORK STATE ARCHIVE.
1. Dialogue script.

THE STATE HISTORICAL SOCIETY OF WISCONSIN.
1. Versions of the screenplay.

UNIVERSITY OF WYOMING. AMERICAN HERITAGE CENTER.
1. *Underground* by Charles Grayson, n.d. 158 pp. (Charles Grayson Collection #6,482.)

USC. WARNER BROTHERS ARCHIVE.
1. Original screenplay by Oliver H. P. Garrett and Edwin Justus Mayer, n.d. 59 p.
2. Plan to rewrite *Underground* with a war background. Robert Lord, September 8, 1939.
Mr. Wallis. 12 p.
3. *The Secret Army* screenplay by Lester Cole, May 25, 1940 (a.k.a. *Underground*). Part 1,
temporary. 24 p.
4. Screenplay by Edwin Justus Mayer, June 20, 1939. Temporary. 181 p. Copy with Lord's
notes.
5. Mayer, Endore. Revised temporary, Part 1, July 29, 1939. 186 p. Mr. Lord's original
copy.
6. Revised temporary, Part 1, July 29, 1939. 155 p. No authors indicated.
7. Second revised temporary, August 11, 1939. 164 p. No authors indicated.
8. Charles Grayson. Part 1, final, January 24, 1941. 159 p.

9. As no. 8. Revised final, February 14, 1941. Various paging. Includes blue revision sheets.

ADDITIONAL SCREENPLAY MATERIAL IN THE FOLLOWING LIBRARIES.
Dartmouth College Library.

UNDER THE VOLCANO. 1984.
Ithaca-Conacine/Universal. Screenplay by Guy Gallo, based on Malcolm Lowry's novel of the same name (London: J. Cape, 1947). Directed by John Huston.

THE AMERICAN FILM INSTITUTE.
1. Guy Gallo, May 1983. 110 p.

AMPAS. GENERAL COLLECTION.
1. Screenplay by Guy Gallo. February 22, 1984. Ithaca Productions. 93 p.
2. Guy Gallo, n.d. William Morris Agency, represented by Erica Spellman. 110 p.

THE BRITISH FILM INSTITUTE.
1. A version of the screenplay.

NEW YORK PUBLIC LIBRARY FOR THE PERFORMING ARTS.
1. Screenplay by Guy Gallo, based on the novel by Malcolm Lowry. Registered with Writers Guild of America, East. *Label:* Return to Paul Kohner, Los Angeles, July 1983, revised, unpaged, 59 scenes [105 p., with page 99 consisting of handwritten notes, not clear]. Photocopy.

UCSB. DAVIDSON LIBRARY.
1. Screenplay by Guy Gallo, based on the novel by Malcolm Lowry, n.d., 110 p.

USC. GENERAL COLLECTION.
1. *Under the Volcano.* A screenplay by Guy Gallo, based on the novel by Malcolm Lowry, n.d. 100 p. Gen 1424.

ADDITIONAL SCREENPLAY MATERIAL IN THE FOLLOWING LIBRARIES.
Emerson College, Mississippi State University, New York Public Library, Stanford University, University of Miami.

THE UNFINISHED JOURNEY OF ROBERT KENNEDY. 1970.
TV. David Wolper. Earlier working title for release: *Journey of Robert F. Kennedy.* David Seltzer, producer; Mel Stuart, director; Huston, narrator. (*Film Dope* lists as *The Journal of Robert F. Kennedy,* 1971.)

AMPAS. JOHN HUSTON COLLECTION. SCRIPT MATERIAL.
1. Television script. 1969. 41 p.

THE BRITISH FILM INSTITUTE.
1. A version of the screenplay.

THE UNFORGIVEN. 1960.
Hecht-Hill-Lancaster/UA. Screenplay by Ben Maddow. Directed by John Huston.

Screenplays in Collections

AMPAS. GENERAL COLLECTION.

1. Screenplay by Ben Maddow, third draft, November 29, 1958. With changes to January 2, 1959. Hecht-Hill-Lancaster. Includes revised pages, various dates, November 1958 to January 1959. Some pages annotated.

AMPAS. JOHN HUSTON COLLECTION. SCRIPT MATERIAL.

1. *The Unforgiven* (temporary title). Screenplay by Ben Maddow, from the novel by Alan LeMay. First draft, September 15, 1958. 131 p. Specially bound.
2. Treatment by Ben Maddow, July 10, 1958. 93 p.
3. Screenplay by Ben Maddow, October 10, 1958. *Top of pages:* 2nd draft, 10/10/58. 41 p. Annotated.
4. Folder with loose sheets, no t.p., no author, continuously paged, 113 p., 3rd draft, 11/29/58. Other pages dated 11/30/58 and 12/3/58. Additional pages follow with revisions, 12/9/58.
5. Third draft screenplay by Ben Maddow, 11/29/58. John Huston's name on cover. 165 p. Includes yellow, blue, and pink pages: variously dated, November 1958 to January 1959. Another copy, but some of the revised pages are not on colored paper. This copy had inserted between pp. 28–29 four photos of Huston in uniform during World War II, one Columbia Pictures publicity still of Walter Huston visiting John on the set of *Rough Sketch* (the early working title for *We Were Strangers,* 1949), and one photograph of Suzanne Flon (1950s?).
6. Another copy of third draft screenplay. Typewritten pages inserted. Some new pages inserted, 3/18/59 and 3/24/59. This copy is heavily annotated with doodles and drawings of horses on the back of some pages. Also in folder, detached, some pages dated 4/22/59; John Huston, 4/23/59, handwritten page. Back cover has additional Huston drawings and doodles.

NEW YORK STATE ARCHIVE.

1. Dialogue script.

USC. BURT LANCASTER COLLECTION.

1. *The Unforgiven.* Burt Lancaster Collection (USC has just inherited the scripts from the estate) has a special bound copy with Burt Lancaster's name stamped in gold on the cover and "Property of Burt Lancaster" label inside front cover. On *t.p.:* Hecht-Hill-Lancaster Present *The Unforgiven,* Released thru United Artists [superimposed on photograph of cast assembled in front of sod house]. Next is the cast and story, following principles in production, with their photographs: James Hill, John Huston, Franz Planer, Dimitri Tiomkin, Ben Maddow, with other credits. *Then the script's t.p.: The Unforgiven,* Final Continuity, by Ben Maddow, Contemporary Productions, Inc., 5/12/59, with the actual still used on the cover, bound in. Following is the script: pp. 1–151. Interspersed in the text are additional stills from the film, bound in.

VICTORY (*Escape to Victory*). 1981.

Paramount. Screenplay by Evan Jones and Yabo Yablonsky. Directed by John Huston.

THE AMERICAN FILM INSTITUTE.

1. *Escape to Victory* screenplay by Evan Jones. The Victory Co., c/o Lorimar Productions, Culver City. *Label:* Goldfarb Lewis Agency, n.d. 128 p.

AMPAS. GENERAL COLLECTION.

1. *Escape to Victory* (the word *Escape* is crossed out). Screenplay by Evan Jones. The

Victory Company, c/o Lorimar Productions, Culver City, California, n.d. 128 p. Photocopy, bound. Yellow highlights of some sentences.

AMPAS. JOHN HUSTON COLLECTION. SCRIPT MATERIAL.
1. *Escape to Victory.* Screenplay by Evan Jones. Second draft. The Victory Company, Burbank, n.d. 128 p.
2. Screenplay by Evan Jones. The Victory Co., c/o Lorimar Productions. Revised March 22, 1980. *Note:* The name "Von Streicher" will be changed to "Von Steiner." *Cover:* Revised 5–22. *Business card clipped to cover:* Dr. Daniel Diaz Mendez, Puerto Vallarta. *Inserted: Escape to Victory* sheet, with characters, their nationality, and page number. 128 p.
3. Screenplay by Evan Jones. Freddie Fields Productions and Lorimar, April 25, 1980. *Cover:* old, April 25, 1980. 134 p.
4. Evan Jones, April 25, 1980. Corrected and revised, May 16, 1980. 134 p. Some annotations. Another copy without annotations.
5. No t.p. *Cover, handwritten:* "Escape to Victory" script as shot (only as far as the start of the game). *Upper right:* J. Huston. 110 p. No author or date. Czech company and address on cover.

THE BRITISH FILM INSTITUTE.
1. A version of the screenplay.

MUSEUM OF MODERN ART. FILM DEPARTMENT.
1. *Escape to Victory.* Screenplay by Evan Jones. The Victory Co., c/o Lorimar Prod., Culver City. *Label:* Goldfarb Lewis Agency, n.d. 128 p.

UCLA. ARTS SPECIAL COLLECTION. GENERAL COLLECTION.
1. *Escape to Victory.* Screenplay by Evan Jones. First draft, n.d. 137 p. *In pencil, top of t.p.:* MP (1981). Indication that the director was Brian Hutton.

USC. GENERAL COLLECTION.
1. *Victory.* On t.p.: *Escape to Victory* (crossed out and *Victory* written in pencil). Screenplay by Evan Jones, April 25, 1980, Freddie Fields Productions and Lorimar, Culver City, California. 134 p.

THE VISITOR (*Il Visitore/Stridulum*). 1980.
International Picture Show. Produced by Ovidio Assonitis. Screenplay by Lou Cimici and Robert Mundy, story by Michael J. Paradise and Ovidio Assosnitis. Directed by Michael J. Paradise (Giulio Paradisi). Huston, actor, Jersey Colsowitz and The Visitor.

AMPAS. JOHN HUSTON COLLECTION. SCRIPT MATERIAL.
1. *The Visitor,* no author or date indicated. Swan American Film Corp., Beverly Hills. 98 p. Some annotations.
2. As no. 1. *On cover, label:* John Huston. 108 p. Some annotations.

A WALK WITH LOVE AND DEATH. 1969.
Twentieth Century-Fox. Screenplay by Dale Wasserman and adaptation by Hans Koningsberger. Directed by John Huston, who also acted, Robert the Elder.

AMPAS. JOHN HUSTON COLLECTION. SCRIPT MATERIAL.
1. Screenplay by Dale Wasserman. Revision of July 1968, 133 p., plus five poems (lyrics?)

bound in front. Also after p. 133, photocopied pages inserted. Heavily annotated with additions, emendations, cross outs, Huston's changes to script and doodles. Spine of specially bound copy stamped: "D. Wasserman and H. Koningsberger."

2. (Novel) Koningsberger, Hans. *A Walk with Love and Death.* New York: Simon & Schuster, 1961. Inscribed "To John Huston—a happy birthday! 5 Aug. 1968 (in Vienna)."

3. Screenplay by Dale Wasserman, n.d. 119 p. Some annotations.

4. Screenplay by Dale Wasserman. *On cover:* Paul Kohner. Dates on pages, 4–11–66. 112 p. While t.p. is obliterated, following t.p. is a note from Wasserman, April 11, 1966: "This is an intermediate script . . . I anticipate approx. two or three weeks' work in competing it as a fully detailed shooting script."

5. Folder of screenplay, loose pages, somewhat consecutive. No author. Dates at top of some pages: July, 1968. 141 p. Heavily annotated.

6. Envelope with designation "Discards #1," with numerous pages, various dates, revisions May to June 1968, marked "JH & GH"; some pages with "DW, JH & GH"; some with only "DW." Some pages marked "Old Version."

7. Envelope with designation "Discards #2," with various paging, dates July 1968. Some pages handwritten; others marked "JH & HK," July 1968; "JH and GH," May and July 1968; revised July 1968, "HK."

8. Envelope contains two screenplays, loose pages.
   a. No t.p. Dates on pages: July 1, 1968. Some pages mark who wrote the script: "DW, JH & GH." Some pages dated July 5, 1968. 132 p.
   b. Screenplay by Dale Wasserman. Revision of May 1968. 28 p. Some pages revised 6/15/68. Annotated.

9. Envelope, "Discards #4." Various paging, handwritten pages, various dates, July 1968. Revisions August 1968; call sheet for August 17, 1968. Another copy of screenplay by Dale Wasserman. Revision of May 1968, loose pages. 119 p.

AMPAS. JOHN HUSTON COLLECTION. SCRIPT MATERIAL. Uncataloged, box 3.

1. Screenplay by Dale Wasserman. Revision of May 1968. 132 p.

2. Script pages, revision of September 20. Various paging, no author. Heavily annotated. (Two copies.)

3. Script pages, various paging, July 1, 1968, with revisions, 7/10/68 and 7/12/68. Dale Wasserman.

UCLA. ARTS SPECIAL COLLECTION. TWENTIETH CENTURY-FOX ARCHIVE.

1. Photocopy of Hans Koningsberger's novel (New York: Simon & Schuster, 1961). 167 p.

2. Draft screenplay by Hans Koningsberger, April 2, 1965. 101 p. Includes some annotations.

3. Koningsberger. Draft screenplay, 1965. 119 p.

4. Screenplay by Dale Wasserman, July 1968. 119 p.

5. Dale Wasserman. Revision of July 1968. 141 p. *Cover:* July, 1968. *Top of page:* July 1, 1968.

6. Revisions received from London, September 24, 1968. Various paging, dated July–August 1968 at top of pages.

7. Revised pages for the monastery location in Italy, October 1, 1968. 13 p. *At top of page 1:* Revision of September 20. Carter De Haven's (producer) initials typed at top of most pages.

8. Dale Wasserman. Revision of July 1968. *Handwritten on t.p.:* This is what was shot. *Cover, handwritten:* Carter De Haven's cutting script. July 1968. Heavily annotated throughout. Various paging. *Top of pages:* Revisions, various dates, July–September 1968.
9. Final shooting script. July 1968 (with revisions of July, August, and September 1968). 82 p. plus pp. 9A–9C.
10. Continuity and dialogue, June 29, 1969.

UNIVERSITY OF IOWA. TWENTIETH CENTURY-FOX SCRIPT COLLECTION.

1. Continuity and dialogue, June 29, 1969.

USC. GENERAL COLLECTION.

1. Dale Wasserman. Various dates: 6/24/68 and 7/10/69. 119 p. Some penciled annotations.

USC. TWENTIETH CENTURY-FOX COLLECTION.

1. Photocopy of Koningsberger's novel (New York: Simon & Schuster, 1961).
2. Draft by Hans Koningsberger, April 2, 1965. 101 p.
3. Dale Wasserman, n.d. 119 p. *On cover:* A John Huston–Carter De Haven Production.
4. Dale Wasserman. Revision of July 1968. 141 p.
5. Revision received from London, September 24, 1968. Various paging. Pages dated July–September 1968.
6. Revised pages for monastery location in Italy, October 1, 1968. 13 p.
7. Dale Wasserman. Revision of July 1968. Various paging. *On t.p. in hand:* This is what was shot. *On cover:* Carter De Haven's Cutting Script, July 1968. Heavily annotated copy.
8. Dale Wasserman. Final shooting script, July 1968 (with revisions of July, August, and September 1968). Various paging.

WATCH ON THE RHINE. 1943.

Warner Brothers. Produced by Hal B. Wallis. Screenplay by Dashiell Hammett from the stage play by Lillian Hellman. Directed by Herman Shumlin. Huston was considered as a possible writer and director. Cast includes Paul Lukas and Bette Davis. A. M. Sperber and Eric Lax's *Bogart* (New York: Morrow, 1997, 180–82) notes Huston's interest in doing the film after *The Maltese Falcon.* USC's Jack Warner Collection indicates some possible interest in his writing and directing this film.

USC. WARNER BROTHERS ARCHIVE.

1. *Watch on the Rhine.* Treatment by Dashiell Hammett and Wallis, 3/9/42. 32 p.
2. Synopsis from the play by Hellman, April 10, 1941.
3. *Watch on the Rhine.* Screenplay by Lillian Hellman, May 20, 1942. 137 p.
4. *Watch on the Rhine.* Screenplay by Dashiell Hammett. Original copy with notes, n.d. 180 p.
5. *Watch on the Rhine.* Screenplay by Dashiell Hammett. *Cover:* Part I, Temporary, April 8, 1942; Part II, 4/27/42, Temporary. 152 p.
6. *Watch on the Rhine.* Screenplay by Dashiell Hammett. Additional scenes and dialogue by Lillian Hellman. Director, Herman Shumlan; producer, Hall Wallis. *Cover:* Final, May 25, 1942. 133 p. (Two copies.)
7. *Watch on the Rhine.* (Dialogue transcript). Copyrighted 1942 by Warner Brothers. Various pages.

ADDITIONAL SCREENPLAY MATERIAL IN THE FOLLOWING
LIBRARIES.
Dartmouth College, Indiana University.

WATERLOO (working titles: *Battle of Waterloo, Soldier of Destiny*). 1970.
Paramount/DDL/Mosfilm. Produced by Dino De Laurentiis. Screenplay
by H. A. L. Craig, Sergei Bondarchuk, and Vittorio Bonicelli. Directed by
Sergei Bondarchuk.

AMPAS. JOHN HUSTON COLLECTION. PRODUCTION FILE.
1. Correspondence indicates that John Huston was designated as director to make the picture in 1967 or 1968. File contains information on script development and preproduction.
   According to Lawrence Grobel (*The Hustons*, 574), "The project fell through when the
   Russians agreed to finance it on the condition that a Russian direct."

AMPAS. JOHN HUSTON COLLECTION. SCRIPT MATERIAL.
1. *Soldier of Destiny: The Story of Marshal Ney* by Charles Grayson. Treatment, n.d. Letter
   inserted from Grayson to Huston, dated 11/29/65.
2. *Waterloo.* Property of Dino De Laurentiis, Cinematografica, Roma. No author or date
   indicated. *Following t.p., Note:* Revisions made by Jean Anouilh. 439 p.
3. First draft screenplay by H. A. L. Craig. Property of De Laurentiis, n.d. *On cover, in pencil:* 1965—beginning 1966. 142 p.
4. Part II (in pencil), March 17, 1966, through June 30, 1966, pp. 143–402 [dates from top
   of pages].
5. *Waterloo,* September 3, 1966. No author. 54 p.
6. Draft screenplay by H. A. L. Craig, September 3, 1966, with John Huston's suggestions.
   90 p. Heavily annotated.
7. Part II, draft, by H. A. L. Craig, 91–208. Includes pink revision sheets.
8. H. A. L. Craig, n.d. 117 p.
9. Same as no. 8. *On cover: Waterloo* (revised), Part One from H. Craig. Most recent as of
   October 1966. 117 p.
10. *Waterloo* by H. A. L. Craig. Final draft, December 1966. 201 p. *Note inserted:* Mr.
    Huston, Here is a fresh copy of the very last corrected version of Harry Craig's *Waterloo*
    for you.
11. Various miscellaneous sheets with handwritten notes; draft introduction received,
    December 12, 1966, 6 p.; narration breakdown, 40 p.

WE WERE STRANGERS. 1949.
Horizon/Columbia. Produced by S. P. Eagle (Sam Spiegel). Screenplay
by Peter Viertel and John Huston. Directed by Huston.

AMPAS. JOHN HUSTON COLLECTION. SCRIPT MATERIAL.
1. Rough sketch. Treatment. No author or date. 18 p.
2. Binder contains various pages from the script. Some are marked: "Rough sketch, Revised
   page, September 9, 1948–September 10, 1948." Handwritten pages of dialogue included.
   Pink pages, August 31, 1948. Second revised page, September 1, 1948, and September 2,
   1948. Heavily annotated.

NEW YORK STATE ARCHIVE.
1. Dialogue script.

WHITE HUNTER, BLACK HEART. 1990.
Warner/Malpaso/Rastar. Screenplay by Peter Viertel, James Bridges, and Burt Kennedy. Produced and directed by Clint Eastwood. Fictionalized account of Viertel's working with Huston on *The African Queen,* based on Peter Viertel's novel, *White Hunter, Black Heart* (London: W. H. Allen, 1954). Eastwood plays the Huston character.

AMPAS. GENERAL COLLECTION.
1. Screenplay by Burt Kennedy, James Bridges, and Peter Viertel. Property of Brigade Productions, Inc. November 1987. 112 p. *Note following last page:* This script was prepared by Warner Brothers Inc. Script Processing Dept. Bound copy.

USC. GENERAL COLLECTION.
1. *White Hunter, Black Heart.* Screenplay by Burt Kennedy, James Bridges, and Peter Viertel, from Peter Viertel's novel, November 1987 [*handwritten:* 11/23/87]. Property of Brigade Productions, Inc. 119 p. Gen. 1936.

WHO WAS THAT LADY? 1960.
Columbia. Produced by Norman Krasna. Screenplay by Norman Krasna, based on his play. Directed by George Sidney. Unrealized project (?). No indication of Huston's involvement.

AMPAS. JOHN HUSTON COLLECTION SCRIPT MATERIAL.
1. *Who Was That Lady?* by Norman Krasna, n.d. Various pages. Play script. *Inserted:* With Mr. George Russell's compliments, London.

NEW YORK PUBLIC LIBRARY FOR THE PERFORMING ARTS.
1. Screenplay by Norman Krasna, final draft, May 21, 1959, 150 p. Includes pink, yellow, and blue revision pages, dated through August 11, 1959.

WILD BOYS OF THE ROAD. 1933.
Warner Brothers. Screenplay by Earl Baldwin. Story by Daniel Ahearn. Contributor to treatment, Cyril Hume. Directed by William Wellman. John Huston and William Wyler worked on versions when at Universal (cf. under *Forgotten Boy* for various possible versions). Axel Madsen, in *William Wyler: The Authorized Biography* (New York: Crowell, 1973, 83), writes that after *Laughing Boy,* Wyler and Huston started working on the Universal property, Daniel Ahearn's story *The Wild Boys of the Road,* which was then sold to First National.

NEW YORK STATE ARCHIVE.
1. Dialogue script.

WISCONSIN/WARNER BROTHERS SCREENPLAY SERIES.
1. A script.*

Note. *The Wisconsin Center for Film and Theater Research, the State Historical Society of Wisconsin, which houses this script, reports multiple version of the screenplay.

WILL ADAMS. 1965–66.
Paramount. Unrealized. Director.

AMPAS. JOHN HUSTON COLLECTION. PRODUCTION FILE.

1. Extensive correspondence on Huston's involvement, including a long letter from Huston to Jules Buck (presumably producer) regarding some serious disagreements and accusations regarding Huston's seriousness on the project. (Cf. Grobel, *The Hustons,* 564, 568–70.)

AMPAS. JOHN HUSTON COLLECTION. SCRIPT MATERIAL.

1. *Will Adams.* Written for the screen by Dalton Trumbo, January 5, 1965. *Cover:* First draft, pp. 1–125, May 6, 1961. 125 p. Includes blue revision pages, some dates, April 1965.
2. Part II, pp. 126–234. First draft. After p. 234, background and research material, pp. A–G. Includes blue and pink revision sheets, dated to 4/30/65.
3. *Will Adams.* Written for the screen by Dalton Trumbo, January 5, 1965. 234 p. plus pp. A–G, research and background material. Includes blue and pink revision sheets, dated through April 30, 1965. Preceding script is a six-page piece by Trumbo entitled "The Mood of the Script and How It Came About," pp. A–F, with copies to Joseph Levine, Howard Koch, Eugene Frenke, Peter O'Toole, and Jules Buck. Screenplay based on same script (45 p.) and a treatment in 1958. In summer of 1964 Mr. Buck gave a copy of the script (45 p.) and treatment to Mr. O'Toole, who expressed interest.
4. *Will Adams.* Written for the screen by Dalton Trumbo, January 5, 1965. *In pen:* Revisions to May 2, 1965, with blue revision pages. 234 p. plus pp. A–G. Includes blue and pink revision sheets to April 1965.
5. Loose sheets, various pages, pp. 1–7, January 8, 1966 (at bottom of page 7). Page 1 is missing. Marked on a fragment of p. 1: "Given John Huston, January 16, 1[966?] by J. Bu[ck]. These 7 p. are preliminary by Dalton Trumbo." *Following t.p.: The Story of Will Adams,* written for the screen. Mailed ordinary post, Dec. 20, 1965; received, Ireland, January 3, 1966. 115 p. plus additional pages—"This is the point at which our intensive discussions ended."—6 p., signed by Dalton Trumbo, London, Dec. 18, 1965.

THE WIND AND THE LION. 1975.

MGM/United Artists. Written and directed by John Milius. Huston, actor, John Hay. A novel based on the film, by John Milius and with the same title, was published in New York, Universal–Award House, 1975.

THE AMERICAN FILM INSTITUTE.

1. *Wind and the Lion,* John Milius, MGM/UA Production. Herb Jeffrey Producer. 2. 111 p.

AMPAS. GENERAL COLLECTION.

1. Screenplay by John Milius, n.d. 102 p. *On t.p.:* Message to Theodore Roosevelt from the Sultan of the Berbas, last of the Barbary Pirates, November 1904. Bound copy.

UCLA. ARTS SPECIAL COLLECTION. GENERAL COLLECTION.

1. No title page, n.d. 111p.

USC. BOYLE AND GENERAL COLLECTIONS.

1. No title page, n.d. 111 p.
2. *Wind and the Lion,* John Milius, March 12, 1974. 109 p.
3. *Wind and the Lion,* John Milius, July 9, 1974. 86 p.

WRITERS GUILD OF AMERICA, WEST.

1. Screenplay by John Milius. 1975.

ADDITIONAL SCREENPLAY MATERIAL IN THE FOLLOWING
LIBRARIES.
Stanford University Library.

WINTER KILLS. 1979.
Avco Embassy/Richert International. Written and directed by William
Richert. John Huston, actor, Pa Kegan. Gladys Hill (Huston's secretary and
collaborator for many years) acts as well, as Rosemary, Pa Kegan's secretary.

AMPAS. GENERAL COLLECTION.
1. Screenplay by William Richert. Winter Gold Productions, Ltd., New York, n.d. 156 p.
Some annotations. Bound copy.

AMPAS. JOHN HUSTON COLLECTION. SCRIPT MATERIAL.
1. Screenplay by William Richert. Winter Gold Productions, n.d. *Cover:* Gladys Hill's
name written at top. 156 p. Inserted between pp. 155 and 156 is a still from the film with
Huston in bed (hospital scene). Also included are Huston's notes, which consists of dialogue between Huston and screen son, Nick, 4 p. Also typewritten pages of some of the
handwritten notes: Scene 335, I, pp. 145–46, with "JH" at top; and II, January 5, 1977,
pp. 145–46, with "JH" at top. These pages do not match the script in the file, but some of
the words are in the final version, spoken by the characters Pa Keegan, Nick, and Cerutti.

UCSB. DAVIDSON LIBRARY.
1. Screenplay by William Richert, based on the novel by Richard Condon. A. Stirling Gold
Ltd., New York, n.d. 145 p.

USC. BOYLE COLLECTION.
1. No date. 156 p. Winter Gold Productions.

WISE BLOOD. 1979.
Ithaca-Anthea/New Line Cinema. Screenplay by Benedict Fitzgerald
and Michael Fitzgerald. Directed by John Huston, who also acted (The
Grandfather).

AMPAS. GENERAL COLLECTION.
1. Screenplay by Benedict Fitzgerald and Michael Fitzgerald. Third draft, December 1978.
129 p. Property of Ithaca Productions, Los Angeles. *Penciled on t.p.:* New Line Cinema,
1979.

AMPAS. JOHN HUSTON COLLECTION. SCRIPT MATERIAL.
1. Screenplay by Benedict Fitzgerald and Peter Michael Fitzgerald. First draft, May 1977.
100 p. Hyland–De Lauer, Los Angeles.
2. Second draft, November 1, 1978. 125 p. (Two copies.) Hyland–De Lauer, Los Angeles.
Third draft, December 1978. 129 p. Property of Ithaca Productions, Los Angeles.
3. Miscellaneous script pages, various paging, heavily annotated. Some pages dated
December 1978. Some pages marked with "B.F." and "G.H."

THE BRITISH FILM INSTITUTE.
1. A version of the screenplay.

UCLA. ARTS SPECIAL COLLECTION. GENERAL COLLECTION.
1. Screenplay by Jerome Kass. 1979. 133 p. *On t.p., handwritten:* D. [circled] John Huston.

UCSB. DAVIDSON LIBRARY.
1. Flannery O'Connor's *Wise Blood.* Screenplay by Jerome Kass. Property of Tony Bill, Biplane Cinematograph, Los Angeles, California, n.d., 133 p.

USC. BOYLE COLLECTION.
1. Flannery O'Connor's *Wise Blood.* Screenplay by Jerome Kass, n.d. 133 p.

WOODROW WILSON. *See* IN TIME TO COME.

THE WORD. 1978.
> CBS-TV. Teleplay by Dick Berg, Robert L. Joseph, S. S. Schweitzer, and Richard Fiedler. Directed by Richard Lang. Huston, actor, Reverend Randall.

UCLA. ARTS SPECIAL COLLECTION. TV SCRIPT.
1. Dick Berg. Show #1. April 1978. 113 p. Includes various drafts.
2. Robert L. Joseph. Hour #3. Second draft. Shooting script. April 1978. Includes revisions. 49 p.
3. S. S. Schweitzer. Hour #4. Second draft. Shooting script. April 14, 1978. 47 p.
4. S. S. Schweitzer. Hour #5. Second draft. Shooting script. April 14, 1978. 50 p.
5. Richard Fiedler. Hour #6. Second draft. Shooting script. April 14, 1978. 44 p.
6. Richard Fiedler and Robert L. Joseph. Hour #7. April 7, 1978. 46 p.
7. Dick Berg and Robert L. Joseph. Second draft. Shooting script. April 1978. Includes various revisions. 57 p.

ADDITIONAL SCREENPLAY MATERIAL IN THE FOLLOWING LIBRARIES.
Thousand Oaks Public Library.

THE WORLD MOVES ON. *See* THE ROARING TWENTIES.

WUTHERING HEIGHTS. 1939.
> Goldwyn/UA. Screenplay by Charles MacArthur and Ben Hecht. Directed by William Wyler. *The American Film Institute Catalog: Feature Films, 1931–1940* lists Huston as a contributing writer.

PUBLISHED SCRIPT.
1. Gassner, John. *Twenty Best Film Plays.* New York: Crown, 1943, 292–331.

AMPAS. JOHN HUSTON COLLECTION. SCRIPT MATERIAL.
1. No t.p. *Cover: Wuthering Heights,* November 28, 1938. *In pen:* By J. Huston and W. Wyler. *First page:* Production Office, Samuel Goldwyn Inc., Ltd. 136 p. plus Epilogue, pp. A–D. Includes blue revision pages, December 1, 1938.

THE BRITISH FILM INSTITUTE.
1. A version of the screenplay.

MUSEUM OF MODERN ART. FILM DEPARTMENT.
1. *Wuthering Heights.* Adapted from the novel by Emily Brontë. First draft continuity by Ben Hecht and Charles MacArthur. Property of Walter Wanger Productions. 119 p. (with changes 126 p.), n.d. Includes revision pages 3/2/37.

NEW YORK PUBLIC LIBRARY FOR THE PERFORMING ARTS.
1. Screenplay, November 28, 1938, No author, 140 p. *On cover in pencil:* Ben Hecht. Includes blue and yellow revision pages, dated various dates, December 1938–January 1939.

NEW YORK STATE ARCHIVE.
1. Dialogue script.

UCLA. ARTS SPECIAL COLLECTION. GENERAL COLLECTION.
1. Gregg Toland's (cinematographer) copy, November 28, 1938. 140 p. Heavily annotated. Includes blue revision sheets, variously dated, December 1938. Indication of start date: "Dec. 5, 1938." Various stars autographed this copy.

UNIVERSITY OF WYOMING. AMERICAN HERITAGE CENTER.
1. *Wuthering Heights,* no author, November 28, 1938, 140 p. (Ted Sherdeman Collection, #66,308.)

ADDITIONAL SCREENPLAY MATERIAL IN THE FOLLOWING LIBRARIES.
Asbury Park Public Library, Dartmouth College, Harvard University, Indiana University, St. Joseph's College.

XVII

Theatrical Activity

Listed below in chronological order are John Huston's theatrical activities. As with his cinematic activity he was a writer, a director, and an actor. In addition to the reference works found in chapter 24, "Bibliographical and Reference Sources," an excellent source of information is the New York Public Library's Performing Arts Library (Lincoln Center). The library in many ways serves as the repository of theatrical activity in New York City for many years. In its files is information on virtually every play performed in New York City. Of particular importance is that the library also holds the collection for cinema. In many times when a film was based on a play very prevalent during the studio years (as still happens today), and was the library's collection will have information on both the play and the film.

Virtually all of the reviews have been reprinted in *The New York Times Theater Reviews, 1920–1970* (New York: Arno Press, 1971), and *Critics' Theater Reviews, 1940–1942* (New York: Critics Theater Reviews, 1943; continued 1943 by New York Theater Critics' Reviews).

THE TRIUMPH OF THE EGG. Play by Sherwood Anderson. Provincetown Playhouse, New York, February 10, 1925. Huston, actor (Father).
Review: *New York Times,* February 11, 1925, 19.

RUINT: A FOLK COMEDY IN FOUR ACTS. Play by Hatcher Hughes. Provincetown Playhouse, New York, April 7, 1925. Directed by James Light. John Huston, actor, Aud Horton, with Sam Jaffe as Lum Crowder.
Review: *New York Times,* April 8, 1925, 24.

ADAM SOLITAIRE. Play by Em Jo Basshe. Provincetown Playhouse, New York, November 6, 1925. Huston, actor (Uncle Arthur).
Review: *New York Times,* November 7, 1925, 19.

FRANKIE AND JOHNNY. Marionette play by John Huston. Republic Theater, New York, September 25, 1930.
AMPAS contains information on requests Huston fielded during the 1950s to use his book as the basis of a musical and for the rights to stage the play. Revived in October 27, 1952, Theater de Lys, New York City (first production); adapted by Jack Kirkland, music by Irwin A. Bazelon, choreography by Vonn Hamilton, and musical direction by Ed Safranski. Unlike the 1930s production this revival was not a marionette play, but the program indicated that the book was by John Huston.
Reviews: *Brooklyn Daily Eagle,* October 29, 1952, Louis Sheaffer; *New York Herald Tribune,* Oct. 29, 1952, 26, Walter Kerr; *New York Journal American,* October 29, 1952, John McClain; *New York Times,* October 29, 1952, 37, Brooks Atkinson; *New York World Telegram and Sun,* October 29, 1952, William Hawkins.

STORM CHILD. Staged by Stagecrafters, Elverhoj Theater, Milton-on-Hudson, July 16, 1935.
This information is extremely doubtful. *New York Times Theater Reviews,* July 16, 1935, 24:1, has a small notice regarding the play by John Huston and R. F. Morris; however, the actual play script in the NYPL Collection lists *Storm Child* by John Houston and Griff Morris, produced at the Copley Theater, Boston, April 17, 1936.

THE LONELY MAN. Play by Howard Koch. Presented by the Chicago Federal Theater, 1937. John Huston, actor.
See Howard Koch's *As Time Goes By: Memoirs of a Writer* (New York: Harcourt, 1979).

A PASSENGER TO BALI. By Ellis St. Joseph. Ethel Barrymore Theater, New York City, March 14, 1940. Directed by John Huston.
Reviews: *New York Herald Tribune,* March 15, 1940, Burns Mantle; *New York Post,* March 15, 1940, John Mason Brown; *New York Sun,* March 5, 1940, Richard Lockridge; *New York World Telegram,* March 15, 1940, Sidney B. Whipple; *New York Times,* March 15, 1940, 26, Brooks Atkinson.

IN TIME TO COME. A play by John Huston and Howard Koch. Mansfield Theater, New York, December 28, 1941. Staged and directed by Otto Preminger.

Play script included in *Best Plays of 1941–1942* (New York: Dodd, Mead, 1942). AMPAS contains information on the play, versions of the play script, and reviews of the play.

Reviews: *New York Daily News,* December 29, 1941, Burns Mantle; *New York Herald Tribune,* December 29, 1941, Richard Watts Jr.; *New York Journal American,* December 29, 1941, John Anderson; *New York Times,* December 29, 1941, 20; *New York Times,* January 4, 1942, sect. ix, 1, Brooks Atkinson; *New York World Telegram,* December 29, 1941, John Mason Brown; *PM,* December 29, 1941, Louis Kroningerger.

NO EXIT (*Huis Clos*). Adapted by Paul Bowles, from Jean-Paul Sartre's play. Produced by Herman Levin and Oliver Smith. Directed by John Huston. Cast includes Ruth Ford, Claude Dauphin, and Annabella. Biltmore Theater, New York, November 26, 1946, and closed December 22, 1946.

AMPAS, John Huston Archive, contain information on Huston's activities in producing the play and a version of the play script with changes. Judith Anderson and Katharine Hepburn were considered for the cast. The file includes the following articles: *Newsweek,* December 9, 1946; *New York Times,* November 27, 1946, 21; *New York Times,* December 22, 1946, Brooks Atkinson; *Time,* December 9, 1946.

Reviews: *New York Daily News,* November 27, 1946, John Chapman; *New York Herald Tribune,* November 27, 1946, Howard Barnes; *New York Journal American,* November 12, 1946, Robert Garland; *New York Post,* November 27, 1946, Richard Watts Jr.; *New York World Telegram,* November 27, 1946, William Hawkins; *PM,* November 28, 1946, Louis Kroningerger; *Saturday Review,* December 9, 1946, John Mason Brown; *The Sun,* November 27, 1946, Herrick Brown.

THE MINES OF SULPHUR. Opera. La Scala, Milan, February 1966. Music score by Richard Rodney Bennett. Directed by John Huston.

AMPAS, John Huston Archive, include production information, articles, and reviews: *Avanti,* February 26, 1966; *Corriere della Sera,* January 27, 1966; *Corriere della Sera,,* February 26, 1966; *Corriere Lombardo,* February 26, 1966; *Gazetta del Popolo,* February 26, 1966; *Il Giorno,* February 26, 1966; *L'Italia,* February 26, 1966; *La Notte Sabato,* February 26, 1966; *Sunday Times,* February 20, 1966, interview by Derek Prouse; "Maestro Huston," *Newsweek,* March 7, 1966, 89.

XVIII

Audio Recordings

THE BIBLE. Original motion picture sound track by Tishiro Mayuzumi, Twentieth Century-Fox Records, 1966.
LP recording.

DICK CAVETT SHOW. INTERVIEWS WITH JOHN HUSTON, PBS, October 21, 1980–October 22, 1980.
Audiotape of television programs. Two cassettes. Holdings, Michigan State University.

50 YEARS OF ACTION. Unedited sound track, interview with John Huston, 1985.
Two sound tape reels, UCLA.

HUMPHREY BOGART IN THE MALTESE FALCON; HUMPHREY BOGART IN LOVE'S LONELY COUNTERFEIT Command Performance Records, 197-?, LP recording. "This record produced expressly for members of the Humphrey Bogart Memorial Society." Also stars Mary Astor and Sydney Greenstreet.

I'M TOO BUSY TO TALK NOW: CONVERSATIONS WITH AMERICAN ARTISTS OVER 70. Audio-Forum, Guilford, Connecticut, 1986. Audiotape, six cassettes. Interviews conducted by Connie Goldman, with John Huston interviewed on cassette no. 3.
The following libraries report holdings: Glendale Public Library, Northeastern University, Phoenix Public Library, Sonoma State University, Southern Baptists Theological Seminary, Thousand Oaks Public Library, University of California at San Diego, University of Maryland.

INTERVIEW WITH JOHN HUSTON, "KNIGHT AT THE MOVIES." October 14, 1958.
Audiotape, Arthur Knight Collection, USC.

INTERVIEW WITH TONY HUSTON ON "THE DEAD," host: Charles Champlin, USC, CNTV 466 Course, January 14, 1988.
Audiotape, USC Collection.

IT'S NOT MY WORK, IT'S MY LIFE, Pacific Radio Archive. 1986. Interview with John Huston. Audiotape.
The following libraries report holdings: California State University at Bakersfield, Cincinnati Public Library, Minneapolis Public Library, State University New York, Buffalo.

JOHN HUSTON INTERVIEWED BY TOM BROKAW, "TODAY SHOW," NBC-TV, May 2, 1980.
Audiotape.

JOHN HUSTON INTERVIEWED BY TOM SNYDER, "TOMORROW," NBC-TV, December 16, 1975.
Audiotape, USC Collection.

KEY LARGO, Lux Radio Theater, November 28, 1949. Old Time Radio, Inc. 197?. LP recording.
Starring Humphrey Bogart, Edward G. Robinson, and Lauren Bacall. No indication of John Huston's involvement in this production.

THE NIGHT OF THE IGUANA: DRAMATIC HIGHLIGHTS FROM THE ACCLAIMED FILM, WITH COMMENTARY BY JOHN HUSTON, Limited Collections Ed. MGM Records, 1964. LP recording. "This album is being privately distributed and is not intended for sale to the public."
The following libraries report holdings: Kansas State University, University of California at Los Angeles, University of Southern Mississippi.

"RECOLLECTIONS OF JAMES AGEE," Radio Program on WBAI Radio Station, New York, 197-?. Huston interviewed by David Osman.
Transcript and one-reel tape available at Columbia University Oral History Research Office (Box 20, Room 801, Butler Library, New York, NY 10027).

THE TREASURE OF THE SIERRA MADRE. Mark 56 Records. LP recording.
Originally broadcast on the Lux Radio Theater, April 18, 1949; starring Humphrey Bogart and Walter Huston; William Keighley, host.

XIX

Production Files

Herewith an inventory of those institutions that hold production material of an archival nature on Huston's films. (For archival information on people professionally related to Huston, *see* chapter 10.) The Academy of Motion Picture Arts and Sciences, the Museum of Modern Art (which also has a separate stills department), and the New York Public Library's (NYPL) Performing Arts Library over the years have developed extensive production files that include a wide variety of material. The academy also contains John Huston's papers (production file material from the Huston Collection, while indicated here, is also summarized in chapter 20; but some of the material may yet be uninventoried at the time of this publication). These institutions' files of particular films include clippings from newspapers and magazines; press books, programs, and other publicity materials; the synopsis, cast and credits; pre- and postproduction information; and then-official studio documents. Often these collections have stills, lobby cards, and posters, which are filed separately. In addition these collections have separate files, including photographs, on John Huston.

Of further interest are the Motion Picture Association of America's Production Code Administration files (often referred to as the Breen Office), which are deposited at AMPAS. These files represent the censorship that was imposed on the industry from 1927 though 1967. In addition to the memos and letters expressing concern about certain aspects in the films—that is, censors' reports—the files also serve as veritable production files for each film with correspondence, reviews, credits, synopsis, and so on.

As the NYPL Performing Arts Library is also a theatrical and music collection, background material is available on those Huston properties that were originally plays, including those plays with which Huston was involved as an actor, a playwright, and a director. In the music division under Richard Rodney Bennett, the composer of *The Mines of Sulphur,* one can find material on the opera that Huston directed at La Scala, Milan.

The University of California, Los Angeles (UCLA), and the University of Southern California are important resources as the former has the Twentieth Century-Fox papers and the latter, the Warner Brothers papers. These studio files often contain memos, daily production reports, contracts, and production stills. Along with other institutions, UCLA also has other production file information, which is so indicated.

Some production files have been transferred to microform. In some cases material are available both in print and microform; in other cases, one or the other. If the Museum of Modern Art (New York) has the production file in microform, the location device is indicated.

Movie memorabilia (posters, stills, and so forth) are avidly sought after by collectors. Major auction houses have periodical auctions, and a number of collector's shows are held throughout the United States during the year. As one might expect Los Angeles, especially the area around Hollywood, has numerous stores that specialize in posters, lobby cards, screenplays, photographs, stills, and other materials. Two collector's publications with listings of dealers throughout the country are: *Collecting Hollywood* (P.O. Box 2512, Chattanooga, TN 37409, 615–265–5515) and *Movie Collector's World* (P.O. Box 309, Fraser, MI 48026, 810–774–4311; Fax: 810–774–4311).

The following abbreviations are used:

AMPAS	Academy of Motion Picture Arts and Science, with AMPAS. General Production File and AMPAS John Huston Collection
BFI	British Film Institute
MOMA	Museum of Modern Art
MPAA/PCA	Motion Picture Association of America. Production Code Administration (located in AMPAS)
NYPL	New York Public Library for the Performing Arts
UCLA	University of California, Los Angeles
USC	University of Southern California, Los Angeles
WISCONSIN	Wisconsin Center for Film and Theater Research, State Historical Society of Wisconsin

THE ACQUITTAL

AMPAS. General Production File

BFI. Stills

MOMA. Stills

NYPL

ACROSS THE PACIFIC

AMPAS. General Production File

BFI. Stills

MOMA. Production File; Stills

MPAA/PCA

NYPL

UCLA. Movie Stills Collection

USC. Warner Brothers Archives

WISCONSIN. Production File

ACROSS THE RIVER AND INTO THE TREES

AMPAS. General Production File

AMPAS. John Huston Collection

NYPL

THE AFRICAN QUEEN

AMPAS. General Production File

AMPAS. John Huston Collection

BFI. Poster, Press Book, Stills

MOMA. Production File; Stills

MPAA/PCA

NYPL

UCLA. Press Books, Press Kits, Other Publicity Material

AGEE

AMPAS. General Production File

MOMA

NYPL

ALFRED HITCHCOCK PRESENTS: MAN FROM THE SOUTH

NYPL

622

ALOUETTE

AMPAS. General Production File

AMPAS. John Huston Collection

NYPL

THE AMAZING DR. CLITTERHOUSE

AMPAS. General Production File

BFI. Stills

MOMA. Production File; Stills

MPAA/PCA

NYPL

USC. Warner Brothers Archives

WISCONSIN

AMERICAN CAESAR

MOMA

ANGELA

AMPAS. General Production File

BFI. POSTER

ANNIE

AMPAS. General Production File

AMPAS. John Huston Collection

BFI. POSTER, Stills

MOMA. Production File; Stills

NYPL

UCLA. Lobby Card Collection, Movie Stills Collection, Press Books, Press Kits,
     Other Publicity Material

APPOINTMENT WITH DESTINY

MOMA

NYPL

John Huston

THE ASPHALT JUNGLE

AMPAS. General Production File

AMPAS. John Huston Collection

BFI. Production File; Stills

MOMA. Production File; Stills

MPAA/PCA

NYPL

UCLA. MGM Set Designs; Movie Stills Collection

BACKGROUND TO DANGER

AMPAS. General Production File

BFI. Stills

MOMA. Production File; Stills

MPAA/PCA

NYPL

UCLA. Movie Stills Collection

USC. Warner Brothers Archives

WISCONSIN

THE BARBARIAN AND THE GEISHA

AMPAS. General Production File

AMPAS. John Huston Collection

BFI. Stills

MOMA. Production File; Stills

MPAA/PCA

NYPL

UCLA. Twentieth Century-Fox Archives, Stills

BATTLE FOR THE PLANET OF THE APES

AMPAS. General Production File

BFI. Press Books, Poster, Stills

NYPL

MOMA. Production File; Stills

UCLA. Lobby Card Collection, Movie Stills Collection; Twentieth Century-Fox Archives, Stills

THE BATTLE OF SAN PIETRO

AMPAS. General Production File

AMPAS. John Huston Collection

BFI. Stills

MOMA. Production File; Stills

NYPL (under *San Pietro*)

BEAT THE DEVIL

AMPAS. General Production File

AMPAS. John Huston Collection

BFI. Stills

MOMA. Production File; Stills

MPAA/PCA

NYPL

UCLA. Movie Stills Collection

BECKET

MOMA. Production File; Stills

MPAA/PCA

NYPL

THE BERMUDA TRIANGLE

AMPAS. John Huston Collection

MOMA

THE BIBLE

AMPAS. General Production File

AMPAS. John Huston Collection

BFI. Poster, Stills

MOMA. Production File; Stills

MPAA/PCA

NYPL

UCLA. Press Books, Press Kits, Other Publicity Material; Twentieth Century-Fox Archives, Stills

BLACK CAULDRON
AMPAS. General Production File

BFI. Poster, Stills.

MOMA. Production File; Stills

NYPL

UCLA. Press Books, Press Kits, Other Publicity Material

THE BLUE HOTEL
NYPL

BOLÍVAR
AMPAS. John Huston Collection

BORSTAL BOY
NYPL

BREAKOUT
AMPAS. General Production File

BFI. Poster, Stills

MOMA. Production File; Stills

NYPL

UCLA. Columbia Stills & Keybooks; Lobby Card Collection; Movie Stills Collection

THE BRIDGE IN THE JUNGLE
AMPAS. General Production File

AMPAS. John Huston Collection

MOMA. Micro Collection 101, C, 4

NYPL

THE BRIDGE OF SAN LUIS REY
AMPAS. General Production File

MOMA. Micro Collection 101, C, 4–6

MPAA/PCA

NYPL

BULLET PARK
AMPAS. General Production File

NYPL

BY LOVE POSSESSED
AMPAS. General Production File

AMPAS. John Huston Collection

MOMA

MPAA/PCA

NYPL

UCLA. Lobby Card Collection

CANDY
AMPAS. General Production File

BFI. Poster, Stills

MOMA. Production File; Stills

NYPL

UCLA. Lobby Card Collection; Movie Stills Collection

CANNERY ROW
AMPAS. General Production File

AMPAS. John Huston Collection

BFI. Stills

MOMA. Production File; Stills

NYPL

UCLA. Lobby Card Collection; Movie Stills Collection; Press Books, Press Kits,
Other Publicity Material

CAPTAIN HORATIO HORNBLOWER
AMPAS. General Production File

BFI. Press Book, Poster, Stills

MOMA. Production File; Stills

MPAA/PCA

NYPL

UCLA. Movie Stills Collection

USC. Warner Brothers Archives

THE CARDINAL
AMPAS. General Production File

AMPAS. John Huston Collection

BFI. Press Book, Stills

MOMA. Production File; Stills

MPAA/PCA

NYPL

UCLA. Columbia Stills & Keybooks; Lobby Card Collection; Movie Stills Collection

CASINO ROYALE
AMPAS. General Production File

AMPAS. John Huston Collection

BFI. Press Book, Poster, Stills

MOMA. Production File; Stills

MPAA/PCA

NYPL

UCLA. Columbia Stills, Keybooks

CATHOLICS
MOMA

CHEYENNE
AMPAS. General Production File

MOMA. Production File; Stills

MPAA/PCA

NYPL

UCLA. Lobby Card Collection; Movie Stills Collection

USC. Warner Brothers Archives

CHINATOWN

AMPAS. General Production File

BFI. Press Book, Poster, Stills

MOMA. Production File; Stills

NYPL

UCLA. Lobby Card Collection; Movie Stills Collection; Press Books, Press Kits, Other Publicity Material

THE COMMODORE MARRIES

NYPL

THE CONSTANT NYMPH

AMPAS. General Production File

BFI. Stills

MOMA. Micro Collection 167, D, 5-E, 2, Title; Stills

MPAA/PCA

NYPL

USC. Warner Brothers Archives

WISCONSIN

CREATIVITY WITH BILL MOYERS

NYPL

DANGER SIGNAL

AMPAS. General Production File

BFI. Stills

MOMA. Micro Collection 188, E, 2–4, Title; Stills

MPAA/PCA

NYPL

USC. Warner Brothers Archives

WISCONSIN

THE DEAD

AMPAS. General Production File

BFI. Press Book, Stills

MOMA. Production File; Stills

NYPL

UCLA. Movie Stills Collection, Press Books, Press Kits, Other Publicity Material

DEATH DRIVES THROUGH

BFI. Stills

DEATH IN A FAMILY

NYPL

THE DECEIVERS

AMPAS. John Huston Collection

MOMA. Stills

DE SADE

AMPAS. General Production File

BFI. Stills

MOMA. Production File; Stills

NYPL

THE DESERTER

AMPAS. General Production File

AMPAS. John Huston Collection

BFI. Poster, Stills

MOMA. Stills

NYPL

UCLA. Movie Stills Collection, Poster Collection

DESTRY RIDES AGAIN
AMPAS. General Production File

BFI. Press Book, Stills

MOMA. Micro Collection 207, B, 1; Stills

MPAA/PCA

NYPL

DICK CAVETT SHOW
NYPL

DIRECTED BY WILLIAM WYLER
AMPAS. General Production File

BFI. Stills

MOMA

NYPL

THE DIRECTORS
AMPAS. General Production File

NYPL

THE DISENCHANTED
AMPAS. General Production File

AMPAS. John Huston Collection

NYPL

DISRAELI
AMPAS. General Production File

MPAA/PCA

NYPL

UCLA. Movie Stills Collection

USC. Warner Brothers Archives

WISCONSIN

DR. EHRLICH'S MAGIC BULLET
AMPAS. General Production File

MOMA. Stills

MPAA/PCA

NYPL

UCLA. Movie Stills Collection

USC. Warner Brothers Archives

WISCONSIN

A FAREWELL TO ARMS
AMPAS. General Production File

AMPAS. John Huston Collection

BFI. Poster, Stills

MOMA. Production File; Stills

MPAA/PCA

NYPL

UCLA. Twentieth Century-Fox Archives, Stills; Lobby Card Collection

FAT CITY
AMPAS. General Production File

AMPAS. John Huston Collection

BFI. Press Book, Poster, Stills

MOMA. Production File; Stills

NYPL

UCLA. Columbia Stills, Keybooks

FORGOTTEN BOY
AMPAS. William Wyler Collection

FRANKIE AND JOHNNY
AMPAS. John Huston Collection

NYPL

USC. Warner Brothers Archives

FREUD: THE SECRET PASSION

AMPAS. General Production File

AMPAS. John Huston Collection

BFI. Poster, Stills

MOMA. Production File; Stills

MPAA/PCA

NYPL

UCLA. Lobby Card Collection; Movie Stills Collection

GEORGE STEVENS: A FILMMAKER'S JOURNEY

AMPAS. General Production File

MOMA

NYPL

GOYA

AMPAS. John Huston Collection

MOMA. Micro Collection 319, B, 2

THE HARD WAY

AMPAS. General Production File

BFI. Press Book, Stills

MOMA. Production File; Stills

MPAA/PCA

NYPL

WISCONSIN

HARROW ALLEY

AMPAS. John Huston Collection

BFI. Design

HASSAN

AMPAS. John Huston Collection

HAUNTED SUMMER
AMPAS. General Production File

BFI. Production File; Stills

NYPL

MOMA. Stills

HEAD ON
AMPAS. John Huston Collection

BFI. Stills

MOMA. Stills

NYPL

THE HEART IS A LONELY HUNTER
AMPAS. General Production File

MOMA. Production File; Stills

NYPL

HEAVEN KNOWS, MR. ALLISON.
AMPAS. General Production File

AMPAS. John Huston Collection

BFI. Posters, Stills

MOMA. Production File; Stills

MPAA/PCA

NYPL

UCLA. Movie Stills Collection; Twentieth Century-Fox Archives, Stills

HELL'S HEROES
AMPAS. General Production File

BFI. Press Book, Stills

MOMA. Micro Collection 356, C, 2; Stills

MPAA/PCA

NYPL

UCLA. Movie Stills Collection

HERE'S LOOKING AT YOU, WARNER BROTHERS
MOMA

HERMAN MELVILLE, DAMNED IN PARADISE
MOMA

HIGH ROAD TO CHINA
AMPAS. General Production File

MOMA. Production File; Stills

NYPL

UCLA. Lobby Card Collection; Movie Stills Collection

HIGH SIERRA
AMPAS. General Production File

BFI. Production File, Stills

MOMA. Production File; Stills

MPAA/PCA

NYPL

UCLA. Movie Stills Collection

USC. Warner Brothers Archives

WISCONSIN

THE HOBBIT
AMPAS. General Production File

MOMA

NYPL

HOLLYWOOD ON TRIAL
AMPAS. General Production File

BFI. Stills

MOMA

NYPL

THE HORSE OF SELENE

AMPAS. John Huston Collection

THE HOSTAGE.

AMPAS. General Production File

AMPAS. John Huston Collection

MOMA Micro Collection 379, C, 56, Title

NYPL

A HOUSE DIVIDED

AMPAS. General Production File

BFI. Stills

MOMA. Micro Collection 379, C, 5–6, Title; Stills

MPAA/PCA

NYPL

THE HUNCHBACK OF NOTRE DAME

AMPAS. General Production File

BFI. Stills

MOMA. Production File; Stills

MPAA/PCA

NYPL

UCLA. RKO Archives; Movie Stills Collection

INDEPENDENCE

AMPAS. General Collection File

AMPAS. John Huston Collection

NYPL

IN THIS OUR LIFE

AMPAS. General Production File

BFI. Stills

MOMA. Production File; Stills

MPAA/PCA

NYPL

USC. Warner Brothers Archives

WISCONSIN

IN TIME TO COME

AMPAS. John Huston Collection

NYPL

USC. Warner Brothers Archives

THE INVISIBLE MAN

AMPAS. General Collection File

BFI. Production File; Stills

MOMA. Production File; Stills

MPAA/PCA

NYPL

IT HAPPENED IN PARIS

BFI. Press Book, Stills

USC. Warner Brothers Archives

JACK OF DIAMONDS

AMPAS. General Production File

MOMA. Micro Collection 416, E, 5–417, A, 4

JAGUAR LIVES

AMPAS. General Production File

AMPAS. John Huston Collection

BFI. Stills

MOMA

UCLA. Poster Collection

JEZEBEL

AMPAS. General Production File

BFI. Production File; Press Book, Stills

MOMA. Production File; Stills

MPAA/PCA

NYPL

UCLA. Movie Stills Collection

USC. Warner Brothers Archives

WISCONSIN

JOHN HUSTON AND THE DUBLINERS

AMPAS. General Production File

BFI. Stills

MOMA

NYPL

JOHN HUSTON: THE MAN, THE MOVIES, THE MAVERICK

AMPAS. General Production File

MOMA

JOHN HUSTON'S DUBLIN

AMPAS John Huston Collection

MOMA

THE JOURNEY OF ROBERT F. KENNEDY

AMPAS. General Production File

MOMA

NYPL (under *The Unfinished Journey of Robert F. Kennedy*)

JUAREZ

AMPAS. General Production File

BFI. Press Book, Stills

MOMA. Production File; Stills

MPAA/PCA

NYPL

UCLA. Movie Stills Collection

USC. Warner Brothers Archives

WISCONSIN

JUDAS

AMPAS. John Huston Collection

KEY LARGO

AMPAS. General Production File

AMPAS. John Huston Collection

BFI. Stills

MOMA. Production File; Stills

MPAA/PCA

NYPL

UCLA. Movie Stills Collection

USC. Warner Brothers Archives; Jack Warner Collection

WISCONSIN

THE KILLERS

AMPAS. General Production File

BFI. Press Book, Stills

MOMA. Production File; Stills

MPAA/PCA

NYPL

UCLA. Movie Stills Collection

USC. Mark Hellinger Archives

KISS THE BLOOD OFF MY HANDS

AMPAS. General Production File

MOMA. Production File; Stills

NYPL

KNOW YOUR ENEMY: JAPAN

AMPAS. General Production File

AMPAS. John Huston Collection

NYPL

THE KREMLIN LETTER

AMPAS. General Production File

AMPAS. John Huston Collection

BFI. Press Book, Poster, Stills

MOMA. Production File; Stills

NYPL

UCLA. Poster Collection; Twentieth Century-Fox Archives, Stills

THE LAST RUN

AMPAS. General Production File

AMPAS. John Huston Collection

MOMA. Production File; Stills

NYPL

UCLA. Lobby Card Collection; Movie Stills Collection

USC. Warner Brothers Archives

LAUGHING BOY

AMPAS. General Production File

AMPAS. William Wyler Collection.

BFI. Press Book, Stills

MOMA. Micro Collection 474, D, 1

MPAA/PCA

NYPL

LAW AND ORDER

AMPAS. General Production File

BFI. Stills

MOMA. Production File; Stills

MPAA/PCA

NYPL

LET THERE BE LIGHT

AMPAS. General Production File

AMPAS. John Huston Collection

MOMA. Production File; Stills

NYPL

THE LIFE AND TIMES OF JOHN HUSTON, ESQ.

NYPL

THE LIFE AND TIMES OF JUDGE ROY BEAN

AMPAS. General Production File

AMPAS. John Huston Collection

BFI. Press Book, Poster, Stills

MOMA. Production File; Stills

NYPL

UCLA. Movie Stills Collection; Poster Collection

THE LIST OF ADRIAN MESSENGER

AMPAS. General Production File

AMPAS. John Huston Collection

BFI. Production File; Press Book, Poster, Stills

MOMA. Production File; Stills

MPAA/PCA

NYPL

UCLA. Lobby Card Collection; Poster Collection

LIVE FROM LINCOLN CENTER. FILM SOCIETY
HONORS JOHN HUSTON

MOMA (filed in general folders of John Huston)

THE LONELY PASSION OF JUDITH HEARNE

AMPAS. General Production File

AMPAS. John Huston Collection

MOMA

NYPL

LOVE AND BULLETS

AMPAS. General Production File

MOMA

NYPL

UCLA. Press Books, Press Kits, Other Publicity Material

LOVESICK

AMPAS. General Production File

MOMA. Production File; Stills

UCLA. Movie Stills Collection; Poster Collection; Press Books, Press Kits, Other Publicity Material

LYSISTRATA

AMPAS. John Huston Collection

THE MACKINTOSH MAN

AMPAS. General Production File

BFI. Press Book, Poster, Stills

MOMA. Production File; Stills

NYPL

UCLA. Movie Stills Collection

THE MADWOMAN OF CHAILLOT

AMPAS. General Production File

AMPAS. John Huston Collection

BFI. Press Book, Poster, Stills

MOMA. Production File; Stills

NYPL

UCLA. Lobby Card Collection; Movie Stills Collection

THE MAGNIFICENT YANKEE

AMPAS. General Production File

MOMA. Production File; Stills

MPAA/PCA

NYPL

THE MALTESE FALCON

AMPAS. General Production File

BFI. Production File, Stills

MOMA. Production File; Stills

MPAA/PCA

NYPL

UCLA. Movie Stills Collection

USC. Warner Brothers Archives

WISCONSIN

A MAN FOR ALL SEASONS

AMPAS. General Production File

AMPAS. John Huston Collection

MOMA. Production File; Stills

MPAA/PCA

NYPL

MAN IN THE WILDERNESS

AMPAS. General Production File

BFI. Press Book, Poster, Stills

MOMA. Production File; Stills

NYPL

UCLA. Lobby Card Collection; Movie Stills Collection

MAN OF LA MANCHA
AMPAS. General Production File

MOMA. Production File; Stills

NYPL

THE MAN WHO WOULD BE KING
AMPAS. General Production File

AMPAS. John Huston Collection

BFI. Poster, Stills

MOMA. Production File; Stills

NYPL

UCLA. Lobby Card Collection; Movie Stills Collection

MARILYN: THE UNTOLD STORY
NYPL

MARIUS
AMPAS. General Production File

NYPL

MATADOR
AMPAS. General Production File

AMPAS. John Huston Collection

MPAA/PCA

NYPL

MIGHTY BARNUM
AMPAS. General Production File

BFI. Stills

MOMA. Production File; Stills

NYPL

THE MISFITS
AMPAS. General Production File

AMPAS. John Huston Collection

BFI. Press Book, Poster, Stills

MOMA. Production File; Stills

NYPL

UCLA. Movie Stills Collection

MR. NORTH

AMPAS. General Production File

MOMA. Production File; Stills

NYPL

UCLA. Poster Collection

MR. SKEFFINGTON

AMPAS. General Production File

BFI. Press Book, Poster, Stills

MOMA. Production File; Stills

MPAA/PCA

NYPL

USC. Warner Brothers Archives

WISCONSIN

MOBY DICK

AMPAS. General Production File

AMPAS. John Huston Collection

BFI. Press Book, Poster, Stills

MOMA. Production File; Stills

MPAA/PCA

NYPL

UCLA. Lobby Card Collection; Movie Stills Collection

USC. Jack Warner Collection

MOMO

AMPAS. General Production File

MOMA

NYPL

MONTEZUMA

AMPAS. John Huston Collection

MOULIN ROUGE

AMPAS. General Production File

AMPAS. John Huston Collection

BFI. Press Book, Poster, Stills

MOMA. Production File; Stills

MPAA/PCA

NYPL

UCLA. Lobby Card Collection

MOVIOLA: THIS YEAR'S BLONDE

MOMA

NYPL

MURDERS IN THE RUE MORGUE

AMPAS. General Production File

BFI. Stills

MOMA. Production File; Stills

MPAA/PCA

NYPL. Movie Stills Collection

MYRA BRECKINRIDGE

AMPAS. General Production File

BFI. Production File, Stills

MOMA. Production File; Stills

NYPL

UCLA. Twentieth Century-Fox Archives, Stills

NAGANA
AMPAS. General Production File

BFI. Stills

MOMA. Micro Collection 588, C, 5; Stills

NYPL

THE NIGHT OF THE IGUANA
AMPAS. General Production File

AMPAS. John Huston Collection

BFI. Press Book, Poster, Stills

MOMA. Production File; Stills

MPAA/PCA

NYPL

UCLA. Lobby Card Collection; Movie Stills Collection

NINA
AMPAS. John Huston Collection

NOTES FROM UNDER THE VOLCANO
AMPAS. General Production File

MOMA

NYPL

OBSERVATIONS UNDER THE VOLCANO
AMPAS. General Production File

MOMA

NYPL

ON OUR MERRY WAY (*A Miracle Can Happen*)
AMPAS. General Production File

BFI. Press Book, Stills

MOMA. Micro Collection 627, E, 3–628, A; 554, D, 1–3; Stills (under *A Miracle Can Happen*)

MPAA/PCA

NYPL

THE OTHER SIDE OF THE WIND

AMPAS. General Production File

MOMA

NYPL

PATTON

AMPAS. General Production File

AMPAS. John Huston Collection

MOMA. Micro Collection 662, A, 4-C, 4

NYPL

UCLA. Lobby Card Collection; Twentieth Century-Fox Archives, Stills

PHOBIA

AMPAS. General Production File

AMPAS. John Huston Collection

MOMA. Production File; Stills

NYPL

PORTRAIT OF THE ARTIST AS A YOUNG MAN

AMPAS. General Production File

AMPAS. John Huston Collection

PRELUDE TO FREEDOM

AMPAS. John Huston Collection

USC. Warner Brothers Archives

THE PRINCE AND THE SHOWGIRL

AMPAS. General Production File

AMPAS. John Huston Collection

MOMA. Production File; Stills

MPAA/PCA

NYPL

USC. Warner Brothers Archives & Jack Warner Collection

PRIZZI'S HONOR

AMPAS. General Production File

BFI. Production File; Stills

MOMA. Production File; Stills

NYPL

UCLA. Movie Stills Collection, Press Books, Press Kits, Other Publicity Material;
Twentieth Century-Fox Archives, Stills

THE PROWLER

AMPAS. General Production File

BFI. Production File; Stills

MOMA. Production File; Stills

MPAA/PCA

NYPL

UCLA. Movie Stills Collection

THE QUARE FELLOW

AMPAS. General Production File

MOMA

MPAA/PCA

NYPL

QUO VADIS

AMPAS. General Production File

AMPAS. John Huston Collection

BFI. Press Book, Poster, Stills

MOMA. Production File; Stills

MPAA/PCA

NYPL

UCLA. MGM Set Designs

THE RED BADGE OF COURAGE

AMPAS. John Huston Collection

AMPAS. General Production File

BFI. Stills

MOMA. Production File; Stills

MPAA/PCA

NYPL

UCLA. Movie Stills Collection

REFLECTIONS IN A GOLDEN EYE

AMPAS. General Production File

AMPAS. John Huston Collection

BFI. Poster, Stills

MOMA. Production File; Stills

MPAA/PCA

NYPL

UCLA. Movie Stills Collection

REMINISCENCES OF A COWBOY

AMPAS. John Huston Collection

MPAA/PCA (released as *Cowboy*)

REPORT FROM THE ALEUTIANS

AMPAS. General Production File

AMPAS. John Huston Collection

MOMA. Stills

NYPL

RETURN OF THE KING

AMPAS. General Production File (under *Lord of the Flies*)

MOMA

NYPL

REVENGE

AMPAS. General Production File

MOMA

NYPL

UCLA. Columbia Stills, Keybooks; Movie Stills Collection; Press Books, Press Kits, Other Publicity Material

THE RHINEMANN EXCHANGE

MOMA

NYPL

RHODES OF AFRICA

AMPAS. General Production File (under *Rhodes*)

BFI. Stills

MOMA. Micro Collection 747, A, 6; Stills

NYPL

RICHARD III

AMPAS. John Huston Collection

MOMA. Micro collection 747, D, C-748, C, 5

NYPL

THE ROARING TWENTIES

AMPAS. General Production File

BFI. Stills

MOMA. Production File; Stills

MPAA/PCA

NYPL

WISCONSIN

THE ROCKY ROAD TO DUBLIN

AMPAS. General Production File

MOMA. Micro Collection 759, E, 2

NYPL

ROOTS OF HEAVEN

AMPAS. General Production File

AMPAS. John Huston Collection

BFI. Press Book, Poster, Stills

MOMA. Production File; Stills

MPAA/PCA

NYPL

UCLA. Lobby Card Collection; Twentieth Century-Fox Archives, Stills

SERGEANT YORK

AMPAS. General Production File

BFI. Stills

MOMA. Micro Collection 814, E, 5 and 815, A, 3-G, 3; Stills

MPAA/PCA

NYPL

UCLA. Movie Stills Collection

USC. Warner Brothers Archives

WISCONSIN

SHAKEDOWN

AMPAS. General Production File

BFI. Stills

MOMA. Micro Collection 822, D, 6; Stills

NYPL

SHERLOCK HOLMES IN NEW YORK

NYPL

THE SHOES OF THE FISHERMAN

AMPAS. General Production File

AMPAS. John Huston Collection

MOMA. Production File; Stills

MPAA/PCA

NYPL

SINFUL DAVEY

AMPAS. General Production File

AMPAS. John Huston Collection

BFI. Press Book, Design, Poster, Stills

MOMA

NYPL

SOAR ON EAGLE

USC. Warner Brothers Archives

THE STORM

AMPAS. General Production File

BFI. Press Book, Stills

MOMA. Micro Collection 892, E, 3; Stills

MPAA/PCA

NYPL

UCLA. Movie Stills Collection

THE STORY OF G.I. JOE

AMPAS. General Production File (under *G.I. Joe*)

BFI. Stills

MOMA. Stills

NYPL

MPAA/PCA

WISCONSIN

THE STRANGER

AMPAS. General Production File

BFI. Poster, Stills

MOMA. Production File; Stills

MPAA/PCA

NYPL

U. WYOMING, American Heritage Center. Stills

TARAS BULBA

AMPAS. General Production File

AMPAS. John Huston Collection

MOMA. Production File; Stills

MPAA/PCA

NYPL

TENTACLES

AMPAS. General Production File

BFI. Stills

MOMA. Production File; Stills

NYPL

UCLA. Movie Stills Collection

A TERRIBLE BEAUTY

AMPAS. General Production File

AMPAS. John Huston Collection

MOMA

NYPL

THEODOSIA: EMPRESS OF AMERICA. *See* PRELUDE TO FREEDOM.

THIS PROPERTY IS CONDEMNED

AMPAS. General Production File

MOMA. Production File; Stills

MPAA/PCA

NYPL

THREE STRANGERS
AMPAS. General Production File

BFI. Stills

MOMA. Production File; Stills

MPAA/PCA

NYPL

UCLA. Lobby Card Collection; Movie Stills Collection

USC. Warner Brothers Archives

WISCONSIN

TOMORROW THE WORLD
AMPAS. General Production File

MOMA

MPAA/PCA

NYPL

TOWARD DEATH
USC. Warner Brothers Archives

THE TREASURE OF THE SIERRA MADRE
AMPAS. General Production File

AMPAS. John Huston Collection

BFI. Stills

MOMA. Production File; Stills

MPAA/PCA

NYPL

UCLA. Movie Stills Collection

USC. Warner Brothers Archives & Jack Warner Collection

WISCONSIN

TUNISIAN VICTORY
AMPAS. General Production File

BFI. Stills

MOMA

MPAA/PCA

NYPL

TYPEE
AMPAS. General Production File

AMPAS. John Huston Collection

NYPL

UNDERGROUND
AMPAS. General Production File

BFI. Stills

MOMA. Stills

MPAA/PCA

NYPL

UCLA. Movie Stills Collection

WISCONSIN

UNDER THE VOLCANO
AMPAS. General Production File

BFI. Stills

MOMA. Production File; Stills

NYPL

UCLA. Movie Stills Collection; Press Books, Presets, Other Publicity Material

THE UNFORGIVEN
AMPAS. General Production File

AMPAS. John Huston Collection

BFI. Press Book, Poster, Stills

MOMA. Production File; Stills

MPAA/PCA

NYPL

UCLA. Movie Stills Collection

VICTORY

AMPAS. General Production File

AMPAS. John Huston Collection

MOMA. Production File; Stills

NYPL

UCLA. Lobby Card Collection; Movie Stills Collection; Poster Collection

THE VISITOR

AMPAS. General Production File

MOMA

NYPL

UCLA. Movie Poster Collection

A WALK WITH LOVE AND DEATH

AMPAS. General Production File

AMPAS. John Huston Collection

BFI. Production File; Poster, Stills

MOMA. Production File; Stills

NYPL

UCLA. Lobby Card Collection; Poster Collection; Twentieth Century-Fox Archives, Stills

WATCH ON THE RHINE

USC. Warner Brothers Archives & Jack Warner Collection

WATERLOO

AMPAS. General Production File

AMPAS. John Huston Collection

MOMA

NYPL

UCLA. Movie Stills Collection; Poster Collection

WE WERE STRANGERS

AMPAS. General Production File

AMPAS. John Huston Collection

BFI. Stills

MOMA. Production File; Stills

MPAA/PCA

NYPL

UCLA. Lobby Card Collection

WHITE HUNTER, BLACK HEART

AMPAS. General Production File

BFI. Production File; Press Book

MOMA. Production File; Stills

NYPL

UCLA. Movie Stills Collection; Press Books, Press Kits, Other Publicity Material

WHO WAS THAT LADY?

AMPAS. General Production File

MOMA

MPAA/PCA

NYPL

UCLA. Lobby Card Collection

WILD BOYS OF THE ROAD

AMPAS. General Production File

BFI. Press Book, Stills

MOMA. Production File; Stills

MPAA/PCA

NYPL

WISCONSIN

WILL ADAMS

AMPAS. General Production File

AMPAS. John Huston Collection

MPAA/PCA

THE WIND AND THE LION

AMPAS. General Production File

BFI. Press Book, Stills

MOMA. Production File; Stills

NYPL

UCLA. Movie Stills Collection

WINTER KILLS

AMPAS. General Production File

AMPAS. John Huston Collection

BFI. Production File; Stills

MOMA. Production File; Stills

NYPL

UCLA. Movie Stills Collection

WISE BLOOD

AMPAS. General Production File

AMPAS. John Huston Collection

BFI. Poster, Stills

MOMA. Production File; Stills

NYPL

WOODROW WILSON. *See* IN TIME TO COME.

THE WORD

AMPAS. General Production File

NYPL

WUTHERING HEIGHTS

AMPAS. General Production File

BFI. Press Book, Stills

MOMA. Production File; Stills

MPAA/PCA

NYPL

UCLA. Movie Stills Collection; Press Books, Press Kits, Other Publicity Material

XX

The John Huston Collection: Production Files at the Academy of Motion Picture Arts and Sciences

One of the most important sources of information on John Huston are his papers, from about 1932 to 1981, on deposit at the Academy of Motion Picture Arts and Sciences (AMPAS), Beverly Hills. The papers after that time have either been destroyed or are dispersed elsewhere. According to Lawrence Grobel, "He also gave me his correspondence and files since 1980 (the previous years were at the library)" (*The Hustons,* New York, Scribners, 1989, xiv). In a conversation that we had with Grobel, he said that much of the material had been destroyed by Maricela Hernandez, John Huston's companion at his death, but Grobel turned over what he had to Huston's children, Tony and Anjelica, through the offices of Paul Kohner, Huston's longtime agent.

The Academy Library prepared an *Inventory to the John Huston Collection, Gift of John Huston, Material Received October 20, 1981,* compiled by Linda Harris Mehr, and supervised by Samuel A. Gill, archivist, in March 1982. We used this archive extensively in researching this book. Some parts of the collection remain uninventoried, and Mr. Gill very kindly provided us access to that material. During our research we were able to identify some unidentified and untitled material, which was then moved to designated files. The Academy plans to do an inventory update of Huston's papers. Its current inventory consists of Production files; Production Research; Script Material: Bound Scripts, Unbound Script Material; General Correspondence Files, Pre-1943 to 1981; St. Clerans; Autobiography; Publicity; Publications; Drawings; Photographs: Productions; Non-Production; Films: Productions—John Huston; Productions—Others; Home Movies; and Walter Huston. As the inventory has not been published (along with other inventories of other archival collections; see chapter 24) and for the most part has to be used in-house, we felt that researchers would find some value in seeing what infor-

661

mation is available in the production files. The other part of the inventory has been extensively detailed in chapter 16, "Screenplays in Collections," and chapter 23, "Huston-Related Films on Film, Video, and Laser Disc."

ACROSS THE RIVER AND INTO THE TREES
Notes regarding preliminary research; pages of dialogue; notes and letters from Gladys Hill about preliminary research; indication of possibility of transferring the story from World War I to World War II; a John Huston letter that the script was three-quarters finished; pages of a script by Huston and Gladys Hill; lists of books on World War II; letters to Huston regarding project; and correspondence with Mary Hemingway on various aspects of doing the film.

THE AFRICAN QUEEN
Correspondence regarding Katharine Hepburn's fees; letters between Katharine Hepburn and Huston regarding reviews of film; map of Kenya; a newspaper clipping reporting that Huston was thinking of Gertrude Lawrence for role and that Bette Davis had tried to get Warner Brothers to buy the rights; and an issue of *ABC Film Review* with an article on Huston.

ALOUETTE
Various telegrams and letters regarding Huston's interest in acquiring rights to the Jean Anouilh play and possible tax and residence problems in Ireland if he did; an indication that Anouilh himself might be interested in doing the script; cables regarding Kermit Bloomgarden and Harold Mirisch on doing the film; talks with Billy Wilder; and Huston's interest in having Suzanne Flon in the film. File contains a copy of *Joan;* play script by Jean Anouilh, translated by Lucienne Hill (with "The Lark" written on the cover).

Note. The published translation of the play in English is *The Lark.* Both Christopher Fry and Lillian Hellman have done translations. A Broadway production of the same name starred Julie Harris.

ANNIE
Casting notes with suggestions for Daddy Warbucks and interviews for Annie and Sandy, the dog; memo to David Begelman regarding possible cinematographers; letter from Jesse Jackson regarding positive image of blacks in film; research, locations, production schedules, pages of scripts, songs to be used, possible cameramen, and costume designers, cable from Budapest in which Huston accepts a deal with Columbia; Robert Mitchum considered for film; long letter from Ray Stark to Huston regarding various aspects of production, breakdown of musical numbers, and timing schedule for scenes; phone bills from Mexico that Huston charged to film; and newspaper articles on making the film.

THE ASPHALT JUNGLE

Casting—letters from actors and agents interested in the film; includes some doodles (faces) by Huston on a telegram; general production correspondence; memos on casting and legal business regarding name of city, street names, names of actors, use of local venues, and production code information; preview comments, Pickwood Theater, Los Angeles, February 16, 1950; letters of congratulations from Ira Gershwin, Howard Hawks, and José Ferrer; and publicity clippings and reviews from newspapers.

THE BARBARIAN AND THE GEISHA

Series of telegrams between Huston and Buddy Adler (executive head of production, Twentieth Century-Fox) regarding casting, John Wayne's salary, the producer, dailies, title of the film, and writers for screenplay; casting notes with requests from various people for roles in the film as actors, technical advisers, and makeup artists; employment agreement between Huston and Twentieth Century-Fox; correspondence with Eugene Frenke (producer) regarding possible titles, the character of Townsend Harris, the employment of Japanese technicians, weather conditions during shooting of film, cutting, publicity, reference to Romain Gary's comments about certain scenes in film, and Wayne's feelings about how he looks in film; letter to Isamu Noguchi regarding casting; advances to Huston and expenses; clipping on various aspects of Japanese life, casting problems, Japanese movie stars, and correspondence between Huston and various Japanese officials regarding assistance in making films; conflicts about screen credit in a letter from Charles Grayson to Huston; credit list; list of Japanese extras; publicity; choice of Japanese locales; and research on various aspects of the film.

BATTLE OF SAN PIETRO

Correspondence concerning Huston's desire to acquire a copy of the film from the Army Pictorial Center, Long Island City, New York, April 29, 1959; discussion about the short version (two reels) and longer version (five reels); memo from Huston to the Chief, Army Pictorial Service, regarding conflicts with officers as he went about making film; notes on San Pietro; RKO's involvement in doing dubbing; memo from Huston to Frank Capra regarding title; art work for title; correspondence and memos from Signal Corps regarding changes in dialogue, censorship, and depiction of the removal of American dead; script; congratulatory letters about the film; publicity releases; research on the 36th Infantry Division and the 143d Infantry Regiment; and recommendations for awards.

BEAT THE DEVIL

Correspondence with Humphrey Bogart regarding acquisition of property, use of color, reactions to first drafts of script, lack of comedy in script, Bogart's and Lauren Bacall's support for Adlai Stevenson for president, interest in Laurence Harvey and Peter Lorre for film, wardrobe, change of title, Anthony Veillers' feud with Romulus Films, and Bogart's

663

obligations to Warner Brothers to do the film before a Hepburn film that Huston was thinking of doing; censorship comments from Motion Picture Association of America (MPAA); correspondence between Huston and Claud Cockburn (author of novel) on Cockburn's attempt at a script; letter to Sol Lida on the film's intent; critical letters about the film after previews; an employment agreement; various documents on location shooting, signing of Jennifer Jones, finishing up *Moulin Rouge* before starting *Beat,* accepting Viertel and Veiller's version of the script, on Romulus's control of the film, on Bogart's approval of Peter Lorre for the film, Huston's severing of relations with Horizon Pictures, on Truman Capote's role in screenplay and with Veiller and Viertel; various letters from David O. Selznick regarding his objections to Jennifer Jones's role in picture, close-ups of her, the beach scene, her accent, the lack of a script, the timing of the production, the use of color, and critiquing various roles in film; "mock" credits; publicity; and reviews.

THE BERMUDA TRIANGLE

Correspondence and information on Huston's role as an actor in the film (playing the father, Edward Martin), his salary, and other arrangements; and a contract in Spanish from Conacine (Mexico) Production Co.

THE BIBLE

Numerous letters and memos from Dino De Laurentiis (producer) regarding his concern about various aspects of the film—notes on scenes, actors, sequences, animals, problems with George C. Scott, on using the music of Igor Stravinsky and Benjamin Britten, close-ups, shooting; correspondence with Darryl F. Zanuck; letter from Huston to De Laurentiis regarding Huston's displeasure with the Tree of Knowledge and serpents; documents on recording changes, suggestions for editing, a special for television, credits, sound effects for the Creation, revoicing of Eve, music needed for certain scenes, and billing for Ava Gardner; letter from Richard Burton to De Laurentiis praising him on film; letter from Huston to Ava Gardner urging her to be in the film; correspondence with Alec Guinness; letter to Charlie Chaplin regarding the film and asking him to portray Noah; notes on accounting and the transport of animals; details on shooting in Egypt; cables from Huston to Ernst Haas (Quito, Ecuador) indicating disappointment with nature scenes (too much pans and zooms, material flat and dull) and suggestions on how to shoot various sequences and what filters to use; travel arrangements, meeting agendas, and salary disputes; Huston on not wanting credit for his contributions to the screenplay; such correspondence regarding music as a letter from Leonard Bernstein that he is unable to help, contact with Jerry Goldsmith, and the music breakdown; extensive notes on script pages; installments of the Noah episode, Huston's suggestions for Noah montage, Garden of Eden cutting notes, Abraham's battle sequence, and various other handwritten notes; extensive information on publicity; reviews; shooting schedule; and call sheets.

BOLÍVAR

Letter and flyer from French camera company describing its product, indicating that the principals understand *Bolívar* will be Huston's next production, and inquiring whether he would be interested in their "anamorphic process 'Dyaliscope.'"

THE BRIDGE IN THE JUNGLE

Letter from Pancho Kohner (director) to Huston on Capricorn Productions letterhead (Mexico), about progress on the film and Huston's schedule for filming.

BY LOVE POSSESSED

Series of cables between Mark Cohen (Huston's attorney) and Huston regarding Huston's interest in doing this picture or *Typee* after the Darryl Zanuck film (*Roots*). Huston indicates his interest if writer mentioned in cable does script (cable or identity of the writer not included), but otherwise he will do *Typee*. Cohen discussed with Ray Stark the use of Lillian Hellman and asked Huston if he would accept Howard Koch as an alternate. Huston's response is a definite NO. Indication that United Artists can not accept Hellman and other aspects of the project.

CANNERY ROW

Letter from Paul Kohner to Huston in which a script is included, and correspondence asks Huston to do the narration and to play the role of Joe Blaikey.

THE CARDINAL

Collection of cables regarding preproductions, report dates, and press showing; premiere engagement; crew call sheet; and clippings regarding Huston in film and reviews.

CASINO ROYALE

Correspondence on various aspects of production—guns, grouse shooting, and crew; letter from Nunnally Johnson regarding possible script contribution; people expressing interest in being in film; letter to Huston from Deborah Kerr regarding the part and the script; letter to Huston from Charles Feldman, about Kerr's refusal (?) and possible alternatives; cable to Huston from Abe Schneider and Leo Jaffe with their best wishes on his participation in the film; and a letter from David Niven complimenting Huston on "what you have dreamed up for Sir J.B.!"

CIRCASIA

Announcement of Circasia '75, "A Circus Fantasy," and a invitation to attend; ringmaster John Huston, sponsored by Variety Club of Ireland; letter describing various events; Huston introduces cameo clowns Eric Clapton, Judy Geeson, Richard Harris, Shirley MacLaine, Burgess Meredith, Milo O'Shea, and Siobhan McKenna; and a program.

THE DECEIVERS
Memo by John Masters to Huston on *The Deceivers;* and a two-page synopsis by AE.M. (Aeneas MacKenzie?).

THE DESERTER
Loan out agreement for Huston.

THE DISENCHANTED
Correspondence with Bud Schulberg regarding Huston's possible interest in doing the film of Schulberg's novel, with Schulberg doing the first draft of the screenplay and the two of them polishing the script; letter from Ad Schulberg to Huston indicating Paramount's possible interest and Jerry Wald writes, definitely interested; also noted possible interest on part of Hal Wallis and David Selznick; and other additional correspondence regarding Huston's involvement in the project.

A FAREWELL TO ARMS
Two files available. Newspaper clippings from mostly the English and Italian press on the conflicts between Huston and David O. Selznick, on their "disagreement over the script," and on Huston's walking away from the film forty-eight hours before the start of shooting; and an extensive file of correspondence and twenty-six memos from Selznick to Huston regarding various aspects of the film, but especially the script. Includes a long memo from Selznick to Huston from March 4, 1957, in which Selznick says additional revisions to the script must stop and work begin; additional memos on other aspects of the movie (children in scenes and so on); and ends with March 18, 1957. The famous sixteen-page memo from Selznick to Huston (excerpted in *Memo from David O. Selznick,* New York, Viking Press, 1972, edited by Rudy Behlmer, and located in the Selznick Papers at the University Texas, Austin) that brought an end to their relationship on the film is not included in the AMPAS Huston papers.

FAT CITY
Correspondence regarding Huston being used in an Aer Lingus ad and working in credit for *Fat City;* correspondence with Leonard Gardner (novelist and screenwriter) on various aspects of script development with Huston's comments; correspondence with Paul Kohner and Rastar on various aspects of the film and a mention of Huston's involvement with *The Hostage* project; letter from Huston expressing interest in having Brando in film; notes on casting, estimated footage for each scene, and the premiere at the Museum of Modern Art; notes on a screenplay version dated November 4 after detailed discussions between Huston and Gardner; publicity,* including clippings from various newspapers regarding the development of project, interviews with Huston, and comments by various critics on Cannes screening; press kit for Cannes screening; and correspondence with Ray Stark on various aspects of the film.

Note. *Additional publicity material is included in an uninventoried part of the archives.

FORGOTTEN BOY

Correspondence indicating that William Wyler would direct the film; references to novels, stories, newspaper articles, and magazine articles on boys cast out on their own because of the depression; memo from John Huston to Henry Henigson, March 29, 1933, requesting books and magazines dealing with the subject; extensive research and compliments from Wyler on article appearing in *New Republic* (March 8, 1933); reference to John Steinbeck's "Their Blood is Strong," an April 1938 story on migratory workers in California; file of memos, including one on Wyler's assignment to do a film with Tom Mix starring; memo to Henry Henigson from Wyler, May 17, 1933, indicating that he was in La Quinta working with John Huston on the project; memo from Henry Henigson to Wyler, April 13, 1933, stating that upon completion of the script's first draft with Huston, Wyler should send a copy to Henigson, who will forward it to Mr. Van Every and then take action.

Note. Production files in AMPAS, William Wyler Collection.

FRANKIE AND JOHNNY

Correspondence regarding Huston's original marionette play and requests by others to use his book and ideas for a musical; letter from Ray Stark to Gwen Verdon in which he encloses Huston's screenplay for *Frankie and Johnny* and suggests that while Huston isn't available perhaps she would be interested in doing a musical based on it; and a cover letter from Ray Stark to Huston regarding a confidential report from Bill Fadiman on the screenplay that Huston and Anthony Veiller developed.

FREUD: THE SECRET PASSION

Letter from Dr. Stephen Black (psychiatrist) to Huston in which he comments on script (nine-page document); budget documents; cost breakdown; casting information including a letter from Shelley Winters in which she expresses her desire to be in the film; censorship from the MPAA regarding various aspects of the film; cutting notes; correspondence from Doc Erickson (production manager); general correspondence including the Freud family's objections to using Ernest Jones's biography on Freud as a basis of the film, photos of Freud, music, and dubbing; general production information, such as correspondence with Freud's nephew, Edward Bernays, regarding family involvement and his work on the scripts; two files of extensive correspondence from William Gordon and script analysis; three-page document from Stephen Grimes (art director) on dream sequences; correspondence with Charles Kaufman (screenwriter) on various aspects of screenplay; various notes and documents on pages from the script and particular scenes; preview comments; publicity clippings; press kits; correspondence from

Wolfgang Reinhardt on various aspects of Jean-Paul Sartre's script; reviews; shooting schedule; correspondence regarding Sartre's involvement with the film, including a long letter from Sartre to Huston indicating his uphappiness with Huston and virtually everything else about the film; correspondence with Mel Tucker regarding script changes, his pleasure with rushes, Huston's displeasure with the title, cuts, length of film, suggestion to have an intermission, street scene, and Jewish aspects; and background on writers' involvement, Sartre's role, credits for writers, and an analysis of various writers' contributions to script.

GOYA

Correspondence regarding Huston's having received a first treatment from Titanus Films and a first draft screenplay by Talbot Jennings.

HARROW ALLEY

Letter to Huston from Keep Films Ltd. regarding the company's desire to have him do *Becket* and be involved in *Harrow Alley;* correspondence with Huntington Hartford to get him interested; budget figures; possible cast; correspondence between Paul Kohner and Ingo Preminger on Huston being the only director considered and on his being dropped since he had not done anything for six months; a follow-up from Preminger to Huston stating that Preminger had rights and wanted Huston to do the film with a great cast—Richard Burton, Peter O'Toole, Alec Guinness, and even Huston; and a letter indicating collapse of project because financing couldn't be raised.

HASSAN

Letter regarding interest by Fox, a possible deal with Buddy Adler, and Huston mentioned as director; and notes from Nigel Balchin (screenwriter) that Sophia Loren, José Ferrer, and James Mason were being thought of for film.

HEAD ON

Agreement regarding Huston's acting in the film, starting date, and correspondence regarding work applications in Canada.

HEAVEN KNOWS, MR. ALLISON

Employment agreement with John Huston; correspondence regarding Deborah Kerr and her wardrobe; memos from Buddy Adler (producer) on the script; shooting schedule; relationship between Deborah Kerr and the Robert Mitchum character; dream sequence; letter from Huston (from Tobago) regarding shooting and Mitchum's attitude; the turtle sequence; and a letter from Jerry Wald praising film.

THE HORSE OF SELENE

Correspondence, including press kit of reviews on Juanita Casey's novel of the same name, Tim Vignoles's option to rights, the cost of film, Juanita Casey's preparing the first treatment, Huston's interest; Hugh Leonard, who was to do screenplay, declines and notes that Huston should be involved in developing the screenplay and collaborating with the novelist; Huston's desire to do film in late summer 1972; and Vignoles asks Huston to be writer, director, and producer.

THE HOSTAGE

Correspondence with Irving Paul Lazar regarding percentange of profits for Brendan Behan's widow, Beatrice; Lazar asking Huston whether he is interested in *Borstal Boy;* and a letter from Rastar to Paul Kohner discussing Huston's involvement with *The Hostage* and *Fat City* and the options that if one doesn't work out Huston will do *Fat City* rather than *The Hostage*.

INDEPENDENCE

Location photos; correspondence with Huston, various dates in 1974 and 1975, regarding preparation for the film; press clippings on shooting the film; possible actors for roles; cast list; shooting schedule, June 16, 1975, to June 25, 1975; press kit.

Note. This file is located in the uninventoried part of the archives.

IN TIME TO COME

Clippings on stage play written by Howard Koch and John Huston, based on Woodrow Wilson and the League of Nations (1941); and reviews.

ISRAELI FILM PROJECT

1971, background materials, all located in an uninventoried part of the archives.

JAGUAR LIVES

Correspondence regarding Huston's involvement with the film as an actor; salary; and a script (transferred to screenplay collection).

JOAN (THE LARK). *See* ALOUETTE.

JUDAS

Cable from John Huston to Paul Kohner indicating extreme interest in Marcel Pagnol's play and in having Marlon Brando act and Pagnol do script; cable from Huston to Pagnol praising his play; letter to a priest from Huston requesting the priest's reaction to the play and following correspondence; additional cables—regarding the project with mention of Brando and Charles Laughton and of a conversation with Burt Lancaster regarding the Centurion role; from Harold Hecht to Huston requesting a copy of play; from Kohner to Huston regarding Allied awaiting the priest's reaction and, barring any serious objection, wanting a conference on how Huston proposes to treat subject matter, location, Brando's unavailability, and whether Montgomery Clift or Gregory Peck might be interested.

John Huston

KEY LARGO
Index to breakdown, final script, November 17, 1947; memos regarding censorship; letter from Huston to Margaret Chase regarding the film, its theme, and his philosophy of filming; production code objections; Jerry Wald memos; note from Lillian Ross (on *New Yorker* letterhead) and allusion to her doing a piece on *We Were Strangers* but magazine vetoed it; fan letters; inserts for script; publicity and review clippings; shooting schedule; and call sheets.

KNOW YOUR ENEMY: JAPAN
Memo listing office items issued to Major Huston; memo to Frank Capra about the film being shipped to him; use of *Mikado* in film; and geographic places.

THE KREMLIN LETTER
Cable from Darryl Zanuck to Richard Zanuck, April 1, 1968, regarding his comments on the first eighty-seven pages of the script; folder on casting with stills, correspondence, and other documents regard film, including analysis of the script (n.d., no authors) and censorship matters.*

Note. *This information is located in uninventoried part of the archives.

THE LAST RUN
Preliminary documentation on various aspects of Huston's involvement with film; memo for record by Lucie Lichtig, Stephen Grimes, and Mr. Fairfax regarding Huston's replacement; details regarding script problems and conflicts with George C. Scott and Huston's removal from the film; and lawyers' letters regarding possible lawsuits.

LAUGHING BOY
Preproduction information as Huston and William Wyler developed project, suggested possibilities for cast, and letters to various people, August 1932. Notes with returned photos, indicating that production had been postponed; location scouting, July 1932, with photos of Southwest, Monument Valley, El Capitan, and Grand Canyon (Wyler in some photos, but not Huston; was he taking the photos [?]); music; and a research file that includes "A Brief Outline of Navajo Customs and Traditions" by Earl Haley, n.d., 9 p.*

Note. *Material located in uninventoried part of the archives. AMPAS, William Wyler Collection, includes correspondence from Oliver La Farge to William Wyler, February 14, 1933 (original sent to Myron Selznick, February 20, 1933), expressing his distress that Wyler nor Universal will do the film.

LET THERE BE LIGHT

Letter from Huston to Gen. W. C. Menninger about the U.S. Army's reluctance to release the film for public viewing; correspondence with *Harper's Bazaar* on its article on the film in the May 1946 issue; additional correspondence from Menninger indicating that the U.S. Army is searching out distribution of the film; Huston's letter to Arthur Mayer of Rialto Theater asking to get him to show the film; Archer Winster's (*New York Post*) letter to Huston praising the film and discussing its seizure before the Museum of Modern Art's scheduled screening; various correspondence regarding the U.S. Army's imposing "for official use only" designation on film; a press release from Museum of Modern Art regarding its series "The Documentary Film" and the War Department's refusal to allow eight films, including *Let There Be Light,* to be shown; a memo from MGM to Huston stipulating that it would store Huston's personal print of film in the library's film vaults for him; and correspondence from Amos Vogel, executive secretary, Cinema 16, that he wants to devote the 1956–57 season to Huston's work, including *Let There Be Light.*

THE LIFE AND TIMES OF JUDGE ROY BEAN

Estimated footage summary; note to Ava Gardner that she will want to do film "on reading this"; staff and crew list; scoring and dubbing schedule; main title, roll up, and paid ad information; letter from the British Board of Censors to Huston regarding objections to certain aspects of the film, especially its violence and the expression *piss off;* press kit with cast and synopsis; and clippings from various newspapers.

THE LIST OF ADRIAN MESSENGER

In the casting file—suggestions, letters and photos from agents promoting actors, letters from actors directly to Huston, and cast tests; correspondence regarding the script, notes about the fox hunt, and Frank Sinatra's agreement to be in the film; memo on location phase; information on set list, movement order, call sheet, looping, tentative finishing schedule, editing, and revised finishing schedule; clippings and reviews; and daily production reports.

LONELY PASSION OF JUDITH HEARNE

Correspondence regarding Huston's interest in acquiring rights; play script submitted to Huston for his consideration; letter from Richard Widmark to Huston on his interest in doing film; and Katharine Hepburn's expression of interest and caveat that she doesn't want to leave the United States.

LYSISTRATA

Letter from Gilbert Seldes regarding his producing the play, his understanding that Huston is interested in doing a film, and his interest in being involved in developing the script; letter from Hans Holzer to Huston asking

Huston to direct the play and film; and Huston's response, indicating some interest.

THE MADWOMAN OF CHAILLOT
Letter from Huston expressing his interest in doing a film of the Jean Giraudoux play; crew list; letter indicating Katharine Hepburn's happiness that Huston was willing to direct film and includes Huston's feelings about the script; and various memos regarding casting.

A MAN FOR ALL SEASONS
Correspondence with Fred Zinnemann in which he expresses interest in having Huston act as Duke of Norfolk, schedule of days Huston would work, his compensation, and the script sent to him.

THE MAN WHO WOULD BE KING
Pages from script; cables regarding rights to material, Clark Gable's possible role in film (cf. also Screenplay section, USC, Clark Gable Archives), and Humphrey Bogart's unavailability; Huston's prologue to the film and his handwriting with typescript; correspondence regarding legal matters on using Rudyard Kipling's material; correspondence on locations and logistics in filming in India and tax liabilities; cable from Huston to Gable indicating the Indian locations being scouted and inviting him on a tiger hunt with one of the maharaja; a piece of stationery with Huston's drawing of a man's face and the film's title as letterhead; cable from Gable to Huston saying that he wanted to join Huston but he was shooting in Hong Kong *Soldier of Fortune;* and follow-up cables regarding Huston and Gable getting together; cast and times of radio broadcast starring Dan O'Herlihy; correspondence with Aeneas MacKenzie and Mark Cohen (Huston's attorney) regarding writing the script with MacKenzie; the preproduction budget; summary of discussion regarding film and notes on possible objections to some aspects of the script; legal documents regarding Huston's role in the film; financing of the film; color equipment available in India; suggested shooting sequences by Stephen Grimes; cast and trip itineraries; draft letter from Huston to David Begelman on various aspects of making the film; letter from Peter Guber to John Foreman regarding changes required after the film's screening at Columbia Pictures; letter from Emmanuel Wolf, president and chairman of Allied Artists Picture Corporation, to Huston indicating some cuts that he would like to see; letters to Huston from Allied indicating box office receipts; publicity clippings and reviews; correspondence with Ray Stark; notes on the possible use of Marlon Brando and Cary Grant; copy of letter to Stark from Grimes regarding shooting and scouting schedules and results of location trip; cable to Richard Burton regarding his being in the film; long cable from Stark to Huston regarding financial arrangements and Huston's tax problems; and MPAA objections and approval of script.*

Note. *Additional production file material is located in uninventoried part of the archives. Included are casting information; summary of meetings in Madrid, August 15, 1974 to August 16, 1974, that Huston and Hill attended; production meetings; movement orders; call sheets; credits; and publicity.

MATADOR

Correspondence of Huston's interest in doing the film with José Ferrer; financial matters; rights to be purchased by Huston Corporation; suggestion for stars from agents; plans to start filming in spring 1953; cable from Mark Cohen (Huston's attorney) indicating purchase of movie rights; and memos regarding other groups wanting to do the film, Barnaby Conrad's interest in buying back the rights, and Ferrer's and Huston's agreement to sell the rights.

THE MINES OF SULPHUR

Correspondence regarding the opera that Huston directed at La Scala in 1966. Includes log of rehearsals taken by Gladys Hill, synopsis of opera, La Scala's program, and Sadler's Wells' opera program.

THE MISFITS

Correspondence with Doc Erickson (production manager) regarding Marilyn Monroe, location sites, production problems, the film's reception at its Reno opening, *Freud: The Secret Passion* and *The Man Who Would Be King,* and the use of Bill Hornbeck and Tom Shaw in film; Huston's interest in G. W. Pabst's "Secret of the Soul"; the Legion of Decency's objections to "fanny slapping" in the film; general information on finishing up the shooting, on setting up Mitchum for film (?), Monroe and Arthur Miller, on negotiations with Gable, and on medical insurance for Huston; correspondence with Bill Harrah regarding the mention of Harrah's in the film; letter from David O. Selznick on how much Jennifer and he loved the film; accounting information; staff list; letters and notes from Miller to Huston regarding various aspects of the script, the use of Marilyn Monroe, and Huston's reactions to the submitted script; Huston's contact with Gable to do the film; Panther Books (London) expressing interest in doing a novelization of the script; clippings regarding the making of the film; narration for a 16mm twenty-minute featurette "The Making of 'The Misfits'"; publicity clippings*; Humane Society concerns; reviews; horse-roping sequence, sketches by Stephen Grimes (art director); galleys for "The Story of the Misfits" by James Goode; and wardrobe and sketches.

Note. *Press clippings on *The Misfits* and other films are also included in the uninventoried part of the archives.

John Huston

MOBY DICK.
With more than forty files available this production file is one of the largest in the John Huston Collection. Numerous letters to Huston regarding the search for a three-mast ship for the film; Viking Press's proposal to Huston about writing a book on making the film; correspondence with Ralph Brinton about the "mechanized whale" and research for the *Pequod* and the New Bedford Harbor; preliminary correspondence with Ray Bradbury in which Bradbury compliments Huston on previous projects, Bradbury's signs to do *Moby Dick,* others' early script developments, Bradbury informs Huston of his progress on various sections of the script, and Bradbury alludes to Huston's being uncomfortable "unless death was near" and to Bradbury's feelings of Huston's parallel with Ahab; correspondence with Tyrus Hillway, associate professor at Colorado State College, in which Hillway indicated historical inaccuracies of certain details of the Bradbury script; various correspondence regarding screen credit, such as whether Bradbury should be sole writer of credit, Huston's surprise that somehow this issue went to arbitration with the SAG (Charles Grayson's and Bob Rossen's names also mentioned), a letter from Bradbury apologizing, continuing controversy in which Huston claims that Bradbury did do an early version himself but that they closely collaborated on subsequent versions, the submission of the script in which markings indicate Bradbury's and Huston's contributions (cf. also chapter 16, "Screenplays in Collections"), and the final arbitration in which both got credit for the screenplay; casting sheet as of April 23, 1954 (Gregory Peck, Leo Glenn, Montgomery Clift as Ishmael, and so on), other correspondence regarding such actors for the film as Kirk Douglas), artists' tests for roles, and responses from various actors interested in parts; correspondence regarding Cinemascope for the film; correspondence with Robert Clarke, National Institute of Oceanographers, regarding his providing "factual" information for ensuring the script's accuracy and his request that his organization and other historical organizations receive credit for their help; personal letters to Huston congratulating him on the film; correspondence with Roald Dahl on his connection with developing the script; notes on meetings; movement orders to Youghal and Cork County; shots for the second unit; discussions on shooting certain scenes; the BBC "script" on the shooting of the film; shooting schedule for mechanical whales and miniatures; shots still to be done to complete film's in-sequence order; comments following continuity of picture screened at Stanley-Warners, March 5, 9 P.M.; Huston's schedules during shooting of the film; Huston's health condition, examinations, and his insurance while shooting the film; numerous correspondence on various aspects of the film with Lehman (Lee) Katz (associate producer), many on letterhead—Associated British Pictures Corporation, Ltd., and Moulin Products Ltd.; information on Friedrich Ledebur (Queequeg); schedules for various locations, the staff required at those times, and scenes to be shot at various locations; main title information with background shots of old whaling photographs and prints; correspondence with Harold Mirisch (Allied Artists Productions); Huston's original letterhead drawings of himself and the whale; shooting sequences; music notes; musical score;

correspondence and notes with Oswald Morris, cinematographer, and drawings outlining lighting aspects; correspondence and a copy of Gregory Peck's contract; information regarding various premieres; official program for world premiere in the guise of an issue of *Time* magazine; program for Hollywood opening, July 2, 1956; publicity and radio interviews (script included); "The Ed Sullivan Show" (script of a "John Huston Tribute" the last week of November 1954 [?]); copies of a "news bulletin" with Huston's drawings and letterhead in progress during shooting; drafts of magazine articles; story board drawings on opening of film; publicity clippings in the press; numerous articles on the film from the *Standard-Times* of New Bedford, Massachusetts; research material on filming at sea in sailing ships; correspondence with the Melville Society; sound, including post-synching for various reels; correspondence with and regarding Orson Welles's role in film; correspondence with Peter Nobel, who wrote Huston about the biography he was writing on Orson Welles, and Huston's response about his experiences working with Welles on the film; special effects, including minutes of notes regarding tank scenes, mechanization of the whale, and other special effects; and correspondence regarding making *Moby Dick* into an opera and play.

MONTEZUMA
Correspondence between Paul Kohner and Eugene Frenke regarding this property and in having Huston involved with generous financial arrangements; reports that Kirk Douglas might be interested; and an issue of the *Hollywood Reporter* that notes Huston's and Douglas's involvement in a project to start shooting in summer 1961.

MOULIN ROUGE
Correspondence between Huston and the MPAA, including the British Board of Censors, regarding censorship of the script; letters to Huston from Ray Bradbury, Dean Rusk, and David O. Selznick with their reactions to the film; publicity clippings; call sheets; correspondence with Oswald Morris; an invitation to the premiere screening; correspondence regarding music, including lyrics by Paul Dehn for "The Banks of the Seine"; and contractual arrangements between Huston and Romulus Films.

THE NIGHT OF THE IGUANA
Memos regarding Gavin Lambert's treatment of the play (80 p.); correspondence among Tennessee Williams, Anthony Veiller, and John Huston regarding their version of the script; correspondence with Ray Stark; correspondence from William Fadiman to Gladys Hill regarding Williams's contributions to the script so that credit can be assigned; notice of tentative writing credits, from January 14, 1964, indicating "Screenplay by Anthony Veiller and John Huston from Broadway play by Tennessee Williams"; notes from Frank Sinatra and others congratulating Huston on the film; correspondence with

675

John Huston

Stephen Grimes (art director) on various aspects of shooting the film; expenses for Huston and Gladys Hill; music breakdown; publicity; reviews; and title drawings, including Huston's doodles (a man's face).

NINA
Correspondence from Hemdale Pictures indicating that the company would like John Huston to play the leading role of Edward Granville and asking for his commitment for five weeks; and the screenplay sent to Huston.

NO EXIT
Documentation on Huston's involvement as the director of the New York stage play—the contract; Paul Bowles doing the adaptation of Jean-Paul Sartre's play, with Thornton Wilder also involved; Huston's interest in signing Katharine Hepburn; Judith Anderson also considered; and reviews.

PATTON
Correspondence from Frank McCarthy (producer) to Huston regarding rights Darryl Zanuck bought to Gen. George Patton's biography, Francis Ford Coppola doing the first draft, Burt Lancaster's interest, Zanuck approaching Paul Kohner to assess Huston's interest and availability, a copy of the biography sent to Huston, a summary of the book; Huston's response detailing his interest and his conflicting prior commitments to *Will Adams* and *Waterloo;* continuing correspondence with interest in having Huston direct; additional scripts sent to Huston; and Richard Zanuck's and Darryl Zanuck's continuing interest in Huston being involved.

PHOBIA
Crew list; correspondence between producers and Huston; immigration application from Canada for Huston to direct *Phobia* from September 10, 1970, to April 30, 1980, for $350,000; anti-Semetic letter regarding the film; memo regarding scene changes; shooting schedule; reshoot schedule; press kit; Andrew H. Malcolm's December 11, 1979, *New York Times* article on Huston: "I Want to keep Right on Going," on location with Huston at the shooting of film and an interview with Huston.

PORTRAIT OF THE ARTIST AS YOUNG MAN
Approach from Amicus Productions, with screenplay enclosed, to determine Huston's interest in directing; pleased with his positive reaction to screenplay, the company asked whether he has any ideas on casting; financial matters; suggestions for cast; and an indication that financing fell through.

PRELUDE TO FREEDOM
Correspondence from M. L. Gunzburg regarding a project the two of them developed, questioning the whereabouts of their early script treatments, and expressing Gunzburg's interest in wanting to resubmit the project.

676

THE PRINCE AND THE SHOWGIRL
Publicity clippings showing that Huston was considered to direct.

QUO VADIS
Correspondence regarding casting; preproduction information about music tempo tracks, breakdown of atmosphere people, the search for an assistant director, wardrobe estimates, start and finish dates for cast, and test scenes; revised shooting schedule, atmosphere people revised, summary atmosphere people, general information regarding travel in Italy, and personnel for Italy from the United States; memo from Huston to Dore Schary asking for Albert Band's services; cable from Huston to Suzanne Flon stating that shooting is postponed until the following spring; Albert Band's reaction to the script; principal male characters; bits and extras; preliminary shooting schedule; and a clipping regarding Huston's directing and Gregory Peck's eye infection, which postponed the film.

THE RED BADGE OF COURAGE
Casting information—various actors expressing interest, memos to Huston from Fletcher Markle and Jose Pasternak, telegrams from Louis Calhern, agents' letters regarding their clients, a letter from Will Geer to Huston, and a screen test list; memos from Huston to Dore Schary regarding an estimate on making the film; crew and cast list; congratulatory letter from Schary to Huston on the film; publicity material; letter to Huston from Gottfried Reinhardt (producer) about MGM's destruction of negative cutouts; letter regarding Audie Murphy's legal problems; and a bound copy of Lillian Ross's *New Yorker* articles (May through June 1952) on the making of *The Red Badge of Courage*, "A Saga of a Monster and a Movie."

REFLECTIONS IN A GOLDEN EYE
Various documents from Ernie Anderson (publicity manager) regarding Huston's methods; information on the Cannes Film Festival; extensive information on the color processing used in the film; editing—"start" and "end" sections on twelve reels of film; various telegrams regarding aspects of the film from Doc Erickson (production supervisor); breakdown of scenes regarding design, costumes, discrepancies with chronological time, and proposed shooting schedule; confidential interoffice memo to Ray Stark from William Fadiman regarding treatment (65 p.) from Doc Erickson to Fadiman and detailed analysis with criticism of the treatment's various aspects; letters about casting, medical certification, and crew list; main title billing; extensive correspondence between Huston and Carson McCullers and correspondence with Virginia Spencer Cox, who wrote the biography of McCullers; some letters and analysis of *Reflections* to Ray Stark, concerns about subject matter, setting, and commerciality of the film; correspondence and telegrams from Charles Chapman Mortimer (screenwriter) regarding travel arrangements and his work on the film; telegram from Huston to Mortimer praising his script;

correspondence and telegrams from Alex North regarding music for the film; telegrams to Benjamin Britten, John Cage, and Samuel Barber to ascertain their interest in doing the score; publicity, clippings, and reviews; correspondence with Ray Stark regarding various aspects of film—casting, reference to Francis Ford Coppola's script, a confidential letter to Elizabeth Taylor regarding her role, and Montgomery Clift's death and his replacement, Marlon Brando; Brando's role, salary, and so on; an MPAA letter to William Fadiman about the script; a letter from Sue Mengers regarding Julie Harris's interest in film; letter to Ray Stark from Gloria Steinem analyzing the script; production schedule, contract and salary disputes, and postproduction work; and correspondence from Elizabeth Taylor on different aspects of the film.

REMINISCENCES OF A COWBOY
Various press clippings—Huston to direct an adaptation of Frank Harris's book, produced by Horizon and released by Columbia, Montgomery Clift and Walter Huston to appear in the film following Huston's directing of *Quo Vadis,* and Peter Viertel to do screenplay; letter to Huston from attorneys notifying him that he had rights to the book; and a later letter to Huston from Julian Blaustein regarding the version of *Reminiscences* released as *Cowboy* (the shooting version did not indicate Huston's involvement, writing credits were to be determined, and Huston professed no involvement with the script).

REPORT FROM THE ALEUTIANS
File contains photographs of and commendations for pilots, some killed on a mission over Kiska; Navy Department communiqués; press releases regarding Dutch Harbor activity; Naval Air Defenders of Alaska decorated; U.S. Army casualties in the Alaskan area; letter from John Huston to General Landrum, November 9, 1942, regarding activities in Adak and the material his cameras covered; travel order to Capt. John M. Huston from Capt. A. E. Minnick, Signal Corps, December 17, 1942, ordering Huston to proceed on or about December 19, 1942, from Washington, D.C., to Hollywood, California, for approximately thirty days' temporary duty in connection with photographic activities of the Signal Corps; War Department document from December 28, 1942, in which the signees agree that they have viewed a restricted motion picture titled *At the Front with the U.S. Army in Alaska* and that they will abide by restrictions of secrecy; memo from the Military Intelligence Service, March 11, 1943, to Maj. Richard W. Maibaum, indicating suggested changes and asking to see the "final" draft and to review it before its release; an annotated script; budgetary matters involving Twentieth Century-Fox and Disney Studios; congratulatory letters to Huston about the film; newspaper clippings; and a personnel roster (n.d., no indication of what film it is, and lists James Wong Howe as cameraman; Jules Buck, still man; Jack McEdwards, unit manager; Meyer Levin or Pvt. Dashiell Hammett, writer; William Mellor, Peter Keene, and George Robert Eyerman, cameramen; but this film may not

be related to the Aleutian film as various filmographies do not show Howe making wartime documentaries).

RICHARD III

Correspondence from Romulus expressing the company's interest in having Huston direct and sending him script; suggestions for cast—José Ferrer, Claire Bloom, Michael Redgrave, John Gielgud, Paul Scofield, and Laurence Harvey; cable from Huston with his commitment; number of cables and letters from Huston trying to get Marlon Brando interested in doing Richard; letter from Brando to Huston declining Huston's offer; and Huston's cable saying he would not participate if Brando was not interested.

ROOTS OF HEAVEN

Preliminary correspondence including four-page synopsis of Romain Gary's novel; photocopy of employment agreement between Huston and Darryl F. Zanuck Productions; correspondence with Patrick Leigh-Fermor (cowriter with Gary), including a lyric by John Huston, "Paddy at Nara," Kyoto, Japan, January 17, 1958 (doggerel, "The Paddy" being Leigh-Fermor); correspondence with Romain Gary, including some script scenes; reviews of the Gary novel; reaction to long synopsis of Gary's novel by Frank McCarthy to Buddy Adler and David Brown, April 24, 1957; transportation order for May 28, 1958, with Huston doodle; reviews; letter from Burt Lancaster to Huston (4 p.) in which he critiques the novel and says that he is unable to do the film; critique on the "scripting of Gary's novel" by Aeneas MacKenzie; visa procedures; correspondence and cables to Huston from Darryl Zanuck and Richard Zanuck; and clippings of reviews.

THE SHOES OF THE FISHERMAN

Correspondence and cables from George Englund* showing that a script was sent to Huston and that he wanted Huston to see a revised script.

Note. *Englund produced the MGM version, released in 1968. No scripts are in the Huston Collection, Screenplay.

SINFUL DAVEY*

Portfolio, with photos, of actors interviewed, including Colin Blakely, Nigel Davenport, Ronald Fraser, John Hurt, Ian McShane, and Charlotte Rampling; cast lists; completion schedule; music "starts" and "ends" with footage; the text of a speech (14 p.) Huston gave to the president of Ireland and others on the occasion of shooting the film in Ireland; correspondence with James Webb (screenwriter), including "rough copy of proposed changes and suggestions," March 30, 1967; Webb's April 10, 1967, notes on Davey Haggart; notes on a conversation with James Webb, April 21, 1967; notes on the Cliff Hanley script, June 1, 1967; and tests for certain scenes.

Note. *The uninventoried section of the archives includes additional production materials, casting, progress reports, call sheets, press notices, and a production schedule.

TARAS BULBA
Two cables—one from Eugene Frenke to Huston stating that he is working on a screenplay of Nikolai Gogol's *Taras Bulba* and that if Huston is interested he should cable his reaction; the second is Huston's response, telling Frenke to discuss *Taras Bulba* with Kohner and then asking Frenke about the *Montezuma* script.

A TERRIBLE BEAUTY
Unrealized project. File* contains correspondence; treatments regarding project based on the 1916 Irish uprising; a number of Paul Kohner letters; clippings, including an article from *Irish Independent,* November 11, 1968, indicating that Huston will do the picture in Ireland; screenplay to be written by Gerald Hanley, who discussed a treatment (60 p.) with Huston (not included in archives); chronology, n.d., no author, 8 p.; note that Charles Wood would be involved if the Hanley script is not good; Huston's notes, December 12, 1968 (2 p.); problems, Gerald Hanley, December 12, 1968 (9 p.); letters to Paul Kohner from David Higham, Hanley's agent, in which caption reads: "The Easter Uprising—Gerald Hanley/John Huston, April 21, 1969, and April 22, 1969."

Note. *This production file is located in the uninventoried part of the archives.

THE TREASURE OF THE SIERRA MADRE
Clippings from trade journals on the Academy Awards; congratulatory letters from Dudley Nichols, Ray Stark, Adolph Deutsch, Rex Ingram, and Abraham Polonsky; report on motion picture equipment, studios, and personnel in Mexico; research department answers to Huston's queries on mining laws in Mexico; wild tracks and post-synchronizations still to be done for the picture; interview schedules; salaries for construction crews; copy of Breen Office letter regarding the script and objections; final cast list; publicity material; reviews; story board sketches; letters from T [Traven?] to Paul Kohner (August 29, 1940), Herbert Kline (October 11, 1941), Paul Kohner (December 29, 1941 [B.T.]), John Huston (September 3, 1946 [B.T.]), and John Huston (September 2, 1946 [B.T.]); letter from Huston to Traven (December 30, 1946) on plans and expectations about the film, that Humphrey Bogart and Walter Huston are on the set, and that Ronald Reagan and Zachary Scott are being considered for Curtin and Lacaud (Cody); Traven to Huston (January 4, 1947) that "Bogart will be great as Dobbs"; Traven to Kohner (November 17, 1941 [?]); Traven to Huston (January 6, 1947); screenplay, business: mining

of gold, with drawings of tent, mining construction (no author or date, but in Traven file); and correspondence with Huston on various aspects of the film, script development, and pages of the script dated February 1947 and signed H. C. (Hal Croves, or Traven?).

TYPEE

Correspondence and cables regarding shooting the film in the South Pacific; letter from Huston indicating the start of operations in June 1957; information on the script and cost; continuing interest on Huston's part; sheet music; cable from Harold Mirisch stating that Stephen Grimes will work on the film; cables from Grimes to Huston about the studio instructing them to stop work on the film; copy of letter or cable from Huston about plane reservation and weather problems, calling off production for year, but still thinking of doing preproduction work; another letter to Huston from Grimes that Allied doesn't appear to be interested anymore, but he is still scouting locations; and a letter from Huston's secretary indicating that the film has been postponed indefinitely.

THE UNFORGIVEN

Employment agreement for John Huston to commence November 15, 1958, from Contemporary Productions, Inc.; letter from Herb Jaffe Associates, Agents, about different actors for the film; letter from Oswald Morris to Huston about the Hecht/Lancaster organization wanting him to photograph the film; and cables regarding pre- and postproduction.

VICTORY

Correspondence regarding various aspects of filming; casting; staff and crew lists; general visa information; people expressing interest in being cast in film; "The Game Plan, 2d Unit Photography," May 26, 1980, shooting days and so on; revised unit list; revised shooting schedule; call sheets; postproduction schedule; publicity; clippings; press kit; color sketches of players in uniform; and a drawing of prisoner of war camp.

A WALK WITH LOVE AND DEATH*

Production budget; British Film Institute/Monthly Film Bulletin articles (February 1977); correspondence on various aspects of the film; letter from Bertrand Tavernier to Huston (received January 1, 1970) about a previous interview that he did with Huston, to be published in *Positif* (previously scheduled for *Cahiers*), and his desire to get the film shown in Paris and to provide publicity for it; releases by Ernie Anderson (publicity) on all aspects of the film, for press and so on; statement by Stephen Grimes; new biographical sketch on John Huston and a chronological account running through 1969; chronological records of Huston's work as a director; biography of Stephen Grimes; biography of other principals, including Ted Scaife; piece on Huston, Hans Koningsberger, and Dale Wasserman; synopsis; Huston on directing his own daughter; and reviews.

Note. *Uninventoried part of the archives includes staff list and historical background material.

WATERLOO
Correspondence about Huston's involvement and speculation when he will be able to make the picture; casting information; correspondence from Huston to Cecil Woodham Smith trying to interest him in working on the screenplay; two-page summary of meeting regarding the film and the discussion about various scenes; notes that Richard Burton was being considered for Napoleon's role; communication between De Laurentiis and Huston regarding various aspects of screenplay development; and memo to De Laurentiis from Samuel Marx on various aspects of script, casting, and his problems with continuing with Huston as the director.

WE WERE STRANGERS
Publicity material; women's group protests that the film is Communist propaganda; review; gifts for the crew; telegram from Peter Kass indicating that John Garfield needs work badly; and memos from David O. Selznick regarding his displeasure with original title, final editing, Jennifer's performance, miserable cutting, and so forth.

WILL ADAMS
Long letter from Huston to Jules Buck regarding accusations against Huston made behind his back regarding the development of screenplay between Buck and Dalton Trumbo; further discussion about other projects; numerous drafts handwritten and typed by Huston regarding the conflicts, some with Huston's doodles and drawings; various cables from Paramount regarding Huston medical exam, for insurance; and Jules Buck, Eugene Frenke, and Mark Cohen's extensive notes on *Will Adams*'s script (4 p.), with further discussion about various options with Paramount from Frenke to Huston.

WINTER KILLS

Correspondence regarding Huston's role in film; script sent; staff and crew list; call sheets; bankruptcy documents regarding the production company; and reviews.

WISE BLOOD

Correspondence on various aspects of the film; letters from Michael Fitzgerald (producer) on getting Huston interested in doing the film; money advanced; principals and their addresses; London Film Festival of the British Film Institute inviting Huston to participate in the 23d London Film Festival, November 15, 1979, to November 30, 1979, with *Wise Blood;* publicity; and reviews.

XXI

Archival Resources

The caption after each name below identifies the films on which Huston and the associated person or studio were related. The person's archival sources are indicated, but these are not necessarily related to the particular film. Huston may not be mentioned in the papers or interviews.

Following are abbreviations of the archival sources:

AFI	The American Film Institute, Los Angeles
AMERICAN	American Museum of the Moving Image
AMERICAN/USC	American Society of Cinematographers Oral Histories, housed at the University of South Carolina
AMPAS	Academy of Motion Arts and Sciences, Beverly Hills
ARIZONA	Arizona Historical Society, Tucson
BOSTON	Boston University
BRIGHAM	Brigham Young University, Provo, Utah
BURBANK	Burbank Public Library
COLUMBIA	Columbia University. Oral History Collection
CORNELL	Cornell University. New York Historical Resource Center
EASTMAN	International Museum of Photography. George Eastman House, Rochester
GEORGIA	University of Georgia
HOLLYWOOD	Hollywood Center for the Audio-Visual Arts, Los Angeles
HUNTINGTON	Huntington Library, San Marino
ILLINOIS	University of Illinois
INDIANA	University of Indiana
IOWA	University of Iowa

Archival Resources

LC	Library of Congress
LONG BEACH	California State University, Long Beach
MUSEUM	Museum of the City of New York
NEWBERRY	Newberry Library, Chicago
NEW YORK STATE	New York State Archives, Albany
NYPL	New York Public Library. Performing Arts Library
SMU	Southern Methodist University
STANFORD/KLEIN	Arthur H. Klein/B. Traven Collection
STANFORD/SKOURAS	Stanford University. Spyros Skouras Papers
SYRACUSE	Syracuse University
TENNESSEE	University of Tennessee
TEXAS	University of Texas, Austin
UCLA	University of California, Los Angeles
USC	University of Southern California
WESLEYAN	Wesleyan University
WISCONSIN	Wisconsin Center for Film and Theater Research
WYOMING	American Heritage Center. University of Wyoming, Laramie
YALE	Yale University

INDIVIDUALS

Buddy Adler. Producer. *Heaven Knows, Mr. Allison.* STANFORD/SKOURAS: Papers.

Brian Aherne. Actor. USC: Interviews on tape, March 17, 1968, Vivien Leigh Dinner, T386.

Edward Anhalt. Writer. *The Madwoman of Chaillot.* AMPAS: Academy Seminar and Tribute transcripts; UCLA: Oral History; USC: Papers.

Samuel Arkoff. Producer. *De Sade.* USC: Interviews on tape, March 18, 1971, Panel, Film and Finance (Film Conference), T445–1.

John Arnold. Assistant director. *Beat the Devil.* AMERICAN/USC, T407.

Mary Astor. Actress. *Across the Pacific, The Maltese Falcon.* BRIGHAM: Papers; COLUMBIA: Oral History.

Fay Bainter. Actress. *Jezebel.* USC: Papers.

S. N. Behrman. Writer. *Quo Vadis.* WISCONSIN: Papers.

Alvah Bessie. Writer. *Hollywood Ten.* WISCONSIN: Papers.

Herbert Biberman. Writer. *Hollywood Ten.* WISCONSIN: Papers.

Charles Bickford. Actor. *The Unforgiven, Hell's Heroes.* USC: Papers.

Henry Blanke. Producer. *The Maltese Falcon, The Treasure of the Sierra Madre, Jezebel, Juarez.* UCLA: Oral History.

Robert Bolt. Screenwriter. *A Man for All Seasons.* WYOMING: Papers.

685

Margaret Booth. Editor. *Annie, Fat City.* AMPAS: Oral History.

Ray Bradbury. Writer. *Moby Dick.* UCLA: Oral History; USC: Interviews on tape, October 26, 1961, Knight (i.e., Arthur Knight), *Moby Dick,* T88, November 21, 1963, T90.

Clarence Brown. Director. *The Acquittal.* TENNESSEE: Papers.

David Brown. Producer, Twentieth Century-Fox. WYOMING: Papers.

Frank Capra. Producer, director. WWII documentaries. WESLEYAN: Papers; USC: Interviews on tape, October 31, 1972, Knight, T458; April 17, 1972, lecture at California Tech., T479.

Edward Carfagno. Production designer, MGM. AMPAS: Oral History.

Charles G. Clarke. Director of photography. *The Barbarian and the Geisha.* AMERICAN/USC, T415; AMPAS: Papers. No indication of Huston in papers.

Jack Clayton. Associate producer. *Beat the Devil, Moulin Rouge.* USC: Interviews on tape, December 14, 1961, Knight, T96.

Montgomery Clift. Actor. *Freud: The Secret Passion, The Misfits.* NYPL: Papers.

Charles Coburn. Actor. *In This Our Life.* GEORGIA: Papers.

Chuck Connors. Actor. *The Deserter.* USC: Papers.

Gladys Cooper. Actress. *Sergeant York.* USC: Interviews on tape, March 17, 1968, Vivien Leigh Dinner, T386, USC: Papers.

Stanley Cortez. Photographer. *Let There Be Light.* USC: Interviews on tape, November 9, 1961, Knight, T91; April 1, 1965, Knight, T177.

Owen Crump. Screenwriter, Army Air Forces Motion Picture Unit. AMPAS: Oral History.

Tony Curtis. Actor. *The List of Adrian Messenger.* USC: Interviews on tape, March 3, 1968, Knight, T284.

Claude Dauphin. Actor. *No Exit* (Broadway play). WYOMING: Collection #8296.

Bette Davis. Actress. *In This Our Life, Juarez.* BOSTON: Papers; UCLA: Oral History.

Olivia De Havilland. Actress. *In This Our Life.* BRIGHAM: Oral History.

Andy Devine. Actor. *Red Badge of Courage.* COLUMBIA: Oral History.

Jack De Witt. Writer. "Man in the Wilderness" script in collection. WYOMING: Papers.

William Dieterle. Director. *Dr. Ehrlich's Magic Bullet, Juarez.* USC: Papers.

Edward Dmytryk. Director. *Hollywood Ten.* COLUMBIA: Oral History; USC:

Interviews on tape, November 16, 1967, Knight, T240; January 2, 1969, T278.

Kirk Douglas. Actor. *The List of Adrian Messenger.* WISCONSIN: Papers.

Philip Dunne. Screenwriter, director, Office of War Information, WWII. AMPAS: Oral History; USC: Papers.

Clint Eastwood. Actor, director. *White Hunter, Dark Heart.* WESLEYAN: Papers.

Arthur Edeson. Film editor. *Across the Pacific, The Maltese Falcon.* AMERI-CAN/USC, T417.

Rudi Fehr. Film editor. *Key Largo, Prizzi's Honor.* AMPAS: Oral History.

Charles Feldman. Producer. *Casino Royale.* AFI.

Robert Flaherty. Documentary filmmaker. COLUMBIA: Oral History.

Henry Fonda. Actor. Acted with Huston in two films and was directed by Huston in *On Our Merry Way.* COLUMBIA: Oral History; USC: Interviews on tape, April 4, 1971, Oscar Hammerstein Dinner, T453; WYOMING: Papers, Collection #4675.

Carl Foreman. Writer. *Hollywood Ten.* COLUMBIA: Oral History.

Gene Fowler Jr. Film editor, editor. *Let There Be Light.* AMPAS: Oral History; USC: Interviews on tape.

Marjorie Fowler. Film editor. AMPAS: Oral History; USC: Interviews on tape.

Karl Freund. Cinematographer. *Key Largo.* UCLA: Oral History.

Hugo Friedhofer. Composer. *The Barbarian and the Geisha.* AFI: Oral History.

Daniel Fuchs. Writer. *The Hard Way.* BOSTON: Papers.

Clark Gable. Actor. *The Misfits.* USC: Papers.

Cedric Gibbons. Art director. *The Asphalt Jungle, The Red Badge of Courage.* AMPAS: Papers. No indication of Huston in papers.

Lillian Gish. Actress. *The Unforgiven.* LC: Papers; MUSEUM: Papers.

Richard Goldstone. Producer, Army Signal Corps, Air Force Motion Picture Unit; MGM. AMPAS: Oral History.

William Goetz. Production executive, MGM. WYOMING: Papers.

Samuel Goldwyn. Producer. AMPAS: Papers.

Ruth Gordon. Actor, writer. USC: Interviews on tape, March 17, 1966, Knight, T197; March 23, 1969, Helen Keller Dinner, T388.

Charles Grayson. Screenwriter. *Underground* script in collection. WYOMING: Papers.

Anton Grot. Art director. *Juarez.* UCLA.

Thomas H. Guinzberg. Writer. COLUMBIA: Oral History.

M. L. Gunzburg. Founder and president, Natural Vision 3-D Corp., developed unproduced project with Huston, *Prelude to Freedom.* AMPAS: Oral History; USC: Papers.

Charles Halton. Actor. *Across the Pacific.* WYOMING: Papers.

Howard Hawks. Director. *Sergeant York.* ARIZONA: Oral History; BRIGHAM: Papers; USC: Interviews on tape, September 7, 1969, History of the Western, T300.

Edith Head. Costumer. *The Life and Times of Judge Roy Bean, The Man Who Would Be King.* AMPAS has an Edith Head Collection, but no indication of Huston connection in this collection; SMU: Papers; USC: Interviews on tape, February 1972, Directors Guild of America Banquet honoring her, T438; May 7, 1972, T480; WISCONSIN: Papers.

Ben Hecht. Writer. *A Farewell to Arms, Wuthering Heights.* COLUMBIA: Oral History; ILLINOIS: Papers; NEWBERRY: Papers.

Paul Henreid. Actor. *The Madwoman of Chaillot.* AMPAS: Papers.

Arthur Hornblow Jr. Producer. *The Asphalt Jungle.* COLUMBIA: Oral History.

John Houseman. Producer. COLUMBIA: Oral History.

James Wong Howe. Cinematographer. *Dr. Ehrlich's Magic Bullet, The Hard Way, The Heart Is a Lonely Hunter, This Property Is Condemned.* AMERI-CAN/USC: Interview, n.d., T400; March 30, 1967, Knight, T271; AMPAS: Papers, Screenplays; UCLA: Oral History.

Clair Huffaker. Writer. USC: Interviews on Tape, October 8, 1970, Knight, T314.

John Huston. Actor, director, producer, writer. AMPAS: Papers, 1932–81.

Walter Huston. Actor. AMPAS: Papers, 1932–81.

Sam Jaffe. Agent-Producer (not the actor). AMPAS: Oral History.

Dean Jagger. Actor. BRIGHAM: Papers.

Maurice Jarre. Composer. *The Life and Times of Judge Roy Bean, The Mackintosh Man, The Man Who Would Be King.* USC: Papers.

Dorothy Jeakins. Costumes. *Fat City.* WISCONSIN: Papers.

Nunnally Johnson. Writer. COLUMBIA: Oral History.

Bronislav Kaper. Composer. *The Red Badge of Courage.*T AFI: Oral History; WYOMING: Papers.

Howard Koch. Writer. *In This Our Life, Sergeant York, Three Strangers,* and theater projects with Huston. AFI: Oral History; USC: Interviews on Tape, March 21, 1971, T445–5; WISCONSIN: Papers.

Howard Kreitsek. Writer. *Breakout.* WYOMING: Papers.

Ring Lardner Jr. Writer. *The Cardinal.* AMPAS: Papers; WISCONSIN: Papers.

Jesse Lasky. Producer. *Sergeant York.* AMPAS: Papers; USC: Interviews on tape, April 6, 1961, Knight, T77.

John Howard Lawson. Writer. *Hollywood Ten.* UCLA: Oral History.

Ricky Leacock. Documentary filmmaker. COLUMBIA: Oral History.

Jack Lemmon. Actor. COLUMBIA: Oral History.

Sonya Levien. Screenwriter. *Quo Vadis.* HUNTINGTON: Papers; WYOMING: Papers.

Barre Lyndon. Playwriter. *The Amazing Dr. Clitterhouse.* AMPAS: Papers.

Charles MacArthur. Writer. *Wuthering Heights.* WISCONSIN: Papers.

Roddy McDowall. Actor. *The Life and Times of Judge Roy Bean.* UCLA: Papers.

William McGann. Special effects. *Key Largo.* USC: Interviews on tape, n.d., T274; spring 1966, Knight, T207.

Aline MacMahon. Actress. COLUMBIA: Oral History.

Ben Maddow. Writer. *The Asphalt Jungle, The Unforgiven.* AMPAS: Academy Seminar and Tribute transcripts; USC: Interviews on tape, n.d. McCann, T68.

Albert Maltz. Writer. *Hollywood Ten.* UCLA: Oral History; WISCONSIN: Papers.

Ralph Meeker. Actor. *Winter Kills.* AMPAS: contract for *Winter Kills;* unpublished autobiography.

John Milius. Writer, director. *The Life and Times of Judge Roy Bean; The Wind and the Lion.* USC: Interviews on tape, April 8, 1972, panel, The Young Filmmaker and the Future (Film Conference), C-6.

Arthur C. Miller. Cinematographer. *The Prowler.* AMERICAN/USC: n.d. T402, 415, 409.

Walter Mirisch. Producer. *Sinful Davey.* WISCONSIN: Papers. *See also under* Studios.

Gordon Mitchell. Actor. *Reflections in a Golden Eye.* WISCONSIN: Papers.

Douglass Montgomery. Actor. COLUMBIA: Papers.

Carlton Moss. Writer, director. Oral History. AMPAS: Papers.

Paul Muni. Actor. *Juarez.* NYPL: Papers.

Joseph Newman. Director, MGM. AMPAS: Oral History.

David Niven. Actor. *Casino Royale.* Photographs. AMPAS: Papers.

Samuel Ornitz. Writer. *Hollywood Ten.* WISCONSIN: Papers.

Gregory Peck. Actor. *Moby Dick.* AMERICAN/USC, n.d. T416; January 1963, Knight, T116; AMPAS: Papers (in process).

Sam Peckinpah. Actor. *The Visitor.* AFI: Oral history; AMPAS: Papers.

Jane Powell. Writer. *Typee* script in collection. WYOMING: Papers.

Otto Preminger. Director. *The Cardinal* and theatrical work with Huston. COLUMBIA: Oral History; WISCONSIN: Papers.

Claude Rains. Actor. *Juarez.* BOSTON: Papers.

Irving Rapper. Dialogue director, assistant director. *Dr. Ehrlich's Magic Bullet, High Sierra, Juarez.* AMPAS: Script Collection; no Huston-related films are in the collection; COLUMBIA: Oral History; USC: Interviews on tape, March 19, 1970, Knight, T307.

Gottfried Reinhardt. Producer. COLUMBIA: Oral History; USC: Interviews on tape, May 4, 1961, Knight, T82.

Gilbert Roland. Actor. *We Were Strangers.* AMPAS: Photos.

Harold Rosson. Cinematographer. *The Asphalt Jungle, The Red Badge of Courage.* AFI: Oral History; AMERICAN/USC: Oral History, n.d., T412/3.

Miklos Rozsa. Composer. *The Asphalt Jungle.* SYRACUSE: Papers.

Morrie Ryskind. Writer. *Hollywood Ten.* WISCONSIN: Papers.

Dore Schary. Studio executive, MGM. *The Red Badge of Courage.* WISCONSIN: Papers.

George Seaton. Director. COLUMBIA: Oral History; WISCONSIN: Papers.

David O. Selznick. Producer. *A Farewell to Arms* and his wife, Jennifer Jones, acted in two Huston films. COLUMBIA: Oral History; TEXAS: Papers.

Vincent Sherman. Director. *The Hard Way.* AFI: Oral History.

Don Siegel. Montages. *Across the Pacific.* AFI: Oral History; BOSTON: Papers; USC: Interviews on tape, January 7, 1971, Knight, T270.

Frank Sinatra. Actor. *The List of Adrian Messenger.* USC: Interviews on tape, February 12, 1967, Cole Porter Dinner, T275.

Murray Spivack. Music and rerecording mixer. RKO, Republic, Twentieth Century-Fox. AMPAS: Oral History.

John Steinbeck. Novelist. STANFORD: Papers.

Max Steiner. Composer: *In This Our Life; Key Largo.* WYOMING: Papers.

George Stevens. Director. AMPAS; USC: Interviews on tape, September 21, 1961, Knight, T84.

James Stewart. Actor. *On Our Merry Way.* BRIGHAM: Papers; INDIANA: Papers.

Edward Sutherland. Director. COLUMBIA: Oral History.

Dimitri Tiomkin. Composer. *Here Is Germany, Let There Be Light, The Unforgiven.* USC: Interview on tape, March 18, 1965, Knight, T171; USC: Papers.

B. Traven. Novelist. *The Treasure of the Sierra Madre.* STANFORD/KLEIN: Papers.

Dalton Trumbo. Writer. *Hollywood Ten.* WISCONSIN: Papers.

John Truwe. Makeup Department, MGM. *The Asphalt Jungle, Quo Vadis, The Red Badge of Courage.* AMPAS.

Albert E. Van Schmus. Production Code Administration staff member. AMPAS: Oral History.

Gore Vidal. Writer. *Myra Breckinridge.* WISCONSIN: Papers.

Jerry Wald. Producer. *Across the Pacific, Background to Danger, The Hard Way, Key Largo.* COLUMBIA: Oral History; USC: Interviews on tape, September 13, 1961, Knight, T83.

Hal Wallis. Producer. Post–Warner Brothers years. *Becket.* AMPAS: Papers.

Raoul Walsh. Director. *Background to Danger, High Sierra.* WESLEYAN: Papers.

Dale Wasserman. Writer. *A Walk with Love and Death.* WISCONSIN: Papers.

John Wayne. Actor. *The Barbarian and the Geisha.* ARIZONA: Oral History.

James Webb. Writer. *Sinful Davey.* WISCONSIN: Papers.

Orson Welles. Actor, writer, director. Various involvements with Huston. INDI-ANA: Papers; USC: Interviews on tape, May 12, 1971, T361; WISCONSIN: Papers.

Perc Westmore. Makeup. *Across the Pacific, Dr. Ehrlich's Magic Bullet, Juarez.* AMPAS: Scrapbooks.

John Wexley. Writer. *The Amazing Dr. Clitterhouse.* WISCONSIN: Papers.

William Wyler. Director. Various projects with Huston. AMPAS: Oral History (from SMU); AMPAS: Papers, early years; UCLA: Oral History; UCLA: Papers, later years; USC: Interviews on tape, January 25, 1962, Knight, T98.

Darryl F. Zanuck. Producer. *The Roots of Heaven.* INDIANA: Papers.

STUDIOS

Columbia Pictures. AFI: Stills; LC, UCLA, Yale: Films.

MGM. AMPAS: Legal Department, Final Cast Credit Sheets, 1937–73, Photography Collection, Reference Photographs (*Note:* Additional material from Turner, including screenplays in process); EASTMAN: Films; LONG BEACH: Music; USC: Scripts.

Mirisch Productions. Producers. *Sinful Davey.* UCLA.

Paramount Studios. AMPAS: Scripts, Press books; UCLA: Films; USC: Research Department.

RKO. UCLA: Papers, Films.

Twentieth Century-Fox. IOWA: Scripts; UCLA: Productions Files, Scripts; USC: Set Stills.

United Artists. WISCONSIN: Papers.

Universal Pictures. AMPAS: Story and Synopsis Log Books (produced and unproduced films); LC: Films; NYPL: Still Books; USC.

Warner Bros. BURBANK; CORNELL; EASTMAN; LC; UCLA; USC, WISCONSIN.

OTHERS
Hollywood Ten. WISCONSIN.

"James Agee Documentary." COLUMBIA.

Scripts submitted for censorship. NEW YORK STATE.

XXII

Archival Institutions

This listing provides information on those institutions mentioned in other parts of this book and additional institutions that may have information on Huston. Only definite hours are given. Academic institutions will vary their hours dramatically depending on the academic year. Some libraries will close during days of the week for various reasons. At least one major film library was closed much of the summer of 1995 because new air-conditioning was being installed. So it is always best to call ahead when making plans, and some of the collections require appointments made in advance. In addition there may be staff changes, and persons may have changed their positions within the organization, or have left the institution. Additional information on academic and archival institutions can be found in *American Library Directory, 1996–97,* 49th ed. (New Providence, N.J.: R. R. Bowker, 1996, 2 vols.), and *Directory of Special Libraries and Information Centers,* 19th ed. (New York: Gale, 1996, 3 vols.).

Academy of Motion Picture Arts and Sciences
Margaret Herrick Library
Center for Motion Picture Study
333 S. La Cienega Boulevard
Beverly Hills, CA 90211
310–247–3036; 310–247–3000 ext. 226
Fax: 310–657–5193
Hours: Monday–Tuesday, Thursday–Friday, 10 A.M.–6 P.M.
Contact: Special Collections—Scott Curtis, Sam Gill, Faye Thompson, Howard Prouty; Film Archives—Ed Carter: 310–247–3036 ext. 231

American Film Institute
Louis B. Mayer Library
2021 N. Western Avenue
Los Angeles, CA 90027
213–856–7654; Fax: 213–856–7754
Hours: Monday–Thursday, 1P.M. –5 P.M. ;
AFI members: 10A.M. –5 P.M.

American Museum of the Moving Image
36–01 35th Avenue
Astoria, NY 11106
718–784–4520; Fax: 718–784–4681
Contact: Eleanor Mish, registrar/manager of the collection

Arizona Historical Society
Research Library
949 E. Second Street
Tucson, Arizona 85719
520–628–5774; Fax: 520–628–5695
Contact: Jerry Kyle, Rose Byrne

Boston University
Department of Special Collections
Mugar Memorial Library
771 Commonwealth Avenue
Boston, MA 02215
617–353–3710
Contact: Margaret Goostray, assistant director; Karen Mix, manuscript technician

Brigham Young University
Special Collections and Manuscripts Department
Harold B. Lee Library
Provo, UT 84602
801–378–3514; Fax: 801–378–6347

British Film Institute
21 Stephen Street
London W1P 1PL, England
0171–255–1444; Fax: 0171–436–7950; 0171–580–7503
Contact: Clyde Jeavons, curator; Graham Melville, cataloguer

Burbank Public Library
Reference Department/Media Project
110 N. Glenoaks Boulevard
Burbank, CA 91502
818–953–9741; Fax: 818–953–8639

California State University, Long Beach
University Library
1250 Bellflower Boulevard
Long Beach, CA 90840–1901
213–985–4026/27; 213–985–5518; Fax: 213–985–1703

Columbia University
Oral History Research Office
Room 801, Butler Library
New York, NY 19927
212–854–2273; Fax: 212–222–0331

Cornell University
201 Olin Library
Ithaca, NY 14853–5301
607–255–4144; Fax: 607–255–9346

George Eastman House
International Museum of Photography and Film
Film Collection
900 East Avenue
Rochester, NY 14607
716–271–3361; Fax: 716–271–3970
Contact: Dr. Jan-Christopher Horak

Huntington Library
1151 Oxford Road
San Marino, CA 91108
818–405–2205; Fax: 818–405–0225

Library of Congress
Motion Picture, Broadcasting and Recorded Sound Division
Washington, D.C. 20540
202–707–5840, 202–707–1000; Fax: 202–707–2371
Contact: Rosemary Hanes, reference librarian

Los Angeles Public Library
Frances Howard Goldwyn Hollywood Regional Library
1623 Ivar Avenue
Los Angeles, CA 90028
213–467–2821; Fax: 213–467–5707

Museum of Modern Art
Celeste Bartos International Film Study Center
Department of Film
11 West 53d Street

New York, NY 10019–5498
212–708–9613/9614; Fax: 212–708–9531
Hours: Monday–Friday, 1P.M. –5 P.M.
Contact: Charles Silver, Ron Magliozzi
Museum Library: 212–708–9433
Film Stills Archives, Mary Corliss: 212–708–9830; Fax: 212–708–9531

Museum of Television and Radio
25 W. 52d Street
New York, NY 10019
212–621–6600; Fax: 212–621–6700
Contact: Monica Weiner, Education Department

Museum of Television and Radio
465 Beverly Drive
Beverly Hills, CA 90210
310–786–1000

Museum of the City of New York
Theater Collection
1220 Fifth Avenue
New York, NY 10029
212–534–1672, ext. 210; Fax: 212–534–5974
Contact: Marty Jacobs
Note: There is a fee for use of the collection.

National Archives
Motion Picture, Sound and Video Branch
8601 Adelphi Road
College Park, MD 20740–60001
301–713–7060; Fax: 301–713–6904
Hours: Monday and Wednesday 8:45 A.M.–5 P.M.;
Thursday and Friday 8:45 A.M.–9 P.M.; Saturday 8:45 A.M.–4:45 P.M.
Contact: Jill Abraham, archives technician

National Archives of Canada
Audio-Visual and Cartographic Archives
344 Wellington Street, Room 1016
Ottawa, Ontario, K1A ON3, Canada
613–995–1312; 613–995–6890; Fax: 613–995–6274
Contact: Caroline Forcier Holloway or Sylvie Robitaille

Newberry Library
60 W. Walton Street
Chicago, IL 60610–3394
312–943–9090

New York Public Library for the Performing Arts
40 Lincoln Center Plaza, at 65th Street (Lincoln Center)
New York, NY 10023–7498
212–870–1630; Fax: 212–787–3852
Hours: Monday, Thursday: Noon–7:45 P.M.; Wednesday, Friday, Saturday:
Noon–5:45 P.M.

New York State Archives
Cultural Education Center, Room 11040
Empire State Plaza
Albany, NY 12230
518–474–8955
Contact: Dick Andress, senior archivist

Southern Methodist University
Central University Libraries
Dallas, TX 75275–0135
214–768–2401; Fax: 214–768–1842

Stanford University Libraries
Department of Special Collections
Stanford, CA 94305–6004
415–723–5553; Fax: 415–725–6874
Contact: Linda Long

State Historical Society of Wisconsin
816 State Street
Madison, WI 53706
608–264–6400; Fax: 608–264–6406
Contact: Laura Jacobs, reference archivist
Note: See also Wisconsin Center for Film and Theater Research.

Syracuse University Library
E. S. Bird Library
222 Waverly Avenue
Syracuse, NY 13244–2010
315–443–2573; Fax: 315–443–2060

UCLA (University of California at Los Angeles)
Arts Library
Dickinson Art Center, 2d Floor
Los Angeles, CA 90024–1517
310–206–5426
Contact: Alfred Willis
Note: Houses the film collection.

UCLA
Arts Special Collections
22478 University Research Library, 2d Floor
Los Angeles, CA 90024–1517
310–825–7253
Contact: Brigitte Kueppers
Note: Houses such special collections as Twentieth Century-Fox.

UCLA Film and Television Archives
Research and Study Center
46G Powell Library
University of California, Los Angeles
Los Angeles, CA 90024–1517
310–206–5388; Fax: 310–206–5392
Contact: Andrea Kalas, assistant manager

University of Georgia Libraries
Athens, GA 30602
706–542–0621; Fax: 706–542–4144

University of Illinois Library at Urbana-Champaign
1408 W. Gregory Drive
230 Library
Urbana, IL 61801
217–333–0790, Fax: 217–244–4358

University of Iowa
Special Collections
The University Libraries
100 Main Library
Iowa City, IA 52242–1420
319–335–5867
Contact: Robert McCown, Special Collections librarian
Note: Collection has Twentieth Century-Fox scripts, 1929–69.

University of Southern California
Cinema-Television Library and Archives of the Performing Arts
Doheny Library
Los Angeles, CA 90089–0182
213–740–7610; Fax: 213–747–3301
Contact: Edward "Ned" Comstock
Warner Brothers Archives: Stuart Ng, Bill Whittington
213–748–7747; Fax: 213–747–3301

University of Southern Indiana
8600 University Boulevard
Evansville, IN 47712
812–464–1896; Fax: 812–465–1693
Note: Houses press kit collection, 1955–present.

University of Tennessee
University Libraries
Special Collections
Hoskins Library
Knoxville, TN 37996–4000
615–974–4480; Fax: 615–974–2708
Contact: Nick Wyman, unit head

University of Texas at Austin
Special Collections
Hobitzelle Theater Arts Library
Austin, TX 78713
512–471–9124; Fax: 512–471–9646
Contact: Dr. Charles Ball, head, Special Collections

University of Wyoming
American Heritage Center
P.O. Box 3924
Laramie, WY 82071
307–766–4114
Contact: Rick Ewig or Jennifer King, reference archivists

Warner Brothers Research Library
5200 Lankershim Boulevard, Suite 100
North Hollywood, CA 91601
818–506–8693; Fax: 818–506–8079
Hours: 9 A.M. to 6 P.M., Monday–Friday, PST
Contact: Anne Schlosser
Note: All services are provided for a fee based on an hourly rate with a minimum
charge. Appointments required.

Wesleyan University
Wesleyan Cinema Archives
Middletown, CT 06459
203–347–9411, ext. 2259; Fax: 203–343–3940
Contact: Leith G. Johnson, assistant curator

Wisconsin Center for Film and Theater Research
412 Historical Society
816 State Street
Madison, WI 53706
608–264–6466; Fax: 608–264–6472
Contact: Crystal Hyde or Maxine Fleckner-Ducey
Note: See also State Historical Society of Wisconsin.

Writers Guild of America, West
8955 Beverly Boulevard
Los Angeles, CA 90048
213–550–1000
Contact: Elizabeth Brenner

Yale University
Film Study Center
305 Crown Street
P.O. Box 174
New Haven, CT 06520
203–432–4604

XXIII

Huston-Related Films on Film, Video, and Laser Disc

A great many of the films on which John Huston worked in some capacity (actor, writer, director; realized and unrealized) are available for viewing in various formats—16 mm, 35 mm, video (for videocassette recorders [VCRs]), and laser disc. An attempt is made here to provide information on the availability of these films, and reference sources are indicated. At the end of the film listing is a directory of associated companies and institutions. Except in a few instances, most 16 mm or 35 mm versions are available either for rent or for viewing at the institutions mentioned. Some commercial suppliers that sell and rent videos and laser discs are listed, but these suppliers are not exclusive. *Leonard Maltin's Movie and Video Guide, 1998 Edition* (New York: Signet, 1997) has a section at the beginning of his book that lists suppliers of videos and laser discs. Also many video rental stores sell videos or provide special order services for customers. In addition, many public libraries have video sections and allow patrons to borrow videos. Videos and laser discs go in and out of print, as books do, but various video stores or other institutions may still have copies.

Eddie Brandt is a particularly good source with a comprehensive supply of a tremendous number of films on video that are now out of print and a collection of films that have not been issued on video. It also rents its stock nationwide (as does Facets); call for details. A number of rental sources are on the internet: Best Video—www.bestvideo.com; Home Film Festival—www.homefilmfestival.com; and San Francisco Video Store—www.levideo.com. Those people lucky enough to subscribe to a cable service that carries Turner Classic Movies (TCM) have access to substantial classic Warner Brothers, MGM, and RKO releases. The more obscure Huston-related films—*Tentacles,* for example—will sometimes show up on TCM. Other movie channels that show "classic" films are American Movie Classics (AMC), Bravo, and the Independent Film Channel (IFC).

Where available, prices have been indicated below. These may change, however, as the video and laser disc go out of print. Library holdings of particular films that are unique or difficult to come by are indicated, where the information was available.

AFI/LC	AMERICAN FILM INSTITUTE COLLECTION HOUSED AT THE LIBRARY OF CONGRESS
AMPAS	ACADEMY OF MOTION PICTURE ARTS AND SCIENCES
BFI	BRITISH FILM INSTITUTE
LC	LIBRARY OF CONGRESS
MOMA	MUSEUM OF MODERN ART
MTV	MUSEUM OF TV AND RADIO, NEW YORK CITY AND BEVERLY HILLS
NATIONAL	NATIONAL AUDIOVISUAL CENTER
UCLA	UNIVERSITY OF CALIFORNIA, LOS ANGELES. FILM AND TELEVISION ARCHIVES
WISCONSIN	WISCONSIN CENTER FOR FILM AND THEATER RESEARCH

ACADEMY AWARDS, 25th ANNUAL—Excerpt. Humphrey Bogart, *The African Queen.*

UCLA. Video.

ACADEMY AWARDS: 58th ANNUAL

MTV. Viewing copy.

ACROSS THE PACIFIC

AFI/LC. Feature, preservation copy; copy available for viewing at LC. Donated by United Artists.

AMPAS. FILM ARCHIVES. 16 mm copy in Huston Archives transferred to Film Archives.

BFI. Viewing copy.

LC. Viewing copies, 16 mm and laser disc; 35 mm nitrate reference copy.

MOMA. Reference copy.

UCLA. 16 mm, 35 mm, video.

WISCONSIN. 16 mm, 35 mm, or ¾-in. video.

RENTALS, 16 mm. MGM/UA, Swank.

VIDEO PUBLISHER. MGM/UA Home Entertainment.

VIDEO SALES. Facets, Movies Unlimited. $19.98.

VIDEO RENTALS. Eddie Brandt, Facets.

LASER DISC PUBLISHERS. MGM/UA and Turner Entertainment released this film as part of a two–laser disc set, *The Bogart Collection,* which also includes *High Sierra.*

THE AFRICAN QUEEN

AMPAS. FILM ARCHIVES. 16 mm, incomplete. Copy in Huston Archives transferred to Film Archives.

BFI. Preservation copy.

LC. Viewing copies, 35 mm, laser disc; reference print, 35 mm.

MOMA. Viewing copy, 35 mm.

UCLA. 16 mm, 35 mm, laser disc.

WISCONSIN. 16 mm, 35 mm, or ¾-in. video.

RENTALS, 16 mm. Arcus Film, Budget Films, Cine Craft, Films Inc., Image Films, Institutional Cinema, Ivy Films, Macmillan Films, Modern Sound Newman Film Library, New Cinema, Swank, Syracuse University Film, Twyman Films, Video Communications, Welling Motion Pictures, Westcoast Films, Wholesome Film Center, Willoughby Peer.

LEASE, 16 mm. Macmillan Films.

VIDEO PUBLISHERS. CBS/Fox Video, Magnetic Video Corp., Regie (France), Time-Life Video and Television, Twentieth Century-Fox.

VIDEO SALES. Facets, Movies Unlimited. $59.98.

VIDEO RENTALS. Eddie Brandt, Facets.

LASER DISC PUBLISHERS. CBS/Fox Video,* RCA Selecta Vision.

LASER DISC SALES. Dave's Video, Facets. $24.98.

OTHER FORMATS. Sound recordings:

Lux Radio Theater, Humphrey Bogart and Greer Garson, Hans Conreid, December 15, 1952. Reissued by Jabberwocky/Mind's Eye, San Francisco; National Recording Co., Glenview, Illinois; Mark 56 Records 668, sound cassette and LP.
Listen for Pleasure, Downsview, Ontario, Canada, LFP 7072, 1981, read by Edward Woodward; Books on Tape, Newport, California, 1986, read by Richard Green, six cassettes, $48.00.

Note. *A limited commemorative edition on laser disc was issued by CBS/Fox Video in 1993. It includes Katharine Hepburn's book and the screenplay (122 pages).

AGEE

AMPAS. FILM ARCHIVES. 16 mm.

LC. Viewing copy, 16 mm.

RENTALS, 16 mm. First run.

VIDEO PURCHASE. James Agee Film Project. No price indicated.

THE AMAZING DR. CLITTERHOUSE

AFI/LC. Feature.

AMPAS. FILM ARCHIVES. 16 mm. Copy in Huston Archives transferred to Film Archives.

LC. Fine-grain master positive.

MOMA. Reference copy.

UCLA. 35 mm.

WISCONSIN. 16 mm, 35 mm, or ¾-in. video.

RENTALS, 16 mm. MGM/UA, Swank.

VIDEO RENTALS. Eddie Brandt.

AMERICAN CAESAR

LC. Viewing copy, ¾-in. video.

VIDEO PUBLISHER. Embassy Home Entertainment, Sultan Entertainment, two cassettes, $24.98 each.

VIDEO SALES and RENTALS. Facets, two cassettes, $24.95 each.

THE AMERICAN FILM INSTITUTE SALUTE TO GENE KELLY

MTV. Viewing copy.

VIDEO PUBLISHER. Worldvision Enterprises.

VIDEO SALES. Worldvision Home Video, Inc.; Movies Unlimited. $19.99.

VIDEO RENTALS. Eddie Brandt.

THE AMERICAN FILM INSTITUTE SALUTE TO JOHN HUSTON

LC. Viewing copy, ¾-in. video.

MTV. Viewing copy.

VIDEO PUBLISHER. Worldvision Home Video, Inc.

VIDEO SALES. Worldvision Home Video, Inc.; Movies Unlimited. $19.99.

VIDEO RENTALS. Eddie Brandt.

THE AMERICAN FILM INSTITUTE SALUTE TO ORSON WELLES
LC. Viewing copy, 2-in. videotape.

MTV. Viewing copy.

VIDEO PUBLISHER. Worldvision Home Video, Inc.

VIDEO SALES. Worldvision Home Video, Inc.; Movies Unlimited. $19.99.

VIDEO RENTALS. Eddie Brandt.

ANGELA
VIDEO PUBLISHERS & SALES. Sultan Entertainment, Simitar Entertainment.
$69.98.

VIDEO RENTALS. Eddie Brandt.

ANNIE
BFI. Preservation copy.

LC. Viewing copy, 35 mm, laser disc.

MOMA. Viewing copy, 16 mm.

UCLA. 35 mm.

RENTALS, 16 mm. Films Inc., Swank.

VIDEO PUBLISHER. Columbia Tristar Home Video, Music for Little People.

VIDEO SALES. Facets, Movies Unlimited. $19.95.

VIDEO RENTALS. Facets, Eddie Brandt.

LASER DISC PUBLISHER. Columbia Pictures Home Video.

LASER DISC SALES. Dave's Video.

APPOINTMENT WITH DESTINY: THE CRUCIFIXION OF JESUS (also
issued as *The Crucifixion of Jesus*)
LC. Viewing copy, 16 mm.

LOS ANGELES COUNTY PUBLIC LIBRARY. Video.

VIDEO PUBLISHERS. American Educational Films, Capitol Communications
(Wolper Productions).

FILM (16 mm). American Educational Films.

THE ASPHALT JUNGLE

BFI. Viewing copy.

LC. Viewing copies, 35 mm, ½-in. video, laser disc.

UCLA. Laser disc.

RENTALS, 16 mm. MGM/UA, Swank.

VIDEO PUBLISHER. MGM/UA Home Entertainment.

VIDEO SALES. Facets, Movies Unlimited. $19.98.

VIDEO RENTALS. Facets, Eddie Brandt.

LASER DISC PUBLISHER. Voyager Co.

LASER DISC SALES. Dave's Video, Facets. $39.95.

BACALL ON BOGART

LC. Viewing copy, ¾-in. video.

UCLA. Video.

VIDEO PUBLISHER. Instructional Video.

VIDEO SALES. Facets, Movies Unlimited. $14.99.

VIDEO RENTALS. Eddie Brandt, Facets.

BACKGROUND TO DANGER

AFI/LC. Feature. Donated by United Artists.

LC. Viewing copy, 35 mm.

UCLA. 35 mm.

WISCONSIN. 16 mm, 35 mm, or ¾-in. video.

RENTALS, 16 mm. MGM/UA, Swank.

VIDEO PUBLISHER. MGM/UA Home Entertainment.

VIDEO SALES. Movies Unlimited. $19.99.

VIDEO RENTALS. Eddie Brandt.

THE BARBARIAN AND THE GEISHA

AFI/LC. Feature.

LC. Viewing copy, 35 mm.

RENTALS, 16 mm. Films Inc., Institutional Cinema, Willoughby Peer.

VIDEO PUBLISHER. CBS/Fox Video.

VIDEO SALES. Movies Unlimited. $19.98.

VIDEO RENTALS. Eddie Brandt.

BATTLE FORCE

BFI. Preservation copy.

VIDEO PUBLISHER. Time-Life.

VIDEO SALES. Movies Unlimited. $19.99.

VIDEO RENTALS. Eddie Brandt.

BATTLE FOR THE PLANET OF THE APES

BFI. Viewing copy.

LC. Viewing copy, 35 mm.

UCLA. 35 mm.

RENTALS, 16 mm. Films Inc.

VIDEO PUBLISHER. CBS/Fox Video.

VIDEO SALES. Facets, Movies Unlimited. $19.98.

VIDEO RENTALS. Eddie Brandt, Facets.

THE BATTLE OF SAN PIETRO

AMPAS. FILM ARCHIVES. 16 mm. Copy in Huston Archives transferred to Film Archives.

BFI. Viewing copy.

MOMA. Viewing copy, 16 mm.

UCLA. 16 mm, video.

RENTALS & SALES, 16 mm. Films Inc., International Historic Films, Kit Parker, National Audiovisual Center.

VIDEO PUBLISHERS. A.R.P. Company; Barr Films; Burbank Video; Cassette Corp. of America; Editions Montparnasse (Paris, France; published 1991)*; Fusion Video; Educational Video Library; Ferde Grofe Films; Hollywood's Attic; International Historic Films, Inc. (IHF); Kit Parker Films; Madacy Music Group; Matinee Classics; National Audiovisual Center; Reader's Digest Association; Time-Life Video; Trans-Atlantic Video; Video Treasures; Viking Video Classics; Western Film and Video, Inc.

VIDEO SALES. Facets, Movies Unlimited. $19.95.

VIDEO RENTALS. Eddie Brandt, Facets.

Note. *Cassette includes *Report from the Aleutians.*

BEAT THE DEVIL

AMPAS. FILM ARCHIVES. 16 mm. Copy in Huston Archives transferred to Film Archives.

LC. Viewing copy, 35 mm.

MOMA. Reference copy.

RENTALS, 16 mm. Budget Films, Films Inc., Images Films, Kit Parker Films, National Film Video, Wholesome Film Center.

VIDEO PUBLISHERS. Columbia Tristar Home Video, Moore Video, Nostalgia Family Video. Previously available from Discount Video Tapes, Inc.; Madacy Video (packaged with *Call it Murder,* a Bogart film [not by Huston]).

VIDEO SALES. Facets, Movies Unlimited. $19.95.

VIDEO RENTALS. Eddie Brandt, Facets.

LASER DISC. Dave's Video (rentals only).

BECKET

AFI/LC.

MOMA. Excerpt.

SALES, 16 mm. Festival Films, Maljack.

VIDEO PUBLISHERS. MPI Home Video, The Video Catalog. Previously available in video from Festival Films.

VIDEO SALES. Facets, Movies Unlimited. $59.95.

VIDEO RENTALS. Eddie Brandt, Facets.

LASER DISC SALES. Facets, Dave's Video. $39.99.

THE BEST OF BOGART

UCLA. 16 mm.

THE BIBLE

AMPAS. FILM ARCHIVES. 16 mm, long version. Copy in Huston Archives transferred to Film Archives.

BFI. Viewing copy.

LC. Viewing copy, 35 mm.

MOMA. Reference copy.

RENTALS, 16 mm. Films Inc. (also anamorphic version), Twyman Films.

VIDEO PUBLISHER. CBS/Fox Video.

VIDEO SALES. Facets, Movies Unlimited. $19.98.

VIDEO RENTALS. Eddie Brandt, Facets.

LASER DISC SALES. Dave's Video, Facets. $69.98.

BLACK CAULDRON

AMPAS. FILM ARCHIVES. Video press kit.

LC. Viewing copy, 35 mm.

THE BLUE HOTEL

RENTALS, 16 mm. Iowa Films, Kent State University Film Center, South Dakota State University Audiovisual Center, Syracuse University Film, University of Illinois Film Department, University of Michigan Media, Utah Media.

VIDEO PUBLISHERS & SALES. Coronet/MTI Films and Video, Karol Video, Monterrey Home Video, $24.95. Previously available on video by Perspect Films.

VIDEO SALES. Facets, Movies Unlimited. $24.95.

BOGIE: THE LAST HERO

UCLA. Video.

BREAKOUT

BFI. Viewing copy.

LC. Viewing copy, 35 mm.

UCLA. 35 mm, video, laser disc.

RENTALS, 16 mm. Arcus Films, Bosco Films, Budget Films, Cine Craft, Film Center, Films Inc., Ivy Films, Kit Parker, Modern Sound, National Film Video, Roas Films, Swank, Welling Motion Pictures, Westcoast Films, Williams Films.

VIDEO PUBLISHER. Columbia/Tristar Home Video.

VIDEO SALES. Movies Unlimited. $12.99.

VIDEO RENTALS. Eddie Brandt.

LASER DISC. Dave's Video (rentals only).

THE BRIDGE IN THE JUNGLE

LC. 1-in. video master.

THE BRIDGE OF SAN LUIS REY (1944 version)

SALE, 16 mm. Classic Assoc.

VIDEO SALES. Movies Unlimited. $14.99.

VIDEO RENTALS. Eddie Brandt.

LASER DISC SALES. Dave's Video. $29.99.

BY LOVE POSSESSED

WISCONSIN. 16 mm, 35 mm, or ¾-in. video.

VIDEO PUBLISHER. MGM/UA Home Entertainment.

VIDEO SALES. Movies Unlimited. $14.99.

VIDEO RENTALS. Eddie Brandt.

LASER DISC SALES. Dave's Video. $34.99.

CANDY

LC. Viewing copy, 35 mm.

UCLA. 35 mm.

RENTALS, 16 mm. Films Inc.

Video not available.

CANNERY ROW

BFI. Viewing copy.

LC. Viewing copy, 35 mm.

RENTALS, 16 mm. MGM/UA, Swank.

VIDEO PUBLISHER. MGM/UA Home Entertainment. Previously from Warner Home Video.

VIDEO SALES. Facets, Movies Unlimited. $19.99.

VIDEO RENTALS. Eddie Brandt, Facets.

CAPTAIN HORATIO HORNBLOWER

BFI. Viewing copy.

LC. Viewing copy, 35 mm; video, laser disc.

RENTALS, 16 mm. Charard, Films Inc., Institutional Cinema, Twyman Films, Westcoast Films.

VIDEO PUBLISHER. Warner Home Video.

VIDEO SALES. Facets, Movies Unlimited. $19.99.

VIDEO RENTALS. Eddie Brandt, Facets.

LASER DISC SALES. Dave's Video, Facets. $34.99.

THE CARDINAL

BFI. Viewing copy.

LC. Viewing copy, 35 mm.

MOMA. Reference copy.

UCLA. 35 mm.

RENTALS, 16 mm. Alba House, Bosco Films, Budget Films, Cine Craft, Charard, Corinth Films, Film Center, Films Inc., National Film Video, Roas Films, Twyman Films, Welling Motion Pictures, Wholesome Film, Williams Films. Anamorphic version: Corinth Films.

VIDEO PUBLISHERS. Home Video; Image Entertainment; Video Treasury. $29.98.

VIDEO SALES. Facets, Movies Unlimited. $59.95.

VIDEO RENTALS. Eddie Brandt, Facets.

LASER DISC PUBLISHER. Image Entertainment.

LASER DISC SALES. Facets, Dave's Video (rentals only).

CASINO ROYALE

AMPAS. FILM ARCHIVES. 16 mm.

BFI. Preservation copy.

LC. Viewing copy, 35 mm.

UCLA. 16 mm, laser disc.

RENTALS, 16 mm. Arcus Films, Bosco Films, Buchan Pics, Budget Films, Cine Craft, Charard Motion Pics, Films Inc., Institutional Cinema, Kit Parker, Modern Sound, Newman Film Library, National Film Video, Roas Films, Swank, Twyman Films, Video Communications, Welling Motion Pictures, Westcoast Films, Wholesome Film Center, Williams Films, Willoughby Peer.

VIDEO PUBLISHERS. Columbia Tristar, Moore Video.

VIDEO SALES. Facets, Movies Unlimited. $14.99.

VIDEO RENTALS. Facets, Eddie Brandt.

LASER DISC SALES. Dave's Video. $29.99.

CATHOLICS
RENTALS, 16 mm. Budget Films, Modern Sound, Syracuse University Film Department, Twyman Films, Wholesome Film Center.

SALES, 16 mm. Carousel Films.

VIDEO SALES. Movies Unlimited, $19.99. Facets reports that the video is out of print.

VIDEO RENTALS. Eddie Brandt, Facets.

CHARLIE CHAPLIN'S SEVENTY-SEVENTH BIRTHDAY (London, April 15, 1966)
UCLA. Hearst Vault Material.

CHEYENNE
AFI/LC. Feature.

WISCONSIN. 16 mm, 35 mm, or ¾-in. video.

RENTALS, 16 mm. MGM/UA.

VIDEO RENTALS. Eddie Brandt.

CHINATOWN
BFI. Viewing copy.

LC. Viewing copy, ¾-in. video.

MOMA. Viewing copy, 35 mm.

UCLA. Laser disc.

RENTAL, 16 mm. Films Inc.

SALES. Cinema Concepts, Super 8 Sound Version.

VIDEO PUBLISHER. Paramount Home Video.

VIDEO SALES. Facets, Movies Unlimited. $19.95.

VIDEO RENTALS. Eddie Brandt, Facets.

LASER DISC PUBLISHER. Paramount Home Video, RCA Selecta Vision.

LASER DISC SALES. Dave's Video, $39.99; Letterbox Version, $49.99.

THE CONSTANT NYMPH
AFI/LC. Feature, preservation copy.

BFI. Preservation copy.

LC. Viewing copy, 35 mm.

UCLA . 35 mm.

MOMA. 1934 British edition.

WISCONSIN. 16 mm, 35 mm, or ¾-in. video.

Video, laser disc, and 16-mm rentals not available.

CREATIVITY WITH BILL MOYERS: JOHN HUSTON
LC. Viewing copy, video.

UCLA. Video.

MTV. Viewing copy.

VIDEO PUBLISHERS. Atlantic Community College, Austin Public Library, Denver Public Library, Kokomo Public Library, Muncie Public Library, North Carolina State Library, University of Michigan.

VIDEO SALES. PBS Video, $49.95. Huston's interview is fourth in the series.

CRUCIFIXION OF JESUS. *See* APPOINTMENT WITH DESTINY: THE CRUCIFIXION OF JESUS.

DANGER SIGNAL
AFI/LC. Feature.

LC. Fine-grain master positive.

WISCONSIN. 16 mm, 35 mm, or ¾-in. video.

RENTALS, 16 mm. Swank.

Video* and laser disc not available.

Note. *In all likelihood, TCM has shown and may continue to screen this film, for it is a part of the Warner Brothers Library, which Ted Turner owns.

THE DEAD
BFI. Viewing copy.

LC. Viewing copy, 35 mm; reference print, 35 mm.

MOMA. Viewing copy, 35 mm.

RENTAL, 16 mm. Kino International.

VIDEO PUBLISHERS. First Rate (England), Festival Films, Kino on Video, Live Home Video, Vestron Video, Video Catalog.

VIDEO SALES. Facets, Movies Unlimited. $14.99.

VIDEO RENTALS. Facets, Eddie Brandt.

LASER DISC PUBLISHER. Pioneer Laser Visions.

LASER DISC RENTALS. Dave's Video.

DEATH DRIVES THROUGH
BFI. Viewing copy.

Video, laser disc, and 16-mm rentals not available.

THE DECEIVERS
VIDEO PUBLISHER. Warner Home Video.

VIDEO SALES. Facets, Movies Unlimited. $19.98.

VIDEO RENTALS. Eddie Brandt, Facets.

LASER DISC SALES. Dave's Video. $29.99.

DE SADE
LC. Viewing copy, 35 mm.

RENTALS, 16 mm. Budget Films, Films Inc., Swank, Video Communications.

Video and laser disc not available.

THE DESERTER

AFI/LC. Feature.

UCLA. 16 mm.

RENTAL, 16 mm. Films Inc.

VIDEO PUBLISHERS (released as *Ride to Glory*): Hollywood Home Entertainment, Paramount Home Video, Simitar Entertainment.

VIDEO SALES. Facets, Movies Unlimited. $19.95.

VIDEO RENTALS. Eddie Brandt, Facets.

DESTRY RIDES AGAIN

AFI/LC. Feature, trailer, reference print available for viewing at LC.

LC. Fine-grain master print (1932 version).

MOMA. Reference copy.

RENTALS, 16 mm. Swank (1932 and 1939 version); Williams Films (1932 version).

VIDEO PUBLISHER. MCA/Universal Home Video (1939 version).

VIDEO SALES. Facets, Movies Unlimited. $14.98 (1939 version).

VIDEO RENTALS. Eddie Brandt, Facets (1939 version).

LASER DISC SALES. Dave's Video. $39.99 (1939 version).

DIRECTED BY WILLIAM WYLER

AMPAS. FILM ARCHIVES. Archival material, restrictions apply.

LC. Viewing copy, 16 mm.

MIDDLEBURG COLLEGE LIBRARY, VERMONT. 16 mm.

UCLA. Video.

THE DIRECTORS GUILD SERIES: JOHN HUSTON

UCLA. Video.

DISRAELI

RENTALS, 16 mm. MGM/UA, Swank.

VIDEO SALES. Movies Unlimited. $19.99.

VIDEO RENTALS. Eddie Brandt.

DR. EHRLICH'S MAGIC BULLET

AFI/LC. Feature, preservation copy, reference print available for viewing at LC.

AMPAS. FILM ARCHIVES. 16 mm copy in Huston Archives transferred to Film Archives.

LC. Viewing copy, 16 mm, 35 mm; 35 mm negative nitrate reference copy.

MOMA. Reference copy.

RENTALS, 16 mm. MGM/UA, Swank.

VIDEO RENTALS. Eddie Brandt.

A FAREWELL TO ARMS (1957 version)

BFI. Preservation copy.

LC. Viewing copy, 35 mm.

RENTALS, 16 mm. Films Inc., Twyman Films.

VIDEO RENTALS. Eddie Brandt.

FAT CITY

AMPAS. FILM ARCHIVES. 16 mm copy in Huston Archives transferred to Film Archives.

LC. Viewing copy, 35 mm.

MOMA. Viewing copy, 35 mm.

UCLA. 16 mm, 35 mm.

RENTALS, 16 mm. Arcus Films, Budget Films, Films Inc., Image Films, Ivy Films, Kit Parker, Modern Sound, National Film Video, Newman Film Library, Swank Motion, Twyman Films, Welling Motion Pictures, Westcoast Films, Wholesome Films Center; Anamorphic version: Twyman Films.

VIDEO PUBLISHER. Columbia Tristar Home Video.

VIDEO SALES. Facets, Movies Unlimited. $19.95.

VIDEO RENTALS. Eddie Brandt, Facets.

FREUD: THE SECRET PASSION

AMPAS. FILM ARCHIVES. 16 mm. Copy in Huston Archives transferred to Film Archives.

BFI. Preservation copy.

LC. Viewing copy, 35 mm.

MOMA. Viewing copy, 16 mm.

OTHER LIBRARY HOLDINGS. 35 mm copy: Hampshire College Library, Amherst, Massachusetts; Southwestern Baptist Theological Seminary Library, Forth Worth, Texas; video: University of Queensland Library, Brisbane, Australia, Australia.

RENTALS, 16 mm. Swank, Williams Films.

VIDEO PUBLISHER. A.B.C. (Sydney, Australia)

VIDEO RENTALS. Eddie Brandt (poor-quality sound).

GEORGE STEVENS: A FILMMAKER'S JOURNEY

AMPAS. FILM ARCHIVES. Archival material; restrictions apply.

LC. Viewing copy, 35 mm, laser disc.

VIDEO PUBLISHERS. Facets Multimedia, Inc.; Public Media Video.

VIDEO SALES. Facets, Movies Unlimited. $29.99.

LASER DISC PUBLISHER. Voyager Co.

LASER DISC SALES. Dave's Video, Facets. $49.99.

VIDEO RENTALS. Eddie Brandt, Facets.

THE HARD WAY (1943 version)

AFI/LC. Feature, preservation copy.

LC. Viewing copy, 16 mm, laser disc.

MOMA. Viewing copy.

STANFORD UNIVERSITY LIBRARY. Laser disc.

WISCONSIN. 16 mm, 35 mm, or ¾-in. video.

RENTALS, 16 mm. MGM/UA, Swank.

LASER DISC PUBLISHER. MGM/UA Home Video (released with *The Man I Love*).

HAUNTED SUMMER

VIDEO PUBLISHER. Media Home Entertainment.

VIDEO SALES. Movies Unlimited, $12.99; Facets reports as out of print.

VIDEO RENTALS. Eddie Brandt, Facets.

LASER DISC. Dave's Video (rentals only).

HEAD ON (*Fatal Attraction*)
VIDEO SALES. Vestron Video. $29.98 (as *Fatal Attraction*).

VIDEO RENTALS. Eddie Brandt (as *Fatal Attraction*).

THE HEART IS A LONELY HUNTER
RENTALS, 16 mm. Arcus Films, Swank.

VIDEO PUBLISHER. Warner Home Video.

VIDEO SALES. Facets, Movies Unlimited. $19.99.

VIDEO RENTALS. Eddie Brandt, Facets.

HEAVEN KNOWS, MR. ALLISON
AMPAS. FILM ARCHIVES. 16 mm. Copy in Huston Archives transferred to Film
    Archives.

BFI. Preservation copy.

LC. Viewing copy, 35 mm.

WISCONSIN. 16 mm, 35 mm, or ¾-in. video.

RENTAL, 16 mm and anamorphic versions. Films Inc.

VIDEO RENTALS. Eddie Brandt.

HERE IS GERMANY
LC. Viewing copy, video.

STANFORD UNIVERSITY. Video.

UNIVERSITY OF IOWA. Video.

RENTALS, 16 mm and anamorphic versions. Film Inc.

VIDEO RENTALS. Eddie Brandt.

HERE'S LOOKING AT YOU, WARNER BROTHERS
LC. Viewing copy, laser disc.

VIDEO PUBLISHER. Warner Home Video.

VIDEO SALES. Facets, Movies Unlimited. $19.95.

LASER DISC SALES. Dave's Video, Facets. $29.98.

HERMAN MELVILLE: DAMNED IN PARADISE
LC. Viewing copy, ¾-in. video.

NEW YORK UNIVERSITY. Video.

RUTGERS UNIVERSITY. Video.

FILM & VIDEO RENTAL & SALES. The Film Co. (Includes thirty-page companion guide).

VIDEO SALES. Pyramid Film and Video. $39.50.

HIGH ROAD TO CHINA
BFI. Preservation copy.

UCLA. Video and laser disc.

RENTALS, 16 mm. Swank.

VIDEO PUBLISHER. Warner Home Video.

VIDEO RENTALS. Eddie Brandt.

HIGH SIERRA
AFI/LC. Feature, preservation print, viewing copy. Donated by United Artists.

AMPAS. FILM ARCHIVES. 16 mm. Copy in Huston Archives transferred to Film Archives. (A second copy of film, part 1 only, was in Huston Archives.)

BFI. Preservation copy.

LC. Viewing copies, 16 mm, video, laser disc.

MOMA. Reference copy.

UCLA. Video, laser disc.

WISCONSIN. 16 mm, 35 mm, or ¾-in. video.

RENTALS, 16 mm. MGM/UA, Swank.

VIDEO PUBLISHER. CBS/Fox Video. Previously available from MGM/UA Home Video.

VIDEO SALES. Facets, Movies Unlimited. $19.95.

VIDEO RENTALS. Eddie Brandt, Facets.

LASER DISC. Dave's Video (rentals only).

LASER DISC PUBLISHERS. MGM/UA and Turner Entertainment released this film as part of a two–laser disc set, *The Bogart Collection,* which also includes *Across the Pacific.*

THE HOBBIT

LC. Viewing copy, ¾-in. video.

MTV. Viewing copy.

RENTALS, 16 mm. Budget Films, Films Inc., Roas Films.

VIDEO PUBLISHER. Warner Home Video, Center for Humanities. Previously available from Solar Home Video.

VIDEO SALES. Facets, Movies Unlimited. $14.95.

VIDEO RENTALS. Eddie Brandt, Facets.

HOLLYWOOD ON TRIAL

BFI. Preservation copy.

LC. Viewing copy, 16 mm.

RENTALS, 16 mm. Corinth Films, Images Film.

VIDEO PUBLISHERS. Corinth Films, MPI Home Video.

VIDEO SALES. Facets, Movies Unlimited. $29.98.

VIDEO RENTALS. Eddie Brandt, Facets.

LASER DISC. Dave's Video (rentals only).

A HOUSE DIVIDED

LC. Viewing copy, 35 mm.

RENTAL, 16 mm. Swank.

Video and laser disc not available.

THE HUNCHBACK OF NOTRE DAME

AFI/LC. Feature, trailer, preservation copy, viewing copy.

BFI. Preservation copy.

LC. Viewing copy, 16 mm, 35 mm.

UCLA. 16 mm, 35 mm.

WISCONSIN. 16 mm, 35 mm, or ¾-in. video.

RENTAL, 16 mm. Films Inc.

VIDEO PUBLISHER. Media Home Entertainment, Video Connection.

VIDEO SALES. Facets, Movies Unlimited. $19.99.

VIDEO RENTALS. Eddie Brandt, Facets.

HUSTON, HEMINGWAY, HEARST NEWSREEL FOOTAGE
UCLA. Video.

HYMN TO ATON

LC. Video.

VIDEO SALES. Phoenix/BFA Films.

INDEPENDENCE

VIDEO PUBLISHER. Eastern National Park and Monument Association.

VIDEO SALES. Facets, Movies Unlimited. $19.99.

IN THIS OUR LIFE

AFI/LC. Feature. Donated by United Artists.

AMPAS. FILM ARCHIVES. 16 mm. Copy in Huston Archives transferred to Film Archives.

LC. Viewing copy, ½-in. video; 35 mm preservation copy.

MOMA. Reference copy.

UCLA. 16 mm, 35 mm, video.

WISCONSIN. 16 mm, 35 mm, or ¾-in. video.

RENTALS, 16 mm. MGM/UA, Swank.

VIDEO PUBLISHER. MGM/UA Home Entertainment.

VIDEO SALES. Facets, Movies Unlimited. $19.95.

VIDEO RENTALS. Eddie Brandt, Facets.

THE INVISIBLE MAN

AFI/LC. Feature, trailer.

BFI. Viewing copy.

LC. Viewing copy, 16 mm.

MOMA. Viewing copy.

WISCONSIN. 16 mm, 35 mm, or ¾-in. video.

RENTALS, 16 mm. Swank

VIDEO PUBLISHERS. MPI Home Video, Karol Video, Valencia Entertainment Corp.

VIDEO SALES. Facets, Movies Unlimited. $19.98.

VIDEO RENTALS. Eddie Brandt, Facets.

LASER DISC SALES. Dave's Video, Facets. $34.99.

IT HAPPENED IN PARIS

BFI. Viewing copy.

JAGUAR LIVES

BFI. Preservation copy.

LC. Viewing copy, 35 mm.

RENTALS, 16 mm. Swank.

VIDEO PUBLISHER. Trans-World Entertainment. Previously available from Interglobal Home Video.

VIDEO RENTALS. Eddie Brandt.

JEZEBEL

AFI/LC. Feature, preservation print, viewing copy. Donated by United Artists.

AMPAS. FILM ARCHIVES. 16 mm. Copy in Huston Archives transferred to Film Archives.

BFI. Viewing copy.

LC. Viewing copy, 16 mm, 35 mm, video.

MOMA. Reference copy.

UCLA. 16 mm, 35 mm.

USC. 16 mm.

WISCONSIN. 16 mm, 35 mm, or ¾-in. video.

RENTALS, 16 mm. MGM/UA, Swank.

VIDEO PUBLISHER. MGM/UA Home Entertainment. Previously available from Key Video, CBS/Fox Video.

VIDEO SALES. Facets, Movies Unlimited. $19.95.

VIDEO RENTALS. Eddie Brandt, Facets.

LASER DISC SALES. Dave's Video, Facets. $34.99.

JOHN HUSTON. 1956. Interview (New Bedford, Mass.).

LC.

JOHN HUSTON. 1961. Interview (United Kingdom).
BFI. Preservation copy.

JOHN HUSTON. 1967. The Levin Interview, Rediffusion TV (United Kingdom).
BFI. Preservation copy.

JOHN HUSTON. 1972. Interview, Granada TV (United Kingdom).
BFI. Preservation copy.

JOHN HUSTON, HEARST NEWSREEL FOOTAGE.
UCLA. Video.

JOHN HUSTON, FRED ZINNEMANN. Unidentified Films.
UCLA. 35 mm.

JOHN HUSTON, A WAR REMEMBERED
UCLA. Video.

JOHN HUSTON AND THE DUBLINERS
BFI. Viewing copy.

LC. Viewing copy, 16 mm, ¾-in. video.

OTHER LIBRARY HOLDINGS (Video). Akron-Summit County Public Library; Austin Public Library; Birmingham-Jefferson Library; Buffalo and Erie County Public Library; Central Pennsylvania District Library Center; Cincinnati Public Library; Cuyahoga County, Eastern Shores Library System; Decatur Public Library; Eugene Public Library; Finger Lakes Library System, Four County System; Hudson Valley Community College; Lincoln County District, Indianapolis-Marion County Public Library; The Library Network, Lincoln Trail System; Minuteman Library Network; National Defense University; Northern Illinois University; Onondaga Community College; Oregon State Library; Pennsylvania Public Library Film Center; Rochester Public Library; Texas A&M University; Thousand Oaks Public Library; University of Scranton; Wichita Public Library.

VIDEO PUBLISHER. Kino on Video. Previously available from King Video.

VIDEO SALES. Movies Unlimited. $29.99.

VIDEO RENTALS. Eddie Brandt.

JOHN HUSTON: THE MAN, THE MOVIES, THE MAVERICK
AMPAS. FILM ARCHIVES. ½-in. video.

LC. 1-in. video master.

UCLA. Video.

VIDEO PUBLISHERS. Instructional Video, Turner Home Entertainment.

VIDEO SALES. Facets, Movies Unlimited. $29.98.

VIDEO RENTALS. Eddie Brandt, Facets.

LASER DISC PUBLISHERS. Image Entertainment, Turner Home Entertainment.

LASER DISC SALES. Facets. $29.95.

THE JOURNEY OF ROBERT F. KENNEDY
AMPAS. FILM ARCHIVES. 16 mm.

MTV. Viewing copy.

UCLA. 16 mm, video.

OTHER LIBRARY HOLDINGS (16 mm). Jacksonville Public Library, Morris County, Rochester Public Library.

RENTALS, 16 mm. Budget Films, Films Inc., Swank Motion, Wholesome Film Center.

Video and laser disc not available.

JUAREZ
AFI/LC. Feature, preservation print, viewing copy. Donated by United Artists.

BFI. Preservation copy.

LC. Viewing copy, 16 mm.

MOMA. Reference copy.

UCLA. 16 mm, 35 mm, video.

WISCONSIN. 16 mm, 35 mm, or ¾-in. video.

RENTALS, 16 mm. MGM/UA, Swank.

VIDEO PUBLISHER. MGM/UA Home Entertainment.

VIDEO SALES. Facets, Movies Unlimited. $19.95.

VIDEO RENTALS. Eddie Brandt, Facets.

KATHARINE HEPBURN AND HUMPHREY BOGART IN LEOPOLDVILLE, THE BELGIAN CONGO, AFRICA (Hearst Vault Material, June 6, 1951) UCLA.

KEY LARGO

AFI/LC. Feature, preservation copy, viewing copy. Donated by United Artists.

AMPAS. FILM ARCHIVES. 16 mm. Copy in Huston Archives transferred to Film Archives.

BFI. Viewing copy.

LC. Viewing copy, 16 mm, ½-in. video; reference copy, 35-mm nitrate negative.

MOMA. Reference copy.

UCLA. 16 mm, 35 mm.

WISCONSIN. 16 mm, 35 mm, or ¾-in. video.

RENTALS, 16 mm. MGM/UA, Swank.

VIDEO PUBLISHERS. CBS/Fox Video, MGM/UA Home Entertainment, Time-Life Video and Television. Previously available from Key Video.

VIDEO SALES. Facets, Movies Unlimited. $19.95.

VIDEO RENTALS. Eddie Brandt, Facets.

LASER DISC SALES. Dave's Video, Facets. $34.99.

THE KILLERS

AFI/LC. Feature, trailer.

BFI. Viewing copy.

KANSAS CITY PUBLIC LIBRARY. Video.

LC. Viewing copy, 16 mm.

UCLA. 16 mm, video.

WISCONSIN. 16 mm, 35 mm, or ¾-in. video.

RENTALS, 16 mm. Swank, Williams Films.

VIDEO PUBLISHER. CIC Video (a French release, but in English).

VIDEO RENTALS. Eddie Brandt.

KISS THE BLOOD OFF MY HANDS

RENTALS, 16 mm. Swank.

Video and laser disc not available.

KNOW YOUR ENEMY: JAPAN

LC. Viewing copy, 16 mm, video.

OTHER LIBRARY HOLDINGS (Video). New York University, Rutgers University, Stanford University, University of Michigan.

RENTALS, 16 mm. Iowa Films, Kit Parker.

SALES. National Audio Visual Center.

VIDEO RENTALS. Eddie Brandt, National Audiovisual Center.

THE KREMLIN LETTER

AMPAS. FILM ARCHIVES. 16 mm. Copy in Huston Archives transferred to Film Archives.

BFI. Viewing copy.

LC. Viewing copy, 35 mm.

UCLA. 16 mm.

RENTALS, 16 mm. Films Inc.

Video and laser disc not available.

THE LAST RUN

LC. Viewing copy, 35 mm.

UCLA. 16 mm, video.

RENTAL, 16 mm. MGM/UA.

Video and laser disc not available.

LAUGHING BOY

VIDEO RENTALS. Eddie Brandt.

LAW AND ORDER

RENTALS, 16 mm. Swank.

VIDEO RENTALS. Eddie Brandt.

THE LEGEND OF MARILYN MONROE

LC. Viewing copy, ¾-in. video.

UCLA. Video.

VIDEO RENTALS. Eddie Brandt.

LET THERE BE LIGHT

MOMA. Viewing copy, 16 mm.

UCLA. Video.

WISCONSIN. 16 mm, 35 mm, or ¾-in. video.

RENTALS, 16 mm. Budget Films, Em Gee Film Lib., IFEX, Image Films, Kino International, Kit Parker, National Audio Visual Center, National Cinema.

SALES, 16 mm. Festival Films, Kino International, National Audio Visual Center, Image Films.

LEASE, 16 mm. Kino International.

VIDEO SALES. Barr Films, Boomerang Publishers, Editions Montparnasse (Paris, France; published 1991), Educational Video Library, Facets Multimedia, Foothill Video, Hollywood Attic, Hollywood Home Theater, Horizon Entertainment, IFEX, International Historic Films, Movies Unlimited, National Audiovisual Center, Nostalgia Family Video. $24.95. Previously available from Budget Films, King Features Entertainment, Kit Parker (video), Tamarelle's French Film House, Victory Video, Video Images.

VIDEO RENTALS. Eddie Brandt, Facets.

THE LIFE AND TIMES OF JOHN HUSTON, ESQ

AMPAS. FILM ARCHIVES. 16 mm.

RENTALS, 16 mm. Indiana Audio Visual Center.

Video and laser disc not available.

THE LIFE AND TIMES OF JUDGE ROY BEAN

AMPAS. FILM ARCHIVES. 16 mm. Copy in Huston Archives transferred to Film Archives.

BFI. Preservation copy.

LC. Viewing copy, 35 mm.

UCLA. 16 mm, video.

RENTALS, 16 mm. Films Inc., Modern Sound, Swank, Twyman Films, Williams Films.

VIDEO PUBLISHER. Warner Home Video.

VIDEO SALES. Facet, Movies Unlimited. $19.98.

VIDEO RENTALS. Eddie Brandt, Facets.

LASER DISC SALES. Dave's Video. $39.99.

LIGHTS! CAMERA! ANNIE!
LC. Viewing copy, ¾-in. video.

LINCOLN CENTER, NEW YORK CITY—World Premiere, *The Night of the Iguana* (Hearst Vault Material)
UCLA. Video.

THE LIST OF ADRIAN MESSENGER
AMPAS. FILM ARCHIVES. 16 mm. Copy in Huston Archives transferred to Film Archives.

BFI. Preservation copy.

LC. Viewing copy, 35 mm.

UCLA. 16 mm.

RENTALS. 16 mm. Swank.

VIDEO PUBLISHER. MCA/Universal Home Video.

VIDEO SALES. Facets, Movies Unlimited. $19.99.

VIDEO RENTALS. Eddie Brandt, Facets.

LASER DISC PUBLISHER. MCA Universal Home Video.

LASER DISC SALES. Dave's Video. $62.99.

THE LONELY PASSION OF JUDITH HEARNE
VIDEO PUBLISHER. Cannon Video.

VIDEO SALES. Facets, Movies Unlimited. $79.98.

VIDEO RENTALS. Eddie Brandt, Facets.

LOVE AND BULLETS
RENTALS, 16 mm. Swank.

VIDEO PUBLISHER. CBS/Fox Video.

VIDEO SALES. Movies Unlimited. $12.99.

LOVESICK
BFI. Preservation copy.

LC. Viewing copy, 35 mm.

RENTAL, 16 mm. Swank.

VIDEO PUBLISHER. Warner Home Video.

VIDEO SALES. Movies Unlimited. $19.98.

VIDEO RENTALS. Eddie Brandt.

LASER DISC SALES. Dave's Video. $34.99.

LUIS BUÑUEL

LIBRARY HOLDINGS. Johns Hopkins University, University of California, Berkeley.

VIDEO PUBLISHER. Project for International Communication Studies, Iowa City, Iowa (in Spanish). University of Iowa, 2222 Old Highway, 218 South, Iowa City, IA 52242-1602. 800–373–PICS (7427).

THE MACKINTOSH MAN

AMPAS. FILM ARCHIVES. 16 mm. Copy in Huston Archives transferred to Film Archives. (Huston Archives had another 16-mm copy.)

BFI. Viewing copy.

LC. Viewing copy, 16 mm, 35 mm.

UCLA. 35 mm, video.

RENTALS, 16 mm. Swank, Williams Films.

VIDEO PUBLISHER. Warner Home Video.

VIDEO SALES. Facets, Movies Unlimited. $14.99.

VIDEO RENTALS. Eddie Brandt, Facets.

THE MADWOMAN OF CHAILLOT

BFI. Viewing copy.

LC. Viewing copy, 35 mm.

UCLA. 35 mm.

VIDEO PUBLISHER. Warner Home Video.

VIDEO SALES. Facet, Movies Unlimited. $29.95.

LASER DISC SALES. Dave's Video. $39.99.

THE MAGNIFICENT YANKEE

RENTALS, 16 mm. MGM/UA, Swank.

VIDEO PUBLISHER. MGM/UA Home Entertainment.

VIDEO SALES. Facets, Movies Unlimited. $19.98.

VIDEO RENTALS. Eddie Brandt, Facets.

THE MALTESE FALCON

AFI/LC. Feature, preservation copy, viewing copy. Donated by United Artists.

AMPAS. FILM ARCHIVES. 16 mm. Copy in Huston Archives transferred to Film Archives.

BFI. Viewing copy.

LC. Viewing copy, 16 mm, 35 mm, video.

MOMA. Viewing copies, 16 mm, 35 mm.

UCLA. 16 mm, video.

WISCONSIN. 16 mm, 35 mm, or ¾-in. video.

RENTALS, 16 mm. MGM/UA, Swank.

VIDEO PUBLISHER. CBS/Fox Video, Magnetic Video MGM/UA Home Video, Time-Life Video and Television, Turner Entertainment Co.

VIDEO SALES. Facets, Movies Unlimited. $19.98.

VIDEO RENTALS. Eddie Brandt, Facets.

LASER DISC PUBLISHERS. CBS/Fox Video, MGM/UA Home Video, RCA Selecta Vision Video Discs, Turner Entertainment Co.

LASER DISC SALES. Dave's Video, Facets. $34.99.

MAN FOR ALL SEASONS

RENTALS, 16 mm. Films Inc., Swank.

VIDEO PUBLISHER. Columbia Tristar Home Video.

VIDEO SALES. Facets, Movies Unlimited. $19.95.

VIDEO RENTALS. Eddie Brandt, Facets.

MAN IN THE WILDERNESS

BFI. Preservation copy.

LC. Viewing copy, 35 mm.

RENTALS, 16 mm. Swank, Twyman Films, Williams Films.

VIDEO PUBLISHER. Warner Home Video.

VIDEO SALES. Movies Unlimited. $14.99.

VIDEO RENTALS. Eddie Brandt.

MAN OF LA MANCHA

RENTALS, 16 mm. MGM/UA, Welling Motion Pictures.

VIDEO PUBLISHER. CBS/Fox Video.

VIDEO SALES. Facets, Movies Unlimited. $19.99.

VIDEO RENTALS. Eddie Brandt, Facets.

LASER DISC SALES. Dave's Video. $49.99.

THE MAN WHO WOULD BE KING

AMPAS. FILM ARCHIVES. 16 mm. Copy in Huston Archives transferred to Film Archives.

BFI. Viewing copy.

LC. Viewing copy, 35 mm.

UCLA. 16 mm, video.

RENTALS, 16 mm. Hurlock Cine-World, Swank.

VIDEO PUBLISHER. CBS/Fox Video, Gaumont Columbia Tristar (Paris, France; French-language version), Warner Home Video.

VIDEO SALES. Facets, Movies Unlimited. $19.98.

VIDEO RENTALS. Eddie Brandt, Facets.

LASER DISC PUBLISHER. CBS/Fox Video, Gaumont Columbia Tristar (French version, 1992).

LASER DISC. Dave's Video (rentals only).

MARILYN: THE UNTOLD STORY

LC. Viewing copy, ¾-in. video.

VIDEO PUBLISHER. ABC Video (no price listed). No indication of being currently available from suppliers.

THE MIGHTY BARNUM

MOMA. Excerpt.

UCLA. 35 mm.

RENTALS, 16 mm. Ivy Films.

Video and laser disc not available.

MINOR MIRACLE (*Young Giants*)

VIDEO PUBLISHERS. Columbia Tristar Home Video, Sultan Entertainment. Previously available from Embassy Home Entertainment.

VIDEO RENTALS. Eddie Brandt.

LASER DISC. Dave's Video (rentals only).

THE MISFITS

AMPAS. FILM ARCHIVES. 16 mm publicity film; 16 mm copy of feature film in Huston Archives transferred to Film Archives.

BFI. Preservation copy.

LC. Viewing copy, video disc.

UCLA. Laser disc.

RENTALS, 16 mm. MGM/UA, Swank.

VIDEO PUBLISHERS. CBS/Fox Video, MGM/UA Home Video, Twentieth Century-Fox Video.

VIDEO SALES. Facets, Movies Unlimited. $19.98.

VIDEO RENTALS. Eddie Brandt, Facets.

LASER DISC PUBLISHER. MGM/UA Home Video.

LASER DISC SALES. Dave's Video, Facets. $39.98.

MR. CORBETT'S GHOST

VIDEO PUBLISHERS. Karol Video, Monterrey Home Video.

VIDEO SALES. Facets, Movies Unlimited. $24.95.

VIDEO RENTALS. Eddie Brandt, Facets.

MR. NORTH

LC. Viewing copy, 35 mm.

VIDEO SALES. Movies Unlimited. $14.99.

VIDEO RENTALS. Eddie Brandt.

MR. SKEFFINGTON

AFI/LC. Feature. Donated by United Artists.

BFI. Preservation copy.

LC. Viewing copy, 35 mm.

RENTALS, 16 mm. MGM/UA, Swank.

VIDEO PUBLISHER. MGM Home Entertainment.

VIDEO SALES. Facets, Movies Unlimited. $19.95.

VIDEO RENTALS. Eddie Brandt, Facets.

MOBY DICK

AMPAS. FILM ARCHIVES. 16 mm. Copy in Huston Archives transferred to Film
  Archives.

BFI. Preservation copy.

LC. Viewing copy, 35 mm.

MOMA. Reference copy.

UCLA. 16 mm.

WISCONSIN. 16 mm, 35 mm, or ¾-in. video.

RENTALS, 16 mm. MGM/UA, Swank.

VIDEO PUBLISHER. CBS/Fox Video.

VIDEO SALES. Bennett Marine Video, Facets, Home Vision Cinema, Movies
  Unlimited. $19.95.

VIDEO RENTALS. Eddie Brandt, Facets.

LASER DISC PUBLISHER. CBS/Fox Video.

LASER DISC SALES. Dave's Video. $34.99.

MOBY DICK: JOHN HUSTON INTERVIEW

AFI/LC. Short, preservation copy.

MOMO

LIBRARY HOLDING. Goethe Institute of San Francisco.

VIDEO PUBLISHER. Taurus Video (Munich, Germany; in German).

MONEY AND MEDICINE
LIBRARY HOLDINGS. Lawrence University, National College of Chiropractic, Toledo-Lucas County Public Library, Texas A&M University.

VIDEO PUBLISHER. Amagin (Erie, Penn.).

MOULIN ROUGE
AMPAS. FILM ARCHIVES. 16 mm. Copy in Huston Archives transferred to Film Archives.

BFI. Preservation copy.

LC. Viewing copy, 35 mm.

MOMA. Reference copy.

UCLA. 35 mm.

WISCONSIN. 16 mm, 35 mm, ¾-in. video.

RENTALS, 16 mm. Budget Films, Em Gee Film Lib., Janus Films, MGM/UA, Swank.

VIDEO PUBLISHER. MGM/UA Home Video.

VIDEO SALES. Facets, Movies Unlimited. $19.95.

VIDEO RENTALS. Eddie Brandt, Facets.

LASER DISC PUBLISHER. MGM/UA Home Video.

LASER DISC SALES. Dave's Video. $39.99.

MOVIE DIRECTOR JOHN HUSTON TALKS (Hearst Newsreel Footage, New York City, May 25, 1950)
UCLA. 16 mm, 35 mm, video.

MOVIOLA: "THIS YEAR'S BLONDE"
BFI. Preservation copy.

LC. Viewing copy, 16 mm.

MURDERS IN THE RUE MORGUE
AFI/LC. Feature.

BFI. Viewing copy.

LC. Fine-grain master positive.

UCLA. 16 mm, video.

RENTALS, 16 mm. Swank, Welling Motion Pictures.

VIDEO PUBLISHER. MCA/Universal Home Video.

VIDEO SALES. Facets, Movies Unlimited. $14.98.

VIDEO RENTALS. Eddie Brandt, Facets.

MYRA BRECKINRIDGE
AFI/LC. Feature.

BFI. Viewing copy.

LC. Viewing copy, 35 mm.

MOMA. 16 mm. Viewing copy.

RENTALS, 16 mm. Films Inc., Twyman Films.

VIDEO PUBLISHER. CBS/Fox Video.

VIDEO RENTALS. Eddie Brandt.

NEWS OF THE DAY 19, no. 217—excerpt, "Red Issue Creates Furor at House
Movie Inquiry, Washington, D.C."
UCLA. Video.

THE NIGHT OF THE IGUANA
AMPAS. FILM ARCHIVES. 16 mm. Copy in Huston Archives transferred to Film
Archives.

BFI. Viewing copy.

LC. Viewing copy, 35 mm, Video.

UCLA. 35 mm.

RENTALS, 16 mm. MGM/UA, Swank.

VIDEO PUBLISHER. MGM/UA Home Video.

VIDEO SALES. Facets, Movies Unlimited. $19.98.

VIDEO RENTALS. Eddie Brandt, Facets.

LASER DISC PUBLISHER. MGM/UA Home Video.

LASER DISC SALES. Facets Multimedia. $39.98.

NOTES FROM UNDER THE VOLCANO
LIBRARY HOLDING. Los Angeles Public Library.

VIDEO PUBLISHERS. Fototronics, K Films Video (Paris, France; in English with French subtitles).

OBSERVATIONS UNDER THE VOLCANO

LIBRARY HOLDINGS. Bibliomation, Inc.; Fairfield Public Library; Lee County Library System; North Adams State College; Ohio State University; Trinity University; University of New England; University of North Carolina; Wayne State College.

FILM PUBLISHER. 16 mm. Christian Blackwood Productions.

VIDEO PUBLISHER. United Pacific Arts Video Records.

VIDEO RENTALS. Eddie Brandt.

ON LOCATION: THE NIGHT OF THE IGUANA (Hollywood and the Stars)

LC. Viewing copy, 16 mm.

ON OUR MERRY WAY (*A Miracle Can Happen*)

LC. Fine-grain master positive of outtakes.

VIDEO RENTALS. Eddie Brandt.

ORSON WELLES: THE ONE-MAN BAND

VIDEO. Location not found. See chapter 14, "Huston on Film," for other details.

THE ORSON WELLES STORY

BFI. Preservation copy.

THE OTHER SIDE OF THE WIND. *See* THE AMERICAN FILM INSTITUTE SALUTE TO ORSON WELLES; ORSON WELLES: THE ONE-MAN BAND; WORKING WITH ORSON WELLES.

PATTON

AFI/LC. Feature.

RENTALS, 16 mm. Films Inc., Williams Films.

VIDEO PUBLISHERS. Fox Video, Time-Life Video and Television.

VIDEO SALES. Facets, Movies Unlimited. $29.98.

VIDEO RENTALS. Eddie Brandt, Facets.

LASER DISC SALES. Dave's Video. Letterbox, $69.99; regular pan and scan, $34.99.

PHOBIA

BFI. Viewing copy.

LC. Viewing copy, 35 mm.

VIDEO PUBLISHER. Paramount Home Video.

VIDEO SALES. Facets, Movies Unlimited. $79.99.

VIDEO RENTALS. Eddie Brandt, Facets.

PORTRAIT OF THE ARTIST AS A YOUNG MAN

RENTALS. 16 mm. Texture film.

VIDEO PUBLISHER. Instructional Video.

VIDEO SALES. Facets, Movies Unlimited. $29.95.

VIDEO RENTALS. Facets, Eddie Brandt.

THE PRINCE AND THE SHOWGIRL

MOMA. Viewing copy.

VIDEO PUBLISHER. Warner Home Video.

VIDEO SALES. Facets, Movies Unlimited. $19.98.

VIDEO RENTALS. Eddie Brandt, Facets.

LASER DISC SALES. Dave's Video. $34.99.

PRIZZI'S HONOR

BFI. Preservation copy.

LC. Viewing copy, 35 mm.

MOMA. Viewing copy, 35 mm.

UCLA. 35 mm, video.

RENTALS, 16 mm. Kit Parker.

VIDEO PUBLISHERS. Paramount Home Video, Summa Video, Vestron Home Video.

VIDEO SALES. Facets, Movies Unlimited. $14.95.

VIDEO RENTALS. Eddie Brandt, Facets.

LASER DISC PUBLISHER. Vestron Home Video.

LASER DISC. Dave's Video (rentals only).

THE PROWLER

UCLA. 16 mm, video.

RENTALS, 16 mm. Ivy Films.

VIDEO PUBLISHER. VCII Home Entertainment.

VIDEO SALES. Movies Unlimited. $29.99.

THE QUARE FELLOW

RENTALS, 16 mm. Films Inc.

Video and laser disc not available.

QUO VADIS

UCLA. 16 mm, 35 mm.

BFI. Preservation copy.

RENTALS, 16 mm. MGM/UA, Swank.

VIDEO PUBLISHER. MGM/UA Home Entertainment.

VIDEO SALES. Applause Productions, Facets, Ignatius Press, Movies Unlimited. $29.98.

VIDEO RENTALS. Eddie Brandt, Facets.

LASER DISC SALES. Dave's Video. $39.99.

THE RED BADGE OF COURAGE

AMPAS. FILM ARCHIVES. 16 mm. Copy in Huston Archives transferred to Film Archives.

BFI. Viewing copy.

LC. Viewing copy, 35 mm, ¾-in. video; archival copy, 35-mm nitrate.

RENTALS, 16 mm. MGM/UA, Swank.

VIDEO PUBLISHER. MGM/UA Home Entertainment.

VIDEO SALES. Facets, Home Vision Cinema, Movies Unlimited.

VIDEO RENTALS. Eddie Brandt, Facets.

OTHER FORMATS. Sound Records, MGM/UA Home Entertainment Group, 1985, LP, Armed Forces Radio Service; in NYPL Rare Books and Manuscripts Department.

REFLECTIONS IN A GOLDEN EYE

AMPAS. FILM ARCHIVES. One reel of original tinting, 35 mm; 16-mm copy in Huston Archives transferred to Film Archives.

BFI. Viewing copy.

LC. Viewing copy, 35 mm.

MOMA. Reference copy.

UCLA. 35 mm.

RENTALS, 16 mm. Twyman Films, Video Communications.

VIDEO PUBLISHER. Warner Home Video.

VIDEO SALES. Facets, Movies Unlimited. $19.98.

RENTALS. Eddie Brandt, Facets.

REPORT FROM THE ALEUTIANS

BFI. Viewing copy.

LC. Video, 16 mm.

MOMA. Viewing copy, 16 mm.

NATIONAL. 16 mm.

UCLA. 16 mm, video.

RENTALS, 16 mm. Budget Films, Images Film.

VIDEO PUBLISHERS. Editions Montparnasse (Paris, France; 1991),* Moore Video, Valencia Entertainment. Previously available from International Historic Films, Kit Parker, Tamarelle's French Film House.*

VIDEO SALES. Facets, Movies Unlimited. $19.99.

VIDEO RENTALS. Eddie Brandt, Facets.

Note. *Cassette includes *Battle of San Pietro.*

RETURN OF THE KING

MTV. Viewing copy.

VIDEO PUBLISHERS. Fast Forward, Video Treasures, Xenon.

VIDEO SALES. Facets, Movies Unlimited. $29.99.

VIDEO RENTALS. Eddie Brandt, Facets.

RETURN TO THE ISLAND

BFI. Preservation copy.

REVENGE

RENTALS, 16 mm. Films Inc.

VIDEO PUBLISHER. Columbia Tristar Home Video.

VIDEO SALES. Facets, Movies Unlimited. $19.95.

VIDEO RENTALS. Eddie Brandt, Facets.

LASER DISC. Dave's Video (rentals only).

THE RHINEMANN EXCHANGE

LC. Viewing copy, 16 mm, chapter 1–3.

RHODES OF AFRICA

BFI. Viewing copy.

RENTAL, 16 mm. Budget Films.

VIDEO PUBLISHERS. Nostalgia Family Video, Sinister Cinema.

VIDEO SALES. Movies Unlimited. $19.95.

VIDEO RENTALS. Eddie Brandt.

RIDE THIS WAY, GRAY HORSE. *See* WALKING WITH LOVE AND DEATH.

THE ROARING TWENTIES

AFI/LC. Feature, preservation copy. Donated by United Artists.

BFI. Viewing copy.

LC. Viewing copy, video.

MOMA.

WISCONSIN. 16 mm, 35 mm, or ¾-in. video.

RENTALS, 16 mm. MGM/United, Swank.

VIDEO PUBLISHER. CBS/Fox Video, MGM/UA Home Entertainment.

VIDEO SALES. Facets, Movies Unlimited. $19.98.

VIDEO RENTALS. Eddie Brandt, Facets.

ROOTS OF HEAVEN

AMPAS. FILM ARCHIVES. 16 mm. Copy in Huston Archives transferred to Film Archives.

BFI. Preservation copy.

LC. Viewing copy, 35 mm.

WISCONSIN. 16 mm, 35 mm, or ¾-in. video.

RENTALS, 16 mm. Films Inc.

Video or laser disc not available.

RUFINO TAMAYO: THE SOURCES OF HIS ART

BFI. Preservation copy.

LC. Viewing copy, 16 mm.

MTV. Viewing copy.

FILM PUBLISHER. Alcon Films.

VIDEO PUBLISHER AND SALES. Mystic Fire Video. $50.00.

SAGA OF WESTERN MAN: CHRIST IS BORN

MTV. Viewing copy.

SATURDAY NIGHT LIVE

MTV. Viewing copy.

SERGEANT YORK

AFI/LC. Viewing copy, feature.

AMPAS. FILM ARCHIVES. 16 mm. Copy in Huston Archives transferred to Film Archives.

BFI. Preservation copy.

LC. Viewing copy, 16 mm, video.

MOMA. Viewing copy, 35 mm.

UCLA. 35 mm.

WISCONSIN. 16 mm, 35 mm, or ¾-in. video.

RENTALS, 16 mm. MGM/UA, Swank.

VIDEO PUBLISHERS. CBS/Fox Home Video, MGM/UA Home Video.

VIDEO SALES. Facets, Movies Unlimited. $19.98.

VIDEO RENTALS. Facets.

LASER DISC PUBLISHER. MGM/UA Home Video.

LASER DISC SALES. Dave's Video, Facets. $39.99.

SHERLOCK HOLMES IN NEW YORK
LC. Viewing copy, 16 mm.

SHOES OF THE FISHERMAN
WISCONSIN. 16 mm, 35 mm, or ¾-in. video.

RENTALS, 16-mm and anamorphic version. MGM United.

VIDEO PUBLISHER. MGM Home Video.

VIDEO SALES. Facets Multimedia, Movies Unlimited. $29.99.

VIDEO RENTALS. Eddie Brandt, Facets.

LASER DISC SALES. Dave's Video. $39.99.

SINFUL DAVEY
AMPAS. FILM ARCHIVES. 16 mm.

BFI. Preservation copy.

LC. Viewing copy, 35 mm.

RENTALS, 16 mm. MGM/UA, Swank.

Video and laser disc not available.

THE STORM
LC. Viewing copy, 35 mm.

THE STORY OF G.I. JOE
BFI. Viewing copy.

RENTALS, 16 mm. Budget Films, Mogul Films.

VIDEO RENTALS. Eddie Brandt.

THE STRANGER

AFI/LC. Feature.

AMPAS. FILM ARCHIVES. 16 mm.

BFI. Preservation copy.

LC. Viewing copy, 16 mm.

UCLA. 16 mm, 35 mm, video.

WISCONSIN. 16 mm, 35 mm, or ¾-in. video.

RENTALS, 16 mm. Arcus Films, Budget Films, Em Gee Film Library, Films Inc., Image Films, Ivy Films, Kit Parker, MGM/UA, Swank, Video Commission, Welling Motion Pictures, Westcoast Films.

SALES. Cinema Concepts, Festival Films, Images Films.

VIDEO PUBLISHERS AND SALES. Adventures in Video Cassettes, Alpha Video Distributors, California Video Distributors, Congress Entertainment, Diamond Entertainment Corp., Facets, Henwood Cinema Services, Goodtimes Home Video, Hollywood Home Theater, Kartes Video Communications, Movies Unlimited, Nostalgia Family Video, Prism Entertainment, Turner Home Entertainment. $29.95.

VIDEO RENTALS. Eddie Brandt, Facets.

LASER DISC SALES. Dave's Video. $34.99.

SUPERSTAR PROFILE: JOHN HUSTON. FRANCE

BFI. Film, Thames Television Transmission Company (U.K., September 16, 1982).

TARAS BULBA

RENTALS, 16 mm. MGM/UA, Swank, Westcoast Films.

VIDEO PUBLISHER. MGM/UA Home Video.

VIDEO SALES. Facets, Movies Unlimited. $19.98.

VIDEO RENTALS. Eddie Brandt, Facets.

LASER DISC PUBLISHER. MGM/UA Home Video.

LASER DISC SALES. Dave's Video. $39.99.

THE TELEVISION MAKERS
LC. Viewing copy, ¾-in. video.

TENTACLES
BFI. Preservation copy.

LC. Viewing copy, 35 mm.

OTHER LIBRARY HOLDINGS. Akron-Summit City Public Library, Beverly Hills Public Library.

RENTALS, 16 mm. Welling Motion Pictures, Williams Films.

VIDEO PUBLISHERS AND SALES. Live Home Video; Vestron Video. $59.98.

THIS PROPERTY IS CONDEMNED
LC. Viewing copy, 35 mm.

RENTALS, 16 mm. Films Inc.

VIDEO PUBLISHER. Paramount Home Video.

VIDEO SALES. Facets, Movies Unlimited. $19.95.

VIDEO RENTALS. Eddie Brandt, Facets.

LASER DISC SALES. Dave's Video. $39.99.

THREE STRANGERS
AFI/LC. Feature, preservation copy.

AMPAS. FILM ARCHIVES. 16 mm. One copy in Huston Archives and another transferred to Film Archives.

LC. Viewing copies, 35 mm, video.

MOMA. Reference copy.

UCLA. 35 mm.

WISCONSIN. 16 mm, 35 mm, or ¾-in. video.

RENTALS, 16 mm. MGM/UA, Swank.

VIDEO RENTALS. Eddie Brandt.

TOMORROW THE WORLD
RENTALS, 16 mm. Film classics.

Video and laser disc not available.

TO THE WESTERN WORLD

BFI. Viewing copy.

THE TREASURE OF THE SIERRA MADRE

AFI/LC.

AMPAS. FILM ARCHIVES. 16 mm. Copy in Huston Archives transferred to Film Archives.

BFI. Viewing copy.

LC. Viewing copies, 16 mm, 35 mm.

MOMA. Reference copy.

UCLA. 16 mm, 35 mm, video.

WISCONSIN. 16 mm, 35 mm, ¾-in.video.

RENTALS, 16 mm. MGM/UA, Swank.

VIDEO PUBLISHERS. CBS/Fox Video, MGM/UA Home Video, Time-Life Video and Television. Previously available from Key Video.

VIDEO SALES. Facets, Movies Unlimited. $19.98.

VIDEO RENTALS. Eddie Brandt, Facets.

LASER DISC PUBLISHER. CBS/Fox Video, MGM/UA Home Video, RCA Selecta Vision Video Discs.

LASER DISC SALES. Dave's Video. $39.99.

TUNISIAN VICTORY

BFI. Viewing copy.

LC. Viewing copy, 35 mm.

RENTALS, 16 mm. Budget Films.

VIDEO SALES. Available on one cassette from Discount Video Tapes, Nostalgia Family Video, Victory Video/Captain Bijou; $24.95. Also available on two cassettes from Columbia Tristar Home Video; no price indicated. Also available from Facets, Movies Unlimited. $29.95.

UNDERGROUND

AFI/LC.

BFI. Viewing copy.

LC. Viewing copy, 35 mm.

WISCONSIN. 16 mm, 35 mm, ¾-in. video.

RENTALS, 16 mm. MGM/UA, Swank.

VIDEO RENTALS. Eddie Brandt.

UNDER THE VOLCANO

LC. Viewing copy, 35 mm.

UCLA. 35 mm, video.

RENTALS, 16 mm. Swank.

VIDEO PUBLISHER. MCA/Universal Home Video.

VIDEO SALES. Facets, Movies Unlimited. $79.95.

VIDEO RENTALS. Eddie Brandt, Facets.

LASER DISC PUBLISHER. MCA Home Video.

LASER DISC SALES. Dave's Video. $39.99.

THE UNFORGIVEN

BFI. Preservation copy.

LC. Viewing copy, 16 mm, 35 mm.

RENTALS, 16 mm. MGM/UA.

VIDEO PUBLISHER. MGM/UA Home Video.

VIDEO SALES. Facets, Movies Unlimited. $14.99.

VIDEO RENTALS. Eddie Brandt, Facets.

LASER DISC PUBLISHER. MGM/UA Home Video.

LASER DISC SALES. Dave's Video. $39.99.

UNITED IN PROGRESS

AMPAS. FILM ARCHIVES. 35 mm.

VICTORY

LC. Viewing copy, 35 mm.

UCLA. 16 mm.

RENTALS, 16 mm. Swank.

VIDEO PUBLISHERS. CBS/Fox Video, Warner Home Video.

VIDEO SALES. Movies Unlimited. $14.99.

VIDEO RENTALS. Eddie Brandt.

THE VISITOR

LC. Viewing copy, 35 mm.

OTHER LIBRARY HOLDINGS. Chicago Public Library; Cleveland Public Library; Contra Costa County; Indianapolis-Marion County Public Library; Libraries Online, Inc.; Mesa Public Library.

RENTALS, 16 mm. Twyman Films.

VIDEO PUBLISHERS. Embassy Home Entertainment, HBO Home Video. VIDEO SALES. Hollywood Home Entertainment, UAV Corporation. $29.95.

VIDEO RENTALS. Eddie Brandt.

WALKING WITH LOVE AND DEATH (*Ride This Way, Gray Horse*)

AFI/LC.

BFI. Preservation copy.

LC. Viewing copy, 16 mm.

A WALK WITH LOVE AND DEATH

AMPAS. FILM ARCHIVES. 16 mm. Copy in Huston Archives transferred to Film Archives.

BFI. Viewing copy.

LC. Viewing copy, 35 mm.

UCLA. 16 mm.

RENTALS, 16 mm. Films Inc.

Video or laser disc not available.

WATCH ON THE RHINE

LC. 16 mm, 35 mm.

UCLA. Video, 16 mm, 35 mm.

VIDEO PUBLISHER. Key Video.

VIDEO SALES. Facets, Movies Unlimited. $19.99.

VIDEO RENTALS. Eddie Brandt.

WATERLOO

RENTALS, 16 mm. Films Inc.

VIDEO PUBLISHER. Paramount Home Video.

VIDEO SALES. Facets Multimedia, Fusion Video, Movies Unlimited. $14.95.

VIDEO RENTALS. Eddie Brandt, Facets.

WE WERE STRANGERS

AFI/LC.

AMPAS. FILM ARCHIVES. 16 mm. Copy in Huston Archives transferred to Film Archives.

BFI. Preservation copy.

LC. Viewing copy, 16 mm.

UCLA. 35 mm, video.

RENTALS, 16 mm. Bosco Films, Kit Parker.

VIDEO RENTALS. Eddie Brandt.

WHITE HUNTER, BLACK HEART

BFI. Viewing copy.

LC. Viewing copy, 35 mm, laser disc.

RENTALS, 16 mm. Swank.

VIDEO PUBLISHERS. MGM/UA Home Entertainment, Warner Home Video.

VIDEO SALES. Facets, Movies Unlimited. $19.98.

VIDEO RENTALS. Eddie Brandt, Facets.

WHO WAS THAT LADY?

RENTALS, 16 mm. Cine Craft, Film Center, Films Inc., Modern Sound, Welling Motion Pictures.

Video or laser disc not available.

WILD BOYS OF THE ROAD

LC. Viewing copy, ¾-in. video.

WISCONSIN. 16 mm, 35 mm, ¾-in. video.

RENTALS, 16 mm. MGM/UA, Swank.

VIDEO RENTALS. Eddie Brandt.

WILD WORLD OF ENTERTAINMENT. THE DICK CAVETT SHOW
MTV. Viewing copy.

THE WIND AND THE LION

BFI. Viewing copy.

LC. Viewing copy, 35 mm.

MOMA. Reference copy.

UCLA. 35 mm, video.

RENTALS, 16 mm. MGM/UA, Swank.

VIDEO PUBLISHER. MGM/UA Home Video.

VIDEO SALES. Facets, Movies Unlimited. $19.99.

VIDEO RENTALS. Eddie Brandt, Facets.

LASER DISC PUBLISHER. MGM/UA Home Video.

LASER DISC RENTALS AND SALES. Dave's Video. $39.99.

WINTER KILLS

LC. Viewing copy, 35 mm.

RENTALS, 16 mm. Films Inc.

VIDEO PUBLISHER. Columbia Tristar Home Video.

VIDEO SALES. Facets, Movies Unlimited, Sultan Entertainment. $14.95.

VIDEO RENTALS. Eddie Brandt, Facets.

LASER DISC PUBLISHER. Nelson Entertainment.

WISE BLOOD

RENTALS, 16 mm. Kino International.

VIDEO PUBLISHER. MCA/Universal Home Video.

VIDEO SALES. Facets, Movies Unlimited. $59.95.

VIDEO RENTALS. Eddie Brandt, Facets.

THE WORD

LC. Viewing copy, 16 mm.

UCLA. Video.

VIDEO SALES. Fries Home Video, Movies Unlimited. $24.95. Previously available from USA Home Video.

VIDEO RENTALS. Eddie Brandt.

WORKING WITH ORSON WELLES

LIBRARY HOLDINGS. Indiana University; Kansas City Public Library; North Carolina School of the Arts; Stanford University; University of California, Berkeley; University of Colorado; University of Hawaii; University of Illinois.

VIDEO PUBLISHERS. Grand Am, Image Entertainment.

VIDEO SALES. Facets. $29.95.

WUTHERING HEIGHTS

AMPAS. FILM ARCHIVES. 16 mm.

BFI. Preservation copy.

LC. Viewing copy, laser disc.

UCLA. 16 mm, 35 mm, video.

RENTALS, 16 mm. Films Inc., Syracuse University Film, Video Commission.

VIDEOS. Facets, HBO Home Video; Home Vision Cinema

Movies Unlimited; Sultan Entertainment. $19.98.

VIDEO RENTALS. Eddie Brandt, Facets.

LASER DISC PUBLISHER. Pioneer Entertainment.

LASER DISC RENTALS. Dave's Video (rentals only).

DIRECTORY

Names, addresses, telephone numbers, and faxes are provided from the best available sources at the time of this publication. Additional information on companies can be obtained from Christopher Scanlon's *Video Source Book,* 19th ed. (New York: Gale, 1997, 2 vols.), especially the "Program Distributors" chapter.

ABC Video
Capital Cities/ABC Video Enterprises
1200 High Ridge Road
Stamford, CT 06905
203–968–9100; Fax: 203–329–6464

Academy of Motion Picture Arts and Sciences
Margaret Herrick Library
Center for Motion Picture Study
333 S. La Cienega Boulevard
Beverly Hills, CA 90211
310–247–3036, 247–3000; Fax: 310–657–5193; Film Archives, Fax:
310–297–3036, ext. 231

Alba House
7050 Pinehurst, Box 40
Dearborn, MI 48126
313–582–2033

American Education Films
162 Fourth Avenue, N., Suite 123
Nashville, TN 37219
615–242–3330

Applause Productions
85 Longview Road
Port Washington, NY 11050
516–883–2825; 800–277–5287; Fax: 516–883–7460

Arcus Film
1225 Broadway
New York, NY 10001
212–686–2216

Baker and Taylor Video
501 S. Gladiolus
Momence, IL 60954
800–775–2300; Fax: 800–775–3500

Bennett Marine Video
2321 Abbott Kennedy Boulevard
Venice, CA 90291
310–821–3329; 800–262–8862; Fax: 310–306–3162

Bosco Films
48 Main Street, Box T
New Rochelle, NY 10802
914–632–6562

British Film Institute
21 Stephen Street
London W1P 2LN
United Kingdom
0171–255–1444; Fax: 0171–436–7950; 0171–580–7503

Budget Films
4590 Santa Monica Boulevard
Los Angeles, CA 90029
213–660–0187

Cannon Video
8200 Wilshire Boulevard, 3d Floor
Beverly Hills, CA 90211
213–966–5600; Fax: 213–653–5485

Carousel Films
241 E. 49th Street
New York, NY 10036
212–683–1660

CBS/Fox Video
1330 Avenue of the Americas, 5th Floor
New York, NY 10019
213–373–4800; 800–800–2369; Fax: 212–373–4803

Center for Humanities, Inc.
Communications Park
Box 1000
Mount Kisco, NY 10549
914–666–4100; 800–431–1242; Fax: 914–666–5319

Charard Motion Pictures
2110 E. 24th Street
Brooklyn, NY 11229
718–891–4339

Cinema Concepts
2461 Berlin Turnpike
Newington, CT 06111
203–667–1251

Columbia Tristar Home Video
Sony Pictures Plaza
10202 W. Washington Boulevard
Culver City, CA 90232
310–280–7799; Fax: 310–280–2485

Congress Entertainment
Learn Plaza, Suite 6
P.O. Box 845
Tannersville, PA 18372–0845
717–620–9001; 800–847–8273; Fax: 717–620–9278

Corinth Films
410 E. 62d Street
New York, NY 10021
212–421–4770

Corinth Video
34 Gansevoort Street
New York, NY 10014
212–463–0305; 800–221–4720; Fax: 212–929–0010

Coronet-MTI Film and Video International
P.O. Box 6005
Buffalo Grove, IL 60089–6005
800–777–8100

Critics' Choice Video
P.O. Box 749
Igtasca, IL 60143–0749
800–367–7765; Fax 708–775–3355

Dave's Video
12144 Ventura Boulevard
Studio City, CA 91604
818–760–3472; 800–736–1659; Fax: 818–760–3818

Discount Video
P.O. Box 7122
Burbank, CA 91510
818–843–3366; Fax: 415–843–3821

Eastern National Park and Monument Assoc.
325 Chestnut Street, Suite 1212
Philadelphia, PA 19106
800–821–2903

Eddie Brandt's Saturday Matinee
6310 Colfax Avenue
North Hollywood, CA 91606
818–506–4242, 506–7722

Em Gee Film Library
6924 Canby Avenue, Suite 103
Reseda, CA 91335
818–981–5506

Facets Video
1517 West Fullerton Avenue
Chicago, IL 60614
312–281–9075; 800–331–6197; Fax: 312–929–5437

Fast Forward
3420 Ocean Park Boulevard, Suite 3075
Santa Monica, CA 90405
310–396–4434; Fax: 310–396–2292

Festival Films
2841 Irving Avenue
South Minneapolis, MN 55408
612–870–4744

Film Center
938 K Street, N.W.
Washington, DC 20001
202–393–1205

Film Classics
P.O. Box 77568
Dockwelier Station
Los Angeles, CA 90007
213–731–3854

The Film Co.
511 Second Street, N.E.
Washington, DC 20002
202–547–4970; 547–5016

Films Inc.
5547 N. Ravenswood Avenue
Chicago, IL 60640–1199
800–323–4222; Fax: 312–878–8648

Fox Video
2121 Avenue of the Stars, 25th Floor
Los Angeles, CA 90087
310–369–3900; 800–800–2FOX; Fax: 310–369–5811

Fries Home Video
6922 Hollywood Boulevard, 12th Floor
Hollywood, CA 90028
213–466–2266; Fax: 213–416–2126

Fusion Video
100 Fusion Way
Country Club Hills, IL 60478
708–799–2073; Fax: 708–799–2350

HBO Home Video
1100 6th Avenue
New York, NY 10036
212–512–7400; Fax: 212–512–7498

Hollywood Home Entertainment
6165 Crooked Creek Road, Suite B
Norcross, GA 30092–3105
No phone number indicated.

Home Visions Cinema
5547 N. Ravenswood Avenue
Chicago, IL 60640–1199
312–878–2600; 800–826–3456; Fax: 312–878–8648

Horizon Entertainment
45030 Trevor Avenue
Lancaster, CA 93534
805–940–1040; 800–323–2061; Fax: 805–940–8511

Hurlock Cine-World
13 Arcadia Road
P.O. Box W
Old Greenwich, CT 06870
203–637–4319

Ignatius Press
33 Oakland Avenue
Harrison, NY 10528–9974
914–835–4216; Fax: 914–835–8406

Image Entertainment
9333 Oso Avenue
Chatsworth, CA 91311
818–407–9100; 800–473–3475; Fax: 818–407–9111

Images Film
300 Phillips Park Road
Mamaroneck, NY 10543
914–381–2993

Indiana University Audio-Visual Center
Bloomington, IN 47405
812–332–0211

Institutional Cinema
10 First Street
Saugerties, NY 12477
914–246–2848

Instructional Media Services
University of Toronto
130 St. George Street
Toronto, Ontario M55 1A5 Canada
416–978–6302; Fax: 416–978–7552

Instructional Video
727 "O" Street
Lincoln, NE 68508–1323
402–475–6570; 800–228–0164; Fax: 402–475–6500

International Historic Films, Inc.
P.O. Box 29035
Chicago, IL 60629
312–927–2900; Fax: 312–927–9211

Iowa Films
University of Iowa
C-5, Seashore Hall
Iowa City, IA 52242
319–353–5885

Ivy Films
165 W. 46 Street
New York, NY 10036
212–382–0111

James Agee Film Project
316 ½ Main Street
Johnson City, TN 37601
615–926–8637; 800–352–5111

Janus Films
1213 Wilmette Avenue
Wilmette, IL 60091
312–256–3200

Karol Video
P.O. Box 7600
Wilkes Barre, PA 18773
717–822–8899; Fax: 717–822–8226

Kent State University Film
Kent, OH 44242
216–672–3456

Kino on Video
333 W. 39th Street, Suite 503
New York, NY 10018
212–629–0871; 800–562–3330; Fax: 212–714–0871

Kit Parker Films
1245 Tenth Street
Monterey, CA 93940
408–649–5573; Fax: 408–649–8040

The Library of Congress
Motion Picture, Broadcasting and Recorded Sound Division
Washington, DC 20540–4800
202–707–5840; Fax: 202–707–2371

Live Home Video
15400 Sherman Way
P.O. Box 10124
Van Nuys, CA 91410–0124
818–988–5060

Macmillan Films
34 MacQuestern Parkway, S.
Mt. Vernon, NY 10550
914–664–5051

Maljack Productions
P.O. Box 153
Tinley Park, IL 60477
312–687–7881

MCA/Universal Home Video
70 Universal City Plaza
Universal City, CA 91608–9955
818–777–1000; Fax: 818–733–1483

Media Home Entertainment
510 W. 6th Street, Suite 1032
Los Angeles, CA 90014
213–236–1336; Fax: 213–236–1346

MGM/UA Home Entertainment
2500 Broadway
Santa Monica, CA 90404–6061
310–449–3000

MGM/United Artists Entertainment
1350 Avenue of the Americas
New York, NY 10019
800–223–0993

Modern Sound
1402 Howard Street
Omaha, NE 68102
800–228–9584

Mogulls Films
1280 North Avenue
Planfield, NJ 07062
201–753–6004

Monterrey Home Video
28038 Dorothy Drive, Suite 1
Agoura Hills, CA 91301
818–597–0047; 800–424–2593; Fax: 818–597–0105

Moore Video
P.O. Box 5703
Richmond, VA 23220
804–745–9785; Fax: 804–745–9785

Movies Unlimited
6736 Castor Avenue
Philadelphia, PA 19149–2184
800–466–8437; Fax: 215–725–3683

MPI Home Video
16101 S. 108th Avenue
Orland Park, IL 60462
708–460–0555; Fax: 708–873–3177

Music for Little People
Box 1460
Redway, CA 95560
707–923–3991; 800–727–2233; Fax: 707–923–3241

National Audio Video
4465 Washington Street
Denver, CO 80216
303–292–2952; 800–373–2952; Fax: 303–292–5629

National Audio Visual Center
5285 Port Royal Road
Springfield, VA 22161
703–487–4603; 800–553–6847; Fax: 703–321–8547

National Film and Video Center
1425 Liberty Road
Edlersburg, MD 21784
800–638–1688

New Cinema
35 Britain Street
Toronto, Ontario M5A 1R7, Canada
Phone number not indicated.

Newman Film Library
1444 Michigan Avenue, N.E.
Grand Rapids, MI 49508
616–454–8157

Nostalgia Family Video
P.O. Box 606
Baker City, OR 97814
503–523–9034

Paramount Home Video
Bluhdom Building
5555 Melrose Avenue
Los Angeles, CA 90038
213–956–8090; Fax: 213–956–1100

PBS Video
1320 Braddock Place
Alexandria, VA 22314
703–739–5380; 800–344–3337; Fax: 703–739–5269

Phoenix/BFA Films
2349 Chaffee Drive
St. Louis, MO 63146
314–569–0211; 800–221–1274; Fax: 314–569–2834

Prism Entertainment
1888 Century Park, E., Suite 1000
Los Angeles, CA 90067
310–277–3270; Fax: 310–203–8036

Roas Films
1696 N. Astor Street
Milwaukee, WI 53202
414–271–0861

Simitar Entertainment
3850 Annapolis Lane, Suite 140
Plymouth, MN 55447
612–559–6660; 800–486-TAPE; Fax: 612–559–0210

Sinister Video
P.O. Box 4369
Medford, OR 97501–0168; Fax: 503–779–8650

South Dakota State University Audiovisual Center
University Station
Brookings, SD 57006
605–688–5115

Sultan Entertainment
116 N. Robertson Boulevard
Los Angeles, CA 90048
310–976–6700

Swank Motion Pictures
201 South Jefferson Avenue
St. Louis, MO 63103–9954
314–534–6300; 800–876–5577; Fax: 314–289–2192

Syracuse University Film Rentals Center
1455 E. Colvin Street
Syracuse, NY 13210
315–423–2452

Texture Film
P.O. Box 1337

Skokie, IL 60076
312–256–4436

Time-Life Video and Television
1450 E. Parham Road
Richmond, VA 23280
804–266–6330; 800–621–7026

Trans-World Films
332 S. Michigan Avenue
Chicago, IL 60604
312–427–4545; Fax: 312–427–4550

Twyman Films
4700 Wadsworth Road
P.O. Box 605
Dayton, OH 45414
513–276–5941

UAV Corporation
P.O. Box 7647
Charlotte, NC 28241
704–548–7300; Fax: 704–548–3335

University of California, Los Angeles
Film and Television Archives
160 Powell Library Building
Los Angeles, CA 90024–1622
213–206–5388
University of Illinois Film Center
1325 S. Oak Street
Champaign, IL 61820
217–333–1360

University of Michigan Media Resources Center
416 Forth Street
Ann Arbor, MI 48109
313–764–5360

Utah Media
University of Utah
Milton Bennion Hall 207
Salt Lake City, UT 84110
801–322–6112

Valencia Entertainment Corp.
45030 Trevor Avenue
Lancaster, CA 93534–2648
805–940–1040; 800–323–2061; Fax: 805–940–8511

VCII Home Entertainment
13418 Wyandotte Street
North Hollywood, CA 91605
818–764–1777; 800–350–1931; Fax: 818–764–0231

Vestron Video
c/o Live Home Video
15400 Sherman Way
P.O. Box 10124
Van Nuys, CA 91410–0124
818–988–5060; 800–367–7765; Fax: 818–778–3125

Victory Video/Captain Bijou
4466 Jeff Road
P.O. Box 87
Toney, AL 35773
205–852–0198; Fax: 205–859–8946

The Video Catalog
P.O. Box 64267
Saint Paul, MN 55164–0267
612–659–4312; 800–733–6656; Fax: 612–659–4320

Video Communications
6555 E. Skelly Drive
Tulsa, OK 74145
918–662–6460
Video Connection
3123 W. Sylvania Avenue
Toledo, OH 43613
419–472–7727; 800–365–0449; Fax: 419–472–2655

Video Treasures
500 Kirts Boulevard
Troy, MI 48084
810–362–9660; 800–786–8777; Fax: 810–362–4454

Warner Home Video
4000 Warner Boulevard
Burbank, CA 91522
818–954–6000

Welling Motion Pictures
454 Meacham Avenue
Elmont, NY 11003
516–354–1066

Westcoast Films
25 Lusk Street
San Francisco, CA 94107
415–362–4700

Western Film and Video
30941 Agoura Road, Suite 302
Westlake Village, CA 91361
Phone and Fax: 818–889–7350

Wholesome Film Center
20 Melrose Street
Boston, MA 02116
617–426–0155

Williams Films
2240 Noblestown Road
Pittsburgh, PA 15205
412–921–5810; 800–245–1146

Willoughby Peer
115 W. 31 Street
New York, NY 10001
212–929–6477

Wisconsin Center for Film and Theater Research
816 State Street
Madison, WI 53706
609–264–6466

Worldvision Home Video
1700 Broadway
New York, NY 10019–5905
212–261–2700

Xenon
211 Arizona Avenue
Santa Monica, CA 90401
800–468–1913

XXIV

Bibliographical and Reference Sources

Listed below are resources used in the research for this book and other references that would be helpful for researchers. As reference works are often cited under author, editor, compiler, institution, or title, cross references are provided in this section.

BOOKS AND PERIODICALS

The Academy Awards Index. See Shale, Richard.

Academy of Motion Picture Arts and Sciences. Inventory to John Huston Collection, gift of John Huston, material received October 20, 1981. Inventory compiled by Linda Harris Mehr and supervised by Samuel A. Gill, archivist, March 1982.

Academy of Motion Picture Arts and Sciences. Inventories to Special Collections. Columbia Pictures: Set List/Set Budget Collection.

Edith Head Collection.

James Wong Howe Collection.

Paul Kohner Collection. Unrealized Scripts (Temporary Inventory).

Ring Lardner Jr. Collection.

Barre Lyndon Collection.

Hattie McDaniel Collection.

MGM Collection. Legal Department Records.

David Niven Collection.

Paramount Collection.

RKO Collection. Photographs, Feature Films.

John Truwe Collection.

Universal Pictures Collection.

United Artists Collection. Photographs, 1950–81.

Hal Wallis Collection.

Perc Westmore Collection.

Academy of Motion Picture Arts and Sciences. Oral History Program. Inventory of Collection. Located in AMPAS.

Academy of Motion Picture Arts and Sciences. *See Union List of Motion Picture Scripts, 1995 ed.*

Allen, E., ed. *A Guide to World Cinema.* London: Whittet Books, 1985.

Allen, Nancy. *Film Study Collections: A Guide to Their Development and Use.* New York: Fredrick Ungar, 1979.

American Film Directors. See Hochman, Stanley.

The American Film Industry. See Slide, Anthony.

The American Film Institute. *Catalog of Holdings: The American Film Institute Collection and the United Artists Collection at the Library of Congress.* Washington, D.C.: John F. Kennedy Center for the Performing Arts, 1978. Fourteen thousand films listed.

The American Film Institute Catalog of Motion Pictures. *See Meet Frank Capra.*

American Film Institute Film History Program—Oral History Transcripts. *See* Mehr, Linda, *Motion Pictures Television and Radio.*

The American Film Institute. Catalog of Motion Pictures Produced in the United States. *Feature Films: 1921–1930*—Kenneth W. Munden, executive ed., New York, R. R. Bowker, 1971, 2 vols.; *1931–1940*—Patricia King Hanson, executive ed., and Alan Gevinson, associate ed., Berkeley, University of California Press, 1993, 3 vols.; *1961–1970*—Richard P. Kfarsur, executive ed., New York, R. R. Bowker, 1976, 2 vols. (Volumes for this series also exist for 1911–1920.)

American Heritage Center, University of Wyoming. *Subject Guides: Performing Arts.* 3 vols. Laramie, Wy.: University of Wyoming, 19—. A copy of this work (undated) is in AMPAS.

American Library Directory: 1996–1997. 49th ed., 2 vols. New Providence, N.J.: R. R. Bowker, 1996.

American Screenwriters. See Clark, R..

American Theatrical Arts. See Young, William C.

An Annotated Catalog of Unpublished Film and Television Scripts at the University of Illinois at Urbana-Champaign. Urbana, Ill.: University of Illinois Library, 1983. Contains 252 scripts from 1920 to 1970, with a majority from 1940 to 1970.

Annual Index to Motion Picture Credits. Edited by B. Woodward. Beverly Hills: Academy of Motion Picture Arts and Sciences, 1988. Issued annually from the mid-1930s. Previously titled *Screen Achievements Record Bulletin. Index to Annual Volumes 1976–1987.*

Armour, Robert. *Film: A Reference Guide.* Westport, Conn.: Greenwood Press, 1980.

Ash, Lee, comp. *Subject Collections.* 7th ed. New York: R. R. Bowker; New Providence, NJ: R. R. Bowker, 1993.

Autera, Leonardo. "Huston e la critica: Bibliografica a cura di Leonardo Autera." *Bianco e Nero* 18, no. 4 (April 1957): 35–47. Annotated bibliography.

The Award Movies. See Pickard, Roy.

Award Winning Films. See Mowrey, Peter C.

Baer, D. Richard. *See Harrison's Reports and Film Reviews.*

Baker, B. *See Film Dope.*

Barson, Michael. *See The Illustrated Who's Who of Hollywood Directors.*

Basden, L. *See The Oxford Companion to Film.*

Batty, Linda. *Retrospective Index to Film Periodicals, 1930–1971.* New York: Bowker, 1975.

Behlmer. Rudy. "In Search of Directors' Paper Trails." *DGA News,* December 1994–January 1995, 50–53. Indexes the locations of director's papers.

Bibliography of Film Bibliographies. Compiled by H. Wulff. New York: K. G. Saur, 1987.

A Biographical Dictionary of the Cinema. See Thomson, D.

Bowles, Stephen E. *The Film Anthologies Index.* Metuchen, N.J.: Scarecrow, 1994.

Bowles, Stephen E. *See Index to Critical Film Reviews in British and American Film Periodicals.*

Brady, Anna, Richard Wall, and Carolynn Newitt Weiner. *Union List of Film Periodicals: Holdings of Selected American Collections.* Westport, Conn.: Greenwood Press, 1984.

Brigham Young University. Harold B. Lee Library. *A Guide to Selected Cinema Holdings of the Arts and Communications Archives.* Provo, Utah: Brigham Young University, 1978.

British Film Catalogue, 1895–1985. See Gifford, D.

The British Film Institute, London. Library. *Catalogue of the Book Library of the British Film Institute.* 3 vols. Boston: G.K. Hall, 1975. Includes holdings of unpublished screenplays.

The British Film Institute, London. Library. *Film Index International, 1972–1994. See Film Index International.*

The British Film Institute, London. National Film Archives. *Catalogue of Stills, Posters and Designs.* London: The British Film Institute, 1982. 574 p.

Brooks, Tim. *See The Complete Directory to Prime Time Network TV Shows.*

Brownstone, David M. *See Film Review Digest Annual.*

Bussinot, Roger. *L'Encyclopedie du Cinema.* 2 vols. Paris: Bordas, 1980.

Bullock, Constance S. *See* The UCLA Oral History Program.

Cahiers du cinéma, index. Paris: S. Toubiana, 1989. Covers issue no. 200 (April 1968) to no. 339 (September 1987).

California, University of, at Los Angeles. Film, Television and Radio Archives. *Film/TV/Radio: A Guide to Media Research Resources at UCLA.* Los Angeles: UCLA Publication Services Dept., n.d.

California, University, University at Los Angeles. Theater Arts Library. *Motion Pictures: A Catalog of Books, Periodicals, Screenplays, Television Scripts and Production Stills.* Edited by Audree Malkin. 2d ed, rev. Boston: G.K. Hall, 1976.

Ciment, Gilles. "John Huston (1906–1987): Biofilmographie." In *John Huston, Collection dirigée,* edited by Gilles Ciment, 180–91. Dossier Positif Rivages. Paris: Editions Rivages, 1988. (Collection Positif-Rivages, no. 2.)

Cineforum, December 1981, 51–60. "Filmografia di John Huston."

Cineforum, December 1987, 27–32. "Filmografia di John Huston."

Cinema: A Critical Dictionary—The Major Filmmakers. See Roud, Richard.

Cinema Press Books, 1920–1940. Cambridge, U.K.: Chadwyk-Healey, 1989–1991. Microfiche. Contains 774 actual press books from eight major studios and a number of smaller independents. From the Archives of the British Film Institute. For a guide to the collections, *see* Cohen, Allen.

Cinema Press Books from the Original Studio Collections. Berkshire, U.K.: Research Publications, 1988. Microfilm. Contains seventeen hundred actual press books (1919–49) from United Artists, Warner Brothers, and Monogram Pictures in the collection of the Wisconsin Center for Theater Research. For a guide to the collections *see* Cohen, Allen.

Clark, R., ed. *American Screenwriters: Second Series.* Detroit: Gale, 1986.

Cohen, Allen. *Film and TV Scripts in the UCSB Library.* Santa Barbara, Calif.: University of California, Santa Barbara, January 1992. Published and unpublished screenplays.

———. *Press Books in the UCSB Library.* Santa Barbara, Calif.: University of California, Santa Barbara, September 1992.

———. *The Wisconsin/Warner Brothers Screenplay Series: A Guide to the Collection.* Santa Barbara, Calif.: University of California, Santa Barbara Library, September 1992.

Columbia University: Oral History Collection. Edited by Elisabeth B. Mason and Louis M. Stern. New York: Oral History Research Office, 1979.

The Complete Actors' Television Credits. See Parish, James R., and Vincent Terrace.

The Complete Directory to Prime Time Network TV Shows, 1946–present. 6th ed., rev. and updated. Edited by Tim Brooks and Earle Marsh. New York: Ballantine Books, 1995.

The Complete Encyclopedia of Television Programs, 1947–1979. Compiled by Vincent Terrace. 2d ed., rev. South Brunswick, N.J.: A. S. Barnes, 1979.

The Critical Index. See Gerlach, John C., and Lana Gerlach.

Contemporary Hollywood Negative Hispanic Image. See Charles Richard Jr., Alfred.

Critics' Theater Review. New York: New York Critics' Theater Reviews, 1940–42; New York Theater Critics' Reviews, 1943–94; National Critics' Reviews, 1994–present.

Darnay, Brigitte T. *See Directory of Special Libraries and Information Centers.*

Davies, Brenda. *See International Directory of Film and TV Documentation Sources.*

DeWitt, Donald L. *See Guides to Archives and Manuscript Collections in the United States.*

Dictionary of Filmmakers. See Sadoul, Georges.

Dictionary of Films. See Sadoul, Georges.

Dictionary of Literary Biography. See Marsberger, Robert E., et al.

Directory of Archival Collections on the History of Film in the United States. See Matzed, Richard.

Directory of Archives and Manuscript Repositories. Washington, D.C.: National Historical Publication and Records Commission, 1978.

Directory of Performing Arts Collections in Greater Los Angeles. Los Angeles: Performing Arts Libraries Network of Greater Los Angeles (PALINET), 1990.

Directory of Special Libraries and Information Centers, 1996. 19th ed., 3 vols. Edited by Gwen E. Tureck. Detroit: Gale, 1996.

Dissertation Abstracts International (DAI). Ann Arbor, Mich.: University Microfilms International, 1938–. Also available on CD-ROM.

Documentary Film Classics. 2d ed. Washington, D.C.: U.S. Government National Audiovisual Center. 1980. Catalogue of films available for sale.

Dumaux, Sally, comp. *Sources for Photographs in the Los Angeles Metropolitan Area.* 3d ed. Los Angeles: Southern California Answering Network, 1980.

Dyment, A. R. *The Literature of the Film: A Bibliographical Guide to the Film as Art and Entertainment, 1936–1970.* London: White Lion, 1975.

Eddie Brandt's Saturday Matinee 1996–1997 Catalog. North Hollywood, Calif.: Eddie Brandt, 1996. (See "Directory" in chapter 23 of this book.)

Educational Film/Video Locator. 3d ed., 2 vols. New York: Bowker, 1986.

Ellis, Jack C., Charles Derry, and Sharon Kern, with research assistance from Stephen E. Bowles. *The Film Book Bibliography, 1940–1975.* Metuchen, N.J.: Scarecrow Press, 1979.

Encyclopedia of Television Series, Pilots and Specials. 3 vols. Compiled by Vincent Terrace. New York: New York Zoetrope, 1985–86.

Enser, A. G. S. *Filmed Books and Plays: A List of Books and Plays from Which Films Have Been Made, 1928–1986.* Aldershot, U.K.: Gower, 1987.

Facets Complete Video Catalog no. 14. Edited by Catherine Foley and Milos Stehik. Chicago: Facets Mutlimedia; distributed by Academy Chicago Publishers, 1996. (See "Directory" in chapter 23 of this book.)

Feature Films: A Directory of Feature Films on 16 mm and Videotape Available for Rentals, Sale and Lease. 8th ed. Compiled and edited under the direction of James Limbacher. New York: R. R. Bowker, 1985.

Fernett, Gene. *American Film Studios: A Historical Encyclopedia.* Jefferson, N.C.: McFarland, 1988.

Fielding, R. *A Bibliography of Theses and Dissertations on the Subject of Film: 1916–1979.* Houston, Tex.: University Film Association, 1979.

Film and Television Collections in Europe. See Kirchner, Daniela.

The Film Anthologies Index. See Bowles, Stephen E.

Film: A Reference Guide. See Armour, Robert.

Film as Literature, Literature as Film. See Ross, Harris.
The Film Book Bibliography, 1940–1975. See Ellis, Jack C.
Film Comment 6 (Winter 1970–71): 104. Fifty filmographies.
Film Dope 26 (January 1983): 19–24. John Huston: Biofilmography.
Filmed Books and Plays. See Enser, A. G. S.
The Film Encyclopedia. See Katz, Ephraim.
The Film Index: A Bibliography. Compiled by Workers of the Writers' Program of the Work Project Administration in the City of New York. 3 vols.: vol. 1—*Film as Art,* New York, Wilson and MOMA, 1941; vol. 2—*The Films as Industry,* White Plains, N.Y., Kraus International Publications, 1985; vol. 3—*Film in Society,* White Plains, N.Y., Kraus International Publications, 1985.
Film Literature Index. Vol. 1, *1975–.* Albany, N.Y.: Filmdex, 1975.
Filmlexicon degle autori e delle opere. 9 vols. Rome: Bianco e Nero, 1958–74. Piece on John Huston, including filmography through 1958 and bibliography.
Film Noir: A Comprehensive Illustrated Reference to Movies, Terms and Persons. See Stephens, Michael L.
Film Noir: An Encyclopedic Reference to the American Style. See Silver, Alain.
"Filmografia de John Huston." *Celluloide* (Revista Portuguesa de Cinema) 11, no. 130 (October 1968): 21–24.
Film Plots. See Neff, J.
Film Review Annual: 1981–95. Edited by Jerome S. Ozer. Englewood, N.J.: Jerome S. Ozer, 1982–96. Includes complete reviews from selected journals.
Film Review Digest Annual, 1976–77. Edited by David M. Brownstone and Irene M. Franck. Millwood, N.Y.: KTO Press, 1978.
Film Review Index. See Hanson, Patricia King.
Film Study: An Analytic Bibliography. See Manchel, Frank.
Film Study Collections. See Allen, Nancy.
Film Superlist. See Hurst, Walter.
Footage 91: North American Film and Video Sources. New York: Prelinger, 1991.
Gartenberg, Jon. *See* New York, Museum of Modern Art.
Gerlach, John C., and Lana Gerlach. *The Critical Index: A Bibliography of Articles on Film in English, 1946–1973, Arranged by Names and Topics.* New York: Teachers College, 1974.
Gifford, D., ed. *British Film Catalogue, 1895–1985: A Reference Guide.* London: Newton Abbot, David and Charles, 1986.
Goble, Alan, ed. *International Film Index, 1895–1990.* Vol. 2: *Directors' Filmography and Indexes.* New York: R. R. Bowker, 1991.
A Guide to Critical Reviews. See Salem, James.
Guides to Archives and Manuscript Collections in the United States: An Annotated Bibliography. Compiled by Donald L. DeWitt. Bibliographies and Indexes in Library and Information Sciences, no. 8. Westport, Conn.: Greenwood Press, 1994.
Halliwell's Filmgoer's and Video Viewer's Companion. 11th ed. Edited by John Walker. New York: HarperPerennial, 1995.
Halliwell's Film Guide, 1996. Rev. and updated. ed. Edited by John Walker. New York: HarperPerennial, 1995.

Hammer, Tad Bentley. *International Film Prizes: An Encyclopedia.* New York: Garland, 1991.

Hanson, Patricia King, and Stephen L. Hanson. *Film Review Index.* Vol. 1: *1882–1949;* vol. 2: *1950–85.* New York: Oryx Press, 1986.

Hanson, Patricia King, ed. *Meet Frank Capra: A Catalog of His Work.* Palo Alto, Stanford Theater Foundation. Los Angeles: National Center for Film and Video Preservation, 1990. A project of the staff of the American Film Institute Catalog of Motion Pictures Produced in the United States.

Hardy, Phil. *The Western: The Film Encyclopedia.* New York, Morrow, 1983.

Harrison's Reports and Film Reviews, 1919–1962. Edited by D. Richard Baer. Hollywood, Calif.: Hollywood Film Archives, 1992. Reprints the weekly newsletter for movie exhibitors and includes short articles with plot summaries for virtually every film released during the period.

Hash, Jay Robert, and Stanley Ralph Ross. *See The Motion Picture Guide.*

Helton, H. Stephen, comp. *Preliminary Inventory of the Records of the Office of War Information (Record Group 208).* Washington, D.C.: The National Archives, National Archives and Record Service, General Service Administration, 1953.

Herbert, Miranda. *Performing Arts Biography Master Index. See Performing Arts Master Index.*

Hochman, Stanley, ed. *American Film Directors, with Filmographies and Index of Critics and Films.* New York: Ungar, 1974.

Humanities Index. New York: Wilson Co., 1974.

Hurst, Walter. *Film Superlist: 1894–1959.* Hollywood, Calif.: Hollywood Film Archive, 1989–94. (Updated version edited by D. Richard Baer.)

The Illustrated Encyclopedia of Movie Character Actors. See Quinlan, David.

The Illustrated Who's Who of Hollywood Directors. Vol. 1: *The Sound Era,* by Michael Barson. New York: Farrar, Straus and Giroux, 1995.

Index to Critical Film Reviews in British and American Film Periodicals. Compiled by S. E. Bowles. New York: Franklin, 1975. Supplementary volume covering 1972–76 published 1979.

International Dictionary of Films and Filmmakers. 3d ed. Detroit: St. James Press, 1997. 4 vols.: vol. 1—*Films,* edited by Nicolet V. Elert and Aruna Vasudevan; vol. 2—*Directors,* edited by Laurie Collier Hillstrom; vol. 3—*Actors and Actresses,* edited by Amy Unterburger; vol. 4—*Writers and Production Artists,* edited by Grace Jeromski. Entries for Huston in vols. 2 and 3.

International Directory of Film and TV Documentation Sources. 2d ed. Edited by Brenda Davies. Brussels: Fédération Internationale des Archives du Film, 1980.

Internationale Filmbibliographie. Bibliographie internationale du cinéma. Edited by H. P. Manz. Munich: Verlagsbuchhandlung fur Filmliteratur, 1981.

International Film Index, 1895–1990. See Goble, Alan.

International Film Prizes: An Encyclopedia. See Hammer, Tad Bentley.

International Film, Radio, and Television Journals. Edited by Anthony Slide. Westport, Conn.: Greenwood Press, 1985.

International Index to Film Periodicals. Edited by Michael Moulds. New York: R. R. Bowker Company, 1973.

International Index to Television Periodicals. London: International Federation of Film Archives (FIAF), 1983–93. Volume 4 covers 1979–90.

Inventory of John Huston Collection. *See* Academy of Motion Picture Arts and Sciences.

Jayanti, Vimala. *See* The UCLA Oral History Program.

The Kael Index. *See* Slattery, William, et al.

Kael, Pauline. *5001 Nights at the Movies*. New York: Holt, 1991.

Katz, Ephraim. *The Film Encyclopedia*. 2d ed. New York: HarperCollins, 1994.

Kirchner, Daniela, ed. *Film and Television Collections in Europe: The MAP-TV Guide*. London: Blueprint, 1995.

Langman, Larry, and Daniel Finn. *A Guide to American Crime Films of the Thirties*. Bibliographies and Indexes in the Performing Arts, no. 18. Westport, Conn.: Greenwood Press, 1995.

Library of Congress. *See* United States. Library of Congress.

Limbacher, James. *See Feature Films*.

The Lively Arts Information Directory. *See* Wasserman, Steven R.

McCann, Richard Dyer, and Edward S. Perry, with special editorial assistance by Milli Moisio. *The New Film Index: A Bibliography of Magazine Articles in English, 1930–1970*. New York: Dutton, 1975.

The Macmillan Film Bibliography. 2 vols. Edited by George Reharuer. New York: Macmillan, 1982. Cover has the subtitle: "A Critical Guide to the Literature of the Motion Picture."

McNeil, Alex. *Total Television: A Comprehensive Guide to Programming from 1948 to the Present*. Harmondsworth, U.K.; New York: Penguin Books, 1980.

McNeil, Barbara. *Performing Arts Biography Master Index*. *See Performing Arts Biography Master Index*.

Magill's Survey of Cinema: English-Language Films. 4 vols. Edited by Fran N. Magill. First series. Englewood Cliffs, N.J.: Salem Press, 1980. Second series, 6 vols., 1981; Annual volumes, 1982–93.

Maltin, Leonard Maltin, ed. *The Whole Film Sourcebook*. New York, Universe Books, 1983.

———. *Leonard Maltin's Movie and Video Guide, 1998 Edition*. New York: Signet, 1997. Includes "Mail-Order Sources for Video."

Manchel, Frank. *Film Study: An Analytic Bibliography*. 4 vols. Rutherford, N.J.: Farleigh Dickinson University Press, 1990.

Manz, H. P. *See Internationale Filmbibliographie*.

Marill, Alvin. *Movies Made for Television: The Telefeature and the Mini-series, 1964–1986*. New York: New York Zoetrope, 1987.

Marsberger, Robert E., Stephen O. Lesser, and Randall Clark, eds. *Dictionary of Literary Biography*. Vol. 26, *American Screenwriters*. Detroit: Gale, 1984.

Mason, Elisabeth. *See Columbia University. Oral History Collection*.

Matzed, Richard, comp. *Directory of Archival Collections on the History of Film in the United States*. Chicago: American Library Association, 1983.

Meckler, Alan M., and Ruth McMullin. *Oral History Collections*. New York: R. R. Bowker, 1975.

Meet Frank Capra. *See* Hanson, Patricia King.

Mehr, Linda, comp. and ed. *Motion Pictures, Television, and Radio: A Union Catalogue of Manuscript and Special Collections in the Western United States.* Boston: G.K. Hall, 1977.

Morris, Peter. *See* Sadoul, Georges.

Motion Picture Association of America. Production Code Administration Files, 1927–1967. Inventory and Collection. Located in AMPAS.

Motion Picture Directors. See Schuster, Mel.

The Motion Picture Guide: 1927–83. 9 vols. Edited by Jay Robert Hash and Stanley Ralph Ross. Chicago: Cinebooks, 1985. Vol. 9, *1927–84;* vol. 10, *Silent Films;* vols. 11 and 12, *Indexes;* annual vols., 1984–95.

Motion Picture Performers. See Schuster, Mel.

Motion Pictures, Television, and Radio. See Mehr, Linda.

Moulds, Michael. *See British National Catalogue; International Index to Film Periodicals.*

Movies Made for Television. See Marill, Alvin.

Movies Unlimited Video Catalog, 1997. Philadelphia, Penn.: Movies Unlimited, 1996. (See "Directory" in chapter 23 of this book.)

Mowrey, Peter. *Award Winning Films: A Viewer's Reference to 2700 Acclaimed Motion Pictures.* Jefferson, N.C.: McFarland, 1994

Museum of Modern Art, New York. *The Film Catalog: A Listing of Holdings.* Edited by Jon Gartenberg. Boston: G.K. Hall, 1985.

National Audiovisual Center. *See Documentary Film Classics.*

National Inventory of Documentary Sources in the United States. Teaneck, N.J.: Chadwyck-Healey, 1983. Part 1: "Federal Records"; part 2: "Manuscript Division, Library of Congress"; part 3: "State Archives, State Libraries and State Historical Societies"; and part 4: "Academic and Research Libraries and Other Repositories."

National Union Catalog of Manuscript Collections. Washington, D.C.: Library of Congress, 1959–61.

Neff, J., ed. Film Plots: *Scene-by-scene Narrative Outlines for Feature Film Study.* 2 vols. Ann Arbor: Pierian Press, 1983, 1988.

The New Film Index. See McCann, Richard Dyer, and Edward S. Perry.

Newsbank. See Review of the Arts, Film and Television.

New York (City). Museum of Modern Art. Library. *Catalog of the Library of the Museum of Modern Art, New York City.* 14 vols. Boston: G.K. Hall, 1976.

New York Public Library. Research Libraries. *Catalog of the Theater and Drama Collections, Parts I, II, III.* 51 vols. Boston: G.K. Hall, 1967–1976. Part 3 reproduces the cards, now housed at the Library's Performing Arts Library, Lincoln Center, and catalogs the library's vast nonbook collection of clippings, production files, press kits, stills, and so on. The years 1977 to date are updated in the library's card catalog.

New York Times Directory of the Film. New York: Arno Press/Random House, 1971.

The New York Times Encyclopedia of Film. 13 vols. Edited by Gene Brown. New York: Times Books, 1984. Includes index. Reprints collection of facsimile articles that appeared in the *New York Times* from 1896 to 1979.

New York Times Film Reviews, 1913–1993/94. New York: New York Times, 1970–96.
The New York Times Film Reviews: A One-Volume Selection, 1913–1970. Edited by George Amberg. New York: Arno Press, 1971.
New York Times Theater Reviews, 1920–1971. New York: Arno Press, 1971.
Nowell-Smith, Geoffrey. *See The Oxford History to World Cinema.*
Oral History Collections. See Meckler, Alan M., and Ruth McMullin.
Ottoson, Robert. *A Reference Guide to the American Film Noir: 1940–1958.* Metuchen, N.J.: Scarecrow Press, 1981.
The Oxford Companion to Film. Edited by L. Bawden. Oxford, U.K.: Oxford University Press, 1976.
The Oxford History to World Cinema. Edited by Geoffrey Nowell-Smith. Oxford, U.K.: Oxford University Press, 1996.
Ozer, Jerome S. *See Film Review Annual.*
Parish, James R., and Vincent Terrace. *The Complete Actors' Television Credits, 1948–1988.* 2d ed., 2 vols. Metuchen, N.J.: Scarecrow Press, 1989–90.
Performing Arts Biography Master Index: A Consolidated Index to Over 270,000 biographical Sketches of Persons Living and Dead, As They Appear in Over 100 of the Principal Biographical Dictionaries Devoted to the Performing Arts. Edited by Barbara McNeil and Miranda C. Herbert. 2d ed. Detroit: Gale Research Co., 1982. (Revised edition of *Theater, Film and Television Biographies Master Index,* edited by Dennis La Beau, 1979 [1st ed.].)
Performing Arts Libraries and Museums of the World. See Veinstein, Andre.
Performing Arts Resources. New York: Theater Library Association, 1974.
Pickard, Roy. *The Award Movies: A Complete Guide, A–Z.* London: F. Meuller, 1980.
Picture Sources 4. See Robl, Ernest.
Positif Index, nos. 1 through 50 (March 1963). Indexes articles on John Huston.
Poteet, G. Howard. *Published Radio, Television and Film Scripts: A Bibliography.* Troy, N.Y.: The Whitson Publishing Co., 1975.
Preliminary Inventory of the Records of the Office of War Information. See Helton, Stephen H.
Primary Cinema Resources. See Wheaton, Christopher D., and Richard B. Jewell.
Prouty, Howard H. *Variety Television Reviews, 1923–1988. See Variety Television Reviews, 1923–1988.*
Published Radio, Television and Film Scripts. See G. Howard Poteet.
Quinlan, David. *The Illustrated Encyclopedia of Movie Character Actors.* New York: Harmony Books, 1985.
Rachow, Louis A., ed. *Theater and Performing Arts Collections.* New York: Haworth Press, 1981.
Readers' Guide to Periodical Literature. New York: Wilson, 1905.
Ragan, David. *Who's Who in Hollywood, 1900–1976.* New Rochelle, N.Y.: Arlington House, 1976.
A Reference Guide to the American Film Noir: 1940–1958. See Robert Ottoson.
Retrospective Index to Film Periodicals. See Batty, Linda.
Review of the Arts, Film and Television. New Canaan, Conn.: Newsbank, July 1979 to date.

Richard, Alfred Charles, Jr. *Contemporary Hollywood Negative Hispanic Image: An Interpretive Filmography, 1956–1993.* Bibliographies and Indexes in the Performing Arts, no. 16. Westport, Conn.: Greenwood Press, 1994.

Robl, Ernest, ed. *Picture Sources 4.* New York: Special Libraries Association, 1983.

Rose, Brian G. *TV Genres: A Handbook and Reference Guide.* Westport, Conn.: Greenwood Press, 1985.

Ross, Harris. *Film as Literature, Literature as Film: An Introduction to and Bibliography of Film's Relationship to Literature.* Bibliographies and Indexes in World Literature, no. 10. New York: Greenwood Press, 1987.

Roud, Richard, ed. *Cinema: A Critical Dictionary—The Major Filmmakers.* New York: Viking Press, 1980.

Rowan, Bonnie. *Scholar's Guide to Washington, D.C., Film and Video Collections.* Washington, D.C.: Smithsonian Institution Press, 1980.

Sadoul, Georges. *Dictionary of Films.* Translated, edited, and updated by Peter Morris. Berkeley: University of California Press, 1965.

———. *Dictionary of Filmmakers.* Edited, translated, and revised by Peter Morris. Berkeley: University of California Press, 1972.

Salem, James. *A Guide to Critical Reviews. Part IV: The Screenplay, from the* Jazz Singer *to* Dr. Strangelove. 2 vols. Metuchen, N.J.: Scarecrow Press, 1966–71. (*Supplement 1: 1963–80,* Scarecrow Press, 1982.)

Sarris, Andrew. *The American Cinema, Directors and Direction, 1929–1968.* New York: Dutton, 1968. (Reprint—New York, Da Capo Press, 1996.) Critical dictionary of American film directors.

Schell, Terri Kessler. *See Video Source Book.*

Scholar's Guide to Washington, D.C., Film and Video Collections. See Rowan, Bonnie.

Schuster, Mel. *Motion Picture Performers: A Bibliography of Magazine and Periodical Articles, 1900–1969.* Metuchen, N.J.: Scarecrow Press, 1971. Supplement no. 1, 1976.

———, comp. *Motion Picture Directors: A Bibliography of Magazine and Periodical Articles, 1900–1972.* Metuchen, N.J.: Scarecrow Press, 1973. Huston appears on pages 199–201.

Script City: 1994 Mega-Catalog. Hollywood, Calif.: Script City, 1994. (Or write: Script City, 1765 North Highland Avenue, Suite 760, Hollywood, CA 90028. [213] 871–0707.) Includes unpublished screenplays for sale.

Screen Achievements Record Bulletin. See Annual Index to Motion Picture Credits.

Selected Film Criticism. Edited by Anthony Slide. Metuchen, N.J.: Scarecrow Press, 1982.

Shale, Richard, comp. *The Academy Awards Index: The Complete Categorical Chronological Records.* Westport, Conn.: Greenwood Press, 1993.

Silver, Alain, and Elizabeth Ward, eds. *Film Noir: An Encyclopedic Reference to the American Style.* 3d ed., rev. Woodstock, N.Y.: Overlook Press, 1992.

Slattery, William J., Claire Dorton, and Rosemary Enright. *The Kael Index: A Guide to a Movie Critic's Work, 1954–1991.* Englewood, Colo.: Libraries Unlimited, 1993.

Slide, Anthony. *The American Film Industry.* New York: Greenwood, 1986.

Slide, Anthony, ed. *See International Film, Radio and Television Journals; Selected Film Criticism.*

Sourcebook for the Performing Arts: A Directory of Collections, Resources, Scholars, and Critics in Theater, Film and Television. Compiled by Anthony Slide, Patricia King Hanson, and Stephen L. Hanson. New York: Greenwood Press, 1988.

Sources for Photographs in the Los Angeles Metropolitan Area. See Dumaux, Sally.

Sources of Mass Communications, Film and Theater Research: A Guide. Madison, Wis.: State Historical Society of Wisconsin, 1982.

Southern Methodist University. Oral History Program. *Oral History Collections on the Performing Arts.* Dallas: SMU, 1984.

Special Collections in the Library of Congress. See United States. Library of Congress.

State Historical Society of Wisconsin. *See Sources of Mass Communications, Film and Theater Research.*

Stephens, Michael L. *Film Noir: A Comprehensive Illustrated Reference to Movies, Terms and Persons.* Jefferson, N.C.: McFarland, 1995.

Subject Collection. See Ash, Lee.

Terrace, Vincent. *See The Complete Encyclopedia of Television Programs; Encyclopedia of Television Series Pilots and Specials.*

Theater and Performing Arts Collections. See Rachow, Louis A.

Thomas, Nicholas. *See International Dictionary of Films and Filmmakers,* vol. 2: *Directors.*

Thomson, D. *A Biographical Dictionary of the Cinema.* 2d ed. London: Secker and Warburg, 1980.

The Time Out Film Guide. 3d ed. Edited by Tom Milne. New York: Penguin, 1993.

Total Television. See McNeil, Alex.

The UCLA Oral History Program. Catalog of the Collection. 18 vols. Compiled by Constance S. Bullock. Los Angeles: Oral History Program, University of California, 1982. Second ed., compiled by Vimala Jayanti, 1992. Incorporates the oral history of the motion picture in America, interviews conducted between 1968 and 1969.

Union List of Film Periodicals. See Brady, Anna, Richard Wall, and Carolynn Newitt Weiner.

Union List of Motion Picture Scripts, 1995 Edition. Compiled by Gregory Walsh et al. Beverly Hills, Calif.: Academy of Motion Picture Arts and Sciences, 1995.

United States. Library of Congress. *National Union Catalog: Audiovisual Materials.* Washington, D.C.: Library of Congress, 1983.

United States. Library of Congress. *Special Collections in the Library of Congress.* Washington, D.C.: U.S. Government Printing Office, 1979.

University of California at Los Angeles. Theater Arts Library. *Motion Pictures: A Catalog of Books, Periodicals, Screenplays, Television Scripts, and Proeducation Stills.* Boston: G.K. Hall, 1976. Previously issued in 2 volumes, 1972.

University of California at Los Angeles, Film and Television Archives. Information available through the UCLA automated catalogs (ORION), MELVYL (University of California), and other databases.

University of Wyoming. American Heritage Center. *See* American Heritage Center.

Variety Film Reviews, 1907–. New York: Garland Publishers (through 1984); New York: R. R. Bowker (1985). Vol. 16 is an index to 1907–1980.

Variety International Film Guide. London: Andre Deutsch; Hollywood: Samuel French, annual. Includes an international film archives section, international film bookshops, posters, and records section, and current magazine section.

Variety Television Reviews, 1923–1988. 15 vols. Edited by Howard H. Prouty. New York: Garland, 1991.

Veinstein, Andre. *Performing Arts Libraries and Museums of the World.* Paris: Centre National de la Recherche Scientifique and UNESCO, 1967.

Video Source Book, 17th Edition, 1997–98. 2 vols. Edited by Christopher Scanlon. New York: Gale, 1995.

Walsh, Gregory. *See Union List of Motion Picture Scripts, 1995 ed.*

The Warner Brothers Golden Anniversary Book: The First Complete Feature Filmography. Compiled and edited by Arthur Wilson. New York: Film and Venture Corp., A Dell Special, 1973.

Wasserman, Steven R., ed. *The Lively Arts Information Directory.* 2d ed. Detroit: Gale Research, 1985.

The Western: The Film Encyclopedia. See Hardy, Phil.

Wheaton, Christopher D., and Richard B. Jewell. *Primary Cinema Resources: An Index to Screenplays, Interviews and Special Collections at the University of Southern California.* Boston: G.K. Hall, 1975. Part four notes the library's collections related to film and television.

Who's Who in Hollywood, 1900–1976. See Ragan, David.

Wiley, M. "Video Guide: John Huston—a Home-video Retrospective." *Premiere* 1 (December 1987):93–94.

The Wisconsin/Warner Brothers Screenplay Series: A Guide to the Collection. See Cohen, Allen.

World Film Directors. Vol. 1, *1890–1945.* Edited by J. Wakeman. New York: Wilson, 1987. Vol. 2, *1945–date.*

Writers' Program of the Work Project Administration in the City of New York. *See Film Index.*

Wulff, H. *See Bibliography of Film Bibliographies.*

Young, William C. *American Theatrical Arts: A Guide to Manuscripts and Special Collections in the United States and Canada.* Chicago: American Library Association, 1971.

INTERNET AND CD-ROM SERVICES

John Huston citations in the Magazine and Journal Articles Database provided by the Information Access Company, available through a number of library automated services, including MELVYL (see below), include Peter Richard's "'The Kremlin Letter,' *Film Comment,* January–February 1997, 74–80." In addition to the citation the full text of the article is provided. This search is just one example of how important electronic resources have become for researchers just in the last few years and are relevant for research on the movie industry. Researchers should consult with librarians in public and academic libraries about access to the various bibliographical databases and resources that are available through the internet.

The magazine database covers more than 2 million citations from 1,500 journals, starting from January 1988. The same company also provides a Newspaper Articles Database in which the *Christian Science Monitor, Los Angeles Times, New York Times, New York Times Book Review, New York Times Magazine, Wall Street Journal,* and *Washington Post* are indexed from January 1982. More than 2.5 million citations have been indexed. These newspapers are available through their own web sites, although there is a fee for service from the *Wall Street Journal.* Some have archival files, but those too may charge for that particular service. The web site addresses are

Christian Science Monitor: www.csmonitor.com

Los Angeles Times: www.latimes.com

New York Times: www.nytimes.com

Wall Street Journal: www.wsj.com

Washington Post: www.washingtonpost.com

The Modern Language Association (MLA) of America publishes the MLA Bibliography. This database covers more than four thousand journals, from 1963, and is updated ten times a year. It is available through the OCLC WorldCat Database.

OCLC is one of two major bibliographical database that has international coverage. WorldCat has seventeen thousand public, academic, and other library members and a database of more than 27 million records. In addition to MLA, its databases also include an index to articles and table of contents from nearly 12,500 journals. *Books in Print* is also available.

The other large bibliographic service is provided by RLIN, which covers 143 research and academic libraries. It contains information about more than 22 million books, periodicals, archival collections, and other kinds of material held in major research institutions.

The MELVYL system represents bibliographic holdings and other databases for the nine campuses of the University of California and other libraries in the state. Its database includes over 9 million titles. MELVYL is available on the web (www.melvyl.ucop.edu), but some the specialized databases require a password.

Access to about one hundred different databases are available in MELVYL. Cambridge and Oxford universities in England are included. The important holdings of the Library of Congress, New York Public Library, Los Angeles Public Library, and the University of Southern California are available through MELVYL, but are also accessible through their own web sites:

Library of Congress: http://lcweb.loc.gov/catalog/browse/

New York Public Library: www.nypl.org/catalogs/catalogs.html (the New York Public Library for the Performing Arts catalog is in the process of being automated)

University of Southern California: http://library.usc.edu

Los Angeles Public Library: www.lap.org.

There are web sites for the Academy of Motion Picture Arts and Sciences (www.ampas.org) and the American Film Institute (www.afionline.org/home.html), but information on their respective libraries—the AMPAS Margaret Herrick Library and the AFI Louis B. Mayer Library—is general in nature. Their catalogs and holdings are not yet automated for online service. The same is true for the Museum of Television and Radio (two locations: New York City and Beverly Hills, California; www.mtr.org/frame.htm) and the British Film Institute (www.bfi.org.uk/ frames.asp); but the BFI does make reference to Film Index International a compilation of its SIFT (Summary of Information on Film and Television) database, which is available on CD-ROM (see below).

The internet contains enormous amounts of information on cinema studies. One printed guide is *Your Personal Net Guide: Your Guide to the Best of Everything on the Net,* edited by Michael Wolff, Kelly Maloni, and Steven Keane (3d ed., New York: Wolff New Media, 1996, 734 p.). Its entertainment section covers "Showbiz, Movies, Television, and Music." "For free updates visit Your Personal Net at http://www.ypn.com." The *Web Magazine* (October–November 1996; www.webmagazine.com) is one periodical resource that reviews five hundred sites in each monthly issue and features a film section.

The Los Angeles chapter of the American Society for Information Science (LACASIS) has conducted a workshop on evaluating web search engines. Information on search engines, metasearch engines, resources used at workshops, other sources of information about search engine evaluation, and summary of evaluation criteria from workshops is available through www.well.com/user/tbw/workshop.htm. This web site provides direct links to a number of search engines and metasearch engines. Some search engines are:

AltaVista: www.altavista.digital.com/

Excite: www.excite.com/

HotBot: www.hotbot.com/

Infoseek: www.infoseek.com/

Lycos: www.lycos.com/

Magellan: www.mckinley.com/

Open Text: www.opentext.com/

WebCrawler: www.webcrawler.com/

Yahoo: http://search.yahoo.com/bin/search/options

Metasearch engines attempt to combine in one place any number of different search engines. Some of them are

CUSI: www.nexor.com/susi/cusi.html

Internet Sleuth: www.isleuth.com

MetaCrawler: www.metacrawler.com/index.html

ProFusion: http://topaz.designlab.ukans.edu/profusion/

Savvy Search: http://guaraldi.cs.colostate.edu:2000/form

WebCompass (CD-ROM published by Quarterdeck:www.quarterdeck.com/). The company claims that more than thirty-five search engines can be searched at once.

Videos and laser discs are also available through the internet. A guide to other sources is provided by "Links to . . . Sites and Resources: Video and Film Stores" (www.mdle.com/ClassicFilms/OtherSites/other4.htm). Other sources are

Best Video: www.bestvideo.com

Facets: www.facets.org/index.html

Home Film Festival: www.homefilmfestival.com

Movies Unlimited: www.moviesunlimited.com

San Francisco Video Store: www.levideo.com

Video Specialists International: www.infinitiv.com/videos1

There are also a number of fee-for-service internet web sites:

Baseline: www.pkbaseline.com (This movie industry–based site provides full text of *Daily Variety, Hollywood Reporter,* and *Weekly Variety.* Biographies on film personalities are also provided. See also CD-ROM Cinemania.)

Hollywood Reporter: www.hollywoodreporter.com. Available separately

IBM InfoMarket: www.infomarket.ibm.com/

Two of the most important CD-ROM services, which are available in a number of libraries are Film Index International and the International Index to Film Periodicals. Film Index International is published jointly by the British Film Institute and Chadwyck-Healey, updated annually, based on the BFI SIFT, and includes detailed information on more than ninety thousand films, with periodical citations for films and personalities. Downloading to diskette is possible at library terminals that provide that service. The International Index to Film Periodicals is published by the International Federation of Film Archives (FIAF). The print edition covers 1972 to 1995. The CD-ROM covers a number of those years and continues the print edition from 1996. Indexes to periodical citations for films and personalities are also provided. Downloading either of these CD-ROM works to diskette is possible at library terminals that provide that service.

Also available on CD-ROM is the *Dissertation Abstracts International (DAI)*. Published by Proquest, it includes doctoral dissertations and some masters thesis from 1861 to 1997.

Two commercial CD-ROMs available for purchase in stores are the All-Movie Guide 2 and Cinemania 97. Published by Corel in 1996 (www.corel.com), the All-Movie Guide 2's total movie list is 100,386. Information on John Huston, for example, includes a biography, filmography, and links to the films with which he was involved. Cinemania 97, published by Microsoft in 1996 (http://cinemania.msn.com/), covers movies, people, and articles, or more than thirty-two thousand items, updated monthly through the internet. Biographical information is provided by *Baseline;* reviews and information from Roger Ebert, Ephraim Katz, Leonard Maltin, Pauline Kael, and *The Motion Picture Guide Annual 1996.* Cinemania also provides links to other information on the internet. Its information on John Huston includes a biography, filmography, awards, and a film clip of Huston and Jack Nicholson from *Chinatown.*

Index

Index

Index

Bolkan, Florinda, 497
Bolt, David, 141
Bolt, Robert, 475–76, 565
  archival resources, 685
Bond, Anson, 510
Bond, David, 73, 76
Bond, Ward, 52, 158, 163, 496
Bondarchuk, Sergei, 495, 609
Bonicelli, Vittorio, 116, 495, 522, 609
Bonneau, Gilles, 98
Boone, Richard, 17, 127, 172, 463
Booth, Margaret, 129, 145
  archival resources, 686
Borbolla, Eduardo, 147
Borde, Raymond, 177
Borgeaus, Benedict, 66, 482
Borman, Moritz, 146, 494
Borstal Boy, 669
  production files, 626
  screenplay, 523
  summary listing, 451
Boschariol, Angelo, 117
Bosnos, Alfred G., 132
Botiller, Dick, 59
Bottome, Phyllis, *Danger Signal,* 455
Bottoms, John, 451
Bouchier, Dorothy, 456
Boulle, Pierre, 449
Boulting, Roy, 492–93
Bourget, Jean-Loup, 210
Bousman, Tracy, 150
Bowker, Ryall, 103
Bowles, Paul, 617, 676
Box, John, 476
Boy and the Bridge, 500
Boyar, Sully, 150
Boyd, Alan, 491
Boyd, Stephen, 117
Boyd, William, 490
Boyer, Charles, 119, 455, 475
Boylan, Mary, 113
Boyle, Robert, 171
Boyum, Joy Gould, 199
Bradbury, Ray, 10, 89, 185, 186, 432, 478,
    508, 571–75, 674, 675
  archival resources, 686
  Green Shadows, White Whale, 1, 206, 412,
    416
  writings on, 416
Bradley, Wilbur, 62
Brady, Frank, 203
Brand, Max, 457
Brando, Marlon, 16, 121, 452, 470, 473, 487,
    666, 669, 672, 678, 679
  writings on, 416
Braun, Zev, 447
Brauss, Arthur, 143
Bray, Dawson, 147
Breaking Point, The (Curtiz), 175
Breakout (Gries)
  articles and reviews, 251–52

  format availability, 709–10
  production files, 626
  screenplay, 523–24
  summary listing, 451
Brecht, Bill, 151
Bredell, Woody, 165
Breen, Edwin J., 79
Breen, Joseph, 206, 552
Brennan, Walter, 163, 506
Brent, George, 57, 157
Bresler, Jerry, 118, 453
Breslow, Lou, 66, 482
Bresson, Robert, 15
Bretherton, David, 171, 453
Brewer, Colin, 133
Brickman, Marshall, 474, 562
Bridge in the Jungle, The (Kohner)
  format availability, 710
  production files, 626, 665
  reviews, 253
  screenplay, 524
  summary listing, 451–52
Bridge of San Luis Rey, The
  articles and reviews, 252–53
  format availability, 710
  production files, 627
  screenplay, 524
  summary listing, 452
Bridges, James, 495, 610
Bridges, Jeff, 18, 37, 129, 172, 497
  writings on, 416
Bridges, Lloyd, 480
Brill, Lesley, 204, 209, 225
Brill, Tony, 613
Brimley, Wilford, 463
Brinton, Ralph, 90, 674
Britten, Benjamin, 664, 678
Brockmann, Hans, 138
Brodaux, Lowell. *See* Gunzburg, M. L.
Brodeur, André, 141
Brokaw, Tom, 619
Bronson, Charles, 451, 474, 491
  writings on, 416
Bronson, Tom, 143
Brontë, Emily, *Wuthering Heights,* 497, 613
Brook, Clive, 109
Brooke, Clifford, 164
Brookfield, Fred, 132
Brooks, John (Joe), 154
Brooks, Richard, x, 8, 24, 70, 465, 470,
    552–53
  writings on, 416
Brown, Bernard B., 165
Brown, Charles D., 67, 165
Brown, Clarence, 445
  archival resources, 686
Brown, David, 519–20, 591, 679
  archival resources, 686
Brown, Everett A., 58, 480
Brown, Joe, Jr., 79
Brown, Jophery, 145

Index

Carafa, Sacha, 128
Cardiff, Jack, 82
Cardinal, The (Preminger), 14
  articles and reviews, 256–57
  awards, 503
  format availability, 711
  production files, 628, 665
  screenplay, 527
  summary listing, 453
Cardona, Rene, Jr., 450, 522
Carey, Harry, 472
Carfagno, Edward, 485
  archival resources, 686
Carliner, Mark, 446
Carlino, Lewis John, 461, 541–42
Carpi, Tito, 491, 597
Carr, Karen, 132
Carrere, Edward, 490
Carrington, Margaret Huston, 2, 3, 5, 15
Carroll, Helena, 23, 154
Carroll, Joan, 492, 599
Carroll, Leo G., 497
Carroll, Madeleine, 487
Carruth, Milton, 480
Carruthers, Ben, 476
Carson, Emily, 454
Carson, Jack, 460
Carson, John F., 204
Carson, Robert, 445, 509–10
  Across the Pacific, 58
Carter, Jean, 76
Carter, Pres. Jimmy, 446
Cartwright, William T., 470
Caruso, Anthony, 59, 75
Caruso, Fred, 171, 497
Caruso, Vana, 116, 121
Casablanca (Curtiz), 4, 32
  writings on, 436
Casey, Juanita, 464, 668–69
"Casey Jones," 498
Casino Royale, 15
  articles and reviews, 257–59
  credits, 118–19
  format availability, 711–12
  production files, 628, 665
  screenplay, 527–28
  summary listing, 453
  synopsis, 119–20
  writings on, 201
Cassell, Wally, 73
Casselman, Louise, 141
Cassidy, Jude, 446
Casson, Lewis, 487
Castelun, Araceli Ladewuen, 147
Catholics
  articles, 259
  format availability, 712
  production files, 628
  summary listing, 453
Cavanaugh, Paul, 490
Cavendish, Constance, 109

Cavendish, Robert, 79
Cavett, Dick, 457, 618
Cellier, Frank, 487
Cervi, Kenneth, 151
Chamberlain, Richard, 475
Champlin, Charles, 619
Chan, Spencer, 58, 68
Chandlee, Harry, 163, 488, 506, 592
Chandler, Helen, 464
Chandler, Jack, 76
Chandler, Mack, 79
Chankin, D. O., 207
Chaplin, Charlie, 454, 664, 712
Chaplin, Geraldine, 497
Charles, Collin, 139
Charlie Chaplin's Seventy-Seventh Birthday,
  454
  format availability, 712
Charnin, Martin, 145, 448
Chartoff, Robert, 451
Chase, Margaret, 670
Chasin, George, 567
Chaumeton, Etienne, 177
Chavez, Carlos, 488
Cheever, John, 524
  Bullet Park, 452
Cherry, Robert, 79
Chester, Tim, 513
Cheyenne (Walsh)
  format availability, 712
  production files, 628–29
  reviews, 259
  screenplay, 528
  summary listing, 454
Chiari, Mario, 116
Chief Thunderbird, 472
Chinatown (Polanski), xi, 14, 19, 412
  articles, 259–62
  credits, 170–71
  format availability, 712–13
  production files, 629
  reviews, 262–64
  screenplay, 528–29
  summary listing, 454
  synopsis, 171
  writings on, 186–87, 188, 194, 195, 200,
    202, 205, 207, 413
Chinn, Anthony, 127
Chodorov, Stephen, 488
Cholmondeley, Lady Margot, 20
Chow, Raymond, 463
Christine, Virginia, 165
Ciannelli, Eduardo, 67
Cilento, Wayne, 145
Ciment, Gilles, 202
Ciment, M., 204
Cimici, Lou, 606
Circasia
  articles, 264
  production files, 665
  summary listing, 454

Index

Citarelli, Enzo, 151
Citizen Kane (Welles), 33, 190
Clapton, Eric, 454, 665
Clare, Mary, 85
Clark, Al, 73
Clark, Candy, 129
Clark, David, 76
Clark, Dolores, 132
Clark, Lyle, 79
Clark, Gen. Mark, 62
Clark, Matt, 131
Clarke, Charles G., 95
   archival resources, 686
Clarke, David, 79
Clarke, Robert, 90, 674
Clayton, Jack, 84, 86, 449, 473–74, 561
   archival resources, 686
   writings on, 418
Cleary, Jon, 463
Clegg, Tom, 90
Cliff, John, 76, 79
Clift, Montgomery, 12, 13, 16, 103, 106, 203,
   467, 485, 589, 669, 674, 678
   archival resources, 686
   writings on, 418
Clive, E. E., 466
Clute, Sidney, 451
Clymer, John B., 464, 532, 546, 577
Coates, Ian, 135
Coburn, Charles, 57, 455, 504
   archival resources, 686
Coburn, James, 452
Cochrane, Michael, 144
Cockburn, Claud (a.k.a. James Helvick), 10,
   521, 664
   Beat the Devil, 86, 449
Codiglia, John, 151
Cody, Harry, 76
Coe, Fred, 491, 597
Coffee, Lenore, 571
Cohen, Lester, 480, 577
Cohen, Mark, 452, 525, 665, 672, 673, 682
Cohn, Elie, 143
Cokes, Curtis, 129
Colasanto, Nicholas, 129
Cole, Bill, 514
Cole, Janine, 142
Cole, Lester, 464, 603
Cole, Stan, 141
Coleman, Marie, 176
Colicos, John, 141, 447
Collier, John, 511, 598
Collins, Dale, 577
Collins, Freeman C., 60, 485
Collins, Leon, 123
Collins, Patricia, 141
Collins, Richard, 211, 486
Collins, Stephen, 486
Colton, John, 471, 472, 557, 558–59
Columbia Pictures
   archival resources, 691

collection of, 764
   writings on, 441
Colvin, Jack, 131
Comandini, Adele, 455, 530
Combs, Gary, 132
Combs, Richard, 198
Commodore Marries, The
   production files, 629
   screenplay, 529
   summary listing, 454–55
Concertina
   screenplay, 529
   summary listing, 455
Condon, Richard
   Prizzi's Honor, 22, 39, 150, 484, 505–6,
   582–83
   Winter Kills, 171, 497, 612
Conery, Candida, 145
Confino, Adolfo, 467
Conklin, Gary, 481, 488
Connery, Sean, 19–20, 27, 37, 135, 454, 496
   writings on, 418
Connor, Edric, 90, 99
Connors, Buck, 462
Connors, Chuck, 457, 531
   archival resources, 686
Conrad, Barnaby, 476, 673
Conrad, William, 165, 486
Conried, Hans, 463
Constant Nymph, The (Goulding)
   articles and reviews, 264–65
   format availability, 713
   production files, 629
   screenplay, 529–30
   summary listing, 455
Conti, Bill, 143
Conversi, Luciano, 117
Cook, Elisha, Jr., 52
Cooke, Alistair, 465
Cooke, Malcolm, 92
Coonan, Dorothy, 496
Cooper, Gary, 6, 163, 506
   writings on, 419
Cooper, Gladys, 51, 109
   archival resources, 686
Cooper, Stephen, ix, 202, 208–9, 225, 449,
   477, 494
Coppel, Alec, 561
Coppola, Francis Ford, 15, 39, 483, 491, 579,
   580, 587, 597, 676, 678
   writings on, 418–19
Corden, Henry, 76
Corey, Jeff, 165
Corlan, Anthony, 125
Corliss, Richard, 194
Corman, Roger, 456, 531
Corrington, John William, 449, 520
Corrington, Joyce Hooper, 449, 520
Cortes, Rafael, 474
Cortez, Stanley, 64, 195, 472
   archival resources, 686

789

Index

Index

Index

format availability, 731
interviews about, 410
production files, 644, 672
reviews, 327–29
screenplay, 566–68
summary listing, 476
synopsis, 136–37
writings on, 182, 187, 188, 191, 194, 199
Manaster, Benjamin, 513
Manchester, William, 447
Manchurian Candidate, The (Frankenheimer),
39
Mancilla, Mario, 68
Mandel, Daniel, 497
Mander, Miles, 456, 497
Mango, Alexander, 107
Mankiewicz, Joseph L., 406, 458, 460, 465,
532
Mankowitz, Wolf, 118, 453, 527–28
Mann, Edward, 62
Mann, Hank, 52
Manning, Hugh, 133
Mannino, Franco, 86
Manson, David, 497
Mantee, Paul, 451
Manzu, Giacomo, 15
March, Fredric, 492, 599
Marchand, Colette, 85, 505
Marchant, Gilbert, 116
Margulies, Stan, 480, 575–76
Marill, Alvin H., 198
Marilyn: The Untold Story
format availability, 731
production files, 644
reviews, 329
summary listing, 476
Marin, Albert, 70
Marin, Jacques, 99
Maris, Mona, 494
Marius
production files, 644
screenplay, 568
summary listing, 476
Markle, Fletcher, 677
Markova, Nadine, 465
Marks, Clarence J., 488–89, 592
Marks, Owen, 67
Marley, John, 480
Marley, Peverell, 477
Marlow, Fred, 76
Marner, Richard, 82
Marolis, Ben, 464
Marquand, Christian, 452
Marsh, Liz, 145
Marsh, Terence, 133, 476
Marshall, Brenda, 448, 455
Marshall, E. G., 137
Marshall, Herbert, 109
Marshall, Peter, 145
Marshall, Ted, 484
Martin, Angela, 145

Martin, Dean, 496
Martin, Edward, 450
Martin, Frank, 469
Martin, Leldon, 79
Martin, Mel, 495
Martin, Strother, 76, 79, 474
Martin, Terry, 142
Martinelli, Elsa, 452
Martinez De Hoyos, Jorge, 451
Martinez Ramos, Juan Angel, 147
Martinez Sosa, Roberto, 147
Marton, Ruth, 499
Martson, Joel, 79
Marx, Samuel, 510, 682
Masina, Giulietta, 475
Maslin, Janet, 486
Mason, James, 19, 133, 461, 668
writings on, 425
Massen, Osa, 448
Massey, Anna, 456
Massey, Daniel, 143
Masson, Luis, 126
Masters, John, 666
Deceivers, The, 456
Matador
production files, 644, 673
summary listing, 476–77
Matheson, Richard, 456, 531
Mathews, Marilyn, 154
Matthau, Walter, 452
Matthews, Lester, 58
Matticks, Billie, 113
Mauldin, Bill, 79
Max, Jerome, 491, 597
Maxfield, J. F., 202
Maxwell, John, 76, 484
May, Jack, 136
May, Loralee, 547
Mayberry, Dick, 68
Mayer, Arthur, 671
Mayer, Edwin Justus, 603
Mayer, Louis B., 9, 176
writings on, 425, 441
Mayes, Wendell, 474
Mayo, Frank, 59
Mayo, Virginia, 453
Mayuzumi, Toshiro, 116, 121, 618
Mead, Roland, 62
Meany, Colm, 154
Mediolo, Enrico, 452, 525
Meehan, John, 493, 602
Meehan, Thomas, 448
Meek, Donald, 160
Meeker, Ralph, 172
archival resources, 689
Megahey, Leslie, 482
Mellor, William, 678
Melton, Frank, 79
Melton, Jeanne, 563
Melville, Herman, 462, 602
Benito Cereno, 23–24

Index

Suskind, David, 542
Sutherland, Edward, archival resources, 691
Swabacker, Leslie, 594
Swanick, Peter, 82
Swanson, Maureen, 85
Sweet Thursday, 452–53
Switzer, Carl, 67
Swofford, Ken, 145
Sydney, Basil, 487
Sylbert, Anthea, 170
Sylbert, Richard, 128, 170
Sylvester, Robert, *Rough Sketch,* 73, 495
Symington, Donald, 137
Syms, Sylvia, 484

Tafur, Robert, 73
Talbot, A., 522
Tall Man's Boy, 472
Talmadge, Richard, 118
Tamarov, Dimitri, 127
Tannen, Terrill, 477, 569
Tapiador, José Maria, 471
Taradash, Daniel, 451
Taras Bulba (Thompson)
  format availability, 743
  production files, 654, 680
  screenplay, 596
  summary listing, 490–91
Tatge, Catherine, 457
Tavernier, Bertrand, 410, 681
Tayback, Vic, 480
Taylor, Clifford, 456
Taylor, Elizabeth, 14, 16, 121, 172, 473, 497, 678
  writings on, 429
Taylor, Frank E., 103, 477
Taylor, John Russell, 184, 211
Taylor, Otis Chatfield, 557–58
Taylor, Renee, 474
Taylor, Robert, 485
Teal, Ray, 76
Tedford, Charles, 528
Television Makers, The, format availability, 744
Tellez-Chauvet, Guadalupe, 451
Tennessee Jim, 79
Tentacles (Hellman)
  articles and reviews, 375
  format availability, 744
  production files, 654
  screenplay, 597
  summary listing, 491
Terrett, Courtnay, 594
Terrible Beauty, A
  production files, 654, 680
  summary listing, 491
Theodosia: Empress of America. See Prelude to Freedom
Theoharous, Theodore, 151
Third Secret, The, summary listing, 491

This Property Is Condemned (Pollack)
  format availability, 744
  production files, 654
  screenplay, 597
  summary listing, 491
Thoeren, Robert, 484
Thom, Robert, 597
Thomas, Brian Anderson, 17
Thomas, Clarence, 446
Thomas, Dolph, 70, 161
Thomas, Gwen, 141
Thomas, Hugh, 79
Thomas, Karen, 462
Thomas, Sam, 591
Thompson, David, 200
  Suspects, 412–13
Thompson, J. Lee, 449, 490, 520, 596
Thomson, Norman, 95
Thorensen, Hallvar, 143
Thorne, Ken, 123
Thorson, Marjorie, 514
Three Strangers (Negulesco), 4–5
  articles and reviews, 375–76
  credits, 164
  format availability, 744
  production files, 655
  screenplay, 597–99
  summary listing, 492
  synopsis, 164–65
  writings on, 181, 193
Tierney, Lawrence, 150
Tillar, Jack, 481–82
Tiomkin, Dimitri, 60, 62, 101, 462
  archival resources, 691
Tischler, Sam, 62
To Have and Have Not (Hawks), 175
To the Western World (Kinmonth)
  articles, 376
  format availability, 745
  summary listing, 492
Tobias, George, 163
Tobin, Niall, 469
Todini, Bruno, 116
Toland, Gregg, 497, 614
Tolkien, J. R. R., 463
  Return of the King, The, 486
Tolkin, James, 137
Tom Jones (Richardson), 16
Tomasini, George, 103
Tomelty, Joseph, 90
Tomkins, Alan, 133
Tomorrow the World (Fenton)
  articles, 376
  format availability, 744
  production files, 655
  screenplay, 599
  summary listing, 492
Tone, Franchot, 487
Tong, Kam, 58
Tonti, Aldo, 36, 120
Torvay, Jose, 68